The
Garland
CLASSICS OF
FILM LITERATURE

REPRINTED IN PHOTO-FACSIMILE
IN 32 VOLUMES

TWENTY BEST FILM PLAYS

John Gassner
&
Dudley Nichols

Volume I

GARLAND PUBLISHING, INC. • NEW YORK & LONDON • 1977

This edition reprinted by arrangement
with Crown Publishers, Inc.

Library of Congress Cataloging in Publication Data

Gassner, John, 1903-1967, ed.
  Twenty best film plays.

  (The Garland classics of film literature ; 13)
  Reprint of the 1943 ed. published by Crown, New York.
  CONTENTS: Gassner, J. The screenplay as literature.
--Nichols, D. The writer and the film.--Riskin, R. It
happened on night. [etc.]
    1. Moving-picture plays. I. Nichols, Dudley, 1895-
joint ed. II. Title. III. Series.
PN1997.A1G32 1977   822'.03   76-52104
ISBN 0-8240-2877-5

Printed in the United States of America

TWENTY
BEST
FILM PLAYS

TWENTY
BEST
FILM PLAYS

Edited by
JOHN GASSNER
and
DUDLEY NICHOLS

CROWN PUBLISHERS
NEW YORK

Copyright, 1943
by
Crown Publishers

IT HAPPENED ONE NIGHT: Screenplay of the Columbia Pictures Corp. photoplay, "It Happened One Night," copyright, 1933, by Columbia Pictures Corp.

HERE COMES MR. JORDAN: Screenplay of the Columbia Pictures Corp. photoplay "Here Comes Mr. Jordan," copyright, 1941, by Columbia Pictures Corp.

MR. SMITH GOES TO WASHINGTON: Screenplay of the Columbia Pictures Corp. and Frank Capra photoplay "Mr. Smith Goes To Washington," copyright, 1939, by Columbia Pictures Corp.

WUTHERING HEIGHTS: Screenplay of the Samuel Goldwyn photoplay "Wuthering Heights," copyright, 1939, by Samuel Goldwyn.

FURY: Screenplay of the Metro-Goldwyn-Mayer Studios photoplay "Fury," copyright, 1936, by Loews, Inc.

THE WOMEN: Screenplay of the Metro-Goldwyn-Mayer Studios photoplay "The Women," copyright, 1939, by Loews, Inc.

MRS. MINIVER: Screenplay of the Metro-Goldwyn-Mayer Studios photoplay "Mrs. Miniver," copyright, 1942, by Loews, Inc.

THE GOOD EARTH: Screenplay of the Metro-Goldwyn-Mayer Studios photoplay "The Good Earth," copyright, 1937, by Loews Inc.

YELLOW JACK: Screenplay of the Metro-Goldwyn-Mayer Studios photoplay "Yellow Jack," copyright, 1938, by Loews, Inc.

MAKE WAY FOR TOMORROW: Screenplay of the Paramount Pictures photoplay "Make Way For Tomorrow," copyright, 1937, by Paramount Pictures, Inc.

ALL THAT MONEY CAN BUY: Screenplay of the R.K.O.-William Dieterle photoplay "All That Money Can Buy," copyright, 1941, by R.K.O. Radio Pictures, Inc.

THIS LAND IS MINE: Screenplay of the R.K.O. Radio Pictures photoplay "This Land is Mine," copyright, 1943, by R.K.O. Radio Pictures, Inc.

REBECCA: Screenplay of the David O. Selznick Productions photoplay "Rebecca," copyright, 1940, by David O. Selznick Productions, Inc.

THE GRAPES OF WRATH: Screenplay of the 20th Century-Fox Film Corp. photoplay "The Grapes of Wrath," copyright, 1940, by 20th Century-Fox Film Corp.

HOW GREEN WAS MY VALLEY: Screenplay of the 20th Century-Fox Film Corp. photoplay "How Green Was My Valley," copyright, 1941, by 20th Century Fox Film Corp.

MY MAN GODFREY: Screenplay of the Universal Pictures photoplay "My Man Godfrey," copyright, 1936, by Universal Production Pictures, Inc.

STAGECOACH: Screenplay of the Walter Wanger Productions photoplay "Stagecoach," copyright, 1939, by Walter Wanger Productions, Inc.

LITTLE CAESAR: Screenplay of the Warner Brothers photoplay "Little Caesar," copyright, 1930, by First National Pictures, Inc.; copyright, 1930, by Warner Brothers Pictures, Inc.; copyright, 1943, by Warner Brothers Pictures, Inc.

JUAREZ: Screenplay of the Warner Brothers photoplay "Juarez," copyright, 1939, by Warner Brothers Pictures, Inc.; copyright, 1943, by Warner Brothers Pictures, Inc.

THE LIFE OF EMILE ZOLA: Screenplay of the Warner Brothers photoplay "The Life of Emile Zola," copyright, 1937, by Warner Brothers Pictures, Inc.; copyright, 1943, by Warner Brothers Pictues, Inc.

THE FIGHT FOR LIFE: Screenplay of the United States Film Service photoplay "The Fight for Life," copyright, 1939, by Pare Lorentz.

Printed in the United States of America

CONTENTS

ACKNOWLEDGMENTS

It would be rank ingratitude on my part if this volume went to press without some acknowledgment of indebtedness to those who made it possible for it to appear.

The value of Mr. Nichols' collaboration must be apparent to the reader, but no cursory acknowledgment can do justice to the generosity of spirit that led him to consent to the collaboration and shoulder some of the burdens.

Mr. Walter Wanger, President of the Motion Picture Academy, who gave his blessings to the project, and Sidney Buchman, Columbia Pictures executive producer and himself one of our most prominent screenwriters, helped to launch the project with their encouragement and with many ensuing kindnesses. Mr. William Morris not only responded encouragingly to the idea but furthered it by making the necessary arrangements and placing the excellent facilities of the William Morris Agency at our disposal. Mr. James Geller furthered the project in its early stages. Major Pare Lorentz's early friendly response was encouraging.

Much gratitude is in order to the film companies mentioned in the screen credits for permitting the use of the screenplays in this book; and in connection with the by no means uncomplicated task of assuring the availability of these screenplays, I owe a special debt of gratitude to Messrs. J. Robert Rubin, Jacob Wilk, Louis K. Sidney, Charles Koerner, David O. Selznick, Frank Capra, Walter Wanger, Julius Cohn, Samuel Goldwyn, John Byram, William Dieterle, John Hay Whitney, Sidney Buchman, and William Dozier for permissions. Also to Miss Gwen O'Brien of Universal Studios, Floyd Henrickson of MGM, George Wasson of Twentieth-Century Fox, Morris Ebenstein of Warner Brothers, John LeRoy Johnson of Walter Wanger Productions, James Polk of Paramount, Jacques Leslie of RKO, and Marvin Ezzel and Pat Duggan of Samuel Goldwyn. And of course I owe a great deal to the authors of the original material, their representatives, and publishers whose names appear on the title pages of the individual screenplays. Generous responses from such writers as Norman Krasna, Dr. Paul de Kruif, Franz Werfel, Pearl Buck, Eric Hatch, Ernest Haycox, and the late lamented Stephen Vincent Benet were a great help.

I owe a great deal as well to Morris Ebenstein for his legal advice and his sage literary counsel; and to my wife Mollie, who sustained my flagging spirits and brought to editorial matters her unfailing perspicacity.

The many details entailed by more clearances than the reader can possibly imagine were handled by Miss Bertha Kaslow, Miss Margerie Lyon, and Mr. Het Manheim of the William Morris Office. Much of the credit goes to the ingenuity and fine feminine perseverance of Misses Kaslow and Lyon.

Finally, special acknowledgment must be made of the initial interest and the cooperation of Crown Publishers and to their editor, Mr. Edmund Fuller, for his painstaking attention to the work in progress.

J. G.

THE SCREENPLAY AS LITERATURE

By JOHN GASSNER

There is now a literature of the screen—the screenplay. If this fact has not been widely recognized, it is only because screenplays have not been properly accorded the dignity of print, a situation that is being corrected to some degree by this book. Naturally, not everything that is set down on paper is worth publishing, but it will be found on very little investigation that film writing already has substantial claims to literary recognition. Anyone who proclaims that the American film has been growing up would do well, indeed, to pay close attention to the written film. Too often his eulogies sound hollow because he can appeal only to the movie public's rather fleeting impression at a movie theatre, where the noteworthy motion picture is sandwiched in between a Grade B picture for the younger generation and a newsreel or a Donald Duck cartoon and flash intimations of the melodramatic or sentimental marvels with which the patrons will be edified next week. Too often, therefore, he can only deliver his panegyric in generalities, as if a string of superlatives constituted an argument. On this matter our native humorist George Ade has some sound advice fetched straight out of his cracker-barrel: "In uplifting, get underneath." And it stands to reason that one way of getting underneath, as well as having some evidence to provide in black and white, is to turn to the screenplays. Most of the talking pictures that have given the American film its claim to distinction have been fashioned out of a body of writing that commands respect as writing: that is, as theme, story, style, and drama. Its form has been shaped by the requirements of cinematic art, which makes it somewhat unique among the forms of writing hitherto familiar to the reader, but it is nonetheless literature that can stand scrutiny. The only question is whether it can be read with gratification. I believe that it can be so read when properly prepared for publication.

Since the essential justification for this book must be found in its contents, perhaps it would be well to rest our case before starting it. If this volume is worth having, it is because we are able to present here many distinguished screenplays representing most types of films produced in America since the arrival of the talking picture. Indeed, the reader will find that the number of screenplays exceeds that indicated by the title of the book. Just as the book was about to go to print an embarrassment of riches appeared, and we availed ourselves of the opportunity to give the reader an extra dividend, so to speak, even if the great bulk of the volume precluded the possibility of using everything we suddenly found at our disposal—for which reason a second "Twenty Best Film Plays" is already in preparation.

The screenplays in this book are neither summarized nor novelized, but are complete—in fact, more complete than the films as they appeared on the screen—and they retain their motion picture form, their shot-by-shot or scene-by-scene development. All that has been ventured in preparing them for publication has been predicated on the fact that a shooting script is intended solely for use in the studios by those who make our films, and that in this form they do not make pleasurable or easy reading. To assure gratification to the reader, and to enable us to realize the literary qualities of the text, the broken typography of a shooting script, useful only to the director and the camera-men, has been dispensed with; very short shots or scenes have been amalgamated on the printed page whenever they are closely related and a transitional phrase can make the relationship clear; and, except for a few sufficiently descriptive terms, technical jargon has been omitted, shooting directions being translated into their visual equivalent as "seeing" directions.

The sole novelty of our approach rests in our departure from the tacit assumption that the public must have a screenplay predigested for it, summarized or disguised as a popular novel. Like any other vital form of writing, a screenplay has its own construction and inner nature—its own unique progression, flow, and expressiveness. Remove these qualities and you have nothing but a humdrum digest of stories that in most instances appeared to far better advantage within the covers of a magazine or book. The nature of our presentation, which I believe to be the first of its kind, is otherwise. We believe that one does not have to destroy a good film play in order to enjoy it thoroughly, and it is my particular ambition to present the screenplays as an interesting contemporary form of literature which has long been due to the reading public—and, of course, also to the movie public, insofar as the two are not the same.

This, however, is no invitation to the reader to gird up his loins for combat with intractable matter, to grit his teeth with a do-or-die resolve that he is participating in an innovation and a difficult enterprise. To expect such exertion would violate the first principle of book making, which is that it must arouse and hold interest, and that it must engross on one or more levels of entertainment. Even the person who has a special interest in films as a subject for study, or as an outlet for his own literary efforts, should not make the mistake of assuming that the form of the screenplay holds some mystery that he will have to unravel with travail and solemnity.

To look for someone who has miraculously escaped seeing at least some films would be tantamount to seeking the proverbial needle in a haystack, and all of us can therefore follow the text as simply the written record of motion pictures. Even the most disengaged reader, who reads only for pleasure, is familiar with modern narrative in the form of concisely written short stories or novels like those of Ernest Hemingway and John Steinbeck. We can, if we wish, follow the screenplays in this book as we would any swiftly moving piece of contemporary fiction; a casual glance will show that on the printed page they consist of two basic ingredients, narrative and dialogue,—the former combining brisk action with crisp description, the latter combining speech with concise indications of how it is delivered. Besides, if we prefer, we can also read the scenarios as plays that happened to be written for the screen rather than for the stage, and that therefore reflect the particular conditions of the motion picture medium. Although, as Mr. Nichols points out, screenplays differ from both fiction and stage drama in a variety of ways, the reader can indulge his conscious preference or his reading habits to his heart's content.

In any event, the book affords him an opportunity to refresh his recollection of many notable films and provides him with a permanent record that he can keep in his library and pick up whenever the spirit moves him—although, of course, only to the extent to which words can serve as equivalents of photographic action. And at this point my preface can come to a timely close for the reader who is eager to turn to the screenplays themselves or, if he prefers, to the expert opinions embodied in Mr. Nichols' Introduction.

I.

If nevertheless I instantly depart from the modesty of a prefatory statement, it is because the more critical or interested reader is entitled to some explanation of the larger aims and evident shortcomings of this enterprise.

When the groundwork was laid down in conversations with the venturesome publishers who initiated the project nearly three years ago, everything seemed simple enough. Twenty American-made screenplays were to be procured by any means at my disposal and were then to be printed with a minimum of purely technical detail. But even after I was fortunate enough to gain the collaborative interest of Mr. Dudley Nichols, than whom no one is more entitled to represent the writing end of screen art, the difficulties seemed virtually insurmountable.

It took fully two years to acquire most of the screenplays for this volume. Not that there was any objection or diffidence on the part of the Hollywood studios but because each movie property is bought under complicated arrangements often involving many authors, publishers, and agents. And additional complications, some arising from wartime conditions, cropped up with maddening frequency. These difficulties were finally surmounted in most cases with the invaluable aid of the friends and associates whose names appear in a list of acknowledgments and elsewhere in the book. If some important or exceptionally attractive films are not included, the reason is in most cases attributable to our inability to untangle a variety of snarls in connection with permissions.

Then the problem of presentation began to provide complications. No two shooting scripts were written in exactly the same form. Nor did they all possess the same degree of amplification as reading matter, as they were not originally written with an eye to publication but for "shooting" purposes. In some, the descriptive and narrative passages were mainly stenographic, in others the transitions between scenes were recorded ultra-mechanically, in still others the form of presentation varied within the text itself. How well this difficulty has been overcome must be left to the reader, and it will only lessen his pleasure if he is made to share the burden of the procedure. I may say only that a great degree of flexibility in the editing seemed the wisest course—not only because, as Mr. Nichols points out, there is no absolute or classic form in which the screenplay must be cast, but also because the differences in form seemed generally appropriate to the individual content and spirit of the films. In the text of *My Man Godfrey*, for instance, the comparative sparseness of descriptive passages only heightens the vivacity and comic stylization of the action and the dialogue. In the documentary film *The Fight for Life,* the repetitions of medical and social detail achieve exactly the effect intended by the film—the monotonous but momentous struggle against mortality in childbirth.

Finally, the movie patron with a very good memory may notice some discrepancies between the text and the film he saw on the screen. In many instances this may be pure illusion. A photographic image is concrete, whereas descriptive words conjure up different pictures in different minds, and the speed of the film image further modifies impressions—often, it has been suggested, by a process akin to hypnosis. Besides, the images on the screen are recalled differently by each of us. If anything, the printed version may serve to present a variety of details more clearly and accurately than they appeared when viewed in the movie theatre. But there are also actual differences between the complete texts of the screenplays marked "Final" in the studios and the films as seen on the screen. Indeed in special cases, where important short or long sequences did not appear on the screen, brackets were used to indicate omissions, though the policy was not followed consistently because it would have proved annoying. The differences arise, of course, from the well-known procedure of cutting the film as originally shot from the shooting script, from which there were also departures during the shooting. With considerable effort it was possible to make the text conform to the picture where such collation seemed imperative. In most instances, it seemed more feasible to present the "final" screenplays intact; they generally had better continuity and documentation in this form, were often more representative of the authors' intention and more illuminating, and more forthright, too, as they had not yet been completely subjected to the taboos with which Hollywood has been saddled. Sometimes, on the contrary, the cutting is made for dramatic improvement on the screen, but such improvement was for the most part immaterial for purposes of reading. In the main, the result of retaining the deleted scenes had the compensating value of enrichment. I am sure that no one reading *Hamlet* is unhappy because the published text does not conform to the abbreviations and modifications employed by David Garrick or Sir Henry Irving in their respective productions of the play.

II.

And now it may as well be admitted that the original purpose of the book was ambitious. It was high time, we thought, to give recognition to a new form of literature. It might not happen that this book would encourage the studios to create more films of distinction, and so well established an enterprise as Hollywood probably needs no accolade from a private individual to bolster its reputation. Nor could the present writer, who has been unidentified with Hollywood if somewhat intimately connected with the legitimate stage, have any reason to act as Hollywood's apologist. But it seemed important to point out the existence of a new form of worthy dramatic writing by presenting some good examples of the art. Anyone familiar with the many radically differing forms of writing for the stage during the past twenty-five centuries—anyone acquainted with the scenarios of the *commedia dell' arte,* the dance recitatives of the oriental Noh plays, the choral drama of the Greeks, and the multi-scened, continually-flowing dramas of Shakespeare and his contemporaries—cannot snobbishly exclude the screenplay as dramatic literature.

To say that the screenplay is only a verbal record of enacted events does not vitiate the argument, as the same point may be pressed, to a degree, against a play by Sophocles or Shakespeare, to which the status of literature has never been denied. The real question is whether the dramaturgy, dialogue, and meaning of a particular film are worthy and pleasurable.

The argument that the scenario requires mechanical means of projection cannot be admitted, because the staging of a play by Shakespeare or Ibsen also involves mechanical devices; even the ever-so-literary Greek tragedies called for mechanics, as when the actor impersonating some god was lowered to the top of the scene building by means of a crane, creating the illusion of his coming from the sky. It is true of course that the screenplay, as written today, embodies ever so many more technical directions than any other piece of creative literature, and these affect the quality of the writing. Reiteration of stock terms—"dissolve," "pan," "long shot," etc.—becomes more tiresome, because more frequent, than the often equally stereotyped directions written for the stage. But this is the machine age and some mechanical terms are its legitimate property; and besides, many of these terms can be translated into better usage. This is also an age of rapid movement—different in this respect from previous centuries as the speed of a Flying Fortress differs from the pace of a horse-drawn chariot; words conveying movement are therefore part of our linguistic equipment and cannot be fastidiously banished as "unliterary."

The difference in speed is particularly apparent in the number of scenes to be found in a screenplay. There may be only one in many stage plays, but a full-length film play uses more than a hundred and fifty scenes; the text of *The*

Grapes of Wrath consists of 265 "shots." But if this were to be charged up as a demerit, by the same token we should have to declare the artistic form of Shakespeare's *Antony and Cleopatra*, which has 42 scenes, inferior to that of *Abie's Irish Rose*. In all periods of genuine creativity, dramatic form has taken its cue from prevailing mechanical facilities. What really matters in art is the transfiguration of reality into the manifestation of essential truth, spirit, and vision.

Even more specious, of course, would be the argument that screenplays are inferior as literature because they are based on "original" material bought from novelists, story writers, biographers and historians. The same reasoning would dismiss the great Attic tragedians as hacks because they helped themselves generously to what the first of them called "slices from Homer's banquet," as well as to the floating literature of legend and tradition. And Shakespeare would then be placed at the foot of the class because he reworked other men's plays and took his plots from such sources as Bandello's short stories and Holinshed's *Chronicles*. All life and all literature consist of borrowings, some conscious, others unconscious; some avowed, some unavowed—and in our day of plagiarism suits and copyright laws they had better be avowed. The entire question of "originality" is, in fact, largely predicated on social attitudes toward literature as a commodity on the market, having a market value. Neither the Greeks nor the Elizabethans were seriously concerned with the question.

What matters ultimately is the use we make of what we borrow: Not merely what we add or subtract, not merely even what individual interpretation we provide, but also how well we shape the material to the unique demands of different forms of art. A completely gratifying movie can never be a mere transcript of a good book, even when the plots are nearly identical. *The Informer* was a creative work as a novel. It was a freshly creative—basically original—work as a screenplay. It is one thing to criticize adaptations when they cheapen or distort a novel or story; and incompetence, commercialism, official and pressure-group censorship, and timidity have often invited such charges quite legitimately. It is another thing to press a case against the creativeness of the filmwriter because his work is based on material in books or plays. Actually, the shoe fits on the other foot, since there is reason for complaining that writers in other fields cheapen their work by trying to trim it for sale to the films—whereas the cinema has raised its standards by resorting to published and stage material. Hollywood's output was greatly improved when it began to pay careful attention to good literature, new and old, instead of relying solely on plots originated by people segregated in a Los Angeles suburb and notoriously disposed toward intellectual interbreeding. This trend may have discouraged the creation of original stories by writers in the studios, but it has been far from catastrophic, and there has even been notable work written directly for films in both story and scenario forms, as evidenced in this book by Norman Krasna's original story for *Fury* and Dudley Nichols' *This Land Is Mine*.

It is true that often too many writers work on the same script, and as a rule the impress of a single creative or recreative personality is to be preferred in a work of art. But the fact is that many a distinguished screenplay is the solo work of some screenwriter. Among such solo efforts we may single out Sidney Buchman's *Mr. Smith Goes to Washington*, Nunnally Johnson's script of *The Grapes of Wrath*, Philip Dunne's *How Green Was My Valley*, and Dudley Nichols' *The Informer*. Recently some writers have even begun to function as producers and directors of their screenplays. In other instances, authors like

Ben Hecht and Charles MacArthur have long worked as a team both for the stage and the screen. In other collaborations where two or more authors are credited with a script, the impress of a dominant personality is sometimes evident to one who is familiar with the work of the writers. Besides, there has been no dearth of acknowledged and unacknowledged collaboration for the stage. We have reason to wonder about how many hands shaped the beautiful religious plays of the medieval communion, and collaboration was frequent in Shakespeare's time. (In 1602 that enterprising Elizabethan "angel" Philip Henslowe lent a certain company five pounds with which to pay "Anthony Munday, Thomas Middleton, Michael Drayton, John Webster, and the rest, for a play entitled *Caesar's Fall.*") Certainly the script of *Mrs. Miniver,* credited to four writers, reveals more distinction and unity of style than many another work for screen or stage credited to a single author. In one way or another the dramatic arts have always involved collaboration; if not between writers, certainly between the writer and those who staged his work. Of course, these remarks are not intended as justification or apology for arbitrary interference with the writers' creative job, but in such instances the results usually expose the misdemeanor.

The fact is that no art form which draws upon so much of the writing talent of the world—even if ridiculously lopped by censorship—could fail to produce literature eventually. In this collection alone—and it includes only half the number of screenplays that might have been included but for lack of space and permissions—the material is drawn from the pens of such writers as Pearl Buck, John Steinbeck, Franz Werfel, Emily Brontë, Paul de Kruif, Sidney Howard, Richard Llewellyn, Jan Struther, Clare Boothe, W. R. Burnett, Daphne Du Maurier, Norman Krasna, and Stephen Vincent Benet. In this collection alone we also encounter, functioning as screenwriters, such able writers as Robert Sherwood, James Hilton, Robert Riskin, Ben Hecht, Charles MacArthur, Dudley Nichols, Nunnally Johnson, Morrie Ryskind, Philip Dunne, Edward Chodorov, Norman Krasna, Sidney Buchman, Francis Edward Faragoh, Dan Totheroh, Stephen Vincent Benet, Talbot Jennings, Vina Delmar, and Anita Loos. Had it been possible to include certain other films, we could have added to this list Lillian Hellman, Paul Green, S. N. Behrman, Clifford Odets, John Wexley, John Howard Lawson, Irwin Shaw, Lynn Riggs, Donald Ogden Stewart, Preston Sturges, Benjamin Glazer, John L. Balderston, Vincent Lawrence, Lawrence Stallings, Joseph L. Mankiewicz, Dore Shary, Claude Binyon, Jo Swerling, Frances Goodrich, Albert Hacket, John Lee Mahin, Gene Fowler, Oliver N. P. Garrett, John Huston, William Saroyan, and many other names. Most of these contributors to screen literature have also written noteworthy books and plays, and many of them—despite reports to the contrary—have returned from Hollywood to again write plays and books.

The greatest mortality is to be found among writers who go to the Coast at too impressionable an age and before a reputation can save them from a barrage of uninspiring assignments. It is at this end of the age curve that the theatre suffers a real depletion of its writing talent. The best writers who have labored almost exclusively for the films have, besides, exhibited in their important films distinctive styles which invariably earmark a creative talent. The breezy vigor of Sidney Buchman, the sympathetic realism of Nunnally Johnson and John Howard Lawson, the crisp humor of Robert Riskin, the cultivated intelligence and introspective power of Dudley Nichols, and the individuality of several other film creators are easily apparent. Many others have fallen by the wayside, for which the conditions of writing for Hollywood are no doubt at least partly responsible, yet people are apt to fall by the wayside anywhere.

As a matter of fact, the writer of this article would be immensely gratified if his book could in some measure establish the rightful place of screen writers among creative artists. In one respect, they have been for some time aware of their right to be considered artists in their own field, and through their Screen Writers' Guild have argued their case with the film studios. Under favorable circumstances they may even have something to say about the final cutting of the film they wrote. It seems to me that their status as creators is unduly jeopardized when their work is cut and patched by someone—no matter how talented—who does not share their creative process, and is compelled to heed mechanical and commercial requirements—and of course censorship. They have even asserted their right, like all writers with a sense of their obligation to society, to speak out individually and collectively on some social issues. But they have been immoderately modest *vis á vis* other writers who publish novels and other books. They have indulged in self-depreciation until their sincerity has been put under suspicion. They are making lots of money, some of them admit, but they express rueful and tense resolves to shake off the golden chains of Hollywood and write a play or novel—as if the publication of a second rate book were an achievement vastly superior to the creation of a first-rate screenplay, to excellent work in a medium in which they are presumably more practiced. They are indifferent to their literary status in careless omissions of the definite article, and lack the prerogatives of authorship. And so it happens that the screenwriter, along with his studio, rarely acquires the unequivocal right to publish a screenplay (as a complete screenplay rather than as a synopsis or as a short excerpt for publicity) or to allow it to be included in a book like the present one. The monetary value may be negligible enough, but not the privilege of being regarded as a writer who has the right to see his work in print when it merits such recognition. Thus it happens that the author of a published novel or play can prevent the literary recognition of a screenwriter, regardless of the importance of the latter's contribution. The creative excellence of Dudley Nichols' and John Ford's film *The Informer,* a thorough filmic recreation of the novel by Liam O'Flaherty, has been widely acclaimed ever since its appearance. Nevertheless, Mr. O'Flaherty has been able to prevent, without explanation so far as I know, the publication of Mr. Nichols' screenplay in a volume of which Mr. Nichols is co-editor. Another injustice on my part —to Lieutenant-Colonel Frank Capra and Robert Riskin, jointly responsible as director and screenwriter for the success of *Mr. Deeds Goes to Town*—resulted from my inability to persuade Mr. Clarence Budington Kelland to allow its inclusion in the book.

It is not my intention to wage any war of extermination against authors who are not screenwriters. As a matter of fact most authors, and the most distinguished of them at that, as well as their representatives and publishers, were generously cooperative. But it seems to me that when a studio pays anywhere from twenty-five hundred to several hundred thousand dollars for permission to film a book and sets a reputable writer to work on it, it should reserve publication rights to the screenplay; at least after a decent interval, and in any volume that would honor achievements in film writing. The screenwriter is entitled to that much credit, and it would give him an encouraging sense of authorship which might be reflected in the craftsmanship of his work. (The public, in turn, is entitled to read a screenplay which has aroused its interest as a film.) It is a grave mistake to deny the screenwriter at least some of the prerogatives and incentives of full-fledged authorship when he has acquitted himself of a creative piece of work. The play *Julius Caesar* was not written by Plutarch. The author of *Hamlet* was not Saxo-Grammaticus.

Undoubtedly the reason for this kind of discrimination against the screen-writer by himself and others has resulted from the fact that it has occurred to few of us that his work, too, is a literary form—and a fresh one. Much the same attitude was once maintained toward the drama, when it was regarded as a mere text for the actor and publication was a matter of indifference. And plainly the screenplay *is* a literary form, and next to distinctive radio drama the most recent one to be developed in modern times. Strictly considered, a shooting script is a swiftly moving drama consisting of dialogue, descriptions, and narrative sections, presented in many scenes—some as short as a flash, others lasting considerably longer, though they are much shorter than scenes in all but the most expressionistic stage plays.

That the dialogue is usually more meagre than in a play or, as a rule, in a novel, is a condition of the film medium, in which visual movement is para-mount. The abbreviation of dialogue is a trend of the times—the eighteenth century art of conversation has regrettably diminished over the years; and, of course, even abbreviated dialogue can be superb, just fair, or downright bad. The descriptions in screenplays are generally brief or even stenographic, be-cause the background of the various scenes will be set up and photographed at the discretion of the director, the costumes will be designed by other artists, the physical appearance of the characters will be fully realized only through the actors in the cast. This is also true of that superb form of literature, the stage play—as perusal of the text of a Greek tragedy or of a Shakespeare quarto or folio will disclose. The practice of writing elaborate descriptions in plays first arose toward the end of the past century, long after the composition of most of the theatre's masterpieces. Nor is there anything except economy of time and paper to prevent a screenplay from having detailed descriptions, and the reader will, as a matter of fact, find them in abundance in such screenplays as *The Good Earth* and *Mrs. Miniver*. (Though, as in the case of stage plays, these are often changed by the director of the production, and by that part of the actor's personality and physical appearance which is more or less immutable!) But drama has never rested its claims on description. Representation of char-acter engaged in action and in reaction; of tensions, crises and climaxes in individual and collective experience; of ideas and meaning rising out of the projected experiences—that is the essence of dramatic literature.

The narrative in a film play is, as a rule, extensive. But it is brisk and is predominantly a record of movement, since film is movement. It reflects the modern age of activity and of constantly stepped up tempo. Moralists and philosophers may regret this state of affairs as much as they please, and they may be justified. But the form of the screenplay stems from modern conscious-ness, as well as from the nature of *motion* pictures, and it is the business of any vital art to employ the idiom and resources of its time. The plays of Shakespeare and his fellow-dramatists, composed in the vigorous and expanding age of Queen Bess, are replete with swiftly moving action in numerous scenes widely separated in time and space, much to the discomfort of purists, as well as with impassioned rhetoric and brisk low comedy. They seemed painfully barbaric to the courtiers of the Bourbons in the seventeenth and eighteenth century who favored the work of Jean Racine and preferred a restraint in art that paralleled the political aims of autocracy. But it would be inept for anyone to regret that Shakespeare did not write *Hamlet* in the leisurely style of Racine. And it would have spelled artistic suicide for an English dramatist to dam the tide of Elizabethan energy on the dynamic stage of The Globe. We do not of course prescribe the speed of the cinema for other forms of art—for the theatre, for instance, but we cannot proscribe the literature of the films, because it possesses such tempo. The narrative portions of a screenplay when not too carelessly written are, in short, artistically right for the medium, and can provide legitimate gratifications.

Needless to say, there is vast room for improvement in the literary composition of a screenplay apart from content. But the improvement is possible, and in some respects is already on the way. Although the length of dialogue in an effective film will always have to be kept within strict bounds, room may be found for those outbursts of passion and thought that form purple patches in the world's great plays. A place may even be found for poetry, for the spare modern kind of poetry written by Robert Frost, and by T. S. Eliot and Archibald MacLeish in their later phases. The excellent screenplay *All That Money Can Buy,* included in this book, would have achieved even greater literary distinction if the late Stephen Vincent Benet had been called upon to put some of its longer passages into the kind of poetry he wrote so well. Already notable are the colloquial vigor and color of such film plays as *The Grapes of Wrath, How Green Was My Valley,* and *Mr. Smith Goes to Washington;* the hortatory eloquence of climactic scenes in *This Land Is Mine, The Life of Emile Zola, Fury,* and *Mr. Smith Goes to Washington;* the poetry of the interne's soliloquy in Pare Lorentz' *The Fight for Life,* as well as the narrative poetry of his other documentary film, *The River,* which recalls Walt Whitman's sweeping lines. By turning to *The Good Earth* in this volume the reader will see how beautifully a screenplay can read—in dialogue, descriptions and all.

There are, in addition, unique possibilities of fluidity, suggestiveness, and emotional scoring in the screenplay—all related of course to the demands of motion pictures. The presence of many scenes is, as previously noted, not a special attribute, as there have been many multi-scened plays (even modern ones, like *Faust* and *Peer Gynt*), and actually the film play merely avails itself of the novel's freely shifting background. What is unique is the flexible alternation of scenes of varying duration, of contrasting shortness and length for emphasis, of suggestion and symbolization. Objects extrapolated from their surroundings can be used with tremendous effect, and a part can speak eloquently for the whole, while routine exposition can be reduced to a flash. A separate "shot" of a pen moving on a piece of paper or of a foot pushing against a door can create an instant sense of expectancy and suspense. A crumpled piece of paper clinging to a man who has sold his friend's life for a small reward may suggest the informer's troublesome conscience more eloquently than an extended verbal analysis. Seemingly unrelated "shots" of objects in quick succession, superimposed on each other or dissolving into each other, may establish a situation, enforce a comment, or convey the essence of an emotion in fresh and startling ways. A poetry of sensations or relations is often achieved by this kind of composition, for which the technical word is "montage." Speech can be shuttled back and forth, or can be supplemented and counterpointed by picturized events, as well as alternated with effective silence while pantomime and visual backgrounds carry on the dialogue's content. The screenwriter knows that he can rely on the new technical resources of sound recording, described by Lewis Jacobs: "An art of sound devices now parallels the art of camera devices: the elimination of all but one voice or sound on the sound track parallels the camera close-up; the mingling of voices or noises corresponds to the double exposure; the traveling of sound is like the panning or dollying of the camera; the elongation of sound beyond normal parallels a lengthy still shot. The dissolve and the fade, the stop-voice and the play-back—these are other sound devices which approximate devices of the camera."

One written "shot" (the equivalent of a scene in a play) can follow another without preparation and intermission for a change of scene, as in a play; without delaying explanation of the transition, as in a novel. One accepts the convention as natural because films habituate us to freedom of movement in time and space. The viewpoint can also be tellingly differentiated for emphasis. The view can be expressively panoramic, distant and fully inclusive ("full shot"), fairly close and partially revealing ("medium shot"), or close and right on top of us (in a "close-up"). The view can also move to and fro, and up and down; it can expand or contract for revelation or emphasis; it can move with a character ("the camera pans with him" is the usual phrase) or precede him. The scene can "fade in" (generally conveying the start of a "sequence," a segment of the story), by the gradual materialization of a scene. It can "fade out," the gradual disappearance of the scene creating a sense of pause or of finality, generally suggesting the end of a sequence. It can dissolve quickly or lingeringly into another image, suggesting not merely a lapse of time but a special relationship with the image that follows. (A man's face is seen scowling and as it "dissolves out" a picture of his being beaten as a child "dissolves in" simultaneously, creating an impression of psychological continuity and relationship.) The shot can "wipe off"—as though a tissue were being peeled off, giving place to another picture, like another, deeper layer of tissue. The scene can be "cut"—that is, concluded abruptly, changed before its logical termination to achieve some staccato effect. Scenes, moreover, can be presented from the viewpoint of different characters, enabling us to see an object or some transpiring action as some character—personally involved or affected—views it, objectively or subjectively.

The viewpoint of the camera excels that of the static spectator or reader, for it is all-seeing and omniscient. The composition of a screenplay is predicated on the fact that the camera can be moved in all directions and that the view on the screen is in continuous movement. The screenplay, too, is movement, of varying speed and duration. The actors are moving, the background is moving, objects are moving, symbols are moving, the angles of vision are moving.

The resources of the motion picture are virtually inexhaustible, and the form and the detail of the screenplay correspond to them. Since the camera that takes the photographs corresponds to the eye of the observer, the "shooting script" visualizes the film for the reader. The directions intended for those who make the film in the studios or "on location" become, in the reading of the script, "seeing" directions. They tell the reader what to see and imagine, or—if he has already seen the film—what to "re-see."

The famous Russian film director Eisenstein scores a fundamental point when he maintains in his book, *The Film Sense,* that many masters of literature expressed themselves in the cinematic manner long before the advent of the film, citing Milton's battle scenes in *Paradise Lost* and Pushkin's narrative poem *Poltava.* In the latter, an episode is given in terse one-line scenes such as

"Too late," someone then said to them,
And pointed finger to the field.
Then the fatal scaffold was dismantled,
A priest in cassock black was praying,
And onto a wagon was being lifted
By two cossacks an oaken coffin.

Examples from many other masterpieces of poetry and prose (Eisenstein also alludes to Maupassant's work) all the way down to Homer could be cited just as easily. In short, there is no intrinsic reason why the film form cannot provide notable literature.

III.

The interest of the screenplays purely as a relatively new literary form would not, of course, matter greatly, and would certainly not justify this volume, but for their content. It is on the grounds of triviality of subject matter, cheapness or triteness of viewpoint, and infrequency of adult attitudes that average Hollywood films have been most severely criticized. There is much truth in these charges, and we can always turn to George Jean Nathan for the pleasures of vituperation. Certain it is, however, that if the blame were to be properly allocated it would rest not only with Hollywood but with the public that clamors for trash, and with the pressure groups that fall into a frenzy whenever a controversial subject appears on the screen. The economic conditions of film making and perhaps our whole way of life would have to be scrutinized. And account would have to be taken of the fact that the film companies have to satisfy different levels of maturity if they are to stay in business. The percentage of people who have cut their wisdom teeth on *Harper's* and the plays of George Bernard Shaw is hardly overwhelming in a weekly audience of over fifty millon.

Nevertheless, no form of art is appraised on the basis of its trashy products. The novel is not dismissed as beneath contempt because of the enormous sale of Horatio Algers. The drama is not relegated to the dustbin because of the preponderance of mediocre farces, vaudevilles and melodramas in its twenty-five centuries of existence as written literature. The artistic pursuit of motion pictures in America is approximately thirty years old, and the sound film started only some eighteen years ago, whereas the theatre has twenty-five hundred years of history behind it. Appraisal of the American film—of its achievements and potentialities—should be reasonably based on *The Informer, The Grapes of Wrath, Fury* and other films like those it has been possible to include in this book, rather than on cinematic claptrap. The scenarist who is supposed to have told his friend that he was all right now that he had just had all his three-syllable words removed couldn't have had anything to do with the films in this anthology or with many other films.

Anyone interested in a comparison of the legend and the reality of Hollywood may be referred to Leo C. Rosten's documented sociological study *Hollywood.* Anyone interested in an account of the development of the film in America should read Lewis Jacobs' excellent book *The Rise of the American Film.* But the existence of a Hollywood reality of work and taste and of rapidly developing standards can be found within the covers of this book. Call these sound films and two or three dozen others from which selections could have been made an oasis in the desert, if you will. But all good art is an oasis.

The growth of the American film started more than a decade before the development of sound despite the prevalence of shallow spectacles, cheap exoticism and slapstick, and even though the screenplay as a literary form was still non-existent; in fact, the early stages of the sound film between 1926 and 1929 were legitimately viewed as a retrogression. We need only recall the advances in narrative technique and in content ushered in by D. W. Griffith between 1914-1917 with *The Birth of a Nation* and with *Intolerance,* which even included a documentary strike sequence that, except for the antimaccassar phrases of the picture's titles, would have been perfectly at home on the most militant

Broadway stage of the 'thirties. We need only refer to the numerous Chaplin films, with their rueful appraisal of the world, and their flashes of brilliant satire; their pity for the underdog; their realization of love-starved and freedom-seeking humanity, and of something more endurable than brass in the human spirit—all expressed in superbly comic terms. Mr. Chaplin's social awareness and evocation of "the still, small voice of humanity" in the sound films *Modern Times* and *The Great Dictator* was strongly anticipated in his earlier eloquently silent work, which reached its zenith in *The Gold Rush* in 1925. And another peak—this time, in realism—appeared with King Vidor's war film *The Big Parade.*

Finally, note must be taken of the changes in manners and outlook. Theda Bara materialized in all her torrid glory, and her vogue brought some recognition of sexuality, no matter how distorted or inept, on the screen. This marked a sharp departure from the pre-war treatments mordantly recalled by Eric von Stroheim as "Plenty of action, combined with the sterile love of a flat-chested, hairless youth for a coy, equally flat-chested maiden whose paroxysm of passion was to touch ever so lightly her sweet virgin lips with one emaciated finger, which in turn was hesitatingly placed on the lips of the shy, almost retreating youth beside her. In the next scene they said, 'I do.'" The post-war woman of the world, successfully embodied in Norma Talmadge and Alla Nazimova, made her appearance at this time and raised such controversial questions as divorce and birth control. Comedy of manners was treated with tartness by the screenwriter Anita Loos, and with urbanity by the director Ernst Lubitsch.

An overwhelming number of puerilities masquerading as sophistication, of Graustarkian romance, of exoticism in the perfervid manner of *The Sheik,* of glorifications of pulchritude and luxury in the early Cecil De Mille manner, provided an uncritical reflection of the post-war era. But a critical view of materialism arose in Eric von Stroheim's melodramas, among which *Greed,* in 1923, was noteworthy for its insistent picturization of corrupting lust for wealth. Edward Everett Horton's filming of George S. Kaufman's *Beggar on Horseback* in the same year satirized this society in terms of "expressionistic" extravaganza. Main Street stodginess and middle-class absorption in money-making appeared in such "silents" as *Babbitt* and *The Show Off.* In 1927 Joseph von Sternberg's *Underworld,* written by Ben Hecht, displayed this materialism on the lower levels of racketeering, and was supplemented by other gangster melodramas that had more than Lon Chaney to recommend them. A year later, King Vidor's memorable film *The Crowd* presented the overlooked side of the boom-intoxicated 'twenties—the existence of grinding poverty and depersonalization in the lives of white-collar workers. Authentic regional picturization appeared in Henry King's story of a young mountaineer *Tol'able David* as early as 1921; and the possibilities of the "documentary," as contrasted with the plot film, came to the fore with Robert Flaherty's *Nanook of the North* and *Moana of the South Seas* which earned him the title of "father of the documentary." And hardly less important was the rise of serious film criticism in the magazines and newspapers.

Nevertheless the development that has given us screenplays appreciable as literature came only with the rise of the "talkie." Although the early director Thomas Ince started the custom of preparing a careful scenario or continuity for films before 1916, the literary screenplay arose only with the expansion of the film's facilities, the introduction of dialogue, the sobering of the public consciousness, and the effect of economic tensions.

The sound film began moving toward maturity in America after 1929, a year significant in the annals of the nation as the beginning of a sobering up process in our national life owing to the stock-market crash and the ensuing years of economic depression and social conflict. Directors and scenarists, who had by now added dialogue to the film's resources and were acquiring facility in fusing speech with movement, began to treat old-fashioned situations with growing freshness; they favored wit and comedy of manners instead of Keystone slapstick, represented complex characters rather than stereotypes, presented unpleasant realities on the stage, and even erratically reflected social issues. The shortcomings were and remain many, the compromises numerous, the harrassments from all sides innumerable. Conservative opinion often held that the films went too far, radicals that they did not go far enough. But memorable sound films began to appear, films worth anybody's seeing and anybody's reading. I am not prepared to say how many swallows make a spring, though I hazard the guess that there should be many. Nor can one pontificate on how much better each of them should sing, though there is hardly a screenplay—and I suppose the same may be said of most distinguished plays and novels—that cannot be charged with this or that fault. But the evidence of growth and the possibility of gratification cannot be seriously questioned, and this collection, I believe, provides some of the evidence in tangible, literary form.

Murder mysteries have abounded in the film mart, because movement rather than reflection is natural to film art; largely no doubt because of the popularity of this type of story in all forms of entertainment, including fiction. The products have ranged from tripe to very choice fare like *The Maltese Falcon*, and exceptional excellence is perhaps most apparent in *Rebecca*. In this screenplay the murder mystery is plainly subordinated to character drama and to psychological complication, such as the fixation of Mrs. Danvers on Rebecca and the motivation of Rebecca's shameless behavior.

Love is another Hollywood commodity, and there is of course no earthly reason why it should not be. Poetry, drama, and fiction have legitimately thrived on this troublesome instinct and its sublimations for thousands of years. Hollywood has failed most distressingly only because it has so often favored sterile simplifications, adopted a false optimism, and avoided the subject of tragic passion, which affords the deepest insights into the abysses of human nature. One dreads to think how drama and fiction would have fared if Euripides, Shakespeare, Flaubert, Dostoevsky and Proust had suffered from the restrictions that hamper the film industry. It is a welcome sign therefore when the screen gives us a *Wuthering Heights*. Emily Brontë's novel is only one of several classics translated into film, and the presence of a *Romeo and Juliet*, a *Little Women*, a *David Copperfield* on the screen has introduced good literature into a once only barbarically articulate medium. But the screenplay of *Wuthering Heights* is distinctive because for once passion—from adolescence to adulthood—has been presented without adulteration. In some respects the film play even improves upon the novel by concentrating upon the central drama in the lives of the possessed lovers and dispensing with some of the Gothic hugger-mugger and exaggerations of the book that was born in the fevered brain of a brilliant recluse.

To date Hollywood has been more inclined to treat the sexual force in its lighter manifestations, but the past decade has marked an advance from the glorifications of Pollyanna, the sentimentalizations, and the melodramatic intensities of the American films' adolescence. In this interment of the banal, Mae West wielded a lusty shovel, and the late Jean Harlow sprinkled the dust— gold dust?—zestfully. The vogue of such bravura pieces as *She Done Him Wrong*, *Hell's Angels*, and *Red-Headed Woman*, with their brashness, frivolity and "gold-digging" materialism, was a social phenomenon open to much criticism.

But they swept away the fatuities of coyness and prudery. The wholesomeness of the new attitude is noted by Lewis Jacobs, historian of the American film, when he declares that it waved aside "the old convention that sex is the handmaid of sin," . . . "culminated in women's assertion of their rights and status in love," and invested modern women "with a new and bolder attitude." The new treatment of the sexes came, in fact, to such a pass that the films could spoof their own formula in *Boy Meets Girl*.—Self-criticism on Hollywood's part, starting in the silent era with *Merton of the Movies*, and *Hollywood*, has always been a wholesome sign.

Finally, love-making, with its tentative approaches, and provocative conflicts, became as modern as the young people of our time—or those in Shakespeare's high comedies . . . when Frank Capra turned out his classic, *It Happened One Night* (1933), and when Gregory La Cava made *My Man Godfrey* two years later. There have been many comedies of sophisticated love since then, and the recent success of that worthy comedy of romance in overcrowded Washington, *The More the Merrier*, and Paramount's *The Major and the Minor*, set against a more juvenile background, shows that the trend is capable of fresh exploitation. The charm of *Pride and Prejudice* owed a great deal to the fact that the screen treatment made the most of Jane Austen's nineteenth century comedy of manners.

The influence of *It Happened One Night* is widely recognized. Its adult approach to love was a welcome departure from saccharine romance. Its American background of tourist camps and travel by bus was refreshing in itself and commendably removed from the luxurious environments which hitherto had been considered indispensable to the proper flowering of romance. The display of temperament on the part of the principals and the discomforts to which they are exposed constituted a gratifyingly anti-romantic orchestration for the romantic melody. Colloquial speech displaced the customary employment of alternately perfervid and mid-Victorian dialogue, and the flavoring of wit, a quality which like good wine ferments slowly in every art, was added for good measure. Native character types appeared on the screen, and these were portrayed in a manner worthy of the realistic approach that had appeared in the better American novels and plays of the previous decade. The voluble drummer Shapeley, for instance, was first cousin to Sinclair Lewis types of the *Babbitt* era and to the hero of George Kelly's stage comedy, *The Show-Off*. With Frank Capra displaying the fullness of his talent for local color, comic portraiture and revelatory incident, *It Happened One Night* proved a signpost on Hollywood's journey from adolescence to maturity, and pointed the way to Morrie Ryskind's *My Man Godfrey* and another Capra-Riskin masterpiece, *Mr. Deeds Goes to Town*.

My Man Godfrey, in this volume, is distinctive because it added to ultra-sophisticated romance an oblique Shavian comment through characterization of the spoiled children of wealth and satire on the obliviousness of fashionable parasites to the realities of unemployment and homelessness. The party sequence in the first part of the film, counterpointed by the picture of the unemployed in the city dump, is an American Walpurgis-Night of decadence not easily forgotten. *My Man Godfrey* presents a sophisticated love comedy overcast with a darker reality. It also belongs to the class of "daffy" comedies favored by the public; but its frivolity has a cutting edge. Its irreverence was shared by a number of other energetic films that upset the apple-cart of convention—*Twentieth Century*, *Theodora Goes Wild* and *Topper*. But the Ryskind-La Cava extravaganza wears its cap and bells with a difference, now and then—if only briefly—suggesting King Lear's "bitter fool."

Domestic life began to be treated without banal tributes to torpid hearths and pallid devotion. The zestfulness of Myrna Loy and William Powell in *The Thin Man* added pepper to the breakfast table for two, and suggested that marriage could be fun. Triangle drama achieved new vitality and validity in this book's *The Women,* which treats domestic drama with penetration, pays heed to the social phenomenon of Reno, and places its personal story of a divorced couple within the framework of a comic exposé of the social set. The continuing standards of bright and tart film comedy have been well exemplified by *The Philadelphia Story, Holiday, You Can't Take It With You, No Time for Comedy, The Man Who Came to Dinner* and Ring Lardner Jr.'s and Michael Kanin's original screenplay *Woman of the Year.*

Fantasy has not been conspicuously pursued by Hollywood, and its grimmer aspects, as exemplified by that remarkable continental film *The Cabinet of Dr. Caligari,* have not appealed to the American palate. But when the reader comes to a *tour de force* like *Here Comes Mr. Jordan* he will find a special flair for the fantastic combined with blithe ingenuity, light-hearted playfulness on the subject of mortality, and satire on familiar realities. In *All That Money Can Buy,* moreover, the fantasy of Daniel Webster's battle of wits with the Devil is the springboard for an exalted affirmation of American democratic idealism. Here screen drama approaches the levels of imagination on which poetry becomes possible and almost inevitable.

The representation of American history and ideals has, in fact, added not a little weight to the screen's output, and can add a great deal more. Thus far *Young Mr. Lincoln* and *Abe Lincoln in Illinois* have commanded respect, and a peak in native historical romance was reached in the unusually vivid *Gone With the Wind* screenplay which Mr. David O. Selznick would have made available for this volume if this had been possible. But neither romances nor tributes to historical figures or the national spirit can suffice. A realistic examination of our past, as well as of the present in relation to our past, is imperative, and an impressive beginning was made by Dudley Nichols' *Stagecoach,* directed by John Ford and presented by Walter Wanger. In film history it is particularly interesting because it exhibits such a marked advance from what was once, in the heyday of William S. Hart, Hollywood's most reliable stock in trade, the so-called "Western" picture that still attracts the million with assistance from Mr. Gene Autry. The "Western," regardless of its superficiality and naiveté, represented the American dream of independence and virility—but on a juvenile level. As *Stagecoach,* as well as a number of other screen stories like *The Plainsman* and *Wells Fargo,* demonstrate, the story of the West is not inherently wedded to puerilities. The pioneering spirit, properly cherished but also studied closely, can enrich the films. But of course this can be accomplished only when realism is wedded to adventure, and when some larger significance is drawn from the material. That *The Ox-Bow Incident,* a searing treatment of a frontier incident, recently focussed attention to the starker aspects of the untamed West is significant, though its ultimate subject was not the frontier but the dangers of the mob-spirit wherever and whenever unleashed. —Related to the affirmation of the "American Way" without delusions of grandeur have also been those backward glances at our life which made *Ah Wilderness!* gratifying and *Our Town* memorable.

Rich possibilities also exist in hemispheric history, especially now that relations with the Latin-American republics have assumed exceptional importance.

The Hal B. Wallis, Warner Brothers production of *Juarez* in 1939 was a notable step in this direction. The burgeoning of the dream of freedom in the mind of the common man and his resolute pursuit of that dream were represented in the swarthy figure of Juarez. Nor did the sympathetic treatment of his opponent, the Archduke Maximilian of Austria, obscure the essential issue. It only stressed the New World's impulse to reject even a well-intentioned despotism which, significantly, loses its benevolence the moment it encounters opposition from the people. The democratic fervor of *Juarez* and the excellent characterizations in the film entitle it to an important place in the cinema's hall of fame. It is unfortunate only that *Juarez* has not been followed by good films on Bolivar, Zapata, and other Latin-American figures. European history might also enhance Hollywood's reputation. In this field, literateness and competence have not been implemented by any profound understanding of historical characters and forces. The *Marie Antoinettes* of the screen, no matter how expert, have too little significance and stay on the lower rungs of mere costume drama.

The biographical film has made many claims to respect and has continued to win credit, as the recent success of the George M. Cohan film *Yankee Doodle Dandy* and the Lou Gehrig film *The Pride of the Yankees* would show. Biography is uniquely suited to the cinema's capacities for visualization and time-space coverage. *Juarez* was preceded by Warner Brothers' *The Life of Emile Zola*, one of the screen's masterpieces. Appearing in 1937, when Nazism was running amok, the film was a timely representation of a case of rampant injustice and of an inspiring struggle against it. Its hero, Zola, moreover, gave rousing confirmation to the ideals of tolerance and to the social responsibility of men of good will in times of hysterical reaction, such as the Dreyfus story exemplified so vividly in the screenplay's indictment of incompetent but nonetheless vicious militarism, of military caste ethics, or want of ethics. This glowing account of Zola's moral courage and struggle for justice against the greatest odds had implications not confined to any single period or place, and a New York newspaper was quick to editorialize on the parallel between the Dreyfus trial and the Reichstag Fire trial. It is finally to the credit of the film that it developed its story without resorting to either extraneous romance or false heroics. With its quartet of distinguished films *Juarez, The Life of Emile Zola, The Life of Louis Pasteur* and *Dr. Ehrlich's Magic Bullet,* Warner Brothers achieved first rank in the field of biographical drama.

Medical biography and history were treated with distinction in *The Life of Louis Pasteur,* in which the struggle for progress in science was not limited to the laboratory but was extended into society, and in *Dr. Ehrlich's Magic Bullet,* which dramatized one of the inspiring chapters of medical research. MGM's *Yellow Jack,* the screenplay of Dr. Walter Reed's struggle against the yellow fever microbe, has been preferred for this collection because of its greater dramatic scope and democratic spirit, because of its picture of the common man's contribution to the mastery of nature by scientific endeavor.

The film play is, of course, an ideal medium for the dissemination of any kind of knowledge, and the possibilities of more direct public education along the lines of the legitimate theatre's "living newspapers" can be explored indefinitely. Already, in fact, some of the most memorable work in American film art has been accomplished in the field of documentary film. These have not been Hollywood enterprises, but the work of private individuals, progressive groups, and the Federal government. Many able pioneers qualify for the historical record—Joris Ivens, Leo Hurwitz, Robert Stebbins, Paul Strand, Herbert Kline, and others. Many stirring films, seen alas by only an infinitesimal portion of the public, deserve honorable mention. Among them were *Spanish Earth* and *Heart of Spain,* showing the background of the Civil War in Spain; Herbert Kline's documentary story of Hitler's march into Czechoslovakia, *Crisis;* and "The 400,000,000," which called attention to China's struggle against Japanese imperialism. They all came while most Americans were still oblivious to the threat of German and Japanese aggression. Documentary films are now invaluable as records of the war and are employed in training our armed forces and making our civilian population aware of imperative realities. The further range of the "documentary" was exemplified by such films as *The City* and the social hygiene film *From Hand to Mouth,* and the beautiful Herbert Kline-John Steinbeck Mexican picture, *The Forgotten Village.*

The undisputed master of this form remains Pare Lorentz, whose work is represented here by *The Fight for Life.* Major Lorentz' film *The Plough That Broke the Plains* for the Resettlement Administration in 1936 gave a graphic account of the agricultural problem caused by periodic droughts and of federal efforts to cope with it. Two years later he filmed the tragedy of erosion in the Mississippi Valley and the work of the TVA (Tennessee Valley Authority), *The River,* which he made for the Farm Security Administration. Documentary films are not as a rule created in a manner which lends itself to representation on the printed page. Improvisation "on location" is often a necessary procedure, even when the director starts with a shooting plan. Major Lorentz went to work on *The River* with a five page plan, but he filmed what he could find. Nevertheless, *The River* belongs to literature, too; for its creator is not only one of the masters of film art but a poet as well. A new medium for the poet may be opened by the documentaries; their narrative may not constitute little plays but they can be literature of a high order. It is not too difficult to imagine the kind of poetic narratives that Robert Frost and Archibald MacLeish could supply.

The Fight for Life, the memorable Lorentz film on obstetrical work and pre-natal hygiene in the slums, fortunately speaks for itself, and its creator's notes on the unique synchronization and counterpointing of speech and music should increase our appreciation of the text. There is a poetry of anguish, humanitarian devotion, and wearing but also exalting struggle in the film that readily communicates itself through the careful record of the shooting script. If there is much repetition in the text it has an appropriately insistent—"ostinato"—quality suggesting the plodding character of the struggle against death in childbirth. It is counterpointed, moreover, by the even more persistent reality of poverty and ignorance.

IV.

If any broad principle has been disclosed in this hasty survey it is that the growth of the American film has been predicated upon developing realism and growing awareness of the individual and his world. Psychological reality, supplemented by objective reality—social behavior, political conflict, economic pressure such as extreme and numbing poverty—was nowhere better represented than in *The Informer,* which is a landmark in the sound film comparable to D. W. Griffith's *The Birth of a Nation* and *Intolerance* in the era of the silent film. It is regrettable that the text cannot be reproduced here. But it has been possible to present the new realism in some of its most important manifestations through *Little Caesar, Fury, Mr. Smith Goes to Washington* and *The Grapes of Wrath.*

A major social reality from the middle 'twenties onward was the organized racketeering that proliferated in the era of prohibition and prosperity, and gangster dramas based on greatly publicized, readily recognizable facts provided an opening wedge for realism. The first important gangster film, and a classic today, is Warner Brothers' *Little Caesar* (1930). As tightly wound as a spring, carefully constructed, and supplied with authentic dialogue, it remains a masterly example of lean and forceful drama. Although it does not examine the social causes of crime, the causation seems to me implicit in many details, and the work might have lost its admirable staccato tempo if the story had been burdened with supplementary material. It is a relentless study of a maniacal egotist in an unwholesome environment which whets his appetite for success by glorifying materialism and holding out material rewards for his ilk. It also touches discreetly, but vividly enough, on the deeper layers of his personality, his insensitivity to women, fateful attachment to his buddy, and jealousy of the latter's girl. This is his tragic flaw, and it is a complexity of character formation substantiated by many impressive studies in criminal psycho-pathology. *The Public Enemy,* which came a year later, *City Streets, Quick Millions, Scarface* and other films achieved various degrees of realism, made some attempt at representing the causes of crime (*Public Enemy* started with a review of the criminal's childhood), and called for remedial action. Later films, after a lull in gangster drama, became more critical and some of them—*They Gave Him a Gun, Dead End,* and *Angels With Dirty Faces*—even paid more attention to the social conditions that produce criminals.

The arc of crime drama also widened to include other aspects of reality. A number of reputable films—*The Big House, The Last Mile, Mary Burns,* the chain gang drama *I Am a Fugitive, You Live Only Once,* and others—presented the criminal as a subject for rehabilitation, and investigated our system of penology. Mob violence, a subject painfully familiar to the American public, has been the subject of thoughtful and powerful treatments like *Fury, They Won't Forget,* and recently *The Ox-Bow Incident.* The most memorable of them, *Fury,* which Fritz Lang directed with stinging power, can be read in this volume. Equally impressive as drama and as social indictment, *Fury* is terrifying realism on any count. The contagion of mass hysteria, the behavior of the infuriated mob when it burns the prison, and the trial sequences are conceived and executed with the touch of a master dramatist, for which Norman Krasna, Bartlett Cormack and Fritz Lang may be duly honored.

The scalpel of realism also began to be applied to other facets of society, such as the professions. Good observation and considerable understanding appeared in studies of the law and courts of justice—*Counsellor-At-Law, The Mouthpiece, Winterset,* etc.; and of medical practice—*Arrowsmith, Men in White, Of Human Bondage, The Citadel* (which was, however, filmed in England for MGM by King Vidor), and the previously mentioned *Yellow Jack.* Questionable aspects of journalism were subjected to critical scrutiny in *The Front Page, Five Star Final, Exclusive* and other films, and the rise of powerful personalities in various enterprises reached a climax in the controversial original screenplay, *Citizen Kane,* written and directed by that prodigy of the legitimate theatre Orson Welles. Even politics was placed on the operating table of the new realism, and the subjects ranged from municipal corruption, as in *I Am the Law,* to matters of national scope, leading into the White House in the case of Walter Wanger's pictures *The President Vanishes* and *Gabriel Over the White House;* and into Congress in the case of the Frank Capra, Columbia Pictures film *Mr. Smith Goes to Washington.* Of these, plainly the most memorable is *Mr. Smith Goes to Washington.*

No one reading Sidney Buchman's masterfully dynamic screenplay, which combines incisive satire with ennobling idealism, can fail to realize how far

Hollywood has advanced within a mere decade. This was no tempest in a teapot, but a case history expanded by clever film technique into an event of national importance. Notable too in this script is the combination of rich colloquialism and eloquence, effectuated in both verbal and—in the Lincoln Memorial sequence—visual terms. A special flair for comic exposé was also apparent in Preston Sturges' *The Great McGinty*.

A further incentive to realism arose in the early 'thirties when the American people were sobered by the calamitous economic depression which persisted despite the optimism of certain public oracles. Vastly important was the field opened by the depression and the problems and conflicts arising out of the dislocation of the economic system. This subject provided a challenge that the films met, for the most part, only obliquely, often superficially, sometimes obtusely. With the "system" under fire, even apologies for big business began to appear on the screen. Theoretically they should have been very good—if one sided with big business, or they should have been very bad—if one stood on the other side of the controversy. Most of them were merely mediocre, a few of them, among which the idealized *House of Rothschild* and *Lloyds of London* will be recalled, had a certain quality. As the conflict between capital and labor sharpened there was also a flurry of anti-union screen dramas roundly denounced by pro-labor and liberal elements. Hollywood even entered the lists against Upton Sinclair during a disputatious depression election. Actually the one brilliant treatment of industry was Charlie Chaplin's satiric *Modern Times*, which, like other Chaplin masterpieces, it is unfortunately impossible to render adequately in print.

The common man's case also managed to slip through the gilded portals in a few films like *Oil for the Lamps of China* and *Slim*, mildly complimentary to labor, and in that delightful comedy of employer-employee relations, *The Devil and Miss Jones*. Noteworthy, too, was the hoboville theme of *My Man Godfrey*, and there was merit in other representations of unemployment like *One More Spring* and *Little Man, What Now?* based on a notable German novel by Hans Fallada that appeared just before the triumph of Hitlerism, which had been prepared by such conditions. The effect on American youth found its counterpart in a film like *Wild Boys of the Road*. The plight of the sharecroppers was another problem of importance, and it is somewhat to the credit of the screen that the tragic struggle should have found expression in even cautious films like *Cabin in the Cotton* and *White Bondage*. On the constructive side, King Vidor's *Our Daily Bread* in 1934 was the best of several plays recommending a return to the soil as a solution for unemployment. *Mr. Deeds Goes To Town*, brilliantly filmed by Frank Capra, incorporated in its charming comedy of a small-town hero who cleverly routs crooked city speculators and lawyers, the plight of dispossessed farmers at a time when the foreclosure of mortgages was becoming a national scandal. Deeds' democratic vivacity and his efforts to remedy the agricultural situation almost get him to be declared mentally incompetent. Robert Riskin's *Mr. Deeds* was a heart-warming, democratic comedy with overtones of true seriousness. Its compulsory absence from this volume is noted with deep regret.

In one instance, Paramount's highly regarded *Make Way for Tomorrow*, the general problem of insecurity affecting even the middle class in our society received moving recognition. It may be read in this anthology as one of our most touching screenplays, both as a mild social drama since it makes a case for old age pensions (lately made into law) and as a simple tragedy of old age. It combines a temperate understanding of both parents and children with heart-breaking pathos. And in another instance, Darryl F. Zanuck's production of *The Grapes of Wrath,* the social scene inspired what Mr. Crowther of the New York Times has acclaimed as America's most distinguished sound film after *The Informer.* Mr. Crowther will be borne out by Nunnally Johnson's screenplay, which the generosity of Twentieth-Century Fox and the Viking Press have made available for the reading public.

As in the case of all creative writing of a superlative degree, *The Grapes of Wrath* pulsates not only as a social document, and not only until the conditions it describes have been temporarily abated or have vanished forever. Its realization of characters who possess the universality of all intensely alive human beings is not sociology but art, in the sense in which the two become interchangeably one. There is an eternal verity here in the fortitude of the suffering but continually struggling spirit of the common man, in the shape of his desires and dreams, and in his capacity for making love flower in the most arid wastes. "And here in dust and dirt, o here, the lilies of his love appear,"—the lines of an English mystic poet, are perhaps more appropriate to this work than the ominous lines about God "trampling out the vintage where the grapes of wrath are stored," which first occurred to the author. Bedrock is reached in this film, and it proves to be as hard as granite and as soft as down.

There is no telling how fruitful the example of this film might have been. It bore fruit in that other Zanuck Twentieth Century-Fox production, the screening of Richard Llewellyn's notable novel of the Welsh mines *How Green Was My Valley,* a less challenging and perhaps too nostalgic but vastly affecting film. This screenplay also exemplified a realistic lyricism in its evocation of family solidarity and comradeship among the miners, a new-won poetry of reality in American films. After years of wandering in a wilderness of illusory manna, Hollywood's advance patrols had not only entered Canaan but begun to strike roots in the soil. *The Long Voyage Home*—Dudley Nichols' film translation of O'Neill's series of sea-plays in 1940—may also be added to the evidence, as may also be the exciting story of revolt against tyranny on the sea, *Mutiny on the Bounty.* Still more recently, too, the zest and invincibility of the common man received a typical Saroyan transfiguration, although charged with facile sentimentality by some critics, in MGM's *The Human Comedy* which William Saroyan wrote directly for the screen. It was subsequently published as a novel, reversing the usual translation of novel into film. Nor must we fail to mention Lillian Hellman's trenchant study of the predatory forces in our social development, *The Little Foxes.*

Steinbeck's *Of Mice and Men,* though of smaller scope than *The Grapes of Wrath,* may be adduced as further evidence of attention to distressing realities. Its picture of migratory workers encompassed the contemporary American scene and was an unidyllic account of travail among the people. By 1940, however, the inner stresses in our society were beginning to be subordinated to international upheavals. There had been an undeclared war in the Orient since 1931 and a mounting cataclysm in Europe since 1933. To the left and to the right of us the world was bursting into flame. For a long time, merely reflecting the apathy of the nation at large, the films paid scant attention. Although there was a flurry of romanticized pictures of soldiering in 1938, distinguished Hollywood films had treated war with disillusionment and pacifistic protest. From 1930, when *All Quiet on the Western Front* appeared, to *A Farewell to Arms,* a memorable film based on Hemingway's novel several years later, Hollywood set a standard for war drama from which any call to arms would have seemed a woeful regression.

Two films possessing distinction, it is true, took account of the seething East. One of them was *The General Died at Dawn,* a melodrama of internal conflict in China written for Paramount by that dynamic dramatist Clifford Odets, leader of the advance guard of the Broadway theatre. Particular merit pertained to Odets' explosive dialogue and vigorous action. At an earlier time this screenplay could have been given to the reader as an example of robust style, but its theme of banditry seemed less appropriate today. The issue of Japanese aggression and its threat to America seemed too remote to our national mentality to be as yet filmed by any major studio, and the subject was left to the little film groups on the fringe of Hollywood. The other film, the superb MGM screenplay of Pearl Buck's *The Good Earth,* which it is a privilege to present in this book, had the singular qualities of a human document. The tenacious Chinese people, who had hitherto appeared largely as melodramatic caricatures on the screen, could at last be known to the American movie public. The Chinese land, hitherto a country of exotic adventure to this public, became known at last as a reality of unceasing tillage and struggle against the elements, as the mother of strong men and women whose hopes and labors are our own. Probably because the background had to be described in more than usual detail for those who filmed the screenplay, the text is one of the most rewarding as reading literature. However, the story content of *The Good Earth* antedated the conflict with Japan.

To say that Hollywood, which included in its personnel an increasing number of wide-awake writers, actors and directors, was oblivious of the European scene would be incorrect. Nazism was engulfing Germany and rolling on to the very borders of France and filtering into Austria. Italian fascism was pouring into Ethiopia and trickling steadily into the Balkans. Then the two tides met during the civil war in Spain, and became one. But the nation's, and so the film capital's, official attitude was one of tenacious neutrality, and the film business still had a foreign market that it would rather not jeopardize. When, in 1938, Walter Wanger produced *Blockade,* John Howard Lawson's impassioned screenplay on Spain, which proved to be the first phase of the present war, he was credited with exceptional courage, and there were some who no doubt considered him foolhardy. Although the film never mentioned the Loyalist and the Franco parties by name, and used spy melodrama and a love story for protective coloration, partisans of either cause took the hint. There was acclamation from one side, denunciation, as well as boycotting, from the other. Walter Wanger deserved much credit but the studios were still betwixt the devil and the deep blue sea when they looked at the political situation in Europe. It was expected more recently that the filming of *For Whom the Bell Tolls* would overcome the difficulties of treating a still controversial subject, but when after some suspensive delay the film finally appeared, its great success and high acclaim from many critics did not remain unchallenged by those who expected Hollywood to take a stronger stand during a war against fascism.

The spread of fascist reaction could not, of course, be averted by nation-wide ostrich tactics. Discreetly Hollywood had even lifted its head in 1936 and 1937, with *The Legion of Terror* and *Black Legion,* to take note of the backwash of fascism in this country. And the infiltration of Nazi espionage was recognized in John Wexley's Warner Brothers film *Confession of a Nazi Spy,* a screenplay written with something of the bludgeoning power that had characterized this author's earlier stage plays *The Last Mile* and *They Shall Not Die.* After the Fall of 1939, moreover, events moved rapidly across the Atlantic, and as Nazi boots and Nazi planes covered more of the surface of Europe American sympathy and concern began to be reflected on the screen—and with receding resort to subterfuges. On a fateful day in December 1941 America herself was forced into a two-pronged war, and henceforth the film industry entered the arena with no holds barred except in the case of still nominally neutral nations. In 1942, according to Mr. Crowther's count* of 291 films of feature length reviewed by him, eighty were "generally concerned with the war," and as no inventory of them can be taken here Mr. Crowther's summation in the *Times* may suffice— not only for 1942 but for 1943, at least up to the date of this writing: "Some have been plain melodramas and comedies about soldiers or spies; some have been tasteless distortions of the cruel realities of the war. And a few have been fine expositions of the things it has done to human lives."

The bulk of the war-pictures fell into three more or less well defined categories—those dealing with Britain's stand against the *Luftwaffe* after Dunkerque, those representing the sufferings and mounting underground resistance of the occupied countries, and those enacting our own active involvement on outlying battlefronts or on the high seas.

The simple human concerns of a people at war were realized in MGM's *Journey for Margaret,* an affecting picture of children during the air assault on Britain. The adult side of the story of English resistance appeared in *Mrs. Miniver.* When the reader turns to this beautifully written, essentially original screenplay based on the characters and background of Jan Struther's book, he may observe many qualities that can give literary value to film writing. What emerges instantly from the film, which is limited only by a certain British upper-class moderation, is the unexpected gathering strength of people who prefer a way of life remote from violence, their unpretentious heroism, the persistence of precious sympathy and grace in the midst of anguish and struggle—the invincible residuum of the sweetly sane and the human.

Among the films that dealt with the more harassed and provoked occupied nations, those that retained the *Mrs. Miniver* values—broadly conceived—have the strongest claims to literary value and remembrance. *Edge of Darkness,* in which a Norwegian town rises up against an overbearing Nazi garrison and wipes it out, is stirringly active but possesses perhaps too little transfiguration of mere event. *The Moon Is Down* is most memorable in its portraits of men whose quiet humanity rises to the white fire of defiance and self-sacrifice; and it is the representation of acts of tyranny repugnant to the conscience of civilization that lifts *Hangmen Also Die* above the level of the usual in war films.

I have preferred to represent the higher levels of creative objectivity and understanding through the more intellectual qualities of Dudley Nichols' original screenplay, *This Land Is Mine,* cited by the Writers War Board as "one of the most eloquent statements of the basic issues of the war," called by John McManus "the first United Nations anti-fascist film," and praised by Howard Barnes as the picture that weighs "the ultimate verities behind the present struggle." Here the setting is universalized though recognizably French, and the presentation of the issues of freedom of thought and government are joined with sound representation of inner conflict in characters when faced with a crisis. A study of a minor Quisling who is not a melodramatic villain, of a timorous schoolmaster who moves waveringly to a hero's and martyr's destiny, of a mother whose fixation upon her son excludes all thought of other people

---

* Mr. Crowther included a few films made in Britain, such as *The Invaders, One of Our Aircraft is Missing* and Noel Coward's *In Which We Serve.* Our account, of course, is limited to American-made pictures.

and of country, a picture of a conqueror who seeks to bind and corrupt a people's will with Machiavellian subtlety as well as with the force of bullets, a glimpse of people whose weakness was responsible for their defeat and whose growing strength will entitle them to the recovery of their freedom—all this pertains to maturity in film creation. This treatment of a subject which could more easily whip Hollywood's melodramatic disposition into an emotional lather may serve as "journey's end" for this altogether too long, if also altogether too rapid, excursion through American film history. The story of our own engagements with the enemy is on the different plane of actual professional war, and cannot be expected, of course, to follow the analytical approach of *This Land Is Mine.* But even in this category, screenplays like *Wake Island,* Nichols' *Air Force,* and Lawson's *Action in the North Atlantic* bear the same mark of adulthood, even if they would not appear to such good advantage as reading scripts. Straightforward, free of bravado and chauvinistic puerilities, they are exalting as well as exciting mementoes of democratic heroism. In time, no doubt, they will be succeeded by works of greater inner penetration and intellectual force, devoted to the present world travail. The American film's record warrants this benign prophecy, which the forthcoming *Watch on the Rhine* and *The North Star,* both by Lillian Hellman, will probably sustain.

V.

In closing, some words to the reader—mostly a summation of what has already been implied—may be in order: No great effort need be made to distinguish between the meaning of the few technical terms incorporated in the flow of the action. What matters is that a certain continuity or relationship is established between one scene and another—a fact that is invariably obvious in the text. A film flows, of course, without interruption, and the division of the screenplay text into numbered parts (this occurs only after a sequence is completed and "fades out") is intended merely for convenience in reading.

In some cases we have by-passed good films that would not read well enough —action films that excelled chiefly in photographic effects, film musicals, and animated cartoons. Some screenplays seemed too close a transcript of a novel or play, two of them were omitted for reasons of political strategy in the war period, others would have caused too much duplication of style and content. Also, as there were no adequate transcripts of the great silent films, the selections start with the year 1930. And of course, it is to be borne in mind that the book confines itself to films produced in American studios. — In any case, I must make it clear that Mr. Nichols is to be absolved from any responsibility for shortcomings entirely my own, but is entitled to a substantial part of any credit that may accrue, as his guidance has been invaluable. The selection of the material was in all cases initiated by me, and there is no immodesty in the presence of his screenplays in the volume. Faults in the preparation of the texts are all mine, too, as Mr. Nichols has been far too busy *creating* films to give his time to the humdrum task of editing them.

The title, selected for its brevity, is, I need hardly add, a misnomer. A more correct, if barbarous, title would read "Twenty of the Best American Film Plays We Were Able to Secure After Two Years of Maddening Effort."

If nothing else has been accomplished, at least the public has been given a number of interesting screen texts in this publishing enterprise, the potential value of which won the approval of Mr. Walter Wanger, president of the Academy of Motion Picture Arts and Sciences. In the illuminating book *Film and Theatre,* published in 1936, Mr. Allardyce Nicoll of Yale University wrote regretfully, "There can be no hope of turning to the text and to the stage directions as we turn to those of a *Hamlet* or *A Doll's House* . . . It is not perhaps too much to dream of screenplays similarly published—not with technical directions calculated solely for the studio but with a re-rendering of these directions in terms of a general reading public." Mr. Nicholl's dream has been fulfilled in part perhaps sooner than he expected, though of course neither he nor the present editor has ever regarded the reading of the text as equivalent to the experience of seeing the film in motion. Whether the dream has been worth fulfilling is a question best left to the reader himself. I am also certain that the screenplays would have read better had their authors themselves prepared them for publication. My own work was severely circumscribed by fear of tampering with the text and losing its cinematic qualities in too free a transcription. But this effort may pave the way for more successful presentations, more confidently recreated. The book is, in a sense, a venture into the unknown. But if the adventure proves even half as exciting and provocative to the reader as it did to the editor, neither of them will have reason for any marked disappointment.

New York, July, 1943.

THE WRITER AND THE FILM
By DUDLEY NICHOLS

Ours is the age of the specialist. In older times, before the Machine, men did specialize of course in the various arts and crafts—but those arts and crafts were not themselves subdivided into specialized functions. The man who painted did the whole job himself: he was a painter. So with the silversmith and the shoemaker and the sculptor. But the Machine changed all that. The painter today has his materials prepared by other people, by specialized craftsmen or tradesmen, and only wields those materials in the final function of creating pictures. The etcher buys his copper plates already prepared and seldom pulls his own prints. The sculptor models in clay and leaves to others the pouring of the mould or the work of the pointing-machine. The writer no longer turns out beautiful manuscripts that may be passed from hand to hand: he pounds out a script on the typing machine and passes it on to his publisher's printing factories. In science and art we have become specialized, narrowing our fields of study and work because those fields have grown too enormous for the single mind to embrace. We are all specialized, for better or worse, and it is only natural that the one new art form which the Machine has produced should be the most highly specialized of all. For the motion picture *is* an art form, whether it be so regarded or not.

By rights this new art form should be controlled by individuals who include all functions in themselves. They should be film-makers. But the functions are too diversified and complex to be handled by the creative energy of one individual. So we break them down into separate crafts—writing, directing, photography, scenic designing, optical printing and camera effects, cutting and assembly of film, composing music, recording, mixing and re-recording, the making of *dissolves* and *fades* and other transitions: into an immense field of works which require the closest and most harmonious collaboration to produce excellent results.

This in effect is detrimental to film as an art form and an obstacle to the development of artists who wish to work in film. It is too much the modern factory system: each man working on a different machine and never in an integrated creation. It tends to destroy that individuality of style which is the mark of any superior work of art. Individual feeling gets lost in the complicated process and standardized products come off the assembly line. I make these remarks by way of preface to point out that there is only one way to overcome the impediments—and that is to learn the whole process, to be a master craftsman within the factory system; to be, in short, a film-maker first and a writer or director or whatever-you-will afterwards.

Of course this poses a dilemma: one cannot under our present system make films without first learning to make films: and the only way to learn film-making is by making films. Hence by subterfuge of one sort or another one must enter the field as a specialized apprentice and try to learn all the other specialized functions, so that the individual may return to his specialty with the full equipment of an artist. A screenwriter should have knowledge of direction, of cutting, of all the separate functions, before his imagination and talent can be geared effectively and skillfully to his chosen line of work. Fortunately we are none of us so competent as we might be, if for no other reason than that Hollywood is too bent on turning out films to take the time to train its artisans to the top of their bent. As a result there is always room for the interested new worker. A writer can find a place, even without knowing much about film-making, and if he has a secret star he may glitter into sudden prominence even without knowing the slightest thing about film-making.

Hollywood is used to taking works of fiction in other forms and translating them into film; and for this and other reasons the talented writer does not feel encouraged to write directly for the screen. This is to be regretted because the screenplay might easily become a fascinating new form of literature, provided the studio heads acquired sufficient taste to recognize and desire literary quality. Yet there have been, there are, and there will continue to be written, screenplays of quality and sincerity; if only because of the dogged efforts of writers and directors who set themselves high goals and persist frequently against their own material interests.

There is one other circumstance which makes it difficult for the screenplay to be enjoyed as a literary form in itself: it is not and never can be a finished product. It is a step, the first and most important step, in the process of making a film. One might also say that a play is not a finished product for the theatre; yet a play relies entirely on the word; idea, character and action are projected by means of the word; and a skillful playreader can enjoy wonderful perform-ances within the theatre of his own imagination. The screenplay is far less a completed thing than the play, for the skilled screenwriter is thinking con-tinuously in terms of film as well as of the word. The filmwriter must be a film-maker at heart, and a film-maker thinks and lives and works in film. That is the goal, the end-result—eight or ten thousand feet of negative patched together to reproduce, upon its unreeling, an illusion of a particular kind and quality. It is that illusion which the film-maker—and in this instance the filmwriter—is pursuing when he begins to gather together his first nebulous conception.

The truth is that a motion picture undergoes a series of creations: first it is a novel, a short story, or a conception in the mind of the screenwriter. That is the point of departure. Next the filmwriter takes the first plunge toward the finished negative by building the story in screenplay form. This rough draft, at least in the case of the present writer, will undergo two or three revisions, each nearer to the peculiar demands of cinema. With luck the director, who must have an equal sympathy for the drama to be unfolded, will be near at hand during the groundwork, contributing cinematic ideas here and there, many of which will not appear in the script but will be remembered or recorded in other notes to be used when the time comes.

Ordinarily, when all ideas of cinematic treatment have been unearthed and the final draft completed, the writer's work is ended and the creation of the projected film moves on into the hands of the director and other specialists; which is most unfortunate for the writer, for his education ceases in the middle of an uncompleted process. Let us, however, follow along with the writer who is able to follow the progress toward film. The second creation of the film is in its casting, which can help or hinder the designed illusion. The novelist is a fortunate artist who creates his characters out of the flesh and spirit of his own imagination; they need never be distorted by being embodied by living beings who necessarily have other traits and characteristics. But the playwright and the filmwriter must have real persons to present their characters—and identity is not to be found. There have been ideal casts, but even the most perfect will alter indefinably the shape and mood and meaning of an imagined drama. Now each of the actors chosen must create his part of the film; and the sum of their parts creates another phase of the film. Implicated in this is the personality of the director, who creates the film by combining (in his own style which may not be the style of the writer) the contributions of the writer and actors.

It is at this point that a peculiar thing occurs, which must be understood to discriminate between the stage and screen. I have never seen this pointed out before, even by film-workers, and it needs to be set down; stage and screen are entirely different media because the audience participates in quite opposite ways. The theatre—and I use the term to embrace both stage and screen—demands an audience. It is not complete without its audience and even derives much of its power from its audience. Every stage actor knows this and has experienced it. The audience identifies itself with the actor, its collective emotions rush out in sympathy or buffet against him with antipathy like an unseen electric discharge—which increases the actor's potential so to speak, permitting him to give back his feelings with increased power, which again returns to him, like the oscillating discharge of an electric machine. It is these heightened moments that create unforgettable experiences in the theatre when the drama is great both in its literary power and in its acting. Here the relationship between the actor and the audience is direct and the intelligent actor can grow by what he experiences, just as the audience does.

Now, curiously, this does not at all exist in the cinema; but it does exist at the stage of cinema-making we are discussing. On the stage of a film studio the actor still has an audience, though a small one: the half-hundred people who comprise "the crew"—grips, juicers, cameramen, script girl, and all the familiar others. But if he acts in such a style as to affect this audience solely he is lost, for his actual audience is miles away and they will see him only through the uncaring single eye of the camera that looks on like a tripod man from Mars. The significant thing is that at this point there is an invisible transition taking place that will break all the rules of the stage and impose new ones of the screen.

The actors are creating a film, not a stageplay, even though it appears they are making a stageplay. We are not cameras, we are living beings, and we cannot see things with the detachment of a lens. In the early days of sound-film I observed many failures because this was not understood. The action seemed good on the sound-stage, but it did not come off on the screen.

The reason is that the audience, the film-theatre audience, participates in an entirely different way with the projected images of a film. This is not so strange if we remember that a motion picture film will give just as good a performance in an empty theatre as in a full one. It will not, of course, be so moving or so amusing to a single spectator as it will to that same spectator in a crowded theatre: members of an audience need each other to build up laughter, sorrow and joy. But the film is unaffected, it does not in itself participate as do the actors on a stage. It is a complete illusion, as in a dream, and the power of identification (which you must have in any form of theatre) must be between audience and the visually projected re-actor.

Unthinking people speak of the motion picture as the medium of "action"; the truth is that the stage is the medium of action while the screen is the medium of reaction. It is through identification with the person *acted upon* on the screen, and not with the person acting, that the film builds up its oscillating power with an audience. This is understood instinctively by the expert film-makers, but to my knowledge it has never been formulated. At any emotional crisis of a film, when a character is saying something which profoundly affects another, it is to this second character that the camera instinctively roves, perhaps in close-up; and it is then that the hearts of the audience quiver and open in release, or rock with laughter or shrink with pain, leap to the screen and back again in swift growing vibrations. The great actors of the stage are actors; of the screen, re-actors.

If anyone doubts this let him study his own emotions when viewing a good film; an experienced film-maker can do this automatically at the first showing of a film, but very likely others will have to go a second time, or check it over in mental review. I recently did this with some lay friends after a showing of Noel Coward's *In Which We Serve,* and it was illuminating to find out that they had been most deeply moved by reactions, almost never by actions: the figure of a woman when she gets news her husband has been lost at sea, the face of an officer when told his wife has died. (And how cunningly Noel Coward had that officer writing a letter to his wife when the radioman entered with the news; the reaction then was continued to the point where the officer goes on deck and drops the letter into the sea, a reaction extended into action, so to speak.) In the same film one of the most affecting scenes was the final one where the captain bids goodbye to the remainder of his crew; and while this appears to be action, the camera shrewdly presented it as reaction: It is the faces of the men, as they file past, that we watch, reaction to the whole experience even in their laconic voices and in the weary figure of the captain.

Now this brings us to the next phase in the making of a film, or next "creation" if you prefer. I have said that a film ensues from a series of consecutive creations, which were enumerated from the first stage of concept to the point where the first recording on film is made. The director, the actors, the art director, the cameraman, the whole crew in fact, have followed after a fashion (but with many inevitable departures in which the writer, if he is fortunate, has collaborated) the final draft of the screenplay. Now you have perhaps a hundred thousand feet of film, the negative of which is safely tucked away in the laboratory while you have for your study a "work print." Now the film is in the cutting room, in a thousand strips or rolls, some strips perhaps only a few feet long, some four or five hundred. Every foot-and-a-half is a second of time in the projection room, and you do not want your finished film to be one second longer than is determined by dramatic necessity. Every good artist, every good workman, has a passion for economy: if you can do a thing in one stroke, don't use two; if a certain mood or atmosphere is essential to the illusion you are after and it requires a hundred strokes, use them. By elimination and rough assembly the cutter patches together a work-print, say, fourteen thousand feet long: two or three miles of strips of film, assembled consecutively on seventeen or eighteen reels. That is the first creation of the cutter.

Now another job begins, one of the most delicate and sensitive jobs of all. Rough cutting was determined by the screen writer but this did not and could not include the interior cutting of the director and cameraman. Since terminology is not yet standardized in film-making, I designate the cutting of the director on the set the "montage," using a word which the Russians apply for all cutting or editing. It is determined by the style of the director, his feeling for photographed images, the way he rests the eye of the audience or gives it sudden pleasures, moving in at different angles on his scenes and characters. Had the writer attempted to anticipate the director and set down all this montage on paper, his script would have become a useless mess; for this interior cutting cannot be determined precisely (though many attempt to do so) before arriving on the set. This manner of shooting and handling the camera must be guided by spontaneous feeling and by discoveries made on the set. I for one have no patience with the growing method of having every camera-shot sketched beforehand so that director, cameraman and actors can work by rote.

It destroys that spontaneity of feeling which is the essence of film art; though of course many films are so unimportant that it does not matter how they are shot: they never were alive at any moment.

To continue following our film through to its finish, you now have a rough assembly which is far overlength, the cutting of which was largely determined by the script and direction. But this is only a provisional arrangement. Everything depends on the final cutting, elimination and rearrangement. And the only compass to guide you in this final orchestration of images is your own feeling. The final test is to project the film on the screen and see how the arrangement you have made affects you. By this time you have grown weary of every foot of the film but you doggedly keep your feeling fresh as the only touchstone, until you have wearily said, "That's the best we can make of it." And I promise you disappointment in every film, for it is far removed from the perfection of imagination, as is everything that is realized.

Yet you have not finished with this scratched-and-tattered work-print, which now looks as tired as yourself. There are two final stages, sound and music recording, and finally the re-recording of the whole thing. Sound is a magic element and part of your design as a screenwriter or director has been the effect of sound. In the case of *This Land Is Mine,* which was directed by a great film-maker, Jean Renoir, one of the focal points of the drama was a railroad yard, and as we could not shoot the action in an actual railroad yard we determined to create it largely by sound. We spent endless days gathering sound-tracks and trying to orchestrate our sounds as carefully as if they were music. And finally came the scoring of the music itself, not a great deal of it but every bar important: choosing Mendelssohn here, Mehul there, original composition for the rest, and getting it re-recorded in a harmonious whole.

At last you have, say nine or ten thousand feet of image-film and a second sound-film of the same length synchronized to the split-second. Every frame of both films is numbered, corresponding with the thousands of feet of negative in the laboratory. You send your final work-prints to the laboratory, the negative is cut, the sound track printed alongside—and you receive your first composite print. And, if the composite print checks, your work is finished and the negative is shipped, ready for countless prints to be made and released through the theatres of the world. This is what you set out to make—or rather help to make—when you began writing your rough draft of a screenplay. And this is what you had to keep in mind all the wearisome while.

All the foregoing must sound tedious—and yet it has been only lightly touched upon. What it shows, and what I meant to show, is why film-makers must specialize. You could not have done this work alone, carried the film through all its successive creations. A hundred specialists have aided you and carried through the work. It is a vast collaboration in which, if you have ever achieved a satisfactory film, you must accept a humble part. Yet the collaboration must always have a dominant will and personality if the work is to be good. Sometimes two people can work together with such sympathy and shared attitude that they can achieve a common style; and these two people must, I believe, be the writer and director.

Undoubtedly this all seems to be an exhausting introduction to an anthology of screenplays, but I feel it is essential to an understanding of what screenplays are and what their intention is. They are not complete works in themselves, they are blueprints of projected films. Many factors may have intervened to make the finished films different from the designed illusion, for better or worse.

The most noticeable feature of a skillful screenplay is its terseness and bareness. This is because the eye is not there, the eye which fills and enriches. Nor does the screenwriter waste time with much descriptive matter or detailing of photographic moods. These have all been discussed at length with the director, art director and others. It is the writer's job to invent a story in terms of cinema or to translate an existing story into terms of cinema. He creates an approximate continuity of scenes and images, suggesting cinematic touches where he can. He will write "close-up" of a character without setting down the most important thing, which is what that character is feeling during that close-up. That is because the context clearly shows what the character is supposed to be experiencing. The director will take care of that. If he is an artist the director will submit the actor to that experience while photographing the close-up, by playing the actual scene out of range of the camera.

Writing for the screen, if long practiced, also seduces one to write dialogue in a synoptic fashion, which may show itself to the eye when printed on a page, but should never reveal itself to the ear when spoken from the screen. Stage dialogue, no matter how wonderful in quality, cannot be directly shifted to the screen; it must be condensed, synopsized. The reason is obvious; on the stage the actor depends for projection upon the word: on the screen he relies upon visual projection. And it is hard to describe visual projection in a screenplay; that must be left to the director and cast.

For those readers who are preoccupied with the technique of screenwriting I should say this volume is most valuable; not for any secrets which can be made manifest in prefatory remarks but for the screenplays themselves. For the motion pictures made from these scripts have been widely distributed and seen, and here one can study the films in their first stage of creation and then compare them with the end-results. Also in the case of adaptations of books, stories and stageplays one may refer to the original source and study the steps of action taken by the screenwriter.

For this very reason, I assume, Mr. Gassner had selected *The Informer* for inclusion in this volume. Unhappily no permission to publish the screenplay has been forthcoming from the author of the original novel; hence the reader, to trace the process of translation from the novel form into terms of film, will have to compare another of these published screenplays with its source material, e.g. *The Grapes of Wrath* or *The Good Earth* or *Wuthering Heights*.

However, almost everyone who is seriously interested in the cinema has seen *The Informer* on the screen, and as the film projects the screenplay with great fidelity I am prompted by Mr. Gassner to explain the method by which I translated Mr. O'Flaherty's novel into the language of film. In 1935 this was in a certain sense an experimental film; some new method had to be found by which to make the psychological action photographic. At that time I had not yet clarified and formulated for myself the principles of screenwriting, and many of my ideas were arrived at instinctively. I had an able mentor as well as collaborator in the person of John Ford and I had begun to catch his instinctive feeling about film. I can see now that I sought and found a series of symbols to make visual the tragic psychology of the informer, in this case a primitive man of powerful hungers. The whole action was to be played out in one foggy night, for the fog was symbolic of the groping primitive mind: it is really a mental fog in which he moves and dies. A poster offering a reward for information concerning Gypo's friend became the symbol of the evil idea of betrayal, and it blows along the street, following Gypo; it will not leave him alone. It catches on his leg and he kicks it off. But still it follows him and he sees it like a phantom in the air when he unexceptedly comes upon his fugitive friend.

So it goes all through the script; some of the symbolism is obvious, much of it concealed except from the close observer. The officer uses a stick when he pushes the blood-money to Gypo at headquarters, symbolic of contempt. The informer encounters a blind man in the dark fog outside and grips his throat in sudden guilt. The blind man is a symbol of the brute conscience, and Gypo releases him when he discovers the man cannot see. But as Gypo goes on to drown his conscience in drink, the tapping of the blind man's stick follows him; we hear it without seeing the blind man as Gypo hears his guilt pursuing him in his own soul. Later when he comes face to face with his conscience for a terrifying moment he tries to buy it off—by giving the blind man a couple of pounds, a lordly sum. . . . But I shall not continue this account of a screenplay that cannot be presented in this book. Sufficient to say that the method of adaptation in this instance was by a cumulative symbolism, to the very last scene where Gypo addresses the carven Christ, by which the psychology of a man could be made manifest in photographic terms. In this case I believe the method was successful. —I might add that I transferred the action of the drama from its original, rather special setting to a larger and more dramatic conflict which had national connotations. Whether that was any gain I do not know. Size of conflict in itself I hold to be unimportant. It is the size of characters within a conflict and how deeply they are probed that matters.

So much for the adaptation. For an example of an original screenplay you may examine *This Land Is Mine*. It is not easy to trace the origin of a story. It is easier to say that a work of fiction happens. But that is not exact, for a story comes into existence because of some inner necessity of the individual. Every human being contains creative energy, he wants to make something. A man may make a chair, or a pair of shoes, a masterpiece of painting, or a pulp-magazine story; precisely what he makes is dictated by his imagination, temperament, experience and training. But the act of creation is dictated by desire. I should imagine this runs through the universe as a law, since it is so with man, and man is a part of the universe. If the Supreme Will desires to build a Universe, the Universe will "happen." It is all a matter of the degree of intensity of desire. A story-teller is passionately interested in human beings and their endless conflicts with their fates, and he is filled with desire to make some intelligible arrangement out of the chaos of life, just as the chairmaker desires to make some useful and beautiful arrangement out of wood. Frustrate those creative desires in man and his forces will be turned toward destruction: for energy cannot remain unexpended, it is not static, it must swing one way or another.

That is one aspect of the motivation of the story-teller. Another motive is the desire to entertain, to communicate one's own personality by holding the delighted attention of others. This might appear to be nothing more than egotism, yet it can rise above self and have an exalted purpose. Jesus of Nazareth could have chosen simply to express Himself in moral precepts; but like a great Poet he chose the form of the parable, wonderful short stories that entertained and clothed the moral precept in an eternal form. It is not sufficient to catch man's mind, you must also catch the imaginative faculties of his mind.

Yet stories for the purpose of entertainment alone are commonplace fiction and can only be redeemed by a dazzling style, a sheer delight in the materials of story-telling, a touch of the poet. The cinema is only in its infancy as an art form, and its usual fate so far has been to be used only for entertainment and making money. Because it is a very costly medium it will continue to be employed for making money until money ceases to be the great desire of the people of the world. Most motion pictures are mere entertainment and accordingly the screenwriter can work only with half of himself: his satisfaction must usually be in artistry of manner, skill in the way he accomplishes his work, without much regard for the content of the film. For this reason the story of serious intention can rarely be written within a film studio; and for this reason serious writers in other fields, novelists and dramatists, have given great aid to the development of the cinema. For the powers-that-be will buy the film rights of a serious novel if it seems to have enough readers, and though the contents of the novel are sometimes perverted by film censorship or bad taste, enough remains to make a notable motion picture. But the screenwriter who desires to make an original story has no readers, at least not for the projected story. If the story proposes to make a serious statement beyond mere entertaining it will seem off the beaten track and the writer will very likely meet opposition. It is for this reason and this reason alone that so few stories of any account *originate* within Hollywood. In France, before the war, the film-makers were largely their own entrepreneurs and for this reason produced many brilliant original works. They were story-tellers functioning freely in the new medium of film.

Nevertheless the serious film-writer cannot resign himself to Hollywood's barriers against original work designed for the screen. The average Hollywood entrepreneur is an intelligent man, and it is up to writers and directors to prove to him that films which probe into the chaos of life can be successful. John Ford made *The Informer* in spite of studio resistance; even after its completion it was held to be a failure and a waste of money by certain entrepreneurs. But the film did go out and make a profit. There *was* an audience for the realistic film. In spite of this and other instances I will say in all fairness that usually the studio heads have been right and the film-makers wrong: because usually the film-makers have not measured up to their task and their responsibilities when granted freedom. They have not measured up or they have wanted both money and freedom, which are incompatible. It is an axiom that no one will pay you to be a free artist. You are hired for profit—that is common sense. Very well, then, you must stop working for salary, you must devote yourself to the task in hand as do the novelist and dramatist, and only be recompensed if the film makes a profit. Economically I believe the writer and director will fare even better with this arrangement than under the salary system. Spiritually they will become whole men and work with integrity.

I have gone into this divagation to illuminate the fact that *This Land Is Mine* was originated and made into film under just such circumstances: Jean Renoir and I had gained the respect and confidence of an unusually intelligent studio head and he gave us complete freedom to make a film, without any other impediment than our own shortcomings.

There are a thousand ways to initiate a film but it may be worth while to set down our process in this instance. We both wished to lift entertainment to a higher level. We believed that a film should say something as well as hold attention. There are many themes knocking about within the head of every writer. Jean Renoir had lately come from Europe and was a volcano of feeling as a result of what he had seen and experienced. We were dissatisfied with the films against Fascism we had seen, because they all seemed distortions which dealt only with the surface of evil. A good film against Fascism ought to seem shocking even to the German and Italian peoples, and we were convinced that the sensational films on this theme made in Hollywood would only be laughed at, as we in America laugh at the Nazi film *Oom Kruger*. Exaggeration misses the point and becomes risible. Only the truth is shocking.

But to accomplish our purpose we knew we had to deal in ideas, to attempt to penetrate to the core of what had happened in Europe, and that was not easy; because ideas need words for their expression and an excess of words is a stumbling-block to good cinema technique. Words are not entertaining to the mass, who need simpler images.

All this while our imaginations were at work, simply because we had addressed ourselves to the task. Finally we began to clothe our ideas in characters. At first the characters had little life, and the film seemed like a morality play (which even the final film is in its essence) . But gradually as the people of our imagination began to grow, they took on more human traits and eccentricities, and the ideas which had begotten them began to sink out of sight into their hearts, where the motivating ideas of every one of us lie hidden. Once the work had progressed this far the drama began to create itself—that is the only way one may describe it. You may stare at white paper, you may walk the floor, but you are obsessed finally and driven on to a conclusion, digging deep or following the contours of your people, according to your capacity. For myself I must say that I discovered many truths about one modern aspect of good and evil by wrestling with the lives of these characters. I discovered how plausible and attractive Fascism can appear to some people, and if we do not face that truth we can never triumph over it. I saw how much of it there was around me, how much of it perhaps in my own heart. That too must be faced if we are to win over evil.

There was no villain in the drama. We had ruled him out at the outset, for there are no villains in life but only human beings embodying elements of good and evil. I should like to be more explicit about the writing of this screenplay, for the guidance of those who may be interested in this form of writing, but I cannot. We did not say, *Now we make this move to bring about that situation, Now we have that action to heighten suspense.* Instinctively the writer who deals with dramatic forms knows how to create character, situation and suspense; but if this is not done almost unconsciously then you are guilty of mere fabrication. It is very easy to analyze the methods of dramatic construction, but I will not bore the reader with such rationalizations: they have been written fully and expertly by William Archer and Prof. George Pierce Baker, to name only two The true guide for the searcher along this line is the work of the great dramatists.

In any case, proceeding as I have lightly sketched above, we finally arrived at the screenplay which you will find within this volume. It does not contain the voluminous notes we made on sets. music and a score of other things. It contains the flaws we had foreseen from the start, a talkativeness that is contrary to my own instinctive sense of cinema. But the ideas had been embodied within characters, their actions and reactions; a conflict of ideas had become a conflict of human beings; it had become a simple drama of good and evil, the conflict of two contradictory drives in the hearts of men—for power and for freedom. Its form had become that of the mystery play—in a sense, the medieval mystery play as well as the modern: men and women, their lives woven together by fate and circumstance, committed certain seemingly inevitable acts which we do not quite fathom or understand; then in the final act the mystery of a man's life is solved by the protagonist and we suddenly understand everything.

It may be interesting to compare this screenplay with the finished film. You will notice many alterations and elisions, which only prove that a screenplay is not a completed thing in itself but only the first (though most important) stage in the creation of a film. We found, for example, that we had to pare down dialogue still further. Not only because the screen is a laconic medium, but because the film had turned out to be a sort of mystery play and we found that here and there the characters told too much about their lives; some things had to be held back to hold attention more tightly. Whole sequences had to be dropped out in the cutting room, because they extended the film beyond its correct artistic length. There is no absolute rule for length—a film determines its own length finally in the cutting room. Our first assembled print was more than fourteen thousand feet in length; our final cut was around 9300 feet, about an hour and forty minutes of running time, an average length for "feature films" nowadays.

This, then, is the genesis of an original film. Each writer and director will originate a story in a different way, but the process described is typical. If there is one grave fault in the approach of Hollywood to a story, it is the tendency to regard a story as an invention, as something cleverly contrived, with the accent on a novel arrangement of actions rather than on characters. A story is always characters, imagined people who take on a life of their own, plus what is in the back of the mind of the author. As the cinema becomes more concerned with human character we shall have better films and a truer approach to comedy as well as tragedy. In the main, Hollywood has hardly touched humor yet, still relying to a large extent on the "gag," which as someone has said "is the wig of wit and not the real hair which grows close to the brain."

I have not attempted to explain the "secrets" of screenwriting—because there are no secrets. There are certain prescribed forms, but the forms are not final. Others will come along and do better work as we come to understand more clearly the peculiar demands of cinema. Meanwhile those people who may become interested in screenwriting as a vocation must study the best examples of screenplays available and then have a try at it themselves. I do not touch on technical jargon, such as *fade, lap dissolve, dolly* or *pan,* because they are quite unnecessary to the craft. And no matter where you write them into your script the completed film will make its own demands in the cutting room and very likely change your imagined plan. This terminology can safely be ignored, it is merely a convenience.

We try to formulate a classical form for the cinema but there are no final rules. Film continuity can be as broken and erratic as a dream, if it is a potent dream and by some inner need requires that sort of continuity. There are really no rules, in spite of what Hollywood will tell you. A film in its continuity is a stream of images and if they combine into an exciting, intelligible whole you have accomplished your purpose. Most film technique today is very imperfect, as we are still groping for the pure form. The cinema is still a giant in chains and a giant who has not even yet stood up and shaken his chains. Those chains are censorship, commercialism, monopoly, specialization—all the faults that are indigenous to industrial society and not just characteristic of the cinema. If control of film production should fall into the hands of government, any government, the old chains will be struck off only to be replaced by heavier ones. And because of the potent propaganda effect of film that is a danger. No art, including the wonderful new medium of sound-film, can serve one set of ideas: it must be free or perish.

IT HAPPENED ONE NIGHT

(A Columbia Picture)

Screenplay by
ROBERT RISKIN

Based on a Novelette by
SAMUEL HOPKINS ADAMS

Produced and directed by FRANK CAPRA

———

C a s t

PETER	Clark Gable
ELLIE	Claudette Colbert
ALEXANDER ANDREWS . .	Walter Connolly
SHAPELEY	Roscoe Karns
KING WESTLEY	Jameson Thomas
DANKER	Alan Hale
BUS DRIVER	Ward Bond
BUS DRIVER	Eddie Chandler
LOVINGTON	Wallis Clark
HENDERSON	Harry Bradley
REPORTER	Charlie Brown
3rd AUTO CAMP OWNER .	Harry Holman
HIS WIFE	Maidel Turner
ZEKE	Arthur Hoyt
ZEKE'S WIFE	Blanche Frederici
STATION ATTENDANT . .	Irving Bacon
GORDON	Charles C. Wilson
FLAGMAN	Harry Todd

Film Editor - GENE HAVLICK

IT HAPPENED ONE NIGHT

PART ONE

* The HARBOR at Miami Beach fades in, providing quick views of yachts, aquaplanes, and luxurious ship-craft lying at anchor in the calm, tranquil waters of tropical Florida. This dissolves to the NAME PLATE on the side of a yacht, reading "ELSPETH II," and this in turn to a YACHT CORRIDOR where a steward is standing in front of a cabin door, near a small collapsible table upon which there is a tray of steaming food. He lifts lids and examines the contents. A heavy-set sailor stands guard near the cabin door.

STEWARD. Fine! Fine! She ought to like this. (*To the guard*) Open the door.

GUARD (*without moving*). Who's gonna take it in to her? You?

STEWARD. Oh, no. (*Turning*) Mullison! Come on!

The view widens to include Mullison, a waiter. His eye is decorated with a "shiner."

MULLISON. Not me, sir. She threw a ketchup bottle at me this morning.

STEWARD. Well, orders are orders! Somebody's gotta take it in. (*He turns to someone else.*) Fredericks!

The view moves to another waiter, who has a patch of bandage on his face.

FREDERICKS. Before I bring her another meal, I'll be put off the ship first.

STEWARD'S VOICE. Henri!

The view moves over to a Frenchman.

HENRI (*vehemently*). No, Monsieur. When I leave the Ritz you do not say I have to wait on crazy womans.

The view moves back to include the Steward and the others grouped around him.

ANOTHER WAITER (*a Cockney*). My wife was an angel compared to this one, sir. And I walked out on *her*.

GUARD (*impatiently*). Come on! Make up your mind!

A petty officer approaches. He is blustering and officious, but the type that is feeble and ineffective. His name is Lacey.

LACEY (*talking quickly — staccato*). What's up? What's up?

There is a fairly close picture of the GROUP, featuring Lacey and the Steward.

STEWARD. These pigs! They're afraid to take her food in.

LACEY. That's ridiculous! Afraid of a mere girl! (*He wheels on the steward.*) Why didn't you do it yourself?

STEWARD (*more afraid than the others—stammering*). Why—I—well, I never thought about—

LACEY (*shoving him aside*). I never heard of such a thing! Afraid of a mere girl. (*Moving to the tray*) I'll take it in myself.

They all stand around and watch him, much relieved. He picks up the tray and starts toward the door of the cabin.

LACEY (*as he walks—muttering*). Can't get a thing done unless you do it yourself. (*As he approaches the door*) Open the door.

We see him next at the CABIN DOOR as the guard quickly and gingerly unlocks it.

LACEY. Afraid of a mere girl! Ridiculous!

Lacey stalks in bravely, the tray held majestically in front of him, while the steward and waiters form a circle around the door, waiting expectantly. There is a short pause, following which Lacey comes hurtling out backwards and lands on his back, the tray of food scattering all over him. The steward quickly bangs the door shut and turns the key as the waiters stare silently.

The scene dissolves to the MAIN DECK of the yacht, first affording a close view of a pair of well-shod masculine feet, as they pace agitatedly back and forth. Then as the scene draws back, the possessor of the pacing feet is discovered to be Alexander Andrews, immaculately groomed in yachting clothes. In front of him stands a uniformed Captain, but Andrews, brows wrinkled, deep in thought, continues his pacing.

ANDREWS (*murmuring to himself*). On a hunger strike, huh? (*A grunt*) When'd she eat last?

CAPTAIN. She hasn't had a thing yesterday—or today.

ANDREWS. Been sending her meals in regularly?

CAPTAIN. Yessir. She refuses them all.

ANDREWS (*snappily*). Why didn't you jam it down her throat?

CAPTAIN. It's not quite that simple. (*He shakes his head.*) I've dealt with prisoners in my time, but this one—

ANDREWS. Absurd! (*Muttering*) All this fuss over a snip of a girl. (*Suddenly*) I'm going down to see her myself.

He leaves with determination, followed by the Captain, and both are then seen walking in the direction of the cabin, Andrews grim.

CAPTAIN. This is dangerous business, Mr. Andrews. After all, kidnapping is no child's play.

But Andrews ignores him and merely stares grimly forward. They arrive in front of the cabin door, where Lacey is brushing himself off, and where a couple of waiters are picking up the last pieces of the broken dishes.

ANDREWS. What's this! What's happened here?

LACEY (*pathetically*). She refused another meal, sir.

ANDREWS. Get another tray ready. Bring it here at once. (*To the guard*) Open the door.

The Guard unlocks the door and Andrews enters.—Then we get a view of the CABIN at the door, as Andrews enters and closes the door behind him. He looks around and his eyes light on his prisoner, following which the view swings over to ELLIE, a beautiful girl in her early twenties. At the moment, she holds a small vase over her head ready to heave it, and her eyes flash angrily. At sight of her new visitor, however, she lowers the vase and sets it on a small table.

ELLIE. What do *you* want?

Andrews doesn't stir from the door.

ANDREWS. What's this about not eating?

ELLIE (*sitting*). I don't want to eat! (*Raising her voice*) And there's one more thing I don't want! Definitely! That's to see you.

She lights a cigarette. Andrews watches her a moment.

ANDREWS. Know what my next move is? No more cigarettes.

ELLIE. Why don't you put me in chains?

ANDREWS. I might.

ELLIE (*now seen at close range*). All right! Put me in chains! Do anything you want! But I'm not going to eat a thing until you let me off this boat!

She stares petulantly out at the blue sky, but Andrews comes over and sits beside her.

ANDREWS (*tenderly*). Come on, Ellie. Stop being silly. You know I'm going to have *my* way.

ELLIE (*moving away*). I won't stand for it! I won't stand for your running my life! Why do you insist on it!

ANDREWS (*still tender*). You ought to know why. Because—

ELLIE (*interrupting*). Yes. I know. (*She's heard it a million times.*) Because I'm your daughter and you love me. Because you don't want me to make any mistakes. Because—

ANDREWS (*joining in*). Because marrying that fool King Westley is—

ELLIE (*snappily*). You're wasting your time. I'm already married to him.

ANDREWS (*sharply*). Not so far as *I'm* concerned, you're not. (*They are interrupted by a knock on the door.*)

ANDREWS. Yes?

The door opens and several waiters parade in with trays of steaming food.

ELLIE (*starting for them; threateningly*). How many times have I told you not to bring any food in here.

The waiters back up, frightened, but Andrews saves them.

ANDREWS. Wait a minute! Don't get excited! This isn't for you. (*To the waiters*) Put it right here.

Ellie glares at her father, and wanders over to the window seat, while the waiters occupy themselves setting the table. Andrews putters around the food, lifting the lids from which tempting aromas emanate. He shuts his eyes, murmuring "oohs" and "ahs."

A close-up of ELLIE shows her, too, drinking in the inviting aromas; and for a moment she weakens. A close view of ANDREWS shows him glancing toward Ellie to see her reaction; whereupon Ellie's face (again appearing in a close-up) freezes. Then Andrews and the waiters come into view.

FIRST WAITER. Anything else, Monsieur?

ANDREWS. No. Everything seems quite satisfactory. I may want some more of that delicious gravy. I'll ring.

WAITER. Very good, Monsieur.

The waiters bow their way out as Andrews pecks at the food.

ANDREWS (*making clucking noise*). Heavenly!

Now Ellie appears in the foreground, with Andrews at the table in the background.

ELLIE (*disdainfully*). Smart, aren't you! *So* subtle.

ANDREWS (*chewing on a mouthful of food*). If Ghandi had a chef like Paul,

it would change the whole political situation in India.

ELLIE. You can't tempt me. (*Shouting unnecessarily*) Do you hear? I won't eat!

ANDREWS (*quietly*). Please. I can't fight on an empty stomach. Remember what Napoleon said.

ELLIE. I hope you're not comparing yourself to Napoleon. He was a strategist. *Your* idea of strategy is to use a lead pipe.

Andrews eats silently while Ellie rants at him, walking around and puffing vigorously on her cigarette.

ELLIE (*muttering*). Most humiliating thing ever happened to me. (*Shuddering*) A bunch of gorillas shoving me in a car! That crowd outside the justice of the peace—must have thought I was a criminal—or something.

A close view of ANDREWS intercuts with part of Ellie's speech. At the end of her speech he smacks his lips, enjoying the food with too great a relish. Then the two are seen together.

ELLIE (*after a pause—strongly*). Where are you taking me?

ANDREWS (*carelessly*). South America.

ELLIE (*aghast*). South America!

ANDREWS. We leave Miami in an hour. Soon's we get some supplies aboard.

ELLIE (*threateningly*). You'll have a corpse on your hands! That's what you'll have. I won't eat a thing while I'm on this boat.

ANDREWS (*buttering bread*). In that event, we won't need so many supplies.

ELLIE (*exasperated*). What do you expect to accomplish by all this? I'm *already* married!

ANDREWS. I'll get it annulled.

ELLIE. You'll never do it! You *can't* do it!

ANDREWS (*now seen close as he speaks between snatches of food*). I'll do it if it takes every penny I've got. I'll do it if I have to bribe that musical comedy Justice of the Peace! I'll do it—if I have to prove that you were dragged in, staggering drunk. You probably were. (*He smacks his lips.*) Mmm—mmm. This filet mignon is divine!

ELLIE (*seen with her father*). What've you got against King Westley?

ANDREWS. Nothing much. I just think he's a fake, that's all.

ELLIE. You only met him *once*.

ANDREWS. That was enough. Do you mind handing me the ketchup?

ELLIE. You talk as if he were a gigolo— or something.

ANDREWS (*rising—reaching for ketchup*). Never mind—I'll get it myself. (*He falls back in his chair.*) Gigolo? Why, you took the word right out of my mouth. Thanks.

ELLIE (*seen closer now, with Andrews*). He's one of the best fliers in the country. Right now he's planning a trip to Japan.

ANDREWS. You're going to finance him, I suppose.

ELLIE. Why not? Look what he's doing for aviation. It takes courage to do what he does. And character! At least he's accomplished something worthwhile. I suppose you'd like to have me marry a business man. Well, I hate business men —particularly if *you're* a shining example.

He grins, not at all offended, knowing she doesn't mean it.

ELLIE. Your whole life is devoted to just one thing. To accumulate more money. At least there's romance in what *he's* doing.

ANDREWS (*unequivocally*). He's no good, Ellie, and you know it. You married him only because I told you not to.

ELLIE (*strongly*). You've been telling me what *not* to do since I was old enough to remember. (*Screaming*) I'm sick of it!

And as Andrews ignores her, she starts moving around the table toward him.— Next she appears sitting on the edge of Andrews' chair, and she throws her arm around his shoulder.

ELLIE (*pleading sweetly*). Aw, listen, Dad. Let's not fight like this any more. I know you're worried about me—and want me to be happy. And I love you for it. But please try to understand. You're not being fair, darling. This isn't just a crazy impulse of mine. King and I talked about it a lot before we decided to get married. Look—why can't we give it a trial—let's say—for a year or so. If it's wrong, King and I will be the first to know it. We can get a divorce, can't we? Now, be a dear, and let me off the boat. Keeping me prisoner like this is so silly.

Andrews has been listening silently throughout the speech, giving no indication of his feelings in the matter.

ANDREWS (*unimpressed*). You'll be set free when the marriage is annulled.

A close-up of ELLIE, her eyes blazing angrily, shows her slowly edging away from her father, while he continues.

ANDREWS' VOICE (*carelessly*). So there's no use being a stubborn idiot.

ELLIE (*hissing*). I come from a long line of stubborn idiots!

ANDREWS (*again seen with her; calmly*). A time will come when you'll thank me for this.

ELLIE (*wildly*). I *won't* thank you! I'll *never* thank you!

ANDREWS. Please don't shout.

ELLIE. I'll shout to my heart's content! I'll scream if I want to.

ANDREWS (*reaching for it*). Ah! Cocoanut layer cake. Nice and gooey, too. Just the way I like it.

He is about to insert the first bite in his mouth when Ellie, her temper vanishing completely, overturns the small serving table, dumping its contents into her father's lap. The movement is so unexpected that Andrews, the fork still suspended near his mouth, stares at her stupefied. What realizing what she has done, his eyes flash in anger.— Dropping his fork, he rises and goes over to her, while she stands facing him defiantly. Without a word or warning, he slaps her a stinging blow across the cheek. For a moment she doesn't stir, her eyes widening in surprise, and staring at him unbelievingly. Then turning abruptly, she bolts out of the door. Andrews remains motionless, his eyes shutting painfully; it is the first time he has•struck her, and it hurts.

ANDREWS (*calling*). Ellie! (*And he starts for the door.*)

Next on the DECK, at the open cabin door, Andrews is seen, staring off at something and an amazed, frightened look comes into his eyes. Then, as viewed from his position at the cabin door, Ellie appears standing on the rail; and with a professional dive, she leaps into the water.

A full view of the DECK reveals the crew and the officers scurrying around, several of them shouting: "Somebody overboard!"

ANDREWS. It's my daughter! Go after her!

CAPTAIN (*shouting*). Lower the boats!

General excitement reigns; several of the crew dive into the water; others release the boat lines. Following this Ellie is seen swimming furiously against the giant waves. Next she appears as a small speck in the distance, while half a dozen of the crew are swimming in pursuit.

At the SIDE OF THE YACHT one of the boats has already been lowered, and two men jump in and grab the oars.— Then men seem to be gaining on Ellie. In the distance several small motor boats are anchored, and over the sides of the boats their owners are fishing. Ellie seems to be headed in their direction.

One of the motor boats appears closer. A middle-aged man sits on the stern, holding lazily to his line, his feet dangling in the water as the boat is tossed around by the turbulent waves. ELLIE is then again seen swimming. She looks back, and the next scene shows the men rowing toward her, and gaining on her. Thereupon we see Ellie ducking under the water.

The middle-aged fisherman is suddenly startled by Ellie's face which appears from under water, right between his legs. Ellie puts her finger up to her lips, warning him to shush, and he is too dumbfounded to say anything. As the pursuing boats come near, Ellie ducks under the water again and the boats scoot right by the fisherman. Then Ellie's head bobs up; she peers ahead of her, and seeing that her pursuers have passed her, she smiles victoriously.

ELLIE (*to the fisherman*). Thanks. (*And she starts swimming toward shore.*)

The scene dissolves to the DECK of the YACHT as Ellie's pursuers clamber aboard, Andrews waiting for them.

A MAN. Sorry, sir. She got away.

ANDREWS (*disappointed but proud*). Of course she got away—too smart for you.

CAPTAIN. What a hell cat. No controlling these modern girls. (*Murmuring*) They're terrible!

ANDREWS (*resentfully*). Terrible! Nothing terrible about her. She's great! Marvelous youngster! Got a mind of her own. Knows just what she wants. (*Smiling*) She's not going to get it though. She won't get very far. Has no money.

CAPTAIN. What about that diamond wrist watch she had on—she can raise some money on that?

ANDREWS (*his face falling*). Holy Smoke! I forgot all about that. (*To the officer by his side*) Send a wireless at once: "Lovington Detective Agency. Daughter escaped again. Watch all roads—air transports and railroad stations in Miami. Have your New York office keep tabs on King Westley. Intercept all messages. Want her back at all costs!"

OFFICER. Yessir.

The view draws in to afford a close-up of ANDREWS staring out at the sea, his face wreathed in a broad smile; then this fades out.

PART TWO

The RAILROAD STATION of an active terminal in Miami fades in. The view moves down to the entrance gate to the trains, passengers hurrying through it; then picks out two men, obviously detectives, who have their eyes peeled on everyone passing through. Then the view affords a glimpse of ELLIE, who stands watching the detectives. This scene wiping off, we see an AIR TRANSPORT, with several planes tuning up in the background. As passengers file through, several detectives stand around in a watchful pose. This scene wiping off, the front of a WESTERN UNION OFFICE comes into view. Several people walk in and out. At the side of the door, two detectives are on the lookout.

This scene also wipes off, revealing the WAITING ROOM of a BUS STATION. Over the ticket window there is a sign reading "BUY BUS TICKETS HERE," and a line forms in front of it. Here too there are two detectives.

FIRST DETECTIVE. We're wastin' our time. Can you picture Ellie Andrews ridin' on a bus?

SECOND DETECTIVE. I told the old man it was the bunk.

The view moves from them to ELLIE, who stands behind a post and is watching the two detectives apprehensively.—As the two (viewed from her position) stand by the ticket window, one of them turns toward her. Thereupon, we see her slipping behind a post, concealing herself. Just then a little old lady approaches her.

OLD LADY. Here's your ticket, ma'am.

ELLIE. Oh, thank you. Thank you very much. (*She takes the ticket and change from the old lady, and hands her a bill.*) Here.

OLD LADY. Oh, thank you. Thank you.

ELLIE. When does the bus leave?

OLD LADY. In about fifteen minutes.

ELLIE. Thank you.

She picks up a small overnight bag from the floor and hurries away. She crosses to the entrance of the waiting room and disappears through the doors. The view then swings over to a telephone booth near the entrance. Clustered around the booth are half a dozen men of varied appearance. The inside of the booth is lighted, and a young man, Peter Warne, waves his hands wildly as he shouts into the phone, although it is impossible to hear what he is saying. A close inspection of the men surrounding the booth (the scene contracting to a close view) reveals them as being slightly and happily intoxicated. A short man approaches the door of the booth.

SHORTY. Hey, what's going on here? I'd like to use that phone.

FIRST MAN (*a reporter*). Shh! Quiet. This is history in the making.

SHORTY. What?

FIRST MAN. There's a man biting a dog in there.

SECOND MAN (*drunker than the rest*). Atta-boy, Petey, old boy! Atta-boy!—

PETER'S VOICE. I'm not going to stand for this any longer. In a pig's eye, you will!—

GROUP. Is that so? That's telling him, Petey old boy.

A close view of PETER WARNE in the telephone booth gives evidence of his having also imbibed freely.

PETER (*shouting into the phone*). Listen, monkey-face—when you fired me, you fired the best newshound your filthy scandal sheet ever had.

And the scene cuts to a New York NEWSPAPER OFFICE where the night editor, Gordon, his sleeves rolled up, sits at his desk, shrieking into the phone.

GORDON. Say, listen, you wouldn't know a story if it reached up and kicked you in the pants. (*Listening*) Yeah? Sure, sure, I got your copy. Why didn't you tell me you were going to write it in Greek? I'd start a new department.

PETER (*again seen close at the phone*). That was free verse, you gashouse palooka!

GORDON (*at the phone in the newspaper*

office). Free verse, huh? (*Shouting*) What the dickens was free about it? It cost this paper a gob of dough. Well, I'm here to tell you, it's not gonna cost us any more.

PETER (*in his phone booth*). That's okay by me! 'Cause as far as I'm concerned, I'm through with newspapers! See? I'm through with stupidity! I'll never write another newspaper story, for you or anybody else, if I have to starve. (*After a pause*) Yeah? What about my novel! When I get through with that—

GORDON (*in his office*). When you get through with that, I'll have a beard down to my ankles. (*At this point, Gordon's secretary enters.*)

SECRETARY. Mr. Gordon—

GORDON (*looking up*). Huh?

SECRETARY. Did you know he reversed the charges on that call?

GORDON. What! (*Into the phone*) Say, listen *you*! When you get back to New York, take my advice and stay f-a-r away from this office—unless you don't care what happens to that funny map of yours. (*He bangs up the receiver viciously and glowers at the phone.*)

In the PHONE BOOTH Peter reacts to the phone being hung up on him. But he goes right on for the benefit of the boys.

PETER (*into the dead phone*). Oh, so you're changing your tune, eh? Well, it's about time. But it's going to do you no good, my tough friend. It's a little too late for apologies. I wouldn't go back to work for you if you begged me on your hands and knees! I hope this is a lesson to you!

He snaps up the receiver with a great pretense of outraged pride, following which the view expands to include his public.

MEN. Atta-boy, Peter. That's telling him, Peter.

The gang is full of admiration for the courageous way he talked to the boss as Peter staggers out of the booth.

PETER. Give me any of his lip, will he? Huh! I guess he knows now what I think of his job. (*Expansively*) Is my chariot ready?

FIRST MAN. Your chariot awaiteth withouteth, oh mighty King.

MEN. Make way for the King. Long live the King. Make way.

With head held high, he struts majestically out of sight, followed by his admirers, following which the scene dissolves to the BUS STATION. His inebriated admirers stand around the entrance to a bus, while Peter stands on the steps, his suitcase in his hand.

PETER (*making a grand speech*). That's right, my friends. Cling to your jobs! Remain slaves the rest of your lives! Scum of the earth! Newspaper men! Not me! When I'm basking in the glorious arms of the Muse—what'll *you* be doing? Chasing news. You miserable worms! For what? A mere pittance! My heart goes out to you. (*With arms extended, and in tremolo voice*) Good-bye. (*And with this he turns his back and enters the bus.*)

MEN (*in the same spirit*). Goodbye, O mighty King! Peace be with you, Courageous One!

ANNOUNCER'S VOICE. All aboard. Philadelphia, New York. All aboard.

GROUP. Look out. Get back. Farewell. Farewell.

PETER. Scram.

The scene cuts to the INTERIOR of the BUS as viewed from the front, the view moving forward, passing the conglomerate unprepossessing human beings who occupy the seats. Every space is taken and the occupants seem hot and uncomfortable, which adds to their uninviting appearances. Mothers cling to crying babies. A Swedish farm hand and his young wife are already busy opening their basket of food prepared for the long journey. A surly-looking hoodlum traveling alone, is slumped in his seat, his cap drawn carelessly over his eyes. The moving view passes these and other characters until it reaches the one unoccupied seat in the car, unoccupied except for several bundles of newspapers.

Standing before the seat is Peter, his suitcase in his hand, speculating as to what disposition to make of the newspapers.

PETER (*calling*). Hey, driver! How about clearing this stuff away!

Several passengers (seen from his position in the back) crane their necks to scrutinize the intruder. Through a glass partition the driver can be seen receiving his last minute instructions from a superintendent, who stands on the running board, their voices indistinguishable. In answer to Peter's request, the driver glances back indifferently, and continues talking to the superintendent. A close view of PETER shows him arching his eyebrows, an amused acknowledgment of the disdainful attitude of the driver. He drops his suitcase and starts forward. Then we see him arriving at the glass partition, and Peter taps playfully on the pane with his fingernails, whereupon the driver turns and pulls the window down a few inches.

DRIVER (*annoyed*). Whadda you want!

PETER (*pleasantly*). If you'll be good enough to remove those newspapers I'll have a seat.

DRIVER (*irritably*). Okay! Okay! Keep your shirt on, young feller. (*With which remark the driver turns away from him.*)

PETER (*looking at the back of the driver's neck for a moment, then confidentially*). Just between you and me, I never intended taking it off.

He wheels around uncertainly and swaggers jauntily down the aisle toward the empty seat. En route he bestows genial smiles upon several of his disgruntled fellow passengers, and he stops in front of a robust lady who at the moment is breast-feeding her baby while a lighted cigarette dangles from her lips.

PETER. Personally, I was raised on a bottle. (*As the woman looks up at him, perplexed*) When I was a baby, I insisted on it. You know why?(*As the woman stares up stupidly*) I never liked the idea of getting cigarette ashes in my eyes.

He moves forward, leaving the woman unable to make head or tail of it; and assuming that he's crazy, she shrugs her shoulders and turns her attention to the baby.

Now PETER arrives at his seat, and whistling softly, raises the window. Unhurriedly, he picks the newspaper bundles up one by one and flings them out of the window. They hit the sidewalk below with a dull thud. Thereupon a close view of the DRIVER shows him reacting violently to Peter's unprecedented cheek, and starting down from his seat.

PETER has now cleared the seat of all the newspaper bundles and still whistling his favorite melody, he picks up his suitcase preparatory to placing it in the rack overhead. At this point, the driver enters the side door of the bus.

DRIVER (*pugnaciously*). Hey, wait a minute!

Peter, his arms holding the suitcase over his head, turns and glances at the driver, a quizzical look in his eyes.

DRIVER (*coming forward*). What do you think *you're* doing!

PETER (*turning*). Huh?

DRIVER (*bellowing*). The papers! The papers! Whadda you mean throwin' 'em out!

PETER. Oh—the papers—

He slowly lowers his arms and deposits the suitcase on the floor.

PETER (*now seen close, with the Driver*). That's a long story, my friend. You see, I don't like sitting on newspapers. I did once and all the headlines came off on my white pants.

DRIVER. Hey, whadda you tryin' to do— kid me?

PETER. Oh, I wouldn't kid *you*. On the level, it actually happened. Nobody bought a paper that day. They followed me all over town and read the news from the seat of my pants.

DRIVER. What're you gonna do about the papers? Somebody's gotta pick 'em up.

PETER (*turning to his suitcase*). It's okay with me. I'm not arguing.

DRIVER (*pugnaciously*). Fresh guy, huh! What you need is a good sock on the nose.

PETER (*turning back to him*). Look here, partner. You may not like my nose. But I do. It's a good nose. The only one I've got. I always keep it out in the open where anybody can take a sock at it. If you decide to do it, make sure you don't miss.

During his speech, Ellie enters from the rear and plunks herself into Peter's seat. Unseen by Peter, she places her small bag beside her.

DRIVER (*answering Peter; weakly*). Oh, yeah?

PETER. Now, that's a brilliant answer. Why didn't *I* think of it? Our conversation could have been over long ago.

DRIVER. Oh, yeah?

PETER. If you keep that up, we're not going to get anywhere.

DRIVER. Oh, yeah?

PETER (*exhausted*). You win!

Smiling, he turns to sit down. But the smile dies on his face when he finds his place occupied by Ellie, who stares out the window.

PETER (*now at close range, with Ellie*). Excuse me, lady—(*slowly*)—but that upon which you sit—is mine.

Ellie glances up at him—then down at her buttocks.

ELLIE (*eyes flashing*). I beg your pardon!

PETER. Now, listen. I'm in a very ugly mood. I put up a stiff battle for that seat. So if it's just the same to you—(*gesturing with thumb*) scram.

ELLIE (*ignoring him—calling*). Driver!

The driver, who has stopped to witness this new altercation, returns.

ELLIE. Are those seats reserved?

DRIVER (*pleased to discomfort Peter*). No. First come, first served.

ELLIE (*dismissing the whole thing*). Thank you. (*Peter, thwarted for a moment, just glares at her.*)

PETER (*also calling*). Driver!

DRIVER. Yeah?

PETER. These seats accommodate two passengers, don't they?

DRIVER (*hating to give in*). Maybe they do—and maybe they don't.

Peter lifts Ellie's overnight bag off the seat and drops it on the floor. Part of her coat covers the small space by her side. This he sweeps across her lap.

PETER. Move over, lady. This is a "maybe they do."

He plops into the seat, the other passengers around them heaving a high of relief. Ellie flashes him a devastating look and deliberately turns her back on him. But Peter suddenly looks down toward the floor, following which a close-up AT THEIR FEET reveals that Ellie's bag on the floor annoys Peter. With his foot he slowly moves it over to her, and Ellie's foot is seen pushing it back, whereupon Peter viciously kicks it over to her side again. Next we see Ellie glaring at him, picking up her bag, and standing on the seat depositing it on the rack overhead. But just then the bus starts forward with a lurch which unbalances her, and she falls backward right in Peter's lap. Their noses almost touch. Their eyes meet, and they glare at each other hostilely. Ellie quickly scrambles off and gets back in her seat, turning her back on him.

PETER (*amused*). Next time you drop in bring your folks.

This dissolves to a COUNTRY ROAD, and the bus sways perilously as it speeds through the night, following which the view dissolves to the INTERIOR of the BUS, revealing Peter slumped in his seat, his hat drawn over his eyes. Ellie has her head thrown back, trying to sleep. But the swaying bus causes her head to roll from side to side uncomfortably, and finally she gives up.

ELLIE (*an order*). Tell that man not to drive so fast. (*At which Peter just cocks his head slightly.*)

PETER. Are you talking to me?

ELLIE. Yes. Tell that man to drive slowly.

Peter stares at her a moment, resenting her officious manner.

PETER (*pleasantly*). Okay.

And much to her surprise, he sighs deeply and relaxes to his former position, shutting his eyes. She glares at him crushingly.

The scene dissolves to another view of the BUS, disclosing the driver, and suddenly the bus comes to a stop.

DRIVER (*sticking his head in to face the passengers*). Rest station! Ten minutes!

The view draws back as some of the passengers rise. The men stretch their legs, and the women straighten out their skirts. A close view of Peter and Ellie then shows her rising. Peter accommodatingly shoves his feet aside for her to pass, and Ellie starts up the aisle. But she suddenly stops; looks back, first at her bag and then at Peter; decides to take her bag with her, and returns to take it. She reaches for it on the rack, Peter watching her, amused.

The scene dissolves to the outside of the REST STATION with several passengers walking briskly back and forth. The place is dimly lit by one or two lamp-posts, and Peter can be seen leaning against one of these posts, smoking a cigarette. The scene moving in, a close view of Peter shows him stealing a glance in the direction of Ellie. And a view, from his angle, reveals Ellie in the shadow of the bus, her bag at her feet. She slowly turns her head toward Peter and then quickly averts it.

PETER (seen close) speculates about her. He glances around the place, and the scene moves about, following his gaze. It takes in the other passengers, all obviously poor and uncultured. The moving view reaches Ellie. The contrast is perceptible. Thereupon, we see Peter reacting with comprehension: No doubt about it! She doesn't belong with these passengers. —Then suddenly he sees something which startles him, and we see what it is: Directly in back of her, the young hoodlum passenger slyly lifts her overnight bag from the ground and starts running with it. Ellie is oblivious of his actions. PETER springs forward.

Ellie sees Peter coming toward her and is perceptibly startled. But Peter whizzes by her, and this amazes her even more. She shrugs her shoulders, perplexed, and resumes her smoking. In a few seconds Peter returns, puffing breathlessly.

PETER. He got away. I suddenly found myself in the middle of the brush and not a sign of the skunk.

ELLIE (seen close with PETER) doesn't know what he's talking about. She looks at him, puzzled.

ELLIE. I don't know what you're raving about, young man. And, furthermore, I'm not interested.

PETER (*taken aback*). Well—of all the— well— (*Hard*) Maybe you'll be interested to know your bag's gone.

At this, Ellie wheels around and stares at the spot where her bag had been.

ELLIE. Oh, my heavens! It's gone!

PETER (*sarcastically*). Yeah. I knew you'd catch on eventually.

ELLIE. What happened?

PETER. That cadaverous-looking yegg who sat in front of us, just up and took it. Boy, how that baby can run!

ELLIE. What am I going to do now?

PETER. Don't tell me your ticket was in it?

ELLIE (*opening her purse*). No, I've got that, all right. But my money. All I have here is four dollars. I've got to get to New York with it.

PETER. You can wire home for some money when we get to Jacksonville.

ELLIE. Why, no—I— (*catching herself*) yes . . . I guess I will.

PETER (*starting out*). I'll report it to the driver. About your bag, I mean.

ELLIE (*quickly*). No. I'd rather you didn't.

PETER. Don't be a fool. You lost your bag. The company'll make good. What's your name?

ELLIE. I don't want it reported!

PETER. Why, that's ridiculous! They're responsible for everything that—

ELLIE (*hotly*). See here, can you understand English! I don't want it reported! (*She starts away.*) Please stay out of my affairs! I want to be left alone. (*With which she disappears from the scene.*)

A close-up of PETER shows him glaring after her.

PETER (*mumbling*). Why, you ungrateful brat!

The scene dissolves to the BUS, where all the passengers are scattering back to their seats; Peter is already seated, when Ellie arrives. —A close view then shows her standing uncertainly for a moment, speculating whether to cross over his legs to get to her place by the window. Peter feels her presence by his side and glances up. She tosses her head and plants herself in the seat in front of him, vacated by the young man who stole her bag. Peter takes the affront with a shrug and slides over gratefully to the coveted spot near the window.

The scene dissolves to a close view of Ellie and a recently arrived fat man next to her. She has her head thrown back in an effort to sleep, but the fat man, his hands clasped over his protruding stomach, snores disgustingly, and the rumble of the flying bus accompanies him. Suddenly the bus careens, the fat man falls against Ellie, and she awakens with a start and pushes him back. The fat man's snoring goes on uninterrupted, and Ellie relaxes again; but in a few seconds the procedure is repeated, and Ellie is beside herself. She looks around for somewhere to flee.

PETER, seated in back of her, in his customary slumped position, opens his eyes slightly. It is apparent he has been watching her for some time, for he grins at her discomfiture. Ellie's head turns in his direction and the grin leaves Peter's face. He shuts his eyes and pretends to be asleep.—Ellie glances at Peter to make certain he is asleep. The fat man falls against her again and it is all she can stand. She starts to rise. Peter sees her coming and deliberately puts his hand on the seat next to him, still pretending to be asleep. Just as Ellie starts to sit, she notices his hand and is embarrassed. Gingerly she picks up his limp hand and places it on his knee. She then slides into the seat, sighing with relief, whereupon Peter opens his eyes and is amused. Slowly his head turns—and he scrutinizes her, soberly and appraisingly. —Ellie slowly turns her head for a glimpse of Peter—and is startled to find him gazing at her. She turns forward, her jaw set forbiddingly.

The scene dissolves to the view of a ROAD. It is dawn, and in the distance, against the horizon, the bus, a mere speck, makes its lone way over the deserted country. This dissolves to a large SIGN, reading "JACKSONVILLE," and then into the BUS affording a close view of ELLIE and PETER. They are both asleep, her head resting comfortably on his shoulder, Peter's topcoat thrown over her. Then the view draws back. The bus is empty except for Ellie and Peter, the last few passengers are just leaving.

PETER's eyes slowly open. He looks down at the head on his shoulder and grins. With a sigh, he shuts his eyes again and resumes his slumber.— Next, at the front of the bus, the DRIVER stands staring at Peter and Ellie in this intimate position, · and his mouth twists knowingly.

DRIVER (*murmuring*). Oh, yeah?

ELLIE stirs, squirms a little uncomfortably, and with a sleepy grunt shifts her position. Just as she settles down, her eyes open. She stares out of the window with unseeing eyes, and then closes them dreamily, giving the impression that, still half conscious, she is trying to recall where she is. Apparently she does, for her eyes suddenly snap open and she lifts her head. Finally (in a scene including Peter), Ellie realizes that she has been sleeping on his shoulder, whereupon she straightens up, embarrassed.

ELLIE. Oh, I'm sorry— (*Feebly smiling*) Silly, isn't it?

She looks around, and her finding herself alone with Peter, adds to her embarrassment.

ELLIE. Everybody's gone.

She lifts her arms to adjust her hat and becomes conscious of his coat over her, which slips. She stares at it thoughtfully for a moment—then at Peter.

ELLIE (*realizing that he put it there*). Oh, thank you. (*She hands him his coat; ill at ease.*) We're in Jacksonville, aren't we?

PETER. Yes.

ELLIE (*nervously*). That was foolish of me. Why didn't you shove me away?

PETER. I hated to wake you up. (*She glances at him speculatively.*) How about some breakfast?

ELLIE. No, thank you. (*She rises, anxious to get away.*) Thank you so much.

Most uncomfortably, she edges away from him toward the front of the bus, Peter watching her leave, his interest definitely provoked.

The scene cuts to the STAND as Ellie emerges from the bus. At the foot of the steps is the driver.

ELLIE. How much time have I?

DRIVER. About a half hour.

ELLIE. I'm going over to the Windsor Hotel.

Peter appears in the door of the bus in the background, and a close view then shows him stopping to listen as he sees Ellie talking to the driver.

DRIVER'S VOICE. The Windsor! You'll never make it in time.

ELLIE'S VOICE. You'll have to wait for me.

DRIVER'S VOICE (*aghast*). Wait for you!

A smile flits across Peter's face; then a wider view shows Ellie leaving the driver.

ELLIE (*as she goes*). Yes. I may be a few minutes late.

She disappears from sight, leaving the driver staring at her, dumbly; and Peter, standing in back of the driver, shakes his head in amazement.

The scene dissolves to the BUS STAND later that morning—at the same spot where the bus had previously been. It is no longer there, however. A huge crowd fills the space, and the view moving down through the crowd, singles Ellie out. She has just arrived and looks around helplessly. Finally she spots a uniformed terminal guard and approaches him.

ELLIE (*now next to the Guard*). Where's the bus to New York?

GUARD. Left twenty minutes ago.

ELLIE. Why, that's ridiculous! I was on that bus—I told them to wait!

GUARD. Sorry, Miss. It's gone. (*And he turns his back on her.*)

Ellie's face clouds. The crowds surge about her. She looks around thoughtfully. Suddenly her eyes open in surprise at something she sees, and the view then moves over to Peter, who sits on his suitcase, looking toward Ellie.

PETER. Good morning.

Peter is in the foreground, the guard is seen in the background. Ellie stares at Peter, perplexed.

PETER. Remember me? I'm the fellow you slept on last night.

ELLIE. Seems to me I've already thanked you for that. (*Turning to guard*) What time is the next bus to New York?

GUARD (*turning*). Eight o'clock tonight.

ELLIE. Eight o'clock! Why, that's twelve hours!

GUARD. Sorry, Miss.

The Guard leaves the scene, and Ellie's disappointment is apparent.

PETER (*sarcastically*). What's the matter? Wouldn't the old meanies wait for you? (*Ellie glares at him, disdaining to reply. This angers him, and he continues hotly.*) Say, how old are you, anyway? Don't you know these buses work on schedule? You need a guardian.

ELLIE (*starting away*). What are you excited about? *You* missed the bus, too.

Peter looks at her a moment before replying.

PETER (*quietly*). Yeah. I missed it, too.

There is a close view of the two. She turns to him. Her interest is provoked by his tone of voice. She glances up into his face.

ELLIE. Don't tell me you did it on *my* account! (*A pause*) I hope you're not getting any idea that what happened last night is— (*She interrupts herself.*) You needn't concern yourself about me, young man. I can take care of myself.

PETER. You're doing a pretty sloppy job of it. (*He reaches in his pocket.*) Here's your ticket.

ELLIE (*surprised*). My ticket?

PETER. I found it on the seat.

ELLIE (*taking it*). Oh, thank you. Must have fallen out of my pocket.

While she is putting the ticket away in her purse, Peter speaks:

PETER. You'll never get away with it, Miss Andrews. (*This is a shock to Ellie.*)

ELLIE (*weakly*). What are you talking about?

PETER. Just a spoiled brat of a rich man. You and Wesley'll make an ideal team.

ELLIE (*bluffing it through*). Will you please tell me what you're raving about!

PETER. You'll never get away with it, Miss Andrews. Your father'll stop you before you get half way to New York.

ELLIE. You must have me confused with—

PETER (*interrupting*). Quit kidding! It's all over the front pages, You know, I've always been curious about the kind of a girl that would marry King Westley.

He pulls a newspaper out of his pocket and hands it to her. Ellie glances at the headline hurriedly.

PETER (*while she reads*). Take my advice —grab the first bus back to Miami. That guy's a phony.

ELLIE (*looking up at him*). I didn't ask for your advice. (*She hands the paper back.*)

PETER. That's right. You didn't.

ELLIE. You're not going to notify my father, are you?

PETER (*looking at her squarely*). What for?

ELLIE. If you play your cards right, you might get some money out of it. (*A disdainful expression crosses his face.*)

PETER. I never thought of that.

ELLIE (*frantically*). Listen, if you'll promise not to do it, I'll pay you. I'll pay you as much as he will. You won't gain anything by giving me away as long as I'm willing to make it worth your while. I've got to get to New York without being stopped. It's terribly important to me. I'd pay now only the only thing I had when I jumped off the yacht was my wrist watch and I had to pawn that to get these clothes. I'll give you my address and you can get in touch with me the minute you get to New York.

PETER (*furious*). Never mind. You know I had you pegged right from the start; you're the spoiled brat of a rich father. The only way you can get anything is to buy it. Now you're in a jam and all you can think of is your money. It never fails, does it? Ever hear of the word "Humility?" No, you wouldn't. I guess it never occurred to you to just say, "Please mister, I'm in trouble. Will you help me?" No; that'd bring you down off your high horse for a minute. Let me tell you something; maybe it'll take a load off your mind. You don't have to worry about me. I'm not interested in your money or your problem; you, King Westley, your father, you're all a lot of hooey to me.

He turns his back on her and leaves. A close-up of ELLIE shows her staring after him, her eyes blazing angrily.

In a TELEGRAPH OFFICE, Peter addresses a girl operator as he drops a telegram on the counter, which she reads.

PETER (*brusquely*). You send telegrams here?

OPERATOR (*recognizing him apparently; sarcastically*). I'm just fine thanks, and how are you? (*Reading*) To "Joe Gordon, care of New York Mail, New York. Am I laughing. The biggest scoop of the year just dropped in my lap. I know where Ellen Andrews is—" (*Looking up, excitedly*) No, do you really?

PETER (*impatiently*). Go on. Go on send the telegram.

OPERATOR. "How would you like to have the story, you big tub of—of—"

PETER. Mush. Mush.

OPERATOR. "Tub of mush. Well try and get it. What I said about never writing another line for you still goes. Are you burning? Peter Warne." Well, that will be $2.60.

PETER. Send it collect.

OPERATOR. Collect?

PETER (*firmly*). Collect.

As the clerk takes the wire from him, the scene fades out.

PART THREE

The BUS TERMINAL fades in. It is night now, and the rain comes down in torrents. People scurry around to get into the buses as the voice of an announcer is heard:

ANNOUNCER'S VOICE. Bus for blah-blah-blah-blah—Charleston—blah-blah-blah—and all points North to New York!

This dissolves to the interior of a BUS, which is practically filled. Peter is in his seat, reading a magazine, while Ellie enters hurriedly from the rear door and starts forward. —As she approaches Peter, she hesitates a second, and deliberately passes him, plunking herself into a seat in the opposite aisle. Peter turns just as she gets seated. He glances at her indifferently.

A close view shows Ellie seated next to a man who sits reading a newspaper which covers his face. Her eyes are fixed forward, her lips set adamantly. A close-up of the MAN next to Ellie makes it plain that he is a typical drummer. At the moment he is absorbed in a serial story, but suddenly he becomes aware of something at his feet, and without lowering the newspaper, his gaze slowly shifts downward. At this, the view moves down until it reaches Ellie's trim ankles. Her feet beat a regular tattoo on the floor; her extreme agitation is evident. The view moves back slowly, taking in Ellie's shapely leg as far as the knee. Then we see ELLIE and the DRUMMER as his gaze is still fixed on her leg. Slowly his face breaks into a lascivious grin, he lowers his paper, and turns for a scrutiny of her face. What he sees apparently delights him, for he drops his paper completely—and smiles broadly.

DRUMMER. Hi, sister— All alone? My name's Shapeley. (*Ellie favors him with a devastating look which is wasted on the drummer.*) Might as well get acquainted. It's gonna be a long trip—gets tiresome later on. Specially for somebody like you. You look like you got class. (*He surveys her from head to foot.*) Yessir! With a capital K. (*He chuckles at his own sally.*) And I'm a guy that knows class when he sees it, believe you me.

A close-up of ELLIE, as Shapeley's voice continues, shows her glancing back at Peter, expecting him to come to her rescue.

SHAPELEY'S VOICE. Ask any of the boys. They'll tell you. Shapeley sure knows how to pick 'em. Yessir. Shapeley's the name, and that's the way I like 'em.

Ellie again looks toward Peter. —But PETER seems to have found something of unusual interest in his magazine . . . and we again see the harassed ELLIE and the irrepressible SHAPELEY, who continues:

SHAPELEY. You made no mistake sitting next to me. (*Confidentially*) Just between us, the kinda muggs you meet on a hop like this ain't nothin' to write home to the wife about. You gotta be awful careful who you hit it up with, is what I always say, and you can't be too particular, neither. Once when I was comin' through North Carolina, I got to gabbin' with a good-lookin' mama. One of those young ones, you know, and plenty classy, too. Kinda struck my fancy. You know how it is. Well, sir, you coulda knocked me over with a Mack truck. I was just warming up when she's yanked offa the bus. Who do you think she was? Huh? Might as well give up. The girl bandit! The one the papers been writin' about. (*He pulls out a cigar, and continues—awed by the recollection.*) Yessir, you coulda knocked me over with a Mack truck. (*He lights his cigar, takes a vigorous puff, and turns to her again.*) What's the matter, sister? You ain't sayin' much.

ELLIE (*intending to freeze him*). Seems to me you're doing excellently without any assistance. (*This, however, only brings a guffaw from the drummer.*)

SHAPELEY. That's pretty good . . . Well, shut my big nasty mouth!

A close-up shows ELLIE enduring more of this as Shapeley's voice continues:

SHAPELEY'S VOICE. . . . Looks like you're one up on me. Nothin' I like better than to meet a high-class mama that can snap 'em back at you. 'Cause the colder they are, the hotter they get, is what I always say.

Now Ellie and Shapeley are seen together, with Peter seen in the background.

SHAPELEY. Take this last town I was in. I run into a dame—not a bad looker, either—but boy, was she an iceberg! Every time I opened my kisser, she pulls a ten strike on me. It sure looked like cold turkey for old man Shapeley. I sell office supplies, see? And this hotsy-totsy lays the damper on me quick. She don't need a thing—and if she did she wouldn't buy it from a fresh mugg like me. Well, says I to myself—Shapeley, you better go to work. You're up against a lulu. Well, I'm here to tell you, sister, I opened up a line of fast chatter that had that dame spinnin' like a Russian dancer. Before I got through she bought enough stuff to last the firm a year. And did she put on an act when I blew town!

Ellie has scarcely listened to him, and has divided her attention between glancing back at Peter and staring at Shapeley as if he were insane—none of which bothers Shapeley. He goes on with his merry chatter, blowing rings of smoke in the direction of the ceiling.

SHAPELEY. Yessir. When a cold mama gets hot—boy, how she sizzles! She kinda cramped my style, though. I didn't look at a dame for three towns. (*Quickly*) Not that I couldn't. For me it's always a cinch. I got a much better chance than the local talent. (*Confidentially*) You see, they're kinda leery about the local talent. Too close to home. Know what I mean?

ELLIE has now reached the point where she could, without any compunction, strangle him.

SHAPELEY'S VOICE (*continuing over this glimpse of her desperation*). But take a bird like me—it's here today—and gone tomorrow. And what happens is nobody's business.

At this she turns helplessly toward Peter, but we see PETER being deliberately oblivious of her presence, following which the three are seen, with Peter in the background.

SHAPELEY. But I don't go in for that kinda stuff—much. I like to pick my

fillies. Take you, for instance. You're my type. No kiddin', sister. I could go for you in a big way. "Fun-on-the-side Shapeley" they call me, and the accent's on the fun, believe you me. (*This is all Ellie can stand.*)

ELLIE (*snappily*). Believe you me, you bore me to distraction. (*But Shapeley merely throws his head back and emits his characteristic guffaw.*)

SHAPELEY (*laughing*). Well, you're two up on me now. (*He holds up two fingers.*)

PETER (*approaching them*). Hey, you!

Shapeley's laugh dies down. He looks dumbly up at Peter, his two fingers still held in mid-air.

SHAPELEY. Huh?

PETER (*indicating his own seat*). There's a seat over there for you.

SHAPELEY. What's the idea?

PETER. I'd like to sit with my—uh—wife—if you don't mind. (*At which Shapeley's face falls.*)

SHAPELEY (*puzzled*). Wife?

PETER. Yeah. Come on—come on!

SHAPELEY (*rising*). Oh, excuse me—(*edging away*) I was just tryin'—you know—to make things pleasant.

And smiling sheepishly, he sidles over to Peter's seat, his two fingers still poised in air. Peter plants himself next to Ellie and totally ignoring her, opens his magazine, and resumes his reading. Then Ellie and Peter are seen close together. She looks up at him.

ELLIE. If you promise not to snap my head off, I'd like to thank you.

PETER (*without turning*). Forget it. I didn't do it for you. His voice got on my nerves.

She feels herself crushed, and ventures no further comment as Peter resumes his interest in his magazine.

A full view of the BUS follows, and there is silence for a while as the bus slows down and comes to a stop. Almost simultaneously a boy makes his appearance, selling magazines and candy.

BOY. Here you are, folks. Candy—popcorn—cigarettes—magazines—

As Ellie and Peter are seen again, she turns and calls to the boy:

ELLIE. Here, boy!

PETER (*turning to her*). What'd you do? Wire one of your friends for money?

ELLIE (*rummaging in her purse*). No. It'd be useless. Father'd get the wire before *they* would.

BOY (*as he enters*). Yes, ma'am?

ELLIE. A box of chocolates, please.

PETER (*to the boy*). Never mind, son. She doesn't want it. (*He gestures with his thumb for the boy to leave.*)

BOY (*puzzled*). But the lady says—

ELLIE. Of course I do. What do you mean—

PETER (*to the boy*). Beat it! (*And the boy, frightened by his voice, leaves.*)

ELLIE (*resentfully*). You have your nerve! (*She starts to rise.*) Here, boy—!

Peter snatches the purse out of her hand and takes the money out. Ellie stares at him dumbfounded.

PETER. A dollar sixty! . . . You had four dollars last night! How do you expect to get to New York at the rate you're going?

ELLIE (*vehemently*). That's none of your business!

PETER (*with finality*). You're on a budget from now on. (*He flings her purse back at her and pockets the money.*)

ELLIE. Now, just a minute—you can't—

PETER. Shut up!

He returns to his magazine, leaving her staring at him petulantly as the scene fades out.

PART FOUR

SOMEWHERE ON THE ROAD at night. This is apparently on the outskirts of a town. Two local policemen and our bus driver stand in the foreground near a police booth. The rain sweeps across their faces as they talk. The passengers in the bus, which stands in the background, stick their heads out, trying to hear what is going on.

FIRST POLICEMAN. You won't be able to pass till morning.

SECOND POLICEMAN. Not even then, if this keeps up.

Peter approaches the group and is then seen with the officers and the driver.

PETER. What's up?

FIRST POLICEMAN. Bridge washed out—around Dawson.

DRIVER. Looks like we can't go through till morning.

SECOND POLICEMAN (*his only contribution*). Not even then, if this keeps up.

FIRST POLICEMAN. Any of your passengers want a place to sleep—there's an auto camp up yonder a piece.

PETER (*interested*). Yeah? Where?

FIRST POLICEMAN (*pointing*). Up yonder. See the lights?

PETER. Yeah.

FIRST POLICEMAN. That's it. Dyke's Auto Camp.

PETER. Thanks.

He dashes toward the bus. Then he appears at the side door of the bus.

PETER (*calling*). Hey, Brat—! (*He is about to enter when he sees Ellie.*)

The view moves to the rear door of the bus. Ellie stands on the bottom step.

ELLIE (*haughtily*). Are you talking to me!

PETER. Yeah. Come on—we're stopping here for the night.

He disappears inside the bus through the side door. With an independent toss of her head, Ellie turns and also enters the bus, but through the rear door.

The scene dissolves to DYKE'S AUTO CAMP. Ellie stands alone on the porch of a small bungalow, sheltered from the rain. Over her head is a sign reading:

OFFICE—Dyke Auto Co.—P. D. Dyke, Prop.

She looks about her restlessly, giving the impression that she has been waiting for someone. Suddenly she is attracted by something and gazes in its direction. Then, as seen by Ellie in a long view, there appears, about twenty yards away, a small cabin, lighted on the inside; and from it Peter emerges accompanied by a man—presumably Mr. Dyke. We cannot hear what is being said; from their movements, however, it is apparent that an exchange of money is taking place. Dyke waves his hand in departure and starts toward Ellie. At the same time, Peter calls to her!

PETER (shouting). Hey! Come on! We're all set. (Saying which he enters the cabin.)

Ellie hesitates a moment, then starts toward the cabin. Now she is hurrying across the open space. En route she passes Dyke.

DYKE (as they pass). Good evening. Hope you and your husband rest comfortably.

Ellie keeps on running, but suddenly she stops dead and looks back at Dyke, following which a close-up of ELLIE shows her eyes opening wide with astonishment. Her impulse is to call Dyke back, to make him repeat what he said—to make certain she heard him correctly. But Dyke is gone, and she turns and glances thoughtfully in the direction of the cabin. Then slowly the corners of her mouth screw up in an attitude of cynicism. So that's it, is it! He has given her no previous evidence of being "on the make"; yet now, with the first opportunity—. Her thoughts, however, are interrupted by Peter's voice:

PETER'S VOICE. Well, Brat—what do you say!

As she doesn't stir, there appears a close-view of PETER standing in the doorway of the cabin, looking toward Ellie.

PETER (impatiently). Come on! Come on! What are you going to do? Stand there all night? (He disappears inside.)

For a long moment, ELLIE is lost in speculation as to how to proceed. Then, tossing her head defiantly, with her lips set grimly, she starts toward the cabin until she reaches it, stops in the doorway and peers in. As she does this, there is a view of the inside of the CABIN, as seen by her at the door. Except for two cots on either side of the room, a few sticks of cane furniture, a small table upon which stands an oil burner for cooking, the place is barren. At the moment Peter is attaching a clothes line across the center of the room. His suitcase is already open.— And now Ellie steps inside, surveying the place contemptuously. But Peter, with his back to her, is oblivious of her presence; and as he works, he hums his favorite melody. Ellie finally breaks the silence.

ELLIE (sarcastically). Darn clever, these Armenians.

PETER (seen close as he turns). Yeah. Yeah, it's a gift. (But he finishes his hammering and turns to his suitcase.)

ELLIE (seen with Peter). I just had the unpleasant sensation of hearing you referred to as my husband.

PETER (carelessly). Oh, I forgot to tell you. I registered as Mr. and Mrs. (The matter-of-fact way in which he says this causes her eyebrows to lift.)

ELLIE. Oh, you did? What am I expected to do—leap for joy?

PETER. I kind of half expected you to thank me.

ELLIE. Your ego is colossal.

PETER (blithely). Yeah. Yeah, not bad. How's your's?

There is silence for a moment, and Peter proceeds with the unpacking of his suitcase. As she watches him, Ellie's mood changes from one of anger to that of sarcasm.

ELLIE (appearing in a close-up, her face disdainful). Compared to you, my friend

Shapeley's an amateur. (*Sharply*) Whatever gave you an idea you can get away with this! You're positively the most conceited—

PETER'S VOICE (*interrupting*). Hey, wait a minute! (*Appearing beside her*) Let's get something straightened out right now. If you've got any peculiar ideas that I'm interested in you, forget it. You're just a headline to me.

ELLIE (*frightened*). A headline? You're not a newspaper man, are you?

PETER. Chalk up one for your side. Now listen, you want to get to King Westley, don't you? All right, I'm here to help you. What I want is your story, exclusive. A day-to-day account. All about your mad flight to happiness. I need that story. Just between you and me I've got to have it.

ELLIE. Now isn't that just too cute? There's a brain behind that face of yours, isn't there? You've got everything nicely figured out, for yourself, including this.

PETER. This? Oh, that's a matter of simple mathematics. These cabins cost two bucks a night and I'm very sorry to inform you, wifey dear, but the family purse won't stand for our having separate establishments. (*He goes back to the business of laying out his things.*)

ELLIE (*starting to leave*). Well, thank you. Thank you very much, but—you've been very kind. (*But the rain outside causes her to hesitate.*)

PETER. Oh, yeah? It's all right with me. Go on out in the storm, but I'm going to follow you, see? Yeah. And if you get tough I'll just have to turn you over to your old man right now. Savvy? Now that's my whole plot in a nutshell. A simple story for simple people. Now if you behave yourself, I'll see that you get to King Westley; if not, I'll just have to spill the beans to papa. Now which of these beds do you prefer? This one? All right.

While he speaks he has taken the extra blanket from the cot and hung it over the clothes line. This manages to divide the room in half.

A close view at the DOOR shows Ellie watching him with interest.

ELLIE (*sarcastically*). That, I suppose, makes everything—uh—quite all right.

PETER (*the previous scene returning*). Oh, this?—I like privacy when I retire. I'm very delicate in that respect. Prying eyes annoy me. (*He has the blanket spread out now.*) Behold the walls of Jericho! Maybe not as thick as the ones that Joshua blew down with his trumpet, but a lot safer. You see, I have no trumpet. (*Taking out pajamas*) Now just to show you my heart's in the right place, I'll give you my best pair of pajamas.

He flings them over to her, and she catches them and throws them on her cot. Throughout the scene she hasn't budged from the door, but Peter now prepares to undress.

PETER. Do you mind joining the Israelites?

ELLIE. You're not really serious about this, are you?

PETER (*seen at close range, going about the job of undressing very diffidently*). All right, don't join the Israelites. Perhaps you're interested in how a man undresses. (*And he hangs his coat over the chair.*) Funny thing about that. Quite a study in psychology. No two men do it alike. (*Now his shirt is coming off.*)

A close view of ELLIE shows her standing stubbornly.

PETER'S VOICE. I once knew a chap who kept his hat on until he was completely undressed. (*Chuckling*) Made a comical picture. . . .

As a scene includes both of them, Peter spreads his shirt over his coat.

PETER. Years later his secret came out. He wore a toupee.

He lights a cigarette diffidently while she remains brazenly watching him, her eyes flashing defiantly.

PETER. I have an idiosyncrasy all my own. You'll notice my coat came first—then the tie—then the shirt—now, according to Hoyle, the pants should come next. But that's where I'm different. (*He bends over.*) I go for the shoes first. After that I—

ELLIE (*unable to stand it any longer*). Smart Aleck!

And thoroughly exasperated, she goes behind the blanket, and plops on the cot. She sits on the edge, debating what to do, feeling herself trapped. Her impulse is to leave, if only to show this smart Aleck he's not dealing with a child, and she rises impetuously and moves to the window.

A close view at the WINDOW shows her looking out. The downpour has not abated one bit, and the heavy raindrops clatter against the window pane in a sort of challenge to Ellie, whose jaw drops. She turns slowly back to the room, and as she does so her eyes light on the cot. It looks most inviting; after all, she hasn't had any rest for two nights. She falls on the cot again, her shoulders sagging wearily. Following this, the view reveals both sides of the blanket. Peter is already in his pajamas.

PETER. Still with me, Brat? (*There is no answer from Ellie.*) Don't be a sucker. A night's rest'll do you a lot of good. Besides, you've got nothing to worry about. The Walls of Jericho will protect you from the big bad wolf.

A close view shows ELLIE glancing over at the blanket. Despite herself, the suggestion of a smile flits across her face.

ELLIE. You haven't got a trumpet by any chance, have you?

PETER gets the idea and smiles broadly.

PETER. No. Not even a mouth organ.

Pulling the covers back, he prepares to get into bed, humming as he does so.

PETER (*humming to himself*).
Who's afraid of the big bad wolf—
The big bad wolf, the big bad wolf.
(*Louder*)
She's afraid of the big bad wolf,
Tra-la-la-la-la—(*He springs into bed.*)

Ellie smiles, and wearily she pulls her hat off her head. She sits this way a moment, thoughtfully; then, determined, she looks up.

ELLIE. Do you mind putting out the light?

PETER. Not at all. (*He leans over and snaps it off.*)

The room is thrown into darkness except for a stream of light coming in the window from the night-light outside the camp. Visible are Peter's face and arms as he stares ceilingward, while on Ellie's side all we can see of her is her silhouette, except for such times as she gets in direct line with the window. There are glimpses of her as she moves around in the process of undressing, and we see, or rather sense, her dress dropping to the floor. She now stands in her chemise; this being white silk, it stands out more prominently against the darkness. She picks up the pajamas and backs into a corner, following which a close-up of her head and shoulders shows her glancing apprehensively toward Peter's side of the room; and holding the pajamas in front of her with one hand, with the other she slips the strap off her shoulders. She flings her "slip" over the blanket.

PETER, on his side of the room, looks toward the blanket, and reacts to the "slip" coming into sight. Then other undergarments join the "slip" on the blanket.

PETER (*hoarsely*). Do you mind taking those things off the walls of Jericho? (*A pause*) It's tough enough as it is.

ELLIE'S VOICE. Oh, excuse me. (*And we see the underthings flipped off the blanket.*)

Ellie's side of the room appears, showing her crawling quickly into bed, pulling the covers over her and glancing apprehensively in Peter's direction—following which a close view shows PETER being very conscious of her proximity. The situation is delicate and dangerous; the room is atingle with sex. He turns his gaze toward the blanket. The view moves to the BLANKET, remaining on it a moment. It is a frail barrier! The view then moves back to Peter, whose eyes are still on the blanket, his face expressionless. A close view of ELLIE, next, shows that she, too, has her eyes glued on the blanket, a little fearfully. She turns her head and gazes at the ceiling for a moment. Then suddenly her eyes widen— and she sits up abruptly.

ELLIE (*seriously*). Oh, by the way— what's your name?

PETER (*seen close; turning his head toward her*). What's that?

ELLIE (*both sides of the blanket coming into view*). Who are you?

PETER. Who, me? Why, I'm the whippoorwill that cries in the night. I'm the soft morning breeze that caresses your lovely face.

ELLIE (*interrupting*). You've got a name, haven't you?

PETER. Yeah. I got a name. Peter Warne.

ELLIE. Peter Warne? I don't like it.

PETER. Don't let it bother you. You're giving it back to me in the morning.

ELLIE (*flopping back on her pillow as she mumbles*). Pleased to meet you, Mr. Warne. . . .

PETER. The pleasure is all mine.

There is silence between them for a few seconds.

PETER. I've been thinking about you.

ELLIE'S VOICE. Yes?

PETER. You've had a pretty tough break at that. Twice a Missus and still unkissed.

Ellie doesn't like the implication, and glares in his direction as Peter's voice continues:

PETER'S VOICE (*meaningly*). I'll bet you're in an awful hurry to get back to New York, aren't you?

ELLIE (*hard*). Goodnight, Mr. Warne. (*She turns over.*)

PETER. Goodnight.

He also turns his head toward the wall, and the scene fades out.

PART FIVE

A long view of the SKY, in the early morning, fades in. In the dim distance there is a speck, which, as it comes nearer, turns out to be an airplane. The drone of its motors becomes louder and louder. Then the view cuts to the CONTROL COCKPIT of the PLANE revealing TWO PILOTS.

FIRST PILOT (*shouting to other*). The old man's screwy!

SECOND PILOT (*who can't hear him*). What's 'at?

FIRST PILOT (*louder*). I said, the old man's screwy!

SECOND PILOT (*nodding his head in agreement*). Yeah!

FIRST PILOT (*cupping his mouth*). The dame's too smart for him.

SECOND PILOT (*nodding again, then leaning over*). How'd you like to be married to a wild cat like that?

The First Pilot grimaces in disgust, grabs his nose between his fingers, and goes through the motion of ducking under water. And as they both laugh, the scene cuts to the CABIN of the plane, a privately built plane which has all the equipment of a passenger ship. Andrews and one of his secretaries, a conservative-appearing man of middle age, lean over a table. This being a closed cabin, the roar of the motors scarcely interferes with the dialogue.

SECRETARY. Here's another wire, sir. This one's from Charleston. (*As there is a close view of the two*) "Checking every northbound train. Also assigned twenty operatives to watch main highways. No success yet. Will continue to do everything possible." Signed: Lovington Detective Agency, Charleston.

ANDREWS. Any others?

SECRETARY. Yessir. (*Holding up stack of wires*) There's a report here from every State along the East coast. Want to hear them?

ANDREWS (*impatiently*). What do they say?

SECRETARY. They're practically all the same, sir. (*He shrugs his shoulders to indicate there is no news.*)

ANDREWS (*muttering*). Amateurs!

SECRETARY. They're the finest detective agency in the country, sir.

Andrews doesn't answer him. He puffs furiously on his cigar, glances out of the window, and turns irritably to a phone by his side. He snaps up the receiver and presses a button, following which the scene cuts to the CONTROL COCKPIT, where a light flashes on the instrument board, and the pilot picks up the receiver.

PILOT. Yes, sir?

ANDREWS (*seen in the cabin*). I thought I made it clear I was in a hurry to get to New York? (*Bellowing*) What are we crawling for!

In the control cockpit, the pilot reacts to the complaint and glances at his speed indicator. We then see the SPEED INDICATOR registering 180 miles an hour. The pilot looks aghast.

PILOT (*yelling into phone*). We've got her wide open, sir.

ANDREWS (*irascibly*). Well, step on it! Step on it!

He bangs up the receiver and stares moodily out of the window. It is plain that he is worried. The view then includes his secretary, Henderson.

HENDERSON. I hope she's all right, sir.

ANDREWS (*sharply*). Of course she's all right. What do you think can happen!

HENDERSON (*intimidated*). Nothing, sir!

ANDREWS. Then shut up about it!

Thereupon the view cuts to a close-up of an airplane motor in rapid motion, and this dissolves to the AUTO CAMP CABIN next morning, a close view showing ELLIE peacefully sleeping. But the drone of the plane overhead disturbs her, and she moves restlessly.

ELLIE (*murmuring in her sleep*). Darn planes—

She squirms around uncomfortably, and finding it impossible to resume her slumber, opens her eyes. The sun pouring in through the window causes her to squint. She sits up and stares outside, puzzled.

Then remembering where she is, she looks toward the other side of the cabin, listening for some sign of life. But there is none, and she relaxes. She falls back on the pillow, pulling the covers over her.

Now PETER enters from the outside with an armful of foodstuffs, which he dumps on the table. He looks toward Ellie.

PETER. Hey—you not up yet? Come on—come on!

ELLIE'S VOICE. What time is it?

PETER. Eight o'clock.

He goes to the blanket which hangs between the two cots and throws something over it to Ellie.

PETER. Here—

ELLIE (*catching the package*). What is it? (*Opening the package*) Why, it's a toothbrush! Thanks. (*Noticing her dress hanging freshly pressed*) You—you had it pressed.

PETER (*getting things ready for breakfast*). Come on! Hurry up! Breakfast'll be ready in no time.

ELLIE. Why, you sweet thing, you. Where'd you get it pressed? (*At this, the view moves with him as he goes to the blanket.*)

PETER. Listen, Brat—I'm going to count ten. If you're not out of bed by then, I'm going to yank you out myself . . .

A close view of ELLIE shows her being stubborn, but alarmed.

PETER'S VOICE (*counting quickly*). One—two—three—four—five—

ELLIE (*panic-stricken*). Why, you bully! I believe you would.

PETER'S VOICE. —six—seven—eight—nine—

ELLIE (*screaming*). I'm out! I'm out!

And she jumps out of bed, throwing the cover around herself, following which Peter is seen going back to the table.

PETER. You'll find the showers—and things—right back of the second cottage. (*At this Ellie sticks her head over the blanket.*)

ELLIE (*aghast*). Outside!

PETER. Certainly, outside. All the best homes have 'em outside.

ELLIE. I can't go out like this.

PETER. Like what?

ELLIE. Like this. I have no robe.

PETER. Here—take mine.

He flings his robe over to her, and she disappears behind the blanket.

PETER. But make it snappy.

Now Ellie has got into his robe, and appears on his side. The robe is too large for her and she makes a comical figure. As she enters, she tries to maintain her customary dignity.

ELLIE (*dignifiedly*). Where'd you say the showers—and things—were? (*Peter turns. When he sees her he laughs.*)

PETER (*appraisingly*). Hey—you're little, aren't you?

ELLIE. Where is the shower?

PETER. Your hair's cute like that. You should never comb it.

ELLIE (*leaving haughtily*). I'll find it myself.

She slams the door viciously, but Peter rushes over to the window to watch her; and as viewed by him, Ellie appears next walking to the showers outside the cabin. She holds her head high and struggles valiantly to maintain as much dignity as she can muster under the circumstances.—Then in the cabin, at the window, Peter watching Ellie, chuckles at her, shaking his head in amusement. He starts toward the table, and the scene cuts to a moving view outside the cabins, with Ellie walking past several cottages on her way to the showers. Several people stop to stare at her until she reaches her destination. There are two wooden shacks adjoining, each having a sign on them; one reads, "Showers—Men" —the other, "Showers—Women." In front of the women's shower there are several unappetizing-looking fat women waiting, and with them is a small girl. Ellie crosses over to the women's shower and disappears inside, the waiting women staring at her, puzzled. A moment elapses and Ellie backs out, being pushed by a woman, part of whose naked body is visible, and whose voice is heard in protest:

WOMAN. Can't a body have some privacy around here?

The women who are waiting chuckle at Ellie's embarrassment as she stands aside. They certainly are making a monkey out of her decorum. The little girl keeps eyeing Ellie, fascinated.

LITTLE GIRL (*pointing*). Don't she look funny, Mama?

Ellie, wheeling on the little girl, crushes her with a devastating look, so that the little girl cringes against her mother's skirt. Ellie goes to the end of the line to await her turn, following which close-ups show the LITTLE GIRL slowly turning her head to look at Ellie, and ELLIE noticing the little girl staring at her, whereupon Ellie sticks her tongue out at her. And, in a scene which includes both, the little girl retaliates by sticking her tongue out also.

This dissolves to a view of ELLIE coming out of the showers. At the same time Shapeley comes out of the men's shower, and upon seeing Ellie, his faces lights up.

SHAPELEY. Hello, sister.

Ellie ignores him, and walks toward her cabin. But Shapeley falls into step with her.

SHAPELEY. Sorry about last night. Didn't know you were married to that guy. Shoulda told me about it right off. (*He chuckles.*) There I was, gettin' myself all primed for a killin', and you turn out to be an old married woman.

The scene cuts to the DOOR OF PETER'S CABIN as Peter comes out, stands in the doorway, and is surprised to see Ellie and Shapeley, who are then seen (from his angle) talking. Thereupon PETER is seen again as his lip curls up a little jealously; he returns to the cabin, following which we again see Ellie and Shapeley walking. He notices the robe she is wearing, and he looks down toward her feet, the view moving down to show Ellie's legs and feet. The pajama legs are seen protruding below the robe, the cuffs of which she has turned up. Then the view moving back up to Ellie and Shapeley, he lifts her robe playfully.

SHAPELEY. Hey, what's this? Wearing Papa's things? Now that's cute. That's what I call real lovey-dovey. Yessir.

ELLIE (*stopping—her eyes blazing*). If you don't get out of here, I'll slap that fresh mouth of yours.

SHAPELEY (*startled*). Sorry—I didn't mean to—

ELLIE (*sharply*). Get out!

SHAPELEY. Okay. I was just trying to make conversation.

Ellie leaves him abruptly, and the scene cuts to the CABIN, where Peter is now busy setting the small table. Ellie enters after a moment, while Peter has his back to the door.

PETER (*without turning*). High time you got back.

ELLIE. I met some very interesting women at the showers. We got to chatting about this and that. You know how time flies.

[She disappears behind the blanket, following which we see Peter's side of the cabin, while Ellie's voice continues from behind the blanket.

ELLIE'S VOICE. We must come back to this place often. You meet the nicest people!

Her head bobs up over the blanket now and again as she dresses.

ELLIE. I saw the little Pussinfoos girl. She's turned out quite a charming creature.

Peter ignores her chatter, except for an annoyed glance once in a while.

ELLIE. Very outspoken, too. Said I looked funny. Wasn't that cute?

PETER. Hurry up and get dressed.

ELLIE (*sticking her head over blanket*). Why, Peter! Don't you want to hear about our lovely friends?

PETER. If you didn't waste so much time on that wisecracking drummer—we'd

have been through with breakfast by this time.

A close view shows ELLIE in the process of buttoning her dress. She looks up, having recognized a tinge of jealousy in his voice, which intrigues her. She starts to the other side of the blanket. Then we see her joining Peter in his part of the cabin.

ELLIE. Well, I hope you're not going to dictate whom I can talk to.

PETER. I know a couple of truck drivers I'd like to have you meet sometime. (*Setting a plate for her*) Come on, sit down.

ELLIE. Thank you. (*Sitting down to the table; referring to the food*) My, my! Scrambled eggs.]

PETER. Egg. One egg—doughnuts—black coffee. That's your ration till lunch. Any complaints?

ELLIE (*cheerily*). Nope. No complaints.

PETER. I'd have gotten you some cream, but it meant buying a whole pint.

ELLIE (*"sweetly"*). Why, you don't have to apologize, Mr. Warne. You'll never know how much I appreciate all this.

PETER (*gruffly*). What makes you so disgustingly cheerful this morning?

ELLIE. Must be the Spring.

PETER. I thought maybe—uh—"believe you me" told you a couple of snappy stories.

ELLIE. He apologized for last night. (*Carelessly*) Said he didn't know we were married.

PETER (*passing her a doughnut*). Just shows you how wrong a guy can be. Doughnut?

ELLIE. Thanks. (*Embarrassed*) You think this whole business is silly, don't you? I mean running away and everything.

PETER (*easily*). No. No. It's too good a story.

ELLIE. Yes, you do. You think I'm a fool and a spoiled brat. Perhaps I am, although I don't see how I can be. People who are spoiled are accustomed to having their own way. I never have. On the contrary, I've always been told what to do and how to do it and where and with whom. Would you believe it? This is the first time I've ever been alone with a man!

PETER. Yeah?

ELLIE. It's a wonder I'm not panic stricken.

PETER. Um. You're doing all right.

ELLIE. Thanks. Nurses, governesses, chaperones, even body-guards. Oh, it's been a lot of fun.

PETER. One consolation; you can never be lonesome.

ELLIE. It has its moments. It got to be a sort of game to try to outwit father's detectives. I—I did it once; actually went shopping without a bodyguard. It was swell. I felt absolutely immoral. But it didn't last long. They caught up with me in a department store. I was so mad I ran out the back way and jumped into the first car I saw. Guess who was in it?

PETER. Santa Claus?

ELLIE. King—King Westley was in it.

PETER. Oh. Is that how you met him?

ELLIE. Um-hm. We rode around all afternoon. Father was frantic. By 6 o'clock he was having all the rivers dragged. (*She has been "dunking" her doughnut throughout this, Peter watching her.*)

PETER. Say, where did you learn to dunk, in finishing school?

ELLIE (*indignantly*). Aw, now, don't you start telling me I shouldn't dunk.

PETER. Of course you shouldn't. You don't know how to do it. Dunking's an art. Don't let it soak so long. A dip and plop, into your mouth. If you let it soak so long, it'll get soft and fall off. It's all a matter of timing. I ought to write a book about it.

ELLIE. Thanks, professor.

PETER. Just goes to show you. Twenty millions and you don't know how to dunk.

ELLIE. I'd change places with a plumber's daughter any day.

But before he can answer, they are interrupted by voices directly outside their window, and the view moves with Peter as he goes to the door, which he opens slightly. Thereupon Dyke is seen in conversation with two men outside the CABIN.

DYKE (*protesting loudly*). You can't go around bothering my tenants. I tell you, there's no girl by that name here. Besides, how do I know you're detectives?

FIRST DETECTIVE. Show him your credentials, Mac. I'll look around.

At this, Peter closes the door and turns to Ellie.

PETER. Detectives!

ELLIE (*petrified*). That's Father at work. What'll I do? (*Appealingly, to him*) Peter, what'll I do?

PETER. Don't look at me. I didn't marry King Westley.

Ellie runs around the room picking up her stuff and murmuring, "Oh, my goodness!" She reaches the window.

ELLIE (*now seen close, at the window*). Maybe I could jump out of the window. (*Tremulously*) Do you think they'd see me?

PETER'S VOICE (*suddenly*). Come here, you little fool!

She starts toward him.— We then see him plunking her in a chair:

PETER. Sit down!

He rumples her hair and sticks a few hairpins in her mouth. He now stands aside and deliberately talks loud enough to be heard outside.

PETER (*practically shouting*). Yeah. I got a letter from Aunt Betty. She says if we don't stop over at Wilkes-Barre she'll never forgive us.

ELLIE (*a close-up showing her staring at him in bewilderment*). What are you talking about?

At this, Peter rushes over to her and clamps his hand over her mouth.

PETER (*with his hand over her mouth*). The baby is due next month—and they want us to come.

Ellie looks up at him, and realizes what he's doing, she nods to him that it's all right, whereupon he removes his hand from her mouth. And now one of the detectives approaches the FRONT DOOR of the cabin. When he hears Peter's voice, he stops to listen.

PETER'S VOICE. She says she saw your sister Ethel the other day, and she's looking swell.

The detective knocks on the door.—At this we again see the inside of the cabin as Peter whispers to Ellie to say "Come in."

ELLIE (*calling*). Come in!

The moment she does, Peter rushes behind the hanging blanket. He has his head stuck over it, waiting for the detective to enter, and the moment the door opens Peter ducks. The detective takes a step inside the room.

PETER'S VOICE (*from behind blanket*). I hope Aunt Betty has a boy, don't you? She's always wanted a boy. I think we'll stop over in Wilkes-Barre this trip, darling. Give the family a treat.

A close view shows Ellie and the detective. They have been staring at each other.

ELLIE (*very sweet, calling to Peter*). There's a man here to see you, Sweetheart.

PETER'S VOICE. Who—me? (*Appearing from behind the blankets; pleasantly*) Want to see me?

DETECTIVE (*who hasn't taken his eyes off Ellie*). What's your name?

ELLIE (*innocently*). Are you addressing me?

DETECTIVE. Yeah. What's your name?

PETER (*stepping in front of him*). Hey, wait a minute! You're talking to my wife! You can't walk in here and—what do you want, anyway?

DETECTIVE. We're looking for somebody.

PETER. Well, look your head off—but don't come bustin' in here. This isn't a public park.

While Peter has been speaking, the second detective and Dyke have entered. They walk over to Peter, the First Detective, and Ellie.

PETER. I got a good mind to sock you right in the nose.

FIRST DETECTIVE. Take it easy, son. Take it easy.

SECOND DETECTIVE (*crowding forward*). What's up?

The Second Detective's eyes fall on Ellie, and he stops to stare at her suspiciously. He takes a photograph out of his pocket which he inspects.

DYKE (*explaining*). These men are detectives, Mr. Warne.

PETER (*shouting*). I wouldn't care if they were the whole police department! They can't come in here and start shooting questions at my wife!

ELLIE (*appearing very domestic*). Don't get excited, Peter. They just asked a civil question.

PETER (*turning on her; very sarcastic*). There you go again! How many times did I tell you to stop butting in when I have an argument?

ELLIE (*sharply; entering into the spirit of the pretense*). Well, you don't have to lose your temper!

PETER (*mimicking her*). You don't have to lose your temper! (*In his own voice*) That's what you told me the last time, too. Every time I step in to protect you. At the Elk's dance—when that big Swede made a pass at you—

ELLIE. He didn't make a pass at me! I told you a million times!

The two detectives and Dyke are seen watching the other two, who are now out of sight.

PETER'S VOICE (*screaming*). Oh, no! I saw him! He kept pawing you all over the dance floor!

ELLIE's VOICE. He didn't! You were drunk!

PETER (*now seen with Ellie*). Oh, so now I was drunk!

ELLIE. Well, you were!

PETER. I'm sorry I didn't take another sock at him.

ELLIE. Yeah, and gotten yourself arrested!

PETER. Aw, nuts! You're just like your old man! Once a plumber always a plumber! There isn't an ounce of brains in your whole family!

ELLIE (*starting to cry*). Peter Warne, you've gone far enough. I won't stand being insulted like this another minute.

Ellie goes over to her cot, and starts picking up her hat and things, whereupon Dyke, very much affected, turns to the detectives.

DYKE. Now look what you've done!

FIRST DETECTIVE (*apologetically*). Sorry, Mr. Warne. But you see, we're supposed to check up on everybody.

SECOND DETECTIVE. We're looking for a girl by the name of Ellen Andrews. You know—the daughter of the big Wall Street mug.

A close-up of ELLIE appears as their voices are heard.

FIRST DETECTIVE's VOICE. Your wife sure looks like her. Don't she, Mac?

SECOND DETECTIVE's VOICE. She sure does.

PETER (*the entire group coming into view*). Well, I hope you find her. (*To Ellie*) Quit bawling! Quit bawling!

The detectives start out, accompanied by Dyke, who is still concerned about the disturbing of his tenants. As they disappear out the door, we hear Dyke's voice:

DYKE's VOICE. I told you they were a perfectly nice married couple.

Their voices die. Peter stands in the middle of the room watching them go. From her side, where she has been stalling, Ellie peers out of the window until the detectives vanish. She starts toward Peter.—

Then they appear together, both staring out until the detectives are well out of sight. Finally, Peter closes the door and turns to her.

PETER (*seriously*). It'll be a dirty trick on Aunt Betty if it turns out to be a girl after all.

This brings laughter from them both. But Peter suddenly sobers, and he looks at her thoughtfully.

PETER. Say, you were pretty good. Jumping in like that. Got a brain, haven't you?

ELLIE. You weren't so bad yourself.

PETER. We could start a two-person stock company. If things get tough—we can play some small town auditoriums. We'll call this one "The Great Deception."

ELLIE. Next week "East Lynne."

PETER. After that "The Three Musketeers." (*He strikes a pose.*) I'd make a great D'Artagnan.

ELLIE. How about Cinderella—or a real hot love story?

PETER. No mushy stuff. I'm running this troupe.

ELLIE (*fighting*). Oh, you are! Who made *you* the manager?

PETER. I did! It was my idea, wasn't it?

ELLIE. You always want to run everything.

PETER. If you don't like it, you can resign from the company.

ELLIE. I refuse to resign!

PETER. Then I'll fire you. I'll do all the parts myself.

They are interrupted by the door being flung open. Dyke sticks his head in the door.

DYKE. Your bus leaves in five minutes.

PETER. Holy jumping—! We haven't started to pack yet!

And they both scurry around, throwing things carelessly into Peter's suitcase, as the scene fades out.

PART SIX

GORDON'S OFFICE fades in, and Gordon is at his desk as his secretary enters.

SECRETARY. Here's another wire from Peter Warne.

GORDON. Throw it in the basket. (*As the secretary starts to do so*) What's it say?

SECRETARY (*reading*). "Have I got a story! It's getting hotter and hotter. Hope you're the same."

Gordon snatches the wire out of her hand and tears it viciously into bits.

GORDON. Collect?

SECRETARY. Yes.

GORDON. Don't accept any more.

The scene dissolves to ANDREWS' NEW YORK OFFICE—a richly appointed place, awe-inspiring in its dignified furnishings, which shriek of wealth. Andrews paces back and forth in back of his desk. Sitting before him is a man of fifty, with very rugged features. He is Lovington, head of the detective agency bearing his name. When the scene opens, Andrews is holding forth:

ANDREWS. Three days! Three whole days! And what have you accomplished!—(*In a close view at the desk*) All you've shown me is a stack of feeble reports from those comical detectives of yours. I want action, Lovington!

LOVINGTON. We can't do the impossible, Mr. Andrews.

ANDREWS. What I'm asking isn't impossible. My daughter is somewhere between here and Miami. I want her found!

LOVINGTON. I've put extra men on, all along the way.

ANDREWS. It's not enough! (*Suddenly*) Are you certain she's not with King Westley?

LOVINGTON. No. He's been trailed twenty-four hours a day since this thing started. He can't even get a phone call we don't know about.

ANDREWS (*who has been pressing several buttons on his desk*). I'm worried, Lovington. After all, something might have happened to her. (*He is interrupted by the entrance of several employees.*)

ONE OF THEM. Yessir?

ANDREWS (*seeing them*). Oh, Clark—I want you to arrange for a radio broadcast—right away—coast to coast hookup! Offer a reward of ten thousand dollars for any information leading to her whereabouts.

CLARK (*leaving*). Yessir.

ANDREWS. Brown—

BROWN. Yessir?

ANDREWS. Send the story out to the newspapers. (*He rips a picture of Ellie on his desk out of its frame.*) Some of the out of town papers may not have a picture of her. Here—wire this to them—I want it to break right away.

As he hands the picture to Brown, the view moves in to a close-up of the PICTURE, which dissolves to a close-up of the same picture in a newspaper, and as the view draws slowly back we see the headline over it, which reads

"DAUGHTER OF BANKER DISAPPEARS
TEN THOUSAND DOLLARS REWARD"

The view then draws back to reveal SHAPELEY reading the newspaper. He stares long and absorbedly at the picture. Then slowly he turns his head toward the rear of the bus, and the view following his gaze, passes a group of men singing "The Man On the Flying Trapeze." They are huddled together, and accompanied by a man who plays a guitar. Then the view continues moving until it reaches Peter and Ellie, who join in the song, and a close-up of ELLIE shows her eyes sparkling as she sings gaily.

SHAPELEY looks back at Ellie, and apparently comes to the conclusion that his suspicions are correct, for he quickly folds the newspaper, casting a surreptitious glance around to make certain he is not being watched. A diabolical smirk spreads over his face.

A full view of the interior of the bus shows most of the occupants joining in the fun, singing. They seem unmindful of the discomfiture caused by the rocking of the bus, which throws them against each other. Then the view draws in to a front seat in which sit a woman and a small boy of ten. The woman's face is haggard and she sways uncertainly, her eyes half closed. Her small son's frightened face peers up at her.

BOY (*in a trembling voice*). What'sa matter, Ma? Don't you feel all right?

The woman struggles valiantly to recover her composure. She presses her son's small hand in a feeble effort at assurance.

A close view of Ellie and Peter shows ELLIE singing more boisterously than the rest, doing the comical song with exaggerated gestures. But suddenly her face clouds, at something she sees.

ELLIE (*touching Peter's arm*). Peter! (*As he turns*) There's something the matter with that woman. She looks ill.

Peter follows her gaze, whereupon we see the WOMAN. Her head rolls weakly, a pained expression on her face.

ELLIE (*again seen with Peter; sympathetically*). I better go over and see her.

PETER. Don't be silly. Nothing you can do. Must be tough on an old woman—a trip like this.

ELLIE (*worried*). Yes.

We see the other passengers around Ellie and Peter enjoying themselves. One of them pokes her.

MAN. Hey, Galli-Curci, come on—get onto it! (*Poking Peter*) You, too, Mc-Cormack.

Ellie and Peter snap into it; they are just in time for the long wail which precedes the chorus:

ELLIE AND PETER (*singing*). "O-o-o-o-h— He flies through the air with the greatest of ease—

This daring young man on the flying trapeze—"

At this the scene cuts to the ROAD. The bus is caught in a muddy road, full of ruts, and at the moment wavers dangerously at an angle. The left front wheel is stuck in a deep hole, and the engine roars and clatters as the driver feeds the gas. Finally the bus moves forward, extricating the wheel; but just as it does, the right front wheel falls into another mud hole on the other side, and this time the bus seems hopelessly stuck,—a close-up of the RIGHT WHEEL showing it revolving desperately, but in vain. The mud splashes in all directions, and the wheel seems to sink deeper and deeper. Thereupon this view cuts to the inside of the BUS. The bus is tilted over at an extreme angle, which has thrown Ellie into a corner on the floor, where she now crouches in an undignified position. She looks like a turtle, her head being invisible.

ELLIE (*sticking her head out*). Thank the man for me, Peter. This is the first comfortable position I've had all night.

Peter, amused, is assisting her to her feet. The guitarist has continued his playing uninterrupted, and as Peter lifts Ellie, he sings:

PETER (*singing*).
"She flies through the air with the greatest of ease.
This darin' young maid on the flying trapeze—(*grunting*)
Her movements are graceful—all men does she please—"

A close view of the WOMAN and the LITTLE BOY now shows the latter terrifiedly watching his mother, whose head sags wearily. Finally she topples forward in a swoon.

BOY (*with a moan*). Ma! Ma! What'sa matter with you? (*Tears stream down his cheeks.*) Somebody help me! Somethin's happened to her!

The music stops abruptly. Everyone looks up, startled. Ellie starts forward, followed by Peter. Passengers closely group around the woman and chatter. "She's fainted. Look how pale she is."

Peter and Ellie step up.

PETER. Get some water, somebody. (*To the boy*) Let me get in here, son.

Ellie goes out of sight to get water. The

boy cries audibly, terror-stricken, but gets out of Peter's way, and Peter lifts the woman up and stretches her across the seat. Ellie comes back with water which she silently hands to Peter, who administers to the woman and when she slowly opens her eyes, makes her drink the water. The woman looks around, bewildered.

PETER (*consolingly*). That's better. You're all right now. Just took a little nose-dive, that's all.

He assists her in sitting up. The boy's wailing is heard, and he now rushes over and throws his arms around his mother.

BOY (*crying*). Ma—oh, gee, Ma—!

His mother clings to him, but still feeling faint, her head sways. Peter looks up at Ellie and gives her a sign to sit down beside the woman.— ELLIE sits down beside her. Peter takes the boy by the shoulders.

PETER. Come on, son. Better give your mother a chance to snap out of it. (*As the boy emits a heart-breaking sob.*) It's all right, son. She'll be okay in a couple of minutes.

He leads the boy away, while Ellie places her arm around the woman.

ELLIE. You'd better rest. It's been a hard trip, hasn't it?

The scene cuts to a close view of SHAPELEY who has his eye peeled on Peter, watching him, and we next see Peter and the boy, who is still sobbing quietly. They are now standing away from the other passengers.

BOY. We ain't ate nothin' since yestidday.

PETER. What happened to your money?

BOY. Ma spent it all for the tickets. She didn't know it was gonna be so much. (*With a new outburst*) We shouldn'a come, I guess, but Ma said there's a job waitin' for her in New York—and if we didn't go, she might lose it.

PETER. Going without food is bad business, son. Why didn't you ask somebody?

BOY. I was gonna do it, but Ma wouldn't let me. She was ashamed, I guess.

Peter reaches into his pocket for a bill, just as Ellie approaches them.

ELLIE. She'll be all right, soon's she gets something to eat.

Peter has extracted a single bill and digs in his pocket for a smaller one. Before he can find anything, however, Ellie takes the one he has in his hand and gives it to the boy.

ELLIE. Here, boy—first town we come to, buy some food. (*Peter glances at his empty hand and then at Ellie.*)

BOY. I shouldn't oughta take this. Ma'll be angry.

ELLIE (*confidentially*). Just don't tell her anything about it. You don't want her to get sick again, do you?

BOY (*a sob in his voice*). No-o. But I shouldn't oughta take the money. (*To Peter*) You might need it.

PETER. Me? Forget it, son. (*Rumpling his hair—smiling*) I got millions.

BOY (*also smiling*). Thanks.

ELLIE (*her arm around the boy*). Come on. Let's go back to your mother.

She leaves with the boy, Peter watching her a moment, impressed by her display of humanness, before turning and leaving the scene, following which a close-up shows SHAPELEY watching Peter, then also rising and starting out.

On the ROAD, the driver is now standing in front of the mud-hole, staring at the sunken wheel dolefully, as several people stray into the scene.

DRIVER. That storm sure made a mess outa these roads.

PETER (*appearing, and seeing the trouble*). Holy Smokes! You'll never get out yourself! Better phone for some help.

DRIVER. Phone for help? (*Unhappily*) We're right in the middle of nowhere. There isn't a town within ten miles of here.

Shapeley is just entering the outskirts of the group. He stops, looks in the direction of Peter speculatively. He has the newspaper stuck in his pocket, which he caresses tenderly. The scene expanding, Peter is then seen leaving the group.

SHAPELEY (*as Peter approaches*). What's up?

PETER. Looks like we're going to be stuck for a long time. (*He starts away.*)

SHAPELEY (*calling to him*). Say, Buddy—

Peter turns, and looks at him quizzically, and the two are then seen close together.

SHAPELEY. Like to have a look at my paper?

He has taken it out and has it opened as he hands it to Peter. The headlines concerning Ellie and her picture shriek out at Peter. This startles him for a moment, but he manages to recover his poise.

SHAPELEY. Travelin' like this, you kinda lose track of what's goin' on in the world.

PETER (*guardedly*). Thanks. (*He glances from the newspaper to Shapeley, wondering how much he suspects.*)

SHAPELEY. If you wanna get anywhere nowadays, you gotta keep in touch with all the news, is what I always say.

PETER (*eyeing him expectantly*). That's right.

SHAPELEY (*pointing to paper*). Take that story there, for instance. Be kinda sweet if we could collect that ten thousand smackers.

PETER (*non-committally*). Yeah — wouldn't it?

SHAPELEY. It's a lotta dough. If I was to run across that dame, you know what I'd do?

PETER. What?

SHAPELEY. I'd go fifty-fifty with *you*.

PETER. Why?

SHAPELEY. Cause I'm a guy that don't believe in hoggin' it, see? A bird that figures that way winds up behind the eight ball, is what I always say.

PETER. What's on your mind?

SHAPELEY (*hard*). Five G's—or I crab the works.

PETER. You're a pretty shrewd baby.

(*Looking around*) We better get away from this gang. Talk this thing over privately.

And the view moves with them as Peter leads the way toward a clump of bushes off the side of the road, Shapeley following. They are concealed from the rest of the passengers.

PETER. Lucky thing, my running into you. Just the man I need.

SHAPELEY (*smiling broadly*). You're not making any mistake, believe you me.

PETER. I can use a smart guy like you.

SHAPELEY (*expansively*). Say listen, when you're talkin' to old man Shapeley, you're talking to—

PETER (*suddenly*). Do you pack a gat?

A close view of the TWO shows the smile dying on Shapeley's face. He looks up quickly.

SHAPELEY. Huh?

PETER. A gat! A gat! (*Feeling him*) Got any fireworks on you?

SHAPELEY (*weakly*). Why—no—

PETER (*carelessly*). That's all right. I got a couple of machine guns in my suitcase. I'll let you have one of them. (*Shapeley is beginning to realize he is in for something he hadn't bargained for, and stares speechlessly at Peter, who continues blandly.*) Expect a little trouble up North. May have to shoot it out with cops.

The perspiration starts appearing on Shapeley's brow (as we see him in a close-up). Peter's voice continues:

PETER'S VOICE (*with emphasis*). If you come through all right, your five G's are in the bag. Maybe more. I'll talk to the "Killer"—see that he takes care of you.

SHAPELEY (*finally finding his voice*). The Killer?

PETER (*seen with Shapeley; watching the latter to gauge the effect of his words*). Yeah—the "big boy"—the Boss of the outfit.

SHAPELEY (*shakily*). You're not kidnapping her, are you?

PETER (*tough*). What else, stupid! You don't think we're after that penny-ante reward, do you? (*Contemptuously*) Ten thousand bucks? Chicken feed! We're holding her for a million smackers.

SHAPELEY (*stammering*). Say, look! I didn't know it was anything like this, see—and—

PETER. What's the matter with you! Gettin' yellow?

SHAPELEY (*raising his voice, pleadingly*). But I'm a married man. I got a couple of kids. I can't get mixed up with—

PETER (*gripping his arm*). Sh-sh-sh—! Soft pedal, you mug!—before I—What're you trying to do? Tell the whole world about it! (*Low and menacingly*) Now listen, you're in this thing—and you're *staying* in! Get me? You know too much.

SHAPELEY (*frightened out of his wits*). I won't say anything. Honest, I won't.

PETER. *Yeah?*— How do I know? (*He reaches into his coat threateningly.*) I gotta good mind to plug you. (*Arguing with himself*) I shouldn't take any chances on you.

SHAPELEY (*breaking down*). You can trust me, Mister. I'll keep my mouth shut.

PETER. Yeah? (*He glares at Shapeley a moment silently, as if making up his mind.*) What's your name?

SHAPELEY. Oscar Shapeley.

PETER. Where do you live?

SHAPELEY. Orange, New Jersey.

PETER. Got a couple of kids, huh?

SHAPELEY. Yeah. Just babies.

PETER. You *love* them, don't you?

SHAPELEY (*sensing the threat; horrified*). Oh, gee, Mister—you wouldn't— You ain't thinkin' about—

PETER (*threateningly*). You'll keep your trap shut, all right.

SHAPELEY (*quickly*). Sure—sure—I'll keep my trap shut. You can depend on me, Mister.

PETER. If you don't— Ever hear of Bugs Dooley?

SHAPELEY. No.

PETER. Nice guy. Just like you. But he made a big mistake, one day. Got kind of talkative. Know what happened? His kid was found in the bottom of the river. A rock tied around its neck. Poor Bugs! He couldn't take it. Blew his brains out. (*Shapeley can't stand much more of this. He is ready to keel over.*)

SHAPELEY. Gee! That musta been terrible (*Righteously*) I guess he had it comin' to him though. But don't you worry about me. I don't talk. I never talk. Take my word for it. Gee, I wouldn't want anything to happen to my kids.

PETER. Okay. Just remember that. Now beat it.

SHAPELEY (*grabbing Peter's hand and shaking it gratefully*). Oh, thanks— thanks, Mister. I always knew you guys were kind-hearted.

PETER (*putting his hand away*). Come on, scram! And stay away from that bus.

SHAPELEY. Sure. Anything you say.

As he says this, he backs away from Peter, following which a close-up of PETER shows a twinkle in his eye and then, as seen by Peter, Shapeley appears walking hurriedly away. When he thinks the distance is safe, he starts running. He slips and falls into the mud, picks himself up, and continues his race for life.

The scene dissolves to the ROAD, at night, with Ellie and Peter walking along. It is apparent they have been trudging like this for a long time.

ELLIE. Poor old Shapeley. You shouldn't have frightened him like that.

PETER. At the rate he started, he's probably passed two state lines by this time. The exercise is good for him.

ELLIE. Yes, I noticed he was getting a little fat lately. (*She grabs her side.*) Ouch!

PETER. What's the matter?

ELLIE (*grimacing*). I was never built for these moonlight strolls. (*Protesting*) Why did *we* have to leave the bus?

PETER. I don't trust that chatterbox.

The scene dissolves to the banks of a narrow STREAM at night. Peter is bending over, removing his shoes, and we see the two closer as they talk.

PETER. First town we hit in the morning, you better wire your father.

ELLIE. Not as long as I'm alive.

PETER. Okay with me, if you can stand the starvation diet.

ELLIE. What do you mean—starvation?

PETER. It takes money to buy food.

ELLIE. Why, haven't you—?

PETER (*interrupting*). Not a sou. I had some before the fainting scene.

ELLIE. You didn't give that boy *all* your money?

PETER. I didn't give him *anything*. *You* were the big-hearted gal. How about wiring your father now?

ELLIE. Never! I'll get to New York if I have to starve all the way.

PETER (*rising—uttering a deep sigh*). Must be some strange power Westley has over you women. (*He now has his shoes off and ties them to each other.*) How do you expect to get there?

ELLIE. To New York?

PETER. Yeah.

ELLIE. I'm following you.

PETER. Aren't you afraid of me?

ELLIE (*confidently*). No.

PETER (*looking at her*). Okay. Hang on to these.

As he bends down in front of Ellie, he gets a firm grip around her legs and throws her over his shoulder like a sack. She squeals, terrified, but Peter ignores this; and with his right hand, which is free, he lifts the suitcase and starts walking across the stream. Ellie's first fright is gone and she now rather enjoys the sensation of being carried by Peter. She lets herself go completely limp, still clinging to his shoes, which she carries by the string. As they walk, the dangling shoes keep hitting Peter's backside.

PETER. I wish you'd stop being playful.

ELLIE (*thereupon holding the shoes out at a safe distance*). Sorry. (*Peter takes several more laborious steps before either of them speaks.*)

ELLIE. It's the first time I've ridden "piggy-back" in years.

PETER. This isn't "piggy-back."

ELLIE. Of course it is.

PETER. You're crazy.

ELLIE (*after a silence for several seconds*). I remember distinctly Father taking me for a "piggy-back" ride—

PETER. And he carried you like this, I suppose.

ELLIE. Yes.

PETER (*with finality*). Your father didn't know beans about "piggy-back" riding.

ELLIE (*another silence before she speaks again*). My uncle—Mother's brother—had four children . . . and I've seen *them* ride "piggy-back."

PETER. I don't think there's a "piggy-back" rider in your whole family. I never knew a rich man yet who was a good "piggy-back" rider.

ELLIE. That's silly.

PETER. To be a "piggy-backer" it takes complete relaxation—a warm heart—and a loving nature.

ELLIE. And rich people have none of those qualifications, I suppose.

PETER. Not a one.

ELLIE. You're prejudiced.

PETER. Show me a good "piggy-back" rider and I'll show you somebody that's human. Take Abraham Lincoln, for instance—a natural "piggy-backer." (*Contemptuously*) Where do you get off with your stuffed-shirt family? (*Turning*) Why, your father knew so much about "piggy-back" riding that he—

In his excitement he wheels around to speak to her, forgetting that as he turns she goes with him. Not finding her at his right, he swings around to his left. Naturally he takes Ellie with him—and realizing his mistake he mutters:

PETER. Aw, nuts!

He proceeds on his way, walking faster than before. They continue this way silently for some time. Finally Ellie breaks the silence.

ELLIE (*persistently*). My father was a great "piggy-backer."

Peter raises his eyes heavenward in thorough disgust, then calmly hands his suitcase to her.

PETER. Hold this a minute.

Ellie takes the suitcase from him, and his hand now free, he delivers a resounding smack on her backside, so that Ellie lets out a yelp.

PETER (*taking the suitcase*). Thank you.

The scene dissolves to the edge of a COW PASTURE, at night, and Ellie and Peter are revealed climbing under a barbed wire fence, following which the scene dissolves to a HAYSTACK, in front. Peter sets his bag down and surveys the layout, Ellie watching him.

PETER (*to himself*). This looks like the best spot.

ELLIE. We're not going to sleep out here, are we?

PETER. I don't know about you, but I'm going to give a fairly good imitation of it.

And he busies himself laying out a bed for her, pulling hay from the stack and spreading it out on the ground. Ellie wanders aimlessly and then moves to a rock, where she sits and watches Peter.

ELLIE (*after a pause; coyly*). Peter—

PETER (*as a close view shows him still arranging her bed; grumbling*). What?

ELLIE'S VOICE. I'm hungry.

PETER (*without looking up*). Just your imagination.

ELLIE (*seen at the rock, while Peter is out of sight*). No, it isn't. I'm hungry and—and scared.

PETER'S VOICE. You can't be hungry and scared at the same time.

ELLIE (*insisting*). Well, I am.

PETER (*as both he and Ellie are seen at their respective places*). If you're scared, it scares the hunger out of you.

ELLIE (*argumentatively*). Not if you're more hungry than scared.

PETER (*impatiently*). All right. You win. Let's forget it.

ELLIE (*after a pause*). I can't forget it. I'm still hungry.

PETER (*tearing his hair; screaming*). Holy Smokes! Why did I ever get mixed up with you!

This brings silence, and he goes on building a bed for her. Then a close-up of ELLIE shows her watching him. Her eyes soften. A very definite interest in him is slowly but surely blossoming, and the fact that he is making her bed adds to the intimacy of the scene. A close view of PETER shows him concentrating on his task, but he pauses a moment and turns to glance at her. It is a devouring look, which he quickly dispels by working more feverishly on her bed.

PETER (*muttering while he works*). If I had any sense, I'd have been in New York by this time. (*He emphasizes his feelings by yanking viciously at the hay as both of them are now seen.*) Taking a married woman back to her husband. Hunh! What a prize sucker I turned out to be. (*He has her bed ready. Without glancing at her*) Come on—your bed's all ready.

She watches him a moment, then rising slowly, starts toward Peter. Then she stands over her bed, surveying it speculatively.

ELLIE. I'll get my clothes all wrinkled.

PETER (*sharply*). Well, take them off.

ELLIE (*shocked*). What!

PETER (*shouting*). All right! Don't take them off. Do whatever you please. But shut up about it.

She flashes him a petulant, offended glance but it is lost on Peter, who has his back to her, and meticulously, she slips to her knees and proceeds to stretch out on the hay. The hay bed is bumpy and hard and she has quite a difficult time getting comfortable; her efforts to do so are accompanied by painful sighs.—A close view shows PETER stopping to watch her, and his look is sympathetic and solicitous.—Then while Ellie groans and sighs and pounds the hay with her palm, Peter steps out of sight. Ellie is unaware of his departure, so busily occupied is she with her makeshift bedding. She squirms around unhappily and finally stretches out, deciding to make the best of it. She lies on her back, her hands clasped under her head, looking up at the stars.

ELLIE (*seen close, as she is lying back on hay bed*). You're becoming terribly disagreeable lately. Snap my head off every time I open my mouth. (*She waits for a reply, but receives none.*) If being with me is so distasteful to you, you can leave. (*Independently*) You can leave any time you see fit. Nobody's keeping you here. (*Martyr-like*) I can get along.

She waits a second and then turns to see what effect this has on him. The fact that Peter is gone doesn't quite register at first. She looks around calmly, then is puzzled, and finally she becomes panicky. She sits up with a start.

ELLIE (*murmuring, frightened*). Peter— (*There is a pause while she listens, but nothing stirs, and there is more apprehension in her voice.*) Peter!

Real terror comes into her face, and she is ready to cry. She gets to her feet.

ELLIE (*with a terrified outcry*). Peter!!

At this he comes running into the scene; under his arm he has a watermelon.

PETER. What's the matter?

ELLIE (*relieved*). Oh, Peter— (*She throws her arms around his neck and sobs freely.*)

PETER (*hoarsely*). What's got into you?

ELLIE (*clinging to him*). Oh, Peter! I was so scared.

With his free hand he removes her arm from around his neck and starts away.

PETER (*setting the watermelon down*). I wasn't gone more than a minute. Just went out to find you something to eat.

ELLIE (*a sob still in her voice*). I know —but—

PETER (*kicking the melon over to her*). Here. Eat your head off.

ELLIE. I don't want it now.

PETER (*vehemently*). Thought you were hungry!

ELLIE. I was—but—

PETER. But what!

ELLIE. I was so scared—that it scared—

PETER (*exasperatedly*). Holy Jumping Catfish! You can drive a guy crazy.

He kicks the melon viciously out of sight, and without any particular preparation or fuss, he flops down on his bed, following which Ellie goes to her bed and lies down, too. Then a close view of ELLIE appears, and at the moment she looks far removed from the spoiled, pampered, self-reliant brat of Alexander Andrews. Instead, she is a helpless baby, clinging to Peter's protective wing. She'd be ever so grateful right now for a little civility on his part, for a little tenderness and understanding, and she glances over at him, hopefully. PETER, however, stares up at the stars, dreamily; and we then see ELLIE turning away from him, disappointed. Still, the minute Ellie turns her head, Peter looks at her out of the corner of his eye, and it's a long and steady gaze. Then suddenly he gets an idea and rises. He finds his topcoat and goes to her.

PETER. Might get chilly later on. (*He spreads it over her.*) Better use this.

As he bends down to tuck her in, their faces are seen in close proximity. Ellie, tremulous and fearful, has her eyes peeled on him. The situation is imminent with danger; anything is likely to happen at this moment; and she is frightened and expectant—she knows how weak she would be, if he suddenly crushed her in his arms. Peter avoids her gaze. He, too, is a bit shaky. The temptation is there and his resistance is waning. He tucks her in and quickly turns away.—Ellie's eyes, however, never leave him. Immediate danger has

vanished, and it leaves her a little regret-
ful.

[A close view of PETER, as he walks over to
a rock and sits down, shows him nervously
taking out a cigarette and lighting it.

> PETER. You've had a lot of men crazy
> about you, haven't you?

ELLIE doesn't respond. She has the scrutin-
izing, speculative look of a girl who feels
herself falling in love with someone who
is practically a stranger to her, as a result
of which she is frightened.—Then a wider
view includes both of them and we see
that Peter, too, fights valiantly against a
mounting interest in this girl, who epi-
tomizes everything he dislikes. He creates
the impression in the following scene, that
in his analysis of her he is trying to dissuade himself from something he is bound
to regret. His attack on her, consequently,
is overly vicious.

> PETER. I guess you've pretty much had
> your own way with them. That's your
> trouble mostly. You've *always* had your
> own way. That's why you're such a mess
> now.

He pauses a second, waiting for a protest,
but Ellie offers none; she is too much absorbed in her own confusing emotions. A
close view then shows PETER taking a long
puff on his cigarette and exhaling the
smoke, watching it vanish before he speaks.

> PETER (*suddenly*). You know what gen-
> erally happens to people like you?—You
> get your values all mixed up. You at-
> tach all the importance to the wrong
> things. Right now, for instance, there's
> only one thought in your mind—to get
> back to King Westley.

He waits for a reaction, but a close view
shows ELLIE absorbed, and she remains
silent. Peter's voice continues.

> PETER'S VOICE. Comical part of it is, it
> isn't what you want at all. In a couple
> of weeks you'll be looking for the near-
> est exit. . . . (*Now seen with her*) Peo-
> ple like you spend all your life on a
> merry-go-round. I guess that's what
> makes you so dizzy. (*He rises and paces
> a few moments.*) You're always chasing
> after something. At least you think you
> are. Truth is, you're just running away.

(*Emphatically*) From yourself, mostly.
'Cause you're miserable. You hate your-
self. The world's full of people like you.
Don't know what they want.

> ELLIE. Do you know?

> PETER. Sure.

> ELLIE. What?

> PETER (*flatly*). Nothing. (*After a pause*)
> Nothing you'd give two cents for.

> ELLIE (*seen close*). Try me.

> PETER'S VOICE. I just want to be let alone,
> that's all. Life's swell if you don't try
> too hard. Most people want to get a
> strangle-hold on it. They're not living.
> They're just feverish. (*Now appearing
> with her*) If they didn't get themselves
> all balled up with a lot of manufactured
> values, they'd find what they want.
> Peace and calm. When you get right
> down to it, what's all the shootin' for,
> will you tell me? After all, you can only
> eat three meals a day, only sleep in one
> bed—(*Looking up*) Right now, that hay
> feels pretty good to you, doesn't it? Sure
> it does. 'Cause you were tired—and it's
> the only thing around.

> ELLIE. You sound like a hobo.

> PETER. I am. I only work when I have
> to. Two years ago I got a notion and
> went to China. There was a war going
> on. Swell! After a while it got stale.
> I went down to Tahiti. Just lay on the
> beach for six months. What could be
> sweeter?

> ELLIE. Doesn't sound very exciting.

PETER, seen close, looks at her for a long
time before speaking:

> PETER. I guess not. I'd have given odds
> it wouldn't mean anything to you. (*He
> goes over and flops down on his own
> side of hay.*) There were moments when
> I had hopes. When I—Aw, I'm wasting
> time— You're destined to be a dope the
> rest of your life. (*Contemptuously*) I
> pity you. Goodnight.

He turns over with a finality that precludes
any further discussion, following which a
close-up of ELLIE reveals that her eyes are
wide open, staring thoughtfully up at the
sky.—The scene fades out slowly.]

PART SEVEN

A ROAD fades in. It is day now, and Peter and Ellie are trundling along. Ellie limps, and wears an unhappy expression on her face.

ELLIE. What are you thinking about?

PETER. By a strange coincidence, I was thinking of you.

ELLIE (*pleased*). Really?

PETER. Yeah. I was just wondering what makes dames like you so dizzy.

ELLIE. What'd you say we're supposed to be doing?

PETER. Hitch-hiking.

ELLIE. Well, you've given me a very good example of the hiking— (*Strongly*) where does the hitching come in.

PETER (*amused at her*). A little early yet. No cars out yet.

She spies a rock and heads for it. Then we see her seated on the rock.

ELLIE. If it's just the same to you, we'll sit right here till they come. (*Peter comes over, sets his bag down, and prepares to wait.*) Got a toothpick?

PETER. No. But I've got a penknife. (*He extracts one from his pocket which he snaps open.*)

ELLIE. Hay—in my teeth.

She points to her front teeth, and Peter flicks the hay out of her teeth.

PETER. There it is. Better swallow it. We're not going to have any breakfast.

ELLIE. Needn't rub it in. (*Peter takes a carrot out of his coat pocket and starts nibbling on it. Ellie looks up at this.*) What're *you* eating?

PETER. Carrots.

ELLIE. Raw?

PETER. Uh-huh. Want one?

ELLIE (*emphatically*). No!! (*As Peter smacks his lips with satisfaction.*) It's a wonder you couldn't get me something *I* can eat.

PETER. You don't think I'm going around panhandling for you. (*He takes a bite.*) Best thing in the world for you—carrots. Had a tough time getting them. If that farmer ever caught me—goodnight!

ELLIE. I hate the horrid stuff.

While she speaks a car roars by at terrific speed. Peter and Ellie both jump up.

PETER. I wish you wouldn't talk too much. We let a car get away. (*Ellie goes back to her rock, despondently.*)

ELLIE. What if nobody stops for us?

PETER. Oh, they'll stop, all right. It's a matter of knowing how to hail them.

ELLIE. You're an expert, I suppose.

PETER. Expert! Going to write a book on it. Called the "Hitch-Hikers Hail."

ELLIE. There's no end to your accomplishments.

PETER. You think it's simple, huh?

ELLIE (*exaggeratedly*). Oh, no!

PETER. Well, it *is* simple. It's all in the thumb, see? A lot of people do it—(*waving*)—like this. (*He shakes his head sadly.*) But they're all wrong. Never get anywhere.

ELLIE. Tch! Tch! I'm sorry for the poor things.

PETER. But the thumb always works. Different ways to do it, though. Depends on how you feel. For instance, number one is a short, jerky movement —(*He demonstrates.*) That shows independence. You don't care if they stop or not. 'Cause you got some money in your pocket, see?

ELLIE. Clever.

PETER. Number two is a wider movement—a smile goes with that one—like this. (*He demonstrates.*) That means you got a couple of brand new stories about the farmer's daughter.

ELLIE. You figured that all out yourself, huh?

PETER. Oh, that's nothing. Now take number three, for instance. That's a pip. It's the pathetic one. When you're broke—and hungry—and everything looks black. It's a long movement like this—(*demonstrating*)—with a follow through.

ELLIE. Amazing.

PETER. Hm? Yeah, but it's no good if you haven't got a long face with it.

In the distance a car is heard approaching, and Ellie looks up quickly.

ELLIE (*excitedly*). Here comes a car!

PETER (*alert*). Now watch me. I'm going to use Number One. Keep your eye on that thumb, baby, and see what happens.

Peter steps forward into the road and does his thumb movement. The car approaches, but speeds right by, spreading a cloud of dust in Peter's face, leaving him staring at the departing car, nonplussed. Thereupon ELLIE (seen close) glances up at him, a satirical expression on her face.

ELLIE (*sarcastically*). I'm still watching your thumb.

Peter is still looking after the car.

PETER. Something must have gone wrong. I guess I'll try number two.

ELLIE. When you get up to a hundred, wake me up.

Another car is heard coming, and Peter steps forward, prepared to hail it. Then this dissolves to a long view of the ROAD as a stream of cars of every description speeds forward ("toward the camera") and vanishes. The view moving in to the side of the road, Peter is seen still in the same spot. He waves his arms, jerks his thumb, indulges in all sorts of gyrations, while Ellie remains slumped on her rock, completely worn out.

Now Ellie watches Peter out of the corner of her eye, her face expressionless. Peter continues his arm waving—but slows down like a mechanical toy which has run out. He finally gets down to just thumbing his nose at the passing vehicles; and then thoroughly wearied, he flops down on a rock near Ellie.

PETER. I guess maybe I won't write that book after all.

ELLIE. Yes. But look at all the fun you had. (*As he glares at her*) Mind if I try?

PETER (*contemptuously*). You! Don't make me laugh.

ELLIE. You're such a smart Aleck! Nobody can do anything but you. I'll show you how to stop a car—and I won't use my thumb.

The scene widens as she rises and steps forward.

PETER. What're you going to do?

ELLIE. Mind your own business.

She lifts her skirt to above her knees and pretends to be fixing her garter. Her very attractive leg is in full display. Almost instantly, we hear the screaming and grinding of quickly applied brakes, and Peter looks up astonished.

The scene wiping off, we then get a close view of Ellie and Peter sitting in the back of an open Ford. It is a broken-down, rickety affair of the 1920 vintage. Ellie grins victoriously up at Peter, who stares ahead of him, glumly.

ELLIE. You might give me a little credit.

PETER. What for?

ELLIE. I proved once and for all that the limb is mightier than the thumb.

PETER. Why didn't you take *all* your clothes off? You could have stopped *forty* cars.

ELLIE. We don't *need* forty cars.

Peter glares at her, and Ellie's eyes twinkle mischievously, following which we get a wider view which includes the driver of the car, Danker. He is a man of about thirty, a heavy set, loose chinned person; at the moment he is singing an aria from some opera. He suddenly stops, turning to Ellie and Peter in the back seat.

DANKER. So you've just been married,

huh? Well, that's pretty good. If I was young, that's just the way I'd spend my honeymoon—hitch-hiking. Y-e-s s-i-r!

And for no reason except that he cued himself into it, he bursts forth into song gustily.

DANKER (*singing*). "Hiking down the highway of love on a honeymoon.
Hitch-hiking down—
Down-down-down the highway
Down—."

Ellie and Peter in the back of the car react to the noise Danker makes.

PETER. Hey, hey, aren't you afraid you'll burn out a tonsil?

DANKER. Tonsil? Me? No! Me burn a tonsil? (*Singing*) "My tonsils won't burn—
As life's corners I . . .

PETER (*giving up*). All right, let it go.

DANKER (*completing his last line*). . . . turn."

The scene dissolves to the front of a LUNCH WAGON on a deserted road, and Danker's car drives into the scene and stops. Then we see Danker turning to Ellie and Peter.

DANKER. How about a bite to eat?

ELLIE (*quickly*). Why, I think that would be—

PETER (*stopping her*). No, thanks. We're not hungry.

DANKER (*sentimentally*). Oh, I see, young people in love are never hungry.

PETER. No.

DANKER (*singing as he leaves them*). "Young people in love
Are very seldom hungry.
People in love
Are very seldom hungry. . . . "

When he is out of sight, Peter glares at Ellie.

PETER. What were you going to do? Gold dig him for a meal?

ELLIE (*defiantly*). Why not? I'm hungry.

PETER. Eat a carrot.

ELLIE. Never! (*She starts out of car.*) I'm going in and ask him—

PETER (*grabbing her arm*). If you do, I'll break your neck.

She looks up at his glowering face, realizes he means it, and wilts under his dominant gaze.

PETER. Let's get out and stretch our legs.

Peter gets out, followed by Ellie, and they walk away from the car. Both are silent. At the DOOR of the LUNCH WAGON, then, Danker comes out and looks around furtively.—Ellie and Peter, as seen by him, appear, walking away, following which the view moves over to the Ford and drops down to a close-up of Peter's suitcase. Now Danker looks about quickly and starts toward his car. He springs into the car, steps on the starter, and is off.

ELLIE and PETER hear the motor. They wheel around, and their eyes widen in surprise.

PETER. Hey!

He flings his coat at Ellie and dashes after the Ford. He is then seen running after it when the car turns around a bend in the road. Peter continues the pursuit. This scene wiping off, the FORD now makes its appearance around the bend, and as it approaches, Peter is seen at the wheel. He looks like he's just been through a fight.— And as Peter rides in, Ellie comes running toward him.

ELLIE (*a note of great relief in her voice*). Oh, Peter! What happened? Are you all right?

PETER. Come on—get in.

ELLIE (*noticing a gash on his cheek*). Oh, you've been hurt! There's a cut on—

PETER (*impatiently*). Come on! Come on! (*At this she runs around to get in the other side.*)

ELLIE (*as she runs*). What happened?

PETER (*as we see them closer*). Just a road thief. Picks people up and runs off with their stuff. What a racket! (*By this time she is in the car.*)

ELLIE. What'd you give him for the car?

PETER. A black eye. (*Thereupon the car moves out of sight.*)

A close view shows Peter and Ellie driving along in the Ford. Peter looks ahead, uncommunicatively. Ellie glances up at him, and it is plain that something's on her mind.

ELLIE (*a little self-consciously*). Look—uh—how are the—uh—carrots holding out? Any left?

Peter glances at her. He knows what a concession this is on her part, and he smiles sympathetically.

PETER (*tenderly*). You don't have to eat the carrots. (*As she looks her surprise.*) Just passed a pond with some ducks in it.

ELLIE (*with a cry of joy*). Darling!

She reaches up and kisses his cheek, and Peter beams happily.

PETER (*looking worried*). Haven't much gas left in this thing. Got to start promoting some. (*Throwing her his coat*) Better take the things out of the pocket of that coat. Ought to be good for ten gallons.

The scene fades out.

PART EIGHT

ANDREWS' STUDY fades in, affording a close view of KING WESTLEY. He answers every description we have had of him. He is a stiff, handsome, stuffed-shirt gigolo. He sits in a chair, leaning on a cane, his gloves loosely in his hand. The view then moves back to reveal Andrews, who, from the opening of the scene, is speaking as he paces around the room.

ANDREWS. I haven't changed my mind, Westley, I want you to understand that! I don't like you! I never have! I never will! That's clear enough, isn't it?

KING. You've made that quite evident—with all your threats of annulment. (*Confident*) Well, it hasn't bothered me for a minute. Ellie and I got married because we love each other. And she's proving it; as far as I'm concerned there's going to be no annulment.

ANDREWS (*hard*). You've got a good thing and you're hanging on to it, huh? (*Andrews smiles in a very superior manner.*) All right, you win. I'll just have to get used to you. I admit I'm licked. But only because I'm worried. I've had detectives all over the country searching for her. I've seen thousands of photographs. Fortune tellers, nuts, every crank in the country has written me. (*Quietly*) Haven't slept one night this week. If I don't find her, I'll go crazy.

WESTLEY. I might have been able to help

if it weren't for you. I've been watched so closely, I—

ANDREWS (*impatiently*). Yes. I know. Well, you can help now. I issued a statement yesterday that I've withdrawn my objections. Begging her to come home. I haven't heard from her. Apparently she doesn't trust me.

WESTLEY. Why should she? After all—

ANDREWS (*interrupting*). All right. That's why I sent for you. (*Pointing to next room*) There's a room full of reporters out there. I want you to make a statement—that you've had a talk with me—that we've reached an understanding—that if Ellen comes home, I won't interfere with your marriage. Will you do that?

WESTLEY. If you really mean it, I will.

ANDREWS (*strongly*). Of course I mean it! I don't care whom she's married to—(*softly*)—as long as I can get her back. (*He starts out.*)

As Andrews opens the door, a number of reporters enter.

ANDREWS. Come in, boys. This is my— uh—this is King Westley. (*Westley rises.*) He has a statement to make.

REPORTERS. Hello, Westley. . . . How do you do. (*They group around him.*)

The scene dissolves to the side of a lonely ROAD at night. First there is a close-up of a newspaper headline, which reads.

ANDREWS WITHDRAWS OBJECTION
Magnate and Aviator Reconciled
"Everything all right. Come home, darling," says Westley.

Then the view draws back revealing that the newspaper is in the hands of Ellie, who sits in the car alone, gazing at the headlines. Then Peter's voice is heard.

PETER'S VOICE. All right, Brat.

At the sound of his voice, she is startled, and she quickly folds the paper and throws it out of sight. She starts to get out of the car.

ELLIE (*as she scrambles out of the car just as Peter comes up to her*). Any luck?

PETER. Yeah. He finally agreed to let us have a room.

ELLIE. What about money?

PETER. Talked him out of it. He thinks we're going to stay a week. I'll have to think of something before morning.

ELLIE. That's swell!

PETER. I'm glad you think so. If you ask me, it's foolish. I told you there's no sense in our staying here tonight. We could make New York in less than three hours.

ELLIE. I couldn't arrive in New York at three in the morning. Everybody's in bed.

PETER (*after a pause*). Okay. (*With a wave of his hand*) Cottage Number Three.

As they start toward it, the scene cuts to the OWNER'S CABIN. The owner of the auto camp and his wife are standing at window, looking out. She is a hatchet-faced shrew. He is meek and docile.

WIFE. There you go—trustin' people again. How many times did I tell you—

OWNER. He looked like an upright young feller to me, Ma.

WIFE. Yeah. They're all upright till they walk out on you.

OWNER. Said he was gonna stay a week.

WIFE. Mebbe.

OWNER. Worst comes to the worst, we got his car for security.

WIFE (*unconvinced*). I don't trust him.

The scene cuts to the inside of a CABIN not unlike the previous auto camp cabin in which Peter and Ellie spent a night. Peter's opened suitcase is on a chair, over which he leans. Ellie walks around, puffing at a cigarette.

PETER (*without looking up*). Well, here we are on the last lap.

Ellie crosses to the window and stares out moodily. Peter removes several things from his suitcase and lays them on the bed. There is a strained silence between them, as both are lost in their own thoughts. A close view of PETER as he putters abstractedly with the contents of his bag creates the impression that he empties it tonight rather ruefully. It somehow spells *finis* to their adventure.

PETER (*strangely*). Tomorrow morning, you'll be in the arms of your husband.

ELLIE (seen close) turns away from the window and looks at Peter. She stares this way for a long moment before speaking.

ELLIE (*in a still, small voice*). Yes. You'll have a great story, won't you?

PETER (*dryly*). Yeah, swell.

Peter takes the rope out of his bag. It is the one used for the "Walls of Jericho" previously. He lays it aside and then, remembering, retrieves it. For a moment he holds it in his hand, speculatively; then turning, proceeds to tack it up. The noise of the tacking attracts Ellie's attention, and Ellie (again seen close) turns and looks toward Peter.

ELLIE. Is that the Walls of Jericho going up?

PETER'S VOICE. Yep! The Walls of Jericho. (*At which she turns back to the window.*)

PETER (also seen close) stretches the rope across the room and tacks the other side.

PETER (*then reaching for blanket*). We certainly outsmarted your father. (*He throws the blanket over the rope.*) I guess you ought to be happy.

There is no response from her, a close view revealing that she quite obviously isn't happy. They are now separated by the blanket, and Peter gets her pajamas from his suitcase and throws them over the blanket.

ELLIE. Thank you. (*There is silence while Peter starts undressing.*)

ELLIE (*suddenly*). Am I going to see you in New York?

PETER (*laconically*). Nope.

ELLIE. Why not?

PETER glances up at the "Walls of Jericho" and after a speculative pause, speaks quietly.

PETER. I don't make it a policy to run around with married women.

A close-up of ELLIE, disclosing only her neck and shoulders, shows her slipping out of her clothes. She pauses—then looks up.

ELLIE. No harm in your coming to see us.

PETER'S VOICE. Not interested. (*At this Ellie's face falls. This is a definite rebuff.*)

ELLIE (*weakly*). Won't I ever see you again?

PETER (seen close) is now getting into his pajamas.

PETER. What do you want to see *me* for? *I've* served my purpose. I brought you back to King Westley, didn't I? (*His mouth screws up bitterly.*) That's what you wanted, wasn't it?

ELLIE is already in bed, staring up at the ceiling.

ELLIE. Peter, have you ever been in love?

PETER crawls into bed.

PETER. I probably did the world a great favor at that. Got two pinheads out of circulation. (*He reaches over and lights a cigarette.*) Cupid thinks he's doing something when he brings two lovers together. What good's that? *I'm* bringing two pains-in-the-neck together. I think I'll start an institution—hang out a shingle.

The view now widens to include both sides of the blanket. Ellie doesn't hear a word of Peter's attack. She is too intent on her own thoughts.

ELLIE. Haven't you ever *wanted* to fall in love?

PETER. Me?

ELLIE. Yes. Haven't you thought about it at all? Seems to me you could make some girl wonderfully happy.

PETER (*disdainfully*). Maybe. (*After a pause*) Sure—sure, I've thought about it. Who hasn't? If I ever met the right sort of a girl, I'd—(*Interrupting himself*) Yeah, but where you going to find her—somebody that's real—somebody that's alive? They don't come that way any more.

ELLIE's disappointment is apparent.

PETER (*seen close*). I've even been sucker enough to make plans. (*A long puff on his cigarette*) I saw an island in the Pacific once. Never been able to forget it. That's where I'd like to take her. But she'd have to be the sort of a girl that'd jump in the surf with me on moonlight nights—and love it as much as I did. (*He loses himself in his romantic contemplations.*) You know, those nights when you and the moon and the water all become one—when something comes over you—and you feel that you're part of something big and marvelous. (*Sighing*) Those are the only places to live. Where the stars are so close over your head that you feel you could reach right up and stir them around.

A close-up of ELLIE at this point shows that she is affected by his stirring description of a heaven—from which she is excluded, as she listens to him continuing.

PETER'S VOICE. Certainly I've been thinking about it. Boy, if I could ever find a girl who's hungry for those things—

PETER (again seen close) has disposed of his cigarette and now stares dreamily heavenward.

PETER. I'm going to swim in the surf with her—I'm going to reach up and grab stars for her—I'm going to laugh with her—and cry with her. I'm going to kiss her wet lips—and—

Suddenly stopping, he turns his head slowly, sensing Ellie's nearness; and the view, drawing back to include Ellie, shows her standing at his bedside, looking down at him yearningly.

Then we see them close together: Peter's face is immobile. Ellie drops to her knees.

ELLIE (fervently). Take me with you, Peter. Take me to your island. I want to do all those things you talked about.

Peter stares at her lovely face. His heart cries out with an impulse to crush her in his arms.

PETER (after a long pause; hoarsely). Better go back to your bed.

ELLIE (simply). I love you.

PETER (arguing with himself). You're forgetting you're married.

ELLIE (tensely). I don't care. I love you. Nothing else matters. We can run away. Everything'll take care of itself. (Begging) Please, Peter. You can't go out of my life now. I couldn't live without you. (In a choked voice) Oh, Peter—

Sobbing, she lays her head on his breast and throws her arms around him.— All is quiet for a moment as Ellie's head rests on his breast, while Peter struggles with an overwhelming urge to pour out his heart to her.

PETER (scarcely audible). Better go back to your bed.

There is a lengthy pause, neither of them stirs. Then Ellie slowly raises her tear-stained face and gets to her feet.

ELLIE (whispering). I'm sorry.

She turns and disappears behind the blanket. Peter remains motionless. Then a close view shows ELLIE, as she gets into bed, sobbing quietly. She hides her face in the pillow to suppress her sobs. It is the first time in her life that she has been so deeply hurt. A close view next shows PETER reaching over for a cigarette, which he lights. All his movements are thoughtful, meditative. He leans back and stares at the ceiling, until we see only the cigarette in his mouth as it emits slowly rising puffs of smoke. This dissolving, the cigarette is seen to be burnt three quarters down, a long, frail ash hanging perilously on. PETER is then seen as he removes the cigarette from his mouth and crushes it in a tray. He leans back on the pillow and for a moment he is quiet. Then glancing over in Ellie's direction, he calls to her:

PETER (softly calling). Hey, Brat—! (A pause) Did you mean that? Would you really go? (He waits for a response, but none comes. He tries again.) Hey, Brat—

He listens—all is quiet. He slips his covers off and crosses to the blanket, and peers over it.—She is asleep. Her tear-stained face rests on the pillow, her arm extends over her head. It is a childlike posture.

PETER is watching her tenderly. He speculates whether to awaken her and decides against it. He starts away.—Peter tiptoes around the room for a few moments, deep in thought. Then as an idea which he has been turning over in his mind begins to take form, he hastily begins dressing.

The scene dissolving, Peter is seen completely clothed and starting for the door when he thinks of something. He turns back, grabs his suitcase, stops to throw a kiss to Ellie, and goes out into the night. Thereupon the scene wipes off, disclosing a GAS STATION along the road at night. Here Peter is talking to a station attendant.

PETER. All I'm asking is enough gas to get me to New York. The bag's worth twenty-five dollars.

MAN (hesitatingly). Yeah, but I got a bag. My wife gave me one for Christmas.

PETER ("high-pressuring" him). Listen, man—I'll tell you what I'll do. When I come back in the morning, I'll buy it back from you and give you ten dollars profit? What do you say?

MAN (*looking at Peter's hat*). I ain't got a hat—

PETER. What?

MAN. I ain't got a hat.

PETER (*promptly putting it on his head*). Well, you got one now.—Come on, fill 'er up.

While he is still talking the scene dissolves to a view of Peter driving furiously, a broad, happy grin on his face, following which several scenes wipe off in succession (denoting the passage of time)—scenes of Peter driving at high speed, causing several cows to amble out of the way; of the CAR driving into the Holland Tunnel, and of the BACK ROOM of a SPEAKEASY where Peter stands in front of a small desk upon which there is a typewriter. Near him is a swarthy Italian.

PETER. Fine! That's fine, Tony. Now get me a drink and make sure nobody disturbs me for half an hour.

ITALIAN (*going out*). Sure. Sure, Pete.

As Peter plants himself in front of the machine, the scene dissolves to a close-up of the typewriter carriage upon which are typed the words:

"—and that's the full and exclusive story of Ellen Andrews' adventures on the road.

As soon as her marriage to King Westley is annulled, she and Peter Warne, famous newspaperman—and undoubtedly the most promising young novelist of the present era—will be married."

The view drawing back, Peter re-reads the last sentence, smiles contentedly, and as he yanks out the sheet, the scene wipes off disclosing the outside of GORDON'S OFFICE, the sign on the door reading: "Office—Mr. Gordon." Gordon's secretary is at her desk as Peter breezes in.

PETER (*rumpling her hair*). Hello, Agnes.

AGNES. Better not go in. He'll shoot you on sight.

PETER (*entering*). I haven't been shot at for days.

In GORDON'S OFFICE, Gordon is at his desk. He looks up when Peter enters.

GORDON (*rising to his full height menacingly*). Get out of here!

PETER (*advancing*). Wait a minute, Gordon—I—

GORDON (*quietly*). Get out!

Peter reaches his side, and grabs him by the arms.

PETER. Joe, listen—

GORDON. Don't "Joe" me.

PETER. Okay, Joe. Listen— You know I've always liked you. Anytime I could do you a great turn—anytime I ran into a story that looked good—I always came running to you, didn't I? Well, I got one now. Those wires I sent you were on the level. It's the biggest scoop of the year. I'm giving it to you, Joe.

GORDON. You mean about the Andrews' kid?

PETER. That's it. (*Tapping his pocket*) I got it all written up. Ready to go. All I want is a thousand dollars.

Upon hearing this GORDON is ready to jump out of his skin.

GORDON. A thousand dollars! (*Furiously*) Get out of this office before I throw you out bodily.

PETER. Don't get sore, Joe. This is something you got to do for me. I need a thousand dollars—and I need it quick. I'm in a jam.

GORDON (*softening*). What's the thousand bucks for?

PETER. To tear down the Walls of Jericho.

GORDON. What!

PETER. Never mind . . . Listen—suppose I should tell you that Ellen Andrews is going to have her marriage annulled.

GORDON. Huh?

PETER. That she's going to marry somebody else.

GORDON. You're drunk.

PETER. Would an exclusive story like that be worth a thousand bucks to you?

GORDON. If it's on the level.

PETER. Well, I got it, Joe.

GORDON. Who's she gonna marry?

PETER (*taking out the story from his pocket*). It's all right here. Give me the thousand and it's yours.

GORDON (*skeptically*). I wouldn't trust you as far as I could throw that desk.

PETER. Wait a minute, Joe. Use your bean. I couldn't afford to hand you a phoney yarn, like that. I'd be crazy. There isn't a newspaper in the country'd give me a job after that! I could go to jail!

GORDON. I'd put you there myself.

PETER. Sure. I wouldn't blame you, either.

GORDON. Who's the guy she's gonna marry?

PETER. I am, Joe.

GORDON (*his eyes widening*). You!

PETER. Yeah.

GORDON. Now I *know* you're drunk. (*He grabs his hat.*) I'm going home. Don't annoy me any more.

PETER (*running after Gordon as the latter starts out*). For heaven's sake, Joe— stop being an editor for just a minute. (*He grabs his arm.*) We've been friends for a long time, haven't we? You ought to know when I'm serious. This is on the level.

Gordon is affected by the sincere note in Peter's voice.

PETER. I met her on a bus coming from Miami. Been with her every minute. (*Hoarsely*) I'm in love with her, Joe.

GORDON. Well, I'll be—

PETER. Listen, Pal—you've got to get this money for me. Now. Minutes count. She's waiting for me in an auto camp outside of Philadelphia. I've got to get right back. You see, she doesn't know I'm gone. (*Self-consciously*) A guy can't propose to a girl without a cent in the world, can he?

While Peter has been speaking Gordon stares into space thoughtfully.

GORDON. What a story! (*Picturing it*) On her way to join her husband, Ellen Andrews falls in love with— (*Alert— grabbing paper out of Peter's hand*) Lemme see that a minute.

He moves to his desk excitedly, and Peter, a gleam of hope in his eyes, joins him, following which the scene cuts to the SHACK of the camp owner and wife in the early morning. The owner is suddenly startled out of his sleep by the voice of his wife calling, "Zeke! Zeke!" He looks up, just as she rushes into the room.

WIFE. I told you! I told you, you couldn't trust him! He's gone!

OWNER. Who?

WIFE. That feller last night, that's who! He was gonna stay a week, huh? Well, he's skipped. Took the car with him, too. We wouldn't have known a thing about it until morning if I hadn't took that magnesia. (*Pulling at him*) Come on, get up, don't lay there. Let's do something about it.

Thereupon the scene cuts to the AUTO CAMP CABIN affording a close view of ELLIE tossing restlessly in her sleep. Suddenly there is a loud banging on the door, and Ellie, startled, awakens.—The pounding continuing, Ellie looks around, frightened. The door suddenly bursts open, and the owner and wife enter. They both glance over at Peter's side.

WIFE. See that. They're gone!

OWNER (*timidly*). Looks like it, don't it? (*Suddenly he sees Ellie.*) Here's the woman, ma.

WIFE (*full of fight—glaring at Ellie*). Oh!!

ELLIE (*in a close view at Ellie's Bed as the owner and his wife come up to her; timidly—sitting up*). What's the matter?

WIFE. Where's your husband, young lady—

ELLIE. Husband?

WIFE. Yes—if he *is* your husband.

ELLIE. Isn't he here?

WIFE. No, he ain't! And the car's gone, too.

ELLIE (*bewildered*). Why, he'll be back.

WIFE. Yeah? What makes you think so! He took his suitcase and everything. (*Ellie is perceptibly startled by this piece of news.*) Kinda surprised, huh? It's just like I told you, Zeke. They ain't married a'tall . . .

There is a close view of ELLIE as the wife's voice continues uninterruptedly:

WIFE'S VOICE. . . . could tell she was a hussy just from the looks of her.

Ellie is lost in thought, trying to adjust herself to the idea of Peter's leaving her like this. She scarcely hears what is being said.

OWNER'S VOICE. Hey! You! Got any money?

ELLIE (*snapping out of her trance*). Why —no.

WIFE (*the three now seen together*). Then—you'll have to *git!*

OWNER. Yeah, you'll have to *git.*

ELLIE. Why, you can't put me out in the middle of the—

WIFE. Serves you right. Oughta be careful who you take up with on the road. You can't go plyin' your trade in my camp.

ELLIE. But can't you wait until morning—

WIFE. Ain't gonna wait a minute.

OWNER. Not a minute!

WIFE. Better start gettin' into your clothes.

OWNER. Yeah.

WIFE (*glaring at him*). Zeke. (*He looks up startled.*) Git!

OWNER (*disappointed*). Yes, Ma.

As Zeke leaves, the Wife plunks herself in a chair, grimly determined to wait until Ellie gets dressed and out.

ELLIE. Can I use your telephone? I want to talk to New York.

WIFE. You ain't gonna stick *me* for no phone calls. You can go down to the Sheriff's office.

The scene thereupon cuts to the EXTERIOR of the AUTO CABIN as Ellie emerges, the Wife standing in the doorway. In the foreground several people are scattered around the courtyard. One woman washes stockings under a pump. A man is changing the tire on his car. Ellie comes down the steps and crosses the courtyard.

WIFE (*shouting to her*). And listen, next time better keep away from here. I run a *respectable* place.

Ellie does not turn, but walks straight forward, trying to maintain her poise. The people in the courtyard turn to stare at her, and one of them snickers.

The scene dissolves to GORDON'S OFFICE as Peter is pocketing the money. Gordon is fondling the story.

PETER. Thanks, Pal. You saved my life.

GORDON (*waving the story*). Okay, Pete. (*He drops the story on the desk and escorts Peter out, his arm around his shoulder.*) For my dough, (*smiling*) you're still the best newspaperman in the business.

They reach the door, which Peter opens. Then they appear at the DOORWAY. Through the open door the secretary stares dumbfounded at their friendliness.

GORDON. S'long, kid. And good luck.

Outside GORDON'S OFFICE, Peter kisses the secretary as he passes through.

PETER. 'Bye, Agnes. You're beautiful. All women are beautiful! (*He goes out.*)

Gordon is immediately electrified into action.

GORDON. Oh, boy! What a yarn! What a yarn! (*Suddenly*) Get me Hank on the phone. Gotta hold up the morning edition.

While he speaks he dashes back to his desk. We then see him in his office.

SECRETARY'S VOICE. There's Hank.

GORDON (*grabbing phone*). Hank! Listen. Hold the morning edition. Break down the front page. Gonna have a completely new layout— Send a couple of re-write men in here. Don't do a thing— I got a story that'll make your hair curl.

During his speech, his other phone has been ringing persistently. He has ignored it until now. He picks up receiver:

GORDON (*into the second phone*). Yeah. Yeah. Don't annoy me. I'm busy. (*He bangs up receiver, and turns back to the first phone.*) Listen, Hank! Dig out all the Andrews pictures. Get Healy out of bed. I want a cartoon right away. (*The second phone rings impatiently, but Gordon ignores it.*) With King Westley in it. He's waiting at the church. Big tears streaming down his face. His bride hasn't shown up. Old Man Andrews is there, too. Laughing his head off. Everything exaggerated. You know —Now snap into it! (*He bangs up the receiver, and grabs the second phone, speaking into it impatiently.*) Yeah. Yeah. What is it?

A close view of GORDON, as he listens, shows his eyes widening with amazement.

GORDON. What!—Ellen Andrews! You're crazy!

This cuts to a TELEPHONE BOOTH where a reporter is seen speaking excitedly.

REPORTER. Yeah. She just phoned her father from an auto camp to come and get her. He's getting a police escort. Westley's going along, too. She's been traveling by bus. The moment she read that her father and Westley made up, she phoned in.

Back in GORDON'S OFFICE Gordon is seen still at the phone.

GORDON. You sure that's right! Say, you haven't been drinking, have you! Okay —grab a car—and stay with them. (*He hangs up the receiver and grabs the first phone.*) Put Hank on. (*Shouting*) Agnes! (*As the Secretary hurries in*) Get me a doctor. I'm about to have a nervous breakdown. (*She stares at him dumbly as he speaks into the phone.*) Hank—forget everything I just told you. I was just having a nightmare! (*He hangs up—and turns to Agnes.*) Call up the police department! Tell 'em to find Peter Warne. Send out a general alarm. I want the dirty crook pinched.

He picks up Peter's story and flings it viciously into the wastebasket.

AGNES (*starting out*). Yessir. (*Two re-write men come in, passing Agnes.*)

MEN. You want us?

GORDON (*wheeling around*). Yeah. Shove everything off the front page. Ellen Andrews just phoned her father—she's coming home. The moment she heard the old man withdrew his objections, she gave herself up. Spread it all over the place. Here's your lead: "Love Triumphant!" Step on it!

MEN (*leaving*). Yessir.

Gordon goes to his desk, mumbling to himself. His eye lights on the waste basket containing Peter's story, and he is about to kick it when he stops. He stares at it thoughtfully, reaches down, lifts it out— runs through it hastily—and then stares into space, deep in thought.

The scene dissolves to an open ROAD, in the morning, as Peter flies over it in his Ford. He beams happily. He passes a gasoline truck and waves cheerily to the driver. This dissolves to a close-up of an AUTO SIREN accompanied by a prolonged wail, then to a ROAD, that morning, as four motorcycles, two abreast, speed forward, followed by a luxurious limousine, which in turn is trailed by a car filled with reporters. Next, in the LIMOUSINE, Andrews is seen in the back seat. He is accompanied by King Westley —Henderson—Lovington, and a police inspector.

HENDERSON. I knew she was safe.

LOVINGTON (*sighing*). Certainly gave us a run for our money. (*But Andrews is too overwhelmed with joy to listen to any of this.*)

ANDREWS (*anxiously*). Can't you get them to go any faster? (*At this the Inspector leans over to talk to chauffeur.*)

This dissolves to a deserted ROAD, Peter at the wheel of his car. His high spirits find expression in his efforts to sing.

PETER (*singing*). "I found a million dollar baby—"

He is interrupted by the song of a meadowlark, whistling its strange melody. Peter listens to it a second time, then answers its call by imitating it. The meadowlark whistles again, and Peter is highly amused.

PETER (*waving his hand—to the meadowlark*). Okay, Pal. Be seein' you.

Just then the sound of sirens is heard in the distance. Peter glances back, and as the sirens come nearer, he pulls over to the side of the road. There follows a full view of the ROAD, with Peter in the foreground at the side as the police cavalcade whizzes by accompanied by the shrieking sirens. Thereupon PETER (seen close) gets an idea.

PETER (*to his Ford*). Come on, Dobbin, old boy. We got a police escort.

He applies the gas and shoots out of sight, following which a full view of the road shows Peter's car trying to catch up with the parade. It outdistances him, however, and we see PETER in the Ford pressing his body forward to help the car make time. His foot pushes the accelerator down to the floor.—But the police cars are now out of sight, and Peter gives up.

PETER (*seen close; to the car—with exaggerated dramatics*). Dobbin, me lad. You failed muh. I'm afraid you're gittin' old.

Thereupon the scene dissolves to a small town ROAD, where at the door of a Sheriff's office a policeman is standing on guard. The reporters hang around in front of him. Several yokels look on. The limousine and motor cycles are at the curb.—And now, in a closer view, at the DOOR the policeman on guard steps aside as the door opens and Ellie, her father, and King Westley emerge. King has his arm around her. The moment they appear in the doorway, cameras click and several reporters surround them.

REPORTERS. Will you make a statement, Miss Andrews? Was it an exciting experience? How did you travel?

ANDREWS (*brushing them aside*). Later, boys, later. See her at home.

They cross the sidewalk—to the waiting limousine, as cameras click.

The scene dissolves to a ROAD, with Peter still driving. He is, however, as before, in excellent form, and is singing lustily. Suddenly, however, his eyes widen and he pulls on his brake; the car screeches and moans—and comes to a stop.

PETER. Take it easy, Dobbin. Remember your blood pressure.

We find Peter directly in front of a slow moving freight train. Several hoboes stick their heads out of a car, and Peter waves to them. The hoboes look puzzled for a minute and then wave back. The view then swings over to an opening between the cars affording a flash of the police parade on the other side, apparently on its way back.

PETER amuses himself by talking to an old flagman.

PETER. Better get that toy train out of here. I'm in a hurry.

The Flagman grins at him in reply. By this time the last car is in sight, and Peter gets all set to move. He stops, however, to wave to a couple of brakemen on the rear platform.

In the meantime, the motorcycles have started forward, and the sirens begin their low, moaning wail. Peter, attracted, turns, and over Peter's shoulder we see the parade starting. As the limousine passes, we get a glimpse of the inside. Ellie lies back on King Westley's shoulder. He has his arm around her as they pass out of sight. Thereupon a close view of PETER shows him reacting to what he saw. He turns his head quickly to stare at the disappearing car, a look of astonishment and bewilderment in his eyes. Slowly he turns his head forward, staring ahead of him blankly; he can't quite make it out. Then gradually the significance of it all strikes him—and his mouth curls up bitterly.

The scene wiping off, a series of NEWSPAPER HEADLINES come into view:

"ELLEN ANDREWS RETURNS HOME."
"MARRIAGE HALTED BY FATHER TO BE RESUMED"
"ELLEN ANDREWS AND AVIATOR TO HAVE CHURCH WEDDING"
"LOVE TRIUMPHS AGAIN"
"PARENTAL OBJECTION REMOVED IN FAVOR OF LOVERS"
"CANNOT THWART LOVE SAYS FATHER OF ELLEN ANDREWS"
"GLAD TO BE HOME SAYS ELLEN"

This dissolves to the ante room of a NEWSPAPER OFFICE. The place is alive with activity, and copies of newspapers are lying around, bearing headlines relating to the Andrews story. Peter, a bewildered, stunned expression on his face, enters and crosses funereally toward Gordon's office.—Several people standing around look up.

PEOPLE. Hi, Pete— Didya see this? Ellen Andrews is back. Gonna marry that Westley guy after all— What a dame! What a dame!

Peter pays no attention to any of this. He reaches Gordon's door, which is open. He walks directly past Agnes and enters the office. She looks up at him, puzzled. Then in GORDON'S OFFICE, Peter walks to Gordon's desk and lays the roll of bills on it. Agnes enters, watching him anxiously.

AGNES. Gordon's out back some place. (*Seeing the money, she looks up, surprised.*)

PETER. See that he gets that, will you, Agnes? Tell him I was just kidding. (*He goes out.*)

As Agnes stares after him, puzzled, Gordon dashes in from a back door.

GORDON. You can't get a thing done around here unless—

AGNES. Peter Warne was just in.

GORDON. Huh? What?

AGNES. Left this money. Said to tell you he was just kidding.

GORDON (*looking at the money*). Where is he?

The scene cuts to the OUTER OFFICE and CORRIDOR, as seen over Gordon's shoulder through the open door. Peter is seen walking out. Gordon hurries after him.

GORDON'S VOICE. Hey, Pete!

At the sound of Gordon's voice, Peter turns, and Gordon comes over to him.

PETER. Hello, Joe. Sorry. Just a little gag of mine. Thought I'd have some fun with you.

GORDON (*understanding*). Yeah. Sure. Had me going for a while.

PETER. Wouldn't have made a bad story, would it?

GORDON. Great! But that's the way things go. You think you got a swell yarn— then something comes along—messes up the finish—and there you are.

PETER (*smiling wryly*). Yeah, where am I?

GORDON (*slipping a bill in his coat pocket*). When you sober up—come in and see me.

PETER (*a whisper*). Thanks, Joe.

He leaves, Gordon watching him sympathetically, and the scene fades out.

PART NINE

[The LAWN of the ANDREWS ESTATE fades in. It is morning and at the moment the place is a beehive of activity. Dozens of butlers and maids hustle around setting tables. Floral decorations are being hung by men on ladders. In the background on a platform, a twenty-piece orchestra is getting ready, accompanied by the scraping of chairs, adjusting of music stands, unpacking of instruments.

The scene cuts to ANDREWS' STUDY: King Westley is seated, and Andrews walks around him. They are both dressed in striped trousers, frock coat, etc.

ANDREWS. Well, here we are; it's all set. You're finally going to be married properly. (*He waves toward the window.*) With all the fanfare and everything. (*Shaking his head*) I still don't know how it happened—but you're going to be my son-in-law whether I like it or not. I guess you're pleased.

KING. Why, naturally, I—

ANDREWS (*drily*). Naturally. (*With vehemence*) You're going to become a partner in a big institution. It's one of the largest in the world.

KING. You talk as if—

ANDREWS. Someday perhaps, you might even take charge.

A close view of ANDREWS shows him looking around his study despairingly.

ANDREWS (*murmuring*). The thought of it makes me shudder.

KING'S VOICE (*confidently*). You might be surprised.

ANDREWS. I hope so. However, that'll take care of itself. (*Taking a new tack*) There's another responsibility you're taking on. One that I'm *really* concerned about.

KING'S VOICE. What's that?

ANDREWS. My daughter.

KING (*the two now seen again; lightly*). Ellie? Oh, she's no responsibility.

ANDREWS. No? Say, listen—I've devoted a whole lifetime trying to tame that wildcat. Toughest job I ever tackled. Ever hear of J. P. Clarkson? Biggest man in the country, isn't he? Well, I tamed *him*. Got him eating out of the palm of my hand. I've browbeaten financiers, statesmen, foreign ministers—some of the most powerful people in the world —but I've never been able to do a thing with her. She's been too much for me. I'm glad you think it's easy. (*He bends over him.*) Now listen—if you'll do what I tell you, perhaps I might develop a little respect for you. You never can tell.

KING. What would you like to have me do?

ANDREWS. Sock her!

A close view of KING shows him looking up, surprised, as Andrews' voice continues.

ANDREWS' VOICE. Sock her at least once a day. Do it on general principles. Make her know *you're* the boss and never let her forget it. Think you can do that?

KING. It's quite an assignment—

ANDREWS. Try. Do me a favor. Try. It's your only chance. And hers, too. Do that for me—and maybe we'll be friends.— (*Muttering*) Maybe. (*He holds out his hand.*) Do we understand each other?

KING (*taking his hand—rising*). Yes, sir.

ANDREWS (*dismissing him*). Fine. I'll see you at the reception.

: withdraws his hand, which he looks at

disgustedly—the result of a jellyfish handshake.

KING. Oh, by the way, Mr. Andrews, I thought of a great stunt for the reception. (*As Andrews looks at him quizzically*) I'm going to land on the lawn in an autogyro. What do you think of tht!

A close view of ANDREWS shows him staring off at King in complete disgust.

ANDREWS. You thought that up all by yourself, huh?

KING (*unabashed*). Why, it'll make all the front pages. A spectacular thing like that—

ANDREWS (*hard*). Personally, I think it's stupid! (*Humoring a child*) But go ahead. Have a good time. As long as Ellie doesn't object.

KING. Oh, no. She'll be crazy about it. Well, see you later. I'm going out on the lawn and arrange for landing space. (*Holding out his hand*) Goodbye. (*But Andrews turns his back on him.*)

ANDREWS. We've done that already.

KING (*smiling*). Yes, of course.

He turns and leaves; Andrews watching him go, shaking his head sadly.

ANDREWS. Autogyro! I hope he breaks his leg.

Andrews starts out, and the scene cuts to the HALLWAY as Andrews enters from the study. A maid coming down the stairs, he calls to her:

ANDREWS. Oh—Mary—

MARY. Yes, sir?

ANDREWS. How is she?

MARY (*hesitantly*). Why—uh—she's all right, sir.

ANDREWS. What's the matter? Anything wrong?

MARY. Oh, no, sir. No different than—

ANDREWS. Yes. Yes, I know. Still in the dumps, huh?

MARY. Yessir. If you'll excuse me, sir— she sent me for a drink. (*She leaves.*)

Andrews stands a moment thoughtfully and then starts up the stairs, following which the scene dissolves to the UPSTAIRS CORRIDOR in front of Ellie's door. Andrews enters and knocks several times. Receiving no response, he gingerly opens the door.] Next Andrews enters ELLIE'S BEDROOM and looks around. The view swings around the room, following his gaze. It focuses on Ellie, who reclines on a sofa, in her bridal outfit, her head resting on the back. She stares moodily, unhappily up at the ceiling. The view then expanding to include both father and daughter, Andrews is seen staring at her a moment sympathetically. He senses some-. thing is wrong.

ANDREWS (*after a pause*). Ellie—

ELLIE (*jumping up with a start*). Oh, hello, Dad.

ANDREWS (*a close view as he goes over to her*). I knocked several times.

ELLIE. Sorry. Must have been day-dreaming. (*To hide her confusion, she reaches for a cigarette.*)

ANDREWS (*with forced lightness*). Well, everything's set. Creating quite a furore, too. Great stunt King's going to pull.

ELLIE (*in a faraway voice*). Stunt?

ANDREWS. Landing on the lawn in an autogyro.

ELLIE. Oh, yes. I heard.

ANDREWS (*Noting her listlessness*). Yes. Personally, I think it's silly, too.

As he continues talking, the view moves with Ellie, who wanders over to a window overlooking the lawn and stares out, lost in thought.

ANDREWS' VOICE (*He goes over to Ellie*). You look lovely. Are you pleased with the gown? (*As Ellie does not seem to hear him, he becomes worried.*) Ellie!

ELLIE (*turning and looking at him blankly*). Huh? (*It just penetrates.*) Oh —the gown— (*Distantly*) Yes, it's beautiful.

ANDREWS (*tenderly*). What's the matter, Ellie? What's wrong?

ELLIE. Nothing. (*She walks over to table and crushes her cigarette.*)

ANDREWS. You've been acting so strangely since you returned. I'm—I'm worried. I haven't bothered to ask you any questions—I— (*Waving his hand toward the lawn*) Isn't all this what you wanted? (*Receiving no answer from Ellie*) You haven't changed your mind about King, have you?

ELLIE (*too quickly*). Oh, no.

ANDREWS. If you have, it isn't too late. You know how I feel about him. But I want to make you happy. You gave me such a scare—I—when I couldn't find you. (*Smiling feebly—meaning his heart*) You know, the old pump isn't what it used to be.

ELLIE (*her hand on his arm*). Sorry, Dad. I wouldn't hurt you for the world. You know that.

She moves away from him and sits on the sofa, and Andrews watches her a moment and crosses over to her. He sits beside her, placing an arm affectionately around her shoulder.

ANDREWS (*tenderly*). Ellie—what is it? Aren't you happy, child?

At this point she finally breaks, and impulsively buries her face on his breast.

ANDREWS (*after a pause, hoarsely*). I thought so. I knew there was something on your mind. (*There are audible sobs from Ellie.*) There—there!

They remain thus quietly for some time. Finally Andrews breaks the silence.

ANDREWS. What is it, darling? (*Receiving no answer*) You haven't fallen in love with somebody else, have you?

As this brings an audible sob from Ellie, Andrews lifts up her chin.

ANDREWS (*looking into her eyes*). Have you? (*Ellie turns her head away, a little ashamed of her tears.*)

Ellie now rises and walks miserably away from him, dabbing her eyes. Andrews, watching her, realizes he has hit upon the truth. He walks over to her.

ANDREWS. I haven't seen you cry since you were a baby. This must be serious. (*Ellie is silent.*) Where'd you meet him?

ELLIE. On the road.

ANDREWS (*trying to cheer her*). Now, don't tell me you fell in love with a bus driver!

ELLIE (*smiling*). No.

ANDREWS. Who is he?

ELLIE. I don't know very much about him. (*In a whisper*) Except that I love him.

ANDREWS (*the great executive*). Well, if it's as serious as all that—we'll move heaven and earth to—

ELLIE (*quickly*). It'll do no good. (*Wryly*) He despises me.

ANDREWS. Oh, come now—

ELLIE. He despises everything I stand for. He thinks I'm spoiled and pampered, and selfish, and thoroughly insincere.

ANDREWS. Ridiculous!

ELLIE. He doesn't think so much of you, either.

ANDREWS (*his eyes widening*). Well!

ELLIE. He blames you for everything that's wrong about me. Thinks you raised me stupidly.

ANDREWS (*smiling*). Fine man to fall in love with.

ELLIE (*whispering*). He's marvelous!

ANDREWS. Well, what are we going to do about it? Where is he?

ELLIE (*sadly*). I don't know.

ANDREWS. I'd like to have a talk with him.

ELLIE. It's no use, Dad. I practically threw myself at him. (*She shrugs futilely.*)

ANDREWS. Well, under the circumstances, don't you think we ought to call this thing off?

ELLIE. No, I'll go through with it.

ANDREWS. But that's silly, child. Seeing how you feel, why—

ELLIE. It doesn't matter. (*Tired*) I don't want to stir up any more trouble. I've

been doing it all my life. I've been such a burden to you—made your life so miserable—and mine, too. I'm tired, Dad. Tired of running around in circles. He's right, that's what I've been doing ever since I can remember.

A close-up of ANDREWS shows him watching Ellie, as her voice continues.

ELLIE'S VOICE. I've got to settle down. It really doesn't matter how—or where—or with whom.

ANDREWS (*seriously—impressed*). You've changed, Ellie.

ELLIE (*seen with Andrews; sighing*). Yes, I guess I have. (*Sincerely*) I don't want to hurt anybody any more. I want to get away from all this front page publicity. It suddenly strikes me as being cheap and loathsome. I can't walk out on King now. It'll make us all look so ridiculous. (*She shrugs resignedly.*) Besides, what difference does it make? (*Inaudibly*) I'll never see Peter again.

ANDREWS. Is that his name?

ELLIE. Yes. Peter Warne.

She starts to walk away when she is attracted by her father's surprise at the mention of the name.

ANDREWS. Peter Warne! (*His hand has instinctively gone to his inside pocket.*)

ELLIE (*noticing this*). Why? Do you know him? (*But Andrews withdraws his hand. Apparently he has changed his mind.*)

ANDREWS (*evasively*). Oh, no—no.

ELLIE (*suddenly anxious*). You haven't heard from him, have you, Dad?

ANDREWS (*obviously guilty*). Why, no. . . . Don't be silly.

ELLIE. Oh, please, Dad—

She has reached into his pocket and has extracted a letter, which she hurriedly opens and reads, following which we see a LETTER in Peter's handwriting. It is addressed to: "Alexander Andrews, 11 Wall Street." It reads:

"Dear Sir:

I should like to have a talk with

you about a financial matter in connection with your daughter.

> Peter Warne."

Ellie is then seen reading and re-reading the note. Her face clouds and then slowly changes to an expression of complete disillusionment.

ELLIE (*her voice strident*). Looks like that was his only interest in me. The reward.

ANDREWS (*taking the note from her*). I'm sorry you read it.

ELLIE. Are you going to see him?

ANDREWS. I suppose so.

ELLIE (*hard*). Certainly! Pay him off. He's entitled to it. He did an excellent job. Kept me thoroughly entertained. It's worth every penny he gets.

She paces agitatedly, Andrews watching her silently. He knows what an awful blow to her pride this must be.—Mary now enters with a cocktail tray which she sets on the table.

ELLIE. Thanks, Mary. That's just what I need. (*She pours herself a cocktail.*)

MARY. Mr. King Westley is on his way up.

ELLIE. Fine—Fine! Have him come in.

ANDREWS (*mumbling*). I'll be going. (*He goes out behind Mary.*)

Ellie swallows her drink and starts pouring herself another, as King enters.

ELLIE (*upon seeing him*). Well, if it isn't the groom himself! You're just in time, King.

A close view of the TWO shows King taking her in his arms.

KING. How are you, Ellie? (*He gives her a kiss, which she accepts perfunctorily. But he insists upon being ardent.*) Are you happy?

ELLIE (*releasing herself*). Happy? Why shouldn't I be happy? I'm getting the handsomest man in captivity. (*Handing him a drink*) Here you are, King. Let's drink. (*She holds her glass out.*) Let's drink to us. (*She drains the glass; pouring another, as she continues:*) We finally made it, didn't we?

KING. You bet we did.

ELLIE. It's up to you now. I want our life to be full of excitement, King. We'll never let up, will we? Never a dull moment. We'll get on a merry-go-round and never get off. Promise you'll never let me get off? It's the only way to live, isn't it? No time to think. We don't want to stop to think, do we? Just want to keep going.

KING. Whatever you say, darling.

ELLIE. I heard about your stunt. That's swell, King. Just think of it—the groom lands on the lawn with a plane. It's a perfect beginning for the life we're going to lead. It sets just the right tempo. (*Handing him a drink*) Come on, King. You're lagging. (*They both drink.*)

In ANDREWS' STUDY, Andrews walks around the room, perceptibly affected by his visit with Ellie. He keeps turning Peter's letter over in his hand, apparently debating in his mind what to do with it. He finally gets an idea—and determinedly crosses to the phone. Then the scene cuts to a HOTEL ROOM. First there is a close-up of a NEWSPAPER—a tabloid bearing a heading which reads: "LOVE TRIUMPHANT."

> "Interrupted Romance of Ellen Andrews and King Westley Resumed, as Father Yields. Wedding Reception to be Held on Andrews' Lawn."

Below this is a page of pictures, and the view turns to each photograph. The first picture is of Ellie and King on a beach. The title over the picture reads: "Where they met." The second picture shows them in the cockpit of a plane, the heading reading: "Where they romanced." The next picture is of a small frame house with a shingle on it reading: "Justice of the Peace." Over the photograph is a caption: "Where they were married." The next picture is of the Andrews yacht, and the title reads: "Where she was taken." Finally, the view moves down to the bottom of the page to a picture of Ellie and King, with her father between them, in front of Sheriff's office. Caption reads: "Where love triumphed."— Over these pictures the phone bell has been ringing.

And now PETER is seen staring, expressionless, at the newspaper. Suddenly he becomes conscious of the phone ringing; he looks up—then goes to it.

> PETER (*into the phone*). Hello. . . . Yes? . . . Who? . . . Oh . . . Why can't I see you at your office?

The scene cuts to ANDREWS' STUDY, affording a close view of ANDREWS at the phone.

> ANDREWS. I leave for Washington tonight. May be gone several weeks. Thought perhaps you'd like to get this thing settled.

This cuts to the HOTEL ROOM where PETER is at the phone.

> PETER. Yeah, but I don't like the idea of walking in on your jamboree. . . . Just between you and me—those things give me a stiff pain.

> ANDREWS (*seen in his office*). You needn't see anybody. You can come directly to my study. I'd appreciate it very much if—

> PETER (*at his phone*). No—no. What the deuce do I want to—

His eyes fall on something, and there follows a close view of a tabloid newspaper, featuring the heading: "Love Triumphant" and containing the pictures of Ellie and King. The view then moves down to feature headline reading "Groom to Land on Bride's Lawn."

> "King Westley plans to drop in an autogyro on the lawn of Andrews estate . . ."

Peter's mouth screws up disdainfully.

> PETER (*into the phone*). Yeah, wait a minute. Maybe I will come over. I'd like to get a load of that three-ring circus you're pulling. I want to see what love looks like when it's triumphant. I haven't had a good laugh in a week. (*He is still at the phone as the scene dissolves.*)

Then the LAWN of the ANDREWS ESTATE dissolves in. It is now filled with guests, who wander around, chattering gaily. The orchestra plays. A captain of waiters in the foreground instructs his men.

> CAPTAIN. I want everything to be just so. When the ceremony starts, you stand

on the side—*still*. No moving around— no talking, *comprenez*?

The view cuts to a ROADWAY leading to the estate, and Peter is seen driving up in his Ford and squeezing in between two Rolls-Royces. The uniformed chauffeurs glare at him. But Peter springs nonchalantly out of his car.

> PETER (*blithely, as he passes them*). Keep your eye on my car when you're backing up, you guys.

And as he goes, the chauffeurs look at each other, surprised. The scene dissolves to ANDREWS' STUDY, where a butler stands in front of Andrews who is seated at his desk.

> ANDREWS. Show him in.

The Butler leaving, a close view shows ANDREWS reaching over and snapping on a dictograph concealed somewhere on his desk. The office coming into view again, we see Andrews rising and awaiting Peter's entrance. After a moment Peter comes in, removes his soft felt hat, and tucks it under his arm.

> ANDREWS. Mr. Warne?

> PETER. Yeah.

> ANDREWS. Come in. Sit down.

Peter advances into the room, looking around curiously. His air is frigid, contemptuous as Andrews studies him, and he makes no move to sit. Andrews waves to a chair and sits down himself. Peter flops into the nearest chair.

> ANDREWS (*seen close with Peter; after a pause*). I was surprised to get your note. My daughter hadn't told me anything about you. About your helping her.

> PETER. That's typical of your daughter. Takes those things for granted. (*Too restless to sit, he jumps up.*) Why does she think I lugged her all the way from Miami—(*vehemently*) for the love of it?

> ANDREWS. Please understand me. When I say she didn't tell me anything about it, I mean not until a little while ago. She thinks you're entitled to anything you can get.

PETER (*bitterly*). Oh, she does, huh? Isn't that sweet of her! *You don't,* I suppose.

ANDREWS (*shrugging*). I don't know. I'd have to see on what you base your claim. I presume you feel you're justified in—

PETER (*seen close now*). If I didn't I wouldn't be here! (*He reaches into his pocket.*) I've got it all itemized. (*And he throws the paper on Andrews' desk.*)

ANDREWS picks up the paper and glances at it. After a moment, he looks at Peter, studying him interestedly; then he returns to the paper, and reads its contents:

"Cash outlay	8.60
Topcoat	15.00
Suitcase	7.50
Hat	4.00
3 shirts	4.50
Total	39.60"

Andrews looks up from the paper. This is a twist he hadn't anticipated, and he doesn't quite know how to handle it.

PETER (*now seen closer with Andrews*). I sold some drawers and socks, too; I'm throwing those in.

ANDREWS. And this is what you want—thirty-nine dollars and sixty cents?

PETER. Why not? I'm not charging you for the time I wasted.

ANDREWS. Yes, I know—but—

PETER. What's the matter? Isn't it cheap enough? A trip like tht would cost *you* a thousand dollars! Maybe more!

ANDREWS. Let me get this straight. You want this thirty-nine sixty in *addition* to the ten thousand dollars?

PETER. What ten thousand?

ANDREWS. The reward.

PETER (*sharply*). Who said anything about a reward!

ANDREWS (*smiling*). I'm afraid I'm a little confused. You see, I assumed you were coming here for—

PETER (*impatiently*). All I want is thirty-nine sixty. If you'll give me a check I'll get out of this place. It gives me the jitters.

ANDREWS. You're a peculiar chap.

PETER (*irritably*). We'll go into that some other time.

ANDREWS. The average man would go after the reward. All you seem to—

PETER. Listen, did anybody ever make a sucker out of you? This is a matter of principle. Something you probably wouldn't understand. (*He burns at the thought.*) When somebody takes me for a buggy ride I don't like the idea of having to pay for the privilege.

ANDREWS. You were taken for a buggy ride?

PETER. Yeah—with all the trimmings. Now, how about the check. Do I get it?

A close-up indicates that ANDREWS has been studying Peter throughout the scene. He is now completely won over.

ANDREWS (*smiling*). Certainly. (*He opens a checkbook and writes it out.*)

While Andrews writes, Peter wanders around the room in an attitude of bitter contempt. Andrews rises and goes to him.

ANDREWS. Here you are. (*As Peter takes the check.*) Do you mind if I ask you something frankly? (*Peter just looks at him without responding.*) Do you love my daughter?

PETER (*evasively, while folding the check*). A guy that'd fall in love with your daughter should have his head examined.

ANDREWS. That's an evasion.

PETER (*putting the check into a wallet*). She grabbed herself a perfect running mate. King Westley! The pill of the century! (*Pocketing wallet*) What *she* needs is a guy that'd take a sock at her every day—whether it's coming to her or not.

A close view of the TWO shows Andrews smiling: Here is a man!

PETER. If you had half the brains you're supposed to have, you'd have done it yourself—long ago.

ANDREWS. Do you love her?

PETER (*going for his hat as he replies*).

A normal human being couldn't live under the same roof with her, without going nuts. (*Going to the door*) She's my idea of nothing!

ANDREWS. I asked you a question. Do you love her?

PETER (*snapping it out*). Yes! (*As Andrews smiles*) But don't hold that against me. I'm a little screwy myself.

He snaps the door open and goes out, following which ANDREWS is seen watching the door, his eyes twinkling, and the scene cuts to the DOWNSTAIRS HALLWAY as Peter comes through, moving on to the front door. But just as he reaches it, Ellie enters, accompanied by half a dozen men and holding a cocktail in her hand. They see each other almost simultaneously, and both stop, glaring.

PETER (*looking her over contemptuously*). Perfect! Now you look natural.

At this Ellie leaves her group and comes toward Peter, and a close view shows them together, glaring at each other.

ELLIE (*icily*). I hope you got your money.

PETER. You bet I did.

ELLIE. Congratulations.

PETER. Same to you.

ELLIE. Why don't you stay and watch the fun? You'll enjoy it immensely.

PETER. I would. But I've got a weak stomach.

He wheels around and goes through the door, Ellie looking after him, her eyes blazing.—The drone of a plane motor outside is heard, and several people rush down the stairs, all excited.

GUESTS. Here comes King! He's just coming down! Hurry up, everybody! Come on, Ellie!

Immediately there is a general excitement, as guests hurry through the hallway on the way to the lawn. But Ellen does not move —she remains staring blankly at the door through which Peter went until Andrews enters from his study.

ANDREWS. I just had a long talk with him.

ELLEN (*her voice breaking*). I'm not interested.

ANDREWS. Now, wait a minute, Ellie—

ELLIE (*sharply*). I don't want to hear anything about him!

She walks away from him, and Andrews, frustrated, looks at her helplessly. Thereupon the scene dissolves to a full view of the LAWN. The orchestra is playing Mendelssohn's Wedding March. The lawn is crowded with guests. In the background we see the autogyro idling. A closer view shows a small platform, serving as an altar. Over it there is an arbor of roses. Back of the altar stands a minister, ready. A reverse view reveals a long, narrow, carpeted pathway leading to the house. Both sides are lined with guests, who are murmuring excitedly. At the moment, King Westley and his best man are marching solemnly toward the altar.—Back of the altar we see a high platform upon which are several newsreel men who are grinding their cameras.

The guests, of whom close glimpses are caught, are now peering over each other's shoulders.—King and his best man have reached the altar, and the music of the wedding march comes to a stop.—The orchestra leader is looking around, apparently waiting for a signal. At the DOOR of the HOUSE a very "prissy" middle-aged man waves his handkerchief and nods his head to the orchestra leader.—The orchestra leader acknowledges the signal by nodding his head—turns to his men—waves his baton, and the orchestra starts playing, "Here Comes the Bride."—The guests whisper to each other excitedly. A great deal of stirring takes place.

The door of the house slowly opens—and a parade of small flower girls emerges. They march, taking each step carefully, while they strew flowers along the path. They are well out of the way when Ellie, on the arm of her father, appears in the doorway.—A view of the guests shows that they cannot contain themselves. Murmurs of "Here she comes," and "Doesn't she look beautiful?" are heard.—The newsreel men on their platform behind the altar bestir themselves. This is what they've been waiting for!

ELLIE and her FATHER (seen close) now

make their way to the altar. Ellie's face is solemn, and her jaws set.

ANDREWS (*whispering out of the side of his mouth*). You're a sucker to go through with this.

Ellie glances at him out of the corner of her eye—and quickly turns forward again.

ANDREWS. That guy Warne is O.K. He didn't want the reward.

Ellie keeps her eyes glued in front of her, remaining expressionless.

ANDREWS. All he asked for was thirty-nine dollars and sixty cents . . . that's what he spent on you. It was a matter of principle with him—says you took him for a ride.

This registers on Ellie and she raises her eyes—but her reaction is only slightly perceptible.

A close view of a GROUP OF GUESTS shows two girls looking enviously in the direction of the bride.

A YOUNG GIRL (*whispering*). I wish I were in her shoes.

SECOND GIRL. Yes. She certainly is lucky.

ELLIE and her FATHER are seen again, and ANDREWS is still whispering to her.

ANDREWS. He loves you, Ellie. Told me so.

This brings a definite reaction, which she quickly covers up.

ANDREWS. You don't want to be married to a mugg like Westley.

At this there is a close view of Westley— there is a satisfied smirk on his face.

ANDREWS. I can buy *him* off for a pot of gold, and you can make an old man happy, and you wouldn't do so bad for yourself. If you change your mind, your car's waiting at the back gate.

Ellie gives no indication of her intentions. Her face remains immobile.—And now Ellie and her father have reached the altar. The 'prissy" man is placing them in position. The big moment has arrived. The guests are all atwitter. But a close view of ELLIE shows that she realizes that her fate is closing in on her. She looks around for a means of escape.

MINISTER (*starting the ceremony*). Dearly beloved, we are gathered together here in the sight of God and in the face of this company to join together this man and this woman in holy matrimony. If any man can show just cause why they may not lawfully be joined together, let him speak now or else hereafter forever hold his peace. King, wilt thou have this woman to be thy wedded wife? So long as ye both shall live?

KING. I will.

MINISTER. Ellen, wilt thou have this man to be thy wedded husband so long as ye both shall live?

Then, seen at the ALTAR, Ellie makes her decision. She reaches down, takes a firm hold on her train and, pushing several people aside, runs out of the scene. Those at the altar look up, surprised, and the most startled of all is KING himself.

KING (*calling after her*). Ellie!

He starts to go after her—but finds Andrews in his way while the outcries of the guests rise in chorus.

GUESTS. What's happened? Where's she going?

On the platform, the Newsreel Men, a look of astonishment on their faces, decide to follow Ellie.

A MAN. Get her, Mac! She's ducking!

And, as viewed by the newsreel men, Ellie is seen in the distance dashing through the gates. The guests stare dumbfounded. Following this, Andrews and King are seen together in the crowd.

KING (*helplessly*). What happened?

ANDREWS (*blandly*). I haven't the slightest idea.

But his mouth twitches as he tries to keep from smiling. As King runs out of sight Andrews gets out a cigar and lights it—a happy smile on his face which he now doesn't try to conceal.

Outside the FRONT GATE Ellie is seen in a fast roadster, as she starts away with a plunge. Her eyes sparkle.—A crowd of people dash up, headed by King. They stop dead when they see the car disappear.—On the LAWN the commotion runs high, and the guests chatter their amazement. A close view of ANDREWS shows him smiling with satisfaction.

The scene dissolves to ANDREWS' OFFICE, where Andrews is regaling himself with a whiskey and soda. He is in a pleasantly inebriated mood when his SECRETARY enters.

ANDREWS (*as he picks up the phone that has started ringing*). Don't want to talk to—don't want to talk to anybody. Don't want to see anybody.

SECRETARY. But it's King Westley on the phone.

ANDREWS. Ooooooh. (*Into the phone*) Hello my would be ex-son-in-law. I've sent you a check for a hundred thousand. Yes. That's the smartest thing you ever did, Westley, not to contest that annulment. That's satisfactory, isn't it? Yeah. Well, it ought to be. Oh I'm not complaining. It was dirt cheap. (*As he hangs up*) Don't fall out of any windows.

SECRETARY (*placing a telegram on the desk*). There's another wire from Peter, sir. They're in Glen Falls, Michigan.

ANDREWS (*reading it*). "What's holding up the annulment, you slow poke? The Walls of Jericho are toppling." (*To the Secretary*) Send him a telegram right away. Just say: "Let 'em topple."

This dissolves to the exterior of an AUTO CAMP very much like the other camps at which Peter and Ellie stayed. The owner's wife is talking to her husband.

WIFE. Funny couple, ain't they?

MAN. Yeah.

WIFE. If you ask me, I don't believe they're married.

MAN. They're married all right. I just seen the license.

WIFE. They made me get 'em a rope and a blanket, on a night like this.

MAN. Yeah?

WIFE. What do you reckon that's for?

MAN. Blamed if I know. I just brung 'em a trumpet.

WIFE (*puzzled*). A trumpet?

MAN. Yeah. You know, one of those toy things. They sent me to the store to get it.

WIFE. But what in the world do they want a trumpet for?

MAN. I dunno.

The scene moves to the cabin occupied presumably by Peter and Ellie. The windows are lighted. There is a blast from a trumpet, and as the lights go out a blanket is seen dropping to the floor, and the scene fades out.

REVISED OPENING SCENE

In the final cut version of the film the opening dialogue sequence, considerably more brief than in the original script, was as follows:

ANDREWS. Hunger strike, eh? How long has this been going on?

CAPTAIN. She hasn't had anything yesterday or today.

ANDREWS. Send her meals up to her regularly?

CAPTAIN. Yes, sir.

ANDREWS. Well, why don't you jam it down her throat?

CAPTAIN. Well, it's not as simple as all that, Mr. Andrews.

ANDREWS. Ah! I'll talk to her myself. Have some food brought up to her.

CAPTAIN. Yes, sir.

ELLIE. I'm not going to eat a thing until you let me off this boat.

ANDREWS. Aw, come now, Ellie. You know I'll have my way.

ELLIE. Not this time, you won't. I'm already married to him.

ANDREWS. But you're never going to live

under the same roof with him. I'll see to that.

ELLIE. Can't you get it through your head that King Westley and I are married? Definitely, legally, actually married. It's over, it's finished. There's not a thing you can do about it. I'm over twenty-one and so is he.

ANDREWS. Would it interest you to know that while you've been on board, I've been making arrangements to have your marriage annulled?

ELLIE. Annulled? I'll have something to say about that and so will King.

ANDREWS. Yes, I expect him to. Ah, the victuals. Come in. Come in.

ELLIE. I thought I told you not to bring any food in here.

ANDREWS. Now wait a minute. This isn't for you. Put it right down here.

ELLIE. Smart, aren't you? So subtle.

ANDREWS. Strategy, my dear.

ELLIE. I suppose it was strategy sending those gorillas down to drag me away from that Justice of the Peace. Your idea of strategy is to use a lead pipe.

ANDREWS. I've won a lot of arguments with a lead pipe.

ELLIE. Outside of the fact that you don't like him, you haven't got a thing against King.

ANDREWS. He's a fake, Ellie.

ELLIE. He's one of the best flyers in the country.

ANDREWS. He's no good and you know it. You married him only because I told you not to.

ELLIE. You've been telling me what not to do ever since I can remember.

ANDREWS. That's because you've always been a stubborn idiot.

ELLIE. I come from a long line of stubborn idiots.

ANDREWS. Well, don't shout. You may work up an appetite.

ELLIE. I'll shout if I want to. I'll scream if I want to.

ANDREWS. All right, scream.

ELLIE. If you don't let me off this boat, I'll break every piece of furniture in this room.

ANDREWS. Here, here, here. Have a nice piece of juicy steak. You don't have to eat it; just smell it. It's a poem.

(End of cut sequence.)

THE WOMEN

(*An M G M Picture*)

Screenplay by
ANITA LOOS AND JANE MURFIN

Based on the Play *The Women* by
CLARE BOOTHE

Produced by HUNT STROMBERG

Directed by GEORGE CUKOR

The Cast

MARY (Mrs. Stephen Haines) .	Norma Shearer
CRYSTAL ALLEN	Joan Crawford
SYLVIA (Mrs. Howard Fowler) .	Rosalind Russell
THE COUNTESS DE LAVE .	Mary Boland
MIRIAM AARONS	Paulette Goddard
EDITH (Mrs. Phelps Potter) .	Phyllis Povah
PEGGY (Mrs. John Day) . .	Joan Fontaine
LITTLE MARY	Virginia Weidler
MRS. MOREHEAD	Lucille Watson
NANCY BLAKE	Florence Nash
JANE	Muriel Hutchison
INGRID	Esther Dale
EXERCISE INSTRUCTRESS .	Ann Morriss
MISS WATTS	Ruth Hussey
OLGA	Dennie Moore
MAGGIE	Mary Cecil
MISS TRIMMERBACK . . .	Mary Beth Hughes
PAT	Virginia Grey
MRS. VAN ADAMS	Cora Witherspoon
DOLLY DE PUYSTER . . .	Hedda Hopper

Film Editor—ROBERT J. KERN

THE WOMEN

PART ONE

As the view fades in we look down toward two female DOGS being led along the sidewalk on leashes. One (a small breed such as a Peke) is coming from the north—the other from the south. Each is led by a woman who is only seen from the knees down. As the two dogs approach each other they begin to snarl. Their leashes tighten. As they pass, both strain to get at each other, their snarls rising in pitch. The hands of one of the women reach down and pick up the snarling little Peke. Following this we see the woman who has picked up the Peke: She is a tall, Junoesque matron—Mrs. Van Adams.

MRS. VAN ADAMS (*to the Peke, as she heads for the entrance to Sidney's, the Peke still growling and barking after its enemy*). Did the bad, bad monster try to fight with Muddy's little girlie? (*By which time she reaches the door and goes quickly inside, the Peke still struggling to get at the other one whose insolent snarls continue.*)

SIDNEY'S RECEPTION FOYER appears as Mrs. Van Adams enters with her dog and heads for the checking room.

THE GIRL AT RECEPTION DESK (*who is in the background—in quiet tones, talking on the phone*). Good morning . . . Sidney's . . . Sorry, madam, but Marie is all booked up. I could give you our new manicurist, Olga . . .

A WOMAN (*who is leaving*). Imagine marrying a title these days! (*Her speech and her companion's are simultaneous with the Receptionist's words on the telephone.*)

HER COMPANION. Imagine! Why for the same money, you could get yourself a baseball team!

WOMAN. And they'd all be nice clean-cut Americans.

By which time Mrs. Van Adams goes into a checking room. Then the ROOM left of the entrance quickly appears as Mrs. Van Adams enters. The room is in charge of a colored maid. There are seven or eight dogs there, all of different breeds and ages, yapping at each other. The maid has one lying on its back while she scratches its tummy.

MAID (*to the dog—talking as Mrs. Van Adams enters*). You sure is sweet and nice, honey, but you certainly needs some perfume on your breath. . . . Good morning.

MRS. VAN ADAMS. Good morning, Olive. (*Distastefully—looking the other dogs over*) Great grief! Wouldn't you think women would leave beasts like those at home?

MAID (*polite and dead pan*). Yes, ma'am.

MRS. VAN ADAMS (*to her Peke in baby talk as she hands it over*). Lilly's different! Lilly's Muddy's little playmate!

MAID (*same as before*). Yes, ma'am.

MRS. VAN ADAMS (*taking a small bottle of Poland water from handbag*). Here's her special drinking water, Olive.

MAID. She don't never want a drink, Mrs. Van Adams.

MRS. VAN ADAMS. Oh, but one never can tell! One day she *may!*

MAID (*polite and dead pan*). Yes, ma'am.

MRS. VAN ADAMS (*heading for the door*). If she cries for me, Olive, just tell her Muddy's getting all booful for her precious little girlie.

OLIVE (*quizzically*). Yes, ma'am. I'll tell her.

As Mrs. Van Adams turns to go, Olive sticks her tongue out at her. Then the RECEPTION ROOM appears quickly as Mrs. Van Adams enters and heads for the Receptionist.

RECEPTIONIST. Good morning, Mrs. Van Adams.

MRS. VAN ADAMS. Good morning. Mrs. Carter and I are being done together. Is she here yet?

RECEPTIONIST. She's in the garden, Mrs. Van Adams.

MRS. VAN ADAMS. Thanks. (*And she heads for the garden.*)

RECEPTIONIST (*to Mrs. Van Adams as she goes*). Mr. Sidney told her to go out there and breathe in a little *spiritual* beauty.

Mrs. Van Adams smiles and goes out. Then the GARDEN materializes as Mrs. Van Adams enters.

MRS. VAN ADAMS (*looking off*). Hello, darling.

VOICE OF MRS. CARTER (*who is out of sight*). Hello, sweet.

As Mrs. Van Adams goes out of sight, we see Mrs. Carter, a companion, another woman slumped in a chair, and a Saleswoman.

SALESWOMAN (*holding up a tiny jar*). . . . and you've no idea what this tiny fellow will do for those stubborn little granular cells of yours.

MRS. CARTER (*mildly interested, taking the jar*). Really? (*Turning, and addressing a companion*) So I said to Hubert last night—I said "exhilarated my eye! You're stiff as a plank and I get that new necklace or else!"

At which point, the First Nurse appears coming down the stairway.

FIRST NURSE (*speaking to the very dejected looking lady, slumped in a chair. She is Mrs. Erskine, who has had a bad night*). Oh, Mrs. Erskine.

A close-up shows Mrs. Erskine looking up blearily.

FIRST NURSE (*approaching her*). We're ready for you.

She helps Mrs. Erskine to rise and they start upstairs, the view moving with them.

FIRST NURSE (*looking at a slip of paper*). You're to have quite a heavy morning— a basic metabolism—a phenolsuphon-

phthalein test and a check up on your specific dynamic action and a capillary fragility.

MRS. ERSKINE (*blearily*). I see. The works!

By which time they reach the DIET BAR, attended by a Dietician in uniform, who is working a Juice Extractor. Two women sit at the bar drinking juice.

MRS. ERSKINE (*speaking to a woman at the bar—a Mrs. Spencer*). Hello, dear.

MRS. SPENCER. How are you, Violet?

MRS. ERSKINE (*as she starts to sit at bar*). Awful! I ate lobster at the opening of the Ritz.

FIRST NURSE. Sorry, Mrs. Erskine—but your metabolism test requires an *empty* stomach.

MRS. ERSKINE. Oh, it won't make a bit of difference. I've already had ham and eggs. (*To Dietician*) Tomato juice. (*Whereupon First Nurse subsides patiently.*)

DIETICIAN (*to Mrs. Erskine—as she works the Juice Extractor*). We're not serving tomato juice plain, madame. Dr. Bleistone feels that a better combination of calcium, Vitamin A, B-1, and D can be achieved by a mixture of pineapple, spinach and passion fruit with just a touch of pomegranate to take care of one's chloasmic spots.

MRS. ERSKINE (*leaning on bar*). Well— go ahead. I'm game.

At which point the Second Nurse appears from the reception room.

SECOND NURSE. Mrs. Spencer—your skin analysis. (*Speaking with great patience*) We've been waiting.

MRS. SPENCER (*rising—to the woman friend who has accompanied her*). Come along, dear, and help me face it.

They start through the door, and the scene moves to the RECEPTION ROOM where the Second Receptionist sits at a desk. She looks up as the nurse ushers in Mrs. Spencer and her friend. Several other women sit on couches, reading various books, while they wait for their appointments. Other women are looking at an exhibition of miniature furniture.

MRS. SPENCER (*spotting the miniature furniture*). Oh, look at Sidney's miniatures.

MRS. SPENCER'S FRIEND. Miniatures! H'm! Sure sign of a petty mind!

RECEPTIONIST (*approaching with great patience*). They've been waiting half an hour, Mrs. Spencer. Would you mind seeing the art exhibit later?

MRS. SPENCER. Oh—all right! (*As they proceed*) Art exhibit, my foot!

The scene moves to the SKIN ANALYSIS ROOM as the Second Nurse shows in Mrs. Spencer and her friend. (The analysis paraphernalia is in the foreground. In the background a woman sitting at a little table is being instructed in the application of make-up by a make-up artist.)

MAKE-UP ARTIST (*to her client*). With your stratum corneum in its present condition, Miss Hicks, it's better for the papillary layers of the skin to use a fatty powder base.

MISS HICKS (*understanding nothing but vastly impressed*). Oh—is it?

SECOND NURSE (*to Mrs. Spencer—setting skin analyzer*). Sit right here, Mrs. Spencer. That's right.

MRS. SPENCER'S FRIEND. How fascinating!

SECOND NURSE (*to Mrs. Spencer*). Now —just hold your face there a moment, and keep absolutely still.

MRS. SPENCER'S FRIEND (*shoving the nurse aside*). Let me see! (*Peering through the instrument*) Good grief! I hate to tell you, dear, but your skin makes the Rocky Mountains look like *chiffon velvet!*

During this speech, the Third Nurse comes through from the reception room on the way to the metabolism room, exchanges a very slight glance with Second Nurse, and goes through the door. Then the scene moves to the METABOLISM ROOM as Third Nurse enters. Here a woman is stretched out on the table with a clamp on her nose and a gag in her mouth. She rolls agonized eyes at the nurse.

THIRD NURSE (*sweetly—looking at watch*). Only half a minute more, Mrs. Miller, and *you can talk again!*

At which point a young girl of sixteen pokes her head through the door, letting in some squealing sounds from the next room.

YOUNG GIRL. Oh! Beg your pardon. I'm looking for Grandma.

As the nurse restrains her annoyance at the interruption she withdraws and the scene moves to a BATHROOM where the young girl closes the door. A big, fat woman, Mrs. Maxwell, is letting out squeals as, hidden by a towel held up by the First Masseuse, she gets into a mud bath. A very pretty young woman sits in the opposite bath tub completely covered, except for her head, by the foam bath.

YOUNG GIRL (*addressing them in general*). Grandma isn't in there.

FAT WOMAN (*annoyed at the intrusion on her privacy*). Well, she isn't in here! Oh, this mud's got worms in it—(*between squeals*)—I know it's got worms in it. I can feel 'em!

FIRST MASSEUSE (*gently*). No, it hasn't, Mrs. Maxwell. Now, don't be a coward!

THE PRETTY GIRL (*the one in the foam bath; mischievously to Mrs. Maxwell*). They're probably more scared of you than you are of them.

YOUNG GIRL (*heading for opposite door*). What's a little worm, Mrs. Maxwell? Up in Harvard and Yale they *eat* them!

MRS. MAXWELL (*as she sinks into the mud*). O-o-oo.

The young girl goes out, and the scene moves to the WAX BATHROOM as the young girl enters. A fat client is seated, her back turned, as the Second Masseuse smears hot wax onto her back.

SECOND MASSEUSE (*to the young girl— trying not to show her annoyance*). Why don't you look for your grandmother out in front, dear?

YOUNG GIRL. Oh, I have. (*Making no move to leave*) Grandma's awful. We never know where she's at.

EUPHIE (*entering with juice*). Potassium and lemon for Miss St. Clair.

SECOND MASSEUSE (*indicating her client*). This is Mrs. Goldstein.

EUPHIE. Oh!

YOUNG GIRL (*to Masseuse—cutting in*). All right I'll try out front. (*She goes out the way she came.*)

SECOND MASSEUSE (*to Euphie—gesturing into the next room*). Miss St. Clair may be in there. (*To her client—soothingly —sweetly*) I know it's hot, Mrs. Goldstein. But just concentrate . . . concentrate on the lovely svelte willowy figure you're going to have . . . maybe.

At this point Euphie goes out and the scene moves to the FIRST MASSAGE ROOM as Euphie enters. Here a very thin woman is stretched out on the table, her body covered by a towel—her neck being soothingly and gently massaged.

EUPHIE. Potassium and lemon for Miss St. Clair.

THIRD MASSEUSE (*gesturing to table*). Put it down please, Euphie. (*Soothingly to her patient*) Just rest, Miss St. Clair! Relax . . . and close your eyes.

MISS ST. CLAIR (*closing her eyes*). All right—but what I wanted to tell you was that I'm going to pull a gun on the big thug just like I did on Judge McCleary. (*At this Euphie just rolls her eyes at Miss St. Clair.*)

THIRD MASSEUSE (*soothingly*). Yes . . . yes . . . yes . . . Miss St. Clair . . . Relax . . . Relax.

By this time, Euphie has gone back to the door and opened it. A dog runs in, barking, and Miss St. Clair and the nurse look up.

EUPHIE (*going for the dog*). Come here, you! You come back here.

The dog opens the swinging door and bounds into the next room, whereupon the scene moves to the SECOND MASSAGE ROOM as the dog bounds in, followed by Euphie. A fat woman is in the hands of a very big masseuse.

EUPHIE (*to the fat woman*). Don't get scared, Madam! I'll catch him. (*To the dog as it bounds into the next room*)

Come back here, you bad girl! You come back here.

FAT WOMAN (*talking simultaneously as the Masseuse starts slapping her with the flat of her hands*). Oh, Hilda! Oh stop! Hilda! I'd rather *lose* my husband and the heck with him! Oh stop! Stop! STOP!

Euphie goes after the dog and the scene moves to the ELECTRIC CABINET ROOM as Euphie enters. (There are two square cabinets and one long one. They are all filled.) The dog has found his mistress and is jumping up and down beside one of the square cabinets.

MISTRESS (*to the dog*). Well—did she find her mama! Yes, of course, she found her mama!

WOMAN (*in the next cabinet to the woman in the long cabinet, talking simultaneously*). That woe-begone lingerie woman you sent me cost me sixty dollars.

WOMAN IN LONG CABINET (*also talking simultaneously*). Darling, I didn't expect you to buy anything. I was just trying to get rid of the creature.

MISTRESS OF DOG (*to Euphie*). Be an angel, will you? And give her some milk.

EUPHIE (*grabbing the dog*). Yes, ma'am.

Sounds of pounding water and screeches go up from the next room.

EUPHIE (*in surprised comment over the racket*). Uhm! Uhm! (*She peeks through the door.*)

The scene moves to the SCOTCH DOUCHE ROOM as Euphie peeks in and the Fifth Masseuse is seen playing the hose on a woman in silhouette who is screeching at the top of her lungs.

FIFTH MASSEUSE (*with supreme tolerance but having to scream to be heard*). Stand still, Mrs. Hildebrand . . . don't move now. . . . How can I make you thin if you don't stand still?

At which point, a woman, Mrs. North, in shorts and bra, sticks her head in from the Sun Room.

MRS. NORTH. Is that Mrs. Hildebrand?

FIFTH MASSEUSE. Yes, Ma'am.

MRS. NORTH (*to the woman being doused*). Don't be a baby Theresa! (*To the Masseuse*). Just make her take it! She's only got six weeks . . . she's going to be married.

FIFTH MASSEUSE. Don't move, Mrs. Hildebrand. Think of your wedding gown. Stand still.

During the above speech Mrs. North withdraws, and the scene moves to the SUN ROOM where there are six tables with sunlight arcs over them. Four of them are occupied by women in shorts and bras attended by the Fourth Nurse. As Mrs. North, entering from the Scotch Douche Room, closes the door, we hear someone calling from up above.

A VOICE. Oh, Ruthie! Ruthie!

MRS. NORTH (*calling up in answer as she mounts the stairs*). I'm coming! (*Speaking down to a woman on the sun table*) My dear! Can you believe it—that absolute old mountain of flesh is going to marry a *jockey!*

WOMAN. Won't her husband fairly turn in his grave!

SECOND WOMAN (*speaking simultaneously*). What's she got in common with a *jockey?*

MRS. ATKINS (*piping up from the sun table*). Horse feathers! (*At which they both laugh.*)

FOURTH NURSE (*looking at her watch—to one of the women who is lying on her stomach*). Sun on your stomach now, Mrs. Gillespie, for your gastro-intestinal pick-up.

During the above, the door of the Shadowgraph Room opens and Mrs. South enters.

MRS. SOUTH. Is this where I get my sun— (*She suddenly breaks off sharply on seeing Mrs. Atkins.*)

MRS. SMITH (*aghast*). Marjorie!

MRS. ATKINS (*equally aghast—sitting upright*). Geraldine!

There is a moment's awful pause as they look at each other, every other woman in the room looking on in abject interest,

when suddenly Mrs. South turns abruptly and whips right out through the same door she came in. Thereupon the scene moves to the SHADOWGRAPH ROOM where a girl of very sloppy posture is standing in front of the shadowgraph machine while the Fifth Nurse is taking a picture. Mrs. South agitatedly starts through.

FIFTH NURSE (*politely*). Aren't you taking your sunbath, madam?

Mrs. South, without deigning to reply, whams out through the other door.

NURSE (*registering mild surprise over Mrs. South's strange mood—then addressing herself to the girl behind the shadowgraph*). Thank you. You may join your exercising class.

GIRL (*coming out from behind the shadowgraph, revealing herself to be in bathing suit*). I can't see why you stand me in back of that machine—my posture has always been perfect.

FIFTH NURSE (*politely*). Quite.

Presently the girl approaches the exercising room, and the scene moves to the EXERCISE ROOM where the Shadowgraph Girl enters and joins the other debs on bars. They stand sideways holding on to a bar with the right hand and resting the right foot on the bar. In the exercise the left foot and left hand are extended.

INSTRUCTRESS. Out—Together . . . Stretch —Together . . . Out—Together . . . Stretch—Together . . . One-Two . . . One-Two . . .

FIRST DEB (*during the instruction*). Isn't it too divine about Constance and Freddy?

SECOND DEB. Simply heavenly, darling. I'm going to wear my new beige.

And now a fat, extremely tailored girl enters with a candid camera.

INSTRUCTRESS (*to the tailored girl—covering her annoyance at the interruption*). Yes, miss?

FIRST DEB (*to Instructress*). Oh, she's all right, Miss Spencer. She's my press agent.

Instructress, hiding her feelings starts counting again as the Tailored Girl starts to snap pictures of the deb.

YOUNG GIRL (*opening the door*). Beg pardon. I'm looking for my grandmother. (*Nobody pays her any attention.*)

SHADOWGRAPH GIRL (*as she starts to exercise*). That mouldy press agent I've got charges me every bit as much as he charges broken down old dowagers.

YOUNG GIRL (*piping up—louder*). Has anybody seen my grandmother. She's Southern.

INSTRUCTRESS. There's someone Southern in there on a bicycle.

YOUNG GIRL (*heading for the opposite door*). Oh, thanks.

The scene moves to the BICYCLE AND ROWING ROOM as the young Girl enters. Three bicycles and two rowing machines are seen; all the bicycles and one rowing machine are in use.

YOUNG GIRL (*to the woman on the bicycle who looks about twenty-eight*). Grandma!

GRANDMA (*pedaling away*). Hello, dear.

YOUNG GIRL. I've been looking all over for you. May I go to the fights tonight?

GRANDMA. Not without me.

FIRST BICYCLIST (*a nice Jewish housewife to the second bicyclist*). And I told Mrs. Mackay—it's the quality of the meat, dear. For myself, I said, I'd go to Blumenthal's Market if I was a Hindoo.

RECEPTIONIST (*coming in*). Is Miss Atkinson here?

WOMAN IN ROWING MACHINE. Next door.

The Receptionist goes out and the scene moves to the ARDENA MASK ROOM which the Receptionist enters. A nurse is giving Miss Atkinson a mask treatment with diathermy.

MISS ATKINSON (*barely able to talk through the mask*). Well, you see, the story of this picture begins when they're only about ten years old and—

RECEPTIONIST (*seeing this is going on forever*). Miss Atkinson, you're to call your broker when you get through.

MISS ATKINSON. Thanks. Well, the story of this picture begins when—

SIXTEENTH NURSE (*politely—trying to stop her*). It won't get so hot if you're quiet.

MISS ATKINSON (*grimly intent on telling plot*). I can stand it. The story of this picture begins when they're only about ten—

A treatment girl enters from the next room.

TREATMENT GIRL (*to Nurse—picking up jar of cream*). Through with this, Elsie? (*Elsie nods*).

Treatment Girl goes out, and the scene moves to the FACIAL ROOM which the treatment Girl enters. A bored-looking deb sits in the midst of a treatment, eating from a box of chocolates.

DEB (*drawling*). Say—if mother comes in here today, don't tell her you saw me. She thinks I'm on a world cruise.

TREATMENT GIRL (*set face and efficient —starts patting her face with cream*). Very well.

DEB (*as a whoop goes up from the next booth*). Who's that?

TREATMENT GIRL. I don't know.

DEB. Take a peek, will you. She screeches just like Mother.

As the treatment Girl goes and looks in, the scene moves to ANOTHER FACIAL ROOM where we see the First Treatment Girl looking in but presently withdrawing. An "Old Girl" of sixty is in a tieup as the Second Treatment Girl is zipping hair off her arm with wax.

OLD GIRL. Ouch! My skin's always been like a baby's. Would you believe I'm forty-two!

SECOND TREATMENT GIRL. Never tell it, Mrs. Gillingswater. You don't look a day over thirty-five.

She starts out and the scene moves to the KITCHEN, which the Second Treatment Girl enters.

SECOND TREATMENT GIRL (*speaks to herself*). The old gasoline truck! Sixty if she's a minute!

FIRST HAIR DRESSER (*who stands getting glass of water at sink*). Who is it?

SECOND TREATMENT GIRL (*contemptuously*). Gillingswater.

FIRST HAIR DRESSER. Oh—that old bag! One more permanent and she won't have a hair left on her head.

SECOND TREATMENT GIRL (*tossing the wax away*). She's got plenty on the arms, baby!

EUPHIE. She sho' does shed, don't she?

SECOND TREATMENT GIRL. She'd better shed that gigolo she's seeing through Art School. (*Sweetly as she goes back into the booth with the fresh wax*) Getting impatient, Mrs. Gillingswater?

EUPHIE (*giggling—looking off after the Treatment Girl*). My oh my! Ain't she the one?

Euphie goes out with the cup of tea on a tray, and the scene moves to the FIRST HAIR BOOTH as Euphie enters with the tea. Mrs. Wagstaff is having a permanent, a pedicure —and a sandwich.

EUPHIE. Here you is, ma'am.

MRS. WAGSTAFF (*not hearing her*). O-o-oo! It's burning my neck.

SECOND HAIRDRESSER. Be brave! It's going to be so worth it, Mrs. Wagstaff!

PEDICURIST. Careful now—you'll smear your beautiful big toe.

MRS. WAGSTAFF. Oh, my ears!

SECOND HAIRDRESSER. Be brave!

MRS. WAGSTAFF. O-o-oo. My nerves— O-o-oo! My foot! (*To Pedicurist*) Oh, my sandwich—

EUPHIE (*moving forward*). Here you is, Mrs. Wagstaff.

MRS. WAGSTAFF (*dismayed*). Tea? How revolting! I wanted a *drink!*

A coy "old girl" in a mud mask sticks her head in the door.

MUD MASK. Oh, pardon. I thought I was here. Why, hello, Mrs. Wagstaff. (*Coyly*) Guess who I am?

EUPHIE. Mustn't talk, ma'am. You'll crack yo'self.

A VOICE (*coming from the adjacent booth*). I wonder if you could be a little more quiet in there?

MUD MASK (*looking up with the others, reacting with curiosity, and whispering to the others*). Here I go! *The Mystery!*

And the scene moves with "Mud Mask" as she crosses the hall and pokes her head into the FOURTH HAIR BOOTH, where a theatrical child sits on a high stool having a permanent and studying a part, mumbling the lines. It is her mother whose voice we heard.

STAGE MOTHER (*to Mud Mask*). Sorry, but Genevieve is getting up in a new part and she has so little time to learn it!

MUD MASK (*impressed*). Oh! How fascinating!

Mud Mask leaves, hurrying down the corridor to break the news of the presence of Little Genevieve.

MUD MASK (*talking to someone out of sight*). A fascinating stage child is in here! Getting a permanent! A stage child! *AN ACTRESS!*

By which time she passes where Sylvia Fowler is getting a manicure from Olga while her hair is drying. She is holding a copy of Vogue in one hand.

OLGA (*quite loud*). It's the newest color, Mrs. Fowler . . . Jungle Red.

Sylvia nods, and goes back to the magazine. She evidently sees something especially interesting and Olga leans forward to look. Olga gazes at it a moment, then leans close again and starts to speak in a lowered voice. And Sylvia listening at first with indifference, suddenly removes her head from the dryer and from her expression it is obvious she is amazed and excited by what Olga is saying.

SYLVIA (*beside herself with delight— piling one question right on top of another*). Are you sure? I can't believe it! Where did you hear it? How d'you know?

During this time the Hairdresser turns off the dryer, removes the net from Sylvia's hair, and starts to comb it out.

OLGA. Well, there couldn't be any doubt about it, Mrs. Fowler. You see I know the—

At which point, a drying machine next to them is turned on, drowning out Olga's voice. But in Sylvia's face, we see a swiftly growing malicious delight, and finally Sylvia can stand it no longer and jumps up excitedly. She grabs her coat, hat and bag, all the time protecting the nails of the hand Olga has just finished, tips the two girls, and rushes out. And the view wiping off, we see a row of five PAY STATION TELEPHONE BOOTHS in a DRUG STORE with Sylvia striding along. She starts toward the first booth, and sees that it is occupied by a woman as are all five. As she reaches the last booth, she hears the door of the first one open and quickly turns and makes a dash for it. But just as she reaches it a large woman obstructs her way and eases herself inside, barely making it, much to Sylvia's annoyance. The next instant, the woman in the last booth emerges, but again, as Sylvia rushes forward, she arrives too late and a package-laden woman beats her to it, giving her a sweet smile as she closes the door, a smile which Sylvia forces herself to return. Grimly now, she takes her position opposite the middle booth.

The CENTRAL BOOTH now appears and Sylvia is seen tapping nervously on the glass door as the woman inside talks on, turning to cast an annoyed glance at the tapper. Finally the woman hangs up and Sylvia pushes into the booth while the woman is coming out, getting them both practically stuck for an instant. Inside, Sylvia sniffs distastefully at the smell of the place, waves her handkerchief to clear it out, then opens her bag, takes out a coin purse, looks in it and finds only two fifty cent pieces. Now begins a frantic search through her bag for a nickel. She takes out vanity case, lipstick, cigarette case, address book, gold pencil, small perfume bottle, key-ring, comb, a small bottle of dental floss, stamp book and more paraphernalia. She finally starts out with the thought of getting change, but seeing the lineup of women, abandons the idea. She searches through the pockets of her coat and although she finds no money, her eyes light up as she feels the round weights which have been put into the lining. She quickly rips open the lining, takes out the weight and breathlessly fits it into the coin box. It works, and with a snooty grimace of triumph she dials the number.

SYLVIA (*at the telephone*). Mrs. Potter, please . . . this is Mrs. Fowler. (*She waits eagerly.*) Edith? . . . Take a grip on yourself! You're going to die! . . . Stephen Haines is stepping out on Mary!

A close-up of EDITH shows her in a negligee —at the phone—bristling with delight, with a nasty tempered little Peke lying in her lap.

EDITH. Are you sure it's true? . . . Tell me about it this instant! . . .

As she listens the scene draws back to reveal the hallway of Edith's New York apartment. It is a large, square hallway with a private elevator door at one side, an archway opening into the drawing room across from it. An open door to the right leads to the dining room and the one to the left to a corridor off which are bedrooms. Edith has seven girls. At the moment, the First Child in the background is skating on roller skates up and down the corridor, rugs cast aside in a heap; the Second Child is going over some scales with a lady singing teacher in the drawing room.

EDITH. . . . How *heavenly!*

At which point, the elevator door slams open, and the Third Child, eleven, pops her head out.

THIRD CHILD (*to Edith*). Boo! I'm an elevator man!

EDITH. Don't frighten Mother, dear. (*The elevator door slams shut with a bang—at which Edith jumps. Then, into the phone*) Go on, darling.

A close-up shows SYLVIA speaking.

SYLVIA. Well—this manicurist—she's perfectly divine—she said to me, "I know something about that awfully rich Mrs. Haines!"

In the HALLWAY Edith is again seen at the phone.

EDITH. Funny how people like that think people like us are rich.

FIRST CHILD (*skating up, throwing her arms about Edith*). Mother, when I grow up, can I be an elephant?

EDITH (*anxious to get rid of her*). Yes, dear. . . . (*As First Child skates happily away*) But, darling! *Suppose Mary should hear about it!* Wouldn't it be awful?

SYLVIA (*seen in another close-up*). Wouldn't it be *ghastly!* If there were only some way to warn her. . . . (*Then indignantly—bridling*) Why, *of course*, I won't tell her! What d'you take me for? I'd die before I'd be the one to hurt Mary like that.

In the HALLWAY, still at the phone:

EDITH. Well it's just all too foul!

At which point Fourth and Fifth Child come running in from the dining room, the latter holding a bird cage.

FOURTH CHILD (*excitedly*). Mother, the canary laid an egg!

EDITH (*trying to listen*). Sh, darling!

FIFTH CHILD. I'm going to boil it for lunch.

EDITH. Darlings!

FOURTH CHILD. You are over my dead body! (*And she starts banging at Fifth Child as the latter races out through dining room.*)

EDITH (*looking at wrist watch*). Good grief! I'll never get out to the country by lunch time.

SYLVIA (*seen in a close-up again*). Won't it be just *too tragic!* Eating Mary's food and knowing *all* about *her husband!*

EDITH (*in the hallway; in despair*). Oh, dear! I'll burst until I get the details, but I've got to see that filthy doctor. My regular check-up, you know. . . . Goodbye, darling.

During the above, a nurse, in uniform, comes briskly from the corridor with Edith's twins in a perambulator, one of which is banging on the side of it with a rattle. She proceeds to the elevator and pushes the button.

EDITH (*rattling the receiver*). Give me Great Neck 8123. (*As the little dog starts to bark*) Don't hamper Mother, pet. (*Yelling off toward music teacher in drawing room*) Miss Phipps! This is a toll call. Can't you tone her down!

As the singing lesson tones down, the elevator door bangs open and Third Child yells from the elevator. "All aboard for the main lobby!"

EDITH (*addressing all the children as the nurse trundles the pram into elevator*). Darlings! Hello. Oh . . . hello. This is Mrs. Potter. Will you tell Mrs. Haines not to wait for me for lunch. I've got to see my doctor, but I'll make it just as soon as I can.

The corner of the LIBRARY in MARY HAINES' COUNTRY HOME appears, revealing Miss Fordyce, Little Mary's governess, answering the telephone. She is tall and thin and very efficient looking, her dark hair being plainly and neatly done in a bun at the nape of her neck.

MISS FORDYCE. Mrs. Haines is out riding now with Little Mary but I'll let her know. Goodbye.

She hangs up, and turning looks out of a window close by, whereupon the view changes quickly to a FIELD as seen from the house. Two horses are galloping toward a fence. One is ridden by Mary Haines and the other by her small daughter. They take the fence and bring their horses to a trot. Then a closer scene reveals that Mary Haines is a beautiful young woman in her late twenties. She is extremely chic, and belongs to a sophisticated world which she enjoys, while at the same time being "on" to its nonsense. Little Mary is about eight years old, but between the two there is a great comradeship, which is enhanced by a mutual sense of humor. At the moment Little Mary is watching her mother as the latter looks off into space, day-dreaming.

LITTLE MARY. Better take on more knee grip, Mother.

MARY (*snapping out of her mood*). Eh?

LITTLE MARY. You've been sitting awfully lax.

MARY (*amused at her daughter's expert criticism*). Have I? (*And she corrects her position.*) Well, professor, how's this?

LITTLE MARY (*watching her expertly*). Better. (*She watches her mother a mo-*

ment longer—then) Your mind hasn't been on your riding this morning, Mother dear.

MARY (*amusedly*). Hasn't it? (*Briskly*) All right! Bet I can beat you to the stables!

Little Mary spurs her horse forward, and the race is on.

The view cuts to mother and daughter racing toward the stables, then to Mary, clearly pulling her mare so that Little Mary can win, and then to the latter looking back over her shoulder as she outdistances her mother.

As Little Mary reaches the stable yard a length or two ahead of her mother, the dogs, Sheba and Babs, bark and jump excitedly.

LITTLE MARY (*greeting the dogs as she approaches*). Look out there, Sheba! Look out, Babs, or I'll run you down! (*Pulling up her horse she turns excitely to Mary who rides up and dismounts.*) Will you tell Daddy I beat you? If I tell him he'll think I'm conceited.

MARY (*laughing—then proceeding to get a small movie camera from the saddle*). He'll be awfully disappointed in *me*!

LITTLE MARY. Oh—but you're so solid with him anyway!

MARY (*laughing and focussing the camera on Little Mary—starting to shoot*). All right. I'll tell him.

As Mary's horse goes into the stable, Little Mary dismounts, her horse following Mary's.

LITTLE MARY (*as the dogs jump up at her making a charming picture*). Down Babs! Be good, now! Down Sheba! (*Running to her mother*) Now, mother, let me take you!

She grabs the camera then walking backward ahead of her mother and the dogs, shoots the picture, as they head toward the house.

MARY (*indicating Little Mary's grip on camera*). Look out there! You're shooting us on the bias.

LITTLE MARY (*alibiing—but with a twinkle*). Oh, I *meant* to! That's artistic!

MARY. That won't fool Daddy. It's what you told him the *last* time. (*She grabs up Babs who keeps getting in her way.*) Didn't she, old girl? Didn't she?

As she fondles the dog, they reach the kitchen door and enter, followed by Sheba and Babs, and the scene moves to KITCHEN where the cook, Ingrid, is at the table pounding some food in a mortar. She is blonde, Swedish, not pretty, but strong and healthy and sensible. She is so fond of Mary that she allows herself certain liberties of criticism, making a little game which both of them enjoy. Little Mary, trailed by the dogs, goes over toward the cooky jar which she proceeds to rifle.

MARY (*then looking into a stewpot on the stove*). Any ideas about dessert for this evening, Ingrid?

INGRID (*intent on her job*). Baked apples.

MARY (*amused*). What? No Charlotte Russe?

INGRID. You'd never eat it, ma'am, and *he* shouldn't!

MARY. Why shouldn't he? (*Taking off her gloves, she goes to the sink and proceeds to pick up some herbs which she expertly starts making into a small bouquet.*)

INGRID. Working hard all day in an office; and nearly every night, too . . . lately.

MARY (*gaily*). That's why he needs to be pampered! And this is our last dinner at home! We'll be two weeks up there in Canada—living like pioneers. I'm going to do the cooking myself—so *you know* what he'll get!

LITTLE MARY (*piping up*). I know! Indigestion! (*As they laugh, she goes out with the cookies, followed by the dogs.*)

INGRID (*wisely*). You can't fool me. You'll cook for him like a French chef all the while you're away. (*As Mary looks sharply up at her*) I was looking for my cook book this morning and I finally found it *in your trunk!*

MARY (*as she puts the bouquet of herbs into the stewpot*). I'll bring it back.

INGRID (*with a twinkle*). I hope. Well—what kind of goo do you want for him tonight?

MARY (*gingerly—as if knowing Ingrid will rebel*). Pancakes Barbara . . . ? (*In answer, Ingrid as if annoyed, starts to mumble disgustedly to herself.*) How about it?

INGRID (*still muttering*). All right, if you say so—but that Adonis figure of his can't last forever without a *little* help from the kitchen!

Mary laughs and goes through the door, and the scene moves with her through the dining room, where Jane, a young and pretty housemaid, is arranging the linen on the luncheon table.

JANE. Mrs. Haines. You spoke about having the linen gone over.

MARY. Oh, yes, Jane. (*As Jane heads for buffet, Mary examines the elaborately decorated table.*) H'm! That ought to knock their eyes out, hadn't it?

JANE. Yes, indeed! I always say you're the most exciting housekeeper, Mrs. Haines.

MARY (*amused as she fusses with decorations*). Thanks.

JANE (*picking up a piece of linen from the stack on the buffet*). There's one piece here I think we might as well throw out.

MARY (*with alarm—rescuing the piece of linen*). Good heavens, Jane! That was a wedding present!

JANE (*laughing—as Mary starts out*). Oh, dear! Well, I'm glad I asked you.

Mary makes her way upstairs, the scene moving with her. At one point she stops and stands a moment, looking at the old wedding present, day dreaming at the happy memories it brings up. Then, realizing she must hurry, she starts upstairs again, humming a little tune, and the view cuts to the DRESSING ROOM, which Mary enters happily, still humming. She puts the old wedding present on a table, gives it a little pat and starts to remove her riding clothes. (*In the background we see Mary's bedroom in which there is a double bed. In the dressing room is a partly packed small*

trunk.) Then she disappears into the adjoining bathroom, and we soon hear the sound of water being turned on in the shower and Mary starting to hum louder, and more happily.

In the DRESSING ROOM Little Mary now enters from Stephen's room, holding a man's mackinaw.

LITTLE MARY. I'm helping you to pack, Mother.

MARY'S VOICE (*from the bathroom as the water is turned off*). Thanks, darling. That's fine!

LITTLE MARY. D'you want to take this old thing along of Daddy's?

MARY'S VOICE (*from the bathroom*). What old thing?

Mary comes in from the bathroom, wearing a robe made of towelling and a bathing cap, her face glistening with water.

MARY (*seeing the mackinaw which Little Mary holds up*). Oh. By all means!

She takes the coat and proceeds into Stephen's room where she starts putting it into a trunk. (*There are a couple of extra bags, some gun cases and other paraphernalia of hunting about.*)

LITTLE MARY (*looking about in the drawer of the trunk*). But Daddy never wears that coat.

MARY. Oh, yes, he does! He wears it whenever he and I go off on trips . . . hunting . . . or fishing.

LITTLE MARY (*picking up some old kodak pictures*). What are these, Mother? (*As Mary looks up, Little Mary takes them to her.*)

MARY (*touched and delighted*). Why, these were taken on our honeymoon!

LITTLE MARY. Were they? Where was your honeymoon?

MARY. Up there in Canada. Where we're going tomorrow. (*Indicating the snapshot*) That's the spot where I caught that very fish! (*Gesturing to the stuffed fish hanging on the wall.*)

LITTLE MARY (*looking at snapshot*). Goodness gracious! (*With reservations—*

as she studies fish) It's not such a *big* fish though, is it, Mother?

MARY (*sorting over hunting equipment as if looking for something*). Well—the big fish aren't always the most important! Oh dear—where's Daddy's cartridge belt?

LITTLE MARY (*picking it up*). Is this it?

MARY. Thanks. (*As she packs the cartridge belt*). You see when I married your Daddy I couldn't fish worth a cent. So he started to teach me. First I learned how to cast a fly. And then I caught *that fish!*

LITTLE MARY. And Daddy said he'd have to have it stuffed . . . in case you might not ever catch another! (*Mary joins in the last sentence and says it with her, proving it to be a family joke.*) Oh, but you *do* catch others!

MARY (*humorously boastful as she goes about packing*). I'll say I do! It's just nip and tuck *now* who brings in the biggest catch, Daddy or I.

LITTLE MARY. Does it make Daddy jealous?

MARY. Of course! We have terrific battles!

LITTLE MARY. Oh, now you're fooling! (*Taking another snapshot to Mary*) Where's Daddy in this one?

MARY. He's taking the picture.

LITTLE MARY. Oh, I see his shadow . . . look . . . there in the snow!

MARY (*warmly — in reminiscence*). That's right! Dear! Dear! How I remember *that* morning. The snow came up unexpectedly during the night and we had to dig our way out of our cabin. Why we were snowbound in camp for two whole days!

LITTLE MARY. Like in a movie?

MARY (*squeezing her*). Yes, darling.

LITTLE MARY (*her eyes sparkling with excitement*). And were your lives in danger?

MARY. Well, no . . . but it was pretty romantic!

LITTLE MARY. Oh. (*Disappointed*) I think that kind of movies are sort of silly, Mother. (*Mary laughs, kisses her and then returns to her dressing room and begins to put on make-up at her dressing table. Little Mary follows her and sits on the floor against the wall.*) Mother?

MARY. Yes, dear.

LITTLE MARY. What do you and Daddy talk about when I'm not around?

MARY (*thoughtlessly—absorbed in her make-up*). Oh . . . everything.

LITTLE MARY. You do an awful lot of laughing. . . . I hear you sometimes. What do you laugh at?

MARY. Little jokes . . . lots of things!

LITTLE MARY. Do you love Daddy better than me?

MARY (*touched—turning to her*). Of course not!

LITTLE MARY. Ingrid says you love him better than anyone.

MARY. It's a different kind of love, darling. You'll understand that when you grow up.

LITTLE MARY. Will I? (*Giving a little sigh—then, with a rising inflection*) Well—*when I do,* I hope that I won't think it's silly.

MISS FORDYCE (*appearing as Mary laughs*). The lunch guests have started to arrive, Mrs. Haines.

LITTLE MARY (*as she runs to closet*). Mother, darling—let me pick out your dress. (*She starts to look over the clothes.*)

MARY (*hurrying with her make-up*). They would be on time today!

LITTLE MARY (*bringing out a plain sweater and skirt*). Here you are, Mother! They'll all be so fancy—why don't you be plain?

As Mary laughs and caresses her, the view cuts to the DOWNSTAIRS HALLWAY, where in a close-up we see Jane opening the door on Edith.

JANE. How'd you do, Mrs. Potter?

EDITH. Hello, Jane. (*The view now expanding to include the others*) Oh, Jane. (*Itching to connect with Sylvia*) Will you tell Mrs. Fowler I'd like to see her a moment.

JANE. Yes, Mrs. Potter.

At which point a Woman's Voice is heard "How's the little Mother?"

As Edith looks up, Nancy comes from the washroom. She is in her early thirties, unmarried; she writes novels and is a very likeable person.)

EDITH (*seeing Nancy*). Oh . . . (*To Jane*) Never mind. (*To Nancy—furious at her interruption, poisonously sweet*) Hello, dear.

NANCY (*grabbing her by the arm, and steering her into the drawing room*). The spider's in the parlor—let's go join her.

They reach Sylvia who stands looking in a mirror fixing her hair. Peggy, a nice and very dumb young woman, very much in love with her husband, sits looking at some magazines.

SYLVIA (*to Peggy*). So I said to Howard, "What d'you expect me to do? Stay home and darn your socks? What do we all have money for? Why do we keep servants?"

NANCY. You don't keep 'em long, goodness knows. (*Sylvia, turning, reveals the front of her dress on which are three "junk jewelry" eyes*) Great guns, what are you made up for? The Seeing Eye? (*She goes to the table and proceeds to pour some sherry.*)

SYLVIA. Better save your cracks for your next book, dear. (*To Edith—significantly*) Well, Edith, you *must have* dashed!

EDITH (*significantly*). I broke every speed record!

They exchange glances; then while awaiting her chance to see Sylvia, Edith dives into a plate of canapes.

EDITH. Thought you were going to Africa to shoot, Nancy.

NANCY (*evasive*). Soon as my book's out.

SYLVIA. Well, darling, I don't blame you. I'd rather face a tiger any day than the sort of things the critics said about your last book.

PEGGY (*to Nancy*). I wish I could make a little money writing the way you do.

NANCY. If you wrote the way I do that's just what you'd make.

SYLVIA. You're not a very popular author, are you, darling?

NANCY. Not with you. (*Holding out glass to Peggy*) Sherry, honey?

Peggy, who doesn't hear her, goes right on looking at the magazine.

EDITH (*grabbing the glass*). I'll take it. Peggy doesn't connect very well.

NANCY. She's in love, bless her. After the child's been married as long as you girls, she may be able to concentrate on vital matters like cocktails.

SYLVIA. Another lecture on the modern woman?

NANCY. At the drop of a hat.

SYLVIA (*to Nancy*). I consider myself a perfectly good wife, Nancy. (*Putting a canape into her mouth*) I've sacrificed a lot for Howard Fowler. (*Savoring the canape*) H'm! A smoked oyster!

EDITH. Don't mention smoked oysters. They turn me emerald green.

SYLVIA (*wearily*). Oh, Edith—you *are* a bore!

EDITH. Lay off my reputation, girls, while I unswallow. (*She hurries out.*)

PEGGY (*picking up a framed photograph*). Isn't Little Mary a dream! I wish *I* could afford to have a baby.

SYLVIA. You never will if your bridge game doesn't improve. (*A quick glance to see that Edith is out of earshot—then:*) I'm devoted to Edith Potter. But she *does* get me down. I don't blame her husband for being bored with her.

PEGGY. Why, what makes you think Mr. Potter . . .

SYLVIA. My dear! He's one of those flirty types . . . you know . . . just *loves* to kiss *all the girls!* I told him off one time! I said to him, "Look here, Phelps Potter, just one more of those little smacks, and I'll go straight to Edith!"

PEGGY. And did you?

SYLVIA. Of course not! I wouldn't say anything to hurt Edith for the world.

NANCY (*handing her a little dish of pecans*). Nuts?

SYLVIA (*poisonously sweet, taking some nuts*). Thanks, dear! Well, heaven be praised, I'm "on" to my husband. I wouldn't trust him on Alcatraz—the mouse.

PEGGY. Oh, Sylvia—you ought not to talk so about him! I think it's disloyal.

SYLVIA. Listen, Peggy, do we know how men talk about *us* when *we're* not around?

NANCY. I've heard rumors.

SYLVIA. Exactly. And while we're on the subject, have either of you wondered whether the master of *this* maison might not be straying?

NANCY. *I* haven't.

SYLVIA. Well, for all you know, Mary Haines may be living in a fool's paradise.

NANCY (*with sarcasm*). You're so resourceful, darling. I ought to go to you for plots.

SYLVIA (*acidly*). You ought to go to *someone!* (*As Edith enters*) All over, dear?

EDITH. False alarm. Have you finished with me? (*She goes to the table and gathers a handful of sandwiches.*)

NANCY (*still studying Sylvia*). Long ago. We're on our hostess.

SYLVIA. I think Mary's very wise to snatch Stephen Haines off to Canada. (*Observed by Nancy, she and Edith exchange glances.*)

NANCY. You just can't bear Mary's happiness, can you, Sylvia? It gets you down.

SYLVIA (*again exchanging glances with Edith*). How ridiculous! Why should it?

NANCY. Because she's contented. Contented to be what she is.

SYLVIA. Which is what?

NANCY. A woman!

SYLVIA. And what are we?

NANCY. Females!

SYLVIA. Really. And what are you, pet?

NANCY. What nature abhors. I'm an old maid—a frozen asset!

EDITH (*eyeing Sylvia significantly—as a ruse to get her alone*). Come on, Sylvia. Let's see what's keeping Mary. (*Eagerly, Sylvia rises.*)

NANCY. Run along, children. (*To Peggy*) Now it's our turn to go on the pan. (*As Sylvia and Edith head for the doorway*) But we needn't worry. You've got a poor man, and I've got no man at all. (*Sylvia shows resentment at Nancy's attack as they go out.*)

The scene moves with Sylvia and Edith who are heading for the dressing room.

EDITH (*excitedly—sotto voce*). I thought I'd never get you alone! I just can't wait to get the low-down!

SYLVIA (*sotto voce*). Sh! (*With a glance back toward the drawing room*) You're going to swoon, my dear, when I tell you! (*By this time they are in the dressing room where they relax in comfort.*) You know I go to Sidney's for my hair. You ought to go there too, pet. I despise whoever does yours.

EDITH (*impatient*). Oh, hurry up!

SYLVIA. Well—this manicurist, Olga, is a riot! (*Showing her nails*) Isn't that divine? Jungle Red!

EDITH. Simply divine. Go on.

SYLVIA. Well—I was looking through Vogue—the one with Mary in the Beaux Art Ball costume—

EDITH (*cutting in*). —in that white wig that flattered her so much?

SYLVIA. Well—that started this girl on Mary and the whole ghastly story rolled out.

EDITH. Is it someone we know?

SYLVIA. No, my dear. That's what's so awful about it! She sells perfume at Black's Fifth Avenue. It wouldn't be so bad if Stephen had picked someone in his own class. But a *beezle!*

EDITH. How did Stephen ever meet a girl like that?

SYLVIA. How do men ever meet girls like that? That's what they live for, the rats!

EDITH. Someone ought to shut that manicurist up.

SYLVIA. On a great piece of scandal *like that?* Not a chance! That girl never stops talking! You know how creatures like that are! They babble, babble, babble, and never let up for a minute! A lot they care whose life they ruin.

EDITH. Isn't it a dirty trick?

SYLVIA. Isn't it foul! It's not as though only Mary's friends knew. We could keep our mouths shut.

EDITH. Of course! I know plenty I never breathe about my friends' husbands.

SYLVIA. So do I!

They exchange a sudden glance of sharp suspicion—then start out.

EDITH. I adore Mary—

SYLVIA. I worship her! She's not only my cousin . . . she's my dearest friend in all the world. Why, we were raised together!

MARY'S VOICE. Break it up, girls.

As they look up the scene moves to a view of Mary coming down the stairway.

EDITH (*as they join her*). Mary, darling. You're so slim I could kill you. (*And they all head for the drawing room.*)

MARY. You won't have to, dear—the diet I'm on is pure poison.

SYLVIA. Diet nothing! Why the woman can eat blubber! How *can* you exercise all day and look so contented?

MARY. It's a trick I learned from the cows.

The scene moves to the DRAWING ROOM as the three enter.

MARY (*apologetic*). Sorry to be late, girls.

NANCY. It's all right, Mary. We haven't had a dull moment. (*She turns to Sylvia.*) Well, Sylvia, feeling better?

SYLVIA. Meaning what?

NANCY. You and Edith look so relaxed. It must have been choice!

SYLVIA (*looking her right in the eye*). It was!

PEGGY (*dumbly—to Nancy and Sylvia*). What are you talking about?

SYLVIA. Nothing. (*To Mary, overly innocent*) How's Stephie?

MARY (*a trace concernedly*). Stephen's not so well.

SYLVIA. Oh? (*Glancing at Edith who has looked up*) What's the trouble?

MARY. Nervous.

EDITH. Phelps has nervous indigestion. You should hear that man rumble. Like a truck on cobblestones.

JANE (*who has now come in*). Lunch is served, Mrs. Haines. (*Mary nods.*)

SYLVIA. There's nothing worrying Stephen, is there?

MARY. Of course not. He's been working rather late these past few weeks—that's all.

SYLVIA. Are you sure it's *work*, darling, and not a beautiful blonde?

EDITH (*afraid Sylvia will go too far*). I'm famished. Let's feed. (*She starts out —the others following her.*)

SYLVIA (*to Mary—relentlessly*). Stephen's a very attractive man, you know.

MARY. Isn't he? I can't imagine why he hasn't deserted me for some glamorous creature long ago.

The DINING ROOM appears as Mary leads the group in and they proceed to the table.

SYLVIA. Well—I wouldn't be sure of Methuselah! I always tell Howard, "If you ever manage to make a fool of me, I'll deserve what I get."

NANCY. You certainly will!

MISS FORDYCE (*entering as the women have seated themselves*). I am sorry to disturb you, Mrs. Haines, but Mr. Haines is on the phone.

SYLVIA (*looking significantly around at the others*). He probably can't get home to dinner.

MARY (*lightly, as she rises*). Probably . . . poor darling. (*Singing as she goes*) Please don't talk about me when I'm gone!

The scene moves with her as she goes to the phone. She reaches the phone and takes the receiver.

MARY. Hello, dear. (*There is a long pause as she listens, then the smile leaves her face.*) Oh, Stephen, what a bore. . . . Yes, I'm nearly packed, darling, but I can unpack again. . . . I know . . . I know . . . (*Trying to buck him up*) Well—don't be disappointed, dear—it will still be nice, a little later on. . . . Maybe you can make an early train out today. I'll meet you at the station, and we'll. . . . Oh, I see. (*Sighing*) I'm sorry, dear. Ingrid was going to outdo herself for you tonight. . . . All right, darling. You'll call me later, eh? . . . Goodbye.

She sits for a moment as sounds of the chatter in the dining room are heard, and Sylvia's shrill laughter rises up. Trying to dispel a sudden, vague sensation of doubt in Stephen, she rises and goes back to the dining room, the scene moving with her.

SYLVIA (*as Mary enters*). You look as low as a swamp, dear. What's up?

MARY. It's really too disgusting. Stephen can't get away to go to Canada.

SYLVIA (*Edith and she looking up at once*). He can't?

MARY (*with a sigh; trying to be philosophical*). Well—so long as our trip's off, I think in the morning, I'll move back to town.

SYLVIA (*significantly*). I certainly would if *I were you*, Mary!

EDITH (*purposely changing the subject—inspecting her salad*). Watercress. (*Making a wry face*) I'd just as soon eat my way across a front lawn.

PEGGY (*piping up*). Sylvia—what did you mean when you said Mary was living in a fool's paradise.

NANCY (*to Peggy, as Mary looks up—trying to protect Mary*). She was trying to make a Nancy Blake wisecrack about marriage. (*To Mary*) She said, "A woman's paradise is always a fool's paradise!"

MARY. That's not bad, is it, Nancy? (*Amused*) Well, Sylvia, whatever I'm living in, I like it. (*As Jane passes muffins to Sylvia*) Take one, dear. No starch. They're gluten.

SYLVIA (*as a backhanded compliment—annoyed at Mary's defiance*). Did you ever know such a *housewife!* (*Examining her nails a moment, then suddenly showing them to Mary*) Mary, how do you like that? (*At this Edith grows tense.*)

NANCY (*not looking*). Too, too adorable.

SYLVIA. You can't imagine how it stays on. I get it at Sidney's—you ought to go, Mary!

EDITH (*protestingly*). Oh, Sylvia.

SYLVIA. A wonderful new manicurist. Olga's her name. She's marvelous! Look, Jungle Red!

NANCY. Looks as if you'd been tearing at somebody's throat.

SYLVIA. I'll be darned, Nancy, if I'll let you ride me any more!

MARY. Now, Sylvia, Nancy's just being clever, too.

SYLVIA. She takes a crack at everything about me. Even my nails!

MARY (*with real interest*). Well, I like them. I really do! (*Patting her hand*) Sidney's. Olga. Jungle Red. *I'll remember.*

And the scene fades out.

PART TWO

A close-up of a SIGN ON THE MAIN DOOR fades in; and the scene, drawing back, reading: "SIDNEY'S"—reveals Mary entering. Peggy is with her, and carries a book from a lending library and a big pocketbook.

MARY (*lightly—as they enter*). . . . So I woke up this morning and decided for no reason at all to have a thorough overhauling.

PEGGY. But why, darling? Stephen adores you just as you are!

GIRL AT DESK (*cutting in, in greeting to Mary*). Yes, Madam?

MARY (*to the girl at the desk*). I'm Mrs. Fowler's friend. I phoned for my appointment.

GIRL. Oh, yes. (*She starts to study the appointment sheet.*)

MARY (*turning to Peggy—amused at her*). Who *said* I was getting overhauled *for Stephen?*

PEGGY (*wide-eyed*). Oh, but you are, aren't you?

MARY (*after a slight hesitation—then smiling, sighing and speaking the truth*). Of course. (*Justified, Peggy smiles back.*)

GIRL (*looking up from the appointment sheet*). Anyone in particular for your manicure?

MARY. Who does Mrs. Fowler's nails?

GIRL. Olga. I'll see if she's free.

PEGGY (*looking at her own nails*). My Johnnie doesn't like Sylvia's Jungle Red. He says *he'd* like to do her nails right down to the wrist, with a big buzz-saw.

MARY (*smiling*). Johnnie's intolerant. Sylvia's all right . . . underneath. I'm fond of her . . . we were kids together. (*Moodily with a sort of nervous little shiver*) It's chilly.

PEGGY. Well—after all, Mary, it's October!

MARY. Yes. It's October! (*After a little pause*) There's something about *this* autumn, Peggy . . . I don't know what

it is . . . something strange . . . as if there might not ever be another spring.

PEGGY (*equally moody*). I know! I get those feelings, too.

MARY (*a little sigh—then—picking up a bottle of perfume displayed on the counter*). Stephen bought me some lovely perfume for my birthday . . . a new one that's called "Summer Rain."

PEGGY. I think Stephen's awfully *sweet!*

MARY (*amused*). Sweet?

PEGGY. Yes. Because he gave you those gorgeous clips . . . and then he *bothered* to get you perfume, too. (*At which Mary smiles.*)

GIRL (*entering*). Olga's ready, ma'am.

PEGGY (*to Mary—briskly*). I've got to hurry. If I don't get this book back to the library before noon, it'll cost five cents more.

MARY (*in parting*). Meet you at the Ritz at one?

PEGGY. At one! (*Putting down the book to look at her wrist-watch*) Oh, dear. it's nearly twelve. . . . Now I'll have to take a taxi to that library!

MARY. To save *five cents?*

PEGGY (*realizing her folly, laughs*). Oh! I'm such a fool! Goo' bye, darling.

MARY (*as Peggy hurries out, smiling after her*). So long.

GIRL. Pretty, isn't she?

MARY (*warmly*). She's a darling!

GIRL (*to Mary—gesturing upstairs*). Right up here, Madame.

As Mary starts to go upstairs she notes that Peggy has forgotten her book in her hurry to return it. She picks it up, looks off after Peggy, sees she has gone and, smiling over her thoughtlessness, starts upstairs with the book.

The scene dissolves to a close-up of the MANICURE TABLE as Mary enters.

OLGA. Good morning, Madam. You're the one, aren't you? (*As Mary sits down*) I love to get a new client. I always think it puts a girl on her mettle. (*As Mary starts to look at the book, Olga glances at it.*) Don't you just love to read? How do they ever think up those plots? Don't soak it yet. (*As Mary goes on reading*) But I suppose anybody's life would be a plot if it had an exciting finish. Who sent you in here?

MARY (*annoyed—wanting to read*). Mrs. Fowler.

OLGA. Oh, Mrs. Fowler. Isn't she a lamb? She's sent me three clients this week. Know Mrs. Herbert Parrish? Well, Mrs. Parrish was telling me that Mr. Parrish came home one night with lipstick on his collar. She said he always explained everything before, but that was something he just wasn't going to try to explain. . . . Soak it. Know Mrs. Potter? I "did" her at her apartment last week. It looks like a reform school. Those seven daughters of hers are absolutely gangsters! Know Mrs. Stephen Haines?

MARY (*looking up from her book*). What? Why, yes, I—

OLGA. I guess Mrs. Fowler's told you about that! Mrs. Fowler feels awfully sorry for her.

MARY (*laughing*). Oh, she does? Well —I don't. I—

OLGA. You would if you knew this girl.

MARY. What girl?

OLGA. This Crystal Allen.

MARY (*in amazement*). Crystal Allen?

OLGA. Yes—you know—the girl who's hooked Mr. Haines. (*As Mary starts violently*) Don't you like the file? Well —this Crystal Allen is a friend of mine. She's really a terrible man-trap. Soak it, please. (*Mary, dazed, puts her hand in the dish.*) She's behind the perfume counter at Black's. So was I before I got fi—left. That's how she met him.

MARY (*still incredulous*). Stephen Haines?

OLGA. Yeah. It was a couple of months ago. Us girls wasn't busy. It was an awful rainy day, I remember. So this gentleman walks up to the counter. Well, Crystal nabs him. "I want some perfume," he says. "May I awsk what type of woman for?" Crystal says, very Ritzy. That didn't mean a thing. She was going to sell him Summer Rain, our feature, anyway. Well, Crystal goes on conning him and batting her eyes. She's got those eyes that run up and down a man like a searchlight, and she puts perfume on her palm and in the crook of her arm for him to smell. So he got to smelling around and I guess he liked it. Since then they've been inseparable—practically every evening. Did I hurt? (*Mary draws her hand away.*) Jungle Red, I suppose. One coat or two? (*She picks up a red bottle.*)

MARY. Never mind. (*She rises and goes to the chair where she has left her purse.*)

OLGA. But I thought that's what you came for. All Mrs. Fowler's friends—

MARY. I think I've got what all Mrs. Fowler's friends come for. (*She puts a coin on the table.*)

OLGA (*reacting to her strange behavior, picking up the coin*). Oh, thanks. Well, goodbye. I'll tell her you were in, Mrs. —?

MARY. Mrs. Stephen Haines.

OLGA. Mrs. —? Oh, gee . . . gee! Gee, Mrs. Haines—I'm sorry. Oh, isn't there something I can do?

MARY. Stop telling that story.

OLGA. Oh, sure . . . sure I will!

MARY. And please don't tell anyone— (*her voice breaking*) that you told it to me . . .

OLGA. Oh, I won't. Gee, I promise! Gee, that would be kind of humiliating for you. Crystal's a terrible girl . . . I mean, she's terribly clever. And she's terribly pretty, Mrs. Haines—I mean if I was you, I wouldn't waste no time trying to get Mr. Haines away from her—(*Mary turns abruptly away.*) I mean . . . well . . . now you *know,* Mrs. Haines!

Olga eyes the coin in her hand distastefully, then suddenly puts it down on the table as Mary turns and goes out.

The scene moves to the KITCHEN OF MARY'S APARTMENT. The telephone is ringing; after a moment, a door is thrown open and Jane, the maid, hurries in, fixing her apron. She crosses to the telephone and takes down the receiver.

JANE. Hel—

She stops, hearing voices, since Mary has already answered upstairs. Jane starts to hang up but decides to listen. As she sits there engrossed in what she is hearing, Ingrid enters; she has evidently followed after Jane and is quite annoyed.

INGRID. Say you! I've had enough of your—(*Stopping as she sees Jane at the phone*) What are you doing, listening like that? Where is your manners?

JANE (*covering the receiver with her hand*). Sh! . . . There's something up— (*And in spite of herself, Ingrid evinces an interest.*)

JANE (*sotto voce—covering the mouthpiece with her hand*). It's Mrs. Haines' mother. . . . She's coming right over and Mrs. Haines don't want her to . . . the old lady says she's *got* to see her *right off.* (*Listening*) She's had to let her come. (*She hangs up—mystified.*) Say—I wonder what's all the excitement! Mrs. Haines looked like she'd been crying this afternoon when she came in from the beauty parlor.

INGRID. You can't keep your nose out of *anybody's* business, can you?

JANE (*as if surprised*). What's eatin' you?

INGRID. I tell you what's eating me. I am sick of the way I catch you gurgling up to my husband.

JANE (*carelessly*). Oh, you're cuckoo! Ford called me in as I was going by the pantry.

INGRID (*sarcastically*). Oh, he called you in!

JANE (*flaring up*). Yes, he did . . . to help him find something.

INGRID (*in a jealous fury*). Well, you stay away from him! He doesn't need you to help him do anything.

JANE. Oh, don't be such a dumb Swede!

INGRID. Dumb Swede, am I? I told you the other day if you didn't keep away from Ford, I'd speak to Mrs. Haines. (*As she goes through the door*) I guess I got to do it.

Jane runs after her, the scene moving with them upstairs.

JANE (*alarmed*). Don't be a sap, Ingrid! I don't want your Romeo! (*As Ingrid goes right on*) Ingrid, if you complain to Mrs. Haines, I'll lose my job.

INGRID. You should think of that before.

JANE (*now in a panic*). Why, I wouldn't *have* the big, conceited smart aleck if he were gold plated on a silver platter!

By this time they have reached Mary's door which is open, and Ingrid taps on it lightly.

MARY'S VOICE. Who is it?

They enter, Jane hurrying in ahead, and the view cuts to the BEDROOM where Mary is using an eye cup as she comes from the bathroom. She has changed to a house dress.

JANE. It's cook, ma'am. She wants to see you . . . about me. (*Mary looks askance at Ingrid.*)

INGRID. I'd like to talk to you *alone,* ma'am.

JANE (*quickly, cutting in*). Don't you believe a word she says, Mrs. Haines! It's all his fault.

MARY (*aware of Jane's distress for the first time*). Whose fault?

JANE. Her husband's. Ford's.

MARY (*surprised*). What's the matter with Ford. He's a very good butler.

JANE. Oh, he does his work, ma'am. But you don't know how he is in the pantry. Always trying to make dates with us girls. He don't mean any harm, but Cook—

INGRID (*cutting in*). You led him on!

JANE. I didn't. (*Bursting into tears*) I've been with Mrs. Haines seven years. She knows I never make trouble downstairs.

And Jane runs out. Mary looks at Ingrid and sees that she, too, is ready to weep.

MARY. Sit down, Ingrid.

Ingrid sits uncomfortably on the edge of a chair and tries to keep back the tears as Mary puts her eye cup in the bathroom and returns.

MARY. Now, tell me what's the matter.

INGRID. Ma'am, you're the nicest I ever had. But I go. I got to get Ford away from that bad girl.

MARY (*very firmly*). Jane is not a bad girl.

INGRID (*bursting into tears*). Oh, course she ain't. It's him that's the trouble! Sometimes I could die, for the shame!

MARY (*leaning over, and putting a friendly comforting hand on Ingrid's knee*). Don't cry. I'll send him away. You can stay.

INGRID. No. I can't do that.

MARY. I'll pay you a hundred dollars. That's more than half of what you and Ford make together.

INGRID. Thank you, Ma'am, but we both go.

MARY. Is that sensible?

INGRID. No. It's plain dumb!

MARY. Then why?

INGRID (*pausing, rocking from foot to foot*). I guess nobody understands. Sure it was no good to marry him. My mother told me he's a ladykiller. Don't marry them, she said. His wife is the lady he kills. Oh, he's terrible. But except for

that, he's a good man. He aways says, "Ingrid, you take the money. You manage good." (*With pride*) Oh, he don't want nobody but me for his wife! That's an awful big thing, ma'am!

MARY (*thoughtful—almost grim*). Is that the thing that really matters?

INGRID. With women like us, yes, ma'am. You give us references? (*As Mary nods*) And don't say nothing about his ways?

MARY. I won't.

INGRID (*moving to the door*). Black bean soup—a fricassee—fried sweets and apple pie for dinner, ma'am. (*She opens the door, where Jane has been eavesdropping, and explodes in a low, fierce voice*). Huzzy!

JANE (*relieved that her job is safe now; quite cheerfully*). Did you hear what she called me, Mrs. Haines?

MARY (*sick at heart*). Please, Jane.

JANE (*laughing*). I'd rather be that any day than have some man make a fool of me!

MARY (*as the doorbell rings and Jane heads out to answer bell*). That's my mother, Jane. Tell her to come up.

JANE (*going out*). Yes, ma'am.

Left alone, Mary goes to the mirror and tries to press away the puffiness about her eyes. Then hearing footsteps, she turns, faces the door, and braces herself for the ordeal of facing her mother.

MRS. MOREHEAD (*as Jane shows her in; bubbling over—cheerily*). Hello, dear. My! My! What lovely callistephus. (*She gestures to the flowers in the vase.*)

MARY (*wanly*). Hello, mother.

JANE (*cutting in*). What will you wear tonight, ma'am?

MARY (*to Jane*). My old black.

JANE (*starting out*). Yes, ma'am.

MARY (*with a little catch*). No, I won't. I'll wear my new pink.

JANE (*going out*). Very well.

MARY (*trying hard to be casual*). You sounded quite excited, Mother. What's on your mind?

MRS. MOREHEAD (*after a pause—throwing off her pretended buoyancy and getting down to earth—significantly*). Plenty! (*She pulls off her gloves and spreads her hands out.*) Jungle Red! *I've* been to Sidney's this afternoon, too.

MARY (*stiffening*). I see. Did you have . . . Olga?

MRS. MOREHEAD. No. But Olga knew who I was—she asked to meet me. She's very upset over the story she blurted out to you.

MARY (*bitterly*). She didn't say it wasn't true, did she?

MRS. MOREHEAD. No . . .

MARY. Oh, Mother, I knew this happened to other people, but . . . (*a break in her voice*) . . . I never dreamed it could happen to *us* . . . we've been so happy together . . . *really* happy.

MRS. MOREHEAD. I know.

Mary suddenly breaks and cries like a little girl. Her mother puts an arm about her.

MRS. MOREHEAD (*comfortingly*). There, there, Baby.

MARY (*wanly*). I'll . . . I'll be all right now . . .

MRS. MOREHEAD (*worried*). You haven't said anything to Stephen yet, have you?

MARY (*dazedly*). No . . . I haven't seen Stephen since I— (*She breaks off—unable to go on.*)

MRS. MOREHEAD. *Then say nothing!*

Astonished, Mary looks up at her; and at this point Jane enters holding out a pink dress on a hanger.

JANE (*as she heads for the other room*). I'll just give it a little touch with the iron.

MARY (*to Mrs. Morehead—trying to keep Jane from sensing her emotion*). Look darling. Sweet, isn't it?

MRS. MOREHEAD. Charming! And very wise of you to wear pink!

MARY (*turning at once to Mrs. Morehead when Jane is out of the room*). Oh, mother, you don't really *mean* I should say nothing?

MRS. MOREHEAD. I do!

MARY (*shocked*). Oh, but, mother—

MRS. MOREHEAD. My dear, I felt the same way twenty years ago.

MARY. Not Father—!

MRS. MOREHEAD. Mary, in many ways your father was an exceptional man. (*Philosophically*) That, unfortunately, was not one of them.

MARY. And did you say nothing?

MRS. MOREHEAD. Nothing! I had a wise mother, too! (*As she leans forward—earnestly*) Listen, dear. This is not a new story. It comes to most wives.

MARY. But *Stephen*—

MRS. MOREHEAD. Stephen is a man. He's been married ten years—

MARY. You mean he's tired of me. (*She goes to the fireplace and lights the logs and hugs herself as if suddenly cold.*)

MRS. MOREHEAD (*taking out her knitting*). Stephen's tired of himself. Feeling the same things in himself. Time comes when every man's got to feel something new—when he's got to feel young again, just because he's growing old—

MARY (*standing facing the fire—dazedly*). But Stephen's not old!

MRS. MOREHEAD (*impatiently—brushing her remark aside*). Oh, of course not! But we women are so much more sensible! When *we* tire of ourselves, we change the way we do our hair, or hire a new cook. Or redecorate the house. . . . I suppose a man could do over his office, but he never thinks of anything so simple. . . . No, dear—a man has only one escape from his old self, to see a different self—in the mirror of some woman's eyes.

MARY. But Mother—

MRS. MOREHEAD. This girl probably means no more to him than that new dress means to you.

MARY. But, Mother—

MRS. MOREHEAD. "But, Mother— But Mother." Good heavens, he doesn't *love* the girl. If he did you'd have felt it yourself, long ago.

MARY (*dejectedly*). Oh, I always thought I would. I love him so much!

MRS. MOREHEAD. And he loves you, Baby. So take my advice! Keep still! Keep still when you're fairly *aching* to talk! It's about the only sacrifice spoiled women like us ever have to make to keep our men!

MARY (*suddenly flaring up—facing her mother and bursting out*). And what if I don't want him under those terms!

MRS. MOREHEAD (*amazed at her violence*). Why, Mary!

MARY. It's all right for you to talk of another generation . . . when women were chattels, and did as men told them to! But this is *today!* Stephen and I are equals! We took each other of our own free will . . . for life! We've always given each other our best! I won't qualify our relationship *now!* It's wrong! *Shockingly wrong!* Women who stand for such things are beneath contempt and I'll never be one of them! Never!

MRS. MOREHEAD (*still amazed at her violence*). Oh, but darling—

MARY (*with absolute finality*). It's all over, Mother! It's finished! *I'm through!*

MRS. MOREHEAD (*gently*). No, it isn't. . . . It'll never be finished while you love him.

MARY (*with pride*). I'll get over that— women do—*they have to!*

There is a pause as Mrs. Morehead clearly shows she is worried.

MRS. MOREHEAD. What are you doing this evening?

MARY. We're dining here—going to the theatre—I've asked the Dearborns. . . . I'll see it through—and then I'll have it out with him. I'll tell him we can't go on together and I'll—

MRS. MOREHEAD (*alarmed*). Mary! You mustn't say a word to Stephen until you've thought this out . . . *and thought it all out very calmly!* (*She puts away her knitting, picks up her coat.*) I'm going right down this minute and get our tickets.

MARY. Tickets?

MRS. MOREHEAD (*with decision*). You're taking me to Bermuda! My throat's bad. I haven't wanted to worry you, but my doctor says—

MARY (*touched at her concern*). Oh, Mother! It's sweet of you, but what can there be between Stephen and me *now!* The thing that made us belong to each other has gone!

MRS. MOREHEAD. There's something more for you to think of *now,* than each other. (*As Mary looks up*) There's your daughter.

There is a pause as this sinks in on Mary. Then she flares up again, though without quite so much vehemence.

MARY. When Mary's old enough to realize, she'll know I'm right.

MRS. MOREHEAD (*studying her—realizing she has hit on the one thing which will cause Mary to pause in her course, and deciding to leave and let her think it over*). Well, do as you wish, darling, but don't forget it's being together at the *end* that really matters! (*She starts away, but stops.*) One more piece of motherly advice. Don't confide in your girl friends.

MARY. I think they all know.

MRS. MOREHEAD. Do *they* think *you* know? (*As Mary shakes her head*) Leave it that way. If you let them advise you, they'll see to it in the name of friendship that you lose your husband and your home. I'm an old woman, dear, and I know my sex. (*Kissing her*) Goodbye.

MARY. Oh, darling—thanks for coming up!

MRS. MOREHEAD. It's rather *nice* to have you need mother again.

Deeply touched, Mary puts her arms about her mother and they stand for a moment in a close embrace, both deeply moved. The phone starts to ring.

MRS. MOREHEAD (*patting her arm*). Better think it over, dear, about Bermuda. Your home . . . *little* Mary's home—is worth putting up a pretty stiff battle for! (*Heading for the door*) Besides, there's nothing like a good dose of being left alone to make a man appreciate his wife.

Mary smiles wanly at her as her mother leaves. Then she turns and takes up the receiver.

MARY. Hello, Stephen. . . . Yes. . . . Oh, you can't? . . . I see . . . (*It's a struggle, but she manages to keep a cheerful voice.*) No, I'm not angry. Beth and Dave will be disappointed not to see you, that's all. . . . No, I won't wait up. (*Then, in a firm tone, making her first move to hold her home together*) Oh, Stephen, I think I'll take mother to Bermuda for a few weeks. She's just been here and she doesn't feel very well, and— (*As she listens*) Well, on the first boat if you don't mind— (*Then, as he tells her he'll try to break his date, a sudden light begins to come into her eyes.*) Oh, don't break your appointment, dear, if it's going to upset your business. . . . All right, Stephen, if you find you *can* go with us tonight, just phone me back! (*She has to steel herself to keep from showing too great relief.*) You needn't dress and we could dine at seven-thirty. . . . Goodbye.

She hangs up, allowing herself a moment of hope that perhaps Stephen is innocent. As she rises, she sees the bottle of perfume, "Summer Rain," which Stephen gave her on that happier day, and reaching down, picks it up and looks at it intently . . . wondering, as the scene dissolves out.

A close view of a BOTTLE OF "SUMMER RAIN" dissolves in, and the view drawing back reveals a dozen or more bottles arranged in display on a counter. Then Sylvia and Edith are revealed skirting the counter on the search for their prey. They come to a salesgirl, who is standing with her back to them reaching for something on the high showcase behind the counter. She has a beautiful figure.

EDITH (*in low tones as she clutches Sylvia's arm*). Gorgeous torso, dear! Maybe *that's* little Crystal!

At this moment the girl turns, and we see that she is a hatchet-face.

SYLVIA. From the neck *up,* I'd say "no."

They move slowly along until they see a good-looking, brassy blonde.

SYLVIA (*sotto voce as she unobtrusively gestures toward the blonde with her thumb*). How about Baby?

EDITH (*spotting the blonde*). Oh! (*Looking her over*) Why, of course! It *couldn't* be anyone else!

SALESGIRL (*entering the scene; to the blonde*). Pat, here's your customer's change.

PAT. Thanks. (*She takes the money and moves off.*)

SYLVIA (*to Edith, signifying they were wrong*). Pat! (*She starts looking around.*)

EDITH (*her gaze still on Pat*). Well— I don't know why he overlooked *her!*

SYLVIA (*significantly, her gaze wandering off out of the scene*). I do!

EDITH. Eh?

SYLVIA (*knowingly—again gesturing off unobtrusively with her thumb, this time to someone out of the scene*). Pipe!

Edith's gaze follows the gesture, her eyes wide open and *she lets out a little whistle,* and the scene moves quickly along the line of the girls' gaze to a close-up of CRYSTAL, who is standing at a telephone.

CRYSTAL (*in lady-like, well modulated tones*). I see, Stephen . . . (*With brave and noble intonation*) Why, I don't mind breaking our engagement, dear . . . that is, I *mind,* of course, but it's such good discipline for my selfishness about you . . .

PAT (*moving in*). Holy mackerel, what a line!

CRYSTAL (*worried*). Sh! (*Pat putting the things away listens with mild interest.*) I was going to surprise you tonight, darling—cook dinner myself in my little apartment . . . (*Pat looks up quizzically.*) . . . Oh you don't know half my accomplishments!

PAT. I'll say he doesn't!

CRYSTAL (*to Pat—sotto voce*). Shut up! (*Speaking into the phone as Pat goes back to her occupation*) But I'll save you a piece of the cake, dear, with a candle on it. (*Pat now stops in her work and looks on in sheer admiration of Crystal's tactics as Crystal goes on.*) Oh —I didn't tell you before, Stephen, because well—I was afraid that you'd do something extravagant . . . (*Pat now leans on the counter taking it all in, absorbed.*) It *is* dear of you to want to be with me on my birthday. But I won't be lonely, honestly . . . And if this rain lets up, my neuralgia will be better and maybe I can . . . Oh it's nothing —nerves . . . I had a rather gloomy letter from home—my little sister . . (*With a choke in her voice*) . . . she's not so well.

PAT (*talking out of the side of her mouth in warning as she looks off toward the aisle*). Look out! here comes old four eyes!

As she speaks, a severe looking Head Saleswoman, wearing glasses, moves into view, her gaze on Crystal.

CRYSTAL (*thinking fast, speaking for the benefit of the saleswoman*). But she'll be all right. I'm going to send her a *very fine new headache cologne which has really done absolute wonders for a great number of my customers* . . . (*She smiles at the saleswoman, who thinking Crystal is talking business, beams back at her and goes on.*)

PAT (*whistling partly in admiration and partly in relief*). Whew!

CRYSTAL (*after a quick glance to see that the saleswoman is out of earshot*). Oh, darling! I couldn't *think* of your disarranging your evening. (*Bravely*) I'll have another birthday next year—

PAT (*amused—sotto voce*). You'll have another *next week!*

CRYSTAL (*annoyed, moving the mouthpiece so that he may not hear Pat*). Oh, I'm not *that* ill, or *that* lonely! Or *that* blue! . . . But if you *could* come just for a few moments—and drink a little glass of sherry to my health . . . (*Her voice breaking with emotion*) Oh, Stephen, I *do* need you! . . . Yes, dear . . . I'll meet you on the corner in five minutes. (*Hanging up*) Goodbye.

PAT. *Since when* are you cooking dinner for *any* chump!

CRYSTAL. Well—I had to do something drastic! (*With indignation as Pat reacts in quizzical admiration*) Why, he nearly stood me up for his wife!

FIRST SALESGIRL (*with mischievous delight—barging up to Crystal*). A couple of *late shoppers* want *you* to wait on them, *dear!*

Crystal looks off—and the view swings to take in Sylvia and Edith in the background sniffing perfumes.

CRYSTAL (*askance*). Me?

FIRST SALESGIRL (*as she starts off*). Yes.

CRYSTAL (*annoyed*). Why *me*? (*The salesgirl merely shrugs in answer.*)

PAT (*cutting in*). Maybe they're slumming.

Crystal shoots her a look and heads for her customers.

CRYSTAL (*to Sylvia and Edith—all charm and efficiency*). Might I be of assistance?

SYLVIA (*covertly looking her over*). Yes. I'm thinking of changing my perfume.

CRYSTAL (*not noting Sylvia's mood or interest*). Would you like something subtle . . . or something more on the "woodsy" order—this, for instance.

EDITH (*piping up—to Crystal*). Is that what you use?

CRYSTAL. Oh, no . . . it's much too expensive for me.

SYLVIA. Nonsense, my dear . . . a pretty girl like you . . . with all the rich men that float in here.

CRYSTAL (*beginning to sense an attack*). I'm afraid when they come to *this* counter they have other women on their minds.

SYLVIA (*brightly*). I shouldn't think you'd let *that* stop you. (*Crystal, now sure of the attack, looks up.*) Oh—here's this new one—Summer Rain. That's the kind Mary Haines is so keen about.

EDITH (*shooting a covert glance at Crystal to note her reaction*). Yes. That's it. (*But Crystal gives no sign of reaction.*)

SYLVIA (*back to Crystal*). A friend of ours, *Mrs. Stephen Haines,* simply dotes on this. Her husband picked it out for her—perhaps you sold it to him . . . Stephen Haines, the engineer?

They both watch avidly for some sign of guilt from Crystal, but she remains steadfastly innocent.

CRYSTAL. I'm afraid I don't remember . . . we have so many men come in.

SYLVIA. Awfully good looking . . . tall, fair and distinguished. . . . I'm sure you wouldn't overlook *him.*

CRYSTAL. I'm sorry, but when one's mind is on one's *own business*—

SYLVIA (*cutting in*). Of course. And as you say . . . *you have so many men!* (*And she picks up a bottle.*)

CRYSTAL (*poisonously sweet*). I wouldn't think that one suggests *your personality* at all . . . it's called "Oomph!"

SYLVIA (*disregarding the jab*). How amusing.

A set of chimes starts playing a refined melody in signal of closing time.

EDITH. What's that?

CRYSTAL (*ready to poison them*). Closing time.

SYLVIA (*to Edith*). The bum's rush in melody, dear! (*She picks up another bottle, reading the label "Feuilles d'Automne,"   and   mispronouncing   the French*) Fui-de-aut-oom.

CRYSTAL. I beg your pardon. (*Pronouncing it perfectly*) Feuilles d'Automne.

SYLVIA (*quickly*). My! You *are* clever! (*She exchanges alarmed glances with Edith.*)

CRYSTAL. Doesn't a woman *have* to be these days? (*Then calling off*) Goodnight, Pat!

PAT (*in hearty co-operation—working an old trick as she passes*). Goodnight, Crystal!

SYLVIA. Oh—I'm afraid we're keeping you. (*Patronizingly, as she picks up a tiny twenty-five cent bottle of cologne*) I'll take this, my dear. (*She hands her a sales slip from another small package.*) There's my name and address. Just charge and send.

CRYSTAL (*sweetly—as she writes in sales book*). Twenty-five cents. My! You *are* getting off economically, aren't you?

SYLVIA (*never batting an eye*). Aren't I? (*And she and Edith start off.*)

CRYSTAL (*glancing at the slip—calls after them*). It'll be out tomorrow, Mrs. Prowler.

SYLVIA (*turning, annoyed but smiling*). Fowler . . .

CRYSTAL (*taking another look at the sales slip*). Oh, *sorry* . . . Mrs. Fowler.

Crystal mumbles as she looks off after Sylvia, but her words are drowned out by the peal of the chimes which rise in crescendo as she slams her sales book shut. The scene dissolves to a view of SYLVIA AND EDITH as they go out, Sylvia is burning with indignation.

SYLVIA. Why the impertinent little upstart. (*Stopping*) If she thinks I'm going to let her get away with that she's— (*And breaking off, she starts back.*)

EDITH (*grabbing Sylvia*). Oh, come along! (*As they start again*) You weren't exactly Pollyanna yourself. It isn't any wonder she got on.

SYLVIA (*bubbling over with indignation*). But *Prowler!* Really! (*She looks back.*) She's laughing! I know it! I can see her!

EDITH (*looking back*). Why I believe she is!

SYLVIA (*as they proceed, both of them looking back*). She called me that deliberately. I'll have her fired! I know the management here! I'll—

At which point they run smack into a parcel truck and fall head first into the bin, their legs sticking out, as the scene fades out.

PART THREE

A BERMUDA scene fades in, then dissolves to a view of PALM TREES as Mary comes from behind a palm tree and executes a handspring.

MARY'S VOICE (*during the handspring*). How'm I doing?

There is a threefold laughter and the scene drawing back reveals that Mary is showing the motion pictures she and Mrs. Morehead have taken in Bermuda. The room is dark, but Mary's face is revealed in the light from the projection machine, the figures of Mrs. Morehead and Little Mary being more dimly outlined.

On the screen, the picture changes to a view of a Bermuda street car, with Mary descending.

LITTLE MARY. Did you like to ride on that funny thing, Mother?

MARY. We *had* to like it.

On the screen a bicycle shot begins.

MARY. Those were our taxicabs. There wasn't a single automobile in Bermuda!

LITTLE MARY. But, Grandma, *you* can't ride a bicycle!

MRS. MOREHEAD. Oh, can't I?

At this point, Mrs. Morehead appears on the screen on a bicycle. As she arrives safely, she can't help showing off a little. She releases the hand from the wobbling handlebar, waving in cautious daring toward Mary who is grinding the camera.

LITTLE MARY (*delighted*). Oh, Grandma, you're a riot!

At this moment, the handlebars swing sharply over, catapulting Mrs. Morehead directly into the line of stacked bicycles, which come falling forward.

MRS. MOREHEAD (*in comic boastfulness*). Riot nothing! I was a *catastrophe!*

The still grinding camera runs up to a view of the bewildered Mrs. Morehead, and we find her seated in a maze of entangled bicycles, with one wheel still ironically spinning right above her head like a surrealistic "halo."

LITTLE MARY (*to Mrs. Morehead*). How did you ever get out of it?

MRS. MOREHEAD. Your mother brushed me up with a dustpan.

By which time the next scene opens, with a close-up of Mary crying.

LITTLE MARY. What were you crying about, Mother?

MARY (*mock tragic*). Something I love very, very much!

The view draws back disclosing Mary on her knees cutting a huge Bermuda onion, the background revealing that the ladies are in a beautiful park having a picnic.

LITTLE MARY. Oh! I know! I know! *Bermuda onions!*

The view then moves to reveal a couple of cute pickaninnies standing close by, watching Mary in mild astonishment, each contentedly munching a huge big onion!

LITTLE MARY. Why didn't *they* cry? Are they onion proof?

MARY. After the first ten thousand, *anyone* is!

On the screen Mary rides toward the camera on a bicycle.

LITTLE MARY. Oh, look at that darling little pickaninny!

MARY (*laughing*). You'd better look *quick!*

At this point the scene suddenly disappears into blackness.

LITTLE MARY. Is that a scene of the pickaninnies at midnight?

MARY. No, dear, that is the most beautiful view of them all—an immense field of gorgeous white Easter lilies in bloom with a quaint little church in the background. But your grandmother forgot one has to take the little rubber cap off the lens! We'd have taken five more reels of blackness if I hadn't finally grabbed it off.

With the words: "Finally grabbed it off," the next scene suddenly leaps on the screen.

It is taken on a boat and Mary is hauling in a fish. She is having quite a time, but she finally lands it and stands proudly with her prey to pose for a really good picture. But during her struggle with the fish, Mary comes too close to the camera for a good picture, and Mrs. Morehead steps back to frame it properly. Steps back and steps back, and just as the picture starts to disclose the size of the fish, a motorboat speeds up into the foreground, the camera swoops up and falls, recording the waters as they close over the lens.

LITTLE MARY (*during fishing shot*). O-o-o-o Mother! What *have* you got on there? He's certainly giving you a run for your money! (*As she sees the fish*) Oh—that fish is as dead as a doornail, Mother! He wouldn't fool *anybody!*

MARY (*laughing*). Well, you can't blame me for trying! Look out now! Here goes the camera overboard!

LITTLE MARY. Oh, Grandma—did you drop our precious camera *in the water?*

MRS. MOREHEAD (*mock indignant*). Precious *camera!* Listen, my child—your precious *grandma* dropped right in after it, clear to the bottom of the ocean.

LITTLE MARY (*aghast*). You *did?*

MRS. MOREHEAD. Well—nearly to the bottom. I know we passed whales on the way up when they pulled me out.

On the screen we now see Mary on a springboard.

LITTLE MARY (*archly—kidding her grandmother*). Why, Grandma, that's quite a good shot. Did you finally *hire* a photographer?

MRS. MOREHEAD. Now, really!

There follows a lovely scene of Mary, showing her lonely and heartsick.

LITTLE MARY (*with a big sigh*). Oh, mother, but you *are* beautiful!

MARY (*with a little laugh—touched*). Bless you!

LITTLE MARY. Weren't you having a good time that day, Mother?

MARY. I was getting homesick for you, dear, until Grandma broke it up. (*And here the film ends.*)

LITTLE MARY. Homesick for *me* or for Daddy?

MARY (*kidding her*). For Sheba.

LITTLE MARY (*kidding right back*). Oh! So—if you'd have taken Sheba with you, you'd have stayed the *whole four weeks you planned on,* eh?

MARY. Longer!

As they both laugh, Little Mary runs to switch on the lights, while Mary starts to take the film from the camera.

LITTLE MARY (*indicating films*). Don't take the pictures out yet, Mother—I'm going to run them for Daddy.

MARY. I ran them for Daddy last night. (*At this point Miss Fordyce enters and waits for recognition.*)

LITTLE MARY (*going to Mary*). Bet Daddy wished he was there when he saw you catch that fish!

MARY (*with an almost imperceptible catch in her voice*). I bet he did! (*Mrs. Morehead watches Mary covertly.*)

MISS FORDYCE. Your music teacher's here, Mary.

LITTLE MARY (*hating to leave*). Oh dear! (*She clings to Mary.*) We missed you so while you were gone, Mother, darling—Daddy and I!

MARY (*pathetically pleased*). Did you?

LITTLE MARY. Yes. (*Snuggling to Mary*) He finally had to take me to the Zoo to cheer me up.

MARY (*laughing as she fondles her*). Oh! What a compliment to *me!*

LITTLE MARY (*abject—hugging her*). I didn't mean it that way, Mother. You're better than all the lions and tigers and elephants in the whole wide world!

MARY (*holding her close*). I know! I know, dear!

LITTLE MARY. I saw Mrs. Potter at the Zoo that day.

MRS. MOREHEAD (*to Little Mary—cutting in*). Who was she visiting with—the snakes?

MARY (*laughing—mildly shocked*). Oh, mother!

LITTLE MARY (*innocently—not getting their meaning*). As a matter of fact she was! (*Mrs. Morehead shoots a look of comical triumph at Mary.*) Mrs. Potter said (*to Mary*) she and Aunty Sylvia would call you up that evening in Bermuda.

MRS. MOREHEAD (*quickly glancing up to Mary*). You didn't tell me they called up.

MARY (*a trace evasive, fussing with projection equipment*). Didn't I? Well, I'm afraid they didn't have anything much worth reporting.

MISS FORDYCE (*patiently*). Mademoiselle is waiting, Mary.

LITTLE MARY. Oh, bother! Well— (*She gives Mary a big kiss, heaves a reluctant sigh, then goes to Mrs. Morehead.*) Goodbye, Grandma, darling.

MRS. MOREHEAD (*kissing her*). Goodbye, dear.

LITTLE MARY (*mischievously*). I'll give you a lesson some day . . . *with the camera!* (*Mrs. Morehead laughs and gives her a little spank as Little Mary runs out singing "Au Claire de la Lune mon ami Pierrot".*)

MRS. MOREHEAD (*waiting for Little Mary's departure—then, significantly, turning to Mary*). Mary, is *that* why we hurried home *ahead of time?*

MARY (*preoccupied with putting the film away, and pretending she doesn't understand*). Why we . . . hurried?—

MRS. MOREHEAD. Yes, was it something those women *said to you* when they called up?

MARY (*laughing and trying to make light of it*). Oh—of course not. You're so suspicious, darling. I'm very *glad* we came home when we did. Stephen has spent every evening with me since I got back.

MOREHEAD (*studying her narrowly*). And you're really happy, dear?

MARY (*a little bit overly emphatic*). Divinely!

MRS. MOREHEAD. Look me in the eye, Mary. (*As Mary looks at her*) Now! Say it again.

MARY (*pathetically—almost with defiance*). I'm divinely happy!

As Mrs. Morehead studies her, unconvinced, Jane enters.

JANE. Mrs. Haines, Mrs. Potter just phoned. She said she'd meet you at the fashion showing.

MARY. Thanks, Jane. (*To Mrs. Morehead briskly—with a sudden change of mood*) Want to go along and watch me splurge?

MRS. MOREHEAD. And listen to Edith Potter? (*With a humorous gesture of negation*) I'd rather have the itch!

MARY (*gently—with toleration*). I'm afraid you don't humor my friends enough, Mother, dear.

MRS. MOREHEAD. It's humoring *some of them* not to cut their throats.

MARY (*laughing*). Mother!

MRS. MOREHEAD (*affectionately putting her hand on Mary's arm*). Now that you're home, dear, promise you'll stay in your own remote little ivory tower, and be very, very noncommittal about yourself and Stephen.

MARY (*laughing*). They won't get a word out of me!

MRS. MOREHEAD. Good! (*Giving her a goodbye kiss—then*) Buy yourself the silliest hat at the showing and charge it to me!

MARY (*calling after her*). Mother, you're an angel and I'll buy myself a perfect scream!

The scene dissolves to a FASHION SALON where groups of smart women are waiting for the show to begin. A commentator is standing in front of the curtain speaking. Tea is being served by waitresses in uniform.

COMMENTATOR. . . . and Mr. Brugere has staged our showing, ladies, in a manner which will demonstrate the fashions of the day *in action.*

The scene cuts to a close view of a GROUP OF WOMEN with Mary, Sylvia, Edith and Peggy in the foreground.

COMMENTATOR'S VOICE. In other words you will see yourselves as you actually go through the movements of your daily occupations, amusements and sports and you will be able to study the flow of the new line as it reacts to the flow of the body. . . . Thank you.

SYLVIA (*speaking simultaneously*). So I said: "Howard, my boy, you'd better stop picking on me! Did you ever see a *man* try on hats? Why, what *you* go through, you'd think a head was something peculiar!"

PEGGY (*to Sylvia*). Sh!

The Commentator bows, there is a smattering of polite applause, the lights start to dim and the music starts, as the fashion showing begins. We see the models parading the new fashions and the women reacting with various degrees of interest to what they see. Then the show comes to a close and the curtain falls. The lights go up and the music rises into a lively crescendo.

The view cuts to the group of women showing MARY, EDITH and PEGGY.

SYLVIA (*beginning her "fishing"*). What did you wear in Bermuda, Mary?

MARY. Slacks. I got dreadfully sloppy.

EDITH. One always does *travelling alone.*

SYLVIA. You'll have to load up on clothes for Stephen. (*Exchanging glances with Edith*) Is he—taking you out much?

MARY (*evasively*). Oh loads. (*Changing the subject with gestures toward the model*) Look, girls. How charming!

PEGGY (*longingly—looking off at a gown*). I'd love to have that!

EDITH (*considering it for herself*). H'm! (*Speaking to a saleswoman, Miss Bachelor, who is hovering near*) Will you call that model with the evening dress.

MISS BACHELOR (*to the model*). Princess Mara . . . show here, please.

Princess Mara enters the scene. She is Russian, regal, soignée.

MARY. What holds it up, Mara? Pure will power?

MARA. And a piece of adhesive tape. You should have it, Mary. You're just what it needs.

MISS BACHELOR. It was Mrs. Potter who called for the dress, Princess.

MARA (*with a look at Edith's figure*). Oh . . . sorry. (*She models the dress.*)

SYLVIA (*barging up*). You'd sell a woman *anything*, wouldn't you, Mara? (*She takes hold of Mara.*) Why d'you wear it wrong? (*Yanking at the gown*) I saw it in Vogue. (*Jerking*) Off here and down there.

MARA (*slapping Sylvia's hand down*). Stop mauling me!

MISS BACHELOR (*reprovingly, in a very low voice*). Princess!

MARA (*to Sylvia*). What d'you know about how to wear clothes?

SYLVIA. *I'm* not a model, Mara, but no one disputes how *I* wear clothes!

MISS BACHELOR (*in a kind of whisper*). Princess Mara, you'd better apologize.

MARY (*to Miss Bachelor*). It's just professional jealousy. They're really good friends.

SYLVIA (*maliciously*). Yes, indeed—she adores the Fowler family! Particularly *my husband!*

MARA. Do you accuse me of flirting with Howard?

SYLVIA (*pleasantly*). No, darling! Only of *trying* to! I'd like to *see* Howard Fowler bat an eye at *any other woman!*

MARA. Well, *I've* seen him and she's *not bad,* either!

SYLVIA (*utterly outraged*). Why you—

MARY (*cutting in quickly to Sylvia, anxious to break them up*). Come, darling. Let's look at lingerie. (*She drags her off, the scene moving with them. Edith and Peggy follow.*)

SYLVIA (*as they go along*). Did you get her innuendo? I've always hated that girl, exploiting her title the way she does. If there's *one* thing I *am* sure of in this life it's Howard Fowler!

They are now in the French Room where several models are parading.

MISS CARTER (*approaching them*). How d'you do, Mrs. Haines . . . Mrs. Fowler . . .

MARY. Hello, Jessica.

SYLVIA (*simultaneously*). Hello, my dear.

MISS CARTER (*to Mary*). Did you have a wonderful time in Bermuda?

MARY. I had a good rest.

SYLVIA (*with unconscious humor*). Howard wants *me* to take a world cruise!

A model parades past them, wearing an exquisite nightgown with a lace coat, followed by Edith and Peggy who are looking it over.

SYLVIA. Oh! Isn't that adorable?

MARY. It's divine! (*To Miss Carter*) Don't tell me the price—but how much is it?

MISS CARTER (*drawing the tag from the model's sleeve*). Two hundred and— (*Looking more closely*) . . . that's right —two hundred and twenty-five dollars.

MARY (*ironically*). It *is* a *nightgown*, isn't it?

MISS CARTER. Oh yes . . .

PEGGY. *I'd* be glad to wear it for an evening dress.

SYLVIA (*to Mary*). Darling, you really should get it . . . if Stephen doesn't notice the nightgown, he'll at least notice the bill.

MISS CARTER. You'll never regret it, Mrs. Haines.

As Mary stands considering the gown, we suddenly hear a woman's voice.

THE VOICE. *I'll take that!*

As they all look up, amazed at the rudeness of the speaker the view swings to show Crystal Allen standing beyond the model. She is so engrossed in looking at the model that she pays no attention to Mary, Sylvia and Edith.

CRYSTAL (*talking to the saleswoman, as she heads away*). I could use a few more gowns on the same order . . . you know . . . imports with hand embroidery.

MISS CARTER (*to Mary*). I'll get it back. (*She starts away.*)

MARY (*calling after Miss Carter*). Please don't bother. (*But by this time Miss Carter has gone.*)

SYLVIA. Oh, Mary! How humiliating!

EDITH. You poor dear . . . I could die for you.

MARY (*surprised at their tones*). What's the matter? I didn't want it. It's much too expensive.

SYLVIA. You don't *know* who she is?

MARY. No. Who?

SYLVIA (*portentously*). That's Crystal Allen!

There is a moment's pause as Mary pulls herself together.

MARY (*without batting an eyelash*). Pretty, isn't she?

EDITH (*looking off at Crystal*). Did you *hear* the brazen thing? At *two-twenty-five* she could use *a few more!*

SYLVIA (*suddenly bursting out*). Mary! Are you going to stand by and let that common little—

MARY (*cutting in with great dignity and just a touch of reprimand*). Sorry, Sylvia! It's time for my fitting.

She turns and heads away, and a close moving view shows Mary hurrying across the big salon and down a corridor where the fitting rooms are. She holds her head high, fighting to keep her poise. As she comes along, her saleswoman, Miss Bachelor, joins her.

MISS BACHELOR (*showing Mary into room*). Right in here, Mrs. Haines. I'll have your fitting sent down directly.

As Miss Bachelor starts away, we see Miss Archer ushering Crystal into the fitting room across from Mary's.

MISS ARCHER (*to Crystal*). In here, Miss Allen.

Mary watches Crystal go inside, the saleswoman following her. Mary is suddenly furious. For a moment she has the impulse to go in and confront Crystal; then she thinks better of it and turns back into the room.

The interior of MARY'S FITTING ROOM, as Mary closes the door, reveals her holding onto the back of a chair, sick and shattered. Suddenly the door opens and a corset model enters. She wears a negligee over her corset and opens her negligee for Mary to see, but very slightly so as not to reveal nudity.

MODEL (*parrot-like*). This is our new one-piece lace foundation garment. (*Pirouetting*) Zips up the back and no bones.

She walks out, Mary having scarcely given her a glance, and the view moves with the model to Crystal's fitting room.

In Crystal's fitting room Miss Archer is trying something on Crystal as the corset model pirouettes.

MODEL. Our new one-piece lace foundation garment. (*Turning again*) Zips up the back and no bones. (*She goes out.*)

MISS ARCHER (*taking up her salesbook*). Will you open a charge?

CRYSTAL. Please.

MISS ARCHER. May I have the name?

CRYSTAL (*quite self-assured*). Allen . . . Miss Crystal Allen . . . The Hotel Viceroy.

MISS ARCHER. May I have your other charges? Saks, Bergdorf, Cartier?

CRYSTAL (*putting it on*). Oh, I'll be opening those in the next few days.

MISS ARCHER. Then may I have your bank?

CRYSTAL. I've no checking account either, at the moment.

MISS ARCHER. I'm sorry, Miss Allen. But we *must* ask for one business reference.

CRYSTAL (*lightly—she was prepared for this*). Oh, of course. Mr. Stephen Haines, 40 Wall—he's an old friend of my family.

MISS ARCHER (*relieved*). That will do. Mrs. Haines is a very good client of ours.

CRYSTAL (*this she hadn't expected*). Oh. (*As the saleswoman writes—Crystal reaches a decision.*) By the way, I've never met Mrs. Haines.

MISS ARCHER. She's lovely.

CRYSTAL. So . . . I'd rather you didn't mention to her that I gave her husband as reference. (*Beguiling*) D'you mind?

MISS ARCHER. Of course not, Miss Allen. . . . We understand.

CRYSTAL (*angrily*). Do you! What do you understand?

MISS ARCHER (*flustered*). I mean—

CRYSTAL. Oh, never mind.

MISS ARCHER. Please, I hope you don't think I meant—

CRYSTAL (*with a charming smile*). Of course not. Oh, it's dreadful living in a strange city alone. . . . You have to be *so* careful not to do anything people can misconstrue. You see I don't know Mrs. Haines yet, and I'd hate to get off on the wrong foot before I've met her *socially*.

MISS ARCHER (*sounding convincing*). Naturally. Women are funny about little things like that. (*And she starts to leave.*)

CRYSTAL. Just a moment. You know that white negligee they had in the showing? The modernistic one?

MISS ARCHER (*at the door*). Oh yes. It's made of spun glass.

CRYSTAL. I'd like to try it on.

MISS ARCHER (*a little astonished that anyone would really buy it*). A—certainly.

She goes out, the scene moving with her into the corridor where she sees Miss Bachelor taking some accessories into Mary's room.

MISS ARCHER (*hailing Miss Bachelor*). Tst! Ethel! I'm going to sell that little glass number for intimate afternoons.

MISS BACHELOR. Good heavens! She'll freeze in it.

MISS ARCHER. Not this baby!

Miss Bachelor grins and enters MARY'S FITTING ROOM, where Mary is now stepping from her own dress into the evening gown she is having fitted, and the fitter is adjusting it.

MISS BACHELOR (*seeing the dress on Mary*). That really suits you, Mrs. Haines!

MARY (*finding it hard to keep her attention on the dress*). Yes . . . it's very nice.

MISS BACHELOR (*anxiously*). Is there something you don't like?

MARY (*making herself take notice*). Oh, no . . . no. It's really charming.

At this moment we hear Sylvia's voice.

SYLVIA'S VOICE. Yoo hoo! May I come in? (*Saying which she barges through the doorway.*)

MARY (*bracing herself*). Sit down, Sylvia!

MISS BACHELOR. I'll get your wrap, Mrs. Haines.

As the fitter and Miss Bachelor leave the room Mary steps to the window, and opens it almost as if she might faint if she didn't get air.

SYLVIA (*waiting for the door to close—then bursting out*). Mary, you *do* know! Why don't you confide in me?

MARY. Will you please keep out of my affairs, Sylvia.

SYLVIA (*with vehemence*). No, I won't! If you think I'm going to stand calmly by and let you hide your head in the sand like an ostrich, you're very much—

MARY (*almost in appeal—cutting in*). Sylvia.

SYLVIA. You're *absolutely* the *only* one in New York who doesn't know *all* about it! Howard says nobody's *seen* Stephen in the Club *in the afternoon* for weeks!

MARY. Sylvia, go away.

At this moment Miss Bachelor returns with the wrap which goes with Mary's gown.

MISS BACHELOR (*standing in doorway and calling to a model in the hallway*). Sally, show that to Miss Allen right there. (*She enters and closes the door.*)

SYLVIA (*to Miss Bachelor—innocently, with one eye on Mary*). Is that *Crystal* Allen across the hall?

MISS BACHELOR. Yes. She's a new customer. . . . D'you know her? She got a lot of money?

SYLVIA. Well . . . I imagine she knows where to get a lot. (*She glances quickly at Mary who sits down suddenly.*)

MISS BACHELOR. She's buying everything she sees . . . regardless. Why, Mrs. Haines, are you ill?

MARY. No, no. I'm just tired.

MISS BACHELOR. I'm afraid you've been standing too long . . . (*hurrying out*) I'll get you a glass of sherry.

SYLVIA. Mary, you'd feel better if you'd talk this out with someone. Stephen is a worm . . . spending money on a girl like that.

MARY. Oh shut up, Sylvia.

SYLVIA. D'you like being made ridiculous before all your friends? Don't be a fool, Mary. *Go in there!*

MARY (*shocked at the thought*). Go in there? I'm going home! (*She starts to take off the dress.*)

Miss Bachelor returns with the sherry. Sylvia takes it from her, pushes her out and closes the door in her face.

SYLVIA (*turning to Mary*). Here, dear . . . you need this. (*Mary, disregarding the sherry, continues to dress.*) Now's your chance to put an end to this thing, Mary. (*Relentlessly*) Go in there and just say a few *quiet* words. Tell her you'll make Stephen's life an absolute tornado until he gives her up.

MARY. Stephen's not in love with that girl.

SYLVIA. All right! Then look where she was six months ago. And look where she is now.

MARY (*still hurrying into her dress*). Sylvia, please let me decide what is best for me, and my home.

SYLVIA. Well—she may be a perfectly marvelous influence for Stephen, but she's not going to do your child any good.

MARY (*turning to her*). What do you mean?

SYLVIA. Far be it from *me* to tell you things you don't care to hear. I've known this all along. Edith wanted me to tell you when we called you up in Bermuda, but did I *utter*?

MARY (*with violence*). What has my child to do with this?

SYLVIA. It was while you were away. Edith saw them . . . Stephen and that creature and little Mary, lunching in the Park.

Mary's heart sinks as she mentally checks Sylvia's words with the story Little Mary told her of meeting Edith in the park.

SYLVIA. She said they were having a hilarious time. That beezle was sitting with her arm around little Mary and kissing her between every bite. When I heard that, I was positively *heartsick*, dear. (*Mary sits down weakly; and Sylvia, seeing she has scored, celebrates by tossing down Mary's sherry.*) But as you say, it's your affair, not mine. (*She goes to the door looking very hurt.*) No doubt that girl will make a perfectly good *stepmamma* for your daughter!

Mary, left alone, rises as if to follow her, then stops. Her common sense dictates she should go home, but now she violently desires to talk. She struggles against it, then, bitterly determined, goes through the door. Then we see the CORRIDOR as Mary comes from her fitting room. Mary crosses the hall. Without a moment's hesitation she knocks on the door of Crystal's room

CRYSTAL'S VOICE. Come in. (*Mary opens the door and goes inside.*)

We get a glimpse of SYLVIA peeping out from another fitting room. She smiles, well pleased, as she sees Mary go into Crystal's room.

CRYSTAL'S FITTING ROOM: Mary has entered and now closes the door behind her. Crystal turns. For a long moment the two women stand facing each other.

CRYSTAL (*uncomfortably*). I beg your pardon?

MARY. I am . . . Mrs. Stephen Haines.

CRYSTAL (*with remarkable poise*). Sorry —I don't think I know you!

MARY. I believe it's my husband you know.

CRYSTAL. Oh. So Stephen has told you?

MARY (*contemptuously*). No. He's never mentioned you. (*And at this point Miss Archer half enters.*)

CRYSTAL (*brusquely*). Stay out of here! (*Miss Archer goes out quickly.*)

MARY. But I've known about you for some time.

CRYSTAL. That'll be news to Stephen. Personally, I'm glad you do know.

MARY. I've kept still because I knew it wouldn't take Stephen long to get fed up.

CRYSTAL. Don't lay any bets on it, Mrs. Haines. I'm not *you!*

MARY (*her voice rising*). You've been seeing my daughter. . . . That's what I came in here to tell you. . . . *I won't have you touching my daughter!*

CRYSTAL. You don't have to get hysterical! What do I care about your brat. . . . I'm sick of hearing about her.

The scene moves to the CORRIDOR where Miss Archer motions for another saleswoman to come and listen. Their ears are glued to the door of Crystal's fitting room.

MARY'S VOICE. You won't have to hear about her any more because you and my husband are not going on seeing each other.

CRYSTAL'S VOICE. That's rather up to Stephen, isn't it?

MARY's VOICE. Completely. So you'd better start making other plans, Miss Allen.

A head woman comes along and the eavesdropping saleswoman draw back. She looks at them suspiciously but goes on. They resume listening. The head woman returns and listens, too.

Again in CRYSTAL's FITTING ROOM.

CRYSTAL. Listen, I'm taking my marching orders from Stephen. He's satisfied with this arrangement. So don't force any issues unless you want plenty of trouble.

MARY. You've made it impossible for me to do anything else!

CRYSTAL (perking up). Have I? That's great!

MARY. You're very confident!

CRYSTAL. The longer you stay in here, the more confident I get about "your" Stephen!

MARY. Stephen doesn't love you.

CRYSTAL. He's doing the best he can in the circumstances.

MARY. He couldn't love a girl like you.

CRYSTAL. If he couldn't he's an awfully good actor! (As Mary winces) I don't know what you've got to kick about. You have everything that matters . . . the name, the position, the money—

MARY. I had those before I married. . . . I'm thinking about Stephen.

CRYSTAL. Oh, can the sob stuff, Mrs. Haines! You noble wives and mothers bore the brains out of me! And I'll bet you bore your husbands too!

MARY (almost laughing at her idea of values). You are a hard one.

CRYSTAL. Oh, I can be soft . . . on the right occasions. What d'you expect me to do? Burst into tears and beg you to forgive me?

MARY. You're just what I expected!

CRYSTAL. That goes double! And listen, Mrs. Haines, I'd break up your snug, little roost if I could. But I don't stand a chance! And don't think it's because your husband isn't crazy about me. It's because he's the kind that lets that old-fashioned sentiment put the Indian sign on him—that's all.

MARY. I'm glad I came in now. . . . I thought you might be really dangerous . . . (Contemptuously) You're not!

CRYSTAL. Look here, Mrs. Haines, this is my room—

MARY. It's yours for the time being—just like everything else you've got. (Gesturing toward the clothes) May I suggest if you're dressing to please Stephen, not that one! He doesn't like circus clothes.

CRYSTAL. Thanks for the tip. But when anything I wear doesn't please Stephen, I take it off.

Mary, suddenly annoyed at herself for crossing words with such a person, turns and goes out, and the scene moves to the CORRIDOR, as the door of Crystal's fitting room opens and the eavesdroppers scatter. Mary comes out and starts with pride and dignity toward her fitting room, when suddenly Crystal appears.

CRYSTAL (slamming the door after Mary). Oh, what the heck!

Mary, paying no attention whatsoever, enters her fitting room. The saleswomen are clearly sympathetic as they look after Mary.

MISS ARCHER. So that's what she calls meeting Mrs. Haines socially.

MISS BACHELOR. Gee, I feel sorry for Mrs. Haines. She's so nice.

NEGLIGEE MODEL. She should have kept her mouth shut. Now she's in the soup.

MODEL. Allen's smart. She's fixed it so anything Mr. Haines says is going to sound wrong.

SALESGIRL. She'll get him sure!

MISS ARCHER. Look at that painted face! She's got him now!

MISS BACHELOR. You can't trust any man. That's all they want!

CORSET MODEL (plaintively). What else have we got to give?

During the above, there appears a big, screen-filling close-up of "THE PAINTED FACE!" (Crystal) Then the scene dissolves to a picture of a VICTROLA as tango music is heard.

INSTRUCTRESS' VOICE. Up—over—up—down. Up—stretch—up—together.

SYLVIA'S VOICE. Of course my sympathies are for Mrs. Haines. They always are for a woman against a man. But she's been awfully stupid about it.

During this the scene moves back to EXERCISE ROOM where there is a mirrored wall, and on the floor a pink satin mat. The instructor is a bright, pretty girl in a pink silk bathing suit. She stands above Sylvia, drilling her in a carefully cultured voice. They both speak at once.

SYLVIA. Imagine her going into that fitting room and facing the creature! I begged her not to . . . I said, "Mary, where's your dignity?" If she'd only make up her mind to get a divorce. It's terrible on her friends—not knowing —for you can't ask them anywhere.

INSTRUCTRESS (louder). Up—over—up—down. Up—stretch—up—together. Up— (She grabs Sylvia's languid limb, giving it a corrective yank.) Ster—retch!

SYLVIA. Ouch, my scars!

INSTRUCTRESS. This is very good for adhesions. Up—

SYLVIA (resolutely inert). Up! This has got me down!

INSTRUCTRESS. Rest a moment . . . (Sylvia groans her relief.) And relax your diaphragm muscles. (Bitterly) If you can. (She goes to the victrola and changes the record to a fox trot.)

SYLVIA. Of course for her daughter's sake, I think Mrs. Haines ought to hang on. (Piously) I know I would.

INSTRUCTRESS. Now on your side. (Sylvia rolls to her side, reclining on her elbow.) Ready? (Snapping her fingers) Up—down—up—down— (Sylvia flops a limp leg, up, down.)

SYLVIA. She never should have faced Mr. Haines with the issue.

INSTRUCTRESS (imploringly). Don't bend the knee, please.

SYLVIA. When a man's got himself in that deep, he has to have time to wade out.

INSTRUCTRESS (straightening out Sylvia's offending member with considerable force) Thigh in, not out.

SYLVIA (pained, but undaunted). But Mrs. Haines never listens to any of her friends.

INSTRUCTRESS. How does she avoid it? Now, please, —up—down—up—down—

SYLVIA (hearing only her own voice and redoubling her efforts and her errors). I tell everybody, whatever she wants to do is all right by me. I've got to be loyal to Mrs. Haines. . . Oh, I'm simply exhausted. (And she flops over flat on her stomach, panting.)

INSTRUCTRESS. We'll try something simple—like crawling up the wall.

Sylvia lifts a martyred face as the instructress changes the record for a waltz.

SYLVIA (scrambling to her feet). What I go through to keep my figure! And do I see red when some fat lazy dinner partner asks, "What d'you do with yourself all day, Mrs. Fowler?" (She sits alongside the wall.)

INSTRUCTRESS. You rotate on your buttocks.

Sylvia rotates, then lies back, her knees drawn up to her chin, the soles of her feet against the wall.

INSTRUCTRESS. Arms flat. Now you crawl slowly up the wall.

SYLVIA (crawling). Way you say that makes me feel like vermin.

INSTRUCTRESS. That shouldn't be much effort. (As Sylvia gives her a suspicious look) I mean, crawling up the wall.

At this moment Peggy enters in an exercise suit, and Sylvia crawls down.

PEGGY. Hello, Sylvia. How d'you do, Miss Peel.

INSTRUCTRESS. How d'you do, Mrs. Day?

SYLVIA. You're late again, Peggy. After all, dear, I'm paying for this course. . . .

PEGGY. You know I'm grateful, Sylvia—

INSTRUCTRESS. Please, ladies. Let us begin with posture. (*Sylvia rises.*) A lady always enters a room erect.

SYLVIA. Lots of my friends exit horizontally.

She and Peggy go to the mirrored wall and stand with their backs to it.

INSTRUCTRESS. Now— Knees apart. Sit on the wall. (*They sit on imaginary seats.*) Relax. (*They bend forward from the waist, fingertips brushing the floor.*) Now, roll slowly up the wall . . . pressing each little vertebra as hard as you can . . . shoulders back . . . heads back. Mrs. Fowler, lift yourself behind the ears. Pretend you're just a silly little puppet dangling on a string. Chin up. Elbows bent—up up on your toes— arms out—shove with the small of your back—you're off!

Sylvia and Peggy, side by side, mince across the room, the scene moving with them.

PEGGY. John's furious with me for letting you pay for this.

SYLVIA. He ought to be darn glad *he's* not paying for it. You still giving him your own little income?

PEGGY. Yes, and he's so proud he resents taking that tiny amount.

SYLVIA. If he resents it, it's only because it isn't more.

INSTRUCTRESS. Tuck under! Now, back please.

They mince backward across the room.

PEGGY (*staunchly*). You don't understand . . . John's awfully clever, and he makes so little—

SYLVIA. Well, if *you're* clever, you'll hang on to your own money. . . . It's the only protection a married woman has.

They are against the mirror again.

INSTRUCTRESS (*imitating Sylvia's posture*). Not this, Mrs. Fowler. (*She demonstrates.*) That! (*Leading Sylvia forward*) Try it please. (*Facing one another, they imitate exercise.*) Now relax on the mat.

The girls stand side by side, arms straight above their heads. At the count of "one"

each drops a hand, limp from the wrist. At "two," the other hand drops, then their heads fall upon their breasts, their arms flop to their sides, their waists cave in, their knees buckle under them and they swoon or crumble, like boneless things, to the mat.

INSTRUCTRESS (*changing the record*). Now ready? Bend—stretch—bend— down—plenty of pull of the hamstrings, please!

At this point Edith lumbers in. She is draped in a white sheet. Her head is bound in a white towel. Her face is undergoing a "tie-up"—that is, she wears broad white straps under her chin and across her forehead. She appears very distressed.

EDITH. Oh Sylvia! Hello, Peggy—

SYLVIA (*sitting up*). Why Edith, what are you doing up here?

EDITH. Having a facial downstairs. Oh, Sylvia, I'm so glad you're here. I've done the most *awful* thing. I—

INSTRUCTRESS. We're right in the middle of our exercises, Mrs. Potter.

SYLVIA (*to the instructress*). Will you tell them I want my paraffin bath now? There's a dear. I'm simply exhausted.

INSTRUCTRESS. But you've hardly moved a muscle, Mrs. Fowler—

SYLVIA (*with elaborate patience*). Look, whose carcass is this? Yours or mine?

INSTRUCTRESS. It's yours, but I'm paid to exercise it.

SYLVIA. You talk like a horse trainer.

INSTRUCTRESS. Well, Mrs. Fowler, you're getting warm.

She goes out. Sylvia gives her a look and turns to Edith.

EDITH. I've done the most *ghastly* thing. Move over. (*She plumps herself down between Sylvia and Peggy on the mat.*) But it wasn't until I got here, in the middle of my facial, that I realized it. I could bite my tongue off when I think of it—

SYLVIA. Well, what is it, Edith?

EDITH. I was lunching with Dolly de Puyster—

SYLVIA (*interrupting*). I know what you're going to say . . . You forgot she's writing a gossip column.

EDITH (*remorsefully*). Exactly! And I told her all about Stephen and Mary—

PEGGY. Oh, Edith! It'll be in all those dreadful scandal sheets.

EDITH. I know—I've been racking my brains to recall what I said—I think I told her that when Mary walked into the fitting room, she yanked the ermine coat off the Allen girl—

SYLVIA. You didn't!

EDITH. Well, I don't know whether I said ermine or *sable*—but I know I told her that Mary *smacked* the Allen girl!

PEGGY. Edith!

EDITH. Well, that's what Sylvia told me!

SYLVIA. I didn't!

EDITH. You did, too!

SYLVIA (*hurt*). Anyway, I didn't expect you to tell it to a cheap reporter.

EDITH. Well, it doesn't really make much difference. The divorce is practically settled.

SYLVIA (*eagerly*). Who says so?

EDITH. You did!

SYLVIA (*patiently*). I said Mary couldn't broadcast her domestic difficulties and not expect them to wind up in a *scandal*.

PEGGY (*angrily*). Mary didn't broadcast them!

SYLVIA. Who did?

PEGGY. *You* did! And you're all making it impossible for Mary. That's just the sort of talk that mixes everything all up.

INSTRUCTRESS (*re-entering*). The paraffin bath is ready, Mrs. Fowler.

SYLVIA (*rises*). Well, don't worry, Edith. I'll give de Peyster a ring. I can fix it.

EDITH. How?

SYLVIA (*graciously*). Oh, I'll tell her you were lying.

EDITH. You'll do no such thing!

SYLVIA (*shrugging*). Then let the story ride. It will be forgotten tomorrow. You know the awful things they printed about—what's her name?—before she jumped out the window? Why I can't even remember her name, so who cares, Edith? (*She goes out.*)

INSTRUCTRESS. Mrs. Potter, you come right back where you belong.

EDITH. Why, you'd think this was a boarding school!

INSTRUCTRESS. But Mrs. Potter, it's such a foolish waste of money—

EDITH. Listen, relaxing is part of my facial.

INSTRUCTRESS (*coolly*). Then you should relax completely, Mrs. Potter, from the chin up. (*She walks out, leaving Edith gasping.*)

PEGGY (*bursting out—as she goes toward the door with Edith*). Edith, I think Sylvia is a dreadful woman! I'm going to tell her so.

EDITH. Oh, she can't help it . . . just her tough luck she wasn't born deaf and dumb. Peggy, take a tip from me— Keep out of other women's troubles. I've never had a fight with a girl friend in all my life. Why? I hear no evil, I see no evil, I speak no evil!

The scene dissolves to a HEADLINE OF A GOSSIP COLUMN

NEW YORK IN A NUTSHELL
by
Dolly de Peyster
SOCIETY MATRON MAULS GIRL FROM THE WRONG SIDE OF PARK AVENUE

The scene moves to the interior of MARY'S BEDROOM where Jane is standing fairly close to a door leading to an adjoining boudoir. She is obviously listening. In her hand is the newspaper, with the headline.

MARY'S VOICE. Suppose my friends *have* been talking . . . it was *you* who gave them something to talk about . . .

There is the sound of a chair being shoved aside and Jane quickly glances guiltily at the paper in her hand, drops it on a chair, and gets out of the room as fast as she can with safety. Then a fast moving scene in the HALL shows Jane coming from Mary's bedroom, and hurrying to the back stairway and down to the kitchen in lickety-split fashion. She almost stumbles into the kitchen, where Maggie is reading a tabloid. As she puts it down we see pictures of Mary and Crystal and more headlines.

JANE (*excitedly*). Well, it's come . . . they're havin' a 'show-down!

MAGGIE. What's happenin'?

JANE. Give me a cup of coffee and I'll tell you. (*As Maggie pours the coffee*) She says he's put her in an "impossible situation." She can't even walk on the streets without being pointed out on account of her picture in all the papers.

MAGGIE. Tch! Tch! And ain't it true?

JANE. So then he blames the whole thing on her girl friends . . . for spilling it all.

MAGGIE. And that ain't far from wrong either!

JANE. Oh dear! It's enough to make you lose your faith in marriage.

MAGGIE. Sit down. Whose faith in marriage?

JANE (*sits*). You don't believe in marriage?

MAGGIE. Sure I do . . . for women. (*Sighing*) But it's the sons of . . . (*Cutting a slice of cheese*) . . . Adam they got to marry. What else did they say?

JANE. Well, Mr. Haines said "I told you I'd give her up and I did. And I was a swine about the way I did it." (*Reaching for a bottle of cream*) How'd'ya s'pose he did it, Maggie?

MAGGIE. Maybe he just said "Scram, the wife's on to us."

JANE. Well, the madam seemed sort of hurt by him saying he was a swine, the way he gave her up. So she said very quiet, "Would you like to go back to her, Stephen?"

MAGGIE. And did he lie in his teeth to *that* one!

JANE. Oh, the way he said he wouldn't, *I* kinda believed him. But the madam says, "You really should make your manner more convincing, Stephen . . ." She tried to sort of laugh but it didn't come off very well. And he says, "Aren't you ever going to trust me again, Mary?"

MAGGIE (*cutting herself a piece of pie*). I hope she said no . . . You can't trust none of 'em no farther than I can kick this lemon pie.

JANE (*getting some jam from a cupboard*). D'you know, he says this girl was really a good girl . . . that's why he feels he owes her something . . . she wouldn't take nothing from him for months.

MAGGIE. She's a clever piece! She'd have to be . . . to get Mr. Haines.

JANE (*returning to the table*). That's just what the madam said. She said "Stephen, can't you see that girl's only interested in you for your money?"

MAGGIE. Tch, tch, tch. I'll bet that made him sore. A man don't like to be told no woman but his wife is fool enough to love him.

JANE. Then Madam brought up about him taking Little Mary to lunch with that creature, and he said that the poor girl just happened to pass by when he and Little Mary were taking lunch in the park.

MAGGIE. That's a laugh!

JANE. Yes! That's the way Madam took it! Then they both got sore and he began to tell her all over what a good husband he'd been . . . and how hard he'd worked for her and Little Mary. And she kept interrupting, saying as a wife she hadn't been exactly a wash-out herself.

MAGGIE (*rising*). Listen . . . anybody that's ever been married knows that line backwards and forwards. (*She goes to get the coffee pot.*)

JANE. Then somewhere in there he says, "Mary, I may have been a heel but you've always been first with me."

MAGGIE. *First . . .* Don't that sound just like a husband?

JANE. That's what *she* thought I guess, because she says kinda hysterical, "Your idea of love and mine are slightly different, Stephen . . . and while you may regard yourself as a *Superman, romantically,* I don't go for being one of a *group,* even if I *am* first." That kinda makes *him* mad and he says, "I don't ask you to be fair to *me,* Mary, but please remember we have a child and we owe something to her." And that's when she *really* blew up.

MAGGIE (*returning with the coffee pot*). Sure. A woman don't want to be kept on just to run a kindergarten.

JANE. Well . . . it finally got to his saying, "You knew about us for weeks . . . why did you wait until now to make a fool of me?"

MAGGIE. As if he needed her help.

JANE. So then suddenly she says, in an awful low voice, "Oh, Stephen, we can't go on like this." And he says, "You're right, Mary . . . we can't."

MAGGIE. Quite a actress, ain't you?

JANE. My new boy friend says I got eyes like Jeanette MacDonald's.

MAGGIE. Did he say anything about your legs? How did it all end?

JANE. It ain't ended. They're still at it—

MAGGIE. What are you doin' down here then? Get back up there and find out who's ahead. We may be out of jobs tomorrow.

Jane is practically shoved out of the room. The scene moves with her as she hurries upstairs and reaches the door to Mary's bedroom where she finds Sheba. Jane hurries into the bedroom, leaving Sheba outside, scratching at the door and whimpering to be let in. Suddenly the door opens and Jane flies out and hurries quickly down the stairs to the kitchen.

The scene now moves to the KITCHEN, where Jane, all excitement, enters and quietly closes the door.

MAGGIE. Well?

JANE. Give me some more coffee. I'm done in.

MAGGIE (*getting coffee*). Relax and tell me everything they said.

JANE. When I went back, first thing I heard was the madam saying, "Stephen, *I* want a divorce!"

MAGGIE. Tch! Tch! *Abdicating!*

JANE. Well, Maggie, you could have knocked him down with a feather!

MAGGIE (*waving the coffee pot*). I'd like to knock him down with this. What'd *he* say?

JANE. He said he didn't blame her . . . how could he? . . . but he wished she'd wait and think things over . . . he told her to go to bed and get some rest . . . he was going out for a breath of fresh air.

MAGGIE (*eating*). The old hat trick.

JANE. So the madam says, "Fresh air! Is the air so much fresher in the Hotel Viceroy?" That's where the girl lives. . . . And he says "Oh, for Heaven's sake, Mary, one minute you never want to see me again and the next I can't even go out for an airing!"

MAGGIE. You oughtn't to let none of 'em out except on a leash. What happened then?

JANE. Well, nothing for a time. He just walked up and down—up and down—

MAGGIE. Tsch, tsch, he was thinkin'.

JANE. Then he said he was going out and I naturally got ready to scoot. But I heard her call "Stephen?" and he stops on the landing and she says "Don't slam the front door—the servants will hear you." So I came down here. Oh, Maggie, I'm so sad for her. Do you think they're really going to break up?

MAGGIE. Well, I don't know. The first man who can think up a good explanation how he can be in love with his wife *and* another woman is going to win that prize they're always giving out in Sweden!

And as the scene brings the gabbing women very close, it fades out.

PART FOUR

A close view of the dog, SHEBA, fades in. As the dog is whining, the scene draws back to a view of MARY's BOUDOIR where Mary is packing and Sheba is watching her and whining miserably. Mary pays no attention and Sheba turns and goes out, the view moving with her to STEPHEN's DRESSING ROOM. Here Sheba sees Stephen's trunk which Jane is packing, taking things from the nearby closet. The dog lies down beside the trunk and eyes the performance mournfully.

Mary enters with a jar of tobacco and some pipes which have evidently been in her room, and she puts them down rather abstractedly. Jane is about to pack an old coat of Stephen's when Mary notices it.

MARY. Oh, Jane . . . I don't think Mr. Haines wants that old coat any longer. (*She stops and thinks.*) Oh well—I guess it isn't any of my business.

JANE (*sympathetically*). Oh, Mrs. Haines!

Mary turns and goes out, Jane looking after her sympathetically, following which the scene moves to MARY's BEDROOM, where her mother is seen putting some perfume in a travelling perfume bottle as Mary enters.

MRS. MOREHEAD. Train leaves in fifty minutes. Give yourself plenty of time . . . the traffic is maddening.

MARY (*harassed*). Stephen's secretary is bringing around more papers to sign. I never knew there *could* be so many.

MRS. MOREHEAD. You've shown everything to your lawyers—

MARY (*trying to close a bag*). Yes . . . they keep saying I'm getting a raw deal—

MRS. MOREHEAD (*alarmed*). But Mary—

MARY. It's not true. Stephen's been very generous.

MRS. MOREHEAD (*putting an atomizer into its case*). I'm sure he has. (*After a pause, emphatically*) You're both making a terrible mistake.

MARY. Mother, please! (*She gets the bag closed.*)

MRS. MOREHEAD (*picking up odds and ends, and putting them away*). You and Stephen have a child, Mary.

MARY (*undoing a package of books*). What good will it do her to be brought up in a home full of quarrelling and suspicion? She'll be better off just with me.

MRS. MOREHEAD. No she won't. A child needs both its parents in one home.

MARY. Please, Mother, every argument goes round in circles. And it's too late now. (*She chooses which of the books she'll take with her and packs them.*)

MRS. MOREHEAD. It's never too late when you love someone. Mary, call this off . . . Stephen doesn't want a divorce.

MARY. Then why doesn't he fight me on it.

She is tossing old letters from her desk into a wastebasket, tearing them across once.

MRS. MOREHEAD. He's not the fighting kind.

MARY (*tearing a letter viciously*). Neither am I.

MRS. MOREHEAD. Blast these modern laws! Fifty years ago when women couldn't get divorces, they made the best of situations like this, and sometimes out of situations like this they made very good things indeed.

JANE (*appearing in the doorway*). Mr. Haines' secretary, ma'am.

MARY. I'll be right down.

MRS. MOREHEAD (*as Jane goes out*). Go bathe your eyes. Don't let that adding machine see you like this. And remember you have to tell Little Mary yet. . . .

MARY. I'll tell her . . . I've been putting it off because—

MRS. MOREHEAD. Because you hope at the last minute a miracle will keep you from making a mess of your life. Have you thought Stephen might marry that girl?

MARY (*very confidently*). He won't do that.

MRS. MOREHEAD. What makes you so sure?

MARY (*closing the desk drawer and rising*). Because deep down, Stephen does love me— But he won't find it out until I've really gone away. (*As she goes*) You'll *make* little Mary write to me at Reno once a week, won't you? . . . and please Mother, don't spoil her so.

MRS. MOREHEAD. Spoil her! You'd think I never raised any children of my own.

The scene moves to MARY'S LIVING ROOM where Miss Watts and Miss Trimmerback are waiting for her. They are very tailored, plain girls. Miss Watts, the older and plainer of the two, is taking papers out of a brief case. The rug is rolled back and pictures are down. Packing boxes stand around. There is a desolate feeling about the room.

MISS TRIMMERBACK. Don't you feel sorry for Mrs. Haines?

MISS WATTS (*bitterly*). I don't feel sorry for any woman who thinks the world owes her breakfast in bed.

MISS TRIMMERBACK. Gee, I wish I could get some poor fish to furnish *me* breakfast in bed. I'm sick and tired of cooking my own and sloshing through the rain at 8:00 a.m. For what?

MISS WATTS. You have your independence.

MISS TRIMMERBACK. A lot of independence you have on a woman's wages. I'd chuck it like that—(*snapping her fingers*)—for a decent home, wouldn't you?

MISS WATTS. The office is my home.

MISS TRIMMERBACK. Some home. (*Suddenly she looks at her.*) I see. The office wife?

MISS WATTS (*defiantly*). He could get along better without Mrs. Haines or Allen than he could without me.

MISS TRIMMERBACK. Oh, you're very efficient, dear. But what makes you think you're indispensable?

MISS WATTS. I relieve him of a thousand foolish details. I remind him of things he forgets, including, very often these days, his good opinion of himself. I never cry and I don't nag. I guess I *am* the office wife. And a lot better off than Mrs. Haines. He'll never divorce me!

MISS TRIMMERBACK (*astonished*). Why, you're in love with him.

MISS WATTS (*as they face each other angrily*). What if I am? I'd rather work for him than marry the kind of a dumb cluck I could get . . . (*almost tearful*) . . . just because he's a *man*.

Miss Trimmerback, who is facing the door, sees Mary coming and her expression warns Miss Watts, who turns quickly. Mary enters and comes toward them.

MARY. Yes, Miss Watts?

MISS WATTS (*collecting herself quickly*). Good afternoon, Mrs. Haines. . . . Here are the inventories of the furniture. Mr. Haines asked if he could have the portrait of Little Mary.

MARY (*looking at the blank space over the mantel*). Oh, but—it's in storage.

MISS WATTS (*laying a paper on the table*). This will get it out. (*Handing Mary a pen*) Sign there. (*As Mary signs, Miss Watts produces another paper.*) The cook's letter of reference. Sign here. (*As Mary signs*) The insurance papers. You sign here. (*Miss Trimmerback signs each paper after Mary.*) The transfer papers on the car. What d'you want done with it?

MARY. Well, I—

MISS WATTS. I'll find a garage. Sign here. D'you care to rent this apartment, Mrs. Haines?

MARY. Well, I thought I might take a smaller one.

MISS WATTS. This gives us power of attorney till you get back. Sign here. (*As Mary signs*) Mr. Haines took the liberty of drawing you a new will.

MARY (*indignantly*). But—really—

MISS WATTS. It's to your advantage, not his. This will cuts Mr. Haines out. Your lawyers neglected that small detail. Sign here.

Mary signs, then as Miss Watts and Miss Trimmerback sign, Jane enters with a box of flowers.

MISS WATTS. We need three witnesses. Your maid will do.

MARY. Jane, please witness this. It's my will.

JANE (*brokenly*). Oh . . . Mrs. Haines . . . (*And she signs, Miss Watts looking at her slightly contemptuous of her tears.*)

MISS WATTS (*gathering up the papers*). You can always make changes in the event of your remarriage. And don't hesitate to let me know at the office if there is anything *I* can ever do for you.

MARY (*coolly*). There will be nothing, Miss Watts.

MISS WATTS (*cheerfully*). Oh, there are always tag ends to a divorce, Mrs. Haines, and you know how Mr. Haines hates to be bothered with inconsequential details. Good day, Mrs. Haines, and a pleasant journey to you.

MARY. Good-bye, Miss Watts. (*As Miss Watts marches toward the door.*) Good-bye, Miss Trimmerback.

MISS TRIMMERBACK. Good-bye, Mrs. Haines. I . . . I wish you weren't going.

Mary just smiles and Miss Trimmerback makes a hurried exit after Miss Watts.

JANE (*sniveling*). Mr. Haines said I was to give you these, Mrs. Haines.

Mary puts a hand on the girl's arm. Jane goes out abruptly and Mary slowly opens the box and takes out a corsage of orchids and a card on which is written:

"What can I say?
Stephen"

For a moment Mary is touched; then with a violent revulsion of feeling, she throws the orchids into the corner. At the same time, Little Mary can be heard clattering down the stairs calling:

LITTLE MARY'S VOICE. Mother . . . where are you, Mother?

MARY (*collecting herself*). Here, dear.

The next moment Little Mary enters the room with Mrs. Morehead. Both are dressed for the street.

MRS. MOREHEAD. All set, dear?

MARY (*grimly*). All set . . . Mary, Mother wants to talk to you before she goes away.

MRS. MOREHEAD (*going out*). I'll wait for you.

MARY. Mary, sit down, dear. (*Little Mary skipping to the sofa, sits down.—There is a pause.—Mary discovers it's going to be even more painful and difficult than she imagined.*) Mary—

LITTLE MARY. Yes, Mother?

MARY. Mary—

LITTLE MARY (*perplexed by her mother's tone which she feels bodes no good to her*). Have I done something wrong, Mother?

MARY. Oh, no, darling, no. (*She sits beside her daughter and takes her two hands.*) Mary, you know Daddy's been gone for some time.

LITTLE MARY (*sadly*). A whole month.

MARY. Shall I tell you why?

LITTLE MARY (*eagerly*). Why?

MARY (*plunging in*). You know, darling, when a man and woman fall in love what they do, don't you?

LITTLE MARY. They kiss a lot—

MARY. They get married—

LITTLE MARY. Oh, yes. And then they have those children.

MARY. Well, sometimes, married people don't stay in love.

LITTLE MARY. What, Mother?

MARY. The husband and the wife—fall out of love.

LITTLE MARY. Why do they do that?

MARY. Well, they do, that's all. And when they do, they get unmarried, you see?

LITTLE MARY. No.

MARY. Well, they do. They—they get what is called a divorce.

LITTLE MARY (*very matter of fact*). Oh, do they?

MARY. You don't know what a divorce is, but—

LITTLE MARY. Yes, I do. Lots of my friends have mummies and daddies who are divorced.

MARY (*relieved, kisses her*). You know I love you very much, don't you Mary?

LITTLE MARY (*after a pause*). Of course, Mother.

MARY. Your father and I are going to get a divorce. That's why I'm going away. That's why— Oh, darling, I can't explain to you quite. But I promise you, when you are older you will understand. And you'll forgive me. You really will. Look at me, baby, please.

LITTLE MARY (*her lips beginning to tremble*). I'm looking at you, Mother— Doesn't Daddy love you any more?

MARY. No, he doesn't.

LITTLE MARY. Don't you love him?

MARY. I—I—no, Mary.

LITTLE MARY. Oh, Mother, why?

MARY. I—I don't know—but it isn't either Daddy's or Mother's fault.

LITTLE MARY. But Mother, when you love somebody I thought you loved them until the day you die!

MARY. With children, yes. But grown-ups are different. They can fall out of love.

LITTLE MARY. I won't fall out of love with you and Daddy when I grow up. Will you fall out of love with me?

MARY. Oh no, darling, that's different, too.

LITTLE MARY (*miserable*). I don't see *how*.

MARY. You'll have to take my word for it, baby, it is. This divorce has nothing to do with our love for you.

LITTLE MARY. But if you and Daddy—

MARY (*rising and drawing her daughter up to her*). Darling, I'll explain it better to you on the way to the train. We'll go alone in the car, shall we?

LITTLE MARY. But Mother, if you and Daddy are getting a divorce, which one won't I see again? Daddy or you?

MARY. You'll live with me. That's what happens when—when people get divorced. Children must go with their mothers. But you'll see Daddy—sometimes. Now, darling, come along.

LITTLE MARY. Please, Mother, wait for me in the car.

MARY. Why?

LITTLE MARY. I have to wash my hands.

MARY. Then hurry along, dear.

She sees the orchids on the floor and as she moves to the door, stoops, picks them up, and goes out. Little Mary stands looking after her, stricken. Suddenly she goes to the back of the chair, hugs it as if for comfort. Then she begins to cry and beat the back of the chair with her fists.

LITTLE MARY. Oh, please, please, Mother dear—oh! Daddy, Daddy darling! Oh, why don't you do something—*do something*—Mother dear!

The scene fades out.

PART FIVE

A view of "The Reno Special" speeding through the night fades in, and the locomotive emits a shrieking whistle as the scene dissolves into a close-up of MARY seated in the drawing room, leaning back with her eyes closed as the beat of the wheels of the train is heard. Presently Mary opens her eyes; and the view moving back reveals her to be in the train's drawing room. And on the seat across from her sits Peggy sobbing softly.

MARY (*to Peggy*). Don't darling. You mustn't! (*She rises and sits on the arm of the seat beside her.*) Please, dear! Don't!

PEGGY (*piteously*). Oh, Mary! Who'd have thought that *I'd* be going to Reno, too!

MARY. There! There! (*As the doorbell buzzes*) Come in. (*The door is opened by the maid on the train, revealing a small box in her hand.*)

MAID (*to Peggy, holding up the box*). Is you the lady that needs the tooth brush?

PEGGY. Yes.

MAID (*giving her the box*). Here you is, ma'am. Guess you made up your mind to come on the trip in a hurry, didn't you?

PEGGY. Yes.

MAID (*smiling*). Ah thought you did. (*To Mary as she starts out*) The Porter'll make your room up next, Mrs. Haines.

MARY (*as the maid goes out*). Thanks.

PEGGY (*to Mary—indicating an open telegram on the window sill*). Mary— did you *hear* from Stephen?

MARY (*looking at the telegram*). No. That's from an old beau of mine.

PEGGY. Oh. You'll be having lots of beaux now, Mary! (*Mary smiles wryly.*) But I won't! I'll never look at another man! When I think of what he said to me! *My* Johnnie!

MARY. I know! I know!

PEGGY. He wouldn't let me buy a car with *my own money!* Just because *he* couldn't afford a car, *I* can't have a car! He wants me to be a slave!

MARY (*tolerantly*). Oh, no, he doesn't!

PEGGY. But he does! The only protection I have is my own little income!

MARY. That sounds like Sylvia.

PEGGY. Well—this time she's right! (*Pathetically*) Oh, Mary! If I couldn't have caught this train to be *with you,* I'd have jumped right in front of it!

MARY (*smiling in spite of herself*). That would have been quite a feat, dear!

PEGGY. Oh . . . I'm such a fool. (*Snivelling afresh*) Maybe Johnnie *is* right!

MARY (*warmly—sympathetically*). Now, now, honey! Cut it out!

PEGGY (*listening a moment to the beat of the wheels—then, talking through her sobs*). Mary! Listen to the wheels. Do they . . . seem to be saying anything?

MARY (*amused*). No.

PEGGY. Doesn't it seem as if they keep saying: "Go back! Go back! Go back!"

MARY (*quickly*). Why don't you go back to him, Peggy? (*And it is apparent that she is asking herself the same question.*)

PEGGY. I can't, Mary! After all *I have my pride!*

MARY. Yes . . . I know! (*Her own pride, too!*)

PEGGY (*rising*). I think I'll try and get some sleep.

MARY. Goodnight, dear.

PEGGY (*kissing her*). Goodnight. I'll see you in the morning. (*She goes out.*)

MARY (*calling after Peggy is out of sight*). If you can't sleep, send for me.

PEGGY'S VOICE. I will.

Mary stands in the open doorway looking concernedly after her, when the maid steps up.

MAID (*to Mary*). Porter's ready now, Mrs. Haines.

MARY (*still lost in sadness over Peggy*). Thanks. (*She sighs and goes out.*)

The view moves with her as she goes along the corridor into the club car, of which her drawing room is a part. (The club car lights are dim, as it is late at night.) There are three women in the car. One is the Countess de Lave, a silly, amiable, middle-aged woman with carefully waved, bleached hair, who is wearing slacks and a sable coat. The second, Miriam Aarons, a breezy, flashy red-head about twenty-eight years old. She is wearing a theatrical pair of lounging pajamas. The third is just anybody, a Mrs. Jones, and besides her is her small daughter. Mary smiles at the little girl—then picks up a magazine and sits down.

LITTLE GIRL (*piping up—to her mother*). Mummy, will Daddy come to Reno?

MRS. JONES (*rising*). No, darling.

LITTLE GIRL. Mummy, where is Daddy?

MRS. JONES (*taking the child out*). He's gone with the wind—*the big, white Zombie!*

As Mary looks after the departing Joneses, shocked, suddenly she hears a voice calling out:

COUNTESS' VOICE. Won't you join me in some champagne?

Mary looks off and the scene reveals the Countess, who has a bottle of champagne on the floor beside her and a glass in her hand.

MARY (*hesitating a moment, then deciding to make the best of matters, and smiling*). Yes . . . thank you . . . I'd love to. (*She rises and joins the Countess.*)

COUNTESS. I'm the Countess de Lave.

MARY. Of course . . . I've seen your picture in the papers.

COUNTESS (*squinting at Mary curiously*). And I've seen *yours*.

MARY. I'm Mrs. Stephen Haines.

COUNTESS. That's right. (*She is obviously recalling the late scandal.*) Those stinking newspaper pictures didn't half do you justice, Mrs. Haines. (*As Mary smiles wanly*) Don't look so *desolée*, my dear. (*She looks across at Miriam, who is lighting a cigarette.*) You, too, dear . . . don't sit in that corner and mope! Get us some glasses from the bar there, and we'll all have a little drinkie.

MIRIAM (*rising to go to the bar*). Right you are!

COUNTESS (*to Mary as she twirls the champagne in the bucket*). Cheer up, Cherie. Wait till you've lost as many husbands as I have. Married, divorced —married, divorced. But ah, L'Amour —L'Amour—where Love leads I always follow.

MIRIAM (*entering with the glasses*). Here we are, Countess.

COUNTESS (*starting to pour the champagne*). Thanks. (*To Mary*) This sweet little thing is going to get her first divorce, too. She's a very dear friend of mine. (*To Miriam*) What did you say your name was, darling?

MIRIAM (*looking a little askance at Mary*). Miriam Aarons.

COUNTESS (*indicating Mary*). This is Mrs. Haines. You know—(*in a semi-whisper*)—yanked the scalp off that Allen woman in a fitting room.

MIRIAM (*brightening up no end*). Oh yeah! (*To Mary, warmly, with camaraderie*) I was afraid you were a wet firecracker, sister! (*And she holds out her hand.*) Shake!

Mary, trying to adjust herself to her company, shakes Miriam's hand, after which Miriam, in a hearty and friendly gesture claps Mary on the back. Mary winces.

COUNTESS (*holding out a glass to Mary*). Take it, dear, and dip that pretty little beakie.

MARY (*smiling*). Thanks.

MIRIAM (*picking up her own glass*). Happy days!

COUNTESS. Happy nights! (*As they all drink—to Mary*) Mrs. Aarons is connected with the stage . . . (*To Miriam*) . . . or is it the circus, my dear?

MIRIAM. It *was* the chorus. . . .

COUNTESS. The chorus! You must tell us all about it sometime. I'll bet you got some great hauls out of our New York boy friends.

MIRIAM. If you mean diamond bracelets in boxes or orchids, that breed died out just before my time.

COUNTESS (*sympathetically*). What a pity! But then *I* never got a sou from anybody except my first husband, Mr. Strauss. He said the most touching thing in his will. I remember every word of it. "To my beloved wife, Flora, I leave all my estate *to be administered by executors* because she is an A-1 *schlemiel.*" Wasn't that sweet?

MIRIAM. Any ladle is sweet that dishes you out some gravy!

COUNTESS. How true! None of my other husbands ever gave me a dime. Ah, l'amour, l'amour! How it can let you down. But then, how it can pick you up again, too, Cherie. (*As Mary laughs, beginning to be really amused, the train starts through a tunnel and the lights in the car turn on more brightly.*) Where's this wretched train taking us?

MIRIAM. A tunnel, dear. We're in the mountains.

COUNTESS. I detest mountains. They remind me of the day Gustav made me climb to the top of an Alp. Gustav was my third husband. (*To Mary*) Want to pour Flora another little drinkie? (*Mary smiles and obliges.*) Anyhow, there we were. And suddenly it struck me that Gustav had pushed me. I slid halfway down the mountain before I realized that Gustav didn't love me any more. (*Gaily*) But Love takes care of its own, Mrs. Haines. I slid right into the arms of my fourth husband, the Count!

MIRIAM. That's the bird you're divorcing now, isn't it?

COUNTESS. But, of course, my dear! What else could I do when I found out he was putting poison in my headache powders?

MARY (*horrified*). Poison! (*Trying to treat the matter lightly.*) I'm afraid you're not a very good judge of *character*, Countess.

COUNTESS. That's the trouble with me . . . I don't pick 'em for their character. (*To Mary*) I'll bet you picked yours for character, didn't you?

MARY. Well . . . partly.

COUNTESS. And where's it got you? On the train for Reno!

MARY (*moodily as the wine begins to take its effect*). On the train for Reno!

COUNTESS. Well—my way, your marriage may not last till death, but it's fun while it holds together and I always think it's cruel to stand around waiting for someone to die. (*To Miriam*) What did you pick yours for, darling?

MIRIAM (*dryly*). Not for character!

COUNTESS. There! You see? No matter *what* you pick 'em for, where does it get you?

MARY (*dazed*). On the train for Reno! (*And she drains her glass.*)

COUNTESS. That's the answer! (*Starting to pour wine*) Well! let's all have another little drinkie to Reno . . . biggest little city in the world. The American Cradle of Liberty!

MIRIAM (*raising her glass*). Reno! Beautiful Emblem of the Great Divide!

The scene moves quickly to a close-up of Mary, as the beat of the wheels swells up. Listening to them, Mary remembers Peggy's words—that they seem to be saying: "Go back—Go back." Tears well into her eyes.

COUNTESS' VOICE. What's the matter, dear? Cat got hold of your tongue?

MARY (*shaking off her mood, raising her glass and speaking with a sort of violent decision as if to drown out the sound of the wheels*). TO RENO!

As she drinks the champagne the steady beat of the wheels swells up louder and louder, and the scene dissolves into a close-up of a SIGN reading:

TO RENO
Ten Miles

then in a long sweep we see the Nevada country-side with a ranch in the foreground with several women in citified cowboy outfits riding horseback in the distance. Then the scene moves to a view of the RANCH—with a sign over the gate reading:

THE DOUBLE BAR T RANCH
Hourly busses to and from Reno

And we see Lucy at the gate, removing mail from the rustic mail box.

LUCY (*singing*).
"Down on old Smokey, all covered with snow,
I lost my true lov-ver from courtin' too slow."

As she starts for the ranch house with the mail the scene moves with her.

LUCY.
"Courtin's pul-leasure, partin' is grief,
Anna false hearted lov-ver is worse thanna thief."

As she nears the doorway, she hears someone calling:

PEGGY'S VOICE. Oh, Lucy.

Lucy looks up, following which Peggy is seen standing in the doorway at the ranch. She is on the verge of tears.

LUCY. Hello, honey. How's tricks?

PEGGY (*in a quavering voice*). Where's Mrs. Haines?

LUCY. Don't know—but she'll be moseyin' around here soon. Fer the whole six weeks she's been here, I ain't never knowed her to be very far away when the mail comes in.

They enter the house, and then we see them coming into the MAIN ROOM where the LANDSCAPE is visible through the windows.

LUCY (*as they enter*). Wish that man of hers would write her a letter, or send her a telegram or suthin',

PEGGY. They're all alike, Lucy! (*Indicating mail*) Anything for me?

LUCY (*putting down the mail on the table*). 'Nary a postcard, dear. You'll miss Mrs. Haines a lot when she goes tomorrow, won't you?

PEGGY. Yes.

LUCY. Land sakes! I ain't finished gettin' her packed yet! Come along, honey. You can mope just as well in her room as anywhere.

Peggy smiles wanly and follows.

LUCY (*as they go toward Mary's room*). How come you didn't git your divorce this mornin' along with Mrs. Haines?

PEGGY. I had to wait for some papers from New York.

LUCY. I see.

They enter MARY'S ROOM, where Mary's trunks are open and her clothes are strewn about.

LUCY (*as she proceeds to pack*). Truth to tell, I'll miss Mrs. H., too. (*As Peggy sits dejectedly on the sofa*) She's about the nicest ever came here.

PEGGY (*suddenly bursting out*). I hate Reno!

LUCY (*dryly*). You didn't come for fun. (*And she goes on packing and singing*) "The grave'll decay you an' change you to dust.
Ain't one boy outta twenty a poor gal kin trust."

PEGGY. You've seen lots of divorcees, haven't you, Lucy?

LUCY. Been cookin' fer 'em for ten years.

PEGGY. You feel sorry for us?

LUCY. Well, ma'am I don't. You feel plenty sorry enough for yourselves. (*Kindly*) Lord, you ain't got much else to do.

PEGGY (*resentfully*). You've never been married, Lucy?

LUCY. I've had three—

PEGGY. Husbands?

LUCY. Kids,

PEGGY. Oh, then you're probably very happy—

LUCY. Lord, ma'am, I stopped thinking about being happy years ago.

PEGGY (*amazed*). You don't think about being happy?

LUCY. Ain't had time. With the kids and all. And the old man such a demon when he's drinkin'. Them big, strong, red-headed men. They're fierce!

PEGGY. Oh, Lucy, he beats you? How terrible!

LUCY (*trying to close the trunk*). Ain't it? When you think what a lot of women right on this here rancho need a beatin' worse than me. (*Heading for the door*) Guess I'll have to get Buck to close this here contraption.

PEGGY. But you *live* in Reno, Lucy. You could get a divorce overnight.

LUCY (*at the door*). Lord, a woman can't get herself worked up to a thing like that overnight.

The Countess' voice is now heard singing: "Whoopie ti yi, get along little dogies, It's my misfortune and none of your own." Lucy looks off toward the prairie and Peggy joins her. Then outside the RANCH HOUSE the Countess, in full western regalia, is seen riding up to the house singing. On her saddle rests a gallon jug.

COUNTESS.
"Whoopee ti yi, git along little dogies. For you know Wyoming will be your new home."

LUCY and PEGGY are seen at the door.

LUCY (*yelling*). Hi yah, Countess?

COUNTESS (*as she gallops toward the front door*). Hello, Lucy . . . Hello, Peggy. (*Pulling up her horse*) Is Mrs. Haines around? (*She starts to dismount.*)

The scene moves with Lucy and Peggy who now head along the porch to the living room.

LUCY. Nope, Countess, but come on in! She'll be here soon, 'cause the mail's come!

PEGGY (*to Lucy as they enter the living room*). Oh, dear! Now *she* wants Mrs. Haines! And I've simply *got* to see Mrs. Haines *alone!*

The view moves to the LIVING ROOM which the Countess enters carrying the jug.

COUNTESS (*to Peggy*). How are you feeling, dear child?

PEGGY. All right.

COUNTESS. Lucy, here's a wee juggie. (*Putting it down*) We must celebrate Mrs. Haines' divorce.

LUCY. Right you are, Countess. (*Lucy proceeds to hustle glasses from a little bar.*)

PEGGY. Oh, Countess de Lave, I don't think a divorce is anything to celebrate.

COUNTESS. My dear, you've got the Reno jumpy-wumpies. Did you go to the doctor?

PEGGY. Yes.

COUNTESS. What's he say?

PEGGY. He said it was—the altitude.

LUCY (*picking up the jug and placing it beside the glasses*).
"If the ocean was whiskey and I was a duck—
I'd dive to the bottom and never come up.
Oh, Baby, Oh, Baby, I've told you before,
The more I drink whiskey, I love you the more!"

COUNTESS (*throwing herself on a couch*). Oh L'amour! L'amour! Lucy, were you ever in love?

LUCY. Yes, ma'am.

COUNTESS. Tell us about it.

LUCY. Well, ma'am, ain't much to tell. I kinda enjoyed the courtin' time. It was as purty a sight as you ever saw, to see him come lopin' across them hills. The sky so big and blue and that brick top of his blazin' like the bejiggers in the sun. Then we'd sit on my back fence and spark. But, ma'am, you know how them big strong, red-headed men are, they just got to get to the point. So we got married, ma'am. And natcherly, I ain't had no chanst to think about love since.

MIRIAM (*entering from outside*). Hello, Countess! How's rhythm on the range?

COUNTESS Simply divine, dear— Gallop, gallop, gallop! Madly over the sage brush.

MIRIAM (*to Peggy*). Hello, sunshine.

PEGGY (*lugubriously*). Hello.

COUNTESS (*to Peggy—sympathetically*). Aw, what you need, dear, is a wee drinkie of this good corn liquor.

PEGGY. No, thanks. (*And she goes to the doorway and leans against it looking mournfully off across the prairie.*)

MIRIAM. Is that invitation general, Countess?

COUNTESS (*proceeding to pour drinks*). Yes, *indeedy*, as we say on the range. (*Handing Miriam a drink*) Let's drink to freedom! By day after tomorrow, I'll be free, free as a bird from that little French stinkeroo. But whither, oh whither shall I fly? (*She tosses down a glassful and gags at its strength.*)

MIRIAM. To the arms of our pet cowboy, darling?

COUNTESS (*modestly*). Miriam Aarons!

MIRIAM. Why, he's plum loco for you, Countess. He likes you better than his horse and it's such a blasted big horse, too.

COUNTESS. Well, Buck Winston *is* nice. So young. So strong. Have you noticed the play of his muscles? Musical! . . . Musical!

LUCY. Land's sake, you don't mean to say his joints squeak!

COUNTESS (*shocked*). Lucy! (*Lucy goes out.*)

MIRIAM. Well—he could crack a cocoanut with those knees. If he could get them together. Say, Countess, that guy hasn't been arousing your honorable intentions, has he?

COUNTESS. Yes, Miriam, but I'm different from the rest of you. I've always put my faith in love. Still, I've had four divorces. Dare I risk a fifth?

MIRIAM. What are you risking, Countess, or maybe I shouldn't ask?

COUNTESS. Helas! I fear I could never make a success of Buck at Newport.

MIRIAM. Why not? They'd have to admit Buck's handsome. But if I had your dough, I'd sell him to radio first.

COUNTESS. Radio?

MIRIAM. Sure! Think how that voice of his might sound cooing into a microphone!

COUNTESS (*thinking it over*). Drifting dreamily over the ether! Why not? I might turn him into a radio star. Ah! L'amour! L'amour! (*She suddenly looks intently at Miriam.*) Look here, Miriam, why don't you open up and tell us your great secret!

MIRIAM (*getting herself another drink*). What secret, Countess?

COUNTESS. About the man in *your* life. After all there *must be* one.

MIRIAM. Well, Countess, I would have spilled it—(*Lowering her voice so that Peggy can't hear her, she gestures toward her with her thumb.*)—but I found out his *wife's* a friend of our palsy walsies.

COUNTESS (*thrilled*). Oh? (*She casts a quick cautious glance toward the daydreaming Peggy, then bustles over to Miriam, whispering.*) Who is it? Tell me!

MIRIAM (*seen in a close-up, looking off toward Peggy, sotto voce*). Ever hear them speak of Sylvia Fowler?

COUNTESS (*nodding excitedly*). Think I have.

MIRIAM. It's the dame's husband—Howard Fowler.

COUNTESS. Fowler?

MIRIAM. Yeah. And all he had to do to get rid of her was— (*At which point

Mary's Voice interrupts with a "Hello, girls.")

And the view cuts to MARY just entering from the kitchen, followed by Lucy who is wiping her hands on her apron. Miriam and the Countess separate. Peggy looks anxiously toward Mary.

MIRIAM. Hello, Queen. How does it feel to be free?

MARY (*overly emphatic*). Great!

MIRIAM. Yah lie.

MARY (*laughing*). Have it your own way. (*Briskly addressing all of them*) As my last official act in Reno, I've cooked the whole supper with my own hands.

PEGGY (*to Mary—anxiously*). Mary— could I see you, please.

MARY. Just a second, dear. (*She turns to Lucy*) Oh, Lucy—

LUCY (*knowing what she wants, picking up a letter from the mail*). Here it is, honey, and it's all you git.

MARY. Thanks— (*Her face falling as she looks at the writing—to Peggy*) This is from Edith. (*And trying not to show her disappointment, she smiles.*) Couldn't mistake that childish handwriting.

At this point the sound of an iron bar beating on an iron ring, such as is used by ranch houses for a bell, is heard.

LUCY (*screaming out the door*). C-o-m-i-n-g! (*To the ladies*) Reckon that's the new boarder, ladies. Got in on the afternoon train from New York. (*She heads for the door and goes out singing.*)
"I went up to the boss and we had a little chat,
I slapped him in the face with my big slouch hat."

MARY (*to Peggy—amusedly*). Listen to this. (*Reading from the letter*) "Darling: That blundering stork has just delivered Phelps and me *another female.*"

PEGGY. *Oh no!* Good heavens! That makes *eight* girls!

COUNTESS (*beginning to be very mellow*). Eight little cherubs! How sweet! Ah l'amour! l'amour! Toujours l'amour!

At which point we hear a voice.

SYLVIA's VOICE. Who the heck's paging l'amour?

They all look up, and the view cuts to the DOORWAY showing Sylvia dressed in a traveling suit, Lucy following her with her hand luggage.

MARY AND PEGGY (*utterly amazed, in unison*). Sylvia! Why Sylvia Fowler!

Both the Countess and Miriam look up in amazement.

SYLVIA (*sardonically—with a grin*). Well—here I am, girls! *Move over!*

Mary and Peggy stare at her too amazed for speech while the Countess and Miriam take her in thoroughly.

LUCY (*indicating the saddle Sylvia carries*). Say—what is this here dude contraption?

SYLVIA. An English saddle. I'd never learn to ride those Western things.

LUCY. H'm! Did you ever see a horse *laugh?*

SYLVIA. Eh?

LUCY (*contemplating saddle*). Well, *you're going to!* (*She gestures with her head toward the mail.*) You got a letter there, lady. (*Starting off*) Want to go to your room now—or stay here and dish with your buddies?

SYLVIA. I'll be along. (*Lucy goes on out.*)

MARY (*to Sylvia—finally able to speak*). Et tu Brute! Good heavens, what a gathering of the clan! (*And she sinks weakly into a chair.*)

PEGGY. Why didn't you wire us you were coming?

SYLVIA (*lighting a cigarette*). My lawyer told me to put nothing *at all* on paper! Well, here I am anyway . . . (*She turns an inquiring eye on the two strange women.*) A member of the big Round-up!

MARY (*regaining her aplomb, proceeding with introductions*). This is the Countess de Lave and Mrs. Aarons . . . Mrs. Howard Fowler. (*Miriam and the Countess exchange glances.*)

SYLVIA (*briefly—taking a quick measure of them*). How'd you do?

COUNTESS. How are you, dear?

MIRIAM (*in unison; a trace constrained*). Pleased to meet you.

MARY (*to Sylvia*). D'you want to tell us what happened?

SYLVIA. Howard Fowler, my dear, the man I trusted with my life . . . has *kicked me out* . . . kicked *me* out . . . for some filthy beezle. (*And at this Miriam somewhat gingerly, starts to leave the room.*)

COUNTESS (*whole-heartedly and significantly*). Oh, don't go, Miriam, darling. We're all girls together! Pour Mrs. Fowler a little drinkie.

MIRIAM (*fatalistically*). Okay. (*And she proceeds to do so.*)

PEGGY. Sylvia—he couldn't have *kicked* you out! Not Howard.

SYLVIA. Is that so? Well—that's all you know about him! The man's a fiend! An absolute Borgia! You couldn't *believe* what he did to me!

MARY. What?

SYLVIA. He *very meekly* and *innocently* picked a quarrel with me one day! So I ordered him out of the house. Did I know he had dictographs hidden all over the place? Did I know I'd given him complete grounds for incompatibility . . . all recorded on discs . . . in the *most awful sounding language?*

COUNTESS (*sympathetic and aghast*). Mrs. Fowler!

SYLVIA. Then he calmly told me that if I didn't go to Reno and divorce him, he'd go to Reno and divorce me! Divorce *me!* Ruin *my reputation!*

MARY (*heartsick over the story*). Oh, Sylvia!

PEGGY. Who *is* the woman, Sylvia?

SYLVIA. Nobody knows . . . Not even Winchell! (*And again the Countess and Miriam exchange glances.*)

MIRIAM (*handing her the drink*). Here you are, sister! Buck up!

SYLVIA. Thanks. (*She takes the drink.*)

COUNTESS (*holding up her own glass*). A little toastie to Cupid, darling, and tomorrow you can start right in looking around.

SYLVIA. You're darn right, I can, Countess! *I* don't intend to sit in a corner and act glum. (*Drinking*) When I think of all I've sacrificed for Howard Fowler!

MIRIAM (*dryly*). Such as *what*, Mrs. Fowler?

SYLVIA (*as she goes over to the mail to get her letter*). I gave him my *youth!* (*Picking up the letter*) H'm. Airmail, special delivery! I bet it's a bill—forwarded to me by Howard—the skunk! (*As she opens it, a clipping falls out, and the Countess picks it up.*) Oh—it's from Carol Hammond. (*To Mary and Peggy as she reads*) My dear, she says Edith Potter's new baby is another catastrophe. Looks like Phelps and has lungs like a bull! (*Reading a little further her eyes pop wide open. Aghast, she starts to look around for the clipping and notes the Countess absorbed in it. To the Countess*) Give that here!

As Sylvia irately grabs the clipping, Miriam takes a quick survey of her ire and starts once more for the door. Just as she reaches it, Sylvia suddenly wheels on her.

SYLVIA (*a dagger in her eye*). *Say you!* Wait a moment! Wasn't your name Aarons?

MIRIAM. What is it to *you*, Mrs. Fowler?

SYLVIA. Stay right where you are! (*She moves around to block the door, then reads from the clipping.*) "Miriam 'Vanities' Aarons has just been Renovated. Three guesses, Mrs. Howard Fowler, as to who she's going to marry."

MARY AND PEGGY (*aghast—in unison*). Miriam!

COUNTESS (*trying to square things*). Ah, Mrs. Fowler—what can one do against L'amour?

MIRIAM. Yeah! Why can't those mouldy rags leave a successful divorce alone?

SYLVIA (*to Miriam*). Why, you dirty, double dealing little—

MARY (*going to her*). Now Sylvia—

SYLVIA (*to Mary—whipping about*). Did you know this?

MARY. Of course not. But why d'you care, Sylvia? You don't love Howard—

SYLVIA (*brushing her aside*). That has nothing to do with it. (*To Miriam, fiercely*) How much did he settle on you?

MIRIAM. I made Howard pay for what he wants; you made him pay for what he doesn't want.

SYLVIA. Why you filthy little—!

MIRIAM (*cutting in*). Don't start calling names, you Park Avenue play girl. . . . I know more words than you do!

Sylvia gives Miriam a terrific smack. There is a moment's horrified pause, nobody making a move or a sound and then Miriam hauls off and slaps Sylvia back. Peggy lets out a shriek, runs to the opposite side of the room and hides her face, during which time Sylvia and Miriam start mauling at each other's hair.

MARY (*seizing Sylvia's arm*). Sylvia, stop it! Sylvia! Stop it this instant!

SYLVIA (*breaking loose from Mary's grip*). Let go of me! (*She pushes Mary who stands shocked, helpless.*)

COUNTESS (*having grabbed Miriam's belt, starts tugging at it*). Miriam, darling! Mustn't be vulgar!

MIRIAM (*still mauling Sylvia*). She asked for it, Countess! Leave me alone! She's got it coming!

And now Lucy enters, and not at all surprised, eyes them expertly.

LUCY. H'm. Pretty evenly matched, ain't they?

They both go down—continuing to maul each other on the floor.

MARY (*frantic*). Oh, Lucy! Do something!

LUCY (*philosophically*). Oh, Lord, ma'am. Leave 'em enjoy theirselves! (*Heading for the door*) I'll go get some smelling salts for the loser.

At which point the Countess pushes Miriam off of Sylvia and sits smack down on Sylvia in order to stop the fray.

SYLVIA (*furious, to the Countess*). Get off of me! You get off of me, you fat old buffalo!

By now Miriam has regained her feet and starts kicking Sylvia in the shins.

MIRIAM (*getting in a wallop*). Take that, you little snake you!

SYLVIA. Ouch! Let go! Let go, you guttersnipe!

PEGGY (*uncovering her eyes and crying out in alarm*). Mary! Call for help, Mary!

MARY (*to the fighters*). I won't have this, you hear! (*She pulls Miriam off and away from Sylvia.*)

SYLVIA (*indicating the Countess*). Will someone get this big moose off of me!

COUNTESS. Take it easy, Mrs. Fowler. (*As she rises*) I was only trying to help in my own way.

SYLVIA (*gaining her feet and making a lunge at Miriam*). You little viper!

MIRIAM (*dodging*). Say—I'm going to get mad in a minute!

She hauls off and directs Sylvia a well-aimed blow. As Sylvia ducks, Mary seizes her, shakes her violently, and pushes her into an armchair.

MARY (*to Sylvia*). That's enough! (*Sylvia starts to wail in fury.*)

MIRIAM. Who's got some iodine?

MARY. In my bathroom. (*To Peggy*) Help her, Peggy.

MIRIAM (*to Peggy*). Yeah. I gotta' be careful of hydrophobia.

She goes toward Mary's quarters and Peggy follows her.

SYLVIA (*blubbering — nursing her wounds*). Oh, Mary, how could you let her do that to me?

MARY (*coldly*). I'm terribly sorry, Sylvia.

SYLVIA. You're on her side! You, my own cousin! . . . After all I've done for you!

MARY. What have you done for me?

SYLVIA. I warned *you!*

MARY (*bitterly*). I'm not exactly grateful for that.

SYLVIA (*hysterical*). Oh, aren't you? Well, you're only getting what was coming to you . . . and plenty of the girls are tickled to death!

MARY (*holding her temper*). On your way, Sylvia! Go on!

Lucy enters with a bottle of spirits of ammonia as Sylvia gives way completely to hysteria.

SYLVIA (*at the top of her lungs—picking up dishes, ash trays, glasses and cigarette boxes and hurling them violently onto the floor*). I hate you! I hate you! I hate you! I hate *everybody!*

LUCY (*taking Sylvia firmly by the shoulders, forcing the bottle under her nose*). Look out, Mrs. Fowler! You got the hy-strikes! (*And Lucy rushes her gasping toward the door.*)

SYLVIA (*to Mary—as she goes out struggling with Lucy*). You wait. Some day you'll need a woman friend. Then you'll think of your treachery to me.

COUNTESS. Poor creatures. They've lost their equilibrium because they've lost their faith in love. (*Philosophically*) L'amour! Remember the song Buck made up, just for me? (*She pours herself a drink and sings.*)
"Oh a man can ride a horse to the range above,
But a woman's got to ride on the wings of love—
Come a ti-yi-yippi—"

She throws the jug over her shoulder and leaves singing as the view moves to a close-up of MARY, showing her utterly heartsick over what she has witnessed. She buries her face in her hands and stands for a moment. Then, removing her hands from her face, she goes to the mail, picks it up and sorts it over in the vain hope that there *may* be a letter for her which was overlooked. But since there is none she sighs, puts the mail down, then heads for her own room, the scene moving with her to the doorway where she looks off:

We now see MARY'S ROOM where Peggy is ministering to Miriam as Mary enters.

MARY (*to Peggy*). You wanted to see me, Peggy.

PEGGY. Yes. (*After a quick glance at Miriam and unable to hold in her news any longer, she bursts into tears.*) Oh, Mary, I'm going to have a baby!

MARY (*catching her by the shoulders*). Peggy!

PEGGY. Oh, Mary! What shall I do?

MARY. Darling, don't cry! That's splendid! (*She gets an idea and straightening up, thinks quickly.*) Peggy—what's John's telephone number?

PEGGY (*quickly*). Eldorado 5-3598. (*Miriam, who is seated on the table, calmly takes up the telephone.*) But, oh, Mary, I can't tell him.

MIRIAM. Why? Isn't he old enough to know? (*At the telephone*) Long Distance, please.

PEGGY. I always wanted a baby. But what can I do with it now?

MARY (*in exasperation*). You can enter it for Groton—

MIRIAM. Or land it with the Marines. (*Telephoning*) New York, Eldorado 5-3598 . . . and make it snappy.

PEGGY. But I can't talk to him, Mary! I wouldn't know how to begin.

MARY. You will when you hear his voice.

PEGGY. No, Mary! I know I'm wrong, but it's no use. . . . You don't know the things he said to me. I have my pride!

MIRIAM. Reno's full of women who have their pride, sweetheart! (*Mary looks sharply up.*) And it's a pretty chilly exchange for the guy you're stuck on! (*Speaking into the telephone*) Mr. Day, please . . . Reno calling . . . Mr. Day? Suffering Saints! He must live by the phone. . . . Just hold the—

Peggy, who has leaped forward, grabs the phone from Miriam.

PEGGY. Hello, Johnnie . . . (*Clearing her throat of a sob*) No, I'm not sick. . . . That is, I'm all right. . . . That is . . . oh, Johnnie, I'm going to have a baby. . . . Oh, Darling, are you? . . . Oh, darling, do you? . . . Oh, darling, so am I! . . . So do I! . . . 'Course I forgive you. . . . Yes, precious. . . . Yes, lamb—on the very next train! . . . Johnnie? (*She throws a kiss into the phone.*) Johnnie, d'you mind if I reverse the charges? . . . 'bye, precious. . . . (*As she hangs up*) I can't stay for dinner, Mary . . . I've got to pack.

MARY. Run along!

PEGGY (*starting to go, then stopping*). When I get back, Mary, I'm going to do everything Johnnie says!

MARY. Good!

PEGGY (*going out*). Oh, I'm so happy, I could cry.

MIRIAM (*turning to Mary*). Well, sister! When are *you* going to get wise to *yourself*?

MARY. Me?

MIRIAM. Yes, *you!*

MARY (*in reminder—with a little gesture of futility*). I was divorced this morning, Miriam!

MIRIAM (*contemptuously*). Aw! A *Reno* divorce!

The telephone rings. Miriam goes to it.

MIRIAM. Hello. . . . No, we completed that call, operator. (*She hangs up and takes a cigarette.*) Listen, Mary—

MARY (*cutting in*). There's nothing you can say I haven't heard!

MIRIAM. Sure? Maybe I got a new slant. I come from a world where a woman's got to come out on top—or it's just too darn bad.

MARY (*wearily*). All right, Miriam. Talk to me all you want! What does it come to? Compromise!

MIRIAM. What the heck! A woman's compromised the day she's born.

MARY. You can't compromise with utter defeat. He doesn't want me.

MIRIAM. How d'you know?

MARY. I've waited every day for word from him. . . . (*Smiling ruefully, she shrugs her shoulders in a big gesture of defeat.*)

MIRIAM. Did you write to *him*?

MARY (*with pride*). Of course not!

MIRIAM. How d'you know *he* hasn't been waiting, *too*? (*Mary looks at her in surprise, the thought never having struck her.*) Aw! I've been through *all* this, sweetheart! I lost my man, too.

MARY (*smiling*). You—?

MIRIAM. It only happened *once!* Got wise to myself after that. Look, how did I lose him? We didn't have enough dough to get married . . . and I had my pride. Heaven knows where I got it. (*She sighs.*) I liked him a lot better than I've ever liked anybody since. Well, what'd my Romeo do one day? Took a little walk-out on me. I made a terrible row! Why shouldn't I? I should! But what I ought not to have done was to run away and leave him in that woman's clutches . . . like a coward. That's what you are, Mary Haines . . . a blithering coward!

MARY (*trying to defend herself*). Because I wouldn't be humiliated?

MIRIAM. Because you ran out of the trenches, *under fire!* (*Mary looks at her —just looks.*) You *deserted* him!

MARY (*with surprise*). *I* deserted *him!*

MIRIAM. Sure you did! D'you think he wants to be in the grip of that red-headed octopus? (*Mary begins to think very hard.*) If you'd have given him half a chance I'll bet he'd have asked you not to get this divorce!

MARY (*a ray of hope beginning to light up her face*). Why, Miriam! He *did* ask me.

MIRIAM (*utterly aghast*). *And you still ran away?*

MARY (*preoccupied, thinking back*). Yes.

MIRIAM (*shrugging her shoulders in utter exasperation, then trying to be tolerant*). Look here, honey, don't you know that we dames have got to be something more to the guy we marry than a school-girl sweetheart? We've got to be a *wife* —a *real* wife! A mother, too, and a pal. *And* a *nurse-maid!* Yeah, and when it comes to the point, sometimes we've got to be a "cutie." (*Dazedly Mary studies her.*) You should have licked that girl where she licked you . . . in his arms!

MARY (*shocked*). Miriam!

MIRIAM. That's where you win in the first round. And if I know men, that's still Custer's Last Stand. (*Thinking very deeply, Mary turns away.*) Shocked you? Okay, sister. But my idea of love is that love isn't ashamed in nothing.

MARY (*putting up one last argument*). That's easy for you to say, Miriam. But cheap and vulgar as that girl is, she's in his blood. I couldn't have stayed in *my home* and faced *that!*

MIRIAM. Why not? Suppose the guy had small pox? You wouldn't have liked to face *that*, either, would you? But you'd have done it for him, *wouldn't you?*

MARY (*increasingly thoughtful*). Yes.

MIRIAM. Well—this jam he's in would make a bad case of small pox look like a carnival. And while the poor guy's floundering around helpless, you remove the *one* protection he's got—his *legal marriage.* (*Startled, Mary suddenly looks up.*) So he's back there stumbling around in the open, delirious and un-protected with a she-wolf in lamb's clothing right on his heels. And not *one* word of comfort out of *you!* Because why? Because you were too busy nursing your two-for-a-nickel *pride!* (*As Mary looks at her—just looks—the telephone rings. Miriam picks it up and answers:*) Yes? (*Exasperated*) No, operator, we completed that . . . You say New York is calling *Mrs. Haines*? It's *Mr. Haines?*

Mary, her hope growing by leaps and bounds, catches her breath for happiness.

MIRIAM (*to Mary, covering the mouth-piece with her hand*). Tell him you'll tear that divorce decree into one million pieces and use it for confetti! (*Mary hurries to the phone and Miriam hands it to her.*) Here!

MARY (*her eyes shining*). Hello . . . hello? Stephen? Oh, it's so good to hear your voice! (*Excitedly*) Yes . . . it went through this morning on schedule. But Stephen, I can . . . (*frightened*) . . . but Stephen! . . . No, of course, I haven't seen the papers. . . . How could I, out *here*? . . . (*After a long pause*) Yes, I'd rather *you* told me. . . . Of course I understand the position you're in . . . (*Another long pause.*) I—I hope you'll both be very happy. . . . No, I have no plans . . . no plans at all . . . Stephen, do you mind if I hang up? Goodbye, Stephen . . . Goodbye . . .

She hangs up and stands utterly crushed as Miriam regards her. There is a pause —then:

MIRIAM (*with sympathy*). He's married her—hasn't he?

MARY. This afternoon. (*And suddenly bursting into tears, she throws herself down on the couch.*)

MIRIAM (*going to her and patting her shoulder—deeply sympathetic*). Sorry I spoke so rough to you, sister.

MARY (*bitterly self-accusing as she sobs her heart out*). It's all right, Miriam. I . . . I've got my pride!

MIRIAM (*comfortingly—as the scene fades out*). There, there, honey! Buck up! Buck up!

PART SIX

The SKYLINE OF RENO fades in, showing a sign in the foreground; it reads "RENO. Biggest Little City in the World." This dissolves to the "BRIDGE OF SIGHS" at Reno and Mary moves into view and looks moodily down into the water. She presently takes off her wedding ring, and holds it a moment looking at it. Suddenly she hears a cheerful voice.

VOICE. Congratulations, lady!

As Mary looks up, a smart looking colored mama steps into sight.

MARY (*smiling wanly*). Thanks.

COLORED MAMA (*as she takes her own ring off*). They say if you spits on yo' weddin' ring you gits *better luck next time!*

MARY (*laughing*). Do they? (*Saying which she drops ring into the water and dazedly starts away.*)

COLORED MAMA (*sympathetically—looking after Mary*). Tsch! Tsch! Tsch! (*Then, brightening up, she addresses her wedding ring.*) Honey, do you' stuff! (*She spits on it and tosses it into the water.*)

The scene now dissolves to the SKYLINE OF NEW YORK in early spring, which in turn dissolves to a CORNER OF MARY'S APARTMENT showing trunks in the background. Mary, in negligee, is helping Little Mary on with her coat. Miss Fordyce stands by, dressed for the street.

LITTLE MARY (*rebellious*). I don't want to visit that woman, mother!

MARY. Sh! You must be nice to her for Daddy's sake.

LITTLE MARY (*throwing her arms about Mary*). Oh, mother. Don't go to Europe!

MARY (*caressing her*). Darling! I'll be back before you know it!

The scene dissolves to a CORNER DECK of an OCEAN LINER in spring showing Mary leaning back in a steamer chair, her eyes closed, musing as Jane comes up.

JANE. You'll be late, ma'am, dressing for dinner.

MARY (*wearily*). I'll have it up here on a tray.

JANE (*amused—with a touch of reprimand*). You aren't feeling sorry for yourself, Mrs. Haines?

MARY (*briskly — laughing*). Thanks, Jane! (*Rousing herself*) I'm coming!

As she starts out, the scene dissolves to the SKYLINE OF LONDON in late spring with Big Ben in the distance booming out the noon hour, and this view in turn dissolves to a London FLOWER STALL showing Mary and a Flower Woman—Mary bending over, smelling some roses as the booming of Big Ben continues.

FLOWER WOMAN (*arranging a corsage bouquet and speaking to a man who stands out of view*). There you h'are, your lordship. My prettiest posies for the prettiest laidy h'I've seen since Michaelmas.

MARY (*laughing as she takes the flowers*). Thank you. (*Addressing the man who stands just out of sight*) And thank *you*, kind sir.

This dissolves into the SKYLINE OF PARIS at night in the middle of summer, with the Eiffel Tower in the distance, which in turn dissolves into the CORNER OF A HOTEL SUITE, the Eiffel Tower visible through the window. Jane sits asleep. Then the door starts to open and she jumps up.

JANE (*to Mary as she enters in a summer evening outfit*). Was he wonderful, ma'am?

MARY (*as Jane takes her cloak*). Martinelli's always good.

JANE (*impatiently*). Oh, not the opera. *The new French beau!*

MARY (*laughing at her*). Oh! (*Kiddingly she kisses her bunched fingers.*) Magnifique!

The scene dissolves to the SKYLINE OF VENICE in the early fall and this dissolves to a view of Mary in a GONDOLA, lying back as

Venetian music is heard. She is now completely cheerful and relaxed.

> MARY (*talking to an unseen man who is facing her*). Attendez, Paul! Cette musique! C'est charmant, n'est pas?

The scene dissolves to the SKYLINE OF NEW YORK. It is late fall and it is raining. This in turn dissolves to a CORNER OF MARY'S CABIN on a French liner, revealing Mary, dressed for landing, standing at the window of her cabin. She is moodily looking off through the rain at the skyline as the liner approaches its dock.

VOICE OF FRENCH WOMAN. Madame.

As Mary looks up, the stewardess approaches from the doorway with a copy of a New York paper.

> STEWARDESS (*handing Mary the paper*). They've just brought the New York papers aboard, Madame.

MARY. Oh, thank you.

The stewardess leaves and Mary glances at the paper. Suddenly she gives a little start and we see next a NEWSPHOTO of Sylvia and Crystal at the races with the caption:

"SOCIETY AT BELMONT
Mrs. Stephen Haines and Mrs. Sylvia Fowler snapped at the paddock."

The paper drops from Mary's hand as we see Mary again. Dazed, she turns and looks out into the rain which, beating down with increased fury, obliterates the skyline, following which the scene dissolves through the sight of water rippling near the ship (as seen through Mary's porthole) into a view of WATER swirling in a BATHTUB. Then as the scene draws up and back Mary is seen giving Little Mary her bath. It is the bathroom of Little Mary's suite, a small, simple bathroom (in contrast to Crystal's, which we shall next see). Little Mary is largely hidden by the tub.

> LITTLE MARY. Hurry up, Mother. I've got to buy my present for Daddy's birthday.

> MARY (*a catch in her voice*). Oh, yes, of course.

> LITTLE MARY (*her heart torn for Mary*). You mustn't feel sad about him, Mother. I think Crystal's really *very* nice.

MARY. Of course she is.

> LITTLE MARY (*earnestly—trying to cheer her mother up*). Anyway, she makes Daddy very, very happy!

> MARY (*really meaning it*). That's good! I'm glad!

The scene now dissolves to CRYSTAL'S BATHROOM where she is lolling in the deep suds of the tub, smoking and reading a magazine. In a niche back of the tub is a gilded French telephone. After a moment, Helene, a smartly uniformed French maid, enters.

> HELENE. Madame has been soaking a whole hour.

> CRYSTAL (*rudely*). So what?

> HELENE. But, Monsieur thinks that—

> CRYSTAL. I *told* Monsieur the doctor ordered me to soak for my nerves.

> HELENE. But Monsieur feels it does not improve your nerves to stay so long in the water, Madame. He suggests that you join him and walk Little Mary to her mother's apartment.

> CRYSTAL. Ye Mackerel! What a cheerful evening! (*Plaintively*) Oh, I'm so bored —(*And she hurls the soap across the room.*)

> HELENE (*in protest*). Madame!

The telephone rings just then, and Crystal looks startled.

> CRYSTAL (*nervously and rudely to Helene*). Get out! (*As Helene—surprised at her tone—looks up*) Get out!

> HELENE. Yes, Madame.

She goes out, leaving the coast clear for Crystal, who now picks up the telephone.

> CRYSTAL. Hello . . . hello, darling. I'm in the tub. . . . I'm shriveled to a peanut waiting for this call . . . And say, listen —don't call me any more today. If there's any calling to be done, *I'll* call you . . . It's safer. . . . Yeah, when I had the phone put in here, I thought I'd have a little privacy, but people barge in and out of this place like it was the Grand Central Station. . . . Maybe it's a good thing you're going to the Coast tomorrow. . . . (*There is a gentle knock*

at the door which Crystal doesn't hear.) It's getting to be too risky. . . . Yeah, I worked too hard to land this meal ticket to make any false moves now. . . . Peace is a whole lot more to me than romance. . . . I'm not going to get out on a limb again *ever!* (*Little Mary enters and stands hesitantly against the door.*) Sure I'll miss you, Baby! . . . I'll say we had fun! (*Startled, she sees Little Mary, then speaks into the phone quickly*) I'll call you back! (*She hangs up—then turns to the child, worried,*) Who told you to come in here?

LITTLE MARY (*politely*). Daddy. He's going to take me home now. I want to say goodnight.

She turns to go. Crystal thinks a moment —then speaks sweetly.

CRYSTAL. Oh, don't go, darling. Hand me that brush.

LITTLE MARY (*gently*). Please?

CRYSTAL. Please.

LITTLE MARY (*handing her the brush*). Goodnight.

CRYSTAL. My you're in a hurry to tell Daddy about it.

LITTLE MARY. About what?

CRYSTAL. My talk on the telephone.

LITTLE MARY. I don't understand grown-ups on the telephone. They all sound silly. Goodnight.

CRYSTAL. Goodnight, who? (*There is a pause.*) You've been told to call me Aunty Crystal. (*After another pause*) Why don't you do it?

LITTLE MARY (*still edging to the door*). Yes.

CRYSTAL. Yes, what?

LITTLE MARY (*lamely*). Yes, goodnight.

CRYSTAL (*angrily*). You sit down.

LITTLE MARY. Oh, it's awfully hot in here. I've got my coat on.

CRYSTAL. You heard me! (*Little Mary sits and begins to squirm.*) We're going to have this out. I've done my—my level best to be friends with you, but you refuse to co-operate.

LITTLE MARY. What?

CRYSTAL. Co-operate. (*Little Mary nods mechanically, but Crystal is exasperated.*) Answer my question. You don't like me. Why?

LITTLE MARY (*rising.*) Well, goodnight, Crystal—

CRYSTAL. I said, why?

LITTLE MARY (*very patiently*). Listen, Crystal, my mother told me I wasn't to be rude to you.

CRYSTAL. For the last time, young lady, you give me one good reason why you don't like me.

LITTLE MARY. I never said I didn't like you.

CRYSTAL. But you don't like me, do you?

LITTLE MARY. No, but I never said so. I've been very polite considering you're something awful.

CRYSTAL. Wait till your father hears this!

LITTLE MARY (*suddenly defiant*). Listen —Daddy doesn't think you're so wonderful—any more!

CRYSTAL. Did he tell you that?

LITTLE MARY. No. Daddy always pretends you're all right. You see, you wouldn't know about such things, but my Daddy's a *gentleman.* He never talks against *any* woman, not even you! But we *understand,* Daddy and I, without ever saying a word to each other.

CRYSTAL. I bet you've done plenty of blabbing to your Mother.

LITTLE MARY (*bridling*). No, I haven't! *It's my job to try and make Mother feel cheerful.*

The telephone rings again and Crystal casts a worried glance toward the instrument, hesitating.

CRYSTAL (*then, in a cold fury*). Get out!

LITTLE MARY (*going to the door, then turning, rather superior*). And *another* thing, I think this bathroom is perfectly ridiculous! Good night, Crystal! (*And she goes out as Crystal grabs the telephone irritably.*)

CRYSTAL. Hello . . . Hello. (*Irately*) I told you *not* to call me! . . . It's too dangerous! That Haines brat was in here. . . . Say, you've been drinking! . . . Yes, you have. You're all lit up or *you* wouldn't want me to be taking chances either! (*At this point Sylvia's voice stops her.*)

SYLVIA'S VOICE. Yooohoo! May I come in?

CRYSTAL (*ready to cut her throat, but calling sweetly*). Just a minute, Sylvia. (*Into the phone*) Here comes more trouble. I'm hanging up now and *don't you dare call back!* Understand? (*She slams the phone—then calls out*) Come in, dear.

The door opens and Sylvia enters.

CRYSTAL (*apologetically*). I was out, in the open when you knocked. Hope you don't mind my being modest.

SYLVIA. You? *Modest?* (*Laughing*) I'll have to tell *that* to my psychoanalyst! (*Posing soulfully before the mirror*) Would you believe it, my dear, I tell him everything!

CRYSTAL. That must be an awful effort.

SYLVIA. Oh, I don't mind discussing myself. But talking about my friends does make me feel disloyal. . . . (*Still primping*) I just saw poor Stephen leaving with Little Mary. He looked awfully tired and worn. Dr. Sylvester says Stephen has a guilt complex.

CRYSTAL. A what?

SYLVIA (*turning and picking up a bath brush*) Want me to give your back a scrub? (*Proceeding to scrub away pretty roughly*) He says men like Stephen can't admit that what they feel for a woman is anything but love.

CRYSTAL. Ow! You're taking my skin off.

SYLVIA. Sorry! He says that's why Stephen *married* you . . . to convince himself your affair had dignity and importance. . . . Isn't that a laugh?

CRYSTAL (*sore*). Say, who are *you* to laugh? *I've* made good with *my* husband! (*Implying that's more than Sylvia did with hers!*)

SYLVIA (*furious*). I don't think that's the way to talk to me after all I've done for you.

Saying which she chucks the brush into the water, purposely causing it to splash into Crystal's eyes.

CRYSTAL (*wincing from the soap*). Done *what?*

SYLVIA. When you married Stephen you didn't know a soul. It wasn't easy to put *you* over.

CRYSTAL. Who said you put me over?

SYLVIA. Why, I've gotten you into some of our best homes!

CRYSTAL. Yeah! For some of their best *insults!* (*Bridling*) Say, who *was* that Mrs. Buck Winston before she married Buck Winston?

SYLVIA. The Countess de Lave . . . Imagine giving up a title to marry that cowhand! I have to laugh when I think of her actually getting him into radio . . . he's positively the chambermaid's delight.

CRYSTAL (*cryptically*). Oh. Is he?

HELENE (*entering*). Mrs. Potter wants you on the phone, Mrs. Fowler. (*She holds the door open for Sylvia to go out.*)

SYLVIA (*bustling toward Crystal's phone*). I'll just take it in here.

Crystal looks alarmed.

HELENE. But it's on the other phone, madame.

Sylvia looks up surprised.

SYLVIA (*immediately suspicious*). Other phone? (*Indicating the phone*) D'you mean that instrument isn't an *extension?*

CRYSTAL (*quickly, putting up a defense*). Stephen does so much business on the phone, I had to get one of my own.

SYLVIA (*increasingly suspicious, she gestures toward the phone*). I'll bet you anything *Stephen thinks* that's an extension!

CRYSTAL (*increasingly furious*). Stephen doesn't mooch around my bathroom!

SYLVIA. That's pretty obvious!

CRYSTAL (*with a slow "burn"*). Better go answer that call.

SYLVIA (*to Helene—having no intention of leaving*). Tell her I'll call her back.

HELENE (*going out*). Very well, Madame.

SYLVIA (*maliciously—turning on Crystal*). Why, you sly little fox. This settles a question that's been on my mind from the very beginning.

CRYSTAL. Say—what are you getting at?

SYLVIA. You put that phone in to talk to a *man!*

CRYSTAL. Don't be ridiculous!

SYLVIA. Oh, don't lie to me! Everybody knew you're not Stephen's type. I never understood why he picked you up in the first place!

CRYSTAL (*absolutely dismissing the subject*). I've got to take a shower, Sylvia. Go and wait in my bedroom.

Sylvia starts for the door, then stops at the dressing table, and picks up the cold cream. (Crystal has now drawn the curtains for the shower and is out of sight.)

A close-up of SYLVIA shows her snooping, and picking up a jar of facial cream.

SYLVIA. I tried this cream. It brought out pimples. (*She goes to the shower. She can see through the curtains.*) My, but you're putting on weight, dear.

At which point, the telephone rings, and Sylvia makes a grab for it.

CRYSTAL (*as we hear her turn off the shower*). Don't you touch that phone!

SYLVIA (*into the phone, putting on a tone which is sickly sweet*). Hello.

As she listens in fiendish glee, her eyes pop wide open. Then Crystal tears out of the shower wrapped in a towel, grabs the receiver, and slams it up.

CRYSTAL (*to Sylvia fiendishly*). What did he say?

SYLVIA. Not a thing, darling! *Not a single thing!* He was *singing!*

CRYSTAL. So *what?*

SYLVIA. "Come a ti-yi-yippi" darling! (*And laughing, she sinks into a chair.*) Oh, Crystal, how could you? Buck Winston—the chambermaids' delight!

CRYSTAL (*with malicious defiance*). You'll never get a thing on me, Sylvia Fowler! Not *one* thing!

SYLVIA. Do I care? I'm mum as an oyster! I don't want Stephen to get onto you. It would give Mary Haines too much satisfaction! (*As Crystal begins to break into a big malicious grin*) So just *you* hang onto *Stephen* and we'll *both* be happy!

CRYSTAL (*still worried*). Will you shake on that? (*She holds out her hand.*)

SYLVIA (*heartily—grabbing her hand*). *Shake!*

As the two shake hands in a sort of diabolic camaraderie, the scene dissolves into MARY'S BOUDOIR in her New York apartment, where Jane is arranging a number of evening wraps on the chaise longue amid sounds of conversation and laughter. And now, Mrs. Morehead sticks her head in the doorway.

MRS. MOREHEAD. Is the coast clear?

JANE (*laughing*). All clear, ma'am. (*As Mrs. Morehead enters*) They've had a very gay dinner party.

MRS. MOREHEAD (*quizzically*). Well I'm *still* glad I went to the movies. (*Taking off her gloves*) Those dreadful women! Why my daughter tolerates them is beyond me!

JANE (*in defense of her mistress*). Well —it seems she cooked dinner for them in Reno the night she got her divorce and so—

MRS. MOREHEAD (*cutting in*). —so she thinks she has to feed them *annually!* Did they all bring the *same husbands* tonight?

JANE (*nodding*). Guess they couldn't get new ones in only two years!

Approaching laughter is now heard in the hall.

MRS. MOREHEAD. Ah—the approach of the innocents! (*Heading for the door*) I'll just give you my share of them, Jane!

Mrs. Morehead goes out as Jane looks off after her, laughing, and at this point Miriam, Mary and Peggy enter.

MARY (*as they enter*). Well, Miriam, how's matrimony? Still making a go of it?

MIRIAM. I'm doing a reconstruction job on Howard Fowler that makes Boulder Dam look like an egg-cup. (*As they laugh at the above, Nancy enters.*)

PEGGY. Oh, Mary, can't we get off to the Casino Roof? Johnnie and I have to be home by four. Little Johnnie always wakes up . . . He said the cutest thing the other day. (*After a dramatic pause*) He said da-da!

NANCY. When does he enter Harvard?

As they laugh Edith enters.

MARY (*to Edith*). Where's Flora?

EDITH. Down in the bar drinking with the men.

MARY (*to Peggy*). Run down and tell her you're raring to go, dear. (*Peggy starts out.*)

MIRIAM (*to Peggy*). What's the hurry? Another snootful and Flora will float up on her own breath. (*They all laugh and Peggy goes out.*)

EDITH (*fixing her hair at the mirror*). Mary, want to hear something about Sylvia?

MARY, MIRIAM AND NANCY (*in chorus*). NO!

EDITH (*continuing right on*). Well, Sylvia's going to that new psychoanalyst—you know—Doctor Sylvester.

MARY. Why, he's a dreadful fake!

EDITH. Yes. Isn't it a scream? And Sylvia's *mad* about him. Know what she pays an hour, just to drool at the man? A hundred dollars!

MIRIAM. It's worth a million! (*They laugh.*)

EDITH (*to Mary*). You ought to make up with Sylvia, dear. She's livid at the way you've high-hatted her, ever since Reno.

NANCY (*speaking up*). I'd rather have Sylvia for a friend than an *enemy*.

MARY (*from her heart*). I hadn't!

Peggy enters, dragging in the Countess, who is a tangle of tulle and jewels and has a slight "edge" on.

COUNTESS. Such a lovely party. It's so wonderful to see all our lives so settled —temporarily. But, Mary, do put that dear darling Freddy out of his misery.

MARY. How? Shoot him?

COUNTESS. No . . . marry him. Ah L'amour . . . L'amour! (*Jane proceeds to help the Countess into her wrap.*)

PEGGY (*to Mary—anxious to get them started*). I'll get your wrap, Mary. Which one?

MARY. I'm not going.

COUNTESS (*suddenly worried*). You're not cross because Buck's had a wee droppie too much?

MIRIAM. Don't be modest, Flora. Your ducky is stinko. (*Jane helps others into wraps.*)

COUNTESS. Mary, do come. This is *really* our farewell party. I'm never coming back to New York.

MARY. What's wrong with New York, Flora?

COUNTESS (*whispering*). Can I trust you?

MARY. Probably not, dear . . . What is it?

COUNTESS (*including the others*). You will keep this just between the four of us? (*Making a quick recount*) . . . the five of us?

MIRIAM. Shoot, Flora . . . it's a nation-wide hookup.

COUNTESS (*as the others gather around*). Remember how Buck was always crooning love songs in my ear? (*Her voice breaking*) Well—he doesn't do it any more!

MIRIAM. Maybe he's saving himself for his microphone.

COUNTESS (*tearful*). Oh, no, he isn't! He's away from home most of the time. And he comes back smelling of some strange perfume.

MARY. Where does he say he's been?

COUNTESS. Visiting his horse. That's why I think it's safer just to keep floating around.

MARY. Poor Flora!

NANCY (*to the Countess*). Never mind, dear. Chin up! (*The Countess straightens with effort.*)

MIRIAM. That's right. Both of them!

COUNTESS. Goodnight, Mary.

MARY. Goodnight, Flora.

COUNTESS (*heading for the door*). Coming, Nancy?

NANCY. Coming. (*To Mary*) I went up against a tribe of Igorotes in Africa so I guess I can take it. Goodnight, sweet.

MARY (*laughing as Nancy goes out*). Goodnight.

EDITH (*to Mary*). Well, since you're not coming, dear, I can tell you that *you'd have bumped right smack into Stephen and Crystal and Sylvia!*

MARY (*facetiously*). No!

EDITH. Yes. They're going to take supper on the roof. Sylvia told me.

PEGGY. Oh, Edith! And you'd have let it happen?

EDITH. They've got to meet sometime. Why not get it over and loosen the tension?

PEGGY (*staunchly*). But you know Mary hates situations!

MIRIAM. Well, I'm not so squeamish. Wait'll you see the cooing fest I'll put on over Howard, for dear, darling little Sylvia.

They laugh.

EDITH (*to Mary*). Goodnight, dear.

MARY. Goodnight.

EDITH. I don't feel much like going myself. I loathe this dress. Phelps says I look as though I were going to sing in it! (*She goes out.*)

PEGGY (*kisses Mary*). Goodnight.

MARY. Goodnight. Love to little Johnnie.

Peggy heads for the door.

MIRIAM (*to Mary*). So long, darling.

MARY (*to Miriam*). Goodbye.

MIRIAM (*turning to Mary at door*). Shall I spit in Crystal's eye for you? (*Mary shakes her head.*) You're passing up a swell chance, Mary. Where I spit, no grass grows ever!

As Mary laughs, Peggy and Miriam go out. Then sighing, Mary starts to strip off her jewels.

MARY. Jane, turn down my bed.

JANE. Yes, ma'am.

Now a strange hissing sound is heard and Mary looks up. Then we see Mrs. Morehead, in her negligee, holding out a perfume atomizer in one hand with which she is squirting perfume all around. Her other hand is occupied with holding her nose.

MARY. Mother! What are you doing?

MRS. MOREHEAD. Fumigating!

MARY (*laughing*). Oh, Mother. (*She starts to unhook her dress and goes out.*)

MRS. MOREHEAD (*putting down the atomizer and calling to Mary*). How do you stand those dreadful women even *once* a year?

MARY (*out of sight*). An object lesson. (*Mrs. Morehead goes to get a cigarette.*)

JANE (*speaking to Mary, who is still out of sight*). Anything more, Ma'am?

MARY. No, thanks. Goodnight, Jane.

JANE. Goodnight. (*Starting out*) Goodnight, Mrs. Morehead.

MRS. MOREHEAD (*picking up a book on the bedside table*). Goodnight. (*As Mary enters in negligee, fastening it as she comes in, showing Mary the book*) Good book?

MARY (*heading for the bed*). Don't know. (*Facetiously*) It seems to be about—love.

MRS. MOREHEAD (*suddenly*). Oh, Mary, I wish you could find—

MARY (*getting into bed*). Some nice man. Haven't we been over that enough times? I had the only one I ever wanted. If it hadn't been for my pride— (*She breaks off.*)

MRS. MOREHEAD (*sitting on the bed*). But *Stephen's* happy, darling. If you'd only *forget* him and start in to—

MARY (*utterly weary of the subject*). Oh, Mother!

MRS. MOREHEAD (*sighing—then putting down the book*). Well, cheer up, Mary. Living alone has its compensations. Heaven knows, it's marvelous to be able to sprawl out in bed like a swastika. Goodnight, darling.

MARY (*reaching for the book*). Goodnight, Mother.

MRS. MOREHEAD (*as she goes out*). Don't read by that light. You'll hurt your eyes.

A close-up reveals Mary propped against the pillows and beginning to read.

MARY (*softly—moodily—reading to herself*). "But if you would seek only love's *pleasure,* then it is better for you to pass out of love's domain into the outside world, where you shall laugh, but not *all* of your laughter, and weep, but not *all* of your tears—"

Mary leans back in contemplation of what she has read. Tears well up into her eyes and she closes them. Presently she hears Little Mary's Voice calling "Mother!" and looks up. Then we see Little Mary standing near the door in her nightgown.

MARY. Darling, what's the matter?

LITTLE MARY (*going to her*). May I crawl in with you tonight?

MARY. But I'm so restless, dear.

LITTLE MARY. I don't mind. (*Proceeding to crawl into the bed*) You know, that's the only good thing about divorce. You get to sleep with your mother. (*As she kisses her*) I taste lipstick.

MARY (*seen close, with the child*). I haven't washed yet. Go to sleep, darling.

LITTLE MARY. You know you're a very sympathetic mother.

MARY. Am I?

LITTLE MARY. Oh yes. So, would you just scratch my back?

MARY. All right . . . but go to sleep.

LITTLE MARY (*after a short silence*). I can't go to sleep, Mother.

MARY (*not taking her very seriously—proceeding with her reading*). You can if you try.

LITTLE MARY. Oh, no, I can't . . . I . . . I have such a big problem.

MARY (*amused, but still not taking her seriously*). Have you?

LITTLE MARY. Which is the most important, Mother—Truth or Honor?

MARY (*putting down her book*). They're equally important, darling. One doesn't exist without the other.

LITTLE MARY. Yes, it does. It does with Daddy. You see tonight Daddy told me a lie.

MARY. Oh, I don't think he did, Mary.

LITTLE MARY. Yes, he did. He did it for an honorable reason, but he shouldn't lie to *me,* Mother, even to save her skin.

MARY. To save whose skin?

LITTLE MARY. Crystal's. (*Mary begins to take an interest.*) You see, walking home tonight, Daddy told me he was going to go up to Canada.

MARY (*her interest increasing*). Canada?

LITTLE MARY. Yes. Up there where you and Daddy held your honeymoon. (*Mary reacts dazedly in surprise.*) So I thought it was about time Daddy stopped pretending to me that he . . . that he likes Crystal.

MARY. But your Daddy does like her—very much.

LITTLE MARY. Oh—that's what he lets on. But if he'd only just break down and tell me he's going up there because he simply can't bear her another day!

MARY. Why, Mary! (*She has now stopped scratching Little Mary's back.*)

LITTLE MARY (*bursting out*). Oh, Mother, he's so miserable!

MARY. *Mary!*

LITTLE MARY. He sits for hours and hours all alone in his study with his head buried in his hands while that silly thing plays *solitaire* with the *radio on.*

MARY. Why haven't you told me about Daddy?

LITTLE MARY. Because you've cried over him just about enough! (*Beginning to be sleepy*) Please keep on scratching, Mother.

MARY (*dazedly starting to scratch her back again*). Sorry.

LITTLE MARY. I told Daddy tonight I was going to tell you.

MARY. What did he say?

LITTLE MARY. He said not to because why would you care how he feels. (*At this Mary catches her breath.*)

MARY (*after a thoughtful pause*). Is . . . Crystal happy, do you think?

LITTLE MARY (*very sleepy*). I suppose she is. She's got somebody she talks to pretty lovey-dovey on the phone. (*As Mary gives a little start*) Don't stop scratching, Mother.

MARY. Do . . . do you know who it is?

LITTLE MARY (*very sleepy*). No, I don't know. *Guess you'd have to ask Auntie Sylvia.* They're together all the time. (*There is a pause—Mary thinks for a moment, very deeply—then suddenly she starts to get out of bed.*) Oh, Mother, what are you doing?

MARY (*ringing the bell on the table*). Go to sleep, darling. (*She starts for her dressing room.*)

LITTLE MARY (*sleepily—sitting up in bed*). Mother, are you going to get dressed?

MARY. Yes, Mary.

LITTLE MARY. You forgot you were invited to a party?

MARY. Almost.

MRS. MOREHEAD (*entering in negligee; to Mary*). Are you ill, dear? I heard you ring.

MARY (*ecstatic—returning from the dressing room*). I never felt better in my life!

LITTLE MARY (*to Mrs. Morehead*). Mother's going to a party, Grandma.

MRS. MOREHEAD. Why, Mary Haines—what *is* all this?

MARY. I've had two years to grow claws, Mother . . . *Jungle red!*

She thrusts out her hands. As Mrs. Morehead reacts mystified, Jane enters in a kimono.

JANE (*a trace surprised*). Did you ring, ma'am?

MARY. Yes. My new evening dress, Jane! And a taxi! Don't stand there gaping! *Hurry!*

As Mrs. Morehead and Jane react in amazement to the intensity of her mood the scene dissolves to a close-up of MARY in the LADIES' DRESSING ROOM of the Casino Roof. Through the large plate glass we see a spectacular vista of New York at night: Manhattan at its brightest!—a panorama such as one would see from the roof of any of New York's skyscraping hotels. Mary, in evening dress, is seated on a chaise lounge, a tabloid in her hand, nervously pretending to read. The lounge is against the windows so that even before the view moves back to reveal the background, we see the lights of New York. Music from a night-club band is heard—and continues throughout the scene. And now as the view draws back, the door starts to open. Mary looks up toward the door with a start, but relaxes as two society glamour girls enter. A maid also appears.

FIRST GLAMOUR GIRL (*aghast*). Did you see those quaint types with the Freulinheisens?

SECOND GLAMOUR GIRL. Yes. What *filthy* looking *outsiders!* Who are they?

FIRST GLAMOUR GIRL. I wouldn't admit if I knew, pet!

SECOND GLAMOUR GIRL. Really—something ought to be done to protect New York.

FIRST GLAMOUR GIRL (*as they walk out*). That's just what I said to Brenda at lunch today.

MARY (*to the maid Sadie, rising nervously*). You don't think Mrs. Fowler *left* the restaurant before I arrived?

SADIE. Oh, I'm sure, ma'am.

MARY. You *know* who she is, don't you?

SADIE. Certainly. (*Disgustedly*) She's famous for the *size* of her tips. (*Looking at her watch*) It's getting pretty late, ma'am. Maybe she's decided not to come.

Mary stands rigid and tense, looking at the door towards the lobby. As Sadie watches her questioningly, a dowager and a debutante come from the wash room.

DOWAGER. It's one thing to *come out!* It's quite another to *go under the table!*

DEBUTANTE. Yes, mother.

DOWAGER. And don't think I didn't overhear that Princeton boy call me an old drizzle-puss either! (*They go into the lobby.*)

SADIE (*sympathetically—broaching Mary with smelling salts*). Sure you wouldn't like these smelling salts, ma'am?

MARY (*distrait*). Oh. (*She takes them mechanically.*) Thanks.

She puts them down and starts to pace while Sadie looks at her, mystified. Peggy enters.

PEGGY. Please come back to the party, Mary. You've been in here over an hour.

MARY (*tensely*). Have I?

PEGGY. Are you waiting for someone?

MARY (*evasively*). I've a headache.

PEGGY. But you'll never lose it in this bad air.

MARY (*deliberating a moment—then in tones which indicate she is giving up whatever she has in mind*). Perhaps . . . you're right. (*She searches in her evening bag, takes out a bill and hands it to Sadie.*) Thank you.

SADIE (*bowled over by the amount*). Oh! Thank *you*, ma'am.

But at this point the door opens and in barge Crystal and Sylvia.

CRYSTAL (*sourly as they enter*). Stephen's in a mood!

SYLVIA (*seeing Mary and Peggy*). Sh!

Crystal, without batting an eyelash, coolly turns away, gives her coat to Sadie and calmly proceeds to fix her make-up.

SYLVIA (*with brazen briefness—to Mary*). How'd you do.

MARY (*covering her tension*). How'd you do.

SYLVIA (*to Peggy*). Hello, Peggy.

PEGGY (*resentful but self-contained*). Hello.

CRYSTAL (*to Sylvia, talking purposely for Mary as she heads for the washroom*). Stephen's going to give me pearls for my birthday. Isn't that sweet of him?

SYLVIA (*to Crystal—also speaking for Mary's benefit, as she follows along*). You've *me* to thank, dear. I told him you'd love them! (*And they disappear into the washroom.*)

PEGGY (*to Mary, anxious to get out*). Come on, Mary. (*And she starts for the door to the lobby.*)

MARY (*having something obviously in mind—and heading for the mirror*). I have to fix my make-up.

PEGGY (*uncomfortable*). Oh, hurry up, before they come back.

MARY (*keyed to a high pitch of tension*). Leave me alone, Peggy!

PEGGY (*surprised*). Why Mary!

As Peggy studies Mary, the two girls who went into the washroom before come out and head back toward the lobby.

FIRST GIRL. So he says "I gotta go home Sunday"—(*stopping to pull up her shoulder straps*)—and I says "Why d'ja got to?" And he says "I'm always expected home on Easter Sunday." And I says "What they expect ya to do? Lay an egg?"

SECOND GIRL. Imagine leaving a girl on Easter! They got no sentiment, the mugs!

PEGGY (*as the door closes on the two girls, turning to Mary—mystified*). Mary! *What are you up to?*

MARY (*as the door of the washroom is opened by Crystal*). Sh! (*Crystal and Sylvia start across the room toward the lobby.*)

MARY (*to Peggy, pretending to be engrossed in her make-up but speaking for Sylvia's benefit*). Did I tell you I'm going to Dr. Sylvester? (*As Sylvia picks up her ears*) My dear—he keeps me *hours* on end and *never sends a bill.* (*Archly*) He tells me the pleasure is all his.

By which time Crystal and the reluctant Sylvia have gone out.

PEGGY (*all at sea*). Why Mary! You never went to Dr. Sylvester in your life!

MARY. Sh!

She turns and trains her gaze expectantly on he door which, sure enough, suddenly opens and Sylvia pops back in.

SYLVIA (*explaining her return*). I'm having a little stocking trouble.

MARY (*politely*). Such a bore.

SYLVIA (*overly casual, as she straightens her stocking*). How are you feeling, Mary?

MARY. Quite well.

SYLVIA (*fishing for information about Dr. Sylvester*). I just heard you say you'd been to the *doctor*.

MARY. Oh! (*Laughing archly*) Jealous?

As Sylvia shows her amazement, Dolly de Puyster enters.

SYLVIA (*bridling*). Why—I'm not interested in Doctor Syl—

PEGGY (*sotto voce—seeing Dolly*). Sh! Dolly de Puyster! (*Mary and Sylvia look up.*)

DOLLY. Hello, girls.

MARY AND SYLVIA (*in unison*). Hello, Dolly.

DOLLY. Know any dirt for the column?

SYLVIA. Not a thing, sweet!

DOLLY (*to Sadie*). Get my coat out, Sadie. (*To the girls—as she heads for the wash room*) Might as well move along! (*Distastefully*) Never knew such a clean spot!

No sooner has Dolly disappeared than Mary turns to Sylvia.

MARY. Don't be coy, Sylvia. It's all over town what a fool you're making of yourself over Harvey Sylvester. (*To Peggy—who has stood by in dumb amazement.*) Come on, Peggy. (*And she starts on out as if she really intended to go.*)

SYLVIA (*sharply*). Wait a moment! (*Having expected this—Mary stops.*) I'd thank you to explain that last crack.

PEGGY (*beside herself*). Girls! Girls! (*Frantically pointing toward the wash room*) Dolly de Puyster!

MARY (*brushing Peggy aside*). Why, you're paying a hundred dollars an hour just to have him *hold your hand!*

SYLVIA (*aghast*). Did Harvey tell you I—

MARY. Of course not. You know very well that Harvey *never* discusses his patients!

PEGGY (*at the end of her wits*). Mary! You're not feeling well! (*She grabs Mary's hand.*)

MARY (*pushing her off*). Let me alone.

PEGGY (*panicky*). I'm going to get Nancy!

MARY (*calling after Peggy*). Come back

here! (*But by this time Peggy has run out.*)

SYLVIA (*with utter sarcasm—facing her*). You haven't seen me in two years, Mary Haines! Where do you *get* all this information?

MARY. Where d'you think? *Out of Crystal!*

SYLVIA (*disbelieving*). You? Out of Crystal?

MARY. Of course! By way of every saleswoman and manicurist in New York, my dear. She's telling *now* that Doctor Sylvester had to grow a Van Dyke beard so *you* can't see him *laughing* at you!

SYLVIA (*starting to think*). Why, that rotten little— (*With sudden anger*) I'll cut her throat!

MARY. You *would* pick her up, darling! You're the only friend she's got! Who else can she gossip about!

SYLVIA (*spitting it out*). She's got Buck Winston! Why doesn't she tell about *him!*

MARY (*gasping with delight as she learns what she's after*). *Buck Winston!* Oh!

She claps her hand over her mouth for fear she has given herself away. There is a pause as Sylvia studies her—then:

SYLVIA (*with gradual understanding*). Why Mary Haines! You *fished* that out of me!

As Mary, breathing hard in her emotion—looks at her—just looks—Dolly de Puyster comes out of the washroom and heads for Sadie who holds her coat.

MARY (*to Dolly—tensely*). Stick around awhile, Dolly! There's something going to pop! (*Sylvia gasps.*)

DOLLY (*bristling with malicious delight*). Good and dirty?

MARY (*to Dolly—wryly*). Do I ever fail you? Go out there and dig up Buck Winston. Ask him what famous "society" matron is crazy about him!

DOLLY (*beaming*). *Well!* (*And throwing her wrap back at Sadie she dashes out.*)

SYLVIA (*to Mary in slowly mounting wrath*). Why you—! *I'll keep him from opening that drunken trap of his if I have to—*

Breaking off, she starts for the door, as it is opened by Nancy and Peggy.

MARY (*to Nancy*). Stop her! Don't let her get out!

NANCY (*her hands on Sylvia's shoulders —pushing her back in*). Where were you going, my pretty maid?

MARY. Peggy—keep that door closed!

Peggy, finally galvanized into action, holds the door closed.

MARY (*quickly—to Sadie*). Have you got any place we could lock her up?

SYLVIA (*breaking loose from Nancy*). Oh, no, you don't! (*She starts to pull Peggy away from the door.*)

MARY (*quickly, warningly, to Sylvia*). Better stay here! I'll tell Crystal what you've *spilled* and *she'll murder you!* (*Stumped, Sylvia stops short.*)

SADIE (*blandly, fishing a key from her pocket*). How about the closet where I keep the dirty towels?

MARY. Superb! (*Sylvia lets out a gasp as Sadie heads for the closet.*)

SYLVIA (*pleading*). I'll stay here, Mary!

MARY. You bet you will! (*To Sadie*) Open it up!

SYLVIA (*to Sadie—as the latter unlocks the door of a closet*). You'd better think of your job, my good woman!

SADIE. Sorry, Mrs. Fowler—I'm thinking of all the *tips* you *never gave me*.

At which she grabs Sylvia and gives her a jerk which lands her in the closet. Mary slams the door—and Sadie locks it.

PEGGY (*during the above*). Mary! *This isn't like you!*

MARY. I haven't even started!

NANCY (*enjoying herself hugely*). Whatever you're up to, *I'm for it!*

MARY (*to Peggy, indicating the door, the handle of which has never ceased jiggling*). Let 'em in.

Peggy releases the door and two society women who were trying to come in, enter.

FIRST SOCIETY WOMAN (*looking daggers at Sadie*). Who locked the door?

SADIE (*now playing her part wtih vim*). It got stuck!

FIRST SOCIETY WOMAN. Oh!

MARY (*to Peggy*). Want to go reconnoitre?

Peggy whisks out. Subsiding, Mary bides her time, Nancy watching her.

FIRST SOCIETY WOMAN (*during the last part of the above dialogue to Second Society Woman, as she primps at the mirror*). Not *three* pounds, my dear?

SECOND SOCIETY WOMAN (*trying to crowd First Society Woman away from the mirror*). Three pounds! Just bananas and milk for one whole week.

FIRST SOCIETY WOMAN (*crowding her out*). How divine! Aren't you ecstatic?

SECOND SOCIETY WOMAN. Yes, but it's such great moral satisfaction. So uplift-lifting for one's character! (*Saying which, she fairly shoves First Society Woman away from the mirror. As First Society Woman reacts annoyed, Miriam bursts excitedly into the room.*)

MIRIAM. Oh, girls! Come out here quick! All heck's broke loose.

MARY (*a triumphant Fury*). I know it has! *I broke it!*

As Miriam shows her amazement.

FIRST SOCIETY WOMAN (*to Second Society Woman as she hurries toward the door*). We're missing something! Hurry!

As they go out, the Countess enters piloted by Edith.

COUNTESS (*tacking*). How *could* Buck do such a thing to me? Oh, the Dr. Jekyll! The Mr. Hyde! Which was which?

MIRIAM. Now, Flora. Calm down!

COUNTESS (*maundering on*). Of all my husbands, Buck's the first to ever disgrace me in public!

MARY (*tense*). What did he do?

EDITH (*to Mary—cutting in while the others interrupt*). Do? He's involved with your *ex-husband's present wife*, dear. *That's all!*

MIRIAM. He confided it in loud drunken tones, darling, to *Dolly de Puyster!*

COUNTESS (*wailing*). They heard him all over the place! Oh, the *publicity!* The *publicity!*

EDITH (*to Mary*). He even spilled dates, *and addresses!*

MIRIAM (*to Mary—helpfully*). I jotted 'em all down on Howard's shirt.

COUNTESS (*wailing*). He said he'd be a cock-eyed coyote if he'd herd an old beef like me back to the Coast.

MARY (*sorry for her*). Flora!

COUNTESS (*to Sadie*). Get me a bromide. (*As Sadie starts for the door*) Put some gin in it.

And now Crystal bursts into the room.

CRYSTAL (*to Sadie—disregarding all of them—blood in her eye*). Is Mrs. Fowler in here?

NANCY. *And how!*

MARY (*to Sadie*). Let her out!

As they all look on in interest, Sadie unlocks the door and opens it. Sylvia, on her knees at the keyhole, falls out, *and a load of dirty towels on a shelf above her spills down on her head.*

CRYSTAL (*to Sylvia, ready to cut her throat*). You've been shooting off your mouth, you rat!

SYLVIA (*to Crystal as she scrambles to her feet*). Oh, I knew you'd lose him——you—you *shop girl!*

CRYSTAL (*contemptuously*). Lose *who?* (*Whipping about she faces all of them.*) You're trying to break up my marriage, you cats! (*Singling Mary*) But get this straight, Mary Haines! You can't stampede me by gossip or the drunken ravings of Buck Winston. You've got to have *evidence!* And Stephen's a gentleman!

MIRIAM. He don't need *that kind* of evidence outside New York.

MARY. Stephen's fed up with you, Crystal, and in your heart *you know it!*

EDITH (*really helpful*). Better take my advice, Crystal, and put your mind on your alimony!

SYLVIA (*contemptuously—cutting in*). Alimony? (*To Crystal*) With what Stephen can get on you, *he won't have to give you a dime!*

There is a moment's pause as Crystal realizes that the pack has closed in on her.

CRYSTAL (*making a last stand, bursting out*). Is that so! Well, what if I didn't *need* alimony? How would you like that?

EDITH (*amazed*). You don't need—

MIRIAM (*cutting in*). What you going to use in its place, sweetheart?

CRYSTAL. Buck Winston! (*Whipping about she faces the Countess.*) Your cowboy and I get along great, Countess! *Just great!* (*As they all gasp in amazement at this bold declaration of guilt, to Mary*) And that dough he earns on the radio is a lot more than *Stephen Haines* will *ever* dig up! (*Going to get her wrap*) Buck and I are tickled to death to be rid of the whole lot of you!

COUNTESS (*wailing*). Oh—the ingrate!

MIRIAM. Cheer up, Flora. Anyhow, this is a *new* kind of a lesson!

SYLVIA. Yes, Flora—don't let your next husband get financially independent.

COUNTESS (*firing a bombshell*). But Buck isn't independent! (*Crystal, now at the door, turns.*)

MIRIAM (*to Countess*). Hasn't he got a contract with Dainty Jella-teen?

COUNTESS. But, darlings, *I* am Dainty Jella-teen! (*There is a pause as this sinks in on all of them, particularly on Crystal.*) Nobody in radio would give Buck a job—the old meanies! I had to *buy out* Dainty Jella-teen! (*Crystal's mouth drops wide open.*)

MIRIAM (*turning to Crystal*). Coma ti yi yippi, Crystal!

SYLVIA (*to Crystal*). *You* can buy it now, dear. And give Buck away with every package!

As Crystal stands there too dazed for any reaction, the door opens and Peggy whams in.

PEGGY (*to Mary—breathless*). Mary—Stephen's out there—he's waiting for you—that is—he wants to know if you'll see him. *Oh, Mary, will you?*

MARY (*her voice ringing out*). Will I? (*As she heads for the coat rack*) I'll say I will! (*As Crystal with a mighty effort—pulls herself together.*)

CRYSTAL (*determined to go down with colors flying*). Welcome to my leavings, Mrs. Haines!

MARY (*calmly*). I'll take them, thank you!

CRYSTAL. *Help yourself!*

Saying this, she wraps her cloak about her and sails out as if in triumph.

SYLVIA. Why, Mary—haven't you any *pride?*

MARY. No pride!

During this, the view moves swiftly to a screen-filling close-up of Mary.

MARY (*proudly*). I left it on the Bridge of Sighs in Reno!

She starts on out—the scene moving with her. As she goes out the door into the corridor, the music rises up in a triumphant love song. The scene continues to move ahead of her as she hurries up the staircase through the corridor to the roof elevators. The view now is too close for us to see anything—anything but Mary's face, as with eyes shining she walks forward toward the unseen Stephen. Now she stops, doubtless seeing him standing there waiting for her. Then the view moves to reveal Stephen's feet coming into view.

MARY'S VOICE. Stephen!

His feet come closer. Quite evidently he is embracing her fervently. The view moves up to show Stephen—to show the embrace! —but Stephen is not to be seen, nor the kiss, for as the view reaches up to his shoulders the scene fades out.

MY MAN GODFREY

(*A Universal Productions, Inc. Production*)

Screenplay by
MORRIE RYSKIND AND ERIC HATCH

Based on the Novel *My Man Godfrey* by
ERIC HATCH

Produced by CHARLES R. ROGERS

Directed by GREGORY LA CAVA

———

The Cast

GODFREY	William Powell
IRENE BULLOCK	Carole Lombard
ANGELICA BULLOCK . . .	Alice Brady
CORNELIA BULLOCK . . .	Gail Patrick
ALEXANDER BULLOCK . .	Eugene Pallette
MOLLY	Jean Dixon
TOMMY GRAY	Alan Mowbray
CARLO	Mischa Auer
MIKE	Pat Flaherty
FAITHFUL GEORGE . . .	Robert Light

Film Editors—TED KENT, RUSSELL SCHOENGARTH

Screenplay of the Universal Pictures photoplay "My Man Godfrey" copyright 1936 by Universal Production Pictures, Inc. By permission of Universal Production Pictures, Inc. and Eric Hatch. Mr. Hatch's story appeared in Liberty Magazine under the title of "1011 Fifth Avenue" and was published under the title of "My Man Godfrey" by Little Brown & Co. in 1936.

MY MAN GODFREY

PART ONE *

A panoramic view of a CITY DUMP discloses a Man standing by a fire. This dissolves, amid a noise of falling junk, to the END OF A TRUCK, from which cans are being dumped. Then shabby men are seen searching the ground for something of value—a bridge over a river, from which boat whistles are heard, forming an indistinct background. Miserable shacks are in the foreground, with makeshift fires in front of them. And now two men dimly appear, one of them approaching the fire at which the other is seated.

MIKE. Hello, Duke.

GODFREY. Hello, Mike. Any luck today?

MIKE. Well, I figured out a swell racket and everything was going great—till the cops came along.

A close-up of GODFREY, a bearded young man, shows him smoking a pipe.

GODFREY. Too bad it didn't work.

MIKE'S VOICE. If them cops would stick to their own racket and leave honest guys alone, we'd get somewhere in this country without a lot of this relief and all that stuff.

GODFREY. Well, Mike, I wouldn't worry —prosperity is just around the corner.

MIKE (starting out). Yes, it's been there a long time. I wish I knew which corner. Well, Duke, I'm going to turn in. Bon soir.

GODFREY (sitting down). Bon soir, Mike.

A long view of the DUMP, Godfrey by the fire in the foreground, shows two cars coming along the street at the top of the dump, and stopping.

Following this we see a STREET: Cornelia and her escort, George, alight, a second car stopping back of the first one.

Then a close view at the CAR shows Cornelia, a proud, beautiful young woman, and George, looking off, following which a pretty girl, Irene, gets out of the second car, and comes forward.

CORNELIA. This is the place, all right. That looks like one of them sitting outside that shack.

GEORGE. It looks like a pretty tough joint to me.

CORNELIA. You stall, Irene. I'll talk to that fellow. (She goes out.)

IRENE. I don't think it's fair of you and Cornelia! I told you about this place.

GEORGE. Well, we got here first.

IRENE. Well, she's not going to get ahead of me. (She follows after her.)

At the DUMP, a bearded, shabby man is crouching by a fire. Cornelia comes down to him, Irene following. The man, Godfrey, rises; there is dignity and intelligence in his demeanor.

CORNELIA. Good evening.

GODFREY (removing his hat). Good evening.

CORNELIA. How'd you like to make five dollars?

GODFREY. How'd—I didn't quite catch what you said.

CORNELIA. How would you like to make five dollars?

IRENE (seen in a close-up) stands waiting— impatient—angry.

---

* The directions and descriptions for this film are scanty. However, no effort has been made, in the editing, to amplify the text, since its sparseness and emphasis on movement and quickly glimpsed detail are conducive to comic effect. The stress is on movement and comic dialogue. The reader can easily imagine for himself the swanky background of the wealthy home in which most of the action occurs, the expensive costumes, and the odd facial expressions and gestures of the smart set. Copyright, 1936, by Universal Production Pictures, Inc.

GODFREY's VOICE. Five dollars?

CORNELIA's VOICE. Five dollars.

We see next CORNELIA and GODFREY, with Irene beyond them.

GODFREY. I don't want to seem inquisitive—but what would I have to do for it?

CORNELIA. Oh—all you have to do is go to the Waldorf-Ritz Hotel with me and I'll show you to a few people and then I'll send you right back.

GODFREY. May I inquire just why you should want to show me to people at the Waldorf-Ritz?

CORNELIA. Oh, if you must know. It's a game—you've probably heard about it—a scavenger hunt. If I find a forgotten man first I win. Is that clear?

We see a close-up of IRENE, watching as a steamer whistle is heard.

GODFREY and CORNELIA come into view again, standing and talking, the steamer whistle sounding again.

GODFREY. Yes—quite clear. Shall I wear my tails—or shall I come just as I am?

CORNELIA. You needn't be fresh. Do you want the five dollars or don't you?

GODFREY. Madam, I can't tell you how flattered I am by your very generous offer.

A close view in front of the SHACK discloses Cornelia looking for help as she backs away.

CORNELIA. George!

GODFREY (*following her, Irene in the background watching*). However, I am afraid I'll have to take the matter up with my board of directors.

CORNELIA. Don't you touch me!

GODFREY. No matter what my board of directors advise, I think you should be spanked.

George approaches, and Irene moves out of sight. Cornelia backs over to an ash pile as Godfrey talks and she suddenly sits down. George helps her up.

CORNELIA. George—do something!

GEORGE. Are you in the habit of hitting ladies?

GODFREY. Maybe. But I am in the habit of hitting gentlemen also—if that would interest you.

CORNELIA. Aren't you going to do anything?

GEORGE. Yes. Let's get a policeman. (*And they disappear.*)

Godfrey turns back, the scene moving over to the shack. He suddenly sees Irene there.

GODFREY. Who are you?

IRENE. I'm Irene. That was my sister Cornelia you pushed in the ash-pile.

GODFREY. How would you like to have me push Cornelia's sister into an ash-pile?

IRENE. Oh, I don't think I'd like it.

GODFREY. Well, you'd better get out of here then.

IRENE. You bet.

GODFREY. Wait a minute! Sit down!

IRENE and GODFREY sit down on the dump, while some men in the background call to him.

IRENE. I'm sitting.

BOB. What's up, Duke? Need some help?

GODFREY. No thanks, boys. I've got everything under control. (*To Irene*) Are you a member of this hunting party?

IRENE. I was—but I'm not now. Are they all forgotten men, too?

GODFREY. Yes, I guess they are maybe. But why?

IRENE. It's the funniest thing. I couldn't help but laugh. I've wanted to do that ever since I was six years old.

GODFREY. You wanted to do what?

IRENE. Push Cornelia in something—a pile of ashes or something. You know— that was Faithful George with her. It isn't really his name, but we call him that, because he gets in everybody's hair. His father's a broker.

GODFREY. That's funny.

IRENE (*laughing*). Cornelia thought she was going to win and you pushed her into a pile of ashes.

GODFREY. Do you think you could follow an intelligent conversation for just a moment?

IRENE. I'll try.

GODFREY. Well, that's fine. Do you mind telling me just what a scavenger hunt is?

IRENE. Well—a scavenger hunt is just exactly like a treasure hunt, except that a treasure hunt is where you find something you want and in a scavenger hunt you try to find something that nobody wants.

GODFREY. Hmm—like a forgotten man.

IRENE. That's right—and the one that wins gets a prize—only there really isn't a prize. It's just the honor of winning, 'cause all the money goes to charity—that is—if there's any money left over. Only there never is.

GODFREY. Well—that clears the whole matter up beautifully.

IRENE. Yes—well, I've decided I don't want to play any more games with human beings as objects. It's kind of sordid when you come to think of it—I mean when you think it over.

GODFREY. Yes—I—I don't know. I haven't thought it over.

IRENE. I don't like to change the subject, but will you tell me why you live in a place like this when there are so many other nice places?

GODFREY. You really want to know?

IRENE. Oh, I'm very curious.

GODFREY. It's because my real estate agent thought the altitude would be very good for my asthma.

IRENE. Oh, my uncle has asthma.

GODFREY. No? Well—now there's a coincidence.

IRENE. Well—I suppose I should be going, shouldn't I?

IRENE and GODFREY start walking along. She takes his hand, and they start away.

GODFREY. It's a good idea.

IRENE. I want to see who won the game —Cornelia, I suppose, again. She's probably got another forgotten man by this time.

GODFREY. You mean—if you took me along with you, that you would win the game? Is that the idea?

IRENE. Well, I might if I got there first —but after seeing what you did to Cornelia, I'm not saying anything.

GODFREY. But you'd win if you got back first with me?

IRENE. It would be awfully nice of you, but I don't like to ask.

GODFREY. Let's beat Cornelia.

IRENE. It wouldn't be asking too much?

GODFREY. You see, I've got a sense of curiosity, the same as you have. I'd really like to see just what a scavenger hunt looks like.

IRENE. But I told you!

GODFREY. Yes—but I'm still curious.

IRENE. Well—come on!

The scene dissolves to a HOTEL BALLROOM full of chatter, with people passing back and forth, men at a bar in close view. A well-dressed man, Blake, moves forward and offers his hand to Bullock, another well-dressed man. They talk and drink.

BLAKE. My name is Blake.

BULLOCK. My name is Bullock.

BLAKE. This place slightly resembles an insane asylum.

BULLOCK. Well—all you need to start an asylum is an empty room and the right kind of people.

We get a close travelling view of the BALL-
ROOM as an elderly woman, Angelica, and
her young, exotic-looking escort, Carlo,
appear moving forward through the crowd.
She is leading a nanny goat and talks constantly. They stop and talk to other couples.

ANGELICA. Oh, good evening, Mrs. Dawson. Look what I found up in the
Bronx.

MAN. A goat—a real goat! (*The people
chatter.*)

At the BAR we again see Blake and Bullock
talking. Bullock looks around.

BLAKE. Take a look at that dizzy old
gal with the goat.

BULLOCK. I've had to look at her for
twenty years. That's Mrs. Bullock.

There follows a close view of Angelica,
Carlo and others with the goat, as she
moves off; and then a full view of the BALL-
ROOM, noisy with chatter, includes the two
men at the bar in the foreground, people
rushing about, Angelica half-way down
the room—shouting.

BLAKE. I'm terribly sorry.

BULLOCK. How do you think I feel?

ANGELICA. Oh, Alexander! Come here!

BULLOCK (*going to her*). All right—all
right, Angelica!

Bullock approaches her, while several
young men come on with a vegetable cart
and go out of sight with it.

ANGELICA. Look at this lovely goat.
Carlo and I found him up in the Bronx.
Isn't he the sweetest little thing?

BULLOCK. He doesn't smell very sweet.

ANGELICA (*to Carlo, explaining breez-
ily*). Alexander never did like animals.

Angelica, with the goat and the rest of
her party, moves to the foreground; then
the view moves back and down the steps
into the next room—Angelica leading the
goat and a kid. People are passing all sorts
of things to the counter where men are
receiving them. An old corset is handed to
one of the receivers—everybody trying to
talk louder than the rest.

ANGELICA. Come on Go-go-go-go! Come
on!

BULLOCK. Are you talking to me or to
that animal!

ANGELICA (*as the others keep on talking and shouting*). I have a goat! I
have a goat!

A close view of the CROWD shows Angelica
and Carlo trying to be heard.

CARLO. She has a goat.

ANGELICA. I have a goat.

A man behind the counter is trying to
make himself heard as a Man (closely
seen) comes on with an old spinning wheel.
It breaks. Then Angelica and Carlo, with
the goat, again appear.

ANGELICA. I have a goat! A goat!

CARLO. She has a goat.

We get a close-up of a MAN, the receiver, in
the foreground talking—the crowd in the
background; the man makes notes.

MAN. I know you have a goat. Henry,
will you come here and get Mrs. Bullock's goat?

Henry comes on, takes the goat, and leaves
with it. Angelica picks up the kid, as she
talks.

ANGELICA. I have a little baby goat, too.

The two receivers are talking as the kid
is being held up. Startled, the Man gives
it to a bellhop, who goes out with the kid.

ANGELICA. Is there anything else we
have to get?

The receiver, checking the goods received,
looks up.

MAN. All you have to get now is one
forgotten man and a bowl of Japanese
goldfish.

ANGELICA. What? Be still, everybody.
What?

MAN (*raising his voice*). I said a forgotten man and a bowl of Japanese goldfish.

ANGELICA (*repeating after the man*). A
forgotten man and a bowl of Japanese
goldfish.

At this Carlo laughs, and they turn to pass through the crowd. Then they appear pushing through the crowd, with Bullock close to Angelica as a man comes in with snow-shoes.

ANGELICA. A forgotten man—a bowl of Japanese goldfish— A Japanese—I can't remember—

BULLOCK (*to her*). I'm going home!

ANGELICA. Oh, what are you talking about?

BULLOCK. I'm talking about going home!

ANGELICA. We've only got two more things to get— A bowl of Japanese men and a forgotten goldfish. What was it, Carlo?

CARLO. Goldfish.

BULLOCK (*leaving, angrily*). I don't know anything about goldfish—but if you want a forgotten man—you'll find me home in bed.

ANGELICA. I can't stop to talk to you now. A bowl of Japanese goldfish. (*Carlo and she go out.*)

Near the ENTRANCE of the BALLROOM as men and women are passing, we see Irene coming forward with Godfrey. She leads him up the steps, the view moving with them.

GODFREY. Are all these people hunters?

IRENE. Oh, no. We work in groups—some are hunters and some are receivers.

GODFREY. Sounds like bankruptcy proceedings.

IRENE. You know, I never thought of that.

GODFREY. Who receives me?

IRENE. I have to take you to the committee. But you don't mind, do you?

GODFREY. I can hardly wait.

ANGELICA (*out of sight*). Wait a minute! Wait a minute! What have you got?

IRENE (*as they stop in the doorway, meeting Angelica*). Oh, this is Godfrey. Has Cornelia got back yet?

ANGELICA. I haven't seen Cornelia. Where did you find him?

In a close view of one SIDE of the ROOM Irene appears with Godfrey, people watching her. Angelica follows her. The view moves to the receiving counter, where she reports to the receiver. (A monkey jumps about, annoying the man at the counter. As they pass a man with sandwiches on a tray, Godfrey takes some.)

IRENE (*answering Angelica's question*). Oh, he's a forgotten man.

ANGELICA. Irene! Irene!

IRENE. Oh, Mr. Guthrie! Mr. Guthrie! Mr. Guthrie—I've got a forgotten man.

GODFREY curiously watches her as she talks.

IRENE. Oh, Mr. Guthrie! This is Godfrey—he's a forgotten man!

MAN (*who hears her amid the shouting*). Listen, Guthrie, he's the forgotten man.

IRENE. His name is Godfrey.

GUTHRIE (*understanding at last*). A forgotten man? Ladies and gentlemen, please—quiet! Quiet. Miss Bullock has the forgotten man. Would you mind stepping up on the platform, please?

A close view in the room shows Irene, Godfrey, Angelica, Carlo and others, Irene talking—the kid on the counter in the foreground.

IRENE. Will you go right up on the platform, Godfrey?

The view moves with Godfrey as he gets up on the platform—still eating a sandwich.

GUTHRIE (*to Godfrey*). Would you mind if I ask you a few questions?

GODFREY. Fire away.

GUTHRIE (*seen in a close-up*). What is your address?

GODFREY (*now seen in a close-up*). City Dump Thirty-Two—East River—Sutton Place.

GUTHRIE'S VOICE. Hmm—rather fashionable over there, isn't it?

GODFREY. In spots.

GUTHRIE (*in a close-up amid much talking*). Is that your permanent address?

GODFREY. Well, the permanency is rather questionable. You see, the place is being rapidly filled in.

GUTHRIE and GODFREY are now eating amid much chatter.

GUTHRIE. May I ask you a personal question?

GODFREY. If it isn't too personal.

GUTHRIE. Are those whiskers your own?

GODFREY (*whimsically*). No one else has claimed them.

GUTHRIE. I must ask that question because one group tried to fool the committee the early part of the evening by putting false whiskers on one of their own group. May I—

GODFREY. It's a pleasure.

GUTHRIE. One more question. Are you wanted by the police?

GODFREY (*dryly*). That's just the trouble —nobody wants me.

IRENE (in a close-up) is smiling with pleasure. She claps her hands approvingly.

GUTHRIE'S VOICE. What a good answer.

IRENE. Splendid, Godfrey.

Now we see Godfrey, Irene and her mother, Angelica, in the foreground.

ANGELICA. You mean nobody wants him —nobody at all.

GODFREY. Nobody.

ANGELICA. Oh, that's too bad!

Next Godfrey and Guthrie appear on a platform—Irene, her mother Angelica, and Carlo with their backs turned in the foreground. Irene gets up beside Godfrey.

GODFREY. On the contrary, I sometimes find it a great advantage.

GUTHRIE. The committee are satisfied. Miss Irene Bullock wins twenty points

for the forgotten man and fifty points extra for bringing in the first one.

CROWD. Speech! Speech!

GUTHRIE. Group Ten wins the silver cup!

IRENE (*receiving the cup*). They want a speech! Turn around, Godfrey.

GODFREY. My purpose in coming here tonight was two-fold. Firstly, I wanted to aid this young woman. Secondly, I was curious to see how a bunch of empty-headed nit-wits conducted themselves. (*Amid the shouting that arises*) My curiosity is satisfied.

There is now a close-up ON THE PLATFORM showing Irene standing beside Godfrey, Guthrie behind them.

GODFREY (*amid more shouting*). I assure you it will be a pleasure for me to return to a society of really important people. (*He goes out.*)

Angelica and Carlo are left standing and talking, as Irene goes off past them.

ANGELICA. What did he call us?

CARLO. Nit-wits.

ANGELICA. Nit-wits—what are they?

We see Godfrey passing through the crowd. He passes through the doorway into the next room, Irene running after him.

MAN. The man's perfect! I've been wanting to say that all night, but I didn't have the nerve.

IRENE (*catching up with him*). Oh, Godfrey! Godfrey! Oh, Godfrey! I'm terribly sorry.

IRENE clings to GODFREY as they move through the room, Angelica following them.

GODFREY. Oh, that's all right.

IRENE. I'd never have brought you here if I had thought they were going to humiliate you. I'm terribly thankful. It's the first time I've ever beaten Cornelia at anything, and you helped me do it.

GODFREY. Well, that makes me a sort of Cornelia beater, doesn't it?

IRENE. You've done something for me. I wish I could do something for you.

GODFREY. Why?

IRENE (*naively*). Because you've done something for me. Don't you see?

GODFREY. No—I don't see. I can use a job if you've got one hanging around loose.

IRENE. Can you buttle?

GODFREY. Buttle?

IRENE. Yes. We're fresh out of butlers. The one we had left this morning.

ANGELICA (*who has been following them; out of sight*). Irene!

ANGELICA appears at the steps and the moving view follows her over to a pillar where Irene and Godfrey are standing.

ANGELICA. They're calling for you in the game room. Don't you want your nice cup?

IRENE. They can keep their cup. I don't want it.

ANGELICA. You can't stand here talking to this man. What will people think?

IRENE. I don't care what they think. Godfrey's going to be our butler.

ANGELICA. He's going to be whose butler?

IRENE. He's going to work for us.

ANGELICA. Why, it's ridiculous! You don't know anything about him. He hasn't any recommendations.

IRENE. The last one had recommendations and stole all the silver.

ANGELICA. Oh, that was merely a coincidence.

GODFREY. People that take in stray cats say they make the best pets, Madam.

ANGELICA. I don't see what cats have got to do with butlers. You mustn't pay any attention to my daughter. She is very impulsive.

IRENE. I'm not impulsive!

ANGELICA. And don't shout at your mother.

IRENE. I will shout—

A woman comes past them, and Angelica turns to her, embarrassed.

ANGELICA. Oh, Mrs. Merriwell! Irene has —(*She continues talking excitedly.*)

MRS. MERRIWELL. You mean it is all over?

ANGELICA. Irene always shouts when she wins. (*The woman leaves them excitedly.*)

ANGELICA (*impatiently*). Well, run along, my good man, just run along. Thank you so much for coming. Thank you so, so much.

IRENE (*firmly*). He will not—

At the ENTRANCE we now see Cornelia coming on with George and a man. They stop.

IRENE (*completing her sentence*). —run along.

GODFREY. I think I'd better—

ANGELICA. My word! There's Cornelia —and she has another one.

We again see, at the ENTRANCE, Cornelia, George and the man, with other people in the background, and then see the three standing at the PILLAR, with Cornelia approaching, followed by George and the Man, a tramp.

IRENE. You're a little late, Cornelia. I've won the game.

CORNELIA (*taken aback*). Oh, you have.

MAN. Now, when do I get my five bucks?

ANGELICA. Your five? (*To Cornelia*) Will you talk to your sister? She wants—

A close-up of GODFREY shows him smiling with amusement.

ANGELICA'S VOICE. —to hire this man as a butler.

CORNELIA (*seen in a close-up; looking at him with interest*). Why not? He might make a very good butler.

GODFREY (*seen in a close-up, smiling faintly*). I am sure I would make a very good butler.

MAN (*seen in a close-up, impatient*). Say, where do I get my five bucks?

Angelica and George go to him.

ANGELICA. What's he talking about?

MAN. My five bucks.

CORNELIA. Oh, I promised him five dollars.

ANGELICA. Give him the five dollars and the bucks, too, and get him out of here, before your sister hires him as a chauffeur. (*George gets out the money and pays the man, who leaves quickly.*) Why did I have to wait till now to find out there is insanity on your father's side of the family. Come along, Cornelia. (*She leaves them.*)

CORNELIA stops before Irene and Godfrey.

CORNELIA. I hope Godfrey is very good at shining shoes. (*She leaves them.*)

GODFREY. I think we'd better drop the whole idea.

IRENE. I should say not. You're going to make the best butler we ever had. (*Putting money in his pocket*) And here —you need some clothes and things.

GODFREY (*embarrassed*). Oh, well, I—

A roll of bills, and silver, fall on the floor at their feet.

Both look down—startled. Godfrey shows her the holes in his pocket and stoops down.

GODFREY. I told Jeeves to lay out my other coat—

We see Godfrey (in a close-up) picking up the money, and then both Irene and Godfrey:

IRENE. You have a wonderful sense of humor.

GODFREY. Thank you. Well then—good night.

People appear passing as Godfrey starts to leave Irene.

GODFREY (*coming back*). Oh! I forgot one question.

IRENE. What—

GODFREY. Where do you live?

IRENE. Oh—1011 Fiftieth—funny—I never thought of that.

GODFREY. No, you didn't. 1011 Fiftieth.

IRENE. Yes.

GODFREY. Well, good-night again.

IRENE. Good-night, Godfrey. (*He leaves and the scene fades out.*)

PART TWO

A KITCHEN fades in. A young woman, Molly, is seated, reading, as footsteps are heard, and soon Godfrey enters, bag and overcoat in hand. He comes forward, and sets down his bag. Godfrey is no longer bearded, and looks trim.

GODFREY. Good morning.

MOLLY. Good morning.

GODFREY. I'm the new—

MOLLY. I know. You're the new—

A close view of GODFREY shows him looking puzzled.

MOLLY (*out of sight; her voice heard*). —butler.

GODFREY. How did you know?

MOLLY (*seen in a close-up; seated*). Oh, there's one every day at this hour.

They're dropping in and out all the time.

Godfrey now comes toward Molly.

GODFREY. Why is that?

MOLLY. Some get fired and some quit—

GODFREY. Is the— (*Puzzled, as he is now seen in a close-up.*) —family that exacting?

MOLLY (*seen in a close-up; holding a paper and a pencil*). No! They're that nutty.

Godfrey is now seen standing—Molly seated.

GODFREY. May I be frank?

MOLLY. Is that your name?

GODFREY. My name is Godfrey.

MOLLY. All right—be frank.

GODFREY (*in a close-up*). You're quite an enthusiast—

MOLLY (*seen in a close-up, busy with paper and pencil*). Don't worry about me. I'm a seasoned campaigner.

Godfrey now offers his hand, and shakes hands with her.

GODFREY. Well—may we be friends?

MOLLY. I'm friends with all the butlers. Sit down. What's a three-letter sea-bird with an "E" in the middle?

GODFREY. Oh—I—I don't know.

MOLLY. You're no help. Say, where did you get the trick suit?

GODFREY. What's the matter with it?

MOLLY. Well, it might look better if you took the rental tag off the coat.

GODFREY. Thanks. Does the butler have quarters here in the house or is it necessary?

MOLLY. You won't need any quarters. Just hang your hat near the door so you can get it quickly— (*The buzzer is heard.*)

We see a BELL above a panel—the number 8 is up.

MOLLY (*out of view; continuing*). —on your way out.

As the buzzer continues ringing, Godfrey rises.

GODFREY. What's that?

MOLLY (*rising hastily*). That's the old battle-axe. She usually rings about this time.

GODFREY. The old battle-axe?

MOLLY. Mrs. Bullock—she's the mother type.

GODFREY. Don't you do anything about it?

MOLLY. Mrs. Bullock or the buzzer?

GODFREY. The buzzer.

MOLLY. Not the first time. If she has a hangover—and she usually has—she'll ring again in a minute in no uncertain terms. Then, brother, you'd better grab her tomato juice and get going. (*As the buzzer sounds again, she goes over to the refrigerator.*) Aw!—there she goes! Now, Cupid, this is your big opportunity.

Molly is now pouring tomato juice into a tall glass.

GODFREY. Shall I take it to her?

MOLLY. You might as well know the worst, and I want to warn you she sees pixies.

GODFREY. Pixies?

MOLLY. You know—the little men. (*The buzzer sounds again.*)

GODFREY. Oh those! Well, I know how to take care of those. Have you any Worcestershire? Yes—here it is.

MOLLY. What are you going to do with that?

Godfrey gets the bottle from the refrigerator and puts some into the glass as they talk. She gives him a tray, and they go to the door.

GODFREY. Do unto others as you would have them do unto you.

MOLLY. What do you want to do—scorch her windpipe?

GODFREY. There's nothing like a counter irritant in the morning. Where do I find her?

MOLLY. Better go this way—it's quicker. The upper landing to the left.

We see the SERVICE HALL, Molly holding the door as Godfrey moves forward with the tray. Then the view moves along the stairway to the main hall as Molly and Godfrey appear. (*The buzzer can still be heard.*)

GODFREY (*as he mounts the stairs*). Just which is her—

MOLLY (*pointing*). That's her cage up there. The first door.

GODFREY. Wish me luck.

MOLLY. Happy landing.

The BEDROOM DOOR is opened by Godfrey, holding the tray, and he looks around as the view moves across to the bed, revealing Angelica, while a tinkle of prisms is heard and soon also music. Then a close-up at the WINDOWS reveals a lamp with prisms on a table —prisms tinkling—swaying. And now a close view at the BED shows Angelica in it—Godfrey approaching with a tray and taking the buzzer cord from her hand.

ANGELICA. What day is it, Molly?

GODFREY. I am not Molly.

ANGELICA. Who isn't?

GODFREY. I'm not.

ANGELICA. Stop jumping up and down so I can see who you are.

GODFREY. I am not jumping.

ANGELICA. That's better. What's your name?

GODFREY. Godfrey.

ANGELICA. Are you someone I know?

GODFREY. We met last night at the Waldorf-Ritz.

ANGELICA. Oh yes—you were with Mrs. Maxton's party at the bar—or were you?

GODFREY. I'm the forgotten man.

ANGELICA. So many people have bad memories.

GODFREY. So true.

ANGELICA (*seen in a close-up; frowning as the music is heard again*). Why do they keep playing that same tune over and over again?

GODFREY (*a close-up showing him standing, tray in hand*) Why do they?

ANGELICA (*while the music continues*). Do they?

GODFREY (*looking around*). Oh—yes— yes. I do—

At the WINDOWS a close view shows the prisms tinkling on the lamp.

GODFREY'S VOICE. In a way—but—

We see the ROOM as Godfrey offers her the glass.

ANGELICA. Always the same tune—over and over again.

GODFREY. May I?

ANGELICA. May you what? Where are you? What's that?

GODFREY. Pixie remover.

ANGELICA (*taking the glass*). Oh—then you see them, too?

GODFREY. We're old friends.

ANGELICA. You mustn't step on them. I don't like them, but I don't like to see them stepped on.

GODFREY (*seen in another close-up, standing*). I'll be very careful. I wouldn't hurt them for the world.

ANGELICA (*holding the glass*). What am I supposed to do with this?

GODFREY'S VOICE. Drink it.

The BEDROOM comes in to view again as Godfrey goes to the window. He closes the shutters, then returns to the bed.

GODFREY. —and they'll go away very quickly—very, very quickly. You must never be rough with them. You must always send them away quietly. Is that better?

ANGELICA. Yes. You're a great help.

Godfrey is standing at the BED with the tray:

ANGELICA (*suddenly*). Go away—go away—shoo shoo— Oh but— Oh—you haven't told me who you are.

GODFREY. I am Godfrey—the forgotten man. I'm the new butler.

ANGELICA. Are you that ugly man with the beard?

GODFREY. The same.

ANGELICA. My, you've changed. I should never have known you.

GODFREY. Thank you.

ANGELICA. You are very comforting. I hope I'll see more of you. Maybe I'd better not drink any more of this. Then you might go away, too. (*He leaves.*)

We see Godfrey on the UPPER LANDING closing the door and the view moves with him as he goes down the stairs. Molly meets him there with a large tray.

MOLLY. Well, I put your hat and valise at the foot of the stairs. You can go out the front way—it's closer.

GODFREY. I think I won the first round.

MOLLY. You mean you're still working here?

GODFREY. I haven't heard anything to the contrary.

MOLLY. Well, you just got by the cub. Try the lioness.

GODFREY. Oh—which is she?

MOLLY. Her name's Cornelia. She's a sweet-tempered little number.

GODFREY. Oh yes, I met her last night.

MOLLY (*giving him the tray*). You've got a treat coming. You never met her in the morning. Second door.

He goes up the other stairs, carrying the tray, opens the door, stops, and looks in. We see Mollie on the STAIRS listening as Cornelia is heard speaking irritably.

CORNELIA'S VOICE. Who are you and what are you doing in here? If I want you to bring my breakfast I'll—

A close view of the UPPER LANDING, as the noise of things being thrown is heard, shows Godfrey in the doorway with the breakfast tray. He closes the door, comes forward, and the view moves with him along the stairs as Godfrey descends and meets Molly.

CORNELIA (*off scene*). Get out! You won't come in here again if you know what's good for you!

GODFREY. I'm afraid I lost the second round.

IRENE'S VOICE (*now heard*). Hey, Molly! Cut out all that noise and bring me some breakfast.

MOLLY. Opportunity never stops knocking in this house. Do you want to try again?

GODFREY. And how is *she* in the morning?

MOLLY. She's not as violent, but she's more insidious.

GODFREY. Okay. (*He goes up again, to the first door, and opens it.*)

MOLLY (*out of sight*). I'll leave your things right up here so you won't forget them.

Irene's BEDROOM: The door opens, Godfrey enters, and the view moves with him over to the bed where Irene is lying.

GODFREY. Good morning. I brought your breakfast.

IRENE (*startled*). Are—are you the new butler?

GODFREY (*holding the tray*). Don't you remember last night?

IRENE (*a close-up showing her looking around, puzzled*). But—what happened to Godfrey?

GODFREY. I'm Godfrey.

IRENE (*the close-up showing her troubled*). Oh—you look so different. What happened to those nice whiskers?

Godfrey puts the tray on the bed—Irene looking at him.

IRENE. Turn around and let me look at you. You're the cutest thing I've ever seen.

GODFREY (*turning*). Thank you. Will there be anything else?

IRENE. Yes. Sit down and talk to me. I like to talk in the morning when your head is clear—especially if you've been somewhere the night before.

GODFREY. Don't you think it would be better if I talked standing?

IRENE. No. Because, if you're uncomfortable, I'd get uncomfortable and forget what I have to say.

GODFREY (*starting to sit down on the bed*). If you insist.

Irene is pleased as Godfrey sits down—they talk.

GODFREY. —but it doesn't seem very good form for a butler.

IRENE. You're more than a butler. You're the first protégé I ever had.

GODFREY (*in the foreground*). Protégé?

IRENE. You know—like Carlo.

GODFREY. Who is Carlo?

IRENE (*now in the foreground*). He's mother's protégé.

GODFREY. Oh.

IRENE. You know, it's awfully nice Carlo having a sponsor, because he doesn't have to work and he gets more time to practice—but then, he never does and that makes a difference.

GODFREY (*again in the foreground*). Yes, I imagine it would.

IRENE. Do you play anything, Godfrey? I don't mean games or things like that. I mean the piano—and things like that.

GODFREY. Well, I—

IRENE. It doesn't really make any difference. I just thought I'd ask. It's funny how some things make you think of other things.

GODFREY. Yes, it is very peculiar.

IRENE. It makes me feel so mature and grown up.

GODFREY. Er—what does?

IRENE. Having a protégé. You're the first one I ever had.

GODFREY. You've never had any others?

IRENE (*in a close-up with him, in the foreground; naively*). No—you're the first one and it's terribly thrilling. Not only does it occupy my mind, but I think it's character building, too.

GODFREY. Uh-huh. Just what does a protégé have to do?

IRENE. Oh—you just go on buttling and I sponsor you. Don't you see?

GODFREY (*with Irene in the foreground*). It's getting clearer.

IRENE. It's really not much work. It gives you something to think of. It's going to be such fun.

GODFREY (*now in the foreground*). I'm sure it's going to be heaps of fun.

IRENE. You see, if Cornelia gets mean or anything, you don't have to do anything about it. You see, I take care of everything. You see, I'm your sponsor and I'll just take a sock at her.

GODFREY. Oh, I hope that's not going to be necessary.

IRENE. I just wanted to give you the idea.

GODFREY. That's fine, but—you see, a protégé has certain responsibilities also. For instance if someone should ring for me now and I didn't answer, that would reflect upon you because you're my sponsor. Don't you see?

IRENE. Yes, I suppose it would. I never thought of that. You don't know how nice it is having some intelligent person to talk to.

GODFREY. It's been very enlightening to me, too.

IRENE. Oh, I just thought of something else. Do you know what you are?

GODFREY. I'm not quite sure.

IRENE (*brightly—in a close-up*). You're my responsibility.

GODFREY (*bowing*). That's very nice.

IRENE (*as he is at the door now*). See you in church.

GODFREY opens the door and starts to go out, bowing.

Down the LOWER HALL Bullock is seen coming forward, and looking off. As viewed from the upper landing leading to the lower hall Godfrey's coat appears on the railing and his bag below it, as he closes the door, Bullock watching from down stairs. Godfrey takes his things and descends the stairs.

GODFREY (*to Bullock*). Good morning.

BULLOCK (*scowling*). Good morning.

GODFREY. Fine morning, sir.

BULLOCK (*descending the lower stairs with him*). Yes—it is a fine morning. Don't be in a hurry. You see, I'm the old fashioned type and I was also middle weight champion when I was in college. I thought you might like to know that before this thing starts. (*He stops him from leaving. Bullock removes his coat and vest.*)

GODFREY. Well, you see, sir, I'm the new butler. I just served Miss Irene her breakfast.

BULLOCK. Do you always take a change of wardrobe when you serve breakfast?

GODFREY (*as Molly enters*). Well—I—I think this young lady can explain.

MOLLY. He really is the new butler, Mr. Bullock. I can't imagine how his things got in the hallway.

BULLOCK. Well, I still don't get it, but if you are the new butler—why didn't you say so?

GODFREY. I'm very sorry, sir. May I? (*He holds Bullock's coat for him.*)

MOLLY. There's a man at the door to see you. I think it's a process server.

BULLOCK (*leaving*). Another one?

MOLLY. Yes, sir.

At the DOOR: Bullock opens it, and admits a man who gives him a paper.

MAN. Well, here I am, Mr. Bullock, with a little present for you.

BULLOCK. Yes—I've heard all that before. Which one of the family is it this time?

MAN. Miss Cornelia. It seems she was feeling pretty gay last night and on the way home she busted up a few windows along Fifth Avenue. I'm sorry to give you that, but girls will be girls.

BULLOCK (*closing the door*). Good-bye.

The LOWER HALL: Godfrey and Molly stand watching. Bullock comes in; he is plainly angry.

BULLOCK. Life in this family is just one subpoena—

MOLLY. Mr. Bullock, there's a hansom cab driver waiting to see you in the kitchen.

BULLOCK. What's he want?

MOLLY. He wants fifty dollars and his horse.

BULLOCK. What horse?

MOLLY. The one Miss Irene rode up the front steps last night.

BULLOCK. Where is his horse? I haven't got it.

MOLLY. It's in the library, where Miss Irene left it.

Bullock opens the LIBRARY DOOR. He looks in, and is startled at hearing a horse neighing. In the HALL Godfrey and Molly look at each other with understanding as the horse neighs again.

MOLLY (*triumphantly as she leaves*). Well—do you begin to get the idea?

The scene fades out and then the DRAWING ROOM fades in, showing Godfrey turning on the lights. He comes forward, as music is heard, and turns on a table light as Cornelia enters.

CORNELIA. Come here, my man. (*Music continues throughout.*)

A close-up next shows them near the WINDOW:

CORNELIA. Do you like your place here —I mean, so far as you've gone?

GODFREY. I find it very entertaining.

CORNELIA. Yes. We are a very entertaining family. You really think you're going to like it here? (*She is definitely provoked.*)

GODFREY. I must admit it's more desirable than living in a packing case on a city dump.

CORNELIA. Oh, that's where I met you, isn't it?

She moves through the room, Godfrey watching her.

CORNELIA. Yes—I remember now. We were playing a sort of a game—a scavenger hunt I think we called it.

GODFREY (*in a close-up*) is seen closely observing Cornelia.

CORNELIA'S VOICE. We needed a forgotten man. I asked you to go to the Waldorf-Ritz Hotel with me and—(*now seen standing close*)—I am just a little bit hazy as to just what happened after that.

GODFREY. I pushed you onto an ash pile.

CORNELIA (*blandly*). Oh, of course you did. It was very amusing. They were nice clean ashes.

GODFREY (*bowing*). I am very sorry, Miss.

CORNELIA (*seated now, laughing*). I didn't mind at all. It was very amusing. Have you a handkerchief?

GODFREY takes out a handkerchief, looking at Cornelia, who is now out of sight.

CORNELIA'S VOICE. There is a spot on my shoe. Will you see what you can do about it?

They look at each other intently (in close-ups), then we see Cornelia seated—Godfrey kneeling—wiping her shoe with his handkerchief.

CORNELIA. I could have you fired you know, but I like to see things wriggle. When I get through with you, you will go back to your packing case on the city dump and relish it. People don't make a practice of pushing Cornelia Bullock into ash piles.

A close view at the DOORWAY discloses Irene, who is listening to Cornelia's voice.

CORNELIA'S VOICE. I'll make your life so miserable—

We see Cornelia leaning forward and Godfrey on one knee. They look off at the DOORWAY where Irene appears again gazing at the scene and moving forward.

Godfrey is now standing—putting his handkerchief in his pocket. Cornelia rises as Irene approaches and sits down.

IRENE. Hello, Godfrey.

GODFREY. Good evening, Miss Irene.

IRENE. I like your new monkey suit.

GODFREY. Thank you for picking it out.

IRENE. You know, it fits you very well for a hand-me-down.

GODFREY. I'm more or less standard, Miss.

IRENE. How do you like my new pajamas?

GODFREY. I think they're very nice.

Godfrey goes out. Irene turns to Cornelia.

IRENE. I heard what you said to Godfrey.

CORNELIA. So what?

IRENE. So what—you leave him alone.

CORNELIA (*rising*). So who's going to make me leave him alone?

IRENE. If you don't you'll get a good sock from me.

CORNELIA. Oh, the physical type.

The sisters move about the room as they quarrel.

IRENE. What I say goes.

CORNELIA. Since when did you start falling in love with butlers?

IRENE (*she and Cornelia both looking furious*). I'm not falling in love with him. He's my protégé.

CORNELIA. Oh, your protégé. That's why you're picking out his suits for him. Suppose father hears about this. How long do you think Godfrey will last?

IRENE. Father isn't going to hear about it.

CORNELIA. You seem terribly sure of everything.

IRENE. If father hears about Godfrey, he's going to hear about you and that sappy college boy.

CORNELIA. I don't know what you're talking about, but if father does hear about it, I'm likely to do a little socking myself.

Cornelia moves away; Irene follows and faces her as Cornelia sits down. Soon Carlo appears in the background.

CORNELIA. So little Red Riding Hood didn't have enough feminine charm to trap a wolf her own age, so she fell in love with the butler and lived happily ever after on the ash pile—if you know what I mean.

IRENE. I know what you mean—if you know what I mean.

Carlo now appears, standing, book in hand.

CARLO. May I come in?

CORNELIA. You're in, aren't you?

CARLO. I've just been reading a very interesting book, "The Greeks of The Middle Ages."

CORNELIA. Irene would like that. You love the middle ages, don't you, dear?

At this point ANGELICA (out of sight) is heard talking baby talk. Then she appears with a dog in her arms, and approaches Carlo.

CARLO (*kissing her hand*). *Marta Gratia.*

ANGELICA. Oh, Carlo! Who's giving the concert tonight?

Bullock enters the drawing room.

CARLO. The great Koraninski.

ANGELICA. Pianist, isn't he?

CARLO. No—cellist.

ANGELICA. What's the difference? It's all music, isn't it? Oh! It's so nice to see you two girls having a pleasant chat. Or is it a pleasant chat?

BULLOCK. Well, well, well! Imagine the Bullocks gathered together all in one room.

ANGELICA. Oh, you mustn't forget Carlo.

BULLOCK (*in an expressive close-up— meaningfully*). I'm not going to forget Carlo.

CARLO (*now standing behind the seated Angelica*). Don't bother about me. I feel like one of the family.

Irene starts toward the doorway. Bullock stops her.

BULLOCK. Don't you go away. (*In a close-up, to Carlo*) You don't mind if I discuss a few family matters, do you, my boy?

CARLO. Oh no, not at all.

ANGELICA. Oh, Alexander—you're not going to bring up those sordid business matters again, I hope.

BULLOCK (*angrily*). I've just been going through the last month's bills and I find that you people have confused me with the Treasury Department.

CORNELIA. Oh, don't start that again, Dad.

BULLOCK. I don't mind giving the government sixty percent of what I make, but I can't do it when my family spends fifty percent.

IRENE. But why should the government get more money than your own family?

ANGELICA. That's what I want to know. Why should the Government get more than your own flesh and blood?

BULLOCK (*dryly—he knows he couldn't possibly explain to them*). Well, it's just a way they have of doing things.

We see Carlo standing back of Angelica in a close view. He drops his book, and cries out:

CARLO. Oh, money, money, money! the Frankenstein monster that destroys souls.

Bullock, looking at him, is startled. Angelica rises. Carlo has his hands over his face.

ANGELICA. Please don't say anything more about it. You're upsetting Carlo.

Bullock, angry, crosses over to Angelica, while Carlo is raving.

BULLOCK. We've got to come to an understanding right now. Either Carlo leaves or I am!

Carlo goes to the windows in the background.

ANGELICA. And what?

BULLOCK. Well, one of us has got to and that's all there is about it!

ANGELICA. Alexander, you're inebriated. You don't know what you're talking about.

Bullock's face shows that he is furious.

BULLOCK. Well, who would know what they're talking about, living with a bunch like this. There is one thing I do know—what this family needs is discipline. I've been a pretty patient man—but when people start riding horses up the front steps and parking them in the library, that's going a little bit too far.

Bullock has crossed to the doorway and addresses himself at this point to Irene.

IRENE. Horses?

ANGELICA (*rising*). Are you insinuating that I rode a horse up the front steps last night?

BULLOCK. Maybe that wasn't a horse I saw in the library this morning.

ANGELICA (*holding the dog, sits down*). Well, I'm positive I didn't ride a horse into the library because I didn't have my riding costume on and I hope you're not insinuating that I should ride a horse into the library without my riding costume on.

CORNELIA (*now seen in a close-up; seated*). It was Irene who rode the horse— up the front steps.

IRENE. What horse?

CORNELIA (*again visible, in a close-up*). Don't try to be innocent. I begged you not to do it.

Irene walks angrily over to Cornelia.

IRENE (*accusingly*). I didn't ride a horse —but if I did ride a horse— Who broke those windows on Fifth Avenue?

CORNELIA. What windows?

IRENE. You know what windows. And how about the college sap? Yah! Yah! Yah!

BULLOCK (*going over to them*). And I don't care who broke the horse or rode the windows up the steps or who yah-

yah-yahed—(*seen in a close-up now; excited*). —This family has got to settle down!

CARLO. Ooooh!

ANGELICA (*out of sight*). Will you stop bellowing! (*Seen standing; indignantly*) Look what you're doing to Carlo.

BULLOCK (*furious*). Hang Carlo!

Irene is now watching Godfrey at the DOORWAY as he brings a tray. She stops him and takes something from the tray.

IRENE. Did you make those yourself, Godfrey?

GODFREY. I helped.

IRENE. Oh, they must be wonderful. I'd like to help some time, if you'll let me.

GODFREY. I'd feel honored.

Now as the family is seated and standing about, Godfrey comes forward—Irene following. They come to Cornelia, while Bullock and Angelica are arguing in the background.

BULLOCK (*out of sight*). You might as well face the situation right now. I've been losing a lot of money lately.

ANGELICA (*out of sight*). You have?

BULLOCK (*now in the scene*). Yes, I have!

ANGELICA (*sitting down*). Maybe you left it in your other suit.

BULLOCK. If things keep on the way they're going now, it won't be long till I won't have another suit. (*He starts to go out.*)

Irene is watching as Godfrey serves Cornelia.

CORNELIA. Which one's poisoned? Thank you.

We see Godfrey with Irene and Cornelia; and the view expands as he brings the tray to Bullock and Angelica.

CORNELIA. While we're on the subject, how about this business of certain people picking up anybody they find on the city dump and dragging them into the house? For all we know, we might all be stabbed in the back some night and robbed.

We see a close-up of Irene—startled, angry. Godfrey is then seen serving Angelica from the tray.

ANGELICA. Who's going to stab who?

We see a close-up of CORNELIA seated—talking.

CORNELIA. We don't know anything about certain people. Someone should speak to Irene about her habit of picking up strays.

Godfrey is still serving Angelica.

ANGELICA. What's a stray?

We see IRENE (in a close-up)—furious.

IRENE. You shut up!

While Godfrey is holding the tray near Angelica, she looks up—startled.

ANGELICA. Me?

IRENE (in a closeup) whirls around.

IRENE. No. Cornelia.

CORNELIA (out of sight). I will not shut up.

Cornelia is seen seated as Irene comes over to her.

CORNELIA. My life is precious to me.

IRENE. Well, it won't be in a minute.

As Godfrey is waiting before Angelica, Carlo, standing in the background, starts toward Godfrey.

ANGELICA. Now, now, children— Come, Carlo, come and get some nice hors d'ouvres.

Irene is standing near Cornelia, who is talking insolently.

CORNELIA. I think we should get our help from employment agencies.

BULLOCK (in a close-up; looking toward Godfrey). I don't know but what I agree with Cornelia.

GODFREY (in a close-up) looks sideways at Bullock. Then we see IRENE (in a close-up) ready to cry.

ANGELICA (out of sight). Whatever are you all talking about?

Cornelia looks delighted. Irene, half crying, crosses the room to her father, and falls crying into his arms.

Now Angelica puts down the dog, goes to Bullock and Irene, and embraces her, while Carlo continues eating, undisturbed.

ANGELICA. You've upset Carlo and now you're upsetting Irene. Don't you remember her breakdown last summer?

CORNELIA (in a close-up). I certainly do. That's why I'm not paying any attention to this.

Godfrey is now serving Carlo in the background.

IRENE. Well, if mother can sponsor Carlo, why can't I sponsor Godfrey?

CORNELIA (out of sight). Godfrey knows I'm not being personal, but after all, none of us would like to wake up some morning stabbed to death.

ANGELICA (as Godfrey moves forward with the tray, Carlo following him for more food). You mustn't come between Irene and Godfrey. He's the only thing she's shown any affection for since her Pomeranian died last summer.

Irene drops down on the couch. Her mother picks up the dog and the view moves to Carlo seated on the opposite couch. Irene is still crying.

ANGELICA (going to Carlo and giving him the dog). Now, Irene, you mustn't have a spell. Carlo, quick! quick! A sofa cushion—here. (She takes a cushion from Carlo.) Come darling. Lift up your head now.

CORNELIA (as George approaches in the background). She's not having a spell. That's old stuff.

As Angelica is still bending over Irene, Irene cries out.

IRENE. Ooooh!

ANGELICA. Now, darling.

BULLOCK. What is all this nonsense?

Angelica is worried over Irene, who is now sobbing.

ANGELICA (*to Bullock*). Please be quiet. You never did understand women. Why don't you get the doctor?

IRENE. I don't want a doctor.

ANGELICA. Do you want an icebag?

IRENE. I don't want an ice-bag. I want to die!

ANGELICA. You mustn't do that now.

CORNELIA (*to George*). She makes me ill. Let's get out of here.

Carlo is now seated before the FIREPLACE, reading, while Angelica is fussing over Irene.

ANGELICA. Carlo—do the gorilla for Irene—it always amuses her, Carlo.

CARLO. I'm not in the mood.

ANGELICA. Stop eating hors d'ouvres and get in the mood. Here.

CARLO (*pettishly*). All right. I'll do it, but my heart won't be in it.

ANGELICA. Irene, be a good girl.

We see BULLOCK watching with utter amazement.

ANGELICA (*out of sight*). Sit up and look at Carlo. You know it always amuses you.

Angelica is now watching Carlo as he puts on his monkey act.

IRENE (*out of sight*). Ooooh!

ANGELICA. Go ahead!

We get a close view of BULLOCK watching—disgusted.

ANGELICA'S VOICE. Go on, Carlo.

The group before the FIREPLACE comes into view, Bullock watching as Carlo puts on the monkey act—Irene lying on the couch, her mother in the background.

ANGELICA. Look Irene—look at Carlo! Ain't that lovely. Isn't he clever, Irene? Come on—

And in successive close-ups we see: CARLO jumping on the couch; IRENE sitting up and staring; CARLO making funny noises; BULLOCK standing there, still more disgusted. This is followed by a full view of the room, with Carlo doing the monkey act and the others watching.

ANGELICA. Father, sit down now. (*Standing up*) Isn't that clever?

Now Carlo is jumping over tables and chairs amid Angelica's laughter as Godfrey enters from the hall, carrying a tray with decanter and glasses. Next, Carlo jumps toward Irene as she lies on the couch, following which he races around and starts toward the door.

IRENE. Ooooh!

ANGELICA (*out of sight*). Look! Ain't that funny? He's going to climb up the door! Look!

Carlo climbs the doors in the background, swinging like a monkey, laughing.

IRENE. He frightens me.

ANGELICA. No, no, darling. You mustn't be frightened. He isn't a real gorilla— he's just playing.

Carlo drops, comes into the room, passes Bullock and Godfrey and goes toward Angelica.

ANGELICA (*laughing*). Darling—look at Carlo!

Carlo picks up her dog and begins looking comically for fleas on the animal amid more laughter.

ANGELICA (*out of sight*). Look darling, isn't he clever?

But Irene is again crying and Angelica bends over her solicitously. Finally Bullock, who has been standing with Godfrey, bursts out in disgust.

BULLOCK. Why don't you stop imitating a gorilla and try to imitate a man?

We see CARLO suddenly looking toward him and dropping the dog.

ANGELICA. You wouldn't know an artist if one came up and bit you.

Bullock addresses himself to Godfrey as he takes the cocktail tray from him, and starts to leave the room.

BULLOCK. This family don't need any stimulant. I'll be in my room and you can repeat this order in thirty minutes. Some day I'm going gorilla hunting—and I won't miss.

We see CARLO at the couch putting on his shoes, and then Angelica bending over Irene, who has stopped crying.

IRENE. Has Cornelia gone?

At the DOORWAY Godfrey turns to leave.

ANGELICA (out of sight). Yes, darling. She's gone.

IRENE (also out of sight), Where's Godfrey?

ANGELICA's VOICE. He's right here. Don't go away, Godfrey. (Godfrey starts back.)

CARLO (standing up). We'll be late for the concert.

ANGELICA. Get my things. I'll be right with you. Godfrey's right here, darling. Godfrey! Come over here so Irene can look at you.

Godfrey approaches Irene.

ANGELICA. Here's Godfrey, darling.

IRENE. Where?

ANGELICA. Right here—look! Say hello to Irene so she'll know who you are.

GODFREY. Hello.

IRENE. Oh, hello, Godfrey.

ANGELICA. And he's promised to stay on, haven't you, Godfrey?

GODFREY. If I'm wanted.

ANGELICA. Of course you're wanted. Isn't he, Irene?

IRENE. Yes. Go away.

ANGELICA. Yes, darling—I'm going. Take good care of her. Yes, Carlo, I'm coming. Good-bye, darling—good-bye.

IRENE (whispering to Godfrey). I'm not really having a spell.

GODFREY. I beg your pardon.

IRENE. I'm not really having a spell.

GODFREY. I'm sorry, but I couldn't quite hear.

He bends close to her as she whispers.

IRENE. I said—I'm not really having a spell. (She kisses him.)

Godfrey straightens up, bows, and leaves. She looks after him.

We get a close view in the PANTRY of Molly busy with glasses as she sends them down the dumbwaiter. She opens the door and addresses the unseen cook.

MOLLY (calling out). Hey, cook, you'd better put this back on the fire. It looks like we've lost most of our customers.

She closes the door as Godfrey enters at the next door.

MOLLY. What's the matter, handsome. Did something frighten you?

GODFREY. What kind of a family am I up against?

MOLLY (dryly). There's some things even I can't answer.

GODFREY. Do they go on this way all the time?

MOLLY (blandly). Oh—this is just a quiet evening.

GODFREY. A quiet evening?

MOLLY (carelessly as he goes out). If I were you I'd get rid of that lip rouge. It makes you look a little like Cupid.

Irene comes in.

MOLLY. You'll find Godfrey in his room.

IRENE. How did you know I wanted to see Godfrey?

MOLLY (airily). I don't know. It just came over me. (Irene goes out.)

A close view in GODFREY's ROOM shows Godfrey wiping his mouth. Irene enters.

GODFREY. You—you can't come in here.

IRENE (moving across the room; Molly seen in the background). Why not? It's our house, isn't it? And after all—one room is just like any other room—besides, I want to talk.

Godfrey appears embarrassed.

GODFREY. I'm terribly sorry but we—we can't talk here.

Irene is now seated on his bed.

IRENE (*pettishly*). Don't you think it's rather indecent of you to order me out after you kissed me?

GODFREY. After I kissed you—did you say?

IRENE (*blithely*). It's funny. This morning you were sitting on my bed and now I'm sitting on yours.

GODFREY. We'll overlook that startling coincidence. (*Pointing to a chair*) will you—er—sit over here?

IRENE. If the bed's not very comfortable to sit on, I'll get you another.

GODFREY (*uneasily*). We'll have our talk here.

IRENE (*sitting down*). Now that I'm your sponsor, if you want a new bed you can have it.

GODFREY (*standing; embarrassed*). The bed's very comfortable, thank you. Much more so than I am at the moment.

IRENE. Any time you're uncomfortable—you just let me know.

GODFREY (*wondering at her*). Er—thank you. Hasn't anyone ever told you about —certain proprieties?

IRENE. Oh, you use such lovely big words! I like big words. What does it mean?

GODFREY. Well, I'll try to simplify it. Hasn't your mother or anyone ever explained to you that some things are proper and some things are not?

IRENE. No. She hasn't. She rambles on quite a bit, but then she never says anything.

GODFREY. Then—you want me to remain on here as butler—don't you?

IRENE. Oh, of course!

GODFREY. Well, I want to justify your faith in me by being a very good butler—and in time perhaps filling the void created by the death of your late lamented Pomeranian.

IRENE. Oh, I've forgotten all about him. He had fleas anyway. Besides you're different. You use big words and you're much cuter.

GODFREY. May I tell you a story?

IRENE. I'd love it.

GODFREY. Once there was a very sentimental little girl, with a very kind heart. And she helped a man who was very grateful. Then she became a nuisance and undid all the fine work she had done.

IRENE. Is it someone you know?

Godfrey rising from beside her, Irene rises and follows him to the door.

GODFREY. Her name is Irene Bullock. And if she were a smart little girl, she would pick out some nice young chap in her own social set and marry him and live happily ever after—and never, never, never enter the butler's room again.

IRENE. You mean I never can come in here again?

GODFREY. Never.

IRENE. But when can we talk?

GODFREY. When I am serving breakfast in the morning, I can say, "Good morning, Miss Irene"—and you can say "Good morning, Godfrey"—but you must never come into my room again.

IRENE (*furiously*). Oh! You'll be sorry!

GODFREY. I'm only trying to be helpful. (*He gets her out of his room, and closes the door.*)

IRENE (*now out of sight*). You're being mean. You're being mean! I'll do something—you just wait and you'll be sorry—you'll be sorry!

As Godfrey listens to her voice, the scene fades out.

PART THREE

A close view in the LIVING ROOM fades in, disclosing Carlo seated at the piano in the foreground playing and singing, Angelica seated in the background.

CARLO. Otchi tchornia! Otchi tchornia! Otchi tchornia!

A closeup of ANGELICA shows her seated, knitting, and looking toward him, enchanted.

CARLO (*again seen playing*). Otchi tchornia! Otchi tchornia!

ANGELICA (*now again seen*). That's a very pretty tune, Carlo. What's the name of it?

CARLO (*seen in a close-up; explaining*). Otchi tchornia! Otchi tchornia— Otchi tchornia.

ANGELICA'S VOICE. Oh! That's the name, too. (*In a close-up*) I thought it was just the words. (*Then as we see them both*) I like it because the words are all the same. It makes it so easy to remember. That's probably why the Star Spangled Banner is so confusing. Nobody seems to know the words.

Godfrey enters carrying a box of roses and a vase, and looks around.

ANGELICA (*out of sight*). Except Godfrey. He seems to know everything. (*Seeing him*) Do you know the words, Godfrey?

Godfrey comes forward carrying flowers and vase as the view moves with him through the room to Angelica. We now see Cornelia and George seated in the background.

GODFREY. The words?

ANGELICA (*out of sight*). Yes, yes. The Star Spangled Banner. Nobody seems to know the words. Do you know them, Godfrey?

GODFREY. I suppose I know as many as the average person.

ANGELICA. Oh, I feel ashamed of myself. I should know them all of course, because after all, my ancestors came over on a boat—not the Mayflower, but the boat after that. What did your ancestors come over on, Godfrey?

GODFREY. As far as I know they've always been here.

ANGELICA. They weren't Indians, Godfrey?

GODFREY. One can never be sure of one's ancestors.

ANGELICA. Well, you know, you have rather high cheek bones.

GODFREY. Yes, ma'am—thank you, ma'am— These flowers came— (*As Irene comes forward, stops, and looks*) for Miss Irene. Where shall I put them?

ANGELICA. You'd better ask her. There she is. Carlo! Did you notice his cheek bones?

GODFREY (*now close to Irene, the two of them in a close-up*). These flowers just came for you, Miss. Where shall I put them?

IRENE. What difference does it make where one puts flowers, when one's heart is breaking.

GODFREY. Yes, Miss. Shall I put them on the piano?

IRENE. Life is but an empty bubble.

ANGELICA (*out of sight*). You don't sound very cheerful (*now seen, mildly disturbed*) for a girl who is giving a tea party.

Cornelia and George now appear seated in the foreground playing backgammon, Irene standing in the background.

IRENE. Why should anyone be cheerful?

CORNELIA. Oh, is Irene giving a tea party?

IRENE (*coldly*). You're not invited.

CORNELIA. I'll invite myself. (*Gaily to George*) Let's stick around, George. (*We see Godfrey arranging the roses as though absorbed in his work.*)

GEORGE (*out of sight*). Sure—why not?

IRENE (*standing by the grill; meaningfully*). All I have to say is that some people will be sorry some day.

ANGELICA (*out of sight*). Naturally, everybody will be sorry some day.

CARLO, who has been playing all the time and continues to play, is seen at the piano.

CARLO. For what?

IRENE. Some people will know for what —and then—it will be too late.

CARLO (*helplessly, plaintively*). This conversation is very confusing.

ANGELICA. Now, now, Irene—you mustn't confuse Carlo—(*now out of sight, since we see only Godfrey putting roses in the vase*)—he's practicing.

CORNELIA (*laughing suddenly*). Do you know any good funeral music, Carlo?

IRENE. Shut up!

CORNELIA. Are you acting for anybody in particular? Godfrey might be interested if he would only turn around and look. I remember that pose so well.

We get a close view of IRENE posed by a pillar—tragically. Godfrey, studiously ignoring them, continues to arrange the roses in the vase.

CORNELIA'S VOICE. I learned it in dramatic school. It's number eight, isn't it?

GEORGE (*also out of sight at this point*). Yeah—that's number eight, all right.

CORNELIA'S VOICE (*as we see Godfrey going about his work indifferently*). Am I spoiling your act, dear?

Irene comes to Cornelia and George angrily.

IRENE. I'll spoil something of yours some day—and it won't be your act. (*She moves angrily away.*)

Godfrey has the roses in the vase, and the view moves with him across the room as he speaks to Angelica, Irene in the background.

GODFREY. Do you suppose Miss Irene would like sandwiches served in here or shall I create a sort of buffet?

ANGELICA. Where do you want the sandwiches served, Irene?

IRENE (*disconsolately*). What is food?

ANGELICA (*Irene now at the doorway, Godfrey moving away from Angelica*). Something you eat, silly. Do you want the sandwiches served in here or don't you?

Godfrey approaches her, then passes her, and goes out.

IRENE. What difference does it make? Some people do just as they like with other people's lives and it doesn't seem to make any difference. (*Cornelia, out of sight, laughs.*)

Angelica laughs. Irene, at the doorway, looks off, following Godfrey's departure, and the scene dissolves into a close view of the ROOM with men and girls leaning on the piano, and a man and a girl playing. The scene then enlarges to include Angelica and others seated at a card table in the foreground.

ANGELICA. What did I call?

GUEST. Five hearts.

ANGELICA. Oh, was it hearts? I meant spades. I can't change, can I. That music has me so confused. Carlo, please.

Irene comes to the foreground among the guests. Van Rumpel approaches and puts his arm about her.

VAN RUMPEL. Hi yah, Irene. Why the shroud?

IRENE. Listen, Van Rumpel, just because some people have a million dollars doesn't mean that they can put their arms around other people.

VAN RUMPEL (*affecting a mock chill*). Brrrr! Where's the bar?

We see Cornelia and George seated on the COUCH as Godfrey comes in, serves them sandwiches and leaves them.

CORNELIA (*to Van Rumpel; cattily*). Don't take her seriously, Charlie. She's been having servant problems lately.

Godfrey comes past Irene carrying the tray.

IRENE. No, thank you. I'm not hungry. (*She follows him as he goes off.*)

Men and girls are seen leaning on the piano—talking, laughing, Godfrey serving them. Irene approaches him, watching. Godfrey presents the tray again.

IRENE. No, thank you.

Godfrey comes over to serve the bridge players, Irene following him.

WOMAN PLAYER. Four clubs.

ANGELICA. No—just a minute Godfrey. By—

At the CROWDED DOORWAY to the HALL, a young man, Tommy Gray, enters, stops and calls, and looks around.

TOMMY. Hello, everybody!

PEOPLE. Hello, Tommy!

ANGELICA looks past GODFREY as he leans toward her with his tray.

ANGELICA. Oh! Tommy Gray! (*Godfrey looks around—startled.*) What's happened to you, Godfrey? Are you ill?

We see Godfrey serving other guests, moving about, as Tommy approaches Angelica.

ANGELICA. Come over here, Tommy, and give Angelica a hug. How's everything in Boston? All the beans and things?

TOMMY (*kissing her hand*). We're rounding them up and putting them in cans as rapidly as possible.

TOMMY (*as Irene is seen standing near the card players*). Hello, Irene, how are you?

IRENE (*morosely*). What does it matter how I am? The—(*out of sight as we see Godfrey serving the guests but glancing around at the group at the card table*)—whole thing is only— (*Irene seen again, being held by the friendly Tommy*)—a delusion.

TOMMY. What thing?

IRENE. You wouldn't understand. (*And she moves away.*)

TOMMY (*bringing a chair over and sitting down*). How about something to eat?

ANGELICA. Oh, Godfrey! Godfrey! Bring Mr. Gray a sandwich.

Godfrey brings the tray up behind Tommy.

ANGELICA (*annoyed*). Oh, come around here. Mr. Gray's not an acrobat. Whatever has come over you? You're beginning to act like the rest of the family.

Angelica questions Godfrey as he leans over with the tray. Tommy looks up, and is startled as he recognizes Godfrey, who looks meaningly at Tommy and leaves.

TOMMY. Hey! Wait a minute!

ANGELICA. What's the trouble?

Tommy without answering, looks around, calls after Godfrey, rises and follows him. Tommy stops Godfrey in the doorway.

TOMMY. Godfrey Parke! You old mug.

ANGELICA (*looking after Tommy*). You know Godfrey?

TOMMY (*standing by Godfrey*). Know him? We went to Harvard together.

A close-up of IRENE shows her staring at them—startled.

GODFREY'S VOICE. I'm afraid you've confused me with someone else, sir. I'm Smith. (*Meaningly*) Remember.

TOMMY. Sure you're Smith—but we did go to college together—

CORNELIA (*seen sitting with George; amused*). Imagine a butler with a college education.

A close-up shows Angelica and the man who sits by her side staring.

TOMMY'S VOICE. He's not really the butler?

CORNELIA'S VOICE. And a very good one.

TOMMY (*as Godfrey stands by him, looking embarrassed*). You mean this is not a gag just for my benefit?

GODFREY. Mr. Gray neglected to tell you that when we were in Harvard together —I was his—(*out of sight, as we see Cornelia, amused, starting forward*)— his valet.

CORNELIA. Was he a good servant, Tommy?

A close-up shows the two men whispering, Tommy amused and puzzled.

TOMMY. Excellent. (*To Godfrey*) What's the idea?

GODFREY (*bowing*). I'll tell you later. Mr. Gray never complained.

TOMMY. When? (*Recovering.*) No. I had very few complaints about Godfrey's work.

GODFREY (*whispering to him*). Tomorrow. That's my day off.

CORNELIA (*coming over to them*). Strange you never gave Mr. Gray as a reference.

GODFREY. Well, I left Mr. Gray under very unusual circumstances.

ANGELICA (*calling from the table; curious*). What circumstances?

GODFREY. I'd rather Mr. Gray told you about that.

ANGELICA'S VOICE. Well, come here. Don't go away—don't go away. Come here and tell us all about it. (*In a close-up; concerned*) You know, Tommy, Godfrey is a very mysterious person.

We get a close-up of Irene looking on, smiling.

ANGELICA'S VOICE. Nobody seems to know anything about him. Don't go away, Godfrey. (*We see the two men and Cornelia standing.*)

TOMMY. No, don't go away, Godfrey. You see, I—I didn't want to say anything about this, but you see Godfrey had been working for us as a butler and—what not—and things had been going along very well, when—(*out of sight, as we see Irene watching*)—when all of a sudden—it happened. (*As we see the group moving along*) Just like that. You're sure you want me to tell

all this, Godfrey? Well, you see, as I said, he'd been working—(*out of sight as we see Angelica and the man listening eagerly*)—for us for some time when one day, he came to—(*we see Irene listening*)—me and said—(*stalling*) Mr. Gray he said—(*Tommy is now seen in the group that watches him*)— I trust my work has always been satisfactory, he said. I said—(*out of sight, as we see Angelica deeply interested and the man by her side very much amused*)—I said, I've never had more satisfactory—(*Irene watching*)—work in all my life. (*We see Tommy with Godfrey trying to keep his countenance.*)— He said, Thank you, Mr. Gray. He was always a very courteous man.

ANGELICA. Godfrey is still extremely courteous. Especially in the morning.

Cornelia comes to them, a light in her eyes.

TOMMY. It's not much of a story—maybe we'd better skip it.

CORNELIA (*brightly*). Oh, Tommy, come on and finish it. You can't stop in the middle.

TOMMY (*at sea, uncomfortably*). Let me see. Where was I?

CORNELIA (*sweetly*). You were telling us how very polite Godfrey was.

ANGELICA. Yes—and that's where I said that Godfrey was still very polite.

GODFREY. Thank you, Mrs. Bullock. It's a pleasure to have you say so publicly.

ANGELICA (*contentedly*). That's my nature, Godfrey. I'll never say anything behind your back that I won't say in public.

TOMMY. That's what I admire about you, Angelica, very much.— Well, anyhow, Godfrey came up to me and said, "I trust my work has been satisfactory." That was about the gist of it, wasn't it, Godfrey?

GODFREY. Those may not have been my exact words, but that was about the gist of it.

CORNELIA (*impatiently, as some men in*

the background laugh). All right. We'll settle for that. You said he was very satisfactory and he said "thank you" and then what?

TOMMY. Naturally I had to take an attitude.

ANGELICA. You don't make sense. What kind of an attitude?

TOMMY'S VOICE (*as we see Irene watching eagerly*). It was the only kind I could take toward a faithful servant— (*We see him talking very seriously.*)— but Godfrey decided in favor of his wife and five children.

A close-up shows IRENE terribly startled.

ANGELICA'S VOICE. Five children?

A close-view shows GODFREY startled, and looking in the direction of Irene.

ANGELICA'S VOICE. What?

Irene starts to go toward them.

TOMMY. Five.

ANGELICA. My—my! Was his wife an Indian woman?

TOMMY. I believe she was rather dark. We used to take her on hunting trips to stalk the game.

Irene goes to Godfrey—horrified.

IRENE. Why Godfrey! Why didn't you tell me you had five children?

ANGELICA. Well, why shouldn't Godfrey have five children? If a woman in Canada can have five children, why can't Godfrey? (*Amid laughter from the guests*) So, you see!

GODFREY (*to Irene*). I owe the creation of my family to Mr. Gray's generosity.

IRENE. Well, if other people can have five children, so can other people.

ANGELICA. Of course they can, but I think two are plenty. And strangely enough—Bullock agrees with me.

IRENE (*having made up her mind; she is shocked and intense*). Listen, everybody. I want to make an announcement. I want to announce something.

GEORGE. Well, what are you going to announce?

IRENE. I want to announce my engagement. I'm going to be married.

GUESTS. Married? To whom? You're going to be married? Married? etc. etc.

IRENE. You'll find out soon enough.

GIRL. Not to Charlie Van Rumpel?

IRENE. Yes. Charlie Van Rumpel. Where is he?

GUESTS. No? Where's Charlie? With all that money! Ooooh!

GIRL. He's at the bar. Let's go and get him.

IRENE. I'm not marrying for money.

We see Charlie and others drinking as two men come to him.

CHARLIE (*to the men*). I've had my arms around her plenty of times before, but this is the first time I ever felt that chill September breeze.

VOICES. Paging Van Rumpel! Paging Van Rumpel!

MAN. Congratulations, old boy.

CHARLIE. Congratulations about what?

MAN. Your engagement, you slug.

CHARLIE. What engagement?

MAN. Why, you're engaged to Irene, aren't you?

CHARLIE. Am I?

MEN. Aw, come on—don't play gaga! Come on!

Now Tommy is standing by the card table, men and girls crowding around Irene and Charlie, Irene clinging to him. He is dazed, puzzled.

CHARLIE. I hear we're engaged.

IRENE. You said it.

CHARLIE. When did it happen?

IRENE. Just now.

ANGELICA (*to Tommy*). What's all the excitement about? What did she say?

TOMMY. I think she's gone and got herself engaged.

ANGELICA (*calmly*). Oh—has she—again? It must be that nice boy in the brown suit. Let's congratulate them.

Angelica goes over to a slender boy.

ANGELICA. This is thrilling. You're a lucky boy. (*The boy looks at her, speechless.*)

In a GROUP we see one man mightily amused as the scatter-brained Angelica is talking to another man.

MAN. I know I am—I'm not Van Rumpel.

ANGELICA. You're not? Which one is he?

MAN. There he is.

ANGELICA. You'll forgive me, I hope.

Irene and Charlie are now being congratulated by a crowd as Angelica comes to them.

ANGELICA. You're Van Rumpel, aren't you?

CHARLIE. Oh, yes—yes.

ANGELICA. Well, you'll take good care of her, won't you?

CHARLIE. I imagine so. My mind's a little cloudy, Irene. I don't even remember proposing.

IRENE. You're always proposing.

CHARLIE. Which one did you take me up on?

IRENE. All of them. (*The crowd laughs uproariously.*)

Now Cornelia faces Irene and Charlie, the others listening.

CORNELIA. How do you suppose Godfrey will feel about your engagement?

IRENE. What's Godfrey got to do with it?

CORNELIA. I wonder.

IRENE (*angrily*). You mind your own business.

We see Godfrey carrying a tray with glasses into the room as the crowd moves to the next room. A man takes the tray from him and carries it to the crowd as George speaks to Godfrey.

GEORGE. All right, Godfrey, let's have those. Come on, everybody. All aboard that's going aboard.

CORNELIA. Aren't you going to congratulate Irene, Godfrey? She just got herself engaged.

GODFREY. I'd be very happy to.

ANGELICA. Godfrey!

Godfrey passes Cornelia, and the moving scene brings him through the crowd to Irene.

ANGELICA'S VOICE. Congratulate Irene!

GODFREY (*solemnly*). May I congratulate you, Miss Irene. I wish you all the happiness in the world.

Irene goes through the hall crying, runs up the stairs, and sits down.

ANGELICA'S VOICE (*coming over*). Just let her alone. She'll be all right in a minute.

Then Charlie and Angelica appear, talking in the crowd.

CHARLIE. Is she mad at me?

ANGELICA. She's not mad at anyone. Don't you know women always cry at their own engagements and other people's weddings.

CHARLIE. Why?

ANGELICA (*going out*). I don't know why—but they just do.

Irene is seated on the stairs as Angelica comes to her. Bullock enters a moment later.

ANGELICA. Irene is so peculiar. She always shouts when she wins and cries when she's happy. Oh, Alexander! You missed all the excitement.

BULLOCK. What's going on?

ANGELICA. Let me think. I knew what it was I wanted to tell you but it slipped my mind.

BULLOCK. What's the matter with Irene?

ANGELICA. Oh yes. That's it. Irene has got herself engaged.

BULLOCK. To whom?

ANGELICA. I don't know—Van something. I think it's that boy with his arm around that girl in pink. He's got lots of money.

BULLOCK. He'll need it.

We see Tommy and Godfrey talking in the crowd, Cornelia watching them closely.

TOMMY. Well, Godfrey, let's you and I have a good cry. How about lunch at my hotel tomorrow?

GODFREY. I guess so. (*Carefully, as he is being observed*) Would you prefer a soda or ginger ale?

TOMMY. Both. Twelve o'clock?

GODFREY. Very good, sir.

Bullock and his wife are talking in the HALL as Godfrey comes through and goes out and Irene, seen through the balustrade on the stairs, is crying.

BULLOCK. Well, if you can just make up your mind just who she is going to marry, I'd like to meet the guy.

ANGELICA. I don't know, Alexander. It's one of those boys in there. Come along.

BULLOCK. All right.

The scene fades out.

PART FOUR

A close view in the BREAKFAST ROOM fades in, disclosing Bullock seated at the table as Godfrey enters.

GODFREY. You're not eating well this morning, sir.

BULLOCK. You notice everything.

GODFREY. Business troubles, sir?

BULLOCK. What made you ask that?

GODFREY. Well sir, butlers can't help picking up scraps of news, shall we say.

BULLOCK (*eating*). We shan't say anything about it.

GODFREY. I thought I might be of some help, sir. I dabbled in the market at one time.

BULLOCK (*dryly*). One dabbler in the family is enough.

GODFREY. Very good, sir. Eggs?

BULLOCK. No, thank you. Godfrey, you seem to be a pretty good sort. Have you noticed anything queer about me lately?

GODFREY. Nothing particularly, sir.

BULLOCK. I sometimes wonder whether my whole family has gone mad or whether it's me.

GODFREY. I know just how you feel, sir. I've felt that way many times since I've been here.

BULLOCK. Then, why do you stay here? I have to—you don't.

GODFREY. It's much more comfortable than living in a packing box on the city dump, sir— Besides—I'm rather proud of my job here.

BULLOCK. You're proud of being a butler?

GODFREY. I'm proud of being a good butler, sir. (*Starting to pour coffee*) And I may add, sir—a butler has to be good to hold his job here.

BULLOCK (*puzzled*). Say—who are you?

GODFREY. I'm just a nobody, sir. More coffee?

The scene dissolves to a COCKTAIL BAR, Tommy seated in the foreground as Godfrey approaches.

TOMMY. Godfrey! here I am. (*Godfrey sees him.*) Turned up at last, eh? I'd begun to think you'd fallen down the kitchen sink.

GODFREY (*shaking hands*). Sorry I'm late, Tommy. It's hard to make beds when they're full of people. (*He sits down.*)

TOMMY. Waiter! You seem to do everything but put out the cat.

GODFREY. I'd do that, too, only we have no cat.

TOMMY (*as the waiter arrives*). The same for me. (*Jovially*) What will you have, Jarvis, my man?

GODFREY. Make it a rousing old lemonade.

TOMMY (*facetiously*). Lemonade? You're sure you can handle it?

GODFREY. Oh yes. I'm the type that can take it or leave it alone. You see, I'm a working man and I have to keep my wits about me.

TOMMY. I'm beginning to wonder if you've got any left at all. Don't avoid the issue. I've been sitting here like a snoopy old maid with her ears flapping in the breeze, waiting to hear the dirt.

GODFREY. What dirt would you like to hear?

TOMMY. Well, when I wander into a Fifth Avenue asylum and see one of the Parke Parkes of Boston serving hors d'houvres, I think I'm entitled to a pardonable curiosity.

GODFREY. Why tell you something that you won't understand? Tommy—you've fallen off so many polo ponies that your brains are scrambled.

TOMMY. But I still want to know why you're buttling when your family is telling everybody that you're in South America doing something about rubber, or sheep or something.

GODFREY. The family has to say something to save its face. You know the Parkes disgrace very easily.

TOMMY. I'd like to see their faces when they find out that you're a butler.

GODFREY. They're not going to find it out.

TOMMY. All right, they're not going to find it out—but come to the point.

GODFREY (*thoughtfully*). Well, there isn't much of a point. You remember the little incident up in Boston?

TOMMY. You still have that woman on your mind?

GODFREY. No, not any more—but I was pretty bitter at the time, so I gave her everything I had—and just disappeared. You know, the Parkes were never educated to face life. We've been puppets for ten generations.

TOMMY. And?

GODFREY. Tommy, it's surprising how fast you can go down hill when you begin to feel sorry for yourself. And boy—did I feel sorry for myself! So I went down to the East River one night, thinking I'd just—slide in and get it over with. I met some fellows living there—on the city dump. They were people who were fighting it out and not complaining. I never got as far as the river.

A close-up at the BAR shows Cornelia and George seated. She looks off and turns to George.

CORNELIA. Will you do me a big favor?

GEORGE. Who do you want killed?

CORNELIA. I'll do my own killing. Just go around the corner and telephone this place and ask for Tommy Gray. When you get him on the wire, keep him there.

GEORGE (*rising*). What's this all about?

CORNELIA. Don't ask too many questions.

GEORGE. Okay. (*He goes out.*)

A close-up at the TABLE shows Tommy and Godfrey seated—smoking.

TOMMY. And so, out of the ruins of Godfrey Parke a new edifice has sprung up in the form of Godfrey Smith.

GODFREY. And I may add—the edifice is going to keep on springing.

TOMMY. You intend to remain a butler?

GODFREY. No. I have some other ideas in mind, but you wouldn't understand those, either, so we won't go into that.

TOMMY. Will you do me a favor?

GODFREY. Maybe.

TOMMY. I have a friend in town—a very eminent brain specialist—I'd like him to examine you.

GODFREY. I'll submit to an examination —if you will also.

TOMMY (shaking hands). That's a bet.

A waiter approaches the table.

WAITER. Are you Mr. Gray?

TOMMY. Yes.

WAITER. You're wanted on the phone.

TOMMY. The phone—what the— Back in a minute, Godfrey.

Tommy rises from the table, leaving Godfrey seated, and goes down the stairs. Cornelia comes up the stairs and sits down beside Godfrey.

CORNELIA. Well, the mystery is solved.

GODFREY. Mystery?

CORNELIA. Yes. Now I know what a butler does on his day off. When you worked for Mr. Gray, were the two of you always so chummy?

GODFREY. You see—I worked for Mr. Gray a long time and—we got to be —er—

CORNELIA. That was under the name of Smith, wasn't it? Or—did I hear him mention the name of Parke?

GODFREY. He may have said that—we used to take long walks in the park. It was a sort of a custom.

CORNELIA. Oh, I see. Well, if you can be so chummy with the Grays, why can't you be chummy with the Bullocks?

GODFREY. I try to keep my place.

CORNELIA. Why? You're very attractive, you know.

GODFREY. As a butler?

CORNELIA. No—as a Smith. You're a rotten butler.

GODFREY. Sorry.

CORNELIA (smiling). Are we going to be friends?

GODFREY. I feel that on my day off, I should have the privilege of choosing my friends.

CORNELIA. You can't go on like this forever. You really like me and you're afraid to admit it.

GODFREY. Do you want me to tell you what I really think of you?

CORNELIA. Please do.

GODFREY. As Smith or—as a butler?

CORNELIA. Choose your own weapons.

GODFREY. You won't hold it against me?

CORNELIA. It's your day off.

GODFREY. Very well.—You fall into the unfortunate category I would call the Park Avenue brat—a spoiled child who has grown up in ease and luxury, who always had her own way and whose misdirected energies are so childish that they hardly deserve the comment even of a butler—on his off Thursday.

They rise as Tommy comes from the stairs.

CORNELIA (rising; furious). Thank you for a very lovely portrait.

TOMMY. Hey! Cornelia—what are you doing here?

CORNELIA. Godfrey and I were discussing tomorrow's menu. (She starts to leave.)

TOMMY. Don't run away.

CORNELIA. I'm in an awfully big hurry. Good-bye. I'll see you down by the ashpile. (She leaves them.)

TOMMY. What did she mean by that?

GODFREY. That's a little joke we have between us.

TOMMY. Oh, I see—a joking butler. What's the matter with that stuff—did it turn your stomach.

GODFREY. No. I think I'll switch. I'm more in the mood.

TOMMY. Now we're getting somewhere. Waiter! Another one of those.

The scene dissolves to the KITCHEN, with Molly seated—darning—as footsteps are heard. Irene enters, carrying a vase of flowers.

IRENE (*coming forward*). He's not back yet, is he?

MOLLY. Not yet.

IRENE. Would you mind putting these flowers in his room? I can't go in there any more.

MOLLY. I can't either.

IRENE. You won't tell him they're from me, will you?

MOLLY. If you don't want me to.

IRENE. I don't want him to know. It's his—do you always sew his buttons on?

MOLLY. Sometimes.

IRENE. I'd like to sew his buttons on sometimes when they come off. I wouldn't mind at all.

MOLLY. He doesn't lose very many.

IRENE. He's very tidy, isn't he?

MOLLY. Yes. He's very tidy.

Irene sits down by Molly.

IRENE. What does he do on his day off?

MOLLY. He never tells me.

IRENE. Oh, he's probably sitting somewhere with some woman on his lap. He's the meanest man I know.

MOLLY (*feelingly*). I think he's very mean.

IRENE. I suppose he's sitting somewhere with somebody on his lap that doesn't care for him at all. As far as I know

maybe his children are there too, calling him—calling him.

We see Molly with Irene, crying.

IRENE. Oh, I can't bear it.

MOLLY (*going into the pantry*). Please don't.

In the PANTRY: Molly appears first, she is crying. Irene follows her—crying. A shadow appears at the door. There is a sound of whistling. Then Godfrey enters whistling. He is drunk and cheerful.

IRENE. You too? Oh, Molly, I know exactly how you feel.

GODFREY. Good evening. How about a quartette?

The girls are crying. When they see him, Molly goes out. Godfrey sings and dances —as Irene also runs out. The scene moves with him as he goes across to his door.

GODFREY (*singing blithely*). Ladies!
"For tomorrow may bring sorrow
So tonight let us be gay!"

We see Angelica in the living room, settled by the FIREPLACE and sewing as Carlo is reading aloud to her.

CARLO (*reading*).
" 'Courage!' he said,
And pointed toward the land,
'This mounting wave will roll
us shoreward soon.'
And in the afternoon they came unto a land
In which it seemed always afternoon."

Irene enters and sits down crying.

ANGELICA. Carlo!

CARLO (*continuing to read*).
"All round the coast the languid air did swoon—"

ANGELICA. What's the matter, darling?

IRENE. Nothing.

ANGELICA. She's been out in the kitchen eating onions again.

CARLO. I like onions. They make me sleep.

ANGELICA. Irene loves onions. When she was a little girl she was always stealing onions from the ice-box. Do you know, sometimes I wonder if my children are all there.

CARLO (*resuming his reading*):
"And like a downward smoke,
The slender stream
Along the cliff to fall and pause and
    fall did seem."

Irene rises and goes out, and the scene dissolves to Godfrey's room. We see him (in a close-up) at the MIRROR fixing his tie and whistling. The scene expands as he goes to the door—drunk—and opens it. The view follows him through the next room, where he puts things on a large tray. At this point Cornelia appears at the stairs in the background; we see her look in his direction and back up the stairs. Then we see her watching in the PANTRY—partly hidden—as Godfrey, fixing a cocktail tray, carries it whistling.

GODFREY. Good evening. (*He opens the door and goes out.*)

A close view of a CORNER OF A ROOM shows Godfrey entering with a large tray, whistling. He removes glasses as Cornelia enters behind him.

CORNELIA (*rudely*). I thought I told you to send that grey satin evening dress to the cleaners?

GODFREY. Gray satin?

CORNELIA. Why can't you do as you're told?

GODFREY. 'S a pleasure. (*He goes out. She starts to the door.*)

The DRAWING ROOM: Angelica is seated with a paper as Godfrey enters. Carlo is on the couch, with a paper over his face.

ANGELICA. It seems to me that every time you pick up a paper, somebody is being murdered or something. Imagine a man drowning his wife in the bathtub?

CARLO. Maybe it's the only way he could get her to take a bath.

ANGELICA (*as Godfrey moves forward; dotingly*). If anyone ever drowned my "booful" in the bath tub, his mama would be very, very cross, yes she would.

Godfrey turns on the light at the table.

GODFREY. Will there be anything else, Madam?

ANGELICA. Well, I haven't asked for anything, so I don't see how I could want anything else.

GODFREY. I beg your pardon. I thought you were Miss Cornelia.

ANGELICA. You thought *I* was Cornelia?

GODFREY. I hope you'll forgive me, madam, but you seem to be looking younger every day, if I may say so.

ANGELICA Well—you certainly may. Thanks very much, Godfrey.

A close view of the SIDE OF A ROOM shows Cornelia at the door looking out. Then the view moves with her over to Godfrey's door as footsteps are heard. Cornelia, entering his room, closes the door, hurriedly crosses the room and hides something under the mattress on the bed. Then she runs back to the door and listens as more footsteps are heard.

Next Cornelia appears in the HALL, stops in the doorway, and sees Godfrey descend the main staircase carrying her gown and going out with it, whistling.

In the LIVING ROOM where Angelica is seated in the foreground, we now see Cornelia entering and addressing her mother.

CORNELIA. Did you send Godfrey upstairs for anything?

ANGELICA. Did I? No, I'm quite sure I didn't. Why?

CORNELIA. Oh—I just wondered.

The scene dissolves to the DINING ROOM with the family seated at the table as Godfrey enters—serving.

A close view at the TABLE shows Godfrey serving Angelica, Irene watching him. Then the view moves around the table to Cornelia as Godfrey offers something to Irene, then moves to Cornelia.

CORNELIA (*intently*). I was in the Sherry Bar today. That place is getting all run down. They're catering to a very low class of people.

ANGELICA. Then you shouldn't go in there, my dear. Irene, what's the matter? You're not eating.

Cornelia is amused as Irene rises, jealous, as Godfrey serves the others.

IRENE. Nobody cares if I starve myself to death.

BULLOCK (*out of sight*). What's the matter with you, Irene?

IRENE. I don't mind dying if other people don't.

CORNELIA. She's in love. Haven't you heard?

ANGELICA. It's probably her engagement. You know, several of my girl friends acted just like that. It has something to do with your chemistry.

CARLO. Maybe her stomach is upset.

IRENE (*abruptly*). Nobody asked you.

There is a crash and Godfrey goes behind a screen—all are startled at the crash of broken dishes. He looks around the screen.

BULLOCK. There go the profits.

GODFREY (*going out*). I beg your pardon.

ANGELICA (*puzzled*). I don't know what's the matter with Godfrey. He's been so peculiar lately. But he did pay me a nice compliment.

IRENE. He's always paying other people compliments.

ANGELICA. Darling—why don't you eat something? Look at Carlo.

We see Carlo eating ravenously.

ANGELICA (*out of sight*). He had two helpings of everything.

BULLOCK. Let her alone. Carlo is eating enough for both of them.

ANGELICA'S VOICE (*admonishing*). Now, Alexander.

BULLOCK. He ought to be strong enough pretty soon to give that concert.

ANGELICA (*as Irene looks sulky*). You can't rush genius.

BULLOCK. He could give a bang-up concert right now with a knife and fork.

Carlo leaves the table and goes out.

ANGELICA (*rising angrily*). Why do you always pick on Carlo? Why don't you pick on someone else for a change? (*She follows Carlo.*)

Angelica is going after Carlo when Cornelia stops her mother.

CORNELIA. Wait a minute, Mother. Come here, Dad. Something terrible has happened.

BULLOCK (*rising*). What is it—what's happened?

ANGELICA. You frighten me. You're as white as a sheet.

CORNELIA (*cautiously*). Let's go into the living room where we won't be overheard. (*They start out.*)

The LIVING ROOM: Carlo is seen seated when the others come in.

ANGELICA. Cornelia, what has come over you? What is it? Aren't you feeling well? Come, sit down here. Let me get you an aspirin or something.

CORNELIA. I'm all right.

BULLOCK. What is it—what's troubling you?

CORNELIA. You remember the pearl necklace I got for my birthday last year?

ANGELICA. Why, yes!

BULLOCK. What about it?

CORNELIA. It's disappeared.

CARLO. Maybe somebody stole it.

BULLOCK. Will you fill your gob full of chicken and keep out of this discussion?

CARLO. I'm only trying to help.

BULLOCK. We don't need your help. (*To Cornelia*) When did you find out about this?

CORNELIA. I put it on my dressing table this afternoon. I went upstairs just now and it was gone.

ANGELICA. My! My! And it cost such a lot of money!

BULLOCK. I'll say it did.

ANGELICA. Well, what are we going to do?

BULLOCK. I'll go call the police.

CORNELIA. Never mind, Dad. I've already called them.

ANGELICA. Oh!

The scene dissolves to a close view of a DETECTIVE, his hat on his head, standing with Cornelia as the scene expands to include the others in the room.

DETECTIVE. Uh-huh— Well, what I want to know is—when did you miss the pearls?

CORNELIA. During dinner I went to my room and they were gone.

IRENE (anxiously). She probably lost them. She's always leaving them around.

DETECTIVE. Nobody asked you anything, lady.

ANGELICA. If you're going to be rude to my daughter, you might at least take off your hat.

DETECTIVE. When we're on criminal cases, lady, we keep both hands free.

Now we see the two detectives and the family. Carlo enters, eating, and one of the officers looks in his direction.

ANGELICA. Do you mean to imply that I'm a criminal?

DETECTIVE. All I know is that it's an inside job.

DETECTIVE (to Bullock). Who's that?

IRENE. It's mother's protégé.

DETECTIVE. No wise cracks. Is that your son?

BULLOCK (sitting down). That? Say, listen. I've made a lot of mistakes in my life, but I'll be hanged if I'll plead guilty to that.

Carlo, in a close-up, looks at them uncomprehendingly.

ANGELICA (out of sight). Stop picking on Carlo.

Molly brings in the tray to the family.

BULLOCK. He wouldn't have time to steal anything. He's always too busy eating.

DETECTIVE. Who are you?

MOLLY (pertly). Guess.

ANGELICA. Where's Godfrey?

MOLLY. He isn't feeling very well. (To the detective) Who are you staring at?

The detective follows Molly and stops her. The second officer joins them.

DETECTIVE. Just a minute, sister.

MOLLY. If I thought that were true, I'd disown my parents.

DETECTIVE. So you've got a passion for jewelry, huh?

MOLLY. Yes—and I've got a passion for socking cops.

DETECTIVE. Where are they?

MOLLY. Most of them in the cemetery.

DETECTIVE. Where's the necklace?

MOLLY. Maybe I swallowed it.

ANGELICA (coming over). You mustn't accuse Molly. She's been with us a long time.

MOLLY. That, in itself, is some recommendation.

ANGELICA. Thank you, Molly.

MOLLY. You're welcome. If you don't mind, flat-foot, I'll turn down the beds. (She goes out.)

DETECTIVE. Who is this Godfrey?

IRENE. He's the best butler we ever had.

CORNELIA. Oh, I'm sure Godfrey didn't take them—although we don't know much about him.

IRENE. Godfrey wouldn't touch those old pearls of yours with a fork.

SECOND DETECTIVE (to Cornelia). Just a minute. What do you mean you don't know much about him?

CORNELIA (*blandly*). You see, we didn't get him from an employment agency. My sister found him on a city dump.

DETECTIVE. Oh, I see.

IRENE (*furiously*). Are you accusing Godfrey?

CORNELIA. I'm not accusing anyone. I want my necklace.

ANGELICA. It's silly to think of Godfrey wearing a pearl necklace.

DETECTIVE. Where is this butler?

CORNELIA. He's probably in his room.

DETECTIVE. Where's that?

CORNELIA. Right this way.

Cornelia leads the officers out, Bullock following them.

IRENE (*running after them*). Oh!

In the PANTRY: Cornelia comes on, followed by officers and others. Irene enters at another door and runs to Godfrey's room. She pounds on the door.

CORNELIA. That's his room over there.

IRENE. Godfrey! Hide 'em if you've got 'em, Godfrey! Hide 'em if you've got 'em! Godfrey!

DETECTIVE (*approaching*). Hey, what kinda joint is this?

IRENE. Look out, Godfrey! Here they come! (*A detective pushes her back and opens the door.*)

The BEDROOM: Godfrey is seen asleep on the bed as they open the door and turn on the light.

GODFREY. Come in. (*They come forward.*)

One of the detectives bends over Godfrey.

DETECTIVE. Where are they?

GODFREY. Where?

DETECTIVE. That's what I said—where?

GODFREY (*sings*). "Where oh where has my little dog gone?"

DETECTIVE. Come on—snap out of it!

(*The second officer comes over, and they pull at Godfrey in the bed.*)

CORNELIA. I suppose you notice he's been drinking?

IRENE. He has not been drinking.

BULLOCK. I don't blame him if he has. This family has probably gotten to him, too.

Godfrey is now sitting up. The officer standing near him, searches.

DETECTIVE. Do you mind if we search your room, Godfrey?

GODFREY. Is somebody lost?

DETECTIVE. There seems to be a pearl necklace missing. Do you know anything about it?

GODFREY (*rising and helping them search*). We must look for it. That's too bad.

CORNELIA. It's too bad for you.

BULLOCK. I wouldn't be too cocksure of everything. This is a serious matter.

CORNELIA (*out of sight*). Well, the pearls couldn't just get up and walk away.

Godfrey goes to the dresser and searches through the drawers. He throws the clothing on the floor. A close-up of IRENE shows her looking at the scene, indignant.

IRENE. She probably threw them out of a taxi like she did last summer.

Godfrey staggers a bit, the detective searching the dresser, the family watching.

GODFREY. Listen. Look under the rug. Maybe that's where I put it.

DETECTIVE. We'll do the searching, Godfrey, old boy.

GODFREY (*looking at the shirt he is holding*). 'S a pleasure.

ANGELICA. It's all very silly. I can understand a woman stealing pearls, but what would Godfrey do with them?

CORNELIA. Look under the mattress.

GODFREY. Yes—there's a dandy place.

We see a close-up of CORNELIA looking on and sneering. Now the group is watching as the detectives tear the bed to pieces. Godfrey, in the background, is looking in a vase of flowers. The bed clothes are being thrown about. The detective turns down the mattress. And now we see CORNELIA startled as she hears:

DETECTIVE (*out of sight*). Well, they're not here.

CORNELIA. But they must be there.

She steps up to the detective, while Godfrey, now seated, watches her ironically.

DETECTIVE. Just a minute, lady. What makes you so sure they ought to be under the mattress?

CORNELIA. Why, I—I read that's where people put things when they steal them.

BULLOCK is frowning—angry. He moves forward.

DETECTIVE'S VOICE. Oh, yeah?

Bullock approaches Cornelia and the detective.

BULLOCK. Say, what are you up to? I'd like to talk to you boys outside, for just a minute, if you don't mind. (*He takes the detectives out with him.*)

A close view at the OPEN DOOR shows Angelica and Irene dazed as Bullock and the two detectives leave the room.

BULLOCK (*looking back*). I'm terribly sorry, Godfrey.

A close-up shows Godfrey seated, a rose in his hand.

IRENE (*out of sight*). I told you so.

A close-up of CORNELIA shows her sullen and angry.

ANGELICA'S VOICE. We're all terribly sorry, Godfrey. Come, Cornelia.

CORNELIA, sullen—angry—starts to leave. She looks back as she starts to close the door, and Irene taunts her as they leave.

IRENE. Yah! Yah! Yah!

A close-up in the ROOM shows Godfrey seated—rose in hand—looking off. He tosses the rose aside.

In the HALL we see Bullock coming forward with the two men. Angelica runs past. Cornelia enters and listens, Irene following her, smiling—triumphant.

BULLOCK. I'm terribly sorry, boys. I want to apologize for my family. They're all slightly hysterical.

DETECTIVE. Yeah. We sorta got an idea of what you're up against.

BULLOCK. I'd like to let the whole matter drop. She's probably mislaid her necklace. As a matter of fact, I'm not certain she ever had one.

DETECTIVE. There's something phoney about the whole thing.

BULLOCK. It's all a mistake. If you don't mind, I'd like to send a little check around tomorrow for the pension fund.

DETECTIVE. Okay, Mr. Bullock. Thanks very much.

BULLOCK (*shaking hands*). Good night.

DETECTIVE. Good night. The whole thing's forgotten.

BULLOCK (*shaking hands*). Good night, boys. (*They go out.*)

BULLOCK turns and faces Cornelia furiously.

BULLOCK. Now, just what have you got to say for yourself?

CORNELIA. Aren't they going to do anything about it?

BULLOCK. No! And it's probably a good thing for you that they're not. And there's something else I want to tell you—if you don't find your necklace, the joke's on you—because it's not insured. (*He goes out.*)

IRENE (*gloating*). Cornelia lost her pearls and I've got mine. Cornelia lost her pearls and I've got mine! Cornelia lost her pearls and I've got mine!

The scene fades out.

PART FIVE

The CITY DUMP fades in, disclosing men about—washing, working, searching while trucks are dumping loads on the pile.

While the noise of trucks is heard, we see some BUILDINGS, Tommy Gray getting out of a car and coming forward. He is followed by Godfrey.

GODFREY. Here we are, Tommy—the village of forgotten men.

Godfrey and Tommy walk down the path on the dump as men watch them passing.

GODFREY. How do you like it?

TOMMY. I don't know but what I prefer Newport.

GODFREY. It's a matter of choice. Unfortunately, these men have no choice. Come along.

TOMMY. I still prefer Newport. What is that delightful aroma?

GODFREY. That's old man river. You get used to it after awhile. (*They disappear near the bottom of the path.*)

A close view at the FOOT OF THE DUMP shows them in the foreground. A dump truck is unloading above them. They stop by the shack Godfrey had lived in.

TOMMY. You mean to say that people really live in this place?

GODFREY. Well, they go through the motions. Tommy, observe yon shack on your left. That was the birthplace of the celebrated butler, Godfrey Smith.

TOMMY. And where are the ashes of Godfrey Parke?

GODFREY. Scattered to the winds!

Mike appears and shakes hands with Godfrey.

MIKE. Hello, Duke! Well, well!

GODFREY. How are you, Mike?

MIKE. How's tricks?

GODFREY. Meet Mr. Gray, Mr. Flaherty.

MIKE. How are you, Mr. Gray. Pardon my wet paw. I was just washing out my lingerie.

TOMMY. That's okay.

MIKE. Hey, Bob, look who's here.

A close-up reveals a man watering a plant in a tin can.

GODFREY (*out of sight*). Hello, Bob!

BOB (*looking around, smiling as he starts forward*). Well, bust my G string.

Bob comes over and shakes hands with Godfrey.

MIKE (*moving away*). Say, thanks for the beans, Duke. They got here just in time.

BOB. If it ain't old Duke himself. The beans was marvelous. Thanks. We ate everything but the cans.

GODFREY. Don't thank me. Thank Mr. Gray. He's got a corner on the bean market.

We see MIKE hanging things on a line as he talks in their direction.

MIKE. Say, is that the same corner prosperity's just around?

We see at the SHACK the four men standing, talking and laughing. Another man approaches; he carries a bundle of wood under his arm.

TOMMY. No. That's another one.

GODFREY. Hello, Arthur.

BELLINGER (*shaking hands with Godfrey*). Hello, Duke.

GODFREY. Meet Mr. Gray—Mr. Bellinger.

BELLINGER. You look as though you had a job, too. What is this, an epidemic?

A MAN (*out of sight, calling*). Hey, Mike! Let's get going.

MIKE. Well, Duke, we've got to run along. This is moving day.

BELLINGER. We've got to help some of the boys move their shacks. The dump trucks are crowding in on us a little. We ought to be in the river by early spring. (*Mike and he leave the group.*)

BOB. Cheer up. We might be able to float by that time.

We see a long view of "SHACKTOWN" as the men leave Tommy and Godfrey.

BOB (*also leaving*). See you again, Duke.

GODFREY. Right.

In a close-up of the SHACK, Godfrey looks at Tommy.

GODFREY. That little fellow with the bundle of wood under his arm is Bellinger of the Second National. When his bank failed he gave up everything he had so that his depositors wouldn't suffer.

TOMMY. Not really.

GODFREY. Really. You see, Tommy, there are two kinds of people. Those who fight the idea of being pushed into the river—and the other kind.

TOMMY. Well, after all, things have always been this way for some people. These men are not your responsibility.

GODFREY. There are different ways of having fun.

TOMMY. You have a peculiar sense of humor.

GODFREY. Over here we have some very fashionable apartment houses—over there is a very swanky night club, while down here men starve for want of a job. How does that strike your sense of humor?

TOMMY. What is all this leading to?

GODFREY. Tommy, there's a very peculiar mental process called thinking. You wouldn't know much about that, but when I was living here I did a lot of it. One thing I discovered was that the only difference between a derelict and a man was a job. Sit down over here

and rest your weary bones. I'll tell you what I wanted to talk to you about.

The two men sit down.

TOMMY. I'll listen, but I still think you belong in a psychopathic ward.

GODFREY. Maybe you're right, but let me tell you my plan, and listen with both ears. I have an idea—

The scene fades out; then a close view of a MAGAZINE COVER—GOTHAM GOSSIP 50 CENTS fades in, as music is heard. The cover is turned, disclosing a picture of Irene and a paragraph. As the paragraph is seen closer, we read:

"PARK AVENUE CHATTER
by Hatton Mann

The Misses Bullock have returned from a long sojourn in Europe where the younger daughter, Irene, (So it is rumored) was sent to forget her latest broken engagement. If Park Avenue knew the name of her real beloved, would everybody be leffing. Cupid strikes in strange places, or words to that effect . . . and heigh-ho . . . "

This dissolves to a close view of the LIVING ROOM, with Angelica, Cornelia and Carlo seated; Cornelia playing with the dog.

CARLO. Did you and Irene have a good time while you were in Europe?

CORNELIA. As good a time as anyone could have with Irene.

ANGELICA. You should be more civil to Carlo.

CORNELIA. Why?

CARLO. Oh, I don't mind. As the French say, "Cherchez la femme."

ANGELICA (*beaming*). That will hold you. Carlo always has a clever answer for everything.

Irene enters, and next we see her seated with Angelica, Carlo standing near them.

ANGELICA. Darling, won't you have some coffee?

IRENE. No, thank you.

CARLO. She didn't eat any dinner, either.

IRENE. *You* had plenty.

CARLO. I can't say anything.

IRENE. You never do.

ANGELICA. Oh darling, what's come over you? We spend good money sending you abroad to forget an engagement and you come back worse off than when you left.

CARLO (*out of sight*). Her liver is probably upset.

ANGELICA. You'd better take a liver pill then.

IRENE. I don't want a liver pill.

ANGELICA. You mustn't get so upset about a broken engagement. You've broken many before and you've never been this way.

We see Cornelia seated before the FIRE-PLACE, amused. She rises.

CORNELIA. It's not her broken engagement. She's upset because Godfrey didn't fall down in a faint when we got in today.

ANGELICA. Why should Godfrey fall down in a faint?

Cornelia sits down and looks at the magazine.

CORNELIA. He didn't make enough of a fuss over Irene to suit her.

ANGELICA. But Godfrey's not the fussing kind. Shhh!

Godfrey enters.

ANGELICA. Oh Godfrey, I was just telling my daughters that you missed them both very much while they were away.

GODFREY. Oh, I did, very much indeed.

CORNELIA. We missed you, too, Godfrey, didn't we, Irene?

IRENE. Yes.

GODFREY. Thanks. I missed you, too.

ANGELICA. Well, it's so nice for everybody to miss everyone else, because then it makes it so nice when they get together again. There, there, darling. It's nice to see you cheerful again. You do have a way about you Godfrey, you really do.

Godfrey goes out as Carlo puts Angelica's wrap about her.

ANGELICA. You know, there's no use denying the fact that Godfrey has a way with him. Well, we must be getting on. Cornelia, cheer her up, like a dear. (*They move on.*)

CORNELIA (*looking at the magazine*). I'm a cinch. Do you feel better now that you know Godfrey missed us?

IRENE. He missed me more than he did you. I could tell by the light in his eyes.

CORNELIA. Why didn't you throw yourself in the man's arms and get it over with?

IRENE. You can't rush a man like Godfrey.

CORNELIA. You're getting pretty old, you know. It's your last chance to get a husband.

IRENE. He's really in love with me. He's just hard to break down.

CORNELIA. I could break him down in no time at all.

IRENE (*rising, angrily*). He wouldn't have anything to do with you.

CORNELIA. How do you know?

IRENE. Because he wouldn't. Don't you try anything.

CORNELIA. I'm not saying I will—and I'm not saying I won't. Come to think of it—Godfrey and I have a little unfinished business.

IRENE (*going out*). Well, you'd better leave it unfinished, unless you want to be wearing a lamp for a hat.

A close view in the PANTRY shows Godfrey washing dishes as Irene enters. He turns to her.

IRENE. Did you mean it when you said you missed me?

GODFREY (*laughing*). Of course I did.

IRENE. I mean did you miss Cornelia and me or just me?

GODFREY. Well, I missed both of you, I guess.

IRENE. Not just me?

GODFREY. Oh, I may have missed you a little more than I did Cornelia. Why?

IRENE. I'm glad—because if you missed Cornelia more, you probably would have missed me less.

GODFREY. Well, that sounds very logical.

IRENE. That's all I wanted to know. You look so cute in that apron.

GODFREY. I'm not trying to look cute. Molly has a cold and I'm doubling for her. (*Irene laughs.*)

GODFREY. What's funny about that?

IRENE. She hasn't got a cold.

GODFREY. No?

IRENE. She's got the same thing I've got; only you won't let me talk about things like that, so I won't because you lose your temper.

GODFREY. No—not seriously.

IRENE. Will you let me do something if I ask you?

GODFREY. What do you want to do?

IRENE. Wipe.

GODFREY. Oh—all right. And you can tell me about your trip.

IRENE. You won't get mad.

GODFREY. Why should I?

IRENE. Because every place I went, everybody was Godfrey—

GODFREY. Every?—I don't want to seem dull, but I do seem to have a little trouble in following you at times.

IRENE. For instance, whenever I'd go into a restaurant in Paris or any place, I'd close my eyes and the waiter was Godfrey, and I'd say, I'm home and

Godfrey is serving me. It made everything taste better.

GODFREY. Why?

IRENE. Haven't you any sense?

GODFREY. I'm afraid I haven't.

IRENE. And when I'd get in a cab I'd say the driver is Godfrey, and this is a chariot and he's taking me up through the clouds to his castle on the mountain.

GODFREY. Suppose you come down out of the mountains and tell me about your trip.

IRENE. Well, we went to Venice and one night I went for a ride in one of those row boats that the man pushes with a stick—not a matador—that was in Spain, but something like a matador.

GODFREY. Do you by any chance mean a gondolier?

Irene is now wiping the dishes—Godfrey washing them.

IRENE. That was the name of the boat, and the man that pushed it sang. It was a beautiful song. I didn't understand it —but it was beautiful.

GODFREY. I see. So you closed your eyes and the man was Godfrey.

IRENE. It was wonderful. I didn't even mind the smells.

GODFREY. It's very convenient to take a trip abroad—without leaving the kitchen.

IRENE. Oh, you have a wonderful sense of humor. I wish I had a sense of humor, but I never can think of the right thing to say until everybody's gone home.

GODFREY. Do you mind if I talk for a little bit while you catch your breath?

IRENE. I'd love it.

GODFREY. While you were away, I've been doing some things also. I've been trying to do things that I thought would make you proud of me.

IRENE. I was proud of you before I went away.

GODFREY. Yes—but I mean—prouder still. You see, you helped me to find myself—and I'm very grateful.

IRENE. You'd make a wonderful husband.

GODFREY. I'm afraid not. You see—I know how you feel about things—

IRENE. How?

GODFREY. Well—you're grateful to me because I helped you to beat Cornelia —and I'm grateful to you because you helped me to beat life—but that doesn't mean that we have to fall in love.

IRENE. If you don't want to—but I'd make a wonderful wife.

GODFREY. Not for me, I'm afraid. You see—I like you very much, but I had a very bitter experience—but I won't bore you with that.

IRENE. Maybe she wasn't in love with you.

GODFREY. Well, maybe not—but that's beside the point. You and I are friends and I feel a certain responsibility to you. That's why I wanted to tell you first.

IRENE. Tell me what?

GODFREY. Well, I thought it was about time I was moving on.

IRENE (*sitting down, startled*). Godfrey!

GODFREY. Now please.

Irene is turning away from him—half crying.

IRENE. I won't cry. I promise.

GODFREY. That's fine. After all—I'm your protégé and you want me to improve myself, don't you?

IRENE. Yes.

GODFREY. You don't want me to be just a butler all my life, do you?

IRENE. I want you to be anything you want to be.

GODFREY. That's very sweet.

IRENE. When are you leaving?

GODFREY. Pretty soon. I'll call you up every now and then. We'll have long chats, and I'll tell you how I'm getting along and we'll have lots of fun together.

IRENE. Are you going back to her?

GODFREY. To whom?

IRENE. That Indian woman.

GODFREY. Indian— Oh! She was just a fabrication.

IRENE. Oh! Then you weren't married to her?

GODFREY. No. She was just a product of Tommy Gray's imagination.

The two now busy themselves washing dishes; Irene looks greatly relieved.

IRENE. Then there wasn't—

GODFREY. No.

IRENE. Then there couldn't have been five children?

GODFREY. Well, naturally.

IRENE. That makes a difference. (*They burst into laughter.*)

The scene dissolves to a close view of the LIVING ROOM, where Cornelia is seated on the couch as Godfrey enters.

GODFREY. Did you ring, Miss?

CORNELIA. You needn't be so formal when we're alone.

GODFREY. Shouldn't that rather increase a butler's formality?

CORNELIA. But you're not a butler.

GODFREY. I'm sorry if I've disappointed.

CORNELIA (*rising*). You might drop that superior attitude for the moment. There's a little matter I've wanted to talk over with you for quite awhile— called, the mystery of milady's necklace or—what happened to the pearls.

We see a close-up of GODFREY and CORNELIA standing and facing each other.

GODFREY. Pearls? Necklace? Oh, you

mean the ones that disappeared last Fall?

CORNELIA. The same.

GODFREY. Didn't they ever turn up?

CORNELIA. Oh yes, of course—but not in *my* possession. I know the first part of the story, but I wondered what you might know about the second part.

GODFREY. I can't imagine.

CORNELIA. I know another story that might interest you. I met some people on the boat coming over, a Boston family—quite distinguished. They know a great deal about a family called—the Parkes. An old Mayflower crowd—very upper crust, too, mind you. Never been a breath of scandal connected with the family.

A close-up in the DOORWAY shows Irene standing—looking at the scene and listening.

CORNELIA (*out of sight*). It would be a shame if they were made the laughing stock of Boston, wouldn't it?

GODFREY. I should hate to see anyone made the laughing stock of any place.

CORNELIA. Let's you and I take a long taxi ride out Van Cortlandt way.

IRENE, listening, looks very hurt.

CORNELIA'S VOICE. We could exchange secrets.

GODFREY (*angrily*). Is that a command?

CORNELIA. As you like. I'll be waiting around the corner.

GODFREY (*pointing*). Which corner? This one or that one?

CORNELIA (*going out*). This corner. It's impossible to exchange intimate secrets here.

Now Irene has her back turned and Cornelia comes toward her.

CORNELIA. The traffic is almost as heavy as at the Grand Central Station. Don't forget, darling—fifteen minutes.

Godfrey turns and comes to Irene as the view moves closer to them. She stops him—crying.

IRENE. Please, Godfrey. You can't go with Cornelia.

GODFREY. But I didn't say I was going any place with Miss Cornelia.

IRENE. But you will. She always gets her own way. She makes everybody do just as she likes.

GODFREY. Why should you care whether I meet her or not?

IRENE. But I do care. That's why. Cornelia's the one who doesn't care!

GODFREY. But I think I should decide those things for myself.

IRENE. I don't want to be annoying, Godfrey, but I— Ooooh! (*She wilts suddenly and faints in his arms.*)

GODFREY (*looking around; desperately*). See here—you—you can't do that. Please —snap out of it. Oooh! This is the craziest family— (*He picks her up and goes out.*)

We see him carrying Irene in the HALL across to the stairs. He runs up with her and opens the door at the head of the stairs. Then we see him entering her ROOM and dropping her on a couch.

GODFREY (*bending over the unconscious girl*). Now, see here, stop this nonsense. Do you hear? If you're faking one of your spells to keep me from meeting Cornelia, you're on the wrong track— do you hear? Do you hear?

Irene on the couch, Godfrey looks off, goes to the dressing table and looks for restoratives. Irene is reflected in the mirror as he smells of the salts. He sees her sitting up —whereupon she drops back onto the couch.

He puts down the smelling salts, goes over to her, and slaps her cheek.

GODFREY. Are you feeling better? No? Godfrey knows how to take care of little Irene—yes, indeed. (*He turns and goes to turn on the lights in her bathroom.*)

A close view in the BATHROOM shows Godfrey opening the shower stall and putting a stool inside the stall. Then he moves toward her.

GODFREY. Just lie there quietly and Godfrey will take care of everything.

Godfrey comes to her—picks her up—talking—puts her over his shoulder and carries her into the bathroom.

GODFREY. Godfrey knows just how to take care of those nasty old faints. That's the girl. Come right up here—there you are. Godfrey will soon fix Irene—yes, indeed. Just leave everything to Godfrey. Godfrey will take care of everything. Now just sit right down there like a good girl—and in just a minute you'll forget that you had any trouble.

He puts her in the SHOWER STALL and puts her down on the stool. He turns on the water, and backs out.

IRENE (*coming to with a scream*). Ooh! Godfrey!

We see Irene in the SHOWER STALL wriggling under the spray, as he moves away.

GODFREY. I thought so. Let that be a lesson to you.

IRENE. Godfrey!

Now Irene runs after him and grabs him. Godfrey, angry, tries to get away from her.

IRENE. Oh Godfrey, don't go away! Oh, Godfrey! Now I know you love me.

GODFREY. I do not love you and you're getting me all wet.

IRENE. You do or you wouldn't have lost your temper.

Angelica appears in the DOORWAY and moves into the ROOM as Irene is clinging to Godfrey. Irene runs to her mother, excited.

ANGELICA. What is the meaning of this, may I ask?

IRENE. Oh, Mother, Godfrey loves me. He put me in the shower!

ANGELICA. Whatever are you talking about?

IRENE. Godfrey loves me! Godfrey loves me!

ANGELICA. Godfrey, I demand an explanation.

IRENE (*jumping up and down the couch*). Godfrey loves me! Godfrey loves me!

GODFREY (*coming past Angelica*). I think, madam, that I had better resign.

ANGELICA (*stopping him*). I think you'd better. That's a very good idea. What do you suppose your father will say to all this?

IRENF Godfrey loves me! I don't care what anybody says—Godfrey loves me.

ANGELICA. See here, young lady. You take a bath and put on some dry clothes and come downstairs immediately. Do you hear?

IRENE (*running to the bathroom; singing*). Godfrey loves me! Godfrey loves me!

ANGELICA. I never heard of anything like this in all my life!

IRENE (*out of sight*). Godfrey loves me!

Following this, there is a close view at the PIANO of Carlo playing, eating, and singing.

CARLO (*singing*). Otchi tchornia—otchi tchornia!

Then there appears a full view of the ROOM, as Bullock enters.

CARLO. Otchi tchornia! Otchi tchornia!

Bullock puts down his hat, notices him, and speaks angrily.

BULLOCK. Shut that thing off!—(*Out of sight, as we get another close view of Carlo, who looks at him*)—I feel gloomy enough as it is.

Bullock sits down. Angelica enters, excited, as Carlo rises from the piano.

ANGELICA. Alexander, something terrible has happened!

BULLOCK. What?

ANGELICA. Godfrey pushed Irene into a cold shower.

BULLOCK. What's so terrible about that?

ANGELICA. And besides, he's in love with her or thinks he is or something. I can't make head or tail out of the whole thing.

BULLOCK. I can't make head or tail out of what you're saying.

ANGELICA. The only thing to do is to send him back where he came from. He never should have come here in the first place. Imagine falling in love with a butler.

BULLOCK (*dryly*). If you're going to feel sorry for anyone, feel sorry for Godfrey.

ANGELICA. Alexander!

BULLOCK. Don't Alexander me—stop fluttering and come to rest. (*She sits down.*) I've got something more important that I want to talk about.

ANGELICA. Don't tell me you're going to talk about those sordid money matters again?

CARLO (*in the background*). Oh, money —money—money!

BULLOCK. Yes, I am—but before I start I'm going to have a little talk with Carlo.

ANGELICA. What are you going to do, Alexander?

Angelica watches as Bullock goes to Carlo.

BULLOCK. This is very private—just for Carlo's ears.

A close-up at the GRILL shows Carlo uneasy as Bullock approaches.

BULLOCK. You don't mind if we have a little chat—Carlo, old boy? You know, for some time, Carlo, I've— (*He leads him out of the room.*)

Next there is a crash outside. Angelica looks up, startled—frightened. Another crash follows. Then Bullock comes in, and goes to her.

ANGELICA. What happened? What did you say to Carlo?

BULLOCK. I said good-bye.

ANGELICA (*absentmindedly*). Did he go?

BULLOCK. Yes. He left hurriedly.

Godfrey and Cornelia appear at the DOORWAY.

BULLOCK (*continuing*). —by the side window.

ANGELICA (*out of sight*). Side window? Side window? Where is he going?

BULLOCK (*out of sight*). I don't know— but he won't be back.

Godfrey and Cornelia are standing. Bullock makes his wife and daughter sit down.

BULLOCK. Now you sit down and do some listening.

ANGELICA. I've never seen you act like this before.

BULLOCK. Sit down!

ANGELICA. What's come over you, Alexander?

BULLOCK. And you're just in time to sit down and do some listening?

CORNELIA. Do you want Godfrey to listen?

BULLOCK. Yes. I want Godfrey to listen. This concerns him, too. You might as well all know, point-blank, we're about broke.

ANGELICA. You mean—we haven't any money left?

BULLOCK. We've got this house—a few odds and ends and that's about all. Not only that—I've lost all of my stock in the Bullock Enterprises—

A close-up at the DOORWAY shows Godfrey standing—waiting—a small packet in his hand.

BULLOCK'S VOICE. Not only that—I've borrowed some of the stockholders' money trying to recoup my losses.

A close view of the SIDE OF THE ROOM shows the two women seated—Bullock standing.

BULLOCK. I don't know where I'm going to end—maybe in jail.

ANGELICA. Oh, Alexander!

BULLOCK (*sitting down*). But if I do end up in jail, it will be the first peace I've had in twenty years—and I don't want any of you to chortle about Godfrey.

A close-up at the DOORWAY shows Godfrey smiling.

BULLOCK'S VOICE. You may all be on the city dump before you're through.

ANGELICA'S VOICE. What are we going to do?

GODFREY (*bowing*). May I intrude, sir?

We see Bullock and the two women seated as Godfrey comes forward.

GODFREY. I'm afraid things are not as bad as you make out.

BULLOCK. What do you know about it?

GODFREY. Well, sir— (*He hands the packet to Bullock.*) I've known for a long time that the Bullock interests were in rather a bad way—I offered to help you once, but you declined that help, so I took the liberty of dabbling in the market on my own account. Here, sir—

A close-up of CORNELIA shows her watching —startled.

BULLOCK'S VOICE. What's this?

GODFREY (*out of sight*). That's most of your stock.

Bullock examines the contents of the packet.

GODFREY. I knew it was being dumped on the market, so I sold short.

ANGELICA. I don't understand—you sold short. You mean gentlemen's underwear?

BULLOCK (*rising*). Wait a minute. Do you mean that you've been making money while I was losing it?

GODFREY. I did it in your interests, sir. The stock has been indorsed over to you.

BULLOCK (*examining papers*). I don't understand. You did this for me?

GODFREY. Well, sir, there comes a turning point in every man's life—a time when he needs help. It happened to me, also and—(*as Bullock sits down, relieved to the point of exhaustion*)—this family helped me. I hope I've repaid my debt. And, if I may add, some of the money went into a project of my own—I hope you won't mind, sir.

ANGELICA. You mean that you did all that on one hundred and fifty dollars a month?

GODFREY (*taking Cornelia's pearls out of his pocket*). Well, hardly. You see, with the aid of Tommy Gray I was able to transmute a certain trinket into gold— then into stock and then back into pearls again. (*Giving them to her*) Thank you, dear lady, for the use of the trinket.

ANGELICA (*rising*). Godfrey! Then you did steal them after all?

GODFREY. Well—I—perhaps Miss Cornelia had better explain to you.

CORNELIA. You win.

ANGELICA. What is this all about anyway?

CORNELIA. I put the pearls under Godfrey's mattress.

BULLOCK stares at them.

GODFREY. Thank you, Miss Cornelia. I wanted you to say that.

ANGELICA. But why?

CORNELIA. You wouldn't understand, Mother. Here, Godfrey, these are rightfully yours.

GODFREY. No, thank you. I've repaid my debt and I'm grateful to all of you.

CORNELIA. If anyone's indebted we are, after the way some of us have treated you.

GODFREY. I've been repaid in many ways. I learned patience—(*out of sight, as we see Bullock sitting, dazed*)—from Mr. Bullock.

GODFREY (*now seen with Cornelia*). I found Mrs. Bullock at all times, shall we say—amusing?

ANGELICA. That's very complimentary of you, Godfrey. Don't forget that you said I looked as young as Cornelia.

CORNELIA. What good did you find in me—if any?

GODFREY. A great deal. You taught me the fallacy of false pride—you taught me humility.

CORNELIA. I don't understand you.

GODFREY. Miss Cornelia, there have been other spoiled children in the world. I happened to be one of them myself. You're a high-spirited girl. I can only hope that you'll use those high spirits in a more constructive way. And so—good day.

We see the DOORWAY TO THE HALL, the curtains blowing, then a close up of CORNELIA, holding the pearls—looking after him. Suddenly she throws aside the pearls and starts to cry.

Angelica is watching Cornelia as she cries and Bullock sits with his head bowed.

ANGELICA. You know, I hate to see Godfrey go. He's the only butler we ever had who understood women.

Godfrey enters the PANTRY, and crosses to Molly, who is standing at the table. He picks up his hat and coat.

GODFREY. Well, Molly, you told me to leave my hat near the door—remember?

MOLLY. I hate to see you leave, Godfrey.

GODFREY (kissing her). Molly, you've been swell.

MOLLY. The house will seem empty.

GODFREY. Well, I guess the best of friends have to part. Will you say good-bye to Miss Irene for me? I don't think I can go through that ordeal right now. You're sweet, Molly. Good-bye. (She opens the door for him, and he goes out. Molly is crying now.)

Irene comes through the HALL into the LIVING ROOM as Cornelia goes past her, crying. Irene stares at her as Cornelia goes by. Irene comes to her father and mother; they are seated and look very doleful.

IRENE. What is it? What's the matter with Cornelia? What's the matter with everybody? Mother, what's the trouble?

ANGELICA (dolefully). He's gone.

IRENE. Who's gone?

ANGELICA. Godfrey.

IRENE. Where?

ANGELICA. And Carlo's gone—out the window. Everybody's gone!

The PANTRY: Irene enters—runs across to Molly, who is crying at the door, and runs back across the room.

IRENE. Oh, Molly, has he gone? Oh, poor Molly. He's not going to get away from me. Order the car—I'll be right down.

The scene dissolves to the DUMP where people are arriving in cars. We see the bridge over the river in the background. (Music is heard throughout the scenes that follow.) Then a close view at a CAR in front of the "NIGHT CLUB" (a building on the dump area) shows a doorman taking bags from a chauffeur. Godfrey alights, and we see him at close range as he talks to the doorman, who turns out to be MIKE.

MIKE. Hello, Duke.

GODFREY. Business looks pretty good tonight.

MIKE. I'll say it is. Mayor Courtney's here with a big party.

GODFREY. Well!

MIKE. I'll have one of the boys bring these down, Duke.

The NIGHT CLUB, with people at tables and at the bar, music playing. Godfrey comes down the stairs, looks around as he passes between tables, and stops at the door to the office and speaks to a man who turns out to be Bob.

BOB. Hello, Duke.

GODFREY. Well, Bob. We can't complain about this.

BOB. Say, we've got the Mayor here with us tonight.

GODFREY. So I heard.

BOB. Big stuff.

GODFREY. Yep. (*He opens the door to the office and starts to go out.*)

The OFFICE, where Tommy Gray is seated at a desk and Bellinger is standing as Godfrey enters.

TOMMY. This is all Greek to me. Here's our wandering butler now. Explain it to him.

BELLINGER (*picking up plans*). Hello, Duke.

GODFREY. Hello, Arthur.

BELLINGER. I've got an estimate from the contractor on your housing plan for the winter.

GODFREY. Yes?

BELLINGER. He figures he can partition off our present building into compartments to take care of at least fifty people. It will cost fifty-eight hundred dollars, but that includes steam heat.

TOMMY. Forgotten men with steam. That sounds like something that ought to be on the menu.

GODFREY. I'll talk with you about it later, Arthur.

TOMMY. Say, I've still got an interest in this company. When do you start paying dividends?

GODFREY. Well, we're giving food and shelter to fifty people in the winter and we are giving them employment in the summer. What more do you want in the way of dividends?

TOMMY. You're the most arbitrary butler I've ever met.

GODFREY. Ex-butler. I quit. I felt that foolish feeling coming on again.

TOMMY. You mean Irene?

GODFREY. What do you know about that?

TOMMY. Nobody knows anything about her love except all of New York and Lower Manhattan.

Godfrey rises and gives Tommy a pen.

GODFREY. Looks like I got out just in time.

TOMMY. Why don't you marry the girl?

GODFREY. No thank you. I've had enough of matrimony.

TOMMY. What's wrong with butlers—lots of society girls run away with their chauffeurs.

GODFREY. Never mind about that. Write me out a check for five thousand dollars.

TOMMY (*sitting down at the desk*). For what?

GODFREY. A new dock, so we'll get some of the yachting trade.

TOMMY. Well, how about an airplane landing? Have you thought of that?

While Tommy, seated at the desk, is writing a check, Godfrey, going to the back, looks out of the big window.

GODFREY. We'll come to that later.

A view of the NIGHT CLUB and RIVER with people moving about as Mike, the doorman, appears: A car stops in the foreground. As Mike opens the door of the car (now seen closely), Irene gets out, and her chauffeur, getting out, goes around the car to Irene and Mike.

IRENE. Say, Mister, what happened to the city dump that was here?

MIKE. Well, Lady, most of it's been filled in.

IRENE. But what happened to all the forgotten men?

MIKE. Forgotten men? We got most of 'em out in time.

IRENE. Don't be fresh. Where's Godfrey?

MIKE. You mean Mr. Godfrey Smith?

IRENE. Yes.

MIKE. Well, lady, his office is right over there where it says "Office."

IRENE (*remembering the shack*). Oh,

just where it used to be. Thank you. Come on, Clarence.

Mike watches as Irene and Clarence enter, Clarence carrying two big baskets of food. Mike stops him.

MIKE. Hey, wait a minute! What is this—a basket party? (*Irene goes on.*)

Irene enters the house, walks past the tables, and sees the Mayor.

IRENE. Good evening, Mr. Courtney.

MAYOR. Good evening, Miss Bullock.

IRENE. Lovely evening, isn't it? Good evening. (*She goes to the office.*)

The OFFICE: Tommy rises.

TOMMY. Well, there you are. Business is fine—I'm stuck—you're nuts and I'm going back to Boston before I disgrace my family.

GODFREY. Good riddance.

Tommy opens the door, and, behold, Irene walks in, smiling.

TOMMY (*smiling at her*). Oh, Godfrey—company has come.

GODFREY looks around from the window.

GODFREY. What are you doing here?

TOMMY. Yes, what are you doing here? Don't let him off the hook.

IRENE. I won't.

TOMMY. You must leave at once, do you hear me?

Tommy pushes Irene away from the door into the office as Godfrey comes forward.

TOMMY (*blithely*). Well, we got rid of her in a hurry. If I can help you in any way, be sure and let me know. (*Tommy goes out, closing the door.*)

IRENE (*moving about and looking around*). Oh, my, how you fixed this place up, Godfrey! It's much nicer than when I was here before.

GODFREY. Oh, you noticed that?

IRENE. Are the forgotten men having a party?

GODFREY. It's their annual reunion.

IRENE. I saw the mayor out there. Is he one of them, too?

GODFREY. He's the guest of honor.

IRENE (*going to the window*). It's a lovely view! You can see the bridge and everything. Is it always there?

GODFREY. Most always.

IRENE (*opening doors*). Oh, you have a kitchen. I'm going to like this place very much. What's over here? Is this where you sleep?

GODFREY. That's the general purpose of the room. Any observations?

Irene turns from the door.

IRENE. Oh, I think it's very cute, but we'll have to change the wallpaper.

GODFREY. What do you mean—*we'll* have to change the wallpaper?

IRENE (*going to him*). I don't like green wallpaper—it makes me bilious.

GODFREY. Well, you won't have to look at it. You're going home right now.

IRENE. But I can't go home.

GODFREY. Why not?

IRENE. I can't go home after what happened.

GODFREY. What happened?

IRENE. You know what happened just as well as I do.

GODFREY. Now, see here—

IRENE. Oh, go on and lose your temper again. I love it when you lose your temper.

GODFREY. Why can't you let me alone? (*He sits down.*)

IRENE. Because you're my responsibility and someone has to take care of you.

GODFREY. I'll take care of myself.

IRENE (*seated near him*). You can't look me in the eye and say that. You love me and you know it. There's no sense in struggling with a thing when it's got you. It's got you and that's all there is to it—it's got you.

Irene and Godfrey look up as they hear a knock at the door.

IRENE. That's Clarence. (*She rises—opens the door—Clarence enters loaded down with baskets of food.*)

CLARENCE. I'm sorry I was delayed, Miss Irene—but I had to go all the way around the back way.

A close-up at the SEAT shows Godfrey seated—smoking his pipe—curious.

IRENE. Put the wood over there.

Clarence follows her with the basket through the room.

CLARENCE. Hello, Godfrey.

IRENE. You can put the groceries right there in the kitchen. Right there, Clarence.

GODFREY. What's the idea?

IRENE. I brought some wood and I brought some food. It ought to last us for a week anyway.

GODFREY. It's a wonder you didn't have the foresight to bring a minister and a license.

IRENE. It's funny. I never thought of that.

Irene is seen standing before Godfrey as the Mayor enters.

MAYOR. May I come in?

IRENE. Oh, Mr. Courtney!

MAYOR. Mr. Gray said there were a couple of people over here who wanted to get married.

A close-up of GODFREY shows him startled—his pipe in hand.

MAYOR'S VOICE. Are you it?

IRENE. Yes, we're it. Can you marry us without a license?

Godfrey is flabbergasted.

MAYOR'S VOICE. Without a li— Well, it may get me into trouble—but—I guess I've known your family long enough to take a chance. Who are you going to marry?

IRENE. Godfrey.

She points at Godfrey. The Mayor goes to him and shakes hands.

IRENE. Oh, this is Godfrey.

MAYOR. How do you do, Godfrey? Er —does your father know about this?

IRENE. Everybody knows about it except Godfrey.

MAYOR. Well, I guess we'd better have a witness.

IRENE (*as Clarence enters*). Oh, sure! Oh, use Clarence. Clarence, you be the witness. Come down here. Stand right here. (*Pulling Godfrey to his feet*) Come on, Godfrey. Now, we're all set.

MAYOR. Join hands, please. Join the right hands.

IRENE (*grasping his hand*). Stand still, Godfrey, it'll all be over in a minute.

The scene fades out.

HERE COMES MR. JORDAN

(A Columbia Picture)

Screenplay by
SIDNEY BUCHMAN AND SETON I. MILLER

Based on a Story by Harry Segall

Directed by ALEXANDER HALL

Produced by EVERITT RISKIN

The Cast

JOE PENDLETON	Robert Montgomery
BETTE LOGAN	Evelyn Keyes
MR. JORDAN	Claude Rains
JULIA FARNSWORTH	Rita Johnson
MESSENGER 7013	Edward Everett Horton
MAX CORKLE	James Gleason
TONY ABBOTT	John Emery
INSPECTOR WILLIAMS	Donald MacBride
LEFTY	Don Costello
SISK	Halliwell Hobbes
BUGS	Benny Rubin

Film Editor—VIOLA LAWRENCE

HERE COMES MR. JORDAN

PART ONE

An ADIRONDACK CAMP fades in: It is a clearing in an Adirondack forest, with a rambling rail fence around it, and log cabins set deep among the trees. Some cars are parked just inside the large gate. The camera moves forward, providing a view of the GATE, and continues moving forward as though we were entering the camp. A large wooden sign nailed to a gate post, announces this to be:

JOE PENDLETON

TRAINING CAMP

As the camera continues its forward movement the scene dissolves to an OUTDOOR FIGHT RING, a rude, temporary affair set in a clearing. In the ring, with protective headgear on and rather heavily dressed, are Joe Pendleton and a sparring partner—at the moment mixing it pretty fast and furiously. (A few people are seated in a makeshift bleacher around the ring. They call ad lib comments to the fighters.) And now we get a closer view of MAX CORKLE AND CHARLIE, with Max, Joe's manager—small, tough and nervously excitable—watching the bout critically. At his side is Charlie, a handler.

MAX (calling to Joe in ring). Get that left workin', Joe! The left!

A close view of JOE PENDLETON reveals him pumping away at his partner. From what can be seen of him under the headgear, he is young, buoyant, good-looking, and at the moment spry as a kitten. Max's snarling comment comes over.

MAX'S VOICE. Move in! Follow up the punch! Get in there!

Joe, while his arms flail, turns to look at Max.

JOE (grinning as he calls out). Okay, Pop!

Joe takes a clip on the chin—and gets his mind back on fighting. This is followed by a view of MAX AND CHARLIE.

MAX (yelling to Joe). Come on—look what you're doin', will you! You're dead on your feet. (Then to Charlie, confidentially) Charlie—that's the next world

champion you're lookin' at! He's terrific!

CHARLIE (with a grin). He'll slaughter Murdock!

A bell clangs.

MAX (calling out). Okay! That's all, Joe!

A FULL VIEW OF THE RING: A handler starts pulling Joe's headgear off—as Joe goes over to Max's corner.

JOE. Gee, Max, only five rounds—I'm not even started. Lemme go a coupla more!

MAX. That's all, I said! Save some of that for Murdock!

Joe slides through the ropes and lands beside Max. Another handler pulls off his gloves. Charlie starts to throw a robe around him.

JOE (with a grin). How'd I look, Pop?

MAX (grudgingly). Just fair. Not enough speed yet.

Joe reaches for a saxophone under the stool in the ring.

JOE. Aw, go on—I'm in the pink, Max!

MAX (pulling Joe's robe around him). What d'ya want to do—get pneumonia? Listen—the next two weeks you got plenty of training to do—see?

JOE. Break down, Maxie—who's your favorite fighter?

Max pulls Joe along, ignoring the question with a scowl.

MAX. Come on—come on—quit clowning. Get your rub.

JOE. Okay, manager.

And now we follow MAX AND JOE, Joe holding his sax.

MAX. Joe—I've decided we're gonna finish training in New York. We're breakin' camp right after lunch.

JOE. Oh, boy! I can fly in this afternoon, huh?

MAX. Now, look—I'm gonna ask you a favor. Leave that plane of yours up here and come back with the gang by train. Will you do that?

JOE. Max, will you stop having kittens every time I go up in the air?

MAX. I can't help it! I don't like this flyin' —I get leary!

JOE (*patting his saxophone*). Now what can happen when I got the lucky sax along? (*Rapturously, looking up at sky*) Boy!—the feeling up there, when I fill my lungs with all that sweet ozone, sit back, and give out with the old horn! You should hear me.

MAX. I don't hear enough of that thing on the ground! (*Pleading*) Joe—the way we're set right now, a couple of weeks from the biggest scrap of your life—and on the way to a cham*peenship*—why take chances?

JOE (*ignoring Max's plea*). Fine thing! Me known as the Flyin' Pug, and the papers'll say "Flyin' Pug Takes Train." Fine thing!

MAX. Joe—

JOE. Meet you in New York at the gym tomorrow—huh?

MAX. Joe, about this flyin'—

JOE (*interrupting by bringing saxophone to his lips*). How about a little of your favorite tune, Max?

MAX. No! Not today!

Joe stops and starts to play, badly, but on the melody.

MAX. Cut it out!

Max starts to run, clapping his hands over his ears, while Joe continues to play.

The scene dissolves to a view of JOE'S PLANE, on an effective cloud skyscape, tooling along in the sunlight. It is a fairly old model cabin plane, the type that an amateur flier would rent for pleasure flying. Then we see the CABIN of the plane, empty except for Joe, who is dressed in comfortable gray trousers, open-necked shirt and cloth, or leather jacket. He has the plane controls locked and is indulging in an industrious practice session with his saxophone, laboriously reading a sheet of music which is propped up in front of him, studiously correcting sour notes which he hits. But a close view of the CONTROL WIRE on the plane tail shows the main elevator control wire vibrating badly, and rapidly fraying—in immediate danger of breaking. And now as JOE is seen at close range in the PILOT'S COMPARTMENT, playing, the music drops from its perch. Joe gives up practice, and instead of picking up the music, settles back and breaks into an old favorite that he knows well. Next the CONTROL WIRE at the PLANE TAIL frays some more— and snaps, with a vicious twang—the elevator dropping, and then THE PLANE does a vicious snap-over and heads downward, starting to spin.

In THE PLANE, Joe, seen close, still clutching his saxophone, fights the controls, trying to bring the plane out of it. He shows no fear, but plenty of exasperation. He keeps on trying. Then through the PILOT'S WINDOW, we see the earth, far below the nose of the plane, spinning like a mad cartwheel. Finally, the PLANE comes partly out of the spin for an instant, then plummets on downward in a screaming tight spin, the noise rising in violent crescendo.

The scene dissolves to a VAST, FLAT PLAIN where JOE and MESSENGER 7013 are walking, behind them a vast, huge, horizonless expanse—not permitting us to establish the place or the time.

Joe's companion, Messenger 7013, is a slight, meticulous, testy fellow, dressed in a kind of uniform that for the moment is baffling. Joe, with his saxophone under his arm and dressed as we last saw him in the plane, is

in a high state of agitation. He keeps twisting his head from the Messenger to his surroundings, and is talking at a rapid rate.

JOE. What do you mean—I'm dead? You
must be crazy! Where we walkin' to?
What's goin' on . . . ?

MESSENGER 7013 (*exasperated*). Now,
Mr. Pendleton—please!

JOE. Listen—you don't make any kind
of sense at all! You got me all mixed up!
You must be a little cracked!

MESSENGER 7013. I'm fast losing patience
with you, Mister Pendleton!

JOE. *You're* losin'—? (*Then*) Look—I
can't be wastin' time with you. I'm due
in New York—I gotta get goin'! Where
do I find a taxi around here, or a—? (*He
stops and looks off.*) Hey!

In the distance, seen from Joe's angle, appear four huge silver airliners on a great
gray expanse. There are no buildings, there
is no horizon. The distant reaches of the
field blend into gray mist.

JOE'S VOICE. A plane! *That's* what I
want!

JOE AND MESSENGER 7013:

JOE (*pointing off eagerly*). One of those
must be goin' to New York! (*Starting
to walk again*) Boy! I'm in luck—!

The Messenger, puffing, starts after Joe.

MESSENGER 7013. Mister Pendleton—*one
moment!*

Joe walks faster, so that the Messenger is
at pains to keep up.

JOE (*calling back*). One moment—nothing! I'm in a hurry, I told you!

A full view of the AIRFIELD, with the four
planes in the background: Forty or fifty passengers are waiting, male, female—old,
young, white, colored—all in everyday
clothes. They are divided into small groups,
each in charge of an Escort. Some of the
passengers are gay, some sad, some introspective. A significant thing is that there
are no relatives to see them off. As the view
comes closer we see the groups, and move
toward the first group near the plane. Mr.
Jordan is standing at the steps leading into

the plane checking passengers off the list
he holds. Jordan is a calm, elderly man of
great dignity and command yet with eyes
that can twinkle warmly on occasion. He
wears a dark business suit, set off by a
small "wings" on the breast. Now the
Escort, who is dressed like Messenger 7013,
approaches with his passengers.

ESCORT. Messenger three thousand eighty-
one reporting, sir. Five passengers.

JORDAN. Territory?

ESCORT. Southeast Australia.

JORDAN (*pencil poised over his list*). Proceed.

ESCORT. Atwater, John—

JORDAN. Check.

ESCORT. Gaylow, William—

JORDAN (*scanning list, mumbling*). Gaylow, Gaylow—(*finding it*)—Check.

ESCORT. Zabel, Frederick.

JORDAN (*looking up testily*). Zabel. That's
Z. You're jumping from G to Z. Haven't
you anyone between?

ESCORT. Yes, sir.

JORDAN (*severely*). Well, then, call them
alphabetically. You've been at this long
enough to know the rules.

ESCORT (*humbly*). Yes, sir. My mistake.
Sorry, sir.

JORDAN. Continue.

ESCORT. Heggie, Alicia.

JORDAN. Heggie, Alicia—check. (*Then*)
Now, that's better, isn't it?

ESCORT. Yes, sir! Ingle, Peter—

Suddenly Joe's voice is heard.

JOE. Hey! Which one to New York?
Who do I see about a ticket?

JORDAN (*looking up annoyed; then to
escort*). What was that name again?

ESCORT. Ingle, Peter—

But Joe's voice breaks in again.

JOE'S VOICE. Hey!. Who's in charge
around here?

Jordan is definitely annoyed now—he drops his list at his side—and looks off.

Joe comes barging in among the group, the Messenger, perspired and nervous, at his heels.

MESSENGER 7013. Mister Pendleton—will you *stop* this commotion!

JOE. What commotion? I'm just asking about a plane!

Jordan moves a few feet toward Joe.

JORDAN. Here—here—what's the trouble?

MESSENGER 7013 (*saluting*). Messenger 7013. No trouble at all, sir.

JOE. No—no trouble *yet*—but there's gonna be *plenty* if I— (*He breaks off; to Jordan.*) Are you the boss?

MESSENGER 7013 (*sharply*). A little more respect, Mr. Pendleton. This is *Mister Jordan!*

JOE (*unimpressed*). Look, Mister Jordan —the next plane leaving for New York— who do I see about a ticket—?

JORDAN (*sharply to Messenger*). What's the meaning of this?

JOE. Meaning of what? I just got through telling you—

MESSENGER 7013 (*ignoring Joe; to Jordan*). A *very* difficult case, sir—fought me tooth and nail all the way up here!

JOE. Fought him! How do you like that? (*To Jordan, indicating Messenger*) Look don't waste your time talking to this little comic; he's got a screw loose! Do you know what he keeps tellin' me— *keeps telling me I'm dead!*

MESSENGER 7013 (*losing patience*). You most certainly *are*—else I shouldn't have taken you!

JOE. Hear that?

JORDAN (*quietly*). I'm afraid you are.

JOE (*with sudden shock*). Are—*what?*

JORDAN. Dead.

JOE (*blazing*). You too? Why, *you* must be as crazy as—!

Joe stops, for Jordan's eyes are on him steadily—and the look in Jordan's face commands silence and respect in Joe.

JOE (*softly; incredulously*). Dead—?

JORDAN (*quickly*). Just a moment, please.

Jordan moves back to former position with the Escort and group, leaving Joe dazed.

JORDAN (*consulting his list; to the Escort*). That last name again.

A close view of JOE AND MESSENGER 7013 reveals Joe in a frightened daze, staring around bewilderedly.

ESCORT'S VOICE. Ingle, Peter.

JORDAN'S VOICE. Ingle—check.

ESCORT'S VOICE. Zabel, Frederick. And that is all, sir.

A full view of the scene, with Jordan making a last check and Joe anxiously looking at him, now appears.

JORDAN. Zabel, Frederick. Check. (*Indicating the plane*) You may proceed. (*Then he calls out*) Next, please!

The Escort moves into the plane after Zabel, and another escort moves up with his passengers. But Joe has started toward Jordan and interrupts the proceedings.

JOE (*reverent; uncertain*). Uh—Mr. Jordan—excuse me. I don't get this—you— —you wouldn't *kid* me?

MESSENGER 7013 (*trying to hold him back*). Mr. Pendleton—!

JOE (*continuing to Jordan*). What I mean is—are you—are you *sure?*

MESSENGER 7013. Of course!!

JOE. But I—I *feel* all right—!

MESSENGER 7013 (*to Jordan*). Pay no attention to him, sir.

Jordan, interestedly observing Joe, takes a step toward him and the Messenger.

JORDAN (*to Messenger—critically*). Is he all you gathered?

MESSENGER 7013 (*morosely*). Yes, sir. I'm sorry, sir.

JORDAN. Name?

MESSENGER 7013. Pendleton, Joseph.

JOE. Not Pendleton Joseph—Joe Pendleton.

MESSENGER 7013. Oh, for heaven's sake, be still!

JORDAN (*scanning list*). Pendleton—Pendleton—

Joe, very upset, tries to glance at the list.

JOE. Gee—I—I *can't* be on any list—

MESSENGER 7013. Quiet—*please!*

JOE. I'm *telling* you—from the way I feel—there's some wires crossed or something—somebody's made a mistake.

MESSENGER 7013. Mistake! Utterly fantastic!

JORDAN (*turning papers*). What did you do? Your occupation? (*Glancing at saxophone*) Musician?

JOE. No—no—just my hobby—like flyin' is. I'm Joe Pendleton—The Flyin' Pug they call me. (*As they look surprised*) Pug—I'm a *prizefighter!*

MESSENGER 7013. You *were* a prizefighter.

Joe gives the Messenger a dazed glance. Jordan suddenly slaps the last page closed and stares at the Messenger disapprovingly.

JORDAN (*sharply*). There's no Pendleton, Joseph, listed.

JOE (*in small excitement*). See! I *told* you—

MESSENGER 7013 (*agitatedly*). Oh, but it—it can't be possible, sir! There must be *some* explanation—

JORDAN (*fixing a critical stare on messenger*). Let's *hope* so, for your sake. I'll see if he's on any newer listing.

And Jordan starts out, Messenger 7013 and Joe tagging at his heels. We follow them toward the huge, silvery blunt nose of the second plane. The co-pilot's window, high above us, looms into the scene; the co-pilot leaning out of the window idly watching the scene below, his earphones shoved up on his head.

MESSENGER 7013 (*as Joe and he follow Jordan*). Oh—he's simply got to be, sir.

JOE. What do you mean—I *got* to be? If I ain't on any list—I ain't on any list!

By this time the three have come into position near the plane, heedless of the interested group of passengers and the escort, who stand nearby.

JORDAN (*breaking in on Joe; calling up to co-pilot*). Mister Sloane—contact the Registrar's office. Ask them for everything they have on Pendleton, Joseph—

CO-PILOT. Yes, sir.

He disappears inside the window. Then in the PILOT'S COMPARTMENT, we see him adjusting earphones and switching on the radio.

CO-PILOT (*into the instrument*). Calling Registrar's office—plane twenty-two calling Registrar's office. Hello— (*Very respectfully*) Mr. Jordan asks if you would please check the name Pendleton, Joseph.

At the PLANE: Joe is a little confident and cocky, although still very nervous.

JOE (*insistently*). I'm trying to tell you fellows—I'm not ready for this place. I never felt better in my life! Why, I'm in the pink! How could I be dead?

Jordan hands the old list to the escort standing by with his passengers.

JORDAN. Here—carry on with the rest of your passengers.

ESCORT (*saluting*). Yes, sir.

MESSENGER 7013 (*increasingly nervous, addressing Jordan*). Really sir—it isn't possible that he could have survived. Why, he was hurtling to earth with the speed of a meteor . . .

JOE. Just the same, I wouldn't have crashed! I'd have pulled that ship out, somehow—*if you'd just left me alone.*

JORDAN (*to Messenger 7013*). You mean to say you took him out of that plane *before* it crashed?

JOE. Yeah—that's what he did!

MESSENGER 7013. Please, Mr. Pendleton—! (*Then to Jordan*) Yes, sir. I know we messengers shouldn't permit our emotions to sway us, but—there he was, plummeting earthward—and such a fine-looking young man—I wanted to spare him the agony of crashing, so I—I—

JORDAN. Unpardonably presumptuous!

JOE. Yeah!

MESSENGER 7013. I'm desolate about it, sir.

JORDAN. What territory do you cover?

MESSENGER 7013. A place called New Jersey, sir—and if it can be arranged, I should very much like to be transferred.

JORDAN. You're new, aren't you?

MESSENGER 7013. Yes, sir, I—I was put on only this morning. This is my first trip.

JORDAN. I thought so. Over-zealousness. Out for record collections. This happens right along with the inexperienced—

MESSENGER 7013. Really? Dear me!

JOE. I'm telling you—it wasn't in the cards. (*Building his confidence; touching his saxophone; with a laugh*) Why, nothing ever happens to me when I've got my lucky sax along.

JORDAN (*indicating the saxophone; to the Messenger*). How did he manage to wangle that thing up here?

CO-PILOT'S VOICE. Mr. Jordan, sir!

They all turn up to the co-pilot.

CO-PILOT (*seen at close view leaning out of the window*). On Pendleton, Joseph: the official record says both his parents are happily withdrawn and awaiting his arrival. Joseph is scheduled to join them the morning of May eleven, nineteen hundred ninety-one.

In JORDAN'S GROUP:

JOE (*in amazed delight*). *Nineteen ninety-one!* Why, that's *fifty years off* yet! What did I tell you!

Jordan looks a hole through miserable Messenger 7013.

JORDAN. It seems you were a bit premature.

JOE. Fifty years more to go! Gee! (*To the Messenger, lightly*) You sure pulled a boner *that* time!

MESSENGER 7013. Oh, dear me! I—I'm afraid I owe you an apology, Mr. Pendleton.

JOE. I'll tell the world you do! But that's all right. No harm done. We all make mistakes. Just take me back and forget about it.

MESSENGER 7013. T-take you back?

JORDAN. Naturally—*take him back*. Return him to the body out of which you so indiscreetly snatched him!

JOE. That's right. And say—could we make it snappy? I gotta meet Corkle—he'll be worried.

MESSENGER 7013. Corkle?

JOE. My manager. I'm in training for the Murdock bout. Gotta keep the body in the pink, you know. Let's go!

MESSENGER 7013. *I'm* the one that says, "Let's go"—if you don't mind, Mr. Pendleton.

They start off.

JOE (*happily*). All right with me. Oh—!

Joe stops, comes back to Jordan quickly, holding out his hand, which Jordan takes.

JOE. I'm sure glad I met you, Mr. Jordan. Thanks for straightening this thing out.

JORDAN. Not at all.

JOE (*with a smile*). Well—be seeing you, fifty years from now—if you're still on the job.

JORDAN (*smiling back; he likes this boy*). I will be.

JOE. So long.

He and Messenger 7013 move off again. But as they pass a group of passengers, waiting to be checked in, Joe's attention fastens on a man of fifty or so.

JOE (*to the passenger*). H'ya, pal. This ain't such a bad place. I wouldn't mind staying only I got a lot of work to do yet. How about you? Did you finish your job?

PASSENGER (*smiling*). Quite. I was glad to come.

JOE. Oh. Well, that's okay then. Well—good luck!

And as Joe and the Messenger move away from the Camera—their figures growing smaller—the scene dissolves to a CLEARING, seen in daylight. JOE AND THE MESSENGER approach—Joe hurried and excited. He breaks into a run, with Messenger 7013 at his side. This small clearing is a natural field with forest rising around it.

JOE (*pointing ahead, calling out*). There's the old crate!

Joe's wrecked plane in the near background appears, and Joe and the Messenger hurry up to it on the run. Then a closer view of JOE AND THE MESSENGER, as they come to a pause, finds them staring into the wreck. Their eyes rove over it quickly—then come to rest, expressing bewilderment, a frown forming on Joe's brow. And we see what he sees ("from Joe's angle") at close range: THE PILOT'S COMPARTMENT. It is empty, and there is no trace of a human being in it.

JOE AND THE MESSENGER: Joe, his frown deepened, turns to look at the Messenger, who is equally nonplussed.

JOE. I—I'm not here! What happened? Where—where is it—I mean—where am I?

MESSENGER 7013 (*recovering slowly; stammering*). Obviously your—your body was removed. Mr. Pendleton—

JOE. Yeah—but where to? Where *to*?

MESSENGER (*confused*). Well, let me think. Perhaps I'd better take you back to Mister Jordan.

JOE (*with a sudden idea*). I know! Corkle! He did it! Ten-to-one he's got me laid out in my own living-room right now—the idiot! Let's go!

MESSENGER 7013. *I* say "let's go"!

Both men start away together—as if on a signal—and as the eye follows them—and

before we can determine whether they ran off across the field or just vanished into thin air—the scene dissolves to:

A RESIDENCE STREET in daylight, as JOE AND MESSENGER 7013 are hurrying along. The same eagerness and drive appear in Joe's face and bearing as before, Messenger 7013 perspiring to keep up with him. It is a street like one in the west Seventies or Eighties—brownstone fronts—and in the background a drugstore on the corner—and maybe a small store or two. A few people pass.

JOE. Boy, we sure get around, don't we? Zip—we're at the crackup; bam—we're here in New York. How do you do it?

MESSENGER 7013 (*severely*). I'll have to ask you not to pry into trade secrets, Mr. Pendleton.

JOE (*laughing*). Okay with me!

Joe's step quickens as he turns his eyes up to the fronts of the houses. Suddenly he heads up one of the sets of stairs, the Messenger on his heels.

JOE. Here we are! Here's home!

He has gone up two steps when a newsboy's voice bawls out:

NEWSBOY'S VOICE. Read all about it! Extra! Joe Pendleton cracks up in plane!

Joe comes to an abrupt stop. Joe and the Messenger remain on the steps as the Newsboy enters the scene, moving fast along the walk, the papers under his arm.

NEWSBOY. The Flyin' Pug killed in crash! Extra!

Joe hops down the couple of steps just as the Newsboy is passing the steps.

JOE (*laughing back at Messenger*). This is a laugh! That's what *he* thinks! (*Reaching for money in his pocket*) Hey—gimme one of them!

The Newsboy isn't conscious of Joe—he keeps right on going and bawling his extra.

NEWSBOY. Extra! Flyin' Pug dies in crash!

JOE (*loudly*). Hey, kid! Paper!

NEWSBOY. Read all about it!

Beside himself, Joe shouts with all his might after the departing boy.

JOE. Hey!

Messenger 7013 has hurried down to Joe's side—and is plucking Joe's sleeve.

MESSENGER 7013 (*breaking in*). Mr. Pendleton!

The Newsboy is gone. His voice fades out as he repeats one of the headlines.

JOE (*turning on the Messenger*). Why, that kid's goofy!

MESSENGER 7013. He can't see or hear you, Mr. Pendleton.

JOE. What? Why not?

MESSENGER 7013. Because you're not in your body. That's simple.

JOE (*startled*). Oh! (*Then quickly*) Yeah —but I can see and hear *him!*

MESSENGER 7013. Yes, of course.

JOE (*confused and alarmed*). Well, *holy smoke!* What are we waiting for? Let's go!!

And Joe and the Messenger make for the steps as the scene dissolves to:

JOE'S APARTMENT LIVING ROOM as Joe and the Messenger move in out of a fairly deep foyer behind them. (We have therefore not seen them actually come in by the front door—leaving to the imagination the question of whether they opened the door, came through it unopened, or simply appeared where we discover them.) Joe, moving into the room, is arrested a few feet inside it by the voice of Corkle.

CORKLE'S VOICE. —if I told him once, I told him a thousand times—

Now there is a full view of the room, with Joe and the Messenger standing some feet inside it. Seated around are three or four men—among them Charlie and Max Corkle —all at the moment in deep depression.

CORKLE. —but no—he's *gotta* fly!

Joe's first impulse on seeing Max is one of delight—since Joe knows he isn't dead and that Max's sorrow is misplaced. Therefore Joe smiles and bounds forward happily.

JOE. Max! Be yourself, pal! Look!

MESSSENGER 7013 (*plucking Joe's sleeve*). Remember—he can't see or hear you.

JOE (*stunned, subsiding*). Oh, I forgot.

CORKLE (*choked*). This washes me up, boys. I'm quittin' the game. I couldn't handle anybody after Joe—

CHARLIE (*softly*). You sure loved that kid, didn't you?

Max turns away to hide his eyes. Joe is affected.

JOE. Gee—poor Max. I wish I could tell him— (*Suddenly staring around in alarm*) Say—I—I don't see me around. Where am I?

He turns and darts off—in the direction of the adjoining bedroom, the Messenger following.

In the REDROOM: Joe and the Messenger enter, staring around swiftly. There is no body in sight.

JOE. What'd they *do* with me?

And Joe rushes back into the living-room.

The LIVING-ROOM: Max walks around, while Charlie is going through some letters in Joe's desk. Joe comes flying in, the Messenger at his heels again, and blurts passionately:

JOE. Max! What did you do with—?

Joe breaks off, remembering again that he can't be heard.

CORKLE. And what a champ he'd'a made! The cleanest kid in the world—with a heart as big as a house—!

JOE (*impatiently, to Messenger*). Can't you ask him what he did with me?

The Messenger shakes his head.

CORKLE (*continuing*). —and how he *wanted* to be a champ. Not like these other palookas—not just for the roar of the crowd and the dough—and his picture in the paper. Not Joe. Know what he'd say sometime? "Max, I gotta knock over that title—because a lotta kids expect me to do it!" That's the kind of thing that was botherin' *him*—

JOE (*his impatience mounting*). How do ya *like* this? Max Corkle, gettin' sentimental! Why don't he stop the gush and *tell* us something?

Charlie holds up some letters.

CHARLIE. Who'd he know out in Kansas?

CORKLE. Some fifth cousins—or something. Was always sendin' them dough. Them—and fifty other people—"A fighter's got to live cleaner'n anybody else," he used to say—"cause kids look up to fellas like that and try to live like 'em—"

JOE (*patience at an end, yelling*). Max! Lay off! Where *am* I?

A knock on the door. Max goes to it and opens it. There stand three kids. The one in front, named Johnnie, carries a small bouquet.

JOE (*impulsively*). Johnnie!

CORKLE. Hello, boys—

JOHNNIE (*chin quivering a little*). Hello, Mr. Corkle! It's—it's awful, isn't it?

CORKLE. Yeah—sure is, Johnnie—

JOHNNIE. He was—swell—Joe was—

CHIP (*the kid behind Johnnie; blurting*). He'd'a licked Murdock—and Gilbert too!

CORKLE. That's how I felt about it, Chip.

Johnnie extends the flowers.

JOHNNIE. We—we brought these. Kinda late. But—but—you see—we didn't know where that place was—you know—the—uh—

CORKLE. Crematory—yeah—

We get a close view of JOE AND THE MESSENGER, their eyes popping.

JOE. Crematory!

CORKLE'S VOICE. Thanks, boys—

JOE (*frantically; to Messenger*). Cremated!

MESSENGER 7013. Oh, dear me!

Joe listens to the next lines (off-scene) in a wild daze.

JOHNNIE'S VOICE. You mean—they really took Joe and—?

CORKLE. Yup—it's all over, fellas—

JOE (*yelling*). Max—you dumb cluck—!

MESSENGER 7013. *Control* yourself, Mr. Pendleton!

JOE. *Control* myself! Do you realize—? What do I do now?

MESSENGER 7013 (*at a loss*). Well, offhand I—I—

JOE (*angrily*). And offhand I oughta—! (*Then*) Come on! We're going back to Mister Jordan!

And again, Joe and the Messenger start forward from the bedroom door, where they have been standing, toward the exit. But before they have taken many steps the scene dissolves to:

JORDAN'S OFFICE, revealing Joe, Messenger 7013 and Jordan, who now is seated at an enormous desk, of unusual design, in an office, which is *not* an office in the accepted sense, but a place whose walls blend off insubstantially and where one is not aware of a ceiling. Joe, the saxophone still hanging from his shoulder, is bending over Jordan's desk dramatically talking right at him, while Messenger 7013 stands by, wringing his hands in great nervousness.

JOE. That's what I said! *Cremated!* While you two kept me up here gabbing, that dumb Corkle finds my body in the plane —and *has me cremated!*

JORDAN. Tsk—tsk—that's *bad!*

JOE. *Bad?*

MESSENGER 7013 (*distraught*). *Most* deplorable, sir! I shall never forgive myself! I—I feel *ghastly!*

JOE. How do you think *I* feel? Wait'll I

get hold of that Corkle! He can't go burning me up and get away with it!

JORDAN. Very bad. This complicates everything.

MESSENGER 7013. I've an idea, sir. Could we have him reborn?

JOE. Nix! I'm not going through that again!

JORDAN (*to Messenger*). No, no. (*Rising tiredly*) Well, I see I'll have to take personal charge of this.

JOE. Now you're talking, Mister Jordan! You got to get busy and *do* something about this.

JORDAN. I intend to. Come along, Joseph.

JOE. Where to?

JORDAN. I'm taking you back.

JOE. But you can't! Didn't we tell you? I haven't got a *body* any more—

JORDAN (*annoyed*). What of it? I'll get you another body.

JOE. You'll do what?

MESSENGER 7013 (*to Jordan; in amazement*). Another *body*, sir?

JORDAN (*testily*). That's what I said. Come along.

He takes Joe by the arm as if to lead him off. But Joe holds back.

JOE (*hotly*). Wait a minute, now—wait a minute. What kind of a deal is this? You fellas aren't shoving anybody else's body off on me. Not on your life!

MESSENGER 7013 (*seeing the light*). Oh, but Mr. Pendleton—if Mr. Jordan says he'll get you a body, it'll be as good as your own—if not *better*.

JOE (*stubbornly; troubled*). There isn't any better! I put in ten years getting that body in the pink. No! Just because you two fumbled the ball is no sign—!

JORDAN (*with authority*). But, Joseph— it's *gone*! Your body doesn't *exist* any more!

JOE (*doggedly*). That isn't my fault. You

fellows can do anything. Now come on— do your stuff!

JORDAN (*kindly*). We shall, Joseph. You may have your choice of a thousand bodies, all excellent specimens.

MESSENGER 7013. A *thousand* bodies, Mr. Pendleton. Think of it!

JOE. I *am* thinking of it, and I say no dice! I want my *own* body—nobody else's!

MESSENGER 7013. Oh, tush! Don't make such a fuss. What is it, after all? A mere physical covering—worth chemically— —*just thirty-two cents!*

JOE. Not mine. It was in the pink, I tell you!

MESSENGER 7013. Oh dear!

JORDAN. Suppose we get started, Joseph.

JOE (*holding back*). Now wait. Let's understand each other before we go running around—

JORDAN. I promise you—we'll keep looking until you find a body you like. Is that fair enough!

JOE. I only want what's coming to me— What I was and what I was going to be —Nothing more, nothing less. And *I expect you to make good*, Mr. Jordan.

JORDAN (*smiling*). I'll do my best, Joe. Come along.

He starts off with Joe.

JOE (*grudgingly, as he goes*). Okay—but I'm warning you—you may be just wasting your time—

JORDAN. I've a *lot* of that.

MESSENGER 7013 (*calling after them*). Goodbye, Mr. Pendleton—the best of luck.

Joe turns, while walking, to call back.

JOE. That sounds mighty weird, coming from *you!*

And as the figures of Joe and Jordan become lost in fog, the scene fades out.

PART TWO

A STREET in an exclusive residence section of Long Island fades in. Along the walk runs a high, grilled fence, through which can be seen the beautiful grounds and home of a big estate. Joe and Jordan are coming along the walk. Joe, his saxophone slung under his arm, is looking around at the surroundings.

JOE (*grinning*). Boy—I thought that Messenger was good at getting around—but you're *terrific*. Russia—Australia—South Africa—now New York. How do you do it? (*As Jordan smiles, Joe adds quickly*) I know. It's a trade secret.

JORDAN. Joe—we've made a hundred and thirty stops—

JOE. We sure made a raft of 'em.

JORDAN. I know how you feel about a *perfect* body. But I've offered you the *cream* of last week's crop—and you've turned up your nose at the lot—

JOE (*in justified protest*). Now, *you* know there wasn't a physique in the whole bunch, Mr. Jordan. And you're not palming off any second rater on me. Just remember—I was "in the pink."

JORDAN. That's becoming a most *obnoxious* color, Joe. Don't mention it again—please.

JOE. Okay—

They have now come to the large gates, and Jordan stops and looks up the long drive-way toward the house. Joe too comes to a halt. He nods in the direction of the house.

JOE. Next stop?

JORDAN. Yes.

JOE (*looking off, appraising the lay-out*). Pretty snazzy place. Who do we size up here?

JORDAN. The owner—Bruce Farnsworth.

JOE. Look, Mr. Jordan—this isn't just another one of those things—?

JORDAN. You'll find this *most* interesting, Joe. (*Joe looks quizzically.*) By *far* the most interesting we've looked into yet.

JOE. Okay. I don't want you to think I'm not playin' ball.

They turn up the driveway.

The FARNSWORTH ENTRANCE HALL: Joe and Jordan, who have already entered, are moving forward into the entrance hall—the front door behind them. The entrance hall is spacious and beautifully furnished, indicating great wealth and fine taste, and Joe is glancing around appraisingly. Now they come to the entrance of the living room and Joe glances into it.

The LIVING ROOM, seen with Joe and Jordan at the entrance, is enormous and richly furnished.

JOE. Whew! Cozy little place.

From offscene, somewhere behind Joe in the entrance hall, are heard the sound of a closing door and approaching footsteps. Joe turns to look, as does Jordan. Suddenly there appears Farnsworth's chief butler, Sisk—a middle-aged fellow, pompous and stuffy—carrying a liquor tray on which are brandy and glasses. He is heading for the living room—right in the direction of Joe and Jordan, whereupon Joe grabs Jordan and pulls him to one side of the living room entrance.

JOE. We better duck!

JORDAN. *Please* stop yanking me around, Joseph! Can't you remember we can neither be—

JOE (*relaxing—finishing the sentence with Jordan*). —seen or heard. (*Smiling*) Yeah. I keep forgetting.

Sisk, the butler, passes right past them into the living room. And now, at close range, Sisk places the liquor tray on a table—and Joe and Jordan advance into the room a trifle.

JOE. Who's that?

JORDAN. Farnsworth's butler.

JOE. Oh.

They watch as Sisk moves solemnly out of

the room again. Jordan has sat down on the piano bench—and during the following aimlessly picks out chords on the piano.

JOE (*when Sisk is gone*). About this Farnsworth. What's the dope?

JORDAN. Well, he's about your age, and fairly husky—

JOE (*looking around*). *My* age—and's got all this?

JORDAN. He inherited it, Joe.

JOE. Oh. (*Flexing his arms*) And he's well set up, huh?

JORDAN. Quite. Played polo a while back—

JOE. Sounds pretty good. Is he dead?

JORDAN. No.

Jordan adds the left hand to his piano and is playing softly.

JOE. *Gonna* die though.

JORDAN. Yes.

JOE. Sick, huh?

JORDAN. Not *really*. He *has* a slightly run-down condition but—

JOE. Oh-oh! (*Indicating luxurious surroundings*) Playboy—wine-women-and-song! Ruins his health! Fine body you're making me a present of—a guy who drinks himself into an early grave—!

JORDAN. No, he didn't—

JOE (*with sarcasm*). No—just *slightly* run-down—and he's gonna *die!* That's all!

JORDAN (*calmly*). He's being *murdered,* Joe.

Joe is aghast—Jordan continues to play.

JOE. Murdered! (*Jordan is unperturbed.*) You mean it's going on right now—?

JORDAN. Yes.

JOE. In this house? (*Jordan nods.*) Who—who's killing him?

JORDAN. His wife—and the man she's in love with—Farnsworth's confidential secretary.

JOE. Nice people you want me to meet— How are they doing it?

JORDAN (*as he continues playing calmly*). They're drowning him in the bathtub.

Joe glances in panic up at the ceiling—then he rushes for Jordan.

JOE. Holy Cow! (*Seizing Jordan's arm*) Come on—let's scram out of here! I'm keeping my nose clean! I'm in enough trouble already!

Jordan stops playing, turns on the piano bench—and shakes Joe's hand off.

JORDAN (*with authority*). *Wait,* Joe—!

Joe stops, speaking in pleading protest.

JOE. Look, Mr. Jordan—you don't think I'm going to change places with a guy who's got a wife like *that* hanging around? I'm not punch-drunk yet!

JORDAN. We'll have to wait here until I collect him, Joe. (*Starting to play again*) It's my job.

JOE. But—how can you sit there playing when—when they're killing somebody? Why can't we call the cops?

JORDAN. I'm afraid they wouldn't pay any attention to us.

Joe is standing at the entrance into the hall —agitated.

JOE. Oh, that's right.

Jordan breaks off at the piano and turns.

JORDAN (*quietly*). It's all over, Joe—

JOE. You mean—he's dead?

Before Jordan can answer, a door is heard to close on the floor above. Joe whirls frightenedly and looks up.

The STAIR BALCONY (seen upward from Joe's and Jordan's angle near the living room entrance): Tony Abbott, Farnsworth's secretary, a handsome, suave fellow—and Julia Farnsworth, a voluptuous brunette—have just come out of a bedroom door. They are nervous and strained, as they stand on the UPPER LANDING. Julia is on the verge of collapse.

JULIA. Tony—I'm frightened!

TONY (*quickly, softly*). Get hold of yourself, Julia.

He starts to lead her along the balcony toward the stairs. In the LIVING ROOM, JOE AND JORDAN, seen at close range, follow the progress of Tony and Julia down the stairs.

JOE (*in a hushed voice*). Those are the two that did it, huh?

JORDAN. Yes. Mrs. Farnsworth and the secretary, Tony Abbott.

Then Tony and Julia come down the stairs and head for the living room, going right past Joe and Jordan, Joe studying them as they go by.

JOE. Gee—to look at her you wouldn't think—

Julia, trembling, stops near Joe, and clutches at Tony.

JULIA. Tony—I—I don't know what's come over me. I have a feeling I can't shake off—that there's something weird —something hanging over us—watching us—

JOE (*softly*). You said it, sister.

Tony leads Julia on into the room, toward the divan and the liquor tray.

TONY. Come now—stop it, Julia!

He begins to pour her a brandy.

TONY (*comforting her; smoothly*). What could be more natural—a glass of warm milk—a sleeping tablet or two—and a very *tired,* dissipated young man—uh— unfortunately—*drowses* off in his bath—

This is too much for Joe.

JOE (*to Jordan*). I've had enough of this! I need some fresh air!

JORDAN. Joe! Wait! Don't go yet!

JOE. No, sir! I don't want any more of *this* mob!

As Joe heads for the entrance hall, he pulls up sharply as Sisk appears in the entrance.

SISK. Miss Bette Logan to see Mr. Farnsworth.

Julia jumps up from the divan, startled; and Joe pauses, looking questioningly back at Jordan, who hasn't moved.

JORDAN. Wait, Joe.

JULIA (*to Tony, tensely, hiding her emotion from Sisk*). I can't talk to her now.

TONY (*calmly*). Of course you can. (*To Sisk*) Show her in.

As Sisk exits, Tony turns at once to Julia:

TONY. It's very simple. Just be sympathetic. I'll be in the study. If she becomes difficult, bring her in to me.

He hurries to a set of doors that lead to the study, and disappears. Julia touches her hair quickly, as Joe turns to Jordan, puzzled.

JOE. Who's this Logan—somebody else mixed up in this murder!

JORDAN. Judge for yourself, Joe.

And at this instant, while Joe's head is turned to Jordan, Sisk reappears.

SISK. Miss Logan.

JOE, seen close, swings his head from Jordan to the entrance. He gasps at what he sees. BETTE LOGAN, seen fairly close, comes to a pause just inside the living room and fastens her eyes on Julia. Bette is a slender, exceedingly beautiful young girl of twenty —a vision Joe might very well gasp at. She is dressed in taste, expensively. The face reveals pride and spirit, and still there is a youthful helplessness about her.

JULIA'S VOICE. Good afternoon, Miss Logan.

BETTE (*stiffly*). How do you do.

A close view of JOE reveals him still in the throes of excitement.

JOE. Gee—she's beautiful!

JORDAN, seen close, simply smiles back at Joe.

JOE (*seen close, continues to look at her*). I didn't see anything like that in heaven, Mister Jordan.

BETTE'S VOICE. I'd like to see Mr. Farnsworth.

Now we have a full view of the room, including all four characters.

JULIA. He'll be right down, my dear.

JOE. Right *down! She* knows he's dead!

Jordan doesn't answer.

JULIA. Won't you sit down?

BETTE. No, thanks. You heard of my father's arrest.

JULIA. Yes. I was terribly sorry. But certainly you didn't come here expecting Mr. Farnsworth to help him?

BETTE. I didn't come to ask for favors. My father isn't guilty of *anything!*

JULIA. Except—he *is* head of Logan and Company—and he *did* float the Bay Ridge securities.

BETTE (*flashing—angry tears in her eyes*). He was in *Europe* at the time! He left everything in Mr. Farnsworth's hands— and Mr. Farnsworth unloaded those worthless securities under my father's name!

JULIA. Why, you're a bit hysterical, aren't you? Let me give you a brandy.

BETTE. No, thanks!

JOE (*impulsively, to Bette*). That's right. Don't take anything from that dame!

JULIA. If you don't believe your father acted of his own accord, you might step into the study—to Mr. Abbott. He has some documents that will convince you. Would you care to see them?

BETTE (*grimly*). Yes—I'd like very *much* to see them.

Julia leads the way for Bette—to the study.

JOE (*agitated*). Gosh, that's a tough spot for that kid! She's got gumption— coming here all alone to battle for her father like that!

JORDAN. She worships him.

JOE. But she's no match for those buzzards! She needs help. She's in trouble! Why don't you get busy?

JORDAN (*quietly*). Farnsworth is the only one who can help her, Joe.

A slight pause—then Joe blurts:

JOE. But he's dead!

JORDAN (*gently*). But you *can be Farnsworth.*

Joe's eyes pop as he stares an instant at Jordan. Then Joe shakes his head as though shaking off a bad punch.

JOE. Wait a minute. I don't get this.

JORDAN. It's simple.

JOE. You mean—you want me to be Farnsworth and have a swell girl like that *hate* me!

JORDAN. You'll make a very different Farnsworth. Spiritually there'll be no change in you—

JOE (*thinking hard*). How do you figure? I couldn't be myself any more—and if a guy isn't himself, what good is he?

JORDAN. *You'll always be yourself, Joe.* You'd merely be using Farnsworth's physical covering—like donning a new overcoat—

JOE. It's got to be *some* overcoat—to last me fifty years!

JORDAN. —but inside that overcoat—it would still be Joe Pendleton thinking and acting and feeling—

JOE. Yeah—but that overcoat—that'll be *Farnsworth.* That's what she'll *see,* and he was a rat! She'll think *I'm* a rat!

JORDAN. Maybe at first—but *eventually* she'll see the soul of Joe Pendleton—because that is never lost. That will always shine through, Joe—no matter what *overcoat* you put on—

Joe walks small circles in extreme agitation.

JOE. Yeah—okay—but—but this run-down overcoat—I mean, this playboy Farnsworth—why, I'd have to give up everything—a crack at the title and— (*Then emphatically*) No, no! I can't do *that!* No, Mister Jordan. I'd like to help her—but not this way—

JORDAN (*gently*). There is no other way.

JOE (*flaring up, in his enormous trouble*). Gee—do you think it's fair to put me in a spot like this!

He moves toward the open door to the study, anxiously looking inside.

In the STUDY, a luxurious, book-lined room: At the desk stand Julia, Tony and Bette, a pile of legal correspondence before them and Bette examining some of it.

BETTE (*throwing the papers down defiantly*). These were forged! Because my father never did a dishonest thing in his life! He couldn't *cheat* a lot of poor people with worthless stock! He couldn't! I want to see Mr. Farnsworth!

JULIA (*calmly*). Mr. Abbott—have Sisk announce Miss Logan to Mr. Farnsworth.

Tony goes to the place near the door where Joe stands looking in, and pulls the bell cord.

JOE (*looking back at Jordan*). What's the idea? She knows he's dead! Why send Sisk?

In the LIVING ROOM, we see JORDAN, with Joe in the background near the study door.

JORDAN. Very convenient. . . . Sisk discovering the body. Joe—you haven't much time to decide—

JOE. Gosh, I—I don't *want* to be Farnsworth, Mr. Jordan!

Julia's voice breaks out in the study, causing Joe to swing his attention back.

JULIA'S VOICE. Miss Logan—you're a stupid child! What would Bruce Farnsworth do for you—or anyone?

In the STUDY, Joe, in the background, is seen looking in through the open door.

JULIA (*continuing*). No crueler man ever lived! A spoiled brat who grew up to be a vicious, selfish adult. Perhaps you think he'll reach into his pocket and pay out five million dollars to redeem those securities—just to make you happy and get your father out of jail! Why, he'd see you both starving first—and enjoy it!

Bette stands grimly, Joe whirls back to Jordan.

JOE. You hear that!

JORDAN'S VOICE. You want to help her, don't you, Joe?

JOE (*in terrible, troubled indecision*). Yes —I do—I *do*—only—

Suddenly at Joe's side, practically in the study doorway, appears Sisk. Joe watches the ensuing action fascinatedly.

SISK. You rang, Madam?

JULIA. Yes. Tell Mr. Farnsworth Miss Logan is here to see him.

SISK. Yes, Madam.

The LIVING ROOM: As Sisk turns from the study door and crosses the living room towards the hall entrance, Joe turns back to Jordan in high excitement.

JOE (*indicating Sisk*). Gosh! He's going up there!

JORDAN. Hurry, Joe—make up your mind.

JOE (*going crazy*). Don't rush me. I—I can't make a step like this without— without figurin'—

Jordan's eyes follow Sisk who is mounting the stairs.

JORDAN. He's not far from the bathroom, Joe.

JOE. Holy smoke! (*Then wildly*) Look— what if I did it—but only *temporary!* I mean—could I be Farnsworth just—just for a little while—till I help this kid out? Could I do *that?*

JORDAN. If you wish it.

JOE. Then, that's *it!* But look now— afterwards you get me out of Farnsworth and—and we find the body I want! You got that *clear* now?

JORDAN. Quite clear.

JOE. Okay! It's a deal!

JORDAN. Come!

And Jordan starts quickly for the entrance hall, Joe, with the saxophone still under his arm, following fast at Jordan's heels. As we follow them, we move into FARNS-WORTH'S BEDROOM as SISK enters from the hall, looks around for Farnsworth and begins to cross to the bathroom door. Dressing gown and other articles are laid out on the bed.

The BATHROOM affords a close view of JOR-DAN AND JOE. Jordan, his back turned to us,

is holding up a large bathrobe—and the figure standing in front of him—his back also
to us—is slowly getting into it. Then JOE
AND JORDAN are seen at close range, facing
us. It is Joe who has been getting into the
bathrobe—and we now see him closing it
around him. On the breast pocket is neatly
initialed: "B.F." Joe's actions are slow, mechanical—as though he were somewhat
dazed.

(NOTE: Joe's physical appearance is in no
way altered now that he is Farnsworth. We,
as an omniscient audience, in on the facts,
continue to see him as he sees himself—
looking at his unchanged soul. The other
characters see him as Farnsworth—as explained shortly by Jordan.)

Joe turns his head slowly and looks down.
It is the EMPTY BATHTUB that he sees, and
the Farnsworth who occupied it is gone off
the face of the earth.

JOE, seen at close range with JORDAN, turns
his head back from the empty bathtub—
wondering, but Jordan, seen over Joe's shoulder, is smiling. Joe lifts his eyes, looks off to
his left side, and is shocked.

Joe's reflection is caught in a full-length mirror—as he himself sees it. He sees himself—
Joe Pendleton—and it is the reason for his
shock. He touches his face.

    JOE. Hey—it's still *me!* I haven't
changed! Look!

A knock on the door.

    SISK'S VOICE. Mr. Farnsworth.

    JOE (*in a panic*). What do we do?
(*Pointing at mirror*) I can't get away
with this! I still look like *me!*

    SISK'S VOICE. Mr. Farnsworth! Are you
there, sir? What's happened?

    JORDAN. Answer him, Joe.

    JOE. Answer! You mean—people can
hear me now?

    JORDAN. Yes.

    JOE. But—if I talk, he'll—he knows the
other guy's voice!

    SISK'S VOICE (*at high pitch, turning
locked door handle*). *Please*—answer me,
sir!

    JORDAN. Go ahead, Joe.

    JOE (*after a pause—taking the plunge—
shouting*). *In a minute!*

A dead pause. Joe waits.

    SISK'S VOICE (*calmly answering*). Yes,
sir.

Joe does an amazed "take," snapping his
head to Jordan, who smiles.

    JORDAN. What *he* heard was—the voice
of Bruce Farnsworth.

    JOE. He did?

    JORDAN. And when you open that door—
what he'll *see* will be Farnsworth.

Joe snaps his head to the mirror.

    JOE (*pointing to his reflection*). But how
come? Isn't that Joe Pendleton—or am I
nuts?

    JORDAN. *Inwardly*, you haven't changed.
You're still Joe Pendleton. And that's
what *we* see. *Outwardly*, you're Bruce
Farnsworth, and that's what *they* will
see.

    SISK'S VOICE. Mr. Farnsworth! A Miss
Logan is here to see you.

    JOE (*calling out*). Yeah—I *know*—!

Jordan shakes his head quickly.

    SISK'S VOICE (*quickly*). I *beg* your par-
don!

    JOE. I mean—I'll be right out—I'll be
right down! (*To Jordan*) Look, you're
kidding me. I—I won't fool *anybody!*

    JORDAN. You'll fool *everybody*. Open the
door, Joe.

A pause. Joe hesitates. Then, holding his
breath, he unlocks the door desperately, and
yanks it open.

The BEDROOM, AT THE BATHROOM DOOR: Joe
enters, Jordan behind him, and stops—facing Sisk, who has stood waiting. Joe's eyes
search Sisk for his possible reaction.

    SISK (*seen at close range as he looks Joe
up and down quickly*). I—I'm sorry for
making such a racket, Mr. Farnsworth.

As JOE, seen close with Jordan standing behind him, listens to Sisk, who obviously is

taken in completely—and as he hears Sisk call him "Mr. Farnsworth," his eyebrows go up. He turns his head ever so slightly to Jordan.

SISK'S VOICE. —but I thought something had happened to you.

JOE. Uh—something *did*, but—it's all right! (*Then quickly*) Oh, Miss Logan! I'll go right down.

He starts past Sisk.

SISK (*as Joe is on his way toward the door*). Mr. Farnsworth, sir! Your clothes!

Joe stops, and looks at himself in bathrobe and bath slippers.

JOE. Oh, well, I better get into something! Give me some clothes.

Sisk flies into action, and hurries over with a pair of socks.

SISK. Please—if you'll sit down, sir—

Joe, bewilderedly, sits in a chair. Sisk kneels and begins the operation of getting Joe into his socks. Joe glances from this embarrassing operation to Jordan. Then he speaks confidentially to Jordan, who has come to a halt near Joe.

JOE (*indicating the kneeling Sisk*). He never batted an eye.

SISK (*glancing up startledly*). I beg your pardon?

JORDAN (*quickly—to Joe*). Remember—people can hear you now.

JOE. Oh, I forgot.

SISK (*looking up again*). Forgot what, sir?

JOE. Uh—nothing.

Sisk works quickly. Joe looks up puzzledly at Jordan. A thought strikes him.

JOE (*blurting*). But they still can't see or hear *you*, huh?

JORDAN. No.

SISK (*in genuine alarm by this time*). Pardon me—*who* can't see or hear *who*, sir?

JOE. Uh—nobody. Just—thinking. Hurry, will you?

SISK. Yes, sir—!

As Sisk rises—and Joe rises with him—and as Sisk starts to pull the bathrobe off the bewildered Joe, we move to the UPPER HALL: JOE AND JORDAN come out of the bedroom and walk toward the staircase. Joe is dressed in dressing gown, trousers, and a scarf around his neck, and there is excitement in his step now.

JOE. "Farnsworth" he calls me—and looking right at me! (*Jordan smiles.*) Gee Whiz—how do you do it, Mr. Jordan?

JORDAN. If there were no mystery left to explore, Joe—life would get rather dull, wouldn't it?

JOE (*laughing excitedly*). You got an alibi for everything! Wow—if we can put this over down there—we're terrific!

They have reached the end of the staircase and now start down briskly.

JORDAN (*with a smile*). You'll get more "terrific" by the minute, Joe.

The LIVING ROOM, revealing TONY, JULIA AND BETTE, who is standing impatiently: Julia is picking up her brandy glass, with an outward show of calm. Inwardly she is tense, casting an anxious glance toward the hall.

JULIA (*with nervous energy; to Bette*). Well! Taking pretty long, isn't he? Perhaps he won't come down at all!

TONY (*cautioningly, to steady her; softly*). Julia.

JULIA, seen at close range now, her nervousness growing, breaks out with a sudden new burst of vehemence against Bette.

JULIA. Why don't you go! There's *no* help for you! Your father's in jail to stay—

Then her eyes glancing off, her voice breaks off as if cut by a knife, and the brandy glass falls from her hands. And there, at the LIVING ROOM ENTRANCE, stands Joe; Jordan standing over to the side—out of the way—to give Joe the entrance. Joe looks into the room tensely, waiting for recognition or otherwise.

Then TONY, JULIA AND BETTE are seen together. Julia is transfixed. Tony's mouth has dropped open and his cigarette dangles from his lower lip. Bette just waits grimly.

JULIA. Bruce!

A slight pause.

TONY (*incredulously, low*). Mr. Farnsworth!

Joe—reacting to their recognition—turns his head quickly to where Jordan stands and smiles fleetingly. Then Joe throws his shoulders back and comes forward.

There is a full view of the LIVING ROOM, as Joe enters slowly, smiling, while Julia is rigid.

JOE (*eyeing Tony and Julia*). Hello.

Neither Julia nor Tony answers. Joe then turns smilingly to Bette.

JOE. Hello, Miss Logan. Glad to see you.

BETTE (*bitingly*). Mr. Farnsworth, I'd like to talk to you privately.

Joe looks up, notes Jordan, who has moved across toward the open library doors and is now standing in the entrance to the study. Jordan indicates the study with a slight bend of the head, and enters it. Joe now turns quickly to Bette.

JOE (*to her*). Sure. (*Indicating the study*) How about—in there?

She hesitates—then with determination turns and walks quickly into the study. Joe pauses, looks at Tony and Julia, and moves measuredly toward the study—always with eyes on Tony and Julia, who are then seen at close range—both rigid—their eyes following his progress across the room. Next JOE is seen close as he approaches the study door, eyes on the two. Just before entering he points to Julia.

JOE. Say—Mrs. Farnsworth looks kinda pale around the gills. She looks like she's going to— (*He breaks off.*)

And JULIA is seen close. Her eyes close dizzily—she rocks—and starts to slump to the floor in a faint.

JOE (*seen close, shaking his head*). She did. (*And he turns away, moving into the study.*)

The STUDY in full view as Joe enters, closing the door after him: (During the following, Jordan takes a deep chair and relaxes in it.) Bette stands on her feet, facing Joe in a belligerent attitude, and Joe is extremely nervous as he starts to feel his way.

JOE (*being very cheerful*). Uh—well!— here we are—uh—sit down, Miss Logan! We—we'll have a nice little talk—

BETTE. Mr. Farnsworth—I came here hoping you'd at least *listen* to me—!

JOE. Listen to you? Why, of course I will—!

The study door opens suddenly and Sisk enters, carrying a tea tray. Joe is amazed.

JOE. What's this?

SISK. Your tea, sir.

JOE. My—tea?

He looks off at Jordan in perplexity.

JORDAN, seen close, is smiling, nodding—saying in pantomime that it's all right.

As the study is again in view Joe turns from Jordan and addresses himself to Sisk:

JOE. Oh, yes. Well—uh—just—just put it down—

Sisk deposits it on a table and starts out, at which point Jordan is seen indicating to Joe to offer some to Bette.

Again the full view of the STUDY as Sisk moves out: Joe, in his high nervous state, bounds around, not able to light.

JOE (*laughing a little*). Tea! That's fine! (*Going to the tray, he starts to pour.*) We'll have some *tea*, Miss Logan. What do you say?

BETTE. No, thanks.

JOE. Aw, now—it'll do you good. You look a little nervous. Go on, sit down. Take it easy. Everything's going to be all right.

She continues to stand, but Joe has poured and starts to lift the cup.

JOE. How'll you have yours—*straight* like this or—?

BETTE (*sharply—a little hysterically*). I don't want any!

Her explosion causes Joe's hand to shake so that the cup drops with a crash into the tray, spilling all over.

JOE. Whoops! (*With a sick smile*) Well —anyway—you—you didn't want any.

A quick exchange of smiles between Joe and Jordan. Before Joe can recover, Bette has opened the attack.

BETTE. I just want one thing—I want you to get my father out of jail!

JOE. That's right—he *is* in jail, isn't he?

BETTE. As if you didn't know!

JOE. Well—I *did*—and I *didn't*—

BETTE (*incensed*). You must know that *you put* him there!

JOE. Yes—that is—*Farnsworth* did. He—he was an awful rat—!

BETTE. *Was?*

Joe is sweating—running circles in his mind.

JOE. I mean—you see—I'm not really Farnsworth—

BETTE. Not Farnsworth!

JOE. Well—you know how it is—for instance—if you was to change coats—I mean—

BETTE. This is hardly the time for *jokes*, Mr. Farnsworth!

Joe looks off helplessly at Jordan, at which point a close view shows JORDAN shaking his head cautiously at Joe.

Joe is struggling to extricate himself—under the puzzled, angry gaze of Bette.

JOE. I—I didn't mean to joke, Miss Logan—

BETTE. Then admit it—you *did* put my father in jail!

JOE. All right—*yes! But*—I didn't have anything to do with it— (*Helplessly entangled*) Look—I—I could explain it to you—but you'd just think I was balmy—

BETTE. I don't understand a word you're saying!

JOE. I was *afraid* of that—

BETTE. You're just trying to put me off—

you're trying to make a fool of me— You think you can laugh me out of it as if I were a child—!

JOE (*quickly*). Now, wait a second. Your father's going to be all right—

BETTE (*continuing—furious*). Another Farnsworth trick! They *told* me there was no use coming here to plead with you—

JOE. Listen—

BETTE. I *knew* you were cruel! But to play with people like this—and *torture* them—!

She rushes for the door—blind with tears of rage. Joe starts after her.

JOE. Miss Logan! Wait! I *promise* you —I'm getting your father out—!

But she is gone—and Jordan, who has risen, calls out as Joe reaches the door, intending to follow her.

JORDAN. Joe!

Joe stops, turns on Jordan angrily.

JOE (*pointing after Bette*). That was swell! I certainly fixed that up. She likes *me* a *lot*!

JORDAN. She will in time, Joe—

JOE. Don't you see? I'm *poison*. I told you. It won't work. Now look, there's just no sense wasting time inside this guy Farnsworth. Get me out of this overcoat —and let's move on, Mister Jordan—

JORDAN. She *is* wonderful though, isn't she?

JOE (*reflectively*). Yeah—gosh—I'd give my right arm to help her if I could— but—

JORDAN. You *promised* you would, didn't you, Joe?

Joe snaps his head to Jordan.

JORDAN. Don't you intend to keep it?

JOE (*suddenly worried*). I *did?*

JORDAN. Yes, the promise to help her father. You can't very well move on until you make good, can you?

Joe thinks hard an instant.

JOE. But—it's no use—I—I don't even know what to *do!*

JORDAN. Bruce Farnsworth can do anything he wishes.

Then Jordan suddenly starts for the door.

JORDAN. I'll have to be leaving you now, Joe.

JOE. What?

He follows Jordan quickly to the door.

JORDAN (*turning, with a smile*). My work's piling up. I have to go back.

JOE. But wait, Mr. Jordan—you can't leave me holding the bag! If I gotta make good—look at this mess—what do *I* know about stocks and finance?

JORDAN. Finance is just a matter of the heart being in the right place, Joe—you'll be surprised how easily it will all come to you—

Jordan starts into the living room, Joe at his heels.

The LIVING ROOM, with JORDAN AND JOE, as Jordan crosses quickly, Joe at his heels.

JOE (*pleading—worried*). Can't you just stick around till I get the hang of things?

JORDAN. I'll be back whenever you *need* me, Joe—

As Jordan is reaching the entrance to the hall, Sisk appears carrying Joe's saxophone. Joe calls after Jordan:

JOE. No—no—wait—!

Joe finds himself confronted with Sisk, who is alarmed. Sisk has stepped in between Jordan and Joe—and Joe is forced to stop. Jordan has disappeared into the entrance hall. Sisk glances in the direction Joe has called.

SISK. Pardon, sir?

JOE. Uh—nothing—!

Then Joe streaks around Sisk and into the entrance hall, Sisk turning in amazement.

In the ENTRANCE HALL as Joe bounds in, looking frantically around for Jordan—of whom there is no trace: Joe, keeping in mind that Sisk is nearby, lowers his voice.

JOE (*in a fierce whisper*). Mister Jordan!

No answer. Joe is breathing fast. He realizes it is hopeless. He hesitates an instant, then re-enters the living room.

The LIVING ROOM, as Joe charges back in: Sisk is standing with the saxophone—trembling a little.

JOE (*angrily*). You *would* have to come barging in just when—

He breaks off and notes the saxophone.

JOE (*sharply*). Where'd you get that?

SISK. Why, in your bathroom, sir. I can't imagine how it got there.

JOE. I *put* it there!

And he eagerly grabs the sax out of Sisk's hands.

SISK. *You—put* it there, sir?

JOE. No wonder I wasn't getting the breaks. Didn't have the lucky old sax.

SISK. I—pardon me—but I—I never saw that before—

Joe starts to walk around troubledly, hugging the sax. Suddenly he stops—with an idea.

JOE. That's it! Tell what's-his-name to come down—

SISK. *Who,* sir?

JOE. The—the confidential—my secretary.

SISK. Mr. Abbott!

JOE. Mr. Abbott—yes. Get him down here—*quick.*

SISK. Yes, sir.

And Sisk starts away fast—out of the room.

JOE (*patting his saxophone—smiling nervously—addressing the instrument*). I knew I'd start clicking—with you around.

JULIA'S BEDROOM: Julia is stretched out on a chaise longue, Tony standing by her with a glass of water in his hand. He puts it to her lips, but she pushes it away.

JULIA. I'm fine now—(*Rising excitedly and starting to pace, shuddering*) It gave me cold chills, Tony! How can he be alive?

TONY. I was *certain* he was dead. I held him under long enough. Then to see him walk into that room, grinning like a hyena—

JULIA. It—it's creepy! (*Then, in sudden alarm*) Do you think he knows what we tried to do?

TONY. Impossible! He was asleep—

A knock on the door. Both jump.

JULIA (*calling out*). Come in.

Sisk enters.

SISK. I beg your pardon. Mr. Farnsworth would like to see you immediately, Mr. Abbott.

A quick exchange of glances between Julia and Tony.

TONY. Very well.

Tony takes a few steps when, from below, comes a sudden, loud wail on the saxophone. Julia and Tony are startled stiff; Sisk jumps with nervousness.

JULIA. What's that?

SISK (*gulping*). A—saxophone.

JULIA. Who's playing it?

SISK. Mr. Farnsworth.

JULIA. Mr. Farnsworth! (*Whirling in alarm to Tony*) He doesn't know how to play a saxophone!

SISK. He evidently does, Madame. It was in his bathroom—and he *put* it there!

JULIA. Tony—I—I'm afraid!

TONY (*quickly*). I'd better go right down.

Tony starts out of the room quickly. The saxophone has played continuously.

The LIVING ROOM: Joe is playing his saxophone—walking about—building confidence by the minute. Suddenly, Tony appears in the entrance, and Joe, in the middle of a note, breaks off. Tony stares.

TONY. You—sent for me, Mr. Farnsworth?

JOE. Yeah. What are you looking at?

TONY. I—I didn't know you played a saxophone.

JOE. That's nothing. A lot of people don't think I do—even when they see me doing it! You'll get used to it.

TONY. Are you sure you're—uh—quite well, Mr. Farnsworth?

JOE. I'm fine and—(*pointedly*)—and *I'm stayin' that way.*

Joe goes into a frowning attitude, which he hopes will pass for a concentration on weighty business matters. Inwardly he is scared and uncertain.

JOE. Now, let's get down to a little business. I got something pretty important on my mind—

TONY (*alert, business-like—breaking in*). Oh, I have a memo from Gibbons. He thinks we should go "long" ten million bushels of July wheat.

JOE (*startled—fumbling*). He does, does he?

TONY. Immediately.

JOE. Ten million bushels of wheat, eh? Where'll we put it?

TONY. How's that?

JOE (*in a spot—resorting to a joke*). Tell you what you do. Order a million gallons of sweet cream. As long as we have the wheat, we might as well eat it.

TONY. Have your little joke, sir—but surely we can't ignore—

JOE (*breaking in severely—with frowning importance*). Never mind that for a minute. I'm interested in just one thing today. This—uh—Logan business. I've been talking to a pal of mine about that—

TONY. You mean J.P. of course.

JOE. No—just J. Jordan.

Tony fishes in his mind for "Jordan."

JOE (*continues quickly*). The whole thing looks pretty bad to me. I want it all straightened out. I want Mr. Logan out of jail!

TONY. With fraud pinned on him like this?

JOE. Pinned. Yeah—who *pinned* it on him?

TONY. Well, naturally—

JOE. That's what I thought! So, let's *un*-pin it. *Anything*—only get him out.

TONY. Mr. Farnsworth—you realize—that puts the entire responsibility on your shoulders. You would have to buy back every share of that worthless stock! And that's impossible!

JOE. Why? Who's got it?

TONY. Why, naturally—small investors all over the country—!

JOE (*thinking hard*). *Small* investors, eh? Nice work. (*Then with sudden sharpness*) Buy all that stuff back! Give those small people every cent they paid for it!

TONY. That will take *millions* of dollars!

JOE. Have I got it?

TONY (*snorting*). Really, sir—!

JOE. *Have* I?

TONY. Many times that amount!

JOE. Then—go ahead!

TONY. But—don't you feel you ought to think this over first, sir?

Joe fastens a look on Tony.

JOE. I *have* thought it over! And get this —you and I are going to tangle plenty— unless you watch your step. So don't try any funny business—and *stay out of my bathroom!*

Λ pause.

JOE. Get going—Mr. Abbott!

Tony swallows and heads for the study— fast. Joe lifts his saxophone and blows a blast that fairly *sweeps* Tony out of the room. As Joe continues to play the scene dissolves to NEWSPAPER HEADLINES, dissolving into each other:

FARNSWORTH CLEARS LOGAN IN
SECURITIES FRAUD

Then:

STOCK SALE ORDER AN ERROR
SAYS FARNSWORTH IN DEFENSE
OF LOGAN

Then:

LOGAN RELEASED!

Then:

FARNSWORTH ORDERS MILLIONS
PAID BACK TO INVESTORS

This dissolves to an OFFICE ENTRANCE on Wall Street, a neat bronze plate at one side of the entrance reading: "FARNSWORTH, LTD." A line of investors, elderly people indifferently dressed and holding certificates in their hands, are waiting to be let in—a few at a time. A few policemen are in evidence to keep order. Then at THE CURB, out of a limousine step Tony and Joe. Joe is dressed in a finely tailored, dark double-breasted suit and wears a bowler hat and carries a cane. He looks around, a little bewildered, and eyes the line of people outside the building. Tony also observes this line.

TONY (*disapprovingly*). It's practically a stampede—to turn in that stock!

JOE (*smiling with satisfaction*). Uh-huh.

TONY. Come, sir—

Joe starts after Tony, who heads into the building. Almost at once they are surrounded by three or four reporters, who fall in beside them.

A REPORTER. Mr. Farnsworth—have you any further statement to make on the Logan securities?

TONY (*quickly*). Nothing now, gentlemen. Mr. Farnsworth is late for his Board of Directors meeting. Please!

And Tony hustles the bewildered Joe into the building, leaving the scene to the reporters, who turn to each other.

SECOND REPORTER. Boy—*that'll* be a hot session!

In an UPPER FLOOR of the building, JOE AND TONY are seen walking briskly—Joe glancing around at the sparkling marble corridor. Suddenly, Tony heads for a door, pushing inside, and Joe, startled, makes a quick stop, turns and follows Tony in.

FARNSWORTH'S OUTER OFFICE is a lavish reception room, with many doors opening off it, and hallways. Several secretaries sit at desks, and as Joe and Tony enter, the secretaries come to attention, calling ad lib "good mornings" in a subdued way. Joe is amazed at the secretaries, the general layout—the labyrinth of doorways and hallways, but Tony, without hesitation, makes for one of the small hallways and Joe, glancing around furtively, follows. He is next seen following obediently at Tony's heels, down the narrow hallway, up to a door marked: MR. FARNSWORTH. Tony pushes it open. Then Joe and Tony enter the OFFICE OF FARNSWORTH'S SECRETARY and cross to another door. Seated there is a middle-aged woman, Farnsworth's secretary, and a young man at another desk.

SECRETARY. Good morning, Mr. Farnsworth.

JOE. Uh—good morning.

Tony pushes into Farnsworth's private office, Joe following. The secretary moves in after them—also the young man.

Tony and Joe enter FARNSWORTH'S PRIVATE OFFICE, and Joe stares around in faint alarm at the most sumptuous office of its kind he has ever seen. He unconsciously takes off his hat, as if in respect to the office. The secretary takes his hat and cane out of his hands, surprising Joe somewhat. The young fellow sticks a flower in Joe's lapel. Then suddenly his secretary pushes some papers into his hands. All these rapid actions startle Joe, but before he has recovered, Tony picks up a portfolio off Joe's desk and hands it to Joe.

TONY. We'd better go right in to the board meeting, sir.

JOE. Yeah—

Tony indicates, "Go ahead," with a gesture of his hand. Joe imitates the gesture—indirectly telling Tony to lead on. Tony starts for one of the doors leading out of the private office. Joe falls into step, not yet fully recovered from his amazement at all the lightning action around him. Next Joe and Tony barge through a SMALL CONNECTING OFFICE, Tony swinging open a door on the opposite side, and standing aside to let Joe enter. Joe moves to the doorway and stops, looking into the next room.

The BOARD ROOM (as seen from Joe's angle in the doorway): It is a large room with a board table in the center. Some ten men of varying degrees of age, are standing around the room, in groups and singly—some with newspapers in their hands. They have been caught in attitudes of violent conversation. Every face, now fixed in Joe's direction, is set angrily and accusingly. And JOE, seen at close range, gulps, and forces a little smile. Then Joe takes an uncertain step forward into the room, whereupon all the men break out at once, moving forward and waving newspapers, and a blast of words is hurled at him.

BOARD MEMBERS.
What in heaven's name have you done?
Have you gone crazy, Bruce?
What is the meaning of this?
Are you trying to ruin this company—?
Will you please explain this insane move?
Do you realize what this will mean—?
You must have taken leave of your senses, Bruce!

JOE. *Hold it!*

A sudden quiet. Joe is getting his bearings.

JOE (*calmly*). One at a time, fellows.

He moves forward toward the table.

FIRST BOARD MEMBER. Bruce, how you could have done an *insane* thing like this!

SECOND BOARD MEMBER. To take the responsibility for this Logan business—publicly!

THIRD BOARD MEMBER. Bruce, something must have happened to you! I—I'm convinced you're *ill!* Your nerves have gone to pieces—!

JOE (*stoutly*). If somebody's honest, that means he's sick, huh?

FOURTH BOARD MEMBER. Listen, Bruce—it's your own money you're throwing away in this case, and we can't stop you! But look what you're doing! You're destroying public confidence in this company! People will now suspect every stock issue we're mixed up in!

JOE (*calmly*). Maybe they're right. I'm going to look into *all* that stuff—and whatever isn't on the level gets tossed out.

CHORUS.
What?
Good grief!
He's stark mad!
What's he talking about?

The first board member comes raging over to Joe, brandishing a newspaper.

FIRST BOARD MEMBER. Have you seen this? The stock quotations!

He slams the paper down on the table in front of Joe, and begins to turn pages violently.

JOE AND THE FIRST BOARD MEMBER are seen together ("a two shot") as the board member turns pages. Joe's eyes are absently on the pages.

FIRST BOARD MEMBER (*as he turns pages*). Look—by this one idiotic gesture of yours, the panic is on in Farnsworth Limited—drops twenty points over night . . . !

Suddenly Joe's hand reaches forward to stop a turning page; he is all attention.

JOE (*sharply*). Wait!

Joe's eyes widen as he grabs at the paper. We see a HEADLINE under the page heading, which reads: SPORTS. Here in bold streamer is the headline:

K.O. MURDOCK MAY GET CRACK AT GILBERT'S
TITLE

and a sub-head:

With Contender Joe Pendleton Out of Picture, Murdock-Gilbert Championship
Bout a Natural

JOE, seen close, lifts his eyes from the page furiously. He crumbles the paper in his fist.

JOE (*bursting out*). They can't do that!

The Board members, seen again in the full scene, are stunned as Joe continues violently:

JOE. They can't brush me off and give Murdock the nod—!

Joe is suddenly heading for the door by which he entered.

TONY (*in alarm*). Mr. Farnsworth! What is it?

JOE. Nothing! Leave me alone!

And Joe is out, paper still clutched in his hand, while the board members and Tony remain stupefied, looking at each other.

Joe goes sailing through the SMALL CONNECTING OFFICE. Then he swings the door to the PRIVATE OFFICE open violently and bounds in. But he pulls up as if hit, and stares off.

JOE. Mister Jordan!

We see JORDAN AND MESSENGER 7013, Jordan seated comfortably in a deep chair, while Messenger 7013, nervous and fidgety, stands at his elbow.

JORDAN. Hello, Joe.

MESSENGER 7013. How do you do, Mr. Pendleton?

Now Joe comes forward quickly into the office, wiping his brow.

JOE (*breathless*). Mister Jordan—you're just the man I got to see!

Joe holds out the paper dramatically.

JOE. Look at this! Talkin' about matching Murdock with Gilbert! Murdock's gotta fight *me* first—and the *winner* was supposed to get a crack at Gilbert and the title!

MESSENGER 7013. Yes, yes—that's exactly what we've come about, Mr. Pendleton!

JOE (*wheeling on Messenger*). I'm not talking to you! You're the guy who fumbled the whole thing. Stay out of this!

Messenger 7013 lifts his eyes to Heaven. Joe turns back to Jordan.

JOE (*waving the paper*). Ya see? Ya see what comes of fooling around with this Farnsworth? I *told* you! Now look Mister Jordan, *we said* I was going to be Farnsworth *just temporary!* When I finished this job, you were going to find me the body I need to fight Murdock. *You promised!*

JORDAN (*calmly*). Yes, I did, Joe.

MESSENGER 7013 (*breaking in violently*). Mr. Pendleton—if you'll stop bellowing and listen a moment! We've found out you are actually intended to be the next world's champion!

Joe stares—then speaks to Jordan in a breathless, small voice.

JOE. Is that a fact?

JORDAN. Yes, Joe.

JOE. How do you know?

JORDAN. Nothing can prevent it.

JOE (*in a sudden burst of jubilance*). I knew it! I told you! I *told* you nothing could stop me!

MESSENGER 7013 (*impatiently*). Yes—yes. Now let's get down to business, Mr. Pendleton. I've scoured the world for the physical specimen you will need. I'm rather worn out, I might add—

JOE. What've you found?

MESSENGER 7013. Well—there's a strapping fellow in Australia—he'll soon be available—motor accident—

JOE. What's his weight?

MESSENGER 7013. One hundred ninety-two pounds.

JOE. Good. What's his reach?

MESSENGER 7013. Uh — seventy-eight inches.

JOE. Not bad. How about his waist, chest, forearm—?

MESSENGER 7013 (*highly irritable*). How would *I* know you'd want all those things!

JOE. I've *got* to have 'em! Well, let's look this Australian guy over. (*To Jordan*) I got this Logan business all polished off. What are we waiting for? Let's go.

Jordan starts to rise out of his chair slowly.

JORDAN. Just as you say, Joe.

Before Jordan is fully up, the door opens suddenly from the secretary's office, and the lady secretary enters quickly, documents in her hands. She stops abruptly on seeing Joe.

SECRETARY. Oh. Excuse me, sir. I thought you were in the meeting—

JOE. No. I—I'm through with the meeting. I'm *all* through. I'm getting right out of here.

SECRETARY. Then—you don't want to see Miss Logan?

JOE. Who?

SECRETARY. Miss Logan. She's waiting.

A small excitement has seized Joe.

JOE. Oh, sure. Sure. Uh—bring her in.

The secretary turns and calls through the doorway into the outer office.

SECRETARY. Will you come in, please?

As Joe holds his position, Bette Logan enters, stops a few feet inside the room and looks penetratingly at Joe. The secretary goes out, closing the door. And JOE, seen close, is staring at Bette—the old feeling on him—as when he first saw her.

First, JORDAN AND MESSENGER 7013 are seen. Jordan, smiling, sits back down slowly into the chair, while Messenger 7013 looks impatiently from Bette to the relaxed Jordan.

MESSENGER 7013. Is this delay necessary, sir?

JORDAN. And quite interesting.

Then Bette and Joe can be seen, with Jordan and Messenger 7013 in the background. Bette comes forward a step, staring at Joe.

JOE (*slowly, reverently*). Hello, Miss Logan.

BETTE (*after a pause; simply*). My father's home—Thank you.

JOE. Well—that's fine! (*Nervously excited*) Uh—won't you sit down?

She doesn't hear the last. She is staring at him steadily.

BETTE. It was a wonderful thing you did. Not only for father. I mean—to give back money to all those people—

JOE (*embarrassed*). Well—of course—it was the only thing to do, wasn't it?

A pause.

BETTE (*on sudden impulse*). I—I'm sorry to keep staring at you like this—

JOE (*attempting a small laugh*). That's okay. I—I'm staring a little myself.

BETTE (*with difficulty; puzzling through*). I—I'm all mixed up—about this. When I went to see you, I expected so little—I had made up my mind about you—and I was terribly rude. I—I always thought I'd be afraid of you. But something happened. You were so different. Strangely enough—when I was trying to hate you most, I couldn't deny there was something warm and friendly —even gentle—in the way you smiled.

JOE (*with a quick glance at Jordan*). Really?

BETTE. In fact—I didn't come here to thank you as much as to—because I had to *see* you again.

JOE (*in excitement*). Well—that's wonderful! (*Suddenly active*) You gotta sit down *now!* Come here.

He takes her arm and forcibly draws her to an upright leather chair.

JORDAN AND MESSENGER 7013 again appear at close range, Jordan smiling, the Messenger most impatient.

MESSENGER 7013. How long does this drivel go on?

JORDAN. A little patience—

MESSENGER 7013. But I have work to do!

JOE AND BETTE: Joe is pushing her into the chair, hovering over her in great excitement.

JOE. Right there—that's it! Say I—I could even get some tea brought in and . . . (*Breaking off; laughing*) No— I guess I'd spill that!

She laughs with him.

BETTE. You know what I told father this was? A miracle.

JOE. Miracle? Why?

BETTE. Well—that a man like Bruce Farnsworth could actually think the way I was brought up to think—about people —that he could have a real feeling for the happiness of others—

JOE. Why not? As good a way to go through life as any other.

BETTE. Yes, that's all I meant. (*Then staring at him again*) Except—when you

find that in somebody, it's a great discovery. (*With a little laugh*) I guess that's why I keep staring. I can't help it. I suddenly feel warm and alive—and happy. It's something in your eyes—and what's behind them—that I keep trying to see. (*She rises suddenly.*) That sounds silly, doesn't it?

JOE. No!

BETTE. I must go now. (*She starts for the door.*)

JOE (*stopping her*). Wait!

MESSENGER 7013 AND JORDAN are seen, the latter calm and smiling. The Messenger lifts his eyes to heaven.

MESSENGER 7013. Great grief!

Joe is breathless with tenseness.

JOE (*softly*). I know what you mean. And when you *make* a discovery like that —it's pretty important, isn't it?—more important than what two people look like —or who they are—or anything else—

BETTE (*puzzled, looking at him*). Of course.

JOE. I mean—even if *she* was a queen— and he could be a—well, maybe just a prizefighter—and the other thing would be all that counts—

BETTE (*softly*). That's how it *ought* to be. Goodbye.

She goes to the door quickly, Joe at her heels.

JOE. Wait—I—I've got to see you again.

BETTE. If you'd care to. Goodbye.

And she goes out fast, closing the door after her.

The PRIVATE OFFICE: Jordan still seated. Messenger 7013 is beside himself with impatience.

MESSENGER 7013. Thank goodness!

As Joe stands entranced at the door, the Messenger walks over and taps him on the shoulder.

MESSENGER 7013. Mr. Pendleton—*your* time may not be valuable—

Joe, jolted out of his trance, whirls toward Jordan.

JOE (*to Jordan*). Mister Jordan! Did you hear what she said! That was *me* she was looking at—Joe! And she likes me—*me!*

MESSENGER 7013 (*appealing to Jordan*). Really, sir—we *have* to get moving.

JOE (*continuing to Jordan*). You *said* she would! You said—just give her time!

Jordan rises slowly, smiling.

JORDAN. Yes, I did. Ready, Joe?

JOE (*confused*). Wait—what do you mean? Oh—this Australian guy!

MESSENGER 7013 (*bitingly*). If you *recall* —yes.

JOE. Hold on a second! I can't do that!

JORDAN (*softly*). Why not?

JOE (*struggling with himself*). Well— don't you see? I—I got her to like me the way I am! Suppose I got running off to Australia now—and do a switch—after I got her used to this Farnsworth! I'd lose her! No—*I* can't take a chance like *that—!* Don't you see what I mean?

JORDAN. Yes, Joe.

MESSENGER 7013. *Mister* Pendleton—

JOE (*with an explosive motion*). Mister Jordan! Look—this guy Farnsworth— he's the same age as me—he had a pretty good body once—played polo you told me—! Why couldn't I build him up physically like I did myself?

JORDAN. Why not?

JOE. Exercise, plain food, plenty of fresh air—!

JORDAN (*smiling*). I'm sure you'd do wonders with him.

JOE. And with what I know about fighting! Sure I would! I can get this body in the pink in no time—and lick Murdock with it! Then I've got the title— and I've got her—

MESSENGER 7013. Mr. Pendleton! Is this *final!*

JOE. You're darn right it is! I'm staying like I am!

He reaches for his hat on the coat rack.

JOE (*in wild excitement*). Excuse me, Mister Jordan! I got a lot of things to do! Thanks. So long— (*He stops at door; to the Messenger*) So long—you! It's *final!* I won't have to be seeing *you* again.

MESSENGER 7013. Thank goodness!

JOE. Ditto!

And Joe is out, leaving the Messenger and Jordan alone.

MESSENGER 7013 (*blowing a breath of relief*). Well! That's off my hands!

JORDAN. In a case like this, you can never be sure.

MESSENGER 7013 (*seen close, startled by Jordan's words, his eyebrows going up*). Oh, dear!

The scene dissolves to the SUN ROOM, where a close view reveals a PUNCHING BAG going like a trip hammer—through intricate maneuvers and rhythms. It fairly sings. As the full scene comes to view ("the camera pulls back") we realize it is Joe punching the bag. He is in trunks and boxing shoes—and sweat shirt. Behind him, we see a room that has been converted into a gymnasium —with rowing machine, wall pulley, medicine ball, exercise bicycle, etc.

Next we see JULIA AND TONY in the LIVING ROOM, standing outside French doors that are curtained. Julia, in morning lounging outfit, and Tony listen in amazement to the tattoo of the punching bag which comes through the doors.

JULIA. You mean to say he was up at six again this morning?

TONY. And started jogging over the countryside. Covered ten miles, he said.

JULIA. Incredible!

Suddenly the punching bag stops and they listen. In a moment they hear a peculiar sound repeated at short intervals—an "ugh" sound—a deep human grunt. In alarm, Julia pushes the door open.

The SUN ROOM, as Julia and Tony burst in: Sisk is hurling the medicine ball at Joe's stomach, Sisk looking a wreck—coat off, tie awry, hair a mess.

JOE (*to Sisk*). Harder, Sisk! (*Pointing to his stomach*) Right in the middle!

JULIA. Bruce!

Joe pauses.

JOE. What's the matter?

JULIA. What's the *matter!* Great heavens —your blood pressure can't stand this sort of thing!

He comes toward her, arm flexed.

JOE. Can't, eh? Feel that arm! That's a muscle *now!* Feel that leg! (*Presents his stomach to Tony.*) Hit me in the stomach—go on—hit me as hard as you can!

TONY (*rearing back*). You'll pardon me, sir.

JOE (*snorting*). My blood pressure's perfect! I'm a little tight in the joints yet— but—

JULIA. Sisk! *Look* at you!

SISK (*getting his coat—puffing*). I can just imagine, Madam.

JOE. He's doing fine. (*To Tony*) I'll take you for a jog in the morning. Do you good— Sisk—get me a bath ready, will you? (*Pointedly, to Julia and Tony*) And I won't need any help taking it.

He starts on the dummy, suspended from the ceiling, and begins to punch it.

JOE (*calling out to Julia and Tony*). Be seeing you.

Sisk goes out—bewildered and still tousled. Tony and Julia glance at each other, troubled.

TONY. Mr. Farnsworth—I *must* tell you, sir—the Board is frantic at your absence. They've *got* to have your decision on Air Carbide—and something has to be done about the "P. & R. Debentures."

JOE. Yes—yes—I'll get to it. We're going to dump a lot of that stuff. We got too many fingers in too many pies. Let's have just *one* thing—and run it right.

TONY. But, Mr. Farnsworth—!

JOE (*yelling*). Can't you see I'm busy?

Julia and Tony back out quickly—closing the door. Joe has never stopped punching the dummy.

In the HALL, TONY AND JULIA are moving away from the French doors.

JULIA (*in an undertone*). Tony—he's gone mad!

Suddenly both stop—and stare off. And now Sisk, still looking bedraggled, is seen followed by Max Corkle, who is glancing around at his surroundings. Then all four characters are included in the scene—as Tony steps in Sisk's path.

MAX. Uh—Mr. Farnsworth?

TONY. No. Who is this gentleman, Sisk?

MAX. Corkle's the name. Max Corkle.

SISK. He says he has an appointment with Mr. Farnsworth.

MAX. Yeah—

TONY (*to Max; with suspicion*). There must be some mistake. I'm Mr. Farnsworth's secretary. You couldn't have an appointment unless *I* had given it to you.

MAX. You don't have to get snooty about it.

TONY. Do you mind stating your business?

MAX (*his voice rising*). Look—I don't know what it's all about! All I know is I got a telegram—(*He searches his pockets*)—from Bruce Farnsworth—telling me to come to this address—!

TONY. Why?

MAX (*shouting*). I don't *know*, I tell you! Aside from seeing his picture in the paper, I don't know the guy from Adam—!

Suddenly a voice comes over the scene.

JOE'S VOICE. Mr. Corkle!

All heads turn.

JOE is seen at close range standing in the doorway to the sun-room, his face lit up.

JOE (*putting on formality*). Will you— uh—step in here, please?

Max, puzzled, walks toward Joe. Tony and Julia are perplexed.

The SUN ROOM, as Max enters, looking around; Joe, smiling, closes the door. Then he makes a lunge for Max and starts pumping his hand.

> JOE. Max! You old son-of-a-gun! How are you! Gee, I'm glad to see you!
>
> MAX. You—you know me?
>
> JOE. *Know* you? I *oughta* know you—you dumb-ox!
>
> MAX (*searching his pockets again*). Uh-huh. Uh—look—I—uh—got a telegram this morning—
>
> JOE. That's right. Take a good look at me, Max. Don't you know me?
>
> MAX (*nervously*). Sure—sure—I know you. Everybody knows you, Mr. Farnsworth.
>
> JOE. Where are your eyes, you sap? I'm not Farnsworth. I'm Joe Pendleton—your Joe!

Max's eyes pop. He starts to back away.

> MAX (*softly*). You're uh—nuts, Mr. Farnsworth.
>
> JOE. Max, listen. I know I don't *look* like Joe any more, but I'm him just the same. And it's all *your fault.*
>
> MAX (*wetting his parched lips*). My fault?
>
> JOE. Yeah. If you wasn't in such a gol-darn hurry to cremate my body, I wouldn't *be* in this jam now.
>
> MAX. I cremated—*you?*
>
> JOE. Well, didn't you?

Max swallows and starts to edge toward the door.

> MAX. Now—uh—just take it easy, Mr. Farnsworth. Uh—pretty *hot* out today, isn't it?

Joe jumps around and bars Max's exit.

> JOE. Oh, no you don't—!

Joe takes him by the lapels and pushes him back into the room, while eagerly talking.

> JOE (*pleading*). You *gotta* believe me, Max! Listen—you know the last trip I took in the plane?—well, something went flooey—the ship started to fall. And then one of those guys that goes around collecting people—he pulled a boner—I wasn't dead at all—but he *thought* I was, see?—so he grabs me outa turn—and while we're arguing about it, you go and cremate me. So then, they got to make good. They gotta find me another body. Get it?

Max is white as a ghost.

> MAX (*gasping*). Sure! Sure! Well then, everything worked out fine! All you need now is a doctor—*the best there is!* (*He makes a bolt for the door.*) Lemme outa here!

Joe makes a dive for him—and clutches Max violently.

> JOE. Gol-darn you, Max! Will you stay put and *listen* to me—!
>
> MAX (*panting*). Look—I'm a very busy man—!
>
> JOE. Listen—so the body they gave me was *this* guy's—he had just drowned in the bathtub—I mean, they held him under—
>
> MAX (*shrieking*). Help!
>
> JOE. Shut up—!

A voice breaks in on them.

> JORDAN'S VOICE. Having trouble, Joe?

Joe swings around, one hand still gripping Max's lapel. Max gets a new shock. He has heard nothing, of course, and follows Joe's gaze in new alarm. For an instant JORDAN appears at the OTHER END OF THE ROOM, standing just inside the doors that lead out to the garden. Then we see JOE AND MAX again.

> JOE (*his face lighting up*). Mr. Jordan!

Max's head twists incredulously from Joe to the direction in which Joe is looking. Max sees nothing.

> JOE. Gee, I'm glad you showed up. I'm having *plenty* of trouble.

Jordan moves slowly and easily into the room. Joe at the same time, starts pulling the alarmed Max toward Jordan.

JOE (*to Jordan*). I can't get *anything* through this guy's head. Tell him what happened, will you? (*Then suddenly*) Oh, this is Max Corkle, my manager—the guy that fixed me *good*. (*To Max*) Max—this is Mr. Jordan. You know those collector fellas I was telling you about? Well, Mr. Jordan's in charge, see?—that's his department.

MAX (*chattering*). Is—is there somebody with us?

JOE. Mr. Jordan!

MAX (*trembling; humoring Joe*). Glad to meet you, Mr. Jordan.

JOE. Oh, I forgot—you can't see him.

MAX. Maybe—if—if I had a—a stiff drink—

JOE. You can't see him because you ain't dead yet.

MAX (*swallowing*). Uh-huh. (*Then, trying to break Joe's hold*) Well—I guess you fellas got some business to talk over —so I'll be mooching along.

JOE (*holding on*). Stay where you are! (*Then, to Jordan*) Mr. Jordan—look—I gotta get this over to Max. He's a swell manager and I need him. I'd feel lost in the ring without him. You gotta make him understand. Maybe, if you could let him see you for a minute—

JORDAN (*quietly*). You can do it yourself, Joe. Try.

JOE. I can? (*Turning on the bewildered Max*) You're gonna believe me if I have to pound you into a jelly. How would I know about Joe, if I wasn't Joe? And listen to this: You've got forty percent of me.

MAX. I have? (*Looking around*) Well, thanks. That's pretty nice. Since when did you give me that?

JOE (*emphatically*). Since that time in Astoria when you saw me put away "Butcher Boy" McKenzie.

Max stares hard, his eyes opening a trifle.

JOE. You told me I had color—I was what the fans wanted—like the Manassa Mauler. Remember?

Max's eyes open wider, his mouth sags.

JOE. How's your sister Rosie—and her three kids? Did the twins get over the measles?

MAX (*staring in panic*). Say—who are you, anyway?

JOE. I'm trying to tell you. I'm Joe—your Joe. I'm in Farnsworth's body because you burned mine, you big stiff! (*Then he has a sudden idea.*) Wait—I'll prove it.

He rushes to a bench and grabs up his saxophone which rests there. He runs back and shoves it up to Max's face.

JOE. Remember this?

Max stares at it, reaching out to touch an inscription on it.

MAX (*reading*). "To Joe—from Max." That's Joe's! I gave it to him! Poor Joe! (*Accusingly*) Where'd *you* get it?

JOE (*shouting*). It's mine, I tell you! Listen—I'll play your favorite piece for you.

Joe starts to play a tune—one we haven't heard before—a maudlin melody as Max listens, hypnotized. After a couple of bars, Joe hits a sour note.

MAX (*out of old habit; blurts*). You *always* hit that note sour—!

Then he realizes what he has said and his eyes pop. Joe breaks off, smiling.

MAX (*gasping*). Joe! It's you! (*Hoarsely*) Joe—!

And Max faints dead away—in a straight back flop.

JOE (*joyfully*). He knows me!

Joe rushes to Max, starting to massage Max's wrists, and Jordan stands benignly smiling.

JOE (*again*). He knows me!

The scene dissolves to the SUN ROOM, revealing MAX sitting up weakly in a chair, a cold towel on his head. Joe is handing him a glass of whiskey. Max blinks his eyes weakly, shakes his head, and takes a long drink. The view expands to show Jordan sitting composedly on the bench, Max's eyes come to rest on Joe.

MAX. This—this ain't a hangover from last night? You're—really Joe?

JOE. Just inside I am, Max. Outside I'm Farnsworth.

Max takes another quick swallow. Then he looks around.

MAX. Is—is that pal of yours still around?

JOE (*pointing*). Right there.

Max squints his eyes in that direction, then gives up.

MAX. He is, huh? Maybe *I'm* somebody else too. Ask him. (*Quickly*) No, no— better not. If I'm in somebody else's body I don't want to know about it!

JOE. Now, look, Max—I'll tell you why I wanted you. They're talking about matching K.O. Murdock with Gilbert—

MAX. Yeah.

JOE. But who did Murdock have to fight first? Who was the other logical contender for Gilbert's title?

MAX. Joe was—uh—*you* was.

JOE. All right. Then fix it for me to fight Murdock.

MAX. What!

JOE. Get me that match!

MAX. Wait a minute. You're crazy. K.O. won't fight *Farnsworth*!

JOE. *Some* way you gotta fix it!

JORDAN (*interposing*). Tell him what the Registrar discovered, Joe—

JOE (*turning in Jordan's direction*). Oh, yeah! That's right!

MAX. Is he talking again?

JOE (*with enthusiasm to Max*). Max—I'll let you in on something. I'm supposed to be the next champ! It's in the book. Nothing can change it.

MAX. Is that what *he* says?

JOE. Yes, and he *knows*!

MAX. Will he insure any bets?

JOE. Max—I'm *telling* you what you gotta do—

MAX (*confused*). Yeah—but—how can I put this over with the Boxing Commission. The regulations bar ghosts—

JOE. I'm no ghost. I got *fifty years* to go yet! It's *Farnsworth* who'll be fighting! Can't you get that through your head?

MAX. Okay!! But Farnsworth—a *banker* —they'll throw me out on my ear.

JOE. Then go to K.O.'s manager, Lefty— offer him dough. *Any* amount.

MAX. Like what?

JOE. What'll it take?

MAX. I don't know. Twenty-five grand— *at least!*

JOE. Whew! That's a lota dough!

JORDAN. Why, just have your secretary write him a check, Joe.

JOE. Sure!

And in a burst of enthusiasm, Joe tears out of the sunroom. We hear him yelling:

JOE'S VOICE. Hey—Abbott!

Casually, Jordan saunters out of the sunroom—into the living room. Max does not see him do this—in fact, he is suddenly conscious of being with someone he can't see. He is immediately alarmed—edges toward the door.

MAX. Excuse me—

Jordan, of course, is not there. Suddenly, Max gets an idea. He closes the door with a show of secretness—lowers his voice.

MAX. Oh—Mister Jordan—I'd like a couple of words with you. It's about Joe. You and me might get together on something—

He comes forward—and during the following he wanders around as if expecting to find Jordan almost anywhere.

MAX (*in lowered voice*). Say—you're here, aren't you? Sure you are. Don't mind me. Little nervous, that's all. I've knocked around the world—and seen just about everything—but this is new. (*He wipes his forehead.*) Would you mind moving a chair or something—so I know you're listening? I'd feel a little more comfortable. (*He waits, but gets no answer or signal.*) Okay—if you don't want to. (*Then—taking the plunge*) Look—if this *is* Joe—I mean—I just got thinking—why, he's sitting pretty—with millions! Now why should he go get himself punched silly trying to be champ? What'll it get him? Certainly no millions. And the way things stand now, I've got forty percent of him. You heard him say that. Well, considering *what he's worth,* forty percent is okay right now. Suppose he takes a couple of hard punches in the ring and goes goofy on me—*and forgets who I am? Then* where'll I stand? What good'll it do *me* —or *him?* See? Why take a chance? So what I want *you* to do, Mister Jordan—

The door opens behind Max, and Joe stands there—listening to Max talk to the air.

MAX. —help me get this fight notion out of his head. Let him stay Farnsworth like he is. I'd make it worth your while—

JOE (*interrupting*). Talking to yourself lately, Max?

Max whirls as if shot.

MAX. Oh! Never do that! (*Recovering*) I—uh—I was just having a little conversation with your friend. It—it was a little one-sided, of course—

JOE. What friend?

MAX. Mister Jordan.

JOE (*indicating living room*). He's sitting in there.

Max does a violent "take."

MAX. What!

JOE (*with a laugh*). You're crackin' up, Max!

Then Joe extends the check to Max.

JOE. Here. Here's the dough. Now, go on—do your stuff. Go right down and see Lefty.

MAX (*staring at check*). Is this good?

JOE. It's perfect. (*Then*) Hey—what was that you were saying about me getting

this fight notion out of my head? What's *that* all about?

MAX (*caught*). Well—now look, Joe—I been thinking—this fight game's a bad racket. If you needed the dough, I'd say all right—but when a guy's got millions—

JOE. You sap! That's not my dough!

MAX. So it's Farnsworth's. And you're Farnsworth. And I got forty percent of *whoever* you are. That gives me *something* to say!

JOE (*hotly*). I'm still *Joe!* And I don't *want* any of that guy's coin. It ought to be given back to the people he swiped it from!

MAX. Are you nuts? Giving back twenty million sabaffles?

JOE. Listen—you dope! We'll make plenty ourselves. Just get me the fights! I've got to be *champ*, Max. And there's another reason. There's a girl. I want to have money that I earned myself—

He throws his arm around Max and draws him into living room.

JOE. Come on now—do as I tell you.

The LIVING ROOM, with Jordan standing— waiting. Joe enters leading Max in.

JOE. Get right down to that Murdock crowd—and set this fight.

MAX. Joe—

JOE. Quit arguing! Another peep out of you, and I'm through with you! (*To Jordan*) Imagine this guy! Give up the title, he tells me!

MAX (*looking around*). Is—is he here?

JOE (*pointing to Jordan*). Right there. (*To Max*) Get going, Max. And call me the minute you get it fixed. I'll be waiting—if I have to stay up all night. Ya hear?

He pushes Max toward the entrance hall.

MAX. Okay—okay. (*He glances back— waves at nothing—that is, Jordan.*) Well —glad to've met you. Can I drop you off some place—? (*Quickly*) No—come to

think of it—I—I'm not going your
way—!

And Max leaves—fast.

JOE (*turning to Jordan happily*). Gee—
thanks a lot, Mister Jordan. That takes
care of everything.

JORDAN. Then you're quite happy, Joe?

JOE. Yes, it's going swell. (*Pinching himself*) I'm getting hard as nails. Oh—and
Bette Logan—I'm seeing her tonight.
She's stopping in for a few minutes—on
her way to the theatre—some papers I
got to attend to for her father— (*Then
suddenly*) She likes me a *lot,* Mister
Jordan!

JORDAN. Well, that's nice, Joe.

JOE. Yeah—only—it's all gummed up. I
mean—I can't even see her. Here I am
—supposed to be married—so naturally
Bette won't come here to visit me—and
I can't take her out for the same reason.
People'd talk.

JORDAN. You'll work that out, Joe.

JOE. Yeah—I got to make some changes
around here—and I'm going to do it
pretty quick! Well—I got to take a bath
—and get a rest—I'm in training, you
know. You don't mind, do you, Mister
Jordan?

JORDAN. No, of course not. I've got to
leave anyway.

He starts in the direction of the sunroom,
Joe following a few steps.

JOE. Gee—*this* is something new—*me*
walking out on *you!* (*Worriedly*) You're
not sore?

JORDAN (*laughing*). Certainly not. Good
luck, Joe.

JOE (*calling after him*). Thanks again,
Mister Jordan!

Joe is about to start for the stairs—but stops.
He heads for the sunroom instead.

The SUN ROOM: Joe enters and goes for his
saxophone. Jordan is gone and as Joe notes
this, he smiles; he is used to it. He pats
his saxophone affectionately, and as he
starts out, blowing a blast on the saxophone
the scene shifts to the BATHROOM as Joe, in

a bathrobe, enters—still tooting the horn. He
pauses, and sees: SISK AT THE TUB (seen at
close range); the tub is filled, and Sisk is
testing the water. Then, the whole Bathroom in view again, Joe's eyes are fixed on
the tub of water. He swallows.

SISK. Your bath is ready, sir.

JOE (*still eyeing tub*). Nix. Make it a
shower my friend.

Joe lifts the saxophone to his lips again.

The UPPER HALLWAY: Julia emerges from
her suite and crosses the hall to Joe's bedroom. She puts her hand on the doorknob,
but a saxophone blast from inside makes
her jump. She recovers—and pushes in.

JOE'S BEDROOM as Julia enters: Almost simultaneously, Joe enters from the bathroom.
He is dressed in a bathrobe—and is blowing
the saxophone. He breaks off in alarm on
seeing her.

JOE. Wha—what are *you* doing in here?

JULIA. I wanted to talk to you, Bruce—

Joe is conscious of being in a bathrobe—and
in a bedroom with her.

JOE. Oh, you do? Well, I'd like to talk
to *you.* I'll get into some clothes—and
see you downstairs.

She approaches him and takes his arm.

JULIA (*lightly*). How silly. Come—sit
down, dear—

JOE (*trying to get loose*). Now, wait a
minute—

She pulls him down.

JULIA. Right here—close to me—for just
a moment. (*Joe squirms.*) One would
think you were afraid to be alone with
me.

JOE (*dryly*). *One* might be right.

JULIA. Darling, don't you think it's time
we were honest with each other—?

Joe rises quickly—and says definitely:

JOE. That's just what I'd *like* to be!

JULIA. Then it seems to me, as my husband, you—

JOE. I'm *not* your husband!

Julia is puzzled.

> JOE (*adding quickly*). What I mean is
> —*spiritually*—we're not married at all.
> We never were.

> JULIA. Why, Bruce—!

> JOE (*wound up*). And it's no use going
> on this way. That's what I had to tell
> you. We're splitting—you and me.

Julia gets up quickly.

> JULIA (*dangerously*). Are we?

> JOE. That's sure!

> JULIA (*trying another tack—going to-
> ward him*). Bruce, dear—this is absurd.
> I realize—you've changed in some way I
> can't understand—but it doesn't matter—
> I still love you—and I won't let you go.

She has put her arms around his neck—and
he throws them off.

> JOE. I'm not *that* dumb! You're in love
> with Tony Abbott. And he's in love with
> you. And that suits me fine. Because
> that's how *I* feel about Bette Logan—and
> as soon as we can *arrange* it—

> JULIA. Bette Logan! That's being *quite*
> honest!

> JOE. You asked for it.

> JULIA. Do you expect me to step aside
> and make Bette Logan a present of *my
> position* and the Farnsworth millions?

> JOE. Oh—those millions! *You're* getting
> pretty honest *now,* aren't you?

> JULIA. I have rights to that money! And
> what's more, I don't intend to sit like
> a fool and watch you throw it away. I
> want some explanation. I want to know
> how far you intend to go.

> JOE. I may give it *all* away. Then we can
> both get a job and go to work.

> JULIA (*blazing*). You can't do that to
> me, Bruce! I'll never let you do it!

> JOE (*with sudden directness*). Listen—
> you try any funny business—you make
> one wrong move—and you'll be sorry.
> Understand?

A pause, as Julia looks at him quietly, and
steadily.

JULIA. Yes. I understand.

She turns and starts out to the door; and as
she swings it open with decision, the scene
dissolves to the study.

The STUDY at night reveals BETTE AND JOE.
Bette, in evening dress and fur wrap—a
stunning sight—has handed some folded
papers to Joe. He glances at them casually,
embarrassed.

> JOE. I—I'll have Abbott take care of these
> in the morning. They'll be signed an'
> everything—just as your father says.
> Don't worry about that—

> BETTE. Thank you.

> JOE. You—uh—you have to go now,
> huh?

> BETTE. The car's waiting. I'm a little
> late.

> JOE (*his eyes roving over her face*). I—
> I wish you didn't. I wish—I wish I could
> stand here and look at you all night. I
> mean—I never saw you gotten up this
> way—and—and it's pretty wonderful.

> BETTE (*laughing*). Thank you. I wish I
> *could* stay a little—

> JOE (*at once excited*). Well, why not?
> Just for a minute!

> BETTE (*looking around troubledly*). I'd
> like to—*any place* but here.

> JOE (*quickly*). I know how you feel. And
> you're right. But—just for a minute—I've
> got so many things to tell you—and so
> many things to ask you—

As he takes her hand and leads her to a
chair the scene dissolves to Julia's sitting
room.

JULIA'S SITTING ROOM, at night, reveals JULIA
AND TONY. Tony sits at Julia's writing table
and is talking on the phone. Julia is at the
window, staring down into the driveway.

> TONY (*into the phone*). A fight manager?
> You're sure?

He hangs up. Julia, with her own thoughts,
whirls from the window.

> JULIA. Her car's still here. She's been
> down there with him an hour! What's
> the meaning of it?

TONY. That doesn't matter. Do you know who Mr. Corkle is . . . ? A *fight* manager!

JULIA. What?

TONY. Twenty-five thousand dollars—to arrange a fight! He intends to enter the ring!

JULIA. He's not *that* mad!

TONY. What else could it mean? This gymnasium downstairs . . . training schedules . . . he's throwing money away in every direction! Where will this stop, Julia? If it keeps up, you'll be a pauper within a month.

JULIA. I can't figure it out. This squandering of money . . . prizefighting . . . and everything else. . . . (*Then*) We could have him declared insane!

TONY (*quietly*). And by the time you brought it to trial, he'd have tossed away every last cent.

JULIA. Then how are we going to stop him?

TONY (*simply*). As we tried to do before except this time there's going to be no mistake. (*A pause*) I'll see to that—tonight.

The STUDY—JOE AND BETTE: She sits watching him, as Joe paces nervously in front of her.

JOE (*with attempted lightness*). —That's what I do most of the time, I guess—think about you and me. I keep figuring—maybe she'd want me *different* some way. And if she does—I'd like to know—

BETTE (*laughing*). I can't think of a single way.

JOE (*walking on clouds*). Well—that's wonderful! Because—nothing else would be worth a hoot if—if you didn't like me.

BETTE. I—I couldn't help doing that—

JOE (*quickly—anxiously*). Yes, but—I've been looking ahead too—and wondering—(*He breaks off.*) Remember that day we said—it only mattered what two people were like inside—?

BETTE. Yes.

JOE. Well—no matter what I did *outside* —(*Laughing*) Funny way to say it, but—! I mean—well—Farnsworth might do all sorts of things with his life. I got a lot of queer notions, you know. Why, I might up and say: "You know what I think I'll do? I think I'll go ahead and be a prizefighter!" (*Quickly*) Do you like prizefighters?

BETTE. I never knew one.

JOE. They're just like anybody else.

BETTE (*slowly—staring at him*). I actually believe you'd like to be one.

JOE. Well—in a way—yes. You can never tell. I *might*.

BETTE. And get all bruised and battered!

JOE (*laughing*). Listen—you say the word—and nobody'll ever lay a glove on me!

She laughs with him. Then suddenly Joe is intense again—

JOE. You see what I mean? Nothing like that would matter, would it? You'd still like me—

BETTE. I always will, Bruce—

JOE. And later on—sometime—it might be *more* than that, Bette—

BETTE (*getting up*). We can't talk that way!

JOE. I'm sorry. You meant, I haven't got the right. But you've got to believe something—she never meant a thing to me. And I've already told her—we aren't going on this way—I want to be free—

Suddenly, glancing off, Joe's eyes are held by something that makes his breath catch, and we see MESSENGER 7013 at close range, standing troubled in the doorway, and looking steadily at Joe. Then back in the study, Joe is seen still staring off, Bette swinging around to look in the same direction. Seeing nothing, she turns back to Joe.

BETTE. What's the matter, Bruce?

JOE (*snapping out of it*). Nothing. What was I saying? Oh—you—you don't have to worry about that. (*Then, impulsively*) Would you excuse me for just a minute?

BETTE. I must *go,* Bruce.

JOE. No—please. I—I just remembered something—*please* wait. I'll be right back—

And he starts quickly for the living room. The Messenger, seeing him coming, retires. Bette watches Bruce go, extremely puzzled by his behavior.

The LIVING ROOM as Joe enters from the library quickly, closing the door. The Messenger gulps nervously. Joe is frightened. He has a premonition of bad news, and keeps his voice in an intense whisper.

JOE. What's the idea—poppin' up like this? I thought I saw the last of you.

MESSENGER 7013 (*wiping his brow—in soft voice*). I—I had hoped so too. As you know—I went through *Hades* to make good my error. And I *thought* I'd had the last of it.

JOE (*whispering*). What's the matter? What do you want?

MESSENGER 7013. It's distressing news, Mr. Pendleton. *You can't use Farnsworth's body any more.*

JOE. What! What are you talking about?

MESSENGER 7013. Just what I said.

JOE. You're crazy! Didn't you tell me I was going to be champ?

MESSENGER 7013. But not with Farnsworth's body.

JOE. Why not?

MESSENGER 7013. It wasn't meant to be that way, Mr. Pendleton.

JOE. Why not?

MESSENGER 7013. Don't keep saying "why not"! You must just *believe* me—

JOE. I'll believe nothing! You can't pull this on me! Why don't you guys get together for once?

MESSENGER 7013. Mr. Pendleton—you haven't much more time to stay in Farnsworth—

JOE. I'm not even listening! Mr. Jordan said okay—and this is how it's going to stay!

MESSENGER 7013. Oh, dear—

JOE (*his voice raised now*). "Oh, dear" nothing! You go on back and tell whoever's pulling this that it's no soap! I'm laughing! See? Now get out of here!

The Messenger has been backing in the direction of the sun room.

JOE (*bearing down on him*). And don't come back! You're just bad news! You keep gumming up everything—!

The library door swings open and Bette enters. Simultaneously, Messenger 7013 disappears into the sun room. Joe turns quickly to face Bette, who is glancing around.

BETTE. Were—weren't you talking in here?

JOE. Uh—yes—I—I was just saying something to Sisk— I'm sorry to keep you waiting. I—I'll take you out to your car.

He takes her arm and starts out with her. He is terribly troubled—and silent, while Bette glances at his face furtively. Then as they start into the entrance hall, the UPPER HALLWAY comes in view, revealing Tony and Julia coming out of Julia's sitting room. They stand listening for sounds from below. Tony is hard-faced and determined. Julia, behind him, is distraught—on the point of hysteria.

The EXTERIOR OF THE FARNSWORTH HOUSE with JOE AND BETTE as he walks with her toward her car: When they are within fifteen feet of it, Joe stops Bette, turns her to face him, and stares at her.

JOE. Bette—

BETTE. Yes—

A pause.

BETTE. Something's happened!

JOE (*trying to be off-hand*). No. No. I was just thinking—believe in one thing, Bette. We—we got a great life ahead—you and me. Nobody's going to take that away from us.

BETTE. Why are you looking at me like that?

JOE. I—I'm just memorizing your face, that's all. I want to memorize everything about you—so—so no matter what happens—I won't forget you.

BETTE. *What* might happen, Bruce?

JOE. Nothing! Don't be scared. Look at me, Bette. You'd never forget me, either, would you?

BETTE. No—never.

JOE. Course you wouldn't! And if anything ever *did happen*— (*Quickly*) It won't, though. It won't! But *supposin'*—you'd never forget me. I mean—the thing you saw in me—you said it was something in my eyes—remember? Well, if some day somebody came up to you—he might be a fighter—and he acted like he'd seen you before—you'd notice that same thing, wouldn't you? I mean—even if you *thought* you did—you'd give him a chance? He might be a good egg!

BETTE (*crying out*). I don't understand you!

JOE (*laughing breathlessly*). I'm just crazy! (*He seizes her in his arms.*) I never want to lose you! That's all I'm trying to say! And I'm never gonna! (*He kisses her swiftly.*) Good night.

He then takes her to the limousine—and helps her in. The car drives off, Joe looking after it. Then he turns back to the house. As JOE comes up the walk, and steps onto the porch, he stops dead—his mouth dropping open. JORDAN is standing in the shadow on the porch—to the side of the front door. His smile is compassionately warm, and his eyes are on Joe steadily. JOE, seen at close range, stands rooted. His premonitions are now deep and swift. Beads of sweat break out on his forehead.

JORDAN's VOICE (*softly*). I'll have to talk to you, Joe.

Jordan's words jolt him from his stupor. He gulps, shakes his head as if to lose his dread, and opens his mouth as if to speak—but can't form words. He lamely indicates the front door—and starts forward. Next Joe opens the front door and enters, Jordan fol-

lowing. Next Joe and Jordan are in the ENTRANCE HALL, walking toward the living room. And in the UPPER HALLWAY, Tony stands on the stairs—listening to Joe's progress. Behind Tony, at some distance, is the frightened Julia.

Through the LIVING ROOM, Joe and Jordan enter the STUDY, and Joe quickly closes the door. He is still sweating, and his heart is pounding with dread.

JOE (*with difficulty*). Wha—what do you want, Mr. Jordan? (*Then, before Jordan can answer*) It—it isn't true, is it? Giving up Farnsworth. You aren't going to ask me to do *that*!

JORDAN (*gently*). It's not up to me, my boy.

JOE (*coming toward Jordan passionately*). But why—*why*? Here we got everything going swell—after all the trouble we went through! I can't leave Farnsworth *now*!

JORDAN. Joe—

JOE (*running on*). You *told* me—I was going to be champ!

JORDAN. You will be, Joe. But on another road.

JOE. Why not with Farnsworth? I got his body in the pink—Corkle's out getting the fight—I'm all ready. Why not with Farnsworth?

JORDAN. It wasn't meant to be that way.

JOE. *That's* no answer!

JORDAN. On the contrary, Joe—it's the *perfect* answer!

JOE. But Bette—I love her, Mr. Jordan—and I got her to love me—as Farnsworth—! You can't ask me to give her up now—and forget her!

JORDAN. No, Joe. If *that* was meant to be —it will be, too.

JOE (*angrily*). No! I can't believe anything you tell me now! No—!

The phone rings. Both look at it an instant. It rings again before Joe jumps for it with sudden alert expectancy.

JOE (*into phone*). Hello! . . . Max! I knew it—it *is*? . . . When? . . . That's great! . . . Yeah . . . No, not tonight. See me tomorrow. Come over early. Nice work, Max! (*He hangs up—comes excitedly toward Jordan.*) Mr. Jordan—Max got the fight with Murdock! Don't you see? That's it! I can't switch now—!

JORDAN. Joe—you haven't much time.

JOE. Don't say that! Listen, Mr. Jordan—please—let me just get through this fight—and work it out with Bette some way! Give me some time. *You* can fix it, Mr. Jordan!

JORDAN. There's no time left at all now, Joe.

JOE (*storming*). Then I say no! No! You're not playing tricks with my life again. I'm staying the way I am!

JORDAN. Joe—you are no more able to stop the course of your destiny than—

JOE. No! We'll *see* about that! If you think you can pry me loose from Farnsworth—just try!

He rushes for the door. When he has taken several steps, he stops—glued to the floor. He tries to heave himself loose—but can't budge.

JOE. Hey! Something's holding me back! I can't move!

JORDAN. Sorry, Joe.

JOE. Lemme go, will you?

JORDAN. You have only a few seconds. You wouldn't get very far.

JOE. Lemme go—and I'll *show* ya!

JORDAN. Very well.

Joe can move. He lunges for the door, his hand on the knob.

JOE (*yelling back exultantly*). Now! Goodbye, Mr. Jordan!

He pulls the door open. We can see a man's arm on the other side of the doorway. The hand holds a gun which is pointed at Joe.

As Joe swings into the hallway, *the gun explodes*. The arm is quickly withdrawn.

JOE, seen close, staggers and spins bewilderedly. He shows no sign of pain—but is conscious of having been hit.

JOE (*in intense wonderment*). Who was it? (*Puzzling it out frantically*) It was *those* two! (*Then, explosively*) Call the police! Never mind—I'll get 'em! (*He whirls toward desk.*)

In the room, as Joe staggers toward the desk, Jordan watches—his expression gentle and sorrowful. Joe grabs up the phone—he is weakening fast.

JOE. Hello—police—

JORDAN (*kindly*). Don't fight, Joe. *Leave Farnsworth!*

The phone drops from Joe's hand. He grabs the desk for support, beginning to slump. He raises his eyes to Jordan.

JOE (*weakly*). This—is—it, huh?

JORDAN. Yes, Joe.

JOE. But—Farnsworth—I got him in the pink. What happens to him now?

JORDAN. Just earthly remains—for *them* to dispose of now.

JOE. And *me*, Mr. Jordan—Joe Pendleton!

JORDAN (*softly*). Why, you and I will be moving again, Joe—searching.

JOE. Oh, Mr. Jordan—Bette—

JORDAN. Joe—*leave Farnsworth*.

Joe sinks to the floor, disappearing behind the desk. Jordan walks slowly to where Joe lies, and looks down at him. Then, Jordan raises his eyes to look off at something, and a close view of the OPEN WINDOW OF THE STUDY reveals Messenger 7013 standing outside and looking in through the open window. His eyes are directed down, obviously at Joe on the floor.

MESSENGER 7013. Have I got *him* on my hands again?

His expression is one of intense dismay as the scene fades out.

PART THREE

The FARNSWORTH HOUSE fades in. It is morning. Max is paying off a taxi driver. Max's air is jaunty—his dress is on the loud side. He throws a bill at the driver.

MAX. Keep the change, buddy. The stuff grows on trees!

And whistling, Max pushes through the gate and up the walk to the house.

At the FRONT DOOR Max pushes the button—still whistling. The door is opened after a moment by Sisk, who is hurried and nervous.

MAX. Ah! The major domo! Good morning, my man!

And Max pushes on in before Sisk can say anything.

The ENTRANCE HALL, as Max saunters in—starting in the direction of the living room.

MAX. Tell the master of the house that Old Faithful is here—with glad tidings!

SISK (*following Max*). Mr. Corkle—I'm sorry—Mr. Farnsworth isn't home.

MAX (*stopping*). How come?

SISK. Well—it seems he went out last night—and never returned.

MAX. What d'ye mean? Where'd he go?

SISK. I don't know. It's all rather strange, sir. He left no word—and he took no clothes of any kind with him.

MAX (*with sudden misgivings*). What *is* this? What's going on here? He said to meet him here early. He wouldn't go running out on *me!*

A voice breaks in on him.

TONY'S VOICE. Mr. Corkle—!

Max whirls to find Tony emerging from the living room.

TONY. —evidently Mr. Farnsworth changed his mind about—*fighting.*

MAX. Evidently you don't know what you're talking about! He might change his mind about everything else—but not about that! I *know!*

TONY. I'd advise you to drop the matter until Mr. Farnsworth sends for you.

MAX. Drop nothing! There's something awful fishy about this! And I'm going to find out *what!*

As Max turns and starts rapidly for the front door, the scene dissolves to a POLICE INSPECTOR'S OFFICE, revealing MAX, the INSPECTOR AND TWO OTHER MEN. Max is addressing the Inspector behind the desk.

MAX (*hotly*). —for four days now—no sign of him! They can't kid *me!* He's disappeared—and *I* say its foul play! *Cause Mr. Farnsworth wants to see me.* And if he could, he *would!* I want you to check every morgue, hospital, hotel, railroad—!

On these last words, the scene dissolves to a NEWSPAPER HEADLINE rolling out:

BRUCE FARNSWORTH DISAPPEARS
Search Begun For Missing Multimillionaire

This dissolves to MAX CORKLE'S OFFICE, revealing MAX AND CHARLIE. Max is on the phone. Charlie, whom we saw in the first scene, sits alongside.

MAX (*into the phone—perspiring*). —Lefty, listen—they got all the police in the country lookin' for him! They *gotta* find him! Gimme another day!

We get a close view of LEFTY, K.O. Murdock's manager, on a phone somewhere else.

LEFTY (*barking back*). No—it's off, Max! Murdock and me ain't waitin' for no screwball millionaire! *Murdock's fighting Gilbert on the seventh!*

He slams up. And back in MAX CORKLE'S OFFICE Max is seen hanging up, dazed and baffled.

The scene dissolves to MADISON SQUARE GARDEN at night. First a POSTER appears at close range:

FOR THE CHAMPIONSHIP OF
THE WORLD

GILBERT
Lou   vs.   MURDOCK
                                              Ralph (K.O.)

Across it is slapped a strip reading: TONIGHT! Noise of traffic comes over—and hubbub of people. Then a crowd is revealed swarming around the entrance to the Garden. Then JORDAN AND JOE appear on the outskirts of the crowd—coming to a stop. Joe gazes off at the poster.

JOE (*troubled*). There goes my fight. You sure got me in a fine mess, Mr. Jordan—weeks now—and no body yet.

JORDAN (*consolingly*). Joe—you shan't be cheated. In the final reckoning, everything will be accounted for. You wanted to see this fight. Shall we go in?

They take just one step when Joe stops to look over the shoulder of a man who has a newspaper spread open—arrested by a NEWSPAPER HEADLINE:

FARNSWORTH DISAPPEARANCE
STILL UNSOLVED
Police Again Questioning Principals

Joe and Jordan (back in the scene) talk right next to the ear of the man with the newspaper. He is not aware of them, naturally.

JOE (*disturbed*). More questioning. They'll be draggin' Bette into it again.

JORDAN. Come, Joe.

They start forward.

JOE (*stopping*). Gee—no wonder—no *wonder* nothing's going right! I haven't got my lucky saxophone! Left it at Farnsworth's. Let's go get it, Mr. Jordan.

JORDAN. Now?

JOE. Yeah—*now*. We got plenty of time before the fight. Come on.

JORDAN. Very well, Joe.

As Joe and Jordan start away from the crowd the scene dissolves to the SUN ROOM of the Farnsworth home at night as Jordan and Joe enter through the open Garden doors; they are already several feet within The room and are making straight for the living room.

JOE. The last I remember it was on the piano in the living room.

When they are near the entrance to the living room, both stop dead—looking ahead. At the same time we hear a voice of authority say:

WILLIAMS' VOICE. —I've called you all together again, because I want to go over every step since the night Mr. Farnsworth disappeared.

And now the LIVING ROOM, seen from Joe's angle, reveals Tony, Julia, Bette and Max, all of them seated, while two plainclothesmen stand in the entrance to the hallway. A toy dog is in Julia's lap. On his feet, walking in circles, is Inspector Williams—an unimaginative man, given to gusts of temper. He is already pretty exasperated.

WILLIAMS. We're going to start all over. Maybe I missed something—or maybe somebody *forgot* something! I'm going to *crack* this case—!

MAX. You better call in Houdini.

Williams throws Max a look. Joe has come forward to the entrance to the room and is staring off at BETTE, of whom there is now a close view as she sits tense, nervous, and a little drawn.

WILLIAMS' VOICE. Miss Logan—(*Bette jumps.*) You said it was approximately eight-thirty when you left Mr. Farnsworth that night—

BETTE. Yes.

Max has risen and is slowly working around the room, now in full view again. At the same time the toy dog jumps off Julia's lap and starts roving around.

WILLIAMS. You brought some papers for him to sign?

MAX, seen close, is working around the curtains near the piano—nudging things as he passes them.

BETTE'S VOICE. Yes—for my father.

MAX (*addressing the curtains*). Psst! Hey, Joe—you here?

WILLIAMS' VOICE. And you didn't hear from Mr. Farnsworth after that?—by phone—or in any way?

BETTE'S VOICE. No.

MAX (*looking under piano*). Joe—for Pete's sake—where are you?

Max is at the piano now, touching the saxophone.

MAX. You aren't on the end of your old sax, are you, Joe?

We get a close view of WILLIAMS, his attention caught by Max; he watches. Then MAX is again seen proceeding with his search. The toy dog, strolling by, catches Max's attention. He addresses the dog.

MAX. Joe—come on—who are you now? —give me a break—

WILLIAMS' VOICE (*sharply*). Corkle!

Max jumps, gulps and stands sheepishly in the room again, fully revealed.

WILLIAMS. Exactly *what* do you think you're doing?

MAX. Looking for Joe.

WILLIAMS. Who's Joe?

MAX. He may be *anybody!* I don't know!

PLAINCLOTHESMAN. Maybe we'd better call the psychopathic.

WILLIAMS. Corkle—are you going to shut up and sit down!

MAX (*sitting*). Okay—but if Joe or his pal Jordan is around, I'm going to find 'em!

WILLIAMS. Who's Jordan?

MAX. He's the guy who put Joe in Farnsworth's body!

WILLIAMS. I *warned* you about this goofy talk, Corkle!

MAX. All right. All right.

WILLIAMS (*striding to Max*). When *you* last saw him, what was he doing?

MAX. Arguin' with some guy from heaven!

WILLIAMS (*savagely*). That's what you'll be doing if you don't cut out the clowning!

MAX. Clowning? After what I've been through? And what do I wind up with? Forty per cent of a ghost. Forty per cent of nothing! And I can't even find that!

JOE is now seen at close range.

JOE (*with a wry smile*). Sorry, Max—

JULIA'S VOICE. Inspector Williams—we'll accomplish *nothing* here! (*Joe turns his head in her direction.*) I can only repeat that my husband's disappearance is neither mysterious nor does it surprise me in the least! When you consider his actions for several weeks' previous—giving away his money—and preparing to enter prizefighting—! He was obviously insane!

BETTE. He was nothing of the kind. I knew him better than any of you! He was fine and generous!

She bursts into tears. Joe takes an impulsive step forward.

JOE. Don't cry, Bette!

JULIA. I can explain the tears, Inspector. The last time I spoke to Mr. Farnsworth, he told me he loved Miss Logan. He wanted to marry her—and asked for a divorce—

WILLIAMS. I see—uh huh.

MAX. You can say "uh huh" again, but it won't get you a thing!

WILLIAMS. Quiet! (*To Bette*) Miss Logan, if he were alive, you feel sure he'd communicate with you?

BETTE. I *know* he would.

JOE (*impulsively*). You *bet* I would!

Max rises in sudden impatience.

MAX. Look—for the last time—you *think* you're looking for Farnsworth, but you're really looking for Joe. *Farnsworth's dead.*

BETTE (*agonized*). I knew it!

MAX. In fact, if you wanna know—he was drowned in the bathtub by his wife and that guy there—six weeks ago!

JULIA (*springing up*). You're mad!

WILLIAMS. Hold it! (*To Max, sarcastically*) So Mr. Farnsworth was drowned in his bathtub, was he?

MAX. Yes!

WILLIAMS. Six weeks ago?

MAX. Right!

WILLIAMS. And he's only been missing *three* weeks!

MAX. I don't care. That's what he told me.

WILLIAMS. Who told you?

MAX. Joe—I mean Farnsworth.

WILLIAMS. Just when did he tell you this?—before or *after* he was drowned?

MAX. *After!*

WILLIAMS (*shouting*). Get hold of him, boys! He's violent!

The plainclothesmen rush for Max.

MAX. Take your hands off me!

BETTE. He *was* murdered! I'm sure of it!

WILLIAMS. Then where's the body?

There is a pause.

JOE AND JORDAN are seen close as Joe turns quickly to Jordan.

JOE. Where *did* they put it, Mr. Jordan?

JORDAN. In the basement refrigerator.

Joe registers this sharply.

WILLIAMS' VOICE (*shouting*). Come on! Any suggestions, Corkle? You got ideas about everything else. *Where's the body?*

Max, in the now again fully revealed scene, indicates Julia and Tony.

MAX. Ask them!

TONY (*quickly*). Why, naturally—we cut it up, stuffed it in a trunk, flew it out over the Atlantic and—

BETTE (*screaming*). Stop it! Stop it!

JOE AND JORDAN: Joe is beside himself at the sight of Bette's torment.

JOE. They're killing her, Mr. Jordan! I can't stand it!

JORDAN. Then, let's leave, Joe. Take your saxophone—

JOE (*torn*). Leave Bette?

WILLIAMS' VOICE (*calmingly*). Now, now —get hold of yourself, Miss Logan.

We hear Bette's sobs.

JORDAN. But—the fight's about to start, Joe.

JOE (*can't make up his mind*). I can't walk out on her this way! (*With a sudden idea*) Wait—it'll be on the radio, won't it?

JORDAN. It's on now.

JOE. Then I can hear it!

WILLIAMS' VOICE. I'd like to ask *you* a questions, Mr. Abbott—

JOE (*to Jordan*). Oh—but how am I going to turn it on?

JORDAN. Mr. Corkle will, if you concentrate on him.

Joe's eyes open wider, he turns in Max's direction and starts to concentrate.

WILLIAMS' VOICE. You said you last saw him right down here, when Miss Logan arrived with those papers.

JOE. Come on, Max! Turn on the radio!

MAX, seen close, pulls out his watch.

TONY'S VOICE. That's correct, Inspector—

MAX (*leaping up*). Holy smoke—it's ten o'clock. The fight's on!

Max rushes for the radio in the room and turns it on.

WILLIAMS' VOICE. Turn that off, Corkle!

MAX. Yeah? Listen—you kept me from *seeing* that fight—draggin' me here—but I'm gonna *listen* to it!

WILLIAMS. Corkle!

The radio blasts out:

ANNOUNCER'S VOICE. —Murdock is crowding Gilbert to the ropes—shoots over a right cross—*ohhh!*—a left jolt to the chin— (*Roar of the crowd*) —*another* right—*another* left to Gilbert's jaw—lightning punches that hit their mark like a bullet. Gilbert throws one high to Murdock's head but it glances off. Murdock comes back with a right cross—a left to the body!

The group is silent and listening. Even Williams is fascinated by the progress of the fight.

We see JOE AND JORDAN, Joe absorbed.

ANNOUNCER'S VOICE. Gilbert isn't even in it! Murdock's toying with him. Wow! He jolted Gilbert with a short right—then a left to the ribs! Gilbert swings wild—can't touch Murdock—misses another left hook. Murdock's crowding Gilbert to the ropes—with lefts and rights—punishing blows— (*There is a roar.*) Gilbert's down! A smashing right that lifted him clear off his feet! The referee's counting—!

The roar of the crowd continues to come from the radio.

JOE. Murdock's dynamite!

JORDAN (*smiling*). I thought you said he was a "palooka."

JOE (*gulping*). He—he's just lucky tonight, I guess.

Max is jumping around excitedly in the room.

ANNOUNCER'S VOICE. Gilbert's up! Murdock rushes him—swarming all over him—whips over a left, a right, another left—now he gets in a hard left hook.

JOE AND JORDAN are seen as another roar comes from the crowd.

JORDAN. Murdock's a great fighter, Joe—and you know it. In your heart, you'd even *like to be like him*.

JOE. Who? Me?

ANNOUNCER'S VOICE. Murdock smashes over a hard right—a left—another right to the head—Gilbert swings wildly and—

A deafening roar.

ANNOUNCER'S VOICE. —*Murdock* is down! He's down—flat on the floor! It looked like a wild punch that only grazed the side of his head—he couldn't even have felt it. But Murdock went down like a shot!

Max and all the others in the room are extremely tense.

MAX. What happened?

JOE AND JORDAN are seen close:

ANNOUNCER'S VOICE. The referee's started the count—one—!

JOE. Why, he was going like a buzz saw!

JORDAN. *He's dead.*

JOE. What? You're crazy! Murdock's got a build like a bull!

JORDAN. They don't know it yet—but *he was shot,* Joe.

JOE. What!

The roar has drowned out the count.

JORDAN. Because he wouldn't throw the fight. He told Lefty and the gamblers he would—otherwise they wouldn't have given him a chance at the championship. But once he got in the ring—

ANNOUNCER'S VOICE (*piercing the roar*). —four—five—

JOE. And they *shot* him! *Murdock*—the finest guy in the game! Gee—I'd like to finish that fight for him—I'd like to be him for just five minutes—!

JORDAN (*quietly*). You can, Joe.

JOE (*staring*). You mean—I can take Murdock's—?

JORDAN. We've just got time to make it! Come!

Joe is about to start out—remembers his saxophone—grabs it off the piano—and as he and Jordan race into the sun room, the scene shifts to—

MADISON SQUARE GARDEN. First there is a close view of the prone figure of MURDOCK—the referee standing over him.

REFEREE. —nine—!

Suddenly the figure leaps up—and, the scene expanding, Gilbert is seen waiting in the neutral corner. Joe flies across the ring to Gilbert—full of fight—the roar of the crowd a frenzied outburst!!

In the FARNSWORTH LIVING ROOM the people —especially Max—are transfixed as the announcer's voice comes over hysterically.

ANNOUNCER. He jumped up!—at the count of nine—*Murdock is up!* Full of fight! One minute lying there like a dead man—now on his feet like a dynamo! It's amazing!

MAX. Wow!

In the GARDEN—THE RING, Joe is charging into Gilbert savagely—to avenge Murdock —ripping Gilbert with punches. The crowd is frenzied. A close view of LEFTY at the ringside reveals him watching Joe incredulously and with fright. His glance goes off to: A close view of TWO PLUG-UGLIES at the ringside. They look from Lefty to each other. One of them tremblingly drops a gun to the floor and kicks it under the ring. Then JOE AND GILBERT are seen close, Joe driving Gilbert against the ropes—slashing him with lefts and rights. And in the FARNSWORTH LIVING ROOM we hear:

THE ANNOUNCER'S VOICE. —a rain of punches to Gilbert's head! Murdock's fighting like a savage—a murderous left —and a *right* to Gilbert's head—then a smashing blow to the body—a paralyzer —Gilbert's rocking dizzily! What a fight! What a comeback for Murdock! Ohh! A slashing right to Gilbert's face—another one—and another!—Gilbert's down!

A deafening roar ensues. And back in the GARDEN—THE RING—the referee is counting over the prostrate Gilbert, JOE, his eyes wild —chest heaving—is watching the count, which the roar drowns out, and LEFTY, at the ringside, is paralyzed with amazement.

In the FARNSWORTH LIVING ROOM:

ANNOUNCER'S VOICE. —eight—nine—ten! Murdock's fight by a knockout! (*The crowd is heard roaring.*)

MAX. What a scrap!

In the GARDEN—THE RING, the referee raises Joe's hand.

REFEREE (*yelling*). —the winner and new champion of the world—*Ralph Murdock!*

Joe's handlers swarm into the ring—flashlights pop—a bathrobe is thrown over Joe's shoulders. He suddenly pushes through them to his own corner and reaches under his stool for his saxophone.

The FARNSWORTH LIVING ROOM:

ANNOUNCER'S VOICE. —will go down in history as the most sensational encounter of all time!

WILLIAMS. All right—now shut that thing off!

Max goes to the radio, to listen to it.

ANNOUNCER'S VOICE. —oh—oh—what's that Murdock picked up from under his stool? *A saxophone!*

MAX. What!

Max is suddenly beside himself.

ANNOUNCER'S VOICE. Imagine that! I didn't notice it there before—

MAX. Saxophone—!

He rushes toward the piano—starts feeling around like a madman.

MAX. It's gone! It was right here! I touched it! He took it! He was here in this room.

WILLIAMS. Corkle—what's come over you!

MAX (*frantic*). Joe! He was here! (*Points to the radio*) That was Joe! That was Farnsworth—!

Bette has jumped up and has seized hold of Max violently.

BETTE (*shaking him*). Mr. Corkle—tell me what you mean!

MAX. Yes! Joe—*Farnsworth!* It's *Joe* you're nuts about—I mean—! Let me go!

And suddenly Max darts out, sailing between the two plainclothesmen.

WILLIAMS. Where you going?

MAX. I'm following that saxophone!

WILLIAMS. Hey—!

But Max is gone.

The scene dissolves to the DRESSING ROOM as a milling crowd pushes in following Joe, Lefty, his handler (Bugs)—and a couple of hangers-on. Joe, in dressing gown, with gloves still on—and carrying his saxophone —is strangely serious and thoughtful, as he is being slapped on the back. Lefty is disturbed and excited. He shouts to a policeman, who is trying to keep the crowd back.

LEFTY. Keep that mob out of here! Get 'em out!

The policeman pushes the noisy bunch out —and finally the door is closed, leaving Joe with Lefty, Bugs (the handler) and a few others.

LEFTY Greatest fight of your life, K.O.! I'm proud of you!

Joe throws a look at Lefty.

BUGS (clapping him on the back). You're champ, Kid! You're champ!

Joe sits on the rubbing table—and Bugs begins removing his gloves. A handler begins putting a small piece of adhesive tape over Joe's eye.

JOE. This guy Murdock is the best.

A HANDLER. I'll say you are!

JOE. Not me—I said *Murdock!*

Lefty and Bugs exchange quick glances. Lefty picks up the saxophone.

LEFTY. How'd *this* get in the ring?

JOE (grabbing it). Gimme that!

LEFTY. You didn't have it when you climbed in!

JOE. I always got it at *all* my fights!

BUGS (with a warning glance at Lefty— humoring Joe). Sure—sure—he's got it at *all* his fights! What a night, kid! You're champ! You're in the dough!

JOE. No—Murdock's not fighting again.

LEFTY. What are you talking about? Why, you're perched on top of the world!

JOE. I ain't perched any place. I don't even know where I go from here—!

A HANDLER. He's woozy—!

LEFTY. It's the punch he took when he went down for the nine count—!

BUGS. Punch, my eye! Gilbert didn't even touch him! How come you dropped, K.O.?

Before Joe can answer, the door is opened violently and Max is trying to force his way past a couple of objecting cops at the door.

MAX (yelling). I got to get in here!

LEFTY. What do you want in here, Corkle?

Max points dramatically at Joe and the saxophone, while a cop tries to restrain him.

MAX (yelling). Murdock—where did you get that saxophone?

LEFTY. Get him outa here!

JOE (suddenly). Let him in!

LEFTY (whirling on Joe). What for? What's Corkle got to do with you?

JOE. Plenty! And you get out, Lefty— you and all of you—get out of here a minute.

LEFTY (angrily). How do you get that way? You know I'm still your manager?

JOE. And a fine crooked manager you turned out to be.

Lefty is stopped. Joe follows up quickly.

JOE. Go on, get out—get out before I sock ya.

They are all, including Lefty, making for the door. Joe follows them and closes the door after them. Then he turns to face Max, who is dazed by all that has just proceeded. Finally Max recovers to point again at the saxophone.

MAX. I asked you, Murdock, where did you get that sax?

JOE. Gee, Max, you never know me.

Max drops back in alarm and stares. Then,

trembling, he starts feeling Joe's arms, legs, and head.

MAX. Are—are you—?

JOE. Yeah, Max. Sure I am.

MAX (*joyfully*). Joe! (*He throws his arms around Joe.*)

JOE. Come on, now, Max—don't faint.

MAX (*repeats*). Joe! (*He backs away.*) What are you doing in Murdock's body?

JOE. Now, take it easy, Max. I just took Murdock's body to help him out. You see, Max, he was shot. (*Now Joe opens his dressing gown to show Max.*) See this?

Max stares at the wound. We cannot see Joe's chest.

MAX. Jehosophat! A fine body you got into. I'd better get a doctor.

He makes a start for the door and Joe grabs him.

JOE. Max! Don't worry. It's nothin'!

MAX. Nothin'! You got a *bullet* in you!

JOE (*impatiently*). How many times do I have to tell ya? The bullet is in *Murdock's* body and as soon as Jordan arrives I'm getting out of it.

Into the room at this moment burst Williams and one of the plainclothesmen.

WILLIAMS. Now, Corkle—what about that saxophone you were following—!

MAX (*pointing to it*). Here it is—and— (*Then indicating Joe*)—there's the guy you're looking for!

WILLIAMS (*looking at Joe—sarcastically*). Oh, it is, eh?

MAX. Yeah—he's Farnsworth!

WILLIAMS. Don't kid me—I know Farnsworth!

MAX. Yeah, I know—only he's not using Farnsworth's body now!

WILLIAMS. Whose body *is* he using?

MAX. Murdock's—but he's really Joe Pendleton.

PLAINCLOTHESMAN. Holy cats!

WILLIAMS (*throwing his hat to the floor*). Will *somebody* talk *sense* around here?

MAX. Listen—if you'll calm down we can clear up this whole Farnsworth case for you. I told you he was killed by Mrs. Farnsworth and Tony Abbott—!

WILLIAMS (*breaking in*). That bathtub routine again! And I still ask—*where's the body?*

MAX (*appealing to Joe*). Where's the body?

JOE (*shrugs*). I don't know. It *might* be in the basement ice box.

MAX (*triumphantly to Williams*). Yeah. Have you looked in the basement ice box?

Williams, for an answer, lays his hand on Max.

WILLIAMS. That settles it, Corkle. You're coming to headquarters!

JOE. Lay off him!

MAX (*to Williams*). Wait! Why don't you find out? And if it isn't there you can take me any place you want to.

WILLIAMS. All right— (*Then to plainclothesman*) Come on, Chuck, this is going to make me look like an idiot, but we'll phone Farnsworth's.

He starts out with Chuck and turns at the door.

WILLIAMS. Don't either of you guys leave the building.

Williams and Chuck have left the door open as they exited. Simultaneous with their exit is the appearance of Mr. Jordan who enters slowly and comes to a stop a few feet inside the room. Max has turned to Joe and is saying pathetically:

MAX. Joe—when is this merry-go-round going to stop? I haven't slept in a month—

Joe, who has already spotted Jordan, is looking past Max and interrupts him to say:

JOE. Mr. Jordan! Hello!

Max whirls in the direction in which Joe is looking:

JORDAN. Hello, Joe.

MAX (*excitedly to Joe*). Joe—is he here?

JOE. Yeah, Max.

Then Joe gently urges Max toward the door with a hand on his shoulder.

JOE. I got to talk to him. Will you wait outside a minute?

MAX (*nervously*). Sure. Sure.

At the door he looks around in all directions and says:

MAX. Nice to see you again, Mr. Jordan.

He makes a feeble gesture in the wrong direction and ducks out fast.

Joe turns at once to Jordan.

JOE. I'm sure glad you're here, Mr. Jordan. Did you see the fight?

JORDAN. Yes, Joe. You did a nice job. You made Murdock very happy. He was told how it came out.

JOE. That's swell.

JORDAN. You fought beautifully, cleanly, scientifically. You make it an art.

JOE (*beaming*). Thanks. I'm back in my old form again.

JORDAN. This is your niche, Joe. This is where you belong—where you were meant to be—*world champion!*

JOE. Not me. Murdock is. I'm glad I could do it for him—but now—*get me out of this*, Mr. Jordan.

JORDAN (*quietly*). Joe.

JOE (*feeling something fateful in Jordan's tone*). Yeah?

JORDAN. You remember I said—you wouldn't be cheated?

JOE. Yeah.

JORDAN. Nobody is, really. Eventually all things work out. There is design in everything. You were meant to be champion. You are. You and Murdock are one—you belong to each other. This is your destiny, Joe. You're back on your own road.

JOE. No, no—wait. You're forgetting about Bette! What good's anything if I can't have her?

JORDAN. That's a chance you have to face. Joe—no matter *whose* body you take. Wasn't that true from the moment you left Farnsworth?

JOE. Yes—yes—I forgot—

JORDAN. But don't worry—you'll have everything that was ordained for you.

JOE. No—I don't like it! I want to find something—I mean—I wanted to be somebody besides just a plain fighter—even though Murdock's a swell guy—and a champ. (*Another idea*) An' I told you —Murdock's champ—not me! (*With finality*) No—I don't like it! Look, Mr. Jordan—if it's all the same to you—let's keep looking till we find the *right* guy!

JORDAN. Will you ever be *sure* he's the right guy, Joe?

JOE. Of course I will! (*Excitedly*) Wait here till I take a shower and dress! Then we can get started! I'll be back in a minute, Mr. Jordan!

Joe rushes into the shower room, stripping off his bathrobe as he goes. Jordan follows a few steps slowly, looking into the shower room. And now JORDAN, seen at close range, is looking off at Joe.

JORDAN (*softly, with authority*). This is your road, Joe. And everything's going to be all right.

As Jordan backs away slowly, we hear the sound of rushing water and Joe's sloshing.

The CORRIDOR, NEAR JOE'S DRESSING ROOM: Lefty, Max, the handlers, Bugs and Williams—all are walking circles. Suddenly, the plainclothesman comes rushing in—and up to Williams.

PLAINCLOTHESMAN. Chief—Pierce found it—Farnsworth's body—in the basement icebox!

WILLIAMS. Holy mackerel! He knew

what he was talking about! (*To plain-clothesman*) Call Pierce back—tell him to arrest Mrs. Farnsworth and Abbott! And send the body to the morgue.

MAX. No! Don't touch it! Joe *may need that body!*

WILLIAMS (*to plainclothesman—too excited to think*). Don't touch it! Joe may— (*Breaking off—glaring at Max, then to plainclothesman*). Come on, Chuck—!

Williams and the plainclothesman dash out. Lefty makes for the dressing room.

LEFTY. What's going on here, anyhow?

MAX. Stay out of there!

Lefty and the handlers continue on in—Max at their heels.

The DRESSING ROOM, as the gang breaks in: Jordan stands with his back against the wall near the water cooler. Joe is in the other room. They are all stunned at not seeing Joe in the room.

LEFTY. K.O.!

MAX. Joe! Where are you?

Bugs has gone to the shower room entrance.

BUGS. Here he is!

Joe steps quietly out of the shower room— in a dressing gown—wiping behind the ears with a towel. He moves slowly as if in a kind of trance.

JOE. What's the row, boys?

MAX. Joe—they found Farnsworth—just like you said!

JOE. I don't get this—I don't know any Farnsworth—

MAX. What are you talking about? (*Then looking around*) Why, where is he?

JOE. Who?

MAX. Jordan!

JOE. What Jordan?

MAX. Joe—don't give me answers like that!

LEFTY. You're out of your mind, Corkle. Stop bothering K.O. Get out of here.

BUGS. Somebody take Corkle to a hospital.

MAX. Me to a hospital? (*He points dramatically to Joe.*) Take him. He's been shot! That's the trouble! He's got fever! He was shot!

JOE. *Who* was shot?

Max rushes for Joe and pulls his robe open. He stares at Joe's chest.

MAX. What happened to it?

LEFTY. To what?

MAX. The mark he had there. The bullet hole. He showed it to me.

JOE (*to Max*). Are you crazy? (*Then to Bugs*) Come on, Bugs. Get me dressed. I got to hurry.

Bugs sets about hurriedly to dress Joe.

MAX (*holding his head*). Wait a minute! I'm going around again! It's that guy Jordan. (*Then to Joe*) Joe—what did he do? What's happened to you?

JOE. What are you calling me "Joe" for?

Then Max stands dramatically under Joe's nose and says in a quavering voice:

MAX. Look at me—take a *good* look. Don't you know me?

JOE. Yeah, I think so.

MAX. Who am I?

JOE. Don't *you* know?

MAX. I have my doubts. *You* tell me.

JOE. You're Max Corkle.

MAX. Yeah. And who are you?

JOE. K.O. Murdock—

MAX. You sure?

JOE (*to the others*). What's the matter with him?

MAX (*to the others*). What's the matter with him?

MAX. Do you know Joe—Joe Pendleton?

JOE (*slowly*). Sure. Pendleton was killed —airplane crash.

MAX. That's right.

JOE. Tough break. He was a fine kid. Strictly on the level.

MAX (*gulping*). He sure was.

JOE (*staring at Max; thinks*). I've heard tell *you* are too.

Joe turns from Max to Lefty. Then he looks back at Max.

JOE. How'd you like to manage me, Corkle?

LEFTY (*belligerently*). How do you get that way?

Joe fastens a level glance on Lefty.

JOE. I made up my mind, Lefty—after that Gilbert deal—you and me were through.

LEFTY. I got a contract! I'm not letting you go!

JOE (*quietly*). You wouldn't want me to tell the world you're a crook, Lefty.

Lefty subsides. Joe turns back to Max and studies him an instant.

JOE. Funny—your dropping around just at the right time. We'll do all right, Corkle—you and me.

MAX (*bewildered—choked*). Yeah, I—

JOE (*stirring, troubled*). Well—I got to be going.

He snatches his hat from a peg and starts out.

BUGS (*anxiously*). Where to, K.O.?

JOE. I—I don't remember exactly, but—

He pauses, halfway to the door. He comes back, picks up the saxophone, as if by habit. Then he pauses to look at it, wondering why he did that. Max comes to him dramatically, trying to solve his horrible confusion.

MAX (*pleadingly*). Joe—I mean K.O.—tell me—is this thing *yours?*

JOE (*slowly—handing Max the horn*). I guess so—sure. Take care of it, will you? (*Then smiling*) Gee, Corkle—you look like you had a bad dream. (*He pats Max's shoulder.*) Snap out of it. We're going to do all right—*Max.*

And he turns and walks out, leaving Max dazed, holding the saxophone. Jordan slowly follows Joe out.

The CORRIDOR shows JOE walking as with the feeling that he is in a hurry, glancing at his watch once—though that tells him nothing. In the background, Jordan slowly follows. We follow Joe as far as an exit, where a light burns over the door. As he approaches this exit, Bette comes from the opposite direction. They almost collide. For an instant they stand looking at each other—without recognition. Then:

JOE. 'Scuse me.

BETTE. I'm sorry.

Again a pause, after which a close view shows JORDAN standing some fifteen feet away, looking intently off at them and smiling. And now we see BETTE AND JOE:

JOE. Looking for somebody?

BETTE. Yes—Mr. Corkle. They said he might be in Mr. Murdock's dressing room.

JOE. Don't—don't I know you?

BETTE (*slowly*). I—don't think so.

JOE. I guess I don't. For a minute, I—I thought maybe I did. Funny—how sometimes you feel you know people.

BETTE (*looking at him steadily*). Yes. (*Then indicating lamely*) Is the dressing room that way?

JOE. Uh-huh.

But she makes no move to go, nor does Joe seem to expect her to. They are both too fascinated by a sense of recognition that refuses to become defined yet holds them.

JOE (*quickly*). Did—did you like the fight?

BETTE. I didn't see it.

JOE. Oh.

BETTE. But I heard it over the— (*She breaks off; she has been staring at his eyes.*) Your eye is hurt.

JOE. It's nothing—just swole a little.

BETTE. It's all red.

JOE. It doesn't hurt. (*Then*) I'm Murdock.

BETTE. Oh.

JOE. Ralph Murdock. And you're—?

BETTE. Logan—Bette Logan.

JOE (*lightly*). Hello. Glad to know you.

BETTE (*smiling*). How do you do.

They laugh at this playful formality—without knowing why. The laughter is a trifle unnatural and strained.

JOE. You interested in the fight game?

BETTE. I knew a man who was.

JOE. Do I know him?

BETTE. Bruce Farnsworth.

JOE. Oh. They—they were just telling me about him. He—he was killed—

BETTE (*choked*). Yes.

JOE. I'm sorry. Was—was he a friend of yours?

BETTE (*quietly—simply—emotion draining out of it.*) I loved him.

JOE. Gee—that's too bad.

BETTE (*after a thinking pause*). Yes. But —I don't know why—but—maybe it was the kindest thing. He was so troubled. I—I don't seem to feel—

She breaks off. Again, now, she is staring into Joe's eyes. She lifts her hand mechanically to his face—touching the bandage over Joe's hurt eye.

JOE (*staring fascinatedly*). Why did you do that?

BETTE (*faltering; embarrassed*). Your bandage was loose. I—I didn't mean to.

JOE (*quickly*). Oh, *it* felt good. —But you were looking at me—somehow like —well—sort of right *through* my eyes—

Suddenly, *the lights dim*—for just a second. The exit light remains on, to hold them in a strange, indistinct light.

BETTE (*in alarm*). What's that!

JOE. Don't be scared! (*The lights come on again.*) Just a warning—all lights out.

BETTE. Oh.

JOE. Funny—in the dark there—your voice sounded like I'd heard it before— but I couldn't remember where—or when. You didn't feel that, did you?

BETTE. Well—yes—I—I felt I was standing high up—looking down at the sea —and someone was swimming toward me—shouting something—something I felt I'd heard long ago—

JOE. I said "Don't be scared."

BETTE. Oh. Did you? (*Then shaking it off; lightly*) People are always thinking they knew someone before—in another existence—

JOE (*smiling lightly too*). Yes. Funnier things than that can happen.

BETTE (*softly*). I—I'd better be going. (*She makes a move.*)

JOE (*impulsively*). Please don't go. (*Then, embarrassed*) It seems like I was in a hurry to meet someone I—I knew. I mean—well—there's a nice little place —Mike's—just around the corner, where I always go after my fights. I wonder if you'd— (*He breaks off.*) But I guess you wouldn't tonight—feeling like you do about *him.*

She is looking off, thinking, remembering.

JOE (*gently insistent*) .I guess not—huh?

BETTE (*slowly*). What was it he said?— if I were to meet a fighter—I was to— (*Looks at Joe and smiles.*) I'd love to go with you, Mr. Murdock.

He is excited. He smiles. He takes her arm gently—and they start out.

And now JORDAN appears at close range. He is smiling after them. He lifts a hand and cocks it in a farewell salute after the manner of Joe, saying softly to himself, in broad imitation of Joe's speech—

JORDAN. So long—champ!

The scene fades out.

REBECCA

(A Selznick International Production)

Screenplay by
ROBERT E. SHERWOOD AND JOAN HARRISON

Based on the Novel *Rebecca* by
DAPHNE DU MAURIER

Produced by DAVID O. SELZNICK

Directed by ALFRED HITCHCOCK

The Cast

MAXIM de WINTER	Laurence Olivier
MRS. de WINTER	Joan Fontaine
JACK FAVELL	George Sanders
MRS. DANVERS	Judith Anderson
MAJOR GILES LACY	Nigel Bruce
COLONEL JULYAN	C. Aubrey Smith
FRANK CRAWLEY	Reginald Denny
BEATRICE LACY	Gladys Cooper
ROBERT	Philip Winter
FRITH	Edward Fielding
MRS. VAN HOPPER	Florence Bates
CORONER	Melville Cooper
DR. BAKER	Leo G. Carroll
CHALCROFT	Forrester Harvey
TABBS	Lumsden Hare
BEN	Leonard Carey

Film Editor—JAMES NEWCOM

REBECCA

PART ONE

A panorama of SKY, CLOUDS AND MOON fades in, accompanied by music.

The view moves down to MANDERLEY GATE and in coming closer picks out the gate in a mist.

> "I's" VOICE* (THE NARRATOR). *Last night I dreamt I went to Manderley again. It seemed to me I stood by the iron gate leading to the drive and for a while I could not enter, for the way was barred to me.*

The scene moves right through the closed gate.

> "I's" VOICE. *Then, like all dreamers, I was possessed of a sudden with supernatural powers and passed like a spirit through the barrier before me.*
>
> *The drive wound away in front of me, twisting and turning as it had always done, but as I advanced I was aware that a change had come upon it. Nature had come into her own again, and, little by little, had encroached upon the drive with long, tenacious fingers.*

The scene travels quickly, in ghostly fashion, well above the drive. The beginning of the driveway is partly overgrown with trees and foliage, and grows more and more overgrown as we move nearer Manderley.

> "I's" VOICE. *On and on wound the poor thread that had once been our drive, and finally there was Manderley—Manderley, secretive and silent. Time could not mar the perfect symmetry of those walls.*
>
> *Moonlight can play odd tricks upon the fancy—and suddenly it seemed to me that light came from the windows . . .*

There is music, and a little wind blows the mist away gradually revealing lights in the upstairs windows. As the Narrator starts again, clouds obscure the lights.

> "I's" VOICE. *And then a cloud came upon the moon and hovered an instant like a dark hand before a face. The illusion went with it and the lights in the windows were extinguished. I looked upon a desolate shell—with no whisper of the past about its staring walls.*

The view starts to move again slowly—closer to the house, revealing for the first time the gaping, black windows. No moonlight is visible now.

We continue moving closer slowly to a gaping, black window in the West Wing, until the view is right on the empty black frame of one window.

> "I's" VOICE. *We can never go back to Manderley again. That much is certain. But sometimes in my dreams I do go back—to the strange days of my life—which began for me in the South of France. . . .*

Simultaneously with these last words, the scene dissolves to a CLIFF TOP, viewed as though we were looking down, WAVES BREAKING ON ROCKS. Then the view moves up to the top of the cliff, where Maxim is discovered standing and looking down.

Next MAXIM's face is revealed at close range—the agonized face of a man staring at the sea below him; then the ocean is viewed over Maxim's shoulder.

MAXIM'S FEET are seen at close range as they take two steps slowly and dangerously nearer the edge of the cliff as if he were going to walk off. And at this point a girl's voice stops him.

---

* This story is the dramatization of a first person narrative related by the second Mrs. De Winter. Except for her formal name, later in the story, she can be known to us only as "I," and is therefore so called throughout.—Ed.

Copyright, 1940, by David O. Selznick Productions, Inc.

"I's" voice. No! Stop!

MAXIM, seen at close range, is startled, and he looks off in the direction of the voice. Then we see both "I" the girl AND MAXIM at some distance. "I" is standing in the path, having come from the other side of a rise of ground and having not yet reached the top of it when she saw him. She stands only partly revealed, frozen to the ground. She is holding a sketchbook in her hands.

MAXIM (*after looking a moment at her*). What the devil are you shouting about? (*Striding toward her*) Who are you? What are you staring at?

"I", seen close, takes a few timid steps forward.

"I" (*timidly*). I—I'm sorry. I didn't mean to stare. But—I—I only thought . . .

MAXIM is seen close, with the ocean as a background.

MAXIM. Oh, you did, did you? Well, what are you doing here?

"I" (*seen close, alone*). I was only walking.

MAXIM AND "I" are now seen together.

MAXIM (*impatiently*). Well, get on with your walking! Don't hang about here screaming!

"I" hurriedly starts to go, the scared expression still on her face.

MAXIM, left alone and seen at close range, looks after her, then looks back at the ocean, and starts to leave in the opposite direction as the scene dissolves to a long view of MONTE CARLO at night, which in turn dissolves to the outside of the PRINCESS HOTEL, the view being even darker and many more lights having come up. Then this dissolves to—

The HOTEL LOBBY, where the strains of a small, string orchestra playing selections from "The Dollar Princess" are heard. The panoramic view moves over to pick up MRS. VAN HOPPER and "I" seated on a divan. Mrs. Van Hopper is surveying the assemblage through her lorgnette and indicating acute distaste.

MRS. VAN HOPPER. I'll never come to Monte Carlo out of season again. Not a single well-known personality in the hotel.

As she says this, she is not addressing her lines to her young companion at all. She sips her coffee and makes a face.

MRS. VAN HOPPER. Stone cold! (*As a waiter passes in back of her, she turns to call*) Waiter, garçon! (*Turning to "I"*) Call him. Tell him to get me some . . .

"I" starts to rise, looking off for a waiter. But Mrs. Van Hopper's expression changes as she looks across the lounge and sees someone.

MAXIM, walking rapidly, comes forward and his progress is halted by Mrs. Van Hopper's voice.

MRS. VAN HOPPER'S VOICE. Why!—It's Max de Winter.

He looks toward her and hesitates.

MRS. VAN HOPPER'S VOICE. How do you do?

MAXIM (*uncertainly, walking toward her and "I",* How do you do?

A close-up of "I", standing up, indicates that she recognizes him as the man she saw on the cliff, and she slowly sits down on the divan again. Then we see all three characters.

MRS. VAN HOPPER (*as Maxim approaches; with effusiveness*). I'm Edythe Van Hopper. It's so nice to run into you here, just when I was beginning to despair of finding any old friends here in Monte.

MAXIM (*seen in a close-up*) is listening and watching "I" out of the corner of his eye.

MRS. VAN HOPPER. But, do sit down and have some coffee. (*To "I"*). Mr. de Winter is having some coffee with me. Go and ask that stupid waiter for another cup. (*"I" starts to rise.*)

MAXIM notices this harsh treatment of the girl as she starts to rise. But before she can get up, he speaks:

MAXIM. I'm afraid I must contradict you. You shall both have coffee with me.

The view widens to include all three as Maxim sits and calls off:

MAXIM. *Garcon!*

WAITER (*coming into the scene*). Oui, Monsieur.

MAXIM (*indicating all three*). Coffee, please.

MRS. VAN HOPPER (*taking up a cigarette case and offering it to Maxim*). Cigarette?

MAXIM. No, thank you.

MRS. VAN HOPPER (*taking a cigarette as she starts talking*). You know, I recognized you just as soon as you came in, though I haven't seen you since that night at the Casino in Palm Beach.

Maxim lights her cigarette.

MRS. VAN HOPPER (*again seen in a close-up with "I" in the background; provocatively*). Perhaps you don't remember an old woman like me. . . . Are you playing the tables much here at Monte? ("*I*" *in the background is looking very distressed at all this.*)

MAXIM (*seen in a close-up over "I's" shoulder; smiling slightly*). No, I'm afraid that sort of thing ceased to amuse me years ago.

MRS. VAN HOPPER (*as she and "I" are seen at close range together*). I can well understand that. As for me, if I had a home like Manderley, I should certainly never come to Monte. I hear it's one of the biggest places in that part of the country and you just can't beat it for beauty.

MAXIM (*seen in a close-up; not answering her, but turning to "I"*). And what do you think of Monte Carlo? Or don't you think of it at all?

"I" (*seen in a close-up, with Mrs. Van Hopper tipped in; embarrassed and tremblingly*). Oh, well—I—I think it's rather artificial . . .

MRS. VAN HOPPER AND "I" are seen together, over Maxim's shoulder.

MRS. VAN HOPPER (*annoyed, interrupting*). She's spoiled, Mr. de Winter. That's

her trouble. Most girls would give their eyes for the chance to see Monte. ("*I*" *looks very distressed at the turn of conversation.*)

MAXIM (*in a close-up*). Wouldn't that rather defeat the purpose?

MRS. VAN HOPPER'S VOICE (*impervious to the dig*). Now that we've found each other again, I hope I shall be seeing something of you. You must come and have a drink in my suite. I hope they've given you a good room. The place is empty, so if you're uncomfortable, mind you make a fuss. Your valet has unpacked for you, I suppose?

MAXIM. I'm afraid I don't possess one. Perhaps you'd like to do it for me?

MRS. VAN HOPPER (*at last embarrassed*). Well—I—I hardly think . . . (*Turning to "I"*) Perhaps you could make yourself useful to Mr. de Winter if he wants anything done. (*Smiling slightly*) You're a capable child in many ways.

The view widens to include the three people.

MAXIM (*rising; with a faint, sardonic smile*). That's a charming suggestion, but I'm afraid I cling to the old motto: "He travels fastest who travels alone." Perhaps you've not heard of it. Good night. (*He bows and exits rapidly.*)

MRS. VAN HOPPER (*in a close-up; with amazement*). What do you make of that? (*Gives a little snort.*) Do you suppose that sudden departure was intended to be funny? (*Rising: to "I", nastily*) Come! Don't sit there gawking! Let's go upstairs. Have you got the key?

"I" (*following*). Yes, Mrs. Van Hopper.

"I" and Mrs. Van Hopper, during the following conversation, cross the lobby toward the lift, the view moving with them.

MRS. VAN HOPPER. I remember when I was younger there was a well-known writer who used to dart down the back way whenever he saw me coming. I suppose he was in love with me and wasn't quite sure of himself. Well, *c'est la vie!*

They have reached the lift by now, when Mrs. Van Hopper turns to "I".

MRS. VAN HOPPER. By the way, my dear, don't think that I mean to be unkind, but you were just a teeny weeny bit forward with Mr. de Winter. Your effort to enter the conversation quite embarrassed me, and I'm sure it did him. Men loathe that sort of thing.

"I" shrivels at this attack.

MRS. VAN HOPPER. Oh, come, don't sulk. After all, I am responsible for your behavior here. Perhaps he didn't notice it. Poor thing! (*As the lift door opens and they walk in*) I suppose he just can't get over his wife's death.

"I" looks at Mrs. Van Hopper but doesn't say anything.

MRS. VAN HOPPER (*explaining*). They say he simply adored her.

By now the door has closed, and the scene fades out.

Now a MENU fades in. It reads:

PRINCESS HOTEL
MONTE CARLO

A page turns, revealing a breakfast menu written in French, and this dissolves to a view of the DINING ROOM OF THE HOTEL, with "I" entering the dining room. We see Maxim seated at his table off to one side as "I" walks quickly to a table and starts to sit down. The head waiter assists her.

HEAD WAITER (*calling off*). Oui, M. Alphonse. Mademoiselle.

Embarrassed and self conscious, "I" starts to unfold her napkin and awkwardly knocks over a small vase of flowers.

"I" (*looking off quickly to see if the waiter has seen her*). Oh!

MAXIM (in a close-up), seated at a nearby table, is attracted by the accident. He looks off, slightly amused, then gets up and starts for "I"s table. Over the scene we hear:

"I's" VOICE. Oh, how awkward of me. What a stupid thing to do. Oh, I'm so sorry. (*To the waiter*) Please don't bother, it doesn't really matter.

MAXIM (*moving into view; brusquely to the waiter*). Leave that—leave that—go and lay another place at my table. Mademoiselle will have lunch with me.

The waiter, with a look at Maxim, goes out.

"I" (*still brushing at herself futilely with her napkin; unhappy*). Oh, no—I couldn't possibly.

MAXIM (*abruptly*). Why not?

"I" (*unable to think of a reason*). Oh, please don't be polite. (*Not wanting to bother him*) It's very kind of you, but I'll be all right if they just change the cloth.

MAXIM. I wasn't being polite. I should have asked you to lunch with me even if you hadn't upset the vase so clumsily. Come along. We needn't talk to each other if we don't feel like it.

She looks at him. He now seems completely calm and reasonable. We follow them back to Maxim's table, where they sit down. The waiter gives "I" a menu.

"I" (*shaking her head*). Thank you very much. I'll just have some—some scrambled eggs.

WAITER. Oui, Mademoiselle. (*He leaves with the menu.*)

We get a close view of MAXIM AND "I" at the table.

MAXIM. What's happened to your friend?

"I". Oh, she's ill in bed with a cold.

MAXIM. Oh. I'm sorry I was so rude to you yesterday. The only excuse I can offer is that I've become boorish through living alone.

"I". Oh, you weren't, really. You simply wanted to be alone, and—

MAXIM. Tell me—is Mrs. Van Hopper a friend of yours or just a relation?

"I". No, she's my employer. I'm what is known as a paid companion.

MAXIM. I didn't know that companionship could be bought.

"I" (*in a close-up, over Maxim's shoulder; smiling*). I looked up the word "companion" in the dictionary once. It said "a friend of the bosom."

During the course of the scene more guests have entered the dining room.

MAXIM. I don't envy you the privilege.

"I". Oh, she's very kind, really—and—I have to earn my living.

MAXIM. Haven't you any family?

"I". No. No, my mother died years and years ago. Then there was only my father —and he died last summer. And then—I took this job.

MAXIM. How rotten for you.

"I". Yes, it was rather because, you see, we got on so well together.

MAXIM. You and your father?

"I". Yes, he was a lovely person—very unusual.

MAXIM. What was he?

"I". A painter.

MAXIM. Ah-a-a—was he a good one?

"I". Well, I thought so, but people didn't understand him.

MAXIM. Yes, that's often the trouble.

"I". He painted trees—at least it was one tree.

MAXIM. You mean he painted the same tree over and over again?

"I". Yes, you see—he had a theory that if you found the perfect thing, place, or person you should stick to it. Do you think that sounds silly?

MAXIM. Not at all. I'm a firm believer in that myself. What did you find to do with yourself while he was—painting his tree?

"I". Oh, I sat with him—and I sketched a little. I don't do it very well though.

MAXIM. Were you going sketching this afternoon?

"I" (*again seen close, over Maxim's shoulder*). Yes.

MAXIM. Where?

"I" (*hesitantly*). Oh, I haven't made up my mind.

The waiter enters and puts the dish of eggs in front of "I".

MAXIM. I'll drive you somewhere in the car.

"I" (*painfully*). Oh, no, please—I didn't mean . . .

MAXIM (*interrupting, and motioning toward eggs*). Oh, nonsense. Finish up that mess and we'll get along. (*During this "I" has not touched her eggs at all.*)

"I" (*in a close-up*). Thank you. It's very kind of you, but I'm not very hungry.

MAXIM'S VOICE. Oh, come on—eat it up like a good girl.

Shyly, rather embarrassed, she lifts a forkful of egg to her mouth, keeping her eyes on Maxim, as the scene dissolves to A TERRACE BALCONY OVERLOOKING MONTE CARLO BAY, with a car parked in the foreground, this in turn dissolving to a view of MAXIM AND "I" with their backs turned as "I" is sketching. Then the view is reversed.

MAXIM (*turning to "I"*). You've taken long enough with that sketch. I shall expect a really fine work of art.

"I". Oh, no, don't look at it—it's not nearly good enough. (*She starts feverishly to rub it out, as he protests.*)

MAXIM (*crossing to other side of her*). Oh, it can't be as bad as all that. Now don't rub it all out—let me see it first.

"I". Oh, no—it—it's the perspective. I never can get it right.

MAXIM (*insisting*). Let me see. Oh, dear!

"I's" SKETCH OF MAXIM comes to view as Maxim's voice is heard:

MAXIM'S VOICE (*in mock gravity*). Tell me, is it the perspective that gives my nose that curious twist in the middle? (*He points with his finger to the nose.*)

"I" (*taking her cue from his mood, smiling back happily*). You're not a very easy subject to sketch.

MAXIM. No?

"I" (*as she answers in her own defense*). Your expression keeps changing all the time.

MAXIM. Does it? (*He walks over toward Camera and bends over parapet.*) Well, I'd—I'd concentrate on the view instead if I were you. It's much more worth while. Rather reminds me of our coastline at home. (*Suddenly*) Do you know Cornwall at all?

"I" (*following him and standing beside him at the parapet*). Oh, yes. I went there once with my father on a holiday. (*Now seen close.*) I—I was in a shop once and I saw a postcard with a beautiful house on it—right by the sea—and I asked whose house it was, and the old lady said "That's Manderley!" I felt ashamed for not knowing.

MAXIM (*seen close; speaking with great bitterness*). Manderley is beautiful—but to me it's just the place where I was born and have lived in all my life. Now—I don't suppose I shall ever see it again. (*His thoughts have obviously gone far away.*)

A close view of the two: There is a silence while "I" thinks of something to say. She looks around for inspiration down toward the shore. Then turning back to her companion, with a great effort, she starts to chat.

"I". We're lucky not to be home during the bad weather, aren't we?

MAXIM. Huh . . .

"I". I can't ever remember enjoying swimming in England until June, can you?

MAXIM is seen at close range reacting strangely as "I" continues without being seen.

"I's" VOICE. The water's so warm here—I could stay in all day. There's a dangerous undertow—and there was a man drowned here last year. I never have any fear of drowning, have you? (*At this,* MAXIM *turns abruptly and strides off some distance.*)

"I", seen at close range, is looking off at the ocean. Upon hearing no response from Maxim, she turns to look at him and finds him gone. A reverse view with the bay in the background, shows her standing astounded, and bewildered. Then a long view brings MAXIM into focus.

MAXIM. Come—I'll take you home.

"I", seen close, looks at Maxim unhappily, unable to understand what she has said to upset him. She gives a little nod as much as to say "all right," and the scene dissolves to MONTE CARLO at night, and then to the HOTEL CORRIDOR, with "I" entering.

MRS. VAN HOPPER'S SUITE: As "I" opens the door and enters the room, she hears:

MRS. VAN HOPPER'S VOICE. Oh, yes, I know Mr. de Winter well. I knew his wife, too. Before she married she was the beautiful Rebecca Hildreth, you know. She was drowned, poor dear— while she was sailing—near Manderley.

We see MRS. VAN HOPPER propped up in bed. Standing beside the bed is a NURSE measuring out some medicine. Mrs. Van Hopper is chattering.

MRS. VAN HOPPER (*continuing*). He never talks about it of course, but he's a broken man! (*Looking at the medicine*) I suppose I better have it. Wretched stuff! Give me a chocolate, quick. (*Noticing that "I" has come into the room*) Oh, there you are. It's about time. (*Her mouth full of chocolate*) Hurry up, I want to play some rummy. (*"I", still standing at the door, is startled, as she absorbs the news of how Rebecca died.*)

The scene dissolves to "I's" ROOM at night. As she tosses and turns in bed, we hear her recollection of Mrs. Van Hopper's words:

MRS. VAN HOPPER'S VOICE. She was the beautiful Rebecca Hildreth, you know. They say he simply adored her. She was the beautiful Rebecca Hildreth, you know . . . I suppose he just can't get over his wife's death. . . . She was the beautiful Rebecca Hildreth, you know. But he's a broken man.

This dissolves into MRS. VAN HOPPER'S SUITE with Mrs. Van Hopper in bed, looking into a hand mirror and fussing with her face. The nurse is busy in the far corner when "I" comes into the room with her tennis racket.

"I" (*entering*). *Bon jour.*

NURSE. *Bon jour.*

MRS. VAN HOPPER (*looking at her sharply*). Well—where are you going?

"I". Oh, I thought I'd take a tennis lesson.

MRS. VAN HOPPER. I see. I suppose you've had a look at the pro and he's desperately handsome, and you've conceived a schoolgirl crush on him. All right, go ahead, make the most of it.

"I" leaves hurriedly, and the scene dissolves to the HOTEL LOBBY at the ENTRANCE as "I" is walking toward the revolving door.

MAXIM'S VOICE. Off duty? (*He comes to her.*)

"I" (*turning*). Oh, yes. Mrs. Van Hopper's cold has turned into 'flu, so she's got a trained nurse.

MAXIM. I'm sorry for the nurse— (*Noticing the tennis racket*) You keen on tennis?

"I". No—not particularly.

MAXIM (*taking racket from her*). That's good—we'll go for a drive.

We follow him as he conceals the racket behind some flowers. Then the scene dissolves to a COUNTRY ROAD with MAXIM AND "I" seen in Maxim's car as they drive along the road. "I" is still a little frightened of Maxim, remembering his strange behavior on the terrace the last time they were together, although she has learned some explanation of it from hearing Mrs. Van Hopper tell of Rebecca's drowning.

Maxim is looking straight ahead, seemingly absorbed in his own thoughts. "I" can't make up her mind whether she's happy or uncomfortable. She steals a shy look at Maxim, but finds out nothing. She steals another look, still discovers nothing and is anything but relieved. While she is looking ahead Maxim turns, looks at her for a moment, then back to his driving. "I" steals

another look at Maxim and this time he catches her. She is slightly embarrassed. He notices her embarrassment and breaks into a smile, really the first indication of the warmth under his hitherto frightening exterior. He pats her hand and "I" smiles tentatively. Then Maxim turns his eyes back to the road and puts his hand back on the wheel, resuming his previous preoccupied expression. "I" still watches him a moment, tentatively, then turns her own eyes back to the road. She gives a little sigh of relief and breaks into her first completely happy smile in her relationship with Maxim, relieved at last at this evidence that he has thawed.

The scene dissolves to MRS. VAN HOPPER'S ROOM, with "I" entering, carrying her tennis racket, and we follow her to Mrs. Van Hopper's bed.

"I" (*smiling, happy*). Good afternoon, Mrs. Van Hopper, how are you feeling?

MRS. VAN HOPPER (*with a malignant smile*). You got on rather well with him, didn't you? (*"I" is startled by this question. She doesn't know how to reply.*)

A COLD CREAM JAR on the bedside table comes to view (a close-up) as Mrs. Van Hopper continues to speak and at the same time her pudgy hand comes into the scene and snubs out her cigarette in the cold cream.

MRS. VAN HOPPER'S VOICE. That pro must have been teaching you other things than tennis. (*Now seen close*) Hurry up, I want you to make some calls. I wonder if Mr. de Winter is still in the hotel.

"I" gives a barely perceptible smile of amusement in reaction to Mrs. Van Hopper's speech "—if Mr. de Winter is still in the hotel," and this dissolves to a letter, which reads:

Dear Mr. de Winter:

Why don't you return my calls, you *naughty* man!

As soon as I get over this nasty old cold, I *promise* to keep you from being bored here in Monte. Because I know that's just what you must be—bored, bored, bored!

In fond friendship,
Edythe Van Hopper

This dissolves to a POOL at night, with images of dancers reflected in the water, and then the view moves up to reveal Maxim and "I" dancing together. Next, the latter is seen (in a close-up) over Maxim's shoulder, enjoying the dance immensely, and MAXIM (then seen over "I's" head) is also enjoying this dance. His partner (again in a close-up) is dancing as if she were in a dream. "I" closes her eyes and sighs girlishly, romantically. Maxim looks at her, smiles at her youthful mood. She slowly opens her eyes and is aware that he is smiling at her. She is quite embarrassed at having revealed how much this moment means to her. And on this, the scene dissolves to MRS. VAN HOPPER'S SUITE.

It is day, and Mrs. Van Hopper is seated in a chair wearing a rather loud dressing gown—a magazine on her lap, and smoking a cigarette, while the nurse is making her bed. The door opens, and "I" comes in dressed in spotless white, ready for tennis.

"I" (*to Mrs. Van Hopper*). May I go now?

MRS. VAN HOPPER (*sharply*). For the number of lessons you've had you ought to be ready for Wimbledon. But this will be your last—so make the most of it. The trouble is, with me laid up like this, you haven't had enough to do. But I'm getting rid of that nurse today, and from now on you'll stick to your job.

"I's" expression becomes slightly desperate.

"I". Yes, Mrs. Van Hopper. (*She turns and hurries away.*)

Mrs. Van Hopper thinks a second, then calls:

MRS. VAN HOPPER. Nurse!

NURSE (*entering*). Yes, Mrs. Van Hopper.

MRS. VAN HOPPER. Are you absolutely sure you left those messages for Mr. de Winter?

NURSE. Why yes, Madame.

MRS. VAN HOPPER. I simply can't believe it. He would most certainly have called me back. Oh, well, poor boy— (*She*

starts to resume her reading.*) I simply hate to see him so alone.

The scene dissolves to a PICTURESQUE SECTION OF CORNICHE ROAD, on which a car is running at a comfortable pace, and there we see MAXIM AND "I" driving through the countryside. Maxim has an expression of calm contentment. "I" looks at him—shyly, wistfully.

"I". You know, I wish there could be an invention that bottled up the memory like perfume. And it never faded, never got stale and then whenever I wanted to I could uncork the bottle and live the memory all over again.

MAXIM (*smiling*). And what particular moment in your young life would you want to keep?

"I" (*embarrassed*). Oh, all of them—all of these last few days. (*Seen close; searching for words*) I—I feel as though I'd—I'd collected a whole shelf full of bottles.

Maxim is silent for a moment.

MAXIM (*seen close; gravely*). Sometimes, you know, those little bottles contain demons that have a way of popping out at you just as you're trying most desperately to forget.

"I" (seen close again) is considerably let down, having gone so far as to practically declare her love. She sits back, depressed. Then Maxim turns and looks at her, seeing that she is depressed and that her mood is changed. She starts gnawing at her fingers.

MAXIM. Stop biting your nails!

There is another moment's silence while "I" broods, embarrassed, and then she blurts out:

"I". Oh, I wish I were a woman of thirty-six dressed in black satin, with a string of pearls.

MAXIM (*laughing*). You wouldn't be here with me if you were.

"I" (*turning to him, abruptly*). Would you please tell me, Mr. de Winter, why you ask me to come out with you? (*Passionately*) Oh, it's obvious that you want to be kind, but why do you choose me for your charity?

Maxim drives for a second and then his temper gets the best of him. The scene draws in close as he stops the car and turns to her.

MAXIM. I asked you to come out with me because I wanted your company. You've blotted out the past for me more than all the bright lights of Monte Carlo. (*Angrily*) But if you think I just asked you out of kindness or charity . . . you can leave the car now and find your own way home. Go on, open the door and get out!

He looks at her. Her face is averted. Tears have started from her eyes. He looks back ahead. Suddenly he reaches in his pocket, pulls out his handkerchief and tosses it into her lap.

MAXIM. Better blow your nose.

She uses the handkerchief, blowing her nose hard.

MAXIM (*gently*). And please don't call me Mr. de Winter. I have a very impressive array of first names. (*He laughs at himself.*) George Fortescue Maximilian. But you needn't bother with them all at once. My family call me Maxim.

She looks at him. He is certainly the most unpredictable person she has ever encountered. Maxim looks back at her for a moment, then suddenly brushes her forehead with his hand.

MAXIM. And another thing. Please promise me never to wear black satin or pearls, or to be thirty-six years old.

"I" (*smiling*). Yes, Maxim.

He puts his finger to his mouth and places a kiss with it on "I's" forehead. She looks radiant as he starts the car, and the scene fades out.

PART TWO

A LETTER fades in. It reads:

"Thank you for yesterday.
                    Maxim."

Then we see "I" arranging some roses and humming happily. She picks up the note and puts it into her purse. Suddenly we hear a scream.

MRS. VAN HOPPER'S VOICE. For the love of Pete! Come here!

"I" goes out hurriedly.

MRS. VAN HOPPER'S ROOM: Mrs. Van Hopper is in bed—a breakfast tray in front of her. She is reading a cable. She looks up at "I" and babbles excitedly:

MRS. VAN HOPPER. What do you think? My daughter's engaged to be married!

"I" (*truly delighted*). Oh, really? How nice.

MRS. VAN HOPPER (*getting out of bed*). We must leave for New York at once.

"I" (seen in a close-up) looks stunned at this command and very distressed.

MRS. VAN HOPPER'S VOICE. Get reservations

on the Aquitania, and we'll take the twelve-thirty train for Cherbourg. Hurry up and get in a maid to help with the packing!

MRS. VAN HOPPER (*as "I" is seen over her shoulder*). We've no time to waste. Go on—and don't dawdle! (*"I" goes out hurriedly.*)

"I's" ROOM: She enters hurriedly, lifts the telephone receiver and sits on the edge of her bed as she speaks into the phone, the view bringing her closer.

"I" (*into the phone*). Mr. de Winter, please. (*A pause—then her face falls with disappointment.*) Oh, he's gone out riding? (*In dismay*) He won't be back 'till noon? Oh! (*We see her great disappointment; then—resignedly*) Well, give me the porter please.

The scene dissolves to a CLOCK ON THE MANTLE, the hands pointing to twelve o'clock, then to MRS. VAN HOPPER'S SUITE, with a maid in the background. The floor of the room is filled with luggage which is just being removed by the porters. There is a general bustling air of departure, tissue paper over the floor, open drawers, etc. "I", dressed in her hat and coat, with her bag in one hand, stands apart from Mrs. Van Hopper, looking very miserable. She turns suddenly to her employer.

"I" (*nervously*). I'll go and see if there's anything left in my room. (*She leaves the room quickly, as we follow her.*)

"I's" ROOM: She runs in, closing the door behind her. She picks up the telephone receiver, the view moving in to afford a near view of her which reveals that she is close to tears. She watches the closed door nervously as she speaks into the receiver:

"I". Has Mr. de Winter come in yet? (*Delighted, but frantic with haste*) He has? Will you connect me with his room, please?

We see MRS. VAN HOPPER'S ROOM as Mrs. Van Hopper impatiently leaves it to go after "I". Then "I's" ROOM returns on the screen as "I", still watching the door, hangs up hurriedly when the door opens and Mrs. Van Hopper stalks in. She is heartbroken because Mrs. Van Hopper has not given her one more minute alone in which to get Maxim on the phone; but springs away from the phone guiltily and tries to cover up.

"I". Oh, I—I was looking for my book. I—I suppose I packed it.

MRS. VAN HOPPER (*impatiently*). Well, come on . . . the car's waiting at the door.

"I" follows her out dutifully but unwillingly, a close view of THE PHONE materializing as they leave. After a second we hear the door close behind them, then hear the outer door close behind them, and the next second the phone starts ringing, as if the operator were ringing back to find out why "I" is not waiting for her call to be completed.

The scene dissolves to the EXTERIOR OF THE PRINCESS HOTEL: The hand luggage is being loaded into a car. Mrs. Van Hopper and "I" come down the steps to the taxi. Mrs. Van Hopper gets in and sits down. "I" gives a final despairing look back into the hotel. Then with sudden decision she turns to Mrs. Van Hopper and says hurriedly:

"I". I'd like to leave a forwarding address—if they happen to find that book.

She has leapt up the steps almost before she has finished speaking. Mrs. Van Hopper opens her mouth to speak angrily but the girl is gone.

The HOTEL—AT THE DESK, "I" speaking to the concierge.

"I". Would you ring Mr. de Winter, please?

CONCIERGE (*picking up the phone*). Yes, Madam. (*Into the phone*) *Cent vingt deux.*

MAXIM'S BEDROOM. The loud sound of running water from the bathroom is heard, then the telephone in the foreground starts to ring. Maxim is splashing in the bathroom, sufficiently loudly to make him fail to hear the telephone.

At the HOTEL DESK, "I" waits nervously while the concierge listens at the telephone. He puts down the phone and shakes his head.

CONCIERGE. There isn't any answer.

"I". Thank you. (*She turns away.*)

At the EXTERIOR OF THE HOTEL Mrs. Van Hopper speaks to a clerk.

MRS. VAN HOPPER. Tell her to hurry up.

COMMISSIONAIRE. Yes, Madam.

And now we see "I" hurrying across the LOBBY toward the DINING ROOM. The head waiter comes to her.

"I". I was looking for Mr. de Winter.

WAITER. Mr. de Winter just ordered breakfast in his room, Mademoiselle. (*"I" hurries out.*)

At the HOTEL EXTERIOR we get a close view of MRS. VAN HOPPER in the TAXI: She is waiting impatiently and looking at her watch.

OUTSIDE MAXIM'S SUITE in the CORRIDOR, "I" is breathlessly arriving at the door. She knocks.

MAXIM'S VOICE. Come in.

She opens the door and is in the little foyer leading to the sitting room, the view moving with her as she crosses the room to Maxim, who comes in the half-open door of the bathroom, attired in trousers and dressing gown, his face still lathered from shaving. He looks in astonishment as he sees who it is.

MAXIM (*wiping the remaining lather from his face*). Hello! What are you doing here? Anything the matter?

"I" advances further into the sitting room and stands awkwardly.

"I". I've come to say good-bye— We're going away.

MAXIM. What on earth are you talking about?

"I" (*coming to him*). It's true. We're going now and I was afraid I wouldn't see you again.

Maxim, stunned, sits on the arm of a chair.

MAXIM. Where's she taking you to?

"I" (*upset*). New York. I don't want to go. I shall hate it. I shall be miserable.

Maxim gets up and starts back to the bathroom, picking up his clothes from a nearby chair.

MAXIM. I'll dress in here. I shan't be long. (*He goes back to the bathroom, leaving the door half open.*)

"I" stands, a lonely figure in the middle of the room. There is a pause. Then we hear Maxim's voice from the bathroom.

MAXIM'S VOICE. Which would you prefer, New York or Manderley?

"I" (*calling back, appealingly*). Oh, please don't joke about it. . . . Mrs. Van Hopper's waiting and—I—I'd better say good-bye now. (*She looks around nervously, worried about the time.*)

MAXIM'S VOICE. I'll repeat what I said— either you go to America with Mrs. Van Hopper or you come home to Manderley with me.

"I" (*still looking puzzled*). You mean you want a secretary or something?

MAXIM'S VOICE. I'm asking you to marry me, you little fool.

"I" looks completely flabbergasted and bowled over at Maxim's proposal. Unable to believe what she has heard, she backs up slightly and sits down on a chair. At this moment there is a knock on the outer door.

MAXIM'S VOICE. Come in. (*"I" looks slightly alarmed.*)

The waiter enters with a table on which breakfast is set.

MAXIM (*at the door to bathroom*). Is that my food? I'm famished. I didn't have any breakfast. (*He turns back into the bathroom.*)

The waiter lays the breakfast out, pulls up a chair, and so forth. Eventually he goes out of the room. Maxim emerges quickly from the bathroom, seats "I" at the table, and then seats himself. He starts to eat his breakfast.

MAXIM. Well, my suggestion doesn't seem to have gone at all well—I'm sorry.

"I" (*leaning forward*). Oh, but you don't understand—it's that—I—well—I'm not the sort of person men marry.

MAXIM (*looking up*). What on earth do you mean?

"I". I don't belong in your sort of world, for one thing.

MAXIM (*laughing a little*). What *is* my sort of world?

"I". Well—Manderley—you know what I mean.

MAXIM. Well, I'm the best judge of whether you belong there or not. Of course, if you don't love me, that's a different thing. A fine blow to my conceit, that's all!

"I" (*seen in a close-up over Maxim's shoulder*) has been far too modest to imagine that Maxim loves her, and where before she has been reticent, now she is overcome with anxiety lest he not know how much she adores him, and she speaks with childlike eagerness and anxiety.

"I". I do love you! I love you most dreadfully! I've been crying all morning because I thought I'd never see you again.

MAXIM (seen over "I's" shoulder) is touched by both her obvious adoration of him and by her childishness. After a moment he speaks:

MAXIM (sincerely). Bless you for that. (He pats her hand and looks at her.) I'll remind you of this one day and you won't believe me. It's a pity you have to grow up. (His mood changes and he covers his emotion, turning back to his breakfast.) All right, then. It's settled. You may pour me out some coffee. Milk and two lumps of sugar, please. Same with my tea. Don't forget. (As "I" pours out the coffee, he continues.) Who's going to break the news to Mrs. Van Hopper—shall you or shall I?

"I" (still scarcely believing it). Oh, you tell her—she'll be so angry.

MAXIM (he pushes his plate away). What's the number of her room?

"I". Oh, she's not there. She's downstairs in the car.

He stretches out to the desk nearby and picks up the telephone.

MAXIM. Hello, give me the desk, please. (A slight pause) You'll find Mrs. Van Hopper waiting outside in her car. Would you ask her—with my compliments—if she'd very kindly come and see me in my room. Yes, in my room.

The EXTERIOR OF THE HOTEL: The reception clerk is standing at the car where Mrs. Van Hopper is still waiting. He puts his head inside the car.

CLERK. Mr. de Winter says please for you to come up to his room.

Mrs. Van Hopper's angry expression suddenly changes to a slightly puzzled yet pleased one.

MRS. VAN HOPPER. Mr. de Winter? . . . Why certainly . . .

She starts to clamber out, assisted by the clerk.

MAXIM'S SITTING ROOM: "I" is standing, waiting for Maxim, who at that minute comes from the bathroom with his coat on. He comes up to her and puts his arm around her shoulder.

MAXIM (looking down at her tenderly). This isn't at all your idea of a proposal, is it? It should be in a conservatory—you in a white frock with a red rose in your hand, and a violin playing in the distance—and I should make violent love to you behind a palm tree.

They have been walking around in a circle while Maxim was speaking. "I" looks up at him a trifle self-consciously.

MAXIM (stopping and embracing her). Poor darling—never mind.

"I" (radiantly happy). Oh, I don't mind.

There is a knock at the door. "I" starts in alarm. Maxim pats her reassuringly.

MAXIM. Don't worry. Don't worry. You won't have to say a word.

Maxim moves to the door and "I" steps over to the right of the door so that she isn't seen by Mrs. Van Hopper when she enters. Mrs. Van Hopper's face is wreathed in smiles. She is chattering rapidly.

MRS. VAN HOPPER (to Maxim; her back to "I"). I'm so glad you called me, Mr. de Winter. I was making a hasty departure— It was so rude of me not to let you know, but a cable came this morning announcing that my daughter is engaged to be married. . . .

MAXIM (quietly). That's rather a coincidence, Mrs. Van Hopper. I asked you up here to tell you of my engagement.

If Mrs. Van Hopper took the time to analyze this unexpected announcement, she would wonder why Maxim de Winter would be confiding in her. But all that she considers now is the fact that she has been let in on some remarkably juicy gossip.

MRS. VAN HOPPER. You don't mean it! Why, how perfectly wonderful! How romantic! Who is the lucky lady?

Maxim merely gestures toward "I." Mrs. Van Hopper turns.

MRS. VAN HOPPER (seen in a close-up) is staring at "I", her mouth open; she is completely flabbergasted.

MAXIM'S VOICE. I apologize for depriving you of your companion in this abrupt way. I do hope it won't inconvenience you too greatly.

Mrs. Van Hopper is recovering slowly. She is furious, but she is trying to disguise it with delight.

MRS. VAN HOPPER. When did all this happen?

"I" (*seen close, over Mrs. Van Hopper's shoulder*). Just now—Mrs. Van Hopper. Just a few minutes ago.

MRS. VAN HOPPER (*as all three are included in the view*). I simply can't believe it! (*Roguishly*) And I suppose I ought to scold you for not having breathed a word of all this to me. But—what am I thinking of—I should give you both my congratulations and my blessings, I'm *very* happy for you both! When and where is the wedding to be?

MAXIM. Here. As soon as possible.

Mrs. Van Hopper is now genuinely thrilled. She sees herself playing a leading role in one of the most widely publicized weddings in social history.

MRS. VAN HOPPER. A whirlwind romance! Splendid! I can easily postpone my sailing for a week. This poor child—(*with a nod toward "I"*) has no mother so I shall take responsibility for all the arrangements—the trousseau, the reception, everything! And I'll give the bride away. ("I" *looks worried by this suggestion.*) But—our luggage! (*She wheels on "I" by force of habit.*)

A close view of MRS. VAN HOPPER AND "I."

MRS. VAN HOPPER. Go down and tell the porter to take everything out of the car.

The scene includes Maxim as "I" seems about to obey.

MAXIM (*putting his arm around "I's" shoulder*). Just a minute. (*He turns to Mrs. Van Hopper.*) We're most grateful to you, Mrs. Van Hopper. But I think we both prefer to have it all as quiet as possible . . . and I couldn't allow you to alter your sailing plans.

MRS. VAN HOPPER (*protesting*). But—

MAXIM'S VOICE. No, no.

Throughout the above Mrs. Van Hopper's disappointment increases and then turns to pique as she realizes her presence is definitely not wanted.

MAXIM (*the three of them now seen; going right on—to "I"*). Dear, I'll go down and see that your luggage is brought back.

"I". Thank you, Maxim.

He looks into her eyes—sees she is no longer afraid to face Mrs. Van Hopper—and goes. "I" walks away from Mrs. Van Hopper, and we follow her to a table where she stands with her back to Mrs. Van Hopper. Mrs. Van Hopper walks to "I", dropping all pretense.

MRS. VAN HOPPER. So this is what has been happening during my illness! (*She smiles unpleasantly.*) Tennis lessons my foot! I suppose I've got to hand it to you for a fast worker. How did you manage it? Still waters certainly run deep!

MRS. VAN HOPPER, now seen close, takes out a cigarette and lights it.

MRS. VAN HOPPER (*suspiciously*). Tell me, have you been doing anything you shouldn't?

She looks "I" up and down appraisingly like a judge at a cattle show.

"I" (*startled, unhappy, and indignant*). I don't know what you mean.

Mrs. Van Hopper shrugs her shoulders, then walks away from "I".

MRS. VAN HOPPER. Oh, well—never mind. I always did say Englishmen have strange tastes. (*She comes to the mirror which hangs on the wall, takes out compact and starts to powder her nose; we see "I" in the reflection.*) But you'll certainly have your work cut out as mistress of Manderley. To be perfectly frank with you, my dear, I can't see you doing it. (*Preening herself*) You haven't the experience, you haven't the faintest idea what it means to be a great lady.

Through the mirror we see "I" watching her unhappily, and Mrs. Van Hopper turns to face "I".

> MRS. VAN HOPPER (*sneeringly*). Of course, you know why he's marrying you, don't you? You haven't flattered yourself that he's in love with you. The fact is—

"I", seen close, is more and more unhappy as Mrs. Van Hopper continues:

> MRS. VAN HOPPER'S VOICE. —that empty house got on his nerves to such an extent he nearly went off his head. He just couldn't go on living alone.
>
> "I". You'd better leave, Mrs. Van Hopper. You'll miss your train.

MRS. VAN HOPPER is seen in a close-up. A queer, twisted smile crosses her face. Then we follow her to the door, "I" watching her leave. Mrs. Van Hopper stands in the open door.

> MRS. VAN HOPPER (*with withering sarcasm*). Huh—Mrs. de Winter. (*With a sour laugh*) Good-bye, my dear, and good luck. (*She exits.*)

"I" stands watching as the scene fades out. Then a VILLAGE STREET—a fairly busy market street—fades in. A flight of steps leads up to a stone building outside which stands Maxim's car. The view moves up until the sign on the building is visible. It reads:

MAIRIE

SALLE

DES MARIAGES

The scene now moves over to a view of Maxim and "I" on the stairs with the mayor shaking hands with them, and then we follow them down the stairs.

Next we see a clerk and the mayor leaning out the window.

> MAYOR (*calling to them*). Monsieur! Vous avez oubliez votre carnet de mariage.

MAXIM AND "I":

> "I". What's he saying?

> MAXIM. He says we've forgotten the proof that we're married.
>
> "I". Good heavens!

We follow them as they run to catch the marriage license which is being thrown at them from the window. Maxim catches the license with the aid of his hat. "I" laughs happily.

They stand with their arms around each other as we hear some shouts. A noisy crowd of children and a few townspeople run into the picture, followed by a wedding group. The bride is in white and carries a sheaf of lilies. Maxim and "I" watch the wedding party pass them, and then start forward to their car.

> MAXIM. Ah, somebody else had the same idea.
>
> "I" (*wistfully*). Isn't she sweet?
>
> MAXIM (*giving her a quick look*). Yes. You'd have liked a bridal veil, wouldn't you?

"I" is getting into the car.

> MAXIM (*giving her a look, and starting off*). Or, at least—

The view moves with him to a flower seller. He pulls a handful of notes from his pocket, saying:

> MAXIM. Madame—Madame—combien c'a fait? Tout de tout? Je vous remercie mille fois, Madame, merci.

He grabs the armful of flowers and hurries quickly back to "I" seated in the car. He thrusts the flowers into her arms.

> "I" (*seen in a close-up, with Maxim tipped in*). Oh, Maxim, how lovely. Oh, how perfectly lovely—

We see Maxim walking out of the scene to go around the car.

> "I" (*continuing*). Oh—how perfectly lovely.

She buries her face in the flowers as the scene fades out.

PART THREE

MANDERLEY GATES fades in. It is day. Maxim and "I's" car enters the scene and drives to the gates, which are opened by the gatekeeper. Maxim waves to the gatekeeper.

GATEKEEPER. Welcome home, Mr. de Winter.

MAXIM. Thank you, Smith.

The DRIVE appears, the trees forming a Gothic arch above. The car rounds the bend, and ahead is a long, gloomy stretch and another bend.

"I" AND MAXIM are seen in the car. "I" is looking ahead, nervously. She suddenly shivers with a strange apprehension, and Maxim looks at her.

MAXIM. Cold, darling?

"I" (*with a tremulous smile*). Yes, just a little bit.

MAXIM. There's no need to be frightened, you know. Just be yourself and they'll all adore you. You don't have to worry about the house at all—Mrs. Danvers is the housekeeper. Just leave it to her.

The length of this drive is oppressive. "I" thinks that beyond each bend she will see the house. Maxim, with a slight frown, looks up at the sky.

MAXIM. Hello . . . starting to rain. (*Big raindrops begin to descend.*) We'd better hurry up. Here. Here—have this. (*He reaches back for a mackintosh.*) Put it over your head.

"I" (*taking it*). Thank you.

The DRIVE AT MANDERLEY (an extremely long view) in the rain. Over their shoulders we see through the windshield, as the wiper goes back and forth cleaning off the rain, the car approaching another bend and then another. At last, the car turns a sharp bend and there, suddenly, is the house. The rain is now falling in torrents but it cannot conceal the imposing building.

"I" AND MAXIM IN THE CAR: The sight of Manderley causes "I" to utter an exclamation. Maxim turns to her, smiles, and waves his hand toward the house.

MAXIM. That's it! That's Manderley!

MANDERLEY, first seen from a moving point of view, and then at closer range, appears; and as the car stops the butler comes running down the steps with an umbrella, while the other man starts to unload luggage from the back. Maxim and "I" rush out under the umbrella held by Frith. Now they mount the steps.

MAXIM. Here we are, Frith. Everyone well?

FRITH. Yes—thank you, sir. Glad to see you home, sir.

MAXIM. This is Mrs. de Winter, Frith.

"I" shyly puts out her hand to Frith.

"I". How do you do?

Frith gives a little bow.

FRITH. Madam.

Then he sees the outstretched hand, hesitates for a second as to what to do, and just as she is about to withdraw it, takes it. Maxim smiles a little at this.

As they enter THE HALL, Frith removes the umbrella. Maxim and "I" stop, looking off. We then get a view of a STAFF OF SERVANTS —lined up in a semi-circle.

MAXIM, FRITH AND "I":

MAXIM (*annoyed*). I didn't expect the whole staff to be in attendance.

"I's" hair has been flattened by the mackintosh, and wisps of hair have become wet and hang down her face.

FRITH (*replying in low voice*). Mrs. Danvers' orders, sir.

MAXIM (*without expression*). Oh. (*He turns to "I" from whom Frith is taking the mackintosh.*) I'm sorry about this— it won't take long.

They start toward the group of waiting servants, with "I" looking more scared every moment. We get the impression of a tableau with Maxim guiding "I" toward the group. We are very conscious of the vastness of the hall with its minstrel gallery and broad, sweeping staircase.

The GROUP OF SERVANTS appears again, and Mrs. Danvers enters the scene, a tall, gaunt woman, and walks forward.

MAXIM'S VOICE. This is Mrs. Danvers.

MRS. DANVERS. (*seen in a close-up, coldly to "I"*). How do you do, Madam. I have everything in readiness for you.

"I", seen close, unprepared for this, doesn't know how to reply.

"I". Oh . . . that's very good of you. I didn't expect . . . anything.

She is playing with her gloves in her nervousness, and the gloves drop. She starts to stoop to pick them up, and after a slight hesitation so does Mrs. Danvers.

MAXIM'S VOICE. I think we'd like some tea, Frith.

FRITH'S VOICE. It's ready in the library, sir.

Mrs. Danvers hands the gloves to "I" with the faintest trace of a smile of scorn. "I" is very unhappy. Mrs. Danvers looks her straight in the eye.

MAXIM'S VOICE. Come along, darling.

As "I" steals a look at Mrs. Danvers and turns away, the view moves up to a close-up of Mrs. Danvers, and as the scorn on her face increases slightly, the scene dissolves to a CLOCK, and then to "I's" SUITE in late evening twilight, "I" AND A MAID being visible:

"I" is seated, dressed for the evening, at the dressing table. The maid is putting away clothes. There is a knock at the door, and "I" looks up eagerly.

"I" (*eagerly, calling*). Oh, Maxim? Come in!

The door opens, and in comes Mrs. Danvers.

"I's" VOICE (*disappointed*). Oh, good evening, Mrs. Danvers.

MRS. DANVERS. Good evening, Madam.

We follow Mrs. Danvers into the room. She

glances at Alice—a glance of dismissal, and Alice goes. "I" picks up a hair brush and starts to brush her hair.

MRS. DANVERS (*standing beside "I"*). I hope Alice was satisfactory, Madam?

"I". Oh, yes, thank you—perfectly.

MRS. DANVERS. She's the parlor-maid. She'll have to look after you until your own maid arrives.

"I" (*looking up*). Oh, but I haven't a maid. I—I'm sure Alice will do nicely.

MRS. DANVERS (*coldly*). I'm afraid that would not do for very long, Madam. It's usual for ladies in your position to have a personal maid. (*Turning back to the room and looking around*) I hope you approve the new decoration of these rooms, Madam.

"I" (*turning to face Mrs. Danvers*). Oh, I—I didn't know it had been changed. I hope you haven't been to too much trouble.

MRS. DANVERS. I only followed out Mr. de Winter's instructions.

"I" (*rising*). Oh, well—what did it look like before?

MRS. DANVERS (*coming closer to "I"*). It had an old paper and different hangings. It was never used much, except for occasional visitors.

"I". Oh, then it wasn't Mr. de Winter's room originally?

MRS. DANVERS. No, Madam. He has never used the *East* Wing before.

She turns and goes out of sight toward the window, where we now see that the curtains are parted. Mrs. Danvers comes up to the window.

MRS. DANVERS. Of course, there's no view of the sea from here.

"I" is looking toward Mrs. Danvers.

MRS. DANVERS. The only good view of the sea is from the *West* Wing.

"I" feels it is time to offer some defense of Maxim's choice.

"I". The room's very charming and I— I'm sure I'll be comfortable.

There is a moment's silence.

MRS. DANVERS (*turning from window to "I"*). If there's anything you want done, Madam, you have only to tell me.

There is an awkward pause. "I" walks toward Mrs. Danvers. Then with an effort at brightness, she asks:

"I". I suppose you've been at Manderley for many years—longer than anyone else?

MRS. DANVERS. Not so long as Frith. He was here when the old gentleman was living—when Mr. de Winter was a boy.

"I". I see. And you didn't come until after that?

There is another slight pause. When Mrs. Danvers speaks it is with a slightly harder and less impersonal tone, and the scene draws into a close-up of her.

MRS. DANVERS. I came here when the first Mrs. de Winter was a bride.

"I", seen moderately close, looks away sharply. For a second we see the effect of the words on her face, then with an effort she summons her courage and walks to Mrs. Danvers directly.

"I". Mrs. Danvers, I do hope we'll be friends. You must be patient with me. This sort of life is new to me. And I do want to make a success of it and make Mr. de Winter happy. So I know I can leave all the household arrangements to you.

MRS. DANVERS (*coldly*). Very well. I hope I shall do everything to your satisfaction, Madam. I have managed the house since Mrs. de Winter's death and Mr. de Winter has never complained.

There is an awkward silence.

The faintest shadow of contempt comes into Mrs. Danvers' face. She turns and walks toward the door which she opens. She turns.

"I's" VOICE. I think I'll go downstairs now.

She walks to the open door, glances at Mrs. Danvers, sees the expression of disdain, and

goes out. Mrs. Danvers follows her out, shutting the door.

In the HALL, down the long passage, the two women go toward the stairs. As they reach the top of the stairs, Mrs. Danvers pauses and points to a door along the broad passage the *other* side of the stairs, the scene now providing a close view of the women.

MRS. DANVERS. The room in the West Wing I was telling you about is there— through that door. It's not used now. It's the most beautiful room in the house —the only one that looks down across the lawns to the sea. *It was Mrs. de Winter's room.*

"I" hesitates while looking at the door. She turns and sees Mrs. Danvers' eyes are fixed on her. Mrs. Danvers turns and moves swiftly out of the picture.—"I" glances back toward the door. And now, looking along the *other* way of the broad passage over "I's" shoulder, we see the mysterious DOOR, the view moving in until we lose sight of "I" and focus only on the door; then the view moves down to reveal, lying against the foot of it, Rebecca's dog, Jasper; and this dissolves to THE DINING ROOM at night:

Centered in the foreground on a plate is a napkin bearing the monogram: "R de W". The monogram is done in an imitation of the same sloping handwriting that later appears in the address book. Then the view moves to reveal "I" unfolding her napkin, after which the scene expands disclosing the whole dining table, with Maxim at the head. Finally, the whole dining room becomes visible, with Frith and Robert removing the service plates and preparing to serve the soup.

The previous scene having faded out, a long view of MANDERLEY in the early morning fades in. It is a beautiful, sunny, peaceful day, and the proximity of the house to the sea becomes visible.

The scene then dissolves to a view of THE DINING ROOM as "I" comes in, carrying her handbag, just as she did at the hotel, and a reverse view shows a stranger seated at the table, near Maxim's place. It is Frank Crawley. He has a great many letters and papers before him, which he is sorting out. He jumps to his feet as he sees "I".

FRANK (*awkwardly and shyly*). Good morning.

"I" (*coming up to him*). Good morning.

FRANK. You're Mrs. de Winter, aren't you?

"I". Yes.

FRANK (*embarrassed*). My name's Crawley. I—I manage the estate for Maxim. (*After a pause*) Awfully glad to meet you.

Another awkward pause ensues, then Frank points to the pile of papers.

FRANK. Fearful lot of stuff piled up while Maxim was away.

"I". Yes, I—I'm sure there must have been. (*Another embarrassed pause*) I—I do wish I could help with some of it.

Now MAXIM (seen over "I's" and Frank's shoulders) comes in, carrying some letters. He has heard "I's" remark. As he walks in, the view includes all three.

MAXIM. Oh, no—Frank never allows anybody to help him. Like an old mother hen with his bills and rents and taxes. Come on, Frank, we must go over these estimates.

FRANK. I'll get my papers. (*He goes out of view to gather up the papers.*)

MAXIM. You'll find quantities of breakfast over there. But you must eat it all, or cook will be mortally offended.

"I" (*smiling*). I'll do my best, Maxim.

MAXIM. I have to go over the place with Frank just to make sure he hasn't lost any of it. But you'll be all right, won't you—

"I". Umhum . . .

MAXIM (*hugging her*). Umhum—getting acquainted with your new home? (*Gives her a quick, perfunctory kiss on the forehead, and turns to go, adding as he turns*) Have a look at the Times—there's a thrilling article on what's the matter with English cricket.

Maxim and Frank go toward the door. Suddenly Maxim turns.

MAXIM. Oh, yes—I—er—my sister, Beatrice, and her husband, Giles Lacy, have invited themselves over for lunch.

"I" (*her smile fading*). Today?

MAXIM. Yes. I suppose the old girl can't wait to look you over. You'll find her very direct. If she doesn't like you, she'll probably tell you so to your face. (*He laughs.*)

It is clear that "I" isn't too anxious to be looked over.

MAXIM. Don't worry, darling—I'll be back in time to protect you from her. Good-bye, darling.

"I". Good-bye, Maxim.

FRANK. Good-bye.

"I". Good-bye. (*She then turns toward the side table.*)

The scene moves with her to the buffet. She lifts the lids of the numerous covered dishes on the heaters. There are eggs, bacon, sausages, and many other good things to eat. The sight of so much food destroys whatever appetite she may have had. The view concentrating more closely on her, she pours herself a cup of tea and takes it to her lonely place at the end of the great table. The newspaper is neatly folded by her place, where we then see her seated.

FRITH AND ROBERT enter the room, and Frith looks toward her.

FRITH. Good morning, Madam.

"I". Good morning, Frith.

Frith crosses to the buffet, glances at the covered dishes, undisturbed, then turns again to "I".

FRITH. Isn't there anything I could get for you, Madam?

"I" (*drinking her tea*). Oh, no thank you, Frith. I'm really not very hungry. Thank you.

Robert appears in the background, going to take the hot dishes out, and she puts down her cup, rises, and starts to go.

FRITH. The paper, Madam. (*He picks up the paper and hands it to her.*)

"I". Oh yes, thank you, Frith.

She takes the paper and starts to go. Robert hurries before her and opens the door. Now the DOORWAY is visible, and as she comes through she slips on the polished floor and almost falls.

FRITH (*trying to catch her*). Madam—

"I" (*lamely*). I—I slipped.

Frith steadies her for a few steps, guiding her by the arm.

"I". Oh, thank you, Frith. (*She walks on, looking about the hall.*) It's big, isn't it?

FRITH. Yes, Madam—Manderley *is* a big place. This was the banquet hall in the old days. It's still used on great occasions, such as a big dinner or a ball, and the public is admitted here, you know, once a week.

"I". That's nice.

She walks on, unable to think of anything better to say until she comes to the library door. Frith watches her.

The LIBRARY: The windows are wide open and the curtains are blowing. She enters and gives a shiver. She crosses to the fireplace and looks about for some matches.

FRITH (*at the doorway*). I beg pardon, Madam.

"I" turns quickly, guiltily. She feels she's been caught doing something she shouldn't.

FRITH. I'm afraid the fire is not usually lit in the library until the afternoon. (*His face is expressionless.*) But you will find one in the morning room. Of course, if you wish this fire lit now, Madam . . .

She goes over to Frith.

"I". Oh, no, Frith—I wouldn't dream of it.

FRITH. Mrs. de Winter— (*He hesitates, fearing that he has been tactless.*)—uh—uh—I mean the late Mrs. de Winter always did her correspondence and telephoning in the morning room after breakfast.

"I". Thank you, Frith.

She goes back into the hall, the view moving with them, when "I" suddenly pauses awkwardly.

FRITH. Is there anything wrong, Madam?

"I" (*hesitating*). Oh, oh—no—er—which way is the morning room?

FRITH (*proceeding to direct her*). It's that door there, Madam—on the left.

"I". Oh yes, thank you.

With Frith appearing in the foreground, her small figure crosses the large hall. Then she comes into the MORNING ROOM. It is a bright and cheerful small room, exquisitely furnished and obviously a woman's room by the quantities of flowers in it. There is a blazing fire, in front of which a dog is lying. She shyly inspects the room.

Next we see the dog, Jasper, getting up from before the fire and ambling out of the room. And a fairly close view shows our Narrator behaving almost as though she were an intruder in the room. She crosses to the writing desk, the scene moving with her, and begins to examine its contents, which include an address book, guest book, and menu book. She looks almost furtively about her. A slight sound from outside makes her start guiltily away, but after a moment she turns back. She picks up the address book, and the view moving down to it, we see the initial "R". She opens it and we see on the flyleaf, written in script, "Rebecca de Winter." The view moves up again as she lowers herself into the chair. She replaces the address book and opens a parchment-bound book lying on the centre of the blotting pad. Suddenly a telephone rings. She starts, and with her eyes still fixed on the open book, lifts the telephone hurriedly. She puts the receiver to her ear, listens for a moment and then apparently repeats what was said to her.

"I". Mrs. de Winter? I'm afraid you've made a mistake. Mrs. de Winter has been dead for over a year. (*As she replaces the receiver, she suddenly realizes her faux-pas and exclaims*) Oh—I mean—I—

She looks up and is startled to see Mrs. Danvers standing in the doorway, regarding her with expressionless eyes.

MRS. DANVERS (*coldly*). That was the house telephone, Madam. It was probably the head gardener wishing instructions.

"I"—at THE DESK—is very nervous, Mrs. Danvers' cold personality making her extremely uncomfortable.

"I" (*making a desperate effort*). Did you want to see me, Mrs. Danvers?

MRS. DANVERS is seen fairly close as the view moves with her to the desk beside "I".

MRS. DANVERS. Mr. de Winter informed me that his sister, Mrs. Lacy, and Major Lacy are expected for luncheon. I'd like to know if you approve of the menu. (*She bends over "I" and, picking up a menu from the desk, proffers it to her.*)

"I" (*without looking at it*). Oh, well— I—I'm sure it's very suitable—very nice, indeed.

MRS. DANVERS (*with expressionless face pointing to the menu*). You notice, Madam, that I've left a blank space for the sauce. Mrs. de Winter was most particular about sauces.

"I" (*seen in a close-up over Mrs. Danvers' shoulder*). Oh—oh, well—let's have whatever you think Mrs. de Winter would have ordered.

Mrs. Danvers prepares to withdraw. She looks steadily at "I".

MRS. DANVERS. Thank you, Madam. (*As she goes she adds*) When you have finished your letters, Robert will take them to the post.

"I". My letters? Oh, yes, of course, thank you, Mrs. Danvers.

Mrs. Danvers goes out and we hear the door open and close again. "I" hesitates—looks around—then opens Rebecca's address book.

We get a close view of a PAGE OF THE ADDRESS BOOK (over "I's" shoulder). In Rebecca's handwriting appear the following names:

Lady Ambasley
189 Knight's Road

Jessica Anthony   Midlone 694
41 Hartley Street South

Alfred Anglin   Midwick 7947
216 Lion Head Lane

Herbert Ainsley   Victoria 1494
622 Hayman Street.

Duchess of Atherton   Berkeley 6419
12 Wingate Place

Sir Nagel Armbruster
Mayfair 1492

Marquis of Anningham   Victoria 7492
3 Palace Court Lane.

She closes the book and picks up another and in doing so accidentally hits a china cupid that is sitting on the edge of the desk. It falls and breaks into many pieces. Horror-stricken, she rises. She is then seen picking up the remains. She rises, doesn't know what to do with the pieces, then looks at a desk drawer.

A close view reveals "I's" HANDS—opening the drawer and putting the pieces of cupid in back of the drawer and shoving envelopes and paper in on top of them to hide them. Then, with the room as a background, she sits down at the desk again. She is completely unnerved and trembling as the scene dissolves.

It dissolves to the HALL, the view revealed down toward the front door, from which Giles and Beatrice are entering. Frith is taking Giles' hat and Beatrice's cape.

BEATRICE. How are you, Frith?

FRITH. Good morning, Mrs. Lacy.

BEATRICE. Where's Mr. de Winter?

FRITH (*going out*). I believe he went down to the farm with Mr. Crawley.

BEATRICE. How tiresome of him not to be here when we arrive—and how typical!

During this the view has swung slowly to reveal "I" in the foreground, her profile seen close at the head of the stairs, shrinking back into the shadows out of view.

JASPER is seen close at "I's" heels and looking up at her. Then we see "I" as the moving view follows her down the stairway and over to the door of the library and stops a few feet from the door which is partially open. She stops to adjust her clothes a little and gives a few frantic pats to her hair. She hears voices from the library.

BEATRICE'S VOICE. I must say old Danvers keeps the house looking lovely. She certainly learned that trick of arranging flowers from Rebecca.

GILES' VOICE. I wonder how she likes it now—being ordered about by an ex-chorus girl.

BEATRICE'S VOICE. Now—where on earth did you get the idea she's an ex-chorus girl?

"I" hesitates, wanting to run away.

GILES' VOICE. He picked her up in the South of France, didn't he?

BEATRICE'S VOICE. What if he did.

GILES' VOICE. Well—I mean to say—there you are.

"I" summons up courage and determines to go in and face them. She pushes open the door and goes in. Glancing over her shoulder through the open door into the room, we see Giles and Beatrice look up as she enters. Giles rises.

"I" (*timidly, and wringing her hands together nervously*). How do you do—I—I'm Maxim's wife.

For a moment they both stare at her, obviously surprised, then Beatrice starts forward.

BEATRICE (*murmuring as she approaches*). How do you do? (*She goes close to "I" and subjects her to close scrutiny.*) Well—I must say—you're quite different from what I expected!

"I" is upset, as well as taken aback by Beatrice's remark.

In a scene including all three, we see "I" shyly shaking the hand Beatrice is holding out to her, as Giles enters into the picture, embarrassed.

GILES (*palpably lying*). Don't be so silly. She's exactly what I told you she'd be. (*He also holds out his hand and shakes very firmly with "I" as he continues.*) Well—how d'you like Manderley?

"I". Very beautiful, isn't it?

BEATRICE. And how do you get along with Mrs. Danvers?

"I". Well, I've never met anyone quite like her before.

GILES. You mean she scares you—she's not exactly an oil painting, is she? (*He laughs uproariously at his own joke.*)

BEATRICE. Giles, you're very much in the way here. Go somewhere else.

GILES (*coughing*). I'll try and find Maxim, shall I? (*He hesitates about leaving.*)

BEATRICE (*reminding him*). Giles— (*Giles then leaves.*)

"I" (*shyly*). I—I—didn't mean to say anything against Mrs. Danvers. It—

BEATRICE. Oh, there's no need for you to be frightened of her. But I shouldn't have any more to do with her than you can help. Shall we sit down? (*Motioning toward seat.*)

"I". Oh yes, yes please.

BEATRICE (*as they sit down*). She's bound to be insanely jealous at first, and she must resent you bitterly.

"I" (*astonished*). But why should she?

BEATRICE (*leaning forward*). Don't you know? I should have thought Maxim would have told you. She simply adored Rebecca!

"I" (seen close, with Beatrice in the background) reacts fearfully to Beatrice's statement and the scene dissolves to THE DINING ROOM with the LUNCHEON TABLE AND THE SEATED GROUP: Beatrice is on Maxim's right, Frank on his left. Giles is on "I's" right. And we first we see BEATRICE AND MAXIM together as Robert is serving Beatrice.

BEATRICE. How are you, Robert?

ROBERT. Quite well, thank you, Madam.

BEATRICE. Still having trouble with your teeth?

ROBERT (*embarrassed*). Unfortunately yes, Madam.

BEATRICE. You must have them out—all of them! Wretched nuisances—teeth!

ROBERT. Thank you, Madam.

BEATRICE (*looking at her dish*). Oh, what a plateful!

Next we see GILES AND "I" as Giles tries to make conversation while eating. Robert comes to them and serves Giles.

GILES. Do you hunt?

"I". No, I don't. I'm afraid I don't even ride.

GILES. Have to ride down here. We all do. Which do you ride—side-saddle or astride? Oh yes, of course, I forgot you don't, do you? You must. Nothing else to do down here.

We see the whole GROUP AT THE TABLE, Robert in the foreground serving Maxim; then BEATRICE AND MAXIM.

BEATRICE. Maxim, when're you going to have parties here again like the old days?

MAXIM (*grimly*). Oh, I haven't thought about it.

BEATRICE. But everyone's dying to see you and— (*She looks off toward "I".*)

MAXIM. Yes, I bet they are.

BEATRICE. Why don't you have the Masquerade Ball again this summer?

MAXIM. Oh, I—er . . .

BEATRICE (*calling down to "I"*). My dear, are you fond of dancing?

"I". Oh, I—I love it, but I'm not very good at it.

GILES. Do you rhumba?

"I". I've never tried.

GILES. You must teach me. (*He turns to Maxim.*) I say, old boy—I've been trying to find out what your wife *does* do.

MAXIM'S VOICE. She sketches a little.

GILES. Sketches! Not this modern stuff, I hope? You know, picture of a lamp shade upside down to represent a soul in torment. (*Suddenly he is struck by a thought and lowers his voice.*) You don't sail, do you?

"I" (*in a strained voice*). No—I don't.

GILES. Well, thank goodness for that! (*He realizes what he has just said, and is dismayed.*) Huh!

There is general consternation about the table. GILES is seen to be very embarrassed. Next MAXIM is seen, staring grimly into space. Then the whole GROUP AT THE TABLE is seen perturbed.

The scene dissolves to the HALLWAY where Beatrice is adjusting her hair before the mirror. "I" is beside her.

BEATRICE. You're very much in love with Maxim, aren't you? Yes, I can see that you are. . . . (*Glancing at "I"*) Don't mind my saying so, but why don't you do something about your hair? Why don't you have it cut. . . . (*Searching for something to suggest*) . . . or sweep it back behind your ears?

"I" holds her hair back behind her ears, turning her head for Beatrice's inspection. The latter looks at her critically.

BEATRICE. No, that's worse. What does Maxim say about it? Does he like it like that?

"I". Well—he never mentions it.

BEATRICE (*looking surprised*). Oh, well —don't go by me. I can see by the way you dress you don't care a hoot how you look. But I wonder Maxim hasn't been at you. He's so particular about clothes.

"I". I don't think he ever notices what I wear.

BEATRICE (*as they start out*). Oh well— he must have changed a lot, then. . . . (*The view moving with them as they start walking*) You mustn't worry about old Maxim—and his moods. One never knows what goes on in that quiet mind of his. Often he gets into a terrible rage —and when he *does*! (*She hints at terrible things.*) But—I don't suppose he'll lose his temper with you. You seem such a placid little thing. (*She puts her arm around "I".*)

With their backs turned, they walk on out of the room. Then we see BEATRICE AND "I" coming through the door, and the moving view brings them to Giles.

GILES. Come along, old girl. We've got to be on the first tee at three o'clock.

BEATRICE. All right. I'm coming!

The scene dissolves to the EXTERIOR OF MAN-DERLEY as Giles, Beatrice, Maxim and "I" come from the house and are on the STEPS.

GILES. Well, good-bye, Maxim, old boy.

MAXIM (*shaking hands with him*). Good-bye, Giles—thanks for coming, old boy.

BEATRICE AND "I" are seen together.

BEATRICE. Well, good-bye, my dear. Forgive me for asking so many rude questions. We both really hope you'll be very happy.

"I" (*almost emotional in her hunger for kindness*). Oh, thank you, Beatrice, thank you very much!

BEATRICE. And I must congratulate you upon the way Maxim looks. We were very worried about him this time last year. But then, of course, you know the whole story.

For a moment "I" doesn't realize the significance of Beatrice's remark, then as she does realize it she starts as though to tell Beatrice that she doesn't know the whole story and to ask Beatrice what she means. But Beatrice is gone and she thinks better of it.

MAXIM'S VOICE. Good-bye, Beatrice.

BEATRICE'S VOICE. Good-bye, old boy.

"I" is seen as Maxim comes to her, Giles and Beatrice having driven off, and puts his arms around her.

MAXIM. Well, thank Heavens they've gone! Now, we can have a walk about the place. (*Looking at the sky*) It looks as though we might have a shower—but you won't mind, will you?

"I" (*happily*). No, but wait a minute—I'll run upstairs and get a coat.

MAXIM. There's a heap of mackintoshes in the flower room. (*He goes up and steps inside the front door, calling inside*) Robert! Robert, run and get a coat from the flower room for Mrs. de Winter, will you? (*He comes back to "I".*) What did you think of Beatrice?

"I". Oh, I liked her very much. But she kept saying I was quite different from what she expected.

MAXIM. Well, what the devil *did* she expect?

"I". Someone much smarter, more sophisticated, I'm afraid. (*She pauses.*) Do you like my hair?

MAXIM (*looking at her in astonishment*). Your hair? Yes, of course, I do. What's the matter with it?

"I". Oh, I don't know. I just wondered.

MAXIM (*looking at her*). How funny you are.

Robert comes out from the house carrying an oilskin coat. Maxim takes it.

MAXIM (*to Robert*). Thank you. (*He starts to put the coat on "I".*)

"I". Do I have to put it on?

MAXIM (*helping her put coat on*). Yes, certainly, certainly, certainly. Can't be too careful with children.

They start down the stairs, leaving Jasper sitting alone.

MAXIM'S VOICE (*as they move off*). Come on, Jasper. Come on and take some of that fat off.

We see Jasper run down the steps.

"I" and Maxim are seen walking over the grounds away from the house; then they appear on the LAWN, coming forward, Jasper with them. Then we see them NEAR THE TOP OF A CLIFF. As they walk along, they come to a fork in the paths leading down to the sea; and Jasper unhesitatingly runs ahead and disappears down the path farthest to the right.

"I" AND MAXIM are seen walking through the estate as Maxim calls

MAXIM. Jasper! Here, not that way! Come here! (*He whistles.*)

We see JASPER as he starts to scamper down the stairs which lead to the beach. Then "I" AND MAXIM appear at close range.

"I". Where does that lead to?

MAXIM (*briefly*). Oh, it leads to a little cove where we used to keep a boat.

"I". Let's go down there.

MAXIM (*irritably*). Oh no, it's a perfectly dull and uninteresting stretch of sand— just like any other.

"I" (*eagerly*). Oh, please.

MAXIM (*seeing her look of disappointment*). Well, all right—we'll walk down and take a look if you really want to.

Thereupon "I" AND MAXIM are seen turning from the top of the palisades down onto the stairs leading to the beach and walking down; then coming down onto the beach in THE COVE. Jasper has disappeared, but they hear his bark from the other side of some rocks.

"I" (*pointing*). That's Jasper! (*Worried*) There must be something wrong —perhaps he's hurt himself.

MAXIM. No, he's all right, dear. Leave him alone.

"I". Don't you think I'd better go and see? (*She turns to go.*)

MAXIM (*angrily*). Don't bother about him, I tell you. He can't come to any harm. He'll find his own way back. (*But she has already left the scene.*)

"I" is then seen climbing over some rocks. MAXIM appears angry, and turning his back strides off. Next "I" appears on the beach.

"I" (*calling*). Jasper! Jasper!

She has now reached the other side of the rocks and is on a stretch of beach in a cove. Shaded by the trees which come down very nearly to the water's edge is a small cottage. She looks around a moment and then sees Jasper at the door of the cottage, where he is scratching at the closed door and whining excitedly.

JASPER is seen AT THE DOOR as he paws it, while the Narrator's voice is heard as she approaches:

"I's" VOICE. Oh, there you are. What do you want in there, Jasper? Come on— come on—come on home. Jasper—Jasper!

We see her face in profile and her hands, as she bends down and takes hold of Jasper's collar.

Suddenly the door behind Jasper begins to open slowly. She watches it, still bending over Jasper, frozen to the spot with horror and fright. As she lifts her eyes in terror, the view moves up and takes in the figure of Ben standing in the doorway, finally revealing his face staring at her in fright. "I", seen close, straightens up.

"I". Oh, I—I didn't know that there was anybody. . . .

BEN is seen in a close-up over "I's" shoulder. The fright on his face dissolves into a foolish smile. He steps out from the doorway and looks down at Jasper.

BEN (*foolishly*). I know that dog. He comes fr' the house. (*He eyes her suspiciously.*) He ain't your'n.

"I" (*patiently*). No, he's Mr. de Winter's dog. Have you anything I could tie him with?

Ben gapes open-mouthed at her. Suppressing her exasperation she looks through the open door and moves into the cottage.

We see THE COTTAGE as she enters the room, and the moving view reveals that the place is completely furnished with bookshelves, table, chairs, and bed sofa. She turns to look around for a rope. Then we see a robe on the floor of the cottage showing initials "RdeW." She is startled at what she sees, and enters the boat room, which is filled with ropes, sails, pots of paint and other paraphernalia. She picks up a short piece of rope and hurries out.

AT THE COTTAGE DOOR outside: Ben is still huddled by the door as she comes out from the cottage.

"I" (*to Jasper*). Come here, Jasper.

BEN (*pitifully and pleadingly, terrified*). You won't tell anyone you saw me in there, will ye?

"I" (*suspiciously*). Don't you belong on the estate?

BEN. I warn't doin' nothin'. I was just puttin' my shells away. (*Now seen in a close-up; looking at her vaguely.*) She's gone in the sea, ain't she? *She'll* never come back no more.

"I" (*seen close; gently shaking her head*). No, she'll never come back. Come on, Jasper.

She looks away in the direction of the rocks, then with a quick glance at Ben, turns to walk toward them. The scene moves with her as she hurries toward the rocks with her head slightly bowed, distressed.

We see the ROCKS as she climbs back onto the other section of beach toward where she had left Maxim; then the BEACH as she, with Jasper on his make-shift leash, comes back onto the beach to find it empty of Maxim. She hurries, Jasper running ahead of her, to the stairs and up them.

AT THE TOP OF THE STAIRS: Maxim sees her approach, turns, and goes out. She comes into the scene, breathless, calling after him.

"I". Maxim! What's the matter? (*She starts out after him.*)

We see Maxim striding angrily ahead, then JASPER running along beside her; she is seen only from the waist down. Then Maxim appears, walking, and she approaches him.

"I". Maxim, I'm sorry I was such a time, but I had to get a rope for Jasper.

Maxim strides forward silently at a still faster pace. The dog lags behind, delaying "I". Maxim turns to look down at him.

MAXIM. Hurry up, Jasper, for Heaven's sake!

"I" (*trying to catch up to Maxim; breathlessly*). *Please* wait for me. . . .

Maxim stops and turns, and comes back a few steps to face her.

"I". Maxim, what is it? You look so angry?

MAXIM. You knew I didn't want you to go there—but you deliberately went.

"I". Why not? There was only a cottage down there and a strange man who was—

MAXIM. You didn't go *into* the cottage, did you?

"I". Yes. The door—

MAXIM (*interrupting*). Well, don't go there again! Do you hear?

"I". Well, why not?

MAXIM. Because I hate the place—and if you had my memories, you wouldn't go there or talk about it or even think about it!

He takes a step away from her.

"I". What's the matter? Oh, I'm so sorry. Please!

He still doesn't look at her for a moment, then steps back toward her again, the view again moving in closer.

MAXIM. We should have stayed away. We should never have come back to Manderley! What a fool I was!

"I". I've made you unhappy. Somehow —I've hurt you. I can't bear to see you like this because—I love you so much. (*She puts her head on his shoulder, holding him close.*)

MAXIM (*tensely, holding her*). Do you? Do you? (*He kisses her, then relaxes his hold.*) I've made you cry. . . . Forgive me. I sometimes seem to fly off the handle for no reason at all, don't I? Come —we'll go home and have some tea and forget all about it.

She smiles up at him through her tears. They start to walk on.

"I". Yes, let's forget all about it.

Automatically she puts her hand in the pocket of the mackintosh and pulls out a handkerchief and puts it to her eyes. She glances down at the handkerchief as she starts to return it to her pocket.

MAXIM. Here—let me have Jasper.

We see the HANDKERCHIEF in her hand, which is marked in the corner with a large embroidered initial "R."

Then as she stares down at the initial with a faraway look, while they are walking, the scene dissolves to a view of MANDERLEY with WAVES BREAKING ON THE ROCKS, and this dissolves to the MORNING ROOM as "I" is seated with her legs curled under her on one of the window seats in the room, and is looking thoughtfully out of the window toward the sea. She looks very disturbed. She turns away from the window, thinking hard. Then she suddenly jumps to her feet and with a determined air crosses to the library.

FRANK CRAWLEY'S OFFICE: She opens the door and walks in. Frank, who is seated at a desk immersed in his work, looks up.

FRANK. Oh, hello—come in.

She approaches him and Frank starts to rise.

"I". Oh, please don't get up, Mr. Crawley. I was just wondering if you meant what you said the other day about showing me the run of things.

FRANK. Of course, I did.

"I". What are you doing now?

FRANK. Notifying all the tenants that in celebration of Maxim's return—with his bride—this week's rent will be free.

"I" (*greatly pleased*). Oh, was that Maxim's idea?

FRANK. Oh yes. All the servants get an extra week's wages, too.

"I". He didn't tell me. Oh—can't I help you? I could at least lick the stamps.

FRANK (*weakly*). That's terribly nice of you. Won't you sit down.

"I". Oh yes—thank you.

Now they sit at the desk, she helping him by licking stamps.

"I". I—I was down at the cottage on the beach the other day, and there was a man there—a queer sort of person. Jasper kept barking at him.

FRANK. Oh, yes—must have been Ben. Excuse me. (*He gets up and goes over to file cabinet as the view widens.*) He's quite harmless. We give him odd jobs now and then.

"I". That cottage place seems to be going to rack and ruin. Why isn't something done about it?

FRANK—AT THE FILE—is seen fairly close. He pretends to busy himself excessively at the file; he answers eventually, but without looking up.

FRANK. Oh, I think if Maxim wanted anything done about it he'd tell me.

"I". Are those all *Rebecca's* things down there?

FRANK (*uncomfortable*). Yes—yes—they are.

"I". What did she use the cottage for?

FRANK (*coming back to desk and sitting down again*). The boat used to be moored near there.

"I". What boat? What happened to it? Was that the boat she was sailing in when she was drowned?

FRANK (*knowing he must answer*). Yes. It capsized and sank. She was washed overboard.

"I". Wasn't she afraid to go out like that—alone?

FRANK. She wasn't afraid of anything.

"I" (*silent for a moment, then*). Where did they find her?

FRANK. Near Edgecombe, about forty miles up channel—about two months afterwards. Maxim went up to identify her. It was horrible for him.

She reflects on this for a moment, trying to imagine the effect on Maxim, then rises from the desk, and walks a few steps away, speaking with her back to Frank.

"I". Yes, it must have been. Mr. Crawley— (*Frank rises to her, but she doesn't turn.*) —please don't think me morbidly curious—it isn't that—It's just that I feel at such a disadvantage. (*Turning to Frank*) All the time—whenever I meet anyone—Maxim's sister, even the servants—I know they're all thinking the same thing. They're all comparing me with her—with Rebecca.

Frank goes to her, anxious to reassure her, and the view moves to bring them close.

FRANK (*very much concerned*). Oh, you mustn't think that. I can't tell you how glad I am that you married Maxim. It's going to make all the difference to his life. And, from my point of view it's— it's very refreshing to find someone like yourself who is not entirely—er—in tune, shall we say, with Manderley.

During Frank's speech she is grateful but embarrassed, not quite able to look him in the eye and not knowing what to say. Then:

"I". That's very sweet of you. I daresay I've been stupid, but every day I realize the things she had and that I lack . . . beauty— (*reaching for words*) —and wit—and intelligence—and, or, *all* the things that are so important in a woman.

FRANK. But you have qualities that are just as important, more important, if I may say so. Kindliness, and sincerity, and, if you'll forgive me, modesty—mean more to a husband than all the wit and beauty in the world.

There is another embarrassed silence. She doesn't answer.

FRANK (*very kindly*). We none of us want to live in the past. Maxim least of all. It's up to you, you know, to lead us away from it.

She looks at him gratefully and smiles a little, relieved.

"I". I promise you I won't bring this up again, but before we end this conversation would you answer just one more question?

Frank, not knowing what is coming, goes on his guard.

FRANK (*quietly, nervously*). If it's something I'm able to answer. I'll do my best.

"I" (*bracing herself slightly for it*). Tell me, what was Rebecca really like?

Frank doesn't answer for a second, as she looks at him eagerly. Then he walks slowly back to his desk and sits down, busying himself with his work. She follows him and sits also, waiting for his reply. He avoids her eyes as he speaks.

FRANK (*slowly, reminiscently, but* not *as if he had been in love with Rebecca*). I suppose—I suppose she was the most beautiful creature I ever saw.

"I" looks ahead a moment unseeingly, then continues licking stamps as the scene dissolves to a view of a MAGAZINE COVER, which reads:

BEAUTY

THE MAGAZINE

FOR

SMART WOMEN

April   Two shillings

The page is turned to an illustration of a woman in a black evening gown: "For the Gala Evening." This dissolves to MANDERLEY HALL at night, with "I", in the dress just seen in the magazine. She is coming downstairs, as we follow her down. Her hair is rather sensationally dressed and beautifully coiffed, and she wears somewhat more lipstick than usual. She is very lovely but not the girl Maxim married. She is very conscious of her clothes and appearance, rather excited by them, but very nervous. She stops in the doorway to the library.

The LIBRARY: Maxim is arranging the projection machine. A portable screen is set up at the other end of the library.

"I" (*nervously*). Good evening, Maxim.

MAXIM (*not looking up*). Hello. The films of the honeymoon have arrived at last. Do we have time, do you think, before dinner? (*He looks up to her.*) What on earth have you done to yourself?

She is seen standing at the door, and as she comes forward we see her in a close-up.

"I" (*casually*). Oh, nothing—I just ordered a new dress from London. I hope you don't mind?

MAXIM (*crossing to her*). Oh, no—no—er—only do you think that sort of thing is right for you? It doesn't seem your type at all.

"I" (*very let down*). Oh . . . I thought you'd like it.

MAXIM (*the cruel male*). And what have you done to your hair? (*She doesn't answer. Maxim sees he has hurt her, and puts his arm around her.*) Oh, I see. Oh dear! Oh dear! Oh dear, I'm sorry. (*Then, insincerely*) You look lovely— lovely. That's very nice for a change. . . . (*Dismissing the whole thing*) Shall we see these pictures?

"I" (*very let down*). Yes . . . (*Without enthusiasm, her thoughts only on her comic failure*) I—I'd love to see them. (*She sits on arm of chair.*)

Maxim goes over and turns out the lights. The room is now lit only by the one lamp and the light from the projector. Maxim is more or less lost in darkness.

We see the SCREEN with Maxim and "I" in the foreground, their backs turned.

MAXIM. Oh, look now. Now look at that . . .

"I". Wasn't it wonderful, darling. Can't we go back there some day?

A PICTURE OF HER appears on the screen.

MAXIM'S VOICE. Of course, of course. Ah, look at you. There, won't our grandchildren be delighted when they see how lovely you were?

A PICTURE OF MAXIM comes onto the screen.

"I's" VOICE. Oh, look at you . . .

MAXIM'S VOICE. O—I—I . . .

"I's" VOICE. Oh, I like that. Look at that.

MAXIM'S VOICE. Yes, very nice.

"I's" VOICE. Oh, remember that?

MAXIM'S VOICE. Yes.

We again see the SCREEN with Maxim and "I" in the foreground, their backs turned.

"I". Oh, I wish our honeymoon could have lasted forever, Maxim.

The film breaks, leaving the screen blank.

MAXIM. Oh, dash it, look. Oh, oh, oh hang it. I've threaded it up wrong as usual—or something.

Maxim crosses and turns on the lights, and just at this time Frith appears in the doorway. Then we see him approaching MAXIM AND "I".

MAXIM (*surprised*). Yes, Frith, what is it?

Frith wears a stiff, solemn expression, his lips pursed. He behaves as though a great tragedy is impending.

FRITH. Excuse me, sir. May I have a word with you?

MAXIM. Yes, come in.

FRITH. It's about Robert, sir. There's been a slight unpleasantness between him and Mrs. Danvers.

MAXIM. Oh dear!

FRITH. Robert is very upset.

MAXIM (*making a face at "I"*). This *is* trouble! (*Turning to Frith and settling himself, slightly annoyed, for a long story*) What is it?

FRITH (*with a nervous cough*). It appears that Mrs. Danvers has accused Robert of stealing a valuable ornament from the morning room. Robert denies the accusation most emphatically, sir.

MAXIM. What was the thing, anyway?

During this we see "I" reacting: frightened, almost speaking, increasingly embarrassed, guilty and uncomfortable as she realizes what she's done to poor Robert.

FRITH. The china cupid, sir.

MAXIM. Oh dear—that's one of our treasures, isn't it? Well, tell Mrs. Danvers to get at the bottom of it somehow—and tell her I'm sure it wasn't Robert.

FRITH (*relieved*). Very good, sir.

As soon as Frith has gone Maxim starts to walk around the table.

MAXIM. Why do they come to me with these things? That's your job, sweetheart.

This only increases her embarrassment. Finally she decides to be brave.

"I". Maxim . . . I wanted to tell you, but I—well, I forgot. The fact is . . . (*She gets it out.*) I broke the cupid.

MAXIM (*coming in to her; very surprised*). *You* broke it? Now why on earth didn't you say something about it when Frith was here?

"I". I don't know. I didn't like to. I was afraid he would think me a fool.

MAXIM. Well, he'll think you're much more of a fool now. You'll have to explain to him and Mrs. Danvers.

"I". Oh, no, Maxim! You do it. . . .

(*Eagerly, like a frightened child*) I'll go upstairs.

MAXIM (*very annoyed*). Don't be such a little idiot, darling. Anybody would think you were afraid of them.

Frith enters, ushering in Mrs. Danvers, who is obviously very angry. They advance toward Maxim and "I".

MAXIM (*obviously very annoyed with the whole thing*). It's all a mistake, Mrs. Danvers. Apparently Mrs. de Winter broke the cupid herself and forgot to say anything.

There is a moment's silence as they all look at her, and she feels like a foolish child.

"I". I'm so sorry. I never thought that I'd get Robert into trouble.

She looks at Mrs. Danvers eagerly, as though to a superior, but Mrs. Danvers returns her look coldly.

MRS. DANVERS. Is it possible to repair the ornament, Madam? (*She looks at "I" as though she had known all along that she was the culprit.*)

"I". No, I'm afraid it isn't. It was smashed into pieces.

MAXIM (*with a mixture of amusement and exasperation, lighting a cigarette*). What did you do with the pieces?

The situation is getting worse and worse for "I". She speaks very quietly, ready to break into tears:

"I". Well I—I put them at the back of one of the drawers in the writing desk.

MAXIM (*really exasperated, turns to Mrs. Danvers*). It looks as though Mrs. de Winter were afraid you were going to put her in prison, doesn't it, Mrs. Danvers? Well, never mind. Do what you can to find the pieces—see if they can be mended, and in any event tell Robert to dry his tears.

MRS. DANVERS is seen in a close-up, with Frith in the background, bowing slightly and going out, but Mrs. Danvers stays, while Maxim in the foreground starts to fix the machine.

MRS. DANVERS (*anxious not to let "I" off the hook so easily*). I shall apologize to Robert, of course. Perhaps if such a thing happens again, Mrs. de Winter will tell me personally and I . . .

MAXIM (*interrupting impatiently*). Yes, yes, all right. (*Dismissing her*) Thank you, Mrs. Danvers.

Mrs. Danvers leaves the room. Maxim goes about the business of repairing the film or of taking off the reel and putting in another, the scene continuing the while.

MAXIM. There, I suppose that clip will hold all right, I don't know.

There is a moment's silence as neither of them speaks. Then:

"I" (*seen in a close-up*). I'm awfully sorry, darling. It was very careless of me. Mrs. Danvers must be furious with me.

MAXIM'S VOICE. Oh, hang Mrs. Danvers! Why on earth should you be frightened of her?

Maxim turns and extinguishes the light. He starts the projection machine.

MAXIM. You behave more like an upstairs maid or something—not like the mistress of the house at all.

"I". Yes, I know I do. But I feel so uncomfortable. . . . I try my best every day, but it's very difficult with people looking you up and down as if you were a prize cow.

MAXIM (*putting the film into the projector*). What does it matter if they do? You must remember that life at Manderley is the only thing that interests anybody down here.

"I" (*again in a close-up*). What a slap in the eye I must have been to them, then. . . . I suppose that's why you married me—because you knew I was dull and gauche and inexperienced and there could never be any gossip about me.

Maxim is suddenly angry. He crosses to her.

MAXIM. Gossip? What do you mean? (*He crosses in front of projector and pulls on the light. He stands towering with suppressed rage above her.*)

"I". Why I don't know. I just said it for something to say. Don't look at me like that! Maxim, what's the matter? What have I said?

MAXIM (*seen in a close-up*). It wasn't a very attractive thing to say, was it?

"I" (*in a close-up*). No. It was rude, hateful.

MAXIM moves over to her.

MAXIM (*coldly*). I wonder if I did a very selfish thing in marrying you?

She is almost sick at her marriage apparently being threatened through this silly incident.

"I" (*her voice almost a hoarse whisper, with fright*). How do you mean?

MAXIM. I'm not much of a companion to you, am I? You don't get much fun, do you? You ought to have married a boy —someone of your own age.

"I" (*interrupting*). Maxim, why do you say this? Of course we're companions.

MAXIM. Are we? I don't know. I'm very difficult to live with.

"I" (*eagerly*). No, you're not difficult! You're easy, very easy. Our marriage is a success, isn't it? A great success! (*He doesn't answer. She continues, pleading,*

desperate.) We're happy, aren't we? Terribly happy?

He still doesn't answer, and his failure to answer is a terrible blow to her.

"I". If you don't think we are happy it would be much better if you didn't pretend. I'll go away. Why don't you answer me?

She looks up at him eagerly. He looks into her face and, not unkindly, speaks:

MAXIM. How can I answer you when I don't know the answer myself? If you say we're happy, let's leave it at that. Happiness is something I know nothing about.

During this speech Maxim has gone down to the light switch. There is a silence.

We see "I", at close range. Lit by the lamp of the projector, she appears crushed. Maxim comes into the scene and starts the projector. He looks at the screen, not at her. She tries to say something, fails, and lowers her eyes.

MAXIM'S VOICE. Oh, look! There's the one when I left the camera running on the tripod—remember?

On the screen appear Maxim's and "I's" laughing faces, as the scene fades out.

PART FOUR

A LETTER fades in. It reads:

"Have gone up to London on some business of the estate.

I shall return before evening, and certainly this brief holiday from me should be welcome.

Maxim"

This dissolves to the MORNING ROOM, with "I" on the sofa, looking out the window. The scene draws back as the maid, Hilda, enters and puts the tea table in front of her. She averts her face from Hilda's gaze, afraid her tears will be noticed.

HILDA. Pardon me, Madam. Is there anything I can do for you?

"I". I'm all right, Hilda. Thank you very much.

HILDA. I'll bring the sandwiches immediately, Madam.

"I" rises, and the view moves with her to another window. Suddenly her attention is arrested as she sees: The EXTERIOR OF THE MANDERLEY WEST WING with Mrs. Danvers in the background closing the window.

Then we see "I" AT THE WINDOW, with HILDA in the background.

"I". Hilda!

HILDA. Yes, Madam? (*Looking up from table where she is finishing setting the tea things*).

"I". The West Wing—nobody ever uses it any more, do they?

HILDA. No, Madam, not since the death of Mrs. de Winter. (*She gives her a curious look and then leaves.*)

"I" suddenly turns and the scene moves with her as she leaves the room. Next we see her coming out into the hall and starting to go up the stairs. Suddenly we hear a door close and footsteps coming toward the top of the stairs. There is the indistinct murmur of a man's voice, followed by Mrs. Danvers'.

MRS. DANVERS' VOICE. Come along, Mr. Jack, or someone may see you.

"I" (seen close now), alarmed at the idea of meeting a stranger, slips into the library and stands just inside the door. We continue to hear them talking:

FAVELL'S VOICE. Well, Danny, old harpy, it's been good to see you again. I've been simply breathless to pick up all the news.

MRS. DANVERS' VOICE. I really don't think it's wise for you to come here, Mr. Jack.

Now we see the dog JASPER as he stands in the hall, listening to the voices.

FAVELL'S VOICE. Oh, nonsense, nonsense. It's just like coming back home.

MRS. DANVERS' VOICE. Shh. Quiet, Mr. Jack.

Next "I" is seen, still standing at the library door—motioning for Jasper to come to her.

FAVELL'S VOICE. Yes, and we must be careful not to shock Cinderella, mustn't we?

MRS. DANVERS' VOICE. She's in the morning room. If you leave through the garden door, she won't see you.

FAVELL'S VOICE. I must say I feel a little like the poor relation, sneaking around through back doors. Well, toodle-oo, Danny.

MRS. DANVERS' VOICE. Good-bye, Mr. Jack, and please be careful.

"I" waits a second, then stealthily tiptoes round to try and get a glimpse of the stranger who she thinks is waiting in the hall. Jasper starts to bark excitedly. He runs toward the window leading into the garden. "I" doesn't look back at him, but motions

with her hand behind her as she continues peering into the hall, trying to quiet him.

"I". Jasper, be quiet.

Suddenly a voice speaks from behind her. She swings round in alarm.

FAVELL'S VOICE. Looking for me?

We get a fairly close view of FAVELL with "I" in the background, her back turned. Sitting on the ledge of the open window, is a very self-assured individual of rather obvious good looks, flashy but with a certain charm for women. He is smiling as he adds:

FAVELL. Oh—I didn't make you jump, did I?

"I" comes away from the door and approaches the window, looking and feeling rather foolish. She says uncertainly:

"I". Of course not. I didn't quite know who it was.

Favell is at the window and "I" in the foreground. He is still sitting on the window ledge. Jasper is jumping up excitedly. Favell leans down to pat him:

FAVELL. Yes, you're pleased to see me, aren't you, old boy? I'm glad there's someone in the family to welcome me back to Manderley. (*Easily to "I"*) And how is dear old Max?

"I". Very well, thank you. (*She is plainly taken aback by his familiarity.*)

FAVELL. I hear he went up to London—left his little bride all alone. That's too bad. Isn't he afraid that somebody might come down and carry you off? ... (*He breaks off as Mrs. Danvers enters room.*) Danny, all your precautions were in vain. The mistress of the house was hiding behind the door.

He laughs—and there is a moment's pause. Then Mrs. Danvers approaches her from behind.

FAVELL (*seen at fairly close range at the window*). Oh, what about presenting me to the bride?

As only MRS. DANVERS AND "I" are seen, Mrs. Danvers performs the introduction almost unwillingly, saying quietly:

MRS. DANVERS. This is Mr. Favell, Madam.

FAVELL adjusts his tie and impudently jumps over the window ledge and into the room, the view bringing him over to "I" and Mrs. Danvers. He holds out his hand to "I" and shakes her reluctant one.

"I". How do you do.

FAVELL. How do you do.

There is a moment's awkward silence. "I" has no idea how to entertain this strange visitor. Her glance falls on the tea table.

"I". Won't you have some tea, or something?

FAVELL (*turning with a broad smile to Mrs. Danvers*). Now isn't that a charming invitation? I've been asked to stay to tea, Danny, and I've a good mind to accept.

There is a warning look on Mrs. Danvers' face. Favell gets the look and grins.

FAVELL. Oh, well, perhaps you're right. Pity, just when we were getting on so nicely. (*He looks down at Jasper.*) We mustn't lead the bride astray, must we, Jasper? (*To "I"*) Good-bye. It's been fun meeting you. Oh, by the way, it would be very decent of you if you didn't mention this little visit to your revered husband. He doesn't exactly approve of me.

"I". Very well.

FAVELL. That's very sporting of you. . . . (*The view moves with him as he walks over to window and jumps over the ledge.*) I wish I had a young bride of three months waiting for me at home. I'm just a lonely old bachelor. (*Looking back into the room*) Fare you well. (*Suddenly he adds:*) Oh—and I know what was wrong with that introduction. Danny didn't tell you, did she? I'm Rebecca's favorite cousin. Toodle-oo. (*He exits rapidly.*)

"I" (seen in a close-up) is looking after him in bewilderment. She turns to look at Mrs. Danvers, but Mrs. Danvers has disappeared. She comes to a sudden decision, and determinedly starts out of the room and into the hall.

Next we see her in THE HALL, starting to ascend the stairs. The view moving with her, she reaches the top of the stairs and turns down the corridor in the direction of the West Wing. She goes directly toward the door of the big room, a close view appearing as she glances round almost furtively while starting to turn the handle. She holds herself in a tense attitude when the wood makes a sound of crackling as it swings on its hinges. Opening it the minimum amount of space she almost sidles in.

REBECCA'S ROOM: Inside the room it is practically dark. The silence is broken only by the ticking of the clock. Just the vague shapes of furniture can be seen lit from the slightly open door through which "I" has come. She comes through the curtains in Rebecca's room, and we follow her past the bed and toward the window. She raises her hand and with sudden resolve pulls the cord which parts the curtains. The flood of daylight reveals an astonishing scene. "I" swings round amazed, as she sees a most elegantly furnished room, expressed in the lightest possible tones—white predominates nearly everywhere. The four poster bed is very regal on its double-stepped dais. The bed is made up with the coverlet folded back. A large spray of lovely fresh white flowers is set in a prominent position. In another part of the room is an ornate dressing table complete with brushes, combs, mirrors, elaborate bottles of perfume, and so forth.

She gazes spellbound as her eyes begin to take in more details of the room. The view begins to sweep round the room, taking in as it goes the cream, silken bedcover, the cream velvet-wrapped posters of the bed, and on the cover, most astonishing of all, the palest grey satin nightdress case with the black initial "R"—down across the very light carpet and past the tall cheval mirror.

She moves on, the view following her past the long cheval mirror to the dressing table —where a picture of Maxim is prominently displayed. She touches the hairbrush lightly. Through the mirror we see the bed reflected—"I" sees it and is drawn toward it. She moves over and finds that she is staring down at the nightdress case which lies on the pillow.

MRS. DANVERS' VOICE. Do you wish anything, Madam?

"I" looks startled, entirely confused. Next MRS. DANVERS is seen entering through the curtains in the room. Then "I" (seen in a close-up) puts a hand behind her back almost like a guilty child and half lowers her eyes. Looking up she swallows slightly and speaks timidly:

"I". I didn't expect to see you, Mrs. Danvers. I noticed that a window wasn't closed, and I came up to see if I could fasten it.

MRS. DANVERS (*coming in to her*). Why did you say that? I closed it before I left the room. You opened it yourself, didn't you? (*She walks over to the window, which she closes, then continues on over to the drapes which she pulls back to let the sunlight stream in.*) You've always wanted to see this room, haven't you, Madam? Why did you never ask me to show it to you? I was ready to show it to you every day. It's a lovely room, isn't it? The loveliest room you've ever seen. (*She moves on through the room.*) Everything is kept just as Mrs. de Winter liked it. Nothing has been altered since that last night.

"I" stands, staring at her, almost as if hypnotized.

MRS. DANVERS (*beckoning to her*). Come, I'll show you her dressing room.

The view moves with them—"I" following automatically, to a small anteroom lined with cupboards. Mrs. Danvers suddenly stops. She indicates the cupboards.

MRS. DANVERS. This is where I keep all her clothes. You would like to see them, wouldn't you?

They move on to the wardrobe closet, which Mrs. Danvers opens. Her eyes light on a chinchilla wrap. She takes it out and holds it out to her.

MRS. DANVERS. Feel this. (*Holds it up to "I's" face.*) It was a Christmas present from Mr. de Winter. He was always giving her expensive gifts, the whole year round. (*She has opened another cupboard, with tiers of shelves and drawers, one of which she opens.*) I keep her underwear on this side. They were made specially for her by the nuns in the

Convent of St. Claire. (*Walks on to another part of room.*) I always used to wait up for her, no matter how late. Sometimes she and Mr. de Winter didn't come home until dawn. While she was undressing, she'd tell me about the party she'd been to—she knew everyone that mattered—and everyone loved her! (*She is now walking over to the dressing table.*)

"I" hesitates, then stops. Her eyes follow Mrs. Danvers' movements. She is now completely under the spell of Mrs. Danvers, who has developed from her queer matter-of-fact tones into a low-voiced fanatic.

MRS. DANVERS. When she'd finished her bath she'd go into the bedroom and go over to the dressing table. (*Her eyes rest on the dressing table.*) Oh, you've moved her brush, haven't you? (*Straightening the brush that "I" had moved*) There, that's better, just as she always laid it down. "Come on, Danny, hair drill," she would say. (*She beckons to "I" to come and sit at the dressing table. "I" automatically obeys.*) And I'd stand behind her like this—and brush away for twenty minutes at a time. (*She pretends to brush "I's" hair. She puts the brush back carefully, then turns and looks toward the bed. "I" looks up furtively, wanting to rise and get away from her. Mrs. Danvers is speaking in a faraway voice, walking over to the bed.*) And then she would say "Good night, Danny" and step into her bed. I embroidered this case for her myself and I keep it here always.

We see the PILLOW on the bed, with the nightcase lying on it. The initial "R" is embroidered on it.

MRS. DANVERS picks up the nightcase and takes the black, chiffon nightgown out of it.

MRS. DANVERS (*feeling the material*). Did you ever see anything so delicate?

She beckons for "I" to come closer. "I's" breathing becomes heavier and heavier as she nears the breaking point. Mrs. Danvers puts her hand inside the chiffon and spreads her fingers.

MRS. DANVERS. Look, you can see my

hand through it. (*She literally compels "I" to look at it.*)

"I" can stand no more. She moves away from Mrs. Danvers. Then we see her stumbling blindly through the curtains, the view following her to the door. She starts to open the door when Mrs. Danvers quietly follows her, the view focussing closely on the two of them.

MRS. DANVERS. You wouldn't think she'd been gone so long, would you?

"I" turns at the door to face Mrs. Danvers, her eyes dilated with fear.

MRS. DANVERS (*her face close to "I's"*). Sometimes when I walk along the corridor I fancy I hear her just behind me— that quick, light step. I couldn't mistake it anywhere. It's not only in this room— it's in all the rooms in the house. I can almost hear it now. (*She is pleased by the effect of her words on "I".*) Do you think the dead come back and watch the living?

"I" (*looking at her wildly, vehemently*). No—no! I *don't* believe it!

MRS. DANVERS (*whispering slightly*). Sometimes I wonder if she doesn't come back here to Manderley and watch you and Mr. de Winter together. (*Intently*) You look tired. Why don't you stay here a while and rest?

Mrs. Danvers turns and walks slowly away from "I".

MRS. DANVERS. Listen to the sea . . . it's so soothing. . . . (*She moves slowly toward the curtains, listening to the sea.*)

"I" looks wildly about the room—as though impelled by an impulse to run amuck—tear it all to pieces. Tears run down her cheeks.

MRS. DANVERS. Listen to it . . . listen . . . listen to the sea. . . .

"I" turns, opens the door, and sidles quickly from the room. The view stays on Mrs. Danvers as we hear the boom of the distant surf and it grows louder and louder. Finally the scene dissolves to a picture of WAVES dashing madly against the rocks, and then to the MORNING ROOM: Rebecca's address book is on the desk and the view moves to

"I" staring at it. She has an expression of wild, hysterical despair. Suddenly she turns —looks all about the room, then back at the desk. She turns the book over so that the monogram is hidden.

We see the TELEPHONE ON THE DESK as "I's" hand comes into view, seizes the phone, and lifts the receiver.

"I" (*into the phone*). Tell Mrs. Danvers I wish to see her immediately.

The scene lengthens as "I" hangs up the receiver and starts, in a rage, to pile other books and papers on top of Rebecca's address book on a corner of the desk. "I's" HANDS are next seen piling things frantically, one on top of the other.

A close view shows "I"—AT THE DESK—"I" yanking the drawer open and starting to pull out Rebecca's lists and papers. Amongst these she uncovers an engraved invitation card, and the CARD appears on the screen. It reads:

Mr. and Mrs. de Winter request the pleasure of Mr. Jack Favell's company at a Costume Ball at Manderley on Thursday evening, June 15th   Ten o'clock

and on it is scrawled in one corner:

Rebecca—
  I'll be there—*and how!*

                    Jack

"I" is seen close as she wipes the tears from her eyes, having heard the door opening. Now MRS. DANVERS appears.

MRS. DANVERS. You sent for me, Madam?

We follow her approaching "I", who looks up, her face grimly set, as though she were ready for a fight.

"I" (*rising*). Yes, Mrs. Danvers. I want you to get rid of all these things.

Mrs. Danvers looks down toward the desk with an expression of anger. "I" stands by the desk, and all the courage, all the determination that she possesses are now in play.

MRS. DANVERS. But these are Mrs. de Winter's things.

"I" (*seen close, with quiet determination*). I am Mrs. de Winter now.

Mrs. Danvers looks at her steadily for a moment, but "I" returns her gaze.

MRS. DANVERS (*with a slight bow*). Very well, I will give the instructions.

She turns to go toward the door to the hall. The sound of an automobile horn is heard, and "I" turns eagerly toward the window. Then we see MRS. DANVERS—AT THE DOOR—at close range. She is just about to exit into the hall.

"I's" VOICE (*coldly*). Just a moment, please.

Mrs. Danvers stops and turns. "I" crosses the room to Mrs. Danvers.

"I". Mrs. Danvers, I intend to say nothing to Mr. de Winter about Mr. Favell's visit. In fact, I prefer to forget *everything* that happened this afternoon. (*She goes out past Mrs. Danvers.*)

MRS. DANVERS (seen in a close-up) simply stands and looks after "I".

The HALL at dusk: Maxim comes in from the front door. "I" runs to him, throws her arms about him, holds him frantically.

"I" (*in his arms*). Oh, Maxim, Maxim! You've been gone all day.

MAXIM (*laughing*). Hey—you're choking me.

They walk together toward the library, their backs turned to us.

MAXIM. Well, well, what have you been doing with yourself?

"I". Oh, I've been thinking.

MAXIM (*smiling*). Oh, what did you want to do that for?

"I". Well, come in here and I'll tell you.

The LIBRARY, with MAXIM AND "I" entering.

"I". Darling, could we have a costume ball—just as you used to?

MAXIM (*surprised*). Now, what put that idea into your mind? Has Beatrice been at you?

"I". No! No! But I feel that we ought to *do* something—to make people feel that Manderley is the same as it always was.

Maxim is silent for a moment, filling his pipe and lighting it.

"I". Oh, please, darling—could we?

MAXIM (*trying gently to put her off*). You don't know what it would mean, you know. You would have to be hostess to hundreds of people—all the County—and a lot of young people would come up from London and turn the house into a night club.

"I" (*pleading*). Oh, yes, but I want to—oh, please. I've never been to a large party—but I could learn what to do—and I *promise* you, you wouldn't be ashamed of me.

He looks into her eyes. Her face is so eager, so appealing that he relaxes and takes her in his arms.

MAXIM (*tolerantly*). All right—if you think you'd enjoy it. You'd better get Mrs. Danvers to help you, hadn't you?

"I". No, no! I don't need Mrs. Danvers to help me. I can do it myself.

MAXIM (*kissing her*). All right, my sweet.

"I" (*while she is being kissed*). Oh, thank you, darling. Thank you. Oh, what'll you go as?

MAXIM (*smiling at her*). I never dress up. That's the one privilege I claim as host. What will you be? Alice in Wonderland—with that ribbon in your hair?

"I" (*happily*). No, I won't tell you. I shall design my own costume all by myself and give you the surprise of your life!

He puts his arm around her, and the scene dissolves to "I's" BEDROOM and a close view of a SKETCH BOOK. It is day. "I's" hand is adding a few strokes to a design for a costume. Next to the sketch on the bed lies an illustrated magazine open to the picture of Joan of Arc which she is copying. Then the view draws back to reveal "I" at her sketching—various illustrated books and magazines scattered about. A knock is heard at the door.

"I" (*preoccupied*). Come in.

MRS. DANVERS enters the room, holding a few slightly crumpled sketches in her hand.

MRS. DANVERS (*coming in to "I"*). Robert found these sketches in the library, Madam. Did you intend throwing them away?

"I". Yes, Mrs. Danvers, I did. They were just some ideas I was sketching for my costume for the ball.

"I's" tone is cold, impersonal—indicative of the new relationship she has attempted to establish with Mrs. Danvers—a relationship of "armed neutrality."

MRS. DANVERS. Hasn't Mr. de Winter suggested anything?

"I" (*hesitantly*). No. I want to surprise him. I don't want him to know anything about it.

MRS. DANVERS. I merely thought that you might find a costume among the family portraits that would suit you. . . .

"I" looks up quickly at Mrs. Danvers, amazed at the change in her tone. She thinks she sees a former enemy who is now suing for peace.

"I" (*rising*). Oh, you mean those at the top of the stairs? I'll go and look at them. (*She goes out, followed by Mrs. Danvers.*)

The scene dissolves to a GALLERY as "I" and Mrs. Danvers are walking along, looking up at the departed de Winters.

MRS. DANVERS. This one, for instance.

She turns and indicates the portrait of Caroline de Winter behind them. "I" turns, so we get their two backs facing it.

MRS. DANVERS. It might have been designed for you. I'm sure you could have it copied.

A close view of "I" AND MRS. DANVERS appears. Anxious to be convinced, "I" looks back at Mrs. Danvers and then to the picture again, uncertainly.

MRS. DANVERS. I've heard Mr. de Winter say this is his favorite of all the paintings. It's Lady Caroline de Winter, one of his ancestors.

"I" remains gazing at the picture as Mrs. Danvers, after a slight pause, moves silently away. "I" speaks with almost a touch of relief combined with delight.

"I". Oh, well, well, well—that's a splendid idea, Mrs. Danvers. I—I'm very grateful.

She looks and discovers Mrs. Danvers has silently left. Thereupon the scene dissolves to an exterior view of MANDERLEY at night, and then to the HALL, with Frank entering the scene, dressed in his school cap and gown, and going out. Following this we get a view of a long TABLE at one end of the hall garlanded and decorated with candles for the ball. On it is set the usual type of buffet supper, served for such an affair as the Manderley Ball—plenty of champagne is in evidence. Behind the table stand a couple of men servants and half a dozen maids ready to wait on the guests when they arrive. Frith is superintending the final touches to the preparations.

FRANK (*approaching Frith*). Everything under control, Frith?

FRITH (*surveying Frank with a fatherly air*). Yes, sir. Thank you. (*Pause*) Excuse me, sir, are you supposed to be a schoolmaster?

FRANK. Oh no—this is just my old cap and gown.

FRITH. Certainly makes a very nice costume, sir—and economical, too.

FRANK (*turning away*). Yes, that was the idea.

We then see the ENTRY HALL, a servant crossing to the door, following which MAXIM appears descending the broad staircase, ready to receive his guests.

As the servant, Robert, opens the door the fog outside is seen for a moment. Giles and Beatrice enter, Giles wearing bowler hat and overcoat over his fancy dress; and Beatrice in a long coat with a handkerchief tied over her head-dress.

GILES (*as he divests himself of his coat*).

'Evening, Robert. Not very good weather for the Ball.

ROBERT. No, sir.

GILES. Very misty on the way.

By this time his coat is off, revealing him dressed in faded white tights with long sleeves and a high neck. Over the tights is an imitation tiger skin. Topping all this for a moment he still retains his bowler hat, as he speaks.

GILES. Very chilly, too.

Beatrice is divesting herself of her handkerchief—and remains in her coat. Long, blonde braids hang down her back.

BEATRICE. Oh, this wig's so tight—they ought to have sent an aspirin with it.

By this time Maxim has joined the two at the door. He surveys them both, particularly Giles, with an amused smile.

MAXIM. Hello.

BEATRICE (*moaning on account of her tight wig*). Oh-h-h—

MAXIM. What's the idea? Adam and Eve?

BEATRICE. Oh, Maxim, don't be disgusting.

GILES. Strong man, old boy. (*Suddenly recollecting something, he turns to Beatrice.*) Where's my weight thing?

MAXIM. What thing?

BEATRICE. You haven't left it in the car, have you?

At this moment their chauffeur appears, carrying a large pair of imitation spherical weights, joined by a painted wooden bar. The way he holds it shows that it has no weight at all.

GILES. Oh, no—there it is.

BEATRICE. Are you the first one down? Where's the child?

MAXIM. She's keeping her costume a great secret, wouldn't even let me into her room.

BEATRICE (*leaving*). Oh, lovely. I'll go up and give her a hand.

The view moves with Giles and Maxim as they go to join Frank in the hall.

GILES. I could do with a drink, huh?

MAXIM (*indicating Giles' costume*). Won't you catch cold, in that thing?

GILES (*taking him seriously*). Don't be silly! (*Fingering his tights*) Pure wool, old boy.

Robert enters the picture carrying the weights.

ROBERT. Pardon me, sir, you forgot this.

GILES. Oh, thank you.

As Robert hands it to Giles it drops out of Giles' hands and bounces on the floor.

The CORRIDOR with BEATRICE: Outside the door of "I's" room, Beatrice is knocking. She starts to turn the handle.

BEATRICE. Here I am, dear—it's Bee. I've come to give you a hand. (*She is obviously dying of curiosity to see "I's" costume.*)

"I" (*calling from inside*). Oh, please don't come in, Beatrice. I don't want anyone to see my costume.

BEATRICE (*she looks a little nonplussed*). Oh, well, you won't be long, will you? Because the—the first people will be arriving any moment. (*She moves away from the door.*)

"I's" BEDROOM with CLARICE seen close, a very young maid, who is kneeling on the floor putting finishing touches to the wide skirt of "I's" fancy dress.

"I's" VOICE. Now, you're sure that's where that should be?

CLARICE. *Yes*, Madam. It's *just* right.

The view moves up from Clarice to reveal "I", dressed in a copy of the striking costume of the painting of Caroline de Winter. She is admiring herself in the mirror, turning her shoulders this way and that.

"I". Oh, isn't it exciting!

CLARICE. Indeed it is, Madam. I've always heard of the Manderley Ball—and now I'm really going to see one. I'm sure there'll be no one there to touch you, Madam!

"I". Do you think so? Now—now, where's my fan?

While Clarice fetches the fan, "I" has a last, loving look at herself, then she takes the fan.

"I". You're sure I look all right?

CLARICE (*reverently*). You look ever so beautiful.

"I". Well, here goes!

She starts toward the door, Clarice darting ahead of her to open it.

The CORRIDOR: The door of "I's" room opens and she emerges. As she comes along the corridor, she pats her hair and fusses with parts of her dress. Her pace increases until she comes opposite the picture. She pulls up for a moment to compare herself with the original. Almost preening herself she adopts the pose of the picture and changing her pace to a dignified one, she starts to move toward the staircase.

Seen from her viewpoint, there now appears a group consisting of Frank, Giles, Beatrice, and Maxim—their backs to her. They are all laughing and talking together. "I's" expression (she is now seen quite close) shows she can hardly contain her excitement at the thought of surprising Maxim. With a light step she starts to descend the stairs. When she reaches the bottom she pauses; she catches her breath—this is going to be her big moment.

Now we see the same group as before— Maxim laughing heartily at some joke—his back still turned. "I" starts to move forward toward them across the floor. The view then moves forward closer and closer toward the group until it has Maxim's back only—then it stops and we hear "I's" voice:

"I's" VOICE. Good evening, Mr. de Winter.

Maxim turns—still laughing and changing to a smile of anticipation on hearing her voice. Slowly the smile begins to fade from his face and he eyes her up and down. A look of deep anger takes its place.

"I" (seen in a close-up): Her expression changes from the excited smile to one of crushed bewilderment. Maxim takes half a step toward her—and speaks fiercely.

MAXIM. What the devil do you think you're doing?

Beatrice's hand flies to her mouth as though she would suppress her own cry of:

BEATRICE. Rebecca . . . oh . . .

"I" is seen gazing with petrified eyes at Maxim; she gestures weakly.

"I". But—it's the picture—the one in the gallery.

Maxim does not reply—he stands, facing her like stone.

"I" (*desperately*). What is it? What have I done?

Maxim takes one step toward her and speaks in an icy tone.

MAXIM. Go and take it off! It doesn't matter what you put on . . . anything will do.

"I" stands motionless—unable to believe what she has heard Maxim say. As Maxim speaks his next words—his voice is louder and harsher:

MAXIM. What are you standing there for —didn't you hear what I said?

"I" looks about her desperately—then suddenly she turns and dashes toward the stairs. Maxim takes a step forward as if he might follow her, but at this moment Robert announces in a loud voice:

ROBERT. Sir George and Lady Moore. (*And then*) Dudley Tennant— (*Again*) Admiral and Lady Burbank, etc., etc.

The first guests are arriving—a flock of about eight. We hear their laughing chatter. Maxim is forced to turn and play the part of host.

"I" is seen reaching the top steps of the stairs. She takes a quick look in the direction of the portrait and then looks about a bit wildly, not knowing what has gone wrong. She sees Mrs. Danvers entering Rebecca's room; and instead of going to her own room, "I" hurries off to the West Wing, losing her hat on the stairs. We follow her until she reaches the door of Rebecca's room—it is just closing. She hurries to it and then, bracing herself with courage, pushes the door open and goes in.

REBECCA'S ROOM: "I" comes into the foreground. Mrs. Danvers, halfway across the room, speaks first:

MRS. DANVERS. I watched you go down—just as I watched her a year ago. Even in the same dress you couldn't compare.

"I" takes a step nearer to her—she looks down at the dress, then back at Mrs. Danvers, speaking almost in a whisper:

"I". You knew it! You knew that she wore it and yet you deliberately suggested *I* wear it! (*With great intensity, following Mrs. Danvers*) Why do you hate me? What have I done to you that you should hate me so?

MRS. DANVERS. You tried to take her place. You let him marry you. (*Tensely*) I've seen his face, his eyes—they're the same as those first weeks after she died. I used to listen to him—walking up and down, up and down, all night long, night after night. Thinking of her—suffering torture, because he'd lost her.

"I" starts to back away toward the bed, staring at Mrs. Danvers with increasing agony. At the climax of Mrs. Danvers' outburst, "I" cries out:

"I". I don't want to know—I don't want to know.

MRS. DANVERS (*following her*). You thought you could be Mrs. de Winter—live in her house—walk in her steps—take the things that were hers. But she's too strong for you. *You* can't fight her. No one ever got the better of her—never, never. She was beaten in the end. But it wasn't a man—it wasn't a woman—it was the sea!

"I" (*unable to bear any more*). Stop it, stop it—oh, stop it! (*She throws herself on the bed, breaking into convulsive sobs*).

MRS. DANVERS (in a close view) stands looking down at the sobbing figure. A new thought comes into her face. She glances round toward the window, opens it, then turning back again to the bed, she speaks with uncanny calmness.

MRS. DANVERS. You're overwrought, Madam. I've opened a window for you. A little air will do you good.

She keeps her eyes on the girl as the scene pulls back to "I", who raises herself from her lying position. Half way up she stares down where her head has been resting. It is the pale grey nightdress case with the black initial "R". She gazes at it in horror.

Mrs. Danvers, seen in a close-up, standing by the open window looking over to the bed, realizes what "I" is staring at. Then "I" slowly backs away from the pillow—off the bed—and moves across toward the window, gasping for breath. Now the scene draws in to a close view of the two at the window. "I" stands at one side of the window and Mrs. Danvers at the other.

MRS. DANVERS (*starting to speak in a low tone*). Why don't you go? . . . Why don't you leave Manderley? (*She leans across until her face is close to "I's".*) He doesn't need you. He's got his memories.

From "I's" viewpoint—we now see the swirling mist—thick enough to avoid showing the actual depth to the ground. Over this, we hear Mrs. Danvers' voice:

MRS. DANVERS' VOICE (*softly, quietly*). He doesn't love you—he wants to be alone again with *her*.

"I's" face (in a close-up) is looking down to the depth below. Mrs. Danvers half whispers into her ear.

MRS. DANVERS (*almost a whisper, insistently*). You've nothing to stay for. You've nothing to live for, really, have you. (*Still insistent*) Look down there. It's easy, isn't it.

"I's" face is more terrified—Mrs. Danvers is half behind her.

MRS. DANVERS. Why don't you? . . .

"I" stares out, hypnotized, then slowly looks down again. In her eyes we see the growing thought of self-destruction.

MRS. DANVERS (*egging her on*). Why don't you? Go on . . . go on . . . Don't be afraid! . . .

We see "I's" head with Mrs. Danvers in the background; then, from "I's" angle, looking down again—the swirling mist. Suddenly the silence and the mist are shattered by an explosion. We hear and see it at the same time. Then another, accented by the strident wailing of a siren; then a third.

"I" stands, frightened and mystified—Mrs. Danvers, startled. From below comes the sound of doors being opened. MANDERLEY, as seen from above, comes to view, the running figures of the guests emerging from the front and side doors of the house. They are hardly discernible in the mist, but we hear their voices:

AD LIBS. Shipwreck! . . . Ship on the rocks. . . . It's a ship aground, sending up rockets . . . Shipwreck! Come on everybody—down to the bay! Notify the coastguard. . . . She's aground!

We see Maxim in the scene and a servant comes up to him and throws a coat over his shoulders.

MRS. DANVERS AND "I"—AT THE WINDOW:

"I" (*frantic*). Maxim! Maxim!

VOICES. Ship's aground . . . come on! Come on, everybody! Come on—come on!

Maxim runs off into the mist. And this is followed by a view of MRS. DANVERS AND "I" AT THE WINDOW:

"I" (*calling*). Maxim! Maxim!

The scene starts to move in closer as "I" turns from the window and looks frantically at Mrs. Danvers, then back down into the fog, then back again at Mrs. Danvers. Then she wheels suddenly and runs past Mrs. Danvers and out of the room—the scene moving to a close-up of Mrs. Danvers' face staring out impassively.

The previous scene dissolves to a CLOCK which indicates the passing of time, and then dissolves to the COVE: In the dim half-light of dawn with shafts of sunlight just beginning to penetrate the blanket of fog, we can vaguely discern the outline of rocks. We hear the pounding of the surf. Vague figures, clad for the most part in oilskins, loom out of the mist. "I" appears scrambling down over the rocks. She meets Ben.

"I". Oh, Ben, have you seen Mr. de Winter anywhere?

BEN (*almost overcome with fright and apprehension*). She won't come back, will she? (*Anxious to be reassured*) You said so.

"I" (*startled at his strange words*). Who, Ben? Who do you mean?

BEN. Uh—the other one.

She is now tense with fright—too frightened to shudder or to answer. She sees Ben gaze toward the shore and looks around in desperation, anxious to get away. She hastens out of the scene.

We next see her climbing over rocks in a background of mist which dissolves to WAVES BREAKING ON THE BEACH, which in turn dissolve to "I" walking through the mist. Frank approaches her and the view draws in to provide a fairly close view of her and Frank.

"I". Oh, Frank, have you seen Maxim anywhere?

FRANK. Not since about half an hour ago. I thought he'd gone back to the house.

"I". No, he hasn't been in the house at all, and I'm afraid something might have happened to him.

There is a moment's silence as she looks curiously at Frank and he shifts a little uncomfortably under her gaze.

"I". Frank, what's the matter? Is anything wrong? You look terribly worried. There *is* something wrong.

FRANK. Well— (*Then, facing it*) The diver who went down to inspect the bottom of the ship came across the hull of another boat—a little sail boat . . .

We see the dawning horror in her eyes as she begins to suspect the truth.

"I". Frank—is it . . . ?

FRANK (*looking her in the eyes*). Yes . . . it's Rebecca's.

She digests this in silence for a moment, then speaks quietly:

"I". How did they recognize it?

FRANK. He's a local man—knew it instantly.

She wants to disbelieve what she has just heard, but her immediate thought is concern for Maxim.

"I". It'll be so hard on poor Maxim . . .

FRANK. Yes. It's going to bring it all back again and worse than before.

"I". Why did they have to find it? Why couldn't they have left it there in peace—at the bottom of the sea?

FRANK (*after a moment, embarrassed*). Well, I'd better get along and arrange some breakfast for the men.

"I". All right, Frank, I'll look for Maxim.

Frank goes off, leaving her standing indecisively for a second. We can still hear shouts from the men helping to raise the boat, and the noise of the waves. She starts to walk hesitantly in the direction from which the shouts come. She scrambles over the rocks and into the cove where the boathouse is.

The BOATHOUSE COVE: She looks across to the cottage. In her face appears the recollection of everything the cottage means to her. Suddenly her attention is arrested as she sees:

The COTTAGE IN A MIST: A lamp is alight in the window of the cottage, and firelight throws flickering shadows on the window pane.

Thereupon we see her determinedly but nervously hurrying toward the cottage and opening the door.

The COTTAGE (viewed over "I's" shoulder in the doorway): She is confronted by the figure of Maxim, sitting, gazing off into space.

MAXIM (*without moving*). Hello—

"I" advances toward him (the view bringing them together), extremely worried. Maxim is still in evening dress. His tails are stained with sea-water, and generally he has a dishevelled look; but it is more than that—he has the air of a man who has come to the end of his tether.

"I" (*as she gets near him*). Maxim—you haven't had any sleep. (*After a moment; tenderly*) Have you forgiven me?

MAXIM (*He comes out of his mood, looks at her fondly*). Forgiven you? What have I got to forgive you for?

"I". For last night—my stupidity about the costume.

MAXIM. Oh, that! I'd forgotten. I was angry with you, wasn't I?

"I" (*shyly*). Yes. (*There is a moment's silence. She looks at him pleadingly.*) Maxim, can't we start all over again? I don't ask that you should love me . . . I won't ask impossible things. I'll be your friend and companion . . . I'll be happy with that.

He rises, goes to her, pulls her to him very closely, his behaviour strangely tense. He looks at her strangely, takes her face between his hands and looks at her, tortured.

MAXIM. You love me very much, don't you? (*Dropping his hands from her shoulders*) But it's too late, my darling. . . . We've lost our little chance of happiness.

"I" (*frantically*). No, Maxim, no!

MAXIM. It's all over now. The thing's happened—the thing I've dreaded day after day, night after night.

The scene moves with them as they walk across the room. Maxim seats himself, and she comes to him and kneels in front of him.

"I". Maxim, what're you trying to tell me?

MAXIM. Rebecca has won.

She looks at him, her worst fears realized: that he still loves Rebecca. After a moment, he speaks again.

MAXIM. Her shadow has been between us all the time—keeping us from one another. She knew that this would happen.

"I" (*gazing at him, speaking in stifled voice*). What are you saying?

MAXIM. They sent a diver down. He found another boat—

"I" (*interrupting, comfortingly, but somewhat relieved*). Yes, I know. Frank told me. Rebecca's boat. It's terrible for you. I'm so sorry.

MAXIM. The diver made another discovery. He broke one of the ports and looked into the cabin. There was a body in there.

She reacts sharply to this, bewildered at the tone of utter fatality with which Maxim speaks.

"I". Then she wasn't alone. There was someone sailing with her and you have to find out who it was—that's it, isn't it, Maxim?

MAXIM. You don't understand. There was no one with her. (*A moment's pause while she looks at him*) It's Rebecca's body lying there on the cabin floor.

"I". No! No!

MAXIM. The woman that was washed up at Edgecombe—the woman that is now buried in the family crypt—that was not Rebecca. That was the body of some unknown woman, unclaimed, belonging nowhere. I identified it, but I knew it wasn't Rebecca. It was all a lie. *I* knew where Rebecca's body was! Lying on that cabin floor, on the bottom of the sea.

"I" (*terrified*). How did you know, Maxim?

MAXIM. Because—(*looking at her*) *I* put it there!

There is a tense pause.

MAXIM (*bitterly*). Would you look into my eyes and tell me that you love me now?

She cannot believe what she has heard. Involuntarily she draws a little apart from him, rises, and goes out of view for the moment. Maxim sees she is stunned, overwhelmed, horrified by what he has told her. He rises and walks away.

As he does so, the scene moves up to a close-up of "I", and then we see MAXIM at close range:

MAXIM (*standing before fireplace, back to camera*). You see, I was right. It's too late.

"I" comes into the scene toward Maxim, her heart jumping in quickened, sudden panic. Maxim turns toward her and takes her in his arms.

"I". No, it's not too late! (*She puts her arms around him.*) You're not to say that! I love you more than anything in the world. . . . Please, Maxim, kiss me, please!

MAXIM. No. It's no use. It's too late.

"I". We can't lose each other now! We must be together—always! With no secrets, no shadows . . .

MAXIM. We may only have a few hours, a few days.

"I" (*pleadingly*). Maxim, why didn't you tell me before?

MAXIM. I nearly did sometimes, but you never seemed close enough.

"I" (*she pulls away, looks at him*). How could we be close when I knew you were always thinking of Rebecca? How could I even ask you to love me when I knew you loved Rebecca still?

MAXIM. What are you talking about? What do you mean?

"I". Whenever you touched me I knew you were comparing me to Rebecca. Whenever you looked at me, spoke to me, or walked with me in the garden, I knew you were thinking, "This I did with Rebecca—and this—and this . . . "

Maxim stares at her, bewildered, amazed, then turns slightly away.

"I" (*taking a step toward him*). Oh, it's true, isn't it?

MAXIM (*amazed*). You thought I loved Rebecca? You thought that? *I hated* her!

"I" (seen in a close-up) is incredulous—with the dawning realization that all this time she has been mistaken in thinking Maxim was in love with Rebecca. The view moves with Maxim as he talks . . . speaking in an almost quiet, reflective voice.

MAXIM. Oh, I was carried away by her—
enchanted by her, as everyone was. And
when I was married, I was told I was
the luckiest man in the world. She was
so lovely—so accomplished—so amusing.
"She's got the three things that really
matter in a wife," everyone said—"breeding, brains and beauty." And I believed
them—completely. But I never had a
moment's happiness with her. (*With a
bitter little laugh*) She was incapable of
love, or tenderness, or decency.

There is exultation in "I's" face as she looks
at him.

"I" (*seen fairly close; almost to herself*).
You didn't love her? You didn't love
her . . .

The scene moves with MAXIM as he still
paces. He lights a cigarette and puffs on it
spasmodically as he continues to talk.

MAXIM. Do you remember that cliff
where you first saw me in Monte Carlo?
Well, I went there with Rebecca on our
honeymoon. That was where I found out
about her—four days after we were married. She stood there laughing, her black
hair blowing in the wind, and told me
all about herself—everything. (*Bitterly;
tensely*) Things I'll never tell a living
soul. I wanted to kill her. It would have
been so easy. Remember the precipice?
I frightened you, didn't I? You thought
I was mad. Perhaps I was. Perhaps I
am mad. It wouldn't make for sanity,
would it—living with the devil?

He comes to a halt and swings around to
her. She looks up at him with deep compassion, as he continues, in desperate self-
accusation.

MAXIM. "I'll make a bargain with you,"
she said. "You'd look rather foolish trying to divorce me now after four days of
marriage, so I'll play the part of a devoted wife, mistress of your precious
Manderley. I'll make it the most famous
show place in England, if you like—and
people will visit us and envy us and say
we're the luckiest, happiest couple in the
country. What a grand joke it will be
—what a triumph" (*Walking to end of
the couch and looking out the window.*)
I should never have accepted her dirty
bargain, but I did. I was younger then

and tremendously conscious of the family
honor. (*He utters a short, bitter laugh.*)
Family honor! And she knew that I'd
sacrifice everything rather than stand up
in a divorce court and give her away,
admit that our marriage was a rotten
fraud. (*Looking at her searchingly*) You
despise me, don't you—as I despise myself. You can't understand what my feelings were, can you?

"I" (*seen closer; with infinite tenderness*). Of course I can, darling. Of
course I can.

MAXIM (*as the scene moves with him*).
Well, I kept the bargain—and so did
she apparently. Oh, she played the game
brilliantly. (*He sits on the end of the
couch.*) But after a while, she began to
grow careless. She took a flat in London
and she'd stay away for days at a time.
Then she started to bring her friends
down here. I warned her, but she shrug-
ged her shoulders: "What's it got to do
with you?" she said. She even started
on Frank—poor, faithful Frank. (*After
a pause*) Then there was a cousin of
hers—a man named Favell.

"I" (*seen close*). Yes, I know him. He
came the day you went to London.

MAXIM (*sitting on couch*). Why didn't
you tell me?

"I" (*seen close*). I didn't like to. I
thought it would remind you of Rebecca.

MAXIM (*rising*). Remind me! As if I
needed reminding! (*The view moves
with him as he crosses in front of her.*)
Favell used to visit her here in this cottage. I found out about it and I warned
her that if he came here again I'd shoot
them both. (*Facing her*) One night when
I found that she'd come back quietly
from London, I thought that Favell was
with her—and I knew then that I
couldn't stand this life of filth and deceit
any longer. I decided to come down here
and have it out with both of them. But
she was alone. She was expecting Favell,
but he hadn't come. She was lying on the
divan—a large tray of cigarette stubs
beside her.

The view moves over to the divan, showing

the tea table and a portion of the divan with a tray of cigarette stubs on it as his voice comes over.

MAXIM'S VOICE. She looked ill—queer. Suddenly she got up—started to walk toward me.

The scene tilts up and moves around the room to the door, then to a fairly close view of Maxim standing with his back to the door.

MAXIM. "When I have a child," she said, "neither you nor anyone else could ever prove it wasn't yours. You'd like to have an heir, wouldn't you, Max, for your precious Manderley?" And then she started to laugh. "How funny, how supremely, wonderfully funny! I'll be the perfect mother just as I've been the perfect wife, and no one will ever know. It ought to give you the thrill of your life, Max, to watch my son grow bigger day by day and to know that when you die, Manderley will be his." (*His voice has sunk to a hoarse whisper.*) She was face to face with me—one hand in her pocket, the other holding a cigarette. She was smiling, "Well, Max, what're you going to do about it? Aren't you going to kill me?" I suppose I went mad for a moment—I must have struck her. She stood staring at me.

The view moves down to the floor, indicating the place where Rebecca had stood.

MAXIM'S VOICE. She looked almost triumphant—and then she started toward me again, smiling. Suddenly she stumbled and fell.

The scene moves over to take in the ship's tackle on the floor.

MAXIM'S VOICE. When I looked down—ages afterwards it seemed—she was lying on the floor. She'd struck her head on a heavy piece of ship's tackle. I remember wondering why she was still smiling—and then I realized she was dead.

"I" (*seen fairly close*). But you didn't kill her—it was an accident!

MAXIM is standing in the center of the room, having backed away in horror from the spot where Rebecca had fallen.

MAXIM. Who would believe me? I lost my head. I just knew I had to do something—anything. (*We follow him to the window where he continues talking, his back turned.*) I carried her out to the boat. It was very dark. There was no moon. I put her in the cabin. When the boat seemed a safe distance from the shore, I took a spike and drove it again and again through the planking of the hull. I opened up the seacocks and the water began to come in fast. I climbed over into the dinghy and pulled away. I saw the boat heel over and sink. I pulled back into the cove—it started raining.

"I" (*coming to him*). Maxim, does anyone else know of this?

MAXIM. No, no one—except you and me.

"I" (*walking away from Maxim*). We must explain it. It's got to be the body of someone you've never seen before.

MAXIM. No, they're bound to know her—her rings and bracelets—she always wore them—they'll identify her body—then they'll remember the other woman—the other woman buried in the crypt.

"I" turns and comes back to Maxim, and embraces him.

"I" (*intelligent, mature, taking command of the situation*). If they find out it was Rebecca you must simply say that you made a mistake about the other body—that the day you went to Edgecombe you were ill, you didn't know what you were doing. Rebecca's dead, that's what we've got to remember! Rebecca's dead. She can't speak—she can't bear witness. She can't harm you any more. We're the only two people in the world that know, Maxim—you and I.

MAXIM (*taking tight hold of her arms; desperately*). I told you once that I'd done a very selfish thing in marrying you. You can understand now what I meant. I've loved you, my darling—I shall always love you—but I've known all along that Rebecca would win in the end.

"I" (*putting her arms round him as if to shield him from everything: almost triumphantly she exclaims*) No—no! She hasn't won. No matter what happens now, she hasn't won!

Suddenly the telephone rings, startling the two. The view moves to the phone, covered with dust, on the table. Maxim comes to the phone, and we see his hand pick up the receiver, as the scene tilts up to Maxim with the receiver to his ear.

MAXIM. Hello—hel—oh—hello, Frank. Yes. Who? Colonel Julyan?

The view draws back, bringing "I" into the scene.

MAXIM. Yes, tell him I'll meet him there as soon as I possibly can. What? Oh, well, say we could talk about that when we're sure about the matter. Yes— (*He puts down the receiver.*)

"I" (*coming to him*). What's happened?

MAXIM. Colonel Julyan called—he's the Chief Constable of the County. He's been asked by the police to go to the mortuary. He wants to know if I could possibly have made a mistake about that other body.

The two of them stand looking at each other, the girl terrified as to what this may mean. Maxim puts his arms around her as the scene dissolves to the MORTUARY, lamp-illuminated, where a group of men including Maxim with his back turned, Colonel Julyan and Frank Crawley, are standing looking down at something not visible in the scene. They turn and come forward.

The THREE MEN: The scene draws back with them to the top of the stairway, through a door, across the corridor, up the stairs and to the exterior. The scene moves with them.

MAXIM (*as they walk*). Well, Colonel Julyan, apparently I did make a mistake about that other body.

FRANK (*leaping in; to Maxim*). The mistake was quite natural under the circumstances. Beside, you weren't well at the time.

MAXIM. That's nonsense! I was perfectly well.

Frank is disappointed at Maxim's refusal to let him help, and looks nervously at Julyan.

JULYAN. Well, don't let it worry you, Maxim. Nobody can blame you for making a mistake. The pity is you've got to go through the same thing all over again.

FRANK. What do you mean?

JULYAN. Oh, there'll have to be another inquest, of course. The same formality and red tape.

FRANK. Oh.

JULYAN (*to Maxim*). I wish you could be spared the publicity of it, but I'm afraid that's impossible.

MAXIM. Oh yes—the publicity!

There is a moment's silence.

JULYAN (*thoughtfully*). I suppose Mrs. de Winter went below for something and a squall caught the boat with nobody at the helm . . . and I imagine that's about the solution of it, don't you think, Crawley?

FRANK (*disguising his eagerness*). Probably the door jammed, and she couldn't get on deck again.

JULYAN (*agreeing*). Yes. Tabb, the boat builder, will undoubtedly come to some such conclusion.

FRANK. Why, what would he know about it?

JULYAN. Oh, he's examining the boat now. Purely as a matter of routine, you know. (*Turning to Maxim*) I'll be at the inquest tomorrow, Maxim. Quite unofficially, you know. We must get together for a game of golf as soon as it's all over, eh? (*Shakes Maxim's hand.*)

MAXIM (*distractedly*). Yes, Colonel Julyan. Good-bye.

As Julyan leaves, the view moves up to Maxim and Frank as Maxim walks distractedly off, Frank, at his side, looking nervously at him out of the corner of his eye. The scene fades out.

PART FIVE

A long vista of MANDERLEY fades in and dissolves to the HALL AT MANDERLEY at night. "I" comes down the stairs, simply attired. As the scene progresses it is apparent that she is self-assured, uninhibited, the mistress of Manderley and Maxim's wife at last. As the scene opens, Frith is approaching from another direction, two or three newspapers in his hand. And as Frith approaches her, the scene moves to provide a close view of both of them.

FRITH (*very sympathetic and respectful*). I have the evening papers, Madam. Would you care to see them?

"I". Oh no, thank you, Frith. And I prefer that Mr. de Winter weren't troubled with them, either.

FRITH. I understand, Madam. Permit me to say that we're all most distressed outside.

"I". Thank you, Frith.

FRITH. I'm afraid the news has been a great shock to Mrs. Danvers.

"I". Yes, I rather expected it would be.

FRITH (*hesitantly*). It seems there's to be a coroner's inquest, Madam?

"I". Yes, Frith. It's purely a formality.

FRITH (*still hesitantly, realizing the significance of his own words, and speaking embarrassedly, but trying pitifully and touchingly to be of help*). Of course, Madam. I wanted to say that if any of us might be required to give evidence, I should be only too pleased to do anything that might help the family.

"I" (*touched*). Oh, thank you, Frith. I'm sure Mr. de Winter will be happy to hear that. But I don't think anything will be necessary.

She gives him a kindly look and walks off as he bows slightly. Then she strolls into the library.

The LIBRARY: Maxim is standing at the fireplace, his back to the door, smoking moodily. He turns as the girl comes in and affects cheeriness.

"I". Maxim.

MAXIM (*tenderly*). Hello, darling.

"I". Oh, Maxim, I'm worried about what you'll do at the inquest tomorrow.

MAXIM. What do you mean?

"I". You won't lose your temper, will you? Promise me that they won't make you angry.

MAXIM (*after a moment*). All right, darling . . . I promise.

"I". No matter what he asks you, you won't lose your head?

MAXIM. Don't worry, dear.

"I" (*worried*). They—can't do anything at once, can they?

MAXIM. No.

"I". Then we've a little time left to be together?

MAXIM. Yes.

"I". I want to go to the inquest with you.

MAXIM. I'd rather you didn't, darling.

"I". But I can't wait here . . . alone . . . I promise you I won't be any trouble to you . . . and I must be near you so that no matter what happens we won't be separated for a moment.

MAXIM. All right, dear. (*Suddenly his mood changes and he becomes savage.*) I don't mind this whole thing—except for you. I can't forget what it's done to you. I've been thinking of nothing else since it happened. . . . (*He lifts her chin and looks her in the face.*) Ah-h—it's gone forever . . . that funny, young, lost look I loved. It won't ever come back. I killed that when I told you about Rebecca. It's gone . . . in a few hours. . . . You've grown so much older.

"I" (*looking up at him, speaking quietly*). Maxim . . . Maxim . . .

He takes her in his arms and crushes her to him; and they kiss "feverishly, desperately, like guilty lovers who have not kissed before . . ." like people who may never kiss again. During this, the scene draws back as far as possible until it reveals their silhouetted figures against the firelight in the great fireplace, and then after a moment, during which the tableau stands still, the scene dissolves to a sign above a door, which reads:

KERRITH

BOARD SCHOOL

1872

Then the scene moves down to a policeman standing in front of the door.

POLICEMAN. Black Jack Brady was his name—the most important arrest I ever made.

The view draws back to reveal a group of people, their backs turned to us, listening to him.

POLICEMAN. It must have been about two years ago, now. Of course, there was no doubt about it—he was hung a month after I caught him. . . . Hullo—wait a minute. (*He turns and peeks through door.*) They've got old Balmy Ben up now.

The CORONER'S COURT, at first disclosing Ben, who is standing in the courtroom being questioned by the coroner.

CORONER'S VOICE. You remember the late Mrs. de Winter, don't you?

BEN. She's gone.

CORONER'S VOICE (*slightly impatient*). Yes—we know that.

BEN. She went into the sea. The sea got her.

During the coroner's next question the view draws back to reveal the courtroom. The coroner is at Ben's side, seated alone at a table. Colonel Julyan sits to his left, and Maxim sits to the left and facing Julyan. In the first row of the crowd of spectators sits "I". Frank sits beside her, and they are listening tensely. Mrs. Danvers sits behind them, with Favell appearing off to one side.

CORONER. That's right. That's right. Now —we want you to tell us whether you were on the shore—

The view moves to Frank, "I", and Mrs. Danvers.

CORONER'S VOICE. —that last night she went sailing.

BEN (*seen along with the other people, including the coroner*). Eh?

CORONER (*repeating patiently*). *Were you on the shore* that last night she went out? When she didn't come back?

Ben's bleary gaze travels round the room. He is obviously scared.

BEN. I didn't see nothing. I don't want to go to the asylum! Them're cruel folks there.

CORONER. Now—now—nobody's going to send you to the asylum. All we want you to do is to tell us what you saw.

BEN. I didn't see nothin'!

CORONER. Come, come, did you see Mrs. de Winter get into her boat that last night?

BEN. I don't know nuthin'. I don't want to go to the asylum.

The coroner looks at Julyan, who nods and shrugs. They have abandoned hope of getting anything from Ben.

CORONER. Very well. You may go.

BEN. Eh?

CORONER. You may go now.

FAVELL now turns and looks forward and waves to someone not seen in the scene.

CORONER'S VOICE. Mr. Tabb.

MRS. DANVERS is now seen looking off toward Favell with a faint smile.

CORONER'S VOICE. Would you step forward, please?

We see the CORONER, MR. TABB, AND BAILIFF. Mr. Tabb is being sworn in.

CORONER. The late Mrs. de Winter used to send her boat to your shipyard for reconditioning?

TABB. That's right, sir.

CORONER. Can you remember any occasion when she had any sort of an accident with the boat?

TABB. No, sir. I often said Mrs. de Winter was a born sailor.

MR. TABB is now seen in "a medium close-up."

CORONER'S VOICE. Now when Mrs. de Winter went below, as is supposed, and a sudden gust of wind came down, that would be enough to capsize the boat, wouldn't it?

TABB. Excuse me, sir, but there's a little more to it than that.

CORONER'S VOICE. What do you mean, Mr. Tabb?

TABB. I mean, sir, the sea-cocks.

We get a glimpse of MAXIM, then a close-up of "I", who realizes that things are starting to go wrong; then the CORONER AND MR. TABB:

CORONER. What are the sea-cocks?

TABB. Sea-cocks—oh, the sea-cocks are the valves to drain out the boat and they're always kept tight closed when you're afloat.

CORONER. Yes?

MR. TABB appears now in a close-up.

TABB (*importantly*). Well, yesterday when I examined that boat I found they'd been opened. (*There is a little murmur from the crowd.*)

We see FRANK, "I", AND MRS. DANVERS, "I" looking toward Maxim, apprehensively; then Maxim looking back at her and giving her a faint smile, impervious to her look of sympathy and appeal.

Then MR. TABB again appears at fairly close range as the coroner continues his questioning.

CORONER'S VOICE. Well, what could have been the reason for that?

TABB. Just this. That's what flooded the boat and sunk her. (*A louder murmur of surprise from the crowd follows this statement.*)

FAVELL, now seen at fairly close range,

realizes something unexpected is happening and begins to do a little fast thinking.

The CORONER AND MR. TABB:

CORONER (*gravely*). Are you implying—?

TABB (*unhappy*). That boat never capsized at all. I know it's a terrible thing to say, sir, but in my opinion she was scuttled. (*With great deliberation*) And —there's them 'oles.

CORONER. What holes?

TABB. In 'er planking.

CORONER. What are you talking about?

TABB. Of course—the boat's been under water for over a year, and the tide's been knocking her against the ridge. But it seems to me them 'oles looked as if she'd made 'em from the *inside*—

"I" steels herself into a sort of rigidity.

CORONER'S VOICE. Then you believe she must have done it deliberately?

We see MAXIM: His face is almost mask-like in his effort to retain an outward show of imperturbability. The hub-bub of excitement from the crowd has grown louder.

The CORONER AND MR. TABB:

TABB. It couldn't have been no accident— not with her knowledge of boats.

Still more excitement from the crowd, and the view moves with the coroner as he leans over to Colonel Julyan.

CORONER. You knew the former Mrs. de Winter very well, I believe?

JULYAN. Oh, yes.

CORONER. Would you have believed her capable of suicide?

JULYAN. No, frankly, I would not. But you never can tell.

The CORONER AND MR. TABB:

CORONER. You may stand down, Mr. Tabb. Mr. de Winter, please.

Mr. Tabb leaves the witness stand, and Maxim walks into the scene to take his place.

CORONER. I'm sorry to drag you back for further questioning, Mr. de Winter, but you've heard the statement of Mr. Tabb. I wonder if you can help us in any way?

MAXIM (*shortly*). I'm afraid not.

CORONER. Can you think of any reason why there should be holes in the planking of the late Mrs. de Winter's boat?

MAXIM (*curtly*). Well, of course, I can't think of any reason.

CORONER. Has anyone ever discussed these holes with you before?

MAXIM. Well, since the boat has been at the bottom of the ocean, I scarcely think that likely.

We hear a little ripple of laughter in the courtroom, and the coroner is annoyed.

CORONER. Mr. de Winter, I want you to believe we all feel very deeply for you in this matter, but you must remember that I don't conduct this inquiry for my own amusement.

MAXIM (*with thinly veiled sarcasm*). That's rather obvious, isn't it?

CORONER. I hope that it is.

"I"—seen in a close-up—wants to protest as she sees Maxim becoming angry.

The CORONER AND MAXIM, both seen fairly close:

CORONER. Then, since Mrs. de Winter went sailing alone, are we to believe that she drove those holes herself?

MAXIM. You may believe whatever you like.

CORONER. Can you enlighten us as to why Mrs. de Winter should have wanted to end her own life?

MAXIM (*irritated*). I know of no reason whatever.

"I"—seen in a close-up—is becoming more and more upset.

CORONER (*now seen in a close-up; looking at Maxim*). Mr. de Winter, however painful it may be, I have to ask you a very personal question. Were relations between you and the late Mrs. de Winter perfectly happy?

"I"—again seen in a close-up—looks as if she were going to be ill as she hears this.

The coroner's voice beating at him, MAXIM (seen in a close-up) looks as if he can't stand another minute of this.

CORONER'S VOICE. Were relations between you and the late Mrs. de Winter perfectly happy?

MAXIM (*furiously*). I won't stand this any longer!

"I" (in a close-up) looks as if she were going to faint.

MAXIM'S VOICE. And you might as well know now . . .

"I" faints and starts to fall to the floor. Frank tries to catch her, and we see Maxim run to her. He helps her up with the aid of Frank.

COLONEL JULYAN AND THE CORONER are seen conferring.

CORONER. We'll adjourn until after lunch. Mr. de Winter, I presume you will be available for us then?

Maxim nods his head to the coroner and then turns his attention to "I"

MAXIM (*tenderly*). I told you you should have had some breakfast. You're hungry —that's what's the matter with you.

She responds to his forced cheerfulness by smiling wanly at him. They turn away as he helps her from the courtroom.

The scene dissolves to the SCHOOLHOUSE, revealing Maxim and "I" coming down the steps. The spectators are also coming out. We see an automobile in the foreground and Mullen, the chauffeur, walks in to Maxim and "I".

MULLEN. Mr. Frith thought you might like to have some lunch from the house and sent me with it.

MAXIM (*pleased*). That's fine, Mullen. Can you pull around the corner?

MULLEN. Very good, sir.

He leaves, and Maxim and "I" start walking.

"I". Awfully foolish of me, fainting like that.

MAXIM. Nonsense. If you hadn't fainted like that I'd have really lost my temper.

"I" (*worried*). Darling, please be careful.

He gives her arm an affectionate, reassuring little squeeze; and they are at the car, where the chauffeur is holding the door open.

MAXIM (*as she gets in*). Darling, wait here a few moments. I'll see if I can find old Frank.

"I" (*sitting back*). Of course, darling. Don't worry about me. I'll be all right.

Maxim has been opening the lunch basket and now pulls out a flask of brandy and hands it to her.

MAXIM. Sure? Here. Have a spot of this. Do you good.

"I" (*taking a drink*). Thank you.

MAXIM. Are you all right?

"I" (*smiling wanly*). Yes, of course.

MAXIM. I won't be long.

"I". Right you are.

Maxim leaves and "I" sits, relaxing for a moment. Suddenly she looks off in dismay.

FAVELL'S VOICE. Hello.

FAVELL sticks his head through the car window.

FAVELL. And how does the bride find herself today? I say, marriage with Max is not exactly a bed of roses, is it?

The view moves to "I".

"I". I think you'd better go before Maxim gets back.

The view draws back as Favell opens the door of the car.

FAVELL. Oh, jealous, is he? Well, I can't say I blame him. But you don't think I'm the big, bad wolf, do you? I'm not, you know. I'm a perfectly ordinary, harmless bloke. And I think you're behaving splendidly over all this. (*Significantly*) Perfectly splendidly. You know, you've grown up a bit since I last saw you. It's no wonder.

MAXIM (*entering the scene*). What do you want, Favell? (*He gets into the car and sits beside "I".*)

FAVELL. Oh, hello, Max. Things are going pretty well for you, aren't they? Better than you ever expected. I was rather worried about you at first. That's why I came down to the inquest.

MAXIM (*annoyed*). I'm touched by your solicitude, but if you don't mind, we'd rather like to have our lunch.

FAVELL (*seen fairly close*). Lunch! I say, what a jolly idea! (*He steps into the car, the scene now including the* THREE.) Rather like a picnic, isn't it? (*He lays down his hat.*) Oh, so sorry. Do you mind if I put this there? (*Without being asked, he dips into the basket, takes a leg of chicken and starts to chew it.*) You know, Max, old boy, I really think I ought to talk things over with you.

MAXIM. Talk what things over?

FAVELL (*seen quite close; eating*). Well, those holes in the planking for one thing —those holes that were drilled from the inside! (*Calling off*) Oh, Mullen!

MULLEN (*appearing at window*). Yes, sir?

FAVELL. Would you, like a good fellow, have my car filled with petrol? It's almost empty.

MULLEN. Very good, sir.

FAVELL. And, Mullen, close the door, will you?

MULLEN (*leaving*). Yes, sir.

FAVELL (*winding up the window of the door*). Does this bother you?

We see MAXIM AND "I" watching Favell, then all three of them.

FAVELL. You know, old boy, I have a strong feeling that before the day is out (*reaching over and taking the bottle from basket*) somebody's going to make use of that rather expressive, though somewhat old-fashioned term, "foul play." Am I boring you with all this? No? Good!

He pours himself a drink and returns the bottle. Maxim and "I" watch him intently.

FAVELL. Well, you see, Max, I find myself in a rather awkward position. You've only got to read this note to understand. (*Reaching into pocket for note*) It's from Rebecca. And, what's more, she had the foresight to put the date on it. She wrote it to me the day she died. Incidentally, I was out on a party that night, so I didn't get it until the next day.

MAXIM (*as he and "I" are seen fairly close*). What makes you think that note would interest me?

The view moves to include Favell.

FAVELL. Oh, I'm not going to bother you with the contents now, but I can assure you that it is not the note of a woman who intends to drown herself that same night. (*He looks at the finished leg bone in his hand; in a mocking, hushed whisper*) By the way, what do you do with old bones? Bury them, eh what? (*Opening the window, he flings the bone away.*) However, for the time being . . . you know, Max, I'm getting awfully fed up with my job as a motor car salesman. I don't know if you've ever experienced the feeling of driving an expensive motor car that isn't your own. But it can be very, very exasperating. You know what I mean—you want to own the car yourself.

Maxim stares across at Favell steadily—we can see he is exercising the utmost control.

FAVELL (*seen more closely now*). I've often wondered what it would be like to retire to the country—have a nice little place with a few acres of shooting. I've never figured out what it would cost a year, but I'd like to talk about it with you. I'd like to have your advice on how to live comfortably without hard work.

At this moment Frank enters behind Favell. Frank looks first of all toward Maxim and "I"—then to Favell.

FRANK (*coldly*). Hello, Favell. (*In a different tone*) You looking for me, Maxim?

MAXIM. Yes. Mr. Favell and I have a little business transaction on hand. I think we had better conduct it over at the Inn. They may have a private room there. (*He comes out from the car.*)

FAVELL (*to "I" as he follows Maxim*). See you later.

MAXIM (*turning back to the car; speaking in a low voice*). Find Colonel Julyan. Tell him I want to see him immediately. (*He turns away.*) Come on, Favell. Let's go.

The INN: Maxim and Favell enter.

MAXIM (*to the proprietor*). Have you a private room, please?

PROPRIETOR. Of course, sir. (*Leading the way*) Through here, sir. Hope this will do, Mr. de Winter.

The view moves with them into a private room.

FAVELL. It's splendid—splendid— (*Looking around*) Exactly like the Ritz.

PROPRIETOR. Any orders, gents?

FAVELL. Yes, you might bring me a large brandy and soda. How about you, Max? (*Generously*) Have one on me. I feel I can afford to play host.

MAXIM. Thanks. I don't mind if I do.

FAVELL. Make it two, will you, like a good fellow?

PROPRIETOR (*leaving*). Very good, sir.

COLONEL JULYAN'S VOICE. Where's Mr. de Winter?

PROPRIETOR'S VOICE. Through the other door, sir.

The view moves with Maxim going to open the door. Colonel Julyan, Frank, and "I" enter. Favell looks surprised.

MAXIM (*motioning toward Favell*). Colonel Julyan, this is Mr. Favell.

FAVELL. Oh, I know Colonel Julyan. We're old friends, aren't we?

The view carries Colonel Julyan over to Favell.

MAXIM. Since you're old friends, I assume you also know that he's head of the police here. I think he might be interested to hear your proposition. Go on, tell him all about it.

FAVELL AND COLONEL JULYAN are seen close.

FAVELL (*nonchalantly*). I don't know

what you mean. I merely said I hoped to give up selling cars and retire into the country.

MAXIM. Actually he offered to withhold a vital piece of evidence from the inquest if I made it worth his while.

A fairly close view of FAVELL AND COLONEL JULYAN:

FAVELL. I only want to see justice done, Colonel. Now that boat builder's evidence suggested certain possible theories concerning Rebecca's death. One of them, of course, is suicide. Now, I have a little note here which I consider puts that possibility quite out of court. Read it, Colonel. (*He hands the note to the Colonel.*)

COLONEL JULYAN (*reading*). "Jack, darling. I have just seen the doctor and I'm going down to Manderley right away. I shall be at the cottage all this evening, and shall leave the door open for you. I have something terribly important to tell you. Rebecca."

FAVELL. Now, does that look like the note from a woman who had made up her mind to kill herself? And, apart from that, Colonel, do you mean to tell me that if you wanted to commit suicide, you'd go to all the trouble of putting out to sea in a boat, and then take a hammer and chisel and laboriously knock holes through the bottom of it? Come, Colonel—as an officer of the law, don't you feel that there are some slight grounds for suspicion?

COLONEL JULYAN (*gravely*). Of murder?

FAVELL (*casually*). What else? (*The view follows him as he moves around.*) You've known Max a long time, so you know he's the old-fashioned type who'd die to defend his honor—or who'd kill for it.

FRANK. It's blackmail, pure and simple!

A fairly close view of FAVELL AND COLONEL JULYAN:

COLONEL JULYAN (*going close to Favell*). Blackmail's not so pure nor so simple. It can bring a lot of trouble to a great many people and the blackmailer sometimes finds himself in jail at the end of it.

FAVELL (*sneering*). Oh, I see. You're go-

ing to hold de Winter's hand through all this just because he's the big noise around here, and he's actually permitted you to dine with him.

COLONEL JULYAN. Be careful, Favell. You've brought an accusation of murder. Have you any witnesses?

FAVELL (*walking around*). I do have a witness.

COLONEL JULYAN. Oh.

FAVELL. It's that fellow Ben. If that stupid coroner hadn't been as much of a snob as you are, he'd have seen that half-wit was hiding something.

COLONEL JULYAN (*with an obvious attempt to control his anger*). And why should Ben do that?

FAVELL. Because we caught him once, Rebecca and I, peering at us through the cottage window. Rebecca threatened him with the asylum. That's why he was afraid to speak—but he was always hanging about and he must have seen this whole thing.

A fairly close view of FRANK, MAXIM, AND "I":

FRANK (*breaking in*). It's ridiculous even listening to all this.

FAVELL (*walking around and standing by a chair*). Ah. You're like a little trades union, all of you, aren't you? (*To Frank*) And if my guess is right, Crawley, there's a bit of malice in your soul toward me, isn't there? (*To the others*) Crawley didn't have much success with Rebecca, but he ought to have more luck this time. (*Turning back to Frank*) The bride will be grateful for your fraternal arm, Crawley, in a week or so—every time she faints, in fact . . .

Maxim moves into the scene and over to Favell. He hits Favell on the chin, stopping his words. Favell crumples and falls.

COLONEL JULYAN'S VOICE (*sharply*). De Winter!

"I" (*screaming*). Maxim, please!

FAVELL (*nursing his jaw, rises*). That temper of yours will do you in yet, Max.

The scene draws back to take in the entire

room. Just as it does so, the proprietor enters with the drinks.

PROPRIETOR. Excuse me, gentlemen.

Favell helps himself to a drink as the proprietor puts them down.

PROPRIETOR. Now, is there anything else?

FAVELL. Yes. You might bring Mr. de Winter a sedative.

COLONEL JULYAN (*shortly to the proprietor*). No, no. Nothing at all. Just leave us.

PROPRIETOR (*looking around, bewildered by the strange atmosphere*). Very good, sir. (*He quickly exits.*)

The scene draws in to a view of Favell and Colonel Julyan over Maxim's head.

COLONEL JULYAN. Now, Favell, let's get this business over. As you seem to have worked out the whole thing so carefully, perhaps you can provide us also with a motive?

FAVELL. Ah, I knew you were going to bring that up, Colonel. I've read enough detective stories to know there must always be a motive. And, if you'll all excuse me a moment, I'll supply that, too. (*He leaves the room quickly.*)

Maxim looks at "I", and sees the great alarm in her face. The moving scene brings him over to her.

MAXIM. I wish you would go home. You ought not to be here through all this.

"I" (*pleading*). Please let me stay, Maxim.

He pats her hand, and smiles at her. They walk over, and "I" sits down in a chair.

FRANK. Surely, Colonel, you're not going to allow this fellow to—

COLONEL JULYAN (*interrupting*). My opinion of Favell is no higher than yours, Crawley, but in my official capacity, I have no alternative but to pursue his accusation.

FAVELL'S VOICE. I entirely agree with you, Colonel.

The scene swings to the door and carries Favell into the room.

FAVELL. In a matter as serious as this we should make sure of every point— explore every avenue and, in fact, if I may coin a phrase, leave no stone unturned. (*He looks past the open door.*) Ah, here she is—the missing link—the witness who will help supply the motive!

As he is saying these words, Mrs. Danvers has stepped into the room and Favell closes the door behind her.

FAVELL. Colonel Julyan—Mrs. Danvers. I believe you know everyone else.

The scene draws in to a closer view of Mrs. Danvers.

COLONEL JULYAN. Won't you sit down? I . . .

FAVELL (*coming in closer; interrupting*). No offense, Colonel, but I think if I put this to Danny she'll understand it more easily. (*Turning to Mrs. Danvers*) Danny, who was Rebecca's doctor?

Mrs. Danvers looks about the room with intense suspicion. Her instinctive feeling is that they are trying to trap her into an admission damaging to Rebecca. She is very much on the defensive.

MRS. DANVERS (*coldly*). Mrs. de Winter always had Dr. McClean from the village.

FAVELL (*urgently*). Now, you heard. I said Rebecca's doctor—in London.

MRS. DANVERS (*obviously lying*). I don't know anything about that.

MAXIM, FRANK, "I", AND COLONEL JULYAN are seen watching and listening intently. Then we see only FAVELL AND MRS. DANVERS:

FAVELL. Oh, don't give me that, Danny. You knew everything about Rebecca. You knew she was in love with me, didn't you? Surely you haven't forgotten the good times she and I used to have down at the cottage on the beach.

MRS. DANVERS (*now seen in a close-up; turning on him with a fierce outburst of suppressed emotion*). She had a right to amuse herself, didn't she? Love was a game to her, only a game. It made her laugh, I tell you. She used to sit on her bed and rock with laughter at the lot of you.

COLONEL JULYAN (*quietly, slowly*). Can you think of any reason why Mrs. de Winter should have taken her own life?

MRS. DANVERS (*stunned*). No, no—I refuse to believe it. I knew everything about her, and I won't believe it.

FAVELL (*eagerly, swiftly, grasping at this*). There, you see? It's impossible. She knows that as well as I do. (*He turns to Mrs. Danvers, pretending great sympathy and talking quietly to her.*) Now listen to me, Danny. We know that Rebecca went to a doctor in London on the last day of her life. Who was it?

MRS. DANVERS (*coldly*). I don't know.

FAVELL (*soothingly*). Oh, I understand, Danny. You think we're asking you to reveal secrets of Rebecca's life. You're trying to defend her. But that's what I'm doing. I'm trying to clear her name of the suspicion of suicide.

COLONEL JULYAN (*stepping forward*). Mrs. Danvers, it has been suggested that Mrs. de Winter was deliberately murdered.

FAVELL. There you have it in a nutshell, Danny. But there's one more thing you'll want to know—the name of the murderer. It's a lovely name that rolls off the tongue so easily—George Fortescue Maximilian de Winter.

Maxim returns Mrs. Danvers' stare. "I", clutching his arm, also looks at Mrs. Danvers. Then we see only MRS. DANVERS AND FAVELL.

MRS. DANVERS (*looking steadily at Maxim, weighing her words very carefully*). There was a doctor. Mrs. de Winter sometimes went to him privately. She used to go to him even before she was married.

FAVELL (*impatiently*). We don't want reminiscences, Danny. What was his name?

MRS. DANVERS (*deliberately*). Dr. Baker— one-six-five Goldhawk Road—Shepherd's Bush.

FAVELL (*triumphantly*). There you are, Colonel. There's where you'll find your motive! Go and question Dr. Baker.

He'll tell you why Rebecca went to him —to confirm the fact that she was going to have a child—a sweet, curly-headed little child.

MRS. DANVERS (*horrified*). It isn't true! It isn't true! She would have told me.

Maxim is controlling his emotions at the revelation. "I" is horrified, worried.

FAVELL. She told Max about it—Max knew he wasn't the father! So, like the gentleman of the old school that he is, he killed her!

There is tense silence—broken at length by Colonel Julyan.

COLONEL JULYAN (*to Maxim*). I'm afraid we shall have to question this Dr. Baker.

FAVELL. Hear! Hear! But for safety's sake, I think I'd like to go along, too.

COLONEL JULYAN. Yes, unfortunately I suppose you have the right to ask that. I'll see the coroner and have the inquest postponed pending further evidence. (*He starts out.*)

FAVELL. I say, aren't you rather afraid that the prisoner—shall we say—might bolt?

Julyan stops, looks at Favell, then at Maxim who returns his gaze, then back at Favell.

COLONEL JULYAN (*leaving*). You have my word for it that he will not do that.

FAVELL (*to Maxim*). Toodle-oo, Max. (*To Mrs. Danvers*) Come along, Danny. Let's leave the unhappy couple to spend their last moments together alone. (*He goes out.*)

Mrs. Danvers throws a cold glance at Maxim and "I", and leaves the room.

The scene dissolves to the EXTERIOR OF THE INN, showing MAXIM, "I", AND FRANK, and the scene moves with them to the car.

"I". Are you sure you don't want me to go with you, Maxim?

MAXIM (*tenderly*). No, darling. It will be very tiring for you. I'll be back the very first thing in the morning—and I won't even stop to sleep.

"I" (*simply, covering her own feelings completely*). I'll be waiting for you.

Maxim kisses her and then helps her into the car. He closes the door of the car himself as Colonel Julyan enters.

COLONEL JULYAN. Ready, Maxim?

MAXIM. Yes.

Colonel Julyan raises his hat to "I" as her car drives off, her face pressed to the window. Maxim and Colonel Julyan stroll off, and as we follow them we find Favell's car standing at the curb behind Maxim's car.

COLONEL JULYAN (to Maxim). You two go on ahead. I'll follow with Favell.

The scene dissolves to a COUNTRY ROAD in the late afternoon, showing two automobiles traveling at a fast rate of speed; then to the EXTERIOR OF DR. BAKER'S HOUSE, with Maxim, Frank, Favell, and Colonel Julyan getting out of the cars and starting up the steps, and then to DR. BAKER'S OFFICE. Favell and Colonel Julyan have their backs turned; Frank, Maxim, and Dr. Baker are facing forward.

COLONEL JULYAN (leaning forward). Dr. Baker, you may have seen Mr. de Winter's name in the papers recently . . .

DR. BAKER. Oh, yes . . . yes . . . in connection with the body that was found in a boat. My wife was reading all about it. It was a very sad case. (To Maxim) My condolences, Mr. de Winter.

FAVELL (in irritated tones). Oh, this is going to take hours—let me . . .

COLONEL JULYAN. Don't bother, Favell. I think I can tell Dr. Baker.

The scene draws in to Dr. Baker and Colonel Julyan.

COLONEL JULYAN. We're trying to discover certain facts concerning the late Mrs. de Winter's activities on the day of her death, October the 12th, last year, and I want you to tell me, if you can, if anyone of that name paid you a visit on that date.

DR. BAKER (shaking his head). I'm awfully sorry. I'm afraid I can't help you. I should have remembered the name de Winter. I've never attended a Mrs. de Winter in my life.

FAVELL (moving in). Well, how can you possibly tell all your patient's names?

DR. BAKER (coldly). I can look it up in my engagement diary if you like. Did you say the twelfth of October?

COLONEL JULYAN. Yes.

The view moves with Dr. Baker as he gets up and goes to the mantle and takes the diary book from it. He goes back and sits down again.

DR. BAKER (looking at the page). Here we are. No—no de Winter.

FAVELL (breaking in). Are you sure?

DR. BAKER. Here are all the appointments for that day. Ross, Campbell, Steadall, Perrino, Danvers, Mathews . . .

FAVELL (excitedly). Danny! What the devil!

We see the whole GROUP:

COLONEL JULYAN. Would you read that name again; did you say Danvers?

DR. BAKER. Yes, I have a Mrs. Danvers for three o'clock.

FAVELL. What did she look like? Can you remember?

DR. BAKER. Yes, I remember her quite well. She was a very beautiful woman—tall, dark, exquisitely dressed.

FRANK. Rebecca!

COLONEL JULYAN. The lady must have used an assumed name.

DR. BAKER. Is that so? This is a surprise. I'd known her a long time.

FAVELL. What was the matter with her?

DR. BAKER. My dear sir—there are certain ethics.

FRANK. Could you supply a reason, Dr. Baker, for Mrs. de Winter's suicide?

FAVELL. For her murder, you mean! She was going to have a kid, wasn't she? Come on—out with it. Tell me what else would a woman of her class be doing in a dump like this?

DR. BAKER (to Colonel Julyan). I take it the official nature of this visit makes it necessary for me to . . .

COLONEL JULYAN. I assure you we'd not be troubling you if it were not necessary.

DR. BAKER. You want to know if I can suggest any motive as to why Mrs. de Winter would have taken her life? Yes, I think I can. The woman who called herself Mrs. Danvers was very seriously ill.

MAXIM. She was not going to have a child?

The view moves to Dr. Baker as he gets a card from the file.

DR. BAKER. That was what she thought—but my diagnosis was different. I sent her to a well-known specialist for an examination and x-rays and on this date —she returned to me for his report. I remember her standing here holding out her hand for the photographs. "I want to know the truth," she said. "I don't want soft words and a bedside manner. If I'm for it, you can tell me right away." I knew she was not the type to accept a lie. She'd asked for the truth and I let her have it. She thanked me and I never saw her again, so I assumed that—

The scene draws back to a larger view of the room.

MAXIM. What was wrong with her?

DR. BAKER. Cancer. Yes, the growth was deep-rooted. An operation would have been no earthly use at all. In a short time she would have been under morphia. There was nothing that could be done for her—except wait.

Favell is horror stricken. He turns his back.

MAXIM. Did she say anything—when you told her?

DR. BAKER. She smiled in a queer sort of way. Your wife was a wonderful woman, Mr. de Winter . . . and, oh, yes . . . I remember she said something that struck me as being very peculiar at the time. When I told her it was a matter of months, she said, "Oh, no, Doctor, not that long."

There is a pause as they all take this news and realize its significance. To Maxim it is an explanation of Rebecca's strange behavior the night of her death. To Colonel Julyan it is a confirmation of suicide. To Favell, who has been crushed by the news

of Rebecca's illness, it is a double blow: the news that the woman he loved had cancer and the upset of his plans. Frank is relieved that the suspense is over, but he, too, is depressed by the revelation of Rebecca's illness. They all rise to leave.

COLONEL JULYAN. You've been very kind. You've told us all we wanted to know. We shall probably need an official verification . . .

DR. BAKER. Verification?

COLONEL JULYAN. Yes—to confirm the verdict of suicide. (*He looks at Favell challengingly, who avoids his gaze.*)

DR. BAKER. I understand. Can I offer you gentlemen a glass of sherry?

COLONEL JULYAN. No, that's very kind, but I think we ought to be going.

They go out of Dr. Baker's office.

The scene dissolves to the EXTERIOR OF DR. BAKER'S HOUSE as Colonel Julyan, Maxim, Frank, and Favell come out.

FRANK. Thank Heaven we know the truth!

COLONEL JULYAN. Dreadful thing—dreadful. A young and lovely woman like that. No wonder . . .

FAVELL (*seen in a close-up; obviously suffering deeply from shock*). I never had the remotest idea. Neither did Danny, I'm sure. (*He shudders.*) I wish I had a drink!

We get a fairly close view of the GROUP.

FRANK. Will we be needed at the inquest any further, Colonel Julyan?

COLONEL JULYAN. No, no. (*With a sympathetic look toward Maxim*) I can see to it that Maxim's not troubled any further.

MAXIM. Thank you, sir.

FAVELL (*trying to be friendly, with fake heartiness*). Are you ready to start back, Colonel?

COLONEL JULYAN (*coldly*). No, thank you. I'm staying in town tonight. (*Pointedly*) And let me tell you, Favell, blackmail is not much of a profession, and we know how to deal with it in our part of the world—strange as it may seem to you.

FAVELL. I'm sure I don't know what you're talking about. But if you ever need a new car, Colonel, just let me know. (*With a cheery salute he leaves the scene.*)

The scene draws in to a closer view of the remaining three men.

MAXIM. It's impossible to thank you for your kindness to us through all this. You know what I feel about it without my saying anything.

COLONEL JULYAN. Not at all. Put the whole thing behind you. (*He puts out his hand.*) Better let your wife know. She'll be getting worried.

MAXIM. Yes, of course. I'll phone her at once, and then we'll go straight down to Manderley. (*He exits.*)

The scene draws in to a closer view of the remaining two men.

COLONEL JULYAN (*to Frank*). Good-bye, Crawley. (*Simply*) Maxim's got a great friend. (*He extends his hand.*)

Frank, embarrassed, takes it. Then Colonel Julyan exits. The moving scene brings Frank to Maxim's car. Maxim enters the scene and Frank helps him with his coat.

MAXIM (*looking straight ahead*). Frank . . .

FRANK. Yes, Maxim?

MAXIM. There's something you don't know.

FRANK (*quietly*). Oh, no, there isn't.

Maxim circles around in back of Frank to the side of the car. The two men stand, facing each other.

MAXIM. I didn't kill her, Frank. But I know now that when she told me about the child, she wanted me to kill her. She lied on purpose. She foresaw the whole thing. That's why she stood there laughing when she . . .

FRANK (*relieved to know the truth*). Don't think about it any more.

MAXIM (*looks at him gratefully*). Thank you, Frank.

They start to get into the car.

The scene dissolves to a PHONE BOOTH revealing a close view of FAVELL.

FAVELL (*talking into the phone*). Hello, Danny. I just wanted to tell you the news. Rebecca held out on both of us. She had cancer! Yes—suicide. (*Bitterly*) And now Max and that dear little bride of his will be able to stay on at Manderley and live happily ever after. Bye, bye, Danny. (*He hangs up the receiver and goes out of the booth.*)

The scene moves with him as he goes to his car. We see a policeman standing by the car. As Favell approaches the policeman speaks:

POLICEMAN. Is this your car, sir?

FAVELL (*swings around on him, still under the stress of his emotion*). Yes.

POLICEMAN. Will you be going soon? This isn't a parking place, you know.

FAVELL (*glaring at him angrily*). Oh, isn't it? People are entitled to leave their cars outside if they want to. It's a pity some of you fellows haven't anything better to do.

As he gets into his car, the scene dissolves to the COUNTRYSIDE, showing MAXIM AND FRANK speeding along in the open car.

FRANK. When you phoned, did she say she'd wait up?

MAXIM. I asked her to go to bed, but she wouldn't hear of it. I wish I could get some more speed out of this thing.

FRANK (*looking at him, observes Maxim's troubled face*). Is something worrying you, Maxim?

MAXIM. I can't get over the feeling something's wrong.

The scene dissolves to a vista of MANDERLEY at night, and a light can be seen going from window to window in the upstairs rooms. Next we see MRS. DANVERS in THE HALL. She has a lighted candle in her hand. The scene moves with her as she goes into the library, where we see "I", sleeping in a chair, with Jasper in her lap. Mrs. Danvers stands a second, staring at them. JASPER, in "I's" lap, looks up. "I" is seen over Mrs.

Danvers' shoulder as Mrs. Danvers turns forward, a mysterious, cunning look on her face which is lit from below by the candle she holds.

The scene dissolves to the COUNTRYSIDE with MAXIM AND FRANK in the car, which comes forward, revealing Maxim driving rapidly with Frank dozing beside him. Maxim looks worried.

MAXIM (*suddenly*). Frank!

FRANK (*startled*). What's the matter?

Maxim pulls the car up with a jerk.

FRANK. Why did we stop?

MAXIM. What . . . what's the time?

FRANK (*looking at clock*). Oh, this clock's wrong—it must be three or four —why?

MAXIM. That can't be the dawn breaking over there!

FRANK. It's in the winter that you see the Northern lights, isn't it?

We see a long vista with a LIGHTED SKY seen through trees. Then MAXIM AND FRANK—IN THE CAR:

MAXIM. That's not the Northern lights. That's Manderley!

The long vista appears, with distant flames seeming to light the sky. Then again MAXIM AND FRANK are seen IN THE CAR: Maxim starts the car, and it goes off down the road in a burst of speed.

The scene dissolves to FRANK AND MAXIM— IN THE CAR, the light in the sky appearing through the windshield. The scene moves with the car and Manderley appears in flames in the background. Then the scene carries them to a view of Manderley burning. The car stops and Maxim and Frank jump out. A group of servants, including Frith and Robert, are watching the burning building.

MAXIM (*rushing in*). Frith! Frith! Mrs. de Winter! Where is she . . .

FRITH. I thought I saw her, sir . . .

MAXIM (*wild with anxiety*). Where? Where? (*He turns and starts off in search of her.*)

Next we see JASPER: He is on a leash. We see "I's" feet and legs showing as she walks with him. The scene tilts up to a close view of "I"—the burning Manderley in the background.

Now the SERVANTS appear with the burning mansion in the background, and Maxim comes to them in his search for his wife. Then we see her (in a close-up) as she looks off and sees Maxim.

"I" (calling to him). Maxim!

As a long view of MANDERLEY burning appears, Maxim and "I" run into each other's arms.

"I". Oh, thank heaven you've come back to me!

The scene draws in to a close view of the two.

MAXIM (*anxiously*). Are you all right, darling?

"I". Oh, yes, I'm all right.

MAXIM (*kissing her, holding her tightly to him*). Are you all right?

"I" (*in alarm*). But Mrs. Danvers . . . she's gone mad! She said she'd rather destroy Manderley than see us happy here.

Suddenly we hear the cry of: "Look! The West Wing!" and then we see the WEST WING. The figure of Mrs. Danvers can be seen moving past the windows, seemingly undisturbed by the fire. There is a wall of flame behind her. The scene draws in to a closer view of Mrs. Danvers through the window.

MAXIM, "I", AND THE SERVANTS in the background are next seen, all looking toward the fire, horrified. Then the burning WEST WING comes into view again and the scene draws in to a closer glimpse of Mrs. Danvers looking around at the fire. There is a triumphant and defiant look on her face. Flames shoot up and around her.

The CEILING is seen falling down. Then there is a closer view of the flames sweeping the room. The scene moves to Rebecca's bed and draws in to a close view of the nightdress case and the initial "R." The flames gradually creep up and start to burn the case. Then as the flames devour the "R" the scene fades out.

WUTHERING HEIGHTS

(A Samuel Goldwyn Production)

Screenplay by
BEN HECHT AND CHARLES MACARTHUR

Based on the Novel *Wuthering Heights* by
EMILY BRONTË

Directed by WILLIAM WYLER

The Cast

CATHY . . . . Merle Oberon
HEATHCLIFF . . . . . Laurence Olivier
EDGAR . . . . David Niven
ELLEN DEAN . . . . . Flora Robson
DR. KENNETH . . . . . Donald Crisp
HINDLEY . . . . . . Hugh Williams
ISABELLA . . . . . . Geraldine Fitzgerald
JOSEPH . . . . Leo G. Carroll
JUDGE LINTON . . . . Cecil Humphreys
LOCKWOOD . . . . . Miles Mander
ROBERT . . . . Romaine Callender
EARNSHAW . . . . . . Cecil Kellaway
HEATHCLIFF (as a child) . . Rex Downing
CATHY (as a child) . . . . Sarita Wooton
HINDLEY (as a child) . . . Douglas Scott

Film Editor—DANIEL MANDELL

WUTHERING HEIGHTS

PROLOGUE

A long view of the MOORS fades in. A violent storm fills the night. Snow has been falling for days. The road and the moors are blanketed deep. The immense, lonely moor looks white, devilish and forlorn. There is no sound but the wind, no sight but the swirl of snow.

Into the foreground of this white wilderness comes the figure of a man toiling through the high drifts. He pauses, blinded by the wind and snow. Then we follow him as, shielding his eyes, he sees a tiny light beyond the road. It is the window of some nearby house, and he starts plunging toward it.

Now the scene cuts to a view of the old MANOR HOUSE that seems half buried not only by the long falling snow but by the years. It is a stone building and it stands like a derelict in the wild night, its windows battered and boarded up, its outbuildings half toppled. Some scrub firs have been twisted into eerie shapes by the eternal wind.

The man comes into view. A crumbling fence halts him and he finds the gate. He pushes against it and it opens a foot, reluctantly, as if held back by invisible hands. He wedges himself into the yard, and as he starts desperately forward for the shelter of the lighted room beyond, the wild barking of dogs rises above the noise of the wind; and a pack of shaggy and wolf-like animals leap through the snowdrifts at the traveler.

Then the scene changes abruptly, and we see the animals harrying the bewildered figure, who fights them off with his heavy stick; and after plunging and falling and recovering himself, he arrives at the manor door.

He knocks, with the dogs still leaping at him. There is no response. He bangs with his stick. And then made desperate by the aroused animals, he opens the door and lunges in.

We follow him into a LARGE ROOM in which a fire burns. Seated in the lamplight, morose and silent, is a group of immobile people. The traveler looks at them in amazement. They offer no greeting, and no hint of hospitality is in their sullen eyes.

Dominating the group, with his back to the fireplace over which hangs a pair of guns, is a dark-skinned, saturnine looking figure, his hair half white. He is a surly, slovenly appearing, half-gypsy half-gentleman character; and on his features is the stamp of an embittered arrogance. This is Heathcliff. After a pause, glaring at the storm-driven intruder, Heathcliff speaks. His voice is edged with anger.

HEATHCLIFF. Who are you and what do you want?

TRAVELER (*beating off one of the dogs*). Call off your accursed dogs.

HEATHCLIFF (*sullenly to the dogs*). Down . . .

He lashes at them with a tall poker from the fireplace. The dogs slink away.

HEATHCLIFF. Gnasher! Wolf! Down. Gnasher! Down, I tell you!

TRAVELER. Are you Mr. Heathcliff?

HEATHCLIFF (*without moving*). Yes.

TRAVELER (*cordially, at first*). I'm Mr. Lockwood, your new tenant at the Grange.

HEATHCLIFF (*with a snarl*). Oh, you are? Well, why aren't you there instead of tramping the moors on a night like this?

LOCKWOOD (*taken aback*). I'm lost. Could I get a guide from among your lads?

HEATHCLIFF (*directly*). No, you cannot. I've only one, and he's needed here.

LOCKWOOD (*taking a stand*). Then I'm afraid I'll have to stay till morning. A mile in this storm is out of the question.

HEATHCLIFF (*shortly*). Do as you please.

Lockwood with growing anger looks at the others in the room: a woman sitting by the fireplace who is crippled and aged; another woman, faded, beaten, middle-aged, her hair and clothes more slovenly than the master's; a doddering old man who simply stands watching in a shadowy corner of the room. Then Lockwood addresses himself to the middle-aged woman.

LOCKWOOD (*with increasing sarcasm*). Thank you for your hospitality. Could you extend it to a cup of tea?

THE WOMAN. Shall I? (*Looking nervously at Heathcliff.*)

HEATHCLIFF (*kicking a log on the fire*). You heard him ask for it.

LOCKWOOD (*after a pause; beginning all over*). I presume this amiable lady is Mrs. Heathcliff?

The woman rises to fetch tea, almost cringing as she passes Heathcliff.

HEATHCLIFF. Yes, this amiable lady is my wife.

LOCKWOOD (*now openly angry*). Would it be taxing your remarkable hospitality if I sat down?

HEATHCLIFF (*wheeling on him savagely*). I hope my hospitality is a lesson to you to make no more rash journeys on these moors. As for staying here tonight, I don't keep accommodations for visitors. You can share a bed with one of the servants.

LOCKWOOD (*with excessive dignity*). I'll sleep in a chair, sir.

Heathcliff starts from the room and then returns. He stares almost sadly at the traveler and speaks as if against his will.

HEATHCLIFF. No, no! A stranger is a stranger. Guests are so rare in this house that I hardly know how to receive them —I and my dogs. (*He turns to the dod-dering old man.*) Joseph, open up one of the upstairs rooms. (*He stares at Lockwood and speaks coldly again.*) Goodnight, sir . . .

LOCKWOOD (*staring back in amazement*). Goodnight.

MRS. HEATHCLIFF is now seen putting the tea before him, her eyes fixed on the receding figure of Heathcliff. Dull fear and a dog-like fascination are in her face.

The scene dissolves to an UPPER CORRIDOR: The doddering servant, Joseph, holding a lantern, walks down a twisting, shadowed passage, Mr. Lockwood following. He comes to a door and pauses. The old man looks behind him as if undecided about something, and then with an odd cackle to himself, opens the door. It opens slowly, creaking on its unused hinges.

Lockwood looks into a bedroom in which stands a four poster bed. The room is musty. Some mildewed books line one of the walls. An oak chest covered with bits of fabric that look like rags, a chair with one leg broken, and an old couch make up the furniture of the room.

JOSEPH. Here's a room for you, sir, the bridal chamber. (*Cackling*) Nobody's slept here for years.

LOCKWOOD (*shuddering*). It's a trifle depressing. Could you light a fire?

JOSEPH. No fire will burn in that grate. The chimney has been clogged for years.

LOCKWOOD. Very well—thank you. Goodnight.

He sits down, removes his shoes and coat, unloosens his cravat. He feels the bed and shivers. It is cold and musty to his hand. He looks around suddenly and sees Joseph still in the doorway, watching him.

LOCKWOOD. I said goodnight.

Joseph closes the door slowly. Lockwood makes a pillow of his coat, places it on the bed and lies down. It is a unique kind of bed with wings and cubby-holes extending down its sides. Lockwood lies with his eyes open for a time staring at the shadows of the strange room and listening to the wind rattling the casement shutter. Then he sits up again. He draws from one of the cubby-holes a volume, thick-coated with dust, and opens it. A pressed flower falls out. He examines the flower, then with a certain tenderness that such things always evoke, he places it gently on the ledge beside him. Now he turns the pages of the book with a rather childish scrawl across them. He comes on a lock of hair pasted to a page. He turns the pages back to the fly-leaf. The writing on it reads:

"Catherine Earnshaw— Her book."

LOCKWOOD turns the pages again, and reads with difficulty the faded writing. His eyelids grow heavy. At last he puts the book aside, pinches out the candle, and closes his eyes for sleep.

The scene having dissolved, LOCKWOOD is then seen sleeping and tossing nervously. Outside the storm has increased its fury. As he sleeps we discover the source of an insistent tapping noise that rises eerily above the storm sounds. A shutter is loose outside the casement window. It bangs monotonously back and forth, almost as if it were desperately summoning someone to wake. And wake Mr. Lockwood does, his eyes opening, his mind still disordered by some vivid and ugly dream. Half aroused, he stares into the shadows of the musty room and his ear catches the banging on the window outside.

The SHUTTER is seen banging in the whirling snow. LOCKWOOD fearfully slips out of the bed and stands, his heart beating and his nightmare still clinging to his senses. The insistent noise continues. He moves toward the window. As he tugs it open, in his half sleep, he hears a woman's voice joining with the screech of the wind. As the snow swirls in through the window, the voice calls out.

VOICE. Let me in! Let me in! I'm lost on the moor!

The words terrify him. He reaches desperately out to grab the banging shutter. As his hand almost touches the shutter he stops, riveted with terror. Instead of the shutter in his grip, he feels a small icy hand closing on his; and outlined in the swirl of snow he sees the dim figure of a woman, pale, her hair streaming in the wind and from her lips again rising the wail that made his heart beat wildly a moment ago.

VOICE. Let me in! I'm lost on the moor . . . Let me in!

As his hand remains gripped by the icy and partly visible fingers in the night, Mr. Lockwood gives way to panic. Out of his half sleep he raises a voice strangled with fright.

LOCKWOOD (screaming). Help! Help! Someone's here. Help! Heathcliff! Heathcliff!

He wrenches himself away from this strange thing that gripped him in the storm outside. Snow sweeps in through the window.

LOCKWOOD. Help! Heathcliff! Hurry . . . Hurry!

The door of the room crashes open and Heathcliff stands revealed, lantern aloft.

LOCKWOOD (unnerved). Someone is out there in the storm—a woman—I heard her calling. She said her name over and over—Cathy. (He brushes his hand over his forehead, repeating in a voice that is not so alarmed.) Cathy . . . (Then recalling the scrawl in the diary, he sighs with relief.) I must have been dreaming. Forgive me, Mr. Heathcliff . . .

Heathcliff seizes his shoulders and holds them in a desperate grip.

HEATHCLIFF (tensely). Get out of this room! Get out! Get out, I tell you!

He pushes Mr. Lockwood out and slams the door. Then he rushes back to the window and thrusts open the shutter. The storm, still rising, sweeps in again more violently than before and Heathcliff, throwing his arms out to the raging night, calls out in a wild, heartbroken voice.

HEATHCLIFF (sobbing). Come in! Come in! Oh Cathy, Cathy . . . do come! Oh do, once more! Oh, my heart's darling! Hear me this time, at last! Hear me . . . Cathy, I love you. Come in to me . . . Come to me. Cathy, my own . . . my own . . .

On the snow sweeping over Heathcliff, the scene changes abruptly to the HALL, revealing Lockwood making his way through the black hall toward the living room; and then to the LIVING ROOM as Lockwood enters. Ellen is there, sitting crone-like by the fire. It is as though she sensed a spirit prowling the moors. Ellen doesn't look up as Lockwood enters but sits staring into the fire. After a moment Lockwood joins her there. He is trembling. Over the scene is heard the sound of Heathcliff's voice. Lockwood listens but the words are indistinguishable.

ELLEN (*without looking at him—cackling*). I didn't think you would stay the night through in that room.

Lockwood glances at her. He is trying to compose himself.

ELLEN (*after a pause*). What happened?

LOCKWOOD. I had a dream. I thought I heard a voice calling. I leapt up and flung open the window. Something cold touched me—cold and clinging like an icy hand. Then I saw her . . . My senses were disordered, and the falling snow shaped into what looked like a phan-

tom. It was nothing.

ELLEN (*slowly*). It was Cathy. . . .

LOCKWOOD. Who is Cathy?

ELLEN. A girl—who died.

LOCKWOOD. I don't believe in ghosts. I don't believe in phantoms, sobbing in the night. I don't believe that life comes back after it has died and calls again to the living.

ELLEN (*looking at him for the first time since he returned to the fire*). Maybe if I told you her story you'd change your mind about the dead coming back. (*She throws a handful of kindling into the flames.*) Maybe you'd know, as I do, that there *is* a force that brings them back, if their hearts were wild enough in life.

LOCKWOOD. Tell me—her story.

ELLEN. It began when I was a young girl, fifty years ago, in the service of Mr. Earnshaw—Cathy's father . . .

The scene fades out.

PART ONE

The exterior of "WUTHERING HEIGHTS," as it was forty years before, fades in. It is a place of tranquility and beauty. In the foreground a young tree is in blossom. The grounds are landscaped; the fences are in repair.

A rider approaches the gate of Wuthering Heights. Another horseman appears at a stile near the road. They hail each other.

The scene cuts (changes abruptly) to EARNSHAW ON HORSEBACK. A boy of nine sits sideways across the pommel. The other horseman, Dr. Kenneth, a kindly, youngish, middle-aged man, rides into view.

DR. KENNETH. Hello, Neighbor Earnshaw! Back from Liverpool so soon!

EARNSHAW. How are you, Doctor Kenneth?

DR. KENNETH (*trotting up to him*). What in the world have you got there? (*He points to the unkempt boy.*)

EARNSHAW (*holding up the boy*). A gift o' God. Although it's as dark as if it came from the Devil. (*As the boy twists*

in his arms) Quiet, my bonny lad. . . . We're home.

DR. KENNETH (*squinting at the boy*). He's a dour looking individual. . . .

EARNSHAW (*as the two walk their horses down the lane toward the house*). Aye, and with reason. I found him starving in the streets of Liverpool, kicked and bruised and nearly dead. I spent two pounds trying to find out who its owner was. Nobody would lay claim to him. Rather than leave him as he was, I brought him home. . . .

They dismount, Earnshaw reaching up to help the boy.

EARNSHAW. Hop down, my lad.

But left alone, the boy clambers into the saddle and starts beating the horse, crying out wildly.

EARNSHAW (*pulling the boy out of the saddle*). Off with you, you imp of Satan! (*To Dr. Kenneth*) We'll soon get those tricks out of him. . . . (*He calls.*) Cathy! Hindley!

Ellen, a woman of twenty, plump, competent, bustling, appears in the doorway.

ELLEN. Welcome home, Mr. Earnshaw. The children will be right down.

She sees the boy and stares at him.

EARNSHAW (*smiling at her expression*). Don't look so shocked, Ellen. He's going to live with us for a while. Give him a good scrubbing and put some Christian clothes on him. He's about Hindley's size.

ELLEN (*eyeing the tattered boy*). Food is what he needs first, from the looks of him, Mr. Earnshaw. . . (*She pinches his arm.*) He's as thin as a sparrow. Come into the kitchen, child.

BOY (*jerking away from her*). Don't touch me . . .

He walks in after Ellen as Dr. Kenneth detains Mr. Earnshaw, who has started to follow.

DR. KENNETH (*gravely*). Friend Earnshaw, aren't you making a great mistake?

EARNSHAW (*stopping, surprised*). In what way, Doctor Kenneth?

DR. KENNETH (*slowly*). I certainly don't think you ought to take him into your home.

EARNSHAW (*almost angrily*). What should I have done—left him to starve like a dog?

DR. KENNETH (*quietly*). Softly, neighbor. I've seen more of life than you. And of children. That's a bad one, with bad blood in him. He's young, but he's full of hate, like a dog that's been kicked— and you'll not smooth him out. He'll bite. He'll bite deeply.

EARNSHAW. That's heartless talk, Doctor Kenneth, coming from you. . . . God sent him to me.

DR. KENNETH (*smiling*). Hold on there.

I delivered all the children that God sent you.

EARNSHAW (*quietly*). Then you may remember that Heathcliff would have been this tyke's age—had he lived.

DR. KENNETH (*gently putting his hand on his shoulder*). Remember that "of such are the Kingdom of God." Heathcliff is safe in His mighty arms.

The two men enter, Dr. Kenneth shaking his head dubiously.

The LIVING ROOM: Mr. Earnshaw stands looking cheerily around.

EARNSHAW (*calling*). Cathy!

Cathy, a little girl of nine, and Hindley, a lad a year or two older, come clattering down the stairs, Cathy leading by two lengths.

CATHY (*embracing her father, who leans over to kiss her*). Papa darling! What did you bring! What did you bring me!

HINDLEY. Hello, father . . . (*He turns his cheek to Mr. Earnshaw to be kissed.*)

EARNSHAW (*opening a package*). Here you are, Cathy. It's what you wanted. But be careful how you use it.

He gives her a riding crop which he removes from his coat.

CATHY (*dancing*). Oh, it's wonderful! It's wonderful! (*She whacks Hindley across the back with it.*)

HINDLEY (*bellowing*). Stop that! Father! Make her stop!

EARNSHAW (*mildly*). Children, children! Here's Hindley's violin. . . . (*He opens a small package.*) One of the best in Liverpool. Fine tone and a bow to go with it. . . .

HINDLEY (*mollified for the moment*). Let me see! (*As Earnshaw presents the violin*) Give me the bow!

He dives into the case as the strange boy comes slouching in, Ellen behind him. He is munching on a bread and butter sandwich . . . eating stolidly, his eyes looking sullenly at the company. Hindley stops and stares.

CATHY (*spying him, and exclaiming*). Who's that!

ELLEN (*to the smiling, expectant Earnshaw*). He was hungry as a wolf. . . .

EARNSHAW (*with mock diplomacy intended to amuse Cathy and Hindley as much as to answer the question in their eyes*). Children, this is a little gentleman I met in Liverpool . . . who has accepted my invitation to pay us all a little visit.

CATHY (*slowly*). He's dirty!

EARNSHAW (*shocked*). Don't make me ashamed of you, Cathy. . . . When he's been scrubbed, Ellen, show him Hindley's room. He'll sleep there . . .

HINDLEY (*flaring*). In my room! He cannot! I won't let him!

EARNSHAW (*very grave*). Children, you may as well learn here and now to share what you have with others—not as fortunate as yourselves. Take charge of the boy, Ellen.

There is a silence in the room as the camera moves from face to face showing Cathy's anger, Hindley's indignation, and Dr. Kenneth's worry.

ELLEN (*at last*). Come along, lad . . . what's your name?

The boy looks silently at Mr. Earnshaw.

EARNSHAW. We'll call him Heathcliff . . .

The boy stands staring. Then, he slowly crosses to Earnshaw, hugs him quickly and impulsively, then rushes from the room, followed by Ellen, as the scene fades out.

PART TWO

As the MOOR fades in we see HEATHCLIFF and CATHY racing two horses over it.

CATHY (*screaming*). Come on, I'll race you to the barn! Whoever loses has to be the other's slave for a whole week.

HEATHCLIFF (*leaning over his horses's neck*). Come on . . . (*Kicking his horse*) Go! Go! Go!

They race, Cathy screaming with laughter, through the sunny field to the barn.

The EXTERIOR of the BARN: Heathcliff wins and jumps from the horse, crying out excitedly.

HEATHCLIFF. I won! I won. You're my slave. You've got to do as I say! You've got to water my horse and brush it down.

CATHY (*taken aback*). Oh, that's not fair. It's too real.

Hindley appears.

HEATHCLIFF (*eyeing him, hostile*). What do you want?

HINDLEY (*taking his horse by the bridle*). This horse.

HEATHCLIFF (*rushing*). You can't have him. He's mine.

HINDLEY (*cruelly*). I don't care. Mine's lame and I'm going to ride yours.

HEATHCLIFF (*shoving him*). You're not!

HINDLEY (*blocked*). Give him to me or I'll go tell my father how you boasted you'd turn me out of doors—when he died.

HEATHCLIFF (*violently*). That's a lie! I never said such a thing!

CATHY (*at Heathcliff's side*). Of course he didn't! Just because papa likes him better than he does you—

HINDLEY (*turning on her*). It's like you to take his part! You won't be happy till he's wormed his way in farther and cheated us out of everything that belongs to us! (*Blazing to Heathcliff*) You never had a father, you gypsy beggar, and you can't have mine!

Heathcliff rushes forward. Hindley picks up a rock.

CATHY (*shouting*). Heathcliff! Look out!

Hindley holds the rock poised to throw.

HINDLEY (*his voice charged with hate*). Don't come near me!

Heathcliff dashes at Hindley and the rock takes him on the head. He falls to the ground and Hindley jumps on him, kicking and slugging him as Cathy leaps up and down screaming.

CATHY. Let him go! You've killed him! Hindley!

She rushes at her brother and pulls him off Heathcliff, who lies silent on the ground.

CATHY. I'm going to tell father! He'll cut you off for this!

HINDLEY (triumphantly). You can't go near father until he gets well. You heard what Dr. Kenneth said. . . . (He gets on Heathcliff's horse and glares at Heathcliff as the latter sits up slowly.) Gypsy scum!

Hindley rides off.

CATHY (holding him, as blood trickles from his mouth). Are you hurt badly? Heathcliff! Talk to me! (At his granite look) Why don't you cry? (She wipes his mouth with her apron.) Heathcliff! Don't look like that!

Heathcliff slowly rises, his eyes glaring dully into space.

HEATHCLIFF (with deadly calm). How can I pay him back? I don't care how long I wait—if I can only pay him back! I hope he won't die before I do—

CATHY (frightened at his look). Shame, Heathcliff! It's for God to punish wicked people. We should learn to forgive.

She is still on the ground.

HEATHCLIFF (miserably). Oh, Cathy—

CATHY (seeing that he is about to break). Come, Heathcliff! (She jumps up, but Heathcliff only shakes his head. Cajoling him out of his mood) Let's pick some blue bells. There are thousands of them on Pennistone Crag.

HEATHCLIFF (shaking his head). No.

CATHY (leading her horse up to him). You can ride Jane.

HEATHCLIFF (as before). No.

CATHY (with pretended gaiety, she curtseys to him). Please, my lord.

HEATHCLIFF (surrendering hard). Cathy —no one but you can make me happy. No one but you in all the world. (Helping her on the mare) Get up there.

She gets up. He walks along out toward the moor, holding onto the stirrup.

The scene dissolves to the MOOR NEAR PENNISTONE CRAG: Cathy is mounted and Heathcliff is walking beside her.

CATHY (happily). Oh, Heathcliff, you should smile all the time. You're so handsome when you smile.

HEATHCLIFF (reaching for her hand; serious and pleading). Cathy. Don't make fun of me.

CATHY (taking his hand and kissing it). Don't you know that you're handsome? Remember what I've always told you? That you're a prince in disguise.

The pony stops walking. They stand outlined against the lonely moor, Heathcliff looking up to her, holding her by the hand.

HEATHCLIFF (shyly). Tell me—tell me again—

CATHY (gaily). It's true, Heathcliff! Your father was Emperor of China and your mother an Indian Queen. You were kidnapped by wicked sailors and brought to England. But I'm glad they did it, because I've always wanted to know somebody of noble birth. Instead of . . .

Heathcliff is laughing now.

CATHY. . . . vulgar little peasants like Hindley.

HEATHCLIFF (trying to join in the game). All the princes I've ever read about had castles.

CATHY (pointing with her new riding whip). There is your castle—there, Heathcliff.

HEATHCLIFF (still struggling with fantasy). You mean Pennistone Crag?

CATHY (haughtily). If you don't see that it is a castle, you'll never be a Prince, Heathcliff . . . (Dismounting) Let's go and take possession.

Together they climb Pennistone Crag—an overhanging rock that stands on the moor, forming a half shelter with its beetling top ledge.

CATHY (*under the ledge of rock*). Oh, it's a *wonderful* castle! Heathcliff, let's never leave it.

HEATHCLIFF (*caught by her mood*). Never in our lives!

CATHY (*ecstatic*). Not even to go back to Wuthering Heights. We'll live here forever—we two against the world! (*Struck by something*) I forgot—I'm still your slave.

HEATHCLIFF (*putting his arm around her*). No, Cathy. You're my queen. Whatever happens out there—here you'll always be my queen!

The scene fades out, and then the LIVING ROOM fades in. It is night. Outside an autumn wind lashes against the house. In the room a fire burns. We see the servant, Joseph, Bible in hand, reading. Ellen sits, staring at the stairs as if waiting, and drying her eyes with her apron. Tense and listening in a chair, sits Hindley. Cathy sits on the floor near the fire and Heathcliff lies prone, chin cupped in his hands, staring at Cathy.

JOSEPH (*reading—he reads throughout the scene*). "Let not your heart be troubled; ye believe in God, believe also in Me. In My Father's house are many mansions: if it were not so, I would have told you. I go to prepare a place for you, and if I go and prepare a place for you, I will come again, and receive you unto Myself; that where I am, there ye may be also. And whither I go ye know, and the way ye know . . ." (*He pauses and dries his eyes.*)

CATHY (*in a whisper to Ellen*). Why doesn't the doctor come down?

ELLEN (*her arm around her*). He'll be down—

CATHY. Maybe—it's happened. Oh, Ellen, I want to go to him.

ELLEN (*sympathetically*). Ssh, darling. . . . The doctor will send for you.

HINDLEY (*in a tense voice*). There's no use going—if he's unconscious . . .

Dr. Kenneth appears on the stairs. He stands at the foot of the stairs and looks sadly at the little group.

ELLEN (*who sees him first*). Doctor . . . How is he?

DR. KENNETH (*after a pause*). He is at peace.

Cathy rises and stares at the doctor.

DR. KENNETH (*continuing*). Send for the parson, Joseph . . .

CATHY (*wailing*). He's dead! He's dead!

DR. KENNETH (*coming over and touching her*). Easy, child. He breathed his last calmly and with his eyes closed. He lies now in a deeper sleep. . . .

HINDLEY (*with sudden mastery*). We're going up, Dr. Kenneth. . . .

Cathy weeps convulsively. Heathcliff has risen. He stands watching Cathy, his face stony.

ELLEN (*holding her*). My poor little one. My poor sweet Cathy. My dear wild little Cathy . . . You're all alone, now. (*She holds her in an embrace.*)

DR. KENNETH (*yielding to Hindley*). You may come up now and pray beside him . . .

The group starts upstairs, and the scene cuts to a close view of the DOOR OF MR. EARNSHAW'S DEATH ROOM: It is opened by Dr. Kenneth. Ellen enters, holding Cathy. Joseph enters. The doctor follows. Hindley stands barring Heathcliff's way.

HINDLEY (*alone outside the door with Heathcliff*). You are not wanted in here.

HEATHCLIFF (*hotly*). He loved me more than he did you!

HINDLEY (*pushing him*). My father is past your wheedling. . . . Go and help the stable boys harness the horse for the parson. . . . (*As Heathcliff hesitates*) Do as you're told. I'm master here, now.

He closes the door on Heathcliff. Heathcliff stands staring at the closed door. He digs his fists into his eyes to keep from weeping. He turns slowly and walks away as the scene fades out.

PART THREE

The MOORS IN SPRINGTIME fade in. Flowers ornament rather than relieve the stark power of the moors. Then the scene moves slowly to the exterior of WUTHERING HEIGHTS: The tree has now reached maturity. Its limbs are tossing and its leaves rustling in the breeze. The house itself is somewhat more weathered than when we saw it last.

And now the scene dissolves to the DINING ROOM of the manor at dusk: It is at the end of dinner. Cathy, now about eighteen, sits at one end of the table, Hindley at the other. Joseph is serving them. Hindley starts to pour himself a glass of wine, but there is scarcely a quarter of a glass left in the bottle.

HINDLEY (*bleary*). Joseph—another bottle.

JOSEPH. That's the third, Master Hindley.

HINDLEY (*quite tipsy*). The third or the twenty-third, bring me another.

JOSEPH (*hesitating*). "Wine is a mocker, strong drink is raging," Mr. Hindley.

HINDLEY (*turning on him*). Stop spouting scripture, and do as you're told, you croaking old parrot.

JOSEPH (*shuffling to the sideboard*). Yes, Mr. Hindley.

Cathy, disgusted, starts to rise as Hindley swills off the quarter glass.

HINDLEY (*with a drunken show of authority*). Cathy! Sit down—until you're excused from the table. (*She sits down and stares.*) Joseph—fill Miss Catherine's glass. (*She puts her hand quickly over the glass.*) Oh, my little sister disapproves of drinking. Well, I know some people who don't.

Heathcliff enters, bearing a huge log. It is another Heathcliff grown to young manhood, dirty, his hair matted, his shirt torn. He looks at no one in the room; nor do the others regard him, least of all Cathy, who keeps her eyes on her plate. Joseph has the bottle open and is at Hindley's elbow, about to pour, when Hindley seizes the bottle and pours his own.

HINDLEY. Heathcliff! (*As Heathcliff drops the log on the fire, and turns dully.*) Heathcliff! Saddle my roan . . . And be quick about it, you gypsy beggar.

Heathcliff moves toward the door.

HINDLEY (*continuing; loudly*). I'm going to Gimmerton.

Heathcliff, passing through the door, pauses momentarily, then goes out.

Hindley eats, with deliberate slowness, a few spoonfuls more of a thick porridge, then he throws down the spoon, gets up rudely, and stalks out of the room. Cathy remains seated—until Hindley's departing steps are heard, and then she rises quickly and goes out.

The scene cuts to the KITCHEN where Ellen at her work, looks up to see Cathy steal across the yard, climb the low stone fence and run toward the moor, then to the STABLE where Heathcliff is saddling a horse. Hindley, followed by Joseph, who carries a lantern, enters.

HINDLEY (*to Heathcliff*). I thought I told you to be quick! (*He glances about.*) Look at the stable—filthy as a pigsty. Is that the way you do your work? Clean it up! I want this floor cleaned and scrubbed, *tonight!*

The scene cuts to the EXTERIOR of the STABLE as Heathcliff leads the horse out into the stableyard. Hindley takes the reins roughly from his hand. He walks deliberately into the mud by the barnyard well.

HINDLEY (*to Heathcliff*). Don't stand there, showing your teeth. Give me a hand up.

Heathcliff hesitates, then joins his hands by the stirrup.

HINDLEY. I want your work done when I come back at dawn. (*He grins.*)

As Hindley starts to climb into the saddle the scene cuts to a close view of HINDLEY's MUDDY BOOT IN HEATHCLIFF'S HANDS.

HINDLEY'S VOICE. You're hoping I won't come back. Aren't you? You're hoping I'll fall and break my neck on the road. Aren't you? Aren't you?

The previous scene returns to the screen and we see Hindley mounting, and leaning over toward Heathcliff.

HINDLEY. Muttering gypsy curses under your breath. Well, in case I don't break my neck—in case I do come back, and your work isn't done, I'll thrash you till my arm drops. (*Hindley rides off.*)

JOSEPH (*to Hindley*). I'll see he does it, Master Hindley . . .

Heathcliff stares after the departing Hindley sullenly, then turns quickly and begins to run.

JOSEPH (*shouting*). Where are you going? Heathcliff! Heathcliff! Come back! Master said for you to clean the stable! Master'll be angry. (*Muttering, Joseph goes toward the house*). "The way of the transgressor . . ."

HEATHCLIFF is seen running across the moor, and we follow him. Then the view cuts to the MOORS AND "CASTLE" and we pick up Heathcliff as he approaches the "castle" rock on the moor. He turns into the ledge shelter. Cathy is sitting there, waiting for him.

CATHY. I heard Joseph. Did he see which way you came?

HEATHCLIFF (*dully*). I don't know.

CATHY. It would be dreadful if Hindley ever found out.

HEATHCLIFF (*snarling in pain*). Found out what? That you talk to me once in a while . . . as if I were a little better than a dog.

CATHY (*hotly*). I shouldn't talk to you at all. Look at you! You get worse every day. Dirty and unkempt and in rags. Why aren't you a man? Why don't you run away?

HEATHCLIFF (*in stunned simplicity*). Run away? From you?

CATHY (*in another world*). You could come back to me rich and take me away! Why aren't you my prince like we said long ago. . . . Why can't you rescue me? Heathcliff!

HEATHCLIFF (*swept away*). Cathy! Come with me now!

CATHY (*after a pause*). Where?

HEATHCLIFF (*on fire*). Anywhere.

CATHY (*slowly shaking her head*). And live in haystacks? And go barefoot in the snow? And steal our food from the marketplaces? No, Heathcliff, that's not what I want.

Over the scene comes the sound of music, which she hears but Heathcliff does not.

HEATHCLIFF (*his rage returning*). Oh, you just want to send *me* off. That won't do. I've stayed here and been beaten like a dog, abused and cursed and driven mad. But I *stayed*—just to be near you—even as a dog. . . . And I'll stay till the *end!* I'll live and die under this rock!

She runs quickly out of the castle, and the scene cuts to the EXTERIOR of the "CASTLE," disclosing Cathy coming around the face of the rock. A faint sound catches her ear. She pauses, listens, then looks across the moor toward the Linton house, which is all alight, and whence is borne, on the changing wind, the strains of a waltz, now faint, now clear. Finally, Heathcliff catches up with her.

CATHY. Do you hear?

HEATHCLIFF (*dully*). What?

CATHY. Music— The Lintons are giving a party. (*Holding out her arms to the lights and music*) That's what I want. Dancing and singing in a pretty world! And I'm going to have it!

Starting to run toward the Linton house, she turns and pulls him along.

CATHY. Come on! When you see it, you'll want it, too!

She runs from the rock and Heathcliff follows her.

The scene dissolves to the EXTERIOR of the LINTON HOUSE at night. It is a beautiful Georgian home, set among well kept grounds. Heathcliff and Cathy appear out of the shadows of the foreground, and move silently toward the garden wall.

This is followed by a view of CATHY and HEATHCLIFF climbing over the garden wall. A dog barks—then as the bark is not repeated, they go on through the garden toward the house. The scene cuts to a WINDOW through which we see a country dance—beaux and ladies fully panoplied. A luxurious interior is shimmering with the light of a hundred little tapers. Cathy's and Heathcliff's heads appear. They peer in through the window.

The scene cuts to a reverse view of them looking through the window. Cathy's eyes are wide with excitement. She says something to Heathcliff, which we cannot hear through the glass. Then we see them outside, at the WINDOW.

CATHY (breathlessly). Look! They're dancing. Isn't it wonderful! All those lights. And the gold on the ceiling. Oh, Heathcliff, if we could dance . . . in there! (Pointing) Isn't she beautiful? That's the kind of dress I'll wear. And you'll have a red velvet coat and silver buckles on your shoes . . . Oh, Heathcliff . . . will we, will we, ever?

Out of sight a dog growls. They look around. The dog begins to bark.

CATHY (in sudden terror). Run, Heathcliff!

We follow her as she runs ahead of Heathcliff back toward the garden wall. Dogs dash out of the darkness after the intruders.

The scene cuts to a GARDEN WALL where Heathcliff is lifting Cathy to the top of the wall; then he climbs up to help her over. Her legs still hang down, and the dogs are leaping at her. As Heathcliff goes to lift her up, one of the dogs sinks his teeth into her ankle, and Cathy screams with pain.

The scene cuts to the BALCONY of the house as the guests come out, Judge Linton and his son Edgar to the fore.

EDGAR (to his father). It must be somebody trying to get in.

JUDGE LINTON (holding him back). Thieves . . . Stay where you are, ladies. (To an old servant, Robert, who has just come up with a lantern) Who is it, Robert?

HEATHCLIFF is fighting off a dog who has sunk his fangs into Cathy's ankle. He is hitting it with a stone, but the dog hangs on.

ROBERT'S VOICE. Hold 'em, Skulker! Hold fast . . .

Judge Linton, Edgar and Robert arrive, with some of the young guests in the rear . . . all bearing fire tongs, canes, and other implements.

CATHY (as the group approaches). Run, Heathcliff, run!

HEATHCLIFF (to the Lintons, who have come up). Call off your dogs, you fools!

EDGAR (loudly, to his father). Father, it's Catherine Earnshaw!

Edgar rushes to the dog. Cathy has swooned with pain.

EDGAR. Off, Skulker! Off! Let go! Here —help me, someone. (Two men help Edgar remove the dog.) He's bitten her badly. Hurry—help me carry her in . . .

They lift her up.

HEATHCLIFF. Take your hands off her!

JUDGE LINTON (pointing to Heathcliff). Who's this with her?

EDGAR (peering). The Earnshaw stable boy.

JUDGE LINTON (as his son and another man carry Cathy indoors.) A fine companion for a young lady . . . Bring him in . . .

Robert takes Heathcliff by the arm. Heathcliff, following Cathy, is unaware of the others.

HEATHCLIFF (*struggling*). Look out how you carry her! Let me . . .

CATHY (*faintly*). Run away, Heathcliff. Run!

JUDGE LINTON (*dominating the group*). Oh, no, you don't . . . Hold onto him, Robert.

They close around Cathy, shouldering Heathcliff aside, and start into the house.

The scene dissolves to the LINTON STUDY as they lay Cathy on a couch. Heathcliff, pushing aside Robert who is clinging to him, runs into the room.

EDGAR (*bending over Cathy's injured leg*). Tell Miss Hudkins to come in with some hot water, at once. Isabella, make some bandages.

ISABELLA (*his sister*). Yes, Edgar. . . . How badly is she hurt?

EDGAR (*active at the couch*). I can't tell, yet.

JUDGE LINTON (*confronting Heathcliff*). Now, young man, let's hear your explanation.

HEATHCLIFF (*white*). If your dogs have injured her, you'll pay for this.

JUDGE LINTON (*flaming*). Hold your tongue, you insolent rascal. I'm a magistrate of this county!

ISABELLA. He's just like the gypsy that stole my pony. Isn't he, Edgar?

EDGAR. Miss Earnshaw, roaming the country with a gypsy stable boy!

JUDGE LINTON. And at night! I'm shocked that her brother would permit it.

EDGAR (*confidentially*). Father, please, she's in pain.

JUDGE LINTON (*reluctantly acceding to Edgar*). Well, pack this rascal off . . .

HEATHCLIFF (*standing his ground*). I won't leave without Cathy. . . .

JUDGE LINTON (*thundering*). Show him the door, Robert. The back door!

CATHY (*faintly*). Let me go! I want to go with him. Heathcliff!

He rushes to her, but Edgar stands in his way.

EDGAR (*curtly*). Get out of here!

Heathcliff makes no move to go—but stands glowering.

JUDGE LINTON (*raging*). Throw him out!

Three servants spring on Heathcliff and start to drag him away. For a moment he does not resist, but then one of the servants cuffs him savagely on the side of the head. With a cry he wrenches himself free. His ragged, dirty figure for a moment dominates the elegantly dressed merrymakers who only stand staring at him.

HEATHCLIFF (*addressing them all—his voice vibrant with rage*). I'm going— I'm going from here and this cursed country *both*!

We get a close view of CATHY as she reacts to this last—and there is a sudden gleam of excitement in her eyes. Then we return to the previous scene:

HEATHCLIFF (*his voice is low, intense*). But I'll be back in this house one day, Judge Linton, and pay you out! I'll bring this house down in ruins around your heads! That's my curse on you! (*Suddenly he spits on the floor.*) On *all* of you!

He turns and goes. There is a moment of horrified silence, followed by a babble of voices: The scoundrel! After him! Get the dogs! Impertinent creature! Throw him out! As this goes on we focus on CATHY, who has half raised herself and is looking after him, a wondering expression on her face.

CATHY (*excitedly*). Good-bye, Heathcliff! Good-bye—I'll be waiting. . . .

PART FOUR

The ROAD at WUTHERING HEIGHTS fades in. Down the road from Thrushcross Grange comes a carriage, drawn by two high-spirited horses. Edgar Linton is driving and Cathy is beside him. We hear her gay laughter as the scene cuts to a close view of EDGAR and CATHY in the carriage.

CATHY (*gaily*). I'm ashamed to confess—I haven't been homesick one tiny moment—and I never spent even a single night away from Wuthering Heights before. . . .

EDGAR. It's my vain foolish hope that you'll be just a little homesick for Thrushcross Grange—just a little. . . .

The EXTERIOR of the HOUSE: The carriage pulls up. Ellen opens the door.

ELLEN (*excitedly*). Cathy! Welcome home! (*She grabs up a shawl and comes rushing out.*) Cathy! Welcome home!

CATHY (*happily*). Ellen! Ellen!

ELLEN (*anxiously*). Don't stir! I'll get Joseph to carry you!

EDGAR (*laughing*). Carry her! Why, she runs like a little goat.

CATHY (*joining in his mirth*). Why, Ellen, I've been dancing night after night.

At this moment, barking frenziedly, the dogs come running into the scene, from around the corner of the house. They crowd around Cathy, jumping up on her excitedly.

ELLEN. Down, Rover! Down! (*She takes in Cathy's costume. Exclaims:*) Look at you, Cathy! You look like a Princess doll. Wherever did you get that beautiful dress?

CATHY (*displaying it*). Edgar's sister loaned it to me. It's so wonderful! Edgar, do come in and have a cup of tea. . . . (*Cathy runs ahead into the house.*)

EDGAR. As soon as the horses have been seen to.

ELLEN (*calling*). Heathcliff! Heathcliff! (*She follows Cathy inside.*)

The scene cuts to the LIVING ROOM, with a close view of CATHY.

ELLEN'S VOICE (*out of the scene*). Heathcliff!

Cathy's gaiety vanishes at the sound of the word. She turns to meet Ellen—who comes forward into sight.

CATHY (*slowly to Ellen*). Heathcliff? Is he here?

ELLEN (*with a grimace*). He came back one night last week with great talk of lying in a lake of fire . . . How he had to see you to live. He's unbearable.

Cathy's face shows pain and disillusion.

ELLEN. Where can he be, the scoundrel? Heathcliff! Heathcliff. (*She runs out toward the kitchen.*)

Heathcliff appears from around a corner of the room, and comes towards Cathy. Each beholding the other's appearance, is dismayed.

HEATHCLIFF (*finally—like a famished dog*). Cathy!

CATHY (*with profound disappointment*). Heathcliff!

HEATHCLIFF. Why did you stay in that house so long?

CATHY. I didn't expect to find you here.

HEATHCLIFF (*as before*). Why did you stay so long?

CATHY (*her disappointment turning to indignation, and her indignation to spite*). Why? Because I was having a wonderful time—a fascinating, delightful, wonderful time. (*As Edgar enters she observes him and adds for Edgar's benefit.*) You might wash your hands and face and comb your hair, Heathcliff, so that I need not be ashamed of you before a guest.

Ellen re-enters, and sees Heathcliff.

ELLEN. Heathcliff! What are you **doing**

in this part of the house? Go look after Mr. Linton's horses at once.

HEATHCLIFF (*rudely*). Let him look after his own horses.

EDGAR. I've already done so.

CATHY. Heathcliff, apologize to Mr. Linton at once.

Heathcliff turns on his heel, and walks off.

CATHY. Bring in some tea, if you please, Ellen.

EDGAR (*anxiously*). Cathy . . .

CATHY. Yes, Edgar.

EDGAR. I simply can't understand why your brother allows that beast of a gypsy to have the run of the house.

CATHY (*evenly*). Indeed . . .

EDGAR (*heedlessly*). Cathy— How can you, a gentlewoman, tolerate him under your roof? A roadside beggar, giving himself airs of equality. How can you?

CATHY (*suddenly*). What do you know about Heathcliff?

EDGAR. All I need or want to know!

CATHY (*flaring up*). He was my friend, long before you.

EDGAR. That blackguard . . .

CATHY. Blackguard and all, he belongs under this roof and you'll speak well of him—or get out . . .

EDGAR. What! Are you out of your senses!

CATHY. Get out, I said . . . Or stop calling those I love names. . . .

EDGAR (*dumbfounded*). Those you love! That stable boy . . .

CATHY. Yes! Yes!

Ellen enters, bearing a tea-service, and to her amazement, hears the angry words flying.

EDGAR. Cathy, what possesses you—do you realize the things you're saying?

CATHY (*beside herself*). I'm saying that I hate you—I hate the look of your milk-white face. I hate the touch of your soft, foolish hands.

Edgar looks curiously at Cathy—as though he were beholding her truly for the first time.

EDGAR (*not raising his voice*). Some of that gypsy's evil soul has gotten into you—I think.

CATHY. Yes.

EDGAR. Some of that beggar's dirt is on you.

CATHY. Yes! Yes! Now get out.

He turns abruptly and goes.

ELLEN (*flabbergasted*). Cathy—

CATHY (*savagely*). Oh, leave me alone— (*And with that she bursts into sobs.*)

The scene dissolves to the MOORS—EARLY MORNING, and we follow CATHY as she walks toward the "castle." Shafts of sunlight pierce through the clouds, now and again, illuminating the landscape.

Then the scene cuts to the "CASTLE," and Heathcliff is there watching intently as Cathy approaches. He is less uncouth than before, but still wild enough. There is no greeting between them as she comes near and drops down beside him. It is some time before a word is spoken.

HEATHCLIFF (*looking out over the moors*). The clouds are lowering over Gimmerton Head. . . .

CATHY. Yes. (*Pointing*) See how the light is changing.

HEATHCLIFF (*after a pause*). You're such a part of all this.

CATHY. Maybe we belong to the moors. (*Impulsively*) You're strong, Heathcliff, you're so strong. Make the world stop right here—make everything stop —and stand still—and never move again—the moors never change—and you and me never change. . . .

HEATHCLIFF. The moors and I will never change—don't you, Cathy.

CATHY. I can't. I can't. No matter what I say or do, Heathcliff, this is me—forever. (*They are quiet for a while.*)

When you went away, Heathcliff, where did you go? What did you do?

HEATHCLIFF (*picking idly at the grass, not looking at her*). I went to Liverpool. One night I shipped for America—on a brigantine going to New Orleans. We were held up by the tide and I lay all night long on the deck, thinking of you and the years and years without you— and I knew I couldn't face it. So I jumped overboard and swam ashore. You're inside of me! Your hands are tight around my heart. I can't—I couldn't live without you— Couldn't breathe! Can you understand it? Can you forgive me!

She touches him gently with her hand, in answer, then looks into his eyes. All the passion she feels toward him, but does not comprehend, surges up within her.

CATHY (*filling her lungs*). Smell the heather, Heathcliff, fill my arms with heather—all they can hold.

Heathcliff hastily snatches a large bunch and thrusts the heather into her arms. She closes her eyes.

HEATHCLIFF. Cathy, you're not thinking of that other world now?

CATHY (*breathlessly*). Don't talk, Heathcliff—all this might disappear.

He piles more heather into her arms as the scene fades out.

PART FIVE

CATHY'S ROOM fades in. Twilight is darkening the windows. Through the windows the moors, mantled with snow, now may be seen. Ellen Dean is helping Cathy dress. An effulgent and highly becoming costume is being buttoned up on Cathy.

CATHY (*fidgeting; impatiently*). Oh, Ellen—aren't you through yet?

ELLEN (*sarcastically*). What's the matter? Supposing you're not ready when he gets here . . . (*With a snort*) Any young man that will come snivelling back to you after the way you treated him—you can keep waiting forever. (*Cathy applies scent to the backs of her ears. Ellen sniffs.*)

ELLEN. What's wrong with him? Sending you perfume! Pah! Hasn't he any pride?

CATHY. I sent my apologies to him, didn't I?

ELLEN (*as she fusses around the young lady*). I can't believe this change in you, Cathy. Just yesterday it seems you were a stupid, harum-scarum child with dirty hands and a willful heart . . .

CATHY (*smiling*). That's my other nature, Ellen. I still have it . . . It used to fly around wild, but now I can coax it into a cage—whenever I want to. . . .

ELLEN (*as she stands off to survey her*). Look at you! You are lovely, Cathy— lovely . . .

CATHY (*amused*). That's a very silly lie. I'm not lovely. What I am is very brilliant. I have a wonderful brain . . .

ELLEN (*sarcastically*). Indeed!

The door opens—Heathcliff stands in the threshold—unobserved for several moments.

The scene cuts to a view of the ROOM from the doorway. Heathcliff's head and shoulder are in the foreground.

CATHY (*quite literally*). It enables me to be superior to myself. . . . (*Philosophically*) There's nothing to be gained by just looking pretty—like Isabella. Every beauty patch must conceal a thought and every curl be full of humor as well as brilliantine. . . . (*She looks into the mirror again—sees Heathcliff's reflection—and turns slowly.*) Since when (*hotly*) are you in the habit of entering my room, Heathcliff?

HEATHCLIFF (*quietly*). I want to talk to you. (*Quietly to Ellen*) Go outside, Ellen.

ELLEN. I will not! I take orders from Mistress Caroline—not stable boys. . . .

HEATHCLIFF (*grimly*). Go outside!

His eyes blaze at the nurse. She hesitates, looking at Cathy for help. Cathy offers none and Ellen retreats before Heathcliff.

The scene cuts to the ROOM, caught from Cathy's angle. Heathcliff slams the door shut after Ellen and turns to Cathy.

CATHY (*sarcastically*). And now that we are so happily alone, Heathcliff, may I know to what I owe that great honor . . . ?

HEATHCLIFF (*after a pause—glaring at her*). He's coming here again.

CATHY. Who?

HEATHCLIFF. You know who! That stupid fop—Linton.

CATHY (*smiling at his jealousy*). You're really unbearable, Heathcliff . . . Utterly unbearable.

HEATHCLIFF. Why are you dressed in a silk dress?

CATHY (*icily*). Because gentlefolk dress for dinner . . .

HEATHCLIFF (*coming closer*). Why are you trying to win his puling flatteries?

CATHY (*meeting him head on*). I'm not a child any more. You can't talk that way to me.

HEATHCLIFF. I'm not talking to a child. I'm talking to Cathy. My Cathy.

CATHY (*with a dangerous smile*). Oh, I'm your Cathy.

HEATHCLIFF (*tensely*). Yes.

CATHY (*exploding*). And I'm to take orders from you—a dirty stable boy. . . . Allow you to select what dresses I shall wear and bow humbly to your horrible, wretched tempers . . .

HEATHCLIFF. Cathy! Where's your heart!

CATHY (*white*). Impertinent—that's what are you! Mr. Linton was right! An impertinent, unmannerly lout!

HEATHCLIFF (*seizing her arm*). Call me names now like the rest of them!

CATHY (*struggling violently*). You had your chance to be something else. Now let me alone!

HEATHCLIFF (*holding her savagely*). Yes—yes, tell the dirty stable boy to let go of you—he soils your pretty dress. But who soils your heart? Who turns you into a vain, cheap, worldly fool. . . . Linton does! You'll let yourself be loved by him because it pleases your stupid, greedy vanity. . . .

CATHY (*working herself free*). Stop it! And get out. . . . Go where I can never see you again . . .

HEATHCLIFF (*blazing*). I will! And this time I'll stay!

CATHY (*as the tinkle of sleigh bells is heard*). It won't do any good. Thief or servant were all you were born to be—or beggar beside a road. Begging for favors. Not earning them, but whimpering for them with your dirty hands.

HEATHCLIFF. That's all I've become to you—a pair of dirty hands. . . . Well—have them then. . . . (*And he slaps her face.*) Have them where they belong. (*He slaps her again, wheels and walks out of the door. He turns in the doorway.*) It doesn't help to strike you.

He turns and goes quickly to the stairs as the sleigh bells are ringing loudly.

The scene cuts to the HALL BELOW. Ellen is opening the door on Edgar. He enters.

EDGAR. Good evening, Ellen.

ELLEN. Good evening, Master Linton.

She takes his hat, helps him with his coat.

EDGAR. I hope I'm not too early.

The scene cuts to the STAIRS as Heathcliff is descending.

ELLEN'S VOICE. Master Linton, Miss Cathy will be right down.

We follow Heathcliff as he goes toward Edgar. He holds his hands, palms forward, as though they did not belong to the rest of his body. Edgar observes him, sees his anguished eyes. Heathcliff goes past Edgar without a word or a look. Edgar stares after him.

ELLEN (*quickly*). If you'll go into the living room, Master Linton.

The scene cuts to the LIVING ROOM. Edgar enters, goes toward the fire. His face is troubled, thoughtful. At the sound of steps on the stairs, somberness vanishes. He turns delightedly to meet Cathy, and bends over her hand with due courtliness. Then, without releasing her fingers, he stands back and regards her.

The scene cuts to HEATHCLIFF'S PLACE in THE LOFT OVER THE STABLE: He climbs in, carrying his hands in the same strange way—as though they didn't belong to the rest of him. He goes to the window, and stands there. Harsh little flakes are whirling about outside. Now, with the same motion as when he struck Cathy, he drives his hands, one after the other, through the window pane, shattering the glass, cutting his hands.

The scene dissolves to the KITCHEN, with Ellen and Joseph. Joseph goes to the door leading to the living room, and listens.

JOSEPH. No music . . . no singing . . . no laughing . . . precious little talk —and what there is, so low you can't make a word out.

ELLEN. Get away from that door, you—

The scene dissolves to HEATHCLIFF'S LOFT: He is lying on the bed, face down, his head on his crossed, bloody hands. The irregularity of his breathing tells us that he is not asleep. Then the sound of hooves on cobbles is heard, and Heathcliff's face turns. He listens, then suddenly gets up and is gone.

The scene cuts to the EXTERIOR of the STABLE as Heathcliff appears; and we follow him as he runs through the snow toward the house; then to the KITCHEN: Ellen is at her work. She looks up to see Heathcliff entering.

HEATHCLIFF, Linton . . . has he gone?

ELLEN (seeing his hands). Heathcliff! Your hands! What have you done?

HEATHCLIFF (monotonously). Has he gone?

Ellen seizes him by the wrists.

ELLEN. What have you done to your hands?

Ellen looks at him intently; realization of what he has done comes over her. She tears a strip off her apron and starts binding his hands.

HEATHCLIFF (as though to himself). I want to crawl to her feet . . . whimper to be forgiven—for loving her—for needing her more than my own life—for belonging to her more than my own soul . . . I want to beg for a smile . . . I don't care if she loves Linton—or whom she loves, if she'll only look at me—and say my name . . .

ELLEN. Oh, Heathcliff—

From the living room comes Cathy's voice.

CATHY'S VOICE (softly). Ellen!

Heathcliff automatically puts his bandaged hands behind him. Observing his action, Ellen nods toward a corner of the room which is in shadow. Heathcliff goes there and stands silently as Cathy enters the kitchen.

CATHY (at the door). Oh, there you are. I didn't know whether you were still up.

ELLEN. Has he finally gone?

Cathy nods. Her face is thoughtful for a moment, but that is only fleeting. She smiles.

CATHY. Ellen, I've got some news for you.

ELLEN (with a worried glance in Heathcliff's direction). The kitchen's no place for that dress. Come into the parlor.

She and Cathy go out of the kitchen.

CATHY. Come along. Can you keep a secret?

The view cuts to the LIVING ROOM as they enter.

CATHY. Sit down and listen. (She pushes Ellen into a chair.) Ellen, Edgar has asked me to marry him.

ELLEN. What did you tell him?

CATHY. I said I'd give him my answer tomorrow.

The scene cuts to the KITCHEN as Heathcliff, who has been listening to their voices, enters the hall connecting the kitchen and the living room; then to the LIVING ROOM.

ELLEN. Do you love him, Cathy?

CATHY. Of course.

ELLEN. Why?

CATHY. Why? That's a silly question, isn't it?

ELLEN (*in the same tone as before*). No, not so silly— Why do you love him?

CATHY (*rather defiantly*). Oh—because he's handsome and pleasant to be with—

ELLEN. Not enough.

CATHY. And because he will be rich some day—and I shall be the finest lady in the county.

HEATHCLIFF'S SILHOUETTE appears in the dark HALLWAY.

ELLEN'S VOICE. Humph! . . . And now tell me *how* you love him.

CATHY. I love the ground under his feet and the air over his head and everything he touches.

Then we are back in the former scene:

ELLEN. What about Heathcliff?

CATHY. Oh Heathcliff—he gets worse every day— It would degrade me to marry him— I wish he hadn't come back—

The candles in the room flicker as though they had been blown by a draft. Ellen gazes out toward the kitchen. Cathy falls silent for a time.

CATHY (*sighing*). It would be heaven to escape from this disorderly comfortless place.

ELLEN. Well—if Master Edgar and his charms and money and parties mean heaven to you, what's to stop you from entering that wonderful domain and taking your place among the Linton angels?

Cathy frowns quickly as her thoughts turn inward. She touches her heart with her palm.

CATHY (*with deep seriousness*). The obstacle is here or wherever the soul lives —I don't think I belong in heaven, Ellen. I dreamt once I was there. I dreamt

I went to heaven and that heaven didn't seem to be my home . . . and I broke my heart with weeping to come back to earth . . . and the angels were so angry, they flung me out into the middle of the heath on top of Wuthering Heights . . . and I woke up sobbing with joy. (*After a pause*) That's it, Ellen. I've no more business marrying Edgar Linton than I have being in heaven . . . but Ellen, Ellen, what can I do?

ELLEN. You're thinking of Heathcliff?

CATHY. Who else? He's sunk so low— he seems to take pleasure in being mean and brutal—and yet—he's more myself than I am. Whatever our souls are made of his and mine are the same—and Linton's is as different as frost from fire— My one thought in living is Heathcliff —Ellen, I *am* Heathcliff— Everything he's suffered I've suffered—the little happiness he's ever known I've had too— Oh, Ellen, if everything in the world died and Heathcliff remained life would still be full for me— (*The sound of hooves on cobbles is now heard.*)

JOSEPH'S VOICE (*from the outside*). Heathcliff! Stop!

ELLEN. He must have been listening.

CATHY (*frightened*). Heathcliff was listening to us? (*Ellen nods.*) How much did he hear?

ELLEN. I'm not sure—but I think to where you said it would degrade you to marry him.

We follow CATHY as she flies to the kitchen door, opens it, and runs out.

The scene changes abruptly to the STABLE YARD:

CATHY (*calling*). Heathcliff! Heathcliff!

JOSEPH (*hurrying toward her*). No use calling for Heathcliff, Miss Cathy. He's run away on Master's best horse.

ELLEN (*framed in the doorway*). Come in out of the snow, Miss Cathy. You'll catch your death of cold.

CATHY (*calling—real terror in her voice*). Heathcliff! Heathcliff! Oh, Ellen, he'll never come back. I know him.

ELLEN. Last time he did.

CATHY. Not this time . . . I know him . . . I know him . . . (*To Joseph*) Which way did he go?

JOSEPH (*pointing*). Over the heath.

CATHY. Saddle the mare . . . quickly.

ELLEN. Cathy, come in. Come in out of the storm.

CATHY. The fool! He should have known I love him . . . I love him . . .

The scene dissolves to the MOORS as seen from a little rise. Below us snow and sleet whirl across the scene.

CATHY'S VOICE. Heathcliff! Heathcliff!

The blizzard whirls and eddies so that for a moment we glimpse Cathy's form. Stumbling, she makes her way toward us. Her dress is torn, her hair disheveled. She runs forward.

CATHY. Heathcliff!

The scene dissolves to the PENNISTONE CRAGS, the ENTRANCE TO THE CAVE: Cathy picks her way among the rocks, stumbles and nearly falls, then at last stands in the entrance of the cave. Sleet lashes down on the rock from above.

CATHY. Heathcliff! Heathcliff!

ECHO (*forlornly the sound of her voice echoing from the depths of the cave*). Heathcliff! Heathcliff!

As Cathy turns away and disappears in the snow, the scene fades out. Then it fades into the HALLWAY OF WUTHERING HEIGHTS at night as Hindley opens the door. He is staggering under his nightly load of liquor. Ellen Dean rushes to him, candlestick in hand. She is in tears.

ELLEN (*rushing to meet him*). Master Hindley! Thank heaven you've come home.

HINDLEY (*drunkenly*). Where's Joseph? Told him to stay awake till I came home . . . does he expect me to unsaddle my horse . . . unmannerly rascal . . .

ELLEN (*clinging to him*). Master Hindley—you've got to go out again. Cathy—Cathy's gone. They're looking for her. Joseph . . . everybody . . .

HINDLEY (*still befuddled*). Gone? Gone where?

ELLEN. In the storm . . . Hours ago. Heathcliff ran away. . . . He took a horse and left and she went running after him.

HINDLEY. Oh, she did. Well—don't stand there with your mouth open like a great fish! Get me a fresh bottle . . . and we'll celebrate.

ELLEN (*moaning*). Master Hindley! She'll die on the moors . . .

HINDLEY (*thrusting her off*). Do as I told you—if she's run after that gypsy scum—let her run. Let her run through storm and hell . . . They're birds of a feather and the devil take them both. . . . Get me a bottle, I told you . . .

The scene dissolves to the MOORS at night. At first we see only the snow, then intermittently, five or six lanterns, widely separated as if a number of people had spread out, searching for Cathy. Near us we hear one of Cathy's dogs yelping. He runs into the scene and for a moment stands revealed as he tries to pick up the scent. Then he is lost in the blizzard again. Faintly we hear voices:

VOICES. Cathy! . . . Miss Earnshaw! Hallo! Hallo!

This dissolves to the MOORS at dawn: The blizzard is nearly dissipated and it is beginning to get light. Seen from the top of a hill are the vast moors—now mantled with snow. Into the foreground come Dr. Kenneth and Edgar. The doctor's lantern is already out and Edgar blows out his.

DR. KENNETH (*shaking his head as he looks over the moors*). I don't know where to look next.

EDGAR (*tensely*). We'll find her. We've got to!

VOICE (*shouting*). Hallo—hallo! Over here!

From all over the moors come shouts and the excited yelping of a dog, hot on the trail. Instantly Dr. Kenneth and Edgar start running up the hill. A moment later another searcher—one of the Linton servants—races past. In the background other figures are converging toward Pennistone Crag and the "castle."

The scene dissolves to the LINTON HOUSE at dawn, revealing Edgar, followed by Dr. Kenneth, carrying Cathy up the steps. The door is opened by a servant, and the view cuts to the HALL as Edgar and the Doctor enter. Cathy lies limp and unconscious in Edgar's arms, her hair dripping, her clothes bedraggled, her face and hands deathly white. As they enter, Isabella appears. She is wearing a robe over her night clothes.

DR. KENNETH (*to a servant*). Some brandy . . . quick.

EDGAR (*to a woman servant*). Get a fire burning in the East room.

Edgar carries Cathy to a large couch before the blazing fire in the study.

DR. KENNETH. . . . And a lot of dry towels . . . hurry.

ISABELLA. Is she all right?

DR. KENNETH. I don't know yet. We'll bring her round first.

ISABELLA. Where was she?

EDGAR. Crumpled in front of the big rock on the moor, with life nearly out of her.

Dr. Kenneth holds a glass of brandy to Cathy's lips, forces a few drops between them, then turns away to put the glass down. The view then moves close to CATHY and her lips form the word: "Heathcliff." The scene fades out.

PART SIX

THE GARDEN of the LINTON HOUSE fades in. It is day. Cathy, in a gay bed-jacket, a quilt over her legs, reclines in a chair, looking very beautiful and convalescent. Dr. Kenneth stands, bag in hand. Having finished his visit, he is giving final instructions to Isabella and Ellen.

DR. KENNETH. Twenty drops in a glass of claret, well warmed, then add a lump of sugar—there's nothing else I can think to tell you. (*As though he had said these things before*) Keep her in the sun. Feed her lots of cream and butter. (*To Cathy*) In another month, Cathy, you'll be as good as new.

CATHY (*smiling*). I feel as good as new already.

DR. KENNETH. Good afternoon.

ISABELLA AND CATHY (*repeating*). Good afternoon.

Ellen walks with him into the house. Then the scene cuts to the LINTON LIVING ROOM as Ellen and Dr. Kenneth enter and walk forward.

ELLEN (*frowning*). She'll be going home soon, Doctor.

DR. KENNETH. What's needed now is peace and orderliness in her life. That's not to be found at Wuthering Heights. (*After a pause—significantly*) Has she mentioned him at all?

ELLEN. She hasn't spoken his name since the delirium passed.

DR. KENNETH. Well, sometimes fever can heal as well as destroy . . . I made some inquiries from the people in the village who knew him.

ELLEN. What did you hear?

DR. KENNETH. No sign nor hint of our precious Heathcliff. He's disappeared into thin air.

ELLEN. Heaven hope.

As they move toward the door, the scene cuts to the GARDEN, revealing ISABELLA AND CATHY.

ISABELLA. Now what was it Dr. Kenneth said—twenty lumps of sugar in a glass of claret and one drop of medicine—or was it twenty lumps of sugar and one drop of claret? Oh, why don't I pay attention! (*She goes out.*)

Cathy looks out of the scene, then cries delightedly:

CATHY. Edgar!

EDGAR is seen entering through the garden gate. He is dressed in riding togs, rather mud-spattered. His appearance is quite in contrast to his somewhat foppish appearance of before. He impresses us more as a man who has work to do than as a love-sick boy. He comes forward smiling.

CATHY. Where have you been all day? I've missed you.

EDGAR (*with a laugh*). This time of year every one of our tenants can find something to complain of. For the last four hours I've been arguing with old Swithin whether or not we should build him a new pig-pen. He decided we should.

Edgar observes that Cathy is partly in the shade now.

EDGAR. Let's move you over to where there's more sun.

He lifts her out of the chair. Isabella picks up the chair, runs ahead, puts it down where the sun is bright. Edgar keeps Cathy in his arms while Isabella arranges the pillows.

EDGAR. I saw Hindley in the village.

CATHY (*a shadow flickers on her face*). Oh . . .

EDGAR. He wanted to know when you could come home. (*Smiling*) I'm afraid I wasn't quite truthful—I told him Dr. Kenneth said it would be months and months. . . .

ISABELLA (*giving the pillows a final touch*). There now. You may put her down.

Edgar does so, tenderly.

ISABELLA. Perhaps Ellen will remember what Dr. Kenneth said about the medicine.

She goes quickly toward the house.

CATHY (*looking after her*). She's such a darling . . . but then, you've all been darlings. Everyone is so nice to me here. (*Then, after a pause, during which she becomes very thoughtful*) Still, I can't remain here forever.

Edgar turns away from her abruptly. She glances up surprised.

CATHY. What's the matter?

EDGAR (*not looking at her*). Naturally I'm kind to you—who wouldn't be? But —Oh, never mind. . . . If I can make

you happy just by being kind, that should be enough for me. After all, what else can I give you?

CATHY. What else? You can ask that? Don't you know what else you have given me? (*Now Edgar's eyes meet hers.*) Why it's your own self you've given me—your strength . . .

EDGAR (*uncomprehendingly*). My strength?

CATHY (*trying to find the words to express the feeling in her troubled heart*). You'd understand if you knew what my life was before. It was like the moors—endless and desolate—and I was lost in them . . . calling for someone in the darkness to save me—and nobody, nobody answered. I couldn't even see the trace of a path. . . . I was so frightened, so alone—so terribly alone. . . .

Edgar looks at her—for the first time he understands her real feelings—he is tensely still.

CATHY (*continuing without looking at him*). Then suddenly you were there—you held out your hand and led me back—to happiness, to a way of living I'd thought I'd lost forever . . . What you said long ago was true. There was a strange curse on me—that kept me from being myself—or at least what I wanted to be . . . from living in heaven. (*She pauses, looking suddenly straight at him*) Now do you understand?

EDGAR (*kneeling before her—taking her hand in his*). Cathy, my darling. . . . Let me take care of you forever . . . Let me guard you and love you . . . always.

CATHY (*taking his head in her hands, searching his face as if the terror of being alone again has seized her*). Would you love me always?

EDGAR (*with all his devotion in his voice and eyes*). Always—always.

As they look into each other's eyes, the scene shifts to a view of ISABELLA coming out from the house with the glass of wine in her hand. She stops in her tracks. And from her angle, some distance away, we see Edgar tenderly embracing Cathy. Then we get a closer view of ISABELLA and find an amused expression on her face. She looks at the glass of medicine in her hand. She shrugs comically, then turns back toward the house, as the scene fades out.

Then GIMMERTON VILLAGE fades in, revealing the village church, the bell of which is pealing lustily. It is a clear early autumn day. The scene dissolves to the EXTERIOR of the CHURCH, viewed toward the nearly closed doors: Around the steps are some twenty to thirty villagers curiously waiting. Three or four little boys and girls are clustered around the door trying to peek in through the crack. An organ is heard playing softly.

LITTLE GIRL (*whispering*). What are they doing now?

LITTLE BOY (*disgustedly*). Oh, everybody's kissing everybody. (*He smacks his lips in derision.*)

At this moment the children scatter and the doors are thrown open by the beadle, very impressive-looking with his staff and uniform.

BEADLE (*gruffly to the children*). Make way there! Make way!

Now from out of the church comes Cathy resplendent in her wedding dress. She clings happily to Edgar's arm as a cheer is raised by the villagers outside.

In the back, behind them, we see Mr. Linton, Isabella, and Ellen in all her finery and with the appropriate tears. Villagers and gentry crowd around Cathy and Edgar.

VILLAGERS. Look at her! Isn't she sweet!

Aren't they the happy pair! And so pretty! What a beautiful dress! Long life to both of you!

Now the BEADLE, appearing at the bottom of the steps, waves to the coachman of a traveling carriage in the background. And the coachman picks up his reins and starts toward the steps. Then this scene cuts to a close view of CATHY AND EDGAR on the CHURCH STEPS.

CATHY (*happily*). Thank you—thank you—I'm very happy—

EDGAR (*beside her—smiling*). Come, Cathy . . .

She starts out, then stops. Her eyes seem to take in all the loutish yokels, one by one, with something frightened in her look.

EDGAR (*taking her arm*). Come, dear . . . Whatever are you staring at?

Cathy comes to with a little shudder and clings to Edgar as we see her gradually closer.

CATHY. A cold wind went across my heart just then. A feeling of doom. . . . (*Smiling at him*) You touched me and it was gone. (*They look at each other. He is anxious, but smiles.*)

EDGAR (*looking around at the cold stones*). It's just the dampness, darling —these old stones—

CATHY (*with sudden ecstasy—clinging to him*). Oh, Edgar, I love you! I do!

The scene fades out.

PART SEVEN

The LINTON STUDY at dusk fades in: Isabella, matured now into a high-spirited young woman, is playing the spinet. Cathy is working before a frame of *petit point*. She is paler and more delicate than before her illness but very lovely in the fulfillment of her dream of being the first lady of the county. Judge Linton and Edgar are over a chessboard, in the last phase of the game. The whole scene is one of domestic tranquility.

EDGAR. I'm afraid you've fallen into a trap, father.

JUDGE LINTON (*making a move*). So I have. My mind isn't what it used to be.

EDGAR (*moving a piece*). There you are. Checkmate.

JUDGE LINTON. Another one?

EDGAR. No, thanks . . . I don't think we'll have time before dinner.

JUDGE LINTON (*rising*). Well, I'll go dress for dinner.

He goes out, and Edgar, too, rises. He

crosses to Cathy, and the two are seen closer. Edgar is solider—more substantial looking than when we last saw him.

EDGAR. I talked to Jeff Peters this afternoon, Cathy, about building a new wing.

CATHY. Yes, dear.

EDGAR (*with heavy whimsicality*). It doesn't look as if we're going to be able to marry Isabella off for another decade or two. She's so particular.

We see ISABELLA at the spinet.

ISABELLA (*tartly*). It's a brother's duty, dear Edgar, to introduce his sister to some other type than fops and pale young poets.

EDGAR (*as the scene widens*). Oh, indeed, Isabella. You want a dragoon . . . eh?

ISABELLA. Yes. With a fiery mustache.

CATHY. Poor Isabella, I'm afraid I got the only prize in the county.

EDGAR (*bowing and kissing her on top of the head*). Thank you, Cathy. As for me, my darling, heaven is bounded by the four walls of this room.

CATHY (*smiling*). Yes, we're all angels. Even my *petit point* hero. I'm just putting wings on him. (*Dogs are heard barking.*)

EDGAR. Speaking of wings, would you like to see Jeff Peters' plans? I'll get them.

CATHY (*as the barking grows louder*). What's the matter with the dogs?

EDGAR (*going out*). Probably one of the servants coming back from the village.

The scene cuts to the EXTERIOR of the GRANGE, revealing a stranger, wrapped in a cloak, his back turned, looking at the house in the gathering twilight, while the dogs sniff and growl around his feet. He stares silently at the lighted windows and the darkening sky for an instant, then goes to the door, raises the knocker and lets it fall twice. There is a pause. Then Ellen opens the door and peers out from the lighted interior.

THE STRANGER. Tell Mrs. Linton someone wishes to see her.

ELLEN (*staring*). Who's that?

HEATHCLIFF (*coming closer*). Don't you know me, Ellen?

ELLEN (*frightened*). Heathcliff! Is it really you?

HEATHCLIFF. Yes. I've come back. Go tell—your mistress.

ELLEN (*greatly disturbed*). It will put her out of her head!

HEATHCLIFF (*wildly*). Go and carry my message.

The LINTON STUDY: Cathy leans back, and surveys her work, while Isabella is playing. Ellen enters, her face white. She comes up to Cathy.

ELLEN (*almost a whisper*). Cathy.

CATHY (*observing her alarm*). Ellen! What is it?

ELLEN. Someone—wishes to see you.

CATHY. Well, you look as if it were a ghost.

ELLEN. It is. He's come back.

CATHY (*apprehensively*). Who?

ELLEN. Heathcliff.

Cathy sits stock still, the heart gone out of her.

CATHY (*after a pause—tensely*). What does he want?

ELLEN. He wants to see you.

CATHY (*slowly*). Tell him—I'm not at home.

Edgar comes back into the room, carrying a roll of plans.

EDGAR (*surprised*). Not at home, Cathy? To whom are you not at home?

CATHY (*obviously pulling herself together*). It's Heathcliff. (*She resumes her needlework with a show of calm.*) It seems he's come back.

EDGAR (*genially*). Well, that's news. Where has he been?

Ellen, about to carry Cathy's message, stops.

ELLEN. America, he said. He's so changed I didn't recognize him.

EDGAR (*essaying a pleasantry*). For the better, I hope.

ELLEN (*bubbling*). Oh, yes! He's quite the gentleman. Fine clothes—a horse—

CATHY (*on edge*). Don't stand there prattling. Tell him that I do not wish to see him.

EDGAR (*putting his arm about her*). Nonsense, Cathy. We can't be that cruel. He's come a long way. And a great gentleman, Ellen says. Let's find out how America has managed to make a silk purse out of our master Heathcliff. Show him in, Ellen.

ELLEN (*leaving*). Yes, Master Edgar.

CATHY (*with a shiver*). Edgar . . .

EDGAR. Yes?

CATHY. It's chilly in here. Put another log on the fire.

EDGAR (*placing the log—and touching her hand*). Darling, your hand is cold. Why be nervous? The past is dead . . . What nonsense, Cathy, to tremble before a little ghost that returns . . . a dead leaf blown around your feet. . . . (*He puts his arm around her.*) You may smile at him without fear of offending me, Cathy, because it's my wife who smiles—my wife who loves me.

Cathy looks at him questioningly. He returns her look with calm assurance on his face.

CATHY (*smiling*). Yes. Yes . . . I was silly. Thank you, Edgar.

They all turn as they hear Heathcliff's steps approaching. He appears in the hall, and advances toward them through the living room to the door of the study. It is indeed another Heathcliff. Not only is he handsomely dressed, but he carries himself with utter assurance—a man who has thrown himself against the world and conquered. He stands staring at Edgar for a moment. Then he bows.

HEATHCLIFF. Mr. Linton.

EDGAR (*quite in command of the situation*). Come in, Heathcliff. How are you, sir?

HEATHCLIFF (*now he turns to Cathy—in a lower voice*). Hello, Cathy.

Cathy returns his look mutely. He looks around the room.

HEATHCLIFF. I remember this room . . .

EDGAR (*looking him over curiously*). Sit down, sir. By the fire. (*Civilly*) A whiskey?

HEATHCLIFF. No, thank you.

EDGAR (*as he sits down*). Well—I've never seen such a change in a man. I'd not have known you, Heathcliff. You seem to have prospered since our last meeting.

HEATHCLIFF. Somewhat.

CATHY. Ellen said you'd been to America.

HEATHCLIFF. Yes.

CATHY. We all wondered where you went.

Isabella has now joined her brother.

EDGAR (*his hand on Isabella's arm*). Oh. Have you met my sister? Heathcliff . . . Miss Linton . . .

HEATHCLIFF (*rising and bowing*). Miss Linton . . .

EDGAR. Well, Heathcliff, what's brought about this amazing transformation? Did you discover a gold mine in the new world, or perhaps you fell heir to a fortune?

HEATHCLIFF. Or perhaps, Mr. Linton, I made it more spectacularly on the English highways, but the truth is . . . I remembered that my father was Emperor of China and my mother an Indian queen, and I went out and claimed my inheritance . . . (*Addressing Cathy —his tone changed—he crosses to couch, and sits.*) It turned out as you once suspected, Cathy, that I'd been kidnapped by wicked sailors and brought to England, that I was of noble birth . . .

CATHY (*a little flutter in her voice*). Are you visiting here long? I mean, in the village?

HEATHCLIFF (*quietly*). The rest of my life. . . . I have just bought Wuthering Heights—the house, the cattle and the moors.

CATHY (*astounded*). What!

EDGAR (*equally floored*). You mean that Hindley has sold you the estate . . .

HEATHCLIFF (*easily*). He's not aware of it—as yet . . . I'm afraid it will be somewhat of a surprise to him when he finds out that his gambling debts and liquor bills were all paid up for him by his former stable boy. . . . Or perhaps he will merely laugh at the irony of it, Mr. Linton.

EDGAR (*coldly*). I don't understand how it happened. How it could have happened without Mrs. Linton hearing.

HEATHCLIFF (*smiling*). Modesty compelled me to play the good Samaritan— in secret, Mr. Linton.

EDGAR (*unable to contain himself*). By Heavens, this is as underhanded a piece of work as I've ever known in this county, Heathcliff!

ISABELLA (*getting up*). Edgar, please . . .

EDGAR (*apologizing to Cathy who still stares at Heathcliff*). If I had only known, Cathy—I knew that Hindley was in financial difficulties but not that his holdings were being stolen from him by a stranger.

HEATHCLIFF (*rising*). I am neither thief nor stranger. Merely your neighbor, sir. Now I'll say goodnight.

CATHY (*tensely*). Wait, Heathcliff! (*She gets up.*) Edgar and I have many neighbors whom we receive with friendship and hospitality . . . And if you are to be one of them you are welcome to visit our home but not with a scowl on your face or an old bitterness in your heart.

HEATHCLIFF (*softly yet bitterly*). Thank you. It occurs to me I have not yet congratulated you on your marriage. I've often thought of it. Allow me to express my delight over your happiness now. Goodnight.

CATHY (*holding out her hand*). Goodnight, Heathcliff.

Heathcliff ignores her hand, bows formally, and goes. They watch without speaking until he has reached the hall.

ISABELLA (*as he leaves*). Edgar, I think you behaved abominably. . . .

EDGAR (*stunned*). What!

ISABELLA (*turning to Cathy*). And you, too, Cathy. I'm dreadfully disappointed in you both.

EDGAR. What in thunder are you talking about?

ISABELLA. You could have been civil, at least.

EDGAR (*sharply*). I conducted myself perfectly, Isabella—and so did Cathy. I am very grateful to you, my dear. (*He embraces Cathy.*)

ISABELLA. You dismissed him as if he had been a servant!

EDGAR (*staring at her*). Don't tell me you thought him anything else, Isabella?

ISABELLA. I thought him fascinating and —and very distinguished.

EDGAR (*slowly*). I hope I've misunderstood you. It's impossible that any sister of mine could consider Heathcliff anything but a surly dressed-up beggar . . . a lout and a boor. I shall take precautions to insure your never seeing him again. Now come to dinner.

At this Isabella walks angrily out of the room. For a moment Cathy does not move, trying to control herself. Edgar watches her intently—then goes to her, and touches her gently. She looks up at him.

CATHY (*shuddering*). I dread the consequences of this visit, Edgar. I greatly dread them.

The scene dissolves to the HALLWAY at WUTHERING HEIGHTS in the morning, a week later: Hindley, drunken and disheveled, is fumbling at the door. He throws it open and paws on the outside at the lock. He calls out.

HINDLEY. Joseph! Joseph!

JOSEPH (*appearing from the stables*). Yes, Master Hindley.

HINDLEY. Where's the key here?

JOSEPH (*helping him look*). Isn't it in the door?

HINDLEY (*railing*). No, and I want it! He's left, and it's our chance!

Joseph follows him inside, and Hindley slams the door.

HINDLEY. We're going to lock him out this time! And if he tries to get in, I'll kill him! Now find the key! And fetch me a bottle of whiskey, too!

JOSEPH (*apathetically*). You've had a bad night, Master Hindley.

HINDLEY. A bad night, you call it. How can I stay sober with that vulture's beak inside me. . . . He struck me in the dark, Joseph. Robbed me! Robbed me of my home and gold. Where's the whiskey?

JOSEPH. Dr. Kenneth has forbidden it, Master Hindley.

HINDLEY. Blast Dr. Kenneth.

HEATHCLIFF (*appearing in the doorway from outside*). Get him what he wants, Joseph.

JOSEPH. Dr. Kenneth has forbidden it— Mr. Heathcliff.

HEATHCLIFF. Do as I tell you. (*Calmly*) What difference to the world if he's drunk or sober—or to Dr. Kenneth?

Joseph is cowed by Heathcliff's intensity. He goes away. Heathcliff stares calmly at Hindley, whose snarl grows wilder.

HINDLEY. Get out! It's too early in the morning to look on the devil.

HEATHCLIFF (*smiling faintly, hanging up his coat, etc.*). Your ingratitude, Hindley, makes me almost sad. All I have done to you, Hindley, is enable you to be yourself. My money has helped you drink and gamble and enjoy the world as you wished and now that you are without a roof of your own, I remember that you once gave me a place to sleep when you might have thrown me out —and I allow you to remain, Hindley, and even provide you with solace— against the doctor's orders. . . . (*He goes into the kitchen, Hindley lurching after him.*)

The KITCHEN: Heathcliff, followed by Hindley, comes in. Joseph is opening a bottle.

HINDLEY (*doggedly*). I'll have Wuthering Heights back, do you hear? I'll be master here and turn you out, as I should have done years ago.

HEATHCLIFF. We're just in time, Joseph. Mr. Hindley is beginning to whine and stutter. He needs fire in his veins—some courage with which to face his unhappy life.

During this Heathcliff has taken the whiskey bottle from Joseph and poured out a good-sized drink. Now he suddenly proffers it to Hindley. The latter breaks off his tirade, seizes the glass and drinks it down.

HINDLEY (*wild with liquor*). I'll have my gold and I'll have your blood, and hell shall have your soul.

Heathcliff laughs. Hindley puts his hand into his open coat, brings out a pistol, waveringly trains it on Heathcliff.

HINDLEY. Laugh now, Heathcliff.

HEATHCLIFF (*simply*). I am.

HINDLEY (*coming toward him*). . . . Because now you're going to die . . .

HEATHCLIFF (*looking at the gun*). All you have to do is shoot.

HINDLEY. They'll thank me for it . . . the whole world. . . . They'll say I did right in ridding it of a rotten gypsy beggar.

HEATHCLIFF. Yes, they'll say that. Shoot and you'll be master again. . . . The country will resound with your courage, Hindley. Go on, shoot, you puling chicken of a man . . . with not enough blood in you to keep your hand steady. (*Coming slowly up to him*) Do you remember that time you hit me with a rock, Hindley . . . And the times you shamed and flogged me as your stable boy. . . . You were a coward then and you are a coward now.

He pushes the drunken man gently. Hindley, off balance, topples back into a chair. His gun clatters to the floor.

HEATHCLIFF (*to Joseph*). Take him out, Joseph . . . find some place for him to sleep . . .

JOSEPH. He's ill. I'll put him to bed.

HEATHCLIFF. Not in the master's room. I'm master here now.

Heathcliff watches Joseph half dragging the drunken Hindley out. He picks up the pistol.

HEATHCLIFF. His gun, Joseph.

JOSEPH. I'll hide it.

A servant appears in the doorway.

HEATHCLIFF. No. A gentleman must not be deprived of his weapons, Joseph. I prefer that he have it always at his side—as a reminder of his cowardice.

Joseph drags Hindley up the stairs.

SERVANT. Master Heathcliff.

HEATHCLIFF (*noticing him for the first time*). What is it?

SERVANT. A lady. She wishes to see you.

HEATHCLIFF (*with sudden excitement*). A lady . . . from where?

SERVANT. The Grange, sir . . .

HEATHCLIFF (*brushing his hat, straightening his coat*). Why didn't you tell me! (*He dashes out of the room.*)

The LIVING ROOM: Isabella in riding costume is standing near the door as Heathcliff hurries in.

HEATHCLIFF (*coming to a stop and staring at her, crestfallen*). Oh. Miss Linton. (*He bows.*)

ISABELLA. I hope I am not disturbing you.

HEATHCLIFF (*regaining his composure*). Not at all.

ISABELLA (*faltering*). I was riding behind the Heights on the moor when my horse went lame . . . and . . .

HEATHCLIFF (*with a smile*). And you brought him here . . .

ISABELLA. Yes.

HEATHCLIFF. That was very wise. It is quite wrong to ride a lame horse. (*Divining that all this is a ruse of some kind*) Shall we look at the unfortunate animal? (*He starts out.*)

A close view of ISABELLA betrays her agitation.

ISABELLA (*quickly*). It isn't necessary. I put him in the stables. He's—he's being taken care of.

Back in the previous scene:

HEATHCLIFF (*pausing and looking at her*). Well . . . let me give you a chair.

ISABELLA. I was furious with my brother —and Cathy, too. I told them so. I thought they acted most shamefully.

He places a chair. Both sit down.

HEATHCLIFF (*staring at her keenly*). Your brother didn't send you with these apologies?

ISABELLA (*startled*). Oh no. He—he has forbidden me to . . . (*She breaks off.*)

HEATHCLIFF (*smiling again*). To speak to me?

ISABELLA. Yes.

HEATHCLIFF. And Mrs. Linton . . . ?

ISABELLA. She is also . . . angry with you.

HEATHCLIFF (*purring*). Then in all the county you are my only friend.

ISABELLA. I—would like to be.

HEATHCLIFF (*getting up suddenly*). It's too fine a day for sitting indoors. We'll celebrate our friendship by a gallop over the moors.

ISABELLA (*remembering awkwardly*). But—but my horse is lame . . . and . . .

We see them closer as Heathcliff speaks.

HEATHCLIFF (*very close*). My dear, your horse is not lame—and never was. You came to see me because you are lonely. Because it is lonely sitting like an outsider in so happy a house as your brother's. Lonely riding on the moors with no one at your side. . . . (*He puts his arm around her.*) You won't be lonely any more.

He kisses her, and the scene fades out.

PART EIGHT

The DRAWING ROOM of the LINTON HOME at night fades in. An elaborate party is in progress. It might be the same party of years ago when Cathy and Heathcliff looked on through the window. As before, the drawing room is aglitter with candles. The guests are dancing a minuet. The scene has about it an archaic charm. The view then changes quickly to the ORCHESTRA, musicians brought all the way from London for the occasion; and this cuts to various glimpses of the dance, conveying the impression of its quaint charm and stilted gaiety.

Now DR. KENNETH AND EDGAR appear, standing by the punch bowl.

DR. KENNETH (*raising his glass*). Your health, Edgar.

EDGAR. Thank you, sir, again . . .

DR. KENNETH (*smiling*). All the pains and ills of life seem worthy the bearing when you look at a scene as beautiful as this, Edgar.

EDGAR (*looking off*). Yes—and when you look at Cathy.

DR. KENNETH. She's quite the belle tonight . . . Hasn't missed a single dance.

EDGAR (*ruefully*). Not one. I'm completely worn out.

The scene cuts to a view of CATHY dancing. She is flushed, gay, enchanting in an all white gown. She carries a huge black fan. We follow her then as she and her partner perform dainty capers of the dance, but their figures are soon lost among others on the floor.

ISABELLA AND HER PARTNER appear dancing in the foreground, and we follow them until they come close.

HER PARTNER. Do you think my dancing has improved since last year? Tell me truly. I've been taking lessons.

Isabella is quite deaf to his chatter. She darts a glance at the wide double-doors in the background as though she were looking—hoping for another's presence there.

HER PARTNER. I say, Isabella, do you think my dancing is improved?

They dance away, her partner still chattering. But his words are indistinguishable.

Now there is an overall, overhead view of the BALL, and the music ends. Applause ruffles the air. Gallants proffer courtly

elbows, and mincing ladies are escorted off the floor. And following this, the scene cuts to a close view of ISABELLA on her partner's arm. Her eyes steal furtively out of the scene and this time she sees that which she has been longing to see. Delight shows instantly on her face. The view moves to HEATHCLIFF framed in the threshold of the room. He is impeccably dressed, altogether a commanding figure. Isabella enters the scene, and goes toward him, making her way through the guests. Heathcliff bows on her approach.

DR. KENNETH (*looking out of scene; frowns; startled. To Edgar:*) Heavens—is that Heathcliff? I'd swear that was Heathcliff . . . the one in the red velvet coat.

EDGAR (*troubled*). Yes, it is.

DR. KENNETH. I can't believe it . . . Cathy having him here . . . it's impossible!

EDGAR (*quickly*). Not Cathy. My sister. A young girl's fancy. One must be careful about it—not to inflame it with too much opposition . . . allow it to spend its irresponsible self harmlessly in a few dances, a few dinners.

The scene cuts to a moving view of HEATHCLIFF AND ISABELLA as they advance into the room.

ISABELLA. I was so afraid you wouldn't come . . . and tonight would have been ruined, if you hadn't . . .

Now it is the man who does not listen to Isabella's words, who keeps looking expectantly out of the scene. And now the orchestra starts up again.

ISABELLA (*joyfully*). Oh, a waltz! Heathcliff, will you? We can hold each other and no one can object . . . Because that's the way it's danced.

HEATHCLIFF (*as the dance begins, looking off; in mock amazement*). It's the way the gypsies dance . . . I'm amazed to see such abandoned ways creep into so fine a house.

ISABELLA (*giggling*). Yes, father says . . . it will undermine the whole of society and turn everybody into . . . profligates . . .

A dandy appears and bows to Isabella.

THE DANDY. Would you honor me, Isabella?

ISABELLA. Oh, thank you, Giles . . . But I don't think I can . . . (*looking at Heathcliff*) and besides . . .

HEATHCLIFF (*quickly*). Nonsense, Isabella . . . let me see you waltz.

ISABELLA (*eagerly*). Will you watch me? . . . (*To the Dandy*) I am ready, Giles.

He takes her stiffly in his arms and they waltz off, Isabella smiling over the dandy's shoulder. Heathcliff looks out of the scene. And now we see CATHY in a group, fanning herself and laughing. Heathcliff approaches.

HEATHCLIFF. You're not dancing this dance?

CATHY. No. I'm nearly exhausted.

HEATHCLIFF. Would the moonlight and a breath of air refresh you?

CATHY (*taking up his challenge*). Always.

He offers her his arm and we follow them to the entrance leading on to the BALCONY, which then comes into view.

CATHY. Are you enjoying yourself, Heathcliff?

HEATHCLIFF. I've had the pleasure of watching you.

CATHY. You're ever so grand, Heathcliff—so strong and handsome. Looking at you tonight I could not help but remember—how things used to be.

HEATHCLIFF (*moodily*). They used to be better.

CATHY (*gaily*). Don't pretend that life hasn't improved for you.

HEATHCLIFF. I don't call it living to hover in fancy clothes outside the gates of somebody else's heaven.

CATHY. Please . . . No melancholy speeches. Let's just stand and watch the moors.

HEATHCLIFF. How can you stand here beside me and not remember? And not know that my heart is breaking for you, Cathy? That your face is the one little light burning in all this darkness. . . . Oh Cathy!

CATHY (*frightened*). Heathcliff! No. I forbid it.

HEATHCLIFF. And do you forbid what your heart is saying to me now, Cathy?

CATHY (*white and trembling*). It's saying nothing.

HEATHCLIFF (*recklessly*). It is! It is! I can hear it louder than the music. Oh Cathy! Cathy!

CATHY. I'm not the Cathy that was. Can you understand that? I'm somebody else. . . . I'm another man's wife and he loves me—and I love him.

His arm is around her. Momentarily she weakens and seems about to faint before the love in his eyes. Her lips part, her eyes close.

HEATHCLIFF. Not he, not the world . . . not even you can stand between us, Cathy.

Cathy turns from him and runs quickly toward the entrance.

The scene cuts to the ENTRANCE: As Cathy starts in, Isabella appears.

ISABELLA. Cathy, have you seen Heathcliff? (*Sighting him*) Oh, there you are. Come darling, it's another minuet —quite suitable to your high moral character. . . .

HEATHCLIFF appears absorbed as Isabella approaches him. In the background stands Cathy at the threshold.

ISABELLA (*hopefully*). Unless you care to sit it out with me?

As Cathy enters the house, Heathcliff looks after her.

ISABELLA (*as he neither moves nor makes any answer*). What's the matter, darling?

Now Heathcliff looks at her. Her words are only an echo in his ears.

ISABELLA. Was Cathy behaving horribly again . . . ? If she were not my sister-in-law, I'd say she is jealous.

Heathcliff regards Isabella queerly. He frowns. An idea takes form and fashion in his brain.

ISABELLA. It's lovely out here, darling. The night air feels like velvet. And how romantic the music sounds. . . .

He is pondering as the scene dissolves into the HALLWAY, and Cathy and Edgar are seen saying goodnight to the last of the departing guests.

GUESTS. Goodnight. Thank you for a most marvelous evening. We had a wonderful time. It was delightful . . .

CATHY AND EDGAR. Goodnight. Goodnight.

The scene then dissolves into ISABELLA's BEDROOM: She is sitting before her dressing table, a gown thrown loosely over her shoulders. She is brushing her hair, slowly, rhythmically, and humming a tune that the orchestra had played that night. She smiles at herself in the mirror. She is the very picture of a young girl who has made her first conquest. She turns at the sound of her door opening quietly. It is Cathy. Isabella shows surprise.

CATHY. Isabella, I want to talk to you.

Isabella knows well enough what is coming. She goes on brushing her hair; making a little yawn.

ISABELLA. What about, Cathy?

CATHY. Heathcliff.

ISABELLA. It's very late—and I have no desire to discuss Heathcliff with you, anyway.

CATHY (*sharply*). Isabella, you behaved disgracefully tonight.

ISABELLA. In what way, may I ask?

CATHY. It was bad enough—your asking him here—but to make a spectacle of yourself—to throw yourself at him . . .

ISABELLA. Catherine! Be careful what you say!

Isabella has risen, and moves as if to pass Cathy. Cathy takes her by the shoulders, shakes her.

CATHY. You fool! You vain little fool!

ISABELLA. Let me pass.

CATHY. I won't be silent any longer. I'm going to tell the truth. You're old enough to hear it. You're strong enough.

ISABELLA. Let me pass, Catherine.

CATHY. Not till I open your eyes.

ISABELLA. My eyes are quite open, thank you.

CATHY. He's been using you . . . Don't you *see* what he's been doing—using you to be near me, to smile at me behind your back—to try and rouse something in my heart that's dead . . . dead! I'll not have it any longer! . . . And I'll not allow you to help him any longer. . . .

ISABELLA (*softly*). It's you who are vain and insufferable. Heathcliff's in love with me.

CATHY (*wildly*). It's a lie!

ISABELLA. It's not a lie. He's told me so. He's kissed me . . .

CATHY (*seizing her arm, digging her nails into her wrist*). He's what!

ISABELLA (*exulting*). He's kissed me. He's held me in his arms. He's told me he loves me!

CATHY. I'm going to your brother.

She almost throws Isabella down in a gesture of rage.

ISABELLA (*hitting every raw nerve*). Go to him. He's asked me to marry him. . . . Tell Edgar that! We're going to be married! That Heathcliff's going to be my husband!

CATHY (*a moaned guttural*). Isabella, you can't! Heathcliff is not a man but something horrible and dark to live with.

ISABELLA (*slowly and cruelly*). Do you imagine, Catherine, I don't know why you are acting so— Because you love him . . .

CATHY (*flaming*). How *dare* you say that!

Cathy flies at Isabella and slaps her viciously. Isabella doesn't flinch.

ISABELLA. Yes, you love him! And you're mad with pain and jealousy at the thought of my marrying him! Because you want him to pine for you and dream of you, to die for you . . . while you live in comfort and security as Mrs. Linton.

CATHY. You little fool.

ISABELLA (*unflinching*). You don't want him to be happy. You want to hurt him, destroy him. But I want to make him happy—and I will . . . I will!

There is a knock at the door. Isabella falls silent. The two women stand looking into each other's eyes. Isabella's are challenging. The knock is repeated.

ISABELLA (*calls*). Come in.

The door opens and Edgar enters looking from one to the other, a slightly puzzled expression on his face.

EDGAR. I heard your voices.

ISABELLA (*controlling her voice*). We were—we were talking over the ball.

Isabella smiles. Edgar doesn't recognize the spite behind her smile.

EDGAR (*dismissing whatever suspicions he may have had as to what they were quarreling about*). Come, Cathy, to bed. There's all day tomorrow for gossip . . . and you look tired—you really do, my dear.

He puts his arm around her. She lets him lead her out. Isabella, smiling, watches after them.

The scene dissolves to the WUTHERING HEIGHTS LIVING ROOM, next morning. The room is in greater disorder than before.

As there comes the sound of knocking at the door, Joseph enters from the kitchen, and disappears into the hall. There is the sound of a door opening, then Cathy's voice is heard.

CATHY'S VOICE. Good morning, Joseph.

JOSEPH'S VOICE. Miss Cathy—Mistress Cathy, I mean. Master Hindley's away.

CATHY'S VOICE. It's Master Heathcliff, I wish to see.

JOSEPH'S VOICE. Oh, I'll try to find him. (*His boots resound on the stairs.*)

Cathy enters the living room, and stands in the disordered midst, looking about, following which the view, now disclosed from another angle, includes the approaching figure of Heathcliff.

HEATHCLIFF. Well, what brings you to Wuthering Heights, Cathy? Does Edgar know? I doubt he'd approve.

CATHY. Heathcliff, is it true?

HEATHCLIFF. Is what true?

CATHY. That you asked Isabella to marry you? (*She waits for his reply. As none comes:*) It is true, then. (*Desperately*) Oh, Heathcliff, you must not do this villainous thing. She hasn't harmed you.

HEATHCLIFF (*stonily*). *You* have.

CATHY. Then punish me.

HEATHCLIFF (*cruelly*). I am going to. When I hold her in my arms . . . when I kiss her . . . when I promise her life and happiness.

CATHY (*horrified*). You'll marry her— for that . . .

HEATHCLIFF. Yes . . . to teach you the ways of pain and to let you taste the hell I am in!

CATHY. Heathcliff . . . if there's anything human left in you, don't do this! Don't make me a partner to such a crime . . . it's stupid! It's mad!

HEATHCLIFF (*quiet; passionate*). If your heart were only stronger than your dull fear of your God and the world, I would live silent and contented in your shadow . . . Cathy! (*He moves to her— but she backs away.*) But no . . . you must destroy me with that weakness you call virtue. (*He takes her arm.*) You must keep me tormented with that cruelty you think so pious.

CATHY (*pulling her arm away*). Let me go!

HEATHCLIFF. Well, after this you can think of me as something else than Cathy's foolish and despairing lover . . . you can think of me as Isabella's husband . . . and be glad for my happiness . . . (*With a terrible smile*) As I was for yours.

She runs out. He looks after her, closes the door and goes up stairs.

The scene dissolves to the LINTON LIVING ROOM at night: Cathy sits in a chair by the fire, nervously watching Edgar as the latter, in a state of considerable perturbation, walks back and forth.

EDGAR (*disbelieving*). Get married! Preposterous! My sister and that adventurer!

CATHY. It's true. What are you going to do?

EDGAR (*resolutely*). Do . . . I shall keep her under lock and key if need be.

He strides out of the living room, and the scene cuts to the STAIRWAY as Edgar ascends.

EDGAR (*calling*). Isabella! (*There is no answer. He calls again—louder.*) Isabella!

The view moves to CATHY standing by the stairs in the lower hall, alarm showing on her face. As the silence from above continues her expression changes from alarm to dread. The scene cuts to another view of the STAIRS, from another angle, with Cathy in the foreground. Edgar appears, and descends the stairs. He holds a sheet of writing paper in his hand, and holds it out to Cathy. It is all she can do to take it from his hand, and read the few scrawled lines.

CATHY (*crying*). You must go after them. Do you hear? Get your pistols and go after them . . . and bring her back. . . . Kill him, if need be . . .

EDGAR. . . . She's no longer my sister. Not because I disown her—but because she has disowned me.

CATHY (*wildly*). You must go after them . . . while there's still time. . . . It cannot be—such a marriage. Do you hear? It cannot be!

Edgar regards Cathy with amazement. He takes a step toward her, stares full into her face, and the truth begins to dawn on him as the scene fades out.

PART NINE

The LIVING ROOM OF WUTHERING HEIGHTS fades in by day: Hindley, sodden and unkempt, is stretched on a couch. He is ill. Dr. Kenneth is sitting at his side.

DR. KENNETH (*amiably*). Hindley, instead of drinking, why don't you just hit yourself over the head with a hammer the instant you get up in the morning? If you hit yourself hard enough you'll stay unconscious all day and achieve virtually the same results you can get through a whole gallon of gin—

Isabella appears in the background and then advances.

DR. KENNETH (*continuing*). —with no wear and tear on the kidneys. (*To Isabella*) Don't you agree with me, Mrs. Heathcliff?

Isabella goes to the couch with a pitcher of water.

ISABELLA (*dully*). What does it matter?

DR. KENNETH (*pointedly*). I had hoped, Mrs. Heathcliff, that it *did* matter—that when you came here things would change.

ISABELLA (*smiling dully*). No, only I changed . . .

DR. KENNETH (*standing up and looking around*). I remember this house when it rang with laughter and love. Goodbye, Mrs. Heathcliff . . . Ask your husband to call another doctor in the future.

Whoever dwells in this house is past my healing arts.

He goes toward the hall, and the scene cuts to DR. KENNETH AND ISABELLA seen coming into the HALLWAY, Isabella following the physician.

ISABELLA (*quietly*). I shall miss you, Dr. Kenneth.

DR. KENNETH (*stopping suddenly and returning*). Isabella, I brought you into the world. And it's a world you're not going to grace very long—if you stay in this house. Dear child, I *must* say this to you. Go back where you belong. Back with Edgar, if only for a month or two. It will mean your salvation—and his.

ISABELLA. Edgar has disowned me . . .

DR. KENNETH. Nonsense . . . that was natural under the circumstances. But he needs you now.

ISABELLA (*coldly*). He does—and why?

DR. KENNETH. Cathy is gravely ill. (*This is a bombshell.*) I'm afraid it's . . . (*shrugging*) well—only a matter of hours. . . .

We now see ISABELLA very close. Her eyes become brilliant, hard as gems.

ISABELLA (*tense*). What is it, Doctor?

DR. KENNETH'S VOICE (*Dr. Kenneth being out of the scene at this point*). Fever and inflammation of the lungs . . . but there's something beyond that—I don't know. I'd call it the will to die.

ISABELLA (*slowly, her eyes wildly lighted*). If she died, I might begin to live.

DR. KENNETH (*staring horrified at her*). Isabella. . . . (*He breaks off, turns and withdraws. Isabella, bursting into tears, sinks to the floor.*)

The scene cuts to a view of HINDLEY.

HINDLEY (*thickly*). Begin to live, eh? In this house—with Heathcliff—nothing can live. Nothing but hate. He gets up with effort, and we follow him as he goes, half staggering, to Isabella. Hate —I can feel it like the devil's own breath on me . . . And you! He hates you worse than he does me . . . He loathes you. Each time you kiss him his heart breaks with rage because it's not Cathy.

The scene changing abruptly, now discloses both ISABELLA AND HINDLEY: He leans over her, whispering:

HINDLEY. Isabella, why don't you do what I've been too weak to do. Kill him!

ISABELLA (*hysterically*). Stop it! I've forbidden you to talk to me about Heathcliff.

HINDLEY (*staring and whispering*). Kill him!

ISABELLA (*panic-stricken*). Stop! Do you hear!

She rises, seizes Hindley, and shakes him.

HINDLEY. Kill him! Kill him! Kill him while there's time to save your immortal soul!

The scene widens to include HEATHCLIFF— who stands listening with apparent approval.

HEATHCLIFF (*smiling*). Well—that's the first lucid talk I've heard out of Hindley for weeks. It's not very Christian talk, but at least it's coherent . . . and seems to make some point. I'm delighted with your improvement, Hindley. (*He turns, hangs up his coat.*)

ISABELLA (*after staring at him*). Heathcliff! I tried to stop him.

HEATHCLIFF (*still smiling diabolically*). Thank you, my dear wife. Your loyalty is touching.

HINDLEY (*snarling*). Your curses will come home to feed on your own heart . . . every agony you've given will return. Laugh, now, Heathcliff . . . There's no laughter in Hell . . . (*And chuckling drunkenly, he leaves the room.*)

ISABELLA (*begging*). Heathcliff, why do you have him here? I can't breathe with him in this house.

Heathcliff silently leaves the hall, and the scene cuts to the LIVING ROOM as Heathcliff enters, Isabella following him.

HEATHCLIFF (*with a sardonic smile*). Existence would be so much less without my boyhood friend under my roof.

ISABELLA (*clinging to his arm*). Oh, Heathcliff, don't you see? You poison yourself with hating him. Darling, send him away and love will come into this house.

HEATHCLIFF (*desperately*). Why isn't there the smell of heather in your hair? (*And he shakes her off.*)

ISABELLA (*on her knees*). Oh, Heathcliff, let me come near you! You're not black and horrible as they all think. You're full of pain. Heathcliff, I can make you happy. Oh, let me. You'll never regret it. I'll be your slave. I'll bring life back to you—new and fresh . . .

He lifts her from her knees where she has fallen beside him in the chair. Her arms go around him. She kisses him.

HEATHCLIFF. Why are your eyes always empty like Linton's eyes?

ISABELLA. They aren't—if you'll only *look* deeper. (*Beseechingly*) Look, I'm pretty—I'm a woman . . . I love you . . . Let your heart look at me once . . .

HEATHCLIFF (*covering his face with his hands, his voice rising in a wail*). Oh, why did God give me life! What is it but hunger and pain? A naked runner in a storm of spears!

The door opens in the background and Ellen appears. Heathcliff sees and stares at her.

HEATHCLIFF (*dully*). What do you want, Ellen? What are you doing here?

ELLEN (*evading him*). I want to speak to Isabella.

HEATHCLIFF (*blocking her*). Then you'll do so in front of me.

ELLEN (*hesitating*). Her brother has asked me to bring her home for a visit.

HEATHCLIFF (*snarling*). Oh, he's lost some of his mucky pride. Well, there's none gone in *this* house.

ELLEN (*quietly, to Isabella*). He needs you with him, Isabella.

HEATHCLIFF (*apprehensively at her tone*). Why? *Why?*

He rises and approaches Ellen, takes her arms, stares deep into her eyes.

ELLEN (*frightened*). Let go of me, Heathcliff.

HEATHCLIFF (*staring—then suddenly*). Cathy! She's ill!

ELLEN (*defiant*). Yes. Master Edgar wants you to come at once, Miss Isabella.

HEATHCLIFF (*wildly*). She's dying! Tell me the truth!

He drops Ellen's arms, turns and walks slowly toward the door, something mechanical in his movements. Isabella rushes to the door, and confronts him.

ISABELLA. You're not going, Heathcliff! She belongs to Edgar. If she's dying, let her die in his arms—where she belongs. Let her die! Let her die!

He raises his hand mechanically as if to strike her, and she stands aside. As he passes her the scene dissolves.

The previous scene has now dissolved into CATHY'S BEDROOM, where she lies pale and motionless in the bed, staring up from her pillow. Beside her, Edgar sits reading from a book.

EDGAR (*reading*).
"Adown the silver walls of Heaven rang
The Voices of the blessed, and round the throne
Of stars the night-enchanted angels sang
The melodies of God, to Heaven known . . .
And yet there was a murmur from the height,
A faraway and wild heartbroken moan.
The wings of Lucifer beat on the night,
The soul of Lucifer wept all alone . . ."

CATHY (*interrupting faintly*). Edgar.

EDGAR (*tenderly*). Shh, darling, you mustn't talk . . .

CATHY (*with a little smile*). Open the window.

EDGAR. It'll be too cold.

CATHY (*with a child's insistence*). I want air. I want to smell the wind.

Edgar goes to the window and opens it a trifle.

EDGAR. Is that better?

CATHY (*breathing deeply and smiling*). Yes. I can smell the heather. Edgar, isn't there a south wind and isn't the snow almost gone?

EDGAR. Yes, it's quite gone down here, darling. . . . Just a few patches left. . . .

CATHY (*dreamily*). The sky is blue and the larks are singing and the brooks are all brimming full. . . . I remember . . . Edgar, will you get me something?

EDGAR (*gently*). What do you want, darling?

CATHY (*with childlike directness*). Some heather. There's a beautiful patch near the castle. I want some from there.

EDGAR (*tenderly and confused*). Near the castle? What castle, my darling?

CATHY (*petulantly*). The castle on the moors, Edgar. Go there. Get me some, please.

EDGAR. You're in a fever, dear. There is no castle on the moors. . . .

CATHY (*her voice rising*). There is! There is! (*Trying to sit up*) It's on the little hill beyond Wuthering Heights.

EDGAR (*worried*). You mean Pennistone Crag . . .

CATHY (*relieved*). Yes! Yes! Please go.

EDGAR. Why do you call it the castle, darling?

CATHY. Because—I was a queen there . . . once. Will you go there, Edgar—will you—and get me some heather?

EDGAR. If you'll sleep while I'm gone—rest, so you'll be better tomorrow.

CATHY. You're so kind—so good.

EDGAR (*bending over her*). My darling . . .

CATHY (*smiling up at him*). You made me the finest lady in the county. Such lovely clothes . . . I've always adored that velvet dress—the most . . . The blue one with the silver sleeves . . . Wasn't it a wonderful dress, Edgar . . .

EDGAR (*torn*). Wonderful when you wore it . . . and you will wear it again —soon, my own sweet Cathy . . .

CATHY. Go now—Edgar, get me some heather so I can have it on my pillow.

EDGAR (*rising*). Sleep, dear Cathy. . . . I'll be back with the flowers you want. Now sleep, my darling . . .

He covers her gently, and she closes her eyes. He leaves the room, and next we see the ENTRANCE HALL as Edgar comes wildly down the stairs. He speaks to an old Servant with hardly controlled panic.

EDGAR. Where's Dr. Kenneth?

The scene dissolves to a view of HEATH-CLIFF, who is forward on his horse, beating it as he speeds over the moors . . . He rides, rides as—through his riding—the scene dissolves to the EXTERIOR of the THRUSHCROSS GRANGE with Heathcliff reining up his sweating animal before the gates. He hurls himself from the steed and rushes to the door. Boldly he seizes the knocker and bangs with it on the door panel. There is a pause. Then the servant opens the door.

SERVANT (*startled*). Mr. Heathcliff!

HEATHCLIFF (*staring into the gloomy interior*). Where is she? Your mistress?

SERVANT. She's not to be disturbed, sir. The master has just gone for Dr. Kenneth!

HEATHCLIFF (*thrusting him aside*). Get out of my way!

He hurries inside and starts up the steps. The servant calls after him vainly.

SERVANT. Mr. Heathcliff . . . ! Mr. Heathcliff!

We follow Heathcliff swiftly up the stairs.

CATHY'S ROOM: She lies on the bed, her eyes closed. The room is peaceful . . . The door opens slowly and Heathcliff stands on the threshold. He stares at her, agony in his eyes, his face drawn and silent. He stares till her eyes open, till her head turns slowly on the pillow and she sees him. For a moment she remains without expression. Then she closes her eyes with a sigh . . . and after holding them shut, opens them again. She still sees him. He is no figure in a fevered dream. Her lips part—she whispers his name.

CATHY. *Heathcliff* . . . (*Faintly*) Come here . . .

HEATHCLIFF (*softly*). Oh, Cathy! Oh, my life! How can I bear it?

CATHY (*a child's wheedling*). Come here . . . come here. I was dreaming you might come before I died . . . you might come and scowl at me once more.

HEATHCLIFF. Cathy . . .

CATHY. Does it hurt so much to see me dying? Well, I'll not pity you . . . How strong you look . . . Ah, Heathcliff, how many years do you mean to live after I'm gone . . .

HEATHCLIFF. Cathy . . . You're my life, you're my soul.

CATHY. Oh, my darling . . .

He strides to the bed. She raises herself. They embrace. They cling to each other, locked in a desperate, agonized kiss that tries to drain the agony out of their hearts. She closes her eyes, swoons away, opens her eyes again, her wasted hands clutching at his shoulders, his face, his head. He sinks on his knees beside the bed and weeps. She raises his face to her, her fingers wildly in his hair.

CATHY. Don't—don't let me go. Oh, if only I could hold you till we were both dead.

HEATHCLIFF. Cathy.

CATHY. Why shouldn't you suffer? I do. . . . I dread to die . . . Heathcliff, I don't want to die . . .

HEATHCLIFF (*in agony*). Cathy—don't speak of death.

CATHY. Will you forget me . . . will you be happy when I'm in the earth? Will you say, "This is the grave of Catherine Earnshaw? I loved her long ago and wept to lose her. But it is all past . . . past." (*Softly*) Tell me . . . tell me . . . will you forget?

HEATHCLIFF (*softly*). I could as soon forget you as my own life! If you die . . . Cathy, if you die . . . there'll be no peace for me, Cathy . . .

CATHY (*smiling*). Poor Heathcliff . . . Kneel down again . . . let me feel how strong you are. (*She has taken his hands with this.*)

HEATHCLIFF (*wrenching away*). Strong enough to bring us both to life . . . Cathy, if you want to live!

CATHY. No . . . I lied . . . because while you held me I forgot what life was . . . I forgot, Heathcliff, that life is not as sweet as this. . . . Oh, Heathcliff, I lied. I want to die . . . to escape.

HEATHCLIFF (*his voice rising in agony*). Why did you betray your own heart? Cathy, why did you kill yourself?

CATHY. Shh . . . my darling, hold me. Just hold me.

HEATHCLIFF (*wildly*). No! I'll not comfort you! You deserve this!

CATHY. Heathcliff—don't break my heart—

HEATHCLIFF. Oh, Cathy, I never broke your heart! You broke it . . . Greedy for the trifles of living. . . . I've lain in the night cursing your wantonness. Cursing and cursing you . . . My tears don't love you, Cathy. They blight and damn you. . . . Cathy . . . Cathy, you loved me . . . What right had you to throw love away for the poor fancy thing you felt for him?

CATHY. Heathcliff—I found out . . .

HEATHCLIFF. Misery and death and all the evils that God or man could have hammered down would never have parted us. . . . You did that alone! You wandered off like a wanton greedy child . . . to break your heart and mine. . . . Oh, the worse for me that I'm strong, and stay alive!

CATHY (*faintly*). If I've done wrong I'm dying of it. . . . Forgive me . . .

HEATHCLIFF. Oh, Cathy, your wasted hands . . . Kiss me again . . . I forgive you what you've done to me. I love you. I love my murderer . . . But *your* murderer—how can I ever forgive her!

The door opens and Ellen enters. She is white-faced, alarmed and breathing hard.

ELLEN. Heathcliff! He's coming . . . Mr. Linton. . . . For Heaven's sake, go. Only be quick. . . .

CATHY (*faintly*). You mustn't go. You can't go . . . It's the last time . . .

HEATHCLIFF (*softly*). I'm not going, Cathy. I'm here . . . I'll never leave you again. . . .

CATHY (*faintly with a crazy childish smile, childish sing-song voice*). I told you, Ellen—when he went away—that night in the rain . . . I told you I belonged to him . . . that he was my life, my being. (*She is ecstatically slipping weeps.*)

ELLEN. Are you going to listen to her ravings?

CATHY (*wailing*). It's true. It's true! I'm yours, Heathcliff . . . I've never been anyone else's . . .

ELLEN (*frantically*). She doesn't know what she's saying . . . You can still get out. Go, before we're done for!

CATHY (*raising herself weakly*). Heathcliff—take me to the window! . . . Let me look at the moors with you once more . . . Oh, my darling . . . once more . . .

HEATHCLIFF (*carrying her from the bed*). Yes . . . yes!

CATHY (*faintly at the window*). How lovely the day looks . . . the sweet blue sky . . . Heathcliff, can you see the Crag? Over there, where our castle is —I'll wait for you till you come . . .

She droops and stiffens in his arms. Heathcliff stands holding her, her night dress trailing and stirring faintly in the breeze.

As he stands, Edgar Linton, followed by Dr. Kenneth, enters in the background. Edgar stands staring at Heathcliff holding the silent Cathy near the window.

EDGAR. Cathy . . . Cathy . . .

He hurries to her. Dr. Kenneth follows, and takes her dangling wrist.

DR. KENNETH. We're too late, Edgar . . .

ELLEN (*wailing suddenly*). Cathy, oh, my wild heart! Cathy . . . She's gone . . . She's gone . . .

EDGAR. Oh! (*He covers his face and weeps.*)

DR. KENNETH (*to Heathcliff*). Place her in the bed, Heathcliff.

Heathcliff stands motionless, holding her. His eyes are centered on space, his face is drawn. No tear or sounds come from him.

HEATHCLIFF (*softly*). She's mine . . .

EDGAR (*weeping*). Cathy . . .

HEATHCLIFF (*as Edgar rises to take her —softly*). Leave her alone. She's mine— now . . . (*He takes her to the bed.*)

DR. KENNETH. You've done your last black deed, Heathcliff. Now leave this house.

EDGAR. There's no use for words, Doctor . . . She's at peace now in Heaven . . . beyond us. . . . Cathy—my own sweet Cathy.

HEATHCLIFF (*to the body as he places it tenderly on the bed*). What do they know of Heaven or Hell, Cathy, who know nothing of life . . . (*As they start to pray, looking at Linton, who is praying beside the bed, his head bowed*) Oh, they're praying for you, Cathy. I'll pray one prayer with them. I repeat till my tongue stiffens—Catherine Earnshaw, may you not rest so long as I live on. I killed you . . . Haunt me then! Haunt your murderer! I know that ghosts have wandered on the earth. Be with me always—take any form— drive me mad! Only do not leave me in this dark alone where I cannot find you. I cannot live without my life. I cannot live without my soul!

The view moves from Heathcliff's face to those of the company in the room, resting on Ellen's face, weeping. Then the scene dissolves to—

(THE EPILOGUE)

ELLEN'S FACE, twenty years later—the face of the Narrator whom we met in the Prologue. She is now telling her story, the story of "Wuthering Heights." She sits beside the fireplace facing Mr. Lockwood, the man who put up for the night at the Heights in the prologue. He has been listening all the snow-bound night to the story of Heathcliff and Cathy . . .

Dissolving in on Ellen's face, Heathcliff's last cry of "haunt me" uttered over Cathy's dead body is still in the air. . . .

And now the old Ellen is leaning forward,

tears again in her eyes as they were twenty years ago.

ELLEN (*to Lockwood*). I can still see and hear that wild hour, with poor Heathcliff trying to tear away the veil between death and life . . . crying out to Cathy's soul to haunt him and torment him till he died.

LOCKWOOD. And you say it was Cathy's ghost I heard . . . ?

ELLEN. Not her ghost—but Cathy's love, stronger than time, still sobbing for its unlived days and uneaten bread. . . . And that one up there who sleeps is Isabella, dragging herself through the shadows of Heathcliff's heart . . .

And as someone rattles the door, Lockwood rises and stares. The door opens, and old Dr. Kenneth enters. He is covered with snow.

DR. KENNETH (*entering*). Hello Ellen! Hello Mr. Lockwood!

LOCKWOOD. What in the world are you doing out this night?

DR. KENNETH. On my way to the Peters —they're expecting an heir—the carriage broke down— (*He goes to the fire and rubs his hands.*) I'm not really needed—there's a young doctor from Leeds attending—but I thought I'd harness up anyway . . . Tell me—has Heathcliff gone stark mad, or am I not to believe my eyes?

ELLEN. What do you mean?

DR. KENNETH. I saw him out on the moor wandering through the snow with some woman.

ELLEN. A woman—you say?

DR. KENNETH (*nodding*). A young woman she seemed—and mad as himself. They were walking through the storm with their arms about each other . . . I've never seen anything so daft in my life.

Lockwood looks from the face of the doctor to the face of the old woman, who catches his eye and nods jerkily.

DR. KENNETH (*continuing*). At first I thought they might be lost in the blizzard—

The scene cuts to ISABELLA in the shadow whence she has come unobserved. Joseph is a step or two behind as Dr. Kenneth's voice is heard.

DR. KENNETH'S VOICE (*continuing*). I shouted at them but they acted as though they didn't hear. So I started my horse over to them . . . (*Reappearing as the previous scene returns on the screen*) The wind had shifted and all was calm long enough for me to see the two of them plain as I see you. I was nearly up to them when all of a sudden old Daisy began to rear and plunge and snort; took the bit in her teeth and clean bolted, dragging me through drifts and cracking the shafts.

ISABELLA (*dully*). You saw him with her . . .

DR. KENNETH (*nodding*). Whoever she is . . .

ISABELLA. Cathy . . .

DR. KENNETH. What are you talking about, my dear?

ISABELLA. He went out during the night. She called him and he followed her onto the moor.

JOSEPH. The devil has snatched him away—snatched them both away forever.

LOCKWOOD (*hoarsely*). We'd better be looking for him. The drifts are over a man's head in some places.

ISABELLA (*wailing*). Look for him! Where? Where?

ELLEN (*clairvoyant*). I know where . . . There's a rock with a cave under it. He's in there.

The scene dissolves to the MOORS, and discloses Lockwood, Dr. Kenneth, and Isabella as they plunge through the snow following tracks which lead toward Pennistone Crag.

DR. KENNETH. They're his tracks all right—but where are hers—the woman's? I could have sworn . . .

As the view moves following the tracks, it dissolves to HEATHCLIFF lying at the Crag, his flesh frosted in death, and this sight dissolves to a series of views of the MOORS as Cathy and Heathcliff beheld them in the springs, summers and winters of their youth, ending with TWO BIRDS hovering over the "CASTLE," then flying away into the winter sky. Then the scene fades out.

THE GRAPES OF WRATH

(A 20th Century-Fox Picture)

Screenplay by
NUNNALLY JOHNSON

Based on the Novel *The Grapes of Wrath* by
JOHN STEINBECK

Produced by DARRYL F. ZANUCK

Directed by JOHN FORD

The Cast

TOM JOAD	Henry Fonda
MA JOAD	Jane Darwell
CASY	John Carradine
GRAMPA	Charley Grapewin
ROSASHARN	Dorris Bowdon
PA JOAD	Russell Simpson
AL	O. Z. Whitehead
MULEY	John Qualen
CONNIE	Eddie Quillan
GRANMA	Zeffie Tilbury
NOAH	Frank Sully
UNCLE JOHN	Frank Darien
WINFIELD	Darryl Hickman
RUTH JOAD	Shirley Mills
THOMAS	Roger Imhof
CARETAKER	Grant Mitchell
WILKIE	Charles D. Brown
DAVIS	John Arledge

Film Editor—ROBERT SIMPSON

THE GRAPES OF WRATH

PART ONE

AN OKLAHOMA PAVED HIGHWAY in daylight. At some distance, hoofing down the highway, comes Tom Joad. He wears a new stiff suit of clothes, ill-fitting, and a stiff new cap, which he gradually manages to break down into something comfortable. He comes down the left side of the road, the better to watch the cars that speed past him. As he approaches, the scene changes to a roadside short-order RESTAURANT on the right side of the road. From it comes the sound of a phonograph playing a 1939 popular song. In front of the eatery is a huge Diesel truck labeled: OKLAHOMA CITY TRANSPORT COMPANY. The driver, a heavy man with army breeches and high-laced boots, comes out of the restaurant, the screen door slamming behind him. He is chewing on a toothpick. A waitress appears at the door, behind the screen.

WAITRESS. When you be back?

DRIVER. Couple a weeks. Don't do nothin' you wouldn't want me to hear about!

We see him climbing into the cab of the truck from the right side. Getting behind the wheel, he is releasing the handbrake when Tom appears at the driver's seat window.

TOM. How about a lift, mister?

DRIVER. Can't you see that sticker?

He indicates a "No Riders" sticker on the windshield.

TOM. Sure I see it. But a good guy don't pay no attention to what some heel makes him stick on his truck.

After a moment of hesitation the driver releases the brake.

DRIVER. Scrunch down on the running board till we get around the bend.

As Tom scrunches down on the running board the driver throws the truck into gear and it moves.

The scene dissolves to the CAB OF THE TRUCK. It is day, and Tom is seated beside the driver, who is surreptitiously eyeing him, trying to confirm some suspicion—an inspection which Tom ignores at first.

DRIVER. Goin' far?

TOM (shaking his head). Just a few miles.

I'd a walked her if my dogs wasn't pooped out.

DRIVER. Lookin' for a job?

TOM. No, my old man got a place, forty acres. He's a sharecropper, but we been there a long time.

DRIVER (after a curious glance). Oh!

Cautiously, the driver's eyes drop to Tom's feet. We see TOM'S SHOES. They are prison shoes—new, stiff and bulky.

Curiosity is in the eyes of the DRIVER as they shoot a swift glance at Tom. TOM is looking straight ahead, with the dead-pan look that prisoners get when they are trying to conceal something. The DRIVER's eyes take in Tom's hands and the stiff coat.

DRIVER. Been doin' 'a job?

TOM. Yeah.

DRIVER. I seen your hands. You been swinging a pick or a sledge—that shines up your hands. I notice little things like that all the time. (After a pause) Got a trade?

TOM (evenly). Why don't you get to it, buddy?

DRIVER (uneasily). Get to what?

TOM. You know what I mean. You been givin' me a goin' over ever since I got in. Whyn't you go on and ask me where I been?

DRIVER. I don't stick my nose in nobody's business.

TOM. Naw—not much!

DRIVER (*a little frightened*). I stay in my own yard.

TOM (*without emotion*). Listen. That big nose of yours been goin' over me like a sheep in a vegetable patch. But I ain't keepin' it a secret. I been in the penitentiary. Been there four years. Like to know anything else?

DRIVER. You ain't got to get sore.

TOM (*coldly*). Go ahead. Ask me anything you want.

DRIVER. I didn't mean nothing.

TOM. Me neither. I'm just tryin' to get along without shovin' anybody around, that's all. (*After a pause*) See that road up ahead?

DRIVER. Yeah.

TOM. That's where I get off.

With a sigh of relief the driver puts his foot on the brake. The TRUCK stops and Tom gets out. He looks at the uneasy driver contemptuously.

TOM. You're about to bust to know what I done, ain't you? Well, I ain't a guy to let you down. (*Confidentially*) Homicide!

The driver throws the truck into gear. He doesn't like this at all.

DRIVER. I never asked you!

TOM (*as the truck moves away*). Sure, but you'd a throwed a fit if I hadn't tol' you.

He looks indifferently after the truck and then starts on foot down the dirt crossroad. A wind has begun to blow.

The scene dissolves to the roadside under a WILLOW TREE in daylight. The wind is still blowing. Sitting on the ground, his back against the tree, Casy, a long, lean man in overalls, blue shirt, and one sneaker, is fixing something on the other dirty sneaker. To the tune of "Yes, Sir, That's My Baby" he is absent-mindedly singing.

CASY. Mmmm he's my saviour.
Mmmmm my saviour,
Mmmmmmmmmmm my saviour now.

(*Looking up as Tom comes down the road*) Howdy, friend.

Carrying his coat under his arm, TOM wipes his face with his cap as he cuts off the road to acknowledge the greeting.

TOM. Howdy.

He stops, grateful for the momentary relief of the shade.

CASY. Say, ain't you young Tom Joad—ol' Tom's boy?

TOM (*surprised*). Yeah. On my way home now.

CASY. Well, I do declare! (*Grinning*) I baptized you, son.

TOM (*staring*). Why, you're the preacher!

CASY. *Used* to be. Not no more. I lost the call. (*Reminiscently*) But boy, I sure *used* to have it! I'd get an irrigation ditch so squirmin' full of repented sinners I pretty near *drowned* half of 'em! (*Sighing*) But not no more. I lost the sperit.

TOM (*with a grin*). Pa always said you was never cut out to be a preacher.

CASY. I got nothin' to preach about no more—that's all. I ain't so sure o' things.

TOM. Maybe you should a got yourself a wife.

CASY (*shakes his head sadly*). At my meetin's I used to get the girls glory-shoutin' till they about passed out. Then I'd go to comfort 'em—and always end up by lovin' 'em. I'd feel bad, an' pray, an' pray, but it didn't do no good. Next time, do it again. I figgered there just wasn't no hope for me.

TOM. I never let one go by me when I could catch her.

CASY. But you wasn't a preacher. A girl was just a girl to you. But to me they was holy vessels. I was savin' their souls. (*Fervently*) I ast myself—what *is* this call, the Holy Sperit? Maybe *that's* love. Why, I love everybody so much I'm fit to bust sometimes! So maybe there ain't no sin an' there ain't no virtue. There's just what people do. Some things folks do is nice, and some ain't so nice. But that's as far as any man's got a right to say.

TOM (*after a moment, figuring there is no percentage in continuing this philosophical discussion, pulls out a flask, which he extends*). Have a little snort?

CASY (*holding the flask*). Course I'll say grace if somebody sets out the food— (*shaking his head*)—but my heart ain't in it. (*He takes a long pull.*) Nice drinkin' liquor.

TOM. Ought to be. That's fact'ry liquor. Cost me a buck.

CASY (*handing back the flask.*) Been out travelin' around?

TOM. Didn't you hear? It was in the papers.

CASY. No, I never. What?

TOM. I been in the penitentiary for four years. (*He drinks.*)

CASY. Excuse me for asking.

TOM. I don't mind any more. I'd do what I done again. I killed a guy at a dance. We was drunk. He got a knife in me and I laid him out with a shovel. Knocked his head plumb to squash.

CASY. And you ain't ashamed?

TOM (*shaking his head*). He had a knife in me. That's why they only give me seven years. Got out in four—parole.

CASY. Ain't you seen your folks since then?

TOM (*putting on his coat*). No, but I aim to before sundown. Gettin' kind of excited about it, too. Which way you going?

CASY (*putting on his sneaker*). It don't matter. Ever since I lost the sperit it looks like I just as soon go one way as the other. (*Rising*) I'll go your way.

They pause at the edge of the shade, squint up at the sky, and then move off.

The scene dissolves to the SURFACE OF A DIRT ROAD by daylight. Leaves are scuttling across it. The top soil begins to fly up. It is not a hard wind as yet, but it is steady and persistent. Tom's and Casy's feet walk into sight.

TOM. Maybe Ma'll have pork for supper. I ain't had pork but four times in four years—every Christmas.

CASY. I'll be glad to see your pa. Last time I seen him was at a baptizin', an' he had one a the bigges' doses of the Holy Sperit I ever seen. He got to jumpin' over bushes, howlin' like a dog-wolf in moon-time. Fin'ly he picks hisself out a bush big as a piana an' he let out a squawk an' took a run at that bush. Well, sir, he cleared her but he bust his leg snap in two. They was a travellin' dentist there and he set her, an' I give her a prayin' over, but they wasn't no more Holy Sperit in your pa after that.

TOM (*worriedly*). Lissen. This wind's fixin't to *do* somepin'!

CASY. Shore it is. It always is, this time a year.

Tom, holding his cap on his head with his hand, looks up . . . The TOPS OF THE TREES are bending before the wind. TOM AND CASY continue walking.

CASY. Is it fur?

TOM (*still looking back*). Just around that next bend.

TOM AND CASY are almost being blown along and dust is rising from the road.

CASY (*lifting his voice above the wind*). Your granma was a great one, too. The third time she got religion she got it so powerful she knocked down a full-growed deacon with her fist.

TOM (*pointing ahead*). That's our place.

The JOAD CABIN is an ancient, bleak, sway-backed building. There is neither sign of life nor habitation about it.

CASY (*looking back*). And it ain't any too close, either! We better run!

A DUST STORM, like a black wall, rises into the sky, moving forward. TOM AND CASY are running, but looking back over their shoulders as the DUST STORM nears. Dust rises from the ground to join and thicken the black wall.

TOM AND CASY are seen racing down the road to the cabin, the wind whipping up the dust. The two men smack open the door and slam it shut after them. The screen begins to grow dark as the storm sweeps over the land. It becomes black.

In THE CABIN, it is black, too, but the sound

is different. In addition to the sound of the wind there is the soft hissing of sand against the house.

TOM'S VOICE. Ma? . . . Pa? . . . Ain't nobody here? (*After a long silence*) Somepin's happened.

CASY'S VOICE. You got a match?

TOM'S VOICE. There was some pieces of candle always on a shelf.

Presently, after shuffling about, he has found them and lights one. He holds it up, lighting the room. A couple of wooden boxes are on the floor, a few miserable discarded things, and that's all. Tom's eyes are bewildered.

TOM. They're all gone—or dead.

CASY. They never wrote you nothing?

TOM. No. They wasn't people to write.

From the floor he picks up a woman's high button shoe, curled up at the toe and broken over the instep.

TOM. This was Ma's. Had 'em for years.

Dropping the shoe, he picks up a battered felt hat.

TOM. This used to be mine. I give it to Grampa when I went away. (*To Casy*) You reckon they could be dead?

CASY. I never heard nothin' about it.

Dropping the hat, he moves with the candle toward the door to the back, the only other room of the cabin. He stands in the doorway, holding the candle high.

In the BACK ROOM the scene moves from Tom at the door across the room to the shadows, where a skinny little man sits motionless, wide-eyed, staring at Tom. His name is Muley.

MULEY. Tommy?

TOM (*entering*). Muley! Where's my folks, Muley?

MULEY (*dully*). They gone.

TOM (*irritated*). I know that! But *where* they gone?

Muley does not reply. He is looking up at Casy as he enters.

TOM (*to Casy*). This is Muley Graves. (*To Muley*) You remember the preacher, don't you?

CASY. I ain't no preacher anymore.

TOM (*impatiently*). All right, you remember the *man* then.

MULEY AND CASY. Glad to see you again. Glad to see you.

TOM (*angrily*). Now where is my folks?

MULEY. Gone—(*hastily*)—over to your Uncle John's. The whole crowd of 'em, two weeks ago. But they can't stay there either, because John's got *his* notice to get off.

TOM (*bewildered*). But what's happened? How come they got to get off? We been here fifty years—same place.

MULEY. Ever'body got to get off. Ever'body leavin', goin' to California. My folks, your folks, ever'body's folks. (*After a pause*) Ever'body but me. I ain't gettin' off.

TOM. But who done it?

MULEY. Listen! (*Impatiently Tom listens to the storm.*) That's some of what done it—the dusters. Started it, anyway. Blowin' like this, year after year—blowin' the land away, blowin' the crops away, blowin' us away now.

TOM (*angrily*). Are you crazy?

MULEY (*simply*). Some say I am. (*After a pause*) You want to hear what happened?

TOM. That's what I asked you, ain't it?

MULEY is seen at close range. Not actually crazy, Muley is a little touched. His eyes rove upward as he listens to the sound of the storm, the sough of the wind and the soft hiss of the sand. Then . . .

MULEY. The way it happens—the way it happen to me—the man come one day . . .

The scene dissolves to MULEY'S DOORYARD. It is a soft spring day, with the peaceful sounds of the country. Seated in a three-year-old touring car is THE MAN, a city man with collar and tie. He hates to do what he is doing and this makes him gruff and curt, to hide his misgivings. Squatted beside the

car are Muley, his son-in-law, and a half-
grown son. At a respectful distance stand
Muley's wife, his daughter, with a baby in
her arms, and a small barefooted girl,
watching worriedly. The men soberly trace
marks on the ground with small sticks. A
hound dog sniffs at the automobile wheels.

THE MAN. Fact of the matter, Muley,
after what them dusters done to the land,
the tenant system don't work no more. It
don't even break even, much less show a
profit. One man on a tractor can handle
twelve or fourteen of these places. You
just pay him a wage and take *all* the
crop.

MULEY. But we couldn't *do* on any less'n
what our share is now. (*Looking
around*) The chillun ain't gettin' enough
to eat as it is, and they're so ragged we'd
be shamed if ever'body else's chillun
wasn't the same way.

THE MAN (*irritably*). I can't help that.
All I know is I got my orders. They told
me to tell you you got to get off, and
that's what I'm telling you.

Muley stands in anger. The two younger
men pattern after him.

MULEY. You mean get off my own land?

THE MAN. Now don't go blaming me. It
ain't *my* fault.

SON. Whose fault is it?

THE MAN. You know who owns the land
—the Shawnee Land and Cattle Company.

MULEY. Who's the Shawnee Land and
Cattle Comp'ny?

THE MAN. It ain't nobody. It's a company.

SON. They got a pres'dent, ain't they?
They got somebody that knows what a
shotgun's for, ain't they?

THE MAN. But it ain't *his* fault, because
the *bank* tells him what to do.

SON (*angrily*). All right. Where's the
bank?

THE MAN (*fretfully*). Tulsa. But what's
the use a picking on him? He ain't anything but the manager, and half crazy
hisself, trying to keep up with his orders from the east!

MULEY (*bewildered*). Then who *do* we
shoot?

THE MAN (*stepping on the starter*).
Brother, I don't know. If I did I'd tell
you. But I just don't know *who's* to
blame!

MULEY (*angrily*). Well, I'm right here
to tell you, mister, ain't *no*body going to
push me off *my* land! Grampa took up
this land seventy years ago. My pa was
born here. We was *all* born on it, and
some of us got killed on it, and some
died on it. And that's what makes it
ourn—bein' born on it, and workin' it,
and dyin' on it—and not no piece of
paper with writin' on it! So just come on
and try to push me off!

The scene dissolves to the BACK ROOM. The
sound of the storm is heard again as Tom
and Casy watch Muley.

TOM (*angrily*). Well?

MULEY (*without emotion*). They come.
They come and pushed me off.

We see MULEY at close range.

MULEY. They come with the cats.

TOM'S VOICE. The what?

MULEY. The cats—the caterpillar tractors.

The scene dissolves to a MONTAGE OF TRAC-
TORS: tractors looming over hillocks, flattening fences, through gullies, their drivers
looking like robots, with goggles, dust
masks over mouth and nose—one after the
other, crossing and recrossing as if to convey the impression that this was an invasion
of machine-men from some other world.

MULEY'S VOICE. And for ever' one of 'em
ten-fifteen families gets throwed outa
their homes—one hundred folks with no
place to live but on the road. The Rances,
the Perrys, the Peterses, the Joadses—one
after another they got throwed out. Half
the folks you and me know—throwed
right out into the road. The one that got
me come a month ago.

The scene dissolves to MULEY'S FARM. We
see the backs of Muley and the two younger
men standing shoulder to shoulder watching
a lumbering tractor headed straight toward
them. It is at some distance. Muley holds a
shotgun. His son has a baling hook. The

son-in-law has a two-by-four. Behind them is their cabin. Frightened and huddled together are the women and children. The roar of the tractor comes closer.

MULEY (*shouting*). You come any closer and I'm gonna blow you right outa that cat! (*He lifts his shotgun.*)

The TRACTOR continues to lumber along, its driver goggled and black of face where his dust mask doesn't cover. MULEY lifts his shotgun to his shoulder, and aims.

MULEY. I *tol'* you!

The TRACTOR stops. The driver takes off his goggles and dust mask. Like the others he's a country boy. His face is sullen. Muley is lowering his shotgun. There is surprise in his face as he recognizes the driver.

MULEY. Why, you're Joe Davis's boy!

He moves forward, followed by his son and son-in-law in the TRACTOR. Davis is wiping his face as they walk toward him.

DAVIS. I don't like nobody drawin' a bead on me.

MULEY. Then what you doin' this kind a thing for—against your own people?

DAVIS. For three dollars a day, that's what I'm doin' it for. I got two little kids. I got a wife and my wife's mother. Them people got to eat. Fust and on'y thing I got to think about is my own folks. What happens to other folks is their lookout.

MULEY. But this is *my land,* son. Don't you understand?

DAVIS (*putting his goggles back on*). *Used* to be your land. B'longs to the comp'ny now.

We see THE WOMENFOLKS. A small girl pulls her mother's dress.

GIRL. What's he fixin' to do, ma?

MA. Hush!

Back to the TRACTOR AND THE MEN:

MULEY (*grimly*). Have it your own way, son, but just as sure as you touch my house with that cat I'm gonna blow you plumb to kingdom come.

DAVIS (*contemptuously*). You ain't gonna

blow nobody nowhere. First place, you'd get hung and you know it. For another, it wouldn't be two days before they'd have another guy here to take my place.

And the tractor roars into slow motion again . . .

We see the HOUSE AND TRACTOR. The womenfolks scamper out of the way as the tractor heads for a corner of the house. It goes over a ramshackle fence and then a feeble little flower bed. Muley and the two younger men walk along. Breathing hard, frightened and desperate, Muley is shouting warnings at Davis, but the roar of the tractor drowns his voice. The dog barks excitedly, snarling at the tractor. THE WOMENFOLKS stand watching, terrified but dead pan, until a cry bursts from Muley's wife.

WIFE. Don't! Please don't!

The little girl begins to whimper.

MULEY. I'm tellin' you!

The TRACTOR moves across the yard, nosing ·a chair out of the way, and with a rending of boards hits a corner of the house, knocking a part of the foundation away. The corner of the house sinks. MULEY lifts his shotgun, aims it, holds it, and then slowly lowers it. As he stands looking at what has happened his shoulders sag. He seems almost to shrink.

The scene dissolves to MULEY, once more in the back room of Tom's old home, as the sound of the storm continues.

MULEY (*dully*). What was the use. He was right. There wasn't a thing in the world I could do about it.

TOM (*bewildered*). But it just don't seem possible—kicked off like that!

MULEY. The rest of my fambly set out for the west—there wasn't nothin' to eat —but I couldn't leave. Somepin' wouldn't let me. So now I just wander around. Sleep wherever I am. I used to tell myself I was lookin' out for things, so when they come back ever'thing would be all right. But I knowed that wan't true. There ain't nothin' to look out for. And ain't nobody comin' back. They're gone —and me, I'm just an ol' graveyard ghost—that's all in the world I am.

Tom rises in his agitation and bewilderment.

MULEY. You think I'm touched.

CASY (*sympathetically*). No. You're lonely—but you ain't touched.

MULEY. It don't matter. If I'm touched, I'm touched, and that's all there is to it.

TOM (*still unable to grasp it all*). What I can't understand is my folks takin' it! Like ma! I seen her nearly beat a peddler to death with a live chicken. She aimed to go for him with an ax she had in the other hand but she got mixed up and forgot which hand was which and when she got through with that peddler all she had left was two chicken legs.

He looks down at Muley.

MULEY. Just a plain ol' graveyard ghost, that's all.

His eyes are dull on the floor. The sound of the dust storm continues strongly.

The scene dissolves to the EXTERIOR OF THE CABIN at night. It is several hours later and the sound of the storm has faded out. Now all is silence as first Tom, then Casy, and finally Muley step out of the cabin and look around. There is still a slight fog of dust in the air, and clouds of powderlike dust shoot up around their feet. All three men have wet rags tied over their mouths and noses.

TOM. She's settlin'.

CASY. What you figger to do?

TOM. It's hard to say. Stay here till mornin' an' then go on over to Uncle John's, I reckon. After that I don't know.

MULEY (*grabbing Tom*). Listen! (*Faint sound of motor*) That's them! Them lights! Come on, we got to hide out!

TOM (*angrily*). Hide out for what? We ain't doin' nothin'.

MULEY (*terrified*). You're *tres*passin'! It ain't your lan' no more! An' that's the supr'tendant—with a gun!

CASY. Come on, Tom. You're on parole.

A CAR approaches at some distance, the headlights moving up and down as the car rides a dirt road.

A PART OF THE COTTON FIELD: Muley leads the way.

MULEY. All you got to do is lay down an' watch.

TOM (*as they lie down*). Won't they come out here?

MULEY (*snickering*). I don't think so. One come out here once an' I clipped him from behin' with a fence stake. They ain't bothered since.

The EXTERIOR OF THE CABIN: The car stops. A strong searchlight flashes on and goes over the cabin.

MAN (*in car*). Muley? (*After a pause*) He ain't here.

The car moves on.

TOM, CASY, AND MULEY lie flat, listening to the sound of the car going away.

TOM. Anybody ever tol' me I'd be hidin' out on my own place . . . !

He whistles, as the scene fades out.

PART TWO

DRIED CORNSTALKS, seen by daylight, fade in. The cornstalks, their roots blown clean and clear of the earth, lie fallen in one direction. This is what has happened to farms that were once rich and green. Then Uncle John's cabin comes into view. It is just after sunup. The air is filled with country sounds—a shrill chorus of birds, a dog barking in the distance. The cabin is of the same general appearance as the Joad cabin but even smaller. Smoke curls from the chimney.

We see a PLATTER ON A TABLE, inside the cabin. The platter is filled with sidemeat. Over the scene comes Ma Joad's voice.

MA'S VOICE. Lord, make us thankful for what we are about to receive, for His sake. Amen.

As she speaks, a man's scrawny hand reaches forward and sneaks out a piece of sidemeat.

Five people are seated around the breakfast table on chairs or boxes. They are Pa, Grampa, Granma, Noah, and Uncle John. Two children, Ruthie and Winfield, stand to the table, because there are no more chairs. Their heads are all bent as Ma, standing with a fork in her hand between the table and the stove, ends the grace. Heads lift and there is a bustle as Ma turns back to the frying pork on the stove and the others truck into their food. Granma points a spiteful finger at Grampa.

GRANMA. I seen you!— You et durin' grace!

GRAMPA (*indignantly*). One little ole dab! —one teeny little ole dab!

RUTHIE AND WINFIELD, though they are shoveling it in, are grinning at Grampa.

RUTHIE (*in a snickering whisper to Winfield*). Ain't he messy though!

GRANMA (*viciously*). I seen him!—gobblin' away like an ole pig!

GRAMPA. Whyn't you keep your eyes shet durin' grace, you ole . . .

NOAH is solemnly studying a handbill. Over his shoulder the HANDBILL can be read:

"800 PICKERS WANTED—WORK IN CALIFORNIA"

We see NOAH AND UNCLE JOHN.

NOAH (*who is a half-wit*). What's it say again?

JOHN. Says plenty work in California— peaches. Eight hundred pickers needed.

Noah frowns at the print.

GRAMPA (*who has mush on his mouth*) Wait'll I get to California! Gonna reach up and pick me an orange whenever I want it! Or grapes. That there's somethin' I ain't *never* had enough of! Gonna get me a whole bunch a grapes off a bush and I'm gonna squash 'em all over my face and just let the juice dreen down offen my chin!

GRANMA (*in a feeble bleat*). Puh-raise the Lawd for vittory!

GRAMPA (*expanding*). Maybe I get me a whole *washtub* fulla them grapes and jest sit in 'em and scrooge around till they was gone! (*Sighing*) I shore would like to do that!

RUTHIE AND WINFIELD are snickering. Ruthie has smeared her face with mush. She pulls Winfield around to see.

RUTHIE (*whispering*). Look. I'm Grampa!

She begins to slobber in mimicry. Winfield snickers. At that instant Ma enters, unobserved, and without a word gives Ruthie a fine wallop. Nobody else pays any attention to the slap as Ma, a bucket in her hand, moves on toward the door. We see her now in the BACKYARD, first at the door, then moving toward the well. She stops dead still, her eyes gazing outward.

TOM is looking at the household goods piled around the yard, to be taken to California. Casy is in the background. Then Tom looks up and sees Ma (out of the scene). His face softens. He moves toward her.

MA (*softly—her eyes closed*). Thank God. Oh thank God. (*In sudden terror as he approaches*) Tommy, you didn't *bust* out, didya? You ain't got to hide, have you?

TOM. No, Ma. I'm paroled. I got my papers.

With a sigh and a smile, and her eyes full of wonder, she feels his arm. Her fingers touch his cheek, as if she were blind. Swelling with emotion, Tom bites his lip to control himself.

MA. I was so scared we was goin' away without you—and we'd never see each other again.

TOM. I'd a found you, Ma.

CASY, with great politeness, turns his back to the scene and keeps well away from it.

TOM now looks around at the dusty furniture piled around the yard.

TOM. Muley tol' me what happened, Ma. Are we goin' to California true?

MA. We *got* to, Tommy. But that's gonna be awright. I seen the han'bills, about how much work they is, an' high wages, too. But I gotta fin' out somepin' else first, Tommy. (*Breathlessly*) Did they hurt you, son? Did they hurt you an' make you mean-mad?

TOM (*puzzled*). Mad, Ma?

MA. Sometimes they do.

TOM (*gently*). No, Ma. I was at first— but not no more.

MA (*not yet quite convinced*). Sometimes they do somethin' to you, Tommy. They hurt you—and you get mad—and then you get mean—and they hurt you again —and you get meaner, and meaner—till you ain't no boy or no man any more, but just a walkin' chunk a mean-mad. Did they hurt you like that, Tommy?

TOM (*grinning*). No, Ma. You don't have to worry about that.

MA. Thank God. I—I don't want no mean son. (*She loves him with her eyes.*)

At the DOOR, Pa is staring toward them, his mouth open.

PA (*almost to himself*). It's Tommy! (*Then shouting inside*) It's Tommy back! (*Heading for Tom*) What'd you do, son—bust out?

INSIDE UNCLE JOHN'S CABIN, all but Granma are staring toward the door. Then all but Granma scramble to their feet, headed for the door.

WINFIELD AND RUTHIE (*in an excited chant*). Tom's outa ja-ul! Tom's outa ja-ul!

GRAMPA. I knowed it! Couldn't keep him in! Can't keep a Joad in! I knowed it from the fust!

The children and Grampa scramble out first, followed hurriedly but less rowdily by Uncle John and Noah. Granma, aware only that there is some excitement, looks interestedly after them but decides against any activity.

GRANMA (*vaguely*). Puh-raise the Lawd for vittory! (*She resumes eating.*)

In the BACKYARD, the prodigal son, mother and father proudly beside him, is having his hand wrung by Grampa, who vainly tries to button various buttons of his shirt, as always. The two children jump up and down

excitedly but are too shy to force themselves into the reception.

GRAMPA (*to Pa*). You know what I al'ays said: "Tom'll come bustin' outa that jail like a bull through a corral fence." Can't keep no Joad in jail!

TOM (*grinning*). I didn't bust out. They lemme out. Howya, Noah. Howya, Uncle John.

NOAH AND JOHN. Fine, Tommy. Glad to see you.

GRAMPA (*to anybody*). I was the same way myself. Put me in jail and I'd bust right out. Couldn't hold me!

As Tom chucks the two children under the chin, the rattling roar of a jalopy causes all to turn to look.

NOAH (*confidentially*). Bust out?

TOM (*shaking his head*). Parole.

The roar increases. A home-built TRUCK comes around the corner of the house. Once a Hudson sedan, the top has been cut in two and a truck body constructed. It is driven now by Al, and on the front seat with him are Rosasharn and Connie. The arrival, as the truck moves into the yard, increases the excitement, and the scene is a little incoherent with the talking and shouting and the noise of the jalopy.

AL AND ROSASHARN. Hi, Tom! Howya doin'?

TOM (*surprised and pleased*). Rosasharn! Hi, Rosasharn! Howya, Al!

GRAMPA (*wildly*). The jailbird's back! The jailbird's back!

OMNES. Hi, Ma! Hi, Connie! Hiya, Grampa!

PA (*to Tom*). That's Connie Rivers with her. They're married now. (*Confidentially*) She's due about three-four months.

TOM (*marveling*). Why, she wasn't no more'n a kid when I went up.

AL (*eagerly as he jumps down*). You bust outa jail, Tom?

TOM (*patiently*). Naw. They paroled me.

AL (*let down*). Oh.

ROSASHARN. Heh'o, Tom. (*Proudly.*) This is Connie, my husband.

TOM (*shaking hands*). If this don't beat all! (*Chuckling*) Well, I see you been busy already!

ROSASHARN (*gasping*). You do not see either!—not yet!

At the whoop of laughter that goes up from all, she turns in a fine simulation of maidenly mortification, and throws herself into Connie's arms, hiding her face against his chest. After a moment of surprise, a slow, happy, fatuous grin begins to broaden his face. He beams, whereupon their delight increases, the men roaring and jeering and slapping their legs, the women making modest efforts to suppress their amusement.

OMNES. Lookut his face! Y'see his face? Lookut Rosasharn! Y'ever see anything like her face when Tom said it? Look around, Rosasharn! Let's see it again!

An automobile horn sounds sharply. Their laughter halted as though cut by a knife, they look off. A TOURING CAR has stopped in the road by the house, the engine still running. One man drives, the other talks.

MAN. Hey, Joad! John Joad!

In the BACKYARD the people are silent, their faces without expression, as all gaze toward the touring car.

MAN. Ain't forgot, have you?

JOHN. We ain't forgot.

MAN. Comin' through here tomorrow, you know.

JOHN. I know. We be out. We be out by sunup.

The touring car's engine is still heard after the men drive off. The Joads watch the car, their heads turning, their eyes following, expressionless.

The scene dissolves to the BACKYARD just before dawn. Now and then a rooster crows. A couple of lanterns light the scene as the men load the truck. It is nearly done, the body piled high but flat with boxes, and more tied on running boards. Al has the hood open and is working on the motor.

Noah, Casy, Uncle John, Connie, Pa, and Tom are at various tasks. They talk as they work.

TOM (*to Pa*). How you get all this money?

PA. Sol' things, chopped cotton—even Grampa. Got us about two hunnerd dollars all tol'. Shucked out seventy-five for this truck, but we still got nearly a hunnerd and fifty to set out on. I figger we oughta be able to make it on that.

TOM (*dryly*). Easy. After all, they ain't but about *twelve* of us, is they?

AL (*proudly closing the hood*). She'll prob'ly ride like a bull calf—but she'll ride!

PA. Reckon we better begin roustin' 'em out if we aim to get outa here by daylight. How about it, John? How you boys comin'? (*He casts a critical eye over the truck.*)

INSIDE THE CABIN, Ma sits on a box in front of the stove. The fire door is open and the light shines out. The room itself has been pretty well stripped, with only trash and discarded things left. In Ma's lap is a pasteboard shoebox and she is going through the meagre treasures stored in it, to see what must go and what she can take with her. Her eyes are soft and thoughtful as each item brings a memory, but not sad. Occasionally she smiles faintly. She pulls out a letter, looks at it, starts to throw it into the fire, then puts it back in the box. Her hand pulls out a PICTURE POSTCARD. We see it in Ma's hand. It is a picture of the Statue of Liberty. Over it: "Greetings from New York City." She turns it over. It is addressed: "Mrs. Joad RFD 254 Oklahomy Territory." In the space for a message: "Hello honey. Willy Mae."

MA, after a moment of studying it, throws the card into the fire. She lifts the letter again, puts it back. She pulls out a worn NEWSPAPER CLIPPING. We see it in Ma's hand. The headline is: "JOAD GETS SEVEN YEARS."

MA drops the clipping into the fire. Rummaging around, she pulls out a small CHINA DOG. We see it closely as before. On it is printed: "Souvenir of Louisiana Purchase Exposition—St. Louis—1904."

MA studies the dog, smiling, remembering something that it meant in her life. Then she puts it in a pocket in her dress. Next she pulls out some pieces of cheap jewelry; one cuff link, a baby's signet ring, two earrings. She smiles at the ring, then pockets it. The cuff link too. The earrings she holds for a moment longer, then looks around to make sure nobody sees, then holds them to her ears, not looking into any kind of mirror, just feeling them against the lobes of her ears, as once perhaps she wore them. Her eyes are grave.

TOM (*from the door*). How about it, Ma?

MA. I'm ready.

Tom disappears. Ma looks at the earrings, and then at the contents of the box. She lifts out the letter again and looks at it. Then, without drama, she drops it into the fire. She watches it burn. Her eyes are still on the flame as she calls.

MA. Rosasharn honey! Wake up the chillun. We're fixin' to leave.

The flame dies down.

In the BACKYARD it is grey dawn. There is a thrill of quiet excitement as they all stand around the loaded truck, hats on, putting on coats. The ones missing are Ma, Rosasharn, the children, and Grampa. Pa is in charge.

PA (*as Ma comes out of the cabin*). Where's Grampa? Al, go git him.

GRANMA (*trying to climb in the front seat*). I'm gonna sit up front! Somebody he'p me!

Tom easily lifts her up the step. The two children come running out of the house, chanting.

RUTHIE AND WINFIELD. Goin' to California! Goin' to California!

PA. You kids climb up first, on top. (*All obey as he directs.*) Al's gonna drive, Ma. You sit up there with him and Granma and we'll swap around later.

GRANMA. I ain't gonna sit with Grampa!

PA. Connie, you he'p Rosasharn up there alongside Ruthie and Winfiel'. (*Looking around.*) Where's Grampa?

GRANMA (*with a cackle*). Where he al'ays is, prob'ly!

PA. Well, leave him a place, but Noah, you and John, y'all kinda find yourself a place—kinda keep it even all around.

All have obeyed and are aboard but Pa, Tom, and Casy, who is watching the springs flatten out.

TOM. Think she'll hold?

CASY. If she does it'll be a miracle outa Scripture.

GRAMPA'S VOICE. Lemmo go, gol dang it! Lemmo go, I tell you!

All turn. In a CORNER OF THE HOUSE Al is pulling Grampa gently but firmly, the old man holding back, and furious. He flails feebly at Al, who holds his head out of the way without effort.

AL. He wasn't sleepin'. He was settin' out back a the barn. They's somepin' wrong with him.

GRAMPA. Ef you don't let me go—

Al permits Grampa to jerk loose and sit down on the doorstep. The old man is miserable and frightened and angry, too old to understand or accept such a violent change in his life. Tom and Pa come up to him. The others watch solemnly from their places in the truck.

TOM. What's a matter, Grampa?

GRAMPA (*dully, sullenly*). Ain't nothin' the matter. I just ain't a-goin', that's all.

PA. What you mean you ain't goin'? We *got* to go. We got no place to stay.

GRAMPA. I ain't talkin' about you, I'm talkin' about me. And I'm a-stayin'. I give her a good goin' over all night long —and I'm a-stayin'.

PA. But you can't *do* that, Grampa. This here land is goin' under the tractor. We *all* got to git out.

GRAMPA. All but me! I'm a-stayin'.

TOM. How 'bout Granma?

GRAMPA (*fiercely*). Take her with you!

MA (*getting out of the truck*). But who'd cook for you? How'd you live?

GRAMPA. Muley's livin', ain't he? And I'm *twicet* the man Muley is!

PA (*on his knee*). Now listen, Grampa. Listen to me, just a minute.

GRAMPA (*grimly*). And I ain't gonna listen either. I tol' you what I'm gonna do. (*Angrily*) And I don't give a hoot in a hollow if they's oranges and grapes crowdin' a fella outa bed even, I ain't a-goin' to California! (*Picking up some dirt*) This here's my country. I b'long *here*. (*Looking at the dirt*) It ain't no good—(*after a pause*)—but it's mine.

TOM (*after a silence*). Ma. Pa. (*They move toward the cabin with him.*)

Grampa, his eyes hurt and hunted and frightened and bewildered, scratches in the dirt.

GRAMPA (*loudly*). And can't nobody *make* me go, either! Ain't nobody here *man* enough to make me! I'm a-stayin'!

All watch him worriedly.

INSIDE THE CABIN:

TOM. Either we got to tie him up and *throw* him on the truck, or somepin. He can't stay here.

PA. Can't tie him. Either we'll hurt him or he'll git so mad he'll hurt his self. (*After thought*) Reckon we could git him *drunk*?

TOM. Ain't no whisky, is they?

MA. Wait. There's a half a bottle a soothin' sirup here. (*In the trash in the corner.*) It put the chillun to sleep.

TOM (*tasting it*). Don't taste bad.

MA (*looking in the pot*). And they's some coffee here. I could fix him a cup. . . .

TOM. That's right. And douse some in it.

PA (*watching*). Better give him a good 'un. He's awful bull-headed.

Ma is already pouring coffee into a can as GRAMPA is seen.

GRAMPA (*mumbling defiantly*). If Muley can scrabble along, I can do it too. (*Suddenly sniffing*) I smell spareribs. Somebody been eatin' spareribs? How come I ain't got some?

MA (*from the door*). Got some saved for you, Grampa. Got 'em warmin' now. Here's a cuppa coffee.

GRAMPA (*taking the cup*). Awright, but get me some a them spareribs, too. Get me a whole mess of 'em. I'm hongry.

He drinks the coffee. Pa and Tom watch him. He notices nothing. He takes another dram of the coffee.

GRAMPA (*amiably*). I shore do like spareribs.

He drinks again.

The scene dissolves to the TRUCK. It is just after dawn. Pa, Tom, and Noah are lifting Grampa into the truck. He mumbles angrily, but is unconscious of what is happening.

PA (*fretfully*). Easy, *easy!* You wanta bust his head wide open? Pull his arms, John.

GRAMPA (*mumbling*). Ain't a-goin', thas all . . .

PA. Put somepin' over him, so he won't git sun-struck. (*Looking around*) Ever'body set now? (*A chorus of responses.*) Awright, Al, letta go!

The engine rattles and roars shakily. Grinning with excitement, Pa sits down and pats Grampa clumsily.

PA. You be awright, Grampa.

The truck starts to move heavily. Casy stands watching it.

CASY. Good-by, an' good luck.

PA. Hey, wait! Hold 'er, Al! (*The car stops.*) Ain't you goin' with us?

CASY (*after a pause*). I'd like to. There's somethin' happenin' out there in the wes' an' I'd like to try to learn what it is. If you feel you got the room. . . .

He stops politely. Pa looks from one face to the other in the truck—a swift, silent canvass—and though no one speaks or gives any other sign, Pa knows that the vote is yes.

PA (*heartily*). Come on, get on, plenty room!

OMNES. Sure, come on, Casy, plenty room!

Quickly he climbs aboard. The truck rattles into motion again.

PA (*excitedly*). Here we go!

TOM (*grinning*). California, here we come!

As they all look back the deserted CABIN is seen from the departing truck.

Now we see the FAMILY IN THE TRUCK, as it snorts and rattles toward the road—a study of facial expressions as the Joad family look back for the last time at their home. Connie and Rosasharn, whispering, giggling, and slappings, are oblivious of the event. Ruthie and Winfield are trembling with excitement. But Tom's and Pa's smiles have disappeared, and all the men are gazing back thoughtfully and soberly, their minds occupied with the solemnity of this great adventure.

In the FRONT SEAT OF THE TRUCK. Al is driving. Granma is already dozing. Ma looks steadily ahead.

AL (*grinning*). Ain't you gonna look back, Ma?—give the ol' place a last look?

MA (*coldly shaking her head*). We're goin' to California, ain't we? Awright then, let's *go* to California.

AL (*sobering*). That don't sound like you, Ma. You never was like that before.

MA. I never had my house pushed over before. I never had my fambly stuck out on the road. I never had to lose . . . ever'thing I had in life.

She continues to stare straight ahead. The TRUCK is lumbering up onto a paved highway.

The scene dissolves to a MONTAGE: Almost filling the screen is the shield marker of the U. S. Highway 66. Superimposed on it is a montage of jalopies, steaming and rattling and piled high with goods and people, as they pull onto the highway, to indicate as much as possible that this departure of the Joad truck is but part of a mass movement of jalopies and families. The signs of towns on U. S. Highway 66 flash past— CHECOTAH, OKLAHOMA CITY, BETHANY.

This dissolves to a HIGHWAY. It is late afternoon. The Joad truck pulls off the paved highway and stops. The men leap down quickly from the truck, all but Pa, who lifts Grampa in his arms and then lowers him slowly, gently into Tom's arms.

In TOM's arms Grampa is whimpering feebly.

GRAMPA. *Ain't* a-goin' . . . ain't a-goin' . . .

TOM. 'S all right, Grampa. You just kind a tar'd, that's all. Somebody fix a pallet.

With a quilt pulled from the truck Ma runs ahead as Tom carries Grampa toward a clump of woods back off the highway. The others get down soberly from the truck, all but Granma, who is still dozing. Cars pass —a fast car passing a jalopy. Tom is letting the old man down gently as Ma adjusts the quilt on the ground. Death is in Grampa's eyes as he looks up dimly at them.

GRAMPA (*a whisper*). Thas it, jus' tar'd, thas all . . . jus' tar'd. . . . (*He closes his eyes.*)

The scene dissolves to an insert of a NOTE. It is written awkwardly in pencil on the flyleaf of a Bible. Tom's voice recites the words.

TOM'S VOICE. This here is William James Joad, dyed of a stroke, old old man. His fokes bured him becaws they got no money to pay for funerls. Nobody kilt him. Jus a stroke an he dyed.

A GRAVE, at night. In the clump of woods, lighted by two lanterns, the Joad tribe stands reverently around an open grave. Having read the note, Tom puts it in a small fruit jar and kneels down and, reaching into the grave, places it on Grampa's body.

TOM. I figger best we leave something like this on him, lest somebody dig him up and make out he been kilt. (*Reaching into the grave*) Lotta times looks like the gov'ment got more interest in a dead man than a live one.

PA. Not be so lonesome, either, knowin' his name is there with 'im, not just' a old fella lonesome underground.

TOM (*straightening up*). Casy, won't you say a few words?

CASY. I ain't no more a preacher, you know.

TOM. We know. But ain't none of our folks ever been buried without a few words.

CASY (*after a pause*). I'll say 'em—an' make it short. (*All bow and close eyes.*) This here ol' man jus' lived a life an' jus' died out of it. I don't know whether he was good or bad, an' it don't matter much. Heard a fella say a poem once, an' he says, "All that lives is holy." But I wouldn't pray for jus' a ol' man that's dead, because he's awright. If I was to pray I'd pray for the folks that's alive an' don't know which way to turn. Grampa here, he ain't got no more trouble like that. He's got his job all cut out for 'im—so cover 'im up and let 'im get to it.

OMNES. Amen.

The scene fades out.

PART THREE

HIGHWAY 66, in daylight, fades in: an Oklahoma stretch, revealing a number of jalopies rattling westward. The Joad truck approaches.

In the FRONT SEAT OF THE TRUCK Tom is now driving. Granma is dozing again, and Ma is looking thoughtfully ahead.

MA. Tommy.

TOMMY. What is it, Ma?

MA. Wasn't that the state line we just passed?

TOM (*after a pause*). Yes'm, that was it.

MA. Your pa tol' me you didn't ought to cross it if you're paroled. Says they'll send you up again.

TOM. Forget it, Ma. I got her figgered out. Long as I keep outa trouble, ain't nobody gonna say a thing. All I gotta do is keep my nose clean.

MA (*worriedly*). Maybe they got crimes in California we don't know about. Crimes we don't even know *is* crimes.

TOM (*laughing*). Forget it, Ma. Jus' think about the nice things out there. Think about them grapes and oranges— an' ever'body got work—

GRANMA (*waking suddenly*). I gotta git out!

TOM. First gas station, Granma—

GRANMA. I gotta git *out*, I tell ya! I gotta git *out!*

TOM (*foot on brakes*). Awright! Awright!

As the truck slows to a stop a motorcycle cop approaches after them. Looking back, Tom sees him bearing toward them. He looks grimly at Ma.

TOM. They shore don't waste no time! (*As Granma whines*) Take her out.

COP (*astraddle his motorcycle*). Save your strength, lady. (*To Tom*) Get goin', buddy. No campin' here.

TOM (*relieved*). We ain't campin'. We jus' stoppin' a minute—

COP. Lissen, I heard that before—

GRANMA. I tell ya I gotta git out!

The cop looks startled, puzzled, but Tom shrugs a disclaimer for responsibility in that quarter.

TOM (*mildly*). She's kinda ol'—

GRANMA (*whimpering*). I tell ya—

COP. Okay, okay!

GRANMA (*triumphantly*). Puh-raise the Lawd for vittory!

As Ma helps Granma out the other side, Tom and the cop exchange a glance and another shrug at the foibles of women and then look studiedly into space.

The scene dissolves to a MONTAGE: superimposed on the marker of U. S. Highway 66 an assortment of roadside signs flashes by:

Bar-B-Q, Joe's Eats, Dr. Pepper, Gas, Coca Cola, This Highway is Patroled, End of 25 Mile Zone, Lucky Strikes, Used Cars, Nutburger, Motel, Drive-Inn, Free Water, We fix Flats, etc.

A HAND-PAINTED SIGN reads: "CAMP 50¢." It is night. We hear the sound of guitar music. In the CAMP GROUND a small wooden house dominates the scene. There are no facilities; the migrants simply pitch makeshift tents and park their jalopies wherever there is a space. It is after supper and a dozen or more men sit on the steps of the house listening to Connie play a road song on a borrowed guitar. The music softens the tired, drawn faces of the men and drives away some of their shyness. In the dark, outside the circle of light from the gasoline lantern on the porch, some of the women and children sit and enjoy the luxury of this relative gaiety. The proprietor sits tipped back in a straight chair on the porch.

We see the JOAD TENT. Behind their truck, a tarpaulin is stretched over a rope from tree to tree. Granma lies asleep on a quilt, stirring fitfully. Ma sits on the ground at her head, fanning her with a piece of cardboard. Rosasharn lies flat on her back, hands clasped under her head, looking up at the stars. The music comes to them pleasantly.

ROSASHARN. Ma . . . all this, will it hurt the baby?

MA. Now don't you go gettin' nimsy-mimsy.

ROSASHARN. Sometimes I'm all jumpy inside.

MA. Well, can't nobody get through nine *months* without sorrow.

ROSASHARN. But will it—hurt the baby?

MA. They use' to be a sayin': A chile born outa sorrow'll be a happy chile. An' another: Born outa too much joy'll be a doleful boy. That's the way I always heard it.

ROSASHARN. You don't ever get scairt, do you, Ma?

MA (*thoughtfully*). Sometimes. A little. Only it ain't scairt so much. It's jus' waitin' an' wonderin'. But when sump'n happens that I got to do sump'n—(*simply*)—I'll do it.

ROSASHARN. Don't it ever scare you it won't be nice in California like we think?

MA (*quickly*). No. No, it don't. I can't do that. I can't let m'self. All I can do is see how soon they gonna wanta eat again. They'd all get upset if I done anymore 'n that. They all depen' on me jus' thinkin' about that. (*After a pause*) That's my part—that an' keepin' the fambly together.

As the music ends we see a GROUP ON THE PORCH STEPS. The men murmur approbation of Connie's playing.

PA (*with quiet pride*). Thas my son-in-law.

FIRST MAN. Sings real nice. What state y'all from?

PA. Oklahoma. Had us a farm there, share-croppin'.

TOM. Till the tractors druv us out.

FIRST MAN. We from Arkansas. I had me a store there, kind a general notions store, but when the farms went the store went too. (*Sighing*) Nice a little store as you ever saw. I shore did hate to give it up.

PA (*profoundly*). Wal, y'cain't tell. I figger when we git out there an' git work an' maybe git us a piece a growin' lan' near water it might not be so bad at that.

OTHER MEN. Thas right. . . . Payin' good wages, I hear . . . Ever'body got work out there . . . Can't be no worse . . .

As they talk, a SECOND MAN, standing on the edge of the group, begins to grin bitterly. He is much more ragged than the others.

SECOND MAN. You folks must have a pot a money.

The GROUP turns to look at the Man.

PA (*with dignity*). No, we ain't got no money. But they's plenty of us to work, an' we're all good men. Get good wages out there an' put it all together an' we'll be awright.

The Man begins to snigger and then to laugh in a high whinneying giggle which turns into a fit of coughing. All of the men are watching him.

SECOND MAN. Good wages, eh! Pickin' oranges an' peaches?

PA (*quietly*). We gonna take whatever they got.

TOM. What's so funny about it?

SECOND MAN (*sniggering again*). What's so funny about it? I just *been* out there! I been an' *seen* it! An' I'm goin' *back* to starve—because I ruther starve all over at oncet!

PA (*angrily*). Whatta you think you're talkin' about? I got a *han'bill* here says good wages, an' I seen it in the papers they need pickers!

SECOND MAN. Awright, go on! Ain't nobody stoppin' ya!

PA (*pulling out handbill*). But what about this?

SECOND MAN. I ain't gonna fret you. Go on!

TOM. Wait a minute, buddy. You jus' done some jackassin'! You ain't gonna shut up now. The han'bill says they need men. You laugh an' say they don't. Now which one's a liar?

SECOND MAN (*after a pause*). How many you'all got them han'bills? Come on, how many?

At least three-quarters of the men worriedly reach into their pockets and draw out worn and folded handbills.

PA. But what does *that* prove?

SECOND MAN. Look at 'em! Same yella han'bill—800 pickers wanted. Awright, this man wants 800 men. So he prints up 5,000 a them han'bills an' maybe 20,000 people sees 'em. An' maybe two-three thousan' starts movin' wes' account a this han'bill. Two-three thousan' folks that's crazy with worry headin' out for 800 jobs! Does that make sense?

There is a long worried silence. The proprietor leans forward angrily.

PROPRIETOR. What are you, a trouble-maker? You sure you ain't one a them labor fakes?

SECOND MAN. I swear I ain't, mister!

PROPRIETOR. Well, don't you go roun' here tryin' to stir up trouble.

SECOND MAN (*drawing himself up*). I tried to tell you folks sump'n it took me a year to fin' out. Took two kids dead, took my wife dead, to show me. But nobody couldn't tell me neither. I can't tell ya about them little fellas layin' in the tent with their bellies puffed out an' jus' skin on their bones, an' shiverin' an' whinin' like pups, an' me runnin' aroun' tryin' to get work—(*shouting*)—not for money, not for wages—jus' for a cup a flour an' a spoon a lard! An' then the coroner came. "Them children died a heart-failure," he says, an' put it in his paper. (*With wild bitterness*) Heart-failure!—an' their little bellies stuck out like a pig-bladder!

He looks around at the men, trying to control his emotions, and then he walks away into the darkness. There is an uneasy silence.

FIRST MAN. Well—gettin' late. Got to get to sleep.

They all rise as at a signal, all moved and worried by the Second Man's outburst. TOM, PA AND CASY move away, worry on their faces.

PA. S'pose he's tellin' the truth—that fella?

CASY. He's tellin' the truth awright. The truth for him. He wasn't makin' nothin' up.

TOM. How about us? Is that the truth for us?

CASY. I don't know.

PA (*worriedly*). How can you tell?

The scene dissolves to a MONTAGE: super-imposed on the shield marker of U.S. Highway 66 and the rattling Joad truck the signs of towns flash by: AMARILLO, VEGA, GLENRIO.

The TRUCK is seen on the HIGHWAY. It is now mountain country—New Mexico. Then it is seen at a GAS STATION. It is a cheap two-pump station, hand-painted, dreary, dusty. Huddled next to it is a hamburger stand. In front of the hamburger stand is a truck labeled: NEW MEXICO VAN AND STORAGE

COMPANY. The Joads are piling out of their truck. Directed by Ma, Noah lifts Granma out. The two children scamper around shrieking because their legs have gone to sleep. Al is preparing to put water in the radiator. Pa takes out a deep leather pouch, unties the strings, and begins calculating his money as the fat proprietor advances.

FAT MAN (*truculently*). You folks aim to buy anything?

AL. Need some gas, mister.

FAT MAN. Got any money?

AL. Whatta you think: —we's beggin'?

FAT MAN. I just ast, that's all.

TOM (*evenly*). Well, ask right. You ain't talkin' to bums, you know.

FAT MAN (*appealing to heaven*). All in the worl' I done was ast!

INSIDE THE HAMBURGER STAND, a standard cheap eatery, Bert is doing the short orders and Mae is handling the counter. A nickel phonograph is playing a tune. Bill, a truck driver, sits at the counter; his partner, Fred, is playing a slot machine.

BILL. Kinda pie y'got?

MAE. Banana cream, pineapple cream, chocolate cream—and apple.

BILL. Cut me off a hunk a that banana cream, and a cuppa java.

FRED. Make it two.

MAE. Two it is. (*Smirking*) Seen any new etchin's lately, Bill?

BILL (*grinning*). Well, here's one ain't bad. Little kid comes in late to school. Teacher says—

He stops. Pa is peering in the screen door. Beside him Ruthie and Winfield have their noses flattened against the screen. Mae looks at Pa.

MAE. Yeah?

PA. Could you see your way clear to sell us a loaf a bread, ma'am.

MAE. This ain't a groc'ry store. We got bread to make san'widges with.

PA. I know, ma'am . . . on'y it's for a ole lady, no teeth, gotta sof'n it with water so she can chew it, an' she's hongry.

MAE. Whyn't you buy a san'wich? We got nice san'widges.

PA (*embarrassed*). I shore would like to do that, ma'am, but the fack is, we ain't got but a dime for it. It's all figgered out, I mean—for the trip.

MAE. You can't get no loaf a bread for a dime. We only got fifteen-cent loafs.

BERT (*an angry whisper*). Give 'em the bread.

MAE. We'll run out 'fore the bread truck comes.

BERT. Awright then, run out!

Mae shrugs at the truck drivers, to indicate what she's up against, while Bert mashes his hamburgers savagely with the spatula.

MAE. Come in.

Pa and the two children come in as Mae opens a drawer and pulls out a long wax-paper-covered loaf of bread. The children have been drawn to the candy showcase and are staring in at the goodies.

MAE. This here's a fifteen-cent loaf.

PA. Would you—could you see your way to cuttin' off ten cents worth?

BERT (*a clinched teeth order*). Give 'im the loaf!

PA. No, sir, we wanta buy ten cents worth, thas all.

MAE (*sighing*). You can have this for ten cents.

PA. I don't wanta rob you, ma'am.

MAE (*with resignation*). Go ahead—Bert says take it.

Taking out his pouch, Pa digs into it, feels around with his fingers for a dime, as he apologizes.

PA. May soun' funny to be so tight, but we got a thousan' miles to go, an' we don't know if we'll make it.

But when he puts the dime down on the counter he has a penny with it. He is about to drop this back in the pouch when his eyes fall on the children staring at the candy. Slowly he moves down to see what they are looking at. Then:

PA. Is them penny candy, ma'am?

The children look up with a gasp, their big eyes on Mae as she moves down behind the counter.

MAE. Which ones?

PA. There, them stripy ones.

Mae looks from the candy to the children. They have stopped breathing, their eyes on the candy.

MAE. Oh, them? Well, no—them's *two* for a penny.

PA. Well, give me two then, ma'am.

He places the penny carefully on the counter and Mae holds the sticks of candy out to the children. They look up at Pa.

PA. (*beaming*). Sure, take 'em, take 'em!

Rigid with embarrassment, they accept the candy, looking neither at it nor at each other. Pa picks up the loaf of bread and they scramble for the door. At the door Pa turns back.

PA. Thank you, ma'am.

The door slams. Bill turns back from staring after them.

BILL. Them wasn't two-for-a-cent candy.

MAE (*belligerently*). What's it to you?

BILL. Them was nickel apiece candy.

FRED. We got to get goin'. We're droppin' time.

Both reach in their pockets, but when Fred sees what Bill has put down he reaches again and duplicates it. As they go out of the door. . . .

BILL. So long.

MAE. Hey, wait a minute. You got change comin'.

BILL'S VOICE (*from outside*). What's it to you?

As Mae watches them through the window, her eyes warm, Bert walks around the counter to the three slot machines, a paper with figures on it in his hand. The truck roars outside and moves off. Mae looks down again at the coins.

MAE (*softly*). Bert.

BERT (*playing a machine*). What ya want?

MAE. Look here.

As he looks we see the COINS ON THE COUNTER. They are two half-dollars.

MAE (*reverently*). Truck drivers.

There is a rattle of coins as Bert hits the jackpot. In his left hand on the machine is a paper with three columns of figures on it. The third column is much the longest. He scoops out the money.

BERT. I figgered No. 3 was about ready to pay off.

The scene fades out.

PART FOUR

The ARIZONA BORDER, in daylight, fades in. It is in a gap in the mountains and beyond can be seen the Painted Desert. A border guard halts the Joad truck. He is not as tough as his words indicate, just curt and matter-of-fact.

GUARD. Where you going?

TOM (*who is driving*). California.

GUARD. How long you plan to be in Arizona?

TOM. No longer'n we can get acrost·her.

GUARD. Got any plants?

TOM. No plants.

GUARD (*putting sticker on windshield*). Okay. Go ahead, but you better keep movin'.

TOM. Sure. We aim to.

The truck rattles into movement.

The scene dissolves to a MONTAGE superimposed on the shield marker of U. S. Highway 66 and the Joad truck. Signs flash by: FLAGSTAFF, WATER 5¢ A GAL, WATER 10¢ A GAL, WATER 15¢ A GAL, and finally, NEEDLES, CALIF.

In the foreground, their backs turned, the Joads stand on and about their truck looking in a long silence at what can be seen of California from Needles. Their silence is eloquent. The faces of the Joads are blank with dismay, for this is an unattractive sight indeed.

PA (*finally*). There she is, folks—the land a milk an' honey—California!

CONNIE (*sullenly*). Well, if *that's* what we come out here for . . .

They look at each other in disappointment.

ROSASHARN (*timidly, to Connie*). Maybe it's nice on the other side. Them pitchers —them little pos'cards—they was real pretty.

TOM (*rallying them*). Aw, sure. This here's jus' a part of it. Ain't no sense a gettin' scairt right off.

PA. Course not. Come on, let's get goin'. She don't look so tough to me!

The Joads and the landscape are seen again. Then the scene dissolves to the BANK OF A RIVER. The camp at Needles is on the bank of the Colorado River, among some willows. We see the men of the family sitting chest-deep in the shallow waters, talking, occasionally ducking their heads under, reveling in this relief. In the background are the towering mountains.

TOM. Got that desert yet. Gotta take her tonight. Take her in the daytime fella says she'll cut your gizzard out.

PA (*to Al*). How's Granma since we got her in the tent?

AL. She's off her chump, seems to me.

NOAH. She's outa her senses, awright. All night on the truck keep talkin' like she was talkin' to Grampa.

TOM. She's jus' wore out, that's all.

PA (*worriedly*). I shore would like to stop here a while an' give her some res' but we on'y got 'bout forty dollars left. I won't feel right till we're there an' all

workin' an' a little money comin' in.

NOAH (*lazily, after a silence*). Like to jus' stay here myself. Like to lay here forever. Never get hungry an' never get sad. Lay in the water all life long, lazy as a brood sow in the mud.

TOM (*looking up at the mountains*). Never seen such tough mountains. This here's a murder country, just the *bones* of a country. (*Thoughtfully*) Wonder if we'll ever get in a place where folks can live 'thout fightin' hard scrabble an' rock. Sometimes you get to thinkin' they *ain't* no such country.

They look up as a man and his grown son stand on the bank.

MAN. How's the swimmin'?

TOM. Dunno. We ain't tried none. Sure feels good to set here, though.

MAN. Mind if we come in an' set?

TOM. She ain't our river. But we'll len' you a little piece of her.

They start to shuck off their clothes. THE MEN, excluding those undressing, form another scene.

PA. Goin' west?

MAN'S VOICE. Nope. We come from there. Goin' back home.

TOM. Where's home?

MAN'S VOICE. Panhandle, come from near Pampa.

PA (*in surprise*). Can you make a livin' there?

MAN'S VOICE. Nope.

The man and his son sit down in the water.

MAN (*continuing*). But at leas' we can starve to death with folks we know.

There is a long silence among the Joads as the man and his son splash water over their heads.

PA (*slowly*). Ya know, you're the second fella talked like that. I'd like to hear some more about that.

TOM. Me an' you both.

The man and his son exchange a glance, as

though the Joads had touched on the deadliest of subjects.

SON (*finally*). He ain't gonna tell you nothin' about it.

PA. If a fella's willin' to work hard, can't he cut her?

MAN. Listen, mister. I don't know ever'thing. You might go out an' fall into a steady job, an' I'd be a liar. An' then, you might never get no work, an' I didn't warn you. All I can tell ya, most of the folks is purty mis'able. (*Sullenly*) But a fella don't know ever'thing.

There is a disturbed silence as the Joads study the man, but he obviously has no intention of saying anything more. Finally Pa turns to his brother.

PA. John, you never was a fella to say much, but I'll be goldanged if you opened your mouth twicet since we lef' home. What you think about this?

JOHN (*scowling*). I don't think *nothin'* about it. We're a-goin' there, ain't we? When we get there, we'll get there. When we get a job, we'll work, an' when we don't get a job we'll set on our behin's. Thas all they is to it, ain't it?

TOM (*laughing*). Uncle John don't talk much but when he does he shore talks sense. (*He spurts water out of his mouth.*)

The scene dissolves to a GAS STATION, at night. The Joad truck, loaded with goods and people, is last gas and servicing before the desert. Two white uniformed boys handle the station. A sign reads: "LAST CHANCE FOR GAS AND WATER." Al is filling the radiator. Tom is counting out the money for the gas.

FIRST BOY. You people got a lotta nerve.

TOM. What you mean?

FIRST BOY. Crossin' the desert in a jalopy like this.

TOM. You been acrost?

FIRST BOY. Sure, plenty, but not in no wreck like this.

TOM. If we broke down maybe somebody'd give us a han'.

FIRST BOY (*doubtfully*). Well, maybe. But I'd hate to be doin' it. Takes more nerve than I got.

TOM (*laughing*). It don't take no nerve to do somep'n when there ain't nothin' else you can do. (*He climbs into the driver's seat.*)

MA AND GRANMA are seen lying on a mattress in the TRUCK. Granma's eyes are shut. Actually she is near death. Ma keeps patting her.

MA (*softly*). Don't you worry, Granma. It's gonna be awright.

GRANMA (*mumbling*). Grampa . . . Grampa . . . I want Grampa . . .

MA. Don't you fret now.

The truck moves off.

We see the GAS STATION again with the truck pulling away. The First Boy, a lad who knows everything, stands looking after them, shaking his head. His assistant is cleaning up the pumps.

FIRST BOY. Holy Moses, what a hard-lookin' outfit!

SECOND BOY. All them Okies is hard-lookin'.

FIRST BOY. Boy, but I'd hate to hit that desert in a jalopy like that!

SECOND BOY (*contentedly*). Well, you and me got sense. Them Okies got no sense or no feeling. They ain't human. A human being wouldn't live like they do. A human being couldn't stand it to be so miserable.

FIRST BOY. Just don't know any better, I guess.

NOAH is seen hiding behind a corner of the GAS STATION. Peering out, he sees that the truck has gone. He turns to walk away into the darkness.

The scene dissolves to a RIVER BANK at night, and Noah is once more seated in the shallow water, splashing, looking up at the mountains, content.

The TRUCK is rattling along U.S. Highway 66, across the desert, in the night. In the DRIVER'S SEAT Tom is driving, Al and Pa are by his side.

AL. What a place! How'd you like to walk acrost her?

TOM. People done it. If they could, we could.

AL. Lots must a died, too.

TOM (*after a pause*). Well, we ain't out a it yet.

RUTHIE AND WINFIELD huddle together in THE TRUCK, eyes wide with excitement.

RUTHIE. This here's the desert an' we're right in it!

WINFIELD (*trying to see*). I wisht it was day.

RUTHIE. Tom says if it's day it'll cut your gizzard smack out a you. (*Trying to see too*) I seen a pitcher once. They was bones ever'place.

WINFIELD. Man bones?

RUTHIE. Some, I guess, but mos'ly cow bones.

MA AND GRANMA are seen agann. The old woman lies still, breathing noisily. Ma continues to pat her.

MA (*whispering*). 'S awright, honey. Everything's gonna be awright.

Then we see the TRUCK still churning along Highway 66 by night. CASY is asleep in the truck, his face wet with sweat. CONNIE AND ROSASHARN are huddled together, damp and weary.

ROSASHARN. Seems like we wasn't never gonna do nothin' but move. I'm so tar'd.

CONNIE (*sullenly*). Women is always tar'd.

ROSASHARN (*fearfully*). You ain't—you ain't sorry, are you, honey?

CONNIE (*slowly*). No, but—but you seen that advertisement in the Spicy Western Story magazine. Don't pay nothin'. Jus' send 'em the coupon an' you're a radio expert—nice clean work.

ROSASHARN (*pleadingly*). But we can still do it, honey.

CONNIE (*sullenly*). I ought to done it then—an' not come on any trip like this.

Her eyes widen with fright as he avoids meeting her glance.

MA AND GRANMA lie side by side. Ma's hand is on Granma's heart. The old woman's eyes are shut and her breathing is almost imperceptible.

MA (*whispering*). We can't give up, honey. The family's got to get acrost. You know that.

JOHN's VOICE. Ever'thing all right?

Ma does not answer immediately. Her head lifted, she is staring at Granma's face. Then slowly she withdraws her hand from Granma's heart.

MA (*slowly*). Yes, ever'thing's all right. I—I guess I dropped off to sleep.

Her head rests again. She lies looking fixedly at the still face.

The scene dissolves to an INSPECTION STATION, near Daggett, California, at night. Obeying a sign that reads: "KEEP RIGHT AND STOP," the Joad truck pulls up under a long shed as two officers, yawning, come out to inspect it. One takes down the license number and opens the hood. The people aboard the truck bestir themselves sleepily.

TOM. What's this here?

OFFICER. Agricultural inspection. We got to go over your stuff. Got any vegetables or seed?

TOM. No.

OFFICER. Well, we got to look over your stuff. You got to unload.

MA gets down off the truck, her face swollen, her eyes hard. There is an undercurrent of hysteria in her voice and manner.

MA. Look, mister. We got a sick ol' lady. We got to get her to a doctor. We can't wait. (*Almost hysterically*) You can't make us wait!

OFFICER. Yeah? Well, we got to look you over.

MA. I swear we ain't got anything. I swear it. An' Granma's awful sick. (*Pulling him to the truck.*) Look!

The officer lights his flashlight on Granma's face.

OFFICER (*shocked*). You wasn't foolin'!

You swear you got no fruit or vege-tables?

MA. No, I swear it.

OFFICER. Then go ahead. You can get a doctor at Barstow. That's just eight miles. But don't stop. Don't get off. Understand?

Ma climbs back up beside Granma.

TOM. Okay, cap. Much oblige.

The truck starts.

MA (*to John*). Tell Tom he don't have to stop. Granma's all right.

The TRUCK moves away on Highway 66.

The scene dissolves to the TEHACHAPI VALLEY, by day. Taking it from the book, there is a breath-taking view of the valley from where Highway 66 comes out of the mountains. This is the California the Joads have dreamed of, rich and beautiful, the land of milk and honey. It is just daybreak, with the sun at the Joads' back. They have pulled off the side of the road and stopped, just to drink in the sight. They are looking almost reverently at the sight before them as they climb stiffly out of the truck.

AL. Will ya look at her!

PA (*shaking his head*). I never knowed they was anything like her!

One by one, they climb down.

TOM. Where's Ma? I want Ma to see it. Look, Ma! Come here, Ma!

He starts back. MA is holding to the rear of the truck, her face stiff and swollen, her eyes deep-sunk, her limbs weak and shaky.

TOM (*shocked*). Ma, you sick?

MA (*hoarsely*). Ya say we're acrost?

TOM (*eagerly*). Look, Ma!

MA. Thank God! An' we're still together —most of us. (*Her knees buckle and she sits down on the running board.*)

TOM. Didn' you get no sleep?

MA. No.

TOM. Was Granma bad?

MA (*after a pause*). Granma's dead.

TOM (*shocked*). When?

MA. Since before they stopped us las' night.

TOM. An' that's why you didn't want 'em to look?

MA (*nodding*). I was afraid they'd stop us an' wouldn't let us cross. But I tol' Granma. I tol' her when she was dyin'. I tol' her the fambly had ta get acrost. I tol' her we couldn't take no chances on bein' stopped.

With the valley for background, Ma looks down on it.

MA (*softly*). So it's all right. At leas' she'll get buried in a nice green place. Trees and flowers aroun'. (*Smiling sadly*) She got to lay her head down in California after all.

The scene fades out.

PART FIVE

A TOWN STREET, by day, fades in. Down a town or small city business street, with quite a bit of traffic, comes the Joad truck being pushed by the Joad men. At the wheel, aiming at a corner gas station, is Rosasharn, frightened and uncertain, with Ma beside her on the front seat. In the back Ruthie and Winfield are delighted with this new form of locomotion. Crossing the street, a policeman falls into step with Tom.

POLICEMAN. How far you figger you gonna get *this* way?

TOM. Right here. We give out a gas.

It is a two-pump station and one of the pumps has a car, with the attendant servicing it. The Joad truck stops by the other pump and Tom, wiping his face with his sleeve, grins and addresses himself to the policeman. The others stand listening solemnly in the background.

TOM. Where's the bes' place to get some

work aroun' here? (*Pulling out the handbill*) Don't matter what kin' either.

POLICEMAN (*patiently*). If I seen one a them things I must a seen ten thousan'.

PA. Ain't it no good?

POLICEMAN (*shaking his head*). Not here —not now. Month ago there was some pickin' but it's all moved south now. Where'bouts in Oklahoma you from?

TOM. Sallisaw.

POLICEMAN. I come out from Cherokee County—two years ago.

ROSASHARN (*pleased*). Why, Connie's folks from Cherokee County—

POLICEMAN (*stopping her wearily*). Okay, ma'am, let's don't go into it. I already met about a hundred firs' cousins an' it mus' be five hundred secon'. But this is what I got to tell you, don't try to park in town tonight. Keep on out to that camp. If we catch you in town after dark we got to lock you up. Don't forget.

PA (*worriedly*). But what we gonna *do*?

POLICEMAN (*about to leave*). Pop, that just ain't up to me. (*Grimly he points to the handbill*.) But I don't min' tellin' you, the guy they *ought* to lock up is the guy that sent out *them* things.

He strolls away, the Joads looking concernedly after him, just as the gas station attendant comes briskly to them after disposing of the other car.

ATTENDANT (*brightly*). How many, folks?

AL (*after a pause*). One.

The attendant regards him in disgust.

The scene dissolves to HOOVERVILLE, by day. A large migrant camp, a typical shanty town of ragged tents and tarpaper shacks, jalopies and dirty children. A dozen or more children pause to watch as the Joad truck lumbers down a dirt incline from the road and stops at the edge of the camp in front of one of the most miserable of the shacks. The Joads regard the camp with dismay.

TOM (*shaking his head*). She shore don't

look none too prosperous. Want to go somewheres else?

MA. On a gallon a gas? (*As Tom grins at her*) Let's set up the tent. Maybe I can fix us up some stew.

The truck moves into the camp through a lane of children.

The scene dissolves to the JOAD TENT. In front of it, Ma is on her knees feeding a small fire with broken sticks. On the fire is a pot of stew. Ruthie and Winfield stand watching the pot. About fifteen ragged, barefooted children in a half-circle are now around the fire, their solemn eyes on the pot of stew. Occasionally they look at Ma, then back at the stew. Presently one of the older girls speaks.

GIRL (*shyly*). I could break up some bresh if you want me, ma'am.

MA (*gently*). You want to get ast to eat, hunh?

GIRL (*simply*). Yes, ma'am.

MA. Didn' you have no breakfast?

GIRL. No, ma'am. They ain't no work hereabouts. Pa's in tryin' to sell some stuff to get gas so's we can get along.

MA. Didn' none of these have no breakfast?

There is a long silence. Then:

BOY (*boastfully*). I did. Me an' my brother did. We et good.

MA. Then you ain't hungry, are you?

The boy chokes, his lip sticks out.

BOY (*doggedly*). We et good. (*Then he breaks and runs.*)

MA. Well, it's a good thing *some* a you ain't hungry, because they ain't enough to go all the way roun'.

GIRL. Aw, he was braggin'. Know what he done? Las' night, come out an' say they got chicken to eat. Well, sir, I looked in whilst they was a-eatin' an' it was fried dough jus' like ever'body else.

Pa and John enter.

PA. How 'bout i'?

MA (*to Ruthie*). Go get Tom an' Al.

MA (*looking helplessly at the children*). I dunno what to do. I got to feed the fambly. What'm I gonna do with these here?

She is dishing the stew into tin plates. The children's eyes follow the spoon, and then the first plate, to John. He is raising the first spoonful to his mouth when he notices them apparently for the first time. He is chewing slowly, his eyes on the children, their eyes on his face, when Tom and Al enter.

JOHN (*standing up*). You take this. (*Handing plate to Tom*) I ain't hungry.

TOM. Whatta ya mean? You ain't et today.

JOHN. I know, but I got a stomickache. I ain't hungry.

TOM (*after a glance at the children*). You take that plate inside the tent an' you eat it.

JOHN. Wouldn't be no use. I'd still see 'em inside the tent.

TOM (*to the children*). You git. Go on now, git. You ain't doin' no good. They ain't enough for you.

The children retreat a step, but no more, and then look wonderingly at him.

MA. We can't send 'em away. Take your plates an' go inside. Take a plate to Rosasharn. (*Smiling, to the children*) Look. You little fellas go an' get you each a flat stick an' I'll put what's lef' for you. (*The children scatter.*) But they ain't to be no fightin'! (*Dishing plates for Ruthie and Winfield*) I don't know if I'm doin' right or not but—go inside, ever'body stay inside. (*The children are back.*) They ain't enough. All you gonna get is jus' a taste but—I can't help it, I can't keep it from you.

She goes in the tent hurriedly to hide the fact that tears have come into her eyes. The children pounce on the pot, silently, too busy digging for the stew to speak.

INSIDE THE TENT they have all finished their stew already.

MA (*bitterly*). I done fine! Now *nobody* got enough!

At the ROAD a new coupe drives off the highway and into the camp and stops. It contains two men. One gets out.

A GROUP OF MEN are squatting in a half-circle, the usual pattern for conversation, but they are silent now as their eyes fix on the man approaching. He is a labor agent.

OUTSIDE THE JOAD TENT the men are looking in the direction of the group. They start to walk toward it.

AT THE GROUP OF MEN: The agent, wearing a flat-brimmed Stetson and with his pockets filled with pencils and dog-eared booklets, looks down at the silent men. All of the men in the camp are approaching slowly, silently. The women give their anxious attention in the background. Among the men who walk up is FLOYD, a grimly disappointed young man.

AGENT. You men want to work?

PA. Sure we wanta work. Where's it at?

AGENT. Tulare County. Fruit's opening up. Need a lot of pickers.

FLOYD. You doin' the hirin'?

AGENT. Well, I'm contracting the land.

FIRST MAN. What you payin'?

AGENT. Well, can't tell exactly, yet. 'Bout thirty cents, I guess.

FIRST MAN. Why can't you tell? You took the contrac', didn' you?

AGENT. That's true. But it's keyed to the price. Might be a little more, might be a little less.

FLOYD (*quietly*). All right, mister, I'll go. You just show your license to contrack, an' then you make out a order—where an' when an' how much you gonna pay —an' you sign it an' we'll go.

AGENT (*ominously*). You trying to tell me how to run my own business?

FLOYD. 'F we're workin' for you, it's our business too. An' how do we know— (*pulling out a handbill*)—you ain't one a the guys that sent these things out?

AGENT (*tough*). Listen, Smart Guy. I'll run my business my own way. I got work. If you wanta take it, okay. If not, just sit here, that's all.

The squatting men have risen one by one. Their faces are expressionless because they simply don't know when one of these calls is genuine or when it isn't. Floyd addresses them.

FLOYD. Twicet now I've fell for that line. Maybe he needs a thousan' men. So he gets five thousan' there, an' he'll pay fifteen cents a hour. An' you guys'll have to take it 'cause you'll be hungry. (*Facing the agent*) 'F he wants to hire men, let him write it out an' say what he's gonna pay. Ast to see his license. He ain't allowed by law to contrack men without a license.

AGENT (*turning*). Joe!

The other man gets out of the COUPE. He wears riding breeches and laced boots, carries a pistol and a cartridge belt, and there is a deputy sheriff's star on his brown shirt. He smiles thinly and shifts his pistol holster as he starts toward the group. THE MEN are watching the deputy approach.

FLOYD (*angrily*). You see? If this guy was on the level, would he bring a cop along?

DEPUTY (*entering*). What's the trouble?

AGENT (*pointing at Floyd*). Ever see this guy before?

DEPUTY. What'd he do?

AGENT. He's agitatin'.

DEPUTY. Hmmm. (*Giving Floyd a looking over*) Seems like I have. Seems like I seen him hangin' around that used car lot that was busted into. Yep, I'd swear it's the same fella. (*Sharply*) Get in that car.

TOM. You got nothin' on him.

DEPUTY. Open your trap again and you'll go too.

AGENT (*to the men*). You fellas don't wanta lissen to troublemakers. You better pack up an' come on to Tulare County.

The men say nothing.

DEPUTY. Might be a good idea to do what he says. Too many of you Okies aroun' here already. Folks beginnin' to figger it ain't maybe *safe*. Might start a epi-

demic or sump'n. (*After a pause*) Wouldn't like a bunch a guys down here with pick handles tonight, would you?

As the agent gets into the coupe FLOYD's thumbs hook over his belt and he looks off, away. TOM's look away is an answer. His thumbs also hook over his belt.

DEPUTY (*to Floyd*). Now, you.

He takes hold of Floyd's left arm. At the same time Floyd swings, smacks him in the face. As the deputy staggers, Tom sticks out a foot and trips him. Floyd is already running through the camp. The deputy fires from the ground. There is a scream. A WOMAN is looking down at her hand, the knuckles shot away.

The COUPE is seen as the agent steps on the gas to get away. As Floyd gets in the clear, the DEPUTY, sitting on the ground, aims his pistol again, slowly, carefully. Behind him Casy steps up, gauges his distance, and then kicks him square in the base of the skull. The deputy tumbles over unconscious. Tom picks up the pistol.

CASY. Gimme that gun. Now git outa here. Go down in them willows an' wait.

TOM (*angrily*). I ain't gonna run.

CASY. He seen you, Tom! You wanta be fingerprinted? You wanta get sent back for breakin' parole?

TOM. You're right!

CASY. Hide in the willows. If it's awright to come back I'll give you four high whistles.

As Tom strides away there is the distant sound of a siren. Casy empties the gun and throws cartridges and gun aside. The men, aghast, have been standing back, worried and excited and apprehensive. They wish nothing like this had happened. The women have gathered around the wounded woman, who is sobbing. Now at the sound of the siren everybody begins to move uncomfortably toward his tent or shack. Al looks admiringly from Casy to the unconscious deputy.

Everybody has disappeared into his tent but Al and Casy. The siren draws nearer.

CASY. Go on. Get in your tent. You don't know nothin'.

AL. How 'bout you?

CASY (*grinning*). *Some*body got to take the blame. They just *got* to hang it on somebody, you know. (*Shrugging*) An' I ain't doin' nothin' but set around.

AL. But ain't no reason—

CASY (*savagely*). Lissen. I don't care nothin' about you, but if you mess in this, your whole fambly li'ble to get in trouble, an' Tom get sent back to the penitentiary.

AL. Okay. I think you're a darn fool, though.

CASY. Sure. Why not?

Al heads for the Joad tent and Casy kneels down and lifts the deputy. He wipes his face clean. The deputy begins to come to. An open car curves off the highway, stops in the clearing, and four men with rifles pile out. The deputy sits rubbing his eyes and Casy stands.

SECOND DEPUTY. What's goin' on here?

CASY. This man a yours, he got tough an' I hit him. Then he started shootin'—hit a woman down the line—so I hit him again.

SECOND DEPUTY. Well—what'd you do in the first place?

CASY. I talked back.

Two of the men have helped the deputy to his feet. He feels the back of his neck gingerly.

CASY. They's a woman down there like to bleed to death from his bad shootin'.

SECOND DEPUTY (*to assistant*). Take a look at her. (*To deputy*) Mike, is this the fella that hit you?

DEPUTY (*dazedly*). Don't look like him.

CASY. It was me, all right. You just got smart with the wrong fella.

DEPUTY (*shuddering*). Don't look like him, but . . . maybe it was. I ain't sure.

SECOND DEPUTY. Get in that car.

With a deputy on either side of him, Casy climbs in the back seat. The sickish deputy is helped into the car. The other man comes running back.

MAN (*proudly*). Boy, what a mess a .45 does make! They got a tourniquet on. We'll send a doctor out.

The car starts. CASY and two deputies beside him are revealed in the back seat. Casy sits proudly, head up, eyes front. On his lips is a faint smile; on his face, a curious look of conquest.

DEPUTY (*angry at the whole business*). But what you gonna do? Must be *thousands* of 'em around here, sore and hungry and living in them dumps. What you gonna do about 'em?

SECOND DEPUTY. You gotta hold 'em down. Hold 'em down or they'll take over the whole country. That's all you *can* do.

DEPUTY (*grimly*). Well, they ain't gonna take over *my* country. I been livin' here too long for *that*. Maybe some a the boys better drop around tonight and give 'em something to think about.

Casy sits with eyes front. AT THE WILLOWS, screened by trees or brush, Tom looks off at the car taking Casy away. Starting at a sound, he withdraws into the brush as the scene dissolves.

IN FRONT OF THE JOAD TENT, at night, Ma stands facing Pa and Al. Rosasharn lies on a pallet, her face in her arms, while Ruthie and Winfield look on, wide-eyed at the family quarrel.

PA (*to Ma*). Leave him alone, Ma—Al's just billy-goatin' around—

AL. Sure! I was just aimin' to meet up with a couple girls I know.

MA. You don't know *no* girls around here. You're lyin', Al. *You're runnin' away!*

PA (*a short flash of momentary but ill-advised belligerence*). Cut it out, Ma, or I'll—

MA (*softly, as she picks up jack-handle*). You'll *what*? . . . Come on, Pa. Come on an' whup me. Jus' try it.

PA (*solemnly*). Now don't get sassy, Ma.

MA. Al ain't a-goin' away, an' you gonna *tell* him he ain't a-goin' away. (*Hefting the jack-handle*) An' if you think dif-f'unt, you gotta whup me first. So come on.

PA (*helplessly*). I never *seen* her so sassy. (*With a touch of bewildered pride*) An' she ain't so young, neither!

AL (*sullenly*). I'd come back—

MA (*eyes on Pa*). But ef you *do* whup me, I swear you better not ever go to sleep again, because the minute you go to sleep, or you're settin' down, or your back's turned, I'm gonna knock you belly-up with a bucket.

They stand staring at each other in silence.

At the EDGE OF HOOVERVILLE, Tom is heading for the Joad tent warily, glancing around constantly, but not running, for that would draw attention to him.

IN FRONT OF THE JOAD TENT again:

PA (*helplessly*). Jus' sassy, that's all.

MA (*angrily*). Sassy my foot! I'm jus' sick an' tar'd a my folks tryin' to bust up. All we got lef' in the *worl'* is the fambly—an' right down at bottom that's all we *got* to have! Ef some of us dies, we can't he'p that—but ain't nobody else runnin' away!

AL. But it ain't runnin' away, Ma. All I wanta do is go away with another fella an' look aroun' for work by ourself—

MA (*blazing*). Well, you ain't a-goin'! Ain't *nobody* else a-goin'! We *got* here an' we gonna *stay* here, together! As long as we got the fambly unbroke I ain't scared, but it's a long bitter road we got ahead of us—(*squaring off*)—an' I'm here to tell ya ef anybody else tries to bust us up anymore I'm a-goin' cat-wild with this here piece a bar-arn!

As she gets ready for whatever . . . IN THE SHADOWS, twenty feet away from the tent, Tom whistles softly.

TOM. Hey, Al!

IN FRONT OF THE JOAD TENT, all but Ma are looking off. Ma still eyes Pa.

AL (*peering into the darkness*). Tom? You can come on. They gone.

TOM (*entering quickly*). We got to get outa here right away. Ever'body here? Where's Uncle John?

JOHN (*from tent*). Here I am.

PA. What's a matter now?

TOM. Fella tells me some a them pool-room boys figgerin' to burn the whole camp out tonight. Got to get that truck loaded—what you doin' with the jack-handle, Ma?

MA, PA, AND AL (*together*). Al's tryin' to go away . . . She jus' got sassy . . . All I aimed to do . . .

TOM (*taking the jack-handle*). Awright, you can fight it out later. Right now we got to hustle. Where's Connie?

There is a silence that stops Tom in his rush of preparation.

MA (*quietly*). Connie's gone. (*Indicating Rosasharn*) Lit out this e'enin'—said he didn't know it was gonna be like this.

PA (*angrily*). Glad to get shet of him. Never was no good an' never will be—

MA. Pa! Shh!

PA. How come I got to shh? Run out, didn't he?

TOM (*looking at Rosasharn*). Cut it out, Pa. He'p Al with the truck. (*He kneels beside Rosasharn. Gently*) Don't fret, honey. You goin' to be awright.

ROSASHARN (*uncovering her face*). Tom, I jus' don't feel like nothin' a tall. Without him I jus' don't wanta live.

TOM. Maybe he'll be back. We'll leave word for him. Jus' don't cry. (*He pats her awkwardly.*)

The scene dissolves to HOOVERVILLE, at night. The jalopies are lumbering up on the road, one after the other, as the migrants scatter before the threatened invasion.

IN THE JOAD TRUCK, Tom is helping Rosasharn into the front seat, beside Ma. The others are aboard except Al. Tom hands Al a wrench.

TOM. Just in case. Sit up back an' if anybody tries to climb up—let 'im have it.

PA (*from truck*). I ain't got nothin' in *my* han'.

TOM (*to Al*). Give 'im a fryin' pan. (*He gets into the driver's seat and starts the truck.*)

In the FRONT SEAT of the truck, Tom drives, Ma sits in the middle, Rosasharn on the other side.

ROSASHARN (*hopefully*). Maybe Connie went to get some books to study up with. He's gonna be a radio expert, ya know. Maybe he figgered to surprise us.

MA. Maybe that's jus' what he done.

TOM. Ma, they comes a time when a man gets mad.

MA. Tom—you tol' me—you promised you wasn't like that. You promised me.

TOM. I know, Ma. I'm a tryin'. If it was the law they was workin' with, why, we could take it. But it *ain't* the law. They're workin' away at our spirits. They're tryin' to make us cringe an' crawl. They're workin 'on our decency.

MA. You promised, Tommy.

TOM. I'm a-tryin', Ma. Honest I am.

MA. You gotta keep clear, Tom. The fambly's breakin' up. You *got* to keep clear.

TOM. What's that—detour?

As he slows down the truck, we see that half of the ROAD is blocked with boards and red lanterns. A group of men swarm around the Joad truck as it stops. A leader leans in Tom's window.

LEADER. Where you think you're goin'?

In the FRONT SEAT of the truck Tom's hand reaches for the jack-handle on the seat at his side but Ma's hand clutches his arm in a steel grip.

TOM. Well—(*then in a servile whine*)—we're strangers here. We heard about they's work in a place called Tulare.

LEADER. Well, you're goin' the wrong way, an' what's more, we don't want no more Okies in this town. We ain't got work enough for them that are already here.

Tom's arm trembles as he tries to pull it away, but Ma holds on tight.

TOM. Which way is it at, mister?

LEADER. You turn right aroun' and head north. An' don't come back till the cotton's ready.

TOM. Yes, sir.

The TRUCK turns around. In the FRONT SEAT Tom is almost sobbing with anger as he maneuvers the truck around.

MA (*whispering*). Don't you min', Tommy. You done good. You done jus' good.

The TRUCK is going back down the road as the scene fades out.

PART SIX

A MONTAGE fades in: superimposed on growing fields hand-made signs flash by: NO HELP WANTED, KEEP OUT—THIS MEANS U, NO WORK, NO HELP WANTED.

Then we see the JOAD TRUCK pulled up off the paved highway, and jacked up while Tom and Al fix a puncture. Ma is seated in the front seat with Rosasharn. Pa and Uncle John are puttering about worriedly.

MA (*thoughtfully*). Sump'n got to happen soon. We got one day's more grease, two days' flour, an' ten potatoes. After that . . . (*Looking at Rosasharn*) An' Rosasharn, we got to remember she's gonna be due soon.

PA (*shaking his head*). It sure is hell jus' tryin' to get enough to eat.

TOM. Fella tells me they's three hunerd thousan' aroun' here like us, a-scrabblin' for work an' livin' like hogs. Can't figger what it is, but *sump'n's* wrong.

A BUICK ROADSTER which has been speeding toward them stops suddenly. Driving it is a husky man, named Spencer, whose manner is amiable and disarming.

SPENCER. Morning.

TOM. Morning.

SPENCER. You people looking for work?

TOM. Mister, we're lookin' even under boards for work.

SPENCER. Can you pick peaches?

TOM. We can pick anything.

SPENCER. Well, there's plenty of work for you about forty miles north, this road just outside Pixley. Turn east on 32 and look for Hooper's ranch. Tell 'em Spencer sent you.

This is electrifying news, as their faces show.

TOM. Mister, we sure thank ya!

As they snap into action to get under way again the scene dissolves to the FRONT SEAT, Al driving, with Ma and Tom beside him. They are all smiles, their faces glowing with excitement.

MA (excitedly). Fust thing I'll get is coffee, cause ever'body been wantin' that, an' then some flour an' bakin' powder an' meat. Better not get no side-meat right off. Save that for later. Maybe Sat'dy. Got to get some soap too. An' milk. Rosasharn's got to have some milk.

TOM. Get some sugar too, for the coffee.

MA. You know, I jus' can't remember when I felt so good before!

AL. Know what I'm a-gonna do? I'm a-gonna save up an' go in town an' get me a job in a garage. Live in a room an' eat in restaurants. Go to the movin' pitchers ever' night. Cowboy pitchers.

The scene dissolves to the ENTRANCE TO THE HOOPER RANCH in daylight. A gravel road leads from the paved highway to the big wire gates, which are enclosed. Along the side of the paved highway are parked a dozen jalopies, the migrants sitting soberly in them. Fifty or sixty other migrants line the gravel road and the junction with the paved highway. Five jalopies are in line waiting to enter the gates. And the scene is overwhelmingly policed. There must be ten motorcycle cops around. Six are dismounted and strolling to keep order among the migrants along the road. Three, their motorcycles roaring, flank the line of five jalopies. As the Joad truck drives up, we see the FRONT SEAT. Tom, Al, and Ma are beholding the scene with bewilderment.

AL. What is it, a wreck?

COP (on motorcycle). Where you think you're going?

TOM. Fella named Spencer sent us—said they was work pickin' peaches.

COP. Want to work, do you?

TOM. Sure do.

COP. Pull up behind that car. (Calling) Okay for this one. Take 'em through.

TOM (the truck moving). What's the matter? What's happened?

COP. Little trouble up ahead, but you'll get through. Just follow the line.

The motorcycle escort forms around the line of six cars and a deafening din is raised, of motorcycles, sirens, and an inexplicable blowing of horns on the jalopies. At the same time, as the gates open and the six cars start through, flanked by the motorcycle cops, the migrants begin spasmodic shouts, but what they say cannot be understood. As the cars move slowly, Tom and Al in the FRONT SEAT are puzzled and worried at the demonstration.

AL. Maybe the road's out.

TOM. I don't know what these cops got to do with it but I don't like it. (Looking out) An' these here are our own people, all of 'em. I don't like this.

AT THE GATES the heckling from the bystanders is spasmodic, not continuous, as the six jalopies in line pass through the gate into the Hooper ranch. Two men stand beside the gates with shotguns. They keep calling.

MEN. Go on, go on! Keep movin'!

The Joad truck passes through the gates. IN THE HOOPER RANCH the six jalopies are halted at the end of a camp street. The houses are small, square blocks, set in line. One, a little larger, is a grocery store. Casually about are men in pairs with metal stars on their shirts and shotguns in their hands. Two bookkeepers are already passing down the cars and jotting down information.

BOOKKEEPER. Want to work?

TOM. Sure, but what is this?

BOOKKEEPER. That's not your affair. Name.

TOM. Joad.

BOOKKEEPER. How many men?

TOM. Four.

BOOKKEEPER. Women?

TOM. Two.

BOOKKEEPER. Kids?

TOM. Two.

BOOKKEEPER. Can all of you work?

TOM. Why, I guess so.

BOOKKEEPER. Okay. House 63. Wages 5 cents a box. No bruised fruit. Move along and go to work right away.

He moves to the next car. The Joad truck starts. . . .

AT HOUSE 63, as the Joad truck pulls up, two deputies approach. They look closely into each face as the Joads pile out. One of the deputies has a long list in his hand.

FIRST DEPUTY. Name.

TOM (*impatiently*). Joad. Say, what is this here?

SECOND DEPUTY (*consulting list*). Not here. Take a look at his license.

FIRST DEPUTY. 542-567 Oklahoma.

SECOND DEPUTY. Ain't got it. Guess they're okay. (*To Tom*) Now you look here. We don't want no trouble with you. Jes' do your work and mind your own business and you'll be all right. (*The deputies walk away.*)

TOM. They sure do want to make us feel at home all right.

Ma and Rosasharn step inside the house. It is filthy. A rusty tin stove resting on four bricks is all the one room contains. Ma and Rosasharn stand looking around at it. Finally:

ROSASHARN. We gonna live here?

MA (*after a moment*). Why, sure. It won't be so bad once we get her washed out.

ROSASHARN. I like the tent better.

MA. This got a floor. Wouldn't leak when it rains.

OUTSIDE, a clerk with glasses appears, pushing a cart loaded with three-gallon buckets.

CLERK. Name?

TOM (*patiently*). It's still Joad.

CLERK (*doling out the buckets*). How many?

MA (*at the door*). Six. (*To Tom*) All y'all go. Me an' Rosasharn'll unload.

With their buckets they shuffle away toward the peach trees—Tom, Pa, Uncle John, Al, and the two children struggling with the enormous containers.

The scene dissolves to the INTERIOR OF HOUSE 63 at night, a lantern lighting the scene. Sitting wherever they can, the Joads have finished their supper of hamburgers. And grateful they are, too, for the meat.

TOM (*wiping his mouth*). Got any more, Ma?

MA. No. That's all. You made a dollar, an' that's a dollar's worth.

PA. That!

MA. They charge extry at the comp'ny store but they ain't no other place.

TOM. I ain't full.

MA. Well, tomorra you'll get in a full day—full day's pay—an' we'll have plenty.

PA (*rising*). You wouldn't think jus' reachin' up an' pickin'd get you in the back.

TOM. Think I'll walk out an' try to fin' out what all that fuss outside the gate was. Anybody wanta come with me?

PA. No. I'm jus' gonna set awhile an' then go to bed.

AL. Think I'll look aroun' an' see if I can't meet me a girl.

TOM. Thing's been workin' on me, what

they was yellin' about. Got me all curious.

JOHN. I got to get a lot curiouser than I am—with all them cops out there.

TOM (*laughing*). Okay. I be back a little later.

MA. You be careful, Tommy. Don't you be stickin' your nose in anything.

TOM (*leaving*). Okay, Ma. Don't you worry.

IN THE RANCH STREET. There is a faint moonlight, but not much, and little sound from the other houses as Tom strolls down the street.

NEAR THE GATE: beyond, cars pass. As Tom approaches the gate a flashlight plays on his face suddenly and a guard rises from a box.

GUARD. Where you think you're going?

TOM. Thought I'd take a walk. Any law against it?

GUARD. Well, you just turn around and walk the other way.

TOM. You mean I can't even get outa here?

GUARD. Not tonight you can't. Want to walk back?—or you want me to whistle up some help and take you back?

TOM. I'll walk back.

The guard watches him as he walks back and then douses his flashlight.

At a SECTION OF WIRE FENCE, watching his chance, moving silently, Tom drops on the ground, on his back, gets his head under the bottom wire, and pushes himself under and outside. Rising, he crosses the paved highway.

AN EMBANKMENT across the road from the wire fence: Tom clambers down it, moving quietly. He picks his way down the shallow ravine.

A TENT: there is a light inside and there are the shadows of figures. In the background, beyond the tent, is the silhouette of a small concrete bridge spanning a small stream. Following a trail, Tom enters and approaches the tent. (The opening is away from him.) IN FRONT OF THE TENT, a man sitting on a box looks up suspiciously as Tom enters. His name is Joe.

TOM. Evenin'.

JOE. Who are you?

TOM. Jus' goin' pas', that's all.

JOE. Know anybody here?

TOM. No. Jus' goin' pas', I tell you.

A head sticks out of the tent. Until he speaks, Tom does not recognize Casy.

CASY. What's the matter?

TOM. Casy! What you doin' here?

CASY. Well, if it ain't Tom Joad. How ya, boy?

TOM. Thought you was in jail.

CASY. No, I done my time an' got out. Come on in. (*He pulls Tom into the tent.*)

INSIDE THE TENT, three other men sit on the ground as Casy brings Tom in. One's name is Frank.

FRANK. This the fella you been talkin' about?

CASY. This is him. What you doin' here, Tommy?

TOM. Workin'. Pickin' peaches. But I seen a bunch a fellas yellin' when we come in, so I come out to see what's goin' on. What's it all about?

FRANK. This here's a strike.

TOM (*puzzled*). Well, fi' cents a box ain't much, but a fella can eat.

FRANK. Fi' cents! They pain' you fi' cents?

TOM. Sure. We made a buck since midday.

CASY (*after a long silence*). Lookie, Tom. We come to work here. They tell us it's gonna be fi' cents. But they was a whole lot of us, so the man says two an' a half cents. Well, a fella can't even eat on that, an' if he got kids . . . (*After a pause*) So we says we won't take it. So they druv us off. Now they're payin' you five—but when they bust this strike ya think they'll pay five?

TOM. I dunno. Payin' five now.

CASY (*soberly*). I don't expeck we can las' much longer—some a the folks ain't et for two days. You goin' back tonight?

TOM. I aim to.

CASY (*earnestly*). Well—tell the folks inside how it is, Tom. Tell 'em they're starvin' us an' stabbin' theirself in the back. An' as sure as God made little apples it's goin' back to two an' a half jus' as soon as they clear us out.

FRANK (*suddenly*). You hear sump'n?

They listen. Then:

TOM. I'll tell 'em. But I don't know how. Never seen so many guys with guns. Wouldn't even let us talk today.

CASY. Try an' tell 'em, Tom. They'll get two an' a half, jus' the minute we're gone. An' you know what that is? That's one ton a peaches picked an' carried for a dollar. That way you can't even buy food enough to keep you alive! Tell 'em to come out with us, Tom! Them peaches is *ripe*. Two days out an' they'll pay *all* of us five!

TOM. They won't. They're a-gettin' five an' they don't care about nothin' else.

CASY. But jus' the minute they ain't strike-breakin' they won't get no five!

FRANK (*bitterly*). An' the nex' thing you know you'll be out, because they got it all figgered down to a T—until the harvest is in you're a *migrant* worker—afterwards, just a bum.

TOM. Five they're a-gettin' now, an' that's all they're int'rested in. I know exackly what Pa'd say. He'd jus' say it wasn't none a his business.

CASY (*reluctantly*). I guess that's right. Have to take a beatin' before he'll know.

TOM. We was outa food. Tonight we had meat. Not much, but we had it. Think Pa's gonna give up his meat on account a other fellas? An' Rosasharn needs milk. Think Ma's gonna starve the baby jus'

cause a bunch a fellas is yellin' outside a gate?

CASY (*sadly*). Got to learn, like I'm a-learnin'. Don't know it right yet myself, but I'm tryin' to fin' out. That's why I can't ever be a preacher again. Preacher got to *know*. (*Shaking his head*) I don't. I got to *ask*.

JOE (*sticking his head in tent*). I don't like it.

CASY. What's the matter?

JOE. Can't tell. Seems like I hear sump'n, an' then I listen an' they ain't nothin' to hear.

FRANK (*rising*). 'Tain't outa the question, y'know. (*He exits.*)

CASY. All of us a little itchy. Cops been tellin' us how they gonna beat us up an' run us outa the country. Not them reg'lar deppities, but them tin-star fellas they got for guards. (*After a pause*) They figger I'm the leader because I talk so much.

Frank's head sticks in the door. His voice is an excited whisper.

FRANK. Turn out that light an' come outside. They's sump'n here.

Quickly Casy turns the light down and out. He gropes for the door, followed by Tom and the other man.

IN FRONT OF THE TENT:

CASY (*softly*). What is it?

FRANK. I dunno. Listen.

There are night sounds but little else to be distinguished.

CASY. Can't tell if you hear it or not. You hear it, Tom?

TOM (*softly*). I hear it. I think they's some guys comin' this way, lots of 'em. We better get outa here.

JOE (*whispering*). Down that way— under the bridge span.

Casy leads the way softly. THE BRIDGE SPAN is seen from the stream as Casy, Tom, and the other men wade carefully toward it.

UNDER THE BRIDGE it is almost black as they creep through the culvert. Just as Casy and Tom step out from under the bridge on the other side, a blinding flashlight hits them, lighting them like day.

VOICE. There they are! Stand where you are!

Halted, uncertain, they stand as three men with stars on their coats and pickhandles in their hands slide down the EMBANKMENT. Two of them hold lighted flashlights.

DEPUTY. That's him! That one in the middle, the skinny one! Chuck! Alec! Here they are! We got 'em!

There are faint responses from a distance. CASY AND TOM are alone. The others have fled. The deputies approach, their lights on Casy and Tom.

CASY. Listen, you fellas. You don't know what you're doin'. You're helpin' to starve kids.

DEPUTY. Shut up, you red—

He swings the pickhandle. Casy dodges but the stick cracks his skull. He falls face down out of the light. The deputies watch for a moment but Casy doesn't stir.

SECOND DEPUTY. Looks like to me you killed him.

DEPUTY. Turn him over. Put the light on him.

Bending over, their bodies hide Casy.

TOM, seen close, is breathing hard, his eyes glistening.

DEPUTY'S VOICE. Serves him right, too.

As the deputies straighten up, Tom steps forward, grabs the pickhandle from the man who felled Casy, and swings. The blow strikes the deputy's arm, sending his flashlight flying, and the scene is in semi-darkness as Tom swings again. There is a grunt and a groan as the deputy goes down. Then all is confusion. Backing away, swinging the pickhandle, Tom bolts, splashes a few yards through the stream, turns and gains a better start by throwing the pickhandle at his pursuers. They duck, and Tom disappears into the night. Other men rush through the scene in pursuit.

THE SECOND DEPUTY is seen bending over the body of the man Tom laid out.

SECOND DEPUTY. Where's that flash?

THIRD DEPUTY. Here.

The light flashes on the man's face.

THIRD DEPUTY (awed). Boy, he's good and dead! You see that fella that done it?

SECOND DEPUTY. I ain't sure—but I caught him one across the face, and believe me, I give him a trade-mark he ain't gonna be able to shake off easy!

TOM is seen crashing through the bushes, his face bloody. The scene fades out.

PART SEVEN

THE EXTERIOR OF HOUSE 63 fades in. It is day. Ma comes down the street with a bundle under her arm and enters the house.

INSIDE HOUSE 63, Rosasharn sits by the window as Ma enters.

MA. Anybody ask anything?

ROSASHARN. No'm.

MA. Stand by the door.

Rosasharn takes her post at the door as Ma rag, and kneels on the floor beside Tom, puts down the bundle, gets a basin and who is under a quilt, with his back alone

visible. She speaks softly, guardedly, as she bathes his face.

MA. How's it feel, Tommy?

TOM. Busted my cheek but I can still see. What'd you hear?

MA. Looks like you done it.

TOM (soberly). I kinda thought so. Felt like it.

MA. Folks ain't talkin' about much else.

They say they got posses out. Talkin' about a lynchin'—when they catch the fella.

TOM. They killed Casy first.

MA. That ain't the way they're tellin' it. They're sayin' you done it fust.

TOM (*after a pause*). They know what—this fella looks like?

MA. They know he got hit in the face.

TOM (*slowly*). I'm sorry, Ma. But—I didn't know what I was doin', no more'n when you take a breath. I didn't even know I was gonna do it.

MA. It's awright, Tommy. I wisht you didn't do it, but you done what you had to do. I can't read no fault in you.

TOM. I'm gonna go away tonight. I can't go puttin' this on you folks.

MA (*angrily*). Tom! They's a whole lot I don't understan', but goin' away ain't gonna ease us. (*Thoughtfully*) They was the time when we was on the lan'. They was a bound'ry to us then. Ol' folks died off, an' little fellas come, an' we was always one thing—we was the fambly—kinda whole an' clear. But now we ain't clear no more. They ain't nothin' keeps us clear. Al—he's a-hankerin' an' a-jib-bitin' to go off on his own. An' Uncle John is just a-draggin' along. Pa's lost his place—he ain't the head no more. We're crackin' up, Tom. They ain't no fambly now. Rosasharn—(*a glance at the girl*)—she gonna have her baby, but *it* ain't gonna have no fambly. I been tryin' to keep her goin', but—Winfiel'—what's he gonna be, this-a-way? Growin' up wild, an' Ruthie, too—like animals. Got nothin' to trus'. Don't go, Tom. Stay an' help. Help me.

TOM (*tiredly*). Okay, Ma. I shouldn't, though. I know I shouldn't. But okay.

ROSASHARN. Here come a lot a people.

Tom puts his head under the quilt. Ma turns, faces the door, her body protectively between Tom and whatever threatens.

BOOKKEEPER'S VOICE. How many of you?

MIGRANT'S VOICE. Ten of us. Whatcha payin'?

OUTSIDE HOUSE 63, the bookkeeper has encountered the newcomers.

BOOKKEEPER. House 25. Number's on the door.

MIGRANT. Okay, mister. Whatcha payin'?

BOOKKEEPER. Two and a half cents.

MIGRANT (*angrily*). Two an' a half! Say, mister, a man can't make his dinner on that.

BOOKKEEPER. Take it or leave it. There's 200 men coming from the South that'll be glad to get it.

MIGRANT. But—but how we gonna *eat*?

BOOKKEEPER. Look. I didn't set the price. I'm just working here. If you want it, take it. If you don't, turn right around and beat it.

MIGRANT (*sullenly*). Which way is House 25?

TOM (*slowly*). That Casy. He might a been a preacher, but—he seen a lot a things clear. He was like a lantern—he helped me to see things too.

MA. Comes night we'll get outa here.

At night, the TRUCK is backed up to the door of House 63; it is already loaded. Ma is speaking in a low voice to Tom, who is peering out from under a mattress in the truck.

MA. It's jus' till we get some distance. Then you can come out.

TOM. I'd hate to get *trapped* in here.

GUARD'S VOICE. What's goin' on here?

Tom disappears. Ma turns, her back to the truck. The guard plays his flashlight on the Joads, who stand watching him ominously.

PA. We're goin' out.

GUARD. What for?

MA. We got a job offered—good job.

GUARD. Yeah? Let's have a look at you. (*He plays his flashlight on the truck.*) Wasn't there another fella with you?

AL. You mean that hitch-hiker? Little short fella with a pale face?

GUARD. I guess that's what he looked like.

AL. We just picked him up on the way in. He went away this mornin' when the rate dropped.

GUARD (*thinking hard*). What'd he look like again?

AL. Short fella. Pale face.

GUARD. Was he bruised up this mornin'? About the face?

AL. I didn't see nothin'.

GUARD (*reluctantly*). Okay. Go on.

Quickly, Al is in the driver's seat, with Ma and Pa beside him. The truck rattles into motion and moves down the street.

AT THE GATES TO THE RANCH another guard flashes a light as Al stops the car.

SECOND GUARD. Goin' out for good?

AL. Yeah. Goin' north. Got a job.

SECOND GUARD. Okay.

He opens the gate and the truck goes through. It turns from the gravel road onto the paved highway.

IN THE FRONT SEAT OF THE TRUCK:

MA. You done good, Al. Just good.

Al shows his pleased pride in her quiet approval.

PA. Know where we're a-goin'?

MA (*shaking her head*). Don't matter. Just got to go—an' keep a-goin', till we get plenty a distance away from here.

The TRUCK is rattling along the highway.

Next, it is day, and the TRUCK is still churning along.

In the FRONT SEAT, Tom is driving, his cap pulled as far down as possible over his wounded cheek. Rosasharn has taken Pa's place and is leaning wearily against Ma's shoulder.

ROSASHARN. Ma . . . you know, if Connie was here I wouldn't min' any a this.

MA. I know, honey, an' just as soon as we get settled Al's gonna set out an' look for him. How 'bout gas, Tommy?

TOM. Full up. Uncle John come through with five bucks he been hol'in' out on us since we lef' home.

The TRUCK keeps moving along.

Then it is night, and the TRUCK is still making distance.

On a COUNTRY ROAD, in grey dawn, with a deafening clank under the hood, the Joad truck pulls to a stop off the side of the road. Al is driving. Asleep in Tom's arm in the front seat, Ma stirs awake as Al turns off the ignition and gets out. He lifts the hood.

TOM. She's hotter'n a heifer.

AL. Fan-belt's shot.

He pulls out the pieces. Tom gets out and takes off the radiator cap. There is a geyser of steam. In the back of the truck the others stand looking on, sleepy-eyed.

TOM (*looking around*). Picks a nice place for it, too, don't she?

They all look around. At first they find nothing in sight. Al and Tom look at each other in disgust.

TOM. Any gas?

AL. Gallon or two.

TOM (*whistling*). Well, looks like we done it this time awright!

ROSASHARN (*standing in truck*). Tommy. (*Pointing*) Some smoke up there.

All look. Tom climbs on the running board the better to see.

TOM. Looks like about a mile. Reckon she'll make it?

AL. She got to make it.

MA (*as they get back in*). What is it?

TOM. Don't know—but it's better'n this.

As Al starts the truck, the scene dissolves to a weather-beaten wooden sign:

PERMANENT CAMP NO. 9
DEPT. OF AGRICULTURE

We see the GATE TO THE GOVERNMENT CAMP, a wide gate in a high wire fence, with a caretaker's shack to one side of the gate. The caretaker stands beside his shack as the Joad truck swings off the road, hits an unnoticed rut that bounces the whole truck off the ground, and stops.

CARETAKER (*mildly*). You hit 'er too fast.

In the FRONT SEAT Al leans angrily out of the driver's window. Tom is keeping his face away from the caretaker's line of vision.

AL. What's the idea of that?

CARETAKER (*chuckling*). Well, a lot a kids play in here. You tell folks to go slow and they liable to forget. But let 'em hit that hump once and they don't forget!

Al starts climbing out. Pa jumps down from the truck.

AL. Got any room here for us?

CARETAKER (*nodding*). You're lucky. Fellow just moved out half-hour ago. (*Pointing*) Down that line and turn to the left. You'll see it. You'll be in No. 4 Sanitary Unit.

MA. What's that?

CARETAKER. Toilet and showers and washtubs.

MA. You mean you got *washtubs*? An' runnin' water?

CARETAKER. Yes, ma'am. (*To Al*) Camp committee'll call on you in the morning and get you fixed.

AL (*quickly*). Cops?

CARETAKER. No. No cops. Folks here elect their own cops. (*To Ma*) The ladies' committee'll call on you, ma'am, about the kids and the sanitary unit and who takes care of 'em. (*To Al*) Come inside and sign up.

As Ma, Pa, and Al look at each other in almost incredulous bewilderment, Tom climbs out of the truck.

TOM. Take 'er on down, Al. I'll sign.

PA. We gonna stay, ain't we?

TOM. You're tootin' we're gonna stay. (*He follows the caretaker into the shack.*)

INSIDE THE SHACK, Tom enters warily, alert for any indication that either his name or his scar may have been learned and telegraphed here. But the caretaker obviously attaches no significance to either. The shack is bare but for a cot, a table, a chair, and an electric light. The caretaker is seated at the table, pen in hand, a soiled ledger open, when Tom enters.

CARETAKER. I don't mean to be nosy, y'understand. I just got to have certain information. What's your name?

TOM (*watching him*). Joad. Tom Joad.

CARETAKER (*writing*). How many of you?

THE JOAD TRUCK is seen in front of its camp site as the Joads descend.

AL. How 'bout it, Uncle John? Gotta pitch this tent.

JOHN (*groggy with sleep*). I'm a-comin'.

MA. You don't look so good.

JOHN. I *ain't* so good, but—I'm a-comin'.

INSIDE THE CARETAKER'S SHACK:

CARETAKER. Camp site costs a dollar a week, but you can work it out, carrying garbage, keeping the camp clean—stuff like that.

TOM. We'll work it out. What's this committee you talkin' about?

CARETAKER. We got five sanitary units. Each one elects a central committee man. They make the laws, an' what they say goes.

TOM. Are you aimin' to tell me that the fellas that run this camp is jus' fellas—campin' here?

CARETAKER. That's the way it is.

TOM (*after a pause*). An' you say no cops?

CARETAKER (*shaking his head*). No cop can come in here without a warrant.

TOM (*marveling*). I can't hardly believe it. Camp I was in once, they burned it out—the deputies an' some of them pool-room fellas.

CARETAKER. They don't get in here. Sometimes the boys patrol the fences, especially dance nights.

TOM. You got dances too?

CARETAKER. We got the best dances in the county every Saturday night.

TOM. Say, who runs this place?

CARETAKER. Government.

TOM. Why ain't they more like it?

CARETAKER (*shortly*). *You* find out, I can't.

TOM. Anything like work aroun' here?

CARETAKER. Can't promise you that, but there'll be a licensed agent here tomorrow mornin', if you want to talk to him.

TOM (*leaving*). Ma's shore gonna like it here. She ain't been treated decent for a long time.

CARETAKER (*as Tom is at the door*). That cut you got?

TOM (*evenly*). Crate fell on me.

CARETAKER. Better take care of it. Store manager'll give you some stuff for it in the morning. Goodnight.

TOM. Goodnight.

As he exits we see the GOVERNMENT CAMP, with Tom coming out of the shack, amazement still on his face. As he walks slowly down the main camp street we share the revelation of the place to him. It is nearly daylight. Roosters crow in the distance. The street is neat and orderly in a military way, its cleanliness in sharp contrast to anything he has known before. Inside the tents people are stirring. In front of one tent a woman is cooking breakfast. A baby is in her arms.

TOM. Good mornin'.

WOMAN. Mornin'.

As he walks on, Tom draws a breath of exultation. As he moves on, looking around, we see the EXTERIOR OF SANITARY UNIT NO. 4, a cheap frame building the purpose of which is pretty obvious. Ruthie, warily alert lest she be caught, is peering in the door. She looks a long time and then she runs out of the scene.

WINFIELD is seen asleep in a quilt on the ground when Ruthie enters and rousts him out.

RUTHIE (*in an excited whisper*). Git up. I got sump'n to show you.

WINFIELD (*sleepily*). Whatsa matter?

RUTHIE (*tugging him*). It's them white things, made outa dish-stuff, like in the catalogues!

He stumbles after her.

THE EXTERIOR OF SANITARY UNIT NO. 4. Ruthie is putting on a bold front as she leads Winfield into sight but she is still alert for interference.

RUTHIE. Come on. Ain't nobody gonna say anything.

WINFIELD. Won't they ketch us?

He follows her into the unit, big-eyed with excitement and apprehension. There is a silence. Then:

RUTHIE' VOICE. Them's where you wash your han's.

Another silence. Then:

WINFIELD'S VOICE. What's these?

RUTHIE'S VOICE (*uncertainly*). Well, I reckon you *stan'* in them little rooms—an' water comes down outa that there little jigger up there—take a bath!

Another silence. Then:

WINFIELD'S VOICE (*excitedly*). Jes' like in the catalogues, ain't they!

RUTHIE'S VOICE (*proudly*). I seen 'em b'fore you did.

WINFIELD'S VOICE. What's this?

RUTHIE'S VOICE (*in alarm*). Now don't you go monk'ing—

There is the sound of a toilet flushing. It is a cheap toilet and it is a loud flush which eventually ends in a long refilling of the tank just as loudly. There is a paralyzed silence. Then:

RUTHIE'S VOICE. Now you done it! You busted it!

WINFIELD'S VOICE. I never—

Terrified, Winfield comes dashing out of the unit but Ruthie grabs him just outside the door. Beginning to cry, he struggles to get away.

WINFIELD. Lemme go! I didn't go to do it!

RUTHIE (*fiercely*). Keep qui'te, will ya! Shet your mouth!

WINFIELD (*weeping*). I never knowed it! All I done was pull that string!

RUTHIE. Lissen. You done busted it. You hear? (*They listen to the refilling of the tank.*) But lissen here. I won't tell nobody, y' understan'?

WINFIELD. Please don't.

RUTHIE. I won't—(*craftily*)—if you won't tell what *I* done!

He nods quickly. Then Ruthie begins to walk away with what she fancies is an innocent, nonchalant stroll, yawning casually. Sniffling a little, Winfield mimics her, a very innocent walk and yawn indeed.

The scene dissolves to a DITCH. Alongside the ditch are some lengths of concrete pipe. Tom and the two Wallaces are in the ditch, Tom and Tim picking, Wilkie shoveling.

TOM (*exulting*). If this don't feel good!

WILKIE (*chuckling*). Wait'll about 'leven o'clock, see how good she feels then!

TOM. Seems like a nice frien'ly fella to work for, too.

TIM. Lotta these little farmers mighty nice fellas. Trouble is they're little, they ain't got much say-so.

TOM. Shore looks like my lucky day, anyway. Gettin' some work at las'.

Mr. Thomas, the farmer, a stocky man wearing a paper sun helmet, enters. His face is worried as he squats down beside

the ditch. What he has come to say has taken some effort and he is still uncertain and annoyed. The men stop work.

THOMAS. Lissen here. Maybe I'm talkin' myself outa my farm, but I like you fellas, so I'm gonna tell you. You live in that gov'ment camp, don't you?

TOM (*stiffening*). Yes, sir.

THOMAS. And you have dances every Saturday night?

WILKIE (*smiling*). We sure do.

THOMAS. Well, look out next Saturday night.

TIM (*suddenly tense*). What you mean? I belong to the central committee. I got to know.

THOMAS. Don't you ever tell I told.

TIM. What is it?

THOMAS (*angrily*). Well, the association don't like the government camps. Can't get a deputy in there. Can't arrest a man without a warrant. But if there was a big fight, and maybe shooting—a bunch of deputies could go in and clean out the camp. (*Unfolding a newspaper*) Like last night. Lissen. "Citizens, angered at red agitators, burn another squatters' camp, warn agitators to get out of the county."

TOM (*sick of the expression*). Listen. What *is* these reds? Ever'time you turn aroun' somebody sayin' somebody else's a red. What is these reds, anyway?

WILKIE (*chuckling*). Well, I tell you. They was a fella up the country named King—got about 30,000 acres an' a cannery an' a winery—an' he's all a time talkin' about reds. Drivin' the country to ruin, he says. Got to git rid of 'em, he says. Well, they was a young fella jus' come out an' he was listenin' one day. He kinda scratched his head an' he says, "Mr. King, what *is* these reds you all a time talkin' about?" Well, sir, Mr. King says, "Young man, a red is any fella that wants thirty cents a hour when I'm payin' twenty-five."

THOMAS (*fretfully*). I ain't talkin' about that one way or the other. All I'm saying is that there's going to be a fight in the camp Saturday night. And there's going to be deputies ready to go in.

TOM. But why? Those fellas ain't botherin' nobody.

THOMAS. I'll tell you why. Those folks in

to being treated like humans. Suppose the Government closes its camps. Suppose too many people pass through 'em. Well, when those people go back to the squatters' camps they'll be hard to handle. (*Wiping his brow*) Go on back to work now. Maybe I've talked myself into trouble, but you're folks like us, and I like you.

TIM (*extending his hand*). Nobody won't know who tol'. We thank you. (*Grimly*) An' they ain't gonna be no fight, either.

They shake hands.

The scene dissolves to the GATE TO THE CAMP, at night. It is Saturday evening, the night of the dance. Glaring electric lights hang over the open gate. Parked jalopies line the highway as the invited guests, small farmers and migrants from other camps and their families, arrive to be greeted and checked by a committee of three men.

COMMITTEE MAN. Ev'nin', ma'am. Who'd you say invited you?

GUESTS. Mister an' Mizz Clark, they ast us.

COMMITTEE MAN. Yes, ma'am. Come right in, ma'am.

There is an air of eager anticipation, of gay celebration, and everyone is in his or her best—the men in clean washed overalls, clean shirts, some with ties, their hair damp and slicked down, the women in their nicest. Through the gate, inside the camp, can be seen the outdoor dance floor, brightly lighted, with the camp musicians already tuning up, and around the dance floor scores of wide-eyed children.

INSIDE THE GATE TO THE CAMP, we see Wilkie and a dark-complexioned man named Jule standing among a group inside watching the arrivals. They watch sharply, eyeing everyone, listening to every credential. As his employer, Thomas, comes through the gate with his wife, Wilkie grins and greets him with a handshake.

WILKIE. Hidy, Mr. Thomas. Hidy, Mizz Thomas.

THOMAS (*sotto voce*). You watching out, ain't you?

WILKIE (*grinning*). Don't you worry. Ain't gonna be no trouble.

THOMAS. I hope you know what you're talking about. (*He moves away, Wilkie grinning after him.*)

We see the DANCE FLOOR, and after three pats of the foot, to get the tempo, the home talent dance orchestra swings into music.

INSIDE THE JOAD TENT, Rosasharn dressed in her nicest, sits gripping her hands together, the music seeming to bring her to the verge of tears.

ROSASHARN. Ma . . . (*Ma turns from drying dishes.*) Ma, I—I can't go to the dance. I jus' can't, Ma. I can't hardly stan' it, with Connie not here—an' me this way.

MA (*trying to cheer her*). Why, honey, it makes folks happy to see a girl that way —makes folks sort of giggly an' happy.

ROSASHARN (*miserably*). I can't he'p it, Ma. It don't make *me* giggly an' happy.

Drying her hands, Ma sits beside Rosasharn and takes her in her arms.

MA (*tenderly*). You an' me's goin' together—jus' you an' me. We're a-goin' to that dance an' we're a-goin' to jus' set an' watch. If anybody says to come dance —why I'll say you're poorly. But you an' me, we're gonna hear the music an' see the fun.

ROSASHARN. An' you won't let nobody touch me?

MA. No—an' look what I got for you.

Smiling mysteriously, Ma fishes in a pocket in her dress and brings out the envelope of her treasures. From it she produces the earrings and holds them up in front of Rosasharn's wide eyes.

MA (*softly*). I used to wear these—when your pa come callin' on me. (*Then as she puts them on Rosasharn's ears*) You'll look pretty in 'em tonight.

They smile at each other, proud in the luxury of ornaments.

Down the road from the GATE a touring car with six men pulls off the pavement and stops. Three men get out. They are bareheaded and dressed similar to the other migrants. They stroll down the highway toward the gate. The other men, deputies, sit watching them.

WITHIN THE GATE:

WILKIE. They tell me you're half Injun. You look all Injun to me.

JULE. No, jes' half. Wisht I was full-blooded. Gov'ment'd be lookin' out for me an' I'd be ridin' around in a Buick eight.

The three men from the touring car are at the gate. Wilkie and Jule watch them.

COMMITTEE MAN. Who give you the invitation?

MAN. Fella named Jackson—Buck Jackson.

COMMITTEE MAN. Okay. Come on in.

The three men stroll past Wilkie and Jule, whose eyes follow them.

JULE. Them's our fellas.

WILKIE. How you know?

JULE. Jes' got a feelin'. They're kinda scared too. Follow 'em an' get a holt of Jackson. See if he knows 'em. I'll stay here.

Wilkie moves after them.

We see the DANCE FLOOR. The musicians are at it and the fiddler is calling the turns.

FIDDLER. Swing your ladies an' a dol ce do. Join han's roun' an' away we go! Swing to the right an' a swing to the lef'. Break, now break—back to back!

Well in front, among the older folks and children who surround the floor, are Ma and Rosasharn, clinging close. A young man stops in front of them.

MA (quietly). Thank you kin'ly but she ain't well.

As Rosasharn's eyes drop, Ma bends toward her, a shy smile on her face.

MA. Maybe you wouldn't think it, but your pa was as nice a dancer as I ever seen, when he was young. (With a little sigh) Kinda makes me think a ol' times.

The three men stroll into sight and stand watching the dancing. One glances at Ma and Rosasharn but does not speak. Ma has smiled back at him.

WILKIE AND JACKSON are seen; removed somewhat from the dance floor they are peering in the direction of the three men.

JACKSON. I seen 'em before. Worked at Gregorio's with 'em. But I never ast 'em.

WILKIE. Awright. Keep your eye on 'em. Jus' keep 'em in sight, that's all. (He moves quickly away.)

We find ourselves INSIDE TIM WALLACE'S TENT. The five members of the central committee, Tim Wallace, chairman, look grave as a 15-year-old boy reports.

BOY. I seen 'em, Mr. Wallace. A car with six men parked down by the euc'lyptus tree an' one with three men on the main road. They got guns, too. I seen 'em.

TIM. Thank you, Willie. You done good. (As Willie exits) Well, it looks like the fat's in the far this time.

FIRST MAN (angrily). What them deppities want to hurt the camp for? How come they can't leave us be?

SECOND MAN. What we oughta do, we oughta git us some pickhandles an'—

TIM (quickly). No! That's what they want. No sir. If they can git a fight goin', then they can run in the cops an' say we ain't orderly—(He stops as Wilkie enters followed by Tom.)

WILKIE. They're here. We got 'em spotted.

There is a grim pause at this news. Tim's eyes go hard.

TIM (to Tom). You sure you got ever'-thing ready?

TOM (calmly). Ain't gonna be no trouble.

TIM (worriedly). You ain't to hurt them fellas.

WILKIE (grinning). You don't have to worry. We got ever'thing arranged. Maybe nobody'll even see it.

TIM. Just don't use no stick nor no knife, no piece a arn. An' if you got to sock 'em, sock 'em where they won't bleed.

TOM. Yes, sir.

TIM. Awright. An' if she gets outa han',

I'll be in the right han' corner, this side the dance floor.

TOM (*blandly*). Ain't gonna get outa han'.

Wilkie makes a mocking military salute as he and Tom exit. The committee men look worriedly after them.

FIRST MAN. Mighty sure a themselves, looks like.

TIM. All I hope, I hope they don't kill nobody.

In front of the JOAD TENT, dressed to kill, is Al, ready for the festivities. He wears a tight-fitting wool suit, a tie on his shirt, yellow shoes, and his hair is damp and slicked down. He rubs his hands together in anticipation as he strolls in the direction of the dance floor.

At ANOTHER TENT, a blonde girl sits on a box as Al enters. Casually he throws open his coat, revealing a vivid striped shirt. This is designed to stun his quarry.

AL. Gonna dance tonight? (*The girl ostentatiously ignores him.*) I can waltz.

GIRL (*aloofly*). That's nothin'—anybody can waltz.

AL (*shaking his head*). Not like me!

A fat woman thrusts her head out of the tent.

WOMAN. You git right along! This here girl's spoke for. She's gonna be married, an' her man's a-comin' for her.

Shrugging, Al winks at the girl and moves on, stepping and moving his shoulders and snapping his fingers in time to the music, a very gay fellow indeed. The blonde girl's eyes follow him. Then she turns and glances cautiously toward the tent.

ON THE DANCE FLOOR, we see Ma and Rosasharn as Tom enters and stands between them. This is during a pause between dances and only a few couples stand on the floor waiting for the music to begin again. We also see the three men very casually looking around—but no more casual looking than Wilkie, standing just behind them, idly whistling.

TOM (*grinning*). She's gettin' prettier, Ma.

MA (*as Rosasharn hides her face*). Girl with a baby *always* gets prettier.

The music starts again, once more the dancers move onto the dance floor. The three men exchange a glance and step casually to the edge of the dancing space, one in the lead. They survey the scene, but for the moment make no further move. The atmosphere is tense.

TOM (*softly*). Excuse me, Ma. (*He moves quietly out of the scene, toward the three men.*)

AL, taking the blonde girl's hand, steps onto the dance floor. Encircling her waist, they begin to dance. They are a smooth, rhythmic couple who move as one being.

AL. Well, you said anybody can waltz. . . . How'm *I* doin'?

BLONDE GIRL. Don't hold me so tight.

AL (*tongue-in-cheek*). Why, I ain't hardly touchin' you!

BLONDE GIRL (*squirming*). You're *ticklin' me!*

AL (*grabbing her still closer*). That comes from not holdin' you tight *enough.*

BLONDE GIRL (*complaining but loving it*). Now I can't breathe.

At this moment the leader of the three men (the other two directly behind him) enters the scene.

LEADER. I'll dance with this girl.

AL (*angrily*). You an' who else?

Behind the three men a solid wall of migrants are closing in quietly, Tom and Wilkie in the middle.

LEADER. Don't gimme no argament— (*A shrill whistle sounds in the distance.*) —you little—

His fist goes back, his left hand reaches for Al's collar. At the same instant Tom grabs him, Wilkie claps his hand over the leader's mouth, at least fifteen other men have similarly collared the other two invaders, and they are all lifted bodily. There is not a sound as the three men, held in iron grips, are whisked from the dance floor and into the crowd.

Two touring cars have stopped in front of the closed GATE and the deputies have drawn guns.

DRIVER. Open up! We hear you got a riot.

CARETAKER. Riot? I don't see no riot. Who're you?

DRIVER. Deputy sheriffs.

CARETAKER. Got a warrant?

DRIVER. We don't need a warrant if it's a riot.

CARETAKER. Well, I don't know what you gonna do about it, because I don't hear no riot an' I don't see no riot, an' what's more I don't believe they *is* no riot. (*Waving toward the dance floor*) Look for yourself.

As the deputies, puzzled and uncertain, look toward the DANCE FLOOR, we see the music, the dancing, the gaiety continuing as if nothing had happened.

WITHIN THE JOAD TENT at night, several hours later: the tent is black, Tom strikes a match. From a piece of wood on the ground or floor he selects one from several cigarette butts and lights it. While he is ding so, he lifts his head suddenly, and listens.

In the CAMP STREET we catch sight of legs walking, the ground lighted from a flashlight. Two pairs of the legs wear state policemen's leather leggings. The third pair are the caretaker's. They stop behind a car. The flashlight plays on the license plate. One of the state cops leans down to copy the license number in a booklet. Then they move on.

TOM has lifted the edge of the tent a trifle, enough to see out by flattening his head on the floor. The LEGS are now seen at the Joad jalopy. The light is on the license plate. The cop leans over and copies the number. They move on.

TOM, lowering the edge of the tent, sits up. Quietly he pushes aside the piece of carpet that covers him. He is wearing his clothes. We see the policeman's CAR at the care-taker's hut. The two policemen get into the car.

CARETAKER. You got no right to arrest anybody without a warrant, you know.

FIRST COP. We'll have a warrant—just as soon as we check with headquarters.

The car drives off, leaving the caretaker looking somberly after it.

WITHIN THE JOAD TENT, his cap on, fully dressed for travel, Tom is tieing the ends of the carpet into a shoulder bundle. Rising, he slings it across his shoulder. As he tiptoes toward the door:

MA. Ain't you gonna tell me goodbye, Tommy?

For a moment he looks into the darkness in her direction.

TOM. I didn't know, Ma. I didn't know if I ought.

She has risen, pulling the quilt around her. He takes her by the hand.

TOM. Come outside.

They go out. Tom leads Ma around BEHIND THE TENT, to a SECTION OF WIRE FENCE. There is a bench there. Tom leads Ma to it and sits her down. He sits beside her.

TOM. They was some cops here, Ma. They was takin' down the license numbers. It looks like somebody knows sump'n.

MA (*softly*). It had to come, I reckon, soon or later.

TOM. I'd like to stay. I'd like to be with ya—(*smiling*)—an' see your face when you an' Pa get settled in a nice little place. I sure wish I could see you then. But—(*shaking his head*)—I guess I won't never be able to do that. Not now.

MA. I could hide you, Tommy.

TOM (*touching her hand*). I know you would, Ma. But I ain't gonna let you. You hide somebody that's kilt a man an' . . . an' you'd be in trouble too.

MA (*touching his face with her fingers*). Awright, Tommy. What you figger you gonna do?

TOM (*thoughtfully*). You know what I been thinkin' about, Ma? About Casy. About what he said, what he done, an' about how he died. An' I remember all of it.

MA. He was a good man.

TOM. I been thinkin' about us, too—about our people livin' like pigs, an' good rich lan' layin' fallow, or maybe one fella with a million acres, while a hundred thousan' farmers is starvin'. An' I been wonderin' if all our folks got together an' yelled—

MA (*frightened*). Tommy, they'll drive you, an' cut you down like they done to Casy.

TOM. They gonna drive me anyways. Soon or later they'll get me, for one thing if not another. Until then . . .

MA. You don't aim to kill nobody, Tom!

TOM. No, Ma. Not that. That ain't it. But long as I'm a outlaw, anyways, maybe I can do sump'n. Maybe I can jus' fin' out sump'n. Jus' scrounge aroun' an' try to fin' out what it is that's wrong, an' then see if they ain't sump'n could be done about it. (*Worriedly*) But I ain't thought it out clear, Ma. I can't. I don't know enough.

MA (*after a pause*). How'm I gonna know 'bout you? They might kill you an' I wouldn't know. They might hurt you. How'm I gonna know?

TOM (*laughing uneasily*). Well, maybe it's like Casy says, a fella ain't got a soul of his own, but on'y a piece of a big soul—the one big soul that belongs to ever'body—an' then . . .

MA. Then what, Tom?

TOM. Then it don't matter. Then I'll be all aroun' in the dark. I'll be ever'-where—wherever you look. Wherever there's a fight so hungry people can eat, I'll be there. Wherever there's a cop beatin' up a guy, I'll be there. I'll be in the way guys yell when they're mad—an' I'll be in the way kids laugh when they're hungry an' they know supper's ready. An' when our people eat the stuff they raise, an' live in the houses they build, why, I'll be there too.

MA (*slowly*). I don't understan' it, Tom.

TOM (*drily*). Me neither. (*Rising.*) It's jus' stuff I been thinkin' about. Gimme your han', Ma. Good-by. (*He climbs over the fence.*)

MA. Good-by, Tom. Later—when it's blowed over—you'll come back? You'll try to fin' us?

TOM. Sure. Good-by.

MA. Good-by, Tommy.

He walks away. She stands looking after him. He's leaving her forever—she knows it. She lifts her hand and waves. She tries to smile. TOM turns, waves, smiles. His lips form the words: "Good-by, Ma." Then he strides away into the darkness.

The scene fades out.

PART EIGHT

The JOAD TRUCK fades in. It stands loaded in front of the Joad tent while Al, Pa, Uncle John, Ma, and the little fellas pile in the last articles in a fury of excitement. Beyond, in the background, another jalopy is being prepared for travel with the same feverish haste. It is day.

AL, PA, JOHN (*ad lib*). Get them buckets on! Somebody tie down that mattress! You little fellas keep outa the way!

MAN (*from other truck, gaily*). What y'all hurryin' so for? Tell me they got twenny days work.

PA. Yes, sir, an' we aim to git in all twenny of 'em.

Other jalopies in the background are being readied for leaving—an excited, hopeful exodus on a new report of work.

AL. Ready, Ma?

MA. I'll get Rosasharn.

PA (*beaming*). All aboard, ever'body! All aboard for Fresno!

Ma comes out of the tent supporting Rosasharn tenderly. For the plumpness has gone from the girl and she is thin again, her face drawn and unhappy, her eyes swollen with weeping and suffering.

MA (*softly*). Try to be strong, honey. Someday it'll be diff'rent—someday you'll have another one. You're still jus' a little girl, remember.

Pa takes Rosasharn's other arm. He and Al and Uncle John help Rosasharn onto the truck. She lies down on the mattress, her face away from them.

PA. Make her easy, John. Watch her.

MA. She'll be awright.

AL (*in the driver's seat*). Ready, Pa?

PA (*as he and Ma climb in the front seat.*) Let 'er go, Gallagher!

The truck wabbles into motion. Al races the engine. It nearly crashes another wheezing jalopy at the corner. When it turns the corner we see the GATE, and a line of loaded jalopies that ride out to the highway. The caretaker waves and the migrants wave back.

CARETAKER. Good luck to you! Good luck, ever'body!

THE JOADS. Good-by, Mr. Conway! Much oblige to you for ever'thing!

The Joad truck turns onto the highway. In the FRONT SEAT Al is driving, Ma in the middle, Pa on the outside.

AL. Twenty days work, oh boy!

PA. Be glad to get my han' on some cotton. That's the kin' a pickin' I understand'.

MA. Maybe. Maybe twenny days work, maybe *no* days work. We ain't got it till we get it.

AL (*grinning*). Whatsa matter, Ma? Gettin' scared?

MA (*smiling faintly*). No. Ain't ever gonna be scared no more. (*After a pause*) I was, though. For a while I thought we was beat—*good* an' beat. Looked like we didn't have nothin' in the worl' but enemies—wasn't *nobody* frien'ly anymore. It made me feel bad an' scared too—like we was lost . . . an' nobody cared.

AL. Watch me pass that Chevvy.

PA (*soberly*). You the one that keeps us goin', Ma. I ain't no good any more, an' I know it. Seems like I spen' all my time these days a-thinkin' how it use'ta be—thinkin' of home—an' I ain't never gonna see it no more.

Ma places her hand on one of Pa's and pats it.

MA. Woman can change better'n a man. Man lives in jerks—baby born, or somebody dies, that's a jerk—gets a farm, or loses one, an' that's a jerk. With a woman it's all one flow, like a stream, little eddies, little waterfalls, but the river it goes right on. Woman looks at it like that.

AL (*at the jalopy ahead*). Look at that ol' coffeepot steam!

PA (*thinking of what Ma says*). Maybe, but we shore takin' a beatin'.

MA (*chuckling*). I know. Maybe that makes us tough. Rich fellas come up an' they die, an' their kids ain't no good, an' they die out. But we keep a-comin'. We're the people that live. Can't nobody wipe us out. Can't nobody lick us. We'll go on forever, Pa. We're the people. (*She says this with a simple, unaffected conviction.*)

The TRUCK, steaming and rattling and churning, passes the Chevrolet and Al leans out of the window and waves a jeering hand at it. As the Joad truck pulls in front, we see Ruthie and Winfield laughing with excitement over the triumph. Even Uncle John shares the general satisfaction. Grinning, he waves. As the truck moves away along the road, all three are beaming and waving. Further along the truck passes a sign on the side of the road. It says NO HELP WANTED.

The scene fades out.

HOW GREEN WAS MY VALLEY

(A 20th Century-Fox Picture)

Screenplay by
PHILIP DUNNE

Based on the Novel *How Green Was My Valley* by
RICHARD LLEWELLYN

Produced by DARRYL F. ZANUCK

Directed by JOHN FORD

The Cast

MR. GRUFFYDD	Walter Pidgeon
ANGHARAD	Maureen O'Hara
MR. MORGAN	Donald Crisp
BRONWEN	Anna Lee
HUW	Roddy McDowall
IANTO	John Loder
MRS. MORGAN	Sara Allgood
CYFARTHA	Barry Fitzgerald
IVOR	Patric Knowles
WELSH SINGERS	Themselves
MR. JONAS	Morton Lowry
MR. PARRY	Arthur Shields
CEINWEN	Ann Todd
DR. RICHARDS	Frederick Worlock
DAVY	Richard Fraser
GWILYM	Evan S. Evans
OWEN	James Monks
DAI BANDO	Rhys Williams
MERVYN	Clifford Severn
EVANS	Lionel Pape
MRS. NICHOLAS	Ethel Griffies
MOTSHELL	Dennis Hoey
IESTYN EVANS	Marten Lamont
MEILLYN LEWIS	Eve March
ENSEMBLE SINGER	Tudor Williams

Film Editor—JAMES B. CLARK

HOW GREEN WAS MY VALLEY

PART ONE

We hear a magnificent choir of men's voices singing one of the great Welsh songs. The voices continue through the opening scene, but more softly when the voice of the Narrator comes in.

We see HUW's HANDS, the hands of a man about sixty, carefully folding some shirts, ties and socks into an old blue cloth. As the hands knot the blue cloth round the clothes, the scene shifts to the window, so that we can see, beyond, a typical WELSH COAL VALLEY, ugly, dirty, dominated by its stacks, cranes and towering slag heap. Not far from the window the great slag heap rises in a broken sweep, high into the sky.

HUW's VOICE (*simultaneous with the unfolding scenes*). *I am packing my belongings in the little blue cloth my mother used to tie around her hair when she did the house, and I am going from my Valley. And this time I shall never return.*

I am leaving behind me my sixty years of memory— Memory.

There is strange that the mind will forget so much of what only this moment is passed, and yet hold so clear and bright the memory of what happened years ago —of men and women long since dead. For there is no fence nor hedge round Time that is gone. You can go back and have what you like of it—if you can remember.

The scene shifts, as if passing through the window, until we are looking up the steep STREET. In the background are the slag heap and the collieries. Moving up and down the street are poorly dressed men, walking bent because of the steepness of the street. The houses are built of quarry stone, grimy and huddled together—an atmosphere of poverty and decay. Finally the entire ugly coal VALLEY spreads before us. Smoke, blackness, poverty.

Then the picture dims slowly down as the Valley, as it once was, appears, fresh and green, each detail in the new scene fitting in with its counterpart in the old. The Chapel, almost hidden in the first scene, now stands bravely in view. Next we see the COLLIERY with only a small slag heap—a splotch of ugly black on the green; then, the CHAPEL dominating the street.

And now we see the COLLIERY with only a small slag heap—a splotch of ugly black on the green.

The Exterior of the CHAPEL is next seen, dominating the street.

HUW's VOICE. *So I can close my eyes on my Valley as it is today—and it is gone— and I see it as it was when I was a boy. Green it was, and possessed of the plenty of the earth. In all Wales, there was none so beautiful, for the colliery had only begun to poke its skinny black fingers through the green. The black slag— the waste of the coalpits—made only a small pile then—and our little Chapel was master of the Valley from where it stood at the head of the street.*

Far down below a man and boy appear, slowly climbing the hill. They are GWILYM MORGAN and his ten-year-old son, the same HUW who is the Narrator of our picture. Both wear the clothes of the period around 1890. They are of a family of coal miners and are attired accordingly. Morgan is smiling down at Huw as the boy struggles to keep up with his father's great strides.

HUW is seen drinking in what his father says. He looks round him as if expecting actually to see the men of whom his father is speaking. Then the two stop on the ridge of the hill, where they are silhouetted against the golden light that bathes the Valley. The wind blows through their hair.

HUW'S VOICE. *Everything I ever learnt as a small boy came from my father, and I never found anything he ever told me to be wrong or worthless. He used to tell me of my Valley and its people—the brave men of Wales who never bowed to Roman or Danish or Saxon conquerors until so many had died that the women could not bear enough children to fill the ranks. The Men of the Valley, long since gathered to their Fathers—became as real to me as if I had met them face to face. But the battles they had fought had been long forgotten and we of my Valley fought a new fight now—to wrest from beneath the green the black wealth of Nature: the coal—which first enriched us and then made us poorer than we had been before. Coal miners were my father and all my brothers—and proud of our trade as our ancestors had been of theirs.*

The scene dissolves, first to the COLLIERY WHISTLE, which is blowing, and then to a section of the colliery, a COLLIERY CUTTING, with IVOR, the eldest of the Morgan sons, punching at the coal face with his pick. He wears a miner's outfit and is blackened and grimy with the coal dust.

HUW'S VOICE. *We were a big family. After my father: Ivor, the eldest—solid and dependable as the mountainside.*

In ANOTHER CUTTING, IANTO, second of the sons, up to his waist in water, is levering out a boulder with a crowbar. Ianto turns at the sound of the whistle.

HUW'S VOICE. *Ianto—who had the devil's own tongue and liked a fight better than the blood in his veins—*

DAVY is seen, pick on shoulder, lantern in hand. He is coming down from one of the cuttings.

HUW'S VOICE. *Davy, the brain of the family—*

OWEN AND GWILYM appear trundling a barrowful of coal.

HUW'S VOICE. *Owen, the dreamer, whom we seldom heard speak—Gwilym, who was named for my father, and yet as quick with his tongue as my father was slow—*

The scene dissolves to the interior of the COLLIERY, where the miners, with Morgan

and his sons prominent, are taking their places in the CAGE. It moves slowly up, revealing some adolescent boys.

At the MINE ENTRANCE. It is day, and the stalwart miners, grimy with coal dust, are coming from the cages and lining up to get their pay. The Morgans again are prominent.

IVOR is seen receiving his pay in gold from the paymaster in his little booth. There are gold coins on the paymaster's counter. Ivor drops one and it rings faintly.

HUW'S VOICE. *Saturday was the great day, for then the men would be paid off as they came off the morning shift.*

In those early days of the colliery, money was easily earned, and plenty of it. And not in pieces of paper, either. Solid gold sovereigns, yellow as summer daffodils— and they rang when you hit them on something solid.

We see the MORGAN HOUSE, where AN-GHARAD, a pretty girl of seventeen, stands in the door looking up toward the colliery. She goes into the house and reappears with a stool which she sets outside the door. After a moment, MRS. MORGAN (BETH) comes out, wearing a snowy white apron, and sits on the stool, spreading the apron.

At the COLLIERY the miners start down the hill in a solid, compact mass. As they approach, one of them, in the foreground, opens his mouth and starts a song. Others immediately join in the rich Welsh harmony.

And now we can see the miners marching DOWN THE HILL, still singing. As they pass each house, a little group breaks off and goes to the house. Morgan and his five grown sons leave the procession and turn in at the little gate of the MORGAN HOUSE. Morgan throws his sovereigns in his wife's lap and passes into the house. IVOR passes next with a smile for his mother, the other brothers following. IANTO tweaks Huw's ear as he passes.

HUW'S VOICE. *My sister Angharad would warn my mother that the men were coming up the hill. On pay day, all the women would dress up specially in their second best, with starched stiff aprons. One of the men would strike up a song.*

Singing is in my people as sight is in the eye.

As the men came up they threw their wages, sovereign by sovereign, into the shining laps, fathers first, sons and lodgers in a line behind. With my father and five brothers working we had forty every week for the box on our mantelpiece.

The scene dissolves to the INTERIOR OF THE MORGAN SHED. The boys have stripped to the waist and are having the grime scrubbed off their backs by their sister and Huw. Buckets of water and towels are in evidence. A pair of GRIMY HANDS is seen. Their owner scrubs at them without avail, leaving the black lines of coal dust.

The boys towel themselves vigorously, with Huw standing on tiptoe to reach Ivor's broad shoulders. HUW looks with distaste at his own lily-white hands.

HUW'S VOICE. *Then the scrubbing—out in the shed. My mother had drawn the buckets of hot water and cold and I used to help my sister scrub the coal dust from my brothers' backs. Most would come off them, but the hands were hopeless. Scrub and scrub, Mr. Coal would lie there and laugh at you. It is the honorable badge of the coal miner and I envied it on my grown-up brothers.*

The scene dissolves to the INTERIOR OF THE MORGAN KITCHEN, where Morgan is seated at the head of his table. His head is raised as his lips move in the act of saying grace. All are standing. We see the bountifully laden table and the expectant family waiting. Huw squirms restlessly, and his father shoots him a look.

Morgan is carving and Beth is ladling out soup for the family. The plates are passed round and the family begins to eat.

HUW'S VOICE. *Then dinner, with my father saying the grace, looking up at the stain in the ceiling, and maybe giving me a look under his brows if I moved. There was always a baron of beef and a shoulder or leg of lamb at my father's elbow. And chickens or ducks or goose—and plenty of vegetables—and the soup. There was a smell with that soup—vital with herbs fresh from the untroubled ground. If happiness has a smell, I know*

it well—for in those days it was all over our house.

There was never any talk while we were eating. I never met anybody whose talk was better than good food.

Beth moves to the stove to lift a lid off a pot. She looks back at her family, smiling.

HUW'S VOICE. *My mother was always on the run—always the last to start her dinner and the first to finish. For, if my father was the head of our house, my mother was its heart.*

The scene dissolves to ANGHARAD washing dishes in the sink. Huw stands with a towel, wiping.

HUW'S VOICE. *After dinner, when dishes had been washed, the box was brought to the table, for the spending money to be handed out.*

We see the INTERIOR OF THE PARLOR, the box on the mantelpiece. Beth lifts down the box, takes it over to the table, and sets it down in front of her husband, who is smoking his pipe. The sons are gathered round. As Morgan opens the box, Huw and Angharad hurry in from the kitchen. Morgan begins to hand out small amounts of money to his children as they step up in order of their age, but first he gives some to Beth, and with it an affectionate kiss.

HUW'S VOICE. *My father used to say that money was made to be spent just as men spend their strength and brains in earning it—and as willingly—but always with a purpose.*

HUW, as the youngest, is last in line. He stands eagerly and expectantly. Morgan gives him a playful frown and then puts a penny in his hand. As soon as he gets the penny, Huw turns and runs from the room like one possessed. Morgan and Beth laugh after him.

Huw reaches the door. He starts out, then stops, hurries back and grabs his cap and runs out once more.

Huw darts out of the house. Then he runs up the street and around a corner.

HUW'S VOICE. *I had my Saturday penny every week.—Out of the house and round the corner—as I had run a hundred times before.*

Huw appears, still running, at the LITTLE GREEN IN FRONT OF THE CHAPEL. He slows down to a respectful walk as he approaches the Chapel, and walks past it, touching his cap politely to a dignified elderly couple.

HUW'S VOICE. *Softly now, for respect for Chapel was the first thing my father taught us.*

As soon as he passed, he breaks into a run once more, reaching A SMALL SIDE STREET, where he runs up to a small bakery and confectionery shop, embellished with a sign:

TOSSALL
BAKERY AND CONFECTIONS

and darts in. A bell jingles from somewhere within the shop. Soon Huw is dancing impatiently from foot to foot before the counter. A benign, elderly woman hands him a package of toffee, which she has all ready for him, and accepts his penny. Huw gives her a polite little bow and turns to leave the shop. He goes out the door, the bell jingling once more. He is cramming the toffee into his mouth and is in heaven. He chews mightily and stuffs in some more. Some of it gets caught round a back tooth and he puts in an exploring finger to straighten it out.

HUW'S VOICE. *Then straight to Mrs. Tossall, the Shop for that toffee which you could chew for hours, it seems to me now, and even after it had gone down, you could swallow and still find the taste of it hiding behind your tongue. It is with me now—so many years later. It makes me think of so much that was good that is gone.*

It was on this afternoon that I first saw Bron—Bronwen— She had come over from the next valley for her first call on my mother—

HUW comes back to his own house. He stops near the gate, looking off down the street. The chewing motion of his jaws slows.

Approaching the gate, walking up the steep hill, is a very pretty girl with a double basket held on her hip, her hat tied under her chin with a gay bit of ribbon.

As BRONWEN approaches the gate we begin to hear her footsteps, the Chapel bell tolling, the rumble of wagon wheels, all the dim murmuring sounds of a little village come to life. Bronwen looks inquiringly at the house, turns in at the gate, which creaks, and stops as she sees Huw. She smiles.

BRONWEN. Is this Gwilym Morgan's house?

Huw, staring at her, nods.

BRONWEN (*smiling*). You must be Huw.

Huw gulps, turns and darts into the house. Bronwen laughs as she moves towards it.

Beth is at the table under the window in the MORGAN KITCHEN, cutting a pie. Huw runs excitedly in.

BETH. What's the matter with you?

Huw cannot speak; he points, gaping, into the parlor.

BETH (*looking up*). Oh—

She puts down her knife, straightens her hair hurriedly, and seeing Bronwen standing outside the door of the PARLOR, goes to meet her.

BETH. Is that you, Bronwen?

BRONWEN (*whispering*). Yes.

BETH. Come in, my child.

She opens the door; Bronwen comes in. Beth kisses her in warm greeting, then stands back to look at her.

BETH. There is lovely you are. I am so proud for Ivor.

BRONWEN (*shyly*). I'm the one to be proud.

BETH (*laughing*). You think well of our Ivor? It seems only a few months since he was scratching round like this one here (*indicating Huw, who is still gaping*) with his mouth open.

She puts a finger under his chin to close his mouth, then takes Bronwen's basket and gives it to Huw.

BETH (*to Huw*). This is Bronwen, Huw, who is to be your sister.

BRONWEN (*with a smile*). We've already met.

She bends down to kiss Huw, who reacts to this with wonder and awe, touching his finger to his cheek.

BRONWEN (*smiling*). Be careful of the basket. There's shortcake in it.

It is less a warning than an invitation to help himself. But Huw's mind is not on shortcake. Then Morgan's voice is heard.

MORGAN'S VOICE (*heartily*). Well—

Morgan comes down the stairs, followed by his sons. He smiles at Bronwen, then crooks a finger over his shoulder.

MORGAN. Ivor—

Ivor comes down the stairs, looking at Bronwen. The brothers grin at him covertly. Morgan, grinning, pushes Ivor toward Bronwen. As Ivor is about to take Bronwen in his arms, Morgan, who has observed Huw gaping, takes him by the back of the neck and leads him toward the stairway. Huw would like to look back, but doesn't dare.

MORGAN (*grinning*). Those things are not for you, my son. You will have your turn to come.

He gives Huw a friendly push up the stairs and goes back into the room.

HUW is seen reluctantly climbing the stairs, stopping occasionally to look wistfully back. He can hear the happy, excited voices of the people below: Ivor's brothers meeting Bronwen, congratulating Ivor.

HUW'S VOICE. *I think I fell in love with Bronwen then. Perhaps it is silly to think a child could fall in love. But I am the child that was, and nobody knows how I felt, except only me. And I think I fell in love with Bronwen that Saturday on the hill.*

The scene dissolves to the EXTERIOR OF THE CHAPEL. It is day. Crowds of people, all dressed in their best, are entering. This dissolves to the INTERIOR, which is packed, men sitting on one side, women on the other.

IVOR is waiting nervously with Ianto beside him and his other brothers behind him.

Bronwen, in her wedding dress, is seen coming up the aisle on her father's arm.

Beth and Bronwen's mother are crying happily into their handkerchiefs. Morgan and Bronwen's father, as the latter steps back from Bronwen to stand beside Morgan, are both perspiring and uncomfortable. The Morgan brothers, with Huw, are standing solemnly.

MERDDYN GRUFFYDD, the minister, is standing at the head of the aisle as Ivor and Bronwen take their places before him. He looks at them with his head on one side, smiling a little, and with something of appraisal in his eyes. They shift a little uneasily.

HUW'S VOICE. *All our Valley came to the wedding, and Bron's valley, too—and Chapel packed so full you could not raise your elbows.*

Ivor had my father's white waistcoat and there is a swell he was with the pinks in his buttonhole. And Bron in her great-grandmother's wedding dress.

My mother and Bron's were crying down in front, and her father and mine looking unhappy in their high collars and top hats. And all my brothers as solemn as a funeral. But the new preacher—Mr. Gruffydd—was not solemn. It was my first sight of him. I remember how he smiled—and looked at Ivor and Bronwen—and waited—and waited—almost as if he would refuse to marry them unless he could learn right there from looking at them that they would be happy together.

The congregation is waiting for the minister to begin the services, some of the elders in the front pews rather startled by Gruffydd's easy informality. GRUFFYDD is still smiling down at Ivor and Bronwen. Then his eyes grow serious and he begins the ceremony.

The scene dissolves to the CHAPEL GREEN. Long tables, loaded with food, have been set up before the Chapel. The happy wedding guests are thronged round the tables, laughing and chatting. Prominent is an enormous wedding cake.

The scene dissolves to the EXTERIOR OF THE MORGAN HOUSE, at night. Celebrants are waiting round with tankards as Morgan swings a bung-starter on a barrel of beer. The beer gushes forth. Morgan begins to fill the tankards, straightening to take an enormous gulp himself. Beth, inside the house, is dispensing tea to the women.

HUW's VOICE. *I will never forget the party after the wedding—and the wedding cake it took two men to lift.*

It was one of the few times I ever saw my father drink too much beer—but if a man cannot get drunk on the night his eldest son marries and gives him a chance for grandchildren, let us all go into the earth and be quick about it. Everyone was drunk that night, and if tea had been beer, the women would have been on the floor, too.

Next we see the GUESTS assembled, singing. Ivor, now in his ordinary Sunday best, is leading them. The MORGAN FAMILY is sitting with others on the porch, Huw sitting with Mr. Gruffydd and his father and mother, all singing. A short distance away, Angharad sits with Ianto, Davy, Owen, and Gwilym. They, too, are singing. Huw looks up at Gruffydd, who is singing with vigor and enthusiasm and GRUFFYDD continuing to sing, gives Huw a little smile. Angharad, seen among her brothers, looks over toward Gruffydd and stops singing as she watches him.

HUW notices that Angharad is not singing. He follows her glance to Gruffydd, looks back at her, then back at Gruffydd, as if he understands the reason for her silence. Gruffydd is oblivious of Angharad's adoring gaze.

HUW's VOICE. *We made a noise to lift the mountain from its base, indeed, and we learned Mr. Gruffydd could sing as well as he could preach. And Angharad could not sing at all for watching him.*

We see ANGHARAD, IANTO and DAVY—Angharad still looking at Gruffydd. Ianto notices that she is silent and gives her a hearty nudge in the ribs. Angharad hastily begins to sing once more.

The crowd is singing under the stars, with lighted windows of the houses round them.

HUW's VOICE. *And round about us the Valley echoed with the happy voices—*

happy, then—all of us—but soon there was to be trouble.

The scene dissolves to the MINE ENTRANCE by day. A mine employee is tacking up a card, headed:

WAGE SCHEDULE
EFFECTIVE AUGUST 3RD

The men gather round. An angry buzz goes up from them. A bitter voice rises.

MINER. Up to our waists in water all week—and paid short today.

Morgan and his sons, along with several other miners, shoulder their way into the forefront of the scene, and read the notice, frowning. Morgan looks up thoughtfully at the mine office.

OUTSIDE THE MINE OFFICE, Christmas Evans, the owner, stands with his manager. They go back into the office. Morgan turns to Ivor, who is beside him.

MORGAN. Ivor—find Dai Griffiths and Idris John and bring them to the office.

Ivor leaves. Morgan turns to go but Ianto detains him.

IANTO. Will we come with you?

MORGAN. No. This is a matter for the older men. Home to your mother and ask her to keep my supper hot.

Davy frowns as Morgan leaves.

DAVY. But—

Ianto puts his hand on Davy's arm, restraining him.

IANTO. Leave it now, Davy.

Both look off after their father with worried frowns.

The scene dissolves to the MORGAN PARLOR. The Morgan boys are sitting tensely, waiting. Beth can be seen in her kitchen in the background, Huw and Angharad helping her. Morgan comes quietly in, and crosses to hang up his jacket. His back is to the boys, but we can see his face. He looks angry and bitter. He pauses without turning as he hangs his coat.

MORGAN (*quietly*). Why aren't you washed?

IANTO. We were waiting for you.

Morgan turns as Beth comes in. Morgan speaks to her kindly.

MORGAN. The cut is only a few shillings. There will still be plenty for all of us. (*Patting her arm*) A bit of supper now, is it, girl?

Beth goes back into the kitchen. Morgan turns to the boys, who are still eyeing him steadily. He is taking his time over satisfying their curiosity. Finally, he speaks:

MORGAN. It is because they are not getting the old price for coal. Come and wash, now.

He starts to go, but Ianto stops him.

IANTO. May we speak, first?

MORGAN. Yes.

IANTO. They have not given you the real reason for this cut.

Morgan's eyebrows go up.

DAVY (*nodding*). We have been expecting it for weeks—ever since the iron works at Dowlais closed down.

MORGAN. What have the iron works to do with us?

IANTO. The men from Dowlais have come to the colliery, willing to work for any wage—so all our wages must come down.

Davy, standing near the box on the mantelpiece, nods gloomily.

DAVY. And this is only a beginning. Watch, now. They will cut us again and still again, until they have this—(*tapping the box*)—as empty as their promises.

MORGAN. Nonsense. A good worker is worth good wages, and he will get them.

IANTO. Not while there are three men for every job.

DAVY (*pressing the point*). Why should the owners pay more—if men are willing to work for less?

MORGAN. Because they are not savages! They are men, too. Like us.

IANTO (*quietly*). Men, yes. But not like

us. Would they deal with you just now when you went to them?

MORGAN (*honestly*). No.

IANTO. That's because they have power and we have none.

MORGAN (*with irony*). How will we get power, then? From the air?

The boys exchange another look, then Davy speaks with deliberation.

DAVY. No—from a union of all the men.

Morgan's lips compress.

MORGAN. Union, is it? (*With studied distaste*) I had no thought I would ever hear my own sons talking socialist nonsense.

DAVY (*hotly*). But it's sense. Good sense. Unless we stand together—

MORGAN (*cutting in*). I have had enough of this talk.

DAVY (*protesting*). But, Father—

Morgan turns his gaze full on him, looking him in the eyes. Davy stares for a moment, then subsides. Morgan, having established his mastery over his sons, returns to his normal tone.

MORGAN. Come and wash, now. Your good mother will be waiting.

Morgan leads the way out, Huw watching with wide eyes, sensing the bad feeling that exists between father and sons.

The scene dissolves to the EXTERIOR OF THE COLLIERY. A rainy day. Huw is going home from school, carrying books. He stops short as he comes to the colliery entrance, looking up to where the checkers are checking the trams loaded with coal that the men push past them. Two of the checkers stand under little sheds. Morgan, the third, is standing in the pouring rain without a shed. Huw stares at his father.

Morgan is grim-faced as he does his job in the pouring rain. Ianto and Davy approach with their trams. They are looking accusingly at their father, who averts his eyes from them. He looks over the coal in their trams, makes a check mark and waves them past. They hesitate a moment, then they go on past. Morgan turns to check a tram pushed by another miner as the scene dissolves to:

The INTERIOR OF THE MORGAN HOUSE. The family is at dinner. They are silent and tense, the boys looking at their father out of the corners of their eyes. He is eating quietly. Davy suddenly jumps to his feet, shaking his fist.

DAVY (*with sudden anger*). Do you think I will let them make my father stand like a dog in the rain and not raise my hands to stop it?

BETH (*scandalized*). Hisht, Davy—

All turn to look at Morgan, who finishes chewing what is in his mouth and then turns to look at Davy.

MORGAN (*quietly*). Who gave you permission to speak?

DAVY (*stubbornly*). This matter is too important for silence. They're trying to punish you—

MORGAN (*cutting in*). It is not more important than good manners.

DAVY (*heatedly*). But what are we going to do about it? You will die of the cold when it comes to snow.

IANTO (*nodding grimly*). Let us all stand together and see how they will act, then.

DAVY. Right. The men will come out if we say the word. All the pits are ready.

At this, Morgan's eyes harden. He speaks with quiet deliberation and emphasis.

MORGAN. You will not make me a plank for your politics. I will not be the excuse for any strike.

IANTO. But if they learn they can do things like that to the spokesman, what will they try and do to the men?

MORGAN. We will see. Be silent, now, and finish your supper.

DAVY (*desperately*). But—Father—

MORGAN (*sharply*). Enough, now.

His manner says plainly that he will tolerate no more of this talk. He begins to eat his dinner. Davy sits down, but Owen slams down his fork.

OWEN. It is not enough!

MORGAN (*sternly*). Owen—

OWEN (*doggedly*). I am sorry, sir—but—

MORGAN (*quietly*). Hold your tongue at table until you have permission to speak.

OWEN. I will speak against injustice anywhere—with permission or without it.

MORGAN. Not in this house.

OWEN. In this house and outside.

MORGAN (*quietly*). Leave the table.

OWEN (*also quietly*). I will leave the house.

He pushes back his chair and rises. Beth puts out her hand to her husband.

BETH. Gwil— (*To Owen.*) Tell your father you're sorry.

OWEN (*stubbornly*). I'm not sorry.

Gwilym suddenly springs to his feet.

GWILYM. I'm with you! We can find lodgings in the village.

BETH (*shocked*). Gwilym!

Morgan sits like a rock, his eyes traveling slowly to his other sons. It is a challenge to them to choose sides and state their intentions. Davy meets his look defiantly, then slowly rises to his feet. Morgan's look passes over to Ianto. Reluctantly, Ianto joins the others.

MORGAN. All of you, then?

They nod silently, in unison.

MORGAN (*quietly*). You have one more chance. Sit down—finish your dinner—and I will say no more.

IANTO (*also quietly*). We are not questioning your authority, sir, but if manners prevent our speaking the truth—we will be without manners.

There is a moment's pause, then Morgan picks up his knife and fork.

MORGAN. Get your clothes and go.

The four boys turn and go slowly toward the stairs, Huw watching breathlessly. Morgan resumes his dinner, outwardly calm, but his hand trembles slightly as it carries his fork to his mouth.

BETH. Oh, Gwilym— (*She begins to sob quietly.*)

Angharad rises and begins to stack the plates. She looks at her father, and then her mother, then puts down the plates.

ANGHARAD (*mutinously*). I'm going with them—to look after them.

Beth whirls on her, her tears forgotten. In her emotion, she slaps Angharad lightly.

BETH. Close your mouth, girl. Get on with your dishes.

She means what she says. Angharad wilts, picks up the plates and goes to the sink. Beth looks up toward the stairs.

In the UPSTAIRS BEDROOM, used by all the boys, with five beds in it, Ianto, Davy, Owen, and Gwilym are packing their clothes in bundles, rolling up their mattresses.

In the KITCHEN Beth turns and goes slowly to the sink after Angharad, her shoulders sagging.

MORGAN and HUW are still at the table. Huw is pretending to eat. Morgan lays down his knife and fork and stares stonily straight in front of him. Huw scrapes his plate with his fork. After a moment, Morgan smiles a little, without looking at Huw.

MORGAN. Yes, my son. I know you are there.

He looks at Huw kindly and fumbles for his pipe. He begins to fill it as the scene fades out.

PART TWO

The UPSTAIRS BACK BEDROOM of the Morgan House fades in. Beth is making Huw's bed in the foreground. Beyond are the bare springs of the four beds of her other sons. She looks at them sadly as she gives Huw's pillow a final pat. We hear a door slam and running feet on the stairs. Beth turns as Angharad comes bursting into the room. Her face is white, her eyes wide with excitement.

BETH. Goodness gracious, girl!

ANGHARAD (*breathlessly*). Mother—the men are coming up the hill!

BETH. What?

She hurries toward the stairs, followed by Angharad. Beth and Angharad emerge and go to the gate of the house, while all the way down the hill on the street toward the colliery, the women are appearing at their gates, looking anxiously off toward the colliery. In the background the men appear, walking slowly and quietly up the hill. There is no singing.

BETH at the gate is looking toward the men with her hand to her mouth. Then her eyes move to the towering slag heap. The conveyor belt in the distance is moving up the slag heap, dumping the slag on the growing pile. As Beth watches, it slows and comes to a creaking stop.

Beth and Angharad are in the foreground, while the other women are waiting at their gates. Some boys are running excitedly ahead of the men. We begin to hear their cries, unintelligible at first, but then coming more clearly.

SHOUTS. Struck work—the men have struck work! It's a strike!

We get flashes of several of the women reacting: careworn faces contract, a tear or two; a stringy woman gathers her two little children protectively under her arms.

The vanguard of the men comes up the hill. Their faces are grim, but determined. Morgan and Ivor are seen approaching Bronwen's cottage. Bronwen is waiting for Ivor. Ivor and Morgan exchange a look, then Ivor goes to join Bronwen, entering the gate without a word. Morgan moves on toward his own house.

GRUFFYDD'S LODGINGS, a small, dingy house in a street down the hill below the Chapel. Gruffydd and Huw come out from the house, climb the few steps to the street level, and stand staring at the men passing up the street. Gruffydd is coatless and carries a book in his hand with his thumb marking the place, as if he had been interrupted during a lesson. Huw is excited and curious, Gruffydd troubled and sad. The men pass Huw and Gruffydd. The Morgan brothers are prominent in the scene. Inasmuch as they are the strike leaders, they are surrounded by a group of eager, gesticulating men.

HUW (*in a whisper*). What does it mean, Mr. Gruffydd?

GRUFFYDD (*soberly*). It means that something has gone out of this Valley that may never be replaced.

Huw is deeply impressed. He looks off again toward the men. Gruffydd puts his hand kindly on Huw's shoulder.

GRUFFYDD. Home to your father and mother, now. They will need you today.

Huw looks up at Gruffydd for a moment, then nods and runs toward his own house.

At the gate of the MORGAN HOUSE Beth, Morgan and Angharad stand watching silently. Huw comes running, crossing in front of his brothers who are approaching up the hill. The brothers pass by the house without stopping or looking over while the depleted Morgan family watches them pass.

The scene dissolves to the EXTERIOR OF THE MINE WORKS. It is day, but there is no smoke coming from the chimneys, and a big crowd of men is gathered silently outside.

In a VLLAGE STREET the men are standing idly about in knots, some leaning up against the walls. Down the street women are sitting dejectedly on their doorsteps. Children play aimlessly about in the streets, with shrill noise and laughter, unconscious of the tragedy that has befallen the village. The sound of the children's laughter begins to fade as HUW'S VOICE comes in.

HUW'S VOICE. *There is strange it was to go out into the street and find the men there in the daytime. It had a feeling of fright in it.*

HUW comes out of his house and looks off down the street. Against a SECTION OF WALL some men are leaning, arguing quietly. They leave, strolling off down the street, leaving a black mark, shoulder high, on the wall.

Again at the SECTION OF WALL, determined looking women are scrubbing off the black marks with buckets of soapy water.

HUW'S VOICE. *All down the hill, along the walls, a long black mark could be seen where men's shoulders had leaned to rub grease. The women would scrub, but soon it was back, for the men had nowhere else to go.*

The scene dissolves to the EXTERIOR OF THE COLLIERY. It is day, and again the men are standing silently before the colliery. They are now wearing overcoats and scarfs. The wind is howling. Music begins to build in the background..

HUW'S VOICE. *Twenty-two weeks the men were out, as the strike moved into winter. Always the mood of the men grew uglier—as empty bellies and desperation began to conquer reason. Any man who was not their friend became their enemy.*

The scene changes to the EXTERIOR OF THE MORGAN HOUSE. A crowd of depressed, ugly shivering men stands outside. A stone is thrown and it crashes through Morgan's window. Simultaneously, the music reaches a climax and stops.

In the MORGAN PARLOR, Morgan is smoking quietly. He does not move as the stone crashes in, spraying glass at his feet. Beth and Huw, in the background, gasp in dismay.

The scene dissolves to the HILLSIDE. It is night, and Huw and Beth, warmly dressed. are moving up the hill. There is a grim. implacable light in Beth's eyes.

BETH (*gasping*). This way?

Huw nods and points. As they come closer to us, a few drops of rain fall on them. Huw turns up his collar against the rain and stumbles on after his mother, who appears not to notice the rain as she moves purposefully up the hill.

The scene dissolves to ANOTHER LOCATION ON THE HILLSIDE, where Beth and Huw are moving steadily on. A flicker of distant firelight begins to play on their faces. The rain is now coming down harder, and the wind is beginning to blow.

Further along the HILLSIDE, while the rain

is still pouring, a union meeting is in progress. The men are crowded round a circle of Druid stones. They have lit several fires and are all warmly dressed against the cold. Now the meeting is breaking up in the increasing rain. The men are headed toward the path that leads back to the village. At the edge of the crowd, some of the men stop as Beth and Huw appear. She moves determinedly past them in the now driving rain, up to some rocks which form an impromptu speaker's stand. Davy, Ianto, Owen and Gwilym are standing there with other men. They look over in surprise as their mother appears and turns to face the moving men.

BETH (*in a loud, strong voice*). Wait! Wait till you have heard me.

The men, surprised, turn to face her.

BETH looks over the crowd. Her eyes are like Joan of Arc's. Davy and Ianto step toward her, but she ignores them. When she speaks, her voice is low and resolute, like a man's.

BETH. I am Beth Morgan. I have come up here to tell you what I think of you all, because you are talking against my husband.

We see the faces of the men. Some look ashamed, some angry and defiant.

BETH. You are a lot of cowards to go against him. He has done nothing against you and he never would and you know it well. For you to think he is with the owners is not only nonsense but downright wickedness. How some of you can sit in the same Chapel with him I cannot tell. (*Fierce-eyed, she looks over the crowd.*) There is one thing more I will say and that is this. If harm comes to my Gwilym I will find out the men and I will kill them with my hands. And that I will swear by God Almighty.

THE MORGAN BROTHERS staring at her, BETH takes Huw by the arm and leads him away. The men part for her as before, looking after her in the pelting rain. The brothers are seen still staring.

The scene dissolves to BETH and HUW making their way down the HILLSIDE in the dark and rain. The wind is beginning to howl fiercely.

Beth and Huw appear on a STEEP BANK ABOVE THE BROOK. They slip on the bank and fall to the rocks on the edge of the brook where some half-melted snow is banked.

BETH and HUW are in the snow. He lies quiet as she struggles to her knees. The rain has plastered her hair across her face. She is white-faced and panting.

BETH. Huw—

He stirs, pulls himself upright. smiles at her, but dazedly.

HUW. Yes—

BETH. Are you hurt?

HUW. No. I'm all right. (*Bravely*) Up a dando now, Mama.

She laughs in her relief.

BETH. Up a dando, is it? And who was up a dando just now and frightening his mother sick?

She looks around, brushing off the snow.

BETH. Where's the bridge?

HUW (*pointing*). Over by there . . .

They start wearily in the direction Huw has pointed.

HUW'S VOICE. *I was wrong then, for in the blackness I thought we were below the bridge and in truth we were above it.*

Again Beth and Huw stumble forward, pausing to get their bearings. Huw points first in one direction, then another. They start off again in the teeth of the gale.

The scene dissolves to a MOUNTAINSIDE. It is still night. Huw and Beth, almost totally exhausted, are stumbling down a steep place. It is raining fiercely and the wind shrieks through the trees above them. Beth is failing visibly. Huw puts his arm around her, struggling to support her.

HUW'S VOICE. *Hours it seemed, and no feeling or sense was in me—but I was crying to God to help me save my mother and I was helped sure or I could not tell where I found the strength—*

The scene dissolves to a BRIDGE, as Beth and Huw stagger toward it. They reach the bridge. Beth clutches at the rail for support. The wood is rotten and breaks under her weight. She pitches forward into the icy water a few feet below the bridge. Huw gives a frightened gasp and throws himself in after her.

IN THE WATER Beth, inert, is slung around by the swift current. Huw struggles closer to her, as the current brings her up against a rocky point. Gasping with the cold Huw brings her head and shoulders clear of the water. He cannot leave the water himself, but must push against her with all his might to hold her clear of the racing stream.

HUW'S VOICE. *So strong was the cold that for minutes I couldn't breathe—*

HUW, his face contorted, is struggling to hold his mother up as he stands shoulder deep in the icy black water. A faint light appears upon Huw and the inert figure of Beth.

HUW'S VOICE. *How long it was I cannot tell, but there was a weariness of time before I saw a light—*

Huw is desperately holding on as the light grows stronger and dark figures appear in the rain. It is a group of men from the meeting, headed by Davy and Ianto. They have a lantern.

Huw turns, his eyes glistening in the light, and opens his mouth to shout.

HUW'S VOICE. *I tried to shout but my voice was gone from my throat.*

Davy, Ianto and the men, not seeing Huw and his mother, start to cross the bridge. Huw's mouth is open. He is trying to shout against the wind, but he cannot make himself heard. He begins to fail, to slip. Beth's head rolls and she almost goes under the water.

Ianto and Davy with the other men are on the bridge. They are about to leave the bridge and pass on when Ianto almost casually notices that the rail is broken. He stops for a second look, holding the lantern high. Huw is straining mightily to hold Beth above the water. Ianto starts to move away, then raises the lantern once more. As he looks down the stream, his eyes widen in horror. He turns and shouts into the storm.

IANTO (*shouting*). Davy—

He puts down his lantern and plunges forward into the water where Huw is giving his last ounce of strength to hold up his mother until Ianto reaches them. As Ianto pulls them to the bank, Davy and the other men are there to help them to safety. The scene fades out.

The MORGAN PARLOR fades in. It is day, and Bronwen is sitting with some sewing, singing softly. The shades behind her are drawn, so that the light in the room is dim. She raises her head and looks toward the wall bed. We see Huw, unconscious and swathed in bandages, lying in the wall bed. As she looks, his eyes open. He turns his head slowly to look at Bronwen. She puts down her sewing and crosses swiftly over to him.

BRONWEN. Oh—Huw— (*there are tears in her voice.*) There is proud I am to have your name. (*She kisses him softly, straightens and smiles down at him.*)

HUW (*with difficulty*). Mother?

BRONWEN (*cheerfully*). Upstairs—and doing well. The doctor is with her now.

He closes his eyes with a little smile. She stands looking down at him with pity and affection. Morgan, Angharad and Dr. Richards come down the stairs and move over to look down at Huw.

BRONWEN (*whispering*). He was awake just now.

DR. RICHARDS (*in a low voice*). He'll do then. But it's beyond me to say why. You are breeding horses in this family, Mr. Morgan. This boy should be in his coffin, for my part.

MORGAN (*smiling*). Then he's a Morgan, is it?

His hands stray gently to Huw's bandaged shoulder. He touches it proudly and lovingly. In the meantime the Doctor is getting into his overcoat, which Angharad holds for him.

DR. RICHARDS. He should be fed now, Mrs. Ivor—a little soup and some warm smile.

Bronwen nods and goes into the kitchen.

Morgan, Angharad and the Doctor go out through the front door.

The Doctor, Angharad and Morgan come out of the MORGAN HOUSE. Morgan closes the door, but not completely. It is left open a crack. Gruffydd comes up the steps, carrying a book.

MORGAN (*to Gruffydd*). Huw was awake just now, and spoke to Bron.

GRUFFYDD (*to Richards*). How long, then, for the little one?

DR. RICHARDS (*pursing his lips*). It's hard to say. His legs were frozen to the bone. A year—two years—quiet like that. But I can't promise he will *ever* walk again—

As HUW's eyes open once more, it is evident that he can hear what is being said outside the door. Dr. Richards' voice comes over:

Nature must take her course—Mr. Gruffydd—

Huw stirs as he hears this. His lips quiver a little; then he looks up. BRONWEN is now in the room with his soup. She looks at Huw anxiously, then hurries to the door.

Bronwen comes out at the FRONT DOOR, closing the door behind her. She addresses herself to the Doctor, with compressed fury.

BRONWEN (*fiercely*). Mind your tongue! I think he heard you.

Disturbed, Morgan, Gruffydd, Angharad and the Doctor look toward the door; then Morgan, Gruffydd, Angharad and Bronwen reenter the house, leaving the Doctor to move down the path.

In the MORGAN PARLOR, Huw is lying in the foreground with eyes bright with tears. Gruffydd comes over, followed by the others, and sits down beside him.

GRUFFYDD (*smiling*). Hello, Huw.

Huw's lips form a soundless "Hello," but his face shows his unhappiness and fear. His eyes turn away from Gruffydd.

GRUFFYDD (*sternly*). Where is the light I thought to see in your eyes? Are you afraid, boy?

Huw turns his mute, appealing eyes back to Gruffydd. Bronwen is shocked by Gruffydd's sternness. She puts her hand on his arm in protest, but Gruffydd shakes it impatiently off.

GRUFFYDD (*relentlessly*). You heard what the doctor said?

A spasm crosses Huw's face and he nods.

GRUFFYDD. And you believed it?

Huw nods again.

GRUFFYDD (*fiercely*). You want to walk again, don't you? (*Huw nods.*) Then you must have faith. And if you have, you *will* walk, no matter what all the doctors say.

Huw looks at him piteously.

HUW (*feebly*). He said Nature must take her course.

GRUFFYDD (*swiftly*). Nature is the handmaiden of the Lord. (*Smiling*) I remember on one or two occasions she was given orders to *change* her course. You know your Scripture, boy?

Huw nods, wide-eyed. Angharad is watching breathlessly, her eyes wide with admiration for Gruffydd.

GRUFFYDD. Then you know that what's been done before can be done again—for you. (*Bending over Huw*) Do you believe me, Huw?

Huw nods again, with shining eyes.

GRUFFYDD (*cheerfully*). Good. You shall see the first daffodil out on the mountain. Will you?

HUW (*weakly, but with a smile*). Indeed I will, sir.

GRUFFYDD. Then you will.

He grins down at Huw, who grins back. Morgan, with tears in his eyes, squeezes Gruffydd's shoulder with emotion and gratitude. Angharad is smiling with starry eyes. Gruffydd shows Huw the book he has brought him.

HUW (*feebly*). "Treasure Island"—

Gruffydd smiles a little as he touches the book.

GRUFFYDD. I could almost wish that I were lying there in your place—if it meant reading this book again for the first time.

Huw looks at the book close to his head with wondering eyes. Gruffydd rises from beside him and goes out of the room. Angharad hesitates a moment, then follows him.

As Gruffydd comes out of the MORGAN HOUSE, Angharad follows.

ANGHARAD (*calling after him*). Mr. Gruffydd—

Gruffydd turns.

ANGHARAD. I couldn't let you go without thanking you.

GRUFFYDD. It was only my duty, girl.

ANGHARAD (*looking at him*). No. It was more than duty.

GRUFFYDD (*his eyes sober*). Yes. He is a fine boy—

He hesitates a moment, looking at her, as if he would like to compliment her personally, but he compromises:

GRUFFYDD. —and you are a fine family.

The look in his eyes is not lost on Angharad. She is still staring up at him with shining eyes. Gruffydd tries to cover his embarrassment.

GRUFFYDD (*gently*). You'd better be going back. You'll catch your death.

ANGHARAD. Yes. (*But she doesn't move.*) Will you be coming to supper soon?

GRUFFYDD. Later—when you are finished with doctors and such.

ANGHARAD (*with a smile*). I will hurry them away then.

GRUFFYDD (*smiling at her*). Good.

He touches his hat and goes, stopping at the gate to look back at her. She looks after him as if unconscious of her surroundings; then she gives a sudden little shudder of cold, drawing her shoulders together. She turns and goes back into the house.

Angharad comes into the MORGAN PARLOR, closing the door. She stands quietly at the door, thinking of Gruffydd. Bronwen, sitting beside Huw, has picked up the book.

She looks up at Angharad with sympathy and comprehension, then turns back to Huw and begins to read.

BRONWEN (*reading*). "Squire Trelawney, Dr. Livesey and the rest of these gentlemen, having asked me to write down the whole particulars about Treasure Island from the beginning to the end, keeping nothing back but the bearings of the island, and that only because there is still treasure not yet lifted, I take up my pen—"

Huw's eyes begin to light up. Bronwen reads on. The scene slowly dissolves to an illustration in "Treasure Island": Jim Hawkins in the crosstrees with Israel Hands, dirk in teeth, climbing the shrouds toward him. Huw's hand leafs the page over.

The scene dissolves back into the MORGAN PARLOR. It is day. HUW, now without bandages, and propped up in bed, is reading, studying, while the normal activity of the house goes on around him.

HUW is seen reading avidly in the MORGAN PARLOR, and superimposed on this picture is a view of the shelf beside the bed. His hands appear, putting the books, one by one, on the shelf:

TREASURE ISLAND
IVANHOE
PICKWICK PAPERS
BOSWELL'S LIFE OF JOHNSON

As the shelf dissolves, Huw sets down his book and listens, looking up. As a sharp tapping is heard, Huw smiles and taps three times on the wall.

HUW'S VOICE. *For months I lay in the wall bed. I learned. I read. All the noble books which have lived in my mind ever since—and always I hoped and kept my faith.*

For the first months my mother was still upstairs and we could talk to each other with tappings—

In quick succession we see Morgan painting the doorjambs, Angharad hanging fresh curtains, while Huw, in his wall bed, is watching.

The scene dissolves into the MORGAN PARLOR, at night, as Ianto, Davy, Owen and Gwilym are standing before their father in the parlor. Huw is in the wall bed in the background, watching. All involved are very serious. The boys look thin and rather ragged.

HUW'S VOICE. *Then my father began to make preparations—for the doctor told him that soon she would be leaving her bed. New tile for the kitchen—whitewash on our doorstep—new curtains and fresh paint—and, for the occasion—another surprise for my mother.*

MORGAN (*quietly*). My sons, I would like to have you back here to live—

The boys stare as Morgan goes on.

MORGAN. —but on one condition. We shall all be lodgers here.

The boys are silent a moment before answering.

IANTO (*quietly*). How can you be a lodger in your own house?

MORGAN. Because I have no authority. No man shall say he is head of a house unless his word is obeyed. You are grown and entitled to your own opinions. So, we will all be lodgers and your mother will care for all of us.

The boys are silent, looking at the floor.

MORGAN. Will you come?

The boys exchange a look and nod.

MORGAN. Good. It will make your mother very happy. Tomorrow, then.

The boys turn and go out.

Again in the MORGAN PARLOR, in the day, Huw, in his wall bed, is looking toward the stairs with shining eyes. We see THE STAIRCASE, which in Welsh houses is covered, and hear Beth's footsteps dimly on the stairs. Then Beth appears at the bottom of the stairs, assisted by Morgan. She is weak and shaky, and whiter than before, but her eyes are shining. She stands at the foot of the stairs, leaning on Morgan's arm, looking at Huw. Then she slowly crosses over to him, leaving Morgan in the background.

HUW'S VOICE. *Then the great day when at last she came down again into her own house. First her footsteps. Strike and hardship and illness all were forgotten. Four months. Only a ceiling between us,*

yet for four months we hadn't laid eyes on each other. Then she was there, watching me with diamonds in her eyes and her hand to her mouth. Whether to laugh or cry, now . . .

Beth's eyes are full of tears, and she is too moved to speak. She sits beside Huw on the bed, devouring him with her eyes. As he looks at her almost white hair, his hand goes up to it and touches it wonderingly.

BETH. The old snow got into it—

She chokes on the words, kisses him fiercely, and then moves back a little from him as if the better to see him. Morgan tiptoes over to the door, opens it a crack and signals with his hand.

Into the PARLOR, as Beth and Huw look up, comes the sound of Ivor's choir singing. Morgan, smiling proudly, comes back to them. Beth looks toward the door with wonder. Morgan gently helps her to her feet and leads her out, Huw looking after them proudly.

In front of the MORGAN HOUSE the singers, led by Ivor, are massed in the foreground, while Beth and Morgan are on the porch in the background. The Morgan boys are seen watching their mother as they sing in the front row. They have bundles of their belongings with them.

BETH is tremendously affected by the singing, and above all, by the sight of her sons and their bundles. The tears stream down her cheeks, then she buries her face in her husband's shoulder.

BETH (*brokenly*). Oh, Gwil—there is a wife you've got—resting in her bed and letting strangers care for her family.

Morgan smiles and twines a strand of her silver hair round his forefinger.

MORGAN. There is a wife I have got, then.

BETH (*rallying*). Go on with you, boy.

The men finish their song and burst into a shout for Beth. Cries of "Speech!" Morgan pushes her gently forward.

MORGAN. Go on—say something.

BETH (*frightened*). What will I say?

MORGAN. You found something to say

last time you spoke. It should be easier now, with friends.

Beth tries to find words, chokes a little, smiles, holds out her hands to the crowd, hesitates, then blurts:

BETH. Come and eat—everyone—

The people cheer again and begin to troop into the house, paying their respects to Beth as they pass. But her eyes are on her sons and the bundles in their hands. Ianto and Davy, followed by Owen and Gwilym, come up and embrace her silently. She looks at Ianto's bundle with bright eyes, smiling through her tears, then assumes a mask of sternness.

BETH. There is disgraceful the condition your clothes are in from the lodgings— (*lifting Davy's trouser leg*)—one more step and we would be seeing the back of your leg.

GWILYM. You should see Owen's. One more step and we'd be seeing the back of his neck, indeed.

OWEN (*pushing him*). Shut up, man.

All go into the house.

In the MORGAN PARLOR, the family and guests are trooping in. Some are already making for the food-laden table. Ianto intercepts Morgan in the foreground, and shows his father a newspaper.

IANTO. Have you seen this?

Morgan takes the paper from Ianto and puts on his glasses to read it. Then, with a twinkle in his eye, he looks over at Huw.

MORGAN. Well— (*Turning to the guests*) Listen, everyone—listen to this!

The guests gather round. Morgan clears his throat importantly.

MORGAN. It seems someone has been getting his name in the paper.

He reads proudly from the paper.

"Handwriting competition. Boys under twelve years of age. First prize of Two Guineas is awarded to Huw Morgan, for an entry of great merit."

A cheer goes up. All eyes turn to Huw in the wall bed. Huw is embarrassed, tries to duck beneath his pillow, but Ianto and Bronwen pull him into the open.

MORGAN. And that boy has been lying there going on four months and no sound from him but laughing and no words but cheerful. (*Taking off his glasses and wiping them*) I will stay over here to tell you what a good son you are, Huw. If I went to you now, I would be acting very silly, I am afraid.

Bronwen kisses Huw gently.

BRONWEN. There is a clever old man you are—

HUW reacts to Bronwen's kiss, embarrassed but happy. His eyes are bright, and he touches his cheek where she kissed him.

This scene dissolves to two men with fiddles and Miss Jenkins, a prim spinster who plays the harp. We see the celebration in full swing. These people are hungry and in want, but they are making the most of the occasion and the Morgan's hospitality. A wide-eyed miner receives a cup of tea and some cake from Angharad.

MINER. Real tea you have.

ANGHARAD. A little weak.

MINER. Weak? Hot water at our house.

Standing near each other are Ianto and Mr. Parry, a bespectacled, ascetic elder who has just finished piling his plate. He takes a mouthful and addresses himself to Ianto.

PARRY. Ianto—I haven't seen you in Chapel lately.

IANTO. I have been too busy.

PARRY. What business, may I ask?

IANTO (*looking at him*). Mine.

At this a hush falls on the people round them.

PARRY (*injured*). Only asking a civil question, I was.

IANTO. And having a civil answer. (*Looking at Parry.*) I have been busy with the union.

PARRY (*shaking his head darkly*). Unions are the work of the devil. You will come to no good end.

IANTO (*like ice*). At least I am not *sitting* on it, talking a lot of rubbish in Chapel.

PARRY. Look here—

IANTO (*with an impatient gesture*). Leave it now, or I will say something to be sorry.

He turns away from Parry and finds himself face to face with Gruffydd, who is regarding him steadily. Morgan, Beth and the other Morgan brothers also move into scene, listening intently.

GRUFFYDD. No. This matter requires airing. Ianto—why do you think we of the Chapel talk rubbish?

IANTO. My remark was not aimed at you.

GRUFFYDD (*smiling, but serious*). Then aim it.

IANTO (*deliberately*). Very well. Because you make yourselves out to be shepherds of the flock and yet allow your sheep to live in filth and poverty, and if they try to raise their voices against it, you calm them by saying their suffering is the Will of God. (*With burning scorn*) Sheep indeed! Are we sheep to be herded and sheared by a handful of owners? I was taught that man was made in the image of God! Not a sheep!

MORGAN. Ianto—Mr. Gruffydd healed Huw.

GRUFFYDD (*still looking at Ianto*). Mr. Morgan—Huw healed himself. (*Then to Ianto.*) I have not expressed my views here because I have had no wish to interfere in a family disagreement.

He looks at Morgan challengingly.

MORGAN (*quietly*). You have my permission to speak.

GRUFFYDD. Well, then, here is what I think. First, have your union. You need it.

We see MORGAN listening intently as Gruffydd's voice is heard.

GRUFFYDD'S VOICE. Alone you are weak. Together you are strong.

We get a glimpse of the faces of Ianto, Davy, Owen and Gwilym, listening.

GRUFFYDD'S VOICE. But remember that with strength goes responsibility—to others and to yourselves. (*He is now visible.*) For you cannot conquer injustice with more injustice—only with justice and with the help of God.

ANGHARAD is seen, listening at the tea urn, lips parted and eyes bright. Silence falls on the little group as Gruffydd finishes. He has obviously made a deep impression both on Morgan and on his sons. Then Parry's lips tighten.

PARRY Are you coming outside your position in life, Mr. Gruffydd? Your business is spiritual.

GRUFFYDD (*quietly*). My business is anything that comes between man and the spirit of God.

PARRY (*glowering*). The deacons shall hear that you have been preaching socialism—

Ianto, always ready for a fight, steps up to Parry.

IANTO. Mr. Parry—

Gwilym moves forward.

GWILYM (*hotly*). Loose the old devil's teeth for him!

Morgan quickly steps between them, pushing Ianto and Gwilym back.

MORGAN (*to Ianto*). He is our guest.

He takes Parry's arm and signals to Beth.

MORGAN (*with a grin*). Beth, give Mr. Parry a pint of home brewed, and put his pipe back in his mouth.

BETH (*militantly*). I will give him a good clout with the frying pan.

Parry, abashed, shuts up. Gruffydd smiles and leaves the little group. Morgan and his sons are looking at each other steadily.

IANTO (*to his father*). Can you and your lodgers agree on what we have just heard.

MORGAN (*simply*). I have no lodgers—only sons.

He puts one arm round Ianto's shoulders, the other round Davy's, and signals to Miss Jenkins.

MORGAN. Now, then, Miss Jenkins—a tune. "Comrades in Arms," is it?

The music starts up gaily. All begin to sing, except Parry, who walks off, shaking his head. Angharad, smiling happily, goes into the kitchen with a stack of used plates and sets them on the sink. Gruffydd moves into the foreground, looking at her through the door. Seeing Angharad inspect her fire, then lift the heavy coal scuttle to refill the range, Gruffydd goes into the kitchen.

In the KITCHEN, Angharad is struggling with the heavy scuttle. The singing is heard as Gruffydd comes up to her. She looks at him with a smile.

ANGHARAD. Oh, Mr. Gruffydd—will we always be in your debt? Now you have made us a family again.

GRUFFYDD (*smilingly*). Here—let me—

He takes the scuttle from her and pours some coal into the stove. She is still looking at him. Gruffydd sets down the scuttle and straightens to face Angharad. She sees that his hands are covered with coal.

ANGHARAD. Oh—your hands—there's a pity—

GRUFFYDD (*grinning*). No matter.

He turns his hands to show her the palms. GRUFFYDD'S PALMS, seen in full view, reveal the telltale black lines of one who has worked as a miner. Angharad takes his hands gently, looking at the palms, then up into his eyes.

ANGHARAD. Have you been down the collieries?

GRUFFYDD. Ten years—while I was studying.

ANGHARAD (*moved*). Ten years—

Then she breaks the mood, becoming very businesslike. She moves over toward the sink.

ANGHARAD. A bit of soap, now.

GRUFFYDD. Please don't bother.

He takes a handkerchief from his pocket and begins to scrub at his hands. Angharad turns back to him.

ANGHARAD. There is a man for you—spoiling your good handkerchief.

Gruffydd grins at her. Angharad gets some soap and a piece of rag.

ANGHARAD. Wait, you. You are king in the Chapel, but I will be queen in my own kitchen.

She returns to him and begins to scrub the coal off his hands. Gruffydd's expression has changed. There is no flippancy in his look now. He waits until she has finished, then suddenly speaks, almost as if against his will.

GRUFFYDD. You will be queen wherever you walk.

Angharad looks swiftly up at him, her heart in her eyes. There is a tense pause.

ANGHARAD (*whispering*). What does that mean?

GRUFFYDD (*looking at her*). I should not have said it.

ANGHARAD. Why not?

GRUFFYDD. I have no right to speak to you so.

Angharad continues to look at him, then smiles a little.

ANGHARAD (*softly*). If the right is mine to give—you have it.

They stand looking at each other, deeply moved. Then Bronwen comes into the kitchen with some more plates. She stops short when she sees them, sensing that she has interrupted something, then proceeds to the sink. Gruffydd smiles at Angharad and goes out, Angharad looking after him. Bronwen stands watching her with sympathy and understanding, whereupon Angharad turns to her a little irritably.

ANGHARAD. Well—what are you staring at?

BRONWEN (*smiling*). Let me have my look, girl. (*Then putting her hand on Angharad's arm*) If I were single again —I think I should try to marry Mr. Gruffydd, shame to me or not.

The scene fades out.

PART THREE

An early morning scene fades in. The moon is still shining, lights are lit in all the houses, and the men, singing, appear to march up to work. "Men of Harlech" is their song.

In flashes, we see: Beth preparing lunch boxes. Huw waving goodbye to his father and brothers from his wall bed. The rusty colliery gates opening. The men lined up at the gates, being checked through. Singing men entering the colliery. The winding-house wheel, creaking from disuse, as it begins to turn. A puff of steam from a long disused chimney. The conveyor-belt starting. Men waving their lamps to the beat of the music as they march.

> HUW'S VOICE. *Then the strike was settled—with the help of Mr. Gruffydd and my father—with a minimum wage and at least a promise of no more cuts. No victory, but it was good to see my mother's face as she made ready the lunch boxes again. The men went back on the early morning shift. Cold it was, and still dark, but in all the village I think I was the only one to stay in bed. Wheels that had grown rusty turned again, spinning wages for the box on our mantel, which had grown so light—work to wipe out the memory of idleness and hardship. The men were happy going up the hill that morning. —But not all of them—for there were too many now for the jobs open, and some learned that never again would there be work for them in their own Valley—*

AT THE COLLIERY GATE, the mine manager, with a piece of paper in his hand, is approaching the guards at the gate. As the miners file in, he checks something against his tally. The guard begins to close the gate in the faces of the men who are still waiting to go in. The gates close, leaving outside the men who have been shut out. Prominent among them are Owen and Gwilym, who are standing grim-faced with the other men, silent, hard-eyed.

The scene dissolves to the MORGAN PARLOR. Morgan, Ivor, Ianto, Davy, Owen and Gwilym are assembled—a council of war. Huw, in his wall bed, is in the background.

> OWEN. It is the same all over South Wales. In Cardiff, the men are standing in line to have bread from the government. (*Shaking his head*) Not for us. We will have our share of the box and go.

MORGAN. Where?

OWEN (*quietly*). America.

Morgan's shoulders sag. He turns slowly to the mantelpiece, takes the box, and sets it down on the table. He opens the cover and stands looking down into it. The others gather round. Morgan slowly takes out two small stacks of sovereigns, setting one before Owen and one before Gwilym. Then Ianto speaks:

> IANTO (*quietly*). My share, too, Owen.

DAVY (*quickly*). And mine.

OWEN. No. Our own. We will take no charity.

IANTO (*roughly*). Not charity, man. Sense.

GWILYM (*stubbornly*). No. Only our own.

Owen also shakes his head with finality. Morgan closes the box with a snap, then turns to Owen and Gwilym.

> MORGAN. Say nothing to your mother. Let this day be over, first.

Suddenly they hear Beth's voice.

> BETH'S VOICE. Never mind saying nothing.

They all turn. The little group stands round the table, taking in Beth as she moves slowly toward them from the kitchen door, where she has been standing.

> BETH. I heard.

Beth reaches Owen and Gwilym. The tears spring to her eyes as she embraces them.

> BETH (*brokenly*). America—America—my babies—

After a moment Morgan gently withdraws Beth from her two sons, holding her in his arms for a moment. He looks at the boys.

MORGAN. Shall we read a chapter, my sons?

OWEN. What shall we have?

MORGAN. Isaiah, fifty-five. "Ho every one that thirsteth, come ye to the waters, and he that hath no money, come ye, buy and eat."

Owen crosses to get the Bible from the shelf on the mantel. Beth, unable to stand any more, moves over toward Huw and sits down on the bed beside him. She is crying. Huw tries awkwardly to comfort her.

BETH (*tragically*). This is only the beginning. Owen and Gwil first—then all of you will go—one after the other—all of you!

HUW (*stoutly*). I will never leave you, Mama—

Beth takes him by the shoulders, and stares into his eyes.

BETH. Yes, Huw. If you should ever leave me, I will be sorry I ever had babies.

HUW (*wondering*). Why did you have them?

BETH (*with a twist of her lips*). Goodness gracious, boy! Why, indeed? To keep my hands in water and my face to the fire, perhaps.

Morgan is seen marking his place in the Bible. His sons are grouped round him. Before Morgan can begin to read, though, they hear a commotion out in the street. They all look up, as they hear loud, excited voices shouting something we cannot distinguish. One of the boys opens the door and all go out in the street.

Morgan and his sons are standing outside the house, as Beth comes curiously out to join them. Approaching the house is about half the village following the figure of Dai Ellis, the postman, who carries a letter high in his hand. The villagers are shouting and chattering to each other.

IANTO. What is it?

MORGAN. They're coming here.

They exchange a look, almost as if this might be a lynching party come to get them. The villagers approach behind the postman. Dai Ellis, his hand trembling with excitement, holds up the letter. He tries to speak but his vocal chords are paralyzed with excitement. He stutters impotently.

IANTO (*impatiently*). What's with you, man?

Ellis finally produces words:

DAI ELLIS (*his voice breaking into a falsetto squeak*). From Windsor Castle it is—

He hands the letter to Ivor. The Morgans, seen as a group, are tremendously excited. Ivor takes the letter. The villagers gather close round as Ivor rips it open with impatient fingers. He begins to read from the letter.

IVOR (*in a trembling voice*). Mr. Ivor Morgan is commanded to appear before her Majesty at Windsor Castle with chosen members of his choir.

A great shout goes up from the assembled villagers. Morgan, powerfully affected, grabs Ivor's shoulder.

MORGAN. To sing before the Queen. (*With quiet pride.*) My son, I never thought to see the beautiful day. (*Then with animation.*) Ianto, Davy—(*to the assembled villagers*)—all of you. Fetch everyone from all the Valleys round. (*To the postman.*) Dai Ellis, get your trap and to town to spread the news. Davy—over to the other collieries—invite everybody—it's a celebration, tell them. Ianto—down to the Three Bells for beer. Open house tonight—for all who will come.

Then his eye catches sight of Owen and Gwilym standing together. There is a break in his voice as he addresses them.

MORGAN. My sons. You shall have a send-off worthy of Morgans.

IN THE STREET, the people are running excitedly off in different directions. Dai Ellis jumps into his trap, which stands in front of the post office, and whips his horse off into a gallop.

The scene dissolves to an exterior view of the VILLAGE at night. The windows are all lit and people lean in them, looking out. The party is assembled. The street is filled with celebrating people. Beer is flowing freely. All are singing the last bars of a gay Welsh song. As the song finishes, Morgan climbs up on the wall in front of the CHAPEL with Ivor. (The choir is assembled in the street.) He holds up his hand for silence. When he gets it he begins to pray, simply and sincerely.

> MORGAN. O Heavenly Father, I give thanks from the heart to live this day. I give thanks for all I have, and I do give thanks for this new blessing. For you are Our Father, but we look to our Queen as our mother. Comfort her in her troubles, O God, and let her mighty worries trouble not more than she shall bear in her age. And let sweetness and power and spirit be given to these voices that will sing at her command. And may Ivor have strength to acquit himself with honour. Amen.

A deep, reverent, "Amen" goes up in the street.

Morgan climbs down from the wall and joins Beth. Then Ivor raises his hand and brings it down sharply. The tenors sing the first line of "God Save the Queen." Sopranos join the tenors with the second line.

HUW is seen in his wall bed, eyes shining. Bron and Angharad are with him. The window is open. Baritones, bass and alto come in with tenor and soprano. The whole CHOIR is seen singing. All the voices are now in.

Morgan is singing along with the choir, but Beth is silent. She is looking steadily, with tears in her eyes, out of the scene. We follow the direction of her glance. THE MORGAN BROTHERS are in the front line of the choir, singing with the rest. We see Owen and Gwilym closely as the anthem goes into its final chords.

The whole VILLAGE is seen as the anthem comes to its close.

The scene fades out.

PART FOUR

The INTERIOR OF THE CHAPEL fades in. Gruffydd is leading the congregation in the closing hymn of the service. The hymn stops and the men begin to pick up their hats.

GRUFFYDD (*soberly*). Will you please remain in your places? There is a meeting of the deacons.

A little buzz of conversation goes up as the people resume their seats. The deacons, mostly elderly men, stalk stiffly up to the front of the Chapel. Morgan is among the deacons. Gruffydd relinquishes his place at the lectern to Mr. Parry and then walks slowly down the aisle, his head bent. He passes Angharad, who is sitting on the aisle, and moves to the back of the Chapel. Mr. Parry, spokesman for the deacons, stands forward.

PARRY (*sternly*). Meillyn Lewis—step forward.

A girl, whom we have not seen before, stumbles past Angharad. She is sobbing violently into her handkerchief, which covers her face. She steps before the assembled deacons.

PARRY (*looking down at her*). Your sins have found you out, and now you must pay the price of all women like you. You have brought a child into the world against the commandment.

ANGHARAD is seen staring, white-faced, shocked and pitying. GRUFFYDD, at the back, is expressionless but manifestly uncomfortable. The faces of the deacons look stern. Morgan alone among them looks disturbed and unhappy.

PARRRY (*continuing*). Prayer is wasted on your sort. You shall be cast forth into the outer darkness till you have learned your lesson. Meillyn Lewis, do you admit your sin?

MEILLYN LEWIS sobs out something like "Yes."

ANGHARAD rises slowly to her feet.

PARRY looks sternly down at Meillyn Lewis.

PARRY. Then prepare to suffer your punishment—

Angharad's voice rings out.

ANGHARAD. Stop it! Stop it! Let her alone —you hypocrites!

It is as if the meeting had been struck by lightning. Meillyn Lewis, mouth open, tears dripping from her eyes, is staring at Angharad. The deacons are also staring, still too amazed to be angry. Then Morgan moves. His face is white with fury. He strides over to Angharad.

MORGAN (*furiously*). Angharad—you—

Gruffydd steps quickly between them. He puts his hand on Morgan's arm.

GRUFFYDD (*looking at Angharad*). Leave it now, Mr. Morgan.

He urges Angharad gently away, Morgan staring after them. Gruffydd and Angharad exit from the Chapel, with all the congregation staring.

Angharad and Gruffydd come out of the Chapel. She is still white and shaken. He looks at her soberly. At a little distance from them an old, poorly dressed woman, Meillyn Lewis's mother, is waiting nervously, holding a baby. Angharad with an angry gesture raises her eyes to Gruffydd's.

ANGHARAD (*passionately*). How could you stand there and watch them? Cruel old men—groaning and nodding to hurt her more. That isn't the Word of God! "Go thou, and sin no more," Jesus said.

GRUFFYDD (*sadly*). You know your Bible too well—and life too little.

ANGHARAD (*stormily*). I know enough of life to know that Meillyn Lewis is no worse than I am!

GRUFFYDD. Angharad!

ANGHARAD. What do the deacons know about it? (*Clenching her fists*) What do *you* know about what could happen to a poor girl when she loves a man so much that even to lose sight of him for a moment is torture!

Her eyes try to hold him, for she is now referring to her own love for him. But Gruffydd will not meet the issue.

GRUFFYDD. It was cruel, but you must realize that the men of the Valleys here have made their homes, lived and died with no help from any government of men—no authority but the Bible. If it has produced hypocrites and Pharisees the fault is with the human race. Men are not angels.

ANGHARAD. They were like devils today! My father, too. (*Accusingly*) And you stood by and let them.

Gruffydd frowns. He is as deeply moved as Angharad, but finds his predicament difficult to explain to her.

GRUFFYDD. It's their Chapel. I am only its servant. If I spoke out now—they could put me out to preach in the hedges with only the sparrows to listen.

ANGHARAD. But you *will* speak out against it?

GRUFFYDD (*nodding gravely*). When the time is ripe. When the ground is prepared. Believe me.

She softens. Their eyes meet and hold. Then both turn as the door of the Chapel opens in the background and Meillyn Lewis stumbles out. She runs to her mother, crying. Other people begin to appear from the Chapel. Meillyn takes the baby and kisses it. She and her mother cling to each other forlornly and start to walk slowly away. ANGHARAD AND GRUFFYDD are looking after them with compassion. With one accord they start to move after Meillyn and her mother. Angharad calls gently:

ANGHARAD. Meillyn—

The scene fades out.

PART FIVE

The MORGAN PARLOR fades in. Huw is reading in his wall bed. Beth is straightening up the room. Huw looks up as sunlight falls across him from the opening front door and his face lights up as he sees Gruffydd standing, framed in the sunlight. There is something portentous in his manner. His face is very grave. Beth moves into the scene. She is surprised to see Gruffydd.

BETH. Good morning, dear Mr. Gruffydd. There is good to see you. Angharad is down to market.

Gruffydd does not move. His eyes remain searchingly on Huw.

GRUFFYDD (*looking at Huw*). I have come for Huw.

BETH (*surprised*). For Huw?

She looks over at Huw, who is smiling. He has sensed why Gruffydd is here. He is smiling—but frightened and a little in awe.

HUW. The daffodils are out, Mama.

BETH (*with her heart in her eyes*). Oh, Huw—

She crosses over to him, clutching her hands in her apron. Then Gruffydd, still with his eyes on Huw, advances.

GRUFFYDD. Where are your clothes, Huw?

HUW. Under my pillow, sir.

BETH. Your pillow?

HUW. For these months—ready for today.

GRUFFYDD (*smiling*). Come you, then— You shall bring back a posy fit for a queen for your brave mother—

HUW (*eyes shining*). Indeed, I will—

Beth is too stunned to move. Gruffydd starts to help Huw out from under the covers, and to retrieve his clothes from under the pillow.

The scene dissolves to the HILLSIDE. It is a bright, windy morning. A patch of daffodils is nodding in the wind. In the background Gruffydd is carrying Huw on his shoulders. Silhouetted against the skyline, they come close to the daffodils. Gruffydd gently lowers Huw to his feet and sup-

ports him there, while both look at the flowers. They smile at each other. Gruffydd carefully releases Huw and moves a few steps away from him, then turns and holds out his hands to Huw.

GRUFFYDD. Now, then—over to me—

Slowly, painfully, Huw moves one leg forward, and brings the other up to join it. Then he sways as if about to fall. Gruffydd steps quickly forward to support him, but Huw waves him away with a grin.

HUW (*a little breathless*). I'm all right—

He takes two more steps, which bring him to Gruffydd. They grin at each other, and Gruffydd takes hold of him.

GRUFFYDD. Enough, now. (*Looking at Huw searchingly, and speaking gravely.*) You have been lucky, Huw. Lucky to suffer and lucky to spend these weary months in your bed. For so God has given you the chance to make spirit within yourself. And as your father cleans his lamp to have good light, so keep clean your spirit.

HUW. How, Mr. Gruffydd?

GRUFFYDD. By prayer, my son. And I don't mean mumbling, or shouting, or wallowing like a hog in religious sentiments. Prayer is only another name for good, clean, direct thinking. When you pray, think well what you are saying, and make your thoughts into things that are solid. In that manner, your prayer will have strength, and that strength shall become part of you, mind, body and spirit.

Huw looks up at him, deeply impressed. Then Gruffydd smiles.

GRUFFYDD. And the first duty of your new legs shall be to carry you to Chapel next Sunday.

The scene dissolves to the CHAPEL with the Morgan family approaching it in the daylight. Morgan and Beth are not in evidence. In the group are Angharad, Ianto, Davy and Huw, who is now limping painfully, with the aid of Davy.

NEAR THE CHAPEL ENTRANCE, IESTYN EVANS, a rather supercilious young man, and dressed—even overdressed—in the height of fashion, is lounging on the Chapel green. He looks over and sees Angharad. He steps forward and raises his hat.

IESTYN. Hello, Angharad.

Ianto and Davy step in front of their sister.

IANTO (*with dangerous quiet*). Who are you talking to?

IESTYN (*casually*). Angharad. Your sister, perhaps.

Ianto knocks him down with one punch. IESTYN, out cold, crashes against the Chapel entrance and winds up sitting on the ground. His fall dislodges the sign announcing the subject of the sermon. It falls across him, bearing the legend:

"LOVE YE ONE ANOTHER"

Ianto, his brothers and Angharad are all looking down at Iestyn. Angharad then goes for Ianto with clawed fingers.

ANGHARAD. You devil.

Davy catches Angharad and pulls her back from Ianto, who looks at his knuckles, then at the fallen Iestyn.

IANTO (*quietly*). I will not have my sister treated like a pit-woman. His father may own the colliery, but if he wants to speak to you, let him ask permission. We have a home and he knows well where it is.

The Chapel-goers are now crowded round Iestyn, who is being helped to his feet by Morgan and Iestyn's father, Christmas Evans. They approach Ianto and the others.

EVANS. Did you hit my son?

IANTO. I did.

MORGAN. Here at Chapel?

IANTO (*looking at Iestyn*). That's where he was. Buttonhole and all.

EVANS. I will have you in court, young man!

IESTYN (*to Ianto, groggy but defiant*). Doubtless you had a reason.

IANTO. Doubtless. And doubtless I will break your neck if I have another reason.

MORGAN. Why did you hit him?

IANTO. Let *him* tell you.

Morgan looks at Iestyn, who speaks after a moment's hesitation.

IESTYN. I spoke to your daughter, sir.

EVANS (*his eyebrows go up*). You *spoke* to her?

IESTYN (*somewhat chastened*). Yes, sir.

Evans turns to Ianto and holds out his hand.

EVANS. Ianto, I am sorry for what I said. (*Glaring at Iestyn*) If a man spoke to Iestyn's sister, murder would be done.

He pushes Iestyn toward Ianto.

EVANS. Now, then—shake hands—no malice anywhere, is it?

They shake hands, but gingerly, like a couple of prize fighters. Then Iestyn bows to Morgan.

IESTYN. I will call to ask your permission tomorrow evening, Mr. Morgan.

MORGAN. Good, I will wait for you.

The sound of organ music, the processional, comes from the Chapel. All adjust themselves and start into the Chapel. Moving toward the entrance, Ianto and Iestyn enter together, walking side by side, but still stiff toward each other. Christmas Evans follows and after him Davy and Huw. Then Beth and Morgan. As Beth and Morgan come close, we see that there are tears in her eyes. Her husband notices them.

MORGAN (*in a whisper*). What ails you, girl?

BETH (*sniffing*). Too young—even to be *thinking* of marriage—

MORGAN (*cocking a humorous eye at her*). How old were you?

BETH (*wiping her eyes*). Much older, boy.

MORGAN. Go on with you, girl. You were younger still than Angharad.

Angharad follows them. She comes face to face with Gruffydd, hesitates a moment, then goes into the Chapel.

The scene dissolves into the MORGAN KITCHEN, at night. ANGHARAD is looking through the open door toward a group in the parlor. Her expression is bewildered and unhappy as we hear Gruffydd's voice.

GRUFFYDD'S VOICE. The bath holds one hundred gallons. "A" fills the bath at the rate of twenty gallons a minute. "B" at the rate of ten gallons a minute.

We see Gruffydd, Morgan and Bronwen coaching Huw, who sits at a table piled with books and papers. Beth sits nearby, busy with her sewing. Gruffydd is giving Huw a problem. Huw takes notes as Gruffydd talks.

GRUFFYDD. "C" is a hole which empties the bath at five gallons a minute. Got it? (*Huw nods.*) How long to fill the bath?

Beth clicks her tongue disapprovingly so that they all turn to look at her.

BETH. There is silly. Trying to fill a bath with holes in it, indeed.

MORGAN. A sum it is, my girl. A sum. A problem for the mind. For his examination into school next month.

BETH (*doggedly*). That old National School. There is silly their sums are with them. Who would pour water in an old bath with holes? Who would think of it, but a madman?

MORGAN (*his eyes seeking heaven*). It is to see if the boy can calculate, girl. Figures, nothing else. How many gallons and how long.

BETH. In a bath full of holes.

She throws her sewing at her workbasket, misses it and throws it again twice as hard. Morgan regards her with an exasperated grin, then turns to Gruffydd, who is smiling covertly.

MORGAN. Now I know why I have such a tribe of sons. It is you. Beth Morgan

is the cause. Look you, Mr. Gruffydd. Have you got something else?

GRUFFYDD. The decimal point, Mr. Morgan.

MORGAN. The decimal point, then— (*with a look at Beth*)—and peace in my house.

BETH (*calmly*). Go and scratch.

She rises, putting her work away. Gruffydd also gets up.

GRUFFYDD (*with a smile*). It is late, now. I will be going. (*Putting his hand on Huw's shoulder*) We will follow the decimal point tomorrow night. (*Bowing to Morgan and Beth*) Good night.

They bid him goodnight and Morgan puts out the lamp on the table, which leaves only the little lamp near Huw's wall bed. He and Beth go up the stairs as Gruffydd goes to the door, signalling to Huw to follow him. Huw hobbles after Gruffydd.

Gruffydd and Huw come out of the MORGAN HOUSE. From his pocket Gruffydd takes a beautiful pencil box which he presents to Huw.

GRUFFYDD. It was mine and my father's.

HUW (*deeply appreciative*). There is beautiful, Mr. Gruffydd.

We see the PENCIL BOX IN GRUFFYDD'S HANDS. The hands slide the lid back and forth.

GRUFFYDD'S VOICE. See how he joined it— and the pattern of grained woods on the lid and round the sides. Labor and love —therefore beauty.

He gives the box to Huw.

GRUFFYDD. It's yours—for when you go to school.

HUW (*in an awed whisper*). Mr. Gruffydd—

GRUFFYDD. Take care of it, then—

HUW (*overwhelmed*). Oh, I will, sir— thank you—

GRUFFYDD. You're having an opportunity none of your brothers had—to get yourself a good education in a good school. Be worthy of it, Huw.

HUW. I'll try, sir.

GRUFFYDD. Good. You will come tomorrow? I promised your father we would make him a frame for the picture Queen Victoria gave to Ivor.

HUW. Yes, sir.

GRUFFYDD (*smiles*). Good night then—and God bless you.

HUW. Good night, sir.

Gruffydd goes down the path. Huw goes back into the house and closes the door.

In the MORGAN PARLOR, Huw is hobbling back over toward his bed, looking at the pencil box with wide eyes. He sets it down beside the bed and begins to undress.

In BETH AND MORGAN'S BEDROOM, at night, Beth, in her old-fashioned nightgown, is just climbing into the double bed and pulling up the covers. Morgan, in an equally old-fashioned nightshirt, is approaching the bed with a lighted candle, which he sets beside the bed.

BETH (*frowning a little*). Gwil—who is in charge of this decimal point?

MORGAN (*pleading*). Look, Beth, my little one, leave it now, or else it will be morning and us fit for bedlam, both.

BETH. But who thought of it?

MORGAN. I don't know. The French, I think.

BETH. Well, no wonder! Those old Frenchies, is it?

MORGAN (*climbing into bed*). There is an old beauty you are. Go to sleep now before I will push you on the floor.

Beth turns over on her side.

BETH (*muttering, as she turns*). With Frenchies and old baths full of holes, what will come to the boy? What will come to the country, indeed?

MORGAN. Let the Old Queen in Windsor Castle worry over that.

Beth, apparently mollified, settles herself in the bed and closes her eyes. Morgan reaches over to pinch out the candle, but before he can do so, Beth's eyes open and she speaks once more.

BETH. Gwil—

MORGAN (*impatiently*). Yes, girl?

BETH (*dreamily*). I wonder does the Queen know about this decimal point?

MORGAN. Well, devil throw smoke!

He pinches out the light.

The scene dissolves to GRUFFYDD'S LODGINGS, at night. It is a combination study, bedroom and carpentry shop. (For woodworking is Gruffydd's hobby.) Now, of course, we can see nothing, for the room is dark. Gruffydd enters, crosses to his desk and lights the lamp upon it. Then he stops short. The light reveals Angharad standing there. Her mood is strange, unnaturally calm. For a moment they are silent.

GRUFFYDD (*quietly*). You shouldn't be here.

ANGHARAD. I couldn't spend another night without knowing. (*Looking up at him with tortured eyes*) What has happened? Is something wrong?

GRUFFYDD. Wrong?

ANGHARAD. You know what I mean. Why have you changed towards me? Why am I a stranger now? Have I done anything?

GRUFFYDD. No—the blame is mine. Your mother spoke to me after Chapel. She is happy to think you will be having plenty all your days.

ANGHARAD (*with a note of scorn*). Iestyn Evans.

GRUFFYDD (*looking at her*). You could do no better.

ANGHARAD (*quietly*). I don't want him. I want you.

GRUFFYDD (*quietly*). Angharad—I have spent nights too—trying to think this out. When I took up this work, I knew what it meant. It meant devotion—and sacrifice. It meant making it my whole life—to the exclusion of everything else. That I was perfectly willing to do. But to share it with another— (*With sudden emotion*) Do you think I will have you going threadbare all your life? Depending on the charity of others for your good meals? Our children growing up in cast-off clothing—and ourselves thanking God for parenthood in a house full of bits? (*Shaking his head with determination*) No—I can bear with such a life for the sake of my work. (*Suddenly savage*) But I think I would start to kill if I saw the white come into your hair twenty years before its time.

Angharad comes close, looking up at him with misty eyes. She understands the significance of his last remark.

ANGHARAD (*softly*). Why?

He doesn't answer.

ANGHARAD (*more insistently*). Why would you start to kill?

Gruffydd averts his eyes. She moves even closer to him.

ANGHARAD. Are you a man—or a saint?

GRUFFYDD (*in a low voice*). I am no saint —but I have a duty towards you. Let me do it.

Angharad realizes that she has made no impression on him.

ANGHARAD (*brokenly—tearfully*). Did I come here to hear sermons about your duty?

He does not move. She stares at him for another moment, then turns on her heel and goes out. Gruffydd stands looking after her.

Angharad comes swiftly out of GRUFFYDD's LODGINGS. We watch her as she rounds the corner. Then she bursts into sobs as she hurries along. The scene fades out.

The interior of GRUFFYDD's LODGINGS fades in. It is day. We see Gruffydd's work bench, at which Huw and Gruffydd are busy making the picture frame. Huw shows Gruffydd the piece he has been working on.

GRUFFYDD. Good. Now a piece for the molding—about two feet.

HUW. Yes, sir.

He hunts around on the bench for a piece of wood and then looks up at Gruffydd.

HUW. Will I ever be rich, Mr. Gruffydd?

GRUFFYDD (*gravely*). You *are* rich, Huw.

HUW. Me? Oh, no, Mr. Gruffydd.

GRUFFYDD. What do you want, then?

Huw is silent, trying to think what he wants.

GRUFFYDD (*smiling*). If you cannot think what you want, think how you would feel if you lost what you have. Your father and mother. Your brothers and sisters. Your home. Would you feel poor if you lost them? (*Huw nods.*) Then you are rich in possessing them. And that is the real wealth, Huw—because it was earned by love.

Huw is deeply impressed by what Gruffydd has said, but he is still struggling with his thoughts about Gruffydd and Angharad. He hesitates a moment, then blurts out:

HUW. But you will never have either kind of wealth! You can't marry Angharad because you have no money.

Gruffydd is startled by Huw's outburst. But as Huw looks up at him challengingly, Gruffydd speaks quietly:

GRUFFYDD (*kindly*). Who has been talking to you, Huw?

HUW. Bron—and—I have heard other talk.

Gruffydd's face goes stern for a moment, then he smiles a little wistfully and lays his hand affectionately on Huw's shoulder. After a moment he turns and goes slowly to the window.

GRUFFYDD is at the window, and Huw in the background is watching him. Gruffydd is silent for a moment, then speaks as much to himself as to Huw.

GRUFFYDD (*quietly, but with bitterness*). Perhaps there is still a third kind of wealth. Perhaps a man is wrong to ask more for himself than the opportunity to serve his God—

The scene dissolves to the EXTERIOR OF THE

CHAPEL on a bright spring day. The Chapel door is seen. The whole Valley is out, in much the same spirit as for Bronwen and Ivor's wedding earlier. The villagers are cheering and throwing rice at a bride and groom emerging from the Chapel. In the close foreground stands a smart, open carriage, driven by a coachman, who is not in too resplendent uniform. Until the bride and groom come close, we do not see who they are. They are ducking, shielding their faces from the rice. The coachman jumps down to help them into their carriage and we see that they are Iestyn and Angharad. Iestyn is smiling proudly. Angharad's face is blank. Iestyn helps her into the carriage and climbs in beside her. He takes her hand possessively.

IESTYN. My darling—you shall have everything in the world.

He kisses her while the celebrants round the carriage laugh and cheer. She responds, but automatically, without any real warmth.

Her eyes go past him back to the Chapel, then the coachman cracks his whip and, with a jerk, the carriage moves out of sight. The celebrants crowd into the foreground waving after the carriage. The people gathered at the Chapel begin to leave, moving down into the street. Near the Chapel door are the last of them, Morgan, Beth and Huw. They start to move slowly away from the Chapel. Beth is crying, Morgan has his arm around her. Huw looks at his mother, then back toward the open Chapel door. His face is very grave. They go out of scene as the door comes into view.

From the door, GRUFFYDD is seen moving methodically about at the front of the Chapel, putting away his book, extinguishing a candle, straightening the cloth on the lectern. He finishes his work and walks slowly forward. As he comes close, we see that his face is grave and self-contained. Gruffydd comes out through the door, gently closing it, turns and goes out of our vision, as the scene fades out.

PART SIX

The INTERIOR OF THE SCHOOL CLASSROOM fades in. It is day. Children, boys and girls, are filing into the classroom as if from recess. A group of them come into the foreground. One of them, Mervyn Phillips, is a rather bullying, heavy type. They stop by a desk and look down. On the desk are Huw's books and the pencil-box given him by Mr. Gruffydd. The boys exchange mischievous looks. Mervyn Phillips takes up the pencil-box and cracks it against the desk. Others begin to tear Huw's books and to pour ink on them. One of the boys looks back over his shoulder.

BOY. Look out, here he comes.

They scatter to their own desks. Huw comes up to his desk. As HUW looks down, his eyes widen, then his fists clench and tears start in his eyes. He looks up and faces them.

HUW. I'll fight you all.

Some of the boys laugh, some sneer at him.

MERVYN PHILLIPS. Dirty coal miner!

HUW. You first.

Then Huw begins to sob, though he tries to fight the sobs back. He tries to mop the pencil-box with his clean handkerchief, then puts the handkerchief to his eyes, leaving a black smudge on his face. His fists clenched,

he starts toward Mervyn Phillips. One of the boys calls out warningly.

BOY. Look out!

All take their seats hastily as the sound of the door opening is heard. JONAS, the master has entered the room. He is an unpleasant man, young, but heavy, and pedantic, with a sneering manner and an affected English drawl. He looks at the class and notices Huw's rumpled, tearful condition. He walks slowly over to him and stands looking down at him. Huw looks defiantly up at him, rising slowly.

JONAS. You are the new boy? (*With an unpleasant smile*) What a dirty little sweep it is.

He pulls Huw's handkerchief from his

pocket and inspects it disapprovingly, holding it daintily between two fingers.

HUW (*rebelliously*). It was clean when I left home—

The smile, as if by magic, leaves Jonas' face.

JONAS. You will address me as "sir" or I will put a stick about you. Now sit down. If you expect to stay with us you will have to be more civilized.

Mutiny wells up in Huw. He glares fiercely at Jonas. Jonas turns away and moves up to the head of the class.

The scene dissolves to the SCHOOLYARD. The children are pouring out for midday recess, a jostling crowd. Huw and Mervyn Phillips approach each other.

MERVYN. Fight me, will you?

He swings wildly at Huw. Huw swings back, but is no match for Phillips. He goes down under a rain of blows, comes up with his nose and mouth bleeding and goes down again. This time Mervyn jumps on him and pummels him on the ground. The boys who have gathered round the fight are all for Mervyn. They cheer him on as he pounds Huw.

The scene dissolves to the EXTERIOR OF THE MORGAN HOUSE. It is early evening. Huw, battered and bedraggled, slowly approaches the house. He carries his broken pencil-box and ink-stained books. His clothes are smudged and torn. His face is a battered mass with a black eye and bloody nose and several cuts. He looks at the front door, then turns and goes past the house to sneak in the back way. He stops at the sound of Davy's voice.

DAVY'S VOICE. Here he is.

Ianto and the other brothers are coming out of the shed, where they have been washing. They come up to Huw. Ianto sees Huw's face and whistles. He lifts Huw's chin. Huw tries frantically to think of a plausible lie.

HUW. I—I fell on the mountain.

IANTO (*grimly*). Did you win?

HUW (*honestly*). No.

Ianto looks at Davy.

IANTO. Where will we find Dai Bando?

DAVY. At the Three Bells, likely.

IANTO. Come.

They leave. Huw turns to the HOUSE. Beth is coming out with a pail of slops. She sees Huw and stares. She puts down the pail and runs to him, taking him in her arms, tears in her eyes.

BETH. Oh, Huw—what have they done to you?

Morgan comes out of the house and crosses to Huw. He looks gravely at his son, then takes him by the arm.

MORGAN. Come with me.

He leads him into the house. Beth, fearful that Morgan is going to give Huw a licking, hurries after him.

BETH. Gwilym—Gwilym—

In the MORGAN PARLOR, Morgan and Huw come in, followed by Beth, protesting. Morgan says nothing. He stops before the mantelpiece, takes down the box and sets it on the table. He takes a few coins from it and looks at Huw.

MORGAN. Are you willing to go back to school tomorrow?

HUW. Yes, sir.

MORGAN. Good. From tonight you shall have a penny for every mark on your face, sixpence for a bloody nose, a shilling for a black eye, and two shillings for a broken nose.

He gives some coins to Huw, Beth already listening with growing disapproval.

BETH. Gwilym—stop it. (*To Huw*) Fight again and when you come home not a word shall you have from me. Not a look. (*Fiercely*) Break your old nose, then! Break your mother's heart every time you go from the house!

MORGAN. A boy must fight, Beth.

BETH. Fight, is it? Another beating like that one and he will be dead.

MORGAN (*smiling*). He has had no beating. A hiding—yes—but no beating. He shall come for more until *he* is giving the beating, is it?

The two are glaring at each other, the first serious disagreement we have seen between them. Then the door opens and Dai Bando comes in with Ianto and Davy. Dai is a prize fighter, short, but as broad as he is tall, with long arms, only one or two teeth in his head. He bears the marks of a hundred fights on his face and wears a patch over one eye. The other eye is a mere slit between puffs. Morgan and Beth turn. Morgan is glad to see Dai, but Beth shows her disapproval from the beginning. Dai, however, is too simple to notice this. He is like a big friendly dog as he comes beaming across to them, walking with the curious, mincing prize fighter's walk. Following Dai now, and throughout the picture, is Cyfartha, a mild little man with violently checked clothes and an enormous curved pipe. He is Dai's manager, second, guide, philosopher and friend.

DAI (*heartily*). Good evening, Mrs. Morgan. (*To Morgan*) Good evening, sir.

CYFARTHA (*to everyone*). Good evening to you.

Morgan smiles pleasantly and shakes hands, but Beth only looks at Dai coldly. Ianto pushes Huw gently toward Dai.

IANTO (*to Huw*). Dai is going to teach you to box.

DAI (*correcting him*). To fight, first. Too many call themselves boxers who are not even fighters. (*Impressively*) Boxing is an art, is it?

Cyfartha nods agreement and pantomimes a punch. Beth lets out an emphatic snort of disapproval. Morgan tries to cover her rudeness.

MORGAN. Get on with you, girl. Won't you offer Dai and Cyfartha a cup of tea, now?

CYFARTHA (*hastily*). No—no. No tea, Mrs. Morgan. In training he is—for the match with Big Shoni. Only beer for him. A pint of your good home-brewed, Mrs. Morgan, is it?

He holds up two fingers suggestively. Beth, with obvious bad grace, moves toward the kitchen, glowering. Dai's manner becomes professional.

DAI (*to Huw*). Now, then. Strip off, boy.

Huw unbuttons his shirt.

At the KITCHEN DOOR Morgan intercepts Beth.

MORGAN (*whispering*). What's with you, girl?

BETH (*in a fierce whisper*). Frenchies— and old baths with holes—and now— prize fighters!

She goes into the kitchen, slamming the door behind her. Morgan shakes his head and goes to rejoin the group. Huw is stripped to the waist. Dai begins pinching and feeling his muscles, poking him in the ribs.

DAI (*frowning*). More in the shoulder, more in the forearm, and his legs want two more pairs like them before they will be enough.

IANTO (*quickly*). Not his fault, Dai.

DAI. No, I forgot.

He shows his one tooth to Huw in a grin of apology, then pats Huw on the back. Cyfartha also pats him.

DAI. Now—hit me by here, boy.

He sticks out his chin and touches it with a stubby forefinger. Huw hesitates. Dai touches his chin again impatiently.

DAI. Go on, boy, hit to kill.

CYFARTHA (*puffing at his pipe*). A sovereign if you will have him on the floor.

Huw, bewildered, and not at all wanting to do it, nevertheless lashes out with his fist. He catches Dai solidly. Dai takes the punch without even blinking.

DAI. Hm. Uses his shoulders well, eh, Cyfartha?

CYFARTHA. I have seen worse.

He punches the air speculatively. Dai goes down on his knees, which brings him down to Huw's height, and squares off in boxing position.

DAI. Now, look you. (*Demonstrating as he speaks*) Never swing round unless you have an opening. Jab first, then hook. The straight left first, is it? Up on your toes with your right near your chin—

As he speaks, he demonstrates. Huw copies his position. They begin to spar, Cyfartha shadow-boxing in the background. Beth reappears with the beer and slams the mugs down on the table.

The scene slowly dissolves to HUW AND MERVYN PHILLIPS squaring off. Huw stands in the correct boxing position he has learned from Dai. Both are stripped to the waist. At the beginning of the fight, Mervyn has the best of it, smothering Huw under his wild swings, but Huw keeps his head—and his feet. He begins to jab Mervyn's unprotected nose with his left. Then, when Mervyn's guard goes up, he catches him with a short right in the wind. Mervyn doubles over and Huw gives him a short left and clear right hook. Mervyn goes down in a heap, with a bloody nose. Huw looks at him in wonder. Wide-eyed, he inspects the fists that have wrought this miracle. Mervyn's sister Ceinwen, a very pretty girl about Huw's age, pushes through the crowd and goes on her knees beside him.

> CEINWEN (*crying*). Oh, Mervyn—Mervyn—

She takes her handkerchief and tries to staunch the flow of blood, then she rises to her feet and confronts Huw with blazing eyes.

> CEINWEN. You've killed him! You dirty little beast, you've killed my brother!

She goes for him fiercely. Huw backs up, trying to fend her off, then an arm comes into view and closes on her shoulder. She stops, looks up, frightened.

> JONAS' VOICE. Softly, now.

Jonas is standing, holding Ceinwen, but looking at Huw. There is a smile on his lips.

> JONAS. Dear me, dear me. So our coal mining friend has been indulging his favorite passion again? (*Then like a lash*) Go to my desk and wait.

The scene dissolves to the INTERIOR OF THE CLASSROOM. Huw and Mervyn are standing at the master's desk. Jonas is not in sight.

> MERVYN (*whispering*). Stuff a book down your trews or he'll have you in blood.

We see the class, watching in awe and anticipation as Jonas comes in swishing a flexible, ivory-headed cane. There are a few nervous twitters from the girls in the class. CEINWEN is seen sitting near the front. She has her handkerchief, covered with her brother's blood, in her hand, and is smiling triumphantly at Huw. HUW, as he catches Ceinwen's look, sets his lips grimly. Jonas comes up to Huw and Mervyn.

> JONAS (*softly to Mervyn*). Will you be so good as to make a back?

Mervyn obediently bends over.

> JONAS (*sweetly*). Thank you. (*Turning to Huw*) Please to bend across his back.

Huw obliges. Jonas swings the cane high in the air, then brings it down ferociously across Huw's back. Huw takes the first lash. His lips tighten a little, his eyes flicker, that is all. We hear the cane descend once more. JONAS' face is twisted with sadistic pleasure as he brings the cane down again and again.

We see the faces of the children as the sound of the blows comes over. Their faces mirror their growing fear and pity at the ferocity of the caning. Last of all, we see Ceinwen. The smile of triumph is slowly going from her face as the blows fall. Her eyes are glued to Jonas' stick, moving up and down with its rise and fall. She begins to pick at her bloody handkerchief.

JONAS brings the stick down, harder and harder. Finally, it breaks. Its ivory head bounces on the floor. Jonas steps back, breathing heavily. Huw slowly and painfully straightens. Mervyn does likewise and stands watching him respectfully.

> JONAS (*in a squeaky, breathless falsetto*). Now, then, fight again. Was just a taste. Teach you manners.

With a motion of his hand he indicates that Huw is to resume his desk. Huw looks him in the eye and Jonas' eyes avoid his look, then Huw turns and slowly makes his way down the aisle to his desk. HUW walks with pain but keeps himself erect. The other children look at him with admiration, respect and pity. Then Huw comes to Ceinwen's desk. He stops for a moment, looking down. She is looking up at him with wide eyes. The handkerchief before her is torn and shredded into little pieces. Then he moves on to his desk, slowly, still erect, and sits down.

The scene dissolves to the EXTERIOR OF THE SCHOOL. The children are passing out through the doors on their way home. Mervyn Phillips and Ceinwen appear, the latter looking round through the crowd for Huw. They stop while she looks. She still clutches the bloody handkerchief. The last of the children pass them. Then she turns to Mervyn.

CEINWEN. Go on, you. I'll be home later.

She goes back into the school.

In the CORRIDOR, Ceinwen passes through toward the classroom. She opens the door and goes in.

In the CLASSROOM, seen from Ceinwen's point of view, Huw is sitting alone at his desk. Ceinwen goes over to him. She looks down at him with great sympathy.

CEINWEN. Are you staying here, then?

HUW. For a little—

CEINWEN. And no dinner?

HUW. No.

CEINWEN. Will I get some for you? My house is close by here.

Huw shakes his head stoically. Ceinwen watches him, with tears in her eyes.

CEINWEN (*impulsively*). Huw Morgan— I will kiss you!

She kisses him warmly. He winces a little as her hand comes in contact with his shoulder. She is immediately full of remorse.

CEINWEN. Did I hurt?

HUW (*stoutly*). No!

CEINWEN. They say you had pieces of carpet down your back.

HUW. Feel if there is carpet.

She touches his back gently. He cannot control an involuntary start.

CEINWEN (*crying*). There is sorry I am. No carpet.

They look at each other in embarrassment for a moment, then Ceinwen speaks softly.

CEINWEN. I've got a robin's egg. Would you like it?

HUW. I have plenty.

CEINWEN. No.

HUW. Yes. Nightingales, too.

CEINWEN. Are there nightingales with you?

HUW (*boasting a little*). Thousands.

CEINWEN. We used to have them here, but the new ironworks burnt all the trees. (*She gives him a winning smile.*) May I come and listen to the nightingales with you?

CEINWEN. May I come and listen to the nightingales with you?

HUW. Yes.

CEINWEN (*excitedly*). When?

HUW (*rather brusquely*). Next summer, girl—when they are singing again.

Ceinwen is rather taken aback by this, but after a moment she recovers her composure. She looks at Huw shyly out of the corner of her eye.

CEINWEN. Have you got a sweetheart, Huw?

Huw is startled and speechless. Making a great effort, he rises, straightens his back and picks up his lunch box.

HUW. I will go home now.

CEINWEN (*horrified*). Across the mountain? Let my father take you—in his trap.

HUW (*rather ungraciously*). No—

CEINWEN. Please, Huw.

HUW (*with determination*). No.

He starts away from her toward the door, leaving Ceinwen hurt and disappointed. Her lip trembles a little at his rudeness.

HUW is standing in the doorway. He looks back at Ceinwen, speaks abruptly:

HUW. I will bring you a nightingale's egg tomorrow.

He goes out. CEINWEN's face lights up as she stands looking after him.

The scene dissolves to the VILLAGE STREET in the early evening. Huw is dragging himself painfully up the hill. He can barely walk, but his eyes are shining with pride. As he passes the Three Bells, Ivor, Ianto, Davy, Dai Bando and Cyfartha come out.

IVOR. Well—the scholar!

He slaps Huw on the neck. Huw winces, almost faints from the blow. Ianto catches him.

DAVY. What, now?

Davy peels the shirt from Huw's back and they stare at it.

IANTO (in a whisper). Did you have that in school?

DAVY. He has cut you to the bone, man. Who was it?

Huw will not answer.

IANTO (quietly). Mr. Jonas, is it?

Still Huw will not answer. Ianto's eyes turn slowly to the others.

IANTO. We will have a word with Mr. Jonas.

They all nod grimly, but Huw turns to face them.

HUW. No! Please, Davy—Ianto—I broke the rule when I fought.

DAVY (pointing to Huw's back). There is no rule for that!

HUW (tearfully). But he had given me warning.

DAVY. Rubbish, boy—

Ianto puts his hand on Davy's arm.

IANTO. Wait, Davy. This is Huw's affair. He shall decide it. (To Huw) Say the word and we will have the bones hot from his body.

HUW. Leave him alone.

Ianto nods slowly. He looks from Huw to his brothers, then back to Huw. A smile touches his lips.

IANTO (softly). I think our baby brother is becoming quite a man.

He takes Huw by the arm and leads him away. The other brothers follow, leaving Dai and Cyfartha looking after them. Dai's one visible eye is gleaming murderously.

CYFARTHA (whispering). Well—I will go to my death!

They go right back into the bar.

The scene dissolves to the INTERIOR OF THE CLASSROOM. Huw enters and approaches his desk. He stops at Ceinwen's desk for a moment, but we do not see what he does there; then he moves on to his own desk. His classmates, his former enemies, are looking at him and smiling. It is evident that he has now won his spurs as one of them. Huw does not return their looks, but keeps his eyes on Ceinwen's desk. After a moment Ceinwen hurries in and goes to her desk. She looks down at it and a pleased smile comes to her face. A nightingale's egg rests on her desk. Ceinwen looks over at Huw, trying to catch his eye. Satisfied that she has found the egg, Huw now keeps his gaze averted from her. Jonas' ruler is seen across this picture.

Jonas moves toward the blackboard with a piece of chalk in his hand. As he begins to draw some diagrams on the blackboard, the door opens in the background. Dai Bando and Cyfartha appear. They stand quietly for a moment, watching Jonas, who does not see them. Dai is dressed in his Sunday best, with a bowler hat. He carries a light cane. Huw's mouth drops open as he sees Dai and Cyfartha. He realizes that something is going to happen. Jonas is in the foreground, Dai and Cyfartha are in the background, as Jonas begins to elucidate in his usual supercilious voice.

JONAS. Yesterday the class made some progress—a very *small* progress—in the matter of linear measurements.

As Jonas talks, Dai minces toward him with his prizefighter's walk. Jonas turns curiously at this interruption.

DAI (affably). Good morning, Mr.—

JONAS. Jonas.

DAI (*beaming*). Mr. Jonas. (*To Cyfartha*) We have come to the right place, then, indeed.

His manner is pleasant, but his eyes are hard as ice. Cyfartha nods.

JONAS. What can I do for you?

DAI. A man is never too old to learn, is it, Mr. Jonas?

JONAS (*puzzled*). No.

He moves forward a little and Jonas backs up a few steps.

DAI. I was at school myself once. A flyweight I was, then, and no great one for knowledge.

He taps Jonas on the chest with a large forefinger.

DAI. But today, different. I am strong for learning.

They have now reached Jonas' desk and Jonas can back up no farther. Dai shoves his still smiling face within an inch of Jonas'.

JONAS (*scared*). What is it you want?

DAI. Knowledge. How would you go about measuring a stick—Mr. Jonas?

JONAS (*quavering*). By its length, of course.

DAI. And how would you take the measure of a man who would use a stick on a boy one-third his size?

Jonas gulps, with dry throat.

DAI (*conversationally*). Now you are a good man with a stick, but boxing is my subject, according to the rules laid down by the good Marquess of Queensberry.

CYFARTHA (*interjecting*). God rest his soul.

DAI. Happy I am to pass my knowledge on to you, is it? Good. From the beginning, then.

He removes his coat and bowler and hands them to Cyfartha, who brushes off the bowler and neatly folds the coat over his arm.

DAI. No man can call himself a boxer unless he has a good straight left—

JONAS (*yelling*). Help—help—

Dai drives a series of pistonlike jabs into his face.

DAI. Not to hurt your man, see? (*Jabbing*) This doesn't hurt. But to keep him off balance—

JONAS. Help! Police—

He manages to deflect one of Dai's jabs with his arm.

DAI (*approvingly*). Good—pretty blocking, there, indeed—but you left yourself open for a right hook.

He illustrates with a stinging hook to Jonas' ear. He would fall, but Dai's grip on his collar keeps him standing.

DAI. You should be able to hook with either hand—for the hook is how you will punish your man—

He illustrates with left and right hooks.

DAI. Shoulder into it—turn your fist as you hit—like that—that—that—

Jonas cries out feebly.

DAI. Keep your guard up, man! Under your chin like this. But watch your man doesn't give you a straight right in the solar plexus—

He pumps one into Jonas' ribs. Jonas' breath goes out with an "oof." His head comes down.

DAI (*going on smoothly*). —bringing your head down to where he will give you the uppercut—

He snaps Jonas' head up with a left uppercut. Jonas, his face a mess, is now moaning inarticulately, sagging in Dai's grip.

DAI. This— (*backhanding Jonas across the nose*) is against the rules—so never use it. Breaks a man's nose.

He surveys his handiwork. Jonas, moaning, suddenly goes limp. Dai shakes him and sighs as he realizes Jonas is out on his feet. He looks at the frightened class.

DAI. Eh, dear—I am afraid he will never be one to learn, eh, Cyfartha?

Cyfartha gloomily shakes his head. Dai picks Jonas up by the collar and the seat of the pants and drops him in the coal box near the stove, slamming the lid on him. As he does so, the door bursts open. Motshill, the Head, and Tyser, a junior master, rush in.

MOTSHILL (*furiously*). You cowardly brute! I will have you in court.

Dai unconcernedly takes his coat from Cyfartha and puts it on.

DAI. What for? Only a lesson it was. (*Settling his bowler*) And now home for a pint, is it? Dusty old place you have got here.

CYFARTHA. Dusty, indeed. A pint would be a blessing of good.

DAI (*tipping his bowler politely*). Good day to you, sir.

Cyfartha also tips his bowler. They go out

of the room. Motshill looks after them. Jonas, a sobbing, bloody, coal-smeared wreck, crawls out of the box.

MOTSHILL (*through tight lips*). Mr. Tyser—be good enough to take Mr. Jonas home.

Tyser takes Jonas out. Motshill faces the pupils, who are all standing.

MOTSHILL. Sit down.

All sit except Huw, who remains standing, white-faced, ready to take his blame.

MOTSHILL (*sternly*). Sit down, Morgan. Huw takes his seat.

Although Motshill's face is still stern, there is the flicker of a hidden smile on his lips. He picks up a book.

MOTSHILL. Now—then—take your "Caesar's Commentaries"—

The scene fades out.

PART SEVEN

The INTERIOR OF A TAILOR SHOP, in daylight, fades in. Huw, attired in his underclothes, is standing being measured by Hwfa, the tailor, and Old Twm, his assistant. Morgan stands watching as Hwfa rolls up his tape with a snap and looks at Morgan.

HWFA. The coat will be perfect. The trews, then. Long trews or short, Mr. Morgan? Shall he be a man or stay a boy?

HUW looks at his father longingly; more than his soul he wants long trews. Morgan strokes his chin, pretending indecision. Then he smiles.

MORGAN. Long trews, of course.

Huw swells with pride. Hwfa briskly begins to assemble his tape measure, pins, etc. Huw climbs quickly into his coat and trousers.

HWFA. Good. Long it is. Come back Wednesday at half past four, and have it hot off the goose.

TWM (*with sarcasm*). And Nan Mardy coming in at the same hour Wednesday for a rain-cloak with black braid and pockets both sides.

HWFA (*angrily*). What about Nan Mardy, then?

TWM (*elaborately casual*). Only saying I was, in case.

HWFA. In case what?

TWM (*suddenly angry*). In case he has his trews about his boot tops and his shirttails above his chin, man!

HWFA. Devil fly off with Nan Mardy. A good look at a shirttail would put life in her.

MORGAN (*breaking in sternly*). Mind your tongue before the boy!

Huw, now finished dressing, is bursting with curiosity. Morgan takes his arm.

MORGAN. Come, Huw. (*To Hwfa*) He'll be here at half past four.

They go out.

OUTSIDE THE TAILOR SHOP. Morgan and Huw come out of the shop.

HUW. Why would it do Nan Mardy good to see a shirttail?

MORGAN. Mind your own business, and Nan will mind hers, and we'll all be better off.

The scene dissolves to GRUFFYDD'S ROOM. Gruffydd and Huw are working at the lathe, repairing Huw's pencil box. Huw is watching Gruffydd under his eyebrows, trying to summon up courage to ask the great question. He absent-mindedly blows some sawdust on Gruffydd, who frowns but is really amused. Huw shows what he has done to Gruffydd.

GRUFFYDD. Good. Now a piece—cross-grained—for the corner there.

But Huw doesn't move.

HUW. Mr. Gruffydd—

GRUFFYDD. Yes—

HUW. Why would it do Nan Mardy good to have a look at a shirttail?

Gruffydd, startled, looks at him.

GRUFFYDD. Where did you hear that?

HUW. From Hwfa, the tailor.

GRUFFYDD (*sternly*). It is a low joke, Huw. I'm surprised at you.

HUW. Is it a joke, then? Dada didn't laugh.

Gruffydd relents as he realizes the boy is in earnest.

GRUFFYDD. It means she is an elderly woman, Huw, with no husband—therefore no children. It means she would be better off with a husband.

HUW. Must she have a husband to have children?

Again Gruffydd looks startled. Huw looks at him, earnestly unconscious of any humor in his remark.

GRUFFYDD. Yes—of course. Bronwen will be having her baby any day now. She has a husband, hasn't she?

HUW (*puzzled*). Yes—Ivor.

GRUFFYDD. And your mother had a husband—your father.

HUW. But why?

Gruffydd studies Huw, looks him up and down, debating whether or not the time has come for Huw to learn something of "the facts of life." Huw senses that something momentous is in the offing.

HUW (*hopefully*). I'm getting long trews.

Gruffydd makes a big decision, then smiles.

GRUFFYDD. Very well, Huw. Then, first things first: there are some things you will know now and some things you shall wait to know. But I will give you this to think about: there are men and women. But before that, they shall be boys and girls, and before that, babies, is it?

HUW. Yes, sir.

GRUFFYDD. And before that, what?

HUW (*puzzled*). Nothing, sir—

GRUFFYDD. Nothing!

HUW. —like in the beginning was the Word.

GRUFFYDD (*nodding*). The Word was with God. And then?

HUW. Then came Adam and Eve.

GRUFFYDD. Good—. So now there was Adam and Eve in the garden and what happened?

HUW. They sinned against the Tree of Knowledge—

GRUFFYDD. Yes. What then?

HUW (*not too sure of himself*). Then came an Angel with a flaming sword and sent them from the Garden.

GRUFFYDD (*nodding*). To earn by the sweat of their brows. And what after?

HUW (*this he knows*). Then came Cain and Abel, and Abel was a good man but Cain killed him.

GRUFFYDD (*laughs*). Wait. Before to kill them, have them first. Adam and Eve we have got. Where did we have Cain and Abel?

HUW. From the Bible, sir.

GRUFFYDD (*a little impatiently*). But where from—to get into the Bible, boy?

There is a slight pause while Huw thinks. Gruffydd prompts him.

GRUFFYDD. Adam was created in the image of God, and Eve from the rib of Adam. But where did Cain and Abel come from?

HUW. They were the sons of Adam and Eve.

GRUFFYDD. Good! Now, what makes a man a father, and why is a woman a mother?

HUW (*deadly serious*). Well, sir, one is with moustache and trews, and the other with smoothness and skirts.

GRUFFYDD (*patiently*). No, Huw. One is a husband and the other is a wife. As Eve was the wife of Adam, and they were the father and mother of Cain and Abel, so a child must have a father and a mother and they must be husband and wife. As there is a time for everything, marriage is the time for having children so—some day—as you will be a man— you will also be a father and the girl you marry will be a mother. Like Ivor and Bronwen today.

Huw nods, dimly comprehending. Gruffydd spins the lathe.

GRUFFYDD. And there you are.

HUW. Is that all, sir?

GRUFFYDD. Is that all? What more then?

HUW. I thought it was something terrible.

Gruffydd's manner changes. His face grows very grave.

GRUFFYDD. It is terrible, Huw. Indeed terrible. Think, Huw—

He rises from the lathe. He is thinking now, not of Huw, but of Angharad and the children he will never have. He moves a few steps away from Huw, leaving Huw, wide-eyed, in the background.

GRUFFYDD (*in a low voice*). To ask the

woman you love to share not only your home, your wealth— (*The thought of Angharad grows stronger.*) —your poverty— (*He pauses for a long moment, drawing a deep breath.*) —but to share the responsibility of creating life in the image of your God. Many lives, perhaps. Think of the miseries and afflictions that can come to those lives beyond the span of your own. Think to have small children in your own likeness standing at your knee, and to know them as flesh of your flesh, blood of your blood, looking to you for guidance as you look to God the Father for yours. Can that be anything but terrible, in majesty and in beauty beyond words?

Huw stands impressed but bewildered.

HUW. But why would it do Nan Mardy good to see a shirttail?

Gruffydd turns, looks at him sternly.

GRUFFYDD. I told you that was a low joke and not worth repeating. Home to your supper, now.

Before Huw can move, the sound of the mine whistle comes over, blowing in a series of short staccato blasts. Gruffydd and Huw exchange a look and run out of the house. In the VILLAGE STREET men and women are running up toward the mine. The whistle blows discordantly, shouting: "Accident." Gruffydd and Huw join the others hurrying toward the mine.

OUTSIDE THE COLLIERY the great winding wheel is slowing to a stop. The cage is coming to the surface carrying a group of miners, among them Ianto and Davy. There is a canvas-covered bundle on the floor of the cage. Ianto and Davy's faces are very grave. Gruffydd and Huw appear, hurrying toward the cage. They meet Ianto and Davy, sensing at once from their expressions that the tragedy concerns them.

IANTO. Ivor—

Huw's eyes widen.

DAVY. Slipped under a tram on the lower level.

They start down the hill toward Ivor's house.

In the STREET, as Ianto, Davy, Gruffydd and

Huw move toward the house, Bronwen appears, walking slowly, with an expression that shows that she has a premonition of what has happened. She clutches Ianto by the arm. He cannot find words to tell her what has happened.

BRONWEN (*breathing it*). Ivor?

Ianto and Davy nod. Bronwen stares, then her eyes close, her knees give way and she faints against Ianto, who supports her.

GRUFFYDD (*to Huw*). Fetch Dr. Richards —quickly!

Huw runs out of sight as Ianto and Davy carry Bronwen into her house.

The scene dissolves to BRONWEN'S PARLOR at night. The only sound in the room is a clock ticking on the mantelpiece. It is between two and three o'clock. Gruffydd, Morgan, Huw, Ianto and Davy are waiting, their eyes on the stairs. All look haggard from their vigil. Beth comes slowly down the stairs. Her sleeves are rolled up. She looks haggard, too, depressed, but indomitable. She walks over to Morgan, who is standing beneath the framed picture of Queen Victoria on the wall, under which hangs the baton the Queen gave Ivor.

BETH (*quietly, with a twist of her lips*). We have our first grandson, Gwil—

MORGAN (*nodding solemnly*). Give one, and take the other.

Beth's eyes blaze. Her voice shakes a little as she replies fiercely.

BETH. Go to that girl up by there and say that to her. She will have an answer for you.

MORGAN. Hisht, now, Beth. Do not kindle the wrath.

BETH. To hell with the wrath! (*As she speaks she lifts her eyes*) And I said it plain to be heard.

The scene fades out.

PART EIGHT

HUW'S GRADUATION CERTIFICATE, held in Morgan's hands, fades in. Then we are in the MORGAN PARLOR. Morgan and Beth are looking at the certificate. Bronwen is sitting in the background with her baby.

MORGAN (*studying the certificate*). Good with honors then. (*Smiles*) Our son is a scholar.

Beth takes the certificate, peering at it with wonder.

BETH. What is this, Huw? I can make no sense with it.

MORGAN (*proudly*). Latin, it is.

BETH. Latin, is it?

She puts down the certificate and takes Huw's head in her hands, looking at him with loving eyes.

BETH. My poor Huw. Have they stuffed your head with Latin, then?

She passes her hand over his head almost as if to see if the knowledge would show in great bumps.

MORGAN. Now, then. What will you do?

To Cardiff to school? The University and then to be a lawyer, is it? Or a doctor?

BRONWEN (*with a twinkle*). Dr. Huw Morgan— Well that will be something special—

BETH (*approvingly*). Yes, indeed—and a lovely horse and trap with a good black suit and a shirt with starch. Oh, there is good, my little one. (*Briskly*) Now, then. A glass of buttermilk for you and all your knowledge.

HUW (*smiling*). Yes, mother—(*with a sideways look at Bronwen*)—and some of Bron's shortcake.

Beth on her way to get the buttermilk, stops and puts her hands on her hips.

BETH. Oh—and my shortcake is to be fed to the pigs, is it?

HUW. No. Only I finished it yesterday, and today is shortcake day with Bron.

Bronwen looks over at Huw with the ghost of a smile.

BRONWEN. I'm sorry, Huw—only currant bread I made today. Nobody to eat it now.

Silence falls on the little group. Bronwen's eyes are shining with unshed tears. She rises and goes toward the door. BRONWEN is at the door, leaning her forehead against the door jamb, holding her baby.

BRONWEN. Oh, mother, I am lonely without him. I put his boots and clothes ready every night. But they are there, still, in the morning. (*Her voice catching on a sob*) There is lonely I am.

She goes out of the house.

Morgan, Beth and Huw look after Bronwen with shocked eyes. Then Beth steps into the kitchen for Huw's buttermilk. She comes back with a glass and pitcher as Morgan and Huw are still looking after Bronwen. Beth pours the buttermilk and gives it to Huw.

BETH. Gwil—I will have Bron here to live—if she will come.

MORGAN (*shaking his head*). Not Bron —one mistress in a house.

He sighs, then taps the graduation certificate on the table.

MORGAN. Now, then, Huw. What will it be?

Huw looks toward the door after Bronwen, then back to his father.

HUW. I will go down the colliery with you, sir.

MORGAN. Have sense, Huw. The colliery is no place for you. Why not a try for a respectable job?

BETH (*snorting*). Respectable. Are you and his brothers a lot of old jailbirds, then?

MORGAN. Leave it now, Beth. I want the boy to have the best.

BETH (*stubbornly*). If he is as good a

man as you and his brothers, I will rest happy.

MORGAN. Beth—I am thinking of the boy's future. It was different in our time. There was good money and fair play for all. (*Tapping the graduation certificate on the table*) And Huw is a scholar. Why take brains down a coal mine?

HUW. I would rather, sir.

Morgan drops his hands with a gesture of helplessness.

MORGAN. Decide for yourself, then. And blame yourself if you are wrong.

HUW. The colliery.

MORGAN. Very well. That settles it— The colliery—

BETH. Good.

MORGAN (*bleakly*). Good. I am going to get drunk.

He turns and walks out of the room. Beth and Huw look after him.

HUW (*abruptly*). Mother—could I go down and live at Bron's?

Beth is startled at first.

BETH. Huw—

Huw understands that it is because she doesn't want to lose another of her sons.

HUW. It's only down the street, mother.

Beth considers the idea.

BETH. Yes—it is not good for her to be alone so much— (*Nods with decision*) Yes, go, Huw—until she marries again, you will do.

Huw, about to rise, stares at her. This possibility had not entered his mind.

HUW. Marry again? Bron?

BETH. Yes, boy—she is young, still. She has years of beauty yet— And no wages going into the house. Another husband, then—quick, too.

Huw thinks a moment, then rises.

HUW. I will go and see her.

He exits.

In BRONWEN'S HOUSE, in daylight, Bronwen is sitting in her rocking chair, rocking slowly back and forth. The baby is in her arms and she is gently stroking its hair. She turns with a sudden brightening of her eyes, as if she half expected Ivor to come in. Then the sadness is back on her face.

BRONWEN. Yes?

Huw comes quietly in. He crosses over to stand looking down at her.

HUW. I am going down the colliery, Bron.

A smile touches Bronwen's lips.

BRONWEN. Well—down the colliery. The old coal will be shaking in its seam.

Huw, however, is still very serious.

HUW. Bron—would you have me in the house to live?

She looks at him with widened eyes.

HUW. And have my wages?

Bronwen shakes her head gently.

BRONWEN. Your home is with your mother.

HUW. It was she who sent me.

BRONWEN. From pity.

HUW. No, from sense. If you put clothes night and morning, let them be my clothes.

BRONWEN (with a little smile). Good old man.

HUW. Yes, or no, Bron?

BRONWEN. Yes.

HUW. Good. I will get my bed.

Huw hurries out.

In the STREET, Huw runs from Bron's house to his own.

The scene dissolves to the MINE ENTRANCE. The day shift is going to work. Among the miners as they pass are Ianto and Huw, who is a breaker boy.

The scene dissolves to the MINE CAGE as it drops down the long shaft. The rough walls of the shaft appear to be moving swiftly up. Huw is prominent among the miners huddled in the cage. There are two or three other boys, slightly older, in the cage.

The scene dissolves, successively, to Ianto and Huw working through the day: Ianto monotonously swinging his pick into the coal face, Huw carrying the coal back and loading it on the tram at the foot of the cutting, piling the slag to shore up the walls as they progress into the seam.

HUW'S VOICE. —to work then, to earn bread for those one loves. To grow pale in the damp underground—to know hours, weeks, and months in the dark, with the dust of the coal settling on you with a light touch you could feel—as though the earth were putting her fingers on you, to warn you that she would have you there, underneath her, on her day of reckoning.

This dissolves to the MINE ENTRANCE, in daylight. The mine cage comes to the surface and the grimy men begin to pile out. Huw and Ianto are getting off the cage. Huw, blinking, draws a deep breath and looks around him as if to drink in the blessed sunlight. Ianto extinguishes his lamp and starts out. Huw follows.

At the PAY WINDOW, the men are lining up to get their pay. Ianto, Davy an Huw are prominent in the group. Huw looks very proud as he moves along in line in front of Ianto and Davy. Then Huw, Davy, and Ianto step up to get their pay. Huw receives his money and moves on, but Davy and Ianto stop at the window. They have received slips of paper with their money. Huw stops and turns back as he sees that something is wrong. They grimly show him their slips of paper.

HUW'S VOICE. To know the blessed relief when the whistle blew and the shift was ended. To stretch aching muscles—and when we came up into the light again, to know with thanksgiving, why we mining people sit out on our doorsteps when the sun is shining.

But I felt a man now in truth, to be coming up among that crowd of men, sharing their tiredness, blacked by the same dust—greeting the light with the same blinking in my eyes, thinking with *the same mind, of them, with them, a part of them. Among men, a man.*

But with my happiness came sorrow. Ianto and Davy, the best workers in the colliery, but too highly paid to compete with poorer, more desperate men.

The scene dissolves to the EXTERIOR OF THE MORGAN HOUSE, in daylight. Ianto and Davy, carrying bundles and wearing their caps, come slowly out of the house. Morgan, Beth, Bronwen and Huw stand in the door looking sadly after them. They come down the path, wave once and trudge away up the street. We follow them until they are out of sight over the hill.

HUW'S VOICE. *In my family now only two to earn wages. My father—and myself.*

The scene dissolves to the MORGAN PARLOR at night. HUW'S ATLAS stands out. The book is opened at a Mercator's Projection of the World. Huw is ruling lines from Wales to America, New Zealand and Cape Town. Now Beth and Morgan are seen looking over Huw's shoulder.

BETH. What is this old spider, now then?

HUW (*smiling*). One line from us to Owen and Gwil. (*He traces the lines with his fingers as he speaks.*) Down to Cape Town to Angharad. Over here to

Ianto—in Canada—here to Davy—in New Zealand—

Huw smiles up at his mother, and puts his finger on the point from which the lines radiate.

HUW. And you are the star, shining on them from this house all the way across continents and oceans.

BETH (*with irony*). All the way? (*A little bitterly*) How far am I shining, then, if you can put it all on a little piece of paper?

MORGAN. A map it is, Beth, my little one —a picture of the world, to show you where they are.

BETH (*grimly*). I know where they are without any old pictures and spiders with a pencil!

She turns to leave them at the table and goes slowly away. She stops, turns and looks back at them.

BETH (*flatly*). They are in the house.

She turns and goes.

Huw and Morgan are looking after her as she goes into the kitchen. The scene fades out.

PART NINE

The EXTERIOR OF BRONWEN'S HOUSE fades in. Huw, grimy and in his working clothes, in a crowd of other miners, comes hurrying down from the colliery and into the house.

The INTERIOR OF BRONWEN'S HOUSE as Huw comes in. He stops suddenly as he sees Matt Harries, a pleasant, raw-boned, not too bright young man, standing in the parlor. He is dressed obviously in his best clothes, which do not fit him very well. There is a rather pathetic bouquet of flowers on the table beside him. He is the picture of a proud and somewhat embarrassed swain. Huw looks at him without enthusiasm.

HUW. Oh—(*then grudgingly*)—Hello—

Matt beams and holds out his hand.

MATT. Hello, Huw.

Huw shakes hands rather unwillingly, look-

ing at Matt with an unwinking and distrustful stare. Matt senses Huw's hostility.

MATT. Calling on Bron, I am, but glad to see you, too.

Huw looks past him at the flowers he has brought, and frowns in disapproval. Bronwen's voice comes from upstairs.

BRONWEN'S VOICE. Is that you, Huw?

HUW (*turning*). Yes.

He goes to the foot of the stairs and up a couple of steps. Bronwen is standing at the railing above and Huw at the foot of the stairs.

BRONWEN. I'm dressing the baby. Will you give Mr. Harries a cup of tea?

HUW (*disapprovingly*). Is he staying for tea?

BRONWEN. Yes.

She goes back to her room. Huw goes back to Harries.

Matt, his back to Huw, is just taking down Ivor's ceremonial baton, given him by the Queen, from below the signed portrait of Queen Victoria, where it hangs over the mantel. He is examining it curiously. Huw takes it from him.

HUW (*looking at the baton in his hands*). The Queen gave it to Ivor when he had the choir to sing for her.

MATT. He was a good man, Ivor.

Huw looks up at him.

HUW. Yes—

He turns the baton in his hands, looking sideways at Matt.

HUW (*in a low voice*). Matt—

MATT. Yes, boy—

HUW. There is something I ought to tell you—

MATT. Yes?

Huw hesitates as if on the point of speaking, then shakes his head.

HUW. No—not my business—

He starts to move away. Matt, following him, catches his arm.

MATT. But what is it, boy?

HUW. Let Bron tell you—

MATT. It is about— (*He stumbles.*) Bronwen—and me—?

HUW (*in a low voice*). Yes—and Ivor—

MATT (*puzzled*). Ivor?

HUW. Bron will never forget him.

MATT (*puzzled*). Of course not—

HUW (*steadily*). And she will never marry another.

Matt is stunned by this.

MATT. Has she told you that, boy?

HUW. Many times.

MATT (*stunned*). But she has said nothing to me.

HUW. No—she would not want to hurt you. But she has told me that you are wasting your time here.

MATT (*whispering*). She did?

Huw is not very good at lying, but Matt's denseness makes up for the lack. Huw nods.

HUW. She told me she was sorry for you.

Matt looks very sad. He grins a sickly grin.

MATT. Well, boy—I—I'm glad you told me. I—(*he stumbles*). Well, goodbye, now.

HUW (*politely*). Won't you stay and see Bron?

But he is hoping that Matt will not.

MATT. No. (*Gulping.*) No—I will go.

Huw nods. Matt picks up his cap, looks at the flowers, and goes. Huw looks after him, with a gleam of triumph, then sobers when he hears Bronwen on the stairs. Bronwen comes down the stairs. Through the door, she sees Matt retreating down the path.

BRONWEN. Where did Matt go?

HUW. He didn't say.

BRONWEN. But why—

HUW. He said to excuse him to you.

Since Huw turns away, a suspicion is born in Bronwen's mind.

BRONWEN. Huw—

HUW. Yes—

BRONWEN. What did you say to him?

HUW (*stalling*). To who?

BRONWEN. Matt Harries—who else?

Huw is obstinately silent. Bron shakes him lightly.

BRONWEN. What did you say, Huw?

HUW (*unwillingly*). I told him lies that made him go.

BRONWEN (*quietly*). Go to his house and fetch him back. Tell him you are sorry.

Huw turns his back to her.

HUW. I'm not sorry—and I won't fetch him back.

BRONWEN. Huw—

Bronwen looks as if she would like to be angry, but there is something pathetic about Huw's jealousy. She cannot be more than a little stern with him.

BRONWEN. He is a good man, and would make me a good husband. Why shouldn't I marry him?

HUW. Because you don't love him.

BRONWEN. He understands that. Love isn't everything. Goodness is something. And bread is something—and a roof for our heads. I can take no more from you and your good father. Would you have my little Ivor go hungry because there is no man to provide for him?

HUW. I will be the man and provide for him.

BRONWEN. No, Huw—when you are a man, your wages will not be for me.

HUW. They will be for you as long as you will have them.

BRONWEN (*with a little smile*). There is a good old man you are. But some day you will be having a wife of your own —and the lucky one she will be—and children of your own, is it?

HUW (*looking at her steadily*). No, Bron.

BRONWEN. Yes, Huw.

She smiles and runs her hand through his hair. He continues to look at her with the same expression.

BRONWEN. Now—let us forget about Matt today and have our tea together.

She goes from the room, Huw looking after her. Unshed tears gradually gather in his eyes. They are not the tears of childhood. They are maturely sad.

HUW's VOICE. *But Bron was wrong. Bron, whom I always loved—from the first time I saw her—until now. That day,*

though I looked with the eyes of a child, I saw into the future of a man. And what I saw then has remained true all my life—I never married.

In this I never changed. But there was change now in my Valley. The slag spread faster and faster now, devouring everything in its path—all the things put in my Valley by man and God.

My Valley—soon to be green no longer—

The scene dissolves to a full view of the VALLEY. The slag heap is now much larger. The Valley is beginning to look as it was in the opening shots of the picture: gaunt trees half buried in the slag. The little brook, now a green-scummed slough, choked with slag. A miner's house as the slag pours in on it, crushing it.

HUW's VOICE. *Then Angharad came back —alone. She would not come to our house, but stayed at the big Evans house at Tyn-y-coed.*

The scene dissolves to the EXTERIOR OF TYN-Y-COED by day, the Evans mansion, which is the largest house in the Valley. Huw is walking up the path to the front door. He uses the great knocker, removes his cap, straightens his tie and shoots his cuffs. The door is opened by Enid, a little country maid. A short distance behind her hovers Mrs. Nicholas, a plumply disagreeable housekeeper in funereal black.

HUW (*politely*). To see Mrs. Evans, please.

ENID. Who is it?

HUW. Huw Morgan.

Inside the HALLWAY, Mrs. Nicholas sweeps forward.

MRS. NICHOLAS. Her brother, is it?

Huw nods and comes in. The maid closes the door. Mrs. Nicholas looks Huw over superciliously.

MRS. NICHOLAS. This way, please.

Mrs. Nicholas opens the drawing room door. Angharad is standing by the window at the other end of the room. Huw goes slowly in, Mrs. Nicholas remaining by the open door.

In the DRAWING ROOM, we see Angharad. She looks older now, and is dressed simply but fashionably. The change in her over the years is more marked than in any other member of the Morgan family. She comes quickly to Huw and smiles at him.

ANGHARAD. Well, Huw.

She kisses him on the cheek. Huw is impressed to meet this grand lady who is his sister. Angharad looks over at Mrs. Nicholas.

ANGHARAD. Mrs. Nicholas, will you bring tea, please?

Mrs. Nicholas curtseys and goes out, leaving the door open. Angharad takes Huw's cap from him and puts it on the window seat.

ANGHARAD. Sit down, Huw. (*He sits. She takes his hand and smiles affectionately.*) There is grown you are—and changed.

HUW. You, too—

Angharad laughs with a trace of bitterness.

ANGHARAD. I look ill and should take care of myself. Everyone coming in the house says so. So you say it and we will be finished with it. (*With an obvious change of subject*) Now tell me the news from here. How are all the boys and girls we used to know?

HUW. The Jenkins girls are married. Maldwyn Hughes has gone to be a doctor and Rhys Howell is in a solicitor's office and sending home ten shillings a week—and—(*looking at her under his eyebrows*)—Mr. Gruffydd is still first up and last to bed.

The emotion shows in Angharad's eyes. She grasps his hand.

ANGHARAD. How is he, Huw?

HUW. Not as he was.

ANGHARAD. Is he ill?

HUW. Inside. In his eyes and voice. Like you.

Angharad slowly rises to her feet, looking down at Huw. Her face has gone white, her eyes are terrible.

ANGHARAD. Go from here.

Huw slowly rises to his feet, takes his cap, then both look across the room. Mrs. Nicholas is standing in the doorway, leading Enid, who carries a tea service. She has evidently been listening. When she sees that they notice her presence, she moves briskly forward.

MRS. NICHOLAS. Now then, Mrs. Evans. Tea, is it?

ANGHARAD. Wait, Huw.

Enid carries the service to a table. Mrs. Nicholas busies herself behind it.

ANGHARAD. Leave it, Mrs. Nicholas. I will pour.

MRS. NICHOLAS (*raising her eyebrows*). Well—*I* always did the pouring for Mr. Iestyn's poor mother.

She raps Enid on the knuckles with her keys.

MRS. NICHOLAS. Thumbs off the plates, Enid.

ANGHARAD (*coldly*). That will do. Not so handy with those keys, or I will have them from you. And I will pour.

MRS. NICHOLAS (*curtseying*). Yes, Mrs. Evans. (*With an oily smirk*) A new mistress is like new sheets, yes. Little bit stiff but washings to come.

She signals to Enid to follow her and leaves the room, closing the door after them emphatically. Huw and Angharad look after them.

HUW. Why do you have her here?

ANGHARAD. Thirty-seven years in the family—or so she tells me sixty times a day. Will you have tea, Huw?

She sighs and seats herself behind the tea service.

Huw is looking gravely down at her.

HUW. You told me to go.

Angharad is genuinely sorry for her outburst.

ANGHARAD. No—stay.

She pats the settee beside her. He comes and sits down next to her. She takes his hand.

ANGHARAD. Huw—I am sorry I was nasty.

HUW. It is nothing, girl.

Angharad looks at him, then turns her head away as her eyes fill with tears. She gets out her handkerchief and dabs at her eyes.

ANGHARAD Eh, dear—I am like an old baby. Oh, Huw—my little one—I tried to tell mother—but I couldn't.

Then she suddenly loses control. The tears come hard now. He puts his arm round her and she sobs on his shoulder. Huw tries to comfort her.

Next we see the KITCHEN—TYN-Y-COED, by day. Mrs. Nicholas and Enid are near the table. At the door are a country couple, a man and woman who have come by to sell eggs. A boy in the background is seen filling the coalbin. Mrs. Nicholas wears an expression of righteous indignation. As she talks, she is picking over the eggs.

MRS. NICHOLAS (virtuously). Not for me to say. Only the housekeeper, I am. Thirty-seven years in the family and living to curse the day.

COUNTRYWOMAN (somewhat bewildered). Well—there is terrible, it is, whatever it is, is it?

MRS. NICHOLAS (holding an egg to the light). It will not surprise me any day to see the old master rise up white from his grave. Only the gravestone is holding him down, I will swear—

ENID. Terrible—terrible, indeed. (Puzzled.) But what—?

Mrs. Nicholas leans to whisper to Enid.

ENID (shocked). Divorce?

The bucolic pair look terribly shocked.

COUNTRYWOMAN. What?

MRS. NICHOLAS. Saying nothing I am, but that is what is in her mind. (To the countrywoman.) I will take a dozen— but to ask a shilling is robbery. (Going on.) She is here without her husband, is it? And why? Because she is in love with this preacher—

COUNTRYWOMAN (shocked). No—

MRS. NICHOLAS. Preacher, I said—Mr. Gruffydd it is.

COUNTRYWOMAN (gasping). Mr. Gruffydd?—Can it be true?

MRS. NICHOLAS. True indeed— But you will never hear it from me.

COUNTRYWOMAN. Oh, I will say nothing, Mrs. Nicholas—

MRS. NICHOLAS (hinting strongly). Oh, no—no—unless you think it is your duty.

Then she takes out her handkerchief and begins to sniffle into it.

MRS. NICHOLAS. Poor little Master Iestyn! A drab from a coal mine fouling his home, and him thousands of miles away!

The country couple shake their heads sadly and go out. After they have gone, Enid turns to Mrs. Nicholas, puzzled.

ENID (timidly). But Mr. Gruffydd has not been near the house—

MRS. NICHOLAS (with scorn). What difference is that, girl? (Brusquely) Get on with your work.

Mrs. Nicholas's tears have vanished and we see her as she is.

The scene dissolves to the MAIN HEADING OF THE COLLIERY. Huw, his eyes blazing furiously, and bleeding from a cut on his lip, is giving a terrific beating to a bigger boy, an adolescent. Huw hits him savagely again and again, knocks him up against the wall of the heading, and then, crying, to his hands and knees. Huw is about to launch himself on his victim again when some miners run into the scene and pull him away, still struggling to get back at the boy.

The scene dissolves to the STREET by day. Huw comes slowly down the hill from the colliery, walking with head lowered and fists clenched. He passes little knots of people who stare at him, some whispering behind his back, but he will not look at them. He comes to Bronwen's house, stops with his hand on the gate and looks over to his own house. From his angle we can see that the door is shut. We then follow Huw as he goes over to his own house and up the path, and to the door. The shadow of a cloud falls over him. He looks up, then goes in.

HUW'S VOICE. *The knives that can be hidden in idle tongues. For generations Morgans had lived in the Valley—and now for the first time our name was touched with slander. As the slag had spread over my Valley, so now a blackness spread over the minds of its people. Our house looked strange to me—and then I knew why. For the first time I could remember, our front door was shut tight in the daytime. At the time it seemed important to me. But later I was to remember this day for another reason. My father—and the shadow of a cloud that fell across our door. If only I had known then—*

In the MORGAN PARLOR Huw's shoulder comes into view as he opens the door. Morgan is sitting there in his mining clothes, lacing up his boots. Beth stands near him. The sunlight from the opened door falls on Morgan as the cloud passes. Morgan rises as Huw comes in, closing the door. He looks over at Huw.

MORGAN. Well, Huw—some trouble with the Philistines, then?

Beth rushes to Huw.

BETH. Oh, Huw—what is it with you? Look at your hands.

HUW. Evan John—(*bewildered and hurt*) —he—he said things about Angharad and Mr. Gruffydd.

BETH (*to Morgan*). Even the children—

MORGAN. You were right, my son— (*To Beth*) I will be back for breakfast.

BETH. You will not go to the Chapel?

MORGAN. No—(*then steadily*)—and if they do this, I will never set foot in the Chapel again as long as I live.

He turns to go.

BETH. I will have brandy broth and the sheets warm on your bed.

Morgan replies with a ghost of his old humor.

MORGAN. There is an old beauty you are.

BETH (*whispering*). Go and scratch, boy.

Morgan goes out of the house. Beth and Huw look after him. Then Huw turns to his mother.

HUW. What is this about the Chapel, mother?

BETH (*looking away*). Tonight—after the service—a deacons' meeting—over Angharad.

HUW (*shocked*). Angharad. But she has done nothing.

BETH (*grimly*). Nothing is enough for people who have minds like cesses with them. (*With tears*) Oh, Huw, my little one, I do hope from my soul when you are grown, their tongues will be slower to hurt.

HUW. But will Angharad have to be at the meeting?

BETH. No. None of us will go. But the disgrace will not stay away.

HUW. I will go, mother.

He goes out. We see him come out of the Morgan house and start for Bronwen's.

OUTSIDE THE COLLIERY. Morgan and the other men of his shift are approaching the cage. Morgan gets in, and gives a signal to the operator out of the scene. The cage goes swiftly down.

The scene dissolves to the INTERIOR OF THE CHAPEL at night. It is jammed full. All the people are in their best clothes, looking righteous. Conspicuous among them are Parry and other deacons sitting near the front. Mrs. Nicholas sits close to them. At the back, Huw, now washed and dressed, comes quietly in and sits on a rear bench. People near him look at him.

People's heads turn as Gruffydd comes in and walks quietly up to the front. He takes his place at his lectern.

Gruffydd is looking gravely down at his congregation. He begins to speak with quiet deliberation.

GRUFFYDD. This is the last time I shall talk in this Chapel—(*with infinite sadness*)—I am leaving the Valley—with regret toward those who have helped me here, and who have let me help them.

(*His voice takes on an edge of scorn.*)
But for the rest of you—those of you who
have only proved that I have wasted my
time among you, I have only to say
this—

We see the congregation waiting. Huw
looks horrified at the thought of losing his
friend.

GRUFFYDD'S VOICE. There is not one
among you who has had the courage to
come to *me* and accuse me of wrongdo-
ing—and yet, by any standard, if there
has been a sin, I am the one who should
be branded the sinner. Will anyone raise
his voice here now to accuse me?

Gruffydd waits, his eyes looking his congregation up and down, then he goes on
with scorn.

GRUFFYDD. No. You are cowards, too, as
well as hypocrites. (*With a change of
tone*) I do not blame you. The fault is
mine as much as yours. The idle tongues,
the poverty of mind which you have displayed mean that I have failed to reach
most of you with the lesson I was given
to teach. (*His glance sweeps the congregation.*) I thought when I was a young
man that I would conquer the world
with truth. I thought I would lead an
army greater than Alexander ever
dreamed of, not to conquer nations, but
to liberate mankind. With truth. With
the golden sound of the Word. But only
a few of you heard me. Only a few understood. The rest of you put on black
and sat in Chapel. (*His voice becomes
scathing.*) Why do you come here? Why
do you dress your hypocrisy in black and
parade it before your God on Sunday?
From love? No—for you have proved
that your hearts are too withered to receive the love of your Divine Master. I
know why you have come—I have seen
it in your faces Sunday after Sunday as
I have stood here before you. Fear has
brought you. Horrible, superstitious fear.
Fear of divine retribution—a bolt of fire
from the skies.

Gruffydd's face is expressive as he goes on
inexorably:

GRUFFYDD. The vengeance of the Lord.
The justice of God. You have forgotten
the love of Jesus. You disregard His

sacrifice. Death, fear, flames, horror and
black clothes.

He takes hold of the lectern with both
hands. His voice shakes a little as he speaks.

GRUFFYDD. Have your meeting, then. But
know that if you do this in the House
of God and in the Name of God, you
blaspheme against Him and His Word.

He steps down from his lectern and walks
quietly down the aisle. The heads of the
congregation turn to follow. Huw is seen
looking after his friend with tears in his
eyes. Then he rises and follows Gruffydd
out. In the Chapel, people are looking at
each other, whispering. A few, friends of
the Morgans, get up and walk out. Parry
goes up in front of the Chapel.

PARRY. Wait—there is a meeting.

Other people get up to leave. One man
starts to go. His wife tries to pull him back
in her seat, but he pulls away and commands
her to follow him with a jerk of his head.
More than half of the congregation walks
out. The others, the righteous ones, sit
looking after them blankly.

The scene dissolves to A CUTTING IN THE COL-
LIERY. Three or four men are working with
picks against the coal face. A boy pushes
a tram with coal through the scene. Morgan
comes into the scene, stops, raises his head
with an expression of alarm.

MORGAN (*sharply*). Hold your picks,
there.

The men stop work at once, looking at
Morgan. Morgan keeps his head cocked as
if listening for something. He steps forward,
still listening, pushing one of the men out
of his way as he looks up at the face.

MORGAN (*quietly*). Get some props.
(*Then urgently*) Quick, man.

One hurries to obey. The faces of the men
are grave.

The INTERIOR OF GRUFFYDD'S LODGINGS at
night: there is only one lamp lit. Gruffydd's
old Gladstone bag and his tin trunk lie
near the door. Gruffydd is cording the
trunk. He himself is dressed for traveling.
He looks up as Huw comes in. Huw's
manner is solemn and dejected.

GRUFFYDD. Well, Huw, I am glad you have come.

HUW. Thank you, sir. (*Hesitating*) Is—is there anything I can do?

GRUFFYDD. There is. You can do me a great service.

He takes his gold watch from his pocket and hands it to Huw.

GRUFFYDD. This watch my father gave me when I entered the ministry. Take it, Huw. It has marked time we both loved.

Huw's eyes fill with tears.

HUW (*whispering*). No—Mr. Gruffydd.

GRUFFYDD (*sternly*). A service, I said you would be doing me.

Huw fingers the watch gently, looking down at it. Then he looks up at Gruffydd. The tears are now on his cheeks.

GRUFFYDD (*leading Huw to the door*). No need for us to shake hands. We will live in the minds of each other.

Huw stops at the door, looking tearfully up at Gruffydd.

HUW. Won't you see Angharad before you go?

Gruffydd pauses. His face clouds with pain. Then he answers gently.

GRUFFYDD. No, Huw.

HUW. She wants you—

Gruffydd studies Huw for a moment, then decides to tell him why.

GRUFFYDD. Yes. Teacher and pupil we have been—but friends always. (*Quietly*) If I should see her—I could not find the strength to leave her again. (*Pausing a moment*) Goodbye, my little one—with love—

As they look at each other, the mine whistle screams once—a short blast. For a moment it does not register on them. Then it screams again. Both look toward the colliery and hurry out into the street.

The EXTERIOR OF THE COLLIERY in the evening is seen from their point of view. The whistle is going in short alarm blasts. People are coming out of their houses, men and women running up the hill toward the colliery. Gruffydd and Huw exchange a look, then start up the hill with the others. In the STREET, Gruffydd and Huw cross, looking up toward the colliery. They are joined by Beth, who comes out of her house. No word is spoken as they come up the street. Bronwen comes out from her house to join them.

OUTSIDE THE THREE BELLS INN: Dai Bando comes out with some others. He is older now and his years in the ring have nearly blinded him. He holds a mug of beer and is quite drunk. Cyfartha, also holding a mug, follows him.

DAI BANDO (*vaguely*). What is it now—fire—flood—what?

CYFARTHA. A cave-in, they're saying.

DAI BANDO. Well. I will put my mouth to a barrel, I will, and sleep drunk for the rest of my days.

He drinks deep and hurls his mug away.

DAI BANDO (*to Cyfartha*). Come—help me up there—

A MAN. What good if you can't see?

DAI BANDO. I can still swing a pick deeper than any—come on—

He starts out of the scene, his hand on Cyfartha's shoulder.

The crowd of villagers is gathered at the entrance of the COLLIERY. The winding wheel in the close foreground is turning slowly. THE MINE CAGE comes to the surface. Able-bodied miners begin to help off those who have been slightly injured in the collapse below. Other people run into the scene and begin to carry bodies and badly injured men from the cage. Women rush forward as the men are led and carried from the cage, anxiously searching the faces of the living and the dead. One utters a cry of joy as she embraces her husband who is only slightly injured. Another, on her knees, bursts into sobs as she finds her man is dead.

Some miners hurry into the CAGE. The manager, holding a paper, comes into the scene and waves his hand. The cage goes swiftly down. We follow the manager as he moves over, passing the dead and badly injured, checking names on the list in his hand.

Huw, Beth, Bronwen, and Gruffydd arrive at the gates of the COLLIERY ENTRANCE. They are looking anxiously for Morgan, glancing at the faces of the injured men being helped away. Beth goes from man to man, looking anxiously, fearfully for her husband. Gruffydd and Huw are pushing their way through the anxious crowd toward the cage. They come close to the manager, with his list.

GRUFFYDD. Gwilym Morgan?

MANAGER. Not yet.

At the COLLIERY GATES people are still running in from the village. A carriage pulls up, driven by a plainly dressed coachman. Angharad gets out. Her clothes are in contrast to those of the miners' wives and daughters round her, but her expression is the same, for she is one of them. She hurries toward the cage and joins Beth and Bronwen, looking quickly at their faces for a sign of hope. Beth, with her eyes glued to the cage which is coming up, grimly shakes her head. Bronwen puts her arm around Angharad.

The CAGE is rising once more. The manager, Gruffydd, and others push forward to help the men off. The miners who just went down emerge, carrying three badly injured men. All are coughing and choking, with smarting eyes.

Beth, Bronwen, and Angharad are inspecting a new batch of injured men as Gruffydd comes up with Huw. He stops short when he sees Angharad and their eyes meet for a moment. Then Gruffydd turns to Beth.

GRUFFYDD. There is no word of him. I will go down this time.

Beth nods at him bravely.

HUW (bursting out). I will go with you.

Gruffydd shakes his head and pushes him back.

GRUFFYDD. Stay with your mother, Huw.

He looks at Angharad and turns to go. Angharad looks after him with tears in her eyes, fists clenched. Then impulsively she runs after him.

AT THE CAGE, which is filling with men to go down, Gruffydd turns as Angharad comes up to him, oblivious of the people around them. Now we see only ANGHARAD AND GRUFFYDD.

ANGHARAD (her heart in her eyes). Come back.

Their eyes meet with a look which cannot be misunderstood.

GRUFFYDD. Yes.

He looks at her for a moment, then turns and enters the cage. Angharad stands looking after him.

Huw suddenly leaves his mother and runs toward the cage, jumping on it just as it starts to move down. Beth gasps at Huw's action, starts to move forward, but Angharad and Bronwen restrain her.

IN THE CAGE, as it moves down, Huw and Gruffydd are in the foreground. Gruffydd does not say anything to Huw, but puts his hand on his shoulder. A voice speaks up behind him.

DAI'S VOICE. I have been so long swilling behind the tap in the Three Bells that not a button will meet on my trews.

Huw turns and sees Dai behind him, now in mining clothes.

HUW. Dai—

DAI. Who is it?

HUW. Huw Morgan—

DAI (with a grin). Huw, is it? (Then reassuringly) We will find your father —no fear. He is the blood of my heart.

IN THE HEADING: the cage comes to a stop at the bottom. Water immediately flows over its floor, for the heading is already half-flooded. Gruffydd, Dai, Huw, and the other miners step down into the swirling water. They begin to cough, their eyes smarting with the fumes.

HUW (looking at the water). To our knees already—

GRUFFYDD. They will have the pumps started soon. Come.

A miner speaks up.

MINER. Bad air. Watch the lanterns.

The lanterns flicker even as he speaks. Gruffydd pays no attention to the warning, but forges ahead. The others, tense and silent, follow, coughing, muffling their mouths and noses with their hands. The little party, lanterns held high, coughing and choking in the fumes, moves down the heading. They come to a slight rise and move up it. The lanterns once more burn steadily.

DAI (*sniffing*). The air is better here.

Gruffydd suddenly stops short, holding his lantern high.

They are faced with a pile of shale and rubble. The roof has caved in. Dai feels for the fall with his hands.

DAI (*in a whisper*). Are they under this? (*He gropes for a pick.*) No eyes needed here. Give me a pick.

GRUFFYDD. Get some props up here.

One of the men hands Dai a pick. Dai waves the others back and begins to dig into the face of the slide with his pick. Gruffydd and one of the other miners move the slag back with help from Huw and the others. Two of them carry up props, ready to shore up the roof as Dai digs.

The scene dissolves into a long view of the VALLEY. The dawn is breaking over the mountains behind the colliery. Back at the COLLIERY, men, women and children are waiting silently, tensely. Some are asleep, propped up against the wall. Beth, Bronwen and Angharad are still waiting, sitting now. Angharad's head is in Bronwen's lap, and Bronwen is gently stroking her hair.

The scene dissolves to the INTERIOR OF THE MINE. The rescue party has made progress. Gruffydd now has the pick, using it not with Dai's strength, but strongly and accurately. He is weary and begrimed. Then Gruffydd stops, staring. We do not see what he sees but he glances back at the others.

GRUFFYDD (*quietly*). Here is one of them.

The others move into the scene, pull away some rocks and bring a body out from under the slag. Gruffydd kneels beside the body, looks searchingly for a sign of life, and shakes his head.

ONE OF THE MINERS (*looking down*). Evan Lewis he was, God rest him.

Dai takes the pick from Gruffydd.

DAI. Stand back now.

He once more attacks the fall.

The scene slowly dissolves to the EXTERIOR OF THE COLLIERY in daylight. Angharad, Beth and Bronwen are waiting as before. Angharad is sitting upright now. The mine manager and two young girls are passing food and drink. One of the girls offers some to Beth. She shakes her head, still staring toward the cages.

Back in the MINE HEADING, Dai and Gruffydd are pulling another miner from under the shale. This one is alive but very weak. Dai, Gruffydd and Huw bend closely over him.

DAI. Gwilym Morgan?

The miner makes a feeble gesture.

MINER. He was just ahead of me—

He goes unconscious. Gruffydd signals to two of the rescue squad.

GRUFFYDD. Take him up to the top.

Dai again takes his pick and attacks the fall. He is growing tired now, his breath coming in short gasps, but his energy seems redoubled. Dai's face is black with dust and is glistening with sweat, his breath coming in short gasps, his great muscles trembling as he pulls loose a boulder and sends it with a mighty heave clattering back along the heading. Then he grabs in the dark and stops short.

DAI. Huw!

Huw and Gruffydd push forward beside him. Dai holds up a grimy, sodden cap.

DAI. Is this his cap?

Huw grabs it from him, examines it and nods. Gruffydd points to the side of the heading.

GRUFFYDD. Up in a stall road.

Dai spreads his great hands helplessly.

DAI. Clear the main or the stall road?

Huw's face shows his tortured indecision.

GRUFFYDD. There is no way to tell—

But even as he speaks, Dai clutches his arm.

DAI. Listen—

Over the scene, faintly, comes the tap-tapping of a pick. Huw, Gruffydd, and Dai stand listening. They are looking up the stall road. Then Dai swings the pick with new strength.

DAI. Stand away, now.

Dai attacks the obstruction with great blows which make the walls shudder. One of the men speaks up nervously.

MINER. Mind the roof, Dai!

DAI (*gasping*). Devil take the roof. God is with us, and time, too.

Dai continues to shatter the rock, Huw and Gruffydd hurling it back as fast as Dai can pick it out. Then Dai suddenly chokes, gasps, and collapses on his hands and knees. His read rolls drunkenly. Since he is utterly spent, Gruffydd takes the pick and attacks the wall. Suddenly the wall in front of them seems to give way. The pick flies from Gruffydd's hands as its point meets thin air. They have now reached a pocket in the fall. Huw looks toward the hole in the wall, picks up the lantern and worms his way through. Gruffydd follows.

Huw and Gruffydd are crouched double as they move forward in the narrow passage, holding their lanterns ahead of them. They go forward, clearing rubble out of their way. They stop, listening. Gruffydd taps with his pick against the rock. They listen again. There is no answer. Gruffydd taps once more, then feebly there are two more answering taps. Huw and Gruffydd turn and crawl painfully toward the sound. They come to another fall. Gruffydd breaks it up with his pick. Huw clears the slag. They crawl through the hole they have made and stop.

Morgan is lying cramped in a narrow place, cut and half-covered by the fallen rock. Huw and Gruffydd crawl swiftly over to him. Morgan, held as in a vise by the pile of rock, is unable to move, except for one hand, near which lies his pick. But his eyes turn to Huw and a faint smile touches his lips.

Huw is staring down at his father. Gruffydd, after looking down, looks quicly up at the crumbling roof above them, then tries gently to dislodge some of the rocks upon Morgan. The wall shakes ominously. There is a faint rumbling. Gruffydd stops, startled, with his hand on the rock and looks down at Morgan. Morgan cannot speak, but manages to shake his head slightly, warning Gruffydd not to move the rock.

Huw, Gruffydd and Morgan are seen as one of the other men crawls through the hole with a lantern. Huw speaks without looking at him.

HUW. Chris—bring some props, quick.

CHRIS. Have you found him?

HUW (*in a sob*). Yes.

Chris, wide-eyed, crawls backward out of the scene.

Huw lowers himself gently down beside his father, brushing the matted hair back from a cut on his father's forehead, cradling his head in the hollow of his forearm. Morgan smiles up at him. Faintly the voices of the choir begin to sing.

HUW'S VOICE. *I knew if we moved one stone, the roof would fall on him, for the Earth bore down in mightiness and above the Earth, I thought of houses sitting quiet in the sun, and men roaming the streets, and children playing, and women washing the dishes, and good smells in our kitchen, all of them adding more to the burden upon him. But for all the weight that crushed him I saw in his eyes the shining smile that came from the brightness inside him, like a beacon light burning on the mountaintop of his spirit, and I was filled with bitter pride that he was my father, fighting still, and unafraid. I felt him make straight the trunk of his spine as he called on his Fathers, and then I could hear, as from far away, the Voices of the Men of the Valley singing a plain Amen—*

Morgan's head moves slightly. He raises his eyes, looking beyond Huw; then his eyes slowly close. Huw sits quiet, holding him, looking at him. The voices of the choir grow louder over the scene, singing in beauty and triumph.

The scene dissolves to the EXTERIOR OF THE COLLIERY by daylight and we see Beth, Bronwen and Angharad. The voices of the choir come over faintly. Beth raises her head as if listening, then speaks very quietly.

> BETH. He came to me just now. Ivor was with him— (*Bronwen turns to look at her.*) They spoke to me and told me of the glory they had seen.

Angharad looks at her mother, then off toward the cages. Her eyes are shining, sadly, but with anticipation.

IN THE COLLIERY. The cage is coming up swiftly, Gruffydd in the foreground, his head held high, a look for Angharad in his eyes. Dai Bando and other miners, weary and dejected, are in the background. Huw is on the floor of the cage, holding his father's head in his lap, looking straight ahead. The cage nears the top, and light from above appears like a halo, first on Gruffydd, then on the heads and shoulders of the men and Huw and his father.

> HUW'S VOICE. *And my mother was right. Men like my father cannot die. They are with us still—real in memory as they were real in flesh—loving and beloved forever.*

The scene dissolves to a full view of the VALLEY as it was in the beginning, beautiful in the sunset.

> HUW'S VOICE. *Can I believe my friends all gone, when their voices are still a glory in my ears? No, and I will stand to say no, and no again. In blood I will say no. For they remain a living truth within my mind.*

The scene dissolves to a close view of BETH at her stove as we saw her in the first sequence, smiling back at her family at the table.

> HUW'S VOICE. *Is my mother gone, she who knew the meaning of my family, and taught us all to know it with her?*

The scene dissolves to a close view of THE MORGAN BROTHERS: as we saw them in the opening sequence, stepping up to throw their wages into their mother's lap.

> HUW'S VOICE. *My brothers, with their courage and their strength, who made me proud to be a man among them?*

The scene dissolves to a close view of ANGHARAD sitting on the porch at the reception following Ivor's wedding, looking off at Gruffydd. Then we see Gruffydd, singing with the rest, smiling over at Huw and Angharad.

> HUW'S VOICE. *Angharad—is she gone? And Mr. Gruffydd, that one of rock and flame, who in teaching me, taught the meaning of friendship?*

The scene dissolves to BRONWEN, swinging up the hill with the double basket on her hip, as Huw saw her first.

> HUW'S VOICE. *Is Bronwen gone, who proved to me that the love and strength of woman is greater than the fists and muscles and shoutings of men?*

The scene dissolves to a close view of MORGAN standing with his glasses on, calling the attention of his family to Huw's prize for penmanship. Then Morgan is seen giving money to Huw after his fight at the school.

> HUW'S VOICE. *Did my father die under the coal? But, God in heaven, he is with me now, in the heat of his pride in my penmanship—in his quick understanding of my troubles—in the wisdom of the advice which I never found to be wrong or worthless.*

MORGAN AND HUW are seen coming up the hill as they did in the opening sequence. They walk up the crest of the hill, Huw struggling to keep up with his father's great strides. Morgan and Huw stand in silhouette, against the golden light that bathes their Valley, with the wind blowing through their hair.

> HUW'S VOICE. *Is he dead? For if he is, then I am dead, and we are dead, and all of sense a mockery.*
>
> *How green was my Valley, then, and the Valley of them that have gone.*

The voices of the choir swell in mighty crescendo.

The scene fades out.

MAKE WAY FOR TOMORROW

(A Paramount Production)

Screenplay by
VINA DELMAR

Based on the Novel *The Years Are So Long* by
JOSEPHINE LAWRENCE
And a Play by
HELEN AND NOLAN LEARY

Produced and Directed by LEO McCAREY

The Cast

BARKLEY COOPER	Victor Moore
LUCY COOPER	Beulah Bondi
ANITA COOPER	Fay Bainter
GEORGE COOPER	Thomas Mitchell
HARVEY CHASE	Porter Hall
RHODA COOPER	Barbara Read
MAX RABINOWITZ . . .	Maurice Moscovitch
CORA PAYNE	Elisabeth Risdon
NELLIE CHASE	Minna Gombell
ROBERT COOPER	Ray Mayer
BILL PAYNE	Ralph M. Remley
MAMIE	Louise Beavers
DOCTOR	Louis Jean Heydt
CARLTON GORMAN . . .	Gene Morgan

MAKE WAY FOR TOMORROW

PART ONE

The exterior of a large OLD-FASHIONED FRAME HOUSE, covered with a blanket of snow, fades in. It is a typical old house in a typical Eastern hamlet situated a hundred miles or so from New York City. GEORGE COOPER is walking with the assurance of familiarity across the few steps that lead up to its wooden porch, and he waits for an answer at the door after he has announced his presence by using the old-fashioned knocker. His wait is very short, for the door flies open almost immediately, framing MOTHER COOPER who smiles with pleasure at seeing him. George is equally pleased.

GEORGE. Hello Ma . . . Gee it's good to see you! (*They kiss.*) And you're looking so well. . . .

MOTHER (*surveying him critically*). So are you, George. I think you're a mite heavier than you were five or six months ago—You looked a little peaked then, I thought. (*By this time George has entered the house and the door has closed.*)

The FRONT HALL of the Cooper home appears as GEORGE comes in and his MOTHER looks at him happily. He takes off his coat and as he hangs it up with his hat on an old-fashioned rack the scene moves over to the rack, which is already very crowded with coats, and two female hats are sitting on a chair beside it.

GEORGE'S VOICE (*as we survey the rack*). I see they all got here before me.

MOTHER (*coming back into view with George*). Yes—but your father waited for you.

GEORGE (*puckering his brow*). What do you mean, Ma? What's this gathering of the clan all about?

MOTHER. I'd rather Pa told you. (*She leads George toward the sitting room, and George follows. They speak as they walk.*) How are Anita and the baby?

GEORGE. They're just fine. But Rhoda's no baby any more. She's thinking of going to college.

By now they are at the archway that leads to the SITTING ROOM, and here we next see

FATHER COOPER, who sits in a big chair, his slippered feet on the ottoman. He is in a smoking jacket and is puffing his friendly pipe. Also there are CORA, NELLIE and ROBERT. The latter is mixing cocktails in a mason jar. They are all looking toward the archway, toward GEORGE, as he and his MOTHER come in.

GEORGE. Hello everybody.

THE GROUP.
Hello George.
H'ya.
Hello there.

GEORGE (*going to his father*). Well, Pa, you're looking as fit as a fiddle.

They shake hands warmly, GEORGE resting one of his hands on the old man's shoulder, as though to suggest a hug which he is too old and too self-conscious to actually execute.

FATHER. Nice to see you, son. Guess it's the first time since — (*He stops to reflect.*)

GEORGE. Well, it's too long, anyway. I don't know where the time goes — (*Looking at his brothers and sisters*) Guess it's the same with all of us. You make plans and somehow —

FATHER. Well anyway you're here now—

NELLIE (*as George drops in a chair beside Nellie*). It's nice for all of us children to be together again, isn't it? It gives me a cozy feeling. I don't care what you say — blood is thicker than water.

ROBERT. Um — and more unpleasant. (*By this time Robert is finished shaking the cocktails. He has unscrewed top from Mason jar and poured some drinks. He offers one to his mother.*) Age before beauty, Ma.

MOTHER (*shaking her head*). It doesn't go well with standing over a hot stove.

ROBERT shrugs and drinks his MOTHER's drink. GEORGE takes his drink and hands his FATHER one. CORA takes hers. Robert finishes pouring into the two remaining glasses, one full, the other one half full. He proffers NELLIE the glass that is half full.

ROBERT. Sorry, Sis — it didn't come out even . . . (*Nellie gives him a look and accepts the short drink. Robert keeps the full one for himself, and raises his glass.*) What do you say?—A toast to the old house!

FATHER. It's not a bad idea. (*Rather ominously*) There was more to what you said than you think. Ain't there, Ma? (*Mother nods, soberly.*) In fact it's very fitting because —

MOTHER. Oh, I wouldn't tell them now, Pa. Wait 'til after dinner. (*But the young folks are not drinking because they are puzzled what this news is that Pa is keeping from them.*)

FATHER. Why not now? . . . That's why we got them down here.

NELLIE. Is it bad news?

FATHER. All depends on how you take it. (*Mother still wishes Father had not brought up the subject at this time.*)

ROBERT. Let's have it.

FATHER. Well — our old house isn't ours anymore. The bank's taking it over. (*This stuns the children. They look toward Father, unbelievingly.*)

GEORGE. What happened, Father?

CORA. You mean you lost it?

NELLIE. That's awful?

MOTHER. Isn't it?

They all look toward FATHER for more explanation. Father enjoys being the center of the scene. He settles back in his chair, lights his pipe.

FATHER (*between puffs*). As you know — I haven't been working — it's almost four years now . . . That's right, four years, isn't it, Ma?

MOTHER (*to the children, corroboratingly*). Four years fifth of June.

FATHER. And you remember the house was mortgaged to the hilt back in twenty-seven. (*The children nod.*) And with everything going out and nothing coming in, I couldn't keep up with the interest. . . . Well—one day I went into the bank—thought I'd talk it over with Randy Barlow — you remember him. Randy Barlow? (*The children nod impatiently. They want to know the story.*) Randy used to keep company with your mother before I cut him out. (*To mother with a twinkle*) Anyway I haven't got a glass eye!

MOTHER. You shouldn't talk that way about Randy.

FATHER (*magnanimously*). You're right. . . . I've met worse.

ROBERT. Never mind that. What did the rat say?

FATHER. Oh, he was nice enough. He told me we could take our time in moving out. In fact—after I signed the papers, he gave me six months—

NELLIE (*relieved*). Oh! Then there's no immediate rush . . . When are the six months up, Father?

FATHER (*simply*). Next Tuesday. (*All look alarmed. There is a pause while this sinks in.*)

GEORGE. That doesn't give us much time. (*To the folks*) What do you think we ought to do?

MOTHER. (*With a kindly voice*). It's too bad you have to do *anything*.

FATHER. It ain't so serious. (*Lying like a Trojan*) This house was too big anyway for your mother to take care of

—and any little place you could find for us would do.

MOTHER and FATHER look at their children to see their reaction—not suspiciously at all —just hopefully, feeling that the kids will come quickly to their rescue, but the expression of the Cooper progeny is a study. They are all shocked and look rather blank at the suggestion of a little place for Mother and Father.

MOTHER (*breaking the silence*). Well— I have things to do — and anyway it doesn't have to be decided this minute.

She smiles at them sweetly, hopefully, and then walks toward the kitchen, leaving a pained silence behind her. Then the scene dissolves to the DINING ROOM, where the lights have just been turned on and the table is all set for dinner. MOTHER is in the dining room, proudly surveying the table. She straightens a fork or two, then she goes over to a built-in sideboard. Out of the drawer she takes a batch of old napkin rings—the kind that used to be on tables, each with the name of one of the members of the family on it. She looks at them reminiscently—then puts one at each place at the table. While she is doing all this voices drift in from the living room and Ma cannot help getting an earful of what is being said.

FATHER'S VOICE. It would only take a very small house — and if each of you children could contribute a little —

ROBERT'S VOICE. A little what?

GEORGE'S VOICE. Don't try to be funny. This is serious. It's as much your problem as anyone else's.

ROBERT'S VOICE. All right. It's my problem. And what do I use for money?

GEORGE'S VOICE. You could shoot yourself and leave the folks your insurance. (*Mother makes a funny little grimace at this horrible suggestion.*)

CORA'S VOICE. Or at least you could listen to Father's plans.

ROBERT'S VOICE. I *have* been listening — listening for an hour — listening to you birds passing the buck to each other.

NELLIE'S VOICE. We're not passing any buck. We simply wonder where the money's going to come from.

ROBERT'S VOICE. I see. I suppose the Salvation Army gave you that dress?

NELLIE'S VOICE. Father, are you going to let Robert talk to me that way?

FATHER'S VOICE (*as if reprimanding a little boy*). Robert, don't talk to Nellie that way.

By this time MOTHER has completed her last touches in fixing the table. She gives it a final look and then goes into the kitchen while the scene moves into the LIVING ROOM.

Here it is plain that the Cooper family is much more upset than before. FATHER puffs on his pipe while GEORGE paces up and down the room, lighting cigarettes and crushing them out after a puff or two. CORA and NELLIE sit on the divan quite rigid and tense. ROBERT seems the only one at ease. He is sprawled out on his back on the sofa, looking calmly at the ceiling, and taking in most of the conversation like an observer on the side-lines.

FATHER. Certainly seems funny. Two of us took care of five of you—but five of you can't take care of two of us.

GEORGE (*trying to be patient*). Haven't we explained it, Pa? If I ever get a few dollars ahead, Anita and I want to send Rhoda to college. Nellie's told you about Harvey's business —

NELLIE. That's right — it's never been worse.

GEORGE (*looking toward Cora for corroboration*). And if Bill doesn't do any better, Cora told you she'll have to go to work herself. (*Cora nods soberly.*)

ROBERT. So I guess I'm the millionaire of the family.

He pretends to look in his pockets for some money he can't find. There is a pause while Pa puffs on his pipe and the children look at each other helplessly and silently until GEORGE finally breaks the silence.

GEORGE. So the house is out—at least for

the time being. (*Mother enters, at first unseen. George keeps on talking. She stands in the doorway, listening with a patient look on her face.*) Maybe in a short while — say a few months — we might be better able to see our way to it . . . We can talk it over and write to Addie in California—but for the moment— (*He sees his mother and speaks in a different, tender tone.*) Hello, Ma.

MOTHER. Are you hungry, everybody? (*The family forces nods and smiles.*) Well, it won't be long now. (*She looks around serenely.*) Does it look like everything's going to be settled all right?

NELLIE. Everything's fine, Ma.

MOTHER. I knew it would be. (*To Father*) You explained to them—didn't you, Pa—that all we want is just a *little* house? (*Father nods. George gives a deep sigh. Will he have to go over all this again? The others exchange looks.*) —Because this place—I must confess— has been pretty large for just one person to take care of. . . . So in a way it will be a relief for me—

GEORGE (*trying to be gentle*). Ma — there can't be any little house right now. (*This is shocking news to Mother. It takes a moment for it to percolate.*)

MOTHER (*unable to hide her disappointment*). Oh! (*Trying to be brave but finding it hard.*) Well — we kind of hoped that—You see Pa and I thought— (*Her voice is a little choked. It wouldn't take much to bring a tear.*)

GEORGE (*understandingly*). I know.

Everyone looks at MOTHER who stands in the doorway, toying with her apron. The bottom is out of her dreams and she is showing it, although she would love not to.

FATHER (*knowing that his wife is broken up*). Say, young lady, you'd better get back in that kitchen before the dinner's spoiled.

MOTHER nods to FATHER understandingly, turns slowly, and goes out of the room while they all look after her slowly retreating figure. After she is gone there is a silence. No one seems to want to speak.

Then PA (seen in a close-up) takes a few puffs of his pipe as he looks in the direction of the dining room. Then he knocks out the ashes and puts his pipe down, slowly gets himself out of the big chair and walks across the room toward the dining room. He is in the ARCHWAY between the two rooms when he pauses, turns around, and looks at his children.

FATHER (*gently*). Listen. When you're getting all excited about how this thing affects you, remember that no matter what you give us, you'll still have your pride!

He looks around to see if this statement sinks in — then leaves. The younger Coopers are stumped for an answer. It is a hell of a situation and they don't like it any more than the old folks do.

MOTHER is now in the KITCHEN, and her heart is no longer in the meal. She is looking in the oven door at a pan of biscuits which are burned black. The room is smoky as a result. She sighs deeply, takes out the pan and turns to put it on the sink as FATHER comes in. He looks at her, and there are tears in her eyes.

FATHER (*putting his arm around her tenderly*). Now—now—you're not going to carry on like that over a batch of burned biscuits! (*She is in his arms. He takes the end of her apron to wipe a tear out of her eye. He smiles at her but she finds it hard to smile back.*) Anyway, I don't allow tears in my house . . . And it's still my house — until Tuesday.

MOTHER looks at him as a smile returns to her face, and she hugs him. That's what she has always liked about him—his cheerfulness and understanding. He caresses her in return. Then she thinks of the dinner and, still in his arms, puts one of her hands in back of her to lower the gas burner on the range.

In the LIVING ROOM GEORGE is snuffing out another cigarette. Now that the folks are not in the room the four younger Coopers have thrown delicacy to the winds and are saying what they think. There is a feeling of tenseness and aggressiveness in the air. Also they are talking louder.

NELLIE. Well, *something's* got to be done! You can't leave them out in the street!

GEORGE. That's exactly what I'm driving at. You and Harvey have no children and you're in a better position than any of us to take them.

NELLIE. But I won't be rushed into—

GEORGE. I'm not rushing you but we've got to get somewhere.

NELLIE. Well, suppose you took Mother —we'll say for three months, and Cora took Dad . . . That'll give me time to talk it over with Harvey—Maybe we can get a larger place—then we can take both of them. (*And Cora nods toward George that this might be all right.*)

GEORGE (*to Nellie*). Now you're talking.

ROBERT (*from his place on the couch*). Better get Nellie to put it in writing.

NELLIE (*bridling*). You might as well call me a liar!

ROBERT (*with a shrug*). Why not?

NELLIE (*hysterically*). I can't stand it! Here I am making a bigger sacrifice than any of you—

FATHER has entered unobserved. He has heard this. He stands listening in the archway.

CORA (*to Nellie*). What do you mean— bigger sacrifice?

GEORGE (*to Nellie*). You're not doing a thing—until you take them—

ROBERT (*spying his father*). Better get the hose, Pa. There's a dog fight.

All turn toward FATHER COOPER, and there is a silence as GEORGE, CORA and NELLIE tell in glares what they have been saying in words. Pa looks them over. Then he comes into the room, calmly eyes each one of his children in turn, and starts talking with suppressed anger.

FATHER. Listen—if it wasn't a reflection on your mother I'd tell you what I think of you. (*Lowering his voice*) You've been shouting so loud she can hear every word you're saying. (*The younger Coopers feel ashamed. Father goes over to his chair and sits down with a sigh and a shrug.*) Personally I don't care what you decide—or how you decide it—but will you have a little consideration for her? . . . The poor thing has been on her feet since six o'clock this morning, working and planning— She even made one of those Floating Islands with a dozen eggs in it because you kids used to love it so. So will you do me the favor of at least fooling her into thinking it was all worth while!

He looks pleadingly at his children. His words have sunk deeply, and they look sheepishly at him. Then MA appears in the room. She has regained her composure and is bravely making the best of this awkward situation.

MOTHER. Whatever you've been talking about—it'll have to wait—because dinner is ready—what there is of it.

THE CHILDREN.
That's swell . . .
And I'm hungry . . .
Lead me to it . . .
This is what I've been waiting for . . .

Meanwhile GEORGE has put his arm around his MOTHER to lead her into the DINING ROOM, and the others follow. They all enter, speaking together.

THE CHILDREN.
Just like old times . . .
I wouldn't have missed this for anything . . .
Which chair is mine? . . .

MOTHER (*proud of the effect the table has on them*). You can all find your own places. (*The various children find their places by consulting the napkinrings while Mother chats on.*) Addie isn't here—but I wrote and told her that I'd set a place for her anyway.

By now they are seated at the table and there is an empty chair which evidently was ADDIE's old place.

GEORGE. Gee, Ma—wish I'd thought of it when I got here! (*His mother looks toward him inquiringly.*) I'd have asked you to make one of those old Floating Islands—

MOTHER beams and shakes her head happily while GEORGE gives his FATHER a sidelong glance, with almost a wink.

MOTHER (*to George*). What a memory you have! (*With a chuckle*) But it's better than mine. I hadn't thought of making one of those for years! ...

She laughs again and looks toward FATHER COOPER with a twinkle in her eye as though she were putting something over on GEORGE. All the Coopers smile. This little gesture of George's has made MOTHER completely happy again. Then the scene fades out.

PART TWO

A close-up of young RHODA fades in as she is putting the tie-back on a new curtain which is very much in taste. She completes this and then steps back a bit to appraise her own work. It pleases her, and she turns to look over the rest of her BEDROOM, the view moving, as seen through Rhoda's eyes, to the various appointments of the room, which looks dainty, modern and new, and contains Rhoda's dainty bed — until a jarring sight is revealed by the moving scene: GRANDMA COOPER asleep in an old-fashioned bed which she might have brought with her from the old home. And now the view moves up to the wall over Grandma's bed where once more there appears an object incongruous to the taste that Rhoda has displayed otherwise. This bit of incongruity is a picture of FATHER COOPER in an old-fashioned frame. Now the view shifts to Rhoda who is looking up at this picture and shaking her head thoughtfully. She would like to do something about it.

A close-up shows her getting a sudden bright idea and looking to make sure that her GRANDMOTHER is sleeping. She picks up a chair and tip-toes over to the picture. Noiselessly she gets onto the chair and manages to get the picture down without waking Mother Cooper. Then she hurries out of the room with it.

The scene dissolves to the LIVING ROOM OF GEORGE COOPER'S HOME as RHODA comes in with FATHER COOPER's picture under her arm. Now she looks around the room as if studying where she might put it. She is caught doing this by ANITA who appears in the entranceway.

ANITA (*a complete happy understanding between mother and daughter apparent at once*). Well! — what are you up to?

RHODA. I just had a feeling that Grandpa's picture really belonged in here.

ANITA (*amused*). Uh, huh! (*She shakes her wise head at Rhoda and then points toward an old-fashioned chair which is out of keeping with the rest of the living room furniture.*) Yesterday, it was this old ancient antique! Today it's Grandpa's picture! (*She places the picture on the old chair. Rhoda pouts, disappointed.*)

RHODA (*flinging herself into a chair*). But I've got Grandma in my room, and that's enough.

ANITA (*warmly*). I know how you love your room, honey. (*Some of Rhoda's fury dies beneath such soft understanding.*) It's tough on all of us — even Grandma, you know—but it's only for three months — then Aunt Nellie will take her.

RHODA (*a bit shame-faced now*). Okay. I'll have Mamie take these back to my room.

ANITA smiles sympathetically at her, then goes over to a bridge table where four hands of bridge are already dealt out. She sits down and starts to study the hands, evidently working out an intricate play.

RHODA. Bridge class tonight?

ANITA (*while playing her cards*). A mob of them . . . and by the way, I haven't seen any of *your* friends lately. What's the matter?

RHODA. Grandma. She talks the arm off everybody I bring around.

ANITA (*occupied with her cards while she speaks*). I know. I've had a taste of that. But you've got to bring your friends home. I won't have you going out with boys I haven't met.

Intent on her cards, she misses the expression which suddenly crosses RHODA's face. And now GEORGE comes in, evidently home from work.

GEORGE. Hello, everybody.

As he gives RHODA a kiss, he spies the picture of FATHER COOPER reclining on the chair.

GEORGE. Oh! Going to put Pa's picture in here . . . That's fine.

RHODA gives her MOTHER an amused look and leaves while GEORGE tosses his hat on a chair and comes across the room to his wife. He kisses her on the nape of the neck and glances at the cards.

GEORGE. Sluff off the diamond and it's a small slam.

ANITA. I'm trying to make a grand slam.

GEORGE (after they both consider the cards in silence for a moment). Say, what about Mother tonight? She'll be in your way, won't she . . . Maybe she could go over to Nellie's.

ANITA. It would be nice, wouldn't it? (And in reply he goes over toward the hallway.)

GEORGE crosses to the ARCHWAY from the living room to the hallway, steps into the hall and peers up and down to see if the coast is clear, then goes to the telephone and dials a number.

GEORGE (at the telephone). I hope I don't get Harvey. Hello, Harvey. How are you, boy? Put Nellie on, will you . . . Hello, Nellie . . . Say, Anita's having her bridge class in tonight and I know Mother will be bored to distraction. I thought—

The LIVING ROOM IN NELLIE'S HOME: Nellie is at the phone. HARVEY in his bathrobe disappears into the bathroom.

NELLIE (into the phone). Oh, George, I am sorry. But Harvey's bought theatre tickets for tonight. (After a pause) Well, you know how it is. We always

entertain people he does business with. I guess that's what it is tonight.

As she speaks HARVEY re-enters from the bathroom and stands listening. NELLIE smiles to him as she listens to GEORGE.

NELLIE (into the phone). . . . Couldn't possibly take Mother tonight, George.

HARVEY's expression immediately sours as he hears that the conversation is about NELLIE'S MOTHER.

HARVEY (in a loud whisper). Tell him you can't take her any time. (As Nellie gestures to him to keep quiet) What's the use of stalling? Tell him I'm not going to have your parents here.

NELLIE (trying to listen and shushing Harvey at the same time). What's that, George? . . . Oh, well, I would if I could.

HARVEY. You'll have to tell him sooner or later. I married you. I didn't marry your folks.

NELLIE (into the phone). No, I couldn't possibly tonight. Goodbye. (She hangs up.)

HARVEY. I didn't ask mine to live here did I? No roof is big enough for two families.

NELLIE. I know, Harvey, but let's not talk about it now. Who are we taking to the theatre tonight?

HARVEY. My mother.

The LIVING ROOM OF ANITA AND GEORGE: GEORGE is back at the bridge table, watching ANITA play the cards. His brow is furrowed.

GEORGE. Mother won't fit in at all, will she? You don't suppose she'd stay in her room, do you?

ANITA. No, I don't see—

ANITA breaks off as she becomes aware of MOTHER COOPER standing in the archway. GEORGE looks, too. It is hard to say how long she might have been standing there.

GEORGE. Hello, Mother.

MOTHER (a quick smile for greeting).

George, I never heard such nonsense in all my life. Trying to get Nellie to take me—and talking of me staying in my room. (*She says this without rancor, and walks over to them.*)

GEORGE (*uncomfortably*). I only thought you'd be bored.

MOTHER (*sinking into a comfortable chair*). Don't you worry about me. Why, people'd think it was pretty funny if I wasn't around. They'd think you were ashamed of me.

GEORGE has not refuted his MOTHER's words —and ANITA's soft heart cannot bear the silence. There is pity in her glance—but her tone is matter-of-fact and believable when she speaks.

ANITA. George was trying to be kind to you, dear. My bridge pupils drive him mad.

MOTHER. I guess you'll never have to explain George to his mother.

ANITA nods, her mouth twisted in a slightly cynical smile. GEORGE still says nothing. Perhaps he is a little ashamed of how willing his MOTHER is to believe the best of him. Anita resumes her card playing.

MOTHER (*to George*). Another day gone without any word of your father. Do you guess he's all right?

GEORGE. Of course he's all right. We'd hear fast enough if he were ill.

MOTHER (*brightening*). I guess that's true.

ANITA (*to George*). I've got your Tux laid out but I couldn't find your shirt. Did you send it to the laundry?

MOTHER (*as George shakes his head no*). I did. (*As Anita and George both look at Mother surprised*) I took them to the laundry around the corner. They have a sign in their window—"Bring your own bundle and save twenty percent." — And besides I don't think George's shirts look as crisp and smart as they should — and this place does lovely work.

GEORGE (*dryly*). Except that the shirt won't be here tonight.

ANITA. Look here, Mother C. I know you like to do things for George. Well, so do I—and though I don't do much talking about it, I like to run my house too.

MOTHER. I only wanted to help. You're so busy playing bridge—

ANITA. I don't play bridge. I *teach* bridge. There's a difference that you would notice if you had to meet the bills in this apartment.

GEORGE (*to end the argument*). Well— it's very simple—I'll just run down the street and buy another shirt. (*He starts leaving, martyr-like.*)

ANITA resumes her bridge playing and GEORGE goes to the hallway.

MOTHER. I could make sandwiches, couldn't I?

ANITA (*without looking up*). They're coming from the delicatessen.

MOTHER (*after a pause*). It's cheaper to make them at home.

ANITA (*patiently*). Yes, dear, but these are fancy and you—er—we couldn't do as well.

MOTHER (*as Anita figures, Mother watches her, thinking this over*). How fancy can a sandwich be?

ANITA (*ever so slightly annoyed by now*). You'll see.

MOTHER. I make them with toast. Is that what you mean — sandwiches on toast?

ANITA (*deciding to explain and get it over with*). No, dear. These will be shaped like the card suits—hearts and spades and so forth. You see? And the cream cheese fillings will be colored in pink and green and it'll look very pretty.

MOTHER. And probably poison everybody.

ANITA. Oh, we may lose a couple of the puny players.

ANITA is absorbed in her cards again.

MOTHER stands near her, kibitzing, but it is very apparent that she knows nothing about bridge and is only being polite. Through the entranceway comes RHODA with MAMIE, the colored maid-of-all-work. Rhoda points to the picture and chair and Mamie starts toward them just as Anita looks up, sensing the awkwardness of the situation. It just doesn't seem to be the thing to do to make an issue of these things while Mother Cooper is on the scene, so the ever-alert Anita is quick to intercede with:

ANITA. Don't touch that now, Mamie. I'll attend to it later.

MAMIE gives RHODA a surprised look and leaves. The incident has called MOTHER COOPER's attention to the picture. Her following remark is practically the .same as GEORGE's was when he saw the picture, only George was most casual while Mother's exclamations show that she is nothing short of thrilled.

MOTHER (joyfully). Oh! Pa's picture. You're going to put it in here . . . That's nice!

At this RHODA looks slyly at ANITA, and a close-up of Anita shows that she knows she is trapped and so puts on her best smile and nods her head in agreement. She gets up from her chair at the bridge table. Then Anita goes over to the picture.

ANITA. I haven't decided just where to hang it.

MOTHER (to be helpful). Over the mantel, don't you think?

ANITA (picking up the picture, while Rhoda watches her with pretended innocence). I guess it would fit there as well as anywhere.

RHODA cannot restrain a giggle, because, to her, ANITA's sentence has a hidden meaning, and MOTHER COOPER looks at Rhoda, wondering why the giggle? Meanwhile Anita has taken the picture over to the mantel.

ANITA. I'll have to just set it here, until I get a hanger.

She places the picture upright on the mantel shelf, then steps back to survey it, but the picture slips off and crashes to the floor, before she can get back to save it. ANITA is embarrassed, MOTHER COOPER perturbed. RHODA looks toward her mother suspiciously.

ANITA. I'm so sorry, Mother C.

MOTHER COOPER shrugs her shoulders, resignedly. She retrieves the pieces and tries to fit them into the broken frame but to no avail. Meanwhile ANITA happens to catch RHODA's eyes on her. She glares at the girl defiantly as though denying she did it on purpose.

The scene dissolves to the close-up of a BLACKBOARD on which, drawn in white chalk, is a square, labeled at each side with the familiar bridge names—North, South, East, West. The view then draws back to show ANITA standing by the blackboard, lecturing in her best classroom manner. She is dressed in an attractive dinner frock, and as she talks the scene expands further, revealing four card tables set up in the living room with four people seated at each table—with the exception of one, where a vacant chair is being held for Anita.

ANITA. Any bid made subsequently to an opponent's bid is known as an over-call or defensive bid. An over-call may be made on a much weaker hand than an original bid—a fact which the partner must bear in mind.

By the ARCHWAY as ANITA talks, MOTHER enters the room. She has taken pains with her appearance, and has on her best dress, a cotton print which was her Sunday afternoon dress back home. She smiles pleasantly and stands uncertainly, waiting for ANITA to pause. It is apparent that she doesn't realize this is a lecture and seems to expect ANITA to finish her little talk in a moment.

ANITA'S VOICE. As a rule it is inadvisable to over-call with two on a four card suit or to over-call with a no trump bid without a double stopper in a suit bid by the opponent.

ANITA at the blackboard, as she carries on, spies MOTHER standing there expectantly. She hopes the old lady will sit down quietly.

ANITA. It requires a stronger hand to over-call an original no trumper than a suit bid. Do not bid over an original two except with great strength.

She looks again at MOTHER—and begins to realize that Mother intends to stand there till she's recognized. She gives up, but is game about it, and smiles as her voice changes from that of a teacher to a charming hostess.

ANITA. Forgive me if I interrupt myself for a moment. I do so want you all to know my husband's mother.

The guests turn to nod in MOTHER's direction, and Mother nods back. Then Mamie, the maid, enters, pushing Mother's favorite old chair. Anita takes the arrival of the hated chair in good grace. Mother indicates for Mamie to leave the chair right here—which is fairly near one of the tables, and Mother sits down happily. Anita sighs, and returns to the black-board.

ANITA (*her professional tone returning*). Each table has an identical deal. Now suppose we play the hand.

ANITA walks over and takes her chair. The voices of the pupils rise in bidding, after which there is silence in the room, as the play starts. Occasionally a player glances at MOTHER, an alien presence, sitting there with her company smile on, eyes bright and eager. And a close view of Mother shows her looking questioningly from one group to another. Maybe she can have a chance to get in on a little conversation now, but the pupils smile absently at her and direct nothing further at her.

MOTHER (*leaning over and looking into the hand of the woman nearest her*). Funny, but you know, with a teacher right in the family I don't think I could learn to play bridge.

WOMAN (*good-naturedly*). You don't care for cards?

MOTHER. Well, maybe a little hearts. I used to play it a lot with my husband. I always gave him the queen of spades. (*Laughing at pleasant recollections*) We called it "Dirty Dora." (*There is a pause —then Mother peers again at the wo-*

man's cards.) By the way, that's a good heart hand—and you don't have "Dora." Let's see who has. (*She begins to glance into other hands at the table.*)

ANITA at her table looks over — sees what MOTHER is doing, and is aghast. She rises hurriedly, smiling apologetically to the others.

ANITA (*leaving the room*). Excuse me for just a moment.

ANITA hurries down the HALLWAY resolutely to RHODA's bedroom door, and opens it. There Rhoda is just putting on her hat and coat as her mother enters.

ANITA. Honey, you're going to the movies alone, aren't you? (*Rhoda, puzzled by her mother's tense manner, nods.*) If you love me, if I've ever done anything for you that you appreciated even a little bit—for heaven's sake, take your grandmother with you.

RHODA. She won't go. She likes the company.

ANITA. I'll fix that.

ANITA goes out again, leaving RHODA frowning worriedly. Then Anita appears at the ARCHWAY and beckons to MOTHER, smiling sweetly as she does so. Mother gets the signal, rises, smiles on the people at the table she is deserting, and moves over to Anita.

ANITA. Mother C.—Rhoda's set on going to a picture tonight . . . Do you think it's all right if she goes alone?

MOTHER. I should say not!

ANITA. Well—would you go with her? Or is that too much of a responsibility?

MOTHER (*after bringing up five children, to ask her this!*). Anita! I'm glad to help you any way I can. (*This is what Anita has been waiting to hear.*)

ANITA. What a load off my mind! (*She beams at Mother*) Will you tell Rhoda?

MOTHER smiles and nods. ANITA gives her hand a pat and then hurries into the bridge room. Mother smiles after her, then the smile disappears as it dawns on her that maybe Anita's motives were not so pure, but she shrugs and starts down the hallway toward RHODA's room.

The scene dissolves to the FOYER OF A MOTION PICTURE THEATRE where MOTHER, RHODA and a dozen or so others are standing waiting for seats. The large door leading into the main part of the theatre is closed and guarded by an elaborately uniformed usher. Then a closer view of Mother and Rhoda, with the usher visible in the background, shows that the worried expression is still on Rhoda's face. It is clear that something is bothering her, but Mother merely looks about with interest.

MOTHER. My, this must be a good picture. Nobody seems to want to leave. (*Rhoda nods, preoccupied.*)

The big door opens and a man comes out. The usher calls out to those waiting, raising one finger.

USHER. One single.

RHODA suddenly gets an idea, takes MOTHER's arm and steers her toward the door.

RHODA. There's a single, Grandma. You go in.

MOTHER. But where will you—

RHODA. Go ahead. I'll get a seat and meet you after the show.

They have reached the door, which the usher holds open. MOTHER, still concerned over the separation, disappears into the darkness. As the door closes behind her, RHODA looks nervously at her wrist watch and hurries back to the main door of the theatre, the usher watching her knowingly.

RHODA (*now by the ticket taker at the door*). Pass-out check, please.

He gives her the check and RHODA, with a backward glance, hurries on out to the street. The scene then dissolves to the FOYER of the theatre, two or three hours later. A few people come out of the big door, and in a moment MOTHER emerges and looks expectantly about for Rhoda. Since there is no sign of the girl, Mother walks on out to the lobby. Mother now stands pretty squarely in the middle of the LOBBY for a moment or two and finds herself in the way of people coming out, so she moves to a far side of the lobby and stands in a secluded corner. From here she can see the entrance to the foyer and also the street curb. It is the door to the foyer from which she expects Rhoda to emerge and she looks toward it every time someone appears. She glances toward the sidewalk from time to time, too — and is amazed to see Rhoda.

At the CURB, (seen from Mother's angle), a car has drawn up in front of the theatre and Rhoda hops out quickly. There is a hurried exchange of hand-waves between Rhoda and the young man at the wheel— and then Rhoda dashes through the lobby, offers her pass check to the ticket taker and goes into the foyer, not seeing Mother,— who is next seen watching this curious performance with a mixture of amazement and disapproval. Then Rhoda walks up to the elaborate usher, who opens the big door for her. She stands in the doorway a minute, presumably looking at the screen, and speaks to the usher.

RHODA. Does he win the girl in the end?

USHER. Yes.

RHODA. Is it sad in any place?

USHER. Sure. Everybody cries when his pal dies.

RHODA. Thanks. (*And she turns to leave.*)

USHER. Just a minute. (*As Rhoda pauses.*) The cartoon was about Molly, the Mule, and there was a newsreel. (*At this Rhoda gives him a big smile and walks nonchalantly out toward the lobby.*)

MOTHER is standing very close to the MAIN ENTRANCE DOOR as RHODA emerges, and Rhoda regards her a trifle worriedly.

RHODA. Have you been standing here long?

MOTHER. Not very long.

RHODA (*relieved*). I got a seat later than you did and I couldn't miss a thing. He's wonderful, isn't he?

MOTHER (*as they move through the lobby to the street, Mother looking at Rhoda steadily*). I don't know. I only caught a swift glance of him as you got out of his car.

RHODA. As I got—Oh. You saw me.

MOTHER nodding, they turn up the sidewalk toward home.

RHODA. Are you going to tell?

MOTHER. You going to do it again?

RHODA. *No . . .* (*A silence, then:*) Are you going to tell?

MOTHER (*simply*). No.

She smiles tenderly and understandingly at RHODA who squeezes her arm, relieved. They walk along in silence, a better understanding between them than before.

The scene dissolves to ANITA's LIVING ROOM where the bridge game is still in progress as RHODA and MOTHER appear in the archway. Everybody smiles toward them in a preoccupied manner, except for Mrs. MacKenzie who addresses them in friendly fashion.

MRS. MAC KENZIE. How was the picture?

MOTHER removes her wraps and leaves them in the hallway as she speaks. RHODA goes down the hallway.

MOTHER. Oh, it was fine. (*She enters the room, and seats herself in her special chair.*) A little sad in places but it had a happy ending. A young man was taking the blame for a friend of his who wasn't a very strong character—(*There are a few dagger-like glances directed toward Mother, but she is blissfully unaware of them.*)—But the girl believed in the young man — I mean, the nice young man, you know—no matter how black things looked — but I guess I oughtn't to tell you all this. It might spoil the picture for you.

Mrs. MacKenzie smiles absently at MOTHER, having turned her attention to her cards again. And at the VARIOUS TABLES, the game continues quietly for a few moments, though ANITA and GEORGE exchange an agonized glance over Mother's return in as fine fettle as ever.

MOTHER. Well, I guess I should go to bed. (*She squints across the room at the clock.*) It's eleven o'clock. (*She stands up.*) Good night, folks.

MR. DALE (*who has turned to the clock in amazement*). It can't be eleven. I'll have to— (*As he sees the clock*) No, it's just ten.

MOTHER. Oh, is it really? My sight isn't —(*she sits down again*)—what it used to be. If it's only ten I can stay up a while.

The other players' eyes wander from MOTHER to MR. DALE, who realizes what he has done and looks swiftly down at his cards. Just then the phone rings and ANITA jumps up to answer it.

MOTHER'S VOICE. When I was younger I had remarkable sight. People used to say to me, "Lucy, I never did see anyone who could see the distance you can see."

ANITA (*at the phone*). Hello . . . Oh, yes, Father C. Just a moment—

On hearing her husband's name, MOTHER jumps up and the scene moves as she rushes to ANITA, who hands her the instrument.

ANITA. I forgot to tell you. He called while you were at the movies.

MOTHER takes the phone eagerly and ANITA goes back to her table. Mother is of the old school of telephone talkers—the shout school. Just a trifle louder and she would need no phone at all.

MOTHER (*into the phone*). Hello—is that you, Bark? This is Lucy, Bark. How are you? . . . I say, how are you? . . . Oh, that's good.

The BRIDGE PLAYERS fold up their cards and sit deathly still with hostility on their faces at this interruption.

> MOTHER'S VOICE. I was worried about you. Why didn't you write? . . . But you ought to write. You know I worry . . . Oh, I'm fine . . .

ANITA's despair is seen to be complete, and GEORGE seethes inwardly.

> MOTHER'S VOICE. Yes, they're very good to me. They've got some friends in tonight, playing cards. Oh, lovely people, Bark . . . (*Now seen at the telephone*) How is Cora? How are the children? Really? How is Bill? . . . Well, how are you? You know what I mean, how is everything? . . . Oh, oh, of course. Three months isn't long, Bark . . . Bark, it's getting cool now. Don't forget your coat when you go out. And if it rains don't go out at all. . . . I'm as happy as a lark. Of course, I miss you, Bark. That's the only trouble . . . I know you do, but don't forget what I said. We'll soon be together for always . . . Don't you worry, Bark. Only please take care of yourself.

The hostility on the faces of the players, who are now seen watching, has changed to one of frank interest.

> MOTHER'S VOICE. I know, I know . . . But I worry about you. After all, it's our first separation in a long while . . . Are you sure you're all right? Are you positive? . . . No, I won't fret if you're sure, Bark.

Some of the players exchange glances as they are touched by the old lady's concern for her husband.

> MOTHER (*again seen at the telephone.*) And you're not worrying, are you? Please don't worry. Well, Bark, it's been good to hear your voice. It must have cost a lot to call me . . . Well, that's a lot. You could buy a good warm scarf for that. . . . All right, Bark. Good night Bark. Good night my — my dear.

> (*She hangs up the receiver slowly. When she turns back to the living room her eyes are misty with unshed tears. She gives them her company smile despite the lump in her throat.*) I think I'll go to bed now, if you'll all excuse me. Good night, everybody.

The hostility has completely left the faces of the people AT THE TABLES. They are now soft — not a person in the room has missed the pathos of the old lady's situation. The men rise — and there is a respectful chorus of "Good night, MRS. COOPER."

> ANITA. Good night, dear,

> GEORGE. Good night, Mother. (*Mother disappears through the* ARCHWAY *into the hallway*).

In the LIVING ROOM, the men seat themselves. Everyone sits silent for a moment, even bridge forgotten in the contemplation of a human tragedy. Then, the play suddenly mechanically begins anew. The cards slip-slap and the game goes on until the scene fades out.

PART THREE

THE KITCHEN OF CORA'S HOUSE fades in. CORA'S HUSBAND BILL and the two boys, RICHARD and JACK, are seated at the kitchen table, Cora, who looks out of sorts, serving them breakfast. The kids are eighteen and ten respectively.

CORA. I don't see why Father can't come to breakfast without having a special call. He knows what time we eat bre—

BILL (*good naturedly.*) Oh, he'll be along. What's the use of being sore at him. He —

CORA. He gives me plenty of reasons. He broke his glasses again yesterday — and it cost me nine dollars for a new pair — And he can't even come to breakfast unless somebody calls him.

We see CORA'S HOUSE, which as well as the adjoining other two, exactly like it, is a two-story frame place — old, shabby, unprepossessing. Father stands on the porch. He is looking down the street — obviously waiting for something. Suddenly he brightens — hurries down the steps, and meets the letter carrier.

FATHER. Got anything for me today?

LETTER CARRIER. Sure have. Bet it's a letter from your sweetheart. (*He hands letter to Father.*)

FATHER. You never spoke a truer word.

The POSTMAN continues on and goes out of sight, and FATHER turns toward the house, studying the envelope with pleasant eagerness as he ascends the steps, entering the house.

FATHER enters from the hallway into CORA'S LIVING ROOM, holding the letter in one hand, fumbling with the other in his inside coat pocket for his glasses. As he draws them out CORA appears noiselessly behind him.

CORA (*sharply*). Father!

He jumps, startled — and his glasses fall to the floor and smash. He stuffs the letter quickly into his pocket — and looks ruefully down at the smashed spectacles.

CORA. Another nine dollars for glasses, I suppose. You must think I'm made of money. (*She walks toward the kitchen door, and Father follows.*)

CORA'S KITCHEN — as CORA enters. JACK is reaching for another pancake. Cora stops him.

CORA. You haven't got time to eat anymore or you'll be late for school. (*Father enters, and goes quietly to his place at table.*)

JACK. Aw, gee —

CORA. You heard me. (*Jack sulks and goes out.*)

BILL (*looking at her*). What's making you so short with the kid?

CORA (*putting a plate of pancakes and a cup of coffee in front of Father*). Father just broke his glasses again but his rich daughter Cora will replace them, though Heaven knows why he has to have them.

FATHER. Because I can't read without them. That's a good reason, isn't it?

CORA. No, it isn't. What do you read that's so important?

FATHER. Well — news — things are happening.

CORA (*with an air of finality*). They'll happen whether you read about them or not.

FATHER. Yes — but I won't know about them — without my glasses.

RICHARD (*grinning because his grandfather has gotten the best of his mother, getting up to leave*). Say, Ma, what about that two bucks? I need a new history book.

CORA. Well — that'll have to wait now. (*She nods toward Father as the reason, and Richard gives Father Cooper a disgusted look.*)

RICHARD. Aw, gee. (*He goes out sulking. There is a pause.*)

FATHER (*pushing his plate back while Cora eyes him hostilely*). Sorry that every move I make around here seems to rock the very foundations of your house. (*With a shake of his head*) I break my glasses — and you may have to take Richard out of school!

BILL (*interrupting as Cora is about to answer; to Cora*). Sit down and drink your coffee. No wonder you're skin and bone with you fretting all the time.

CORA. I have enough to fret about, haven't I? If it isn't one thing it's another.

FATHER (*to Cora*). You stayed at my house twenty-three years and I didn't do as much yelling —

CORA. You didn't have anything to yell about.

FATHER. Oh, I didn't, huh? You got a pretty short memory, young lady. You aggravated me and plenty, too. I guess we were supposed to be pleased when you ran around with every Tom, Dick and Harry and used to stay out half the night when other girls were home at half-past nine. (*Cora looks very funny — Bill stops eating to look at her, with a peculiar expression — and she avoids his eye.*)

FATHER. You have no answer for that, have you? Of course I knew there was no harm in you when you took that trip to Philadelphia with people I'd never seen or heard of. But believe me, I had to do some tall talking when folks said there weren't any such people. I had to —

BILL (*interrupting*). Say, this is all news to me.

FATHER. That was before you knew her. (*To Cora*) All thunder breaks loose when I smash my glasses but you cost me plenty —

CORA. Oh, Father, that's enough now.

FATHER. Sure, it's always enough when somebody is telling home truths. When I mowed the lawn up the street to get enough money to telephone Ma, you nearly had a fit. You said what will people say but, by golly, I remember even if you don't what they used to say about you. (*Father gets up and leaves, Bill still looking with narrowed eyes at Cora, who has not met his glance once.*)

BILL (*rising*). I have to go now — but I'll see you later. (*Looking at her steadily a moment*) Every Tom, Dick and Harry, eh? (*And he stalks out of the kitchen.*)

The scene dissolves to THE OUTER OFFICE OF GEORGE'S SUITE containing his secretary's desk, a coat tree and a few chairs. MISS BRAMLEY, his secretary, is writing something on a pad, and MOTHER is seated near her with a package in her lap.

MOTHER. I don't want you to trouble him on my account.

MISS BRAMLEY We'll tell him you're here, anyway. (*She has finished writing on the pad, tears off the piece of paper and goes out with it.*)

GEORGE'S PRIVATE OFFICE: GEORGE sits behind his desk, looking very business-like and authoritative. Three men are seated, listening very attentively as he speaks. MISS BRAMLEY enters unobtrusively during his speech, puts a slip of paper in front of him, but he doesn't look at it immediately and goes on talking.

GEORGE. I know from practical experience what I'm talking about, gentlemen. I worked for the Claremont people and I know their burner isn't what you're looking for. On a big deal like yours — (*His eyes stray toward the note.*)

GEORGE is startled by the message,—which reads: "Your mother is here." Then he looks up at the men before him and continues lamely —

GEORGE. On a big deal like yours — that is, on a real big deal like yours, our burner wouldn't do you a bit of good... (*He catches himself, laughs at his own embarrassment.*) I mean to say, the Claremont heater is just what you want

— er — *our* heater is just what you want.

He smiles at the men, and they smile politely back. Then he turns to MISS BRAM-LEY.

GEORGE. Take her to lunch, will you? Some nice place.

MISS BRAMLEY nods and withdraws. George looks back at the men, still a trifle rattled.

GEORGE. Where was I?

THE OUTER OFFICE: MISS BRAMLEY rejoins MOTHER.

MOTHER. I hope you didn't bother him on my account.

MISS BRAMLEY. Oh, no, he wasn't bothered at all. He said to tell you he's sorry about being so busy.

MOTHER. I wouldn't have come at all only it's his birthday —

MISS BRAMLEY. Really?

MOTHER (*amazed.*) Didn't you know? You see — when I got up this morning George — I mean, Mr. Cooper — had already left the house — and since he's not coming home to dinner tonight, I thought I'd bring his present here.

MISS BRAMLEY. I'm glad you told me about his birthday. I'll have to get him something, too. Maybe some handkerchiefs.

MOTHER. That's what I've brought him. Made them myself. Rolled edges and initials. Pretty hard on the eyes.

MISS BRAMLEY. Maybe I'll get him a tie. We could have some lunch and then you might help me pick one out —

MOTHER. I was figuring on having lunch with Geor— with Mr. Cooper.

MISS BRAMLEY. We'll starve waiting for him to finish his business in there.

MOTHER. No, I can wait.

MISS BRAMLEY studies her for a moment, sees she means it and scribbles another little note.

MISS BRAMLEY (*She goes to George's door again*). Excuse me.

GEORGE'S PRIVATE OFFICE:

GEORGE (*To one man*). I'm glad you asked me that question. It gives me pleasure to answer it, though I must admit that if I represented any other oil burner company in America your question would embarrass me.

MISS BRAMLEY has entered during his speech, putting the note before him. George is not glad to see her. He glances at the note, which now reads "Won't go with me. Will wait for you."

GEORGE scribbles something swiftly on the bottom of MISS BRAMLEY's note and hands it back to her. She nods and goes out — but this time through another door leading to the corridor.

GEORGE (*looking back at men*). That question you asked me is one that both Mr. Henning and I are always proud to answer. Er— what was it again?

IN ANOTHER OFFICE: MISS BRAMLEY appears alone, talking into the phone.

MISS BRAMLEY. Mr. Cooper wants to know if you'll take your mother to lunch — if he paid for it?

The scene cuts to ROBERT'S ROOM, an untidy place; ROBERT, in a dressing gown, is speaking into the phone.

ROBERT (*pleased at the thought of some-one paying for his lunch*). You tell my brother I'll be right over.

GEORGE'S PRIVATE OFFICE:

GEORGE. On a great project like yours you can't afford to gamble. That's why I'm so anxious to see you install our burner. Of course, there is a purely selfish reason, too, but primarily —

MISS BRAMLEY enters through the private door, and GEORGE looks up at her hopefully. She slips a new message in front of him, which reads "Your brother is coming at once."

GEORGE sighs with relief and as MISS BRAMLEY goes back toward the outer office, he turns to the men with new life.

GEORGE. Our burner is the greatest brother—I mean burner—in the world and that's the truth!

The scene dissolves to the OUTER OFFICE where Miss Bramley sits at her desk, rapidly devouring a sandwich and a glass of milk as she and Mother converse.

MISS BRAMLEY. I wish you had at least taken a glass of milk. I feel like a pig sitting here eating without you—

MOTHER. As long as Robert's coming to take me to lunch I'll wait for him but I think it's awful about George working during lunch hour.

MISS BRAMLEY (*munching on her sandwich*). How do you like living in New York?

MOTHER. Oh, all right. Of course, I'm not really a stranger to it. Mr. Cooper and I spent our honeymoon here fifty years ago.

A man nearly as old as Mother enters the room. He is obviously prosperous and greatly respected. Miss Bramley swallows a chunk of sandwich fast and wipes her mouth swiftly with a paper napkin.

MISS BRAMLEY. Good afternoon, Mr. Henning.

HENNING. Good afternoon. Cooper in there with the Corbin Block men?

MISS BRAMLEY. Yes, Mr. Henning.

HENNING. Tell him to come out but don't let them know I'm here.

MISS BRAMLEY. Yes, Mr. Henning.

She swiftly writes another note and walks into George's private office. A few seconds elapse during which Mr. Henning waits impatiently. Once or twice his eyes fall upon Mother. When they do she starts a timid little smile but he always looks away again. She is quite impressed by the great Mr. Henning. George enters with Miss Bramley who closes the door behind them. Mr. Henning begins to speak at once and George is a bit distressed, as there has not been time for him to even say hello to Mother. She smiles at him and waves her hand slightly.

HENNING (*excitedly*). Cooper, I got news I wanted to tell you about immediately. Those birds in there aren't going to Claremont. They've been to Claremont. I know the figures Claremont gave them and now there isn't any reason—

GEORGE (*interrupting uncomfortably*). Mr. Henning, I want you to meet my Mother. Mother, this is Mr. Henning. (*He feels pretty miserable about the whole thing and knows now that he debated too long whether or not there should be an introduction.*)

MOTHER (*rising*). Pleased to meet you, Mr. Henning. (*She smiles sweetly.*)

HENNING (*briefly*). Oh, how do you do.

MOTHER. You don't seem like a stranger to me—that is not really. George has spoken so much about you.

HENNING. That so?

MOTHER. Oh, yes. (*To George*) Haven't you, dear? Tell me, Mr. Henning, how is he doing?

HENNING. He's doing all right, I guess.

MOTHER. I'm glad to hear that. I'm sure he always tries his best. That's one thing I'll say for George. He may not be brilliant but he is conscientious.

HENNING (*smiling absently at her and turning back to George*). Cooper, the deal's in the bag if we can offer the same figure as Claremont did with more service and a better guarantee. Washburn has got the whole story. Have you quoted them any—

Now ROBERT walks into the office and George's despair shows upon his face.

GEORGE (*glumly*). Mr. Henning, this is my brother, Mr. Robert Cooper, Robert, Mr. Henning.

HENNING (*annoyed but polite*). How do you do? (*He and George both sense the awkwardness of the family being present while they are trying to transact important business.*)

ROBERT. How are you? (*He turns to Mother, and gives her a hug.*) Well— a man's best friend is his mother.

His very original remark gets no reaction from any of them except Mother, who smiles happily.

MOTHER (*to Henning*). He's the funny one in our family. (*Henning gives no reaction, and there is an awkward pause.*) Well, goodbye, George, and Mr. Henning and (*indicating Miss Bramley*) you, too, dear. (*She turns toward the door.*) Oh, I nearly forgot. (*She comes back and hands George his birthday present.*) Happy birthday, dear. (*She kisses him.*)

ROBERT. I nearly forgot, too. Happy birthday, Brother.

Henning feels it is the thing to do and shakes hands with George — both feeling a little foolish.

GEORGE (*unhappily*). Thanks, both of you. Mother, this is very sweet of you.

MOTHER. Don't mention it. (*She starts for the door and falters.*) Oh. (*George and Robert leap toward her and help her into a chair.*) I felt so woozy there for a second. I guess it was missing my lunch and the terrible trip down here. I changed cars three times and I got lost and—

GEORGE. Oh, Mother, why didn't you take a taxi?

MOTHER. I only had fifteen cents.

GEORGE (*looking off nervously at Henning*). Why, I gave you five dollars just a few days ago.

MOTHER. I know, dear. I sent it to your father. (*Mr. Henning's indignant reaction to this, seen at close range, is pretty noticeable.*)

GEORGE (*almost, but not quite, sunk*). But I meant it for pocket money for you. Why did you send it to Father?

MOTHER. So he could spruce up a little and maybe get a job. (*George is sunk now. He inquires no further and is afraid to look at Mr. Henning.*)

ROBERT. Well, come on, Mother. I'll get you the best lunch money can buy. (*He pantomimes for George to give him some money which George does. Then he links his arm through his mother's and starts off.*)

MOTHER. Well, goodbye, everybody. Thanks for everything and—(*to George*) —happy birthday again, dear.

GEORGE. Oh, thank you, Mother. (*Robert and Mother go out and Miss Bramley, carrying a sheaf of papers, follows them out.*)

HENNING. Nice mother you've got, Cooper.

GEORGE. I certainly have.

HENNING. Well, then why aren't you nicer to her?

GEORGE. What?

HENNING. You heard me just as plainly as I heard everything she said. Quite innocently she gave you away, Cooper. I don't think you're doing your best for her.

GEORGE. I am though. I'm doing my level best.

HENNING. Well, I don't think so. She wrung my heart. She's a very brave woman, Cooper. If my son treated me in such an off hand manner it would kill me. My son doesn't make me chase after him, he chases after me. It's "Father, can I do this for you. Father, can I do that for you." He's wonderful to me—

GEORGE. Yes, I know he is, Mr. Henning. I know your son very well and sometimes I wonder—

HENNING. You wonder what?

GEORGE. If he'd be such a model son if you didn't have five million dollars to leave. (*Hesitating*) But of course he would be. What was it you came in to tell me, Mr. Henning, about the deal?

A new expression came upon MR. HENNING's face when GEORGE brought up the question of his money. Some of his assurance and pride died and he looks a little older and frightened now, perhaps never again will he be as sure of his son as he was a few minutes before.

HENNING. The deal?

GEORGE (*gesturing toward his private office*). The Corbin Block men.

HENNING (*vaguely*). Oh, yes, the Corbin Block men. Well, you know. Sell them if you can. Let me hear how it comes out.

GEORGE starts into his office, in fact he has his hand on the knob of the door when HENNING stops him. Evidently the Corbin deal has not erased the jolt that George's frankness gave him.

HENNING. Say, Cooper—would you treat your mother any better if she had a lot of money?

GEORGE (*simply*). Well, I don't know, Mr. Henning. All I know is that when people have a lot of money their children are awfully nice to them.

He smiles politely at his boss and walks into his office, closing the door behind him, and leaving HENNING bewilderedly scratching his head. George has given him something to think about.

The scene dissolves to the MAIN STREET OF A SMALL TOWN revealing FATHER walking along the sidewalk with purpose. He pauses before an employment agency with a blackboard out in front listing the jobs open for the day. Another man, perhaps half Father's age, also stands reading the listings.

Both are then seen closer as Father squints up at the blackboard — but can't make things out without his glasses. He moves up closer to the board, then further away —but it's no use. At length he resorts to a move his pride had prevented him from doing at once.

FATHER (*to the other man*). Broke my glasses this morning and can't see a thing. Mind telling me what's written on the board?

MAN. Well, it's the lineup of what jobs they got in there today.

FATHER. Any bookkeepers wanted?

MAN. No. Why? Were you a bookkeeper?

FATHER (*indignantly*). I *am* a bookkeeper. (*After a moment's pause*) It doesn't say anything about bookkeepers there, eh?

The man shakes his head, whereupon Father nods politely and goes on his way down the street. Then he is seen entering a SMALL SHOP, on the window of which is the lettering: B. RABINOWITZ, CIGARS AND STATIONERY.

RABINOWITZ' STORE—a small, old-fashioned shop selling newspapers, cigarettes, magazines and penny candy: Behind the counter is an old Jewish man with skull cap and beard. In front of the magazine display are two camp stools, with boxes heaped upon them. RABINOWITZ is waiting on a woman customer as Father enters and, seeming to notice Father only with his subconscious mind, he steps over to the stools, and removes the boxes from one so that Father may sit down. He also hands Father a morning paper—talking to the customer all the while. Father sits holding the paper, and it is plain that Father's arrival here is a daily occurrence and a well-formed habit to both the old men.

RABINOWITZ. Then if you order the paper by the week, Mrs. Carr, I save it for you no matter how many people are asking for it—and that way there is no disappointments.

CUSTOMER. All right. Do you want to be paid weekly or monthly?

RABINOWITZ (*shrugging*). So what difference does it make? If you're honest by the week I guess you can be honest by the month, too—so we make it by the week.

The customer leaves and Rabinowitz walks over to Father by the MAGAZINE RACK. Rabinowitz clears the other chair and sits down. He gestures toward the newspaper he has handed Father.

RABINOWITZ. What do you think of all that stuff about—

FATHER. I couldn't read the paper. I broke my glasses this morning.

RABINOWITZ. What! Again! (*He smiles faintly.*) What did Cora say this time?

FATHER. You should have heard her! Or did you? She hollered loud enough.

RABINOWITZ. And you say it's nice to live with your children.

FATHER. Well, it is, Mr. Rabinowitz, in a way. I hope I didn't give you the wrong impression about Cora. She's a fine girl and I guess I'm pretty bothersome to have around.

RABINOWITZ. Um. (*He nods as though in full agreement, but he has his own opinion about Cora and about living with one's children.*)

FATHER. All my children are pretty fine and I'm proud of them.

RABINOWITZ. I'm proud of mine, too. They leave me alone. They don't need me and I don't need them. I got enough to live from the store and I got Sarah, and I make a little music with my violin. That's all I want from life and I got it.

FATHER. Well, my life is just the same as yours except that I don't have a store, my wife's three hundred miles away, and I can't play a violin.

A small boy enters the shop and RABINOWITZ gets up to serve him.

BOY. I want a penny's worth of jelly beans and a stick of gum.

Rabinowitz moves about behind the counter serving his customer, and as he does so a close view of FATHER shows him taking Mother's letter from his pocket and looking at it. He looks off in the direction of Rabinowitz, considering whether or not he should ask him to read it aloud. Then the boy goes out with his purchase, and Rabinowitz comes back toward his chair, the scene moving with him, whereupon Father hastily stows the letter away.

FATHER. You know — I sometimes feel that children should never grow past the point where you have to tuck them into bed every night.

RABINOWITZ. That's right — when they get older and you can't give them as much as other children—they're ashamed of you—and if you give them everything

— put tnem through college — they're ashamed of you.

FATHER. I guess the world is filled with what you call "Schlemiels" — and somebody has to raise them. (*They both chuckle.*)

RABINOWITZ (*waxing poetical*). Maybe children only follow the laws of nature after all . . . take the birds . . . in the spring they build a nest for their young — they feed them — protect them — and when the little ones are old enough to fly — they're gone — leaving Mama-bird and Papa-bird plenty to schmoose about.

FATHER (*chuckling*). And if they ever happen to fly back over the old nest again — Mama-bird and Papa-bird better look out.

A woman enters the newsstand with a little boy in tow. As Rabinowitz rises to wait on her he pantomimes to Father as if saying "here's an old bird and a young one," and he chuckles.

WOMAN. Have you "Sincere Confessions" for November? (*Rabinowitz hands her a magazine, pockets a coin she gives him, and rejoins Father.*)

RABINOWITZ (*shaking his head*). I'll miss our talks when you go away, Mr. Cooper — but I'll be glad for you to be with your wife again.

FATHER. Thanks — and I'll be with her soon.

RABINOWITZ (*nodding.*) Sure. Sure. (*After a pause*) Maybe you could be with her sooner — and right in this town. (*As Father looks at him questioningly*) There's a lawyer — Mr. Hunter from New York. He just bought the Harrison farm and he'll need caretakers — a man and his wife.

FATHER. Caretakers? Why, that's the same thing as being a servant.

RABINOWITZ (*shrugging his shoulders and spreading his hands in a typical racial gesture*). So it's the same as being a servant.

FATHER. My children would have a fit.

RABINOWITZ. So let them have a fit. You and your wife would be together and you'd be earning your own living again.

FATHER. It's nice of you to suggest it, but you understand, don't you? (*Again Father pulls letter from his pocket, and looks at it longingly. He does not conceal the letter but sits with it in his hand.*)

RABINOWITZ. What difference does that make? Maybe it would be a home for the rest of your life but, say, everybody's got to do what he thinks best.

FATHER. Mr. Rabinowitz, I wonder if you'd do me a favor.

RABINOWITZ. Sure. Why not?

FATHER (*handing the letter to Rabinowitz*). It's from my wife. Would you mind reading it on account of —

RABINOWITZ. Is that a favor, Mr. Cooper?

He settles his own glasses upon his nose, while Father sits with a smile of expectancy on his face.

RABINOWITZ. Ready? (*Seen close as he starts reading.*)

"Thursday night. Dear Bark: I have been thinking of you all day and have wanted to talk to you worse than ever before. They say that you don't miss people so much after a while but I think I miss you more than I did at the beginning of our separation. Do you realize that when you get this letter it will be George's forty-sixth birthday? It seems like yesterday that he was born. We were so happy then that it hurts to remember it (*Continuing to read as Father is seen listening with emotion.*) . . . I hate to give in and sound so weak but you understand me and won't think less of me and this is just between us two."

RABINOWITZ pauses, looks up at Father, who squirms uneasily in his chair. After a second, he nods for Rabinowitz to continue reading.

RABINOWITZ (*continuing*). "Harvey and Nellie know a woman who is in the home for aged women here. They thought it would be nice for me to know her so that I'd have someone my own age to talk to, so Nellie took me there to meet her. Oh, Bark, that home for the aged is so dreary and dismal. It was all I could do not to ask Mrs. Timmons how she stood it. Nellie kept saying how lovely the place was. I thought she said it to cheer Mrs. Timmons up but she kept saying it after we left so I guess she really thought it was nice. (*Rabinowitz gives Father a look, wondering if Father can sense between the lines. Then he continues to read.*) Poor Nellie! She hasn't been herself at all lately. Her doctor wants her to have a complete change. Nellie said Europe. She is very worried — not about herself — but because that would mean she couldn't take us like she promised. But I told Nellie her health comes first. Oh, Bark, dear, I am so sad. What is to become of us? If only something would turn up so that we could be together, I love you so that—" (*He pauses, folds the letter, hands it to Father, avoiding his eyes.*) Maybe you'd better wait till you have your glasses fixed.

FATHER pockets the letter, rises stiffly, and leaves the store. Rabinowitz stares after him a moment. With the back of his hand he rubs at his eyes, then rises, and walks to the back of the store. A curtain divides his business quarters from his living quarters. He parts the curtains and looks into the room beyond.

RABINOWITZ (*calling softly*). Mama. (*Receiving no reply, he calls again with a note of terror in his voice.*) Mama!

Into the living room seen through the curtains, a fat, pleasant-faced Jewish woman emerges from another room.

MRS. RABINOWITZ. So what do you want?

RABINOWITZ (*smiling sheepishly as he stands by the curtains*). I just wanted to look at you, Mama.

MRS. RABINOWITZ (*appealing to the walls*). He wanted to look at me. In the middle of the day with work to be done, he wants to look at me.

RABINOWITZ (*looking at her as though she were the most beautiful woman alive*). Yes, Mama — I wanted to make sure you were here.

And the scene fades out.

PART FOUR

GEORGE'S LIVING ROOM fades in. It is night, and Mother is sitting working on a hooked rug. George and Anita enter from the hallway, dressed to go out, and Mother looks up at them with a sweet smile.

MOTHER. All ready to go? You both look awfully nice.

ANITA. Thanks, Mother C. Are you going to be all right?

MOTHER. Of course I am.

GEORGE. Are you sure? You know Rhoda's going out, too.

MOTHER (*nodding*). This isn't the first time you've left me alone. Go ahead. Don't worry about me.

ANITA (*hopefully*). You'll be busy with your rug, won't you?

MOTHER. Well, no. My head started to ache a little while ago and I'm going to stop. But I'll find something to do. There's always the radio — Oh, it isn't working, is it? I'd forgotten. Well, no matter. You go and enjoy yourselves. Don't even think about me.

GEORGE (*a little crushed*). Well, good night, Mother.

ANITA. Good night. (*She raises her voice and calls.*) Good night, Rhoda!

MOTHER. Good night, children. Have a good time. Oh, Anita.

ANITA. Yes, Mother C.

MOTHER. There's bicarbonate in the house, isn't there? I feel just a mite as though I'd have dyspepsia tonight.

ANITA. There's bicarbonate, dear, in the medicine chest.

MOTHER. Well, just so I know in case it gets bad. Go ahead now. Enjoy yourselves.

They go out looking less exhilarated than when they came from their room. MOTHER sits alone for a moment and then RHODA, fully dressed for the street, enters from the hallway. Rhoda takes out her make-up case, examines herself in the glass and fixes up her lips.

MOTHER (*looking up at her*). I hope that the boy you're going out with tonight gets you home earlier, Rhoda.

RHODA. He's not a boy. He's thirty-five.

MOTHER. Thirty-five? That's a dangerous companion for a young girl.

RHODA. You think so, huh? I guess you haven't been out with any collegians lately.

MOTHER. But at least among boys of your own age, dear, you'll find the one who you'll finally fall in love with and marry.

RHODA. I'm going to look around a bit before I marry. I don't want to buy the first pair of shoes I try on.

MOTHER. But a man doesn't want a girl who's been going around with everybody. Men get together and talk about girls.

RHODA. Sure, and then they all make a dash for the one who's been mentioned most. (*She hands her fur coat to Mother, who holds it for her to slip into.*) Listen, Toots — a man marries the girl he falls in love with. If she's O.K. that's his luck. If she isn't he marries her anyhow.

MOTHER'S VOICE. But a fine man falls in love with a fine girl.

RHODA. Say, I've seen swell fellows walking down the aisle with girls who have done everything but murder. Don't kid yourself about good behavior getting you anything but long quiet evenings at home. (*To finish the subject*) Next lecture at half-past Tuesday. (*She looks in the mirror to fix her hat.*)

MOTHER. Well — I won't be picking on you much longer, Rhoda — You'll have your room to yourself again right soon.

RHODA (*interested*). Have you some kind of a plan, Grandma?

MOTHER (*seen close*). Well, I haven't but your grandfather has. His letter says he is negotiating a piece of business with some lawyer and if it works out satisfactorily everything will be all right.

RHODA (*shaking her head at her Grandma*). Why kid yourself, Grandma? He can't get a job — he's too old —

MOTHER: I still have faith in your grandfather's ability.

RHODA. But that's just fooling yourself. Why don't you face facts, Grandma.

MOTHER. Rhoda, when you're seventeen and the world is beautiful, facing facts is just as slick fun as dancing or going to parties but when you're seventy you don't care much about dancing and you never think of parties anymore and all the fun you've got left is pretending that there ain't any facts to face. So would you mind if I kind of went on pretending?

For once Rhoda hasn't any answer — stands looking at her grandmother. In the silence the bell rings three times as a signal. Rhoda goes slowly and thoughtfully out, and MOTHER bends her head again over the hooked rug.

The scene dissolves into the LIVING ROOM of a FARMHOUSE as MR. HUNTER and FATHER enter from a hallway. Mr. Hunter is expensively dressed and has the extreme poise and self-confidence that money brings. The room is cozy and informal, furnished in Colonial style.

MR. HUNTER. I'm sorry, I've forgotten your name.

FATHER. Cooper's my name, Mr. Hunter. Barkley Cooper.

HUNTER. Oh, yes, Cooper. Sit down, won't you? (*Father sits down and the two old men, in a closer scene, regard each other critically.*)

HUNTER. Where is your wife?

FATHER. She's down in New York with my oldest son.

HUNTER. You understood, didn't you, that I have to have a couple? (*Father nods.*) Yes.

HUNTER. Is your wife a good cook?

FATHER. None better.

HUNTER (*smiling pleasantly*). I feel a little at sea. Usually Mrs. Hunter does the hiring of — (*Father winces and Hunter uses a word other than the one he had expected to use.*) — people. She won't be able to get here for another week and I want the house running on oiled wheels when she comes. (*Father is beginning to look thoughtful. Since Hunter almost used the word "servant" Father's mind has been wandering out of the room.*) For years we've been going to Florida for the cold months and we're a little anxious for winter sports again.

FATHER. Always wanted to see Florida myself. Do much fishing down there?

HUNTER. (*surprised at this applicant's casualness*). Why, yes, I fished practically every day.

FATHER. Caught some big ones I'll bet.

HUNTER. Yes, I did. If you are going to work here I'll be able to show you some pictures of a monstrous fish that my son-in-law landed.

FATHER. That'll be just fine. I'd like to see them. I always say the next best thing to traveling is looking at pictures.

MR. HUNTER is again taken aback at the conversational tone of this applicant; he hesitates a moment, then proceeds, in business like fashion.

HUNTER. Well, let's talk a little business, now. First of all, is your wife healthy? Will she be equal, I mean to running the house without a hitch and coping with all the housework?

FATHER (*miserably*). I figured maybe I could do that and let her just do the cooking.

HUNTER. One person can't do all the housework in a house this size. Besides, she'll have to carry breakfast trays to Mrs. Hunter and if she's sickly or weak —

FATHER. No, she's well.

HUNTER. She'll have to do a little washing too, and Mrs. Hunter is very particular. She doesn't like floors mopped. She wants them scrubbed and she says that the windows must be washed weekly and then there's the oiling of the furniture and the floor polishing and the white woodwork to be washed down. Now do you think your wife could do all that?

FATHER. What do you think I married — a mule? (*Hunter is startled. It takes him a second to get his bearings and when he does his humor comes to life and he laughs.*) I am sorry, Mr. Hunter. I guess I ought to apologize but I spoke without kind of thinking what I said.

HUNTER. How long have you been doing this kind of work?

FATHER. Well, to tell you the truth —

HUNTER. You've never done it before. That's what I thought. (*He looks at Father steadily.*) What happened? A bad investment? (*Father gives him a quick, surprised look.*) They nearly got me in twenty-nine. (*He sighs.*) It can happen to anyone.

FATHER. Well, we weren't in your class, Mr. Hunter, but we had our home and now — I'm kind of bewildered. (*Father passes his hand over his brow.*) I ought to be glad to take your job if you'll have me but when I think of my wife —

when you said scrubbing and about the trays — She's never had to — it's different when it was her own. I guess I'm kind of a fool. (*He gets to his feet.*)

HUNTER (*also rising*). No, you're not. I understand. (*He smiles at Father as they face each other.*) Drop in again some day and I'll be glad to show you those fish pictures.

FATHER (*dully*). Thank you. (*They start for hall.*)

In the HALLWAY, as the two men enter, FATHER is walking almost like a man in a dream. He is confused and frightened, and he looks both; he is not certain why he threw a job away so lightly. Hunter opens the front door, and extends his hand.

HUNTER. Good-bye.

FATHER (*shaking blankly*). Good-bye, and thank you again. (*He goes out. Hunter watches him walk down the path, shaking his head thoughtfully, then closes door.*)

OUTSIDE THE FARMHOUSE: FATHER comes down the steps, down the pathway to the gate. As he does so, a big, pleasant-faced Negro couple, approach. They smile at Father and the man speaks.

NEGRO. Is you Mr. Hunter?

FATHER shakes his head and gestures toward the house. The couple start up the pathway. Father pauses reflectively, realizing the compliment they've paid him — straightens up, feels to see if his tie is in place, and walks proudly out of the gate.

The scene dissolves to THE LIVING ROOM OF CORA'S HOUSE, where Bill sits on a chair near the couch — on which Father is lying, well blanketed. CORA is handing him some medicine which he gulps down, making a wry face.

FATHER. I wish your mother was here — she'd get me on my feet so fast it would make your head swim.

CORA. Now all you've got is a little cold. What's the use of alarming Mother? (*She glances off toward a window.*) Now who on earth is that just drove up?

BILL (*rising and going to the window*). It's the doctor.

CORA (*slightly dismayed*). For heaven's sake! He got here fast enough. Walk out and meet him, Bill.

Bill crosses to the hall, and goes outside. Then he appears outside, hurrying down the steps and to the Doctor's car at the curb.

BILL. Good morning, Doctor. (*The doctor is a young man, brisk and businesslike. They walk back to house together.*)

DOCTOR. Good morning, Mr. Payne. Who's ill?

BILL. It's my wife's father. Just a little cold, I guess — but we wanted you anyhow. We can't afford no long illness and sometimes that's what comes from neglect. (*They enter the house.*)

In the LOWER HALLWAY: As Bill and the Doctor enter, Cora's voice is heard from upstairs.

CORA'S VOICE. Right this way, Doctor.

Bill looks upstairs in surprise, and the Doctor starts up, the scene moving and showing Cora leaning over the banister. Bill joins her at the head of the stairs.

Cora ushers the Doctor along the UPPER HALLWAY — into CORA'S AND BILL'S BEDROOM, where FATHER is seen comfortably ensconced now in a double bed. The doctor puts down his hat, hurrying over to Father as Cora stands near-by. Father is shivering so badly that the bed nearly shakes.

DOCTOR. How long has he been shivering like that?

FATHER. Just since you drove up and she made me run through the house in my bare feet and night-shirt.

DOCTOR. Well, we'll have a look at you.

FATHER. My wife knows more medicine than all of you young doctors —(*The Doctor pops a thermometer into Father's mouth and Father takes it right out.*) — will ever know.

CORA. Put that thermometer back in your mouth. (*Father obeys.*)

DOCTOR (*opening his bag and getting out a stethoscope*). We'll see what his chest sounds like.

BILL'S VOICE (*from outside*). Cora!

CORA. Excuse me. (*And she leaves the room.*)

CORA hurries down the STAIRWAY, and joins BILL in the downstairs hall.

CORA. What do you want?

BILL. I wanted to talk to you when the old man wasn't around. Do you think we ought to send for your mother? I'm kind of sorry for him.

CORA. Well, so am I but we haven't any room—and if she ever got up here it wouldn't be easy to separate them again. (*Bill nods in complete agreement.*) George would try to talk us into keeping her — and Nellie's run out on her bargain—I burn when I think of her— and Addie's doing nothing to help—

BILL. Yeah, what about Addie?

As Cora and he look at each other thoughtfully, Father upstairs raises his voice peevishly—

FATHER'S VOICE. My wife knows how to take care of a cold. Why didn't they send for her instead of you? (*Cora looks apprehensively at Bill, then hurries back upstairs.*)

In CORA'S BEDROOM, the doctor has the stethoscope on FATHER'S bare back.

FATHER. That thing is freezing cold.

DOCTOR (*as Cora enters and watches*). Say ninety-nine.

FATHER. What for? That can't cure a cold. I'd sooner say twenty-three to you but I guess you're too young to know that means skiddoo.

CORA (*as the doctor looks at Cora in annoyance*). Father behave yourself. Say ninety-nine.

FATHER. Darned if I will. I'd feel like a fool. I'm too old to play games with the neighbor's youngsters, Cora.

CORA (*as the Doctor glares at him*). You mustn't mind him, Doctor.

DOCTOR. It's quite all right. Going around as I do, I meet all kinds of patients. (*To Father*) Come on, Mr. Cooper, say ninety-nine.

FATHER. I will not. And I'll bet you haven't got a lot of patients. (*Looking up he catches Cora's eye. He ignores its message—and speaks belligerently.*) Why the heck should I say ninety-nine?

DOCTOR (*victoriously*). Thank you. (*The Doctor takes his stethoscope and hands it to Father to humor him.*) You can hold it yourself—right over your heart, please.

The Doctor turns away from Father, and Father presses the stethoscope against the Doctor's left side. The Doctor listens unconscious of Father's little joke.

DOCTOR (*addressing Cora*). His heart beat's a little fast—but anyone can see he's quite agitated—he gets excited very easily—I'll prescribe something. (*Now he notices Father's little joke. It flusters him to be caught, and he tries to be at ease.*) Oh, it's nothing to be alarmed about. It's normal enough.

FATHER (*to the Doctor*). Maybe you ought to give up your practice and go away.

The doorbell rings and Cora hurries out of the room, leaving the Doctor looking at Father exasperatedly.

In the UPSTAIRS HALLWAY at the head of the stairs, Cora calls down.

CORA. Bill, answer the door! (*As there is no answer. Cora speaks to herself.*) He must have gone out. (*She starts downstairs.*)

In the LOWER HALL by the front door, as CORA enters and opens the door: The caller is MR. RABINOWITZ, but Cora does not know him, and speaks coolly.

CORA. Yes?

RABINOWITZ. Excuse me. My name is Rabinowitz. I have the paper store down on Graham Street.

CORA. We have a boy who delivers them to the house.

RABINOWITZ (*smiling*). I wasn't trying to do business but it's a good idea. You are Cora, no? (*Cora nods.*) Your father speaks of you. It is on account of him I come like this. I heard he was sick.

CORA. A slight cold. It's nothing.

RABINOWITZ. *So.* (*Nodding his head solemnly.*) Could I see him?

CORA (*with the stairway visible in back of her*). It would be impossible right now. The doctor doesn't want him to have any visitors. Visitors would upset him.

The DOCTOR appears behind her, having just come down the stairs. He has heard only her last statement.

DOCTOR. It's more likely that your father would upset the visitors. Certainly they won't hurt him.

At this Cora opens the door wider and grudgingly admits Rabinowitz.

CORA. As long as the doctor says so, go ahead. It's the room right at the head of the stairs.

Rabinowitz starts upstairs, carrying a small can. Cora sees the Doctor is examining his hand.

CORA. What's the matter, Doctor?

DOCTOR (*with dignity*). Nothing to be alarmed about, Mrs. Payne. I was looking at your father's throat and he bit me.

CORA. Oh, I'm sorry he's behaved so badly.

DOCTOR. Keep him in bed and put mustard plasters on his chest.

CORA (*breaking in*). Doctor, this cold of his—and the winter weather coming and everything—wouldn't it be splendid if I could send him to California?

DOCTOR. It certainly would be splendid if you could send him almost anywhere.

CORA. I was sure you'd say that, Doctor. All along I've felt that Father couldn't stand these awful winters and that California would be so much better and inasmuch as I have a sister out there —

DOCTOR (*picking up his obvious cue*). I see—yes—I think it would be best all around. (*Cora looks at him thankfully.*)

In CORA'S BEDROOM: RABINOWITZ is sitting at FATHER'S side, while Father, sitting up in bed, is eating something directly out of the can we saw Rabinowitz carrying upstairs.

FATHER. This soup is wonderful, Mr. Rabinowitz. I can feel it warming me through and through.

RABINOWITZ (*smiling kindly*). Sure, it's wonderful. My wife made it as soon as she heard you were sick. Just like me, she wants you should get well.

FATHER (*with guile*). Now if someone would only call my wife—

RABINOWITZ. Your daughter can take care of you. Maybe she don't want her Mama around kibitzing. (*At this point Cora enters the room, carrying a bowl with some mustard and flour.*)

CORA. Well, I've got to fix your mustard plaster. I think—what are you eating?

FATHER. Some soup Mrs. Rabinowitz made for me.

CORA (*without looking at Rabinowitz*). That's fine, isn't it? The neighbors think I don't feed you properly, I guess. Well, don't eat any more of it . . . How do I know what's in it?

RABINOWITZ. There's nothing in that soup but good chicken. My Sarah makes —

CORA. Your Sarah can mind her own business. I never heard of such a thing. I cook for my father—

RABINOWITZ. You should live until you can cook like my Sarah.

FATHER is looking from one to the other anxiously but he never stops eating the soup throughout the argument.

CORA. Father, don't you put any more of that in your stomach—

FATHER. I'm afraid it's all gone, Cora.

CORA. You mean you ate all that mess?

RABINOWITZ (*jumping up*). Mrs. Payne, never have I been so insulted. For myself I don't care, but Sarah — she worked —

CORA (*angrily*). Well, you can go home and tell her that my father ate every bit of her fine soup. If he's sick tonight, she can come and take care of him!

RABINOWITZ (*walking toward the door*). Goodbye, Mr. Cooper.

FATHER. Goodbye. Thanks for coming and thanks for the—(*as Cora glares and he ends lamely*)—thanks.

Cora begins to mix the mustard plaster, and as she leans over her work Father watches her distastefully. He takes his eyes off her aimlessly and suddenly reacts brightly to something out of sight—and then in the MIRROR OF THE DRESSER (as seen from Father's angle) we see RABINOWITZ' reflection, as he stands in the doorway and uses his hands to pantomine the act of telephoning. Cora, bent over her work, doesn't see what goes on, but Father grins happily, and nods to Rabinowitz who is seen in the mirror smiling, nodding back, then disappearing.

The scene dissolves to ANITA COOPER'S LIVING ROOM where ANITA, wearing a negligee, is pacing nervously up and down. She looks distressed and worried. MOTHER walks in, and watches her with interest and pity.

MOTHER. Why don't you sit down, Anita. You'll have yourself worn to a frazzle.

ANITA. But she could have telephoned or something — (*With sudden terror*) Don't you see that something terrible has happened? I know Rhoda so well that I know she wouldn't do a thing like this willingly. She's met with an accident or— (*Mother looks at Anita but says nothing, and as Anita breaks off she looks away from her and stares thoughtfully at the floor. Anita takes a second to pull herself together.*) I'd better finish dressing in case George wants me for anything.

Anita goes out, but Mother remains, thinking her thoughts, and soon the phone rings and Mother answers it.

MOTHER (*at the phone*). Yes — this is Mrs. Cooper . . . What? Don't talk so fast . . . Oh heavens — you want the other Mrs. Cooper. Wait a minute. Hello—hello!

She rattles the hook up and down, and listens. ANITA reappears, struggling into the negligee. The party on the other end gone, Mother hangs up.

ANITA. Who was that?

MOTHER. Some woman. She called about Rhoda. She thought it was you speaking.

Mother is very distressed. She wants to say something else but does not seem to know how to frame her words, and Anita knows that Mother is holding something back from her.

ANITA (*anxiously*). But what did she say?

Mother looks at Anita gravely, and is about to answer her when she sees that MAMIE has entered and is all ears, whereupon she pantomimes to Anita to go with her into another room where they can be alone, and the scene dissolves into ANITA's BEDROOM where Anita is changing into her street clothes during the conversation.

MOTHER. You don't know how awful I feel about this, Anita.

ANITA. Let's not talk about it if you don't mind. At least not until we know more.

MOTHER. But I have to talk about it. I feel a little guilty, Anita. I feel I'm to blame a little bit. You see, I could have told you and maybe I should have told you—

ANITA (*pausing in her dressing, and looking sharply at her*). Told me what?

MOTHER. That Rhoda wasn't always just absolutely honest.

A close view of ANITA shows her watching MOTHER sharply.

MOTHER'S VOICE (*continuing*). One night when she and I went to the movies she met a boy you didn't know—

ANITA. Why didn't you tell me then?

MOTHER'S VOICE. I promised Rhoda that I—

ANITA (*hotly*). You promised Rhoda? How did you dare to assume such a responsibility?

MOTHER (*meekly; now seen with Anita*). She promised that she'd never—

ANITA. What she promised is beside the point. You had no business keeping her actions a secret from me. She's my child, not yours.

MOTHER. But you were so busy—

ANITA. With my bridge and things — Oh, I thought you'd get to that sooner or later. This is my fault because I try to get a few extra dollars together. If it's anybody's fault I know who to blame. Why did Rhoda stop inviting people to the house? Why did she start meeting them outside?

MOTHER (*bewildered*). I'm sure I don't know, Anita.

ANITA. Well, I'm going to tell you. It was because you liked to entertain them. They were her friends but you did most of the talking.

MOTHER. Anita, I didn't know I was doing anything wrong.

ANITA. But you must have known you were doing something wrong when you deliberately concealed Rhoda's actions from me. You must have known that you were doing what you certainly had no right to do.

ANITA has finished dressing now. She puts her hat on, slips on her coat, and picks up her purse as MOTHER stands watching her. There is silence while this goes on. As Anita turns to leave the room Mother stops her.

MOTHER. Anita, I'm sorry. I want you to know that I understand about everything you've said just now. You're so worried about Rhoda—You don't mean to be nasty—so there's no hard feelings.

But there *are* hard feelings, nevertheless, as is evident when ANITA looks at her. Just then the phone rings.

ANITA. I'll answer the phone from now on. (*She dashes out, followed by Mother.*)

In the LIVING ROOM, ANITA picks up the phone, Mother behind her.

ANITA. Hello . . . Yes, this is Mrs. Cooper . . . Oh. (*Impatiently to Mother*) It's for you. (*She hands Mother the phone and goes out.*)

MOTHER (*at the phone*). Hello . . . Can you speak louder or something? . . . Who are you? . . . Oh, oh, good heavens! . . . Well, is it serious? How much temperature has he got? . . . Is he coughing? She's keeping him in bed, isn't she? Of course I'll come. Right away. I'll leave this minute. Thank you very much . . . Yes. Thank you. Goodbye.

She hangs up, and stands there helplessly, wondering what the first move should be; then she reaches for the phone again.

The scene dissolves to a TICKET WINDOW IN THE DEPOT: Mother is arguing with the TICKET-SELLER, who makes every effort to be kind, but is beginning to look exasperated—for a long line has formed behind Mother.

TICKET SELLER. I can't do it, Madame. I'm sorry, but it's impossible.

MOTHER. But I can give you my son's name and address and he will positively pay you tomorrow. I tried to get my children on the phone — I wouldn't bother you, only my husband is so ill—

TICKET SELLER. So you said—but don't you see there's nothing I can do? This isn't *my* railroad, you know. (*Tears appear in Mother's worried eyes, and the ticket seller softens.*) I'll tell you what. You go over to that counter where it says Traveler's Aid Bureau—(*pointing to a far-off corner of the depot, behind Mother*) — and tell that woman over there your troubles. Maybe she'll help.

The scene shifts to the MAIN OFFICE OF THE HENNING OIL BURNER CO. as the elevator doors open and GEORGE steps out. He does not look as though the world has treated him well today—there is a weary droop to his shoulders and he looks a little old and very tired. He walks through an aisle of typists, who turn and look at him as he passes, noting his weariness. Then he hurries through his OUTER OFFICE. Now in his PRIVATE OFFICE, he goes immediately to his desk, seats himself dejectedly, and sits for a moment with his face buried in his hands. He looks up as MISS BRAMLEY enters with a sheaf of papers which she lays before him, and he looks at them wearily.

GEORGE. Do all these things need my attention?

MISS BRAMLEY. I'm afraid so — (*She pauses and then continues diffidently.*) Mr. Cooper—is there any word of your daughter?

GEORGE (*wearily*). Yes. Her mother and I just took her home.

MISS BRAMLEY. Oh, I'm glad she's safe. (*She looks at him with pity for he is so tired and she has a message for him which she hates to deliver.*)

GEORGE. Anything else, Miss Bramley?

MISS BRAMLEY. Yes, there is. (*She swallows hard . . .*) The Traveler's Aid Bureau telephoned. Your mother is down at Grand Central. (*As George nods wearily*) They said she was trying to get a ticket to go somewhere or other and that she hasn't any money— not even carfare back up town. (*George sinks back in his seat.*) Couldn't I go? You're so tired.

GEORGE. I am tired. Would you?

He takes out his wallet and peels off a bill which he hands her. She starts to leave the office as HENNING, who is all business, comes in. MISS BRAMLEY goes out leaving the men alone.

GEORGE (*wearily*). Yes, Mr. Henning.

HENNING (*brusquely*). About that big order to Billingsgate and Company. It's too important to leave to a man like

Wilkins — so if you'd handle it personally—

MISS BRAMLEY (*returning, wearing her hat and coat*). Mr. Cooper. Your brother-in-law Mr. Harvey Chase is here to see you. (*George looks sheepishly at Henning.*)

HENNING (*disgusted to George*). I'll see you later. (*He dashes out.*)

GEORGE (*wearily*). Show him in.

HARVEY (*coming in as Miss Bramley goes out*). Hope I haven't picked the busiest day to come in. It would be just like me to pick the worst possible day.

GEORGE. That's right.

HARVEY (*helping himself to a seat*). Well, it's a little difficult to begin. After all I'm not really a relative and this is a family affair but I said to myself last night "After all," I said to myself, "I'm Nellie's husband."

GEORGE. And?

HARVEY. Well, I said to myself, "I wonder if George would mind a few suggestions from a man who isn't really a relative."

GEORGE. Don't forget after all you're Nellie's husband.

HARVEY. You're right. That's just what I thought. So I came here to make a suggestion.

GEORGE. So?

HARVEY. It's about your mother's situation. You don't mind, do you? Of course, it's none of my business—

GEORGE (*as Harvey flounders*). Look, it's none of your business. You're Nellie's husband—You came here with a suggestion—Those three things we have definitely established. I'm a busy man. Let's get on. What's the suggestion?

HARVEY (*at close range*). Well, it costs five hundred dollars, so you can see the women aren't abused. They get good food and good beds—

GEORGE'S VOICE. What costs five hundred dollars? Who gets good—

HARVEY. The Cadwallader Home for Aged Women. Your mother'd meet other old ladies there and make friends and she'd be happy.

GEORGE (*now seen with Harvey; evenly*). You're suggesting that my mother go to an old ladies' home?

HARVEY (*innocently*). Yes. I'd put up the five hundred dollars.

GEORGE (*with quiet rage*). That's awfully decent of you, Harvey.

HARVEY. Yes, isn't it? I—I didn't mean that. I didn't mean it was decent of me, I only meant I was trying to do the proper thing, you know.

GEORGE. What suggestion have you regarding my father? Would you like to have him buried alive?

HARVEY (*laughing boisterously*). That's funny. Bury him alive. That's real good, George. (*His eyes suddenly fall on George's unsmiling, angry face and he is sobered.*) But seriously, George, I thought if I took care of your Mother, the rest of you could get together and sort of — that is kind of take care of your father.

GEORGE. Thanks awfully, Harvey, but we can take care of Mother, too.

HARVEY. Now you're sore. You always get sore, George, at the littlest thing I say. It was the way I said it, I guess. I always have trouble expressing myself.

GEORGE. Well, I don't. Get out. (*As Harvey looks at him in astonishment.*) Get out! What's the matter with you? Can't you even understand words? (*He stands up and Harvey retires swiftly to the doorway.*)

HARVEY. All right but if you change your mind, you know where to reach me. (*Then he goes out without waiting to see if George has a reply.*)

The scene dissolves to the LIVING ROOM OF GEORGE AND ANITA, in the evening. GEORGE is pacing up and down, looking even more tired, and depressed than he did in the afternoon. MOTHER sits on the edge of a chair. RHODA is slumped into another chair, sulkily.

GEORGE. Mother, why don't you quit worrying? Didn't Cora say that his temperature is normal now?

MOTHER (*miserably*). It may be up again tomorrow and, anyway, your father doesn't like his doctor.

GEORGE. Well, his temperature is normal tonight.

MOTHER. It may go up again tomorrow.

RHODA (*very bored—moving restlessly in her chair*). This is where we came in.

GEORGE (*concluding the scene*). Don't be borrowing trouble, Mother, I'm going to see if Anita wants anything. (*Mother stands up as if she'd like to go along with him.*) I'd better go alone. (*He walks out toward the hall — Mother watching him, a bit hurt.*)

In ANITA'S BEDROOM, ANITA is lying in bed, crying softly into the pillow. GEORGE enters, sits down beside her, and gently puts his arm around her.

GEORGE. Now Honey, stop it. You're just going to make yourself ill.

ANITA (*turning to look at him*). I can't seem to help it. (*She dabs at her eyes.*)

GEORGE. Now, now, Mrs. Claire promised not to mention Rhoda's name in the case and everything's going to be all right. (*Anita looks up at him with the expression of a woman who understands her husband. She sees that he is talking silly, optimistic prattle to cheer her up and she knows that it would be ungrateful of her to reveal the fact that he's not deceiving her.*) I'm just worried about you. I've never seen you give in so completely,

ANITA. But everything's gone wrong. I care as much about your Mother as a daughter-in-law can, but—

GEORGE (*surprised at the mention of his mother*). What has Mother to do—Oh, she told me something about a little argument. Forget it, dear.

ANITA. There's no place for your Mother to go since Nellie backed out and Rhoda positively refuses to bring her friends home while she's here. What are we to do?

GEORGE. I don't know, dear.

ANITA. Look at this business today. It couldn't have happened if Rhoda had been entertaining at home like she used to do. I used to know her men friends and I knew what was going on, but now — (*Anita turns her face into the pillow again, and George sits by her looking very worn and serious.*)

GEORGE. I know. (*He pats Anita gently.*) I remember Rhoda used to have the house full of her friends.

ANITA (*turning and speaking desperately*). And she has to have those friends again, George. She has to. Don't you see? What happened today is just a sample. She'll move away from us next. She'll get a job and an apartment of her own.

GEORGE. Those things happen, don't they?

ANITA. And we're helpless to stop it. We can't turn your mother out in the streets and still she's chasing Rhoda away from us. Oh, isn't there anything we can do?

GEORGE (*dully*). I don't know. Maybe. Maybe there is something. Stop crying, Anita. We'll see.

And with this the scene fades out.

PART FIVE

The LIVING ROOM OF GEORGE AND ANITA fades in on a late afternoon. The radio is on pretty loud, playing some hot jazz while RHODA dances to it with evidently nothing else on her mind. Finally Mother appears in the doorway, and Rhoda sees her.

RHODA (*without letting up in her dancing*). I'm sorry Grandma, did I wake you up?

MOTHER. That's all right . . . any mail?

RHODA, still dancing, points to the table on which there is some mail, and MOTHER goes to it. A close-up shows Mother at the table, looking over the mail, rather casually, until she comes to a certain letter. She looks at it for quite a long time. We see the LETTER, which is addressed to GEORGE COOPER, and in the left-hand upper corner is printed the place from which it came, in bold type: CADWALLADER HOME FOR THE AGED.

MOTHER shakes her head in sober thought. It is all she can do not to open the letter. She finally puts it back on the pile unopened but all too well she senses its contents. All the while out of sight, the radio has been "jazzing it up" and RHODA can be heard chiming in with the music of the radio. Then Mother mechanically goes over to a chair, sits down, and starts to knit. Her mind is still on the letter.

As ANITA and GEORGE come in from the street they seem in fairly good spirits — much freer than previously. Mother nods toward them.

ANITA. Good evening, Mother C.

GEORGE. Hello, Ma.

RHODA (*with a fresh salute to her folks*). Hi!

George sits down while Anita goes over to the table where the mail is lying. She picks it up to glance over it while Mother watches her out of the corner of her eye. She comes to the Cadwallader letter, walks over, and hands it to George. George opens the envelope and reads the letter while Anita watches him and Mother pretends to be busy with her knitting. Rhoda is still enjoying the radio, her actions and youthful nonchalance unconsciously heightening the drama that is going on. George finishes the letter, slips it into his pocket and nods to Anita as if to say that all is okay, and Anita sighs in reply. George looks toward his mother, who pretends to be engrossed in her knitting.

ANITA (*to Rhoda*). Rhoda . . . (*She pantomimes for Rhoda to leave with her and Rhoda is about to start.*)

GEORGE (*to Rhoda*). Turn that darn thing off, will you?

Rhoda turns off the radio and goes out with her arm around Anita, leaving George in the room with his Mother. There is a pause while Mother knits.

MOTHER (*to break the silence*). I spoke to your father today, George. He told me he's perfectly well again.

GEORGE (*after a long strengthening drag on his cigarette*). But we want to keep him well, Ma, and it can't be done in this climate. Cora's doctor told her that Father positively has to go where there's no hard winters and—and—on account of Addie living in California and—

MOTHER. He's going out there to live?

GEORGE. Well, it's for his health, dear.

MOTHER. Yes, of course. I want him to be well. There isn't anything I want more, unless it's that you children should be healthy and happy.

GEORGE (*swallowing hard*). Cora wanted Addie to take both of you, but Addie says she can't.

MOTHER. As long as she'll take Father, that's enough. I'm strong. I can stand anything. (*After a pause*) Well—he'll be leaving soon.

GEORGE. Yes, I guess so.

MOTHER. Maybe I'll be able to see him to say—goodbye.

GEORGE. Of course, dear.

He turns to an ashtray to put out his cigarette, then lights another one immediately. He gets up and starts to pace the floor, puffing nervously at his cigarette.

MOTHER, seen alone, suddenly knows that the hour of doom has struck. Everything has become painfully, blindingly clear to her. For a moment she looks frightened and heartsick—but while GEORGE smokes, she gets herself under control. Then they are seen together, Mother watching him closely. She is ready.

GEORGE (*sitting beside her on the couch*). Mother, I've something else to tell you, too.

MOTHER (*after studying his unhappy face*). There's something I'd like to tell you first.

GEORGE. Let me while I can, Ma. Tell me later.

MOTHER. It's simply this. I don't want to hurt your feelings, but I haven't been too happy here. It's lonesome in this apartment all day with everyone gone. Would you mind terribly if I decided to leave you and go to the Cadwallader Home?

GEORGE (*thunderstruck*). Mother!

MOTHER. It's a fine place and I'd make friends my own age—

GEORGE. Mother, I—

MOTHER. Let me finish, dear. Once I thought your father and I would be able to get together again. I see that it's never going to turn out that way. And so I want to go to the home. (*He looks at her with his heart in his eyes—as Mother smiles bravely.*) I'm glad that's over. I hated to tell you as much as you would have hated to tell me anything like that. (*After a pause*) Oh, there's just one thing more, dear. I'd like to stay here till your father's on his way to California. He's funny about some things, you know. He'd never believe that the home's a grand place. He's a little old-fashioned, your father is. Those places seem terrible to him.

(*After pausing*) Don't let him know I'm going. Tell Nellie and Cora and the others that he must never know. This is one thing that has to be handled my way.

GEORGE. Yes, Ma. Anything you say.

MOTHER. Let him think I'm staying on with you and Anita. You can always forward my letters to the home. It'll be the first secret I've ever had from him and it'll seem mighty funny. (*She looks at George but he does not meet her gaze. He is too miserable. Mother is silent for a time, but when she speaks it is with the same lightness she has used throughout the scene.*) I think I'll go to bed now if you don't mind, dear. I'm very tired. (*She stands up and stoops to kiss him on the forehead.*) Here's another secret just between us two. You were always my favorite child. Goodnight. (*George, weak and looking beaten, stares up at her.*)

Mother stands, straight and strong, with courage in her eyes and on her smiling mouth. She turns and starts from the room. But she sways a little as she reaches the archway. George sees this—leaps to her side, and puts an arm about her. Mother smiles a little apologetically.

MOTHER. Floor's a little slippery, I guess.

In the HALLWAY, George leads her gently to her room, and she goes in without a word. As the door closes, George enters the room next door—his and Anita's BEDROOM. Here Anita is standing at the window as he enters. She turns and looks at him expectantly. He goes over to her and sinks his head in her arms.

GEORGE (*his weary back turned*). Well, that's that. As the years go on you can look back at this day and always be very proud of me.

Anita mechanically strokes his head but the tender touch of her hand is belied by the strange light in her eyes which of course George cannot see. She is thinking perhaps that she would have regarded him more highly in the years to come if he had had backbone enough to insist that his mother remain with them. Then the scene fades out.

PART SIX

RHODA'S ROOM fades in, revealing MOTHER, her hat and coat on, standing there watching a couple of furniture movers take out her old-fashioned bed. As the bed goes out, MAMIE comes in.

MAMIE. You wanted to see me, Mrs. Cooper?

MOTHER. Yes, Mamie—but I didn't want to speak to you with those men listening. I'm going now—

MAMIE (*being awfully gay*). Down to meet the bus, huh? (*Mother nods.*) An' won't you be glad to see your husband?

MOTHER. Oh, yes, indeed. When I come back for my valise tonight you won't be here, so I wanted to say good-bye to you now and thank you for—

MAMIE. Land sakes, Mrs. Cooper, there's nothing to thank me for.

MOTHER (*handing her a little package*). I knitted you a scarf, Mamie. It'll be something to remember me by and I'll remember you because you were always so nice to me. (*Mother looks around the room slowly, her eyes bright with unshed tears.*) Well, good-bye.

MAMIE. Good-bye, Mrs. Cooper — and thanks very much. Good luck to you.

Mother smiles at her and goes to the hallway. Mamie stands by Rhoda's door and watches as Mother walks slowly down the hall and out the main door of the apartment. Then Mamie shakes her head mournfully and stands for a moment, lost in deep and confusing thought.

The scene dissolves to a SMALL PARK in the late afternoon, and MOTHER and FATHER are seen walking along the little winding by-paths. As they come closer, their conversation becomes audible. Father is consulting his watch.

MOTHER. What time does your train go?

FATHER. Half past nine.

MOTHER (*brightly*). Then will you stop looking at your watch when we have five whole hours?

This dissolves to another PATH in the PARK, where the two are walking.

MOTHER. I figure that everyone's entitled to so much happiness. Some get it in a lump and others have it spread thin all through the years.

FATHER. The whole trouble is I was a failure. You wanted me because I knew a couple of jokes and could play the mandolin, but there wasn't much room in the business world, Lucy, for that kind of a fellow.

MOTHER. I've never regretted my choice and I won't let you call yourself a failure. I think *I* slipped up somewhere, though I tried always to be a good wife and mother. But if I'd been all that I thought I was, things would be different now.

They stroll on out of earshot, and then the scene shifts to still another PATH IN THE PARK.

FATHER. You're right. We did have a lot out of life, didn't we? We had a nice home and our health. It was fine, Lucy.

MOTHER. Sure, it was. Our trouble was we expected too much. We wanted everything.

FATHER. I'd settle now for one little room and you.

MOTHER. But California will be so good for your health.

FATHER. You sound like Cora. So far I've never been west of Philadelphia and she's got me sick of orange groves and palm trees already.

MOTHER. Oh, Bark. (*She laughs and he watches her amusement with pleasure.*)

FATHER. Guess I can still make you laugh, Lucy.

They reach the gateway of the little park and walk out to the sidewalk of a STREET.

As they walk, Father notices that Mother is limping a little.

FATHER. What's the matter?

MOTHER. New shoes. That's the worst of getting all togged out — you can't wear your old shoes.

FATHER. I'm sorry I walked you around so —

MOTHER. Got to break them in sometime and I wanted you to see me in my new winter things. Don't they look nice?

FATHER. I never saw any clothes yet that didn't look nice when you were wearing them.

They are now walking by a row of stores. Suddenly Father pauses and Mother follows his eyes to — a CHEAP HABERDASHERY SHOP in the window of which is a card which reads: MAN WANTED. And now they are standing before the haberdashery shop.

FATHER. Wouldn't it be a joke on California if I was the man?

He yanks at his necktie, smooths down the front of his coat, and walks into the shop. MOTHER walks to the window and stands looking in. After a few seconds, she draws back away from the window and with what is for her unaccustomed swiftness, retreats to the curb — and even has her back to the shop as FATHER emerges. Wordlessly they continue their walk down the street. They now round the corner of another street, an impressive avenue with a bank building on the corner. A poster in the bank window attracts their attention, and they pause to look at it. We see THE POSTER with MOTHER AND FATHER standing before it. It shows an old couple, beautifully dressed, sitting at a fireplace in an elaborate room, listening to a handsome radio. The poster is captioned:

"SAVE WHILE YOU ARE YOUNG, AND YOUR OLD AGE WILL BE SECURE."

FATHER. This is a fine time to tell me. (They move on down the street.)

THE WINDOW OF AN AUTOMOBILE SHOWROOM comes into view, with a good, medium-priced car glittering brightly with newness.

MOTHER and FATHER approach, and pause to admire it.

FATHER. That's the kind of thing I always wanted to buy for you.

MOTHER. What on earth would I do with it? It would be useless to —

FATHER. Sometimes I wonder if it isn't smarter to buy useless things than to put your money in so-called solid investments.

In the AUTOMOBILE SHOWROOM, two salesmen are standing idly about. They see the old couple through the window.

FIRST SALESMAN. See that old couple out there? It's always those kind have a million bucks salted away. Well — I'm going out and pry them loose from some of it. (He picks his hat up from a nearby chair and walks out whistling.)

At the AUTOMOBILE SHOWROOM WINDOW: Father and Mother do not notice the salesman as he comes through the door. He walks up to them very politely, raises his hat, and smiles most engagingly.

SALESMAN. Good evening. I noticed you admiring the car and I wanted to point out a few features of it you might have missed.

MOTHER. It's a beautiful automobile.

SALESMAN. Yes, isn't it? We of the company are very proud of it. As I looked at you through the window I said to my friend in there, now those two people know a fine piece of work when they see it.

FATHER. (pleased). We were admiring it all right.

SALESMAN. And no doubt you were thinking how foolish it is to let all the beautiful things in life escape you.

FATHER. (awed). I did say something of that kind.

SALESMAN. Of course you did, Mr.—

FATHER. My name's Cooper. Barkley Cooper.

SALESMAN. It's a pleasure to meet you, Mr. Cooper. (He smiles at them both.)

Mrs. Cooper, I presume. My name's Ed Weldon. You don't know me from Father Adam but you can judge something of my character when I tell you that I am permitted to represent this automobile. The car sells itself. When I tell you people that it's the mechanical wonder of the age, you'll be surprised, but when you ride in it and feel how smooth a car can run, you'll be astonished.

As this speech is being spoken, a beggar comes along and moves close to them. The salesman casually drops a quarter into the beggar's hand and quickly looks to see how FATHER and MOTHER like his generosity. Their expressions show that they're pleased with him.

MOTHER (*smiling gently*). I don't expect we'll get to ride in it.

SALESMAN. Why not? Have you a little time right now? (*Father and Mother exchange wondering glances.*) I'd just like you to see what a peak of perfection automotive engineering has reached. My car is at the curb. It's exactly like this one.

Mother and Father look toward the curb, at which there is an attractive sedan.

SALESMAN'S VOICE. How about it?

MOTHER (*appearing with Father and the Salesman.*) Oh, we really couldn't. We were going to dinner at our son's house.

SALESMAN. I'd be glad to take you there.

FATHER. No, you needn't bother about that.

SALESMAN. Well, a ride up the Drive perhaps?

FATHER and MOTHER look at each other again. Each is waiting for a definite word or action from the other.

MOTHER (*smiling at the thought of so pleasant a prospect*). We really couldn't, Bark.

FATHER. Well, I don't know why not.

SALESMAN. That's the proper spirit.

He takes Mother's elbow and the three of them walk down to the curb. The salesman opens the rear door and Mother gets into the car. Father follows. They lean back against the upholstery.

MOTHER (*in the rear seat*). Isn't it awful? The children are waiting for us.

She looks around with happy appreciation at the appointments of the car. The window next her is rolled down — and she sticks her head out in an effort to look down at the wheels.

FATHER. Let 'em wait.

SALESMAN. I think I'd better put this robe around you.

He leans into the car and carefully tucks the automobile blanket about them, Mother is charmed by this attention. As the salesman gets into the driver's seat, he turns back to address them.

SALESMAN. Now notice the way this car drives. It's positively the smoothest thing on wheels. (*He starts the motor — and they roll away.*)

This dissolves slowly into ROBERT COOPER'S APARTMENT in the late afternoon. Not much of an apartment, to be sure, but it has a combination living-dining room and the gateleg table has been opened and is set in the middle of the room. The table is ready for dinner with glasses and china all set out. GEORGE is reading the evening paper. ROBERT is lying on a couch talking on the telephone and NELLIE and CORA, both with dish-towels pinned on them in place of aprons, move in and out adding things to the table.

GEORGE (*glancing at his watch*). I wonder what's keeping the folks?

CORA (*coming in from kitchen*). I thought they'd be here long before now. I hope nothing's happened to them.

ROBERT (*bitterly*). What could happen to them that's any worse than—

NELLIE. They could have been hit by an automobile.

ROBERT. The crack still goes.

CORA. That roast'll be just right in about fifteen minutes. I hope they're here by then.

NELLIE. I hope so too. When I cook a dinner —

GEORGE. Who cooked a dinner?

NELLIE. I did. Cora only helped and I burned my hand and splashed fat on my dress because that bonehead — (*indicating Robert*) — has neither servants nor aprons. Anyhow the dinner will be good.

CORA (*walking to window*). I wish they'd come.

The scene cuts to the moving SEDAN at dusk. MOTHER and FATHER are sitting back in the car enjoying the ride tremendously. They are on Riverside Drive and they enjoy being part of the steady stream of traffic. The SALESMAN is minding his driving and they are luxuriating as though they were the rich couple in the bank advertisement being driven by their chauffeur. The look of peace and enjoyment is plain on their faces.

MOTHER. Pretty nice, isn't it, Bark?

FATHER. Yes, indeed.

MOTHER. Warm enough?

FATHER (*nodding*). Are you?

MOTHER. Oh, yes, I'm very comfortable. Only I hope the children aren't worried about us. We really should —

FATHER (*looking out at the river*). Do you remember we took a ride up the Hudson when we came to New York on our honeymoon?

MOTHER (*fully aware that he has purposely ignored her remark*). Of course I remember.

FATHER (*seen closer with her*). I always intended that we'd do it again some day, but we didn't get anywhere much after our honeymoon, did we? I guess you and I haven't been away from home together since — (*He pinches his brows thoughtfully — then looks at her in amazement.*)—our honeymoon.

MOTHER (*shaking her head*). It doesn't matter, Bark, I had the children.

FATHER. Yes — and I ran out to chat with the men in the evenings, but you

stuck home and sewed and — and — It kind of hurts now to think how selfish I was.

MOTHER (*brightly*). I'm trying to recall the places we went on our honeymoon. We went to the theatre twice I remember.

FATHER. Three times. We went to a matinee once.

MOTHER. So we did, and we went to the museum. Do you remember?

FATHER. Sure I do. I wonder if the Hotel Vogard's still standing?

MOTHER. Oh, yes. I asked George about it when I first came to live here.

FATHER. It was a real nice place and real nice people owned it, too. (*Then with sudden inspiration.*) Say, Lucy, what about going down to take a look at it?

MOTHER. Why, Bark, we couldn't.

FATHER. Why not? Who's to stop us?

MOTHER (*hesitatingly*). The children —

FATHER (*to the salesman*). Say, Mr. Weldon, do you know where the Hotel Vogard is?

SALESMAN. Down on lower Fifth Avenue.

FATHER. Do you suppose you could take us there?

SALESMAN. I certainly could. Say, how do you like this car's performance? Isn't it smooth and —

FATHER. It's perfect, Mr. Weldon. Never rode in a better automobile in my life. (*The salesman's face lights up with assurance of an immediate sale.*)

This dissolves to the VOGARD HOTEL as the car drives up. A liveried doorman opens the car door. The hotel is very expensive looking, though it still retains the charm of other years.

MOTHER and FATHER step out, staring, enchanted, at the hotel.

MOTHER. It's good to see it again.

The SALESMAN steps out too. Of course, he

is unaware of the memories the hotel has awakened in the old folks.

SALESMAN. Do you think you'd be interested in buying a car like this?

FATHER. In buying one? Oh, no, we couldn't buy an automobile but, say, we appreciate the compliment.

SALESMAN. Why not? A car is no longer a luxury. It's a necessity.

MOTHER (*wonderingly*). Were you expecting to sell us an automobile? Oh, I am sorry we took your time. We thought you were really proud of the automobile and sort of wanted to show it off. But we didn't touch anything in it—

The SALESMAN looks from one to the other of the old people. He is convinced by MOTHER's sincerity. He takes the situation like a sport and grins engagingly.

SALESMAN. I'm glad you enjoyed it. It was a pleasure for me, too. I hadn't a thing to do and as a matter of fact you were right in the first place — I only wanted to show the car off.

MOTHER. That makes me feel better. Goodbye. And thank you.

SALESMAN. You're more than welcome. Goodbye. (*He gets into the car, and drives off.*)

FATHER (*scarcely noticing the salesman's departure.*) Goodbye. Well, let's go in. (*They start toward the entrance.*)

THE LOBBY OF THE HOTEL: MOTHER and FATHER enter. A hat-check girl approaches them. Father hands her his hat automatically. Mother eyes the girl and the whole layout.

MOTHER. Been a lot of changes. They've done away with the fountain. (*The girl looks at her in amazement, as though to say — "Fountain? What fountain?"*)

FATHER. You know I'd like to see Mr. Norton again. You remember we told him we'd come here the next time we were in town.

MOTHER. Do you think he'd remember us?

FATHER (*testily*). Of course he would. Didn't we all drink wine together the night we left for home? (*To the hat check girl.*) Ask Mr. Norton to come here a minute.

GIRL. I'm afraid I don't know any Mr. Norton.

FATHER. You must be very new here. Mr. Norton just owns this hotel, that's all. Tell him Mr. Cooper wants to see him. Barkley Cooper. I've known him fifty years. (*The girl walks away looking very perplexed.*)

MOTHER. Come on, Bark, let's look around. We've only got a few minutes—

FATHER. I suppose Mr. Norton'll find us.

As MOTHER and FATHER move through the LOBBY, their eyes are interested, wondering at the many changes. They pause by a bright attractive sign over an archway. It reads: BLACK AND WHITE ROOM.

FATHER. I wonder what's in there?

MOTHER. A reception room fixed up in black and white, I guess. Let's look. (*They enter timidly through archway.*)

MOTHER and FATHER appear in the archway of the resplendent BAR ROOM, and stand transfixed. A few people look at them unconcernedly. Since no one shows surprise or hostility, Father is encouraged.

FATHER. Like a little drink of something, Lucy, to warm you up maybe?

MOTHER. I don't think so — but you go ahead.

FATHER (*in a low voice*). Ladies are drinking here. A little glass of sherry wouldn't do you a bit of harm. (*They move toward the bar.*)

As MOTHER and FATHER come close to the BAR, a pleasant-faced barman looks up at them and smiles—and their last feeling of shyness evaporates immediately.

BARMAN. What'll it be?

FATHER. Well, now —

BARMAN (*helpfully*). Cocktail, maybe?

MOTHER. Yes, Bark, you try a cocktail. I bet you'd like it.

FATHER. How about you? You'd like one yourself. That's why you're egging me on. (*To Barman*) Two cocktails.

BARMAN. What ki — Say, how about old-fashioneds?

FATHER. Why not? Two old-fashioneds it is — for two old-fashioned people.

The scene dissolves to ROBERT'S APARTMENT. GEORGE and CORA are standing at the window. ROBERT is now glancing over the evening paper. NELLIE comes out from the kitchen. It is evening now — the lights are on.

NELLIE. That roast'll be ruined.

GEORGE. I'm not worried about the roast. I'm afraid something happened to Mother and Father.

ROBERT. If it didn't, Nellie will never forgive them.

CORA. I should have brought them right up here.

GEORGE. Of course. That was the plan.

NELLIE. Has he any money on him?

CORA. He has his ticket and fifteen dollars to buy his meals on the train. I wanted to keep the ticket and the money but, no, Bill gave it to him.

NELLIE. You don't suppose they could have been kidnapped. (*George looks exasperated at such stupidity.*)

ROBERT. Imagine how glad they'd be to find somebody who really wanted them.

The scene dissolves to the HOTEL VOGARD BAR. There is a fine looking middle-aged man with FATHER and MOTHER. He is smiling in friendly fashion and Father and Mother are smiling, too, pleased with the warmth of his personality.

FATHER. I should have known the minute I walked in that Elmer Norton didn't own this hotel any more. That fountain was his pride and joy. He never would have —

MANAGER. The Crenshaw Hotel Chain has owned the Vogard since shortly after the war, but that doesn't mean, Mr. and Mrs. Cooper, that we aren't just as glad to see you as Mr. Norton would have been.

MOTHER. I think it was just awful nice of you to bother to see us.

MANAGER. Not at all. The hotel's friends are my friends. You'd better hurry along with that drink, Mrs. Cooper. Your husband and I are one up on you.

MOTHER. Well, you just go ahead. I kind of like to linger.

FATHER (*looking at her affectionately*). Having a good time, Lucy? (*She nods, and Father turns to the manager.*) You wouldn't think, would you, that she was the mother of five children?

MANAGER (*with pretty convincing surprise*). Not really?

FATHER. She's a grandmother, too.

MANAGER. Well, that I just can't believe.

FATHER. It's kind of hard even for me to believe. Fifty years go by pretty fast.

MANAGER. Only when you're happy. How many children have you?

FATHER. We have five of them.

MANAGER. I'll bet they've brought you a lot of pleasure.

MOTHER is about to nod complacently but she is shocked by FATHER's swift answer to the Manager's remark.

FATHER. And I'll bet you haven't any children.

MANAGER (*smiling*). Well, I'm sure it was Mrs. Cooper then who made fifty years go so swiftly.

FATHER. Yes, it was. Best thing I ever did marrying her. Randy Dunlap was courting her at the same time I was, but I looked like the best buy, so she took me. (*He laughs as Mother reproaches him with her eyes.*) Randy Dunlap's the banker in our town now. I got his girl but he's got my house.

MOTHER. Oh, Bark, how you go on.

MANAGER. I guess you're ready for that drink now, Mrs. Cooper. (*He signals the barman.*)

MOTHER. I never thought I'd be sitting here drinking like this. You know ladies didn't use to and we were such babies in the big city. You'd never believe it if I told you — Why, the first Thursday we were here on our honeymoon we started for the museum —

FATHER. That was Wednesday. (*To Manager*) Why do women always get the week days mixed up? (*To Mother*) It was Wednesday. I remember it well. We started out — (*He turns back to the Manager and Mother silently forms the word Thursday — so that the Manager and not Father can see it.*)—and got lost right away.

MOTHER (*as the barman puts the drink before her and she sips it at once*). But it was Thursday. Look, Bark, we got married on —

FATHER. Tuesday.

MOTHER. No. It was to have been on Tuesday but we postponed it so my sister could get there, don't you remember? She got snowbound up in New Hampshire. She was visiting that girl with the buck teeth who married that fellow — you know, he was related to the people who had a daughter down south. Well, the point is we were married Wednesday instead of Tuesday.

FATHER. That isn't the point at all. We were trying to settle what day we went to the museum.

MOTHER. Oh, that was a Thursday.

MANAGER. I'm sure it must have been, Mrs. Cooper. I wonder if you'd excuse me now? If you want anything just ask for it and let me know if you don't get it.

FATHER. It was nice of you to spend so much time with us.

MANAGER. It was my pleasure. Goodbye. (*He smiles engagingly and hurries away.*)

MOTHER (*picking up her drink and taking another little sip*). My, those cocktails are good.

FATHER (*anxiously*). Turn around here, Lucy. Let me look at you.

FATHER (*As Mother turns wonderingly toward him.*) You're not getting tipsy, are you?

MOTHER. Why, Bark!

FATHER. Say — Betty Botter bought a batch of bitter butter.

MOTHER. I've never been able to say that and you know it. (*They both laugh.*)

FATHER. You know, Lucy, I often wonder what I'd do if I was a young fellow nowadays. I guess I'd have to be a bachelor. There's no girls around that a man would want to take a second look at.

MOTHER. Oh, Shucks, Bark, there's plenty of mighty pretty girls.

FATHER. None as pretty as you were and, do you know what? (*As Mother shakes her head*) You've held your looks better than anyone I know. Right now I don't see anybody who looks any better to me than you do. (*He casts his eyes down the length of the bar.*) No, sir, I still fell sorry for Randy Dunlap.

MOTHER. You're sweet, Bark.

FATHER. So are you.

They look into each other's eyes and they are alone. The bar, the people and the laughter are forgotten for MOTHER and FATHER. There is nothing in the world for them except the lovelight they see in each other's eyes. There are smiles on their faces as they capture a moment out of time to hold for the rest of their years. Then the spell is broken at last.

MOTHER. Bark, we should be going.

FATHER. Why?

MOTHER. Because the children are waiting for us. Nellie is cooking dinn —

FATHER. How many dinners did you cook for her? How many times did we wait for the children and when did they ever stop doing something that pleased them so that they could hurry home to us?

MOTHER. I know, dear, but —

FATHER. We're not going to Robert's. (*Mother looks shocked and amazed.*) We're not going. We're having fun Lucy, we're together and certainly we have some rights.

Father looks around — and the scene dissolves to a TELEPHONE BOOTH, with Father at the phone and Mother standing directly outside the booth. The door to the booth is half open so that she can hear everything that he is saying.

FATHER. Hello, Cora . . . Yes, this is your father . . . remember me? (*He gives Mother a wink, and she is astounded at his attitude. She doesn't know whether to smile or what.*) No, there hasn't been an accident — except that we're having a good time . . . . Your dinner? . . . . Well, isn't that, too bad! . . . . No, I'm not fooling — we're not coming to dinner . . . . You heard me! . . . Well — how often have you children disappointed your mother and me? . . . Oh, ain't that too bad! — I'm sure you and Nellie went to a lot of trouble cooking it. . . . it sounds swell — a roast, huh? . . . And everything's all ready? . . . And you don't know what to do with it. . . . Well, I'll tell you. (*He pantomimes to Mother to excuse him, closes the door to the phone booth so that mother and the audience cannot hear him. Mother watches him proudly.*)

In ROBERT'S APARTMENT, a close-up of CORA shows her shocked at the telephone. Then back at the BOOTH, Father hangs up the phone, comes out, and links his arm in Mother's.

FATHER (*very gallantly*). Shall we join the others, Mrs. Cooper?

The scene moves with them into the main dining room. The head waiter comes up and starts to show them to a table.

This dissolves to ROBERT'S APARTMENT where the four Coopers are looking rather stunned. George is walking up and down uneasily.

GEORGE. Let's not go to the train. They don't want us.

CORA. But we have to say goodbye to Father.

ROBERT. George is right. Let them alone. It would be a kindness that we can all do for them. It won't cost us a cent.

NELLIE. I feel terrible.

ROBERT. Funny, isn't it. All along we've known that probably we're the most good-for-nothing children ever raised but it never bothered us particularly till we found out that Father knew it too.

This dissolves to the MAIN DINING ROOM of the HOTEL VOGARD where FATHER and MOTHER are seated at a table with demitasses before them and empty plates upon which their dessert was served. There is also a bowl of fruit on the table. Father and Mother are very happy and their eyes sparkle with the joy of the moment as an orchestra plays slow, sweet waltz music.

FATHER. That's the best dinner I ever had that you didn't cook.

MOTHER. It ought to be good. (*She looks around and lowers her voice.*) Those dinners cost three and a half dollars apiece. Seven dollars for two. It said right out on the bill of fare.

FATHER (*carelessly*). It's worth it.

MOTHER. I hope Cora gave you plenty —

FATHER. Of course she did. Want to dance?

MOTHER. Why, Bark, I never thought about it. It would be nice, wouldn't it? (*They rise, and move toward the floor.*)

MOTHER and FATHER appear on THE DANCE FLOOR, and do a few turns of an old-fashioned waltz — but the orchestra concludes the waltz number. There is a moment's pause, then it recommences with a sultry rhumba number. Mother and Father pause, look at each other helplessly, look at the intricate maneuvers of the few other couples on the floor — and return disappointedly to their table.

The leader of the ORCHESTRA, however, has seen the old couple — and he watches them as they walk off disappointedly.

By their TABLE, the WAITER is just leaving, having cleared away their dishes and left two small cordials. They sit down, and are so intrigued by their cordials that they forget their disappointment over the short-lived waltz.

MOTHER. Should we drink these, do you think?

FATHER. Well, I guess they weren't brought just to tantalize us. (*Tasting his*) It's good. Tastes like catnip.

MOTHER (*tasting hers*). I never tasted catnip — but I'll take your word for it. (*They laugh a little, and drink again.*) I suppose it's proper to take a little drink like this after dinner.

FATHER (*finishing his*). If it isn't, I've made a terrible mistake.

By the ORCHESTRA, the leader motions to one of his musicians to step down and lead for a moment. Then he slips off the platform and disappears into a door nearby. He appears next in a small ANTEROOM off the dining room, and goes swiftly to a pile of music resting in a cabinet — runs through it hurriedly — finally comes to something that pleases him, and goes out again.

FATHER AND MOTHER at the table are laughing.

FATHER. I forgot that till you just mentioned it now.

Suddenly the strains of "Sweet Genevieve" are heard, and they look at each other, almost holding their breath.

MOTHER. We could dance to that, Bark.

FATHER. We did often enough. (*They rise, and go to the dance floor.*)

MOTHER and FATHER start to dance — graceful, very old-fashioned. Several other couples who are dancing now mark time and watch Father and Mother — their old

faces bright with happiness as they sway to the familiar melody. They draw nearer to the orchestra platform, and as they do so, there is a moment's pause in the music — then a newer waltz is heard.

ORCHESTRA LEADER (*at a microphone on the platform*). This is Carlton Gorman, saying good evening to you from the main dining room of the Hotel Vogard. Put aside your cares, for here is sweet music . . .

MOTHER (*watching interestedly with Father*). Oh, that's how they broadcast. What he's saying is going all over America. Just imagine.

ORCHESTRA LEADER'S VOICE. The familiar strains of "Moonbeams on Manila" tells you once again that it is nine o'clock and all is well.

But at this the happiness dies out of the faces of the two old folks. They look at each other quickly — then walk wordlessly toward their table.

AT THEIR TABLE, Father signals the waiter, who presents the check. Father glances at the addition and puts ten dollars on the tray. The Waiter walks away and Father helps Mother into her coat. The Waiter returns, and Father takes some of the change, leaving some of it on the plate. They walk toward the door, their backs held straight and stiff, their pride refusing to let them droop in the presence of strangers.

The scene shifts to the TRAIN STATION where MOTHER and FATHER are following a redcap who is carrying Father's valise. There are many people in the station — but Father and Mother see none of them. They walk along, each wrapped in thought. As they reach the track entrance, Father shows his ticket and they pass. On the PLATFORM by the waiting train the redcap hurries ahead, rushes into one of the cars and reappears without the valise. Father hands him a coin and the redcap leaves. Then Mother and Father move to the car.

FATHER (*gloomily*). Well, I guess this is it.

MOTHER. It looks like a very nice train. I hear they serve good food on trains.

(*As Father nods*) So don't starve your-self. Eat well. It'll help build you up. (*They stand looking at each other.*) Give my love to Addie and tell her to take good care of you.

FATHER. You'll probably see her yourself soon. I'll get a job out there, Lucy, and I'll send for you right away.

MOTHER (*drawing her breath in quickly and looking into Father's eyes*). I don't doubt that, Bark. You'll get a job. Of course you will, but it might not be right away on account of you having to build yourself up first.

From somewhere now comes the ominous voice: "All aboard . . . "

FATHER. Good-bye, Lucy dear.

MOTHER. Good-bye, darling.

They kiss, and he starts to board the train, Mother watching after him longingly. He gets a premonition of some kind and turns around on the step to face her again.

FATHER. In case it should happen that I don't see you again, it's been very nice knowing you, Miss Breckenridge.

MOTHER. And in case I don't see you— for a while—I want to tell you that it's been lovely. Every bit of it. The whole fifty years. (*They stand looking at each other.*) I would sooner have been your wife, Bark, than to have been anybody else on earth. I was always mighty proud of you.

FATHER (*gravely*). Thank you, Lucy.

Now there is a pause—an agonizing silence . . . all that can be said in this short time has been said. Mother merely looks at Father and tries bravely to smile.

MOTHER (*her voice none too steady*). Get going, will you, Bark?

FATHER nods, smiles fondly at her, and starts into the train. In a second he appears at the window—he sits down and waves out to her. She waves back—they smile and nod to each other.

VOICE. All abo—oard!

Suddenly the train gives a lurch—and it is serious now. There is just time for one quick wave. FATHER's face moves on out of sight. She doesn't quite get to throw that last kiss—for the train is gone. She stands with her back turned, her eyes straining into the distance; she stands so for a few moments. There is the soft, low howl of the train whistle coming from the distance; the train is out of sight now. MOTHER turns, squares her shoulders and walks, alone and lonesome, down the platform, toward her future. Then the scene fades out.

LITTLE CAESAR

(*A Warner Brothers Production*)

Screenplay by
FRANCIS EDWARD FARAGOH

Based on the Novel *Little Caesar* by
W. R. BURNETT

Directed by MERVYN LeROY

***

The Cast

"RICO" BANDELLO (Little Caesar)	Edward G. Robinson
JOE MASSARA	Douglas Fairbanks, Jr.
OLGA STASSOFF	Glenda Farrell
THE "BIG BOY"	Sidney Blackmer
POLICE SGT. FLAHERTY . .	Thomas Jackson
PETE MONTANA	Ralph Ince
TONY PASSA	William Collier, Jr.
ARNIE LORCH	Maurice Black
SAM VETTORI	Stanley Fields
OTERO	George E. Stone

LITTLE CAESAR

PART ONE

A FOREWORD appears on the screen.

> *The first law of every being, is to preserve itself and
> live. You sow hemlock, and expect to see ears of
> corn ripen.—Machiavelli.*

The EXTERIOR of a FILLING STATION fades in; it is night. A closed car drives up to the filling station, the proprietor of which can be seen inside. A slight figure gets out of the car while the driver stays at the wheel with the motor running. The light in the station goes out as there are two or three shots in the darkness. The slight figure unhurriedly emerges from the station and steps into the front seat of the car. The door slams, the motor roars, and the car careens out of the service yard into the street on two wheels.

This dissolves into a close-up of a CLOCK FACE with a hand turning back the clock hands from 12:05 to 11:45, and as the view draws back the clock is seen to be at the end of a LUNCH WAGON COUNTER. Caesar Bandello, alias Rico, drops silently from the counter on which he has been kneeling to tamper with the clock and turns to Joe Massara, his friend, who is seated in the foreground at the counter:

RICO (*with a nod of his head toward clock*). How's 'at?

JOE (*grinning his appreciation*). Got to hand it to you, Rico. The old bean's working all the time.

Now a sleepy cook appears from a compartment behind the range, yawning widely.

COOK. What'll it be, gents?

JOE (*amiably*). Spaghetti and coffee for two.

RICO (*without directly looking at the Cook*). Forget my coffee. (*Silently, drawling, addressing Joe pointedly*) I don' wan' it to keep me awake. It's pretty late.

Joe nods his head significantly, indicating that he has understood Rico's purpose.

JOE (*carelessly*). Oh, can't be so terrible late. (*To Cook*) Got a watch on you, bo?

COOK (*indicating the clock*). Eleven forty-five.

JOE (*also looking there*). That means quarter to twelve in any language. (*Playfully poking Rico in ribs*) Well, how 'bout that java?

RICO (*shrugging*). All right. Seein' as how it ain't midnight yet.

The Cook nods, then goes out of view, following which a close-up shows Rico picking up a discarded Chicago newspaper and becoming interested in a story. He looks with disgust at a cheap ring which he twists on the little finger of his left hand, then turns to Joe. Thereupon a close view shows Rico showing Joe the newspaper story, which reads:

"Underworld Pays Respects
to Diamond Pete Montana."

Joe glances swiftly at the story, and looks questioningly at Rico:

JOE. Well, what's that gotta do with the price of eggs?

RICO (*snatching away paper*). A lot. Big time stuff! (*Musing*) "Diamond Pete Montana." He don't have to waste his time on cheap gas stations. . . . *He* don't have to waste his time on hick cops. . . . He's in the Big Town, doin' things in a big way.

JOE (*jerking his thumb at the newspaper*). Is that what you want? A party like that for you, Rico? "Caesar Enrico Bandello Honored By His Friends?"

Rico straightens up and draws a deep breath, and his jaw sets grimly as he stares into vacancy. He mutters as though talking to himself:

RICO. I could do all the things *that* fellow does. More! When I get in a tight spot, I shoot my way out of it. Like tonight . . . sure, shoot first— argue afterwards. If you don't the other feller gets you. . . . *This* game ain't for guys that's soft!

The clatter of dishes placed on the counter by the Cook arouses him from his reverie. Joe attacks his food with enjoyment, but Rico disregards his for the time being, studying the paper.

A full view of the room shows the Cook coming forward, sitting down in a chair and leaning back and he is asleep almost at once. Thereupon Rico looks up from the paper at the cook, and having made sure that the man is asleep, Rico slips off the stool and, with lithe swiftness, glides to the end of the counter and resets the clock. Then Rico goes back to his place. His face, now seen close, is stony as he rejoins Joe, but the latter grins at him with huge appreciation of his cleverness.

JOE (*whispering*). Great!

They eat in silence for a while. Then Joe lifts his head.

JOE (*wistfully*). Yeah, there's money in the Big Town, all right. And the women! Good times . . . somethin' doin' all the time . . . excitin' things. Gee, the clothes I could wear. (*Grasping Rico's arm with sudden seriousness; his voice becoming colored by an almost pathetic yearning*) I ain't made for this thing. Dancin' . . . that's what I wanna do.

RICO (*frowning, his voice full of contempt*). *Women . . . dancin' . . .* where do they get you? (*He shakes his head violently.*) I don't want no dancin' —I figure on makin' other people dance.

Joe looks at him admiringly, and claps him on the shoulder. There is evidently a strong feeling of friendship between them.

JOE. You'll get there, Rico. You'll show 'em.

RICO. Maybe. (*Suddenly sitting up straight, speaking with new-found determination*) Yes, I'll show 'em! This was our last stand in this burg, Joe. We're pullin' out!

JOE (*with a certain timidity*). Where we goin'?

RICO (*with a vague wave of his hand*). Oh . . . east . . . That's it, east. Where things break big!

The sound of a distant police siren, which gradually grows louder during the scene, makes the two men prick up their ears. Then Rico stands up, leaning far over the counter looking for the garbage receptacle. Spotting it, he takes the plates of spaghetti and deftly slides the remainder of the food into the pail. Sitting down he raps loudly on the counter with his cup, and at this the Cook, heavy-eyed with sleep, stumbles to his feet and comes to them.

JOE. More coffee, please.

The Cook takes the cups and fills them at the urn. He hears the police siren and stands listening, but with a shrug he turns to the counter and places the cups before the customers.

COOK. Anything else?

JOE. Two apple pies.

The Cook shoots the pie onto the counter, then listens to the siren. Then, as a wider view of the room comes into sight, the Cook appears from behind the counter and goes to the door, Rico and Joe deliberately paying no attention to him or the siren. And now as the siren screams outside and fades away, the Cook steps aside and two policemen come into the lunch wagon. He speaks to the first, while the other draws his gun and stands blocking the doorway.

COOK. What's the matter, Charley?

The Cop does not take his eyes off Rico and Joe who swing around on their stools when he speaks.

COP. Two cheap crooks held up a filling station on Eighth Street and shot Dinny Graham. We found their car around the corner.

COOK. Hurt him?

COP. Plenty!

A close view centering on the first cop, Rico and Joe, shows Joe sliding off his stool, but the Cop abruptly motions for him to stay where he is.

COP. Where you guys from?

JOE. Allendale. We didn't do nothing. Our car is out in front—the little roadster.

Joe does the talking, and there is no element of fear in either his or Rico's attitude. In fact, Rico assumes a negligent pose, with one elbow on the counter and regards the cops with subtle derision while he combs his sleek black hair, of which he is inordinately proud. This is a characteristic gesture with him. He keeps the comb in his upper vest pocket—in reaching for it his hand is only an inch away from the butt of an automatic, carried in a shoulder holster.

A wider view toward the clock appears as the Cook, nervously afraid of the consequences of a gun battle in his place, turns to the cop. Rico and Joe look at their alibi—perhaps it will work without having to bring up the subject themselves.

COOK. What time did it happen, Charley?

COP. Five minutes to twelve. (*He looks at Rico and Joe.*) How long you guys been here?

COOK. They been eating in here since 11:45.

The Cop glances up at the clock in the background, and pulling out his watch he compares the time. The clock is right.

COP. Pretty lucky for them . . . If you see anybody suspicious, let me know.

The Cops leave. The Cook closes the door and returns to his seat behind the counter, and Joe and Rico start on their pie.

JOE (*now seen closer with Rico, between mouthfuls*). Whew! That was close. You got me kinda jumpy when I seen you reachin' for the . . . (*He finishes the sentence by pantomiming Rico's former action of reaching for his armpit.*)

RICO (*shrugging*). Maybe I should o' done it, too. (*Patting his gun*) That's all I got between me and them—between me and the whole world. . . . (*He pushes his plate away with the half-finished pie.*) Let's go.

Rico rises from his stool. The paper is still before him. Once more he looks at it. Then, with sudden decision, he quickly draws the cheap ring from his finger and throws it into a cuspidor.

JOE. What're you doin' that for?

RICO. No more phonies for me. . . . Big shots don't wear 'em! (*On his way to the door*) Ready?

Joe tosses some change on the counter and the scene fades out.

PART TWO

The "CLUB PALERMO" SIGN going on and off fades in, and then dissolves into SAM VETTORI'S OFFICE, affording a close view of a game of solitaire partly laid out on a table. Two thick, heavy hands can be seen hovering over the table, placing the rest of the cards from a greasy, worn deck.

RICO'S VOICE. . . . and that's all there is to it. I beat it East, like I told you. I wanna run with your mob if you'll let me. What d'you say?

The hand goes on placing, and there is silence from its owner. During this, the scene moves up to the face of SAM VETTORI as he sits there still dealing the cards off the dirty deck. Sam's eyes are on the cards before him, and he appears to be paying

no attention to the unseen Rico, whose voice we hear again.

RICO'S VOICE (*with pleading earnestness*). You won't be sorry for lettin' me in, Mr. Vettori. I'll shoot square with you. . . . I'll do anything you say. . . . I ain't afraid of nuthin'!

Now Sam Vettori slowly raises his eyes to the still unseen man before him as he speaks.

SAM. So you think you're a hard guy, huh?

A wider view includes RICO as he stands before Sam's table, looking at the other with a certain determination.

RICO. Gimme a chance to show you.

SAM. What d'you know about me?

RICO. I got told enough. How you run things this end of town. (*With a wide wave of his hand which indicates the rest of the room*) 'Bout this here Club Palermo—how it's your front. I heard plenty!

SAM (*placing the cards*). Maybe you're good with a rod, too, huh?

RICO. Quick with it, that's what I am. And sure.

SAM (*pausing for the first time with his cards*). Well, that don't go around here. That's old stuff. This ain't the sticks.

RICO. I get you!

Now Sam rises. Stepping closer to Rico he looks into the other's face and speaks in a hard, uncontradictable voice:

SAM. All right! You stick around. But I'm the boss and I give orders. And when we split, we split my way. And no squawks. Get me?

RICO (*a flash of joy lighting up his face*). Sure, Mr. Vettori!

SAM (*now indicating the room with his thick thumb*). Come on, meet the boys. . . . They're A-1, every one of 'em. . . . That's Tony Passa . . . he can drive a car better than any mug in town. . . .

We see Sam and Rico go toward the open door of the office. Beyond the door, not very far in the background, is a gaming table with a bright droplight over it. Seated around the table are several men, some of them in shirtsleeves, playing cards. TONY PASSA, OTERO and SCABBY are among them. During the walk to the door, Sam continues with a nod of his head in the direction of the table:

SAM. . . . and that's Otero. He's the goods all right. An' Scabby—what a smart guy! An' that's Killer Pepi . . .

A close view at the DOORWAY leading into the other room shows Sam and Rico coming in.

SAM. Boys—I want you to meet a new guy who's gonna be with us. This is—

The "Boys" look up from the card table, but Sam has forgotten Rico's name.

RICO. Caesar Enrico Bandello.

SAM. Little Caesar, eh?

He digs him playfully in the ribs and the scene fades out.

PART THREE

A NEWSPAPER HEADLINE fades in. It reads:

NEW CRIME COMMISSION HEAD
DECREES END OF GANGSTER RULE

A SUBHEADING reads:

Alvin McClure Promises Drastic
Measures Against Thugs

Then this dissolves into an impressionistic view of a ROULETTE WHEEL SPINNING, which in turn dissolves into the FOYER of ARNIE's GAMBLING HOUSE at night as we see first the shadow of a hand, falling against a blank wall—the fist closed, the forefinger pointed. After a second the view moves over to LITTLE ARNIE, standing with RITZ COLONNA. It is Arnie's hand that we see reflected in the shadow—and with arm shot out, forefinger extended, he is pointing toward the gambling room, as yet unseen.

ARNIE (*in a lowered voice*). That's your man. I don't know who he is and I don't want to know. But he's too lucky for *my* house. . . .

Little Arnie's MAIN GAMBLING ROOM is then

seen from Arnie's angle as he and Ritz see it now. This is the usual gambling den, with card and roulette tables, and the whirring click of roulette wheels rises above the noise of a crap game in the background. Then, back in the FOYER, Arnie is seen giving Ritz a significant glance.

ARNIE (*lowering his voice*). Wait till he gets downstairs.

RITZ. Oke, Boss! (*Bending closer; in a confidential whisper*) Sam Vettori is still waiting for you in your office.

Arnie frowns and clicks his tongue with a measure of irritation.

ARNIE. All right. I guess I'll *have* to see him. Wonder what he wants here.

With that, he turns on his heels and walks to the door of his office, which is at the other end of the foyer opposite the door through which we had seen the gambling room.

Then a close view of ARNIE AT THE DOOR, just as he is about to open it, shows Arnie turning once more toward Ritz Colonna, who is now out of sight.

ARNIE (*in a low voice*). Say, Ritz, better stick with me! Let that other guy go— I'll need you in here. That Sam Vettori is a no good guy.

RITZ (*with an understanding glance*). You said it, Boss! (*Gently pushing Arnie aside*) Better let *me* go first. . . . (*He opens the door, and they enter.*)

ARNIE'S OFFICE: Sam Vettori's heavy bulk is now seen in an easy chair as Ritz enters, followed by Arnie. Rico, somewhat better dressed than previously, is standing in a strategic position between the door and Sam. Now his hand instinctively goes toward his armpit—he is ready! But Sam waves to him as though saying, "Cut that!" and Rico lowers his hand.

SAM (*without rising—with a measure of amiability*). Lo, Arnie! Surprised to see me in your joint?

ARNIE. Maybe I won't be, after you tell me what you want here.

Arnie sits down at his desk, and Ritz plants himself near him, without sitting

down; he is studying Rico from under drawn eyebrows. Rico stares back, and the two men continue to glare at each other sullenly during the conversation between Sam and Arnie.

SAM (*bending forward in his chair*). I'll tell you all right, Arnie. Diamond Pete asked me to come up. He's coming up too.

ARNIE (*surprised, but agreeably so*). Pete Montana?

SAM (*nodding*). That's who!

ARNIE. Well, if Pete wants you here, it's gotta be all right with me.

Through the same door where ARNIE and RITZ had come in, DIAMOND PETE MONTANA now enters with a bodyguard of his own, KID BEAN and another "mug." MONTANA is well-dressed in a rather loud fashion and sports plenty of jewelry to live up to his soubriquet "Diamond." At this entrance Little Arnie Lorch rises from his seat behind the huge desk and Sam Vettori also heaves his bulk out of his easy chair. Their manner toward Montana is distinctly deferential. He greets them with limp handshakes.

MONTANA. Hello, Arnie! Hello, Vettori!

ARNIE. How are you, Pete—how are you?

SAM. Hello, Boss!

Montana opens his coat, and loosens his muffler (it is winter and all the characters are wearing heavy overcoats where necessary). Arnie reaches for a box of cigars and offers it to Pete, who accepts one silently. Arnie signally omits offering the box to Sam—but Sam reaches over nevertheless and takes one of the cigars.

SAM (*with a touch of sarcasm*). Thanks, Arnie.

Arnie looks at him noncommittally, and remains silent.

MONTANA (*with an indulgent gesture, indicating the chairs to Arnie and Sam, who are still standing*). Sit down, boys. I got somethin' to tell you—a message from the Big Boy . . .

The lifted eyebrows of Sam and Arnie

indicate that this is unusual and important. A certain awe is on their faces as they sit down, waiting for Montana's words as he perches himself on a corner of the desk.

MONTANA (*warming to his speech*). Now listen, here's the lowdown . . . (*He pauses dramatically, while Arnie and Sam draw their chairs nearer in listening attitudes.*) The Big Boy says . . .

Rico leaves the other bodyguards standing in a group away from the desk and draws closer to the big shots. Arnie's glance falls on him, and Arnie stops Montana with a wave of his hand:

ARNIE. Just a minute, Boss! (*Turning sharply to Rico*) Say you! Nobody asked you to be buttin' into this, did they? Screw, mug!

Rico looks at him, flashing back:

RICO. You ain't givin' me orders!

ARNIE (*jumping up*). Oh! You're a fresh guy!

He starts to take a punch at Rico. Instinctively Rico's hand shoots to his armpit, but Sam quickly intervenes:

SAM (*scared*). Take it easy, Rico. You wait out there for me!

RICO (*shooting Arnie a glance full of hatred, and going out*) That's jake with me, Boss!

Arnie gives Ritz a sign, and the latter follows Rico out. Only Pete Montana's bodyguard remains on the scene near the three principals.

Then a close-up of Montana shows him speaking with a certain pompousness and a sense of superiority.

MONTANA. Now listen, boys. (*He bends forward, extending his forefinger.*) Watch this guy McClure—what's head of the new Crime Commission. He's puttin' on the screws and no mistake about it. . . .

A close view shows Arnie and Sam listening with due solemnity—nodding their heads at each point that Montana emphasizes with his heavy fist on the desk.

MONTANA. The Big Boy wants me to tell you to put chains on your gorillas for the next few months, 'cause if any of 'em go too far, it'll be just too bad.

ARNIE (*laughing, somewhat incredulously*). He can fix anythin'. That's why he's the Big Boy.

MONTANA (*shaking his head*). Stop kidding yourself. Nobody can square nothin' with McClure, not even the Big Boy. Li'l jobs—that's different. We can spring guys for them. But shootin's . . . ? *No sir!* (*He stands up and starts to button his coat as he addresses Sam.*) It's guys like that torpedo of yourn that cause all the trouble. . . . (*He jerks his thumb toward the door through which Rico had left as Arnie grins, and nods appreciatively.*)

SAM. Who, Rico? He's all right. A li'l too quick on the trigger but that's 'cause he's new.

MONTANA. Well, it's us that'll swing with him if he shoots at the wrong time.

He pulls his derby hat down over his eyes, and starts for the door, Arnie solicitously opening it for him. Then in the FOYER, facing the door of the office, Ritz Colonna and Rico are seen standing, their hands in their pockets, cigarettes hanging limp from the corners of their mouths. From under lowered eyelids they are watching each other in silence. Just now the door opens and Montana comes out, followed by Arnie, Sam and Montana's bodyguard.

MONTANA. Now remember what I told you. (*He struts to the door, and stops in front of Rico. He surveys him with a hard glance.*) And you—you take it easy with that cannon.

A close-up of RICO shows him looking at the great MONTANA with adulation, then his expression changing to harshness, his eyes dropping from Montana's face, which is unseen in this close-up.

MONTANA'S VOICE. You hear me?

Following this we see Rico's glance stopping at a large horseshoe pin in Montana's cravat, then dropping to a large flashy ring.

RICO (*meekly*). Yes, Mr. Montana!

With a lordly gesture, Montana, now seen with the others, takes his leave, his bodyguard following him.

MONTANA. S'long boys.

THE OTHERS. Good night.

As Montana and his bodyguard walk out, Arnie turns to Rico, casting a malicious sidelong glance at Vettori:

ARNIE. Leave your gat home on the pianna next job you pull. Yeah, park it next to your milk bottle!

Rico hardens again, and Sam swings around, growling:

SAM. G'wan! Run your own mob, Arnie—I'll take care of mine!

There is no love lost between him and Arnie. The latter starts to make a sharp retort, but Rico steps up to him, smiling evilly:

RICO. Yeah, I'll park it! I don't need no cannon to take care of guys like you, Mr. Lorch. (*He turns and follows Sam.*)

A close-up shows ARNIE staring blankly after Rico as the view fades out.

ARNIE (*muttering*). He's gonna get up in this world—yes he will! A coupla feet higher than he wants to—if the rope don't break. . . .

PART FOUR

Through a fading-in menu heading—THE BRONZE PEACOCK—the view dissolves into the main room in The Bronze Peacock, a smart North Side Night Club. The room is richly decorated in excellent taste, and the guests are mostly in dinner clothes. A good orchestra is playing a dance number, and people are dancing amid a general movement of waiters and guests.

Then the scene is the DANCE FLOOR where JOE and OLGA STASSOFF are dancing. As they come into sight the view follows them in a close-up. Joe is immaculately dressed in tails and Olgo wears a stunning evening gown. The girl looks up at the boy with a melting expression in her eyes.

OLGA (*softly*). Gee, I thought you weren't coming at all! I kept on looking at that door and saying to myself: "He forgot all about me. . . . " (*But she smiles at him as though courting his reassuring denial.*)

JOE (*smiling back at her*). Not a' chance, Baby! Wouldn't I be a sap to miss out on such a swell break—'specially with a dame like you for a partner?

OLGA. We oughtta make a swell team, you and me. That's what I told my agent, too, when he brought you 'round. (*Pressing his arm; anxiously*) Do your best, will you, Joe? The manager is eyeing you up. I want him to like you.

JOE. Just watch me! He's gonna get an eyeful.

A close view shows DE VOSS standing near the dressing room entrance. He is a sleek

maitre d'hotel—proud of his establishment, and as he follows the movements of the young couple he smiles with approval. Viewed from his angle, the long DANCE FLOOR then comes into view and as the music rises to a crescendo, Joe, taking advantage of a clear spot on the floor, is seen executing a graceful movement ending in a spin. The orchestra stops; there is desultory hand clapping for another encore; the dancers drift toward their tables. Then Joe and Olga are seen heading for DeVoss.

A close view of DE VOSS shows him being approached by Joe and Olga, the latter breathing quickly after her exertions. She is holding Joe's hand and pulls him to DeVoss, questioning eagerly.

OLGA. Well, I got hold of a real hoofer for a partner, didn't I, Mr. DeVoss?

DeVoss runs an appraising eye from Joe's glossy hair to his immaculate boots. There is no doubt that Joe qualifies, but De Voss stalls, teasing the girl, who is on tenterhooks and looks at him pleadingly:

OLGA. He's an elegant dancer. We'd panic 'em, working together.

DE VOSS (*smiling*). You're not trying to sell him now, Olga? (*Laughing, to Joe*) Well, young fellow, a hundred a week ought to buy you. That's more than I usually start them with.

JOE (*laughing*). Can't get no limousines with that, but it ought to buy me a lot of gas till I get paid enough to buy a car to go with it.

Olga looks at the two men, delighted, as DeVoss laughs.

OLGA. Gee, thanks, Mr. DeVoss! You won't be sorry for this.

DE VOSS (*chucking Olga under the chin*). Olga, when are you going to give me a chance to do something I *can* be sorry for?

She takes Joe's arm and leads him toward the dressing room, DeVoss looking after them, pleased.

Joe and Olga come into the girl's DRESSING ROOM, which they are to share from now on. It is a cozy place with a dressing table, day-bed, and a chair or two; pictures of a few movie stars are on the wall. Joe, smiling over his success, starts to sit down, but Olga stops him as her manner undergoes a decided change. She holds him by the lapels of his coat and looks up, and a close-up shows Olga studying the boy narrowly.

OLGA. So it's you and me from now on. Well, I'm glad and I ain't ashamed to tell you. It's no use kidding . . . I guess you know by this time how I feel about you. That's all right with you, isn't it? (*Her voice softens, and an anxious note creeps into it.*) Or have you got another girl? A steady, I mean?

We see them together now in the DRESSING ROOM as Joe looks at her steadily and laughs provocatively.

JOE. Hundreds of 'em. Sure! Only . . . (*suddenly putting his arms around her*) . . . what's the difference? This is gonna be *real*, huh? We'll make it . . . mean something . . .

OLGA (*softly*). Yeah, Joey. Let's!

JOE. 'Cause I need somebody . . . somebody like you . . . awful bad . . . Do you believe me, Olga?

OLGA. I want to believe you. . . .

Joe takes the girl in his arms and kisses her, and Olga's arms go around him. In doing this, she touches the gat under his left arm and draws away.

OLGA (*pointing to the gun; frightened*). What's that? What you got there, Joe?

Joe casually takes the big automatic from its holster and slips it into the dressing table drawer, Olga's eyes going wide at sight of the gun.

OLGA (*whispering*). What are you doing with that?

He stares at her grimly, takes her by both arms, and pulls her face close to his.

JOE. Can't you forget you seen it? It won't make no difference . . . not between us, Olga. Don't you worry, Babyface. It's just a little good-luck charm I carry with me. . . .

Olga wets her lips and nods, and Joe releases her. The girl looks at him with a different expression now—there is a glint of frightened admiration in her eyes. But she speaks stubbornly:

OLGA. That your racket?

JOE (*uneasy, but with a smile on his face*). Maybe . . .

OLGA. I suppose I got no right to ask you. But now that we got an understanding . . . Joe, couldn't you . . . leave it . . . ? (*She shakes her head bravely, as though speaking the words to herself.*) No, I suppose I *haven't* got the right. . . .

JOE. What would be the good of you asking, Kiddy? Once in a gang . . . you know the rest . . .

OLGA (*with all the confidence of her love*). I don't want to know. Maybe it can be different this time—if we try . . .

JOE. I never seen the guy could get away with it. . . .

She places her head against his shoulder, and as he puts his arm around her, the scene fades out.

PART FIVE

An ELECTRIC SIGN:

"CLUB

PALERMO

DANCING"

fades in and dissolves to VETTORI's OFFICE. (The Club Palermo in Little Italy belongs to SAM VETTORI. An upstairs room is the headquarters of the gang. It has a closet and a concealed sliding panel leading to back stairs and an alley.)

SAM VETTORI, as usual, is sitting at a table playing a game of solitaire. Grouped around him are OTERO, KILLER PEPI and TONY PASSA. Tony is boyish; Otero has the perfect poker face—he is a little Mexican; Killer Pepi is a huge, hairy, ferocious Sicilian. Leaning against another table, which is at some distance from Sam's, is RICO. It is significant that he is standing alone, keeping apart from the group that has gathered around Vettori. And during the early part of the scene, while the rest of them are intent on Sam's words, Rico continues to study a sheet of paper which is in his hand. As a closer view of the GROUP comes into sight, Sam, placing the cards, continues a conversation apparently begun some time ago.

SAM. But we gotta be careful. Little Arnie is interested in this here club and if it gets out who pulled the job. . . .

KILLER PEPI (*interrupting*). Aw, nobody will be wise to us! They're careless 'cause they never been tapped.

SAM (*uneasily*). Just the same, I don't like this whole business.

TONY (*very nervously*). I don't neither, Sam! Cross my heart, I don't. (*Looking around with instinctive fear*) I couldn't sleep last night . . . I was that worried. . . . I don't wanna take chances—not now, the way they're closin' down on us . . .

A close-up of RICO shows him looking up from his paper, a sneering expression coming over his face as he turns on Tony:

RICO. What's the matter, Tony? Gettin' yellow?

As the office comes back into view Tony is seen bristling and casting an anxious glance at Rico—but his eyes droop under the steely scrutiny of the other.

TONY (*whining*). Aw, it ain't that . . . only . . . well, gee whiz, none of us want to hang, do we?

RICO (*firmly*). You'd like to quit, wouldn't you? You'd like to run out on us, wouldn't you? You're yellow, you dirty . . . (*And he takes a step toward Tony, who retreats, his eyes wide with fear.*)

Sam who has been watching this scene from under lowered eyebrows, now barks at Rico:

SAM. Hold on, Rico! (*Glowering as Rico reluctantly stops*) Where'd you get that yellow stuff? If you're so anxious to know who's yellow, I'll tell you. It's Joe Massara, your pal. That's why he didn't show up tonight.

RICO (*savagely*). Joe'll be here. Just 'cause he's late. . . .

SAM (*waving*). Yeah, I know all about it. Well, I'll just give him ten minutes more. . . . Then we'll see . . . (*He pulls out his heavy gold watch and glances at it. But Rico steps up to the table, and plants himself in front of Sam.*)

RICO. Listen, Sam. Joe is all right. He's the best front man in the world. He can go into a swell hotel and order a suite —a suite—and it's all right. Without Joe we can't pull this job and you know it.

During this speech, Rico has been emphasizing his remarks by fluttering the sheet of paper in his hand. Sam, who had been more concerned with his cards than with listening to Rico's speech, now looks up.

SAM (*narrowing his eyes*). What's that paper?

RICO (*as he and Sam are seen fairly close*

together). It's this layout I been fig-urin' out with Scabby . . .

SAM. This here night club job?

RICO. Yeah.

SAM (*amiably*). Let's see it a minute!

Unsuspecting, Rico hands over the docu-ment. Sam, without looking at it, suddenly rips the paper in two and throws it on the floor. Rico's face darkens, and his fists clench.

SAM. Until I say different, nobody's goin' to plan for this mob but me. Savvy?

Rico stands for a second, glowering. It seems as though he were about to spring at Sam the next moment. Then he drops his hands, turns, and walks away.

In a large view of the room Sam is seen laughing and looking up at the gangsters around the table as though seeking their support, but the men seem embarrassed, ill at ease; only Tony forces a weak smile. In the background Rico is seen striding to the door, which is heavy and has a shutter in it; then Rico goes out.

SAM (*resuming his cards*). Now get on to this, . . . you, Tony, will handle the bus and . . .

Rico, having come out of the door, is now standing at the head of the STAIRCASE, anx-iously peering down the steps. For a while he is alone, then Joe comes leaping up the stairs, skipping two at a time. Joe is dressed in a form-fitting velvet-collared blue over-coat; his natty derby hat is at an angle.

JOE. Hello, Rico.

With a wide grin of greeting he shoots out his hand. But Rico disregards this.

RICO. I told you to be here at 8:30.

JOE (*obviously not telling the truth*). Well . . . you see . . . I was busy . . . rehearsing and . . . you know how it is!

RICO (*darkly*). Yeah, I know how it is! They've been sayin' it in there . . . (*He jerks his thumb in direction of door.*) Only I didn't believe 'em, see! They're crazy when they call you— yellow! (*He says the last word with significance, looking hard at Joe.*)

JOE (*nervously; with an abrupt move-ment of his hand, as though waving aside the accusation*). Aw, tell 'em to . . .

He doesn't finish the sentence, but with sudden anxiety in his voice, he bends closer to Rico.

JOE. What's the big rush for, anyway?

RICO (*as he and Joe are seen closer; af-fecting a careless manner, though with a sharp, hard expression on his face*). It's a li'l job we need you for. A li'l job at the—Bronze Peacock. (*Again there is sinister emphasis on the last two words; he is watching Joe's face closely.*)

JOE (*his mouth drops open, eyes di-lated; he backs up a step*). What do you mean? You kidding me or something? (*Feverishly grasping Rico's arm*) But how can I take the chance? They're my friends—everybody knows me.

RICO (*coldly*). That's why. Nobody will suspect *you*. Don't stall, Joe.

JOE (*desperately*). I ain't stallin'. You gotta let me out of it, Rico. You gotta. I don't want to . . . I'm workin' steady . . . can't a guy ever say he's *through*?

RICO (*carefully measuring his words*). You're gonna be in on it and you'll like it. The time is to be sharp midnight on New Year's Eve.

JOE (*with almost a shriek*). I won't . . . I can't. (*Instantly cringing as Rico pushes his face closer to him. A cun-ning note comes into Joe's voice.*) I can't . . . don't you see . . . ? I'll . . . gee, I'll be workin' New Year's Eve . . .

RICO (*straightening with a curious gleam in his eyes, and with a nod toward the door*). This is the joint where you work! Don't be forgettin' it either . . . (*Turning to the door, and commanding over his shoulder*) Come on! (*And Joe, pale, quaking, follows him.*)

In SAM VETTORI'S OFFICE the group is seen again, close. Sam is still dealing the cards; now he looks up.

SAM. Maybe it ain't so hot, though. Maybe we can't buck Little Arnie.

At this point Rico walks in, with Joe a step behind him.

RICO. *I* can.

SAM (*shrugging*). You're too good, that's what. (*Now he notices Joe.*) You were in a hurry to get here all right. Maybe this kinda work ain't to your liking, huh?

Joe lowering his eyes, bites his lips, and Rico hastily answers for him.

RICO. Joe is all right, Sam. He's in with us.

Again he looks sharply at Joe, and Joe feeling the challenge of the eyes, looks up, then turns his eyes away once more, answering in a low voice:

JOE. Yeah, I'm in with you . . .

A close-up of Sam shows him, with an energetic movement unusual to him, suddenly shoving the cards off the table. Reaching in his pocket, he produces a rolled-up map.

SAM. Well, let's see . . . Here's the way I doped out this thing. . . . (*He slides the map on the table, lays his thick forefinger on it, then he looks at Rico.*) I—Sam Vettori! Not you, Rico . . . nor nobody else . . . that's clear, ain't it?

We see the GROUP again: Some of them are bent over the table—only Rico is standing, his manner aloof as he looks down on the plan, and there is the semblance of a cynical smile on his lips. Joe is also at some distance from the table, nervously lighting a cigarette.

SAM (*now poking the plan with his finger*). Here's where you stand, Otero. . . . This is your spot, Killer . . . Rico is over here. . . . That's plain, ain't it?

RICO. Sure! Only . . . (*With a definite sneer now, he pokes a quick finger at the paper.*) Who stands here, Yeah, the back door . . . ? Kinda forgot that, didn't you?

From Sam's puzzled face, it is plain that he is caught unawares. He scratches his head, then takes out his fury on Rico.

SAM. I'm still bossin' this job, you . . . One more crack outa you . . .

OTERO, grinning widely, is next seen poking Tony in the ribs.

OTERO (*winking*). Big smart guy, Rico. Lotta brain, you betcha my life. . . .

TONY (*with a nervous half-smile*). Yeah, but I'm scared, Otero, honest to goodness I'm scared. . . .

OTERO. You craz'. Rico, he come with us. . . .

SAM (*continuing, as the* GROUP *as a whole is seen somewhat close*). You, Joe, will be in the lobby at five minutes after twelve. . . .

A close-up of JOE shows him listening to Sam as his words continue.

SAM'S VOICE. And give us the high sign if everything's O.K.

Joe's face twitches; and instinctively he opens his coat and starts fingering his holster, which is significantly empty just now. Then his figure dissolves into a close-up of JOE in exactly the same position. But now he is dressed in tails again and his hand, that had been examining the empty holster in the former shot, is now slipping a gun into it. The revolver in its place, he draws his coat tight over it.

Then we see the BRONZE PEACOCK DRESSING ROOM where Joe is now alone. With a last glance in the mirror, and a final adjustment of his tie, Joe crosses to the door, opens it and slips out.

The scene cuts to the MAIN ROOM, where LITTLE ARNIE LORCH is entertaining a party of friends at a prominent table near the dance floor. The noise has materially increased with the approach of New Year; the decorations are appropriate to the New Year; signs and transparencies of "Happy New Year" are prominently displayed. Little Arnie's friends are a vulgar, boisterous lot. They are drinking champagne. Arnie feels important and is a trifle tight.

A closer view shows LITTLE ARNIE's woman —known as Blondy Belle—wanting to propose a toast; but no one will listen to her and she nudges Arnie, whereupon the gambler starts to shout authoritatively.

ARNIE. Ho! Let's have quiet, gang. Blondy's gonna give a toast!

ANOTHER VOICE. Ssh! Blondy's gonna turn a new leaf . . .

A DRUNKEN VOICE. Yeah, a loose leaf.

The bunch at the table stop their gabble and turn bleary eyes on the blonde who tries to stand up, thinks better of it and speaks her piece from her chair.

BLONDY. Here's to the guy what invented New Years! And here's to Little Arnie —may he never be left in the Lorch!

This *bon mot* is greeted with a shout of laughter. Blondy grins with pride at the reception accorded her wit. Arnie slaps her on the back as he would a man, then pulls out a huge roll of bills and gives her fifty.

ARNIE. Here—catch!

BLONDY. Dollink! May you never die— much!

After this magnanimous gesture he looks around the club; and the entrance of a party on the other side of the dance floor catching his eye, he turns squarely around in his chair to see better.

From Arnie's angle a party of three men and two ladies are seen sitting down at the table across the dance floor. Then a closer view of the same group shows that they are middle-aged, quietly dressed, with an air of authority and culture. The host is a big, distinguished-looking man with iron gray hair and firm, clean-cut jaw. His name is ALVIN MC CLURE and he is head of the Crime commission. One of the ladies is his wife.

A close view now discloses Little Arnie talking to DeVoss, with Blondy listening.

ARNIE (*pointing*). Holy Moses, lamp McClure . . . the Crime Commission buzzard. Bring 'im over and I'll buy 'im a lemonade!

De Voss doesn't like the idea at all and tries politely to dissuade Arnie.

DE VOSS. Some other time, Arnie.

BLONDY (*nastily butting in*). Go on, De Voss, do as you're told or we'll wreck your gilded joint. Maybe we ain't good enough to associate with those high-hat mugs . . . ?

A close view centers on De Voss and Mc-Clure. McClure greets the night club proprietor as a friend, and DeVoss tries to be ingratiating.

MC CLURE. Good evening, De Voss. Quite a party.

DE VOSS. Thank you, Mr. McClure. Er— -—er—Mr. Lorch, one of my financial backers, would like very much to meet you. May I bring him over?

McClure frowns thoughtfully—the name is vaguely familiar.

MC CLURE. Lorch? Lorch? (*And he straightens with a jerk, demanding coldly*) I didn't understand that persons of his type were connected with this place. (*Rising*) I'm sorry, Mr. DeVoss, but you might inform "Mister" Lorch that we're—leaving! I came to this place under a misapprehension, obviously.

The ladies start to gather their wraps, McClure impatiently helping them.

FIRST LADY (*obviously his wife*). Alvin, dear, isn't it a bit extreme to get into such a huff . . . ? We're being rather conspicuous. . . .

MC CLURE (*irritably*). Do you expect me to fraternize with crooks?

De Voss is seen now with Little Arnie and Blondy.

BLONDY (*a glass poised in her hand, ready to throw it at De Voss*). Well, where is the guardian angel?

DE VOSS (*agitated*). Say, Arnie, I certainly put my foot in it. McClure is leaving!

ARNIE. Yeah? Well, let 'im go and take a flying jump at the moon!

But at this point a whistle is seen being blown, then another whistle is seen, and still another, until the screen is full of them. A New Year is born! The sound of the whistles makes Blondy (in the reappearing scene) forget the quarrel. She lets out a yell and grabs Arnie around the neck, giving him a sloppy kiss.

BLONDY. Happy New Year and see how you like it! (*And DeVoss gets away in the excitement.*)

A full view of the room shows the air filled with confetti and serpentine. The noise is terrific, practically drowning out the whistles from outside. The close-up of a CLOCK shows the HANDS pointing to 11:55. Then the FOYER comes into full view, showing Joe standing at the top of the steps leading to the main room. He draws the heavy curtains, partially shutting out the racket from inside. Turning, he glances coolly around. The only people here are employees—two check girls, a waiter, a cashier and a cigar clerk. Joe starts for the cigar counter.

A close view of the CHECK GIRLS appears. One of the check girls watches Joe with longing eyes and remarks to her co-worker:

> CHECK GIRL. Gosh! That Joe Massara is a hot looking guy.
>
> SECOND CHECK GIRL (*nodding agreement; with eyes rolled skyward*). Mmm! Yum—yum!

We see the CIGAR COUNTER as Joe stands beside the waiter who is getting cigars for a party inside. The clerk looks at Joe while the waiter picks up the cigars.

> JOE. A package of Egyptian Ovals. Make 'em tobacco!

He flips a dollar bill on the counter. The waiter looks up at the spendthrift—these cigarettes are expensive. The clerk sticks his head in the case, fishing for the cigarettes. At this point Joe and the Waiter have their backs to the door.

The MAIN DOOR of the foyer comes into view as, with Rico slightly in the lead, the three gunmen come through the front door. Their overcoat collars are turned up, their mufflers shroud the lower halves of their faces, hats are pulled down so only the eyes show. Rico has his automatic in his hand—OTERO prominently displays the evil-looking shotgun. Tony carries a gun and some canvas sacks. The view moves as they come into the room and separate fanwise, Rico making for the office door, Tony for the Cashier, and Otero staying near the entrance.

Now JOE is seen close, wheeling around, throwing his hands into the air as if on a signal, and yelling.

> JOE. It's a hold-up!

The waiter turns and nearly collapses, his tray falling with a clatter. The Clerk staggers back against the wall, and in the background the hands of the check girls pop into the air.

> RICO (*out of scene*). A mind reader, ain't you? Well, keep 'em steady!

(We see nothing of the gunmen with the victims. They are always just out of sight except perhaps for the muzzle of a gun, a hand or their shadows.)

A close-up next shows the Cashier, an elderly, frightened man. His hands are above his head, he gasps like a fish as Tony's voice, trying to be tough, is heard:

> TONY. Fork over, Pop, fork over.

The Cashier lowers his hands and the scene moves down to show him begin dumping money into a canvas sack held by Tony, only the latter's hands being visible. A close view shows De Voss' ASSISTANT, a Czech with a swarthy complexion, appearing in the door of the office. A look of incredulous amazement sweeps over his face, his hands leap up, and he slumps against the door-jamb. Rico's shadow appears beside the Czech and we hear his voice:

> RICO (*out of sight*). Quick you! I want a look in there.

A drunk comes in the door and we follow him. He evidently runs smack into Otero and his shotgun. A lugubrious expression comes into his face, he bows and takes off his silk hat. Then his hands go into the air and he sidles along to back up against the wall, trying hard to keep his balance.

> DRUNK (*while putting up hands; with a beatific expression*). Very—happy— New Year . . . !

A close view discloses JOE and the WAITER in the Foyer. Joe is quite brave—even to the point of kidding. He speaks loudly:

> JOE (*loudly*). Wow—a nice little celebration we're having! Fine little celebration. . . .

He smiles at the Waiter, who looks hastily away with agonized eyes as if to say to Otero: "I can't help what that bird's saying."

Otero is seen close near the door as Tony backs into the Foyer. The boy has the money sacks under one arm. The other hand swings a gun unsteadily around the arc of the room. Otero is a statue—only his quick piercing eyes move, but Tony is gradually losing his nerve. Next, a close view shows RICO backing out of the office door, stuffing a wad of bills in his overcoat pocket—his pockets bulging. He snaps the door shut, then whips around and runs into the Foyer.

Now the MC CLURE PARTY comes through the curtains from the main room and stops petrified in the FOYER as Rico's intimidating voice calls out:

RICO (*out of sight*). Stand right there! All of you!

Two of the men and both women put up their hands, but MC CLURE hesitates. Suddenly one of the ladies faints and falls, hitting her head with an audible thump, and slips down the steps. This is too much for McClure, who gives a bellow of rage and reaches for a gun.

MC CLURE. You dirty, low-down . . .

A gun roars out of sight. McClure takes a couple of steps, a dazed expression on his face, and pitches forward, arms outflung.

A close view at the MAIN DOOR next shows Otero holding the door open for Rico, who is slowly backing to him, his gun raised, a feral expression on his face. There is no doubt as to who fired the shot. Rico whisks through the door and they vanish. (Tony has disappeared earlier.)

A full view of the interior of the BRONZE PEACOCK appears as a woman screams, and everyone rushes for McClure, a crowd forming around him. Joe makes for the back of the building. There is confusion!

OUTSIDE THE BRONZE PEACOCK Tony, who has already started the car, is seen close. Tears are streaming down his face; he is completely unnerved. Otero is on the running board, holding the door open for Rico, who barges into sight. Tony cannot get the gears meshed, and Rico slaps him hard across the face.

RICO. What's the matter, losing your nerve?

The boy shivers—a single sob escapes him —but the blow acts like a dash of cold water. He throws the gears into second and the car leaps away.

OLGA is now seen in the DRESSING ROOM.

Joe staggers through the door, his face chalk-pale, his hair disarrayed.

OLGA. What's the matter? Joe . . . what happened?

Joe supports himself with one hand on the dressing table. He is terrified through and through.

JOE. It's all right . . . nothing . . . (*Trying to compose himself, forcing a certain calmness which doesn't quite come off*) The joint's been held up. . . . They . . . they shot McClure!

OLGA (*with frantic fear in her voice*). JOE!

JOE (*with a faint, painful smile*). Well . . . now you know . . . (*And he drops into a chair.*)

Olga, drawing back, stares at him in horror.

OLGA (*quaking*). It was you . . .

Joe's face distorts under the direct accusation, and he jumps as if to rush at her, as if to force her to be quiet.

JOE. No . . . that's a lie . . . I . . .

OLGA (*her voice harsher now*). YOU shot McClure!

JOE (*his face twitching with fear*). I didn't . . . I swear I didn't. It wasn't me that shot him—it was . . .

But before he can complete the sentence, he catches himself; he shuts his eyes, with lips compressed as though to choke back the truth. Then his hands drop inertly to his sides and he mutters:

JOE. I don't know who . . . (*Picking up his head with a certain bravado*) But it's our hips for this job, all right!

With that, he gets to the drawer, pulls it open, and hastily drops the revolver into it, again shutting the drawer. But he hasn't the energy to leave the dressing table this time, and just stands there staring at his own image in the mirror. A close view next appears: Joe's body is excluded from the view—only his face is visible, as reflected by the mirror. . . . His eyes stare ahead of him, full of hopelessness and misery. After a while Olga comes up behind him, places her arm around his neck—her face also appearing in the mirror, her cheek pressed close to Joe's.

OLGA. Maybe everything will be all right, Joey. . . . Maybe he wasn't hurt badly! But you're through with that bunch!

You don't belong, Joe . . . you're not that kind. You'll never go near them again.

JOE (*sadly shaking his head as the scene fades out* . . .). You can't go back on the gang!

PART SIX

The PALERMO OFFICE shows VETTORI standing in the foreground, mopping his face with his bandana and looking at Rico, who is emptying his pockets of money. It is quite a pile—and he adds the contents of the canvas sacks to it. In the background OTERO locks the riot gun in the closet—which holds a regular arsenal—then he takes off his overcoat, unconcernedly walks to the table and sits down.

Now a close view shows that Vettori senses something wrong. There is nothing jubilant in the attitude of Otero and Rico—who should be gay after a successful job.

VETTORI (*sweating with excitement*). Well? Well? Everything go off all right? Tell us, for the love of . . .

RICO (*without looking up from counting the money*). Sure all right! I had to take care of a guy.

Vettori falls into a chair with a thump—as though his legs had suddenly lost their strength—his eyes bulge—his face grows purple with rage.

VETTORI. A guy? Who—who—was it?

RICO. McClure!

Sam, seen in a close-up, appears to be having an apoplectic seizure. Inarticulate, he bangs on the table with both hands. Finally he manages to gasp with hoarse rage:

SAM. What did I tell you, Rico? Didn't I say to make it clean? Didn't I say no gun-work? You . . . you . . . *Amore de dio* . . . (*He chokes with rage.*)

A close view shows RICO white with anger.

RICO. You think I'm gonna let a guy pull a gat on *me*? He tried to get me! See? That's the way you gotta play this game.

Vettori makes an elaborate, tragic gesture —rocking in his chair as if in pain.

SAM (*wringing his hands*). The head of the Crime Commission! The Big Boy can't do us no good—not this trip—

they'll get us dead sure now . . . What am I gonna do?

Rico continues automatically to count the money. He speaks over his shoulder, without looking up:

RICO. Maybe you better go and give yourself up. You're slippin', Sam.

SAM (*still too frantic to react to the insult, and suddenly reminded of something—his voice trembling*). And Tony? Where is he?

OTERO (*answering for Rico*). Gettin' rid of the car—Tony nervous . . . bigga' baby, Tony . . .

The scene cuts to an ALLEY, only faintly illuminated by a solitary street lamp. Tony's car drives up, veering dangerously. All at once something seems to go wrong with it; it swerves to the curb and comes to a dead halt as the engine dies. Then a close view of TONY at the wheel shows his face twitching with terror, and he is seen fumbling with the gear shift. His hands shake so that he is unable to mesh the gears. Again and again he tries; and now he is sobbing aloud—his whole body is shaken. Then abandoning his task in panic, he quickly yanks the door open and starts running down the street.—Next the view moves with Tony as he runs, flattened against the walls of the building—his knees giving way under him—his loud sobbing increasing as he staggers along. . . .

This cuts back to the PALERMO OFFICE where Rico is still at the table, automatically counting the money. Grouped around the table are Sam, Scabby, Otero and one or two unnamed gangsters. Sam, his head buried in his hands, is keening, his mumbled words not distinguishable. Now, from outside, there is the sound of footsteps—someone is running up the stairs, and all present glance toward the door. Then moving past the group at the table to the door the view stops at where the club's bouncer, BAT CARILLO, is standing. He closes the door, the men facing him tensely.

BAT. Flaherty and two other dicks downstairs, boss. They're coming up.

At this Rico whips off his coat and wraps the money in it.

RICO (*in command of the situation*). Stay there, Otero! (*To Sam*) They won't know nothing unless they picked Tony up—give 'em the salve. I'll be right there, listening.

Sam, scared to death, still sits with his head buried in his palms, and Rico nudges him viciously.

RICO. Snap out of it, you!

The view follows him as he runs lightly across the room and slips into the passage behind the secret panel. All others remain in their places. Sam, hastily starts spreading his cards on the table as usual.

There is a knock on the door. In response Vettori nods and Carillo opens it. Flaherty and two other detectives step in, their right hands in their overcoat pockets. Sam waves for Carillo to leave and the bouncer goes out. Flaherty walks over to Sam, while the other detectives stay by the door. Sam dreamily plays solitaire without so much as a glance at the "flat-foot." A closer view follows, including Sam, Flaherty and Otero. Flaherty hasn't a thing on this gang and is only fishing for information, but he is tough.

FLAHERTY. Happy New Year, boys! There's a lonesome touring car down the street. Do you know anything about it?

Sam effectively conceals his inward fears, laughs and shakes his head—from this question he knows Flaherty is not hot on the trail.

SAM. I got a good cafe business. I don't know nothing about automobiles what's been left.

FLAHERTY. You might know if some of the smart young guys who hang around here had anything to do with it, wouldn't you?

Sam shakes his head. Otero then asks a leading question.

OTERO. Wasn't anybody in it?

FLAHERTY. Yeah, one guy—but not when we got there. He beat it—we got a good description of him, though!

A close-up of RICO in the passageway shows him sitting cross-legged on the floor with his head against the door, listening to the conversation. A flashlight is trained on the money in piles on his coat on the floor. In the center of it is his automatic—ready—as he keeps on counting. His face is harsh. This is succeeded by a close view of the GROUP in the office as Vettori speaks convincingly:

SAM. I keep telling you—I don't know nothing about it!

Flaherty stares hard at him for a long moment, then his glance flicks around the room. But there is nothing suspicious here, and he turns to the door, addressing the other detectives.

FLAHERTY. Let's get going. As long as Vettori doesn't know anything about it.

The other two detectives step outside. Flaherty, however, pauses in the doorway.

FLAHERTY. Oh, say . . . you heard the news, Vettori? (*As Sam looks at him silently*) Somebody got Alvin McClure over at the Bronze Peacock.

SAM. McClure! That's terrible. Some guys are sure careless with the lead. What a tough break for Arnie!

FLAHERTY (*grimly; seen in a close-up*). It's going to be a tough break for a lot of birds! Well, so long . . . I forgot to wish you fellows a Merry Christmas! (*And he closes the door.*)

The PALERMO OFFICE comes into full view again and we see Sam walking over, shooting the bolt on the door and peeping through the little lookout window. Rico comes out of his hiding place and spreads his coat and the money on the table, and Sam joins him. Both men show the effects of the strain. Otero is unmoved; Scabby and the others come nearer. Then a close view shows SAM dropping into a chair—his nerves frayed.

SAM. It's Tony . . . I can't get 'im. . . . The kid's a great driver . . . must o' lost his nerve. . . . (*He sighs heavily, shakes his head, then speaks wearily:*) Well, let's see the color of that money . . . (*He puts out his hand. But Rico, standing at the other end of the table, suddenly puts a guarding arm over the money which is lying on the table in stacks.*)

RICO. Not so fast, Sam. I got my own ideas of a split, this trip! And you can take it my way or leave it. We ain't beggin' you!

SAM (*abandoning his customary lassitude, jumping up*). Yeah? Well, I bossed this job and I get my split the regular way or else . . .

RICO. How'd you boss this job? By sittin' here in your office drinkin' wine? Well, that don't go no more. Not with me, it don't. We're done. I been takin' orders too long from you!

SAM (*an ugly, menacing look on his face*). And you'll keep on takin' orders, too—or you'll get out so fast that . . .

RICO (*interrupting him*). Maybe it won't be *me* that gets out . . .

SAM. Guess the boys got something to say about that!

The whole GROUP comes into view, and as Sam and Rico are standing, they occupy places on the opposite sides of the table. Sam, as he finishes his last sentence, looks challengingly at the gang. But the gang, one by one, slowly moves over to Rico's side of the table, the men silently ranging themselves behind him. There is not a word

spoken. Rico stands there, a triumphant half-smile lighting up his face. Sam's face drops.

SAM. Oh! That's it, eh?

RICO. That's it, all right. You've got to where you can dish it out, but you can't take it no more. You're through!

Sam's face hardens, and he stares at the gang. For a while he doesn't seem able to believe the situation.

RICO. Well?

SAM (*slowly*). The split's O.K. with me, Rico!

RICO (*turning to gangsters behind him*). How about you, boys?

Otero, Scabby and Bat reply simultaneously.

THE GANG. It's O.K. with us, *Boss!*

A close view then shows RICO stepping up to SAM.

RICO. No hard feelings, eh, Sam? We gotta stick together. There's a rope around my neck right now and they only hang you once. If anybody gets yellow and squeals—*my gun's gonna speak its piece.*

SAM. No—no hard feelin's. If this is good with the boys, it's good with me!

tero sticks his head into sight.

OTERO. Can I go see my woman now, *boss?*

RICO (*with an indulgent wave of his hand*). Sure! Now don't spend all your money on her, Otero. You worked hard for it . . .

An appreciative laugh from the unseen gang rewards this, as the scene fades out.

PART SEVEN

MA MAGDALENA'S FRUIT STORE fades in at night. MA MAGDALENA, is an old, fat, ugly Sicilian hag. She is a notorious fence and the confidante of half of Little Italy. For a blind she runs a small basement fruit store, behind which are her office and living quarters. She is sitting in the rear of her shallow shop and as the view fades in, the cry of a newsboy is coming close.

NEWSBOY. Extra! Extra! Crime Commissioner shot!

A newsboy crosses the store to Ma and sells her a paper. As he goes away, Rico enters and passes the boy who goes out, slamming the door behind him. Ma Magdalena takes one look at Rico's set face, rises and motions him into the back room. She hobbles after, on her stick. The newspaper is still in her hand. He doesn't speak; only by a surreptitious motion of his hand does he beckon to her to follow him.

MA MAGDALENA'S OFFICE comes into close view. One wall of the small room is lined with shelves of canned goods. A makeshift desk-like affair and a litter of odds and ends are visible in the place.

MA (*perching on chair at desk, throwing down her newspaper, and looking inquiringly at Rico*). Well, Rico, business good?

Rico pulls out his split, peels off a few bills which he returns to his pocket and hands the bulk of the money to the old woman.

RICO (*smiling*). Can't complain. Here . . . salt this away with the rest.

MA (*while deftly counting the money*). Had a big New Year's Eve, did you?

RICO (*with satisfied expression*). Plenty big.

MA (*having finished counting, she looks up*). Twenty-seven hundred.

RICO (*nodding*). That's right. How much have I got now, all told?

MA (*looking ceilingward, her face screwed up as she figures, counting on her fingers*). Lemme see . . . 'Twas thirty-one hundred—then the two grand you gave me a week ago—and now this pile. . . . (*Looking at Rico*) Seven thous' eight hundred.

RICO. Good enough. Hang on to it good, Magdalena. Never know when I'm gonna need it. There'll be lots o' fun, startin' tomorrow.

MA (*shrugging*). Good, you know what to do if things get too hot. . . .

RICO. The hideout all fixed up?

MA. Look at it yourself . . .

We get a close view of the HIDEOUT, a very narrow room, not much larger than a closet, containing a cot and a chair.

MA's VOICE. Best hideout in the world. . . . Nobody find you here . . . !

In the OFFICE, RICO, seen close, nods approvingly. Then Ma swings the shelves back in place, moves to Rico and taps him on the shoulder with her stick.

MA (*wheedling*). Look, Rico, ain't you got a nice little girl who wants a big diamond?

RICO (*scornfully*). Me buy a diamond for a Jane from a fence?

MA. You are cold, Rico. Don't care for anything except yourself—your hair and your gun.

Ma shakes her head and makes a clucking noise. She thinks this man is not human.

RICO (*smiling*). I might like a diamond for myself—like big shots wear . . . (*As the old hag's face lights with avarice*) One o' these days. Maybe soon . . . (*Now Rico notices newspaper on Ma's desk, and with a nod indicates it.*) Here, lemme see that . . . !

Ma with a knowing, crooked smile, hands him the paper, on which the large display type headline emblazoned across the front page is visible. Rico takes up the paper, and starts reading it with interest. A close-up reveals the headline, which reads:

"THUGS KILL CRIME COMMISSIONER IN NIGHT CLUB HOLDUP."

Rico grunts and his hands fold the paper so as to be able to read the story properly. A portion of the NEWSPAPER appears next; it reads:

"The thug who shot Alvin McClure was described by one eye-witness as a small, unhealthy-looking foreigner."

A close-up shows RICO'S FACE filled with annoyance.

RICO. Where do they get that unhealthy stuff? I never been sick a day in my life.

Irritated, he crumples the newspaper and throws it on the floor as the scene fades out.

PART EIGHT

TONY'S FLAT fades in. This is a combination living and bedroom in one of those wretched tenement houses that are typically Little Italy. The apartment itself perhaps consists of a bedroom and a kitchen in addition to his room, but we do not see the other chambers at this time. Tony's bed is made up on a pulled-out davenport. As the view fades in, he is lying on it, fully dressed. It is early morning. A feeble city sun sends its rays through the cracks of the window shades now drawn over the two small windows of the room.

A close view shows TONY lying on the bed. He is asleep, but a nightmare seems to be torturing him—his face moves convulsively and he tosses about, occasionally throwing his entire body into the air. Now, suddenly with a shriek, his eyes open, instant terror takes possession of his face, and he jerks himself upright on the bed. Crouched against the wall, he sits there, his eyes darting back and forth as though looking for hidden enemies. Then, satisfied that he is alone, he seems to quiet down a bit, and with the back of his palm wipes away the perspiration that has gathered on his forehead. Then with trembling hands, he searches his pocket for cigarettes. Finding the crumpled package, he pulls out a cigarette and with unsteady hands lights it. But after a puff or two, he leaps up from the bed.

Then we see him nervously moving the cigarette between his lips, walking up and down the tiny room. Now, unable to stand the torture of his thoughts any longer, he jerks the cigarette out of his mouth and throws it on the floor, viciously crushing it under his heel.

TONY (almost shrieking the words). Oh, God! I can't stand it . . . I can't . . .

The door opens quietly and MRS. PASSA, an old Italian woman with a parchment-like yellowed face, comes in. She is fully dressed for the street.

MRS. PASSA (coming forward, with a look of concern). What's matter, Antonio? Why you no sleep?

Tony comes to a halt, and merely stares at his mother.

MRS. PASSA. You sick, maybe?

TONY. Yes . . . no . . . I don't know. . . . (Bursting out irritably) Can't a guy get up when he wants without having to answer a lot of fool questions . . . ?

MRS. PASSA (slowly nodding her head through this speech). You stay out late, Tony? You drink lotta wine?

TONY (turning away). Oh! Lemme alone . . .

Mrs. Passa looks sadly at the boy as his back is turned.

MRS. PASSA (after a pause). Listen, Antonio, I leave spaghetti on stove. Yes? When you feel better, eat some, eh? Do you good.

She starts toward the door again, but at this Tony wheels around and speaks frantically:

TONY. Where you going, Ma?

MRS. PASSA (spreading her hands). I go to work.

TONY (hanging on desperately). It's early yet. . . . You don't have to go . . .

MRS. PASSA. I got to go see Mrs. Mangia . . . she has new baby. Only think! That will be six.

TONY (with a sickly smile). One is too much . . . a bad egg like me is . . .

MRS. PASSA (a softer look coming into her eyes). You ain't a bad egg, Antonio. You are only lazy. You go with bad boys . . . (Stepping closer, her tone full of reminiscent tenderness) You was good boy, Antonio. . . . You remember when you sing in choir with Father McNeil . . . You in white, remember?

Tony's face suddenly becomes rigid and his eyes stare off into the distance.

TONY (whispering). Father McNeil . . .

MRS. PASSA. The church was beautiful . . . you little boy with long hair . . . the big candles . . . flowers . . . remember, Antonio?

The verbal picture has a terrific effect on

Tony. Inner sobs shake him. His lips twitch, and he grasps his mother's arm as he says, almost hysterically:

> TONY. Don't go away, Ma . . . I don't want you to go away . . . don't leave me . . .

> MRS. PASSA. Antonio! (*Her hand goes out to caress his hair.*) No, no . . . I stay . . . I no go to work . . . I . . .

But Tony cannot bear her touch. He shrinks away—and his voice is harsh again as he snaps:

> TONY. Oh, go right ahead, go! I'm all right—sure I'm all right . . .

Mrs. Passa, repulsed, lets her hand drop. She sighs, then slowly, without a word, she turns and goes to the door. At the door she turns back and looks at her son as though expecting his summons again. But Tony is silent, and he again fumbles for a cigarette, which he sticks into his mouth without lighting. Mrs. Passa goes out.

A close-up of TONY shows him whispering to himself: "Father McNeil . . . " and the view dissolves to a STREET NEAR A ROMAN CATHOLIC CHURCH at dusk. It is snowing. For a while no one is seen in the picture. Then a solitary figure slowly walks into it, headed down the street. Then a close-up shows TONY, his head still lifted as he stares hard ahead of him, as though seeking encouragement. Now he nods, twice, to himself. He has reached a decision, and starts forward.

And now the STREET comes into view and OTERO is seen lurching into it. He is patently drunk; he is almost reeling as he hails the boy jubilantly:

> OTERO (*at the top of his voice*). Hey, Tony!

Tony stops, notices Otero—and his figure seems to shrink as he draws his head between his shoulders, looking out of frightened eyes at the Mexican. But Otero lurches up to him, slapping him on the shoulder with a great show of friendliness.

> OTERO. Ha! Where you been? I look all over . . . Rico—he say come and get your split.

Tony shakes his head. He is unable to utter words.

> OTERO (*staring at him*). What's matter, Tony? You don't want split, huh? You craz'?

> TONY (*softly*). I ain't crazy, Otero, but I don't want no split.

> OTERO. Listen, Tony . . . Rico know you lose your nerve. Be a man, Rico say. That is good. Be a man. You no better be yellow.

The words seem to strike Tony with especial force—and he starts biting his lips, wringing his hands in silent agony. Otero laughs, and again he slaps the boy on the shoulder.

> OTERO. Look at me! I am Ramon Otero, a great, brave man. I ain't afraid nobody or nothing. And Rico—he my friend. I love him with a great love. I, Ramon Otero, love Rico with great big love.

During the main part of the speech Tony remains silent. But before the Mexican has finished his oration, Tony turns and starts walking away.

Having come to the end of his harangue, the Mexican notices that Tony has left him. Now he hurries after him.

> OTERO (*catching up to Tony*). Hey, Tony, where you go, huh? . . .

> TONY. To church.

> OTERO (*alarmed*). Church . . . you mean . . . go . . . confess?

Tony nods assent and continues toward the church. Drunk as he is, Otero realizes what the other is doing and is stunned by the discovery.

> OTERO (*shooting out his hand after Tony as though to stop him*). Hey, Tony, you mustn't. . . . Tony, please, not talk to the Priest. . . . (*But Tony is rapidly walking away.*)

> OTERO (*crying out in alarm*). Tony . . . Tony . . . no tell nothing to nobody . . . Tony, please.

Tony quickens his pace, and hurries away from Otero. Then the view dissolves into the PALERMO OFFICE: Rico, Sam and Scabby are in the room, also Bat Carillo, when Otero bursts in. The excitement seems to have sobered him and he is quite coherent as he rushes up to Rico and tells him the news:

OTERO (*gasping with excitement*). I found Tony . . . but it's too late. He's craz', craz'—I tell 'im, be a man . . . but he just shake his head and go to the Priest. . . .

Shocked by this intelligence, the gangsters look at each other. They are all aghast. Only Rico nods knowingly, as though he had expected this.

SAM (*gasping*). The Priest?

RICO. Well, I guess that's it. What'd you expect of a guy that's been a choir boy . . . ? We ain't got any time to waste.

SAM. It's only the Priest! Confession— that's all!

RICO. Yeah, I know. I'm as religious as you are any day! But a guy who'll talk to the Priest will talk to other people, too. Get yourself a can, Sam, and let's go.

SAM (*suddenly putting a palm over his face with an expression of horror, whispering:*) Not me! Take . . . take Scabby . . .

RICO (*impatiently*). Scabby's no good!

SCABBY (*a look of relief spreading over his face*). No, I'm no good!

RICO (*now looking hard at Otero*). Can you drive, Otero?

Otero hesitates a moment, looks at Rico as though he were also about to refuse, then nods:

OTERO. Yes . . .

RICO. All right, there's no other way out. . . . We'll use the black roadster. . . . (*He quickly dashes for the door, Otero following him.*)

The scene dissolves to the STREET BEFORE THE CHURCH. It is still dusk, and the snow falls faster now. A black roadster, hugging the curb, approaches and slows down near the church. A close-up of the ROADSTER then shows Otero and Rico peering through the windshield—the car is barely crawling. Otero points, and Rico's face becomes as grim as death. He lifts the big automatic which has been resting on his knee.

Tony appears on the sidewalk—and starts walking up the church steps. Then Rico's voice is heard:

RICO (*out of sight*). Tony!

As the boy whips around, there is a fusillade of shots. Tony falls without a sound. The gears of a car scream—the exhaust roars.

PART NINE

A STREET fades in. It is day, and a typical Italian procession is slowly moving down the street. In the van is an Italian band—confined to brasses—playing a slow, mournful funeral march. Following this comes the hearse, richly laden with flowers, wreaths, floral blankets, and inscribed ribbons. Behind the hearse, there are a number of closed automobiles—limousines, of the kind furnished by undertakers for such processions.

The funeral procession is seen from another angle, and a few of the motor cars are included and a section of the hearse. Now the legends on the ribbons are more clearly distinguishable and bear such routine inscriptions as "REST IN PEACE" and "GATES AJAR." Individual names can also be seen on the ribbons: "SAM VETTORI," "RAMON OTERO," "MOTHER," "ST. MARY'S YOUNG MEN'S CLUB," "ALUMNI ASSOCIATION P. S. 25." The funeral march continues.

A close view of MRS. PASSA'S AUTOMOBILE, driven by a uniformed chauffeur, shows MRS. PASSA, Tony's mother, in the back seat.

Next to her is old MA MAGDALENA. Both women are dressed in black. Mrs. Passa is sobbing aloud.

MRS. PASSA (*between her sobs*). Tony . . . Tony . . . Why do you go away like this, why you leave me . . . ?

MA MAGDALENA (*taking hold of her arm, softly*). Ssh! No cry, Mrs. Passa . . . please . . . you no can help . . .

MRS. PASSA (*keening*). Why I not die? First my husband . . . then the baby . . . now Antonio, he go too! Why I raise them? Why I see them grow? . . .

Tony, he didn't hurt nobody . . . He was good . . . Why? Why?

This cuts to a similar LIMOUSINE and a close view shows KILLER PEPI, BAT CARILLO and SAM seated.

SAM. We're gonna plant the kid right. That'll look good.

BAT. See all them flowers . . . ! That hearse is sure decked out pretty . . .

SAM. Well, this wasn't no time to be tight with money. Tony deserved a swell send-off. Poor kid!

KILLER PEPI. But Rico's wreath beat them all. Big like this . . . (*Spreading his hands to illustrate*) And all it said on it was: "TONY"—not even Rico's name.

BAT. Yeah, Rico's no piker.

SAM. Tony looks like he was asleep . . . don't look a bit changed . . .

BAT. Beats me how they do it.

This cuts to a close view in a TAXICAB, parked on a side street—unnoticed. In the back seat are Joe and Olga. Joe's face is white, drawn. He is nervously puffing at a cigarette, fingering it feverishly from time to time. Olga holds on to his left arm with both her hands.

JOE (*suddenly flinging the cigarette out of the window, and starting to hammer his knee with a nervous, impotent rage*). What'd they have to do it for? Why couldn't they let him alone? Who'd he ever harm? Oh, the dirty . . .

OLGA (*still holding on to his arm, now drawing closer to him*). We shouldn't have come, Joey. I begged you not to come. You're getting excited and its all for nothing. . . . *You* can't help poor Tony any more!

JOE. I had to come. I had to see them taking him away . . . (*Now raising his voice to a tragic pitch*) They forced him into that job. . . . He was scared. He didn't want to go . . . (*With a final bitter outburst*) Like me. Tony was like me. I didn't want to go neither . . . they forced me . . .

OLGA. That was your last job, Joey. We'll go away . . . I told you we'll go away.

We can get bookings all over the country . . .

JOE (*his face drawn in fear*). But they'll get me. You watch and see. Once in a gang, always in a gang. They'll get me the way they got Tony . . .

OLGA (*sternly*). No! I can save you. I'm going to take you away!

JOE (*suddenly breaking down*). Yes! Let's try . . . I can never look them in the face again. Not after this . . . I'll do anything rather than go back to the mob. I'll dig ditches . . . anything . . . (*Very eagerly; a cunning quality coming into his voice*) We won't go right away, though, Olga. That would give it away . . . I'll just lie low first . . . keep on dancing at the club . . . and stay away from Rico. Then when the coast is clear, you and me beat it . . .

Olga, her face beaming with happiness, strokes his arm tenderly, and the scene cuts to a close view of Rico and Otero seated in the back seat of a car. For a second or two they are silent.

OTERO (*finally*). Just the same, it's hard on his old lady . . .

RICO. Well, it's Tony's own fault. I didn't want to do it, did I?

OTERO. No, you had to do it, Boss.

RICO (*nodding*). I had to do it. When you're in this racket you gotta take your chances. Tony was a good kid, but he was weak. There's no room for that kind. It was to be us or him—so it had to be *him!* This is a tough game—you gotta know how to take it and how to give it!

OTERO (*suddenly pointing to sidewalk through window*). Look, Rico, there's Flaherty, the bull!

This cuts to a close view of FLAHERTY standing on the sidewalk. He is in plain clothes. With hands stuck in his pockets, he is studying the funeral procession as it goes past him. In the background are idle spectators, loiterers, and passersby. And a view of the STREET, shows Rico's car passing, Flaherty smiles ironically and waves his hand with mocking, elaborate courtesy. Next in RICO's LIMOUSINE a close view shows Rico, bent to the window, seeing

Flaherty and perfunctorily waving back, somewhat irritated.

OTERO. Things must be gettin' pretty hot, Boss. What's he want?

RICO (*shrugging*). Aw, he's just stallin'. Hasn't got a thing on me . . .

They sit in silence for awhile until a long piercing scream is heard from the outside, instantly followed by drawn-out crying. Rico looks out of narrowed eyes; Otero shivers, and crosses himself.

OTERO. Tony's old lady . . . she sure is taking it hard.

RICO (*with a look of disgust on his face*). That's a woman for you.

Otero's face becomes mild for a moment. Then he speaks in an apologetic soft voice:

OTERO. Well . . . Tony was her son . . .

Rico raises his eyebrows with an expression equivalent to a shrug, then pulls out his watch and looks at it.

RICO. Gee, we're movin' slow.

OTERO. We got plenty o' time. That banquet don't start till eight.

RICO (*nodding; then relaxing and settling back in his seat*). Too bad Tony won't be there . . .

As Otero nods, the scene fades out.

PART TEN

The ELECTRIC SIGN: "CLUB PALERMO DANCING" fades in.

Next we see a MAN'S HAND, about to open a program. Just now his thumb is resting on the cover—the owner of the hand seems to be studying it. The hand is wearing a ring either exactly resembling, or similar to, the ring worn by Pete Montana in Arnie's office previously. The program which the man is apparently studying is a semi-stiff cardboard affair, with two embossed angels holding an equally embossed shield in midair. Printed on the shield is:

"TESTIMONIAL BANQUET
FOR
MR. CAESAR ENRICO BANDELLO
GIVEN BY
THE PALERMO BOYS"

Dangling from the shield are two entwined ribbons, embossed, and the legend:

"FRIENDSHIP—LOYALTY"

Below the shield, between the ribbons, are two turtle doves, cooing. The whole cover has a rich frosting of golds, silvers, reds and blues.

Now the hand slowly turns the page, disclosing the advertising section. This is divided into half- and two-quarter page advertisements. In the upper half is printed:

"COMPLIMENTS TO A TRUE PAL
MR. C. BANDELLO
FROM A TRUE PAL
MR. SAM VETTORI"

In the left-hand quarter:

"TO RICO:
REMEMBER THE RIVER
REMEMBER THE BROOK
REMEMBER THE FRIEND
WHO ADVERTISED IN THIS BOOK
BAT CARILLO."

In the right-hand quarter:

"COMPLIMENTS OF
JOE SANSONE (K.O.)
'Lightweight King of Little Italy'
and
HIS LADY FRIEND
MISS ANGELINA VECCHIONI"

The hand turns to the next page. This section is divided into three ads, each one taking up one-third of the page. The uppermost one says:

"BE A SPORT—DRESS TO KILL"
DRESS SUITS FOR HIRE
Tuxedos used at this banquet, exclusively rented by us.
COMPLIMENTS TO MR. BANDELLO AND THE PALERMO BOYS
PARIS-ROME STYLE OUTFITTERS
642 Fairmont Avenue"

And in the ad below this:

"THE HELPING HAND
UNCLE'S
That's all!"

The third ad, occupying the bottom space, reads:

"MA MAGDALENA
FRESH FRUITS AND VEGETABLES
TO RICO
A GOOD MAN HARD TO FIND!"

Now as the hand turns the page again, the view moves so as to include RICO'S FACE. Rico is dressed in a tuxedo—obviously hired and while not grotesquely ill-fitting the suit is by no means a perfect fit.

RICO (*as the conversation, shouts and laughter of the unseen guests rise*). It certainly is a swell lookin' battin'-order! That Scabby is a clever guy to get it up so good-lookin' with gold on it an' everythin' . . .

SAM. It cost all the boys plenty money.

Now the view moves back, disclosing the banquet table in all its magnificence. Then as the scene moves back further, the various guests seated on both sides of the long table come into view. All the members of the gang are present—Rico is seated in the place of honor at the head of the table; on his left the Big Boy, Sam Vettori on Rico's right; then Otero, Scabby, Killer Pepi, Bat Carillo, Kid Bean, Ottavio Vettori, Blackie Avezzano, and others. (Joe Sansone is an ex-lightweight, slender, small, with cauliflower ears; Ottavio Vettori, Sam's cousin, a husky Americanized Italian about twenty-one; Kid Bean is a Sicilian, dark as a negro. The others are the usual gangster type.)

Every other seat is occupied by the ladies of the gang—cheap, semi-prostitute, blondined, over-dressed types; there are, however, no women around Rico. Dangling from the chandeliers are red, green and white streamers. On the wall above Rico's head is an orange and blue square banner, very much like a college varsity affair, inscribed with the simple legend: "CLUB PALERMO," accompanied by an equally gigantic monogram embodying the two letters, "C" and "P."

In a general view of the celebrants the gang and their ladies are now busily eating. There is much indistinguishable conversation, various rough pranks are being played by the guests. Rolls, and occasionally salt cellars and spoons and knives are thrown around; a handspring is performed on the

top of a chair by one of the younger members of the gang; an amorous scene is being played between a lady and her boy friend. The din is terrific.

A close view at the head of the table next shows SAM VETTORI rising and, banging the table, rapping for silence. When comparative quiet prevails, he shouts at the top of his voice:

SAM. What the Sam Hill! Ain't this a fine way to act at a banquet? What do you think you are—a couple gas-house yaps? Cut the chatter—Scabby's gonna make a speech.

There is a close view of a section of the TABLE with Ottavio, a Girl, and Killer Pepi.

OTTAVIO (*making a noise like a goat*). Baa! Baa!

A GIRL (*sitting next to him*). Gosh! Ain't that cute!

KILLER PEPI. Oh, that ain't nothin'. (*Putting three fingers in his mouth, he blows a tremendous blast.*)

OTTAVIO (*screaming*). Wow! The cops! Baa! Baa!

The scene cuts back to the head of the table as SCABBY, seen close, stands up. He is manifestly ill at ease, embarrassed. He fidgets a long time before launching into his speech:

SCABBY. Well, fellows, you all know what we're here for, so what's the good of me tellin' you all 'bout it? Rico is a great guy an' . . . Well, gee whiz, Rico, I don't know how to talk fancy but— (*Pulling a platinum and diamond watch out of his pocket, and awkwardly dangling it on its chain*) . . . this here is for you, see? From the boys!

And there is a close view of the DIAMOND AND PLATINUM WATCH with the inscription "TO OUR STANDARD BEARER AND LEADER— FROM THE PALERMO BOYS"

A VOICE (*coming over the scene*). Come on! Everybody clap like . . .

We see the BANQUET HALL where bedlam has broken loose. Chairs are overturned, napkins waved, plates crashed against the table . . . the women scream, the men cheer wildly. Ottavio jumps up on his chair, and, acting like a college cheer-leader, gives the signal.

OTTAVIO. What do you say, boys? Three cheers for Rico!

Led by Ottavio, comes a regular college cheer, "RICO! RICO! RICO!" accompanied by catcalls, whistling, and applause. A close view of RICO shows his face beaming with pride as he stands up and waves for silence.

RICO. All right, if you birds want me to make a speech, here you are. I want to thank you guys for this banquet. It sure is swell. The liquor is good so they tell me, I don't drink it myself, and the food don't leave nothing to be desired. I guess we all had a swell time and it sure is good to see all you guys gathered together. Well, I guess that's about all. Only I wish you guys wouldn't get drunk and raise Cain, as that's the way a lot of birds get bumped off.

Rico sits down amid prolonged applause. Now Scabby runs up behind Rico's back and bends close to him, speaking:

SCABBY. A coupla newspaper guys, Boss. They wanta take a flashlight. It's for the Sunday section of the paper.

RICO (*indulgently but obviously pleased*). All right. Let 'em come! They'll have to make it snappy . . . (*And he pulls out his comb and starts combing his hair.*)

The photographer and the flashlight man take up their positions in the foreground of the full view of the banquet hall. Farther back, the gangsters sit up, posing for all they're worth. There is a general fixing of ties, hasty smoothing of hair, and sprucing up. The photographer waves, the flashlight goes off . . . a cloud of smoke, through which we hear Ottavio's scream:

OTTAVIO. Eeeh! I'm shot!

There is laughter at this, and then the scene cuts to the STAIRCASE where Flaherty, seen close, with another detective, is coming up the stairs, and this view cuts back to the BANQUET ROOM where Rico is now sitting in his place and Big Boy is leaning toward him.

BIG BOY. That was a bad play, Rico, that flashlight. They may pick you up on that.

RICO (*shrugging and laughing*). Aw, what do I care? Don't I want people to see what the boys think of me?

SAM (*tapping him on the shoulder and looking around*). But say, where's your pal, that dancer guy, Joe Massara?

Rico's face darkens instantly. His expression shows that the same thought must have been troubling him all evening.

RICO. He didn't come. He hasn't been around for a long time.

SAM (*insinuatingly*). He hasn't quit on you, Rico?

RICO (*sullenly*). Shut up, Sam—you tend to your business and let me tend to mine.

Now there is another close view of FLAHERTY and the other cop coming into the room. Flaherty stands at the door-frame, folds his arms on his chest, and looks into the room, and this cuts back to a close-up of Rico turning to Big Boy.

RICO. What does that bull want here? I'll show him where he gets off. (*Angrily rising, he pushes back his chair and starts off.*)

BIG BOY. Careful, Rico!

A close view of FLAHERTY still at the door shows him exchanging a few words with the other cop in a low voice. They both smile. Now Rico stalks toward him.

RICO (*brusquely*). Well, who invited you here?

FLAHERTY (*looking over Rico's new finery with deliberate insolence*). Getting up in the world, aren't you, Rico?

RICO (*feet planted wide apart*). What's that to you?

FLAHERTY (*still pleasantly*). Gosh, nothing. I'm glad to see you decked out like this. You see, I got my eye on you, Rico. Don't forget that I'm your friend—I like to see a young fellow getting up in the world. Well, so long!

RICO. Fall down the steps, will you?

FLAHERTY (*still pleasantly*). Thanks! (*He turns to go, but as he reaches the door, he turns back to Rico.*) Say, somebody threw a brick in Meyerblum's window last night . . . you don't happen to know anything about a platinum and diamond watch that was stolen, do you? In case you hear about it, let me know . . .

Rico, taken aback, is really at a loss for an answer. But Flaherty turns again, and goes through the door, leaving Rico to stare after him as the scene fades out.

PART ELEVEN

A NEWSPAPER PICTURE fades in. It reproduces the flashlight photograph taken at the banquet, the caption under the picture reading

" 'LITTLE CAESAR' BANDELLO GIVEN
TESTIMONIAL BY FOLLOWERS."

This dissolves into the BRONZE PEACOCK LOBBY where Little Arnie and DeVoss are present. Little Arnie is comfortably seated in an arm-chair near the telephone booth, smoking a heavy black cigar. DeVoss is standing before him, hands in pockets, a worried expression on his face. In Arnie's hand we see the newspaper carrying the flashlight photograph. Now he throws it on the floor, annoyed and disgusted.

ARNIE. A banquet, huh? Rico got far . . . too far! So now he's got to stop . . . I'm saying he's got to stop . . .

DE VOSS. Oh, Arnie, are you fellows going to start another scrap? What's the use of my paying heavy money to you for protection if there's never any peace?

ARNIE. Don't you worry, DeVoss. There'll be peace soon enough. I'm saying Rico's got to stop—so he's gonna stop, see! He's been nosin' in on my territory, and that's all wet with me.

A close view shows JOE standing on the other side of the telephone booth, which effectively conceals him from Arnie and DeVoss. He is listening to their conversation with rapt attention. Then the view cuts back to the LOBBY as Little Arnie, now seen close, bends forward and speaks menacingly, emphasizing his remarks with an extended forefinger:

ARNIE. I'm sittin' here, see? I'm sittin' here quiet, smokin' a cigar, see? But a coupla my boys ain't sittin' here . . . they're out lookin' for Rico. And they got their gats with 'em, too. Catch on? And once they find 'im, it won't be no banquet Rico gets—it'll be a wake!

DE VOSS (shaking his head). Well, Arnie, you know best. I never met Rico. I

don't know what he looks like . . . but I do want a little less excitement around here for a change . . .

ARNIE (rising and laughing). There won't be no excitement, after today . . .

He and DeVoss start walking off, and they are next seen crossing the lobby, toward DeVoss' office into which they disappear. Joe Massara, from behind the telephone booth, is watching them closely. Now, as the door closes behind the two men, Joe rushes into the telephone booth, and hastily drops a nickel into the slot. At this moment Olga enters the lobby. As she is only a few steps away from the booth, she hears the bell ringing, and glances at the telephone booth. When she sees Joe, she comes to a halt.

JOE (in the booth). Phelps 2284. . . .

As Olga hears the voice and the number she picks up her head in astonishment, her face darkens, and she hurries toward the booth.

A close view shows JOE clicking the receiver now. Apparently he is having trouble obtaining his connection. Then he is seen again talking quickly.

JOE (forcefully). Otero! This is Joe Massara. I just got a straight tip. Look out for Rico. Little Arnie's after him.

At the CASHIER'S DESK in Club Palermo Otero is then seen staring stupidly at the hand telephone for an instant. Then he drops it on the floor and turns excitedly to Bat Carillo, who is standing beside him.

OTERO (out of breath). Where's Rico?

BAT. Got me! He ain't showed up yet!

OTERO. Come on, we gotta find him!

They go out, on the jump, and a waiter comes into view and retrieves the telephone.

A large TOURING CAR with closed curtains is next seen driving slowly past the Club Palermo. There is little movement in the street as behind the car rattles a big white milk wagon. Following this a close view shows RICO at the corner newsstand, picking up about ten copies of the same paper. The youngster who is in charge of the stand looks at him in surprise.

NEWSPAPER VENDOR. Gee, you takin' all them papers, Mr. Rico?

RICO (*smiling proudly*). Sure—ten! Ain't I got my pitcher in 'em?

Next RICO is seen pausing in the lighted display window to look at his watch. It glistens in the light, and he regards it proudly. Replacing it, he buttons his coat and takes two or three steps. Then he sees a touring car coming toward him, becomes suspicious, and stops. Suddenly he darts into the doorway and stands there, reaching for his gun.

The touring car comes closer, and slows down. In it are two women. The car doesn't stop, but slowly continues, hugging the curb. It passes on and behind it, at some distance, comes a milk wagon. A close view then shows Rico lifting his eyebrows in surprise and relief as he looks after the car. His face is turned after the touring car as he steps out from behind his shelter.

RICO (*to himself*). Well, that's one on me . . .

Now a close view of the MILK WAGON reveals the presence of two Detroit gunmen and RITZ COLONNA, Little Arnie's bodyguard, who is driving. As Ritz sees RICO he points and yells to the other:

RITZ COLONNA. There he is—in front of that store . . .

He slaps his feet on the accelerator and the motor roars. Then the STREET reappears and knowing, too late, what is coming, Rico wheels around, all the time tugging vainly at his gun. It sticks. The milk-wagon drones into high speed, and three streams of fire shoot from the wagon as it sails

past. Rico is hit and falls. Above the sound of the shots is the crashing of glass as the machine guns ploy into the windows. The thugs are shooting too high in their eagerness.

A regular knot of men boils out of the Club Palermo. Bat, Otero, Pepi, Kid Bean and others, all with drawn guns. Curious waiters and some of the bolder guests follow them.

A close-up at the STORE shows Rico struggling to his feet, putting one hand to his shoulder where he has been wounded. A twisted grin appears; and he yells mockingly after the vanished assailants who have left the sidewalk littered with fragments of plate glass from the windows.

RICO. Fine shots you are!

On the street there is a long view of Rico surrounded by his men and a crowd collects from every direction. From the opposite direction Flaherty, the second detective and a huge policeman push their way to Rico. A closer view then shows the two detectives and the huge policeman meeting Rico and his gang in the crowd. Flaherty grins in a tantalizing fashion; Rico looks at him sourly.

FLAHERTY. So, somebody finally put one in you?

RICO. Not enough to hurt.

FLAHERTY. The Old Man will be glad to hear it. He takes a lot of interest in you.

RICO. Tell him the cops couldn't get me no other way, so they hired a couple of gunmen.

The crowd laughs at this sally—to the crowd Rico is a great man, afraid of nothing. The big policeman is writing a report in his notebook.

FLAHERTY (*still grinning*). If I hadn't been on the force I'd have taken the job cheap.

RICO. Listen, Flaherty, did you ever stop to think how you'd look with a lily in your hand?

FLAHERTY. No, I never did. I been at this game for twenty-five years and I've got better guys than you hung—and I never got a scratch.

RICO. Don't think you're ever gonna take a ride with me, huh?

FLAHERTY. When we take a ride together, I'll have the cuffs on you.

RICO. No buzzard like you'll ever put no cuffs on Rico— Come on, boys!

Rico and his mob start moving toward the entrance of the Palermo; and a close-up of FLAHERTY shows him looking after Rico, grimly.

FLAHERTY. I'll get that swell-headed mug if it's the last thing I ever do.

This cuts to a close view of the interior of the MILK WAGON as Ritz Colonna, bent over the wheel, is driving furiously, the two other men behind him.

RITZ. You saps! Wait till Arnie hears of this. . . .

FIRST GANGSTER. Aw . . . I hit 'im, didn't I?

RITZ. You couldn't hit a barn door, you hick!

This cuts into the CLUB PALERMO OFFICE, affording a close view of Rico, beginning to take off his coat and vest. His arm is starting to stiffen, and Killer Pepi helps him.

PEPI. Gee, Boss, I'm sorry. I should o' been with you. You mustn't never go out alone.

Then Scabby approaches Rico with a basin of water and a doctor's kit, cutting away his shirt and next starting to wash the wound—Rico enduring this stoically. We see Otero hurrying up to Rico, who is standing there biting his lips as though in great pain, while Scabby is deftly bandaging his shoulder, binding the arm against the body.

OTERO. It was Little Arnie, Rico. Joe Massara got the tip and called up. We no could get you in time.

A close-up of RICO shows him expressing surprise as he hears the name.

RICO. Oh! Joe, huh? Well, I didn't think he cared enough. . . . It was white of him, all right. Maybe I'll go to see him. . . . (*Lost in thought*) Yeah, I ought to give him a chance to be in on the next job. . . .

The view enlarging somewhat we next see that Scabby has finished the bandaging, and with a last encouraging pat on Rico's shoulder he lets go.

SCABBY. I didn't study medicine for nothin', did I? If they hadn't got after me and taken away my license . . . (*He sighs reminiscently.*)

Rico, his wound attended to, again becomes the man of action. He wheels around, facing the gang.

RICO. I'm going to see Little Arnie tonight! (*Pointing to the various characters as he names them*) I want Killer Pepi, Otero, Kid Bean and Bat to go with me. . . .

On this speech the scene dissolves into a close-up of a GUN in Killer Pepi's hand shoved hard into the middle of a man's back. Then we see that Rico and his men are at the STEEL DOOR which guards Little Arnie's gambling joint. A fear-paralyzed lookout shrinks away from the automatic which Killer Pepi presses against his body.

PEPI (*threatening*). Listen, Handsome. You tell the doorman we're all right or you won't be tellin' nobody nothin' no more.

As the man nods dumbly, Rico and his men crowd into the corners so as to be out of the sight of the doorman when he looks through the wicket. Otero knocks, the shutter opens, and in it appears the familiar face of the doorman.

LOOKOUT (*huskily*). These birds are all right.

The door swings open and before the astounded doorman can open his mouth, he is covered by Otero. The others rush in after him.

In the GAMBLING HOUSE LOBBY, seen fairly close, the doorman has an agonized look. He is sure they are going to kill him for his part in the attack on Rico, but Rico, whose arm is bound beneath his coat, merely speaks to him.

RICO. Where's Arnie?

The doorman gasps like a fish out of water but no words come, his eyes merely flick toward the private room. Rico's glance follows his.

RICO. In the office?

With hands stretched above his head, the doorman bobs his head in an imbecilic fashion, whereupon Rico, Otero, Bat and Killer Pepi move toward the office.

Kid Bean stays behind guarding the look-out and the doorman who back up against the wall. "The Kid" leans against the steel door from where he can cover the gambling room. And now at the OFFICE DOOR Rico briefly outlines his plan of campaign.

RICO. Bat, you stay here and don't let nobody in. Pepi, if the door's locked, do your stuff. Otero and I will cover you.

Pepi twists the handle of the door, but since it is locked, Pepi, placing his huge shoulder against it, throws all of his stupendous bulk into a savage heave. The door springs open and Pepi falls into the room. With drawn gun Otero leaps after him, and Rico follows.

A close view inside the office shows three startled men rising halfway out of their chairs, they are Little Arnie and his hired killers from Detroit. Then Rico and his men are seen surrounding Arnie and his gangsters. Arnie, with indescribable fright showing in his face, is standing, with Killer Pepi's gun pressed against his back; and the two gangsters are half-collapsed in their chairs, watching the muzzles of the guns that guard them. Rico steps close to Arnie, his hat solicitously removed.

RICO (*suavely*). Hello, Arnie! How's business?

The enemy are covered from either side of the room by Otero and Pepi as Rico pulls a chair up to the desk and sits down, calmly taking the center of the stage. And a close-up next shows LITTLE ARNIE sinking into a chair and sitting with his mouth slightly open. As a rule he is imperturbable, but this cyclonic entry is too much for him; his mask slips, revealing a pale, terrified countenance, and he blusters helplessly:

ARNIE. What's the game?

Then a close view of Rico and the Arnie group shows Arnie turning to his gorillas.

ARNIE. I don't know what's wrong, but it's a private row. You guys beat it!

The Detroit gangsters, only too willing, start to get out of their chairs, but they settle back when Rico speaks:

RICO. Sit still! You guys are *invited* to this *private* party.

DETROIT GANGSTER (*sneering, though without moving*). Suppose we don't want to stay, see?

With his maddening smile, Rico looks from Otero to Pepi, then back to the enemy.

RICO (*pleasantly*). I wouldn't stop you for the world, but those boys of mine have itching fingers.

There is a long pause in which the Detroit mugs and Arnie shift uncomfortably in their chairs. Then Rico breaks the silence.

RICO. Arnie, you oughtta had better sense than to hire a couple of outside yaps! Especially bad shots! (*Then, seen in a close-up—thrusting out his square jaw*) You hired these mugs. They missed. Now you're through. If you ain't out of town by tomorrow mornin', you won't never leave it except in a pine box! (*As Arnie, completely unnerved, actually trembling, doesn't reply*) I'm takin' over this territory . . . from now on, it's mine.

ARNIE (*now seen with Rico; bitterly*). You're growin', Rico. This is what you been after all the time, eh? I saw it in your eyes the first time I met you. . . . (*With unaccustomed bravado*) You're a rat, Rico. But if you think you can muscle in on me like you did on Sam Vettori, you're off your nut. I guess you forgot all about Pete Montana?

This, for an instant, stops Rico, and his face assumes a worried expression as his mind weighs the possible consequences of running up against Pete Montana. But his face hardens.

RICO. And how's "Diamond" Pete gonna stop me? He may be your boss, but he ain't mine.

ARNIE (*sneering*). Sam didn't feel that way about him. Sam knew who gave orders!

RICO. Sam was too soft. "Diamond" Pete could scare him. But I ain't no Sam! Sam is through . . . now you're through, too!

A close-up of RICO shows him staring impersonally at Arnie; there is a close flash of ARNIE'S STICKPIN, and then we see that he is studying Arnie's fancy stickpin. Having impressed the design on his mind, Rico's glance lifts to Arnie's face.

RICO. Nice stickpin you got, Arnie! I'll have to make a note of it . . . (*Showing him his hand*) See my ring? Nothin' phony about my jewelry . . .

And the DIAMOND RING on Rico's finger that comes into close view is seen to be an exact replica of the ring worn by Pete Montana. Arnie, without glancing at the ring, just stares at him as Rico laughs:

RICO. Better quit the racket, Arnie. You got so you can dish it out, but you can't take it no more.

Rico motions to his men, turns and walks out. Otero follows. Pepi backs out, covering the boss. Arnie does not move. The two Detroit gunmen sit slouched in their chairs, looking at the desk. The moving view passes through the door as Killer Pepi starts to chuckle. His chuckling rumbles into a roar of laughter as the scene fades out.

PART TWELVE

A SOCIETY COLUMN NOTICE fades in; it reads

"Mr. Arnold Lorch, of the North Side, has just left for Detroit where he intends to spend the summer. He was accompanied by two of his Detroit friends, who have been in Chicago for a short stay."

This item dissolves to the PALERMO OFFICE where some of the gangsters are gathered around SCABBY, who has the newspaper in his hand. The society item is Scabby's work, and he is hailed as a hero by Pepi, Sam Vettori, Bat and Kid Bean. The others roar with laughter and slap Scabby on the back. The Palermo office dissolves now to MA MAGDALENA'S OFFICE, where the repulsive old woman chuckles over the joke at her desk. This in turn dissolves to the PEACOCK DRESSING ROOM, where DeVoss shows the paper to Joe. Both laugh. DeVoss is tickled to think that he is rid of LITTLE ARNIE. But Joe makes a vital comment which turns DeVoss into a thoughtful mood—he is probably dropped from the frying pan into the fire.

JOE. That means you have a new partner—Little Caèsar.

This dissolves to a close-up of FLAHERTY reading the notice and smiling grimly; then his eyes narrow, and the view dissolves to RICO'S ROOM, a dingy room in Little Italy, for Rico has not yet thought of moving into more pretentious quarters. Rico is lying on his bed, in a loud bathrobe—he is not sleeping, merely resting; Otero is seated in a chair, smoking. And now OTERO is seen looking at a newspaper in his hand, then addressing Rico admiringly:

OTERO. Now you're famous, Rico. Everybody laugh at Scabby's story.

RICO (*in a close-up as he lies on his bed*). Yeah, Little Arnie took an awful walloping, all right. You see, Otero, 'tain't no use bein' scared of any of these big guys. The bigger they come, the harder they fall. Yeah, I ain't doin' so bad in this business so far . . . (*And he absent-mindedly fingers his scarf-pin, instantly seen in a close-up that reveals its similarity to the one that Arnie wore the previous night.*)

Rico smiles, apparently thinking of his victory, when there is a knock on the door. Otero leaps across the room—standing at one side of the door, out of range of anyone shooting through the panel. He looks anxiously back to Rico who should not be disturbed. Rico props himself on his good elbow—gazing at the door.

OTERO. Who's there?

RITZ COLONNA'S tough voice answers—but it is not familiar enough to be recognized.

COLONNA. A couple of right guys to see Rico.

RICO. Duck, you "right guys," because I'm going to count three. . . .

ANOTHER VOICE. Hold your horses. This is Pete Montana.

Rico recognizes Montana's voice and motions for Otero to unbolt the door. Otero obeys—standing half behind it with his gun ready. Montana and his bodyguard enter and Otero drags up the only two chairs in the room, placing one at the bedside, the other a little distance away. Montana sits down beside the bed; his bodyguard takes the other chair; Otero squats on the floor, back against the wall behind them.

The brazen assurance and air of authority which so far have characterized Montana seem somewhat lacking as the scene comes closer. His manner is a bit hollow. He and Rico eye each other steadily, then Montana breaks the short silence.

MONTANA. I been watching you, Rico. Any guy that can muscle in on Sam Vettori and Little Arnie is on the up and up with me. The Big Boy thinks the same way. He sent me to talk things over with you!

Rico's mind works at lightning speed— what is this preliminary to? It is unusual, to say the least, for a big shot to make any advances. Then he begins to sense the truth —Montana is getting soft, and with this knowledge his arrogance grows.

RICO (affably). Thanks. I ain't lookin' for no trouble with you, Pete.

MONTANA. I guess we got the wrong steer, then. Some wise guys told us you was going to edge into my territory.

RICO (yawning before answering calmly). Them guys don't know what they're talking about.

A close-up of MONTANA shows his eyes opening, then narrowing wickedly; he is going to test Rico.

MONTANA. You know I used to work Little Arnie's territory and by rights it's mine.

The reaction is swift. Rico sits up and swings his feet over the edge of the bed, bringing his face close to Montana. Rico

evidently has put the fear of death into all the gang leaders, for Pete draws away slightly and adds hastily:

MONTANA. But I don't muscle in on no right guy, see? It's yours now, Rico.

RICO. It's mine and I won't stand for no cutting in.

Montana laughs and answers with the air of a king bestowing largess, trying to keep up his position:

MONTANA. There won't be no cuttin' in —Maybe we can team up on a couple o' jobs.

This is a tremendous concession for a man of Pete's standing and Rico is amazed. He glances toward Otero, and a close-up shows the little Mexican's eyes popping; he grins widely—his idol has outfaced the great Montana. Then a close-up of RICO AND MONTANA shows Rico rising and Montana following suit.

RICO. You and me can do business.

Montana offers his hand—they pump arms briefly—and Rico looks down at the other's manicured fist, whereupon the ring on Montana's little finger comes into view—it is a flashy diamond and emerald creation.

Rico now glances at his own, similar ring in satisfaction, then looks up at Montana. The latter withdraws his hand.

MONTANA. I guess we'll go. If you need any advice, come to me.

RICO. Much obliged. A new guy has a lot to learn.

The ironic tone of his voice causes Pete to look sharply at the little man, but Rico's face is blandly innocent.

Otero unbolts the door and Pete leaves, his bodyguard following him. Otero shoots the bolt and turns to Rico, who is staring into space—envisioning much greater worlds to conquer. The Mexican sums up the situation:

OTERO. *He's scared* of you.

RICO (*seen in a close-up; laughing aloud as the scene fades out*). Otero, you said a mouthful. He's soft. He's got so he can dish it out, but can't take it no more! It's my turn now! There's no stopping me!

PART THIRTEEN

Some time later, as RICO'S ROOM fades in:

OTERO (*helping Rico to dress*). Look, Boss, you're getting up in the world. Ain't none of us ever been asked to eat with the Big Boy at his dump. Nobody ever crashed the gates but Pete Montana—see what I mean? You don't want the Big Boy to think you ain't got no class.

RICO (*feeling uncomfortable—the suit is too big for him*). Yes—they rig you up better than this in the stir. You're crazy if you think I'm going out looking like this.

OTERO (*convincingly*). You look fine, Boss.

RICO. Yes—all I need is a napkin over my arm.

Otero tips the mirror for Rico to get a full length view of himself, and Rico is won over.

RICO. I guess it don't look so bad.

This dissolves to the LIVING ROOM of the "BIG BOY'S" APARTMENT. Rico hands his hat and gloves to the butler. He hesitates about shaking hands with the Big Boy, but the Big Boy crosses to meet him. The host looks at Rico's swell outfit and his eyes twinkle.

BIG BOY. Rather lit up tonight, aren't you, Rico?

RICO (*self-consciously*). Yeh—I thought I'd better put on my monkey suit.

BIG BOY. That's right, Rico. May as well learn now.

His host laughs and motions Rico to a seat. Rico takes a long look around the room before sitting down.

RICO. Some dump you've got.

BIG BOY. Yeh—I sure paid for it. See that picture over there? That set me back fifteen thousand dollars.

RICO (*aghast—whistling*). Them solid gold frames sure cost dough!

The butler wheels in the tea wagon with drinks.

BIG BOY (*patronizingly*). Will you have a cocktail or a dash of brandy?

RICO (*shaking his head*). Not me. Never touch the stuff. Never!

The butler passes a humidor full of cigars, and Rico takes one, lights it and tips back his chair.

BIG BOY. I'm gonna talk and you're not going to hear a word I say. See?—This is inside dope and if it gets out it'll be just too bad for somebody.

RICO. You know me.

BIG BOY. All right, get this. If I didn't think a lot of you I wouldn't be asking you to come to eat with me. You're on the square, Rico, and you're a comer. You got the nerve and you're a good, steady, sober fellow . . . Pete Montana is through . . .

RICO (*almost leaping out of his chair*). Yeh? And I thought he was such a big guy!

BIG BOY. He has seen his day. If he puts up an argument it'll be just too bad.

RICO. I'll say so.

BIG BOY. If I said that you're a Pete Montana from now on—that you were to take over his territory and handle it in addition to your own, would you shake on it?

RICO (*beside himself*). Would I? *Would I!*

BIG BOY. All right. It's set! I'm doing a lot for you, but when I get you planted I want plenty of service.

RICO. You'll sure get it.

BIG BOY (*lifting his glass as the scene fades out*). Permit me, then, to drink to the new Boss of the North Side.

PART FOURTEEN

RICO'S NEW APARTMENT fades in and Rico is seen walking up and down the room like a proud peacock, and addressing Otero.

RICO. I knew it was coming. I knew he had his eyes on me. Let me tell you— it's not only Pete Montana that's through—but the Big Boy himself. (*As a close-up shows him reflecting, then expressing confidence in his future*) The Big Boy himself—he ain't what he used to be, neither. Pretty soon *he* won't be able to take it and then . . . *watch me!*

The butler comes into the LIVING ROOM.

BUTLER (*announcing*). Mr. Massara to see you, sir.

RICO. Send him in.

As the Butler leaves, Rico hastens to a chair at the fireplace, sits down, quickly takes out another Panatela, unwraps it, and inserts it in his mouth; all this is done very obviously to impress Joe. Now JOE enters, stops in the doorway, and takes in the apartment, letting his gaze rest on each object individually, Rico watching him from out of the corner of his eyes.

JOE. Gee whiz, Rico . . . what a palace!

Rico, who has pretended not to notice the other's entrance, now looks up.

RICO (*with an air of boredom*). Oh, hello, Joe! Yeah, it's a good joint. What you expect—ain't I got twenty grand tied up in it?

JOE (*coming nearer*). Hello, Otero! How do you feel, baby?

OTERO. First rate.

RICO. Sit down, Joe.

JOE (*as he goes to fireplace, and takes chair*). You sure I'm good enough to sit in such a swell chair? (*He sits down.*)

RICO. Cut the comedy, Joe. (*Turning to Otero*) Screw, Otero. I gotta talk to Joe private.

OTERO (*with an obliging smile*). Sure. (*He crosses to door, while Rico offers the box of cigars to Joe.*)

RICO. Cigar, Joe?

JOE. Thanks!

By which time Otero has gained the door and gone out.

RICO (*closely studying Joe*). Well, surprise you to hear from me? I sorta thought it would be nice to have a little talk . . . like old times.

JOE (*ill at ease, and trying to assume an air of innocence*). It certainly is nice to see you . . . especially like this!

RICO (*surveying Joe*). You're lookin' good, too, Joe. Only a little too fat, maybe. Livin' easy, kinda?

JOE (*smiling*). Not *that* easy . . . Dancin' is no cinch.

RICO (*with a queer half-smile*). But you ain't complainin'?

JOE (*fearing what is to come, his smile dying away*). No, I ain't complainin'.

RICO. That's good. (*He sits back in his chair.*) You're right about dancin'. Nothin' like relaxation. Yeah, dancin' is fine for a—side-line. (*He looks at Joe from under drawn eyebrows, studying the effect of his words upon him.*)

JOE. What's the difference, Rico? As long as I ain't kickin', why should you kick?

RICO (*stroking his chin*). Who's kickin'? Only, should a young guy like you be wastin' his time? I kinda took a pride in you, Joe . . . brought you into the gang . . . pushed you ahead . . . But now you're gettin' to be a sissy.

JOE (*uneasily shifting in his chair as he is seen closer*). We gonna start that again? Can't you just forget about me?

RICO (*with a certain softness in his voice, as both men are seen in a close-up*). How can I forget about my pal, Joe? We started off together—we gotta keep on goin' along together. Who else have I got to give a hang about? (*Now he jumps up and goes over to Joe.*) I need *you*, Joe. Just before you came, I was over to see the Big Boy. He handed me the whole *North Side*. But it's too big for one man to handle alone . . . I need somebody—a guy like you—somebody I can trust, somebody to work in with me.

JOE (*shaking his head*). It can't be me, Buddy. I've quit.

Fierce rage takes possession of Rico's face and he grabs Joe by the shoulder:

RICO. You didn't quit! Nobody ever quit me. Get that! You're still in my gang. I don't care how many fancy dames you got stickin' on to you. That skirt can go hang. It's *her* that's made a softy outa you.

JOE (*a menacing look coming into his face*). You lay off Olga, Rico!

RICO (*furiously*). I ain't layin' off her. I'm after her. She an' me can't both have you. One of us has gotta lose—an' it ain't gonna be me! There's ways of stoppin' that dame . . . !

As he says the last sentence, he makes his old significant gesture of reaching for his gun.

JOE (*terror-stricken as he interprets the movement*). You're crazy! Leave her out of this . . .

RICO (*his face distorted with rage now; fairly shrieking*). It's curtains for her, see? She's through . . . she's out of the way . . . that's what she is!

JOE (*drawing back; almost insanely*). You're lyin'. You wouldn't . . .

RICO. I *wouldn't?* I'll show you . . . that dirty, painted-up . . .

JOE (*almost shrieking*). I love her! We're in love! Don't that mean nothin' to you?

RICO. Nothin'! Less than nothin'! Love —soft stuff! When she's got you, you ain't safe . . . you know too much. I ain't takin' no chances. You're stayin' here!

JOE. I'm not!

RICO (*gripping his shoulder*). You move an' it's suicide . . . suicide for *both* o' you!

A close-up of JOE alone shows him almost paralyzed with fear. He sinks back against the chair, and drops into it. He shuts his eyes and puts a guarding hand up against his face.

JOE (*hoarsely*). No . . . no, no . . .

A look of evil satisfaction is on Rico's face as he is seen close. He stands over the boy, closely studying him. He is about to say something, as the telephone rings from outside the room. Irritated, Rico glances toward the door. Then he starts off, with a suspicious glance at Joe. Joe rises, but instantly Rico turns and roughly thrusts him back in his chair.

RICO. Don't you move or I'll . . .

Joe, limp, remains in his chair as Rico goes out through the door leading to the bedroom. Then a close-up of JOE, as he sits, shows him trembling in his chair, his face moving convulsively.

JOE. No . . . no . . .

From the other room can be heard Rico's voice at the telephone, his words unintelligible.

JOE (*hysterically*). No . . . Olga . . . no . . .

Suddenly he jumps up, looks around, indescribable fear on his face—once more he looks at the door from behind which Rico's voice is heard . . . and blindly dashes toward the door. . . . He bursts through it as Rico's words still continue on the telephone, and the scene fades out.

The LIVING ROOM of OLGA'S APARTMENT fades in—in the late afternoon. This is a modest enough, very orderly little room. As the view fades in, Olga is nervously walking up and down the room.—From the impatient little noises she makes with her tongue, from her manner of repeatedly glancing at her wrist watch, from her occasional slapping of her palm against the knuckles of her other hand, we are instantly aware of her impatience and agitation. Now, apparently unable to control herself any longer, she rushes to the telephone, and a close-up shows her calling into the telephone.

OLGA. Greenhill 0139.

There is a moment's wait, during which she bites her lips, her face again and again assuming a tense, listening expression. Finally there is a voice at the other end.

OLGA (*her voice trembling with excitement*). Bronze Peacock? This is Olga Stassoff . . . yes, Olga . . . Mr. DeVoss? Listen, has Joe been around there? (*Her face drops, the answer is apparently disappointing.*) Oh! . . . I just thought . . . He's been gone all afternoon . . . went to see Rico. . . .

It is plain that DeVoss is trying to calm her fears, because Olga now answers.

OLGA. It's just that I'm worried . . . I don't know why . . . but he was to be here an hour ago and hasn't come yet . . . I'm afraid . . .

DeVoss again says something. Now Olga essays a little laugh, passing her hand over her forehead:

OLGA. Yes, I suppose it's all right . . . It was just a funny feeling I had . . . Thanks, Mr. DeVoss. Good bye! (*She limply puts down the receiver.*)

Now, from outside a bell is heard, and its sound is a distinct shock to Olga, who jumps up in instant terror. She holds her hands to her breast, gasping for breath. Olga is then seen hurrying across the room to the DOOR. This door opens directly on the staircase landing, without a hallway—a not uncommon feature of old-fashioned apartment houses. She tears the door open.

As Olga is opening the door, Joe bursts in, out of breath, his face pale as a sheet. He tries to speak, but words fail to come from him. He stands in the doorway for a second, his hand on the outside knob, then thrusts himself into the room, closing the door behind him. He leans with his two palms against it. He stares at Olga with eyes wide open, clouded by terror.

OLGA. Joe . . . Joey . . . What is it? What's the matter?

Joe gasps for breath. Then his hand shoots out, the words wheezing out of him:

JOE. We gotta go . . . Come on, . . . hurry!

OLGA. But Joe, you're . . .

JOE (*frantic with fear*). What are you standing there for? Didn't you hear me? Hurry! Hurry!

OLGA. Yes, Joey . . . Just let me get my things . . . (*Going up to him, putting her hand on his arm in sudden alarm*) Honey . . . you're going to faint in a minute.

JOE (*thrusting her arm away, almost hysterically; shaking his head*). No, I'll be all right. . . . Let's get out of here . . . We . . . Rico . . .

His voicing of the name seems to bring back memories of his visit. His face distorts, his eyelids droop—he sinks against the table standing next to the wall.

OLGA (*herself blanching at the name*). What'd he do to you. Oh, I knew it! Didn't I know it?

JOE (*desperately struggling to overcome his dizziness; his voice rising and falling away; feverishly*). He, Rico, . . . told me you and I gotta quit . . . That he'll kill you 'less I stick with him . . . I ran away . . . Don't you see we gotta go . . . ? Anywhere! Any place . . . out o' town . . . so long as we get away . . .

During his speech, Olga stands before him, slowly shaking her head. Now Joe stares at her.

JOE. No? You're . . . not . . . coming?

OLGA. No! That's not the way!

JOE (*grasping her arm*). Olga, we've got to . . . You don't know that guy . . . You're . . . Olga . . . Please . . .

OLGA. No! Sit down, Joey . . . We've got to think . . .

JOE (*shrieking*). I don't want to think. I don't want to sit down. You're . . . you're comin'. (*He moves as though to grab her arm.*)

OLGA (*catching his hand and pinning it down against his body. There is a great firmness and determination in her voice*) Don't you see that would be no use? Where could we go? Where could we run to? There's no place he wouldn't find us. (*Staring at Joe fixedly*) Only one thing for us to do. *Flaherty!*

JOE (*his jaw dropping—staring at the girl. Then:*) You crazy? Do you think that'd save us? *Flaherty!* That's worse than suicide. I can't do it, I won't do it . . . not if both of us have to die a million times . . .

OLGA (*firmly*). *I* can do it! The gang must go. Rico must go. I want my happiness. I want you. We'll never have any peace till Rico is gone . . . I'm *going* to do it!

Olga starts toward the bedroom where the telephone is, and Joe, guessing her intention, tries to stop her.

JOE. Olga . . . stay here . . . don't . . .

But she is quicker than he is . . . gets into the bedroom and slams the door shut before he can stop her. Then a close-up shows Olga locking the door while Joe is pounding on the other side.

JOE'S VOICE. Olga . . . open the door . . . don't call Flaherty . . . Olga; please . . . Rico'll kill us both.

OLGA (*now at the phone*). Park 1000 . . . (*As Joe is pounding and yelling*) Headquarters? I want Sergeant Flaherty!

As he hears the name, Joe in the LIVING ROOM, renews his efforts to batter down the door.

OLGA (*seen close in the* BEDROOM). Sergeant Flaherty? This is Olga Stassoff . . . I've got Joe Massara with me . . . in my apartment, 17 Edgelow Drive. . . . He wants to talk to you . . . Hurry . . .

As she lets the telephone drop and sinks back exhausted the scene cuts to a close-up of FLAHERTY who is just replacing the receiver on its hook. He stares into the mouthpiece for a moment, lost in thought. Then a smile comes to his face and he turns to his partner:

FLAHERTY. Come on, sweetheart!

SECOND DETECTIVE (*rising; yawning*). Who's giving the cocktail party?

FLAHERTY (*with immense satisfaction in his voice*). Joe Massara.

The other detective's eyes open wide in surprise, and he whistles softly.

FLAHERTY (*examining his own holster*). Got the artillery on you?

The scene cuts to OLGA'S APARTMENT where Joe is sunk in his chair, his face buried in his hands.

JOE. You shouldn't have done it . . . you shouldn't have . . .

OLGA (*who is standing near the table*). There was no other way . . . no other right way . . .

JOE. It's the rope for me.

OLGA (*firmly*). No! Not if you turn State's evidence. We'll make them promise that . . .

The scene cuts to the EXTERIOR OF OLGA'S APARTMENT HOUSE, one of many in a row of brownstone fronts. A machine draws up. As it slows down, and before it has a chance to stop, two men jump out of it and dash up the stoop. Only then does the machine come to a halt.

Next the HALLWAY comes into view. Olga's house is a "walk-up" affair, and the dark, winding staircase, is full of obscuring shadows. The two men are rushing up the steps . . . and it is still impossible to see who they are. Then the scene returns to OLGA'S LIVING ROOM where Joe now sits up in his chair . . . he is hearing the footsteps outside.

JOE (*his teeth chattering with fright*). It's them . . . (*He jumps up and cowers against the wall.*)

OLGA (*also listening*). Yes. (*She starts for door, giving Joe's hand a passing touch.*) Stick it out! You can do it!

JOE (*catching hold of her hand*). Wait . . . Olga, I . . .

But it is too late. At this moment the door bursts open, under the battering strength of OTERO'S shoulder. Instantly he steps through the crack . . . followed by Rico.

OTERO. There he is . . . the yellow double-crosser . . . Give it to 'im, Rico!

A close view shows OLGA reeling back, then frantically throwing her arms around Joe.

She is about to scream, but her terror is so great that the sound freezes on her lips.

A close-up of RICO shows him reaching into his pocket, then slowly raising his hand. The muzzle of the gun, sticking through the cloth of the pocket, is pointed at Joe. Rico's face is twisted into a terrifying mask of pain.

A close-up of JOE shows him standing against the wall, his arms spread out. In the failing light of the afternoon he resembles a figure crucified. He shuts his eyes, waiting for the shot.

As OLGA's LIVING ROOM again comes into view, Olga is about to rush at Rico, who still stands there with his gun poised, watching Joe. But Otero, similarly aiming his pocketed gun at her, holds her in check. Joe now staggers, he stumbles, he is on his knees, eyes closed; his arms again shoot out in front of him in a piteous gesture.

    JOE (*screaming*). Shoot! Shoot! Get it over with!

But Rico draws back—his hand drops—he cannot pull the trigger.

    RICO (*in a gruff voice, to Otero*). Let's go, Otero . . . *I can't!*

    OTERO (*shooting Rico a look full of surprise that instantly changes to hatred*). You're gettin' soft, too!

He wheels around, jerks out his gun and fires at Joe. Rico hits the little man's arm up just in time and the bullet goes wild. Joe staggers back, holding his wounded shoulder.

The scene cuts to the EXTERIOR of the APARTMENT HOUSE as another machine stops and Flaherty and his partner, accompanied by a third detective, jump out of it. At this moment a shot rings out above, followed by Olga's scream. The three detectives halt for an instant, look up toward the window from where the sounds issued, then dash up the steps, disappearing through the door of the house. Then the view cuts back to the LIVING ROOM as Rico is wresting the automatic away from Otero, his look menacing the Mexican.

    RICO. Gimme that, you . . .

The Mexican seems to be putting up a fight—the two men struggle for the possession of the gun. Rico succeeds in tearing the weapon from the Mexican and they dash to the door. But at this moment, from outside, we hear voices:

    FLAHERTY'S PARTNER'S VOICE. What floor?

Rico stops short, stares at the door, like an animal at bay. Now, from outside, another voice answers the first:

    FLAHERTY'S VOICE. The third! Come on, boys!

Rico leaps back, wheels around, and dashes to the window, Otero after him. A close view at the WINDOW shows Rico hastily throwing up the window, and crawling through, followed by Otero. Outside the window a fire-escape is visible.— Now the FIRE ESCAPE comes into view and Rico, with unbelievable agility, is dashing down the iron steps, Otero in his wake.

In OLGA's ROOM, Flaherty and the two detectives have just dashed in. Flaherty stops short, and rushes up to Joe, who is cowering, still holding his shoulder.

    FLAHERTY. They get you, Joe? Who was it?

Joe looks up at the cop, defiance in his eyes. Then he suddenly looks away.

    OLGA (*shrieking*). Otero . . . It was Otero . . . He and Rico! (*Dramatically pointing to window*) There!

A close-up shows FLAHERTY, with a snap of his fingers commanding the other two detectives:

    FLAHERTY. Get 'em, boys!

The two detectives yank out their guns, rush to the window and, crawling through, disappear. Then Flaherty turns to Joe:

    FLAHERTY. Well, Joe—ready to talk now?

Joe answers nothing, keeping his eyes on the floor, but a close view shows Olga rushing up to Flaherty.

    OLGA (*beating her breast with her fist to give emphasis to her excited exclamation*). I'll talk! It was Rico's gang that held up the Bronze Peacock. . . . It was Rico that shot McClure . . . the dirty, low, sneaking . . . (*Her voice rising*) Joe will tell you! Ask him! He knows it was Rico. . . .

FLAHERTY (*stepping close to Joe*). Let's have it, Joe. Was it Rico?

Joe is silent. Flaherty's eyes challenge him. Unable to tear his eyes away from the almost hypnotic gaze of the detective, Joe finally drops his eyes. Almost perceptibly he nods his head; then he nods once more. A look of triumph comes over Flaherty's face; he nods, and dashes to the telephone.

FLAHERTY (*now seen in a close-up at the phone*). Park 1000 . . . (*He waits for a second, then speaks rapidly into the mouthpiece.*) Hello—Jack? Round up the Palermo gang—I got enough on 'em to use a mile of rope—Anyway—*get Rico!*

This dissolves into the EXTERIOR of the POLICE STATION: Two emergency police cars, loaded to the running boards with reserves, tear out of the station, sirens screaming. The cops are armed with riot guns. This view dissolves to a SIGNAL BOX where a policeman is listening to a message over the phone and blowing his whistle loudly at the same time. He hangs up, snaps the box shut and runs out, motioning for a second officer to follow.

Now Rico and Otero are seen running toward the corner of an alley and a street. They halt as a police siren is heard in the distance.

RICO (*looking around suspiciously*). Now we got to watch our step. The cops are sure to be cruising around this street.

They step to the corner—nervous—dangerous; then Rico halts for an instant:

RICO. This is what I get for liking a guy too much . . . !

Rico and Otero dash straight across the STREET, looking neither to left nor right, aiming for the alley on the other side. But halfway to their destination a policeman appears out of a doorway three or four houses away and starts running toward them, blowing his whistle and tugging at his gun.

COP. Halt!

The two gangsters instantly take to their heels and beat it for the shelter of the alley, where Otero takes a flying shot at the officer, who keeps on. Then a few yards down the alley Otero stops, waits for the cop to appear, and shoots when he barges around the corner of the building. The cop staggers forward three or four steps and drops to his knees. He has been hit in the leg. Then he is seen calmly steadying his gun with both hands and firing from the kneeling position at the fleeing men in the background.

At the ALLEY, Otero is seen twisting sideways, looking at Rico in surprise, stopping and dropping his gun. He keeps on walking, holding his stomach. Forgetting everything else, even the bullets which continue to sing close to them—Rico puts his arm around the little man and holds him up. But after a few steps, Otero pulls away.

OTERO (*with dog-like devotion*). Run, Rico, run. They got me. I can't feel nothin'.

Rico swings him over his shoulder and starts to run heavily, keeping a telephone pole between him and the disabled cop who is still shooting, while the sound of police sirens is coming from every direction. Rico dodges around the angle of a board fence.

OTERO (*hitting him feebly in the face*). Let me down. Get away yourself. I'm done for!

Reluctantly Rico places Otero on his feet. The little man gives the boss an eloquent look, spins around and falls flat on his back. As the scene widens, Rico is seen leaping a board fence. Then policemen charge around the corner and spread out as skirmishers when they see Otero's body.

This dissolves into the SIGN

"CLUB
PALERMO
DANCING"

It is toward evening and the sign is flashing on and off. Through the sign the view then dissolves into SAM'S OFFICE where Sam is sitting playing solitaire. In the background can be seen Killer Pepi, Kid Bean and a few lesser members of the gang. These other boys are seated at a table, shooting crap, accompanying the game with shouts.

THE GANG. "Hey, keep your hands off that dough!"
"That's mine!"
"Aw, rest your jaw!"

Now the door is torn open and Scabby rushes into the room, breathless.

SCABBY (*almost screaming*). Sam . . . !

Sam, without looking up, speaks casually:

SAM. 'Lo, Scabby! Wanna bottle o' wine?

SCABBY. Wine? (*Rushing up to Sam, screaming*) Joe Massara. . . . They nabbed him on the McClure business and he squawked . . . !

There are excited exclamations from the boys, and they all gather around the table. Sam's jaw falls and he runs his hands over his face in a bewildered way.

SAM (*with a groan*). Oh!

SCABBY (*continuing*). Rico tried to get 'im and now the bulls are after *him*. . . . They got Otero . . . !

KILLER PEPI (*in a hushed whisper*). Otero!

A silence falls on the group for an instant. Next Kid Bean lets out an inarticulate cry of terror, runs to the closet door and, wrenching it open, grabs an automatic and small box of ammunition. The others follow suit. Only Sam sits quietly, his face still covered with his hands.

SCABBY (*impatiently taking hold of his shoulder*). Sam! Don't you get me? It's all off! What are you sittin' there for?

SAM (*shrugging his shoulders*). What else can I do? No use running. They'd get me anyway.

SCABBY. You're outta your head! Get up! Let's beat it!

SAM. No use . . .

SCABBY. You fool, you're gonna . . .

Now a siren is heard from outside and Scabby, no longer in a mood to argue, starts for the closet arsenal.

SAM (*calling after him*). Scabby, if you get away . . . pop Rico for me. It's his doin' . . . He muscled in on me. . . .

He's busted us all. Pop him, Scabby, for old Sam!

Scabby, instead of answering, rushes over to Sam and thrusts an automatic into his hand.

SCABBY. Here . . . be a man!

One or two of the boys have by this time gained the secret panel. There is a sudden rush of feet on the stairs—then a volley of shots bursts out. Next Bat Carillo runs into the room. He sticks his hand around the doorjamb and lets go the remainder of a clip. The shots are answered from outside.

BAT. The bulls!

Bat dashes across the room, toward the secret panel. As he does so, he fires two or three more shots. Scabby jumps through the panel, after Bat, sliding it in place behind him. Then Sam, dazed and petrified, puts his back to the wall and faces the door. Flaherty steps cautiously into the room—sees Sam with the gun and steps back.

FLAHERTY (*calling from the hall*). Sam— better give up—drop that gun before we start shooting!

Sam obeys—the gun making a loud clatter on the floor. Flaherty comes into the room holding his service revolver in front of him. He beckons and two big cops appear.

FLAHERTY (*indicating Sam*). Put the cuffs on him!

Sam stupidly holds out his hands, speaking with a final flash of cunning.

SAM. You ain't got nothin' on me!

FLAHERTY (*laughing grimly*). No? Nor on Rico, either. He's next!

And Flaherty runs out of the room as the cops snap the bracelets on Sam's wrists. Then the scene dissolves to MA MAGDALENA'S FRUIT STORE, where Ma Magdalena is talking to a patrolman. Another cop comes out of the office. Both men have drawn guns.

SECOND PATROLMAN. I looked every place. Nobody here.

FIRST PATROLMAN. Listen, Ma. If you see Rico or the other little guy you'd better let us know pronto!

The old hag bobs her head, and the police go out, Ma snarling after them, following which Rico's head appears in the office door.

RICO. Sssssss.

Ma turns, sees Rico and hobbles to him as fast as she can move. Then we see MAGDALENA'S OFFICE as Rico steps back and the old woman comes in. She looks shrewdly at him.

MA. So, you sneaked in the back way? Well, you got yourself in a nice fix.

RICO (*grinning*). Who told you?

MA. The police were just here searching the place.

Rico's expression changes, and his face falls into lines of worry and sorrow.

RICO. They got Otero.

Ma Magdalena only shrugs and moves across the office to open the secret door to the hideout, Rico following her.

RICO. I'm going to stay here a day or two. Then I'll want a car!

Rico goes through the narrow entrance into the cubbyhole and switches on the light. Thereupon we see the HIDEOUT with Ma Magdalena who stands in the opening holding onto the swinging shelves. Rico makes a swift survey of the tiny room and sits down on the cot.

MA. It's gonna cost you big, because I'm takin' big chances.

RICO (*in the grand manner*). Well, you got ten grand I planted here. Help yourself.

Ma edges the door closed. She knows that Rico is wholly at her mercy and she means to take full advantage of it.

MA. I'll give you a hundred and fifty dollars when you're ready to start.

Rico is instantly aroused. The hag closes the door to a mere slit.

RICO (*angrily*). You're crazy. I need plenty. Most of my dough is cached in my apartment and there won't be no chance of gettin' it.

MA. One hundred and fifty's all you get. Take it or leave it.

RICO (*enraged, starting toward her as if to strangle her*). Why, you dirty, double-crossin', thievin' old hag—I'll—

MA. I'm the only one knows where it's hid. (*Backing away from him*) Go ahead—kill me and you'll never get out of town. (*Through the crack of door*) One hundred and fifty is all you get!

The door is slammed shut. Rico springs toward it, all his fury exhausting itself as he bangs with his fists on the closed door as the scene fades out.

PART FIFTEEN

The CLUB PALERMO SIGN fades in. It is dead, no longer flashing on and off. Most of the electric bulbs are broken or completely gone. Several of the letters are missing. Broken bits of wires hang loose from the sign. The glass portions of it are broken, the tin casing dented.

The view moves down to the MAIN DOOR. Over the padlocked door is the painted sign "CLUB PALERMO"—weather-beaten, dirty. On the door, both windows are cracked, and the curtain hangs loosely, flapping in the wind. On one of the windows there is a sign reading:

"TO LET
APPLY TO OWNER
MA MAGDALENA
FRUIT AND VEGETABLES
101 FRONT STREET"

This dissolves into the EXTERIOR of a LODGING HOUSE affording a close view of the DOOR: This is another door, totally different in character—really just a niche in the wall with a dark hallway behind it. Suspended over the door on chains which creak rustily is the sign: "CLEAN BEDS 25c." This this dissolves into the INTERIOR of the LODGING HOUSE, a dark, murky, evil-looking place. Two long rows of cots fill the room, with hardly enough space to walk between them. In a corner of the room, under a feeble, yellowish, single electric light, sit three nondescript men, their chairs tilted against the wall. The one in the middle is reading a newspaper. The cots are mostly filled—only a few of them are still empty. The room is silent, except for an occasional snore, a mumbled word or two, the creaking of a cot.

The view moves past a few of the beds, showing the occupants. Most of them are lying with their clothes on—the effect is one of squalidness, misery. The view then comes up to the three men sitting against the wall, and at closer range one of them is seen smoking a battered old corncob pipe; the middle one, an old man with bleary, near-sighted eyes, is holding a newspaper close to his face; the third man is sitting with his eyes closed, chewing tobacco.

MAN WITH PIPE. And you knew him?

MAN WITH PAPER. I knew 'im. He was always no good. He was mean, Sam Vettori was, so now he got what was comin' to him!

THIRD MAN (*impatiently*). Well, what's it say in the paper?

MAN WITH PAPER (*painfully reading the items*). "FORMER GANG LEADER FAINTS ON SCAFFOLD. After a futile battle in courts, Sam Vettori, former gang leader, today presented a pitiful figure as the hangman's noose was placed around his neck."

Now the view moves over to a bed a foot or two away from the group with the paper, and a close-up shows RICO lying on a bed in his clothes. These clothes are ragged—there is a battered cap near him; a week's stubble covers his face. He rises, leans on his elbows—snorts with contempt and mutters to himself: "Faints, eh . . . ? He always was yellow. He could dish it out but he could never take it . . ." He giggles with a drunken leer on his face. Then he produces a whiskey bottle, drinks, and speaks, still to himself: "They could say a lotta things 'bout me in the old days, but they couldn't call me yellow . . . !"

Now the voice of the old man floats over this close-up of Rico.

VOICE OF MAN WITH PAPER. Listen . . .
"LITTLE CAESAR HAS NEVER BEEN FOUND. He is hiding like a rat in his hole. The once swaggering braggart of the under-

world wilted in the face of real danger and showed the world his cowardice, thus contradicting his oft-repeated boast that he could dish it out and take it too. When the moment arose, Rico couldn't take it! Meteoric as his rise from the gutter has been, it was inevitable that he should return there . . . "

VOICE OF THE MAN WITH PIPE. Just the same, he was the real leader of that gang.

VOICE OF MAN WITH PAPER. Don't you believe it! Sam was rotten but *he* was the real hand. Rico didn't have the nerve and he didn't have the brains. . . . He was yellow, like the paper says. That's what Rico was . . .

As Rico hears these words, he springs into a sitting position on the bed—an ugly, threatening expression coming to his face. He leaps up, and is about to start toward the group. Then, his face clouding, he looks at the whiskey bottle still in his hand, looks at it long and nods his head as though saying to himself: "I'm not the same man any more! This is the cause of it!" Then his eyes run down his clothes, his entire figure, and dropping the whiskey bottle on the bed, he starts toward the group.

MAN WITH THE PAPER (*now seen in the Group*). He was no good . . . No, sir, he couldn't take it, nohow!

Rico approaches and for an instant there is the old firmness in his face. His voice is strong as he shoots out his hand with the imperious command:

RICO. Let's have that paper!

The Old Man looks up in surprise, is about to resent this, but Rico's look defeats him and without a word, he hands over the paper.

A close-up shows RICO reading the paper, and the item reads:

"LITTLE CAESAR HAS NEVER BEEN FOUND. He is hiding like a rat in his hole. The once swaggering braggart of the underworld wilted in the face of real danger and . . . "

Rico's nervous hands crush the paper savagely—his rage dominating him. He stares at it; and as he stares, another item dissolves in. He imagines he reads:

"LITTLE CAESAR FACES DEATH WITH
CONTEMPT.
Bandello exhibits the cold nerve of an underworld king as he stands on the scaffold, flinging a laughing challenge into the . . . "

A close-up of RICO shows that the thought suddenly elates him with an almost insane longing to see himself as a hero—a superman in the face of death . . . His eyes gleam . . . a crazy smile illumines his face. . . .

Now Rico suddenly pulls himself together —takes another look at the paper—crushes it, flings it at the old man. Turning, he dashes out of sight. The three men are seen staring after him and then the scene dissolves into the EXTERIOR of a POLICE STATION at night as Rico pauses in front of it. He has been soft too long for his bravado to last. There is a mental struggle and his ego wins—though an element of fear remains. He heads hesitatingly into the station.

INSIDE THE POLICE STATION: This is an outlying station on the south side. It is nearing midnight and the Desk Sergeant is alone, writing in a big ledger. Rico, rubbing his hands in the warm air, is seen walking toward the desk. He stops in front of the Sergeant, who does not look up. Rico coughs, and the Sergeant raises his eyes—one swift glance.

SERGEANT (*gruffly*). Outside! All filled up. You can't flop here, tramp.

A reporter joins them, coming from a small room inside the building. He looks disdainfully at the tramp and leans against the desk, prepared to bait the defenseless hobo.

A close view shows Rico looking appealingly from the Sergeant to the Reporter, then back to the former. He does not know what to do in the face of this unexpected reception.

RICO (*faintly*). But . . .

SERGEANT (*belligerently*). You gonna get out or do you want to get thrown out?

A close-up shows RICO unable to understand it, and he makes a funny little helpless gesture.

RICO (*great sincerity*). Take me. I'm givin' myself up. I am Rico.

SERGEANT. Rico? What d'ya mean— Rico?

RICO. Little Caesar! That's who I am.

SERGEANT (*laughing*). Yeah! I'm Napoleon!

The Sergeant points his pen at the ragged apparition and speaks to the Reporter:

SERGEANT (*laughing*). That's one for your paper.

They both laugh. The Reporter comes close to Rico, sniffs his breath, and makes an exaggerated shudder. Then he points to his own head with a twirling motion of his finger.

REPORTER. Plain bugs, Sergeant. Rico never took a drink in his life. Besides, he's hiding down in South America, spending the million bucks he got away with.

SERGEANT (*half rising from his chair, with an air of finality*). I'll give you three to get outside!

Stunned, Rico looks from one to the other, then slowly turns and shambles toward the door.

SERGEANT (*to the Reporter*). That's the sixth guy in the last year who's come in here full of sheep-dip and said he was Rico.

Rico starts to open the door but stops, thinks a moment, then fishes in his vest pocket and pulls out the diamond ring. The sight of it seems to transform him and he makes his last dramatic gesture. With a sweep of his arm, he throws the ring at the Sergeant.

RICO. All right, but give that to Detective Flaherty with Rico's compliments. He'll remember it! (*There is something of his old voice in the words. He pulls the door open and disappears.*)

A close view shows the ring rolling over and over down the Sergeant's slanting desk and finally falling on the floor. The Sergeant gets out of his chair and grunts as he bends to pick it up. He looks casually at it and hands it to the reporter.

SERGEANT. Want some ten-cent store jewelry?

The Reporter starts to toss it back, then becomes aware of the weight of the ring and examines it closely with growing excitement.

REPORTER. Ten-cent store your grandma! This is real. This . . . Rico's ring! Where'd he go? (*He starts for the door on a run.*)

The Sergeant gazes after him with open mouth, beginning to feel uncomfortable. Deciding to take no chances, he rings the bell loudly for the reserves and picking up the phone, he speaks quickly into it:

SERGEANT. Give me Flaherty at Headquarters in a hurry!

The view dissolves to a STREET in the city's industrial section as Rico is walking along, his shoulders hunched against the wind. The scream of a police siren is heard faintly. On ANOTHER STREET then a police car comes careening around a corner on two wheels, its siren screaming, and a close view of the BACK SEAT discloses Flaherty and two other detectives.

DETECTIVE. Are they daffy at that Kenwood Station, or do you think it's really him?

FLAHERTY (*grimly*). I don't know. But I'm not taking any chances. If it's Rico, I'm going to shoot first and ask questions later.

THIRD DETECTIVE. That's how Rico always does business.

The STREET. RICO is seen still trudging along. As the police siren grows louder, he stops, looks over his shoulder, in the direction of the sound—and starts to walk again. He is passing a large illuminated billboard: "The Laughing, Singing, Dancing Success, Joe Massara & Olgo Stassoff in TIPSY TOPSY TURVY at the Grand Theater."

Then the BACK SEAT of the POLICE CAR, which is moving at a high rate of speed, comes back into view, and Flaherty is seen noting something in the street.

FLAHERTY (*excitedly*). There he is. It's Rico all right— Pull up, Ed.

Brakes scream as the car comes to a sudden stop; Flaherty and others quickly get out. Then RICO comes into view. He stands near the billboard; and we see the police car and the three detectives behind him. They are advancing toward him with drawn guns.

FLAHERTY (*seen in a close-up, advancing with his gun drawn*). Stick 'em up, boy. And keep 'em up.

A close-up shows an enigmatic grin playing around the corners of Rico's mouth. He shrugs his shoulders, and starts to reach toward the inside of his coat. And a close-up of FLAHERTY shows him firing three or four shots.

RICO is then seen falling—and his hand clutches a comb! The view then expanding, Flaherty and the others run into sight as Rico lies half-sprawled, half-propped up against a corner of the billboard.

RICO. Hello, Flaherty—you buzzard. I told you you'd never put no cuffs on me!

FLAHERTY (*seeing the man is dying*). You should have stuck 'em up when I asked you to.

Rico defiantly grins up at him and feebly tries to get his hand up high enough to comb his hair. A spasm of pain racks his whole body. Then a close-up makes it apparent that RICO is dying.

RICO (*gasping*). Mother of Mercy—is this the end of Rico?

RICO'S HAND comes into close view: The nerveless fingers slowly relax their grip on the comb. Rico is dead.

The scene fades out.

FURY

(A Metro-Goldwyn-Mayer Production)

Film Play by
BARTLETT CORMACK AND FRITZ LANG

Based on a Story by
NORMAN KRASNA

Directed by FRITZ LANG

Produced by JOSEPH L. MANKIEWICZ

———

C a s t

KATHERINE GRANT . . .	Sylvia Sidney
JOE WHEELER	Spencer Tracy
DISTRICT ATTORNEY . .	Walter Abel
KIRBY DAWSON	Bruce Cabot
SHERIFF	Edward Ellis
"BUGS" MEYERS	Walter Brennan
TOM	George Walcott
CHARLIE	Frank Albertson
DURKIN	Arthur Stone
FRED GARRETT	Morgan Wallace
MILTON JACKSON . . .	George Chandler
STRANGER	Roger Gray
VICKERY	Edwin Maxwell
GOVERNOR	Howard Hickman
DEFENSE ATTORNEY . . .	Jonathan Hale
EDNA HOOPER	Leila Bennett
MRS. WHIPPLE	Ester Dale
FRANCHETTE	Helen Flint

FURY

PART ONE

A view of STATE STREET, CHICAGO, fades in. It is night, and the street is comfortably filled with a leisurely moving, after-dinner crowd. Couples, and here and there an abstracted bum, are window-shopping. Then the view focusses on JOE WATSON and KATHERINE GRANT, his girl—average, middle-class, decent citizens of their country and their time, which is today. Joe wears an old, light raincoat, and is munching at salted peanuts from his pocket. Rounding a corner of a store that has a bronze plaque reading MARSHALL FIELD & COMPANY, they stop before a window display of a bedroom suite and accessories with a mannikin in bridal gown and a placard "For the Fall Bride."

JOE (*grinning at the display*). What d'ya say, kid? Are we movin' in?

KATHERINE (*smiling*). How many times do you want me to say yes?

JOE. Every time you say it, it's like the first time. My heart starts beatin' like I just run around the block. (*His grin fades into an expression of mock seriousness.*) Them slippery little rugs is out— man's liable to break his neck on 'em.

KATHERINE grabs his arm as they saunter down the street.

KATHERINE. Why, *Mister* Watson! Are you planning on doing a lot of running in the living room?

JOE. Yeah. After you.

KATHERINE. The rugs are out.

JOE. And them twin beds, too.

KATHERINE. Out like a light.

They grin at each other, and JOE, in his delight, tosses peanuts into his mouth with great rapidity.

KATHERINE. Hey. I like peanuts, too.

JOE. I thought you hated 'em.

KATHERINE. I did, once.

JOE. What changed your mind?

KATHERINE. I love you. You love peanuts. All right, so I love peanuts.

JOE (*grinning*). That wins.

They stop, and he gives her some peanuts. It begins to rain.

KATHERINE. It's raining— (*She lifts her face to it.*) It feels swell against your face.

JOE (*looking at her*). Tonight of all nights, it's gotta rain.

KATHERINE (*quickly*). Don't talk about it.

JOE. What am I gonna do after you're gone?

KATHERINE. Joe—

JOE. I'll be walkin' like this down a street, an' where are you?

KATHERINE. I'll be here, Joe. (*There is a momentary pause.*) Do you like moving pictures?

JOE (*gloomily*). I couldn't live without 'em.

KATHERINE. Come on.

As they move off, the scene dissolves slowly to the BALCONY of a movie palace, and KATHERINE and JOE appear pressed close together in the end of an aisle next to the wall. Her head is leaning over on his shoulder. From the screen far, far below comes the excited, indistinct voice of the describer of a football game. The voice stops quickly, and we next see the SCREEN which Katherine and Joe are watching: A news-reel is on, the "shot" being that of a football game ending. It changes to the interior of a banquet hall, where WILL VICKERY is already on his feet and is talking, but we do not hear him until the announcer's voice stops.

ANNOUNCER'S VOICE. Will Vickery, political leader of the Independent Party, addressing a recent campaign banquet.

A closeup of VICKERY reveals a typical Western statesman, with a twang in his voice and a professional trick of shoving out his jaw when he says "American."

VICKERY. The American people, dedicated to equality and justice for all, want no Communism, Fascism, or any other such dandruff in their hair! Like our vigilantes of old, we shall continue in this Democracy to settle things in our own way, by continuing to place our trust, in the sense of *fair play* and *common sense* of the American People!

The view changing back to the BALCONY as the news-reel ends to applause, JOE applauds enthusiastically. The noise subsides and the between-pictures lights go up a little.

JOE. Attaboy! (*To Katherine*) Let the people take care of themselves—he's got the right idea—

The man next to JOE (a distinctly American type) objects with a snort.

OBJECTOR. I'll take vanilla! "The American People!" (*He makes a pht-t sound.*)

JOE (*bridling*). What's the matter with the American people?

OBJECTOR. Sheep, palsy—sheep.

JOE (*belligerent*). I suppose it wasn't the people who made this country what it is today?

KATHERINE (*pulling his arm*). Sh-h! Joe—

OBJECTOR. I hope it's satisfied.

From the row ahead a very harrassed-looking man turns his head.

MAN. Look. I come here to see the pitchers. I'd like to see the pitchers—if you don't mind—

KATHERINE (*distressed*). Joe! It's almost time. We've got to go.

JOE (*as he gets his overcoat from under the seat*). If you don't like it in this country why don't you go back where you came from? (*He rises with Katherine.*)

OBJECTOR. Not me, Buddy. I come from Scranton, P-a.

OTHERS. *Sh-h! Quiet!* Scram, you!

The scene dissolves to the EXTERIOR OF THE MOVIE PALACE. The rain has stopped. JOE and KATHERINE appear coming down a stairway and crossing the lobby, Joe buttoning his overcoat, his hat askew on his head. Katherine straightens his hat as she reproves him gently.

KATHERINE. Darling, don't fight everybody else's battles—

JOE (*interrupting*). You'd think some o' these sourpusses didn't belong to the human race at all! Well, I do; and I'm proud of it. In this country, anyway.

KATHERINE. They're not in love—

JOE. Don't I know it.

Passing the lobby display posters and the box-office, they have come to the SIDEWALK. JOE puts out his hand.

JOE. It's stopped raining.

KATHERINE. The stars are coming out. It's very beautiful, now—

JOE (*uncomfortably*). It's — it's almost time. I hate to say it—

KATHERINE (*her eyes still on the stars*). Then, don't— (*He takes her arm, and they move off silently.*)

The CORNER of another street, leading to a more deserted section: Still silently, slowly, constrained, they walk on. They catch each other stealing a look at one another, and smile, tremulously, then look away. JOE hauls in a deep breath, his hands clenching and jamming rigidly in his pockets. They round the corner, and then appear on the deserted street, which is dim in the light of a single street light. Still silent, they pass through the cone of light, and start to cross the street, under "Elevated" tracks.

Now they pass under the "L" tracks, but unable longer to resist, stop and seize the protection of the shadows of one of the steel structures to cling to each other and kiss with desperate longing. Overhead a train pounds by, like their tumultuous blood.

The scene dissolves, amid the sound of a locomotive, to a TRAIN SHED, where a huge engine is being backed up to its train. Its coupling clicks as it hooks onto the first car. Then the railroad station LUGGAGE CHECKING COUNTER appears. It is an old station such as the Santa Fé Dearborn Street Station, Chicago. There is a grating separating customers of the checking counter from the rest of the room. An attendant comes from the racks with a suitcase and a handbag, and swings them on the counter to Joe. Katherine is waiting opposite the grating.

ATTENDANT (*yawning*). Twenty cents.

Joe tosses down coins that ring on the tin counter, and takes the bags. In swinging the bags down from the counter and turning, the pocket of his overcoat catches on the jagged end of a baggage truck and it rips. Joe, setting down the bags, lifts up the tear in his coat.

JOE (*ruefully*). Now how d'y' like that!

KATHERINE. Oh, dear! Give me— (*She takes the smaller bag, lifts and rests it on the top of the grating while she snaps it open. She tries to locate something.*) Where is— Oh, here it is. (*She finds and removes a small sewing kit, then returns the bag to Joe.*) Come on. I'll sew it.

JOE (*masculinely embarrassed*). Here? Aw, no, not—

KATHERINE (*interrupting*). Come on! (*She moves to the luggage step, sits down on the step, and opens the sewing kit.*) You'd just let it go, I know you would. Sit down.

JOE (*hastily*). No, honest I'd remember—

KATHERINE (*firmly*). Sit down.

The conquered male, JOE lifts his eyes to heaven, sighs, and sits beside her. She pulls the torn pocket to her. Joe steals a look around.

KATHERINE (*sewing*). All I've got is blue thread.

JOE (*interrupting*). Blue?

KATHERINE. Yep! Blue.

A train Announcer's voice is heard rolling out its monotonous call.

TRAIN ANNOUNCER'S VOICE. Train Number Eighteen, for Kansas City, Albuquerque, etc.

JOE (*during calling of the stations—relieved*). There! Y'see! Come on! (*He jumps up.*)

KATHERINE. That's not my train. Sit down! (*He sits. She tries to smile.*) I'm hard to get rid of.

JOE. Like my right arm, only I need you more. Aw, Kath—I'll come for you the minute I get that old bank balance up as far as the third floor—and a kitchenette. (*She smiles up at him affectionately.*) This waiting is—awful. After all, we're human. (*Two warning whistles of the locomotive start shrieking.*) Why couldn't you stay with your job here? At least we could—

KATHERINE (*interrupting*). We've been over that, darling. There's a better job there. And I can be saving for us, too.

JOE (*sighing*). I know. (*He stares off gloomily as Katherine finishes her sewing.*)

The train Announcer's voice is heard again.

TRAIN ANNOUNCER'S VOICE. Train Number Twenty, for—

The Announcer comes into view and passes on, his voice continuing as the scene dissolves to a flash of the LOCOMOTIVE with its steam hissing out, and this dissolves to the CANDY AND NEWS CART in the train shed as Joe is collecting a package of candy, two apples, and a magazine or two. He picks up a bottle of eau de cologne.

JOE. How much for this smellum?

CLERK (*grinning at him*). Four dollars—

JOE (*paying*). It ain't for me, wise guy. I'm seeing a young lady off—

He puts it in his pocket and turns, colliding with people — mostly farm or poorer middle-class types—and porters, amid much chatter and noise. Then, Joe, AT THE STEPS TO THE PULLMAN CAR comes to Katherine.

JOE. I got you some little mementums.

KATHERINE (*smiling — but wistfully*). Memen*toes*, darling, 'toes! Not 'tums. I've told you so often!

JOE (*trying to make a joke*). It's a habit from—from having braces on my teeth when I was a kid. (*He stares at her as if he were going to cry.*)

KATHERINE. You're s-still a kid, a lot of you is, and—(*gripping his hands tightly*) I love it, and I—love you, and—(*taking a tissue-paper wrapped plain gold band, old-fashioned wedding ring from her pocket*)—here! I got you a "mementum" too. (*Joe takes it awkwardly.*) Look inside.

As he lifts it to look, a close-up shows the RING bearing a faint engraving in old-fashioned script which reads, "Henry to Katherine . . . "

JOE'S VOICE (*spelling it out*). "Henry to Katherine."

KATHERINE'S VOICE. It was mother's wedding-ring. I was named after her, so I — Turn it around.

We see the ring turn in JOE's fingers, and read on the opposite inside, engraved, " . . . Katherine to Joe," the words "To Joe" in different style lettering.

JOE (*now seen with Katherine — his words stumbling*). I—Kath—hon— (*He can't go on. He tries the ring on. It is too small for his large fingers.*) Have to wear it on my little finger.

He puts it on, and as he does so, the locomotive (out of sight) lets off a whistle and a snort.

CONDUCTOR'S VOICE. All abo-o-a-r-d—

The locomotive bell begins to ring. JOE and KATHERINE cling together, and kiss hastily.

JOE. I'll come for you soon!

KATHERINE. Soon, Joe—soon!

She breaks away from him and runs up the steps of the car. Then KATHERINE appears in the WINDOW of the Pullman car, straining for a last sight of him. She smiles gamely, and waves. He comes into view, and reaches up as if to grab her hand through the window. The train begins to move, and JOE backs up, waving. Then the cars pass him, and we see the successive squares of light cast by the moving windows of the train as it slowly picks up speed. Joe gulps, and unconsciously strokes the ring on his little finger, then finally turns away.

The scene dissolves to the exterior of the RAILROAD STATION. Rain is bucketing down again as JOE appears, and he turns up his overcoat collar, standing under the protective marquee. He absently tears the corner of the waxed-paper peanut sack. He dumps the peanuts in his overcoat pocket and, still absently, eats a couple, feeling pretty forlorn. A closed truck, its tailboard down, is at the curb.—Under a station baggage truck near Joe is a mongrel dog, protecting itself from the downpour, and Joe absently whistles to the dog.

JOE. C'm here, Rainbow. (*The dog comes to him, sits down, and looks up.*) Y'need a shave.

He tosses the dog a peanut, and it catches it in its mouth.

JOE (*grinning*). You think you're pretty good, don't ya? (*He tosses a peanut into the air, and catches it in his mouth.*) How's that, big shot?

At the sound of the starting of the motor of the truck at the curb, JOE turns.

JOE (*to the dog, ruefully*). Sorry. My car is leaving.

The dog looks after him as he leaves, and it barks and runs after him.—Then JOE appears as he begins to drive his own truck.

The dog runs after it. He jumps up into it and crawls into Joe's lap.

> JOE (*grinning*). What's the attraction? Do I smell like a hamburger? (*His grin fades a little.*) I know. You figure maybe I feel the same way you do. Lonely and wet and small— (*He pats the dog's head.*) An' you're right, pooch, you're right—

The scene dissolves to the HALL of a cheap flat-building, in which JOE is living with two brothers. Joe and the dog come up the last few steps of a stairway and stop before a door. He gestures "Quiet!" to the dog, as if not to waken a sleeper inside, gets out his keys and unlocks the door. As he begins to open it, the scene changes to the lighted but empty LIVING ROOM of a cheap, furnished flat with an in-a-door bed down, dishevelled, with some tossed-aside newspapers and a towel on it.

> JOE'S VOICE (*coming from the hall*). Ah-h, that Charlie! Always leaving lights on!

JOE enters followed by the dog. On his way to the bedroom of the flat he passes the in-a-door bed, stoops, picks up a pyjama jacket from the floor, tosses it onto the bed, and tiptoes on to the bedroom door. He cautiously opens it. But the room is dark, except for a square of dim light through the window, beyond which is the top of a telegraph pole and wires.

In the BEDROOM (as seen by Joe) there are two beds, with a small table between them. They are unoccupied and, in contrast to the in-a-door, have not been slept in. Joe goes to the wall-bracket over the table, and snaps on the light. He looks at his wrist-watch, glances at one of the empty beds, and notices — between a photograph of Katherine and a couple of books on Automotive Mechanics and a cheap alarm clock —a note written in pencil. He lifts it up, and its contents appear at close range. It reads:

> "Gone to movie with Charlie.
>   Tom"

And suddenly there is the sound of a drunken laugh and of indistinguishable words.

Joe's hand drops with the note and he listens.

> CHARLIE'S VOICE. Here—come on. Straight ahead. You're walkin' backwards!

As Joe moves to the doorway leading to the living room, he hears:

> TOM'S VOICE. I — I'm a-all right.

In the LIVING ROOM (as seen by Joe) CHARLIE, the older brother, is placing TOM, the younger, who is fairly drunk, against the wall. Charlie is 23, lean, and "fly," dressed just a bit too carefully, too loudly. Tom is 19, an ordinarily nice boy. They do not see Joe.

> CHARLIE. Now hold it!

As he turns to close the door the dog comes to them, and Tom blinks stupidly at it, while Charlie closes the door.

> TOM. Charlie. Where'd y' get the dog?

> CHARLIE (*laughing*). Ah, there's no dog. You're drunk. (*He gets out a cigarette.*)

> JOE'S VOICE (*from the other room*). Went to the movies, uh? (*He is sarcastic.*)

Charlie hesitates a moment, and gives a resigned look to heaven, realizing that they've been caught with the goods — on their breaths. As Joe comes into the room, Charlie lights his cigarette, goes to the bureau beside the in-a-door bed, and without removing his hat, changes shirts during the scene. He wears no undershirt.

> TOM. H-h'lo, Joe! (*Trying to pull himself together, but stuttering a little*) Kath'rine get away a-all right? (*He starts for the bedroom.*)

> JOE. Yeah.

> TOM. That's fine! (*Unable to make the bedroom he drops unsteadily to sit on the in-a-door bed.*) I'm fine, too. (*He pulls himself up, oscillates a moment, then makes a slanting bee-line for the bedroom.*) I feel awful. (*And he goes into the bedroom.*)

> JOE (*turning on Charlie*). Now, listen, Charlie—

> CHARLIE (*without turning*). We just had

a couple of drinks after the show. The kid's gotta have some fun. He can't take it, that's all.

TOM's VOICE. Who can't take it?

They turn to see TOM holding himself, precariously unsteady, with one hand on the door.

TOM (*continuing*). I'd've been all—all right—

JOE (*going to him, taking his arm*). Okay, Tommy. C'mon.

TOM (*trying to excuse himself to Joe*). —but Mr. Donelli—

JOE's face instantly is grim, and he turns toward CHARLIE.

JOE. Donelli, uh? Donelli.

He helps TOM into the bedroom, closes the door and goes slowly to CHARLIE.

JOE. So you took the kid to Donelli's, huh?

CHARLIE is finishing dressing, waiting for the explosion.

CHARLIE (*slicking down his hair with a preparation*). All right! I been waitin' for it.

JOE. You're waitin' for the undertaker, or the cops, the kind o' life you lead— running errands for that racketeer. But you're goin' to leave Tommy out of it!

CHARLIE (*turning—conciliatory*). Joe. I know. But we met Donelli and he invited us up for a drink. Isn't it better for Tom to meet somebody who can do him some good?

JOE. "Good!" "Good!" I'm only glad Dad an' Mom can't see the "good" you're doin' yourself!

CHARLIE. Can that Sunday school stuff! D'you think I'm goin' to ride to heaven on thirty a week from some sweat shop? Be a workin'-stiff all my life, like you? Times've changed.

JOE. Yeh, they've changed all right. The People are *against* you monkeys now, and—

CHARLIE (*interrupting insolently*). The People ain't doin' so good themselves. I'd like to know what's so hot about *you?* Crazy in love with a swell girl and can't make enough money to get married on!

JOE (*hot*). Leave Katherine out of it!

CHARLIE. Then leave me out of it! Stop livin' my life for me!

JOE. I wouldn't live your life for anything in the world!

CHARLIE. Okay, Reverend—okay! (*Going to the door*) You keep on puttin' your shoulder to the wheel, an' don't forget to turn the other cheek! Some day you're gonna wake up outa that dream, an' brother, are you gonna have a hangover! Me, I got no time to bother with ya any more! I'm through—

He yanks open the door, and goes out, banging it after him. JOE rubs both hands wearily over his head, sighs, and goes toward the BEDROOM. Here the light has been left on. TOM, coat half off, is sprawled heavily asleep on one of the beds. We do not see Joe come in, but hear the sound of running water. Then Joe comes between the beds with a soaked towel, lays it across Tommy's forehead, then sits on the opposite bed, looking with some bitter gloom at the boy . . . The dog comes to him, pawing his knees, and Joe absently pats its head.

The scene cuts to a POOL-HALL, a large room with pool and billiard tables and racks. One side has windows, barred on the outside, which look into an alley. Along this wall runs a low counter with several telephones on it behind which, during the day, work the men who take bets. Dope sheets and charts are on the wall. A large blackboard is ruled off into divisions that bear the names, in white paint, of the country's race-tracks — the name "Santa Anita" is in newer paint. A few consumptive loafers are playing pool, and drinking beer, in auras of cigarette smoke, but most of the chairs are stacked and a Negro is mopping the floor. CHARLIE is crossing the room to a door at the further end, before which a "mug" of the bodyguard type is tilted back in a kitchen chair. (There is a clock on the wall over this door.)

BODYGUARD (*yawning*). H'lo, Charlie—

CHARLIE (*moving toward the back-room*). Hi.

The BACK-ROOM: It is an office with flat tables, a typewriter, and adding machine. Two men are at the table checking figures against names and addresses. Charlie takes off his coat.

ONE MAN. H'lo, Charlie.

THE OTHER. Here, kid. One sheet's all ready. (*He hands Charlie a list and continues checking.*) Bellows, $79 and Archer, $165—Wertheimer, $816—Halstead, $75 . . . (*He continues reading off names and figures.*)

Without replying, Charlie takes the list to the adding-machine, and adds up its figures. As the paper begins to roll from the machine to the accompaniment of its clicking sound, and as a PAPER curling from the top of the adding-machine comes into view, the scene dissolves, through the rhythmic sound of machines and of a moving belt, to an AUTO-ASSEMBLY FACTORY, next day. JOE, in overalls and jumper, is at his job on a moving belt that carries monotonously past him a succession of similar motor parts, on each of which he performs some operation. Joe nicks a finger on one of the parts, jerks back his hand, shakes the finger, looks around and calls to the foreman. The foreman, distinguished by lack of overalls and jumper, comes in to him. Joe shows the foreman his finger and indicates that he wants to fix it. The foreman nods and, as Joe goes, takes his place at the belt.

The scene cuts to the LOCKER-ROOM of the factory. It has unfinished cement walls and tin lockers. At two opened lockers two watchmen — special police — are changing their clothes, the outgoing one—young and strapping—into a street suit, the incoming one—a lanky, gaunt man—into a uniform and gun-belt and holster. The Special Police badge on his jacket identifies him.—Joe passes as they are talking.

OUTGOING WATCHMAN. Well, my wife dreamed about the horse, and it was number seven which is lucky for me. So I put five on the nose, and when she passed me at the rail there I swear she *barked* at me!

INCOMING WATCHMAN. Well, if you're stopping at Donelli's today—

The scene cuts to the FIRST AID ROOM, which is separated by a partition wall from the lockers beyond. There is an enamelled table, a large First-Aid kit with a Red Cross sign, and a placard such as are in factories warning employees to take no chances with minor injuries. JOE, having his cut finger taped by a nurse, jerks his head around at the sound of "Donelli," and listens.

INCOMING WATCHMAN's VOICE. — slap two down for me on Discovery in—

OUTGOING WATCHMAN's VOICE. Not me, pal. Donelli's is gettin' raided at eleven-thirty this mornin'.

JOE stiffens, glances quickly around at the clock, the involuntary movement jerking his finger away so that the nurse asks:

NURSE. Hurt?

JOE (*turning back to her*). No—no.

He looks up again anxiously, and a close-up of the enamelled CLOCK on the wall shows that it is eleven o'clock.

INCOMING WATCHMAN's VOICE. Who cares? When one a' them places go down, two o' them come up.

The scene cuts to the LOCKER ROOM as the watchman goes on.

OUTGOING WATCHMAN. My brother-in-law's a stenog' at Headquarters an' gave me the tip. They're crashin' it at eleven-thirty when Donelli's collections come in.

JOE passes hurriedly, the watchman mildly observing his haste. Then he appears coming down the factory STAIRWAY with a precipitous clatter, following which we see the Foreman at the MOVING BELT in the factory looking around, at his watch, and scowling in annoyance.

The scene dissolves to the POOL HALL—at the door to the back room, from which come the sounds of bets being placed, names of horses, ringing of phones, and chatter. The bodyguard is in the chair at the door, talking to a harassed Joe.

> BODYGUARD (*getting out a cigarette*). I don't care who y'are. Nobody goes in there between eleven and twelve.

Joe looks up at the clock, which reads 11:26.

> JOE (*desperate*). Listen—

The bodyguard lights a cigarette, and Joe takes advantage of the diversion to jump to the door. He opens it and calls in.

> JOE. Charlie!

The bodyguard has leaped up, and catching Joe's shoulder spins him back. Joe lifts a fist to smash him, but CHARLIE appears in the door.

> CHARLIE (*to the bodyguard*). Okay. It's my brother. (*The bodyguard shrugs and moves out of sight as Charlie exasperatedly exclaims*) Now what?

A man—a sleek "mug"—appears in the door.

> MUG (*at Charlie*). How long's Donelli gonna have to wait for them figures?

> CHARLIE. Just a second. (*The mug shoves the door shut.*)

In the BACK-ROOM, as the MUG is turning back into the room, several men are sorting a profusion of money on the table into denominational stacks, calling out their amounts as they hand them to DONELLI, himself, who puts them into a small satchel. Beside him at the table a man notes the amounts on a long list. Donelli is a slim, elegantly dressed bandit with a weasel's face and precise diction. He is smoking a long, thin cigar.

> DONELLI (*smiling*). The big chief was wondering down at the meeting this morning whether the — er — barbers oughtn't to need a little protection next.

At this point, however, the rising wail of a police-car siren stabs into the scene, following which we see JOE AND CHARLIE crossing the ALLEY between the pool hall and a drugstore as a police car filled with plainclothesmen swings into the alley from the street, its siren shrilling. Another police car passes, headed for the entrance to the pool hall.

In the POOL HALL the bodyguard is trying to get into the door to the back-room.

> BODYGUARD (*shouting*). Lam! (*But a detective grabs and spins him back.*)

In the BACK-ROOM DONELLI, his cigar still between his teeth, and his gang turn from this door to the alley door with a rush, but it is swung in and the other carload of detectives piles in. The racketeers weave back toward the door to the poolhall, but see that it is blocked there, too.

> DETECTIVE LIEUTENANT (*to Donelli*). Up they go, Nick! You an' your whole outfit's on your way to playin' ten years of solitaire —!

Now JOE and CHARLIE appear near a lamppost in the street.

> CHARLIE (*with relief*). Whew! (*Joe slaps him understandingly on the back.*) Thanks, Joe.

> JOE. Forget it. Go on home. I got to get back to work . . . Don't forget to feed the dog!

The ascending wail of the sirens comes closer and the two police cars, with the racketeers and detectives, pass Joe and Charlie. Then the scene dissolves to the BEDROOM, where the alarm clock shows 2:04. It is running, its ticks coming into the silence of the scene. On the table is a water glass and a can of soda bicarbonate. Charlie's arm and hand are moving to simulate passage of police cars across the screen, and he is making a "whoo-o-sh" whistling sound in mimicry of the sirens, as he tells Tom, who is sitting on his bed, staring up at him, what happened.

> CHARLIE. — and went past me like that. And — (*his voice dropping to a more serious note*) — out o' my life, too, believe me . . . that Joe . . . what a swell guy he is . . .

Tom rises, to reach for the glass, slightly losing his balance for a moment from his hangover.

> TOM. What'll you do now? (*He gets*

down the rest of the water, replaces the glass and falls to the bed again.)

CHARLIE (*after a moment, lighting a cigarette*). I got a couple o' hundred saved up . . . but what'll I do with it? . . . if I'd only learned something — (*picking up one of the books on mechanics*) — instead o' just hangin' around places. (*He drops books, almost incoherent with self-reproach.*) Joe was always learning. With me givin' him the horse-laugh. Big joke! . . . On me. Now I'm back on my heels, and he's the only one o' the three of us with a job. (*As he sits on the edge of the bed, the dog barks.*) Excuse me. The four of us.

He gives a little laugh. The dog barks again and looks toward the door, and Charlie follows his look and starts with surprise. JOE appears, moving toward the door of the bedroom. He is in his street clothes and overcoat, a bundle wrapped in newspaper under his arm. His face is set, his manner depressed.

CHARLIE'S VOICE. Hel-*lo*, Joe!

TOM'S VOICE (*simultaneously*). Joe!

JOE (*depressed*). Hello, kids.

He enters between the two beds and tosses his bundle to his bed, passing CHARLIE and TOM absent-mindedly and standing still for a moment, his back turned. Charlie and Tom feel something is wrong, and their gladness at seeing him leaks away.

CHARLIE. Anything wrong?

JOE. Give me a cigarette.

As he takes one from Charlie, he gazes at the photograph of Katherine on the table. The dog raises itself on its hindlegs, its forefeet against Joe's knees. He pats its head abstractedly.

JOE. Nothing's wrong—(*again glancing at photograph*) except — (*He twists the cigarette between his fingers, breaking it.*) I got fired. (*He turns, going toward the window.*)

TOM. Wh-*what*?

CHARLIE (*jumping up*). You got — what?

JOE (*turning back to them; with a forced shrug*). Well, there's nothing so startling about gettin' fired now'days, is there? That's happened to plenty.

CHARLIE. But why? What happened? What'd you do?

JOE. I broke the rules. I left the plant without tellin' teacher! After a year of comin' early an' leavin' late — goin' to school nights so I could — (*He breaks off.*) Aw, what's the use —

CHARLIE. An' it was on account o' me —

JOE. Oh, we'll get a job. This month. Next month. We won't starve. Only — (*with a faraway look*) Katherine . . . She'll have to wait — even longer now.

The scene fades out.

PART TWO

KATHERINE'S ROOM in Capital City at twilight fades in. It is a rented, furnished combination bedroom-living-room on the second floor of an old-fashioned house. There is a bay window with a window-seat that overlooks a backyard and garden, and beyond it an alley. A potted cactus plant is on the window-seat. The bed is in an alcove. There is a radio, which is playing a sentimental melody. The window is closed.

KATHERINE is at a table correcting the last of a pile of school copy-books, fountain pen in her right hand, and a burning cigarette resting on an ash tray near her left hand. She lays the last copy-book on top of the others, absently crushes out the cigarette, and rises. Lifting her arms over her head, she stretches to get the crick out of her

back, and walks to the radio and snaps it off; then she goes to the window, opening it. Outside, the trees have only a few leaves, for it is Fall. A light breeze stirs the lace curtains.

The YARD comes into view (as seen by Katherine). It has a little garden, and at one end stands an old shed. A strapping young negro is polishing up his old taxi-cab. The cab has painted on it in faded lettering CAPITAL CITY CAB CO. And below it in small letters the slogan "Best In The West." A negro woman's voice rises in song.

NEGRO WOMAN'S VOICE. "Oh, carry me 'long
Dere's no more trouble for me . . ."

The negro looks around over his shoulder and grins toward the rear of the OPPO-SITE YARD — where a young negro woman is removing laundry from a clothesline. She smiles and waves to the man as she sings:

NEGRO WOMAN. "I's gwine to roam
In a happy home
Where all de darkies are free."

KATHERINE smiles wistfully, her mood bitter-sweet, then goes to her bureau and gets out an old candy box, opens it, and takes out a packet of letters tied together with a ribbon. She goes to an easy chair beside the window, under a floor lamp, sits down, and removes the last few letters on the bottom of the packet. She opens and begins to read the bottom one, while the singing of the negroes finishes.

A closeup of the LETTER from Joe, in his handwriting, reads:

". . . and now who knows *when* I'll be able to come for you. But I've got my chin up. . ."

Her hand drops the letter, and brings another one up. She turns the first page and we read on the third of the closely written pages:

". . . and right after Christmas we got the big idea. We put together all we had and bought an option on. . ."

The scene dissolves to the exterior of a SERVICE STATION, a run-down old service-station garage — in winter; and this dissolves to the closeup of ANOTHER LETTER, attached to which is a folded newspaper clipping. Joe's writing reads:

". . . and in March Santa Claus came, but not with reindeers — ponies! See attached mementum!"

Over this can be heard KATHERINE's voice saying tenderly "Memen*to*, Joe—memen*to!*" Her hand folds down the clipping, which is that of a newspaper photograph of a race-track and grandstand in the process of construction. Its caption says: "NEW RACE-TRACK UNDER WAY." In heavy pencil on it Joe has drawn an X and an arrowed line leading off, with the pencilled words "Here is our garage!"

This dissolves to the exterior of the SERVICE STATION in the Spring. New pumps have been installed, and the place is painted. Tom is putting water in the radiator of a car, while Charlie is giving it gasoline. Joe is finishing wiping off the windshield. He takes money from the driver as a second car pulls up. and Joe switches over to the second car.

This dissolves to a closeup of a LETTERHEAD, giving the name of the garage — "Square Deal Service Station." JOE's writing is in pencil this time. Its beginning reads:

"Honey, hooray! We paid off for the garage today and are capitalists. . . ."

KATHERINE's hand turns the page, so that we see its end, which reads:

". . . and the whole family is fine and dandy.
            All my love,
                    Your Joe.

P. S. Speaking of the family, it turns out that my dog, Hash, is no gentleman!"

This dissolves to the SERVICE STATION in summer, and beside a newly painted dog-house lies JOE's DOG, surrounded by puppies only a few days old, and this dissolves to a closeup of ANOTHER LETTER, badly type-written, the lines reading:

". . . bank account is going up like a July thermometer. Soon, honey, soon!"

In KATHERINE's ROOM, it is now dark except for the lamp lit beside her. With a little smile, her thoughts far away, she murmurs, "soon," dropping the letter. There is a knock on the door.

KATHERINE (*awaking from her trance*). Come in.

The landlady of the rooming house comes in to her, a letter in hand.

LANDLADY. It's a Special Delivery this time, Miss Grant. They fetch 'em faster than when I was a girl, but I guess their insides don't change.

KATHERINE. I hope nothing's happened! (*She quickly opens letter, reads the first lines, and cries happily.*) He's coming, Mrs. Whipple! He's coming! (*She reads further, her voice breathless with emotion.*) — wedding license — marriage — He's bought a car! (*She turns the page of the letter.*) Look! (*She shows the landlady a mounted snapshot, enclosed in the letter; and a closeup of the snapshot, as the landlady looks at it, shows Joe, in his garage uniform, beside a rebuilt roadster.*)

This dissolves to the GARAGE in October. It is bathed in sunshine. We see Joe's car and the dog in the seat next the driver's. She has a dog-collar on, and is barking. Over the sound of the motor are heard Charlie's and Tom's voices· "Give Katherine a kiss for me . . . Happy Landing, fella!"

The scene draws back as Joe's overcoat is tossed to the seat beside the dog. JOE is getting in behind the wheel while CHARLIE and TOM, in their service-station clothes, slap him affectionately on the back. Joe's spirits are high.

CHARLIE. Look out for Indians out there!

Tom makes the Indian call with the palm of his hand against his mouth.

JOE (*throwing in gear — to Charlie*). Keep your chin clean — and take care of the kid!

CHARLIE. You can trust me! An' Hash! (*The dog looks around at him.*) Hash— you take care o' Joe!

ALL. Goodbye — Goodbye — 'Bye, Joe!

The DOG barks, and the car drives off, leaving CHARLIE and TOM waving goodbye and laughing. And the cause of their laughter becomes clear when the rear of JOE'S CAR comes into view.—It is hung with brotherly gifts of old shoes and a couple of banging tin cans. A sign reads: "DON'T MIND ME — I'M CRAZY — I'M ON MY WAY TO GET MARRIED!"

Then follow flashes of Joe's movement toward the west: The outskirts of CHICAGO, the Industrial District with its steel mills. JOE'S CAR crossing a BRIDGE over the MISSISSIPPI RIVER. COWS grazing, and the countryside. Then a little GROVE of trees off the highway comes into view.

It is twilight, and a small campfire, with a grill bearing a coffee pot, is burning beside the car. JOE is sitting on the running-board of the car, reading a newspaper, while the dog is sniffing the air. She gets a scent, and with a little bark, runs into the trees.

Joe is popping peanuts into his mouth as he reads. We see the banner headline on the front page:

"KIDNAP RANSOM PAID!"

JOE (*distastefully, half to himself as he turns a page*). War and strikes and crime and — taxes. (*He shoves the pages of the paper together and drops it on the runningboard as excited barking from the dog is heard, whereupon Joe looks in the direction of the sound.*) Hey — Hash! — Hash! (*As the barking continues, he rises.*)

Joe comes to some BUSHES in the grove, pushing the branches aside as the barking continues.

JOE. Where are ya?

We see a small RABBIT in a trap: The dog is in a frenzy, worrying the frightened animal.

Joe appears at another clump of BUSHES, sees the dog and the rabbit, and approaches alertly.

JOE. Hey — *stop* that! (*He bends, and his foot pressing open the trap he lifts up the trembling rabbit. The dog jumps at him, barking, but Joe pushes it off with his leg.*) Get away! (*Patting the rabbit*) You're okay, Baby. (*To the dog, still barking and jumping*) How'd *you* like to be caught in a dirty trap like that? (*He bends, and with one leg keeping off the dog, frees the rabbit which leaps off.*) Good luck!

The dog starts to chase the rabbit, but JOE stops her.

JOE. *Sit down!* ... Get civilized. (*Trembling with eagerness to be off, nevertheless the dog sits.*) You're goin' to meet Katherine tomorrow, an' after the way I've talked you up what'd she think o' you?

In KATHERINE'S ROOM that night KATHERINE is unwrapping packages she has just brought home, and eagerly addressing the landlady:

KATHERINE (*unwrapping one of the packages*)—and some wienies for his dog. (*Giving the landlady another package*) And then an avocado for him — they call 'em alligator pears and cost a fortune back East — d'you think he'll like it?

LANDLADY (*laughing*). He won't know *what* he's eatin' for bein' with you again. What time'll I make lunch for?

KATHERINE (*her words coming fast with anticipatory excitement*). I'm taking the bus to Sycamore Corners on the main road — I wrote him I'd meet him at eleven at that hot dog stand there — so we'll be back by noon, sure. G-golly, Mrs. Whipple, I can hardly stand it. Over a year now —

In the GROVE, JOE is now coming into the car again, addressing the dog,

JOE. Now lie down and behave yourself. (*He drops to the runningboard and picks up the paper again. But the contrast of its matter with his own happy expectancy is too much for him. He shakes his head at it, drops it, paces a moment, then abruptly snaps a finger.*) I got it! (*Turning to the dog*) What d'y' say we drive all night, get to her before she leaves to meet us, an' *surprise* her — eh? (*The dog barks.*) Swell! Get your hat! (*He steps to the fire, gets the coffee pot and grille — giving a S-s-s! sound as he almost burns his fingers, and kicks sand on fire; he also kicks the newspaper over to the fire.*)

A close-up shows the NEWSPAPER dropping on the embers, browning and searing over some live coals, as the motor starts and the car drives away. We see that the paper's sub-head reads:

"FAMILY EMISSARY PAYS $70,000 TO GANG BUT CHILD NOT RETURNED"

Part of the body of the news story below, set in bold-face type, reads:

"Brought in one of the snatcher's cars, which he described as a 1932 Ford with an Illinois license, to a lonely shack, F. T. Maguire, emissary of the frantic parents of the kidnapped child handed over the ransom bills to two other men of the gang. During the transaction, Maguire heard from the next room the voice of a woman quieting a barking dog.

After checking the packages of bills...."

A tongue of flame bursts through the paper, crinkling it.

Next we see JOE and his dog in the car, moving down an old road, the windshield of the car specked with gnats and dust particles.

The sun is shining brilliantly and though the dog is sleeping, Joe is half singing, half humming a song. But he sees something down the road ahead and breaks off. In the distance, (as seen by Joe) a man with a shotgun held crooked and ready in one arm is standing on the right side of the road, his other arm raised in a "Stop" gesture. The view moves to him with a rush, as if it were the car, and stops with a sound of braked wheels and throwing-out of gear. Beyond this man an old, travel-stained open automobile is at right angles across the road, blocking it. A fat young driver—JOHN is his name—is at its wheel, and in front of it, on the left side of the road is another determined man, feet planted apart, also with a shotgun ready. The first man is a typical small town person, of about thirty, with a loose old vest hanging open over suspenders and a shirt buttoned at the neck but minus a necktie, with watery eyes under an old felt hat. His name is "BUGS" MEYERS; and he is not too bright.

"BUGS." Stop your motor, Buddy!

As "Bugs" walks around to Joe, the dog growls. The man comes to a stop beside him, his gun menacing.

"BUGS." An' keep your both hands up on the wheel there.

Joe puts his other hand on the wheel.

JOE. What is this—a holdup?

"BUGS." You weren't lettin' any grass grow under your wheels, were y'?

JOE (*relieved, grins*). Oh. Speedin'. I was in a hurry to—

"BUGS" (*interrupting*). Illinois (*he pronounces it "—oise"*) license plates, uh?

J'E. Sure, Chicago. (*Bewildered.*) Say, what *is* this? (*His hand automatically leaves the wheel.*)

"BUGS" (*quickly*). Keep that fist up there!

JOE (*putting hand back on wheel; exasperated*). I haven't got a gun, if that's what you mean. Peanuts won't kill y', will they? (*"Bugs" reacts to "peanuts."*) I haven't had any breakfast yet.

"BUGS." *Salted* peanuts?

JOE. Yeah. Why?

"BUGS." *I* ain't answerin' the questions, Buddy. *You* are. (*Motioning with gun barrel*) C'mon. Get out.

JOE (*getting mad*). What for?

"BUGS" (*with a flash of nasty cruelty*). 'Cause I tell y' to! (*Calling*) Wilbur, you c'm here an' drive this car. I'll take him with me an' John.

JOE (*boiling*). What right—

"BUGS." Shut up! Y'can pow-wow with the Sheriff. We ain't had any breakfast yet, ourselfs.

As Joe gets out of the car, the scene dissolves to a close-up of LETTERING in suncracked paint on an old two-story frame building:

SHERIFF'S OFFICE
Sage County

and below it, in fresher paint against a scraped background, indicating a new incumbent:

TAD HUMMEL, SHERIFF.

This dissolves to the SHERIFF'S OFFICE — a back room in the old frame building that also houses the town jail, at the end of which is a wide, iron-barred window that overlooks a courtyard. The SHERIFF — a slow-speaking American of fifty, long, lean and muscular, with a loose carriage, a flat jaw, and firm, dry neck, wearing a loose blue serge suit without vest—is leaning back in his swivel chair questioning Joe, who is sitting tense in a chair across the desk from him. His dog is lying on the floor beside him, ears alertly cocked. On the desk are papers, a cardboard placard face downward, a package of cigarettes, a small bowl of salted peanuts, and the Sheriff's broad-brimmed black felt hat. At one end of the desk is a prune-like woman of forty with tight grey hair and nose glasses—the office stenographer, who is making a shorthand transcript of the examination. "Bugs," his hat pushed back, is lounging on the bench. —Joe is concerned, and still bewildered, but not anxious, as he continues giving information.

JOE. —from Chicago. I left four days ago—Tuesday.

SHERIFF (*quite amiably*). Well, Mr. — er —

STENOGRAPHER (*very precisely, glancing at her notebook*). Wheeler . . . Joseph Wheeler.

She removes her glasses, breathes on them with a "Whoo-oosh" sound of expelled breath that causes Joe to look, startled, at her, and vigorously polishes the lenses with a handkerchief.

SHERIFF (*remembering*). Yeah . . . Wheeler. (*He leans back in the chair, crooking a leg over an arm of it.*) Where were y' last night, Mr. Wheeler, if y' don't mind?

JOE (*more at ease*). I was drivin' all night last—

SHERIFF (*interrupting*). On that old road?

JOE. I got lost, tryin' to find a short cut to Capital City, to—

SHERIFF (*interrupting easily*). And the night before last?

JOE. Camping out.

SHERIFF (*as if remembering something*). Excuse me a second. (*He leans forward and picks up a sheet of paper that has been face downward on his desk, and lifts it, turning it to read. Then pointing*

to a pack of cigarettes, he asks amiably:)
Smoke?

JOE. No, thanks.

SHERIFF (*shoving the bowl with nuts across to Joe and asking casually as he starts to read the sheet of paper*). Some peanuts?

There is a close-up of a SHEET OF PAPER, on which is written:

STATE POLICE LABORATORY
CONFIDENTIAL TO ALL SHERIFFS
CHIEFS OF POLICE

Microscopic examination of envelope of ransom letter in Peabody case discloses bits of salt and husks that indicate it was carried in pocket containing salted peanuts.

JOE'S VOICE (*expansive with relief*). Now you're talkin' my language, Sheriff. I've had that habit ever since I was a kid. My old man used to bring 'em home to me—I got used to havin' 'em around—(*Seen again with the others in the office*) There're always some salted peanuts in my pocket! (*His hand takes some peanuts from his pocket and he smilingly shows them.*)

SHERIFF (*dropping the sheet of paper, abruptly sharp*). Wheeler, where'd you say you spent the night before last?

JOE (*startled by his change in manner*). Camping out.

SHERIFF. Why?

JOE. Why—for the— (*A bit angered by the sudden grimness of the Sheriff's face and attitude*) Is it a crime to give yourself some fresh air after livin' in a smoky city all your — Look! What am I suspected of, anyway? I got a right to know!

The sheriff thoughtfully lifts the placard from his desk, turns it face upward, and reversing it, slides it across the desk to Joe. Joe takes it and reads. Then he looks up from the placard, incredulous.

JOE. *Me* (*Indignant*) That's the craziest thing I ever— (*He stops, aghast.*)

SHERIFF. It makes pretty good sense, seems to me.

JOE. Just because I was in a car like that? There're thousands of cars like—and in Illinois, too. (*Helplessly*) It's a big state.

SHERIFF. It's not only the car. Your description kind o' fits. Read it . . . About five feet eight . . . Solid . . . Broad shoulders . . . Light hair . . .

JOE. But that'd fit a million men!

SHERIFF (*shoving the confidential laboratory note over to him*). Read that. (*Joe's eyes drop to the paper, and he reads.*)

JOE (*exclaiming angrily*). Am I the only peanut eater in the country? (*Pointing to the bowl of peanuts*) You, yourself—

SHERIFF (*interrupting with some contempt*). I never ate peanuts in my life!

JOE (*after staring at him a moment*). I get it . . . (*He becomes intense again.*) Check up on me, why don't y'? You can phone my brothers in Chicago. They'll—

SHERIFF (*interrupting*). We'll check all right. That's what I'm here for. Mind showin' me what y' got in your pockets there?

JOE (*jumps up*). I should say not! — That I don't mind, I mean. (*He begins to go through his pockets. He drops his keys, a couple of dishevelled handkerchiefs, his car license, his peanuts, and his pocketbook before the Sheriff.*) Keys — handkerchiefs — my license — money, what there is of it—and peanuts.

SHERIFF (*having taken a printed list of serial numbers of banknotes from his desk drawer.*) "Bugs"! (*As "Bugs" comes over to him, the dog growls at him.*) Check—(*counting the money in the pocketbook*) these—eighty—eighty-five — hundred and forty-three — check these bills against the—(*handing him the list of numbers*) numbers o' those ransom banknotes.

"BUGS." You've come to the right man, Chief— (*He goes to the roll-top desk.*)

JOE (*kidding*). You're sure he's only gonna check those, Sheriff?

Watching Joe surreptitiously the while, the Sheriff relaxes.

SHERIFF (*leaning back in the chair*). You're prob'ly right as rain, Wheeler — though one o' the nastiest crooks I ever did see was one o' the most innocent lookin'. But then that one was a woman.

He glances mildly at the stenographer. Joe joins in his laugh—which is broken by an exclamatory whistle from "Bugs." They turn, to see "Bugs" jump up from the roll-top desk, and come to the Sheriff, the list of numbers and one of Joe's five-dollar bills in his hand. The dog growls at him menacingly.

JOE (*to the dog, patting her head*). Sh-h-h.

"BUGS" (*showing a bill and one of the numbers on the list to the Sheriff*). Here! Under the five-dollar series there. See! L-496-773-08-B. And on this bill o' his the same thing. L-496-773-08-B.

JOE (*thunderstruck*). But it can't—

SHERIFF (*to "Bugs," his lips compressed with seriousness now*). Rip up that car o' his. Might be some more o'—(*tapping the bill against desk*)—these hidden there.

JOE stares at the five-dollar bill, too dumbfounded to speak.

"BUGS" (*nodding and starting for the hall*). Man, is *this* goin' t' be a sensation!

SHERIFF. Keep it to yourself!

The dog barks and flies at "Bugs'" legs. He pushes her away with his foot, and goes out.

SHERIFF (*to Joe*). And keep that dog quiet. Here! (*Opening desk drawer, he takes out a piece of old clothesline and tosses it to Joe.*) Tie it up.

JOE (*tying the clothesline to the dog's collar, and squatting to tie its other end to the radiator*). I guess she's about as worried about this as I am. (*Half to himself*) If I hadn't tried a short cut, an' stuck to the main road—

The scene cuts to a close-up of a CROSS-ROADS SIGN atop a post, reading:

SYCAMORE CORNERS
BUS STOPS HERE EVERY HOUR

Over this comes the sound of the brakes of a bus stopping, and the view dissolves to a HOT-DOG STAND. Dust is coming in from the departing East-bound bus, which has dropped KATHERINE before the hot-dog stand. She approaches the aproned owner of the place who is sweeping dust from the plank walk in front of the lunch counter. The cross-roads sign declares that CAPITAL CITY is 22 miles distant in the direction from which the bus came.

KATHERINE (*looking down the road, away from Capital City*). Any good-looking young man from Illinois been looking for a good-looking girl here yet?

OWNER (*grinning*). Where's the good-lookin' girl?

KATHERINE (*happily*). She'll be along in a minute—

OWNER. The good-lookin' young feller ain't here yet, either.

KATHERINE (*gaily*). He will be! (*And she looks down the road again.*)

The scene cuts back to the SHERIFF'S OFFICE where JOE, his face strained with anxiety, is twisting the ring on his finger, as he exclaims.

JOE (*excitedly*). Let *me* telephone Chicago, then! (*Getting an idea*) or better than that, I can phone my— (*But catching sight of a placard on the desk, he breaks off short.*)

A closeup of the PLACARD reveals a line which reads:

"AND A YOUNG WOMAN ACCOMPLICE."

Joe, with the placard before him, thinks a moment, shaking his head "no." The view drawing back, discloses the SHERIFF watching him alertly.

SHERIFF. Phone your what?

JOE (*finally*). Phone my brothers. I'll pay for it.

SHERIFF (*crisply*). If you *are* mixed up with this gang it wouldn't be very smart o' me to let y' phone 'em. (*He pushes a buzzer button on his desk.*)

JOE. Look! Please! I got that bill in change someplace. I told you! A store— gas station— I don't know! Take me back over the road with you. I can prove—

"BUGS" returns, causing him to break off.

"BUGS." Nothin' in the car.

The lock-up keeper comes in from the hall.

SHERIFF. Take care o'—(*indicating Joe*) —this stranger here, Frank, and go through his clothes. (*To Joe*) Sure you haven't forgot anything, Wheeler?

JOE (*unstrapping his watch*). My watch —(*resentfully*)—and this ring. It's too tight to take off—but maybe you could *cut* it off—why not?

SHERIFF. I'll have to hold you, Wheeler, for the District Attorney. But you'll get a square deal. (*To the stenographer*) You can type that now, Myrtle.

The stenographer collects her pencils and notebook.

LOCK-UP KEEPER (*to Joe, nodding toward door*). That way.

JOE starts to speak, but feels it's useless and goes to the hall door, dazed. The dog begins to bark.

JOE (*faint smile at the dog*). Sh-h. Hash! Sh-h! (*To the Sheriff*) She'll be all right.

He goes out to the hall, the lock-up keeper following him, and they disappear down the hall.

"BUGS." Looks like we got holt o' some-thin', Sheriff—(*going to the hall door*) I'll be at the barber shop down the street.

The scene dissolves to a close view of the screen door of a BARBER SHOP, as seen from inside, showing a revolving barber pole outside. "BUGS" comes in.

"BUGS." Howdy.

The BARBER SHOP is a traditional small-town shop, with two chairs and washbasins, a shoe-shining stand, a small cash register on the cigar counter, and chairs for waiting customers.

In the first chair, being hot-towelled preparatory to being shaved by HECTOR, the elderly proprietor, is MR. JORGENSON, a business-man with a belly and a scrawny neck. In the next chair, a Swedish-looking barber is cutting the hair of a young man, a teacher.

PROPRIETOR (*having turned to greet "Bugs"*). Hi, Buggsy.

JORGENSON (*to the Teacher*). —an' let me tell *you*, Professor, if you young geniuses at the high-school keep trying t' fill our children's heads with these radical ideas, we parents'll have to get a law!

TEACHER (*laughing easily*). It's not possible to get a law that denies the right to say what one believes. In peace times, anyway.

JORGENSON. Who says so?

TEACHER. The Constitution of the United States.

The slap of a Negro shoeshine boy's polishing rag puts an exclamation mark to the speech.

JORGENSON. I don't believe it!

THE OTHER BARBER. You sh'd read it sometime. You would be surprised.

PROPRIETOR (*indignantly*). Now enough o' that now, Sven—

THE OTHER BARBER (*seriously, to Hector*). I *had* to read it, to become an American. You never had to b'cause you was born here.

"BUGS," waiting on the bench, tosses aside the magazine he has been reading, and complains.

"BUGS." Say, Hector, why don't ya get the next issue o' this magazine? I'd like to find out who *won* the Willard-Dempsey fight? (*He laughs at his own joke.*)

JORGENSON (*seeing "Bugs"*). How're y', Meyers? You still at the Sheriff's office?

"BUGS." Yep. I turned Democrat in a

hurry when that store o' mine went broke.

JORGENSON. Anythin' new on this awful Peabody case?

"BUGS" (*affecting nonchalance*). Oh-h, I don't know.

JORGENSON. You public servants quit playin' cards all day and maybe you'd bring somebody to justice once in awhile.

"BUGS" (*nasty*). Oh, yeh? What w'd y' say if I told y' I just raked in a guy who may know somethin' about these kidnappers? Me an' the Sheriff are givin' him the works . . .

THE OTHER BARBER. What d' y' s'pose it is makes people do things like snatchin' that kid? Nutty, I guess. Uh?

PROPRIETOR (*philosophically as he shaves Jorgenson's neck—to the Teacher*). Well, now I'll tell y'. People get funny impulses. If y' resist 'em, you're sane; if y' don't, you're on the way to the nuthouse, or the pen'.

JORGENSON (*growling*). At the taxpayer's expense.

PROPRIETOR (*turning away from the Teacher to Jorgenson*). Mr. Jorgenson, you're one.o' the levellest heads in the county. Would you b'lieve that in the twenty years I been strokin' this razor acrost throats here that many a time I've had a impulse to cut—(*his middle finger touches Jorgenson's Adam's apple*)—their Adam's apples *wide open*? Just like—(*slashes with his razor over Jorgenson's throat*)—that! Yes, sir!

Behind him there is laughter from "BUGS." He turns his head.

"BUGS" (*grinning*). How about it, Hec? Do ya feel an impulse comin' on? (*He laughs loudly.*)

PROPRIETOR (*turning again at his work;—seriously*). Impulses is impulses! (*Turning back to speak to Jorgenson*) It's like a itch you got t' scratch— (*He breaks off, gaping down, and the view drawing back, discloses that the chair is empty. After blinking, bewildered, he looks toward the door, seeing the screen door swinging wildly. Mr. Jorgenson has flown.*)

The scene dissolves to a WALL TELEPHONE, and against the wall under it is a tabouret. The phone bell is ringing lightly on a high-pitched note. As the ringing stops, instantly, as if it were a continuation of the sound of the bell, music begins faint and slow, with a hollow throbbing as if from very distant drums. The effect is of being conscious of this music rather than actually hearing it. It is expressing the creeping, but inevitable menace of gossip and rumors. We see the PROPRIETOR'S WIFE, in housedress and apron, with her sleeves rolled up and a long wooden spoon sticky with batter in her hand, coming to the phone. She kneels on the tabouret in answering the phone, being too short to otherwise reach it.

PROPRIETOR'S WIFE (*into the phone*). Hello? What's that, Hector? What's that? Mr. Jorgenson—? (*A flood of excited talk from the other end stops her.*)

And now the Proprietor in the BARBER SHOP is agitatedly explaining into the hand phone —near which, on the wall, is a mirror.

PROPRIETOR (*full of worry*). . . . my oldest customer! All on account o' that "Bugs" Meyers from the Sheriff's office tellin' a cock-an'-bull story about his capturin' one o' that Peabody kidnappin' gang—(*The Proprietor's wife hears this; and breathes out an excited "Ah!"*) — an' my explainin' my own perfectly nat'ral impulses to cut people's Adam's apples—

The scene moves to the WIFE at the phone. She speaks hurriedly.

PROPRIETOR'S WIFE (*into the phone*). Now jus' you calm down, Hector, an' don't you worry. I got somethin' on the stove, precious. Call you back. Bye, bye—

She hangs up, jumps down from the tabouret, and — the scene wipes off, revealing a small BACK PORCH on the second floor, with a window of the adjoining flat within reaching distance. The Proprietor's wife comes out onto the porch, leans over the railing, reaching with her wooden spoon for the adjoining kitchen window. She makes it, raps the spoon thereon, and the window is raised by the neighboring housewife.

PROPRIETOR'S WIFE (*excitedly*). Mrs. Tuttle! Of all things! My husband just phoned they've arrested a man . . .

The scene cuts to the NEIGHBOR'S KITCHEN. Beside a kitchen table on which some food is being prepared sits Fanny, a turkey-necked woman with a long, sharp nose. She has her hat and coat on, and a half-empty market basket in her lap, having dropped in for a chat. She cranes her neck and points her nose toward the open window. The woman who opened the window comes to her.

NEIGHBOR WOMAN (*in a loud whisper*). Fanny! That barber's wife says this morning they caught a man on the old road who . . .

Fanny stands up, clutching her market basket, and there is a close-up of the half-empty MARKET BASKET over which continues the Neighbor Woman's voice.

NEIGHBOR WOMAN'S VOICE. . . . they suspect . . . knows somethin' about this kidnapping.

FANNY'S VOICE. No!

The view draws back from the market basket, disclosing FANNY now standing with two other women—one of them horse-faced—in the MARKET where she is declaiming, while the expressive music grows louder.

FANNY. I got it on the highest authority! They've arrested one o' that kidnapping gang.

TWO OTHER WOMEN. Good! . . . You don't say.

FANNY. He tried to escape, but they captured him all right. (*To a Clerk who approaches and shows her two cabbages*) I'll take three of those. (*The Clerk goes out of sight; calling after him*) And a pound o' prunes!

TWO OTHER WOMEN. What else? . . . Who is he? . . . What's his name?

FANNY (*smugly*). I can't tell you anymore. It was only told me in strictest confidence!

HORSE-FACED WOMAN (*gabbling with eagerness*). But, darling, you *know* I'm as silent as a tomb!

The scene dissolves through a close view of a COOP OF LIVE CHICKENS AND GEESE, which are squawking and setting up a hubbub, to a GROUP OF SIX DIFFERENT WOMEN surrounding a quiet young housewife. The Horse-Faced Woman is obviously the dictator of the flock. They are all talking at once, their words indistinguishable under the noise of the squawking poultry and the loud music. Suddenly the chatter and the music stop, and in this dead silence, we hear the young wife expostulating.

YOUNG HOUSEWIFE. But are you sure he's not innocent?

HORSE-FACED WOMAN. My dear young woman! In *this* country, people don't land in jail unless they're guilty. (*The chattering and music shrills into a cacophony of agitated sounds as all the women pounce on the Young Housewife, their mouths working in speech.*)

The scene cuts to JOE'S CELL. JOE is knocking on the bars of his cell door with his clenched fist, the ring on his finger making a ringing sound as it strikes the metal. The lock-up keeper comes in answer.

JOE. Has the Sheriff phoned to my brothers yet?

LOCK-UP KEEPER (*amiably.*). I don't know. (*He turns and goes, saying*) You'll hear somethin' one way or the other in due time.

Joe starts to speak, but closes his mouth and turns helplessly.

In SYCAMORE CORNERS, KATHERINE is sitting at the lunch counter. The Owner of the place is setting a cup of steaming coffee in front of her.

KATHERINE (*anxious—looking down the road*). I hope nothing's happened. It's the first time he's ever come West, so maybe—

OWNER (*interrupting, laughing*). Well, I ain't heard o' anybody bein' tomahawked or scalped in the neighborhood for some time now, so I guess he's in no more danger here in God's country than he'd be in at home.

The scene dissolves to a closely seen display of FLASHING KNIVES, ROPE, SICKLES, and other objects outside a hardware store. We hear two sharp reports, like pistol shots, and as the view draws back, revealing the exterior of the HARDWARE STORE, we see a square-jawed Farmer, testing a whip.—In the doorway, the store clerk is talking to two men, one a miner in high-laced boots.

CLERK. —my wife's sister phoned her that a friend o' hers told her that this guy was cocky as a bronco about it. All he'd answer was, "Le' me phone my Lawyer."

MINER. Sure! That's the racket o' those big-town attorneys, helpin' these skunks beat the law.

FARMER (*deadly serious*). They won't beat it with any jury I'm ever on, sir! And if *all* o' us people just had the courage o' our convictions, these vermin would vanish like—like spit on a hot stove! (*And he snaps the whip venomously to punctuate the speech.*)

In an ARCADE, next, a group of men, including ranchers, are discussing the case. A fat and sentimental elderly rancher, visibly affected, is dominating them. (The sound of the underlying music becomes higher, more disjointed, more menacing.)

RANCHER. I lifted that kid onto her first pony with these hands—taught her to ride—She was the prettiest little thing you ever saw!

A NEWSPAPER OFFICE WINDOW comes into view. On its plate glass is painted: "SAGE COUNTY NEWS-BEE." (The music simulates the buzzing of hundreds of gossip-disseminating bees.)

This dissolves to the NEWSPAPER OFFICE. Standing at a littered old roll-top desk behind the window is a reporter—a nonchalant young man in shirtsleeves and vest, with hat pushed back on his head and some papers in his right hand. He is telephoning.

REPORTER (*into the phone*). —with only that rumor to go on. (*He listens.*) You phone the Associated Press Office there, will you? The whole town's buzzin' like a hornet's nest!

The scene dissolves to the ENTRANCE TO A BAR-ROOM. There are knots of men and loiterers buzzing about the case, their words indistinguishable.

Then the scene moves past these knots of people, and the BAR-ROOM comes into view. There are the customary bottles and glasses that equip a bar, and a hand-inked placard reads:

TODAY'S SPECIAL
CALVES BRAINS & MASHED POTATOES
45c

The placard is stuck against the wall above and behind the bar—which wall we see to be the blackboard, with faded stock symbols, of an abandoned brokerage office. There is a GROUP at the bar—and it is dominated by "BUBBLES" DAWSON, a broad-shouldered loafer of twenty-six, and a notorious trouble-maker. He is surrounded by three satellites, and is dropping a handful of nickels on the bar.

DAWSON. Set 'em up for the boys, Oscar. Four beers.

BARTENDER. Last time after you played the slot machine it was full o' telephone slugs!

DAWSON (*sarcastically*). Ain't that a shame!

A VOICE. Say Dawson, I hear they gave that guy your favorite cell at the jail.

DAWSON (*angrily*). Next time I get in it'll be for beatin' up on you!

His pals laugh admiringly at this retort, and while the scene draws back from them we hear rising from the hum of conversation in the room an excited voice.

VOICE. —but what if it'd been *your* daughter? Answer me that!

By now the view has disclosed at the bar next to DAWSON's group a mutton-necked gentleman, with a despondent mustache, named BURMEISTER, who is talking with his neighbor, MR. DURKIN, who is "Merely-A-Tailor." Mr. Burmeister is drinking rye and water; the Tailor, beer.

BURMEISTER. —and while I didn't vote for Hummel for Sheriff, his promptness in catching this kidnapper is most commendable.

MERELY-A-TAILOR (*nodding vigorously*). They can't try him too quick for me.

Simultaneously a man appears between BUR-MEISTER and DAWSON, and taps Dawson's arm with the end of a folded newspaper, indicating for him to move aside. This gentleman is a fat beer-belly of fifty-five, and heavy with dignity. His name is PIPPEN.

PIPPEN (*to Dawson, patronizingly*). If you don't mind.

DAWSON (*loudly, for the benefit of his pals*). Excuse me for livin'.

MERELY-A-TAILOR (*smirking as he recognizes one of his important clients*). Mr. Pippen. (*He moves aside, offering Mr. Pippen his place.*) By the way, I have some new English flannels in for—

PIPPEN (*interrupting*). Later, Durkin, later. (*To the Bartender*) My usual, Oscar. (*Immediately, clearing his throat, to Burmeister, who has greeted him with a "Hello, George"*) We've been discussing at the Chamber of Commerce luncheon about what a great publicity break our capturing this Chicago fellow's going to give our little city—assuming, of course, the — uh — leaders of the community see he's brought to justice.

BURMEISTER (*nodding his head gravely*). We'll see to *that,* all right, all right! We'll go to the sheriff and get it straight from him!

The scene cuts to JOE'S CELL where JOE is pacing tensely. He goes to the barred door, grips the bars, as if to call out, but does not, and jerks away to continue pacing, straining—straining as if to *wish* himself free. This dissolves to a close-up of the DOG — standing, still tied to the radiator, moving his head as if listening, as the SHERIFF is heard.

SHERIFF'S VOICE. I'm tryin' to locate the District Attorney, and we'll get at the truth as fast as possible, but till we do, one way or the other—

And now the SHERIFF'S OFFICE comes into view. (The clock reads 4:03 o'clock.) The Sheriff is in his desk chair, facing DAWSON, PIPPEN, BURMEISTER, MERELY-A-TAILOR, and another citizen named GARRETT, who are

standing, their hats in hand. The Stenographer is busy at the roll-top desk.

SHERIFF (*leaning back in the swivel chair as he finishes*). —I haven't any right to make a statement.

BURMEISTER (*jerkingly*). Ordinarily, Sheriff, yes. But—uh—there's a pretty nervous feeling in town, and the—er—community feels—thinks—

DAWSON. We got a right to know about this kidnapper!

SHERIFF (*interrupting sharply*). I don't *know* he is a kidnapper yet, and so neither do you.

DAWSON. What're y' doin', Hummel, tryin' t' protect this weasel?

Messrs. Pippen and Burmeister look at Dawson, startled at his gall.

SHERIFF (*after a moment, during which he drapes a leg over the arm of his chair*). That's pretty comical, you cockroach—you teaching *me* law-and-order. You've been stirrin' up only trouble for law-and-order hereabouts ever since you put on long pants. (*He turns quietly to the others; and speaks coldly.*) Anything more I can do for you gentleman?

PIPPEN. No offense meant. I'm sure we can count on you, Sheriff, to keep everything ship-shape, I'm sure. Good afternoon.

The men start out, Dawson turning back to protest.

DAWSON. It's an outrage a man can't stick up for law-and-order without being—

SHERIFF (*interrupting*). *Men* do stick up for it.

DAWSON. I'll tell you one thing, Hummel! My friends won't be satisfied with what —(*pointing after Burmeister and Pippen*)—*those* pillars o' society tell 'em! (*He goes closer, more belligerently, to the desk.*) An attack on a girl hits us ordinary people where we live! An' we're goin' to see that politics don't cut any ice!

SHERIFF (*his voice rising in some temper*). I'm goin' to see that a lot o' half-baked rumors don't, either . . . Now high-tail out o' here! And behave yourself. Or I'll have the County take you —and all your relatives—off the dole!

Dawson opens his mouth angrily, closes it, turns sharply and, ostentatiously putting on his hat, goes out, slamming the door. The Sheriff takes a chew of tobacco, rises, and, thoughtful, looks out the window, to see perhaps twenty men and youths in knots, Dawson amidst them. We cannot hear their jabber, but their attitude is excited. The Sheriff purses his lips, his expression becoming more serious. He turns and walks slowly up and down.—Suddenly there is the sound of the crash of glass behind him. He stops, turns quickly, as a stone heaved through the window drops at his feet. He sees a jagged hole in the window. Outside, the last of the men are running off. The Sheriff stoops, picks up the stone, tosses it in his hand, his jaw tightening.

> SHERIFF (*finally*). Myrtle! . . . Get the Governor on the phone.

The scene dissolves to the GOVERNOR'S OFFICE—a large room with heavy mahogany furniture, an American flag, and, in a corner, a State flag on its gold-tipped pole, but draped in such a manner as to be unidentifiable.—A portly, but efficient heavy-set man in ordinary business clothes, the GOVERNOR is at his desk listening at the telephone, while with one hand he signs signatures to papers placed one after another before him by the male secretary standing at his side.

> GOVERNOR (*into the phone*). Certainly, Hummel—certainly . . . Very wise of you to let me know the situation . . . I'll have the militia ready for any merited emergency. (*Pleasantly*) I'm sure you will! Keep me informed. (*He hangs up, and snaps a dictaphone key.*)
>
> ANOTHER SECRETARY'S VOICE (*from the dictaphone*). Yes, Governor?
>
> GOVERNOR (*into the dictaphone*). Have the Adjutant-General get two companies of militia ready for possible riot duty down at Sage.

The scene dissolves to the BAR-ROOM, where the air is now smoke-filled. Among the crowd at, and standing with their backs to, the bar are DAWSON, his satellites, a

STRANGER, GARRETT, DURKIN, THE RANCHER (whom we heard say that he taught the Peabody girl to ride) — all drinking. Raptly intent on them is an adenoidal youth of nineteen, with a silly stare — the town idiot, called Goofy. Dawson is smouldering.

> DAWSON. What'd they rip up his auto back o' the jail there for if it wasn't to find some o' that ransom dough?
>
> ANOTHER (*simultaneously*). I heard there was five thousand of it in —
>
> ANOTHER (*interrupting*). Ten thousand, they tell me!
>
> GARRETT (*eager to be "in" on things*). I heard the first thing he did was phone Chicago for his lawyer.
>
> GOOFY (*pulling Dawson's arm to get his attention*). Maybe he paid the money to the Sheriff to go free on bail.
>
> DAWSON. Ah-h, shut up, Goofy. (*He pushes him away.*)
>
> DURKIN. Hey! Here's "Bugs" Meyers. He ought t' know. Ask him.
>
> OTHERS. That's right! . . There's an idea! C'm here, Buggsy! . . Have a drink. . . ("*Bugs*" *is pulled in to them.*)
>
> "BUGS" (*modestly*). Well — just one if y' insist. (*Swelling a little under this sudden popularity*) What's bitin' you fellas? What d' y' want t' know? (*He drinks, leaning his back against the bar.*)
>
> GARRETT. There's a little argument as t' the amount the Sheriff found in the kidnapper's car.
>
> "BUGS" (*snickering*). I hate t' disappoint ya, fellas, but we didn't find anything in his car. We ripped it to pieces, but —
>
> DAWSON (*interrupting*). Go on-n, we know y' found that ransom money in that car!
>
> STRANGER. Yeh! Ten grand. Hid under the seat. That's what the lock-up keeper's wife said —
>
> "BUGS." What does *she* know? *I* tore up the car, myself! I ought t' know if any money was there. "Ten Grand," my eye . . . All this Wheeler had on him o'

that ransom money was *one* five dollar bill!

There is a sudden hush as this sinks in, broken by a sneer of triumph from Dawson.

DAWSON. Ha! There y' are! (*Vengefully*) Who does *that* make a liar out o'? Wait'll I shove that down the Sheriff's throat. Come on, boys! We'll give him a little serenade!

MEN. Yea-a, Dawson! . . . Attaboy! . . . Come on! . . .

There are cat-calls and whistling.—"Bugs," alarmed, sneaks out.

GARRETT (*trying anxiously to restore order*). Quiet! *Quiet!* (*Lifting his hands for quiet*) Everybody's gettin' too excited. The Sheriff's okay! (*The hubbub diminishes a little.*) This is none o' our business.

STRANGER (*shouting maliciously*). No? I'll tell y', if I lived in this town, I'd make it my business. What are you eggs? Soft-boiled, that you don't stick up for a kidnapped girl?

There is absolute silence. Then Garrett turns to him suspiciously.

GARRETT. Who're you?

STRANGER. Just passin' through. I been up at Capital City strike-breakin' for the street-car company. Maybe y' need some help here, too.

GARRETT. Not from mugs like you!

DAWSON (*pushing in to him*). Lay off, Garrett! The Sheriff made a monkey out o' you, too, didn't he? This—(*indicating the Stranger*)—guy's right. We ought t' be ashamed o' ourselves, that a stranger has t' show us the ropes.

MEN. He's right! . . . Yea-a! . . . What'll we do? Let's do something—Hop to it. (*Cat calls! Shrill whistling! Stamping of feet!*)

The view sweeps through the crowd picking up a welter of milling men—their hands, their mouths, but in lights and shadows. An emotional youth jumps to a chair and — as the expressive turbulent, discordant music (heard throughout the scene) abruptly stops — he yells out.

YOUTH. C'mon! Let's have some fun!

As the others acclaim him, the scene dissolves to the exterior of the BAR-ROOM. The crowd is now emerging, but in chunks, not closely packed yet, for it has not yet coalesced. It's mood is picnicky. DAWSON and the STRANGER are in the middle of the crowd. Then idlers and passers-by appear, running between cars to join the moving crowd of men beyond. And now, seen through ARCADES and COLONNADES in the street, the crowd is marching in more orderly fashion, with DAWSON and the STRANGER in the lead. Youths run in from the sides, joining them. Pedestrians stop, staring. (The music is now simulating the tread of marching feet tramp — tramp — tramp — tramp. It continues through the following scenes with the same beat — tramp, tramp, tramp. We do not see the marching men again, but their presence is felt through the undercurrent of the tramping music.)

This is followed by flashes of Pedestrians — men and women — stopping to look, and following with their heads the movement of the unseen crowd, whose tramp, tramp, tramp is increasingly relentless; there is a flash of an old spinster looking out the window of a house, craning her neck down the street. Then a STREET CORNER appears, and here a shopping woman, an angular MOTHER of fifty-five, carrying packages, has stopped and is regarding the unseen crowd suspiciously. Suddenly her eyes pop, and she darts toward the right side emerging on the other — pulling by one hand a startled youth.

MOTHER (*shrilly, while she smacks the young crusader on the cheek — dropping one of her packages*). You come right home with me, Henry Wasserman! Your father'll 'tend t' you!

YOUTH. But, Mother, they're goin' t' ride somebody on a rail!

A goggle-eyed small boy among the onlookers, who has been watching her, politely picks up her fallen package for her. She snatches it from him and in an excess of upset, smacks his face, too.

THE SHERIFF'S OFFICE comes into view, the music distant but still throbbing with the ominous beat of approaching feet. The Sheriff, the Stenographer, and two other Deputies, including Milt, the young driver of the car that blocked Joe on the road, are listening to "Bugs" who, out of breath, and wiping his forehead under his pushed-back hat, is finishing explaining about the crowd. The Sheriff now wears a pistol, sagging in its holster at his belt.

"BUGS." . . . I cut across fences and — got a head start, but — they'll be here in a couple o' minutes!

SHERIFF. I expected it. (*Half under his breath, a bit nervous with anxiety — looking for a list on his desk*) Myrtle, get Capital City on the phone . . . Where's that Special Deputy list I made out? . . . Did I tell you to get me the Governor? . . . (*He finds list.*) Wait, Myrtle. First call up the men I've checked on this list! (*He gets out a ring of keys and tosses it to the Third Deputy.*) Get the tear gas bombs! Two apiece!

The DEPUTY goes out of sight, as the Sheriff goes to the rifle rack, and opens it, taking the rifles out. During this, Myrtle's voice begins to phone for the Special Deputies. On ANOTHER STREET some people appear on the outskirts of the unseen crowd — two rough-looking young men, their arms locked in those of an older flashy woman between them. In the background are groups of the crowd in movement, some now carrying sticks. The trio in the foreground is hilarious, evidently from the bottle which one of the men is finishing off. He tosses the bottle away out of sight.

In JOE'S CELL, JOE is standing listening, and he turns a little, trying to understand the faraway tread, not realizing what it means. Half automatically, he looks at the barred window of the cell.

We see the JAIL: It is the two-story frame building against which we saw the Sheriff's office sign. Its windows are barred. A few steps lead up to the double door. TWO DEPUTIES, young MILT, and a grizzled OLD-TIMER (who, we later learn, was a Vigilante in the old days) are on either side of the steps, with rifles. On the highest step stands the Sheriff. (The view moves toward them as if it were the approaching crowd, and the music grows louder, then stops when the moving view stops and frames the Sheriff and his group in the doorway.) There is an ominous silence. The Sheriff opens his mouth to speak, but immediately there comes a jangle of cat-calls, jeers, whistling, booing from the still unseen crowd.

In JOE'S CELL, startled, JOE jumps up to the cell window, pulling himself up by the bars. Then, Joe's face comes up behind the bars of the CELL WINDOW (as seen from the outside). The cat-calls come in. His eyes stare bewildered. And now the STREET (as seen by Joe through the bars) is packed with the cat-calling crowd. A fourth of it is women, the rest, milling men and youths. At the head of the mob stand DAWSON, the STRANGER, the FARMER, and GARRETT. Dawson nudges the Stranger as the cat-calls stop.

STRANGER. Sheriff, we want t' talk t' this Wheeler guy.

The Sheriff steps down. He is slowly chewing his tobacco. His hands are behind his back.

SHERIFF. Boys—keep out o' this. There's no positive proof the man you want to — talk to is guilty, or innocent, either. The District Attorney is checking on him now. But whichever he is, he's under the protection o' the law. (*Cat-calls and jeers greet him. The Sheriff's hands come up from behind his back. One arm waves "Quiet" at the crowd. Then his hands rest on his hips.*) As long as I stand here, you can yell yourselves hoarse. But you won't see this man. (*More cat-calls.*)

VOICE. Then y' won't stand there long!

ANOTHER VOICE. We'll move y'! (*Louder cat-calls and whistles.*)

SHERIFF (*through the hubbub*). Well! (*Loudly*) Then I ought t' tell you, men — the militia is on its way! (*The hubbub dies down.*)

The CROWD stands in silence. It looks startled, shocked. Its tension is stopped in mid-air.

The scene cuts to the ARMORY COURTYARD in Capital City. Two trucks loaded with uniformed militia men, equipped with rifles and tear-gas bombs for riot duty, are waiting, motors running. Behind them, other trucks are loading. The CAPTAIN in command is nervously smoking a cigarette. A LIEUTENANT is hurrying toward him, a folded sheet of paper in his hand.

LIEUTENANT (*handing over the message*). Orders to stop, sir. Telephoned from the Governor's office.

The Captain opens the message, and reads it with a start of surprise.

CAPTAIN. Stop? (*He looks up.*) But—

In the GOVERNOR'S OFFICE, the GOVERNOR, completing the movement and speech of the Captain of Militia, is asking:

GOVERNOR. —*why, Oscar?*

OSCAR VICKERY (the politician whom Joe and Katherine saw in the newsreel in Chicago) is sitting draped on the edge of the desk, cutting the end off a cigar with a pocket-knife.

VICKERY (*without looking up.*) Because people resent troops movin' in on 'em. Hurts their pride. When the papers phoned me about this little ruckus in Sage, I calmed 'em down. But —(*looking up, with a chuckle*)—knowin' how — er — conscientious you are, Bert — I came right over. And mighty glad I was in time to stop you, too! You could cut our political throats with this tin soldier stuff in an election year.

We see the exterior of the JAIL — at night, with the SHERIFF and the heads of the crowd visible in the headlights of parked autos. The Sheriff is grimly standing his ground, and still trying to calm the crowd.

SHERIFF (*conciliatory*). I ask you once more — for the sake o' all of us — go home. You're in no condition to do anybody any good. You'll all wind up bein' sorry for this.

In the crowd (as seen by the Sheriff), the stranger sticks his paw in his pockets and idly spits an answer.

GARRETT (*indignantly*). Why didn't you tell us about that five dollar bill in your office? We gave you the chance!

VOICE BEHIND. Protectin' the kidnapper!

DAWSON. Now you'll see "men" act!

A middle-class matronly woman of thirty-five pushes through to cry at the Sheriff.

WOMAN. What about our duty as mothers? In the old days sheriffs were on our side —

The scene cuts to a view of the SHERIFF'S GROUP, in which THE OLD-TIMER (a former vigilante) is listening with excitement, as the Woman's voice continues.

WOMAN'S VOICE (*coming over the Old-timer's reaction to her "old days" argument*)—not on the side o' crime!

THE OLD-TIMER (*stepping forward*). I'll tell y' about the ol' days. We was Vigilantes in them times b'cause there wa'n't any law nor order in this land. We made the law. To *git* order. An' we got it. An' now you idiots want t' bust it down. I'm *agin* y', an' I'll fight y' like I fought b'fore t' make this terr'tory somethin' t' be proud of!

The view now includes the SHERIFF'S GROUP —the SHERIFF in the center of the steps, the OLD-TIMER beyond him, MILT, the young deputy, in the foreground — and the front of the mob around twenty feet from the Sheriff, including the STRANGER.

STRANGER (*to the Old-Timer*). We don't need you to teach us history, Rip Van Winkle!

OLD-TIMER (*starting forward angrily*). You young whelp—

SHERIFF (*keeping him back*). Easy!

Two new armed deputies come out the door and join the defenders on the steps. At the same time, a feverish young woman, without hat, with a lock of hair dangling, and carrying an infant in one arm, runs in from the edge of the crowd, faces Milt, and pointing at him shrills.

WOMAN. You stick in with this kidnapper, Milt Grimes, an' you better not c'm home t'night!

MILT looks sheepish, uncomfortable. There are laughter and jeers from the crowd which begins to wave forward, slowly.

SHERIFF. Go back! Listen to me!

The CROWD is seen listening with growing and wrathful antagonism. A youth yells from the middle of the mob.

YOUTH. "Popeye" the Sheriff man-n-n! (*He is supported by laughter from the crowd.*)

SHERIFF'S VOICE (*indistinguishable over the noise of the crowd*). You're divin' in over your heads, men! Listen to reason! Stop acting like a lot of hysterical— (*His voice disappears under the swollen objecting and muttering of the mob.*)

In the CROWD, beside a lamp post, is a woman with a market basket, her arm locked in her husband's. We see a man's feet clinging to the lamp post above their shoulders. One of the mob behind the woman notices the basket and sneaks a tomato therefrom. And just as we again hear the voice of the Sheriff — "I'm warnin' you! Don't make me use force!"—the tomato thief draws back his arm in a baseball pitch motion.

SHERIFF (*concluding*). You're not up against just us here. More deputies, with more tear-gas an' rifles are inside!

Whi-i-*ish!* In comes the tomato and hits him on the cheek and neck. Instantly there is silence. The SHERIFF, without taking his eyes off the crowd, wipes off the mush with one motion of his left hand.

VOICES (*raised*). Let 'im have it! . . . Let's go! . . . Give it to 'im! (*The mob waves forward.*)

The CROWD is then seen through the bars of JOE'S WINDOW, surging toward the jail, and in the cell JOE now drops from clinging to the window and comes to the cell door, grabbing the bars of his cell door.

JOE (*shaking them as he shouts*). Lock-up! Guard! Come here! Hey, you! I want to talk to the Sheriff! Lock-up!

The scene changes to the HEAD OF THE STAIRS at the door to the cell block. (A stairway that is broken by a landing below leads down to the main hall of the jail.)

On the stairway the lock-up keeper is standing listening apprehensively to the voices and running footsteps of deputies below.

VOICE (*heard over the yelling of the crowd*). Get out more o' those tear-gas bombs . . . Where's the rest o' those deputies? . . . You hurt? Shall we shoot?

SHERIFF'S VOICE (*loudly*). No shooting! More bombs!

JOE'S VOICE (*desperately*). Where's the Sheriff! Lock-up! . . . Lock-up! . . . Bring the Sheriff! *Let me talk to somebody.* I can prove I'm all right! Lock-up! I can explain everything!

JOE is seen at the CELL DOOR. He is crying excitedly.

JOE. I don't want that mob on me! Tell the Sheriff to phone my girl! She's the one I wanted to call up. I didn't want to get her mixed up in it, that's all. Tell the Sheriff to call her up. She's waiting for me. She'll tell you who I am! Her name's Katherine Grant—

At SYCAMORE CORNERS, KATHERINE is inside a TELEPHONE BOOTH—dropping three nickels for a call, the receiver at her ear. The owner of the hot-dog stand passes with a cup of steaming coffee and doughnuts.

Outside on the ROAD, the owner brings coffee and doughnuts to the driver of a passenger bus drawn up before the stand.

OWNER. Ten cents.

The driver tosses him a dime and starts to eat and drink. At the same time, an open car with a moving-picture camera on a tripod, equipment and men in the back seat, pulls in with a screech from the opposite direction. The chief cameraman beside the driver leans out and cries.

CHIEF CAMERAMAN. This way to Sage?

OWNER. Straight ahead.

The car speeds hurriedly on.

DRIVER (*giving a whistle of admiration*). Boy! Them newsreel guys 're sure on their toes. They must've got wind o' this before it happened!

OWNER. What's happened?

The scene cuts to the TELEPHONE BOOTH as KATHERINE comes from the booth, terribly anxious.—The owner's wife is busy at the counter.

KATHERINE (*to the owner's wife*). I phoned where I live. There's no word of him!

OWNER'S WIFE. Oh, he had a puncture, I s'pect. Everything'll be all right—

We hear the sound of the departing bus and the owner approaches.

OWNER (*shaking his head*). Tch, tch, tch! The things that happen! They got somebody they suspect o' that kidnappin' at Sage. Fella name o' Joe Wheeler—

A close view of KATHERINE shows her staring dazedly.

OWNER'S VOICE (*continuing*). —and a mob there's trying t' make him confess.

Katherine comes to. She turns to them.

KATHERINE. Joe Wheel—Joe? But that's impossible! (*Her voice rising*) He never hurt a hair of anyone's head in his life! ... Where's a car? I've got to get there! Lend me *your* car—please! I've *got* to get to him!

OWNER. Miss, the boy's got my car in town. I'm—

KATHERINE When's the next bus?

OWNER. Ain't any more.

KATHERINE. What'll I do? I've got to go to him! (*She looks from one to the other of the bewildered couple in helpless terror.*)

In the GOVERNOR'S OFFICE: The GOVERNOR is in his desk chair. Leaning over the desk is VICKERY, punctuating his words with one hand.

VICKERY. —a question of *practicality*, Bert, not of flagwaving! Of *common sense!*

GOVERNOR. Common sense should have told me not to listen to you!

VICKERY. That Sage crowd was just out for a lark. You'd be a *laughin'*-stock, marchin' troops in t' wake up a town

that's gone to bed after it's got its steam blown off.

GOVERNOR (*after a moment*). If I don't respect the law, how can I ask the people to? (*He rises resolutely.*) I'm ordering the militia to Sage before it might be too late! (*And he clicks open a key of the dictograph.*)

Now the area in front of the jail is littered with missiles, rocks, stones, pieces of broken chairs, bricks. The SHERIFF and DEPUTIES are on the steps and before the jail, tear-gas bombs in hand. A few gas clouds are in the air, indicating that this is merely a momentary lull in the defense of the jail. The Sheriff, his hat gone now, shouts.

SHERIFF. Here they come again! Aim at their feet! Don't throw too far!

The SHERIFF and the DEPUTIES heave their bombs; they strike just out of sight, and as their gas rises the crowd waves through it into view, surging to and fro as it throws stones and insults.

THE CROWD. We'll get him! We'll get you! We'll get you!

Inside the WINDOW of a house a newsreel crew is photographing the scene.

CHIEF CAMERAMAN (*enthusiastically*). Boy, oh boy, oh boy, oh boy, oh boy! What a shot this is ... We'll sweep the country with this stuff! Film's gone! Reload! Be sure you use that hyper-sensitive film! (*His first assistant reloads his camera.*) Snappy! ... And, Bill, get me the telephoto lens!

THIRD ASSISTANT (*running in; excitedly, hurriedly*). Where's the hand camera? (*He kneels and opens a case and takes out a 30mm hand camera.*)

CHIEF CAMERAMAN. Where's Tony?

THIRD ASSISTANT. Taking stills. (*As he gets out a "Bell and Howell" and rises with it*) I got a spot for some swell close-ups.

CHIEF CAMERAMAN (*slapping him on the back*). That's fine! But take care o' yourself! This mob *eats* cameramen!

FIRST ASSISTANT (*having reloaded; calling*

from camera). Camera ready! Quick, Ted! They're tryin' to hit the Sheriff!

CHIEF CAMERAMAN (*running toward the window*). Get the close-up lens!

The DEPUTIES are now falling back into the jail. The OLD-TIMER is bleeding from a gash on his forehead. Two deputies come in—their eyes streaming from the effect of the bombs. A stone hurtles in, striking another deputy. The SHERIFF is the last to back in. He throws his last bomb, while shouting—

SHERIFF. Lock the door!

Helped by the other deputies he gets the double-doors slammed to and locked.

A DEPUTY (*with a rifle*). I c'n get 'em through a window.

He shoves the bench from the wall under one of the barred windows—its pane broken by stones.

SHERIFF. No shooting! More bombs— (*Stones come through the window.*)

THE DEPUTY. We're almost out o' bombs!

OLD-TIMER. Where's—that—militia?

Fists and feet are banged and kicked against the door, outside.

YELLING FROM OUTSIDE.
Open that door!
We'll get y'!
We'll bust it in!
We mean business!

SHERIFF (*to the Deputy*). Get upstairs with what bombs're left, and keep 'em away from the door! (*More stones crash through windows.*) Keep away from those windows! (*Seeing the Old-Timer limping back from the window and crossing scene*) You hurt bad, ol' timer?

OLD-TIMER (*indignantly*). Not by them idiots!

SHERIFF (*to the other deputies*). Any o' the rest o' y' hurt?

DEPUTIES. Not me!
No, sir.

ANOTHER. Nothin' important — just my head! (*He rubs his head.*)

SHERIFF. Where's Ralph? Where's Milt?

A DEPUTY (*nearby behind him*). His wife took 'im home.

SHERIFF. Ah-h-h, the yellow — (*seeing Myrtle outside scene*) — Myrtle! What in Ned're *you* doin' here?

A close view of MYRTLE shows her passing the open doorway to the Sheriff's office. She stops.

SHERIFF'S VOICE. I told you t' go home!

MYRTLE (*precisely*). I've been trying to get the Governor on the phone. But those sons of Cain've cut the wires. I'd better stay around and tend to my job—

In the JAIL HALL the SHERIFF suddenly stops. Outside, the yelling voices have diminished until it is quiet, and the sudden silence worries the Sheriff.

SHERIFF. Wait a minute. What does that silence mean?

DEPUTY. Maybe they're— (*He starts to look out a window.*)

SHERIFF. Quiet!

They all stop and listen. There is a moment of heart-breaking silence, then the sound of a *thud* from outside, followed after a short wait by another, and another— *thud . . . thud . . . thud.*

There is a flash of JOE listening to the sound. Then we see at the JAIL FRONT DOOR —outside—that the thuds are being made by the end of an uprooted lamp-post held and pounded against the door like a battering ram by men of the mob.

In the JAIL HALL—as the *thud . . . thud . . . thud* continues, the SHERIFF turns to the lock-up keeper.

SHERIFF. Go up and lock those cell-block doors — both o' 'em! (*To two deputies*) You! Get filing cabinets—desks—pile 'em up against the door. Don't take the new ones — (*Seeing "Bugs"*) Bugs! Get that fire hose ready!

In the CELL-BLOCK ENTRANCE, the view including iron barred doors at the head of the stairs and the one leading into the cell-block, beyond which we see cells, (including

Joe's, the lock-up keeper now locks both doors.

SHERIFF'S VOICE (*heard over the thud—thud*). We'll drown the rats! Give me those bombs! No matter what happens, don't shoot!

At the JAIL FRONT DOOR—outside—the men continue to sway the lamp-post at the door, one of them giving them the rhythm.

MAN. He-*ave* . . . he-*ave*.

On a COUNTRY ROAD, half-walking, half-running, and stumbling now and then, KATHERINE is trying to get to Sage, trying to stop passing motorists. She sees a car coming behind her, waves her arms, desperately crooks her thumb toward Sage in the hitch-hiker's gesture. It passes her. Clenching her teeth, she stumbles on after it, panting with the strain.

In JOE'S CELL we see JOE desperately shaking the bars of his cell. He throws himself . . . his shoulder . . . against the bars in a frantic effort to escape. The other coat shoulder is already torn from his hurling it against the wall.

JOE (*shouting between the sound of two thuds from below*). Can't anybody hear me? Let me out! I'll talk to them! . . . Give me a chance! . . . Let *me* talk to 'em! Give me a chance! . . . Don't you hear me?

At the JAIL FRONT DOOR — inside — the SHERIFF has planted himself, holding a bomb. "BUGS" is beside him . . . with the fire hose ready.

SHERIFF (*hoarse*). Y'ready, Boys?

DEPUTIES (*almost toneless with tension*). Yes, sir . . . Yes, sir.

Thud! The door begins to give way behind the office furniture now piled against it. The door breaks in. The last gas bomb is thrown. From outside comes a sustained shout of victory from the mob.—Through the cloud of gas, the head of the crowd piles in through the jagged doorway, stumbling over the furniture, shoving it aside. Water spurts from "Bugs'" hose, momentarily knocking back the first ones of the mob. The Sheriff and remaining deputies try to fight off the men with rifle butts.

JOE, in his cell, is in a state of rigid, trance-like waiting. He is half crouched in a fighting position, his eyes on his cell door. He is listening, terror-stricken to the noise of the fight below.

On the COUNTRY ROAD, a plumber in a small old truck headed toward Sage, stops.

KATHERINE. *Please* take me to Sage!

PLUMBER. Hop up, young lady—

He helps Katherine to the seat beside him, and the truck starts off.

Now the SHERIFF is defending the STAIRWAY. But he is knocked down from behind with a stick of wood. With DAWSON, GARRETT, and "MERELY-A-TAILOR" in the lead, men rush over him up the stairs. Then we see the STAIR LANDING where the lock-up keeper stands, pressed against a wall.

DAWSON. Give us those keys!

LOCK-UP KEEPER. I ain't got 'em.

GARRETT. Nothin's goin' t' happen to you, Lem. Give us those keys!

ANOTHER. All we want's this Wheeler!

LOCK-UP KEEPER. I ain't got the keys, I tell—

DAWSON (*menacing him with a chunk of wood*). Stick 'em up! (*Up go the lock-up keeper's arms, and Dawson searches him.*)

JOE, in his CELL, is looking through the bars at the Keeper. Joe is waiting for the keys to be taken from the Keeper. He is white with terror, but holds a leg of his broken stool (which we see behind him) gripped ready in his fist.

The LOCK-UP KEEPER still has his hands up, and DAWSON concludes his search by slapping his pockets for possible concealment places.

DAWSON (*threateningly*). Where are they?

The LOCK-UP KEEPER opens his mouth, but too frightened to speak, points toward the iron-barred door up from the landing. A close-up discloses the KEYS on a jail turn-key's ring, and the view draws back and up from them and on through the bars of the door, to take in the upper part of the stairs from the landing as DAWSON and the men rush in and up to the door. One of the men tries to reach the keys behind the barred door with a picket from a fence, but they are out of reach. The men try to open the door. Men grab the bars, shaking them in a fury of frustration.

VOICES (*shouting — beside themselves*). Get the lamp-post . . . we'll break it down! . . .

DAWSON. We haven't got any time. Those militia 'll be here. We'll smoke 'im out!

OTHERS. Yea-a! . . . That's it! Let's go, men! . . . Get some wood! . . . Bust up somethin'! . . . Get them nice new desks an' break 'em up . . . there's some straw down in the cellar! (*Some of the men pile back downstairs for fuel.*)

In the SHERIFF'S OFFICE now men are wreck-ing the office to get fuel—papers, contents of filing cabinets, chairs, a wastebasket. The scene is one of senseless depredation. —At the CELL-BLOCK DOOR, men are then seen piling paper and wood and pieces of furniture against the door. — Outside the open door to the SHERIFF'S OFFICE, two mem-bers of the mob are trying to angle a table with one leg broken off out of the door— as Joe's dog leaps over the table, half of its torn rope dragging from its neck. — And now we see the DOG sneaking through the feet of the mob, edging along against a wall —leaping over an empty space—

VOICE. There's his dog! . . . Grab 'im! . . . Stop 'im! . . . Don't let that dog out . . . keep her here with *him!*

A stone flies at the dog, but misses. Feet are turning in pursuit. The dog disappears behind the feet. There is a yowl of pain from the dog, but we see her again as she hurriedly limps up the stairs, shaking with fear.

VOICE (*shouting*). There she is! . . . Don't let 'er out! . . .

The pile of "fuel" against the first CELL-BLOCK DOOR is higher. The dog leaps to the top of the pile, and as men strike at her

with pieces of furniture and wood, without hitting her, she squeezes through the bar and jumps to the floor. Then she gets through the second barred door and runs straight for JOE's cell. — Here Joe drops the leg of the stool, and the dog leaps into his arms.

JOE. H-h'lo, Hash. H'lo. (*The dog licks at his face.*)

Beyond the growing "fuel" pile at the first CELL-BLOCK DOOR, the men are crying—

MEN. Let the dog go. Give it to 'im! . . . Wheeler, they can't parole y' out o' this!

At the TOWN'S OUTSKIRTS now the plumber's small, dirty truck, with KATHERINE beside the plumber, is coming to a stop at a cross-roads sign that points to SAGE.

PLUMBER. I turn off here, but—(*as Kath-erine hurriedly gets down*) — it's only a half mile over thataway, right—(*point-ing*)—there, where the heavens 're red. Look! Must be a pretty big fire in Sage.

With a terrified catch of breath, Katherine starts to run out of the scene.

PLUMBER (*offended*). *Well,* young wo-man — y' might 've said "Thank you"!

Then successive scenes show KATHERINE running in a FIELD, across RAILROAD TRACKS —stumbling and catching herself, past BACK YARDS and a chicken-coop as the surround-ing light becomes brighter, and past RESI-DENCE HOUSES, the light beginning to flicker against her face. She stops, her breath tor-tured. She sees—

The JAIL—appearing at a distance at the end of the street. Flames are licking out of the first floor windows, and the hall is a blazing furnace. The surrounding crowd is now quiet, staring at the flames breaking through the roof—but not on the cell-block side.

VOICE (*from the outskirts of the crowd*). Let it burn—the taxpayers 'll have to build it again!

KATHERINE pushes herself through the out-lying groups of the crowd until she stops by a lamp-post and looks up. Seeing some-thing, her face freezes in stark terror. At the same time others in the crowd see and gesticulate to each other, and point in the direction of her gaze.

VOICE. *There he is!*

A close view at JOE's CELL WINDOW—from which smoke curls out—discloses JOE's agonized face.

VOICES FROM BELOW. There he is! . . . Look at him! . . . I see him! . . .

A close-up of KATHERINE shows the fingers of her right hand clutched against the lamp-post, her eyes wide with speechless terror. Then in a GROUP IN THE CROWD, a haggard woman of uncertain age is seen staring up at the window. Suddenly she falls on her knees, chanting wildly.

WOMAN. I am the resurrection and the life, saith the Lord—I am a stranger with thee and a sojourner, as all my fathers were . . . Oh, God, forgive him . . . and forgive us our trespasses, as we forgive them—

In ANOTHER GROUP we see Men and Women (one of the women, prominent here, is later known as the Prim Woman), with faces distorted by the emotional beating the spectacle is giving them.

A close-up of a YOUTH shows him abstractedly eating a hot-dog as he gapes open-mouthed in the direction of the window—and a hatless WOMAN is seen holding up her infant to see the sight. Several louts are also looking up, and one of them, staring fascinated at JOE's face, suddenly reaches down, grabs up a stone, and throws it.

MAN. Drive 'im back! . . . Get back in there! . . . Get back, Wheeler! . . . What are ya lookin' for—the Peabody girl? . . . (*Others grab up stones, and throw them.*)

Stones and rocks strike the bars, driving JOE back, and he disappears from view while smoke continues to pour out of the window of his cell.

KATHERINE is next seen standing rigid as before. For the first time she is able to overcome her numb terror sufficiently to try to cry out. But only faint, almost indistinguishable sounds come.

KATHERINE. No . . . no. (*Her hand loses its grip on the lamp-post. She wavers a moment, then slumps in a faint, dropping like a stone.*)

The window of JOE's CELL is empty—except for smoke billowing out. But now, as the crowd is still staring up at the burning jail, a boy's voice breaks in.

BOY'S VOICE. Jiggers! The—(*indistinguishable words*)—are comin'!

Some of the group turn to see a boy running toward them.

BOY (*pop-eyed with excitement*). Soldiers 're comin'! Four trucks of 'em!

VOICES (*as the whole crowd is seen next*). Beat it! . . . The militia! . . . Soldiers! . . . Beat it!

There is panic in the crowd now and it begins to disperse hastily.

VOICES. Run! . . . Make y'rself scarce! . . . Militia! . . . Beat it! . . . Which way they comin'? . . . How many? . . .

In this group—being passed by running, stumbling men and women—are the MINER and a pal in similar work clothes.

MINER. I got an idea! They're not goin' to get him out!

He gets some short dynamite sticks from receptacles sewn into his jumper.

PAL (*realizing what the Miner is going to do*). That's the stuff! We can fix it so they won't even be able to find the jail! (*Running people have passed them until now the two men are standing almost alone.*)

KATHERINE is seen lying unconscious by the lamp-post in the street as running feet of men and women pass her.

MAN'S VOICE. Wait! . . . Here's somebody.

WOMAN'S VOICE. Help her up.

An elderly man and woman bend down and lift her up. Then as the sound of the running feet diminishes—there is a momentary silence. And suddenly there is a roaring explosion.

The scene dissolves to the STREET with four

army trucks in the background. A company of militia is formed, and they are counting off, their Captain at their head.

MILITIA. —One—two—three—four . . .

One—two—three—four . . . One—two—three—four.

Then the scene slowly fades out.

PART THREE

The GOVERNOR'S OFFICE fades in. VICKERY is irritably arguing with the GOVERNOR, who is harassed by a stricken conscience. There is a folded newspaper on the desk. Vickery's brief case is beside him.

GOVERNOR. Oh, Will—stop it!

VICKERY. It was a lesson to the whole nation that in this State there's still some of the spirit of our fathers!

GOVERNOR. For the last three days, you've been rattling campaign slogans over this, Will! The very spirit of government has been violated, and the State disgraced in the eyes of the world by this brutal outburst of—of lust for vengeance! And I blame myself. I let you talk me down. That mob could have been stopped if assistance had been given the local officers in time.

VICKERY. Oh, forget it! The reformers'll cuss around for awhile and then start cussing something else. (*Getting a batch of letters and telegrams out of his brief case*) These letters and telegrams backing up that statement I gave out — congratulations, ninety percent of 'em!— (*picks up some of the telegrams, and quotes*)—"Finest thing that's been heard of in years" . . . "Congratulations—"

GOVERNOR (*interrupting*). I wonder what kind of letters we'll get when it's known that Wheeler was *innocent!*

VICKERY (*squirmingly trying to find words to excuse himself*). Uh—ah—uh —I know . . . But when I gave out the statement I didn't know that!

GOVERNOR (*seizing newspaper from his desk*). This story's on every wire in the world right now! (*He tosses the paper at the Senator.*)

A close-up of NEWSPAPER HEADLINES shows a double line banner across the front page which reads:

KIDNAPPERS CAUGHT: CONFESS!
"G" MEN NAB WHOLE GANG!

and a sub-head explains:

HELEN PEABODY AND RANSOM
MONEY RETURNED HOME
AS SPEEDY JUSTICE
PROMISED

The view moves to a story lower down on the right-hand side of the page. Its double-column headline reads:

INNOCENT MAN LYNCHED:
BURNED ALIVE BY MOB

And now the LIVING ROOM — back of Joe's service station — comes into view. It is night. — CHARLIE is standing staring down at a Chicago newspaper in his hands. Its headline reads, in much larger type than the previous headline:

INNOCENT MAN LYNCHED!
BURNED ALIVE BY MOB!

He crumples the paper viciously and throws it down.

CHARLIE (*half to himself with dogged fury*). Yeah . . . Yeah! *Now* he's innocent. Yeah!

He paces up and down, and we hear only his tortured breathing, while TOM is sitting, wilted, on a bed, staring at the floor.

TOM. I can't get it out o' — my head . . . Can't get any sleep. . . . When I close my eyes — (*He rises, goes to the window, stares outside, — and turns again.*)

CHARLIE. I don't understand why we haven't heard anything from Katherine. I guess she must be like all the rest. He gets into trouble, an' she takes a run-out powder —

TOM. When I think how happy he was when he left —

CHARLIE. Stop it!

He drops to the bed. Silence. One of Hash's puppies comes in to his feet. He stoops, picks up the pup, and carries it to the door to the next room which is ajar. He shoves the door open with his foot, and goes in. In the OTHER ROOM, the other pups are around an empty bowl. Charlie kneels, and places the pup with the others.

CHARLIE (*calling — but tiredly*). Is there any o' that milk left?

TOM'S VOICE. What? . . . Oh, yes . . . I'll see.

Tom comes in a moment later with an almost empty bottle of milk. Charlie pours it into the bowl, and the pups lap it up. He puts down the bottle, looking at the pups.

CHARLIE (*abruptly vicious — with an expulsion of breath*). If I could only get at them dirty rats — if I could only get my hands on 'em! (*He looks at his brother.*) We're gonna go out there, Tom — we're gonna get them skunks, we're gonna kill them the way they killed Joe!

TOM. Whatever you say, Charlie — and *when*ever —

VOICE (*behind him — ice cold*). That's five-and-ten-cent-store talk.

After a paralyzed moment, they turn and stare, and next (as seen by them) a figure stands silhouetted in the open doorway to the other room — CHARLIE AND TOM stare as if seeing a ghost. Finally Tom gets out an almost indistinguishable word.

TOM. J-Joe . . . Joe. (*With a strangled shout*) Joe!· (*And he rushes forward.*)

CHARLIE (*coming to him*). Joe — J-Joe?

JOE (*curtly*). Pull down the shades.

His voice is ice cold, without any of the sparkle and warmth that characterized it before — the voice of someone back from beyond. The brothers stand immobile.

JOE (*hard*). I told y' to pull down the shades.

Tom goes out of sight, Charlie still staring at Joe, and we hear the sound of window-shades being pulled down. When the second shade is down, Joe moves stiffly forward without even glancing at Charlie, and goes out of sight. Tom approaches timidly looking to Charlie. Neither can understand Joe's behavior. Automatically Charlie switches on the light near the door. As Joe turns into view again, his jerk is sharp, but awkward with pain, his right hand going, with a smothered gasp, to his left arm. His face is drawn with suffering, his eyes sunken and burning feverishly. He never moves his left arm, which hangs limp.

JOE (*in a low, harsh voice*). Turn off that light.

The light goes out, and in the dim light Joe turns and sits down on a chair.

JOE. Y' know where I've been all day? In a movie. (*Charlie and Tom look at each other.*) Watchin' a newsreel . . . Of myself. Gettin' burned alive. I watched it ten times — or twenty — over and over again, don't know how much. The place was packed. They liked it. They get a big kick out o' seein' a man burned to death. A *big* kick —

He laughs, and it is an unpleasant sound. He drops his eyes to the floor, where we now see the PUPPIES around their bowl.

JOE'S VOICE. What an explosion. It blew out the cell door and killed — the dog. She didn't suffer. She was dead — right away.

Charlie and Tom still stare at him.

JOE. I got out down a rain-pipe. Almost burned my side off — I could smell myself burn! Got away in the dark, swam across the river there, and hid in the country. I stole these clothes. There wasn't much left o' mine. (*With an ironic laugh*) The law took 'em.

CHARLIE (*sitting on the foot of the bed away from Joe*). It's awful. I feel like th-thanking God or something —

TOM (*tender*). 'D you get — burned bad?

JOE. Yeah. But that don't hurt me. Ya can't hurt a dead man. Because I'm dead. Everybody knows that. The whole country. Yeah. I'm dead. Y' remember me preachin' to you to be decent? To live right? "Live right!" I tried to — and to like it, and people, and — (*with a sudden outburst*) — they won't let you! You were right, Charlie. Donelli was right, *every*body was right, except me. I was wrong! But now I know. And I'll get 'em —

CHARLIE (*eagerly*). Sure! We'll get a lawyer and have 'em —

JOE (*interrupting*). What? Arrested? For disturbin' the peace? Or for settin' fire to a jail, maybe? No, boys. That's not enough for me! I'm burned to death by a mob o' animals. I'm legally dead and they're legally murderers. That I'm alive's not their fault. But I know 'em. A lot of 'em. And they'll hang for it. Accordin' to the law that says . . . if you kill somebody you have to be killed yourself! . . . But I'll give 'em the chance they didn't give me. They'll get a legal trial. In a legal courtroom. They'll have a legal defense, and a legal judge . . . A legal sentence, and a legal death. (*A long pause*) But I can't do it myself. A dead man can't file charges. You'll have to do it for me. (*He takes from his pocket a page torn from a book.*) See this. I tore this page out of a law book in the Public Library. (*He shows them the page.*)

A closeup of the torn out PAGE from the law book, in the dim light of the room, reads — the light growing brighter:

526. *Killing by lynch law is murder in the first degree.*

When the object is to inflict capital punishment by what is called lynch law, all who consent to the design are responsible for the overt act.*

*State v. Wilson (1871) 38 Conn.

The paucity of cases here cited and the known prevalence of lynching suggests the almost universal acquiescence in lynch law and the want of serious effort to bring such murderers to justice.

This dissolves to a view of the gutted skeleton of the JAIL and its foundations (the debris has been cleared away), and then

to a BACKYARD where some school-boys, one of them (Albert) with an air-rifle, are playing around a tool-shed and a collection of grocery boxes and berry crates.

SCHOOL-BOY (*protesting*). Heck, le' *me* be the Sheriff for once in this game, will y'?

ALBERT (*who has the air rifle*). No, I'm the Sheriff! It's my rifle, ain't it? (*To the objector*) Go on now. Get in there an' holler like you was in a burning jail! The rest o' you c'n be the crowd an' I'll heroic'lly keep y' back.

SCHOOL-BOY (*giving in*). Well, gee, don't you guys throw real stones this time. Just pretend.

WOMAN'S VOICE (*calling at this point*). *Al-ber-t!*

The boy "Sheriff" stiffens, and listens to his mother at an OPEN WINDOW as she calls out.

ALBERT'S MOTHER. For the las' time, you stop playin' that awful game, or I'll phone your father! (*She slams down the window.*)

In the KITCHEN, the two Neighbor Women are there, with hats on, one the PRIM WOMAN whom we saw looking eagerly on at the lynching, the other, the WOMAN WHO PRAYED. Albert's Mother slams the window.

ALBERT'S MOTHER. It's a problem what to do with one's children in this day and age! That ground there was hardly cooled off before every boy in the neighborhood was playin' — (*swallowing*) — that game. (*She takes a pot, sits down, and resumes shelling peas into it.*)

WOMAN WHO PRAYED. My husband says it'd be a blessing if the community would forget — (*lowering her voice*) — what happened. It just leaves a bad taste, and reminds everybody what — as the Minister said Sunday — would be better forgiven and forgotten.

ALBERT'S MOTHER makes a "You're telling me!" gesture.

PRIM WOMAN. I'm glad *we're* out of it! We were at the ranch last week-end, y' know! (*Remembering her in the crowd at the jail, we know she is lying.*) So this — (*sniffing*) — District Attorney hasn't anything to question *us* about!

WOMAN WHO PRAYED. It's — it's a shame such an officious — er — District Attorney, from the Capital, has to stir up everything by holding such an investigation! And at the new hotel, too!

PRIM WOMAN. It'll ruin the business in that nice new cocktail room!

The front doorbell rings, interrupting her. Immediately the women stiffen, looking at each other apprehensively . . . The bell rings again.

ALBERT'S MOTHER. The mailman was just here! (*It rings again.*) Shall I go? (*Again a ring, insistently*) Yes — yes — I'm coming.

She goes out of sight. The others remain on edge with anxious expectation a moment.

PRIM WOMAN. I really have *so* much to do. I think I'll go now.

WOMAN WHO PRAYED. Yes, Mrs. Poole — me, too. (*They dart out the back door.*)

At the FRONT DOOR, ALBERT'S MOTHER opens the door slightly, as the bell rings again.

ALBERT'S MOTHER (*with a sigh of relief*). Oh! It's you, Mrs. Garrett.

A younger woman, with her coat thrown on over her house dress, and strained with anxiety under her faded prettiness, steps in.

MRS. GARRETT. Have you heard anything from the hotel? Fred's been down at that investigation for so long — I wondered if your husband had phoned or — or anything?

ALBERT'S MOTHER takes her in reassuringly, puts the chain on the door, and soothes her.

ALBERT'S MOTHER. Now, don't you worry, Mrs. Garrett! Nobody's going to cut off their nose to spite their face by naming *names* in this — this —

MRS. GARRETT. But if anyone does talk — what will happen?

ALBERT'S MOTHER. Nobody's going to

talk. (*Confidentially*) The responsible business men have decided it's a *community* and not an *individual* thing! So everybody's got to stick together, against this — uh — District Attorney.

In the PARLOR of a hotel suite we see the DISTRICT ATTORNEY, a young man of intense vitality. He is talking to CHARLIE and TOM.

DISTRICT ATTORNEY (*pacing restlessly, smoking a pipe*). Every move I make bumps into a stone wall. (*Charlie starts to exclaim "But — "*) Sure, they're guilty. The way they cleared away the debris of the jail in jig-time proves it. Smart of 'em, too. Because the way — the ashes and—so forth—vanished down the river makes it impossible for me to produce a corpus delicti or any part of it. And they know the law requires proof, first, that someone was killed.

CHARLIE. But everyone knows Joe was— (*swallowing*)—burned there. Why can't you —

DISTRICT ATTORNEY (*interrupting*). Knowing's not proving. The sheriff's still in bed, unable to be questioned. The whole town's tongue-tied. Under wraps. Protecting its own. Naturally! (*He paces again.*)

TOM. But — ask anybody! They'll tell you —

DISTRICT ATTORNEY (*a little irritably*). Before I can charge anyone with murder, I have to prove that a murder was committed. And I can't even find anyone who'll swear that *at the time the jail burned, your brother was in it at all.* Sorry, boys, I've got to go back tonight—

CHARLIE (*passionately*). But—but you've got to try 'em! It's your duty! You can't quit! *Some*body must've seen Joe in there!

DISTRICT ATTORNEY. Sure! But no one will admit it! With one person who'd *swear under oath* he saw your brother in that burning jail, I'd go before the Grand Jury tomorrow! But — (*He lifts and drops his hands helplessly.*)

Next we see KATHERINE's ROOM at night. In the light of a table lamp KATHERINE is sitting at the window, gazing straight ahead of her as she was when in reverie over Joe's letters. But she is wearing a dressing gown now, and is pale, with her hair a little disarranged. She is comatose under the hypnosis of shock. On the table next to her is a tumbler of medicine with a piece of paper over its top, and on the paper a spoon.

In the small HALL outside the door leading to Katherine's room, the Landlady waits anxiously as a Doctor — an old family physician — comes from Katherine's room carrying his little black bag. He carefully closes the door.

LANDLADY. ·What — what d' y' think, Doctor?

DOCTOR. Now don't you worry, Mrs. Whipple. You're takin' fine care of her. Don't worry. (*The Landlady takes up his coat from a hall chair and helps him on with it.*) Thank you — thank you — Keep her quiet — quiet. And lots o' that nourishin' broth o' yours. (*He takes up his bag and hat from the small hall table as he goes on to the door to the outer hall, passing to the kitchen, where we see broth cooking on the stove.*) If we could only get her to talk, it'd be a help. I'll look in tomorrow.

LANDLADY. Thank you, Doctor. Goodbye. (*She lets him out.*)

Next we see TOM leading an unwilling CHARLIE up, Tom arguing as they come up the STAIRWAY in the house in which Katherine rooms.

TOM. But at least we can look her up and find out about her for him, can't we?

CHARLIE. Who wants to know about a dame like that? *He* don't — (*The Doctor passes them, coming down.*) And neither do I. Let her go!

TOM (*stubbornly*). I don't believe she ran out on him. We got an hour till train time, so we might as well *try*. We can ask, anyway.

By this time, they are at the head of the stairs, and Tom, leaning forward to corroborate the name on one of the two cards over the bell, pushes it.

CHARLIE. *I'll* do the talkin'.

The door is opened a little by MRS. WHIPPLE. Tom removes his hat, but Charlie keeps his on.

CHARLIE. Miss Grant live here?

MRS. WHIPPLE (*uncertainly*). She's sick, and can't talk to anybody.

TOM. Well — our name's Wheeler. We're —

MRS. WHIPPLE (*starting, as she interrupts*). Oh! . . . *His* brothers? (*Opening the door wide*) Oh, come in! (*As she gets them in*) Maybe you can —

In the small HALL, the Landlady closes the door. Charlie rather grudgingly takes off his hat.

CHARLIE (*suspiciously*). What's the matter with her?

MRS. WHIPPLE (*anxiously*). She's pretty bad. (*Feelingly*) I'm so sorry about your brother. It was awful. Wasn't it?

CHARLIE. That's all right.

MRS. WHIPPLE. Heaven only knows if what I've figured out 's true — you see, she hasn't talked to anybody, not even to me, so maybe I'm wrong — but *I* think — when she came home so queer after bein' away all that day and night — the night Joe — Excuse me. I got t' callin' him Joe, myself, she talked about him so much — (*She stops, confused.*)

CHARLIE (*gruffly*). That's okay. Go on.

MRS. WHIPPLE. Well — what *I* think is . . . after waitin' so long at where she was going t' meet him there she must 've read — what happened — in the newspaper on her way back. Shock, the doctor said, that paralyzed her thinkin', kind of, so that she's not — well, not *right*, even yet, poor thing. (*She is close to tears. Charlie fumbles embarrassedly with his hat.*) Oh, young men, why must people be so cruel t' each other?

TOM. Maybe if we'd see her —

MRS. WHIPPLE. Maybe it'd help her. Yes. (*She motions them on down the hall, Charlie hanging up his hat.*)

In KATHERINE'S ROOM: We hear the door being carefully opened. Then the shadows of the brothers, followed by that of the Landlady, appear in the room; then Charlie and Tom and the Landlady themselves enter. Tom opens his mouth to speak to Katherine, but closes it again, and looks to Charlie.

CHARLIE (*with an effort, after a pause*). H'lo, Katherine. Katherine . . . It's Charlie.

TOM (*eagerly*). And Tom.

But she does not seem to hear.

LANDLADY (*lifting her hands to let them fall helplessly*). This's the way she's been ever since she came home.

TOM. Katherine! Don't you remember us? We came from . . . We're Joe's brothers. *Joe*, Katherine! (*He receives no answer.*)

LANDLADY. Y' see. The same's ever. (*Remembering*) Lands alive! Excuse me a second. I got broth on the stove! (*She hurries out.*)

TOM (*whispering*). Charlie, look. She *is* sick. Maybe if we told her Joe's al—

CHARLIE (*interrupting, turning as if overheard*). Shut up!

TOM. She can't hear. But it's not fair to her not to know. It might help— (*He stops.*)

CHARLIE. Le' me think!

He nervously gets out a cigarette, finds a match, strikes it, and lifts the flame to the cigarette. There is a choked cry from Katherine, and the boys turn sharply. A close-up of KATHERINE shows her staring at Charlie, her eyes big with fear, following which there is a close-up of the FLAME OF CHARLIE'S MATCH (as seen from Katherine's view); and this dissolves to a suggestive flash of the CELL WINDOW with JOE's frantic face behind the flames; for this is what the lighted match signifies in her disturbed state of mind.

Now Katherine rises, swaying a little, gripping her chair with one hand, as her lips form words, and then stammer weakly.

KATHERINE. *Joe.* (*Then crying out*) Joe!

Charlie, dropping his cigarette and match, steps quickly to her and steadies her.

CHARLIE. No, it's Charlie! *Charlie,* Katherine. And Tom —

LANDLADY (*entering anxiously*). What is it?

TOM (*motioning her to be quiet without looking at her*). Sh-h.

CHARLIE. Joe's brothers. Try to remember, Katherine. Joe's brothers!

KATHERINE (*with a great effort*). Charlie. Tom. (*Almost too weak to be heard*) Oh, Charlie . . . I saw him . . . I saw him . . . behind those flames . . . in that burning jail—(*her voice breaking*) his face—

She chokes up, and the landlady rushes to her to help lower her to the chair.

LANDLADY. Quiet, dear. That's all over now. Calm yourself.

Katherine is crying, but weakly; she is so exhausted by the snapping of the constriction in her head and heart.

CHARLIE. You — you *saw* him? (*Taking a step forward*) You saw Joe there?

LANDLADY (*stroking her hands*). Sh-h — sh-h —

KATHERINE. He was in such agony — behind those bars . . . and those flames . . . His poor face . . . that mob yelling . . . They were throwing stones . . . Then I don't know . . . I can't remember. . . .

Sobs, the breaking of her blocked emotion, stop her.

CHARLIE (*whispering*). The witness . . . (*repressing his tight elation*) . . . we've got 'em!

The scene dissolves to the DISTRICT ATTORNEY'S OFFICE. The DISTRICT ATTORNEY is seated behind his desk; KATHERINE is standing before him.

DISTRICT ATTORNEY (*pointing a pencil at her*). —And *you're* the one piece of evidence I needed! (*He rises and comes around the desk to her.*) This won't be very pleasant for you, Miss Grant.

KATHERINE (*quietly*). It wasn't very pleasant for Joe either —

DISTRICT ATTORNEY (*his hand on her*

shoulder). It will mean examination and cross-examination on the witness chair. It will mean saying things and explaining things that you haven't even dared think about—it will mean going through everything you went through all over again.

KATHERINE. That doesn't matter. I'll never stop going over it as long as I live — (*She pauses a moment, fumbles with her bag, and then looks up at him quickly.*) I don't want anything as blood-thirsty as an eye for an eye, or a life for a life, or whatever it is the law demands. I'll leave those details to you and Charlie and Tom. But part of that mob were women, Mr. Adams! And those men — they have wives, some of them — they have women who love them the way I loved Joe! I want those women to suffer. I want those women to feel what I felt — watching Joe in that jail —feeling my heart and soul and life crackle and burn to ashes in that flame! I want the woman who held up her baby to think about never seeing that baby again. I want those wives to remember the strength in their husbands' arms and the touch of their hands, and the way their eyes crinkled when they smiled — just before they were killed. I want all of them to know what it is to be empty inside — everything gone that matters to them. Not to be able to cry, not to be able to think, not to want to live — *why* live without him?! (*She pauses for an instant, then adds quickly*) You needn't worry about me, Mr. Adams. When does the trial begin?

The scene dissolves to JOE's HIDEOUT in Capital City—A cheap one-room third-floor back. JOE is in his raincoat, and has his hat on. CHARLIE and TOM are in the room.

JOE. I'll make 'em suffer. I'll get 'em now, all right!

CHARLIE. But why'd you have t' come here t' Capital City, Joe? Why didn't y' stay in Chicago? They'll have your pictures in all the papers here, once the trial starts. Somebody'll see you! . . .

JOE (*still the cold, fixed voice*). Yeah? Nobody'll see me — because I'll be hiding. But I gotta be here — (*lighting a cigarette*) — on the scene. D'you think I want t' have t' wait for letters from you? (*He exhales the smoke as he speaks.*)

TOM (*trying again something he's failed at so often before*). Charlie, I think Joe's right. It's natural, him wantin' to hear everything soon as possible . . . and maybe someday he'll want t' see—(*glancing at Charlie*)—Katherine . . . *Katherine!* She's so unhappy, and — I think Joe ought t' —

He lets his voice run down, as it is evident that Joe's mind is still on its one-line track. Tom shrugs — "What's the use?"

JOE (*continuing*). I want to hear everything they say. I want t' see them squirm the way they made me. I want t' see *them*—at the end of a rope! (*He laughs, and his laughter is ugly.*)

The DISTRICT ATTORNEY'S OFFICE — revealing a flat top desk, with shelves of law books in the wall behind it. On the desk is Vickery's hat. The District Attorney is lounging, rather negligently it seems, in his desk chair, playing with a pencil and smoking a pipe. But his thin smile and hard eyes belie his attitude. And now, across the front of the desk comes Vickery, chewing an unlighted cigar.

VICKERY. Adams, you can't force this trial! You're bending your office over backwards to get those two Wheeler brothers and that girl a private revenge that's as — cold-blooded as that — uh — rioting was!

DISTRICT ATTORNEY. My taking up this case has everything to do with the law, and nothing with revenge.

VICKERY. You'll never get a jury down there!

DISTRICT ATTORNEY (*smiling*). I know that. Naturally the people of Sage would be — er — prejudiced . . . That's why I've asked for a — change of venue, here. (*He half-smiles at Vickery's perturbation.*)

VICKERY. Ah-h, this is impossible! I've got to hold this party together in this State, Adams! These — these star-spangled heroics o' yours'll blow it a mile high!

DISTRICT ATTORNEY (*grimly, angry now*). I've got to proceed with this case, as my oath of office requires!

VICKERY (*finally, smoothly*). You an' your wife — that boy o' yours — in college now, isn't he? You like to eat, don't you, Adams?

DISTRICT ATTORNEY. Sure, Oscar. But some o' the things people have had to eat in this country lately haven't agreed with their stomachs.

VICKERY. But — (*laughing it off*) — who can you name? You can't try a townful o' John Does just to pull yourself to heaven on a publicity stunt.

DISTRICT ATTORNEY. John Doe is not going to trial, Will . . . but *twenty-two* citizens of Sage, who I can prove are guilty . . .

And now we see a COURTROOM, and the VIEW moves up to the TWENTY-TWO DEFENDANTS, Men and Women. The voice of the DISTRICT ATTORNEY is concluding his opening address.

DISTRICT ATTORNEY'S VOICE. . . . of murder in the first degree!

The defendants, including DAWSON, GARRETT, DURKIN—the WOMAN WHO HELD UP THE BABY at the lynching, are seen oddly self-assured, even cocky. Armed police guards and one woman bailiff flank them. The voice of the District Attorney continues.

DISTRICT ATTORNEY'S VOICE. Because the law declares that in a lynching all who consent to the design are responsible for what took place . . . *all who participate are responsible for the act!*

The DISTRICT ATTORNEY comes into view. He is speaking standing in front of the table at which sit two assistants, Katherine, Charlie and Tom.

DISTRICT ATTORNEY (*continuing*). This may seem harsh. But when a mob takes it upon itself to identify, try, condemn and punish, it is a destroyer of a government that patriots have died to establish and defend! . . . Every decent person in this country feels the importance of this case!

There is a full view of the SPECTATORS: Jamming every seat are the families and relatives of the defendants; some local "society," slumming for a "thrill"; hill-billies; ranchers; Myrtle, Katherine's Landlady; and the usual avid trial fans. More than half of the spectators are from Sage. Spectators pack the rear aisles, and stand packed about the door. The tension is great.

DISTRICT ATTORNEY'S VOICE. . . . And the proof is, the way the nation is hanging on the outcome of this trial! Has jammed this courtroom full! Has brought here the . . .

The view moves over to the PRESS BENCH where young and middle-aged men and women are busily scribbling — making notes — chewing gum — at their long wooden bench.

DISTRICT ATTORNEY'S VOICE. . . . representative of every news-service and important paper in the country . . .

Superimposed at this point are the "heads" of famous American newspapers — N. Y. Times, Chicago Tribune, Denver Post, etc.

DISTRICT ATTORNEY'S VOICE. . . . Not only our own press, but the . . .

The view now reveals the representatives of the Foreign press, including one Japanese, over which are superimposed, as before, "heads" of foreign papers — London Times, Berlin—, Rome—, Tokio—, etc.

DISTRICT ATTORNEY'S VOICE. . . . correspondents of the great news-services and papers abroad . . . And at this time I'd like to commend the . . .

We see the JUDGE AND BENCH, a microphone is hanging in the foreground. The Judge is a white-haired, ascetic American of the old school.

DISTRICT ATTORNEY'S VOICE. . . . judgement of this Honorable Court in permitting the broadcasting of this trial. And in this way removing these courtroom walls . . .

Then follow flashes of LISTENERS AT RADIOS, one flash dissolving into another.

1. A group of typical Yankee farm-hands in a village post-office, listening. An old boy with a Yankee beard nods vigorous agreement.

DISTRICT ATTORNEY's VOICE (*coming over these "shots"*). . . . so that a waiting world may hear what we do here to prevent the repetition of such inhuman crimes!

2. In a city office, a girl stenographer is listening wide-eyed. A man tries to whisper to her, but she shoos him to let her listen.

DISTRICT ATTORNEY's VOICE (*continuing*). No lynching can be justified . . . though sometimes attempts are made to whitewash them by citing the confessions of, or proofs of guilt against the by now silent corpse.

3. In a bar in a business district, solid business men are gravely listening.

DISTRICT ATTORNEY's VOICE (*continuing*). But *no* one can dare defend the lynching of an *innocent man!*

4. A group of Negro workmen is listening to a radio in an old auto.

As the District Attorney's Voice says "innocent man," the scene dissolves to JOE's HIDEOUT, where JOE is sitting hunched intently over a small, cheap radio, listening with a fixed grin of satisfaction.

DISTRICT ATTORNEY's VOICE. The law is the only safeguard against "an eye for an eye," "a tooth for a tooth" and blind chaos!

We again see the COURTROOM as the District Attorney concludes.

DISTRICT ATTORNEY. American democracy and its system of fair play for the rights of individuals under the law is on trial here, ladies and gentlemen of the jury . . .

The JURY is seen to be seriously intent as the District Attorney's voice continues.

DISTRICT ATTORNEY's VOICE. . . . on trial against mobocracy, that tramples and spits upon those rights. The American people have a stake in the proceedings here. You must answer, therefore, not only to this court — but to them. To this end, you must be guided not only by your common sense, but by your patriotism.

As the District Attorney goes back to his table, all the spectators come into view, and then we see the area in front of the spectators. — At the Defense table are two local lawyers and an associate whose more sophisticated bearing indicates a big city. They have their legal paraphernalia on the table. (The local lawyers will be termed here First Defense, and Second Defense, and the other, Associate Defense.) The First Defense smiles a little, and as the applause subsides, rises.

FIRST DEFENSE. As Counsel for these defendants, Your Honor — ladies and gentlemen of the jury — I must point out that my clients are not on trial for treason against any philosophy of government, as our esteemed District Attorney seems to think. They are on trial for murder . . . a charge that you will see vanish in thin air here . . . as the State, to cover up its own criminal negligence in not protecting this innocent man it speaks of . . . proceeds in this savage attempt to kill as scapegoats these — (*gesturing toward the defendants*) — twenty-two bewildered souls!

The DEFENDANTS are seen absorbing his words with smug modesty. There is the beginning of applause, quieted by raps of the Judge's gavel. Back in the full view of the court, the First Defense continues.

FIRST DEFENSE. There is only *one* question at issue here. Did these men and women, or any one of them, commit murder, or did they not? These defendants have pleaded not guilty to the charge of murder! . . . We are ready, Your Honor.

JUDGE (*to the District Attorney*). Are you ready, Mr. Adams?

The District Attorney now rises.

DISTRICT ATTORNEY. With the permission of the Court, and of my friends for the Defense — and — (*gesturing toward the Associate*) — their — er — experienced associate . . . (*The Associate toys with the thin gold watchchain curving over his well-tailored stomach, and represses a little smile.*) . . . brought from the city of New York . . . I'll reverse the usual order of procedure . . . (*as the Associate looks up quickly — interested*) . . . and instead of establishing the crime itself, first establish the whereabouts of the accused during the commission thereof.

The First Defense makes a movement as if to object, but the Associate puts a hand on his arm, stopping him.

The REPORTERS are seen next. One, a bored sophisticate from a big city, whispers to the girl reporter beside him.

SOPHISTICATED REPORTER. He's stalling for time. From what *I* hear he *can't* prove the crime.

DISTRICT ATTORNEY'S VOICE. As its first witness, the State calls — Edna Hooper.

SOPHISTICATED REPORTER. Where's the body?

GIRL REPORTER. From the looks of this town, it might be any one of the inhabitants.

At the WITNESS ROOM DOOR a bailiff is calling.

BAILIFF. Edna Hooper.

A fat, dumpy, fluttering, little woman comes in and is gestured by the bailiff to the stand. The Clerk waiting with the Bible there swears her in.

CLERK. You do solemnly swear that you will tell the truth, the whole truth, and nothing but the truth, so help you God?

EDNA. I do.

She gives a flirt of her head to reassure herself, and sits down in the witness chair, carefully arranging her skirt. The District Attorney approaches her.

DISTRICT ATTORNEY. Your name?

EDNA. Miss Edna Hooper.

DISTRICT ATTORNEY. Your residence, Miss Hooper?

EDNA. Twenty-three Catalpa Avenue, Sage.

DISTRICT ATTORNEY. Sage is the town, is it not, where this lynching took —

FIRST DEFENSE'S VOICE. Objection!

The District Attorney merely smiles a little, and does not turn, but Edna's head jerks, frightened, toward the DEFENSE TABLE, where the First Defense Attorney is rising to explain.

FIRST DEFENSE. Objection as incompetent. The question assumes the truth of a fact in issue.

JUDGE. Sustained. Strike it out.

The Court Reporter strikes out the question.

DISTRICT ATTORNEY (*smiling*). Exception . . . I'll rephrase the question. Sage is where the jail burned down on the night of October 26th last, is it not?

EDNA. Yes, but I certainly had nothing to do with —

DISTRICT ATTORNEY (*interrupting mildly*). You are not on trial, Miss Hooper. Your occupation in Sage, please?

EDNA. I am a courtourier and modiste.

DISTRICT ATTORNEY. By "courtourier and modiste" you mean you are a dressmaker, do you not? It's just the difference between a dress shop and a gown shoppe —

The jury chuckles. Without their realizing it, the District Attorney is putting them at their ease. The scene cuts back to the WITNESS STAND.

DISTRICT ATTORNEY. On the afternoon and evening of the day in question, Miss Hooper, you were employed in your capacity as — er — courtourier at the home of (*raising his voice*) Frederick Garrett in Sage, were you not?

We see GARRETT among the defendants. He is strained, hanging on the answer.

EDNA'S VOICE. I was.

At the WITNESS STAND, still mildly, the DISTRICT ATTORNEY proceeds.

DISTRICT ATTORNEY. What were you — er "courtouriering" there, please?

EDNA (*a-flutter*). Well — something for the baby. (*In some desperation*) You know.

DISTRICT ATTORNEY. I don't know, but I can imagine. (*Laughter greets this sally.*) Who was in the house beside yourself?

EDNA. The baby and Mr. and Mrs. Garrett.

DISTRICT ATTORNEY. And this Mr. Garrett is the same Frederick Garrett who is one of these defendants here?

EDNA (*firmly*). Yes!

DISTRICT ATTORNEY (*turning toward the defendants*). Will Frederick Garrett stand, please?

In the GROUP OF DEFENDANTS Garrett rises, gritting his teeth.

DISTRICT ATTORNEY's VOICE. This man, charged with murder . . . is the Frederick Garrett who, by the testimony of your eye-sight, Miss Hooper, was at home that Saturday afternoon and evening, then? (*He turns his back on her and goes out of sight for the moment.*)

EDNA (*swallowing*). Yes!

The District Attorney is now leaning back against the table.

DISTRICT ATTORNEY. I will remind the witness she is under oath, and ask her again — Edna Hooper, will you *swear* that during the hours when — (*picking up indictment from table and slapping it against his palm*) — this indictment charges that this defendant, Frederick Garrett, among others, murdered Joseph Wheeler . . . will you swear that during those hours Garrett was peaceably in his own house?

A close view shows GARRETT tense; he wipes some perspiration from his forehead. A view of MRS. GARRETT among the spectators discloses that she is anguished. She looks at her husband, then toward the witness. An old hill-billy with watery eyes is sitting next to her. Then MISS HOOPER is seen pulling herself together.

EDNA. Yes!

There is the sound of an "Ah-h!" of relaxed relief from the room.

DISTRICT ATTORNEY. That's all, thank you.

Surprised, Edna looks at him, then rises,

and the bailiff shows her the door. The District Attorney, however, turns before he reaches his chair, and stops her.

DISTRICT ATTORNEY. Oh, Miss Hooper! (*As she turns*) Isn't it true that for years you have been a close friend of, and, before she was married, roomed with — Mrs. Garrett?

FIRST DEFENSE (*rising*). Don't answer that!

Miss Hooper and the District Attorney turn at this.

DISTRICT ATTORNEY (*with innocent surprise*). But this is a witness for the State, sir, not for the Defense!

FIRST DEFENSE. I simply meant to — uh — object to — uh —

DISTRICT ATTORNEY (*smiling*). I withdraw the question.

A close-up of the CLOCK in the courtroom shows that it is 11:45. The large hand moves quickly twice around the dial, and as it starts around the third time, the WITNESS STAND comes into view. Franchette, a buxom, overdressed blonde of thirty-five, is on the stand.

DISTRICT ATTORNEY. Your occupation in Sage, Miss Franchette, please?

FRANCHETTE. I'm hostess at the Green Light Inn.

DISTRICT ATTORNEY. The one down by the tracks, you mean?

FRANCHETTE. If you're insinuatin' my place ain't respectable an' genteel —

DISTRICT ATTORNEY (*interrupting*). Not at all. The seventeen townspeople of Sage who have preceded you as witness here have painted a picture of the respectability and gentility of that charming town that's above my poor power to add to or detract. But you just said "*my*" place, Miss Franchette. You are, then, the proprietor as well as the hostess of the Green Light Inn?

FRANCHETTE. It's my place — if that's what you mean.

DISTRICT ATTORNEY. That's just what I mean —

The DISTRICT ATTORNEY takes a memorandum from his Assistant.

DISTRICT ATTORNEY. Will the defendants whose names I read, stand? (*He refers to the memorandum, and calls the names.*) Dawson — Piper — Lopez — and Durkin.

These defendants rise, all cocky except the anxious Mr. Durkin.

DISTRICT ATTORNEY. Miss Franchette, you recognize these men?

FRANCHETTE. I mos' cert'nly do!

DISTRICT ATTORNEY. Did you see them at any time between five and nine p.m. October 26th in Sage and if so, where?

FRANCHETTE. They were all in my place — in the cafe — from six to, oh, ten-eleven, anyhow.

A close view shows an OLD LADY among the spectators craning her neck toward the defendants with pained bewilderment. Then among the defendants, DURKIN is seen making an appealing, anguished gesture for forgiveness to the Old Lady we just saw among the spectators — *his wife.* A bailiff motions him to sit down.

DISTRICT ATTORNEY'S VOICE. What were they doing during all this time?

FRANCHETTE'S VOICE. Same as everybody else — talkin' an' drinkin' —

DISTRICT ATTORNEY (*back in the court scene*). What makes the presence of *these* particular men stick in your mind?

FRANCHETTE (*taking a deep breath*). B'cause, for once Mr. Dawson paid the bill. (*This is greeted with laughter, abruptly quieted by Judge's gavel.*)

DISTRICT ATTORNEY. You mean, by "Mr. Dawson," this defendant *Kirby* Dawson — (*Referring to memorandum, as if to himself*) Oh, yes — two years in jail — not identified with any church —

But at this the First Defense springs up.

FIRST DEFENSE. Objection!

DISTRICT ATTORNEY. Sorry. I was only thinking out loud. (*Back to his witness*) — this defendant Kirby Dawson,

according to — (*snapping his memorandum*) — these notes also known as "Bubbles" . . . for once paid the bill! (*Suddenly — speaking fast*) But he or somebody else didn't pay you to concoct this alibi for him and his friends by any chance, did they?

FIRST DEFENSE. Objection!

JUDGE. Sustained. Strike it out.

The First Defense smiles, and makes a silent remark to the Associate from New York, who smiles and shrugs. The District Attorney turns from Franchette to the jury.

DISTRICT ATTORNEY (*mildly*). I wonder if I haven't been calling the Defense witnesses by mistake! Perhaps we're all dreaming, ladies and gentlemen — and there was no lynching in Sage! (*Some laughter greets these remarks.*)

Next, in THE PRESS ROOM, we see the Radio Broadcaster, sitting with earphones on — beside his mixing apparatus and microphone.

ANNOUNCER (*over the laughter*). . . . proves that the District Attorney hasn't lost his sense of humor, in spite of the fact that during the last five hours his attempt to establish the presence of the defendants at the scene of the lynching has either failed or been ridiculed by the defense.

In JOE'S HIDEOUT, JOE is seen still listening to the radio.

JOE (*almost inaudibly between his teeth*). Wait! . . . Just wait!

ANNOUNCER'S VOICE (*from Joe's radio*). Every witness has sworn to an unshakable alibi that the defendants were somewhere else . . . Thaddeus Hummel, Sheriff of Sage County, is now on the stand!

The scene cuts to THE WITNESS STAND. The SHERIFF is in the witness chair.

DISTRICT ATTORNEY. Can you identify any or all of these defendants as having been in the mob that stormed your jail and *burned it thereby burning your prisoner, Joseph Wheeler, to death* —

DEFENSE. Objection! To the latter part of the question as assuming a fact not yet proved.

DISTRICT ATTORNEY. I will change the question to who "stormed your jail and burned it," then.

SHERIFF. No, sir. I cannot identify them.

Over this scene comes a murmur and buzz of excitement from the spectators. Then at THE PRESS BENCH (with the door to the press-room back of it), three or four reporters scramble up and hurry, with their notes, into the press-room.

DISTRICT ATTORNEY (*again seen questioning the Sheriff*). Can you, then, tell me the names of anyone other than these defendants among those rioters?

SHERIFF. No, sir. They must've been men from out o' town. (*We feel from him how hard it is for him to lie.*)

DISTRICT ATTORNEY. Oh, I see. "Foreigners." (*Turning toward the jury*) I will remind the jury of the easy habit of putting onto "foreigners" events that disturb our conscience . . . Or perhaps it was a roving band of — red-skins. Indians, I mean.

SHERIFF. The only red-skinned thing I saw was that tomato that plopped me in the face and made a fool o' me! (*Laughter comes from the spectators. The Judge raps for quiet, and the noise subsides.*)

JUDGE. I must remind the spectators of the dignity of this court. We are here after truth, not entertainment —

DISTRICT ATTORNEY. An injury you suffered put you to bed for a week, Sheriff. How did that happen?

SHERIFF. The deputies who stuck with me — most of 'em disappeared! — and I were holding off the mob with tear gas and rifle butts as best we could when I was slugged on the skull from behind and —

DISTRICT ATTORNEY (*interrupting*). You said "slugged" — "tear gas" — "rifle butts" — "mob." After all, this was an attempted lynching then!

FIRST DEFENSE. Objection!

DISTRICT ATTORNEY (*turning sharply*). The question was entirely proper!

FIRST DEFENSE (*rising*). I disagree! (*Forgetting himself, he addresses the District Attorney.*) Your constant use of the word "lynching" in this case —

DISTRICT ATTORNEY. If Counsel's ears were as quick as his objections, he'd know that I said *"attempted"* lynching!

FIRST DEFENSE. If the State's evidence was as breath-taking as its sarcasm, which I suggest is being employed to hide from the jury the failure of its own witnesses to back up its hollow case — (*There is a sudden burst of single-handed applause.*)

VOICE (*croaking*). Hooray!

We see an old HILL-BILLY among the spectators.

HILL-BILLY. Hollow 's a busted jug 's, what it is!

Defeating attempts on both sides of him to quiet him, the old geezer, who is evidently a relative of one of the defendants, is clapping his horny hands enthusiastically. Other applause begins to resound, quickly stopped by two loud raps of the JUDGE's gavel.

CLERK'S VOICE. Order in the Court!

The Judge is rapping a third time.

CLERK. *Order in the Court!*

A bailiff is going after the old Hill-Billy. With surprising calm — an important characteristic of his that fits with his fine old face — the Judge orders:

JUDGE. Remove that man!

The bailiff jerks the Hill-Billy into the aisle and begins to throw him out. From across the aisle, a dignified FARMER arises to protest.

FARMER. Uncle Billy's right! This is a shame against the good name of our town!

JUDGE (*banging his gavel*). Bring that man before the court! (*As the Farmer is hustled toward the bench, the Judge speaks.*) I will order you held in contempt, with a fine of one hundred dollars or ten days in the county jail. (*To the Clerk*) Enter the order.

FARMER. I protest against this injustice!

JUDGE. The fine will be two hundred dollars or thirty days. (*The Farmer's jaw drops. He is pulled away.*) A trial for murder is the most solemn occasion upon which men can be called to perform a public duty. Any further demonstration and I shall order the courtroom cleared. (*To the Attorneys*) Proceed.

ASSOCIATE DEFENSE (*coming into view*). Your Honor, the State's own witnesses have not been able to identify these defendants as having even been at the scene of the crime alleged in this indictment! We must insist that the State give us facts instead of tittle-tattle here!

The DISTRICT ATTORNEY comes into view, his face grim.

DISTRICT ATTORNEY. Your Honor, in the last 49 years, 4,176 human beings have been lynched by hanging, burning, cutting, in this proud land of ours . . . a lynching about every four days! . . . and only a handfull ever brought to trial. Because their supposedly civilized communities refused to *identify them for trial,* thus becoming as responsible, before God, at any rate, as the lynchers themselves! I did not put these representative citizens of Sage on the stand to prove anything, Your Honor, and ladies and gentlemen of this jury, except that on their *oaths to tell the truth,* and *nothing* but the truth, so help them God, they are — liars! (*There is a confusion of murmuring and movement, quieted by the Judge's gavel.*) . . . And that their contempt of truth shall not go unpunished I shall ask *their* indictments, for *perjury* . . . on-the-same-evidence-that-in-one-minute-*will-prove* the identity of these defendants with that of 22 active members of the mob that stormed and burned the jail and lynched Joseph Wheeler! . . . I shall introduce that evidence now.

JOE, in his hideout, sitting at the radio, grins. The noise from the Spectators comes into the room. It is followed by a silence. Then the Judge's voice is heard.

JUDGE'S VOICE. What is this evidence, Mr. District Attorney?

At the BENCH the DISTRICT ATTORNEY is seen going up to the JUDGE. He speaks to him so quietly that we do not hear. After a moment the Judge looks up.

JUDGE. Counsel for the Defense, please.

FIRST DEFENSE comes in, and joins the palaver. From his excited gestures it is plain that he is disagreeing. He turns and beckons. The ASSOCIATE comes to them, and joins the argument.

In THE PRESS ROOM, we see the RADIO ANNOUNCER broadcasting.

ANNOUNCER. While the Judge is hearing attorneys' arguments over the admission of some mysterious evidence, folks, I'll take this opportunity to remind you that you are listening to this trial through the courtesy of Nomake Mefat — the magic dessert. (*His Assistant hurries over to him with a note on a piece of paper, which the Announcer glances at and reports into microphone.*) Flash, folks! Against the objection of the Defense, the Judge has just admitted this evidence, whatever it is. The District Attorney —

The Defense Attorneys are returning to their table, the Associate shrugging to indicate "that's all we could do!" One of the District Attorney's assistants looks down the center aisle, raises a hand, snaps a finger as if calling some one's attention, and beckons. Spectators' necks crane around to look down the aisle. Then more heads are seen craning around toward the door to the corridor. It opens, and two men push in and wheel down the aisle a contraption covered with a sheet. The spectators' necks follow the object as it moves down the aisle. — And now the contraption, without being unwrapped, is tightened by its crew to the floor. Another man comes from the direction of the Press Room unrolling a cable. The other District Attorney's assistant hurries down the aisle toward the outer door, the spectators following him with their eyes. The back wall of the room has an improvised curtain that slides aside to reveal a moving-picture screen. There are excited whispers, and exclamations of

"Look!" "What's that?" interrupted by the knocking of the Judge's gavel.

JUDGE'S VOICE. Again I warn the spectators . . .

We see the JUDGE at the BENCH now banging his gavel.

JUDGE (*firmly*). . . . against any demonstration! At the slightest sign of disorder, I will unhesitatingly clear this court!

The view then draws back, revealing the DISTRICT ATTORNEY, who turns to the JUDGE.

DISTRICT ATTORNEY. We are ready, Your Honor.

JUDGE. Proceed.

The scene now discloses that the unwrapped contraption is a moving picture projection machine. It is surrounded by its crew.

DISTRICT ATTORNEY (*turning*). State's Exhibit A! A film record taken by Ted Fitzgerald at Sage in his regular course of employment as a news-reel cameraman. (*The lights dim. The camera starts to whir, its lights hitting toward the back wall.*) Defendant number one — Kirby Dawson . . .

A close-up shows DAWSON losing all his cockiness. He stares, suddenly afraid.

DISTRICT ATTORNEY'S VOICE. . . . who according to the testimony was in the Green Light Inn during the hours of the commission of this crime.

DAWSON's head, in spite of itself, turns to see — himself on the SCREEN — in the picture being projected — at the head of the men ramming in the door of the jail. The scene on the screen jumps to a pile of grocery crates, wood, etc., under one of the jail windows — on which DAWSON is pouring a can of fluid.

DISTRICT ATTORNEY'S VOICE. A stop-action of the scene.

The scene on the screen in the court "stops-motion" to show DAWSON motionless. The silver ribbon of poured fluid is of course motionless, too. Over it Dawson's face is contorted with sadistic intent, as motionless as Dawson himself is now, his mouth gaping half open with fear.

DISTRICT ATTORNEY'S VOICE. Defendant number two — Mrs. Sally Humphrey . . .

The view moves to MRS. HUMPHREY, among the defendants. She stares at the screen.

DISTRICT ATTORNEY'S VOICE. . . . who, according to the testimony, during the hours of the commission of this crime was on the farm of her fiancé a hundred and twenty miles from Sage . . .

On the SCREEN: In the mob before the jail is a hatless woman, not very clearly seen, who is swinging a burning rag around her head.

DISTRICT ATTORNEY'S VOICE (*continuing*). . . . though the record proves that at this time she was a member of the rioting mob. She is the figure swinging that burning rag around her head. We identify her by stop-action and enlargement of the same shot.

The picture on the screen jumps to a "stop-action close-up" of SALLY HUMPHREY. — Silence. — The picture moves again to show her tossing the flaming rag. Then the picture jumps to the piled-up wood we saw before as the lighted rag lands on it and flames blaze up.

DISTRICT ATTORNEY'S VOICE. The first brand that transformed that jail into a blazing stake for Joseph Wheeler!

A close view shows SALLY HUMPHREY in the court staring helplessly.

DISTRICT ATTORNEY'S VOICE. Defendant number three — Frederick Garrett . . .

The view moves to GARRETT, whose shaking hand fumbles at his forehead.

DISTRICT ATTORNEY'S VOICE. . . . who, according to the testimony was "peaceably" at home during the hours of the commission of this crime.

GARRETT stares straight ahead, not daring to turn.

On the SCREEN: In the picture we see two Sage firemen in uniform fighting off indistinguishable members of the mob for possession of their fire-hose. The flickering light cast by the flames of the burning jail is over them.

DISTRICT ATTORNEY'S VOICE. The fire department courageously tried to extinguish those flames, but overwhelming numbers fought them back, while in the meantime . . .

The picture jumps to GARRETT, who with an axe is chopping at the fire hose, on the ground, cutting it so that water spouts forth.

DISTRICT ATTORNEY'S VOICE. . . . the defendant, Frederick Garrett, "peaceably" armed with an axe, destroyed the efforts of the officials to save the life of an innocent man! The enlarged stop-action . . .

The picture jumps to a "stop-action" of the scene.

DISTRICT ATTORNEY'S VOICE. . . . proves the defendant's guilt.

There is a short silence as the picture is seen. Then it is abruptly broken by the scream of a woman among the spectators. And the scream we heard is now seen to have come from MRS. GARRETT, who is standing up and pushing off the restraining hands about her as she cries out.

MRS. GARRETT (*on her feet now*). No — no! It's not true! It's not! It's not! It's not! He — he —

She faints, and there is confusion in the dim light. Voices cry: "She's fainted!" "Get a doctor!" Everything is pell-mell. The Clerk's voice calls out: "Order — order in the Court!" The Judge's gavel is banging too.

At the PRESS BENCH, every reporter is trying to get into the press room at once — jumping over their bench, knocking over chairs, spilling papers and pencils. Over this comes the Clerk's voice calling for order, the gabble in the room, the rapping of the gavel. The noise is overpowered by the District Attorney's voice.

DISTRICT ATTORNEY'S VOICE (*insistently pressing on*). Defendant number four — Richard Durkin . . .

The scene cuts to the PRESS ROOM. A shelf has been built out from one wall on which are telegraph instruments, typewriters, telephones, and masses of "copy" and copypaper. Telegraph operators are in kitchen chairs, before their keys. The reporters are still piling in, trying to get the story on the wires. And this scene dissolves to flashes of NEWSPAPER HEADLINES such as:

"IDENTITY OF 22 PROVED!"
"GALLOWS LOOM FOR 'LYNCHERS'!"
"NO HOPE FOR SAGE OFFENDERS!"
"ADAMS SCORES DRAMATIC COUP!"

This dissolves to JOE's HIDEOUT. First a close-up shows JOE's HAND playing abstractedly with a cord, slip-knotting it, drawing it like a noose, tightening and loosening it. Then the view draws back to disclose that JOE is at the window staring out at murky rain — that fixed half-grin still on his face. It is the cord hanging from the old, cracked window-blind he is handling. Newspapers litter the room. His eyes glance around slightly at some interruption. Then we see TOM coming hesitantly to him.

JOE. Why ain't Charlie with you? Where is he?

TOM. He took Katherine home. She's — she's —(*There is a pause.*) Joe. (*Receiving no answer*) Joe, *why* don't you let us tell Katherine — that you're — you're — here. (*He makes a helpless little gesture.*) If you'd see her sitting there all day, and havin' to hear about your — she's been wonderful — Joe, she must love you an awful lot —

JOE (*interrupting harshly*). Shut up and get over to that courtroom. And remember everything. *Every*thing! Last night you left out three things that were in this morning's papers.

TOM (*tired*). All right, Joe . . . All right.

He turns and he goes to the door to the outer hall, picking up his hat. At this moment JOE speaks suddenly.

JOE. Too much depends on her at the trial. If she had the slightest idea . . . about me . . . she'd crack-up under cross-examination.

TOM. Okay. (*He turns up his coat-collar.*)

JOE. Take my raincoat. It's rainin' cats and dogs. (*Tom blinks at him in surprise at this evidence of feeling.*)

TOM (*with a wavering smile*). Gee, Joe, you —

JOE (*interrupting*). *Take it!* (*Tom, afraid of him again, hurriedly takes the coat and opens the door.*) And be careful *you* don't crack-up, either. (*With an ugly little chuckle of satisfaction*) I know twenty-two rats that're kinda nervous today.

A close view of the DEFENDANTS shows them sitting helplessly.

FIRST DEFENSE'S VOICE. While the fact that false witness was borne here is as great a shock to us as to the court —

The COURTROOM, next seen, has been cleared.

FIRST DEFENSE. Your Honor, I must re-iterate that our clients are not on trial for watching a fire, for setting a fire — (*The District Attorney looks up. His attention caught, looks at his watch, and whispers to his Assistant, who shrugs "I don't know," and then at some order of the District Attorney gets up and leaves the scene.*) — or for bashing in a jail door, but for the *murder* of one Joseph Wheeler, which the state has not proved!

KATHERINE, CHARLIE, and TOM now appear shoving into an ELEVATOR, in the COURT-HOUSE.

CHARLIE (*nervously*). C'mon, c'mon! We're gonna be late!

TOM. These street-cars are jammed! An' you can't get *into* this place.

OPERATOR'S VOICE. That's all — that's all!

TOM (*to Katherine*). You feel better to-day?

KATHERINE (*managing a game smile and patting his arm*). I feel fine. I've been waiting for this day.

Her hand stops patting him, as something about the raincoat attracts her attention — though only vaguely.

OPERATOR'S VOICE. Second floor . . . Traffic court.

The elevator stops and some people leave while others enter the elevator. Katherine tries to plumb her memory to bring something back, but fails, and frowns a little abstractedly. She looks at her hand, then

to the raincoat. The fact that it is JOE's raincoat begins to seep into her conscious-ness. To assure herself, she steps back a little. — A close-up discloses the RAINCOAT POCKET with the rip that she sewed in the Chicago railroad station so long, long ago.

CHARLIE'S VOICE. Got a cigarette, Tom?

TOM'S VOICE. Sure.

His hand goes into the raincoat pocket, then surprisedly pulls out something that he raises to his face. He opens his hand, seeing some fragments of salted peanuts there. — A close-up then shows KATHERINE staring at the peanuts, something beginning to dawn, but very vaguely, in her face. TOM gives a self-conscious little laugh and tries to cover-up.

TOM. Peanuts. I like 'em. (*Offering her his hand*) Want some?

KATHERINE opens her mouth to speak, but the Operator's Voice stops her.

OPERATOR'S VOICE. Judge Hopkins' Court!

The elevator stops, and Katherine, Tom, Charlie and others go into the corridor. Katherine is still gazing at the raincoat with a worried little frown. As newspaper photographers take flashlights of her, the Assistant of the District Attorney pushes in.

ASSISTANT. Oh, there you are! Hurry, Miss Grant, please! The District Attor-ney needs you.

In the COURTROOM, the First Defense is seen addressing the jury.

FIRST DEFENSE. . . . the last the Sheriff, the lock-up keeper, or any one else saw of him was *before* the fire! I must in-sist on my question: Who proves that Joseph Wheeler was in that jail at the time it burned?

Katherine, Charlie, and Tom are being brought in by the Assistant just in time to hear these last words of the First Defense. Katherine stops, hanging on his words. The District Attorney comes to her, saying "Are you ready to take the stand?" But she does not hear, her mind being entirely centered on her vague suspicion.

FIRST DEFENSE. The lock-up keeper threw the keys down in the jail. Isn't there the possibility that the prisoner angled for those keys, unlocked his cell door, and escaped the back way? We say that possibility exists! It's up to the State to prove it false!

JUDGE'S VOICE. Is the State prepared to proceed?

DISTRICT ATTORNEY. We call Katherine Grant to the stand.

JOE in his hideout is seen again listening at the radio. The Clerk's Voice is heard swearing Katherine in.

KATHERINE'S VOICE. I do.

Again that ugly smile of anticipation creeps into JOE's face as he hears this.

DISTRICT ATTORNEY'S VOICE. State your name, occupation, and residence, please.

KATHERINE (*in the witness stand*). Katherine Grant. I'm a teacher in the Washington Public School here. I live at 96 Oak Street.

DISTRICT ATTORNEY. With your parents, Miss Grant?

KATHERINE. My father and mother are dead.

DISTRICT ATTORNEY. Your relationship to Joseph Wheeler was — ?

KATHERINE. We were going to be married.

The DEFENDANTS are seen as a group. The woman defendant who held the baby up to see the burning jail is moved.

KATHERINE'S VOICE. He was on his way to me. We were going to be married here and drive back to Chicago for our wedding trip in his car, with his dog. He'd sent me a picture of it.

At the WITNESS STAND, the DISTRICT ATTORNEY is very gentle as he continues.

DISTRICT ATTORNEY. Now tell the jury in your own way what happened October 26th.

KATHERINE. I fixed a little lunch of things I thought he'd like . . . with flowers on the table . . . and — and some salted p-peanuts. He was always fond of peanuts. (*She rubs her forehead vaguely as if again struggling to connect something.*)

DISTRICT ATTORNEY. Are you able to go on, Miss Grant?

KATHERINE (*coming to*). Certainly I can go on. — I went to meet him at Sycamore Corners. On the way, I bought him some neckties for a present . . . he liked blue, and men don't buy those things for themselves — you know how they are. And then . . .

JOE at the radio, is listening with strained nervousness, as he hears her.

KATHERINE'S VOICE (*going on*). I stopped at the minister's to remind him Joe and I would be there at four o'clock all right, and not to forget . . . (*Joe presses his hands over his ears to keep from being touched.*) We'd been away from each other so long. More than a year. (*He drops his hands for a moment.*) And I — I loved him so . . .

Unable to stand it longer, JOE jumps up, savagely snaps off the radio, and paces as if in a trap. Desperation to hear — hear everything — however, beats him and he snaps the thing on again — only to hear:

KATHERINE'S VOICE. . . . I saw him — in the burning window, behind the bars . . . his poor face . . .

Again he shuts it off and unconsciously twists the ring on his finger, possessed with the necessity of hearing the lynchers' progress toward the rope, but afraid of the effect on him of Katherine's voice. He catches sight of his face in the old mirror on the wall and sees that he is sweating, tormented.

The view in the COURTROOM moves to a close-up of the FIRST ROW DEFENDANTS. Their faces, eyes, are as tormented as Joe's. Over this Katherine's voice comes in, and the view stops at the WOMAN we saw in the newsreel.

KATHERINE'S VOICE. They were screaming "There he is!" . . . It looked like he was trying to get out the window . . . but the bars — they threw stones . . . hitting him . . . driving him back in the flames.

The WOMAN DEFENDANT is seen cracking under the strain.

JOE'S FACE is seen in the mirror. Then he pulls himself away from staring at it, and goes to the radio. He hesitates, then decisively snaps it on again, expelling a sigh of relief that it is not Katherine's voice he hears.

DISTRICT ATTORNEY'S VOICE. I turn the witness over to the Defense.

At the WITNESS STAND, the Associate is cross-examining.

ASSOCIATE DEFENSE (*gently*). Miss Grant, if you'll allow me I'll just ask you to think over with me a question or two . . . You were naturally — agitated — when you heard this — (*waving a hand in search of the word*) — this — gossip — that the man you loved was being held as a suspect in jail at Sage.

KATHERINE (*her attitude different now; sarcastically*). How gently you put things —

ASSOCIATE DEFENSE. And all the way hitch-hiking to Sage, afraid you'd be too late, this shocking picture naturally became more plain in your head, so that when you finally reached the jail you expected to see him there, did you not?

KATHERINE. Yes.

ASSOCIATE DEFENSE. According to the fact of psychology that under great emotional stress the mind sees what it has expected to, whether the thing is actually there or not, is it not possible that you did not see Joseph Wheeler, but only the image of him your imagination had created in your head?

KATHERINE. No! I saw him. I *saw* him! Burning to death there! (*She stops, trembling a little.*)

ASSOCIATE DEFENSE (*very gently*). You can see that picture now, too, can't you?

KATHERINE. I'll always . . . see it.

ASSOCIATE DEFENSE. So perhaps after all, it *was* an hallucination of your tortured mind you saw there, just as you see it here?

KATHERINE (*tiredly*). What is it you want me to say — yes or no? I tell you — I *saw* him!

ASSOCIATE DEFENSE. *Can you, from your own personal knowledge, swear that Joseph Wheeler is dead?*

KATHERINE. Why, no — that is, yes — I mean, one can assume —

ASSOCIATE DEFENSE (*interrupting*). Excuse me, but that is exactly what must *not* be assumed, but *proved!* The State is asking the lives of twenty-two people for one!

KATHERINE (*emotionally*). I don't *care* about the lives of twenty-two people! They won't bring back the one life I cared about. I only wish I hadn't fainted. I wish I could have gone in there to him — with him — (*She cries, sinking her head into her hands.*)

ASSOCIATE DEFENSE (*pausing a moment*). That's all, Miss Grant. (*He helps her from the stand, then turns to the jury.*) I will remind the jury that under the law, lives must not be taken on assumptions, but on facts! Where is the corpse of Joseph Wheeler?

DISTRICT ATTORNEY (*coming in fighting*). Witnesses have testified that before the jail site was cold they cleaned it up and dumped the debris into the river. In that way they got rid of the body of their victim or of anything that remained of it!

ASSOCIATE DEFENSE. The law is that corpus delicti must be established! At least by fragments of that human body or of articles known or proved to have been worn by the deceased! It has *not* been proved, and cannot be proved that Joseph Wheeler is dead! On the contrary, there is the admitted possibility that Joseph Wheeler *did* escape . . . *is alive today!*

JOE is again seen at the radio as he listens.

ASSOCIATE DEFENSE'S VOICE. Perhaps with memory gone — as this girl experienced — but nevertheless alive!

In the COURTROOM:

> ASSOCIATE DEFENSE (*turning to the Judge*). And in the absence of convincing proof of corpus delicti, Your Honor, I move that this indictment be set aside and the charge against these defendants be dismissed!

The DEFENDANTS are seen swallowing eagerly; all show revived hope — except the Woman. She wordlessly shakes her head "no — no" a little.

At the radio, JOE awaits the Judge's answer in dread.

> JOE (*uncontrollably, harshly*). Come on — come on! (*He is taut with tension.*)

At the BENCH, the Judge is announcing his decision now.

> JUDGE. I shall take the motion for dismissal under advisement till tomorrow and hear the State's arguments then. (*He rises.*)

JOE, furious, grabs up the radio with both hands and smashes it to the floor.

The scene dissolves to a close-up of JOE's PHOTOGRAPH filling the front page of a tabloid, showing him in a happy mood, as different as possible from his expression in the last scene. The headline blares,

> "IS THIS MAN ALIVE?
> ASSERT WHEELER LIVES
> DEFENSE CLAIM WHEELER STILL ALIVE"

and this dissolves to a close view of KATHERINE, in her room, regarding the photograph with a confused and bothered frown.

The COURTROOM — comes into view — the area in front of the spectators' seats. — The clock is at 11:20. The defendants and jury are in their places. But the Judge is not on the bench. Though the attorneys, reporters, bailiffs, and Court Reporter appear negligently relaxed as they await the delayed opening of Court, there is a shivery feeling of expectancy over the room that makes it tense under its cloak of ease. Some of the men are smoking, some are reading, and eagerly discussing, the morning newspapers. The District Attorney is laughing in friendly fashion with the First Defense and Associate as he idly knocks out his pipe on a newspaper on the table, takes it apart and cleans it. Their professional antagonism is quite absent.

> DISTRICT ATTORNEY. Any team that can score three touchdowns in one quarter deserves to win a football game —

> ASSOCIATE DEFENSE. I'm not interested in your alibis. Where's the dollar you owe me?

The District Attorney laughs, and hands him a bill. The Sophisticated Reporter passes the defendants, a folded newspaper under his arm. A defendant leans forward, reaching for the paper.

> DEFENDANT. Le' me look at that, will y', Bud? (*The Reporter gives him the paper.*)

> SOPHISTICATED REPORTER. Why don't some of you chumps crash through with a confession? You'd only get "life" that way, and I could get back to New York!

> DAWSON (*swelling*). B'cause we're innocent, that's why! Look at the paper!

> SOPHISTICATED REPORTER (*innocently*). So you believe what you read in the papers? My, my! (*He goes out of sight.*)

At the DEFENSE TABLE, the First Defense, looking at his watch, is nervous.

> FIRST DEFENSE. Where d' you suppose the Judge *is?* It's eleven-thirty —

The Associate Defense shrugs "I don't know!" A bailiff comes in, handing two law books to the District Attorney.

> BAILIFF. He's been in his chambers since nine.

We see the DEFENDANTS looking at the newspaper, and they are maliciously happy. One of them, next to the Woman, is holding the paper.

> DEFENDANT. "Alive" . . . Smart lawyers we got, uh? (*He shoves the paper under the rigid Woman's downcast eyes.*) C'mon, Ellie — look 't it.

> WOMAN DEFENDANT (*who is haggard with sleeplessness*). I don't want t' see it. I see that face all the time.

> ANOTHER DEFENDANT. Look! (*He points.*)

We see the DEFENSE TABLE, from the defendants' view. A different bailiff is speaking low to both Defense and District Attorney, who look at each other inquiringly, then rise, and follow the bailiff to the door to the Judge's chambers. The snatches of conversation and sounds of movement in the room quiet down as everyone looks after the attorneys. Reporters skip after them, asking, "What's up?" "Anything new?" The bailiff, keeping the reporters back, opens the door and the attorneys go in.

CHARLIE AND TOM are seen sitting together in the otherwise deserted spectator section. Charlie, a newspaper in his hand, eagerly pokes Tom to look at the attorneys going into the Judge's chambers. Charlie watches with a half-smile of surety, Tom fixedly, biting his under lip, nods nervously.

In the JUDGE'S CHAMBERS there is a bust of Lincoln on the bookcase. The Judge is standing, without his robe, behind his desk, facing the three attorneys. A newspaper, and open law books are on his desk. He has a folded letter in his hand, and its envelope and a small object wrapped in tissue paper, before him.

JUDGE (*to the attorneys*). This came to me Special Delivery two hours ago, gentlemen. Read it, and give me your opinions, please.

CHARLIE AND TOM are seen in the spectator section.

CHARLIE. They're readin' it now.

TOM (*nervously*). What d' y' think they'll do?

CHARLIE. I don't know. (*Seeing someone, he slouches behind the newspaper.*) Sh-h! (*Katherine approaches them.*)

KATHERINE. I waited for you.

Charlie lets her pass, so that she sits between them.

TOM (*lamely*). We didn't know what t' do . . . these pictures . . . and everything in the papers . . . they — (*He stops.*)

KATHERINE. I saw the papers.

CHARLIE. Ah-h, they're crazy, with that stuff about — him — being alive!

KATHERINE (*tiredly, half to herself*). It

would be crazy . . . If I could only stop thinking.

TOM (*distressed for her*). I know. It's—

CHARLIE (*quickly, to Katherine*). Want t' go to a movie tonight?

TOM (*protesting*). Charlie, how c'n you— (*Recovering*) I mean, there's nothing good playing tonight.

KATHERINE (*as if trying to convince herself*). But if he weren't dead he'd have told *me* . . . let me know *some*how . . .

Charlie and Tom watch her fearfully. But there is the sound of a gavel rapping three times, and they look up.

BAILIFF'S VOICE. Oyez, oyez! Hear ye, hear ye! The Supreme Court is now in session, the Honorable Judge Hopkins presiding.

Charlie, Katherine and Tom rise, Charlie letting Katherine pass.

CHARLIE (*to Tom, whispering behind her back*). Don't leave her alone! (*They follow her.*)

The Judge takes the bench. The people sit down. At the Defense table the First Defense is whispering to the Second Defense, who begins hurriedly to look up references in law books there, and to make notes of them. Katherine, Charlie and Tom take their places at the District Attorney's table.

JUDGE (*to the jury*). Ladies and gentlemen of the jury, I have received an object which, if authentic, must be considered as evidence in this case. As to its authenticity, I am not permitted to have an opinion. But that you may decide for yourselves, I have, over strong objections by Counsel, asked the District Attorney to present it to you. (*He gestures toward the District Attorney.*)

DISTRICT ATTORNEY (*coming to the jury with an envelope*). This is a Special Delivery letter postmarked in this city at . . . eleven P.M. last night, and addressed "Judge Daniel Hopkins, Hall of Justice, Courtroom 10." (*He picks up the letter as he explains.*) The communication is not hand-written. It is formed by letters cut from a newspaper and pasted together to spell words. . . .

It is, ladies and gentlemen, the confession of a tortured conscience . . . Listen . . . (*Reading*) "I can't hide the truth any longer. I am a citizen of Sage, who helped clean up the jail mess. In the ashes I found this enclosed ring. Nobody knew it, so I was keeping it for a memento— (*He hesitates an instant over the word.*) —memento (*Katherine, sitting between Charlie and Tom, lifts her head as if hearing a faraway voice.*) but it is upsetting my conscience, so I am getting it off my chest. I don't dare sign this or I would probably get lynched myself . . . A Citizen of Sage."

Dropping the letter to his table, he picks up the ring. Charlie slides the letter toward himself, and bending over it reads it.

DISTRICT ATTORNEY. I now call your attention to the ring, its gold, melted and mis-shapen as if by fire!

FIRST DEFENSE (*jumping up*). Objection! You require expert testimony as to that!

JUDGE. Sustained.

The DISTRICT ATTORNEY raises the ring close to his eyes and deciphers.

DISTRICT ATTORNEY. Inside the ring is an engraved inscription, reading—I can decipher only the words . . . "Henry . . . to . . . K—" the next letter could be an "o," or "a" — perhaps an "e" — but the rest is melted out. But after that word I plainly read, in a different style of engraving . . . "to Joe"! . . . obviously meaning —

FIRST DEFENSE (*on his feet again*) Objection!

JUDGE. Sustained.

FIRST DEFENSE. Since when have anonymous letters become gospel in law? Who can say that that ring was actually the property of Joseph Wheeler? What proof is there that it was really found as that concocted letter would have us believe? Who sent that letter? Anonymous! We all know what to expect from anonymous — a man afraid to sign his name!

KATHERINE is staring at the letter lying before her on the table, and a close-up brings its contents clearly in sight.

FIRST DEFENSE'S VOICE (*continuing*). I don't believe in this "citizen of Sage"! I believe that this fraud is a fabrication of some soul poisoned with hostility toward these defendants!

The Voice of the First Defense grows fainter as the words of the letter fade dizzily, except one of them, which looms plainly. It is the word *"mementum."* The word rushes closer and closer to us, larger and larger, until it seems to explode with the violence of its shock to Katherine's brain.

Katherine's lips part as if to cry out. She makes a sudden movement to stand up, but Charlie strikes his hand out and gripping her arm keeps her down. Terribly afraid, she stares at him.

DISTRICT ATTORNEY. The State recalls Katherine Grant to the stand.

She looks at him, haunted, then back to CHARLIE. There is silence. Then Charlie nudges the girl. She rises abstractedly and starts for the witness stand. The defendants' heads follow KATHERINE's progress to the stand. They are dumb with shock. The jury's heads likewise point after her, keen with expectancy.

DISTRICT ATTORNEY. I remind you, Miss Grant, that you have already sworn to tell the truth. (*Handing her the ring*) Have you ever seen this ring before?

KATHERINE (*taking the ring*). Yes. (*She seems dazed.*)

DISTRICT ATTORNEY. Where? And when?

KATHERINE. In the railroad station in Chicago . . . as I was leaving to come here . . . I gave it to Joe.

DISTRICT ATTORNEY. What did Joseph Wheeler do with the ring when you gave it to him?

KATHERINE. He put it on . . . his little finger. It was too small for any other finger.

DISTRICT ATTORNEY. How can you be sure this ring is the one you gave Joseph Wheeler and saw him put on his little finger there?

KATHERINE. Because . . . it was my mother's, and had engraved in it "Henry" — my father's name — "to

Katherine," which was my mother's name, too. After the "Katherine" in the ring I had engraved "to Joe," and —

An hysterical scream, off, interrupts her. The Woman Defendant's voice comes in.

WOMAN DEFENDANT'S VOICE. We did it! We did it! Tell her to stop!

The view swings abruptly and, to express the sensational impression caused by the woman's hysterical collapse, darts to the WOMAN DEFENDANT. She is half-standing, half-leaning against the man next to her. The panicky defendants try to quiet and pull her down.

WOMAN DEFENDANT (hysterical). I can't stand it any more, I can't stand it! I want to confess — I threw stones at him, I helped kill him! We all helped kill him — we're guilty!

The matron and a bailiff try to remove her, but her outburst continues as the view swings, passing the PRESS BENCH, where the reporters are strained with excitement, then rests on TOM AND CHARLIE. Both are standing staring at the Woman, Tom trembling with sympathy. Tom makes a movement as if to go to her, but Charlie forces him down to his chair. The view swings back to the PRESS BENCH, where the reporters are falling over themselves trying to get in to the Press Room. News photographers are taking flashlight pictures as best they can. The Woman is pulled past them, still crying out to Katherine —

WOMAN DEFENDANT. Let me talk to her, let me tell her I didn't mean to — let me ask her to forgive me!

The view swings, passing the bench and resting on KATHERINE, who is standing rigid at the witness chair, staring in the direction of the frantic Woman. The tumult and the voice of the Woman continue.

WOMAN DEFENDANT. Forgive me! Please forgive me!

The view swings to the DISTRICT ATTORNEY AND JURY, which is on its feet, gaping in the direction of the WOMAN being taken out.

WOMAN. Forgive me . . . forgive us all . . . we didn't know . . .

Her voice cuts off as she is removed, and the room is suddenly quiet. The District Attorney turns to the jury, and points after the Woman.

DISTRICT ATTORNEY. *There* is your answer to this case, ladies and gentlemen! (*He turns toward the Judge.*) Your Honor, the State rests!

The scene dissolves to the COURTROOM CORRIDOR — a corner with a window, below it a bench — KATHERINE and TOM are seen sitting on the bench. CHARLIE is standing, resting a foot on it. The boys are lunching on "hot-dogs," but while Charlie eats heartily and with relish, Tom has no stomach for food. Katherine is staring at the floor.

CHARLIE (swallowing). What a break! (*He takes a bite of his hot-dog.*) What a day.

TOM. I wish I hadn't seen that woman cave in like that.

KATHERINE. She sentenced herself to die when she cracked, didn't she? I mean, we've got them now, haven't we? They haven't got a chance.

CHARLIE (through a mouthful). Not a Chinaman's! (*He eats the last of his hot-dog. For the first time, Katherine looks at him.*)

KATHERINE. That letter. That was what cinched it for us, wasn't it?

CHARLIE (slowly). Yeah. Why?

KATHERINE. It was certainly lucky for us that letter showed up, wasn't it?

TOM. Stop talkin' about it! I mean, where does it get ya?

KATHERINE (ominously quiet — to Charlie). Why didn't you tell me Joe's alive? (*There is a pause.*)

CHARLIE. What're you talkin' about? Are you crazy?

KATHERINE (quite steadily). I know he's alive!

CHARLIE (grabbing her wrists). Will you shut your mouth? (*He glances fearfully around lest they be overheard.*)

KATHERINE (trying to pull away). You can't keep me quiet. *Where is he?*

What's happened to him? Does he realize what we've *all* done?

CHARLIE (*gritting with suppressed fury, afraid that someone will hear*). You saw him. You saw him in that fire. You testified. Not me. Why ask me? I wasn't there. Ah-h, you're losin' your mind again!

A long view of the CORRIDOR INTERSECTION (as seen by them) shows VICKERY and the ASSOCIATE DEFENSE passing, deep in conversation. The Associate lifts and drops his hands helplessly, indicating "no use."

KATHERINE is again seen with CHARLIE AND TOM. Katherine is agreeing tiredly.

KATHERINE. Of course . . . You're right. (*Half rubbing her forehead*) I don't know wh-what's the matter with me. Of course you're right. And he's dead. But I haven't slept for so, long . . . (*Rising abruptly*) I want to go. I can't listen to any more of it. I want to go home!

The scene dissolves to JOE'S HIDEOUT at night. JOE is pacing, elated, whacking his fist into the palm of his hand triumphantly — but winces, as though he hurt himself, and we see that the little finger of his left hand is bandaged. Outside there is a distant rumble of thunder. Behind him the door opens and he jerks around, but relaxes as CHARLIE and TOM come in with evening newspapers. Tom shuts the door. Charlie tosses the papers on the table, on which are three bottles of beer, one having been opened, and plates for three, and in the center a pile of sandwiches, pickles, olives, and such delicatessen.

CHARLIE. There're the papers . . . A celebration, uh?

Tom, in a lethargy of depression, sits down near the door and slumps with abstraction.

JOE. You bet your life! (*Chuckling*) I heard it over that radio in the lunchroom.

CHARLIE (*warningly*). Your picture's in every paper. (*He goes out of sight.*)

JOE (*after him*). Who cares? I got 'em. That was some idea, that ring idea I got, eh? (*He goes to table and pours drink.*) That knocked 'em . . . (*To Tom*) Come on, kid. Sit down! . . . Knocked 'em for a loop, *that* did! A loop around their necks!

He drinks, and Tom, like a whipped dog, sits down at the table with lowered eyes. Charlie approaches, without a coat now, drying his hands on a towel.

CHARLIE. I had some time gettin' rid o' Katherine's hysterics. She's not sold you're dead, y'know.

JOE. Don't make me laugh! (*To Tom*) Go on, baby — have some beer.

Tom pours a drink but doesn't touch it.

CHARLIE. I'm tellin' ya — it was that letter you wrote that made her jump. I don't know what, but —

JOE. Aw, you're just tryin' to make yourself important! Katherine suspicious! You're daffy!

CHARLIE. *I'm* daffy, huh? Look at your radio! I tell ya, that letter —

JOE (*interrupting, insulted*). That letter was the best idea I ever had! It cost me almost my finger gettin' that ring off, but it'd've been worth the whole hand — both hands!

CHARLIE (*to Tom*). Tom, why don't you stick with me? You know as well as — (*Tom makes a "drop it" gesture.*) You're right. What's the use fightin' with him. (*He takes a bite. Again to Joe*) Anyway, she's home now. We got the landlady t' put her to bed. (*He eats.*)

JOE (*staring ahead, reliving in his head the trial*). That must've been some sensation when that woman collapsed. (*There is a sound of thunder. Tom looks at him, drops his eyes again.*) Yeh! They could stand seein' me burned to death all right, but they can't stand a good, honest trial. (*There is a first flash of lightning outside.*) They probably'll collapse all over the place when they're marched up those gallows' steps. I hear there's thirteen of 'em.

The sound of thunder is now nearer.

TOM (*jumping up violently*). Cut it out, will you? I can't stand it! I can't hear about it any more! You haven't been there watching those people — you didn't see that woman — you didn't look in their eyes —

JOE (*scornfully*). You yeller little welsher! Feelin' sorry for those lynchers are ya?

There is another flash of lightning.

TOM. You're as bad as them! *You're lynching me!*

CHARLIE(*to Joe*). It's gettin' me, too! If I hadn't started the whole thing — oh, I was with you, then! But I got a rotten feelin' you talked me into somethin' . . . An' believe me if I knew how to get out of this mess — I don't know what I'd do!

JOE (*raging*). All right. Why don't ya snitch on me, then, both of ya!

CHARLIE. Nobody's talkin' about that!

TOM. I *am!* I can't stand it any longer! Be human Joe! (*Almost supplicating*) We can get out o' the country — start over again. But let's tell 'em the truth! Let's tell 'em you're alive.

JOE (*yanking out his gun, holding it over them*). I'd *kill* ya first!

There is silence. Then a calm voice comes in.

VOICE. You might as well kill me, too.

JOE and the brothers jerk around.

KATHERINE is in the open doorway. There is a lightning flash and thunder over her.

Joe stares blankly at her. Then he whirls on Charlie.

JOE (*viciously*). So you told her, huh? You brought her here, you lyin' —

KATHERINE'S VOICE (*interrupting*). No, Joe. I followed them. I knew you were alive when I saw your letter. (*She comes to him.*) Why not kill me, too? Do a good job of it, what does it matter? Twenty-two, twenty-three, twenty-five — (*Seizing his arms*) Joe, look at me!

JOE (*throwing her off*). No!

KATHERINE. I'm sorry. I didn't mean to talk that way. (*She speaks to him gently,*

quietly.) Joe, I — I understand how you feel, and I understand why you feel that way. Joe, when I thought you were dead and when I thought of what killed you, I wanted to kill, too. I wanted a revenge every bit as complete as what you want. But now I don't. Now that you're alive, now that we're together, I want happiness again. I want what we've always promised ourselves —

JOE. You oughta have a couple of violins play when ya talk like that. I know what I want — an' I'm gettin' it.

KATHERINE. But, Joe, you're hanging twenty-two people for something they didn't do.

JOE. Oh, no I'm not. I'm hangin' twenty-two rats for somethin' they *did* do, for somethin' they can't drive outa their minds, outa their hearts, outa their souls! Why did we throw rocks at him, why did we drive him back into the fire, why didn't we give him a chance, why did we think we were God Almighty!

KATHERINE. Stop talking like that! You — you're petrified with hate!

JOE. Sure I am, and I love it! I love hate — that's funny — love hate —

He turns from her. Katherine looks at Charlie and Tom, then follows Joe.

KATHERINE. Joe. These are twenty-two human beings.

JOE. Yeah.

KATHERINE. They live and breathe, and love and laugh, and cry, just like everybody else.

JOE. Like me, for instance, in that jail.

KATHERINE. They're not murderers — they were part of a mob. If they acted singly, that would be different — one person can be motivated by reason, by thought. But a mob doesn't think — it hasn't time to think.

JOE. But the guy in jail — he can think, can't he? He can lie awake all night thinkin', can't he? Until what he's thinkin' about makes him want to cry, and yell, and hide, and beat his head against a wall! All right, it's his turn now — let them know what it is to be lynched!

KATHERINE. Don't you think they *do* know, by now? Don't you realize that what you felt for one night, for a few hours, they've faced for days and nights and weeks! Afraid of each other, of their wives, of their children, of them-*selves* — wishing with all their souls that they had that day to live over again! And Charlie and Tom — can you stop feeling sorry for yourself long enough to know what *they* went through! They love you, Joe, and because they love you, you make them murder for you! Something to think about for the rest of *their* lives! (*She pauses.*) Joe. I didn't want to live when I thought you were dead. I wanted to be dead too. Don't you see — we can still be together, and be happy. Let me go with you to the Judge — and then, let's start all over again.

JOE. Sure, kid. We'll start all over again. After the hangin'.

Katherine looks at him for a moment; then turns and starts for the door.

JOE. Don't go, Katherine — (*He tries to smile.*) Let's — let's sit down and have some fun — eat and drink and — and — (*His smile fades.*) Stop thinkin' about *them!* Why don't you think about *me!*

KATHERINE. I am thinking about you — about what a swell guy you were, when you were alive.

JOE. When I was — alive?

KATHERINE. You're dead now, Joe. You know that, don't you? If those people die, Joe dies. Wherever you go in the world, whatever you do. (*She pauses.*) I couldn't marry you now, Joe. (*Her voice breaks.*) I couldn't marry a dead man!

JOE. All right, then, all right! You don't want any part of me, you've made that clear! Well, I don't want any part of you, either! I don't need anybody!

KATHERINE. I'll always love you, Joe. That's something I can't do anything about. Maybe this is crazy — but I can't

help thinking we'd all be better off if you hadn't escaped from that jail!

JOE. Okay, so that's what you can't help thinkin'! Who cares? Say, what am I doin' here, anyway, talkin' to you three? This is a big night for me, and I should be out celebratin'! That's what I'm gonna do—celebrate! Alone! From now on, I'm gonna do everything alone!

He grabs his hat and coat and rushes to the door. The other three stand transfixed, watching him. He pauses at the door and turns to them.

JOE (*seriously, quietly*). They killed my dog, didn't they? (*He slams out of the door suddenly.*)

The scene dissolves to the JAIL at night, and the view in the dim light passes the men defendants' cells. We do not see them, but hear from one cell sobbing; from the next one a prayer; next the view picks up a defendant clinging hopelessly to a grating, his head bowed between lifted arms; and from the next cell we hear restless footsteps and see the form of a man moving up and down. There is a flash of lightning, then thunder again.

Then the scene dissolves to the JUDGE's CHAMBERS at night. It is raining heavily outside. In a flash of lightning, the JUDGE is standing with his hands in his pockets at the window, gazing into the night. The room is lighted only by a desk lamp.

BAILIFF'S VOICE. Your Honor . . . (*The Judge does not hear, and the bailiff approaches him.*) Your wife, Your Honor.

JUDGE (*turning*). What? . . . Oh. What was it, Lee?

BAILIFF. Your wife is here, sir.

JUDGE. Ask her to come in, please. (*He comes slowly to the desk, where many law books are open, and his robe is lying over a chair. His wife comes to him with a package wrapped in newspaper, and a basket. — She is a motherly woman.*) Now — now — now, my dear, you oughtn't to be out in this rain. (*He kisses her on the cheek, and turns to the bailiff.*) You can go, Lee . . . Any reports from the jury room?

BAILIFF. Not since they took that last ballot at ten o'clock, sir. But the newspaper boys're all bettin' ten to one on a conviction.

The Judge sighs, and sits down. The bailiff goes out, closing the door.

JUDGE'S WIFE (*unwrapping the package and disposing of its contents*). I brought your rubbers, Dan.

JUDGE (*abstracted*). What? Oh. Thank you, dear . . .

He goes out of sight. His wife opens the basket and gets out some sandwiches and a thermos bottle of coffee she has brought.

JUDGE'S VOICE. Twenty-two people—with wives, husbands, parents, children — Sometimes it's hard to be a judge. (*He comes into view again; gazes at the bust of Lincoln; then noticing the food, he pats her hand.*) Oh, you shouldn't have bothered to — (*He goes to the window.*)

JUDGE'S WIFE. I know how you hate that cooking they send up from that lunchroom. (*She looks after him.*) Dan . . . Have you made up your mind what you'll do if the verdict is guilty, Dan?

JUDGE (*nodding slowly, looking out of the window*). Yes . . . I shall have to sentence them to die. (*There is a flash of lightning. He turns around.*) It's the law, dear. (*A peal of thunder follows the lightning flash.*)

The scene dissolves to a BEER GARDEN at night. JOE is sitting alone at a small round table with a checked tablecloth. A glass of beer is in front of him. Around and behind him are scores of other tables, packed tightly together, but all vacant, though their glasses and dishes indicate the patrons are dancing. Eight musicians in Bavarian costume are playing before a painted backdrop showing a Bavarian landscape. Their music is hearty with happiness. Dancing couples pass the orchestra. Joe takes a drink of the beer, but distastefully sets it down with annoyance, and looking around signals and calls.

JOE. Hi — waiter! (*An aproned waiter comes in to him.*) This stuff's too weak for me . . . Get me some Bourbon, straight, will y'?

WAITER (*shaking his head "no"*). Sorry, but with the kind o' license we got it's against the law.

The music stops, amid applause, laughter and talk.

JOE. Then . . . give me my check.

WAITER. I'm sorry, sir, you feel —

JOE (*interrupting*). That's all right. It's just too — noisy . . . for me. (*Other people come in to their tables, packing the spaces between tables.*) I don't like such a crowded place.

The scene dissolves to a CHEAP BAR. JOE is sitting at the bar, alone now, with his hat and raincoat on. A glass of straight whiskey is before him, but he is staring at the bar, not drinking. The place is silent. His hand vaguely pushes his hat back on his head, he looks to the left and right, but the bar is still vacant except for him. He downs his whiskey, and says.

JOE. Gee, what a lonesome place! Don't you have any . . . music . . . or anything, here? (*The Barkeeper comes to him.*)

BARKEEPER. Sorry. We don't have music here.

JOE. Well . . . Give me another Bourbon.

The Barkeeper takes a bottle, fills the glass, and goes. Joe looks straight ahead. A man's hand taps Joe's shoulder, and frightened, he jerks straight and around. Joe sees a tout with a derby hat on and a cigarette drooping from his mouth.

TOUT (*with an oily smile*). All alone, Bud?

JOE (*confused*). Yes. No — no — yes. I mean — (*He laughs a little, relaxing.*) Why?

As the tout bends down to whisper in Joe's ear, the scene dissolves to a CHEAP NIGHT CLUB, and Joe is dancing with a girl in a crowd of dancing men and women, youths, older men, and girls in cheap evening dresses. He is laughing, as if forcing himself to. The music is cheap jazz from a mechanical piano. It finishes, and the crowd returns to the cheap boxes against the wall. Joe takes his girl to a box. There are two half-finished highballs on the table, and Joe drinks.

GIRL (*looking at him curiously*). Your face is kind o' familiar. Were you ever here before?

JOE. Not me. First time here. But you're okay, baby. What's your name?

GIRL (*sliding her chair closer to him*). It's "Joyce," here, but — (*intriguingly*) — it's "Katherine," to you.

JOE (*jumping up*). What d' y' mean, "to me"? Why'd you say that?

GIRL (*staring at him*). Because Katherine's my real name. Say, what's the matter with you?

JOE (*confused and hurriedly explaining*). Nothing — except that liquor y' serve here maybe. It's so hot I think I'll — go out for awhile.

As the girl gapes at him, he turns and hurries away.

Next JOE comes out of the ALLEY DOOR of the night club. A high wind has risen with the stopping of the rain, and Joe, in his raincoat, bucks against it with lowered head. Joe turns irresolutely, and seeing a taxi, calls.

JOE. Hey — taxi! (*He turns toward it.*)

The driver of the TAXI is at the curb now getting out and opening the door as JOE approaches, bucking the wind.

JOE. Say, where can a guy have some fun?

DRIVER. Leave it t' me, Sport! Hop in!

JOE gets into the taxi, and the Driver slams shut the door. A close-up then shows JOE staring straight ahead. As the taxi starts, there is the sound of the Driver clicking the meter on, and the cab moves off. The tick-tick-tick of the meter comes in, until it is the only sound to be heard. Joe suddenly straightens, noticing something ahead of him: A close-up of the TAXI METER comes into view. The figures are 20. The 0 moves up, everything but these numbers growing dizzy as this last number becomes a 2 — *in his head*. The 22 looms bigger and bigger as the tick-tick of the meter goes relentlessly on.

A close-up of JOE shows him blinking stu-pidly. He strikes his forehead with the heels of his palms as if to drive the number out of his feverish brain. He leans forward, calling to the driver:

JOE. Let me out!

The cab grates to a sudden stop. Then Joe piles out of the taxi at a STREET CURB, fumbling for change.

JOE (*to the driver*). I changed my mind. Rather t-take a walk. It smells good in your face after the rain. (*He gives the driver some change and goes.*)

DRIVER (*looking after him, shaking his head*). Screwball.

The scene dissolves to a STREET as JOE comes along it in the wind. He now notices a display in a show window and goes to the window, where he sees a display of a bedroom suite, with twin beds and furnishings reminiscent of those in the window display when he walked with Katherine before she took the train to the West. A placard announces "for the newlyweds." As he stares at the display there is a slight rustle of the wind, and the noise dissolves into:

KATHERINE'S VOICE (*gay*). Are you planning on doing a lot of running in the living room?

Joe listens, jerks around, but there is no one there. He looks around afraid, then says half to himself, with a shaky little laugh:

JOE. G-gee, I'm crazy . . . hangin' around empty streets. I need some crowds — people —

The noise of talk, laughter and distant music rises, making him turn. He sees a cheap COCKTAIL BAR entrance where a drunk is waving good-bye and talking back to an unseen man behind the open door, from which come the sounds of revelry.

DRUNK. Bye-bye, Jeff. (*Laughing*) Bye-bye.

Joe approaches the entrance as the chuckling drunk leaves. He stops to look at the signs outside, and opens the door, hearing again the sound of music, laughter and revelry. There is a semi-circular curtained windbreak about the door. Joe comes in and stops short, staring at the small, completely empty room. But the sound of voices and revelry goes on. A Negro bar-keeper is listening at the small radio at the bar from which the programme is coming. He glances at Joe, and calls:

NEGRO (*switching off the radio*). Come in, Mister. What'll yo' pleasure be, sir?

JOE (*uneasily looking around*). Straight bourbon.

The Negro pours him a drink which JOE gulps down. The clock begins to strike and continues till it has struck twelve times.

NEGRO. Midnight . . . an' another day! (*He tears off a sheet of the calendar which reads 20, but discloses on the next sheet 22. Joe gapes at the damnable number.*) Two pages must've got hanged together.

Staring at the 22, JOE gets out a quarter, drops it to the bar, and rushes out.

The scene dissolves to a STREET where JOE wanders along — to be jerked up by the sight of a passing policeman, to avoid whose glance at him he turns quickly toward another show window where he sees, in absolute contrast to his mood, a window filled with a charming, beautiful floral display. Ghostly forms seem to materialize at Joe's back, looking over his shoulder. They have the faces of DAWSON, the WOMAN, and others of the defendants. He stands motionless, hearing whispering voices.

VOICES. Do a good job of it, what does it matter? Twenty-two, twenty-three, twenty-five —

JOE is rigid, his eyes stricken, not daring to turn. With an effort he jerks around . . . The misty forms have disappeared. Behind him appears the neat lettering on the glass, FUNERAL DIRECTORS. He tries to shake off his dread, but frightened, looks up and down the street, then sucks in a deep breath and starts off. But with him is the sound of many feet. Abruptly, he stops, listens . . . Nothing. — Letting out his breath, he starts on. — Again the feet pursue him. He stops again. He jerks around. With a half-smothered sob, he grips at his throat, fearful of taking another step. He looks up and down the street, but sees only the empty sidewalk, in deep shadows

Joe, fearing the dark, steps out into the middle of the street, looks around again, listens, and then goes out of sight. But over the empty street comes the sound of those awful, following feet. — Then JOE is seen walking faster and faster, not daring to turn, followed by the sound of the pursuing feet, and this dissolves to ANOTHER STREET. He is frankly running now to escape the rattle of the ghostly feet, that he cannot shake off.

The scene dissolves to the DOOR at JOE's building — a poor tenement. Joe, hurrying, tremblingly gets the door open, and goes in, kicking it behind him shut. (Still the rattling feet follow him.) Then we see him on the STAIRWAY, and Joe races in fear up the stairs to his hideout. The ghostly feet follow him, clapping against the stairs like those of skeletons, nearer and nearer. At last he is at the DOOR of his hideout. The light is off in the room. He storms in, the rattling almost on top of him. He slams the door, locks it, straining a shoulder against it to keep the sound out. He screams in panic.

JOE. Katherine! . . . *Katherine!*

But the noise of the skeleton feet is still around him, and instinctively his hand gropes for and switches on the light. He stumbles back from the door. — Instantly with the coming on of the light the sound of the feet has vanished, and there is absolute silence.

JOE (*hoarsely*). *Katherine!* . . . (*He hesitantly turns around.*)

We see the deserted room as Joe's voice resounds.

JOE'S VOICE (*strained*). Don't . . . leave me . . . alone.

Then there is the thud of a falling body heavily striking the floor.

The scene dissolves to the COURTROOM. The JUDGE is on the bench, counsel for the defense and the DISTRICT ATTORNEY are at their tables, the reporters are alert at their bench. The defendants' eyes are strained on the door to the witness room — from which the jury is filing back into its box.

At the JURY BOX, the jury is extremely grave as it takes its seats. They look as if they'd been up all night. The foreman has a sheaf of paper verdict forms in his hand. — The DEFENDANTS watch the jury with dread. The Woman who collapsed is among them, a matron with her.

The last of the jury (seen from the defendants' view) sits down, and there is a trembling silence over the courtroom. The Judge turns toward the jury.

JUDGE. Ladies and gentlemen of the jury, have you agreed upon the verdict?

The foreman rises, the forms in his hand.

FOREMAN. We have, Your Honor.

The DEFENDANTS are seen hanging motionless on the foreman, except that one man wipes the perspiration from his forehead, and one of the women rips her handkerchief. Their eyes shift to the judge.

JUDGE's VOICE (gravely). You will hand the verdict to the bailiff.

The defendants' eyes shift to the FOREMAN AND JURY. The bailiff approaches, takes the forms from the foreman, turns and hands them to the Judge. The Judge's face is expressionless as he examines the verdicts to assure their propriety in form, and then hands them to the clerk standing before the bench.

We see the whole COURT, everybody tense. In utter silence, the clerk begins to read.

CLERK (unemotionally, but loud). "We, the jury, find in the case of the People of the State versus the following defendants charged with the murder of one Joseph Wheeler as set forth in the indictment: Jasper Anderson . . . not guilty." (There is movement along the press bench, two reporters at the door quickly signalling "thumbs-up" into the press room.)

Defendant Jasper Anderson's jaw drops with astonishment at his unbelievable good luck, and he rises. The monotonous clerk's voice continues:

CLERK's VOICE. "Gilbert Clark . . . not guilty."

Clark, who in extreme tension was sitting next to Anderson, relaxes. Jasper Anderson grabs his hand and pumps it. The defendant on his other side congratulates him. It is obvious that the defendants now believe that they are going to be freed.

CLERK's VOICE (still emotionless). "Oliver Cobb . . . guilty."

This "guilty" strikes like lightning, instantly paralyzing the hopes of the defendants. They are struck motionless, staring unbelievably at the clerk.

CLERK's VOICE. "Kirby Dawson . . . guilty."

The defendants stare, uncomprehendingly.

CLERK's VOICE. "Frederick Garrett . . . guilty."

Now the spell paralyzing the defendants breaks. The next defendant gives way, sliding from his chair to his knees, grabbing the chair next to him for support, resting transfixed with despair as he hears:

CLERK's VOICE. "Walter Gordon . . . guilty . . . Jerome Harris — "

The next defendant, Jerome Harris, jumps up to cry hoarsely.

HARRIS. No — no!

CLERK's VOICE (continuing, emotionless). ". . . . guilty."

HARRIS (shouting raspingly). No — no! Not me! I'm not guilty! I'm not!

A bailiff pulls him down. Simultaneously, the defendant behind Harris jumps up.

NEXT DEFENDANT (beside himself). Go on — go on — get it over with!

Others rise with him, and the bailiffs try to force them down, struggling with them. The woman defendant rises.

WOMAN. Go on — go on! I'm guilty! I burned him! Go on! I'll pay!

CLERK's VOICE (over all this commotion). "William Hull . . . guilty . . . Milton Jackson . . . guilty . . . Richard Keller . . . guilty."

DAWSON has been glancing around, trapped. Abruptly, he breaks loose with the mad hope of escaping — darts between the struggling knots of bailiffs and defendants, and jumping over the partition fronting the spectators' seats, tears up the aisle out of sight.

The whole courtroom is on its feet, transfixed, except for the reporters and bailiffs and attachés trying to quiet the excited defendants. Dawson is jumping over some of the empty seats, into the aisle and heads toward the door leading to the corridor, with bailiffs chasing him and closing in from the sides. He evades them, but abruptly stops in his tracks, dumb with staring shock. There is a sudden stupefying silence over the whole room, as everyone stares, stricken. Dawson's eyes bulge, his jaw drops, and he stumbles backward, in his eyes a look of incredulous fright.

JOE appears against the half-open door. Behind him in the corridor are two policemen. Joe's expression is set with earnestness. He comes slowly down the aisle, passing Dawson, now held by the bailiffs, but not giving him a glance, and he continues down the aisle.

Now Joe passes the defendants, who shrink back from him in superstitious fear; passes the tables of Defense and District Attorney; and comes to the Judge standing behind the bench. Joe looks up at him.

JOE. Your Honor, I'm Joseph Wheeler.

Immediately there is a rustling movement of excitement over the room. Some reporters break for the press room, and photographers begin to flashlight him.

JUDGE (sharply). Keep your seats.

The reporters subside against their will.

DISTRICT ATTORNEY (coming out of his shock). I demand that this man be placed under arrest —

JOE. That's all right with me, Your Honor. But can I say something first?

JUDGE. Go on —

JOE (after a pause). First of all, I know I arrived just in time to save the lives of these twenty-two people. I can't help that. That isn't why I'm here. I didn't want to save them yesterday and I don't want to today. They're murderers. I know the law says they're not because I'm still alive, but that's not their fault. The law doesn't know that a lot of things that were very important to me — silly things like a belief in justice, and an idea that men were civilized, and a feeling of pride that this country of mine was different from all others — the law doesn't know that those things were burned to death within me that night. So it would be silly for me to stand here and say I'll forgive and forget. (He pauses, looks toward Katherine, Charlie and Tom, and then continues.) I came here today for my own sake. I came here because I couldn't stand being alone. Maybe what I'm saying doesn't make sense to you, but my thoughts are all jumbled up, and I've got to tell them as they come to me. I thought I could have my revenge, and that then I could start to live all over again. I didn't believe Katherine when she said I couldn't. Katherine — is the young lady who was going to marry me. (He pauses.) I still don't know whether I was right or wrong. Those people were wrong, they're wrong now, and they'll always be wrong. But maybe it's done them some good. I don't know. All I know is that the only way I could go on living was to come here today. And all I want is to start again and — and maybe some day Katherine and I —

He has been fumbling in his pocket during the very last part of the speech, and as he says the last words, his eyes rest on what he has pulled out of his pocket. — And a close-up of JOE's HAND shows, nestled among tobacco crumbs and fuzz, a solitary salted peanut.

JOE. I guess that's about all I can say. (He pops the peanut into his mouth.)

The scene cuts instantly to a close-up of KATHERINE. Her eyes dimmed with tears, her face aglow in recognition of the Joe she fell in love with, she moves toward him, smiling her forgiveness.

KATHERINE. Joe —

She moves closer and closer until her face, smiling with a tremendous happiness, blots out everything and the picture fades out.